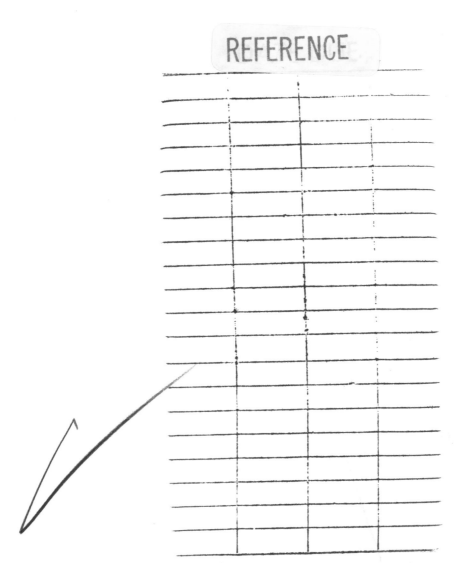

MARK TWAIN
A TO Z

THE ESSENTIAL REFERENCE
TO HIS LIFE AND WRITINGS

R. Kent Rasmussen

Foreword by Thomas A. Tenney, editor
Mark Twain Journal

☑®

Facts On File, Inc.

AN INFOBASE HOLDINGS COMPANY

To my father, mother and Kathy, with love
and

To my most patient readers
and most charitable critics,
whose appreciation for what
I have put into this book
will not, I hope, be diminished by
what I have left out

Mark Twain A to Z:
The Essential Reference to His Life and Writings

Copyright © 1995 by R. Kent Rasmussen

Facts On File, Inc.
460 Park Avenue South
New York NY 10016

Library of Congress Cataloging-in-Publication Data
Rasmussen, R. Kent.
Mark Twain A to Z : the essential reference to his life and
writings / R. Kent Rasmussen ; foreword by Thomas A. Tenney.
p. cm.
Includes bibliographical references (p.   ) and index.
ISBN 0-8160-2845-1
1. Twain, Mark, 1835–1910—Dictionaries. 2. Authors,
American—19th century—Biography—Dictionaries. I. Title.
PS1331.R37 1995
818′.409—dc20   94-39156

Facts On File books are available at special discounts when purchased in bulk quantities for businesses, associations, institutions or sales promotions. Please call our Special Sales Department in New York at 212/683-2244 or 800/322-8755.

Jacket design by Nora Wertz

Map by Dale Williams

This book is printed on acid-free paper.

Printed in the United States of America

VB VC 10 9 8 7 6 5 4 3 2 1

CONTENTS

ACKNOWLEDGMENTS

After a quarter century of research in various fields, I can attest to the fact that people connected with Mark Twain studies *are* special. Everywhere I have gone, I have found warm welcomes and a generous desire to share information. Before continuing, however, let me say without reservation that I could not have finished this project without the help of Kevin Bochynski—who does not think it strange to follow a hobby to excess. Aside from patiently answering my questions, furnishing research materials, reading manuscripts and generally encouraging me, he has given me a friendship that I shall long treasure. Another wonderful friend that this project has found for me is Tom Tenney. Blessed with the sense of humor that one hopes to find in Mark Twain scholars, he has been generous with information and advice and has gone out of his way to make me feel a part of Mark Twain studies.

Most roads to Mark Twain lead through the University of California at Berkeley and the Mark Twain Project, where Bob Hirst and his staff extended to me the spirit of collegiality for which they are well known. I found a similarly generous spirit at Hannibal's Mark Twain Boyhood Home and at Hartford's Mark Twain House.

The many others who have helped and encouraged me in various ways include Dahlia Armon, JoDee Benussi, Derek Burke, Julie Castiglia, Christopher Ehret, Michelle Fellner, Noelle Heenan, Michael Patrick, Casey Peters, Rikki Poulos, Erik Rasmussen, Virginia Rubens, Susan Schwartz, Barbara Staten, Michael Sutherland, Chuck Swift and Johnna Swift. And, of course, I owe special thanks to my wife Kathy and my parents for their love and for helping to make my work possible.

While most of what has gone into this book derives from my own reading of Mark Twain, it should be obvious that it also draws heavily on the painstaking research of others. My select bibliography cannot cite everyone whose work I have used, so I must instead extend my thanks to Mark Twain scholars generally. I would also like to single out the two best reference works yet published on Mark Twain: Tom Tenney's *Mark Twain: A Research Guide,* and Alan Gribben, *Mark Twain's Library.* Finally, I am grateful to the WordPerfect Corporation for making available the word-processing and databasing software that enabled me to finish this project in three years instead of six.

INTRODUCTION

Anyone already familiar with Mark Twain's writings and complex life knows that a single reference book about him—even one as large as this—cannot encompass everything about him that one might wish to know. During his 75 years, he traveled throughout America, lived in all its major regions and spent more than 13 years abroad. He raised a family, launched careers as a printer, miner, journalist, lecturer and publisher, and became personally acquainted with many of the leading figures of his time. On top of all this, he wrote millions of words in travel letters, sketches, stories, essays, polemics, novels and plays. In addition to the classic fictional narratives that he contributed to our literature, he wrote at length about the places he visited, the people he met and countless issues that concerned him. Within his lifetime, he published dozens of books, and he died leaving behind material enough for dozens more.

Since the "A to Z's" of Mark Twain clearly range over far more territory than this book can cover, I have elected to concentrate on hard factual information and leave analysis and interpretation to others. In any case, so much of what passes as "common knowledge" about Mark Twain is erroneous or unsubstantiated that there is a compelling need to get the facts straight. I have brought to my work a skepticism of the Received Truth as well as a hunger for answers to almost every imaginable question about Mark Twain. The questions I address here, however, are mostly of the *who, what, where* and *when* variety, rather than the *how*'s and *why*'s. *Mark Twain A to Z* describes Mark Twain's major writings (and many of his minor works) in detail, identifying characters, places and incidents and telling exactly where they appear. It also covers places he visited and lived in, people he knew, steamboats he piloted, publications he wrote for, and many other important elements in his life.

While I have drawn on considerable secondary literature about Mark Twain, I have tried, wherever possible, to find answers to my questions about him in his own writings, instead of others' descriptions of them. *Mark Twain A to Z* brings to its subject an intense, integrated examination of Mark Twain's writings. I have carefully read each of his works at least four times, I have listened to many of them on audiotapes and I have made extensive use of a computer to database information and search more than three million words of electronic texts.

Instead of being drawn into debates about the number of teeth in a horse's mouth, I prefer to count the teeth myself and move on. In fact, I have done essentially that more than once. For example, the many divergent published estimates of how often the word "nigger" appears in *Huckleberry Finn* prodded me to do the obvious thing: use my computer to *count* the times.

The attention that this book distributes among Mark Twain's writings is deliberately uneven. In general, it looks most closely at the works most often read. For this reason, *Tom Sawyer* and *Huckleberry Finn* are treated nearly exhaustively, while a work such as *Christian Science* receives perfunctory attention. On the other hand, the inherent complexity or special textual problems of a less-read work has often moved me to give it more space than it might otherwise merit. For example, *Following the Equator* is Mark Twain's least-read travel book, but I give considerable space to explaining its complex relationship with *More Tramps Abroad*, its British counterpart.

My basic approach to defining entries and assigning headwords to them has been to place information where readers are most apt to seek it. Wherever possible, I define entries around discrete rather than collective subjects. For example, information about the illustrator Dan Beard can be found under "Beard," not "illustrators." In the matter of book titles, I suspect that most readers will look for Mark Twain's novel about Joan of Arc under "Joan," rather than under *Personal Recollections of Joan of Arc*—the book's full title—so it is entered as *Joan of Arc, Personal Recollections of*. Likewise, *Pudd'nhead Wilson* goes under "Pudd'nhead," not *The Tragedy of Pudd'nhead Wilson; Huckleberry Finn;* goes under "Huckleberry," not *Adventures of Huckleberry Finn;* and so on. This approach also simplifies cross-referencing and places several book titles closer to related entries. Extra help may be found in the index.

The names of both real and fictional persons are entered under their last names, when known, such as "Clemens, Olivia Langdon" and "Sawyer, Tom." Persons best known by their pseudonyms are entered under the names by which readers are most likely to seek them, such as Artemus Ward, Josh Billings or Dan De Quille (also with last names first). Fictional characters whose last names are unknown, such as *Huckleberry Finn*'s Jim, are entered under their first names. In such cases, titles and honorifics are ignored for purposes of alphabetizing; thus "Aunt Polly" (whose last name is not known) goes under "Polly, Aunt." In contrast to human beings, animals, ships and steamboats are entered under their full names. For example, both the dog "Andrew Jackson" and the steamboat "*A. B. Chambers*" go under the "A's." Newspapers are entered under their full masthead names, which generally include the name of the city in which they were published. This system has the advantage of grouping related entries closely together, such as the *Hannibal Courier, Hannibal Journal* and *Hannibal Western Union*.

Mark Twain A to Z presents detailed synopses of most of Mark Twain's major works. Their purpose is not to serve as substitutes for reading the original works, but to provide material that is sufficiently detailed to be useful for serious study and reference. The synopses account for the most important details in each chapter, relegating as much information as possible to other entries, which are indicated by cross-references. Many synopses contain supplemental information, such as dates and corrected names; such information is always enclosed in parentheses to differentiate it from what is actually in Mark Twain's texts.

Mark Twain's travel books present special synopsizing problems, as they mix fact and fiction and typically lack clear and consistent narrative voices. For example, the second part of *Life on the Mississippi* describes Mark Twain's trip on the Mississippi River in 1882, but it would be a mistake to assume that its narrator is necessarily Mark Twain himself. The narrator of chapter 30 who describes rising early to watch sunsets may well be Mark Twain, but who is the narrator of chapter 32 who met the fictional Karl Ritter in a Munich dead house? To avoid reading more into the texts than is actually there, I often employ the inelegant but inclusive term "the narrator."

To avoid cluttering the book with "see also" and "q.v.," I have worked all my cross-references into the text and marked them with SMALL CAPS. For example, "Bloodgood Haviland CUTTER" denotes an entry titled "Cutter, Bloodgood Haviland." Cross-references indicate topics that add *relevant* information to the entries in which they appear. Some subjects are rarely cross-referenced, however, because readers may take for granted that entries on them exist. Such subjects include Mark Twain's best-known books and most famous characters (Tom Sawyer, Huck Finn and Jim), members of his immediate family, and places that are closely associated with him—such as Missouri, the Mississippi River, Hannibal and Hartford.

Within biographical entries on real persons, the dates and locations of birth and death are the most precise that I can find. The abbreviation "c." (*circa,* or "about")

indicates an informed estimate, while a question mark (?) indicates less-informed guesswork. The abbreviation "*fl.*" (*flourit,* or "flourished") indicates the years within which something concrete is known about a person's life. For example, the entry on George Ealer gives only "*fl.* 1850s" because that decade is the only period for which I have information about him. Since Ealer was a licensed pilot when Mark Twain knew him in the 1850s, it is safe to assume that he was born at least two decades earlier; however, since readers can infer the same thing themselves, no purpose would be served by giving Ealer's dates as "*fl.* 1830s–1850s."

Most entries on individual works contain figures for total numbers of words. Some figures I have estimated by counting and extrapolating, but most derive from computer counts of electronic texts (e-texts). Many of the figures given in *Mark Twain A to Z* differ significantly from previously published estimates. However, while I consider my numbers the more accurate, I would caution that definitive word counts are impossible. Different editions of Mark Twain's texts often vary in length. Furthermore, there will always be disagreement on what constitutes a word. For example, is "stage-coach" one word or two? If it is one word, how should "stage coach" be counted? Should numbers and abbreviations count as words? Such questions should be raised, but I am not convinced they need be answered.

It is generally known that Mark Twain was born Samuel Langhorne Clemens. He did not adopt his pen name until he was 26 and then was both "Mark Twain" and "Sam Clemens" through the rest of his life. Knowing when to stop calling him "Clemens" and start calling him "Mark Twain" has long bedeviled writers. For the sake of simplicity, I refer to him throughout this book as "Mark Twain," trusting that readers will know to whom I refer. Similarly, I should add here that I also often use "Mark Twain Papers" anachronistically in order to simplify cross-references, hoping that readers who find their way to the entry under that heading will be satisfied by its explanation.

I believe it is a testament to Mark Twain's uniqueness that several years of intense study and writing have only increased my interest in him. Virtually everything about this extraordinary man fascinates me. Surely, such another man has never lived. I have more questions about him now than when I started, and I fully intend to update *Mark Twain A to Z* in future editions. Meanwhile, I hope that this book will enhance other people's interest in Mark Twain, and I hope too that its readers will not allow its inevitable omissions to spoil their appreciation of its substantial contents.

R. Kent Rasmussen
Thousand Oaks, California

FOREWORD

"If I'd a knowed what a trouble it was to make a book," Huck wrote, "I wouldn't a tackled it." If Kent Rasmussen had any such doubts along the way, he overcame them, and all of Twaindom is in his debt for this remarkable guide to the great author's life and works—the more remarkable because it is the work of a single author.

One happy result of this single perspective is evenness and consistency: all the details a reader needs are there in every entry, and the entries never contradict one another in statements of fact. Throughout, Kent Rasmussen is aware of the kinds of questions the reader is likely to ask, takes nothing for granted in the reader's prior knowledge of Twain, and presents the hard facts where a reader would be most likely to look for them.

Here are the dates, places, and people presented clearly, without a word wasted. Major and interesting characters are described, and placed in the works in which they appear. The works themselves are summarized, and often with that important extra step taken: There are original contributions in the analysis of the relationship between *Pudd'nhead Wilson* and its precursor, "Those Extraordinary Twins," for example, and in a chapter-by-chapter comparison of *Following the Equator* and its slightly longer English counterpart, *More Tramps Abroad*.

Mark Twain deserves the attention he receives from the world of scholarship. His life reflects that of our nation, from frontier days to the beginning of the modern age. When Sam Clemens was born in 1835, our flag had 24 stars and Andrew Jackson was president. Clemens had many lives: river boy, printer in New York and Philadelphia (in his late teens), steamboat pilot, Confederate soldier (for about two weeks), western prospector, reporter, lecturer, and travel writer in a day when tourists were less common and less numerous. He enjoyed the new times as they came: he went up in a balloon (in Paris, in 1879), had one of the first telephones in a private home, and invested in one of the first typesetting machines (the wrong one). In his writings he predicted television, predicted that the energy of the twentieth century would be atomic, and—less happily—anticipated the horrors of modern warfare.

His path crossed those of historical figures—some from a distance, as when he described Charles Dickens and Jefferson Davis. He actually met Czar Alexander II, and dined with both Kaiser Wilhelm II and the Prince of Wales (later King Edward VII). He knew Ulysses S. Grant well, arranged the publication of Grant's *Personal Memoirs*, and had the satisfaction of paying Grant's widow the largest royalty check that had ever been written. A few weeks before Twain died, he was playing miniature golf with Woodrow Wilson in Bermuda.

The characters Twain created are here—virtually every character in *Tom Sawyer* and *Huckleberry Finn*, with citation by chapter and verse. There are even word counts of Twain's works, done by a patient computer. Perhaps there is a law of diminishing returns for human effort, but Rasmussen's machine never became tired or bored with details, and left him free for the work he does so well: careful analyses, gracefully presented, with a full awareness of how the works and their contexts are related to Twain's life and times.

Those times are well set down in a comprehensive chronology by years—a time-line showing where Samuel Clemens lived, what was going on in his life and writing, and some of the more significant literary and historical events of the period.

Not yet exhausted by his exhaustive enterprise, Kent Rasmussen seeks new Twain worlds to conquer; we can only watch, and be grateful.

Thomas A. Tenney
Editor, *Mark Twain Journal*
Charleston, S.C.

MARK TWAIN IN AMERICA

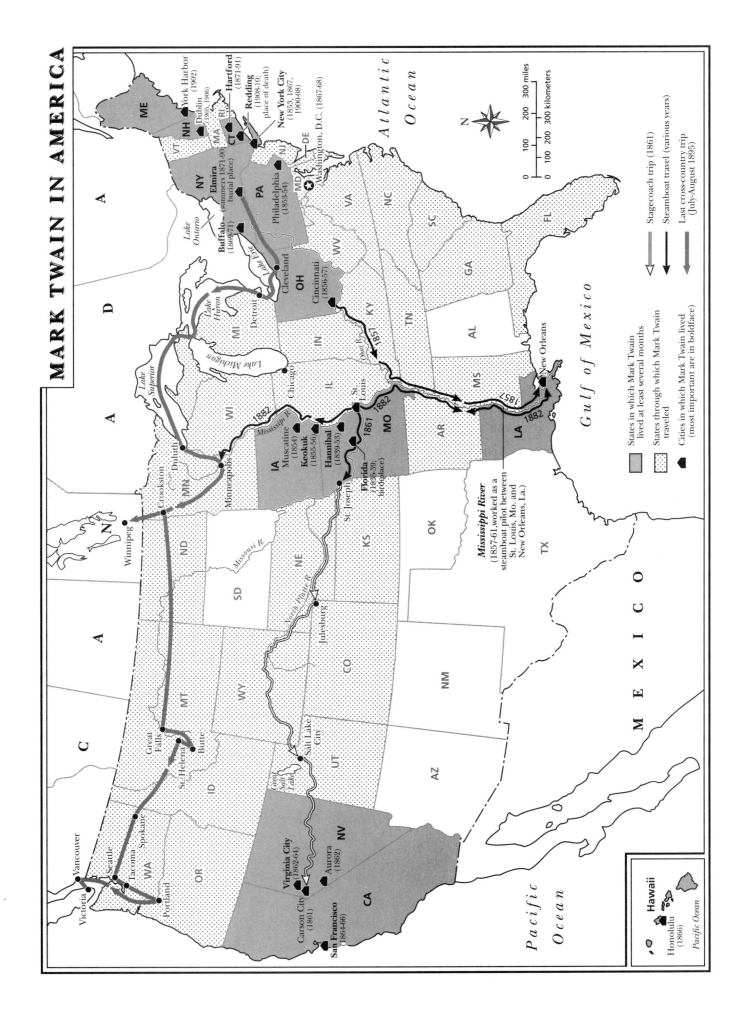

Legend

- Stagecoach trip (1861)
- Steamboat travel (various years)
- Last cross-country trip (July–August 1895)

States in which Mark Twain lived at least several months

States through which Mark Twain traveled

Cities in which Mark Twain lived (most important are in boldface)

Mississippi River (1857–61; worked as a steamboat pilot between St. Louis, Mo. and New Orleans, La.)

Cities and dates

- New York Harbor (1902)
- Dublin (1905, 1906)
- Hartford (1871–91)
- Redding (1908–10; place of death)
- New York City (1853, 1867, 1900–08)
- Elmira (summers 1871–99; burial place)
- Buffalo (1869–71)
- Philadelphia (1853–54)
- Washington, D.C. (1867–68)
- Cleveland
- Cincinnati (1856–57)
- Detroit
- Chicago
- St. Louis
- Muscatine (1854)
- Keokuk (1855–56)
- Hannibal (1839–53)
- Florida (1835–39; birthplace)
- St. Joseph
- Duluth
- Crookston
- Minneapolis
- Winnipeg
- Julesburg
- Salt Lake City
- Great Falls
- St. Helena
- Butte
- Vancouver
- Victoria
- Seattle
- Tacoma
- Spokane
- Portland
- Virginia City (1862–64)
- Aurora (1862)
- Carson City (1861)
- San Francisco (1864–66)
- New Orleans

Hawaii
- Honolulu (1866)

Pacific Ocean

Atlantic Ocean

Gulf of Mexico

Pacific Ocean

C A N A D A

M E X I C O

CHRONOLOGY

Year	Residences & travel	Personal & business	Writing & publishing	Family & friends	Literary events	Historical events
1835	(June) John M. and Jane L. Clemens settle with family in Florida, Mo.	(30 Nov.) Samuel Langhorne Clemens is born in Florida		(June) John M. Clemens runs store with John A. Quarles; (25 Nov.) Andrew Carnegie is born	Alexis de Tocqueville, *Democracy in America*; (27 July) Giosue Carducci is born; (4 Dec.) Samuel Butler is born	Andrew Jackson is president; (9 Apr.) Belgian King Leopold II is born; (15 Nov.) Halley's Comet attains perihelion
1836	lives in Florida; (21 May) John M. Clemens purchases house on Main St. in Florida	begins life frequently ill		(18 Feb.) sister-in-law, Susan Crane, is born	Charles Dickens, *Pickwick Papers*; (25 Aug.) Bret Harte is born; (11 Nov.) Thomas B. Aldrich is born	(2 Mar.) American settlers declare Texas independent; (15 June) Arkansas enters the Union as a slave state
1837	lives in Florida			(Jan.) John M. Clemens joins commission to develop Salt River; (18 Mar.) grandfather Ben Lampton dies; (6 Nov.) Clemens becomes a county judge; (1 Dec.) Laura Hawkins is born	Charles Dickens, *Oliver Twist*; (10 Feb.) Alexander Pushkin dies; (1 Mar.) W. D. Howells is born; (5 Apr.) Algernon Charles Swinburne is born	(4 Mar.) Pres. Martin Van Buren is inaugurated; (18 Mar.) Grover Cleveland is born; (17 Apr.) J. Pierpont Morgan is born; (20 June) Victoria becomes queen of England
1838	lives in Florida			(27 May) Joseph H. Twichell is born; (13 June) brother Henry Clemens is born; (18 Jul) Helen V. Kercheval is born	Charles Dickens, *Nicholas Nickleby*; E. A. Poe, *Arthur Gordon Pym*; (26 Mar.) W. E. H. Lecky is born	transatlantic steamship service begins; (21 Apr.) naturalist John Muir is born; (28 May) Victoria is crowned queen of Britain
1839	lives in Florida; (Nov.) John M. Clemens sells his Florida property, moves family to Hannibal			(17 Aug.) sister Margaret Clemens dies; (15 Oct 1839) Norval Brady is born	H. W. Longfellow, *Voices of the Night*; Frederick Marryat, *Diary in America*	(1 Mar.) Hannibal is incorporated as a town; (Nov.) abolitionists form national party
1840	lives in Hannibal, Mo.	(c. Apr.) begins attending first school in Hannibal		(1 Jan.) H. H. Rogers is born; (27 Sep.) Thomas Nast is born	J. F. Cooper, *The Pathfinder*; R. H. Dana, Jr., *Two Years Before the Mast*; (2 Apr.) Emile Zola is born; (2 June) Thomas Hardy is born	(27 Sep.) Edward Whymper is born; (Nov.) William Henry Harrison is elected president
1841	lives in Hannibal; (13 Oct.) John M. and Jane L. Clemens transfer titles of Hannibal property bought from Ira Stout two years earlier to James Kerr			Jane L. Clemens joins Presbyterian church; (28 Jan.) H. M. Stanley is born; (Sep.) John M. Clemens sits in circuit court jury that sends abolitionists to prison	R. W. Emerson, *Essays*; J. F. Cooper, *The Deerslayer*; Dickens, *Barnaby Rudge*; *Punch* begins in London	(4 Mar.) Pres. W. H. Harrison is inaugurated; (4 Apr.) Harrison dies and John Tyler becomes president
1842	lives in Hannibal			(approx.) Orion Clemens begins working in St. Louis; (Jan.) John M. Clemens trades a slave for 10 barrels of tar; (12 May) brother Benjamin Clemens dies; (Oct.) James Paige is born	Dickens, *American Notes*; Alfred, Lord Tennyson, *Morte d'Arthur and Other Idylls*; (11 Jan.) William James is born; (24 June) Ambrose Bierce is born	(May) John C. Frémont begins four-year exploration of the Rocky Mountains; (28 July) solar eclipse is observed over the United States
1843	lives in Hannibal; (c. June–Aug.) spends the first of about five consecutive summers on the Quarles family farm near Florida	(Sep.) stumbles over corpse of a murder victim in his father's office		John M. Clemens is elected justice of the peace	Charles Dickens, *A Christmas Carol*; (15 Apr.) Henry James is born	large-scale westward migration begins; (1 July) U. S. Grant graduates from West Point

Year	Residences & travel	Personal & business	Writing & publishing	Family & friends	Literary events	Historical events
1844	lives in Hannibal	(Apr.) contracts measles by climbing into Will Bowen's sickbed during epidemic	EVENTS IN HIS FICTION: (summer) approximate time period of *Tom Sawyer*	grandmother Pamela Goggin Clemens dies; (Sep.) John M. Clemens becomes justice of the peace; (12 Oct.) G. W. Cable is born	Alexandre Dumas, *The Count of Monte Cristo*; Charles Dickens, *Martin Chuzzlewit*; (16 Apr.) Anatole France is born; (11 Sep.) Basil Hall dies	(24 May) Samuel Morse sends first telegraphic message; (27 June) Joseph Smith is murdered in Illinois; (22 Oct.) Millerites await the world's end on Hannibal's Lover's Leap; (12 Nov.) James K. Polk is elected president
1845	lives in Hannibal; takes first steamboat ride, to St. Louis; (21 Feb.) Missouri charters Hannibal as a city	(24 Jan.) sees William P. Owsley murder Samuel Smarr	EVENTS IN HIS FICTION: approximate period of *Huckleberry Finn*; (fall) Percy Driscoll and Col. Essex die in *Pudd'nhead Wilson*	(c. 6 Nov.) Hannibal town drunk Jimmy Finn dies; (27 Nov.) Olivia Langdon (Clemens) is born in Elmira, N.Y.	J. J. Hooper, *Some Adventures of Captain Simon Suggs*; Benjamin Disraeli, *Sybil, or the Two Nations*; (23 Oct.) Sarah Bernhardt is born	Irish potato famines accelerate migration to America; (4 Mar.) Pres. James Polk is inaugurated; (29 Dec.) Texas joins the Union
1846	lives in Hannibal; family sells its furniture to raise money			(Sep.) John M. Clemens tries to sell his Tennessee Land; (Nov.) chairs committee promoting road to St. Joseph; (Nov.) becomes candidate for circuit court clerk	J. G. Whittier, *Voices of Freedom*; Herman Melville, *Typee*; (15 Aug.) California's first newspaper begins publication in Monterey	Neptune is discovered; (26 Feb.) Buffalo Bill Cody is born; (13 May) U.S. declares war on Mexico; (14 Jun.) Americans in California revolt against Mexican rule; (28 Dec.) Iowa becomes the 29th state
1847	lives in Hannibal; (12 Apr.) Orion Clemens leases Hannibal home property from James Clemens	(spring) works at odd jobs; (14 Apr.) begins attending John D. Dawson's school; (Aug.) with John Briggs and others, finds a fugitive slave's corpse; (fall) works for the Hannibal *Gazette*	EVENTS IN HIS FICTION: approximate time when *The Gilded Age* opens	(24 Mar.) John M. Clemens dies; (23 Apr.) court names Orion Clemens administrator of father's estate; (Aug.–Sep.) Clint Levering and "Dutchy" drown in Hannibal	Herman Melville, *Omoo*; H. W. Longfellow, *Evangeline*; Charlotte Brontë, *Jane Eyre*; Bram Stoker is born	Missouri charters Hannibal–St. Joseph railroad; (11 Feb.) Thomas A. Edison is born; (24 July) Mormons enter Salt Lake Valley; (5 Sep.) Jesse James is born
1848	lives in Hannibal; (summer) moves into Joseph Ament's home	(c. 30 May) goes to work as apprentice for Joseph Ament's *Missouri Courier*	EVENTS IN HIS FICTION: approximate time of "Tom Sawyer's Conspiracy" and "Huck Finn & Tom Sawyer Among the Indians"	(c. Dec.) Tom Nash is permanently crippled by fall through broken ice on the Mississippi	Emily Brontë, *Wuthering Heights*; William Makepeace Thackeray, *Vanity Fair*; (9 Aug.) Frederick Marryat dies; (8 Dec.) J. C. Harris is born; (19 Dec.) Emily Brontë dies	(24 Jan.) discovery of gold in northern California begins Gold Rush; (2 Feb.) Mexican War ends; (7 Nov.) Zachary Taylor is elected president
1849	lives in Hannibal	(approx.) stops attending school regularly; (June) cholera epidemic hits Hannibal region		(13 Aug.) brother-in-law Charles Jervis Langdon is born; (15 Nov.) Dick Stoker arrives at Jackass Hill	Henry David Thoreau, "Civil Disobedience"; Francis Parkman, *The Oregon Trail*; Dickens, *David Copperfield*; (28 May) Anne Brontë dies; (3 Sep.) Sarah Orne Jewett is born; (7 Oct.) E. A. Poe dies	Pacific Railroad is chartered in Missouri; (28 Feb.) first ship of gold seekers lands in San Francisco; (5 Mar.) Pres. Zachary Taylor takes office; (17 May) fire ravages St. Louis, Mo.
1850	lives in Hannibal	(c. Apr.) joins Cadets of Temperance; (Sep.) works on Orion's newspapers; (c. 19 May) sees Melicent Holliday shoot an intruder; (c. Dec.) yellow fever epidemic hits Hannibal	EVENTS IN HIS FICTION: approximate time period of *Tom Sawyer Abroad*	(3 May) Orion Clemens sells part of the family's Tennessee Land; (summer) Orion returns to Hannibal and starts the *Western Union*; (21 June) Dan Beard is born	Nathaniel Hawthorne, *The Scarlet Letter*; (26 Mar.) Edward Bellamy is born; (13 Nov.) R. L. Stevenson is born	(27 Jan.) Samuel L. Gompers is born; (9 July) Millard Fillmore succeeds Zachary Taylor as president; (9 Sep.) California becomes a state

Year	Residences & travel	Personal & business	Writing & publishing	Family & friends	Literary events	Historical events
1851	lives in Hannibal; (June) cholera epidemic hits Hannibal	(Jan.) begins working for his brother Orion as a printer; (29 Dec.) runs newspaper while Orion is away	PUBLISHES: sketches in Philadelphia's *Saturday Evening Post*; (16 Jan.) "A Gallant Fireman," in the *Western Union*	(Sep.) Orion Clemens buys Hannibal *Journal* and merges it with the *Western Union*; (c. 20 Sep.) sister Pamela marries William A. Moffett; (24 Sep.) Charles L. Webster is born	Nathaniel Hawthorne, *The House of the Seven Gables*; Harriet Beecher Stowe, *Uncle Tom's Cabin* (serial); Herman Melville, *Moby Dick*; (8 Feb.) Kate Chopin is born; (21 Feb.) Mary Shelley dies; (14 Sep.) J. F. Cooper dies	(8 July) solar eclipse is observed over the United States; (25 Aug.) Ballarat strike begins Australian gold rush
1852	lives in Hannibal	occasionally runs newspaper while Orion is away	writes for the Hannibal *Journal*. PUBLISHES: (May) "The Dandy Frightening the Squatter" in the *Carpet-Bag*; (Sep.) uses first pen name, "W. Epaminondas Adrastus Perkins"	(29 Apr.) uncle John Quarles sells Florida, Mo. farm; (1 July) niece Annie E. Moffett is born; (23 Sep.) Carroll Beckwith is born	William Makepeace Thackeray, *History of Henry Esmond*; Ivan Turgenev, *A Sportsman's Sketches*; (Dec.) the *Golden Era* begins publication	(26 Feb.) *Birkenhead* sinks off South Africa (called "*Berkeley Castle*" in *What Is Man?*); (3 Jul.) Congress votes to establish a mint in San Francisco; (2 Nov.) Franklin Pierce is elected president; (2 Dec.) Louis Napoleon proclaims himself Emperor Napoleon III
1853	(June–Aug.) leaves Hannibal for St. Louis; (19–24 Aug.) goes to New York City; (24 Aug.–c. 20 Oct.) works in New York City; (c. 20 Oct.–Feb. 1854) works in Philadelphia	(before 5 Mar.) fire guts Orion Clemens's newspaper office; (6–13 May) runs the Hannibal *Journal* while Orion is away; (June–Dec.) works as itinerant printer in St. Louis, New York City and Philadelphia	(Dec.) corresponds for Muscatine *Journal* from Philadelphia. PUBLISHES: (May) poems in the Hannibal *Journal*. EVENTS IN HIS FICTION: (June) Capello twins arrive at Dawson's Landing in *Pudd'nhead Wilson*; (19 Dec.) train of "Cannibalism in the Cars" is snowbound	(7 Jan. 1853) Karl Gerhardt is born; (23 Jan.) Hannibal town drunk dies in jailhouse fire; (22 Sep.) Orion Clemens sells the *Journal* and moves to Muscatine, Iowa	William Lewis Herndon, *Exploration of the Valley of the Amazon*; Nathaniel Hawthorne, *Tanglewood Tales*; Charles Kingsley, *Hypatia*	Nook Farm is founded at Hartford, Conn.; (4 Mar.) Pres. Franklin Pierce is inaugurated; (14 July) New York City's Crystal Palace exhibition opens; (23 Sep.) Crimean War begins
1854	(Jan.) works in Philadelphia; (c. 16 Feb.) visits Washington, D.C.; (c. Mar.) returns to New York City; (spring) goes to Muscatine, Iowa; (summer–June 1855) lives in St. Louis	works as *jour* printer	writes travel letters to Orion's newspaper	(19 Dec.) Orion Clemens marries Mary Eleanor Stotts	B. P. Shillaber, *Life and Sayings of Mrs. Partington*; Charlotte Yonge, *The Little Duke*; Henry David Thoreau, *Walden*; (16 Oct.) Oscar Wilde is born	Crimean War continues; (28 Feb.) Republican Party is formed at Ripon, Wis.
1855	(Jan.–June) in St. Louis; (June) goes to Keokuk, Iowa; (June–July) visits Hannibal and Florida, Mo.	(c. 15 July) makes first attempt to become a pilot	writes occasional travel letters to Orion's newspapers	(June) Orion Clemens moves to Keokuk, Iowa, and buys a printing office; (14 Sep.) niece Jennie Clemens is born	Q. K. Philander Doesticks, *Doesticks: What He Says*; Walt Whitman, *Leaves of Grass*; Frederick Douglass, *Autobiography*; H. W. Longfellow, *The Song of Hiawatha*; (31 Mar.) Charlotte Brontë dies	Elmira Female College opens; (2 Mar.) Alexander II becomes emperor of Russia
1856	(Jan.–Sep.) lives in Keokuk, Ia.; (c. 15–24 Oct.) moves from Keokuk to Cincinnati, Ohio	(17 Jan.) gives first public speech, at printers banquet in Keokuk; (5 Aug.) announces that will go to the Amazon	(Oct.–Nov.) writes "Thomas Jefferson Snodgrass" letters for the Keokuk *Daily Post*	(17 Mar.) Katy Leary is born	(15 May) L. Frank Baum is born; (26 July) G. B. Shaw is born; (1 Dec.) San Francisco *Morning Call* is founded	(1 Feb.) Crimean War ends; (21 Apr.) the first railroad bridge across the Mississippi River connects Rock Island, Ill., and Davenport, Iowa; (4 Nov.) James Buchanan is elected president

Year	Residences & travel	Personal & business	Writing & publishing	Family & friends	Literary events	Historical events
1857	(Jan.–Feb.), lives in Cincinnati boarding house; (28 Feb.) leaves Cincinnati for New Orleans aboard the steamboat Paul Jones; (Apr.–Dec.) lives on the Mississippi River	(4–11 Mar.) is a cub pilot on the Paul Jones; (Apr.–Dec.) cubs on the Crescent City, Rufus J. Lackland, John J. Roe, William M. Morrison, Pennsylvania and D. A. January	(14 Mar.) writes last "Thomas Jefferson Snodgrass" letter		Gustave Flaubert, Madame Bovary; Thomas Hughes, Tom Brown's Schooldays; (Nov.) Atlantic Monthly begins publication; (3 Dec.) Joseph Conrad is born	(4 Mar.) Pres. James Buchanan is inaugurated; (6 Mar.) Dred Scott decision voids Missouri Compromise; (10 May) Indian Mutiny; (11 Sep.) Mountain Meadows Massacre in Utah
1858	lives on the Mississippi River; (Jan.) on the New Falls City; (Feb.–June) Pennsylvania; (July?) Alfred T. Lacey; (Aug.) John H. Dickey; (Dec.) White Cloud and New Falls City; (Dec.) Aleck Scott	(May) is infatuated with Laura Wright; (c. June) observes Donati's comet; (5 June) after fighting with pilot William Brown, leaves the Pennsylvania in New Orleans—eight days before its boilers explode		(Feb.) Henry Clemens becomes a mud clerk on the steamboat Pennsylvania; (21 June) Henry dies from injuries in the Pennsylvania explosion; (7 Dec.) Susan Langdon marries Theodore Crane	O. W. Holmes, The Autocrat of the Breakfast Table; H. W. Longfellow, The Courtship of Miles Standish; Charles Darwin, Origin of the Species; (18 Dec.) Territorial Enterprise begins publication in Genoa, Nev.	(Aug.) first transatlantic cable is completed; (9 Oct.) Overland Mail stage connects San Francisco and St. Louis; (27 Oct.) Theodore Roosevelt is born
1859	lives on the Mississippi River; (May–Oct.) pilots on the Alfred T. Lacey, J. C. Swon, Edward J. Gay and A. B. Chambers	(9 Apr.) receives steamboat piloting license; works steadily on the river	PUBLISHES: (17 May) "River Intelligence" by "Sergeant Fathom" in New Orleans Crescent		Dickens, A Tale of Two Cities; Alfred, Lord Tennyson, Idylls of the King; (22 May) A. Conan Doyle is born; (28 Nov.) Washington Irving dies	railroad links Hannibal to St. Joseph, Mo.; (28 Jan.) Nevada's Comstock Lode is discovered; (30 July) Hank Monk takes Horace Greeley on immortal stagecoach ride; (16 Oct.) John Brown raids Harpers Ferry
1860	lives on the Mississippi River; (25 Mar.–July) pilots on the City of Memphis; (July) visits Keokuk; (28 July–31 Aug.) on the Arago; (19 Sep.) joins his last steamboat, the Alonzo Child	(26 Dec.) petitions St. Louis Masonic lodge for membership; (Mar.) renews piloting license	PUBLISHES: (30 Aug.) "Pilot's Memoranda" in St. Louis Missouri Republican	Olivia Langdon receives water cure treatment; (5 Nov.) nephew Samuel E. Moffett is born	George Eliot, The Mill on the Floss; (17 Jan.) Anton Chekhov is born; (9 May) James Barrie is born; (c. Nov.) Territorial Enterprise moves to Virginia City, Nev.	(3 Apr.) Pony Express begins; (6 Nov.) Abraham Lincoln is elected president; (20 Dec.) South Carolina secedes from the Union
1861	(24–29 Jan.) in New Orleans on the Alonzo Child; (25 Apr.) at St. Louis; (late Apr.) visits Hannibal; (8 May) returns to New Orleans on the Child; (c. 14–21 May) returns to St. Louis as passenger on the Nebraska; (18 July) goes to St. Joseph with brother Orion; (26 July –14 Aug.) goes to Nevada, by stagecoach; (Sep.) visits Esmeralda; (Dec.) prospects at Unionville	(20 Mar.) renews piloting license; (c. 25 Apr.) piloting career ends when the Civil War stops river traffic; (21 May) joins St. Louis Masonic lodge; (June) campaigns with Confederate irregulars around Marion County; (c. 6 Aug.) meets Brigham Young; (1 Oct.–29 Nov.) clerks for Nevada Territorial Legislature	(Jan.–June) writes story on ghost life on the Mississippi	(27 Mar.) Pres. Abraham Lincoln signs Orion Clemens's commission as secretary to the Nevada Territory; (Apr.) Joseph Twichell enlists as regimental chaplain of the 71st New York Infantry; (10 July) A. B. Paine is born	Charles Dickens, Great Expectations; George Eliot, Silas Marner; Charles Reade, The Cloister and the Hearth; (18 Jan.) E. W. Kemble is born; (21 Mar.) Petroleum V. Nasby letters begin; (24 Sep.) Territorial Enterprise begins daily publication	(Jan.) five Southern states secede; (18 Feb.) Confederacy organizes; (23 Feb.) Texas secedes; (2 Mar.) Nevada and Dakota become territories; (4 Mar.) Lincoln is inaugurated; (12 Apr.) Civil War begins; (8 July) James W. Nye begins organizing Nevada Territory; (30 Aug.) Union proclaims martial law in Missouri; (Oct.–Nov.) Nevada legislature convenes
1862	(c. 15–29 Jan.) goes from Unionville to Carson City with two companions; (Feb.–Aug.) mines at Aurora, Nev.; (Aug.) visits Mono Lake with Calvin Higbie; (Aug.) settles in Virginia City, Nev.	(Sep.–May 1864) works for Virginia City Territorial Enterprise; (Nov.–Dec.) covers the Nevada legislature for the Enterprise	PUBLISHES: (c. Apr.–Aug.) "Josh" in the Enterprise. (4 Oct.) "Petrified Man" hoax	(Mar.–June) Olivia Langdon is treated for partial paralysis; (12 Aug.) C. L. Webster accidentally kills another child; (27 Dec.–24 July 1863) Orion Clemens is acting governor of Nevada Territory	Victor Hugo, Les Misérables; Ivan Turgenev, Fathers and Sons; Artemus Ward, His Book; (24 Jan.) Edith Wharton is born; (6 May) Henry David Thoreau dies; (11 Sep.) O. Henry is born	(5 May) Mexico defeats French invasion force; (22 Feb.) Jefferson Davis is inaugurated president of the Confederacy; (9 Mar.) Monitor and Merrimac meet; (25 Apr.) Admiral Farragut occupies New Orleans; (17 Sep.) Battle of Antietam

Year	Residences & travel	Personal & business	Writing & publishing	Family & friends	Literary events	Historical events
1863	lives in Virginia City, Nev.; (May–July) visits San Francisco; (c. Aug.) visits Lake Tahoe; (Sep.) visits San Francisco	(2 Feb.) adopts pen name "Mark Twain"; (8 July) speaks at Virginia City hotel opening; (26 July) loses possessions in Virginia City hotel fire; (11 Dec.) addresses Nevada legislature's "Third House"	(c. June) writes occasionally for *San Francisco Call.* PUBLISHES: (20 Sep.) "Curing a Cold"; (26 Oct.–mid-Dec.) reports on Nevada Constitutional Convention; (28 Oct.) massacre hoax	(12 Nov.) Olivia Langdon begins keeping a commonplace book; (22–24 Dec.) Artemus Ward visits Virginia City	Jules Verne, *Five Weeks in a Balloon*; Charles Kingsley, *The Water Babies*; (20 Sep.) Jacob Grimm dies; (24 Dec.) William Makepeace Thackeray dies	(1 Jan.) Emancipation Proclamation; (18 May–4 July) siege of Vicksburg; (1–3 July) Battle of Gettysburg; (16 Oct.) Grant takes command of the Union's western armies; (19 Nov.) Lincoln speaks at Gettysburg
1864	(29 May) leaves Nevada with Steve Gillis; (May–Dec.) lives in San Francisco; (Dec.–Feb. 1865) prospects in Tuolumne and Calaveras counties	(Jan.) elected "Governor of the Third House" by Nevada journalists; (summer) meets Bret Harte; (c. 6 June–10 Oct.) works for *San Francisco Morning Call*; (12 June) delivers presentation speech at Maguire's Opera House	PUBLISHES: (Feb.) sketches in the *New York Mercury*; (Oct.–Dec.) "Whereas" ("Aurelia's Unfortunate Young Man"), "The Killing of Julius Caesar 'Localized'" and "Lucretia Smith's Soldier"	(1 Feb.) niece Jennie Clemens dies; (Feb.–Mar.) Adah Isaacs Menken visits Virginia City; (6 Mar.) Capt. Isaiah Sellers dies; (May) Reuel Gridley auctions flour sack in Nevada to raise money for the Sanitary Commission	D. R. Locke, *The Nasby Papers*; Dickens, *Our Mutual Friend*; Verne, *A Journey to the Center of the Earth*; John Ross Browne, *Crusoe's Island*; (19 May) Nathaniel Hawthorne dies; (28 May) C. H. Webb founds the *Californian* in San Francisco	(10 Mar.) Grant takes command of all Union troops; (10 Apr.) France makes Maximilian emperor of Mexico; (31 Oct.) Nevada becomes a state; (4 Nov.) Lincoln is reelected; (10 Dec.) Sherman's army reaches Savannah, Ga.
1865	(22 Jan.–late Feb.) stays at Angel's Camp; (25 Feb.–Mar. 1866) lives in San Francisco	(8 Feb.) participates in Masonic meeting at Angels Camp, Calif.; (Jan.) pocket-mines at Angel's Camp, Calif.; (8 Nov.) feels earthquake in San Francisco	writes for San Francisco publications; (Feb.) begins jumping frog story. PUBLISHES: (May) "Advice for Good Little Girls"; (July) "Advice for Good Little Boys"; (Nov.) "Jim Smiley and His Jumping Frog"	(2 Jan.) William Dean Phelps is born; (3 June) Dr. J. R. Newton treats Olivia Langdon; (4 Aug.) brother-in-law William A. Moffett dies; (13 Dec.) Joseph Twichell becomes pastor of Hartford's Asylum Hill Church	Josh Billings, *His Sayings*; Lewis Carroll, *Alice in Wonderland*; Leo Tolstoy, *War and Peace*; Mary Elizabeth Dodge, *Hans Brinker*; Charlotte Yonge, *The Prince and the Page*; (30 Dec.) Rudyard Kipling is born	(4 Mar.) Lincoln begins second term; (9 Apr.) Civil War ends; (14 Apr.) J. W. Booth shoots Lincoln; (14 July) Edward Whymper ascends Matterhorn; (10 Dec.) Leopold II becomes king of Belgium; (18 Dec.) 13th Amendment ends slavery
1866	lives in San Francisco; (7 Mar.–July) sails to Hawaii as Sacramento *Union* correspondent; (19 July–13 Aug.) returns to San Francisco; (15 Dec.) sails for New York; (30 Dec.) crosses Isthmus of Nicaragua	(2 Oct.) gives first lecture on the Sandwich Islands in San Francisco; (11 Oct.–27 Nov.) on 16-engagement lecture tour in northern California and western Nevada; (Dec.) meets Capt. Edgar Wakeman	(20 Dec.) writes first of 26 letters to *Alta California*, from aboard the *America* in the Pacific. PUBLISHES: (19 July) *Hornet* account of the *Hornet* disaster	(c. May) Orion Clemens leaves Nevada; (10 Oct.) Olivia Langdon undergoes Swedish Movement Cure in New York City	W. D. Howells, *Venetian Life*; Fyodor Dostoyevsty, *Crime and Punishment*; T. J. Dimsdale, *Vigilantes of Montana*; (21 Sep.) H. G. Wells is born	Reconstruction Era begins in the South; (3 May) clipper ship *Hornet* sinks in the Pacific; (29 May) Hawaii's Princess Victoria Kamamalu dies
1867	(1–12 Jan.) sails to New York; (Jan.–June) lives in New York City; (c. 5 Mar.–15 Apr.) visits Midwest; (10 June) sails on the *Quaker City*; (20–23 June) at the Azores; (29 June–1 July) Gibraltar; (4–13 July) France; (14 July–11 Aug.) Italy; (14 Aug.) Greece; (17 Aug.) Turkey; (21–28 Aug.) Russia; (30 Aug.–7 Sep.) Turkey; (10–30 Sep.) Holy Land; (2–7 Oct.) Egypt; (c. 18–25 Oct.) Spain; (11–15 Nov.) Bermuda; (19 Nov.) New York City; (Nov. 1867–late Feb. 1868) lives in Washington, D.C.; (late Dec.) revisits New York City	(1 Mar.) signs up for *Quaker City* cruise; (26 Mar.) meets H. M. Stanley in St. Louis; (early May) spends a night in a New York jail; (25 Mar.–9 Apr.) on lecture tour in Midwest; (6 May) delivers first New York City lecture at Cooper's Union; (late Nov. 1867–Feb. 1868) private secretary to Sen. William M. Stewart; meets U. S. Grant; (27 Dec.) meets Olivia (Livy) Langdon in New York City; (c. 31 Dec.) takes Livy to hear Charles Dickens read	writes travel letters to the *Alta California*; (June–Oct.) writes travel letters from the *Quaker City* excursion. PUBLISHES: (May) *The Celebrated Jumping Frog of Calaveras County, and Other Sketches*; (1 Dec.) is invited by Elisha Bliss, Jr. to write a book on *Quaker City* voyage	(Mar.) Orion Clemens revisits his birthplace, Gainesboro, Tenn.	Bret Harte, *Condensed Novels*; Horatio Alger, Jr., *Ragged Dick*; O. W. Holmes, *The Guardian Angel*; A. D. Richardson, *Beyond the Mississippi*; Karl Marx, *Das Kapital*; (7 Feb.) Laura Wilder is born; (6 Mar.) Artemus Ward dies; (27 May) Arnold Bennett is born; (14 Aug.) John Galsworthy is born; (19 Nov.) Dickens begins final American tour	(1 Mar.) Nebraska joins the Union; (30 Mar.) U.S. purchases Alaska; (19 June) Mexican troops execute Maximilian; (1 July) Canada becomes a Dominion within the British empire; (27 Oct.) Garibaldi begins march on Rome

Year	Residences & travel	Personal & business	Writing & publishing	Family & friends	Literary events	Historical events
1868	(Jan.–late Feb.) lives in Washington, D.C.; (late Jan.) visits Hartford, Conn.; (11 Mar.–2 Apr.) sails to California; (c. 22 Apr.) lectures in northern California and western Nevada; (6–29 July) returns to New York; (Aug.–Nov.) moves between Washington, New York City, Elmira and Hartford; (17 Nov.–3 Mar. 1869) lectures through the East	(5 Jan.) meets Harriet Beecher Stowe; (late Jan.) meets Joseph Twichell; (May) sees hanging in Virginia City, Nev.; (24 May) meets Ned Buntline; (2 July) gives farewell lecture in San Francisco; (Aug.–Sep.) courts Livy in Elmira; (26 Nov.) is secretly engaged to Livy; (16 Oct.) signs book contract with Bliss	(May–June) completes *Innocents Abroad*; (4 Aug.) delivers manuscript to Bliss; (c. Oct.) writes "Boy's Manuscript." PUBLISHES: (Feb.) "The Man Who Put Up at Gadsby's"; (Feb.) "The Facts Concerning the Recent Resignation"; (May) "My Late Senatorial Secretaryship"; (Nov.) "Cannibalism in the Cars"	(14 Aug.) John Mead Howells is born	Louis May Alcott, *Little Women*; Bret Harte, *The Luck of Roaring Camp*; Fyodor Dostoyevsky, *The Idiot*; James Redpath forms lecture bureau; (23 Feb.) W. E. B. Du Bois is born; (14 Mar.) Maxim Gorky is born; (July) *Overland Monthly* begins publication	(24 Feb.) House of Representatives votes to impeach Andrew Johnson; (28 July) 14th Amendment grants citizenship to former slaves; (3 Nov.) U. S. Grant is elected president
1869	(Jan.–Mar.) continues lecture tour in Midwest; (May–June) visits Elmira and Hartford; (Aug.–Oct.) rooms in Buffalo, N.Y.; (Nov.–Dec.) visits Boston	(Jan.) falls on ice in Iowa City; (4 Feb.) engagement to Livy is formally announced; (12 Aug.) buys interest in the Buffalo *Express*; (1 Nov. 1869–21 Jan. 1870) on 45-engagement lecture tour; (Nov.) meets W. D. Howells in Boston	(May–June) corrects *Innocents Abroad* galleys. PUBLISHES: (July) *Innocents Abroad*; (Aug.–Oct.) "A Day at Niagara," "Journalism in Tennessee," "Legend of the Capitoline Venus," "Around the World" letters, etc. in the Buffalo *Express*	(4 Oct.) Charles Langdon leaves on round-the-world trip	Thomas B. Aldrich, *The Story of a Bad Boy*; Charles Dickens, *Mystery of Edwin Drood*; W. E. H. Lecky, *A History of European Morals*; Bret Harte, *The Outcasts of Poker Flat*; (2 Dec.) A. D. Richardson dies	(4 Mar.) Pres. U. S Grant is inaugurated; (10 May) Union and Pacific railways meet at Promontory Point, Utah; (15 Oct.) "Cardiff Giant" is unearthed in New York; (17 Nov.) Suez Canal opens
1870	(4–21 Jan.) completes lecture tour in New York; (3 Feb. 1870–Mar. 1871) lives in Buffalo, N.Y.; (5 July) visits Washington, D.C.; (Oct.) visits Fredonia	(Jan.) sues C. H. Webb over copyright of jumping frog book; (2 Feb.) marries Olivia Langdon in Elmira; (July) is photographed by Mathew Brady; (15 July) contracts with Elisha Bliss to write *Roughing It*; (Dec.) settles dispute with Webb	(27 Aug.) begins *Roughing It*. PUBLISHES: "A Medieval Romance," "A Curious Dream," "A Ghost Story," etc. the Buffalo *Express*; (May 1870–Mar. 1871) monthly column for the *Galaxy* includes "Political Economy," "Goldsmith's Friend Abroad Again," and "How I Edited an Agricultural Paper Once"	(23 Feb.) Anson Burlingame dies; (6 Aug.) Jervis Langdon dies; (29 Sep.) Emma Nye dies in Mark Twain's home; (12 Oct.) Charles Langdon marries Ida B. Clark; (7 Nov.) first child, Langdon Clemens, is born prematurely in Buffalo; (24 Nov.) Reuel Gridley dies; (13 Dec.) Orion Clemens begins working for Elisha Bliss	Bret Harte, *The Luck of Roaring Camp*; C. D. Warner, *My Summer in a Garden*; John Hays, *Castilian Days*; Jules Verne, *Twenty Thousand Leagues Under the Sea*; (5 Mar.) Frank Norris is born; (9 June) Charles Dickens dies; (5 Dec.) Alexandre Dumas (père) dies; (18 Dec.) H. H. Munro ("Saki") is born	(Jan.) Thomas Nast begins attacking Boss Tweed in *Harper's Weekly* cartoons; (19 July) Franco-Prussian War begins; (27 Sep.) Henry Comstock commits suicide in Montana; (12 Oct.) Robert E. Lee dies; (Nov.) Laura D. Fair's first murder trial begins in California; (Dec.) diamonds are discovered in South Africa
1871	(Jan.–Mar.) lives in Buffalo; (18 Mar.–Sep.) stays in Elmira with family while looking for home in Hartford and visiting New York City and Washington, D.C., on business; (1 Oct.) rents house in Hartford's Nook Farm; (16 Oct.–Mar. 1872) on lecture tour through the East	(7 Jan.–Aug.) sends J. H. Riley to South Africa to gather material for book on diamond fields; (2 Mar.) puts Buffalo home and newspaper interests up for sale; (Nov.) meets Thomas B. Aldrich; (31 Dec.) meets "Sociable Jimmy" in Paris, Ill.	(Jan.) assembles *Sketches, New and Old*; (15 May) considers himself "half done" with *Roughing It*; (8 Aug.) delivers first draft of *Roughing It* to Bliss. PUBLISHES: (Feb.) *Mark Twain's (Burlesque) Autobiography*; (Dec.) *Roughing It*	(Feb.) Livy contracts typhoid fever; (Mar.–Apr.) Joseph T. Goodman visits Hartford; (17 Sep.) J. H. Riley dies; (21 Nov.) Livy's niece Julia Langdon is born	Joaquin Miller, *Songs of the Sierras*; Lewis Carroll, *Through the Looking-Glass*; George Eliot, *Middlemarch*; Walt Whitman, *Democratic Vistas*; (Feb.) Bret Harte moves to the East Coast; (summer) W. D. Howells becomes editor of the *Atlantic*; (1 Nov.) Stephen Crane is born	(28 Jan.) Crimean War ends; (22 Feb.) *Quaker City* sinks near Bermuda; (27 Oct.) Boss Tweed is arrested for fraud; (10 Nov.) H. M. Stanley meets David Livingstone in western Tanzania
1872	lives in Hartford; (Jan.) lectures in Midwest and East; (Mar.) in Elmira with family; (May) visits Mary Fairbanks in Cleveland; (July–Aug.) vacations at New Saybrook, Conn.; (21 Aug.–26 Nov.) goes to England alone	(12 Mar.) discusses Orion Clemens's fraud charges with Elisha Bliss; (Sep.) speaks in London; (Sep.–Oct.) meets with Charles Kingsley, Charles Reade, H. M. Stanley and John Ross Browne	(Sep.–Oct.) collects notes for proposed book on England. PUBLISHES: (Feb.) *Roughing It*. EVENT IN HIS FICTION: (9 June) date of Charlie Williams's bogus letter in *Life on the Mississippi*	James W. Paige files patent application for typesetting machine; (Mar.) Orion Clemens returns to Keokuk; (19 Mar.) daughter Susy Clemens is born in Elmira; (2 June) Langdon Clemens dies in Hartford	W. D. Howells, *Their Wedding Journey*; Samuel Butler, *Erewhon*; Jules Verne, *Around the World in Eighty Days*; Thomas Hardy, *Under the Greenwood Tree*; (31 Jan.) Zane Grey is born	(6 Mar.) first Tichborne trial ends in London; (Sep.) Laura D. Fair is acquitted in second murder trial; (5 Nov.) Pres. Grant is reelected over Horace Greeley; (19 Nov.) Boss Tweed is convicted of fraud; (29 Nov.) Greeley dies

Year	Residences & travel	Personal & business	Writing & publishing	Family & friends	Literary events	Historical events
1873	lives in Hartford; (16 Jan.) signs deed to Nook Farm property in Hartford; (22 Mar.) adds strip of land to property; (17 May–2 Nov.) goes to England with family; (late July–Sep.) visits Scotland and Ireland; (c. 8 Nov.–Jan. 1874) returns to England with C. W. Stoddard for lecture tour	(Feb.) joins Hartford's Monday Evening Club; (10 June) attends Tichborne Claimant trial in London; (June–July) meets Robert Browning, Ivan Turgenev, Herbert Spencer, Anthony Trollope, Lewis Carroll, and other literary figures in London; (24 June) patents self-pasting scrapbook; (Aug.) meets Dr. John Brown in Edinburgh, Scotland; (Oct.–Dec.) lectures in England	(Jan.–Apr.) writes The Gilded Age with C. D. Warner. PUBLISHES: (Mar.) J. C. Hotten's pirated edition of The Choice Humorous Works of Mark Twain; (July) "Shah Letters" in the New York Herald; (Dec.) The Gilded Age. DRAMATIC ADAPTATION: (18 Feb.) John Augustin Daly opens Roughing It in New York City	Abraham A. Z. Curry dies	J. S. Mill, Autobiography; Leo Tolstoy, Anna Karenina; (15 Jan.) Edward Bulwer Lytton dies; (8 May) J. S. Mill dies; (14 June) John Camden Hotten dies	(Jan.) Kansas senator Samuel C. Pomeroy is accused of bribery; (9 Jan.) Napoleon III dies; (4 Mar.) Pres. Grant begins his second term; (Apr.) second Tichborne trial opens in London; (Sep.) financial panic closes American stock exchanges for 10 days
1874	lives in Hartford; (13–26 Jan.) sails from England to Boston; (Apr.) goes to Elmira with family; (25 June–c. 15 July) in Hartford; (c. Aug.) visits family in Fredonia, N.Y.; (19 Sep.) family moves into unfinished Hartford house	(8–9 Jan.) lectures in Leicester and Liverpool, England; (June) pays Gilbert B. Densmore $400 for script of play about Col. Sellers; (Sep.) begins rehearsing The Gilded Age in New York City; (12 Nov.) with Twichell, begins hiking to Boston from Hartford; ends up taking a train; (15 Dec.) attends Atlantic banquet	(June) begins writing Tom Sawyer; (late Oct.) begins writing "Old Times on the Mississippi." PUBLISHES: (Apr.) authorized edition of Choice Humorous Works; (July) "A Curious Pleasure Excursion"; (Nov.) "A True Story"; (Nov.) "Sociable Jimmy"; etc. DRAMATIC ADAPTATION: (16 Sep. 1874–Jan. 1875) The Gilded Age runs in New York City	(Feb.) Joe Goodman sells the Territorial Enterprise; (Mar.) W. D. Howells, Thomas B. Aldrich and James Osgood visit Nook Farm; (8 June) daughter Clara Clemens is born in Elmira; (Dec.) Paige gets his first typesetting machine patent	Thomas Hardy, Far from the Madding Crowd; (25 Jan.) W. Somerset Maugham is born; (3 Feb.) Gertrude Stein is born; (26 Mar.) Robert Frost is born; (29 May) G. K. Chesterton is born	(17 Jan.) Chang and Eng Bunker, the "Siamese Twins," die; (28 Feb.) the Tichborne claimant is convicted of perjury; (25 Oct.) Britain annexes Fiji; (30 Nov.) Winston Churchill is born on Mark Twain's 39th birthday
1875	lives in Hartford	(Apr.) attends H. W. Beecher trial in Brooklyn	(July) finishes writing Tom Sawyer; (5 Nov.) delivers Tom Sawyer to Elisha Bliss. PUBLISHES: (Jan.–June and Aug.) "Old Times on the Mississippi" (serial in the Atlantic Monthly); (July) Sketches, New and Old; (Oct.) "The Curious Republic of Gondour"	George Griffin becomes Clemens family butler; (8 May) Edgar Wakeman dies; (June) Dan De Quille writes book about the Comstock Lode in Hartford; (8 Sep.) Annie E. Moffett marries C. L. Webster	Mary Baker Eddy, Science and Health; (4 Aug.) H. C. Andersen dies	(11 Jan.–2 July) H. W. Beecher is tried for adultery in Brooklyn; (5 Apr.) P. T. Barnum is elected mayor of Bridgeport, Conn.; (26 Oct.) fire destroys Virginia City's business district
1876	lives in Hartford	(30 Sep.) speaks in behalf of Rutherford B. Hayes in Hartford; (c. 27 Oct.) helps form Hartford's Saturday Morning Club; (Nov.) does public readings from own works in Brooklyn, Boston, New York and Providence, R.I.; (30 Dec.) contracts with Bret Harte and Charles T. Parloe to produce Ah Sin	(June) writes 1601; begins research work for The Prince and the Pauper; begins Huckleberry Finn; (Oct.–Nov.) writes Ah Sin with Bret Harte. PUBLISHES: (Feb.) "A Literary Nightmare" ("Punch! Brothers, Punch!"); (June) "The Facts Concerning the Recent Carnival of Crime in Connecticut"; (9 June) Tom Sawyer (in London); (Dec.) "The Canvasser's Tale"; (Dec.) Tom Sawyer (in Hartford)	graves of John Marshall Clemens and Henry Clemens are moved in Hannibal; (18 Jan.) Moncure Conway visits Hartford; (25 Feb.) uncle John Adams Quarles dies; (Dec.) Bret Harte writes "Thankful Blossom" at Mark Twain's home	Dan De Quille, The Big Bonanza; C. D. Warner, My Winter on the Nile; (12 Jan.) Jack London is born; (8 June) George Sand dies	(10 Mar.) A. G. Bell achieves the first electric transmission of a human voice; (29 May) Turkey's Sultan Abdul Aziz is deposed; (25 June) Indians led by Chief Sitting Bull annihilate G. A. Custer's Seventh Cavalry at Little Big Horn, Mont.; (4 July) the United States celebrates its centennial birthday; (7 Nov.) national election for president leaves neither Rutherford B. Hayes nor Samuel Tilden a clear winner

Year	Residences & travel	Personal & business	Writing & publishing	Family & friends	Literary events	Historical events
1877	lives in Hartford; (late May) goes to Bermuda with Joseph Twichell; (June–Aug.) stays at Elmira with family, while making frequent trips to New York City and Hartford	(late July) rehearses *Ah Sin* in New York City; (late Nov. or Dec.) has telephone line to Hartford *Courant* installed in home; (17 Dec.) speaks at Boston banquet honoring Whittier's 70th birthday	(23 Nov.) outlines *The Prince and the Pauper.* PUBLISHES: (Sep.) *A True Story and the Recent Carnival of Crime.*; (Oct. 1877–Jan. 1878) "Some Rambling Notes of an Idle Excursion." DRAMATIC ADAPTATIONS: (7 May) *Ah Sin* opens in Washington, D.C.; (31 July–Sep.) *Ah Sin* runs in New York	(23 Aug.) John T. Lewis stops a runaway carriage at Elmira; (July) Thomas Nast turns down Mark Twain's offer to go on joint lecture tour	Henry James, *The American*; Sarah Orne Jewett, *Deephaven*; C. D. Warner, *In the Levant*	(5 Mar.) Pres. Rutherford B. Hayes is inaugurated after disputed election; (July–Aug.) coal miners and railroad workers strike; (29 Aug.) Brigham Young dies
1878	lives in Hartford; (11 Apr.) sails for Europe with family; (12 Apr.–11 Aug.) in Germany; (12 Aug.–16 Sep.) Swiss and French Alps; (16 Sep.–14 Nov.) Italy; (15 Nov. 1878–27 Feb. 1879) Munich, Germany	(8 Mar.) contracts with Frank Bliss for book about Europe; (4 July) speaks at Heidelberg University	(late Nov.) writes "The Stolen White Elephant"; PUBLISHES: (Mar.) "The Loves of Alonzo Fitz Clarence and Rosannah Ethelton"; (Mar.) *Punch, Brothers Punch! and Other Sketches*; (May) "About Magnanimous Incident Literature"	Sam Bowen dies; Bret Harte is appointed an American consul in Germany; (7 Feb.) son-in-law, Ossip Gabrilowitsch, is born; (19 Dec.) Bayard Taylor dies	Edgar Wakeman, *The Log of an Ancient Mariner*; W. E. H. Lecky, *A History of England in the XVIIIth Century*; Thomas Hardy, *The Return of the Native*; (6 Jan.) Carl Sandburg is born; (20 Sep.) Upton Sinclair is born	(12 Apr.) Boss Tweed dies in prison; (2 June) assassin wounds Kaiser Wilhelm I; (7 Nov.) theft of Alexander T. Stewart's corpse inspires Mark Twain's "The Stolen White Elephant"
1879	(28 Feb.–10 July) in Paris with family; (10–19 July) visits Belgium and the Netherlands; (20 July–23 Aug.) in England; (23 Aug.–3 Sep.) sails from Liverpool to New York City; (Sep.–Dec.) in Hartford; (Oct.) visits Elmira	makes balloon ascent in Paris; (21 Mar.) meets Pres. Léon Gambetta; (Apr.) gives "Some Thoughts on the Science of Onanism" speech; (summer) meets Henry James, James Whistler and Charles Darwin; (Oct.) promotes building a monument to Adam in Elmira; (13 Nov.) speaks at Chicago banquet honoring Gen. Grant; (3 Dec.) speaks at Boston breakfast for O. W. Holmes	(Jan.) works on *A Tramp Abroad.* PUBLISHES: (Mar.) "The Great Revolution in Pitcairn"	(Sep.) U. S. Grant returns to America after two years abroad	G. W. Cable, *Old Creole Days*; Henry James, *Daisy Miller*; Henrik Ibsen, *The Doll's House*; A. Strindberg, *The Red Room*; (1 Jan.) E. M. Forster is born; (4 Nov.) Will Rogers is born	(Jan.–Aug.) Zulu War in South Africa; (14 Mar.) Albert Einstein is born; (28 June) Congress authorizes commission to improve Mississippi River navigation
1880	lives in Hartford; (July–Oct.) in Elmira	begins investing in Paige compositor; (Feb.) invests in Kaolatype; (16 Oct.) gives welcome speech when U. S. Grant visits Hartford; (26 Oct.) speaks in behalf of James Garfield's presidential candidacy	(Jan.–Sep.) writes *The Prince and the Pauper*; (7 Jan.) delivers *A Tramp Abroad* to Elisha Bliss. PUBLISHES: (Mar.) *A Tramp Abroad*; (June) *1601* (privately printed); (Aug.) "Edward Mills and George Benton: A Tale"; (Sep.) "Mrs. McWilliams and the Lightning"	(27 June) Helen Keller is born; (26 July) daughter Jean Clemens is born in Elmira; (28 Sep.) Elisha Bliss dies; (19 Oct.) Katy Leary becomes Clemens family maid	G. W. Cable, *The Grandissimes*; Lew Wallace, *Ben Hur*; Fyodor Dostoyevsky, *The Brothers Karamazov*; Emile Zola, *Nana*; (8 May) Gustave Flaubert dies; (22 Dec.) George Eliot dies	(2 Nov.) James Garfield is elected president
1881	lives in Hartford; (4 June–4 Aug.) with family, vacations at Branford, Conn.; (Aug.–Sep.) in Elmira; (12 Sep.) visits mother in Fredonia, N.Y.; (26 Nov.) goes to Montreal to ensure Canadian copyright for *The Prince and the Pauper*	redecorates home; (17 June) meets G. W. Cable; (Apr.) makes C. L. Webster his business manager; (18 July) gives Webster power of attorney in his publishing interests	(Feb.) finishes *The Prince and the Pauper.* PUBLISHES: (Nov.) "A Curious Experience"; (Dec.) *The Prince and the Pauper*	(5 Mar.) Karl Gerhardt goes to Europe to study sculpture, subsidized by Mark Twain	J. C. Harris, *Uncle Remus*; Henry James, *Portrait of a Lady*; Thomas B. Aldrich becomes editor of the *Atlantic*; (4 Feb.) Thomas Carlyle dies; (9 Feb.) Fyodor Dostoyevsky dies	(4 Mar.) Pres. James Garfield is inaugurated; (13 Mar.) Czar Alexander II is assassinated; (2 July) Garfield is shot in Washington, D.C.; (19 Sep.) Garfield dies and Chester A. Arthur becomes president

Year	Residences & travel	Personal & business	Writing & publishing	Family & friends	Literary events	Historical events
1882	lives in Hartford; (18–20 Apr.) goes to St. Louis with James Osgood and Roswell Phelps; (20–28 Apr.) goes to New Orleans by steamboat; (6–21 May) goes by steamboat to Minnesota; (14–17 May) visits Hannibal; (22–24 May) returns to New York; (Aug.) visits Elmira	(10 Mar.) asks U. S. Grant to intercede with Pres. Chester Arthur in behalf of W. D. Howells's father; (10 Apr.) contracts with Osgood to publish book on the Mississippi; (30 Apr.) meets J. C. Harris in New Orleans	(c. Jan.) begins biography of Whitelaw Reid; (June) works on Huckleberry Finn. PUBLISHES: (June) The Stolen White Elephant, Etc.; (Dec.) "The McWilliamses and the Burglar Alarm"	(c. 13 Feb.) Dan Slote dies; (11 May) Dr. John Brown dies; (June) Jean Clemens has scarlet fever; home is quarantined; (7 Aug.) Lem Gray dies in explosion of the Gold Dust	Charles Heber Clark, The Fortunate Island; W. D. Howells, A Modern Instance; (6 Jan.) R. H. Dana, Jr. dies; (24 Mar.) Longfellow dies; (27 Apr.) R. W. Emerson dies; (6 Dec.) Anthony Trollope dies	(3 Apr.) outlaw Jesse James is killed in St. Joseph, Mo.; (9 Apr.) Barnum's elephant "Jumbo" arrives in New York City; (19 Apr.) Charles Darwin dies; (2 June) Garibaldi dies
1883	lives in Hartford; (May) visits Canada with Osgood to establish Life on the Mississippi copyright; (summer) in Elmira with family	(July) invents history game	(Jan.) finishes Life on the Mississippi; (July) writes "1,002nd Arabian Night"; (July) finishes Huckleberry Finn; (Oct.) works on play Colonel Sellers with W. D. Howells. PUBLISHES: (May) Life on the Mississippi	(4 Apr.) Cable visits Hartford; (15 Nov.) Matthew Arnold visits Mark Twain in Hartford	R. L. Stevenson, Treasure Island; (13 Feb.) Richard Wagner dies; (3 Sep.) Ivan Turgenev dies	Joseph Pulitzer buys the New York World; (14 Mar.) Karl Marx dies; (26 Aug.) Krakatoa erupts in Indonesia (an event alluded to in The American Claimant)
1884	lives in Hartford; (c. July–Aug.) in Elmira with family; (Nov.) lectures in the Eastern states with G. W. Cable; (Dec.) lectures in the Midwest; (10 Dec.) spends day in Toronto	(Feb.) visits U. S. Grant in New York; (May) learns to ride a bicycle; (May) founds Charles L. Webster & Co. publishing firm; (June) campaigns for Grover Cleveland; (July–Aug.) sits for bust by Karl Gerhardt; (18 Nov.) offers to publish U. S. Grant's memoirs	(Jan.) begins novel set in Hawaii; (July) begins "Huck Finn and Tom Sawyer Among the Indians." PUBLISHES: (Dec.) extract of Huckleberry Finn in Century Magazine; (Dec.) Huckleberry Finn (London)	(winter) children contract mumps; (May) U. S. Grant's stockbrokerage fails; (25 Nov.) Pres. Arthur and Frederick Douglass meet during backstage visit to Mark Twain and Cable in Washington, D.C.	G. W. Cable, Dr. Sevier and The Creoles of Louisiana; Helen Hunt Jackson, Ramona; (11 Apr.) Charles Reade dies	(28 Mar.) Barnum imports a "white elephant" from Siam; (22 Apr.) United States recognizes King Leopold's Congo regime; (26 Aug.) Ottmar patents the linotype machine; (4 Nov.) Grover Cleveland is elected president
1885	(Jan.–11 Feb.) continues lecture tour with G. W. Cable in the Midwest; (13 Jan.) visits Hannibal; (28 Feb.) ends lecture tour in Washington, D.C.; (late Aug.) visits Onteora	(27 Feb.) contracts to publish Grant's Memoirs; (c. 1 Mar.) visits Pres. Grover Cleveland; (20 Mar.) makes C. L. Webster a partner in his publishing company; (18 Aug.) patents "Mark Twain's Memory Builder"; (19 Nov.) discusses copyright with Cleveland; (30 Nov.) receives 50th-birthday greetings from many literary figures; (1 Dec.) Webster & Co. issues first volume of Grant's Memoirs	PUBLISHES: (Feb.) Huckleberry Finn (New York); (Dec.) "The Private History of a Campaign That Failed." DRAMATIC ADAPTATION: (14 Mar.) Livy's adaptation of The Prince and the Pauper is staged	(May) Osgood's publishing company declares bankruptcy; (23 July) Grant dies	W. D. Howells, The Rise of Silas Lapham; Henry James, The Bostonians; (22 May) Victor Hugo dies; (12 Aug.) Helen Hunt Jackson dies; (14 Oct.) Josh Billings dies	(5 Feb.) Belgium's King Leopold II creates the Congo Free State; (4 Mar.) Pres. Cleveland begins his first term; (15 Sep.) the elephant "Jumbo" is killed by a train in Canada
1886	lives in Hartford; visits New York City frequently on business; (26 June–4 July) takes family to Keokut for family reunion; (mid-July–mid-Sep.) in Elmira with family	(21 Jan.) revises partnership contract with Webster; (28 Jan.) addresses Senate committee on copyright; (Feb.) forms partnership with Paige to develop latter's compositor; (28 Apr.) makes Fred J. Hall a partner in Webster & Co.; (25 Aug.) sells patent rights in Kaolatype	(Jan.) begins Connecticut Yankee. DRAMATIC ADAPTATION: Colonel Sellers is produced in Hartford	(Mar.) W. D. Howells's daughter Winifred dies; (9 Dec.) H. M. Stanley speaks in Boston, introduced by Mark Twain	R. L. Stevenson, Dr. Jekyll and Mr. Hyde; H. Rider Haggard, King Solomon's Mines; W. D. Howells, Indian Summer; Howells becomes editor of Harper's Magazine; (16 Feb.) Van Wyck Brooks is born; (15 May) Emily Dickinson dies; (16 July) Ned Buntline dies	(4 May) Haymarket Square labor riot in Chicago; (3 July) a Mergenthaler linotype machine begins setting type for the Chicago Tribune

Year	Residences & travel	Personal & business	Writing & publishing	Family & friends	Literary events	Historical events
1887	lives in Hartford; (Sep.) in Elmira	Webster & Co. begins seven-year decline toward bankruptcy	PUBLISHES: (Apr.) "English As She Is Taught"; (Dec.) "A Petition to the Queen of England." DRAMATIC ADAPTATION: Colonel Sellers as a Scientist	(2 Mar.) cousin James J. Lampton dies; (13 Apr.) nephew Samuel E. Moffett marries Mary Emily Mantz	Arthur Conan Doyle, A Study in Scarlet; Thomas Hardy, The Woodlanders; (10 Apr.) John T. Raymond dies; (19 Nov.) Emma Lazarus dies	(8 Mar.) H. W. Beecher dies; (21 June) Britain celebrates Queen Victoria's Golden Jubilee
1888	lives in Hartford; (Sep.) in Elmira	(Feb.) makes Fred J. Hall manager of Webster & Co. as Webster withdraws; (c. 19 Apr.) meets R. L. Stevenson in New York City; (June) visits Thomas A. Edison's lab; receives honorary degree from Yale	PUBLISHES: Mark Twain's Library of Humor; (Jan.) "Meisterschaft"	(18 Mar.) David Gray dies; (6 Sep.) Theodore Crane suffers a stroke and (Nov.–Dec.) convalesces in Mark Twain's home; (c. 25 Dec.) Webster retires from Webster & Co.	Edward Bellamy, Looking Backward; Rudyard Kipling, Plain Tales from the Hills; Emile Zola, Le Terre; (15 Feb.) P. V. Nasby dies; (6 Mar.) Louisa May Alcott dies; (15 Apr.) Matthew Arnold dies	(12 Mar.) blizzard devastates Atlantic Coast; (6 Nov.) Benjamin Harrison is elected president over Grover Cleveland
1889	lives in Hartford; (mid-June–Aug.) in Elmira with family	(c. Aug.) meets Rudyard Kipling in Elmira; (Oct.) asks Joe Goodman to find investors for the Paige compositor; (Dec.) signs a new agreement with Paige; (c. Dec.) accused by Charles Heber Clark of plagiarism in Connecticut Yankee	(May) finishes Connecticut Yankee. PUBLISHES: (Dec.) Connecticut Yankee. DRAMATIC ADAPTATION: (24 Dec.) The Prince and the Pauper opens in Philadelphia	(July–Sep.) Paige delays testing of his typesetting machine with further dismantling; (3 July) Theodore Crane dies	J. M. Barrie, A Window in Thrums; B. Björnson, In God's Way; (8 June) Gerald Manley Hopkins dies; (12 Dec.) Robert Browning dies	(4 Mar.) Pres. Benjamin Harrison is inaugurated; (14 Nov.–25 Jan. 1890) Nelly Bly beats the 80-day round-the-world record of Jules Verne's fictitious Phileas Fogg; (6 Dec.) Jefferson Davis dies
1890	lives in Hartford; (c. July–16 Sep.) vacations at Onteora in the Catskills with family; (19 Aug.) visits mother in Keokuk; (early Nov.) attends mother's funeral in Hannibal; (late Nov.) attends mother-in-law's funeral in Elmira	(12 Jan.) meets Edward Bellamy at Hartford; (Jan.) responds to Charles Heber Clark's plagiarism charges; (June–Aug.) busy with Paige compositor, in which he buys all rights	PUBLISHES: (Feb.) "A Majestic Literary Fossil." DRAMATIC ADAPTATIONS: (20 Jan.) The Prince and the Pauper opens in New York; (1 Mar.) the play goes on tour; (12 Apr.) the play opens in London	Joe Goodman visits East Coast three times promoting a capital-stock company for the Paige compositor; (Oct.–Apr. 1891) Susy Clemens attends Bryn Mawr College; (27 Oct.) Jane Lampton Clemens dies; (c. Nov.) Jean Clemens has first epileptic seizure; (28 Nov.) mother-in-law, Olivia L. Langdon, dies	William James, The Principles of Psychology; Rudyard Kipling, The Light that Failed; Knut Hamsun, Hunger; Conan Doyle, The Sign of the Four; (25 Nov.) B. P. Shillaber dies	(July) Idaho and Wyoming enter the Union; (25 Sep.) Mormon Church bans polygamy; (29 Dec.) Indians fight their last major battle with federal troops at Wounded Knee, S.D.
1891	(Jan.–June) ends residence in Hartford; (6–14 June) closes Hartford house and takes family to Europe; (June–July) in France; (Aug.) Germany; boats down the Rhone; (Sep.) Switzerland; (15 Oct.–1 Mar. 1892) Berlin	markets "Mark Twain's Memory Builder"; (Feb.) rheumatism forces him to write with his left hand; (mid-Feb.) stops payments on the Paige compositor; (23 Mar.) speaks at Bryn Mawr; (June–Sep.) visits European health spas	(Feb.–2 May) writes The American Claimant; (late Oct.) translates Der Struwwelpeter. PUBLISHES: (Aug.) "Luck"; (Nov.–Mar. 1892) six travel sketches in the New York Sun; (Dec.) "Mental Telegraphy"	(10 Feb.) James Redpath dies; (27 Feb.) Frances Nunnally is born; (7 Apr.) Barnum dies; (26 Apr.) C. L. Webster dies	Ambrose Bierce, Tales of Soldiers and Civilians (In the Midst of Life); Thomas Hardy, Tess of the D'Urbervilles; Oscar Wilde, The Picture of Dorian Gray; (12 Aug.) James Russell Lowell dies; (28 Sep.) Herman Melville dies	(14 Feb.) Gen. William T. Sherman dies; (4 Mar.) U.S. Congress adopts the International Copyright Act
1892	(Jan.–Feb.) in Berlin; (Mar.) vacations at Menton, France, with Livy; (Apr.–May) travels through Italy; (June) settles family in Bad Nauheim, Germany; (mid-June–early July) Germany; (mid-June–early July) returns to New York alone; (late Sep.–mid-June 1893) lives near Florence, Italy	(20 Feb.) dines with Kaiser Wilhelm II at the Berlin home of his cousin, Mollie Clemens von Versen; (summer) meets Edward, Prince of Wales in Germany	(June–Dec.) writes "Those Extraordinary Twins." PUBLISHES: (Jan.–Mar.) The American Claimant in New York Sun (serial); (Apr.) Merry Tales; (May) The American Claimant (book)	(25 Jul.) Moses Sperry Beach dies; (12 Nov.) Dr. Abraham Reeves Jackson dies	Rudyard Kipling, Barrack Room Ballads; Conan Doyle, The Adventures of Sherlock Holmes; (26 Mar.) Walt Whitman dies; (7 Sep.) John Greenleaf Whittier dies; (6 Oct.) Alfred, Lord Tennyson dies	(1 Jan.) Ellis Island opens as immigration center in New York; (23 Oct.) World's Columbian Exposition opens in Chicago; (8 Nov.) Pres. Cleveland is reelected; (2 Dec.) Jay Gould dies

Year	Residences & travel	Personal & business	Writing & publishing	Family & friends	Literary events	Historical events
1893	(Jan.–mid-June) family stays at Florence; (22 Mar.–late May) goes to America and back on business; (late Apr.) visits Chicago; (early May) visits Elmira; (28 June) settles family in Berlin; (29 Aug.–7 Sep.) sails to New York with Clara; (29 Sep.–Mar. 1894) rooms in New York City; (late Dec.) goes to Chicago with H. H. Rogers	(fall–winter) many public appearances earn him the sobriquet "Belle of New York"; (mid-Sep.) meets Henry H. Rogers again in New York City; (late Dec.) with Rogers's help, negotiates with Paige about compositor	(25 Feb.) ships *Pudd'nhead Wilson* to Fred J. Hall; (14 Apr.) finishes "Extracts from Adam's Diary"; (July) revises *Pudd'nhead Wilson*. PUBLISHES: (Feb.) *The £1,000,000 Bank-Note and Other Stories*; (Sep.) "Is He Living or Is He Dead?"; (Nov.–Jan. 1894) *Tom Sawyer Abroad* in *St. Nicholas Magazine* (serial); (Nov.) "The Esquimau Maiden's Romance"; (Dec.–June 1894) *Pudd'nhead Wilson* in *Century* (serial); (Dec.) "Traveling with a Reformer"	(21 Sep.) Clara Clemens sings at an Elmira concert	*Golden Era* ceases publication; Ambrose Bierce, *Can Such Things Be?*; Stephen Crane, *Maggie: A Girl of the Streets*; Oscar Wilde, *A Woman of No Importance*; (15 Jan.) *Territorial Enterprise* suspends publication; (8 Nov.) Francis Parkman dies	(17 Jan.) Americans in Hawaii establish a provisional republic; (4 Mar.) Pres. Cleveland begins his second term; (27 June) New York Stock Exchange crashes
1894	(Jan.–Mar.) in New York City; (7 Mar.–14 Apr.) returns to family in France; (14 Apr.–9 May) goes back to New York City; (9 May–14 July) returns to France; (14 July–mid-Aug.) in New York City; (late Aug.–Feb. 1895) in France	(Jan.–Mar.) gives frequent speeches and readings in New York City; (6 Mar.) gives power of attorney to H. H. Rogers, who assigns his copyrights to Livy; (Apr.) Webster & Co. goes into bankruptcy; (Oct.) Paige compositor is tested at the Chicago *Herald*, where it proves impractical as a commercial device	(summer) writes "A Scrap of Curious History." PUBLISHES: (18 Apr.) *Tom Sawyer Abroad* (book); (July–Sep.) "In Defense of Harriet Shelley"; (Nov.) *Pudd'nhead Wilson* (book)	(11 Jan.) Kipling visits Mark Twain in Hartford; (4 July) Abel Fairbanks dies; (8 Sep.) posthumous son-in-law, Jacques Samossoud, is born	Rudyard Kipling, *The Jungle Book*; G. B. Shaw, *Arms and the Man*; (7 Oct.) O. W. Holmes dies; (3 Dec.) R. L. Stevenson dies	(24 June) Italian anarchist assassinates French president M. F. Sadi-Carnot; (1 Nov.) Nicholas II becomes czar of Russia; (Dec.) French army court-martials and convicts Alfred Dreyfus
1895	(Jan.–Feb.) in Paris; (23 Feb.–4 Apr.) returns to New York alone; (4 Apr.–11 May) in London; (c. 11–20 May) sails from England to New York with family; (late May–14 July) at Elmira with family; (14 July–22 Aug.) goes overland to British Columbia with Livy, Clara and James B. Pond; (23 Aug.) sails from Vancouver; (30 Aug.–1 Sep.) anchors off Honolulu; (c. 10 Sep.) stops at Fiji; (16 Sep.–1 Nov.) lectures in Australia; (6 Nov.–13 Dec.) lectures in New Zealand; (17 Dec.–5 Jan. 1896) returns to Australia	(Jan.) abandons all interest in the Paige compositor; (23 Apr.) contracts with R. S. Smythe for world lecture tour; (23 May) makes publishing agreement with Harper & Brothers; (14 July–15 July 1896) undertakes round-the-world lecture tour; (summer–fall) troubled by carbuncles during lecture tour	(Jan.) finishes *Joan of Arc* and *Tom Sawyer Detective*. PUBLISHES: (Apr. 1895–Apr. 1896) *Joan of Arc* (serial); (Sep.) "Mental Telegraphy Again"; (3 Oct.) "How to Tell a Story." DRAMATIC ADAPTATION: (8 Apr.) *Pudd'nhead Wilson* opens in Hartford; (15 Apr.) play moves to New York City	(20 Feb.) Frederick Douglass dies; (31 Mar.) meets Helen Keller; (4 Apr.) is honored at dinner given H. M. Stanley; (14 July–Aug. 1896) Susy and Jean Clemens stay at Elmira	Stephen Crane, *The Red Badge of Courage*; Henryk Sienkiewicz, *Quo Vadis*; H. G. Wells, *The Time Machine*; Oscar Wilde, *The Importance of Being Earnest*; Joseph Conrad, *Almayer's Folly*; (4 Nov.) Eugene Field dies; (27 Nov.) Alexandre Dumas (fils) dies	(25 Feb.) Cuban revolt against Spain begins; (20 July) U.S. warns Britain against armed intervention in Venezuela; (5 Nov.) Roentgen discovers X-rays; (29 Dec.–2 Jan. 1896) L. S. Jameson leads abortive raid into South Africa's Transvaal republic
1896	(6–13 Jan.) sails from Australia to Ceylon; (14–20 Jan.) sails to Bombay; (20 Jan.–1 Apr.) lectures through India; stops in Ceylon; (c. 4–15 Apr.) crosses Indian Ocean; (16–28 Apr.) rests	(Jan.–Mar.) lectures in 12 Indian cities; (May–July) lectures throughout South Africa; (26 May) meets Paul Kruger; (31 Dec.) reaches new agreement with the American Publishing Co. to issue a	(24 Oct.) begins *Following the Equator*; (Nov.) writes "The Enchanted Sea-Wilderness." PUBLISHES: (May) *Joan of Arc* (book); (Aug.–Sep.) *Tom Sawyer, Detective* (serial); (Nov.) *Tom*	(14 May–6 June) Livy and Clara stay in Durban as Mark Twain lectures through South Africa; (8 June) Frank Mayo dies during *Pudd'nhead Wilson* tour; (15 Aug.) Livy and Clara sail for	Thomas Hardy, *Jude the Obscure*; Edmund Rostand, *Cyrano de Bergerac*; Anton Chekhov, *The Seagull*; (15 Jan.) Mathew Brady dies; (1 July) Harriet Beecher Stowe dies	(4 Jan.) Utah becomes a state; (6 Jan.) Jameson Raid causes Cecil Rhodes's Cape government to fall; (20 Mar.) revolts against Rhodes's chartered company begin in

Year	Residences & travel	Personal & business	Writing & publishing	Family & friends	Literary events	Historical events
	in Mauritius; (28 Apr.–6 May) sails to South Africa; (6 May–15 July) lectures through South Africa; (15–31 July) sails to England; (c. 27 July) stops at Madeira; (Aug.–Sep.) stays in Guildford, England; (c. 5 Oct.–July 1897) rents London house	uniform edition of his books	*Sawyer Abroad/Tom Sawyer, Detective and Other Stories*	home from England; (18 Aug.) Susy Clemens dies in Hartford; Mark Twain receives the news in Guildford; (1 Sep.) Dorothy Quick is born; (9 Sep.) Livy, Clara and Jean rejoin Mark Twain in England		Rhodesia (Zimbabwe); (6 Apr.) modern Olympics open in Greece; (16 Aug.) gold is discovered in the Klondike; (3 Nov.) William McKinley is elected president
1897	(Jan.–July) in London; (late July–Sep.) in Weggis, Switzerland; (28 Sep. 1897–20 May 1898) rents a suite in Vienna's Hotel Metropole	(June) tells a journalist that reports of his death are exaggerated; (July) rejects James B. Pond's offer of $50,000 for 125 lectures in America; renews copyright of *Innocents Abroad*; (Sep.–May 1898) is lionized in Vienna; (28 Oct.) witnesses fracas on the floor of the Austria-Hungary Reichsrat	writes "Tom Sawyer's Conspiracy"; (Apr.–May) finishes *Following the Equator*; (May–) begins many works that he will never finish; (late July) "Villagers of 1840–3"; (fall 1897–Jan. 1898) "The Chronicle of Young Satan" and other versions of the "Mysterious Stranger." PUBLISHES: (Mar.) *How to Tell a Story and Other Essays*; (Nov.) *Following the Equator*	(5 Aug.) James Hammond Trumbull dies; (11 Dec.) Orion Clemens dies	Joseph Conrad, *The Nigger of the Narcissus*; Bram Stoker, *Dracula*; John Galsworthy, *From the Four Winds*; Rudyard Kipling, *Captains Courageous*; H. G. Wells, *The Invisible Man*; (11 Jan.) Bernard DeVoto is born	(4 Mar.) Pres. William McKinley is inaugurated; (27 Apr.) U.S. Grant's body is reinterred in a New York City mausoleum
1898	(Jan.–May) in Vienna; (25 May–14 Oct.) in summer house at Kaltenleutgeben; (16–27 Aug.) vacations at Salzkammergut with family; (c. 15 Oct.–26 May 1899) lives in Vienna's Hotel Krantz	(Jan.–Apr.) speaks in Vienna; (Jan.) meets Sigmund Freud; (Mar.) learns from H. H. Rogers that his creditors are paid off; (16 Mar.) meets Jan Szczepanik; (17 Sep.) attends Empress Elizabeth's funeral in Vienna	(Apr.–July) begins *What Is Man?*; (late July) "Concerning the Jews"; (c. Aug.) "The Great Dark"; (Nov.–Dec.) "Schoolhouse Hill"; (Dec.) "The Man That Corrupted Hadleyburg." PUBLISHES: (Mar.) "Stirring Times in Austria"; (Nov.) "From the 'London Times' of 1904"	Clara Clemens studies music and meets Ossip Gabrilowitsch in Vienna; (16 Mar.) Dan De Quille dies; (8 Dec.) Mary M. Fairbanks dies	Emile Zola, *J'accuse*; Henry James, *The Turn of the Screw*; H. G. Wells, *The War of the Worlds*; (14 Jan.) Lewis Carroll dies	(24 Apr.–26 July) Spanish-American War; (12 June) insurgents declare the Philippines independent; (12 Aug.) U.S. annexes Hawaii; (10 Sep.) Austrian empress Elizabeth is assassinated; (8 Nov.) Theodore Roosevelt is elected governor of New York
1899	(Jan.–26 May 1899) lives in Vienna; (23–29 Mar.) visits Budapest; (26–30 May) visits Prague; (June–July) in London; (mid-July–Sep.) in Sanna, Sweden with family; (c. 1 Oct.–Oct. 1900) lives in London	(25 May) has a private audience with Emperor Franz Josef I of Austria-Hungary; (late Mar.) speaks in Budapest; (June–July) speaks frequently in London; (4 July) meets Booker T. Washington	(May–Oct.) writes "The Chronicle of Young Satan." PUBLISHES: (Jan.) begins issuing the collected *Writings of Mark Twain*; (Sep.) "Concerning the Jews"; (Dec.) "The Man That Corrupted Hadleyburg"	(7 June) John Augustin Daly dies; (July–Sep.) Jean Clemens is treated for epilepsy in Sweden	Frank Norris, *McTeague*; Winston Churchill (American), *Richard Carvel*; G. B. Shaw, *Caesar and Cleopatra*; Leo Tolstoy, *Resurrection*; (22 May) Edward Bellamy dies; (18 July) Horatio Alger, Jr. dies	(19 Sep.) France pardons Alfred Dreyfus without vindicating him; (11 Oct.) South African (Boer) War begins; (21 Nov.) U.S. Vice-president Garret A. Hobart dies
1900	(1 Jan.–July) lives at 30 Wellington Court in London; (July–Oct.) lives at Dollis Hill near London; (6–14 Oct.) sails to New York City; (Oct. 1900–Oct. 1901 lives at 14 West 10th St., New York City; (late Oct.) attends C. D. Warner's funeral in Hartford	(2 Mar.) meets W. E. H. Lecky; (Mar.–Sep.) speaks frequently in London; (Oct.–Dec.) speaks frequently in New York City; (12 Dec.) introduces Winston Churchill to his first American lecture audience in New York	(June–Oct.) works on "The Chronicle of Young Satan." PUBLISHES: (Jan.) "My Boyhood Dreams"; (June) *The Man That Corrupted Hadleyburg and Other Stories and Essays*; (Oct.) *English As She Is Taught*	(20 Oct.) Charles Dudley Warner dies; (12 Nov.) Ossip Gabrilowitsch makes his American concert debut in New York	Sigmund Freud, *The Interpretation of Dreams*; Theodore Dreiser, *Sister Carrie*; Joseph Conrad, *Lord Jim*; (5 June) Stephen Crane dies; (25 Aug.) Friedrich Wilhelm Nietzsche dies; (30 Nov.) Oscar Wilde dies	(14 June) Hawaii becomes a U.S. territory; (6 Nov.) Pres. McKinley is reelected with Theodore Roosevelt as his vice-president

Year	Residences & travel	Personal & business	Writing & publishing	Family & friends	Literary events	Historical events
1901	lives in New York City; (21 June–19 Sep.) summers at Saranac Lake, N.Y., with family; (Aug.) sails on the *Kanawha*; (late Sep.) visits Elmira; (Oct. 1901–July 1903) lives in Riverdale, N.Y.	(Jan.–Dec.) speaks often in New York City; (27 Feb.) addresses New York State legislature on osteopathy; (Mar.) with Livy, attempts to communicate with Susy through a spiritualist; (9–10 May) speaks at Princeton; (20 Oct.) receives honorary degree from Yale; (31 Dec.) meets A. B. Paine	(c. Feb.) begins "The Secret History of Eddypus, the World-Empire"; (29 Aug.) "A Double-Barrelled Detective Story." PUBLISHES: (Feb.) "To the Person Sitting in Darkness"; (Apr.) "Extracts from Adam's Diary"; (Dec.) "The Death Disk"	(22 Jan.) Clara Clemens makes concert singing debut in Washington, D.C.; (17 Apr.) H. H. Rogers buys the yacht *Kanawha*	Frank Norris, *The Octopus*; Winston Churchill, *The Crisis*; Rudyard Kipling, *Kim*; Thomas Mann, *Buddenbrooks*; (24 Mar.) Charlotte Yonge dies	(1 Jan.) Commonwealth of Australia is founded; (22 Jan.) Queen Victoria dies; Edward VII becomes king of Britain; (23 Mar.) Frederick Funston captures Filipino leader Emilio Aguinaldo; (14 Sep.) Pres. McKinley dies a week after being shot; Theodore Roosevelt becomes president
1902	lives in Riverdale, N.Y.; (late Jan.) visits Elmira with family; (13 Mar.–9 Apr.) travels overland to Florida and cruises the western Caribbean with Rogers on the *Kanawha*; (mid-Apr.) buys house in Tarrytown, N.Y., and puts Hartford house on the market; (29 May–7 June) visits Hannibal, Springfield and St. Louis, Mo.; (24 June–Oct.) at York Harbor, Me. with family; (Oct.) returns to Riverdale; (late Nov.) visits Elmira	invests in American Plasmon Co.; (30 May) is photographed by his Boyhood Home in Hannibal; (4 June) receives honorary degree from the University of Missouri; (25 Oct.) marches in Woodrow Wilson's installation as president of Princeton; (Nov.) hires Isabel Lyon as a secretary	(Nov. 1902–Oct. 1903) works on "No. 44, The Mysterious Stranger." PUBLISHES: (Jan.–Feb.) "A Double-Barrelled Detective Story" (serial); (Mar.) "The Californian's Tale"; (Apr.) "Does the Race of Man Love a Lord?"; *A Double-Barrelled Detective Story* (book); (May) "A Defense of General Funston"; (July) "The Five Boons of Life"; (Nov.) "Amended Obituaries"; (Dec.) "Was It Heaven? or Hell?"; "The Belated Russian Passport"	(22 Apr.–12 Aug.) Clara Clemens goes to Europe alone; (5 May) Bret Harte dies; (14 July) Cyril Clemens is born; (Aug.–Dec.) Livy becomes seriously ill and spends long periods of isolation from Mark Twain; (7 Dec.) Thomas Nast dies; (23 Dec.) Jean Clemens contracts pneumonia	Theodor Mommsen receives the first Nobel Prize for Literature; Joseph Conrad, *Youth*; Joe Goodman, *The Archaic Maya Inscriptions*; A. Conan Doyle, *The Hound of the Baskervilles*; Rudyard Kipling, *Just So Stories*; (5 May) Bret Harte dies; (18 June) Samuel Butler dies; (29 Sep.) Emile Zola dies; (25 Oct.) Frank Norris dies; (14 Nov.) G. A. Henty dies	(26 Mar.) Cecil Rhodes dies; (20 May) Cuba becomes independent; (31 May) South African War ends; (11 Dec.) Marconi transmits the first transatlantic radio signal
1903	(Jan.–1 July) lives in Riverdale; (early July–Oct.) at Elmira with family; (24 Oct.) takes family to Italy; (9 Nov.–June 1904) lives in villa in Florence	allowed to see Livy briefly at long intervals; (Apr.) spends five weeks in bed with bronchitis; (May) sells Hartford house; (mid-Sep.–23 Oct.) negotiates contract making Harper & Bros. his exclusive publisher; (5 Oct.) visits Susy's Elmira grave	PUBLISHES: (Apr.) *My Début as a Literary Person with Other Essays and Stories*; (Dec.) "A Dog's Tale"	Livy's illness worsens; (21 June) James B. Pond dies	Bjornsterne Bjornson receives Nobel Prize for Literature; Henry James, *The Ambassadors*; Jack London, *The Call of the Wild*; G. B. Shaw, *Man and Superman*; (22 Oct.) W. E. H. Lecky dies	(May) E. D. Morel and Roger Casement agitate against King Leopold's Congo regime; (3 Nov.) Panama declares its independence from Colombia; (17 Dec.) Wright brothers achieve powered heavier-than-air flight at Kitty Hawk, N.C.
1904	(Jan.–June) lives in Florence; (28 June–13 July) sails from Naples to New York with daughters; (18 July–Sep.) stays in Lee, Mass.; (Sep.–June 1908) lives at 21 Fifth Avenue, New York City	(Apr.) is forbidden to see Livy; (13 Oct.) executes his last will; (Dec.) sells Tarrytown house; (late Dec.) spends about three weeks in bed in New York City	(Jan.–June) works on "No. 44, The Mysterious Stranger"; (mid-Jan.) begins dictating his autobiography. PUBLISHES: (Jan.) "Italian Without a Master"; (Apr.) "Extracts from Adam's Diary"; (Aug.) "Italian With a Grammar"; (Sep.) *A Dog's Tale* (book); (Dec.) "Saint Joan of Arc"; (Dec.) "The $30,000 Bequest"	W. D. Howells receives honorary Oxford degree; (15 Jan.) sister-in-law Mollie Clemens dies; (8 Apr.) Clara Clemens sings at a Florence concert; (10 May) H. M. Stanley dies; (5 June) Livy dies at Florence; Jean Clemens resumes epileptic seizures; (July) Clara has a nervous breakdown; (July) Clara enters a sanitarium; (14 July) Livy is buried in Elmira's Woodlawn Cemetery; (31 July) Jean is injured in accident on a horse; (31 Aug.) sister Pamela Moffett dies	Frédéric Mistral and José Echegaray y Eizaguirre receive the Nobel Prize for Literature; James Barrie, *Peter Pan*; Joseph Conrad, *Nostromo*; W. H. Hudson, *Green Mansions*; Jack London, *Sea Wolf*; A. B. Paine, *Th. Nast, His Period and His Pictures*; (2 July) Anton Chekhov dies; (22 Aug.) Kate Chopin dies; (26 Sep.) Lafcadio Hearn dies	(8 Feb.–Sep. 1905) Russo-Japanese War; (14 July) Paul Kruger dies; (8 Nov.) Theodore Roosevelt is elected president

Year	Residences & travel	Personal & business	Writing & publishing	Family & friends	Literary events	Historical events
1905	lives in New York City; (late May–21 Oct.) stays at Dublin, N.H.	(Aug.) sees Clara for the first time in a year; (late Nov.) dines at the White House with Pres. Theodore Roosevelt; (5 Dec.) is honored by a 70th-birthday banquet at Delmonico's in New York City; (18 Dec.) speaks in New York City at benefit for Russian Jews at which Sarah Bernhardt performs	(Feb.) finishes writing *King Leopold's Soliloquy*; (May) writes "3,000 Years Among the Microbes"; (late Sep.) "A Horse's Tale." PUBLISHES: (Feb.) "From My Unpublished Autobiography"; (Mar.) "The Czar's Soliloquy"; (Apr.) "A Humane Word from Satan"; (July) "A Monument to Adam"; (Sep.) *King Leopold's Soliloquy*; (Dec.) "Eve's Diary"	(10 May) Clara Clemens has an appendectomy; (26 Nov.) Jean Clemens tries to kill Katy Leary during an epileptic attack; (Nov.) Clara moves into Mark Twain's New York home	Henryk Sienkiewicz receives the Nobel Prize for Literature; Edith Wharton, *House of Mirth*; G. B. Shaw, *Major Barbara*; (15 Feb.) Lew Wallace dies; (24 Mar.) Jules Verne dies; (21 Aug.) Mary Mapes Dodge dies	(22 Jan.) Tsar's troops fire on strikers in St. Petersburg, Russia, on "Bloody Sunday"; (5 Sep.) Russo-Japanese War ends
1906	lives in New York City; (late Jan.) visits Washington, D.C.; (Feb.) attends Patrick McAleer's funeral in Hartford; (late May–18 Oct.) rents house at Dublin, N.H.; (Aug. and Oct.) cruises with Rogers on the *Kanawha*; (early Dec.) visits Washington, D.C.	(Jan.–Dec.) speaks frequently in New York City; (29 Jan. and 7 Dec.) addresses congressional committees on copyright in Washington, D.C.; (Apr.) buys land near Redding, Conn., for a new home; (8 Apr.) meets H. G. Wells; (Dec.) begins wearing white suits in public	(May–June) revises *What Is Man?*; PUBLISHES: *The $30,000 Bequest and Other Stories*; (June) *Eve's Diary* (book); (July) "William Dean Howells"; (Aug.) "A Horse's Tale"; *What Is Man?*; (Sep.–Dec. 1907) "Chapters from my Autobiography" (serial)	(10 Jan.) A. B. Paine joins Mark Twain's household to write his biography; (18 Jan.) Jean Clemens attempts to kill Katy Leary maid during an epileptic attack; (6 Apr.) Maxim Gorky arrives in America; (26 Sep.) Bloodgood Haviland Cutter (the "Poet Lariat") dies; (c. 20 Oct.) Jean Clemens enters a private institution in Katonah, N.Y.	Giosue Carducci receives Nobel Prize for Literature; Ambrose Bierce, *The Cynic's Word Book (The Devil's Dictionary)*; Upton Sinclair, *The Jungle*; John Galsworthy, *The Man of Property*; (12 Jan.) Dixon Wecter is born; (23 May) Henrik Ibsen dies; (29 Sep.) Henry Nash Smith is born	(3 Feb.) George Harvey proposes Woodrow Wilson as a presidential candidate; (18 Apr.) earthquake devastates San Francisco; (12 July) French court vindicates Dreyfus
1907	lives in New York City; (2–10 Jan.) goes to Bermuda with Joseph Twichell and Isabel Lyon; (May–Oct.) stays in Tuxedo Park, N.Y.; (8 June–22 July) makes last transatlantic trip to England, with Ralph Ashcroft; (23 Sep.) sails into Hampton Roads, Va., aboard the *Kanawha*	(Jan.–May, Nov.–Dec.) speaks frequently in New York City; (16 Jan.) hosts dinner party for Helen Keller; (26 June) receives honorary degree from Oxford University; (June–July) speaks in London; (3 July) lunches with James Barrie, Max Beerbohm, and G. B. Shaw	PUBLISHES: (Feb.) *Christian Science*; (Oct.) *A Horse's Tale* (book); (Dec.–Jan. 1908) "Extract from Captain Stormfield's Visit to Heaven." DRAMATIC ADAPTATION: (Mar.) Vitagraph film "A Curious Dream"	Jim Gillis dies; (19 Mar.) Thomas B. Aldrich dies; (17 July) John Briggs dies; (22 July) H. H. Rogers has a stroke; (Aug.) Dorothy Quick visits Mark Twain at Tuxedo Park; (15 Nov.) Moncure Conway dies	Rudyard Kipling receives the Nobel Prize for Literature; Henry Adams, *The Education of Henry Adams*; Joseph Conrad, *Secret Agent*; Maxim Gorky, *Mother*; (7 Sep.) Sully Prudhomme dies	Nicolai Lenin leaves Russia; (27 Sep.) New Zealand becomes a dominion in the British Empire; (16 Nov.) Oklahoma becomes a state; (Dec.) Pres. Roosevelt sends the "Great White Fleet" around the world
1908	(Jan.–18 June) lives in New York City; (late Jan.–early Feb.) goes to Bermuda; (24 Feb.–11 Apr.) returns to Bermuda with H. H. Rogers; (18 June) moves into last home, at Redding, Conn.; (7 Oct.) begins calling Redding home "Stormfield"	(Jan.–May) speaks frequently in New York City; (Feb.) plays golf and socializes with future president Woodrow Wilson in Bermuda; (Apr.) organizes "Angelfish Club" of young girls; (18 Sep.) burglars break into Stormfield; (14 Oct.) helps dedicate Redding's Mark Twain Library; (14 Nov.) gives Ralph Ashcroft and Isabel Lyon power of attorney over his business affairs; (22 Dec.) organizes Mark Twain Company	(May) begins revising *Life on the Mississippi*	(May–8 Sep.) Clara Clemens goes to Europe to study singing; (June–Sep.) "Angelfish" girls are guests at Stormfield; (1 Aug.) nephew Samuel E. Moffett drowns; (26 Sep.–Jan. 1909) Jean Clemens goes to Germany to be treated for epilepsy; (Oct.) Clara leases flat in New York City; (mid-Oct.) Laura Hawkins Frazer visits Stormfield	Rudolf C. Eucken receives the Nobel Prize for Literature; Kenneth Grahame, *The Wind in the Willows*; E. M. Forster, *A Room with a View*; Kenneth Grahame, *The Wind in the Willows*; (3 July) J. C. Harris dies	(24 June) former president Grover Cleveland dies; (20 Aug.) Leopold II hands over the Congo Free State to Belgium; (3 Nov.) William Howard Taft is elected president

Year	Residences & travel	Personal & business	Writing & publishing	Family & friends	Literary events	Historical events
1909	lives near Redding; (18 Nov.–20 Dec.) goes to Bermuda with A. B. Paine	(Apr.–July) removes Isabel Lyon and Ralph Ashcroft from the household; (9 June) delivers his last public speech, at a Baltimore girls school; (July) diagnosed with heart disease (17 July) makes Paine his business manager; (Dec.) rumored to have died; (11 Dec.) collapse of Plasmon Company wipes out his investment	writes (Oct.–Nov.) "Letters from the Earth"; (late Dec.) "The Death of Jean." PUBLISHES: (Jan.) "A New Planet"; (Apr.) *Is Shakespeare Dead?*; (Oct.) *Extract from Captain Stormfield's Visit to Heaven* (book); (Dec.) "A Fable" and "Marjorie Fleming: Wonder Child." DRAMATIC ADAPTATION: Biograph films "The Death Disk"	(Jan.–Apr.) Jean Clemens lives in sanitoriums; (18 Mar.) Isabel Lyon marries Ralph Ashcroft; (26 Apr.) Jean moves into Stormfield; (19 May) H. H. Rogers dies; (6 Oct.) Clara Clemens marries Ossip Gabrilowitsch at Stormfield; (11 Dec.) Clara and Ossip sail for Europe; (24 Dec.) Jean dies at Stormfield; (29 Dec.) Paine and his family move into Stormfield	Selma Lagerlöf receives the Nobel Prize for Literature; H. G. Wells, *Tono-Bungay*; (24 Mar.) John Millington Synge dies; (10 Apr.) Algernon Charles Swinburne dies; (23 Apr.) C. W. Stoddard dies; (18 May) George Meredith dies; (24 June) Sarah Orne Jewett dies	Joan of Arc is beatified; (17 Feb.) Geronimo dies; (4 Mar.) Pres. William H. Taft is inaugurated; (11 Sep.) Halley's Comet is photographed nearing the sun; (17 Dec.) Belgian king Leopold II dies
1910	lives near Redding; (5 Jan.–14 Apr.) goes to Bermuda on last trip outside of the U.S.	(5 Jan.) sees W. D. Howells for the last time; (21 Apr.) dies at sunset at Stormfield; (23 Apr.) Joseph Twichell conducts funeral service in New York City; (24 Apr.) is buried in Elmira's Woodlawn Cemetery	PUBLISHES: (Feb.) "The Turning Point in My Life." DRAMATIC ADAPTATION: (Mar.) Edison releases *A Mountain Blizzard*, adapted from *Roughing It*	(17 Apr.) Clara Clemens returns to Stormfield; (24 Apr.) Harmony Twichell dies; (7 May) Elinor Howells dies; (18 Aug.) only grandchild, Nina Gabrilowitsch, is born at Redding, Conn.	Paul Johann Ludwig von Heyse wins Nobel Prize for Literature; W. D. Howells, *My Mark Twain*; E. M. Forster, *Howard's End*; (26 Apr.) Bjornsterne Bjornson dies; (5 June) O. Henry dies; (26 Aug.) William James dies; (29 Sep.) Winslow Homer dies; (7 Nov.) Leo Tolstoy dies	(19 Apr.) Halley's Comet reaches perihelion; (6 May) Britain's King Edward VII dies; (1 July) the Union of South Africa is formed; (Nov.) Mexican Revolution begins; (4 Dec.) Mary Baker Eddy dies

A. B. Chambers STEAMBOAT on which Mark Twain was a PILOT. A 410-ton side-wheeler built in 1855, the *Chambers* worked the MISSOURI RIVER in the spring and summer months and the Lower Mississippi the rest of the year. Between October 26, 1859 and February 24, 1860, Mark Twain made three or four round-trips on the boat between St. Louis and New Orleans under Captain George W. Bowman. His fellow pilots included Will BOWEN and James C. DeLancey. On September 24, 1860, the *Chambers* sank on a snag near St. Louis.

Abblasoure Fictional English village in *Connecticut Yankee.* Located in the kingdom of BAGDEMAGUS, Abblasoure is about 10 miles south of the VALLEY OF HOLINESS. After Hank MORGAN and King ARTHUR visit the "SMALL-POX HUT" near Abblasoure and see the manor house burn down, they stay with the charcoal burner MARCO and his wife just outside the village (chapters 29–34).

Abdul Aziz (February 9, 1830–June 2, 1876) The sultan of TURKEY (1861–76), Abdul Aziz visited Paris in early July 1867, when Mark Twain saw him with Emperor NAPOLEON III. A month and a half later, Abdul Aziz was in CONSTANTINOPLE when Mark Twain was visiting Turkey. A passage in *Innocents Abroad* that Mark Twain wrote long after traveling through Abdul Aziz's empire calls the sultan a weak, stupid, ignorant and dissipated tyrant who believes in the ARABIAN NIGHTS and opposes every form of progress (chapter 13). In 1876, Abdul Aziz was deposed and died under suspicious circumstances.

Abelard and Héloise Legendary 12th-century lovers. A noted French theologian, Peter Abelard (1079–1142) was a 38-year-old priest when he eloped with Héloise (c. 1098–1164), the teenage niece of Canon Fulbert. After the outraged Fulbert had Abelard castrated and Héloise put in a convent, the lovers maintained a chaste correspondence until Abelard's death. In the early 19th century, their remains were entombed at Paris's national cemetery, which Mark Twain visited in July 1867. Most of chapter 15 of *Innocents Abroad* is a BURLESQUE of their story that he wrote after returning from Europe. His stated purpose is to prove that tears shed for the tragic lovers are wasted because Abelard was a "dastardly seducer" of the innocent Héloise and his "nameless mutilation" was a morally just act of revenge.

"About Play Acting" Essay written in mid-1898 about *The Master of Palmyra,* a 20-year-old play by German dramatist Adolf von Wilbrandt (1837–1911) that Mark Twain attended in VIENNA. The bulk of his essay summarizes the four-hour play's complex plot about a Christian woman of Roman times who, after repeated reincarnations, concludes that life is meaningless. Marveling at the rapt attention and patience of the Viennese through such grim fare, Mark Twain argues that a large audience for tragedy must exist. He uses the play list from a New York newspaper of May 7, 1898 to make the point that too much fare is light comedy—"mental sugar" that will bring on "Bright's disease of the intellect." For a tonic, he suggests *The Master of Palmyra* and recommends that New York should have at least one theater devoted to tragedy.

The essay first appeared in New York's *Forum* in October 1898 and was later collected in *The Man That Corrupted Hadleyburg and Other Essays and Stories* (1900).

"About Smells" Essay on Christian class prejudice published in 1870. Mark Twain reports reading that the Reverend T. De Witt Talmage publicly complained about having to endure the "bad smells" of working-class parishioners in his Brooklyn church. He reminds Talmage that heaven probably admits not only working-class men, but even blacks, Eskimos, Tierra del Fuegans, Arabs and others. "All things are possible with God." He suggests that if Talmage "were sitting under the glory of the throne" and a working man such as Benjamin FRANKLIN entered heaven, Talmage "would detect him with a single sniff and immediately . . . ask to be excused." Mark Twain adds that Talmage would not have enjoyed keeping company with Christ's disciples, either, as he could not have stood their "fishy smell." He concludes by offering the hope that Talmage does not represent modern Christian character.

The 660-word essay first appeared in the May 1870 GALAXY. Not collected in any early standard edition, it was collected in *The Curious Republic of Gondour and Other Whimsical Sketches* in 1919 and in the MARK TWAIN PAPERS project edition *What Is Man? and Other Philosophical Writings* (1973).

Abraham (*fl.* **1860s**) Mark Twain's Maltese guide (dragoman) in the HOLY LAND. In September 1867, Mark Twain and seven companions contracted with Abraham to take them from BEIRUT through SYRIA and PALESTINE over 20 days. Abraham quickly assembled a caravan with 19 servants, 26 pack mules, riding horses, food, tents, iron beds, tables and other comforts. He charged each man one pound ($5) a day, receiving half his fee at Beirut and the balance at JAFFA. In contrast to many guides with whom he dealt, Mark Twain found Abraham honest, competent and polite. *Innocents Abroad* mentions Abraham by name only in chapters 41 and 45 and calls him "FERGUSON" in chapters 45, 47, 51 and 57.

actors At least 15 actors have portrayed Mark Twain on the screen, including several who appear only to introduce stories. Karl Formes, for example, is Mark Twain in the silent film *A Connecticut Yankee in King Arthur's Court* (1921). Royal Dano (1922–1994) appears as Mark Twain at the beginning and end of the 1975 television dramatization of *Huckleberry Finn.* Several productions have been about Mark Twain's own life. In the 1944 feature THE ADVENTURES OF MARK TWAIN, Jackie Brown plays Mark Twain at 12, Dickie Jones (1927–) plays him at 15 and Fredric March (1897–1975) plays him as an adult. James Whitmore (1921–) provides Mark Twain's voice in the 1985 claymation feature THE ADVENTURES OF MARK TWAIN.

In the 1979 television play MARK TWAIN: BENEATH THE LAUGHTER, Dan O'Herlihy (1919–) portrays Mark Twain near the end of his life. Jason Robards (1922–) plays him at the same age in MARK TWAIN AND ME (1991). Several television plays have adapted his semi-autobiographical works with characters representing Mark Twain or his narrative personas. David Knell, for example, is "Sam" in *Life on the Mississippi* (1980) and Gary McCleery is the "second lieutenant" in *The Private History of a Campaign That Failed* (1981). In a 1959 episode of television's "Bonanza," Howard Duff (1917–1990) portrays Sam Clemens at the time he came to NEVADA. The following year, James Daily (1918–) and Andrew Prine (1936–) portrayed Mark Twain at two different stages of his life in a television adaptation of *Roughing It.* Craig Wasson (1954–) is "Mark Twain" in the 1983 production of *Innocents Abroad.*

Other actors given screen credit as "Mark Twain" include Leslie King in *Broadway Broke* (1923), Charles Gerson in *Pony Express* (1925) and Ronald Adam (1896–1979) in *The Man with a Million* (1954). Of the many professional impersonators of Mark Twain, the best known is Hal HOLBROOK.

Adam and Eve Mark Twain had a lifelong fascination with the Bible's first man and woman—whose story is told in the first three chapters of Genesis. Among the hundreds of references to Genesis in Mark Twain's writings and speeches, nearly a hundred concern Adam and Eve. He also wrote several long sketches and stories

focusing on them; these have been dubbed his "ADAMIC DIARIES." Several themes recur in these works.

Since the Bible portrays Adam as our first and only common ancestor, Mark Twain enjoyed calling him his only "celebrity ancestor." "CAPTAIN STORMFIELD'S VISIT TO HEAVEN" alludes to Adam as the most popular figure in heaven. Mark Twain also enjoyed developing the idea that Adam is neglected and deserves special attention. "A MONUMENT TO ADAM" recalls his effort to have a memorial erected to Adam's memory in ELMIRA. As our first ancestor, Adam also began the chain of accidents that determine each person's life—an idea that Mark Twain develops in "THE TURNING POINT OF MY LIFE" (1910).

Mark Twain was also interested in the moral responsibility of Adam and Eve for their Fall. "EVE SPEAKS" attempts to show that they should not have been held responsible for eating the forbidden fruit, since they

Lester Ralph's depiction of Eve offering Adam an apple in the Garden of Eden.

had no experience and no moral sense. Thanks to their Fall, however, Adam gave us labor, sin and death—a point that Mark Twain makes repeatedly, especially in his Pudd'nhead Wilson MAXIMS. Mark Twain also used Adam and Eve to develop the theme that life is meaningless without companionship, a point that he makes especially strongly in EVE'S DIARY.

Adamic Diaries   Collective term for Mark Twain's various ADAM AND EVE writings. "EXTRACTS FROM ADAM'S DIARY" (1893) and EVE'S DIARY (1905) are light and comic in tone, written for specific audiences, with little attention to religious issues. Later pieces, such as "THAT DAY IN EDEN," "EVE SPEAKS" and "Papers of the Adam Family" (c. 1905–6), are pointed satires on Christian beliefs.

Adams, Cholley   Character in *A Tramp Abroad*. A hardswearing young man from western New York, Adams introduces himself to the narrator and his friends as they are walking in BADEN-BADEN (chapter 20). He has been in Germany for nearly two years to study horsedoctoring but is becoming homesick while struggling to learn GERMAN and Latin. Adams resembles two other talkative young Americans in chapters 27 and 38.

Adams, George Jones (1813, New Jersey–May 11, 1880, Philadelphia, Pennsylvania)   American messianic leader. Adams began his career in the 1830s as a Methodist preacher and amateur actor in Boston. In 1840, he joined the MORMON church and was sent as a missionary to England, where he became interested in returning Jews to PALESTINE. A gifted orator, he rose rapidly in the Mormon Church after returning to the United States and became close to Joseph Smith, the church's founder, in Illinois. After Smith was killed in 1844, Brigham YOUNG expelled Adams from the church.

By 1860, Adams was in MAINE leading his own Church of the Messiah, which shared many Mormon practices. To fulfill his Zionist dream, he persuaded 160 people from around Jonesport to sell their possessions, give the proceeds to him and follow him to Palestine. When he and his followers arrived at JAFFA in September 1866, they found that the Turkish government had not approved their application to establish a colony. They stayed, but their work was handicapped by their inability to own land, their unfamiliarity with local agricultural conditions, and various health problems. After a year, it was clear that Adams's colony could not prosper. Poor advice, failed prophecies and drunkenness undermined his authority. By June 1867, followers who had money were leaving; others sought help to finance their departure. When the QUAKER CITY arrived in September, Moses BEACH advanced $1,500 to their relief fund and the ship carried about three dozen colonists to Egypt, whence they made their way home. Mark Twain exaggerates the magnitude of the colony's failure in both his

original letter to the NEW YORK TRIBUNE and chapter 57 of *Innocents Abroad*.

Meanwhile, Adams remained at Jaffa with his family and 13 followers for another eight months, and later resettled in Philadelphia. Shortly before he died, he unsuccessfully sought affiliation with the Reorganized Church of Jesus Christ of Latter-day Saints, which had broken away from Brigham Young's church.

Adams, Henry (Hal)   Narrator of the "THE £1,000,000 BANK-NOTE." At the start of his narrative, Adams is 27 years old, "alone in the world" and a skillful miningbroker clerk in SAN FRANCISCO. An accident lands him in LONDON without friends or funds, but two eccentrics draw him into an experiment that leads him to fame and fortune. Along the way, he wins the hand of Portia LANGHAM—who happens to be the stepdaughter of one of the eccentrics. Adams never deliberately misrepresents himself, but he succeeds because people assume that he is other than what he really is. In this regard, he fits Mark Twain's claimant mold. Indeed, his pseudoaristocratic rank is affirmed by gossip columns—which call him the "vest-pocket monster." At a dinner party, Adams pulls rank on ordinary English aristocrats—with names like BLATHERSKITE, Newgate and Shoreditch—by claiming direct descent from ADAM.

Adams's story has interesting parallels with Mark Twain's life. He is about the same age that Mark Twain was when the latter arrived in the East from San Francisco—where he had enjoyed "a butterfly idleness" while waiting for his Nevada MINING interests to bring him a fortune (*Roughing It*, chapter 58). Also like Mark Twain—who was known as the Wild Humorist of the Pacific Slope when he came east—Adams is regarded by London society as something of a freak. And, just as Mark Twain won the hand of Olivia Langdon though he could not satisfy her father's request for references, Adams persuades Portia's stepfather to overlook the same failing.

"Adam's Soliloquy"   Sketch written in early 1905 and first published in EUROPE AND ELSEWHERE. In modern New York City, the spirit of ADAM muses over a dinosaur skeleton in a museum. He is puzzled because he cannot remember having named this creature. He recalls taking up the question with Noah, who will not explain why this creature was left off his ark. Later, Adam sits outside, watching passersby. He is struck by the fact that a baby he sees is identical to the first baby born in the world; he further marvels over the fact that its mother has the same look of devotion that Eve had when gazing at her own baby 300,000 years earlier. Adam strikes up a conversation with the young mother, who tries to guess his identity. When he reveals that his name is Adam, she is puzzled by his having only one name—like the "original." He asks if she has ever seen the original, but she says that seeing him would scare her badly. Adam asks why she should be scared by seeing her own kin—an idea she thinks "prodigiously funny." Adam is proud of his wit.

Mark Twain wrote this 2,500-word sketch shortly after completing "THE CZAR'S SOLILOQUY" and KING LEO-POLD'S SOLILOQUY. Although the piece remained unpublished during his lifetime, it appears to have revived his interest in ADAM AND EVE and inspired him to fresh work on the ADAMIC DIARIES.

Adler, Private Franz Character in *Life on the Mississippi*. In a tale told in chapter 31, Adler is a German-American cavalryman who kills Karl RITTER's wife and daughter while robbing Ritter's house with his cousin Private KRUGER, in NAPOLEON, Arkansas. Ritter uses a FINGERPRINT to track Adler and Kruger down, then spares Kruger and kills Adler. Years later, however, he finds Adler alive in a Munich dead house and learns that it was actually Kruger he killed. Ritter gets his revenge by watching Adler die slowly.

Admiral, The Old Character in *Roughing It*. A recently retired whaling captain sailing to HAWAII aboard the AJAX, the Admiral appears in chapter 62 as a beloved and respected defender of the weak whom other passengers shun because of his overbearingness. When he argues about the causes of the CIVIL WAR, he is like ANDREW JACKSON—the bull-pup of the JUMPING FROG STORY: once he gets hold of an opponent, he never lets go. His fatal weakness is that his arguments rest on a complex tissue of lies; his power is broken when the soft-spoken WILLIAMS counters his invented history with even bigger lies.

Mark Twain loosely modeled the Admiral on a fellow *Ajax* passenger named Captain James Smith (1800–1877), a former whaler recently retired from the Hawaiian navy.

Adolphus Fictitious name in *Huckleberry Finn*. In chapter 24, the KING has Huck pose as his English servant and calls him "Adolphus" to impress Tim COLLINS. Although Huck presumably goes by this name throughout the entire WILKS episode, it is used only once.

The Adventures of Colonel Sellers (1965) Abridgement of *The Gilded Age*, edited by Charles NEIDER. On the rationale that the only parts of the original novel worth reading are those written by Mark Twain, NEIDER reduced C. D. WARNER's chapters to synopses. He left Mark Twain's own chapters intact, but overlooked his contributions to Warner's chapters.

The Adventures of Mark Twain (1944) Feature film chronicling Mark Twain's life. In the tradition of the "biopics" of its time, Alan LeMay's screenplay attempts to account for every major turning point in Mark Twain's life. The resulting narrative not only rearranges the order of events, it uses revised sequences to supply logical motivation. Under Irving Rapper's direction,

Mark Twain is depicted as a well-intentioned innocent. The film's story line should be compared to the sequence of actual events in Mark Twain's life.

SYNOPSIS

Young Sam Clemens (Jackie Brown) is a mischievous typesetter working for the newspaper of his brother Orion Clemens (Russell Gleason). After Sam outrages Orion with something that he has printed, he flees to the Mississippi River to apprentice as a PILOT. He suffers briefly under the tough tutelage of Horace BIXBY (Robert Barrat), then suddenly becomes the adult Clemens (Fredric March), a full-fledged pilot. While on the river, he meets Charles LANGDON (William Heary) and sees the cameo portrait of Langdon's sister, Livy (Alexis Smith). With the encouragement of his pal, Steve GILLIS (Alan Hale), he quits piloting to take up prospecting in the West. His goal is to become rich enough to marry Livy.

When his prospecting career flops, Clemens becomes a reporter for the VIRGINIA CITY TERRITORIAL ENTERPRISE. During this period, he and Gillis challenge a champion JUMPING FROG owned by Bret HARTE (John Carradine), of nearby ANGEL'S CAMP. Afterward, Clemens writes up a story about the contest and signs it "MARK TWAIN." He then learns that the CIVIL WAR has begun and rushes home to support the South. Meanwhile, J. B. POND comes to Virginia City searching for the author of the jumping frog story.

As war ravages the country, Mark Twain's jumping frog story helps keep the nation laughing. Afterward, Pond finally locates Clemens and persuades him to take up LECTURING. From this moment, Clemens is known to everyone as Mark Twain. When he delivers his first lecture in NEW YORK CITY, W. D. HOWELLS (Douglas Wood) tries to meet him, but since Charles and Livy Langdon are in the audience, Mark Twain ignores Howells in favor of Livy. He then accompanies the Langdons directly to ELMIRA, where Livy quickly falls in love with him. After winning the approval of her father, he marries Livy and moves to BUFFALO, where he starts writing popular books. His son, Langdon Clemens, is born, but dies in infancy.

Each time Mark Twain faces a major crisis, Livy encourages him to return to his writing in order to exercise his unique gift as a humorist. After the fiasco of the WHITTIER birthday speech, he turns to finishing *Huckleberry Finn*. Meanwhile, he begins pouring money into the PAIGE COMPOSITOR. This investment, and his publishing house, Charles L. WEBSTER & COMPANY, are failing. H. H. ROGERS (George Lessey) warns him that he is headed for BANKRUPTCY. Although Mark Twain knows that publishing the memoirs of U. S. GRANT will guarantee financial disaster, he opts to go ahead.

Once his bankruptcy is certain, Mark Twain declares that he will pay off his creditors in full by making a round-the-world lecture tour. Leaving Livy and his daughters behind, he tours with Pond, unaware of how gravely ill Livy is. The lecture tour ends after he earns enough to get out of debt. He rushes to rejoin Livy in FLORENCE, Italy. He is distressed by her weakened health, but gives in to her demand that he go to England to accept the honorary degree offered by OXFORD UNIVERSITY. After he returns, Livy dies. His own death comes not long afterward, when HALLEY'S COMET reappears. As his spirit leaves his body, Tom Sawyer and Huck Finn beckon to him to run off and play.

The Adventures of Mark Twain **(1985)** Feature film directed by Will Vinton using animated clay figures in a technique known as "claymation." Susan Shadburne's script adapts Mark Twain's life and writings to a story line similar to that of TOM SAWYER ABROAD. Tom Sawyer (voice of Chris Ritchie), Huck Finn (Gary Krug) and Becky THATCHER (Michele Mariana) are unhappy stowaways on an airship that Mark Twain (James Whitmore) is piloting. He is trying to catch up with HALLEY'S COMET, but the children think he is leading them all to destruction.

Claymation lends itself well to fluid transfigurations of objects, such as a frog emerging from the pages of a book. The technique also lends itself well to relatively seamless transitions from straight narrative to dramatizations of episodes from Mark Twain's writings. These include the JUMPING FROG story, "CAPTAIN STORMFIELD'S VISIT TO HEAVEN," and the diaries of ADAM AND EVE. Special attention is given to parallels between Adam and Eve and Mark Twain's relationship with his wife Livy. There are also many subtle details, such as the jettisoning of the PAIGE COMPOSITOR to shed weight.

The craft's exterior resembles a STEAMBOAT, while the interior recalls the fantastic submarine in Jules Verne's *Twenty Thousand Leagues Under the Sea*. A particularly apt use of claymation comes in a sequence taken from "THE CHRONICLE OF YOUNG SATAN," in which Satan manufactures tiny human beings and animals from clay.

Africa Mark Twain visited Africa in two widely separated trips. While cruising the MEDITERRANEAN on the QUAKER CITY in 1867, he spent time in TANGIER and EGYPT; he also saw Algiers from its harbor. These experiences fill four chapters of *Innocents Abroad*. Three decades later, he finished an around-the-world lecture tour at the opposite end of the continent. After resting for two weeks on MAURITIUS in April 1896, he stopped in Mozambique and then spent more than two months in SOUTH AFRICA—a period covered in the last nine chapters of *Following the Equator*.

Despite his experience in Africa and the fact that he grew up strongly influenced by African-American culture, Mark Twain made little use of explicitly African settings or references in his fiction. His works occasionally use such ethnic labels as "Bushmen" or "Zulu" as examples of presumably primitive or exotic peoples; otherwise, his references to Africa are mostly cursory.

Tom, Huck and Jim fish from their balloon craft over a Saharan oasis as lions watch, in Tom Sawyer Abroad.

Examples include chapter 27 of *The Gilded Age*, which calls Corruptionville the best missionary field "outside the jungles of Central Africa," and an allusion in chapter 24 of *Connecticut Yankee* to a hermit who has gone to Africa's Sahara Desert. In *Huckleberry Finn*, the word "Africa" appears just once: in chapter 41, a neighbor of the Phelpses alludes to Jim's "secret Africa writ'n." A similarly brief, but more substantive, allusion appears in chapter 14 of *Pudd'nhead Wilson*, in which ROXY tells her son that their illustrious ancestors include "a nigger king outen Africa." Mark Twain's only extended use of African settings occurs in *Tom Sawyer Abroad* (1894)—a story he tentatively called "Huck Finn in Africa"—which concerns a balloon voyage across North Africa.

After the turn of the 20th century, Mark Twain grew increasingly outspoken against imperialism. While he had mixed feelings about Britain's proper role in the South African (Boer) War, he was unreservedly opposed to the ruthless commercial exploitation of the Congo Free State—and denounces it in KING LEOPOLD'S SOLILOQUY.

"The Aged Pilot Man" BURLESQUE poem in chapter 51 of *Roughing It*. An 800-word ballad in 28 stanzas,

"The Aged Pilot Man" extols the heroism of Dollinger, a PILOT of 40 years' experience on the Erie Canal. The poem's narrator recalls going to Albany with his parents when a summer storm suddenly erupts. Their mule-drawn canal boat plows on in the raging tempest as mounting perils fill the passengers with alarm. The stoic Dollinger repeatedly calms them with the admonition, "Fear not, but trust in Dollinger, and he will fetch you through." The joke, of course, is that the canal is shallow and only slightly wider than the boat, which scarcely requires a pilot. After steering it through such perils as a low bridge, torrential rain, curves in the canal and shoal water, Dollinger meets his match when the canal springs a leak, bringing the voyage to jarring halt. The day is saved, however, when a farmer quietly lays a plank out to the boat, allowing its passengers to *walk* ashore.

According to *Roughing It*, Mark Twain originally wrote this poem for the WEEKLY OCCIDENTAL, a Nevada literary newspaper that expired before the poem was published. He adapted its form from "The Raging Canal," a comic ballad by Pete Morris (1821–?) and was partly inspired by Samuel Coleridge's "Rime of the Ancient Mariner." Dollinger himself appears to be modeled on Isaiah SELLERS, an immeasurably proud steamboat pilot of about 40 years' experience. *A Tramp Abroad* (1880) adapts Dollinger's story in an account of a fictional raft trip down Germany's NECKAR River (chapter 14). Like Dollinger, the raft's captain is a 40-year veteran.

Ah Sin, The Heathen Chinee Play produced in 1877. The only major writing project on which Mark Twain collaborated with Bret HARTE, *Ah Sin* is a four-act play set in a mid–19th-century CALIFORNIA mining camp. Its title character is a Chinese laundryman whom Harte had made famous in his poem "The Heathen Chinee." In late 1876, Harte stayed at Mark Twain's Hartford home while working on the play. At the end of the year, they signed a contract to produce it with Charles T. Parsloe, an actor noted for his Chinese impressions. The play opened in WASHINGTON, D.C. the following May. Though moderately well received, it closed after one week. On July 31, Augustin DALY opened a new production in New York City that ran for four weeks. A chaotic mixture of broad comedy and drama, the story revolves around the resourceful Ah Sin, who manipulates gullible miners in order to solve a supposed murder mystery. It badly needed revisions, but its squabbling authors could not get together to provide them. Frederick ANDERSON edited the play's first published version in 1961.

Aileen Mavourneen Narrator of "A DOG'S TALE" (1903). The offspring of a female collie and a male St. Bernard who takes her name from a popular song, Aileen learns patience and a loving philosophy of life from her mother, then is sold to a family named GRAY.

Her happiness seems perfect when she has her own puppy—apparently sired by an Irish setter named Robin Adair; however, she dies of a broken heart after her master kills her puppy in a scientific experiment.

Aix-les-Bains Health spa on the southeast shore of eastern FRANCE's Lake Bourget, about 40 miles south of Geneva. When Mark Twain took his family to Europe in June 1891, they went almost directly to Aix to enjoy the sulfur baths that had been famous since Roman times. Pleased with the relief that the baths brought for the pain in his arm, Mark Twain liked almost everything about the town. He praised it lavishly in "Aix, the Paradise of the Rheumatics," which appeared in the *Illustrated London News* the following November and was reprinted in the NEW YORK SUN in December.

Ajax Ship on which Mark Twain sailed to HAWAII in 1866. Recently built to be a warship, the *Ajax* was a 2,000-ton screw-propelled steamer with sails and accommodations for 60 passengers. Its owners, the California Steam Navigation Company, invited Mark Twain to be a guest on the vessel's inaugural voyage from San Francisco to Honolulu in January 1866; he declined, but covered the event for the VIRGINIA CITY TERRITORIAL ENTERPRISE. Afterward, he accepted the SACRAMENTO UNION's offer to write letters from Hawaii and sailed on the *Ajax*'s second voyage on March 7. Making as many as 300 miles on good days, the ship reached Honolulu on March 18—less than half the time Mark Twain spent on his return voyage on the *Smyrniote*. The *Ajax* proved unprofitable, however, and made no further Hawaiian runs for its company.

Mark Twain's first three Hawaii letters give a full account of the *Ajax* voyage; the briefer account in chapter 62 of *Roughing It* is built around an anecdote about two fictitious passengers, WILLIAMS and the Old ADMIRAL. The cruise was Mark Twain's first ocean voyage. Though it was initially rough, possibly making him seasick, he greatly enjoyed it and made at least 35 more ocean voyages.

Alden, Henry Mills (November 11, 1836, Mt. Tabor, Vermont–October 7, 1919, New York, New York) Chief editor of HARPER'S MAGAZINE from 1869 until he died 50 years later. Alden had great influence over the magazine's content and often worked with Mark Twain over the last decade of the latter's life. He sat next to Mark Twain at the 70th birthday banquet that HARPER'S WEEKLY threw for him in December 1905, and Mark Twain spoke at a lunch in Alden's honor three months later.

Alden, Jean François Fictitious translator of *Joan of Arc*. "Alden" is credited on the title page of the novel with translating Sieur Louis DE CONTE's ancient French into modern English. A thousand words of prefatory remarks by "the translator" sum up Mark Twain's esteem for JOAN OF ARC. Mark Twain adds modern commentary to the novel in footnotes attributed to the translator in chapters 12, 22, 30 and 35 of book 2 and chapters 2, 5, 11 and 16 of book 3. He may have named Alden after Henry Mills ALDEN, the editor of HARPER'S MAGAZINE, in which *Joan of Arc* was serialized.

Aldrich, Thomas Bailey (November 11, 1836, Portsmouth, New Hampshire–March 19, 1907, Boston, Massachusetts) Poet, novelist, dramatist, editor. Aldrich spent part of his childhood in New Orleans and was later a journalist in New York City. During the CIVIL WAR, he served as a correspondent at the front. In 1881 he succeeded W. D. HOWELLS as editor of the ATLANTIC MONTHLY, resigning in 1890 to concentrate on his own writing. He is best remembered for *The Story of a Bad Boy* (1869), a novel drawing on his childhood. His lead character, "Tom Bailey," is a forerunner of Mark Twain's Tom SAWYER: both characters hate Sunday school, sneak out for midnight adventures, imitate heroes of books, camp out with friends on an island and grow lovesick over a girl. Mark Twain read Aldrich's book shortly after it was published, but claimed not to have been influenced by it and to have disliked its prose style.

Thomas Bailey Aldrich. (W. D. Howells, Literary Friends and Acquaintance, *1902)*

Mark Twain and Aldrich met in November 1871, after corresponding for several months. They remained friends the rest of their lives, and Mark Twain spoke at Aldrich's memorial service and remembered him in "MY BOYHOOD DREAMS" (1900).

Aleck Scott (Alexander Scott) The last STEAMBOAT on which Mark Twain served as a cub PILOT. A 709-ton side-wheeler built in 1848, the *Scott* was well known and comparatively old by the time Mark Twain served on it. Between December 13, 1858 and February 27, 1859, he may have made three round-trips between St. Louis and New Orleans on the boat. He definitely made two such trips between March 1 and April 8, 1859—when he received his pilot's license. It was on the *Scott* that his pilot Horace BIXBY and Captain Robert A. Reilly tricked him into thinking a deep-water crossing was dangerously shallow—an incident described in chapter 13 of *Life on the Mississippi*. The boat is also mentioned by name in the next two chapters, and it figures in several of the book's original illustrations. After the start of the Civil War, the boat was acquired by the Union government.

Alexander II (April 29, 1818, St. Petersburg, Russia–March 13, 1881, St. Petersburg) Emperor of RUSSIA. Alexander succeeded his father, Nicholas I, as czar during the CRIMEAN War and had a long reign noted for social reforms—particularly his March 1861 edict freeing serfs from many legal disabilities. Unable to satisfy competing pressures for reform, however, he was eventually assassinated.

On August 26, 1867, Mark Twain was among the QUAKER CITY passengers whom Czar Alexander received at his summer palace near YALTA, where the American consul read a brief speech that Mark Twain had written. *Innocents Abroad* describes the meeting in chapter 37, condensing the more detailed account of Mark Twain's original letters to the SAN FRANCISCO ALTA CALIFORNIA. Contrary to the book's version of how the meeting with the czar came about, it appears that it was not arranged until the ship landed at Yalta. Daniel D. LEARY, one of the *Quaker City*'s owners, hoped to sell the ship to the czar, but did not succeed.

On June 6, 1867, a Pole named Berezowski shot at Alexander in Paris. Mark Twain visited the city a month later and saw the spot where the assassination attempt occurred. Chapter 14 of *Innocents Abroad* makes fun of what a great tourist attraction the bullet's mark in a tree will become; the anecdote seems to anticipate the preface to *Connecticut Yankee*, in which the narrator inspects an ancient bullet hole in the armor of Sir SAGRAMOR LE DESIROUS at Warwick Castle.

Alfred T. Lacey STEAMBOAT on which Mark Twain PILOTED. After Mark Twain left the PENNSYLVANIA in New Orleans in June 1858, he returned up the Mississippi River on the *Lacey*, two days behind the *Pennsylvania*. He was on the *Lacey* when he learned of the *Pennsylvania's* explosion that killed his brother Henry Clemens. He mentions the *Lacey* in accounts of the incident in *Life on the Mississippi* (chapter 20) and in IS SHAKESPEARE DEAD? (part 1).

Incomplete evidence suggests that in July Mark Twain made a round-trip on the *Lacey* when Barton S. BOWEN and George G. EALER were its pilots and John P. Rodney its captain. Firmer evidence suggests that the *Lacey* was the first steamboat on which Mark Twain worked as a licensed pilot. From mid-May 1859, he and Bowen were copilots under Rodney on a round-trip between St. Louis and New Orleans.

Alison, Catherine (Cathy) Central character in "A HORSE'S TALE" and narrator of chapter 4. Born in SPAIN of an American father, George Alison, and a Spanish mother, Cathy lives in FRANCE (possibly in ROUEN), until she is nine, when both her parents die. Her aunt Mercedes then sends her to western America to live with her bachelor uncle, General Thomas Alison, who is about to retire from the army. There Cathy conquers everyone with her vivacity, kindness and sense of justice. The soldiers adopt her and make her an officer, and she becomes close to Buffalo Bill (CODY) and his horse SOLDIER BOY. Despite being everyone's pet, she remains unspoiled and popular among other children.

Cathy has learned English and Spanish from her parents; she also speaks French and some German and Italian. In the West, she begins learning Indian languages, but is not good at formal studies and makes errors resembling those cited in "ENGLISH AS SHE IS TAUGHT" (chapter 5). She also loves using big words that she does not understand. Descended from a Virginia family on her father's side, Cathy identifies with her mother and thinks of herself as Spanish. After her uncle retires, he takes her to her aunt's home in Spain, where she chooses to remain. About six months later, she sees her beloved horse Soldier Boy gored in a bullfight ring. When she rushes to his side, she is gored to death herself.

While Cathy has the athleticism and daring of a rugged boy, she also exhibits such strongly feminine traits that the family servant, Mammy Dorcas, theorizes that she is "twins," in which the boy twin is submerged. Cathy's combination of gentle and martial qualities closely resembles Mark Twain's depiction of JOAN OF ARC, whom—like Cathy—he modeled physically and temperamentally on his daughter Susy Clemens, adding his daughter Jean's love of animals. When Mark Twain submitted his manuscript to HARPER'S MAGAZINE, he included a photograph of Susy on which he wanted the illustrator to model Cathy.

Allbright, Charles William Background figure in the "RAFT CHAPTER" of *Huckleberry Finn* and *Life on the Mississippi*. In a ghost story that Huck Finn overhears aboard a giant raft, Allbright is a baby boy who was killed by his father, Dick ALLBRIGHT. The ghost story concludes with the baby's discovery in a barrel. When Huck himself is discovered aboard the raft, he wins the crew's sympathetic laughter by giving his own name as "Charles William Allbright." The name of another character in *Life on the Mississippi*, Charlie WILLIAMS, may be related to this one.

Allbright, Dick Central character in a ghost story told in the "RAFT CHAPTER" of *Huckleberry Finn* (chapter 16) and *Life on the Mississippi* (chapter 3). Huck Finn sneaks aboard a giant raft and hears a man named Ed tell about Allbright, a fellow boatman whom he knew five years earlier. Three years before that, Allbright choked his infant son to death and put his body in a barrel that later followed him and brought misfortune on his crewmates. When the captain of Ed's raft brings the barrel aboard, Allbright's dead son, Charles William ALLBRIGHT, is found inside. Allbright wraps the baby in his arms, jumps off the raft and disappears.

Alonzo Child Last STEAMBOAT on which Mark Twain worked as a PILOT. A 493-ton side-wheeler, the *Child* was built in Jeffersonville, Indiana for the MISSOURI RIVER trade around 1856. After leaving the ARAGO, Mark Twain joined the *Child* at St. Louis in mid-September 1860—just as it was switching over to the Lower Mississippi River trade. From then until May 8, 1861, he made nine or 10 round-trips to New Orleans. He suffered what may have been his only major mishap as a pilot during an upriver trip on the *Child*. On November 1, 1860, he ran the boat aground about 70 miles north of New Orleans while racing another boat in hazy smoke. During this period his copilots included Horace BIXBY, Sam BOWEN and Will BOWEN, and he served under two captains, David DeHaven and James O'Neal. He and Will Bowen left the boat in New Orleans in early May 1861, after the CIVIL WAR started. The *Child* was converted to an ironclad Confederate warship, the *Arkansas*, and eventually ran aground after reputedly making its way through the entire Union fleet.

Decades later, Mark Twain used the *Alonzo Child* as an 1860 setting for "Newhouse's Jew Story."

alpenstock Long iron-pointed staff carried by hikers in the ALPS. *A Tramp Abroad* often mentions alpenstocks as objects of ridicule. Chapter 25 describes how tourists often carry them as trophies, with their names and the places they have visited burned into them.

Alps European mountain system stretching from southeastern FRANCE to Slovenia and Croatia, encompassing parts of ITALY, SWITZERLAND, Liechtenstein, GERMANY and AUSTRIA. In 1878 Mark Twain traveled extensively through the French and Swiss Alps, which figure prominently in *A Tramp Abroad*. The following year and during the early 1890s, he crossed the Alps several times while traveling between Italy and Germany and Austria.

Amaranth Fictional STEAMBOAT in *The Gilded Age*. In chapter 4, Si HAWKINS takes his family up the Mississippi River on the steamboat *Boreas,* which races with the *Amaranth.* The latter blows its boiler after ignoring its head engineer's warnings, and the *Boreas* picks up 39 wounded persons and 22 dead bodies. Ninety-six persons are missing—including the parents of Laura Van Brunt, whom the Hawkinses adopt. Years later, it is learned that Laura's father survived the accident (chapter 10).

The location of this accident poses a problem. In writing about it, Mark Twain was doubtless thinking of the PENNSYLVANIA's 1858 explosion near MEMPHIS, which he called the "Good Samaritan City." In chapter 4, he alludes to "Good Samaritans" helping the *Amaranth*'s injured and mentions a Memphis physician; however, since the Hawkinses are traveling *north* from Tennessee on the *Boreas,* they should be nowhere near Memphis when the *Amaranth* explodes.

Ament, Joseph (c. 1824–?) Hannibal printer. In May 1848, when Ament was about 24, he moved to Hannibal from nearby PALMYRA and brought with him the *Missouri Courier,* a newspaper that he had published for several years. He merged the *Courier* with the local *Gazette* and took on Mark Twain as an apprentice. Mark Twain's AUTOBIOGRAPHY says that he was taken from school and apprenticed to Ament the moment that his father died, and he gives a colorful account of privations he endured under Ament's miserly employment. John M. Clemens died in March 1847—more than a year before Ament came to Hannibal; Mark Twain's recollection of *when* he joined Ament must therefore be wrong. He appears to have joined Ament in 1848 or 1849; in January 1851, he left Ament to work for his brother's HANNIBAL WESTERN UNION. Ament went back to Palmyra with the *Courier* in 1855.

The American Claimant (1892) Mark Twain's sixth novel. Generally regarded as an unsuccessful blend of sharp social SATIRE and farce, *The American Claimant* is loosely built around Colonel Mulberry SELLERS, whom Mark Twain created for *The Gilded Age*. Its story had an unusual evolution. After Mark Twain and C. D. WARNER published *The Gilded Age* in 1873, an unauthorized dramatization from their novel was staged. Mark Twain bought the rights to this play, which stressed an eccentric characterization of Sellers. A decade later he persuaded W. D. HOWELLS to collaborate with him on a new play, which they called *Colonel Sellers as a Scientist.* This play, which emphasized Sellers's bizarre inventions, flopped, but Mark Twain remained interested in its theme. In early 1891, he began turning the play into a

novel. Once he began writing, however, he found another theme more compelling. Long interested in claimants—such as his distant relation Jesse LEATHERS, who claimed to be the rightful Earl of Durham—he made claimants the story's new center. The only significant elements of the play that he kept pertain to Sellers's inventions. In just over two months he completed the novel, convinced that he had created a sure success.

SYNOPSIS

A 66,000-word story in 25 chapters, *The American Claimant* opens 15 years after the events of *The Gilded Age,* and takes place over at least two months. Its story involves several of the earlier novel's characters, notably Colonel Sellers, the claimant of the novel's title. Sellers is an eccentric American inventor and dreamer who fancies himself the rightful Earl of ROSSMORE. Most of the action in which he is involved tends toward farce. The other central character is Lord BERKELEY, an English viscount who is heir to the current Earl of Rossmore. Berkeley comes to America prepared to trade his hereditary rank for the chance to make his own way in an egalitarian republic free of aristocracy. His story line tends toward heavy social satire, as he tests his personal renunciation of aristocratic privilege in the democratic society he hopes to find in America. Berkeley's path inevitably crosses that of Sellers, generating an intricately interwoven plot filled with confused identities.

Although the novel opens with a disclaimer announcing that no weather will be found in the book to avoid intrusions on the narrative, weather proves to be the central theme at the end of the book.

Chapter 1
The story opens in ENGLAND's Cholmondeley Castle, where the Earl of ROSSMORE and his son BERKELEY discuss Berkeley's intention to go to America to "change places" with Simon LATHERS, a distant relative whose claim to be earl he accepts. Rossmore concedes that while "morally the American tramp *is* the rightful Earl of Rossmore; legally he has no more right than his dog." He accedes to Berkeley's going to America, confident that the trip will sour him on his idealism. Meanwhile, a letter arrives from Mulberry SELLERS in America, who announces that Lathers has died, making him rightful earl.

Chapter 2
The scene switches to an earlier moment in America, where Sellers—not yet an earl—is in his Washington, D.C. home. He is working on a complex mechanical toy and is surrounded by cheap portraits of distinguished Americans labeled with the names of former "Earls of Rossmore." His library also displays a map labeled "Future Siberia," with fancifully named cities. The large house is run-down and sparsely furnished, but otherwise tasteful. Washington HAWKINS, a friend he has not

seen in 15 years, arrives as a congressional delegate from the Cherokee Strip.

Chapter 3

Polly SELLERS, the colonel's wife, fills Hawkins in on Sellers's activities over the past 15 years. We also meet the old family servants, JINNY and her husband Dan'l, and learn more about Sellers himself. He completes his game, which he calls "Pigs in the Clover," and tells Hawkins that he thinks there might be a few hundred thousand dollars in it. This figure impresses Hawkins, but Sellers is more interested in his latest invention: the scientific materialization of departed spirits. Within three days he expects to perfect his process and begin calling up the dead. He dazzles Hawkins with the possibilities—such as replacing New York City's living policemen with dead ones, at half the cost. He predicts that there are billions in the scheme; however, he cannot scrape together $3.40 to pay a bill collector who comes to the door.

Hawkins tells Sellers about One-Armed Pete, a Cherokee Strip bank robber with a $5,000 reward on his head, whom he saw on a train headed to Baltimore. Sellers drafts a plan to capture Pete, beginning with a personal ad that he places in a Baltimore newspaper.

Chapter 4

Sellers and Hawkins discuss how they will spend their reward money until Polly quiets them. The next day Sellers takes the plans of his new game into town to patent it, while Hawkins takes the game itself into town to see if it has commercial possibilities. A Yankee furniture repairer is interested in producing the game, but can pay nothing down, so he offers to pay a five-cent royalty on each 25-cent game he sells. After having the man draw up a contract, Hawkins dismisses the subject from his mind.

When Sellers gets home, he excitedly announces that his cousin Simon Lathers and his brother have died, leaving him the rightful Earl of Rossmore. He cables his daughter, Sally SELLERS—whom he now calls "Lady Gwendolen"—to return home from college to help mourn. The next day he sends the cable that the Earl of Rossmore receives in chapter 1. He also asks authorities in Lathers's Arkansas village to embalm the Lathers brothers and ship them C.O.D. to Rossmore. He arranges elaborate family mourning observations and renames his house "Rossmore Towers."

Chapter 5

Glad to get away from her snooty, rank-conscious classmates, Sally arrives home seven days later. In studying *Burke's Peerage*, Sellers finds that the Rossmore earldom was founded by William the Conqueror and that it ranks third in England. Meanwhile, he receives a cable from One-Armed Pete answering his ad and promising to come to Washington in 10 days. The next day, Sellers ships the remains of the Lathers brothers to England, while Lord Berkeley simultaneously starts for America.

Chapter 6

When the Lathers brothers arrive in England, Rossmore reluctantly gives them a formal funeral and has them interred in the family plot. Back in America, Sally leads a double life: By day, she is sensible and democratic Sally Sellers, working to support the family; by night, she is romantic "Lady Gwendolen."

After One-Armed Pete arrives in Washington, he sends Sellers instructions to meet him near the New Gadsby Hotel the next day. That night, Sellers and Hawkins visit Pete's hotel to spy. Hawkins spots Pete boarding an elevator in his western clothes, but does not notice Viscount Berkeley boarding the elevator.

Chapter 7

In his hotel room, Berkeley records "impressions" of his travels in his journal. He is distressed to find that Americans treat him deferentially everywhere he goes just because of his title. That night, he is awakened by a call that the hotel is on fire. Saving only his journal, he rushes down the hallway, snatches an outfit from another room and puts it on. It is a gaudy cowboy suit that attracts considerable attention outside. He goes off and finds new lodgings.

The next morning Berkeley examines the pockets in his new clothes and finds over $500 in cash. When he reads a newspaper report that *he* died a hero in the hotel fire, he decides to let the error stand so that he can start a truly new life. Since he is officially "dead," he no longer needs to find the American Claimant.

Chapter 8

Sellers reads the report of Berkeley's death in the newspaper, which also reports that a one-armed man was seen headed for certain death during the fire. Unconcerned by the possibility that Pete has died, Sellers promises to "materialize" him so that they can still collect the reward money. After breaking the news of the latest death of a kinsman to his family, Sellers goes to the hotel to claim Berkeley's body for shipment to England.

Chapter 9

At the hotel, Sellers and Hawkins find five charred, unrecognizable bodies. When officials point out that three reports of Berkeley's death place him in spots other than where these bodies were found, Sellers and Hawkins fill baskets with ashes from each of the three places where Berkeley may have died. At home, Polly joins Sellers in sitting up with the ashes, but refuses to let her husband put them on display in the front room.

Chapter 10

Berkeley, now feeling free for the first time, banks most of his newfound money in a way that will make it impossible for him to retrieve it. He keeps wearing the gaudy Western clothes, hoping their rightful owner will find him. While at the bank, he invents a new name for himself: "Howard Tracy." He cables his father to report that he is unhurt, to tell him that he has taken a new name, and to say good-bye. With limited money and no identification, he must now survive on his own.

That evening Berkeley attends a lecture at the Mechanics' Club Debate. The first lecturer attacks Matthew ARNOLD, arguing that irreverence is one of the American press's greatest qualities. The second speaker praises the great achievements of inventors who lacked college educations. Berkeley leaves, thrilled by the arguments for egalitarianism.

Chapter 11
In searching for a job, Berkeley finds that he has no chance without political backing. To get closer to common people and conserve his resources, he moves into a cheap boardinghouse run by Rachel Marsh and her husband. The Marshes' attractive daughter Hattie Marsh surprises Berkeley with her relaxed openness and teaches him how Americans use titles such as "lady."

Berkeley meets Barrow, who believes that aristocratic privilege survives in England only because of the acquiescence of society as a whole. The mass of the people need only declare themselves dukes and duchesses and laugh the nobility into oblivion.

Chapter 12
At his first boardinghouse supper, Berkeley has trouble adjusting to the stench of old cabbage. The landlord Marsh shocks him with his undemocratic tyranny over a young unemployed tinner, Nat Brady. Nevertheless, Berkeley concludes that he is living in a house that is a "republic" in which everyone is free and equal. When Berkeley later boards a streetcar, Sellers and Hawkins see him and recognize One-Armed Pete's clothes. Sellers thinks that Berkeley is the materialized form of One-Armed Pete that his experiment has called up.

Chapter 13
Unable to find work or even join a labor union, Berkeley is becoming desperate. As he grows surly, other boardinghouse residents turn away from him and tease him. However, after a bullying amateur boxer named Allen picks on Brady, Berkeley whips Allen easily, regaining the respect of the other boarders. Meanwhile, his financial situation is so bad that he cables his father, on the pretext of telling him his new name.

Chapter 14
To cheer up Berkeley, Barrow takes him to the Mechanics' Club, where a blacksmith named Tompkins denounces the English aristocracy. Berkeley's conscience burns, but afterward Barrow demolishes Tompkins's argument, which he says ignores the "factor of human nature."

Chapter 15
When Marsh reminds Berkeley the next day that he has not paid his weekly bill, Berkeley discovers that he has been robbed—as have other residents since Allen disappeared. To buy time, Berkeley tells Marsh that he expects a cable from home. Marsh's sarcastic reply drives Berkeley to blurt out that his father is an English earl. Everyone is too stunned to know how to react; however, Marsh will not let Berkeley leave the house to fetch his cable, so Brady volunteers to go. After Brady returns with a cable, everyone is breathless as Berkeley opens it. His father's message has one word: "Thanks." Berkeley is spared further embarrassment when Barrow offers to pay his bill.

Chapter 16
Barrow tells Berkeley that he has found work for him if he can paint details in pictures. Barrow introduces Berkeley to a German named Handel who paints human figures from tintypes, and to an old sailor, Captain Saltmarsh, who paints cannons and backgrounds. Their problem is that each man can paint nothing else; since their customers want variety, they need help.

Chapter 17
Berkeley's spirits sink as he waits for a cable from his father. After a week, he decides to join the painters. They are so pleased with a hearse he paints on a canvas that they make him a full partner. As he paints cats, hacks, sausages, tugs, pianos, guitars, rocks and other things, the painting business booms and Berkeley's self-esteem rises.

Back at Rossmore Towers, Hawkins despairs because One-Armed Pete has failed to show up as Sellers promised. To cheer up Hawkins, Sellers shows him a new invention: his "Cursing Phonograph," for use by sea captains too busy to swear themselves. Another of Sellers's inventions is a decomposer that produces sewergas for home use in lighting; he hopes to have the system adopted in the White House so that it will catch on.

Chapter 18
Sellers reveals his biggest project to Hawkins: a plan to liberate RUSSIA by buying Siberia and using its political prisoners to start a revolution.

When Sellers sees Berkeley strolling by his house, he congratulates himself on getting his "materializee" to come. Berkeley, meanwhile, notices that he is at the American Claimant's home. Sellers invites Berkeley in, tells him that he is expected, and makes some remarks intended for One-Armed Pete that are inscrutable to Berkeley. After Berkeley identifies himself as an artist, Sellers engages him to restore paintings and leaves him to work alone.

Chapter 19
Sellers and Hawkins wonder why this materialization of One-Armed Pete has *two* arms and speaks with an English accent. Sellers concludes that he has materialized an ancestor of Pete and proposes materializing him "down to date." Once One-Armed Pete is under their control, they will have him confess every crime he ever committed and then collect a fortune in rewards.

When Polly asks about Berkeley, whom she sees painting in another room, she surprises Sellers and Hawkins by mentioning that she has seen him eating apples—impossible behavior for a materializee.

Chapter 20

When Sellers's daughter Sally arrives and meets Berkeley, it is love at first sight. She invites him to stay for dinner, but he declines in order to go out and buy decent clothes. The next day, Berkeley returns in a new suit.

Chapter 21

Sally and Berkeley work in different parts of the house, and they are desolate apart from each other. As a result of a mixup, Sally goes to a friend's house for dinner, while Berkeley dines at her house. When she returns, a quick exchange of glances tells her and Berkeley that their affection is mutual. When they are finally alone, they embrace and kiss; Hawkins accidentally sees them and is appalled by the idea that Sally is kissing a "materializee."

Chapter 22

Despondent over what he has just seen, Hawkins cannot understand why no one else notices the brimstone stench emitted by Berkeley. When Sellers joins him, he puzzles over the mystery of a materializee eating solid food. He also confesses to liking Berkeley too much to "degrade" him to a burglar, so he and Hawkins agree to sacrifice their hopes for reward money and leave Berkeley as he is.

Sally tells Berkeley that her father's claim to be an earl is a "sham" and that she no longer wants to be called "Gwendolen." She asks Berkeley if he wants to marry her only because of her rank. Suppressing the urge to laugh, Berkeley swears that he loves her only for herself, then asks her how *she* feels about aristocracy and nobility. He is relieved to learn that she does not disapprove of real titles. This line of questioning re-opens her doubts about Berkeley's sincerity, since she still worries that he is after her father's earldom.

Chapter 23

That night Berkeley writes his father, telling him that he is ready to renounce his quest in America and that he intends to marry the American Claimant's daughter. After receiving the letter, Rossmore immediately leaves for America in order to deal with matters personally.

Over the next 10 days, Berkeley's spirits rise and fall with Sally's shifting moods as he paints a portrait of Sellers in "a peer's scarlet robe." Berkeley eventually learns that Sally has been acting oddly only because she still thinks that he is after her father's earldom. They reconcile, but Berkeley tries to prove his point by telling her that *he* is the son of an English earl. This only angers her. His claim seems completely illogical and he has no proof. When he further identifies himself as the son of the Earl of Rossmore, Sally grows even angrier. Berkeley leaves with the understanding that he should not return without proof of his claims.

Chapter 24

During 10 miserable days of waiting for his father's cable, Berkeley confides in Barrow, who humors him. Sally, too, is miserable throughout this period. Meanwhile, Hawkins and Sellers learn that Sellers's "Pigs in the Clover" games are sweeping the nation, with factories working night and day to supply them. Hawkins is ecstatic, but Sellers is indifferent and tells him to hunt up the Yankee who makes the games and collect the royalty money—half of which Hawkins can keep. Sellers then returns to working on a temperance lecture. Dissatisfied with his previous lectures on temperance, he suspects that his problem is lack of experience with alcohol, so he gets drunk in order to study the results. However, he gets so sick that he must stay in bed for several days and he misses his lecture.

Once Sellers recovers, he finds that Hawkins has banked enough money for him from his game that he can take Polly to England to press his claim for the earldom. They pack and leave for New York.

After her parents leave, Sally asks Hawkins for advice about Berkeley. Hawkins cannot tell Sally what he really thinks, namely that Berkeley is a materialized spirit, so he invents a story calculated to make her reject Berkeley. Hawkins tells Sally that Berkeley is a "dissipated ruffian" from the Cherokee Strip whose real name is "Spinal Meningitis Snodgrass," that he is the son of an idiot doctor, and that his brother is named "Zylobalsamum Snodgrass." Despite the terrible picture of Berkeley that Hawkins paints, Sally concludes that "he has no friend but me, and I will not desert him now." She asks Hawkins to find Berkeley and bring him to her.

Chapter 25

Hawkins goes straight to the telegraph office and cables Sally's parents to return from New York because she is "going to marry the materializee." Meanwhile, a note arrives at Rossmore Towers saying that the Earl of Rossmore will arrive that evening. Berkeley arrives the same evening, hoping only to see Sally. When he is alone with her, she drops references to the Snodgrass family. After failing to get a rise of out him, she finally asks if he is the son of Dr. Snodgrass. Just as it appears that Sally and Berkeley are again reconciled, Berkeley's father appears and finds them embracing. When Rossmore asks his son for a hug, Sally realizes that Berkeley really is an earl's son and says that she will *not* have him. However, after a long private talk with Sally, Rossmore gives his approval to the marriage, which she is now willing go through with.

Meanwhile, Hawkins talks with Berkeley, who convinces him that he (Berkeley) is not a materialized spirit. Once everyone is together again, plans are made for a quiet wedding at Rossmore Towers, and Sellers and Rossmore became great friends. The Sellerses plan to go to England to visit with Rossmore, but Sellers misses the train and Hawkins reports that he is off on a new scheme and will join the others later. In a note he has left to Hawkins, Sellers explains that since making an offer to purchase Siberia with the big money he expected from his materialization scheme, he is concerned that if the czar suddenly accepts, his credit will suffer when he cannot meet the payment. He is therefore going to San Francisco to test a new scheme with the Lick telescope; he plans to reorganize the Earth's climates by controlling sunspots to shift climates around. For example, he wants to buy Greenland and Iceland, then move one of the tropics to the Arctic Circle, which he will convert into a tropical resort.

PUBLISHING HISTORY

After writing this book in early 1891, Mark Twain serialized it in the NEW YORK SUN's Sunday edition from January 3 to March 27, 1892. It also appeared in various McClure Syndicate magazines and in England's *Idler*. Charles L. WEBSTER & COMPANY and CHATTO & Windus both published *The American Claimant* as a book later the same year. A later HARPER volume, *The American Claimant and Other Stories and Sketches,* combines the novel with most of the stories previously published in MERRY TALES. Since its original publication, *The American Claimant* has rarely been reprinted, except in uniform editions of Mark Twain's works. The MARK TWAIN PAPERS project has tentatively scheduled a corrected edition within a "late tales" volume planned for the year 2002. Dan BEARD illustrated the first American edition of the book, and Hal Hurst illustrated the *Idler* serialization. The Chatto & Windus edition combined Beard's and Hurst's illustrations. Beard apparently was responsible for the Rossmore family motto, *Suum Cuique,* which appears in several illustrations, including the original cover. It is a Latin phrase that loosely translates as "To each, his own."

American Publishing Company   Founded in Hartford on April 10, 1865—the day after Lee surrendered at Appomattox—the American Publishing Company began as a conservative SUBSCRIPTION-BOOK house. In its first two years, it issued just three titles—including a Bible. Elisha BLISS joined the company in 1867 and soon transformed it into a bold operation, publishing many titles and embracing genres such as humor previously untapped by subscription publishers. One of Bliss's first moves was to invite Mark Twain to write a humorous book about his QUAKER CITY cruise. The success of the resulting *Innocents Abroad* (1869) began a period of steady growth for the company that lasted into the mid-1880s.

As Bliss expanded the company, he created such subsidiary imprints as F. C. Bliss, R. W. Bliss, Belknap and Bliss, Columbian Book Company, and Mutual Publishing Company. During its first two decades, the company published about 80 books—a huge number for a

subscription publisher—by writers including Josh BILLINGS, Dan DE QUILLE, Bret HARTE, Joaquin MILLER, A. D. RICHARDSON, J. H. TRUMBULL, C. D. WARNER and C. H. WEBB. Meanwhile, it also published all of Mark Twain's important books through 1880: *Roughing It* (1872), *The Gilded Age* (1873), *Sketches, New and Old* (1875), *Tom Sawyer* (1876) and *A Tramp Abroad* (1880). With sales of over 300,000 copies, Mark Twain books were the company's mainstay; and unlike typical subscription books, they enjoyed steady long-term sales.

After a fling with his own publishing company, Charles L. WEBSTER, Mark Twain returned to the American Publishing Company to publish *Pudd'nhead Wilson* (1894) and *Following the Equator* (1897). His friend H. H. ROGERS then worked out a deal with the company that allowed HARPER'S to issue Mark Twain's back titles in a uniform set. By this time, the subscription market was dying and the American Publishing Company was surviving largely on its own uniform Mark Twain editions. In 1903, the company was sold to Harper's.

"The American Vandal Abroad"   Topic of Mark Twain's 1868–69 LECTURE tour. From mid-November 1868 through early March 1869, Mark Twain traveled through the Midwest and the East delivering more than 40 lectures on the subject of the 1867 QUAKER CITY cruise. Drawing heavily on material that would be published a few months later in *Innocents Abroad,* he presented a lighthearted recap of highlights from his travels, offering humorous anecdotes about northern Italy, Greece and Russia and somewhat more somber material on the Holy Land and Egypt. He defined an "American vandal" as the average American who travels abroad—a person not elaborately educated, cultivated or refined, but one who goes everywhere, is at home everywhere and is always self-possessed. The vandal is also an incorrigible relic-gatherer—the kind of person who removes stones from Christopher Columbus's house.

The lecture tour opened in Cleveland, where Mark Twain was assured the support of the *Herald,* owned by the husband of his friend Mary FAIRBANKS. He received mostly favorable reviews, as well as useful publicity for his forthcoming book. After *Innocents Abroad* was published, he abandoned the "American Vandal" topic in his lectures. Truncated versions of the lecture—which doubtless varied from performance to performance—have often been reprinted.

Innocents Abroad does not develop the concept of the "American vandal," but it does touch on it. For example, a subtitle of chapter 41, which discusses the *Quaker City* passengers' allegedly frustrated attempt to pillage relics at EPHESUS, is "Vandalism Prohibited." Mark Twain first wrote about insensitive "specimen collectors" in his 1866 letters from HAWAII that depict his fictional companion "Mr. BROWN" as a relic-grabber. Brown even tries to make off with the lava on which Captain COOK was killed. Other allusions to relic-grabbing and graffiti-writing "vandals" can be found in chapters 15, 28 and 45 of *Innocents Abroad* and at the end of "CAPTAIN STORMFIELD'S VISIT TO HEAVEN."

Anderson, Frederick (1926–January 1979) Editor of the MARK TWAIN PAPERS (1964–79). Anderson was a library staff member at the University of California at Berkeley when Henry Nash SMITH became editor of the Mark Twain Papers there in 1953. Smith made Anderson his assistant, then turned over the general editorship to him in 1964. Over the next 13 years, Anderson oversaw the complex development of the project's long-term publishing plans, built a staff of professional editors and then saw the project's first volumes through publication. After he died suddenly in 1979, Smith returned to the project as interim general editor until Robert HIRST assumed leadership the following year.

Books that Anderson edited or coedited include *Mark Twain of the Enterprise* (1957), *Selected Mark Twain–Howells Letters* (1968), *Mark Twain: The Critical Heritage* (1971), *A Pen Warmed Up in Hell: Mark Twain in Protest* (1972) and the first two volumes of *Mark Twain's Notebooks & Journals* (1975).

Andrew, Father Minor character in *The Prince and the Pauper*. Andrew is a Roman Catholic priest who has lived in OFFAL COURT since King HENRY VIII closed his monastery. Responsible for what little education Tom CANTY has, he would also have taught Tom's sisters, were they not afraid to become literate. John CANTY kills Andrew when the latter tries to protect Prince EDWARD (chapter 10).

Andrew Jackson Dog mentioned in the JUMPING FROG STORY. The property of Jim SMILEY, Andrew Jackson was a small, unimpressive bull-pup, but had real genius as a fighter in money matches. He allowed opponents to bully-rag and throw him around, but once the money was all up, he would seize hold of the other dog's hind legs and hang on until it quit. His career ended tragically when he confronted a dog with no hind legs; after losing badly, he limped away and—like *Huckleberry Finn*'s Emmeline GRANGERFORD—died of a broken heart when his unique talent failed him.

Angelfish Nickname for girls whom Mark Twain admitted to his private "Aquarium Club." After turning 70, he sought to fill his need for grandchildren by forming friendships with young girls whom he later called "Angelfish," after a beautiful fish he had seen in BERMUDA. From 1906 until he died, he admitted more than a dozen girls to his informal club; he corresponded with them frequently and often had one or two girls—and their mothers—as houseguests. His first Angelfish was a 14-year-old English girl, Dorothy Butes, who often visited him in NEW YORK CITY in 1906. During his 1907

trip to ENGLAND, he added Frances NUNNALLY and Dorothy QUICK to his group.

By April 1908, Mark Twain counted 10 "angelfishes." When he moved to REDDING several months later, he organized his club more formally by writing rules declaring himself its "admiral" and setting such membership qualifications as sincerity, good disposition, intelligence and "school-girl age"—a critical requirement. His rules also declared that the chief purpose of his new house—which he then called "INNOCENCE AT HOME"—was to accommodate club members. He made his BILLIARD room the club's official headquarters and gave various parts of the house piscine nicknames, such as "the Fish-Market." Hungry for correspondence, Mark Twain threatened to suspend any girl who went three months without writing to him. Three hundred of the letters that he exchanged with girls are in *Mark Twain's Aquarium: The Samuel Clemens Angelfish Correspondence, 1905–1910* (1991), edited by John Cooley.

While Mark Twain's correspondence and activities with Angelfish girls appear to have been entirely chaste, any elderly man pursuing pretty little girls gives the appearance of impropriety. When Clara Clemens returned from Europe in September 1908, she disapproved of the Angelfish and forced her father to cut back his contacts with them. Shortly before he died, Mark Twain was rumored to have behaved improperly with a girl in Bermuda named Helen Allen, but evidence for this is inconclusive. After his death, Clara discouraged publication of anything concerning the Angelfish. On her behalf, A. B. PAINE asked Elizabeth Wallace not to publish any "affectionate" photographs of Mark Twain with young girls in her book about Mark Twain in Bermuda.

Angel's Camp (Angels Camp) Town in CALIFORNIA'S CALAVERAS COUNTY in which Mark Twain spent nearly a month in 1865. Named after Henry Angel, who discovered gold in a local creek in 1848, Angel's Camp started as a placer-mining center during the California GOLD RUSH and later shifted to quartz-mining. Mark Twain visited the town during a stagnant period, but by the mid-1880s, it developed into a premier gold-producing region. After another 30 years, however, most of its mines were closed.

On January 22, 1865, Mark Twain went north from JACKASS HILL, in nearby TUOLUMNE COUNTY, to Angel's Camp with Jim GILLIS, who had a claim there. During their first week, heavy rains confined them to Tryon's Hotel; they spent the next three weeks prospecting, with little success. Throughout this time—especially during the rainy week—Mark Twain exchanged yarns with locals, notably Ben COON, and left with a NOTEBOOK filled with story ideas. Chapter 61 of *Roughing It* briefly describes this period.

Among the tales that Mark Twain eventually wrote from his Angel's Camp and Jackass Hill notes are the JUMPING FROG STORY (1865), the stories of Jim BLAINE and his grandfather's ram and of Dick BAKER and his cat TOM QUARTZ in *Roughing It* (1872), Jim Baker's BLUEJAY YARN in *A Tramp Abroad* (1880), the ROYAL NONESUCH of *Huckleberry Finn* (1884) and "THE CALIFORNIAN'S TALE" (1892). The earliest version of the jumping frog story sets the narrative in BOOMERANG, for which later versions substitute the name "Angel's Camp." The narrator calls the place a "decayed mining camp"—the same term *Roughing It* applies to the Tuolumne camp (chapter 60).

Angel's Camp was officially incorporated as "Angels" in 1912, but still uses its original name. Now a town of about 2,400 residents, it stands on California's Highway 49. The town's high school is named after Bret HARTE and it calls its athletic teams the Jumping Frogs. Since the late 1930s, the town has held an annual "Jumping Frog Jubilee" in conjunction with the May county fair.

Apthorps Family mentioned in *Huckleberry Finn.* In chapter 28, Huck persuades Mary Jane WILKS to leave town for a few days to stay with the LOTHROP family. However, he tells her sisters that she has gone to see Hanner PROCTOR across the river. He adds that she will also visit the wealthy Apthorps, hoping to persuade them to come to the auction that the KING is planning.

The Arabian Nights Collection of tales that had a profound influence on Mark Twain. *The Arabian Nights Entertainments,* also known as *A Thousand and One Nights,* is a body of 264 Persian and Arabian tales that has become a classic of world literature. By the mid-15th century, its tales were collected and standardized; their translation into French in the early 18th century introduced them to the West. In 1840, Edward William Lane published a three-volume English translation—a copy of which Mark Twain later owned.

The FRAME of the Arabian Nights is the story of Scheherezade, the wife of King Shahriyar of India. After his first wife betrayed him, Shahriyar went mad; to avenge himself, he took a new wife each night and had her beheaded the next morning. Scheherezade stays alive by telling Shahriyar a new tale each night, saving its conclusion for the following night. Her stories do not end until the 1,001st night, when Shahriyar loses his desire to kill her.

Many of Scheherezade's tales are familiar throughout the world: Aladdin and his magic lamp, Ali Baba and the 40 thieves, Abou Hassan the sleeper, Sinbad the sailor and others. The tales are filled with witches, genies, flying carpets and winged horses, as well as beautiful princesses, dashing desert horsemen, camel caravans and heartless kings. Their magic, romance, exotic settings and strange characters have long contributed to Western perceptions of the East as "mysterious." Mark Twain had a lifelong fascination with the Arabian Nights; their influence can be seen in scores of passages throughout his writings. As early as March 1852, he alluded to the Arabian Nights in a description of the CAVE near Hannibal. More difficult to assess, but perhaps even more important, is the extent to which the fanciful tales influenced his own imagination. *Tom Sawyer,* for example, may be unusual in lacking clear allusions to the Arabian Nights, but their spirit can be found in the novel's many flights of fancy.

By the mid-1860s, Mark Twain was regularly dropping Arabian Nights references into his writings. When he went on the QUAKER CITY excursion in 1867, he used the Arabian Nights as a kind of yardstick with which to measure the Near Eastern cultures he encountered. *Innocents Abroad,* the book resulting from that voyage, is filled with allusions to the Arabian Nights, from a description of TANGIER in chapter 8 to the travelers' arrival in DAMASCUS in chapter 44. Chapter 13, for example, calls the Sultan of Turkey, ABDUL AZIZ, an ignorant believer in "gnomes, and genii and the wild fables of the Arabian Nights." In chapter 38, the sight of a camel train evokes forgotten boyhood dreams about the Arabian Nights. A passage that he wrote in a letter to the SAN FRANCISCO ALTA CALIFORNIA calls MILAN'S cathedral "an Aladdin's palace."

Although *Tom Sawyer* lacks clear allusions to the Arabian Nights, Tom is familiar with the stories. In *Huckleberry Finn,* he leads his GANG against an imaginary caravan of Spanish merchants and rich Arabs (chapter 3). To everyone but Tom, the caravan appears to be a Sunday-school picnic; Tom explains the discrepancy as an enchantment performed by magicians and genies. Huck suggests getting their own genies to fight back, so Tom puts him to work rubbing a magic lamp. After hours of rubbing, Huck concludes "that all that stuff was only just one of Tom Sawyer's lies." Despite his rationality, Huck is not above using the Arabian Nights to make a point, though he tends to get his details wrong. In chapter 23 of *Huckleberry Finn,* he tells Jim that King HENRY VIII "used to marry a new wife every day, and chop off her head the next morning." The summer that Mark Twain finished writing *Huckleberry Finn,* the Arabian Nights were much on his mind. He also wrote a long burlesque, "1002D ARABIAN NIGHT," but this was not published during his lifetime.

Arabian Nights themes are particularly evident in *Tom Sawyer Abroad* (1894). As Tom, Huck and Jim fly over North Africa, Tom cites passages from the Arabian Nights in chapters 7, 9, 12 and 13. Mark Twain's visit to INDIA in 1896 rekindled his own memories of the Arabian Nights. Chapter 38 of *Following the Equator,* for example, describes Bombay as "the Arabian Nights come again." Additional passages citing the Arabian Nights appear in chapter 60 of *Life on the Mississippi,* chapter 10 of "IS SHAKESPEARE DEAD?," chapter 5 of "WHAT IS MAN?" and elsewhere.

Arago STEAMBOAT on which Mark Twain served as a PILOT. A 268-ton side-wheeler completed in March 1860 in Brownsville, Pennsylvania, the *Arago* was a "roving" steamer. Mark Twain made one round-trip on it between St. Louis and New Orleans, between July 28 and August 31, 1860. He apparently did not get on well with Captain George P. Sloan and his mate, and left the boat. Before he joined the ALONZO CHILD, the *Arago* left from St. Louis, hit a snag, and sank near Goose Island on September 8, 1860. The boat was, however, refloated and put back into service.

The *Arago* may have taken its name from François Arago (1786–1853), a French scientist and statesman.

Arkansas Character in *Roughing It*. A "stalwart ruffian," Arkansas terrorizes people trapped by a flood at HONEY LAKE SMITH's station in Nevada (chapter 31). His reign of terror ends abruptly when the innkeeper's wife confronts him with scissors and gives him a tongue-lashing. As a blustering bully humiliated by an ostensibly weaker person, Arkansas resembles the Old ADMIRAL of *Roughing It* (chapter 62), the tough-talking raftsmen in *Huckleberry Finn*'s "RAFT CHAPTER" and a Hannibal man whom Jane L. Clemens faced down when Mark Twain was a boy. After writing *Roughing It*, Mark Twain began to dramatize the "Arkansas" episode but did not finish the play.

Arkansas Originally part of Missouri Territory, Arkansas separated in 1819 and was admitted to the Union as a slave state on June 15, 1836—seven and a half months after Mark Twain was born. The act creating Arkansas as a territory spelled its name "Arkansaw"—a form Mark Twain often uses in his writings. On the outbreak of the CIVIL WAR, Arkansas joined the Confederacy. Mark Twain first visited Arkansas in early 1857, during his maiden steamboat trip to New Orleans. Over the next four years he went past it scores of times and doubtless made many brief stops there.

Arkansas is the setting for much of the second half of *Huckleberry Finn*. Huck first mentions it by name in chapter 17, when he tells the GRANGERFORDS that he comes from southern Arkansas. After leaving the Grangerfords' KENTUCKY plantation in chapter 18, Huck and Jim's raft would not have taken more than a few days to reach Arkansas, but it is not until chapter 21 that Huck reveals they are in Arkansas. Meanwhile, chapter 20 is set in a river village called POKEVILLE that could be either in Arkansas or across the river, in Mississippi. In chapter 21 the raft comes to BRICKSVILLE—the only town in the novel explicitly placed in Arkansas. From there, they continue south to the unnamed town where they meet the WILKS family; it could be either in Arkansas or across the river. Their final landing is at PIKESVILLE, near the PHELPSES' farm. *Huckleberry Finn* does not make it clear in what state the Phelpses live; however, *Tom Sawyer, Detective* specifies they are in Arkansas (chapter 1), where most of this later story is set. Assuming that the Phelps farm of *Tom Sawyer, Detective* is the same as that of *Huckleberry Finn*, Arkansas is the setting of *Huckleberry Finn*'s conclusion,

as well as the beginning of the story's immediate sequel, "HUCK FINN AND TOM SAWYER AMONG THE INDIANS."

Arkansas also figures in several other stories. After ROXY allows her son to sell her back into slavery in *Pudd'nhead Wilson*, she ends up on an Arkansas plantation from which she escapes and makes her way back to Missouri (chapter 16). *The American Claimant* alludes to a fictional Arkansas village called "Duffy's Corners," where Simon LATHERS and his brother are killed (chapter 1). Elsewhere, Mark Twain evokes Arkansas's name as a symbol of backwardness. In *Connecticut Yankee*, for example, Hank MORGAN compares the CAMELOT WEEKLY HOSANNAH with "Arkansas journalism." *Innocents Abroad* compares VENICE to an "overflowed Arkansas town" (chapter 22).

Arnold, Matthew (December 24, 1822, Laleham, England–April 15, 1888, Liverpool, England) English writer. The son of Thomas Arnold, the headmaster of Rugby School, Matthew Arnold was a school inspector. He first gained renown as a writer of poetry and became a professor of poetry at Oxford (1857–67). He later wrote mostly prose works on literature, religion, and social and political issues. During lecture tours in the United States in 1883–84 and 1886, Arnold irritated the American press by criticizing the failings of American culture. His book *Discourses in America* (1885) came out of his first visit.

Mark Twain entertained Arnold and his family during their visit to Hartford in November 1883, but he later saw Arnold as a symbol of English cultural snobbery and wrote venomous rebuttals to his criticisms of America that remained unpublished. Some of this material he worked into *The American Claimant*, whose fictional Lord BERKELEY attends a lecture in which Arnold's critiques of America are demolished (chapter 10).

In early 1887 Mark Twain was incensed by Arnold's savage criticism of General GRANT's grammar in his *Memoirs*. In April, he replied to Arnold in a speech to Hartford's Army and Navy Club. Citing as his authority another English writer's book on grammar, he blasted the "grammatical crimes" that Arnold himself committed in his attack on Grant. Arnold's last book, *Civilisation in the United States* (1888), also offended Mark Twain, who is believed to have channeled much of his anger against Arnold and the English into *Connecticut Yankee* (1889).

"Around the World" Series of articles in the BUFFALO EXPRESS. In October 1869, Mark Twain's future brother-in-law, Charles J. LANGDON, began an around-the-world trip with an Elmira college teacher named Darius Ford (1824–1904). Ford agreed to write letters about his travels that Mark Twain would rewrite for the *Express* under the title "Around the World." From then until March 1870, Mark Twain wrote 10 articles, only two of which were based on Ford letters. Two articles were based on invented travels; the rest derived from Mark Twain's own experiences in California and Nevada—several of which he later revised for *Roughing It*.

Arthur, King Character in *Connecticut Yankee* and the chief figure in the national epic of England's early Middle Ages. Arthur has not been proven to be historical, but some historians regard him as a Celtic warrior who became legendary fighting the Saxons. By the 12th century, he was being transformed by romances into an epic figure: the king of all of Britain, endowed with great courage, wisdom and magnanimity. Arthur's importance in later literature grew until he became the central figure in such romances as MALORY's *Le Morte d'Arthur* and TENNYSON's *Idylls of the King*. In these epics

Dan Beard's depiction of King Arthur for Connecticut Yankee *reflects Malory's heroic image of the legendary figure.*

and others, Arthur becomes king after receiving the magic sword Excalibur from the Lady of the Lake, and meets his downfall after discovering that his wife GUENEVER is adulterously involved with his best friend, Sir LAUNCELOT.

Of all the characters in *Connecticut Yankee*, only Hank MORGAN appears more frequently than Arthur. Mark Twain adapts Arthur from Malory, retaining the legendary character's essential nobility and strength, while portraying him as a dimwitted daydreamer insensitive to his subjects' welfare. Hank's relationship to Arthur is a central thread in the narrative. He first meets the king at the court in chapter 2 and becomes his first minister in chapter 6. Thereafter, Arthur has an active role in almost every chapter except those pertaining to Hank's mission with SANDY. In chapter 27, Arthur and Hank set out to tour the kingdom and are together continuously through chapter 38. Hank last sees Arthur two chapters later, before going to Gaul. After he returns to England, he learns that Arthur and Launcelot are waging a great civil war (chapter 42). Arthur's end comes much as it does in Malory, with Arthur and MORDRED killing each other in battle. Arthur's death then gives Hank an excuse to proclaim England a republic, setting in motion the novel's final confrontation.

Though Hank describes Arthur as his own age—about 40 in chapter 40—Hank tends to look on him as a father figure. He never neglects to show him proper deference even after becoming the kingdom's most powerful person. Hank claims not to respect Arthur as a king, but admits to admiring him as a *man*—particularly after Arthur risks his life to help a peasant family dying of smallpox (chapter 29). Immediately after this noble deed, however, Arthur disgusts Hank by suggesting they help capture the same family's sons, who have escaped the oppressor responsible for ruining the people Arthur has just helped.

Most actors who have portrayed King Arthur in screen adaptations of *Connecticut Yankee* depict him as considerably older than the character described in the novel. They include Charles Clary (1921), William Farnum (1931), Cedric Hardwicke (1949), Boris Karloff (1955), Richard Basehart (1978), Kenneth More (1979) and Michael Gross (1989).

Ashcroft, Ralph (1875–1947) Business adviser. A native of Liverpool, England, Ashcroft met Mark Twain in 1903, when he was treasurer of the American PLASMON Company. Over the next few years, he helped Mark Twain in a dispute with the company and accompanied him to England. At some point, he became Mark Twain's paid business adviser. In late 1907, he suggested registering "Mark Twain" as a trademark in order to protect copyrights—an idea that led to the formation of the MARK TWAIN COMPANY, in which Ashcroft became an officer in late 1908. By this time, Mark Twain had so much confidence in Ashcroft and Isabel LYON, his own private secretary, that he gave them power of attorney over his business affairs.

Clara Clemens distrusted Lyon and tried to get Ashcroft to ally with her against the woman. Possibly hoping to quell Clara's fears that Lyon had marital designs on Mark Twain, Ashcroft married Lyon himself on March 18, 1909. Mark Twain attended their wedding, but soon lost confidence in both of them. Under Clara's prodding, he accused them of financial mismanagement and forced them out of his household in April. Later he revoked their legal authority and prepared "The Ashcroft-Lyon Manuscript," a massive document to use against them if they made legal trouble in the future. There is, however, no evidence that Ashcroft or Lyon ever abused their trust.

During the summer of 1909, Ashcroft returned to England in a failed attempt to revive the Plasmon business. Four years later, he and Lyon moved to Montreal, Canada, where they separated during the 1920s.

"As Regards Patriotism" Brief essay written around 1900 and first published in EUROPE AND ELSEWHERE (1923). Mark Twain contends that in America patriotism has become an official religion: the "love of country, worship of country, devotion to the country's flag and honor and welfare." He goes on to argue that if people were trained to think for themselves, they would develop a true form of patriotism, one growing out of reason and honest feelings.

Athens The capital of GREECE was supposed to be a highlight of the QUAKER CITY's scheduled itinerary, but when the ship reached the city's harbor on August 14, 1867, local officials, fearing CHOLERA, would not let anyone go ashore. Bitterly disappointed, the passengers could only see the Acropolis through spyglasses as their ship lay anchored far from shore. That night, however, Mark Twain, Dr. Abraham JACKSON, Colonel William R. Denny and Dr. George Bright Birch slipped ashore and made their way to the Acropolis and back. Moses S. BEACH and Henry Bullard duplicated their feat later that night, but two other men failed and barely escaped arrest.

Chapter 32 of *Innocents Abroad* contains an embellished account of the Acropolis adventure, replete with armies of yapping dogs trailing the men, armed guards popping up out of the vineyards, and mournful faces of ghostly statues staring at the trespassers. The chapter also has a lyrical picture of the ancient Parthenon watching over Athens under the moonlight. Mark Twain included the episode in his "AMERICAN VANDAL ABROAD" lecture, which chided tourists who take relics from historic ruins—a sin of which he may not have been innocent himself. The MARK TWAIN PAPERS project's collection includes a marble head that he may have brought back from the Acropolis.

Atlantic Monthly Literary magazine founded in 1857 by James Russell Lowell (1819–1891), its first editor. Initially based in BOSTON, the *Atlantic* began as a forum for leading New England writers. In 1861, James T. Fields (1817–1881) became editor; he hired W. D. HOWELLS as his assistant five years later and turned over chief editorship to him in 1871. Thomas Bailey ALDRICH succeeded Howells in 1881 and was followed by Horace E. Scudder (1890–98), Walter Hines Page (1898–99), Bliss Perry (1899–1909) and Ellery Sedgwick (1909–38).

The elevation of the midwesterner Howells to the editorship marked the beginning of the magazine's transformation into a national literary journal. Howells solicited contributions from westerners and southerners, while calling attention to new American talent and to leading European writers. Howells was personally responsible for introducing Mark Twain to *Atlantic* readers when he published "A TRUE STORY" in the November 1874 issue. Mark Twain's real breakthrough, however, came the following year, when the *Atlantic* serialized "OLD TIMES ON THE MISSISSIPPI."

Mark Twain's other contributions to the *Atlantic*—all published during Howells's editorship—include "THE CURIOUS REPUBLIC OF GONDOUR" (October 1875), "PUNCH, BROTHERS, PUNCH!" (February 1876), "THE FACTS CONCERNING THE RECENT CARNIVAL OF CRIME IN CONNECTICUT" (June 1876), "THE CANVASSER'S TALE" (December 1876), "SOME RAMBLING NOTES OF AN IDLE EXCURSION" (October–December 1877), "THE LOVES OF ALONZO FITZ CLARENCE AND ROSANNAH ETHELTON" (March 1878), "About Magnanimous-Incident Literature" (May 1878), "The Recent Great French DUEL" (February 1879), "THE GREAT REVOLUTION IN PITCAIRN" (March 1879), "Unconscious Plagiarism" (February 1880), "A Telephonic Conversation" (June 1880), "EDWARD MILLS AND GEORGE BENTON: A TALE" (August 1880) and "Mrs. MCWILLIAMS and the Lightning" (September 1880).

Atlantic Ocean Mark Twain crossed the North Atlantic about 25 times, made five round-trips to BERMUDA, and sailed along America's eastern seaboard on voyages to and from Central America and on pleasure cruises aboard H. H. ROGERS's KANAWHA. He first saw the Atlantic while working in NEW YORK CITY and other Eastern cities in 1853–54, then again in January 1867, when he returned from California by way of NICARAGUA. In June 1867, he began his first transatlantic voyage, a five-month cruise to the MEDITERRANEAN on the QUAKER CITY. He returned to CALIFORNIA from New York in March 1868, sailing down the Atlantic coast to the Caribbean and Central America; he followed the same route when came back in July.

In 1873–74, Mark Twain made two round-trips to ENGLAND. He crossed the Atlantic to GERMANY in April 1878 and returned from Liverpool, England 16 months later. In June 1891, he took his family to FRANCE. Over the next four years, he made five round-trips across the Atlantic to look after business concerns at home as he faced BANKRUPTCY. Except for one crossing to New York with his daughter Clara in August 1893, he made all these trips alone. In May 1895, he brought his family back from Europe and began a lecture tour that would take him across the United States and the PACIFIC OCEAN and back to England by way of SOUTH AFRICA. His trip from Cape Town to England in July 1896 was his only South Atlantic voyage.

Mark Twain's next Atlantic crossing came in October 1900, when he returned to the United States after a five-year absence. In late 1903, he took his family to ITALY, by way of GIBRALTAR, returning in June of the following year. On June 8, 1907—exactly 40 years after sailing on the *Quaker City*—he left New York on the *Minneapolis* on his last trip to England, from which he returned in July aboard the *Minnetonka*.

During his last years of writing, Mark Twain drew on his vast sailing experience in nightmarish stories about sea voyages. "THE GREAT DARK," for example, is about a microscopic ship sailing in a drop of water whose crew thinks they are in the North Atlantic.

"Aurelia's Unfortunate Young Man" Sketch originally published in 1864. The anonymous narrator of this sketch has received a letter from a young lady in San Jose (California) calling herself Aurelia Maria who is confused by the conflicting advice she is getting. Her story follows.

At 16, she met and fell in love with Williamson Breckinridge Caruthers, a man from New Jersey six years older than she. They became engaged and everything seemed to be going well until Caruthers contracted

Aurelia's young man in an advanced state of deterioration.

virulent smallpox; after he recovered, his face was pitted like a waffle-mold. Aurelia considered breaking off their engagement, but decided to give her betrothed another chance. The day before the wedding was to take place, however, Caruthers fell down a well and had a leg amputated above the knee. Aurelia gave him another chance. On the Fourth of July, he lost an arm when a cannon exploded prematurely; three months later, a carding machine pulled out his other arm. Though devastated by Caruthers's alarming depreciation, Aurelia decided to bear with him.

As their next wedding date approached, Caruthers contracted erysipelas, which blinded him in one eye. Aurelia's friends insisted that she break off her engagement, but she said that Caruthers was not to blame and set a new wedding date. This time Caruthers broke his remaining leg and had it removed. After the nuptials were again rescheduled, Caruthers was scalped by Owens River Indians (of the eastern Sierra Nevada).

Aurelia is now perplexed. Her parents oppose her marrying Caruthers because he lacks property and cannot earn a living, so she asks the narrator for advice. The narrator suggests that she buy Caruthers a wig, a glass eye and wooden limbs, and give him another 90 days to go without an accident. If he succeeds, she should marry him; if he fails, he will probably finish himself off.

PUBLISHING HISTORY

Mark Twain's original sketch, titled "Whereas," appeared in the CALIFORNIAN on October 22, 1864. Its original form is about 2,300 words in length. He revised the sketch for publication in his first book, THE CELEBRATED JUMPING FROG OF CALAVERAS COUNTY, in early 1867, but by the time the book appeared, someone else—probably Charles Henry WEBB—had cut just over half the text from its opening and retitled the result "Aurelia's Unfortunate Young Man." Mark Twain retained this title in future reprintings, each of which contained additional revisions. The version now most frequently reprinted is the one that originally appeared in SKETCHES, NEW AND OLD (1875).

Though "Aurelia" was an uncommon name in the 19th century, W. D. HOWELLS had a younger sister with this name.

Aurora Historic MINING town of western NEVADA in which Mark Twain lived in 1862. The center of the old ESMERALDA district, Aurora is 12 miles east of Bodie, a noted California ghost town. It arose quickly after silver deposits were found in August 1860. In September the following year, Mark Twain visited Aurora to buy mining claims. When he returned in April 1862 to work the claims, 2,000 miners lived in the town, with dozens more arriving daily. Over the next five months he worked his claims with little success.

Roughing It devotes several chapters to Mark Twain's Aurora period, but refers only to "Esmeralda"—the name more commonly used at that time. Chapter 40 relates a fantastic story, suggesting that Mark Twain and his partner Calvin HIGBIE laid claim to a "BLIND LEAD" that would have made them both millionaires, had they not lost it through carelessness. While Mark Twain was in Aurora, he lived on his brother's money and ended up working in a quartz mill for $10 a week. The total amount of time he spent there is uncertain, as he occasionally ventured outside the district to places such as MONO LAKE. After about two months in Aurora, he began writing humorous letters to the VIRGINIA CITY TERRITORIAL ENTERPRISE that he signed "JOSH." Just as his financial condition bottomed out, the *Enterprise* offered him a job. In September 1862, he walked 130 miles from Aurora to Virginia City to take up the position.

A year after Mark Twain came to Aurora, its population doubled, and may have peaked at 10,000. By 1870, Aurora was a substantial town, but it declined rapidly when it was realized that its mines were exhausted. Most miners were gone by 1880, and only 100 residents remained in 1908. It originally had many substantial structures, but they were dismantled for their building materials. Today, little remains but foundations. The cabin in which Mark Twain was thought to have lived became a popular tourist attraction in the early 1900s; it was later moved to Reno, where it was eventually destroyed.

Aurora had a peculiar administrative history. When Mark Twain was there, it was considered to be in California and was the seat of MONO County. In 1864, however, a border survey discovered that Aurora was just inside Nevada. Mono County moved its seat to Bridgeport and Aurora became the seat of Nevada's Esmeralda County. After Aurora declined, Esmeralda moved its seat to Goldfield and Aurora itself ended up in Mineral County.

Australia   Between mid-September 1895 and early January 1896, Mark Twain spent more than two months in Australia on the second major leg of his round-the-world LECTURE tour. At that time, Australia comprised seven separately governed British territories. Though Mark Twain traveled only along the continent's southern fringes, he visited all its regions except Queensland and Northern Territory.

After crossing the PACIFIC OCEAN with his wife and daughter Clara on the Australian steamship WARRIMOO, Mark Twain reached Sydney, the capital of New South Wales, on September 16, 1895. He spent 10 days there, then went by train to Melbourne, Victoria's capital city, where he stayed two weeks. On October 11, he took a train to South Australia's capital, Adelaide, then worked his way back to Victoria. After another stay in Melbourne (October 26–31), he sailed to NEW ZEALAND, stopping briefly at Tasmania's chief town, Hobart (No-

vember 1). On December 17, he returned to Sydney for several days before leaving for CEYLON on the steamship *Oceana*. After layovers at Melbourne and Adelaide and an overnight anchorage off Albany in Western Australia, he last saw the continent as the *Oceana* entered the open sea on January 5.

At the moment Mark Twain visited Australia, American relations with Britain were strained over a British dispute with Venezuela about the latter's border with British Guiana. Nevertheless, he was warmly received by mostly full houses throughout Australia as his agent Carlyle SMYTHE accompanied him. Still fresh and comparatively energetic, Mark Twain found much in Australia that fascinated him. More than a quarter of *Following the Equator* is devoted to the continent.

Following the Equator uses "Australia" and "Australasia" almost interchangeably, though the latter is a collective term that encompasses Australia, New Zealand and their island neighbors. It is not always possible to tell in which sense Mark Twain intends "Australasia"; in some passages it is clearly a synonym for Australia—as when calling the Melbourne Cup the "Austral*asian* National Day" (chapter 16).

The Australian chapters begin with a critical analysis of labor recruitment in Queensland (chapters 5–6), a northeastern colony that Mark Twain missed visiting because his health could not stand its tropical heat. The book's main Australia chapters (9–11, 12–25, 27–29) reflect Mark Twain's interest in the continent's economic prosperity—particularly its MINING industry; its early history as a convict settlement; its subjugation of native peoples; and its unusual wildlife. His admiration of the amazing tracking abilities of native Australians probably helped inspire "A DOUBLE-BARRELLED DETECTIVE STORY."

Austria   Mark Twain spent nearly two years in Austria during the 1890s. At that time it was the center of the Hapsburg dynasty's Austro-Hungarian Empire, which included what became Hungary and Czechoslovakia after World War I. He first entered the empire in August 1891, when he visited Bohemian health spas that are now within the Czech Republic. During the summer of 1893, he passed through western Austria while traveling between BERLIN and FLORENCE, and stayed at Innsbruck and Krankenheil.

In late September 1897, Mark Twain returned to Austria with his family and settled in VIENNA, its capital city. Over the next 20 months, he was close to several tumultuous events that reflected the political strains in the empire. On October 28, he personally witnessed a brawl on the floor of the national Reichsrat that helped topple the government of Count Kasimir Badeni (1846–1909), who favored elevating Czech to the same status as GERMAN in Bohemia and Moravia. Over the next month, Mark Twain wrote "Stirring Times in Austria," a long essay describing the fracas and analyzing Austrian politics. It was published in HARPER'S MAGAZINE the following February. Nearly a year later, while Mark

Twain was spending the summer in KALTENLEUTGEBEN near Vienna, Empress Elizabeth was assassinated by an Italian anarchist in Switzerland. Mark Twain took his family into Vienna to witness her state funeral and then wrote "THE MEMORABLE ASSASSINATION." On May 25, 1899, two days before he left Vienna, he had a private audience with Emperor Franz Josef (1830–1899).

Mark Twain's time in Austria was one of his busiest writing periods. Works that he completed and published include "THE MAN THAT CORRUPTED HADLEYBURG," "DIPLOMATIC PAY AND CLOTHES" and "FROM THE 'LONDON TIMES' OF 1904." He also worked on his "MYSTERIOUS STRANGER" stories that are set in early Austria, began WHAT IS MAN?, and wrote "THE GREAT DARK," "SCHOOLHOUSE HILL," and other manuscripts that have been published posthumously.

"The Austrian Edison Keeping School Again"   Essay on Jan SZCZEPANIK that Mark Twain wrote while in VIENNA in early 1898 and published in London's *Century* magazine the following August. A Polish inventor running a large Viennese laboratory, Szczepanik was noted for his contributions to the development of a primitive form of television known as a telelectroscope. Several years earlier, while a schoolmaster in Moravia, he developed a method of photographically copying patterns onto textiles. As a schoolmaster, he was exempt from military duty; however, he got into trouble with the government by failing to register for service when he left teaching to concentrate on inventing. Instead of removing him from his lab to perform his military service, the government sentenced him to return to his Moravian village every two months to teach half a day. Mark Twain notes that if Szczepanik were to live until he was 90, these bimonthly trips would add up to *more* than three years of time lost from his laboratory—a point he promises to bring to the government's attention. Mark Twain also used Szczepanik as a character in a story, "FROM THE 'LONDON TIMES' OF 1904."

Autobiography House   Original name for the REDDING, Connecticut house that Mark Twain later called "STORMFIELD." He chose the first name because he built the house with money earned from the chapters of his AUTOBIOGRAPHY published in the NORTH AMERICAN REVIEW. Shortly before occupying the house in June 1908, however, he changed its name to "INNOCENCE AT HOME."

autobiography, Mark Twain's   As a literary form, autobiography can encompass narratives, journals, memoirs and letters. Generally, however, it is seen as a connected narrative story of an author's own life that provides introspective commentary. Although Mark Twain wrote and dictated half a million words of material that he called "autobiography," he left little that meets the form's narrow definition. Nevertheless, his

Mark Twain dictated much of his autobiography from his Venetian bed while living in New York City in 1906. (Courtesy, Library of Congress, Pictures & Prints Division)

manuscripts—which are now held by the MARK TWAIN PAPERS project—have spawned five major "autobiography" publications.

Before examining Mark Twain's explicitly autobiographical texts, it is important to note that much of his writing, including his fiction, is autobiographical in nature. The opening chapters of *The Gilded Age* (1873), for instance, adapt the story of his own family's coming to Missouri before he was born and recreate his early childhood environment there. In *Tom Sawyer* (1876), Mark Twain expands this description of his early milieu and depicts many incidents that happened to him during his youth. One of the closest things to true autobiography that Mark Twain ever wrote is the first part of *Life on the Mississippi* (1882), which vividly describes his coming of age as a cub steamboat PILOT in the late 1850s. "THE PRIVATE HISTORY OF A CAMPAIGN THAT FAILED" (1885) gives an embellished account of his brief CIVIL WAR experience (1861). *Roughing It* (1871) continues this story with a fuller but equally embellished account of his years in the Far West (1861–66). His other travel books cover briefer periods of his life. *Innocents Abroad* (1869) details his five-month journey to the Mediterranean in 1867, and *A Tramp Abroad* (1880) describes highlights of his European travels in 1878–79. The latter chapters of *Life on the Mississippi* recount his return visit to the river in 1882, and *Following the*

Equator (1897) describes his round-the-world LECTURE tour of 1895–96.

Most of Mark Twain's travel books, as well as many of his short works, contain significant autobiographical fragments. For example, *Innocents Abroad* describes his discovery of a corpse in his father's office when he was a boy (chapter 18), and *A Tramp Abroad* recounts an incident during his first steamboat trip (chapter 10). *Life on the Mississippi* recalls his residence in ST. LOUIS during the early 1850s (chapter 51) and adds poignant memoirs of his youth in Hannibal (chapters 53–56). In *Following the Equator* he tells how an incident he observed in Bombay, INDIA took him back to his youth, when he saw people abusing slaves; this recollection leads him into a discussion of his relationship with his father and a time when he saw a slave killed (chapter 38).

Mark Twain began consciously writing "autobiography" in 1870, when he wrote an essay on his family's TENNESSEE LAND. Over the next quarter century, he added more sketches on his life and on people he had known, setting aside most of these pieces without thought of publishing them. (Note that the BURLESQUE AUTOBIOGRAPHY, which he published in 1871, has nothing to do with his real autobiography.) His interest picked up during the mid-1880s, when he wrote several long passages about his relationship with General GRANT. When the AMERICAN PUBLISHING COMPANY issued the first uniform edition of his books in the late 1890s, Mark Twain wrote a brief autobiographical introduction that his nephew, Samuel E. Moffett, revised for publication.

In 1906, Mark Twain resumed his autobiography in earnest and began dictating passages to secretaries regularly. By this time, his biographer, A. B. PAINE, was installed in his household, where he assisted in this work. Mark Twain continued these dictations intermittently until 1909, when he also wrote "THE TURNING POINT OF MY LIFE," an essay summing up his entire life, and "THE DEATH OF JEAN," which he called the "final chapter" of his autobiography.

Mark Twain liked to boast that he had discovered a new method of creating autobiography by simply talking about whatever interested him at the moment. The inevitable consequence of this discursive approach is that his dictations wander aimlessly. Some recall incidents from his youth, others recall people he has seen recently. Rarely, however, does he try to link passages together into a coherent narrative. His autobiography includes scores of unconnected memoirs, sketches of people he knew and essays on various subjects. Several stretches of his dictations are simply extracts from a manuscript written by his daughter Susy Clemens, to which he added comments. Another part of his "autobiography" comprises the 21,000-word essay IS SHAKESPEARE DEAD?, which he published as a book in 1909.

Mark Twain also believed that he was creating the first completely honest autobiography ever written. He described what he was doing as speaking "from the grave," since he expected to be dead long before it was published. After George HARVEY approached him about serializing parts of his autobiography in the NORTH AMERICAN REVIEW, however, he published about 100,000 words in 25 installments as "Chapters from My Autobiography" (September 1906–December 1907). Meanwhile, he continued his dictations, until he left about half a million words of material for Paine to publish after his death. After incorporating extracts of this material in his biography of Mark Twain in 1912, Paine assembled *Mark Twain's Autobiography,* which HARPER'S published in two volumes in 1924. The 195,000 words of this edition include passages that appeared previously in the *Review,* as well as a few chapters that Paine published in HARPER'S MAGAZINE in early 1922. Paine's introduction to the book implies that it contains everything from Mark Twain's autobiography worth publishing. The material is actually a carefully selected and discreetly edited collection of Mark Twain's most nostalgic and cheerful material. After Bernard DEVOTO became editor of the Mark Twain Estate, he reexamined the manuscripts and decided that Paine had left out

Mark Twain around 1870, when he began writing his autobiography. (Courtesy, National Archives, Still Picture Branch)

far too much. Further, he believed that the additional passage of time had lessened the sensitivity of much of what Mark Twain had written about other people. De-Voto selected about 150,000 words from the original manuscripts and *Review* articles that were not in *Mark Twain's Autobiography;* these he published as MARK TWAIN IN ERUPTION in 1940.

Two decades later, Charles NEIDER decided that it was time to put everything into something like traditional chronological order. After selecting passages from all the earlier publications, he imposed a drastic re-arrangement that approximates a chronologically ordered autobiography, and published the result as *The Autobiography of Mark Twain* in 1959. After another three decades had passed, Michael J. Kiskis collected the *North American Review* chapters into a new book titled *Mark Twain's Own Autobiography* (1990). Using the same text and arrangement as the *Review,* Kiskis argues that since the magazine articles are the only version of the autobiography that Mark Twain himself saw through publication, they are closer to what he intended his autobiography to be than any of the previous book editions. Appendixes in Kiskis's edition include a chronological summary of Mark Twain's autobiographical writings and a table detailing the relationships between the *Review* chapters and Paine's, DeVoto's and Neider's editions of the autobiography. Of the four autobiography editions published as books, Kiskis's contains the fullest index.

After 25 magazine installments and four published books, the history of Mark Twain's autobiography remains unfinished. A major challenge now facing the Mark Twain Papers project is to prepare something approximating a definitive edition of a work that by its nature can never be "definitive." At present, the project expects to publish a two-volume edition of the autobiography in 1998 that will finally include *all* of Mark Twain's autobiographical writings.

"The Awful German Language" Originally published as an appendix to *A Tramp Abroad* (1880), this 7,530-word essay is a comic analysis of GERMAN, exaggerating the idiosyncrasies of a language that even a gifted person needs 30 years to learn. It begins with the narrator's visit to HEIDELBERG Castle, whose museum keeper wants to add the narrator's German to its curiosity collections. Resenting this slight, the narrator examines German's perplexities and finds that no other language is as slipshod. German has 10 parts of speech—all troublesome. An average German sentence occupies a quarter of a newspaper column, contains all 10 parts of speech, is filled with compound words not in dictionaries and treats 14 to 15 difficult subjects, each within its own parenthesis—and its verb comes last.

German's unpleasant features include splitting verbs in two—putting one half at the beginning of a chapter and the other half at the end; its frightful personal pronouns and adjectives; and distributing genders to its nouns without rhyme or reason, so that a turnip has sex, while a girl does not. Also, some German words are so long that they have a perspective. German does have some virtues, however, such as capitalizing all nouns. Also, words are spelled as they sound, and the language contains some very powerful words.

Averse to pointing out faults without suggesting remedies, the narrator proposes several reforms. He would leave out the dative case; move verbs closer to the front; import stronger words from English; redistribute the sexes according to the will of the Creator; do away with long compounds; and discard everything in the vocabulary but *Zug* and *Schlag.* He concludes with the German Fourth of July oration that he delivered before the Anglo-American Students Club.

Azores Atlantic island group of volcanic origin, located about 740 miles west of Portugal, which has owned the islands since the mid-17th century. The QUAKER CITY was to land at the largest island, San Miguel, but to avoid a storm, it instead anchored at the port of Horta on the island of Fayal on June 21, 1867. After two days of exploring this lush island, the passengers voted to skip San Miguel and go directly to GIBRALTAR. Chapters 5–6 of *Innocents Abroad* describe the islands, whose population Mark Twain puts at 200,000 people.

Baalbek (Baalbec) Ancient town in Lebanon. Located about 40 miles east-northeast of BEIRUT and a similar distance north of DAMASCUS, Baalbek originated as a center of Baal worship and developed into an important city in Greek and Roman times. After visiting Baalbek on September 12, 1867, Mark Twain made it the subject of chapter 43 of *Innocents Abroad.* He was impressed by the immense size of Baalbek's building stones and later nicknamed a broken-down horse "Baalbec" because it was "such a magnificent ruin."

Bacon, Sir Francis (January 22, 1561, London–April 9, 1626, Highgate, England) English statesman and philosopher. During a long political career, Bacon served under ELIZABETH I and became lord chancellor under James I. He is better remembered, however, as an essayist and philosopher who challenged Aristotelian philosophy and established the importance of inductive reasoning from direct observation in science.

During the mid-18th century, the idea arose that Bacon's contemporary William SHAKESPEARE could not have written the plays attributed to him. A century later, a theory was advanced that Bacon was the true playwright. Based entirely on circumstantial evidence, this still-popular theory overlooks the fact that Bacon never wrote blank verse. Mark Twain considers the "Baconian theory" in IS SHAKESPEARE DEAD? (1909). While he stops short of accepting Bacon as the author of Shakespeare's plays, he believes that the weight of evidence points in that direction. Chapter 9 explores the Baconian theory in detail, but chapter 1 sums up Mark Twain's conclusions: "I only *believed* Bacon wrote Shakespeare, whereas I *knew* Shakespeare didn't."

Mark Twain also uses Bacon as a character at Queen Elizabeth's court in *1601.*

Bad Nauheim Town in western GERMANY with saline thermal baths, about 24 miles north of Frankfurt. Mark Twain lived there with his family from early June through late September 1892. Soon after settling in with his family, he went back to the United States alone on a business trip lasting several weeks. After returning to Germany, he spent a generally pleasant summer in Nauheim writing sketches and beginning his novelette, *Tom Sawyer Abroad.* At the end of September he moved his family to FLORENCE, Italy.

Baden-Baden Resort town in southwestern GERMANY's BLACK FOREST region, Baden-Baden is noted for its hot springs. From late July through early August 1878, Mark Twain used the town as a base from which to visit the region. Chapter 21 of *A Tramp Abroad* describes Baden-Baden as "an inane town, filled with sham, and petty fraud, and snobbery," with good baths.

Bagdemagus, King Background figure in *Connecticut Yankee.* Bagdemagus (Bademagu in some Arthurian legends) never appears in the narrative, but is mentioned several times. In chapters 29–34, Hank MORGAN and King ARTHUR pass through ABBLASOURE and CAMBENET in Bagdemagus's tributary kingdom near the VALLEY OF HOLINESS. Chapter 9 calls him *Sir* Bagdemagus, a knight whom Sir GARETH bests in a tournament, as well as father of Meliganus—who may be the Sir Meliagraunce who stabs Hank in chapter 44. Chapters 33 and 40 call him *King* Bagdemagus and the latter lists him as a member of the Bessemers baseball team.

Baker, Dick or Jim Character in *Roughing It* (1872) and *A Tramp Abroad* (1880). Chapter 61 of *Roughing It* describes *Dick* Baker as a 46-year-old California pocket-miner who has become a victim of 18 years of unrequited toil and blighted hopes. Gentle, patient and big-hearted, he is given to mourning the loss of his wonderful cat TOM QUARTZ, whom he thinks may have been supernatural. Baker tells how he once accidentally blew Tom Quartz sky-high while blasting a mine shaft.

This same character reappears as *Jim* Baker in chapters 2–3 of *A Tramp Abroad,* which describes him as a middle-aged, simple-hearted California miner who has learned the languages of the birds and beasts. Here Baker relates one of the most famous of Mark Twain's tall TALES, the BLUEJAY YARN.

By his own admission, Mark Twain modeled Baker on his prospector friend Dick STOKER. As a storyteller, however, Baker is more similar to Stoker's partner, Jim GILLIS—who invented the original versions of these tales, making Stoker their hero. Mark Twain—who often had trouble keeping character names straight—probably was thinking of Stoker when he called Baker "Dick" in *Roughing It,* and of Gillis when he called him "Jim" in *A Tramp Abroad.* His confusion persisted to 1907, when he recorded an autobiographical passage identifying Stoker as the "*Jim* Baker" of the Tom Quartz tale. He also added that Stoker never owned a cat.

baksheesh (bucksheesh)   Near Eastern term for gratuity or cash gift. Usually rendered *baksheesh* in English, the word has roots in Persian. Mark Twain mentions "bucksheesh" more than 30 times in the last third of *Innocents Abroad,* expressing his exasperation at being constantly assailed by beggars and petty opportunists throughout the Near East during his 1867 trip.

Ballou   Character in *Roughing It.* In chapters 27–33 and 39, Ballou is a hard-working 60-year-old blacksmith and veteran miner who accompanies the narrator and others from Carson City to HUMBOLDT and back. He is based on Cornbury S. Tillou, a 40-year-old French blacksmith who accompanied Mark Twain to Humboldt in December 1861. A lover of big words, Ballou constantly spouts malapropisms. He calls weary horses "bituminous from long deprivation" and a dog "meretricious in his movements." He gives up drinking coffee made with alkali water, calling it "too technical for him" (chapter 27). Despite his pompous destruction of the language, Ballou is clearheaded enough to recognize that the "gold" the narrator finds in chapter 28 is mica. On the return journey in chapter 31, he is the first to realize that the travelers have been following their own tracks in the snow.

Ballou's fondness for big words that he does not understand is shared by the mother of AILEEN MAVOUREEN in "A DOG'S TALE."

Balum   Background figure mentioned in *Huckleberry Finn.* In chapter 8, Jim tells Huck about a time when a dream told him to give his last 10 cents to a man named Balum—nicknamed "Balum's Ass"—to invest. This man gave the money to the poor, expecting a hundredfold return. Mark Twain's "BURLESQUE AUTOBIOGRAPHY" alludes to an ancestor named "Balum's Ass" who belonged to a "collateral branch" of his family.

The Biblical Balaam was a heathen soothsayer with a miraculous talking ass summoned by the king of Moab to invoke a curse upon Israel (Num. 22–24).

Baniyas   Ancient Syrian town. Located at the headwaters of the JORDAN RIVER, near DAN, Baniyas was known as Caesarea Philippi during the Roman era. After camping there on September 17–18, 1867, Mark Twain describes the place as "execrable village" in *Innocents Abroad* (chapter 45). His letter to the NEW YORK TRIBUNE calls Baniyas "Baldwinsville," a name he finds easier to remember.

bankruptcy   On April 18, 1894, Mark Twain's publishing firm, Charles L. WEBSTER & COMPANY, entered into voluntary bankruptcy in New York, shortly after he arrived from FRANCE. He could not make payments on the firm's debts of $160,000, and the Mount Morris

Bank foreclosed. His business affairs had been in decline for several years. Aside from Webster's publishing problems, he had sunk a fortune into the PAIGE COMPOSITOR, an invention doomed to total failure. Economic conditions in America generally were poor; the collapse of New York's stock exchange the previous June had begun a national panic, making it nearly impossible for Mark Twain to find investors to bail out his sinking company.

Despite Webster's failure, Mark Twain himself never declared personal bankruptcy. Thanks to the intervention of H. H. ROGERS, he got his wife, Olivia Clemens, recognized as Webster's primary creditor and had his valuable literary copyrights assigned to her. Few of his 96 creditors pressured him heavily, and almost all agreed to accept 50 cents on the dollar for what they were owed. Mark Twain determined, however, to pay them in full. To this end, he undertook his most ambitious LECTURE tour in 1895–96—a trip that took him around the world and provided material for his final travel book, *Following the Equator*. By early 1898, he had paid all his firm's debts in full—a feat that elevated his public image to heroic stature.

As Mark Twain was growing up, fear of bankruptcy was never far from his mind. His father, John M. Clemens, had died virtually bankrupt, leaving his family mired in poverty and hoping to be rescued by their "TENNESSEE LAND." Figurative usages of words such as "bankrupt," "destitute," "pauper" and "poverty" permeate Mark Twain's writings, and some of his characters—such as Judge HAWKINS in *The Gilded Age* and Colonel SELLERS in *The American Claimant*—are saddled with past bankruptcies. As Mark Twain was facing his own business failure, he wrote *Pudd'nhead Wilson*—whose plot turns on the undeclared bankruptcy of Percy DRISCOLL. The counterpoint to Mark Twain's financial pessimism is his interest in quick-wealth themes, such as are found in "THE £1,000,000 BANK-NOTE" (1893), "THE MAN THAT CORRUPTED HADLEYBURG" (1899) and "THE $30,000 BEQUEST" (1904).

Whatever lessons bankruptcy may have taught Mark Twain were not deeply imprinted. As soon as he regained solvency, he looked for new investment schemes. Although he lost more money on PLASMON and other investments, he managed to leave an estate that was valued at nearly half a million dollars after he died.

Barnes, Tommy   Minor character in *Huckleberry Finn.* The youngest and most timid boy at the first meeting of Tom Sawyer's GANG, Tommy falls asleep as the bloodthirsty would-be pirates discuss massacring the families of members who betray their secrets (chapter 2). When the older boys tease him, he threatens to tell their secrets. Instead of having Tommy's family slaughtered, however, Tom Sawyer buys his silence for five cents.

Barnum, Phineas Taylor (July 5, 1810, Bethel, Connecticut–April 7, 1891, Bridgeport, Connecticut)   Legendary showman. Barnum won wealth and fame through a long career of exhibiting curiosities, staging hoaxes and manipulating publicity. His flair for exaggeration and self-promotion were examples that clearly influenced Mark Twain's own career. In 1835, Barnum became famous with his first great hoax—an old woman he exhibited as George Washington's 161-year-old childhood nurse. He followed with the "Feejee Mermaid" (a monkey and fish sewn together), the genuine midget Tom Thumb, the SIAMESE TWINS and other sensations. By the early 1840s, he had a wildly popular museum in New York City with permanent displays and stage shows.

Mark Twain was aware of Barnum from at least 1853, when he first visited New York. Like Barnum, he would win fame for himself with hoaxes and make outrageous exaggeration a personal trademark. When Barnum was running for Congress in Connecticut in early 1867, Mark Twain twitted him in articles in the SAN FRANCISCO ALTA CALIFORNIA and the New York Telegram. At the same time, he severely criticized the quality of exhibits in Barnum's museum, which was gutted by fire in 1865. By coincidence, Barnum helped rebuild his collections by sending John Greenwood Jr. to the Mediterranean on the same June 1867 QUAKER CITY cruise that Mark Twain took. In 1871 Barnum turned to developing a traveling circus that he called the "Greatest Show on Earth." A decade later, it merged with James A. Bailey's circus and scored a big success with the elephant JUMBO, which Barnum billed as the last living mastodon.

For most of his life, Barnum lived in or near Bridgeport, CONNECTICUT, about 50 miles southwest of Hartford, where Mark Twain lived from 1871 to 1891. During this period, the two men exchanged visits and letters. Both were popular lecturers, and Barnum particularly enjoyed attending Mark Twain's performances. Barnum's first Bridgeport house was an extravagantly ornate Oriental structure called "Iranistan," which he built in 1848. It burned down in 1857, long before Mark Twain knew Barnum; however, its example probably helped embolden Mark Twain to build his own ornate house in Hartford. Mark Twain was probably thinking of Iranistan when he wrote Connecticut Yankee, which opens with Hank MORGAN awakening in sixth-century England; he sees a "vast gray fortress, with towers and turrets" and asks if he is in Bridgeport. Dan BEARD, who illustrated Connecticut Yankee, later lived on a farm that Barnum had owned near REDDING.

According to A. B. PAINE, one of Mark Twain's favorite books was Barnum's autobiography (1855 and many editions)—a memoir of such revealing honesty that it nearly wrecked Barnum's career. Six months before Barnum died, he inscribed a copy of his last book, Dollars and Sense; or, How to Get On. The Whole Secret in a Nutshell, to Mark Twain.

Mark Twain worked references to Barnum's reputation as an aggressive collector of curiosities into "THE CAPITOLINE VENUS" (1869), "THE STOLEN WHITE ELE-PHANT" (1882) and "THE MAN THAT CORRUPTED HADLEYBURG" (1899). Chapter 64 of Following the Equator has a long anecdote about Barnum's attempt to buy SHAKESPEARE's birthplace—something that Barnum actually attempted to do in 1844. Claiming to have known Barnum "well," Mark Twain accepts a story that Barnum personally told him and credits him with saving Shakespeare's birthplace from ruin by forcing the British to establish an endowment to protect it.

Bartley, Widow Minor character in *Huckleberry Finn*. The Widow Bartley is mentioned in chapters 24–25 as a friend of the late Peter WILKS. In chapter 27 Huck sees her just before Wilks's funeral.

Batavia Steamship on which Mark Twain crossed the ATLANTIC OCEAN several times. After his first visit to England in 1872, he sailed home on the *Batavia* in November. The ship was damaged in a hurricane, but its crew braved gale conditions to rescue the survivors from another ship crippled by the storm. Afterward, Mark Twain wrote a report on the rescue that helped win the men official recognition. In late May 1873, he returned to England aboard the *Batavia* with his family and returned with them on the same ship in late October. *A Tramp Abroad* mentions the *Batavia* several times as the ship on which a talkative young American came to Europe (chapter 27). Mark Twain also recalls sailing on the *Batavia* in "THE GREAT DARK" and in an essay, "About All Kinds of Ships" (1893)—which compares its passenger comforts unfavorably with those of more modern vessels.

Bates, Edward (September 4, 1793, Belmont, Virginia–March 25, 1869, St. Louis, Missouri) President Abraham LINCOLN's first attorney general and the first cabinet member from west of the Mississippi. Mark Twain's brother Orion Clemens worked in Bates's ST. LOUIS law office during the 1840s and helped Bates campaign for Lincoln in 1860. After Orion asked for help in finding a federal job, Bates got him appointed secretary of NEVADA Territory. The appointment's timing was fortuitous: Orion needed travel money just as Mark Twain was looking for somewhere new to go. With Mark Twain paying their STAGECOACH fares, the brothers left for Nevada in July 1861—a trip that would change Mark Twain's life dramatically.

Beach, Emma (Emeline) (1850–1924) The daughter of Moses S. BEACH, Emma was one of Mark Twain's closest friends during the early stages of the QUAKER CITY voyage in 1867, and he later listed her among the eight passengers he wanted to keep as friends. He solicited her help while he was writing *Innocents Abroad* and corresponded with her as late as 1905. In 1891 Beach married the artist Abbott H. Thayer (1849–1921).

Beach, Moses Sperry (October 5, 1822, Springfield, Massachusetts–July 25, 1892, Peekskill, New York) Passenger on the QUAKER CITY excursion. The son of Moses Yale Beach (1800–1868), who bought the NEW YORK SUN in 1838, Beach took over the newspaper in 1852. He made it profitable, but is noted more for his advances in print technology—such as rolled-paper feeding—than for his editorial policies. In early 1868, he sold the *Sun* to Charles A. Dana and retired.

A next-door neighbor of Reverend Henry Ward BEECHER in Brooklyn, Beach was a prominent member of Beecher's church. After Beecher announced that he would not participate in the *Quaker City* excursion in early 1867, Beach worked hard to make the cruise succeed. In the absence of other "celebrities," he and Mark Twain were the voyage's best-known participants, as well as its only professional journalists. Under the punning title, "A Father's Letters to His *Sun*," Beach wrote 37 letters on the voyage for his paper. He also paid the way for the excursion's unofficial photographer, William E. James.

Beach and Mark Twain were friendly during the voyage, but not close, and their paths rarely crossed ashore. Beach and his daughter, Emma BEACH, were among the passengers who left the ship at GIBRALTAR to travel to Paris through Spain. While most passengers were meeting Russia's czar at Yalta, Beach was still in CONSTANTINOPLE. Beach is among the few passengers whose full names are mentioned in *Innocents Abroad*. Chapter 58 makes it clear that "Mr. Moses S. Beach" personally paid the entire cost of sending all the destitute followers of George J. ADAMS home. In a letter to the SAN FRANCISCO ALTA CALIFORNIA, Mark Twain identifies Beach and Henry Bullard as the "two other passengers" whom *Innocents Abroad* credits with sneaking ashore at ATHENS (chapter 32).

Bear Creek Stream in Hannibal, Missouri. Bear Creek passes through southern Hannibal, about a half mile from Mark Twain's BOYHOOD HOME. During his youth, it was big enough for steamboats to enter at high water. An early surveyor dubbed the stream Hannibal Creek before the town itself received the name. The region around the creek later became Hannibal's main railroad and industrial area, and modern development now covers most of its lower course.

Mark Twain learned to swim in Bear Creek and was among the many boys who ignored an 1845 municipal ordinance against swimming within the city limits. He saw two friends—including "DUTCHY"—drown there, and claimed to have twice nearly drowned in the creek himself. Chapter 55 of *Life on the Mississippi* offers a colorful description of Bear Creek.

Beard, Daniel Carter (June 21, 1850, Cincinnati, Ohio–June 11, 1941, Suffern, New York) Illustrator, author and outdoorsman. Born into an artistic family, Beard grew up around Cincinnati, Ohio and Covington, Ken-

Dan Beard's depiction of the Yankee tweaking the British lion's nose may symbolize Connecticut Yankee *as a whole.*

tucky, where he developed a lifelong interest in wilderness skills. He began drawing at an early age and sold his first picture to HARPER'S MAGAZINE when he was 18. Ten years later he went to New York City to begin a successful career as a freelance commercial artist. He later had a second career as an author of boys' books on outdoor life. His *American Boy's Handy Book: What to Do and How to Do It* (1882) was popular for decades. By 1894 he was teaching what he claimed was the world's first animal-drawing course, at New York's School of Applied Design. He became editor of *Recreation* magazine in 1905 and founded the Sons of Daniel Boone, a group that he merged with the Boy Scouts of America on its founding in 1910. He was later a Boy Scout national commissioner and associate editor of *Boys' Life* magazine. In tribute to his work, a mountain near Alaska's Mount McKinley is named after him.

Beard's connection with Mark Twain began in mid-1889, when the latter was finishing *Connecticut Yankee*. Impressed by Beard's illustrations in a magazine story, he had Fred HALL invite him to illustrate his new novel. After reading the manuscript three times, Beard met Mark Twain and received broad latitude to choose his picture subjects and treatments. Over the next few months he produced 400 drawings. He enjoyed adapting real faces to his drawings, and modeled *Connecticut Yankee*'s Hank MORGAN on George Morrison, a photoengraver near his studio. Working from photographs, he gave Sarah BERNHARDT's face to a page boy, actress Annie Russell's to SANDY, and financier Jay GOULD's to a slave driver. He also used the faces of Queen VICTORIA, the Prince of Wales (EDWARD VII), Kaiser WILHELM II, and Alfred, Lord TENNYSON, and even gave his own face to a drunken reveler in chapter 3. Beard's use of important personages as models offended some people, but Mark Twain was immensely pleased with his carefully crafted and wryly humorous work—particularly after being disappointed by E. W. KEMBLE's work in *Huckleberry Finn*. He later called Beard "the only man who can correctly illustrate my writings, for he not only illustrates the text, but he also illustrates my thoughts."

Over the next decade, Beard illustrated *The American Claimant, Tom Sawyer Abroad*, "THE £1,000,000 BANK-NOTE," "THE ESQUIMAUX MAIDEN'S ROMANCE," "TRAVELING WITH A REFORMER" and other short pieces, and he was the most prolific illustrator in *Following the Equator*.

Perhaps in keeping with Mark Twain's tribute, Beard's illustrations often go beyond the author's text. *Connecticut Yankee*'s final illustration is a prime example. Unhappy with the narrative's allowing Hank Morgan to die, Beard drew a corrective collage: Death bends over a prostrate Father Time, whose broken hourglass is at his side; in the background Hank—in modern clothes—is with Sandy and their baby. Beard later explained that since Death had choked off Time, Hank would be reunited with his family. A possible indication of Beard's influence on modern readings of *Connecticut Yankee* is the tendency of dramatic adaptations to end with Hank and Sandy reunited in Hank's own time.

Shortly after Mark Twain turned 70, he spoke to a Society of Illustrators banquet at which Beard—the society's president—had a girl dressed as JOAN OF ARC enter in full armor and give Mark Twain a wreath. A few years later Mark Twain became Beard's neighbor at REDDING, Connecticut. Beard designed a wreath for Mark Twain's funeral and published a eulogy to him in the *American Review of Reviews*. His autobiography, *Hardly a Man Is Now Alive* (1939), includes a long memoir of Mark Twain.

Beard's brother James Carter Beard (1836–1913) was also an illustrator. Two pictures that he drew for Albert RICHARDSON's *Beyond the Mississippi* were reused in *Roughing It*.

Beckwith, [James] Carroll (September 23, 1852, Hannibal, Missouri–October 24, 1917, New York, New York) Portrait painter. Beckwith was born a block and a half from Mark Twain's BOYHOOD HOME the year before Mark Twain left Hannibal. Later described as Hannibal's "second most famous citizen," he grew up in Chicago and studied art in New York and in Paris, where he shared a studio with John Singer Sargent in the mid-1870s. He spent the summer of 1890 at the ONTEORA Club in the Catskills, where he painted a portrait of Mark Twain smoking a corncob pipe that is now displayed at Mark Twain's Hartford house.

Becky Thatcher House Hannibal landmark, located at 209–211 Hill Street, facing the Mark Twain BOYHOOD HOME and the MARK TWAIN MUSEUM. The former home of Laura HAWKINS, the house takes its name from Becky THATCHER, whom Mark Twain modeled on Hawkins. In 1952 a local businessman rescued the house from demolition and had it restored to its 19th-century appearance. Now privately owned, it is open to the public, with its second floor maintained as it was during Hawkins's childhood. Its first floor is a book and souvenir shop that offers one of the largest selections of Mark Twain–related publications in the world.

Beecher, Henry Ward (June 24, 1813, Litchfield, Connecticut–March 8, 1887, Brooklyn, New York) Protestant minister. One of 13 children of Lyman Beecher (1775–1863), Henry Ward Beecher became pastor of Brooklyn's influential Plymouth (Congregational) Church in 1847. He was an outstanding speaker and became nationally famous as a spokesman for middle-class Protestantism. In early 1867, he helped his parishioner Charles C. DUNCAN plan a grand cruise through the Mediterranean and the HOLY LAND for which Mark Twain signed up. Although Beecher wanted to visit Palestine to help in his writing of *The Life of Jesus the Christ*, he never promised personally to go on the cruise. Nevertheless, his expected participation seemed to assure the cruise's success. When he finally announced that he was definitely *not* going, 40 of his parishioners canceled their own reservations, nearly scuttling the excursion. Another parishioner, Moses S. BEACH, helped salvage the trip, which Duncan captained on the steamer QUAKER CITY.

Mark Twain attended Beecher's church in February 1867, but appears not to have met Beecher formally until the following January, when Beecher gave him some advice that led to his signing with Elisha BLISS to publish *Innocents Abroad*. Around this same time, Mark Twain met Beecher's sister Isabella Beecher HOOKER, who would later help his family move to Hartford, Connecticut, where he became a neighbor of another sister, Harriet Beecher STOWE. In later years, Mark Twain often saw Beecher when Beecher visited his sisters in Hartford.

In early 1875, Beecher was the defendant in a sensational adultery trial. Mark Twain attended the trial in April; his private notes indicate he doubted Beecher's innocence. Although the trial ended in a hung jury, Beecher's clerical reputation was largely unscathed. Two months before he died, Beecher contracted with Mark Twain's firm, Charles L. WEBSTER & COMPANY, to publish his autobiography. That book was never written, but the company later published William Beecher's *Life of Henry Ward Beecher* (1888).

Beecher, Thomas Kinnicutt (February 10, 1824, Litchfield, Connecticut–1900, Elmira, New York) Pastor of the Park Church in ELMIRA, New York (1854–1900). The brother of Henry Ward BEECHER and Harriet Beecher STOWE, Beecher was both minister and close friend to the family of Jervis LANGDON, who lived across the street from his church. A ruggedly unconventional Congregational minister, Beecher was known for his independent, nonsectarian views and was an honored figure in Elmira. He also became a close friend of Mark Twain—who often attended his church while visiting Elmira. Along with Joseph TWICHELL, Beecher officiated at Mark Twain's marriage to Olivia Langdon in 1870 and at Susy Clemens's funeral in 1896.

Beirut Lebanese port city. Though nominally under Turkish rule, Beirut was effectively a British and French protectorate when Mark Twain arrived on the QUAKER CITY on September 9, 1867. The ship remained there for six days as many of its passengers began overland journeys. Mark Twain and seven companions left for BAALBEK on the second day. Chapter 41 of *Innocents Abroad* briefly describes Beirut.

"The Belated Russian Passport" Short story written by Mark Twain at YORK HARBOR, Maine in the summer of 1902 and published in HARPER'S WEEKLY on December 6, 1902. Though this story has been read by some as a SATIRE on bureaucracy, it seems more likely that Mark Twain's main object was simply to write a marketable story with a fast pace and an ironic ending. It may have grown out of Mark Twain's own experience of entering RUSSIA without a valid passport in 1867—an incident described in chapter 35 of *Innocents Abroad*.

SYNOPSIS

The story opens at a great BERLIN beer garden, where a crowd of American students is bidding farewell to Alfred Parrish, a YALE student about to return home. His friends encourage him to extend his holiday travel to St. Petersburg, RUSSIA, but he confesses that he is far too timid to do that. An older man overhearing this conversation introduces himself to Parrish as Major Jackson. Claiming to know St. Petersburg—as well as every official between Berlin and there—well, he pushes Parrish into accompanying him there that very night, by scooping up Parrish's train tickets and cash and taking off to exchange them. Parrish survives the first of what will be a series of increasingly severe anxiety attacks when the major returns after a long delay. Parrish's self-confessed "girlish" nature makes the ensuing journey an overwrought nightmare for him.

Jackson hustles Parrish off to the Russian consulate to get him a visa. The consul is out, so he leaves Parrish's passport, asking a clerk to have it approved and mailed to St. Petersburg. The clerk warns that this is risky, as a government edict mandates that anyone caught in Russia without a passport will be sent to Siberia for 10

years. Since this conversation is conducted in Russian, Parrish does not know the peril the major is getting him into until their train journey is well under way. Parrish panics, and his sufferings increase when the major makes him sneak past a nearsighted inspector when they reach the Russian frontier.

After they reach St. Petersburg, a new crisis arises when Parrish cannot produce a passport at their hotel. The major takes him to the head of the secret police, Prince Bossloffsky, and manages to push his way in. The prince throws Parrish into deeper despair by reminding him of the edict about Siberia; however, the major persuades the prince to grant Parrish a 24-hour delay so he can collect his passport from the mail train.

Too nervous to sleep that night, Parrish writes his mother a letter as a kind of last will. The next day he and the major nervously await the mail train from Berlin under the watchful eyes of two policemen. When they overhear Englishmen in the dining room mention that the train is delayed, the major drags Parrish off to the American legation to get a new passport. When they reach the shabby legation office, they find that the minister is away on vacation. They now have only 30 minutes until the prince's deadline, and the secretary of the legation will not grant Parrish a passport because even the major knows too little about him to vouch for him. Suddenly, the secretary starts asking Parrish increasingly detailed questions about where he had once lived in New Haven, Connecticut. Finally, the secretary exclaims that *he* will vouch for Parrish, because he himself once lived in the same New Haven house that Parrish's family once owned.

Belford, Charles (April 25, 1837, Cork, Ireland–December 19, 1880, Ottawa) Canadian book publisher. In 1857, Belford emigrated to CANADA with two younger brothers. He took up journalism in Toronto, where he became editor of the *Leader* (1867–71) and the *Mail* (1871–78). In 1876, he and his brothers formed Belford Brothers, a publishing company specializing in cheap reprints of American and British authors—whose works were not protected by Canadian copyright laws. Belford's first Mark Twain publication was *Tom Sawyer* (1876), which he issued before the American edition appeared. In 1878, Belford retired from publishing because of poor health and devoted his remaining energy to Conservative politics.

Belford Brothers and its successor companies published the first book edition of Mark Twain's "OLD TIMES ON THE MISSISSIPPI" (1876) and a sketch collection titled *An Idle Excursion* (1878), as well as reprints of SKETCHES, NEW AND OLD (1879), *A Tramp Abroad* (1880) and *Roughing It* (1880). The firm's success inspired other Canadian publishers to follow its example in pirating American authors. Canadian piracy hurt Mark Twain financially, leaving him with a special resentment against Belford. His unfinished story "Captain Simon Wheeler" has a criminal character named Jack Belford.

Belgium Mark Twain visited Belgium twice but wrote little about the country. He spent several days on its coast while covering the Shah of Persia's visit to Europe in June 1873; his resulting articles—collected as "O'SHAH"—briefly describe Ostend. In July 1879, he spent about four days in Belgium with his family—a visit he dismisses in one line of chapter 50 of *A Tramp Abroad*. A quarter century later, he became interested in the exploitation of the Congo Free State by Belgium's King LEOPOLD II.

Bell, Levi Character in *Huckleberry Finn*. A lawyer friend of the recently deceased Peter WILKS, Bell is in Louisville, Kentucky on business when the KING and DUKE arrive in his village posing as Wilks's brothers in chapter 24. Bell and Dr. ROBINSON lead the effort to find the truth when two more men claiming to be Wilks's brothers appear in chapter 29. Bell proposes a handwriting test. That fails to settle the matter, so he proposes exhuming Wilks's body to see if it is tattooed, as the newly arrived Harvey WILKS claims.

Bemis, George Character in *Roughing It*. A passenger on the STAGECOACH from St. Joseph to Carson City, Bemis is mentioned by name in chapters 2, 4, 7, 12 and 13. As a somewhat oafish traveling companion whom the narrator meets on his trip, he resembles the "Mr. BROWN" and "BLUCHER" characters of Mark Twain's other narratives. Bemis makes the narrator nervous by carrying an old "Allen" revolver, which he handles carelessly, and tells an amazing story about being chased up a tree by a buffalo (chapter 7). His final appearance is in Salt Lake City, where he gets drunk on "Valley Tan" and goes to bed with his boots on (chapter 13).

Ben, Uncle Name mentioned in *Huckleberry Finn*. In chapter 20, Huck invents a story to show the KING and DUKE why he and Jim are rafting down the river. He tells them that he, his father, younger brother Ike, and Jim were going downriver to live with his Uncle Ben, south of NEW ORLEANS, when his relations were killed in an accident.

Benton, Senator Thomas H. (March 14, 1782, Hillsboro, North Carolina–April 10, 1858, Washington, D.C.) Missouri's leading politician during Mark Twain's youth, Benton began practicing law in St. Louis in 1815 and was elected to the Senate when Missouri gained statehood six years later. Known for supporting sound-money policies during his five terms in the Senate, he was a strong Unionist and came to oppose slavery. After losing his Senate seat in 1850, he won election to the House of Representatives two years later, but failed in a bid for Missouri's governorship in 1856. Despite being a pro-Unionist, he remained a staunch Democrat and opposed the new Republican Party in

Bemis unloads his Allen revolver on the tree-climbing buffalo in chapter 7 of Roughing It.

1856, even though his own son-in-law, John C. Frémont, was the Republican candidate for president.

In *Tom Sawyer*, a "Senator Benton" creates a sensation when he visits ST. PETERSBURG on the Fourth of July (chapter 22). The episode is possibly inspired by an incident from Mark Twain's childhood. In the fall of 1849, the HANNIBAL JOURNAL reported that Senator Benton was coming to town to speak, but he apparently never arrived. His failure to show may have left Mark Twain permanently resentful. *Innocents Abroad* gives the fictional name "Benton House" to a Midwestern hotel that may be the world's worst (chapter 57). Another

"Senator Benton" is a minor character in the unfinished story "Which Was the Dream?"

Benton's grandnephew, also named Thomas Hart Benton (1889–1975), was a Missouri artist who helped create the school of American Regionalism. Known for realistic portraits of ordinary people, he illustrated *Life on the Mississippi* for the Limited Editions Club in 1944.

Berkeley, Lord Kirkcudbright Llanover Marjoribanks (Howard Tracy) Major character in *The American Claimant.* An English viscount just under 30 years old, Berkeley is the son and sole heir of the Earl of ROSSMORE, whose title is challenged by a distant relative in America. Intelligent, honest and fair-minded, Berkeley has powerful democratic egalitarian impulses. He accepts the claimant's case and wants to go to America to swap places with him. Once there, he hopes to make a new life for himself in a land of equality. Against his father's wishes, he heads for WASHINGTON, D.C., where the new American claimant, Colonel Mulberry SELLERS, lives.

Though Berkeley remains committed to the *idea* of equality, his experiences in America teach him that *practicing* equality is a different matter. He misses the respect that aristocratic status brought him, and he is confused and unsettled by the many evidences of inequality that he observes. By the end of the story he is ready to return to England and resume his privileged life.

Berlichingen, Götz von (1480, Jagsthausen, Württemberg–July 23, 1562, Hornberg) Legendary German knight who lost a hand and was nicknamed "Götz of the Iron Hand." From 1497 to 1528, Berlichingen fought almost constantly in GERMANY's small wars and eventually retired to a castle on the NECKAR River. Alternately regarded as a patriotic hero and an outlaw, he was noted for both his lawless daring and his chivalry. His posthumously published autobiography (1731) inspired Göethe's first major play, *Götz von Berlichingen* (1773), which made Berlichingen a folk hero. Still staged annually at Berlichingen's birthplace, the play became notorious during the 19th century for a line of dialogue that has Berlichingen tell an enemy to kiss his rear end.

Mark Twain learned about Berlichingen from reading Göethe and worked several fanciful references to him into *A Tramp Abroad,* which calls him a "fine old German Robin Hood." When the book's narrator rafts down the Neckar, he stays in a HEILBRONN inn that still has the hook on which Berlichingen hung his iron hand when he stayed there (chapter 11); the story is not credible, however, since the inn does not go back to Berlichingen's time. More obviously preposterous is the narrator's claim to have hired Berlichingen's old carriage and horse (chapters 12 and 14). In chapter 15, the narrator and his companions pass Berlichingen's Hornberg castle during their raft trip.

Berlin Capital of GERMANY. Mark Twain first visited Berlin in 1891, 20 years after it had become capital of the German Empire and experienced a period of rapid growth and modernization. In mid-October, he and his family settled in an apartment on the Körnerstrasse. This residence proved unsatisfactory, however, so his wife secured lodgings at the Hotel Royal on Unter den Linden in late December, while he was in America on business. The family remained there until the following March. They also spent two weeks in Berlin in May–June 1892 and four days there in June–July 1893.

Mark Twain enjoyed greater attention in Berlin than he had received anywhere outside of LONDON. Invited constantly to state dinners and cultural and social events, he also gave several public readings. In February 1892, he dined with Kaiser WILHELM II at the home of a Clemens cousin who was married to a Prussian general. Aside from translating SLOVENLY PETER, he wrote little while in Berlin. The last of his six letters to the NEW YORK SUN was "The German Chicago," an essay praising Berlin's modernity and efficiency.

Bermuda British colony in the ATLANTIC OCEAN, about 640 miles from the United States, on the same latitude as Savannah, Georgia. Aside from HAWAII, Bermuda was the first and last foreign shore on which Mark Twain set foot during his life. He first saw the island when the QUAKER CITY touched there on its outward passage in mid-June 1867; the ship also stopped there for five days during its return passage in November. Mark Twain doubtless shared his fellow passengers' enthusiasm for Hamilton's sparkling clean port after spending months in the untidy port cities of the Mediterranean.

Mark Twain's first extended visit to Bermuda was in May 1877, when he spent four days there with Joseph TWICHELL. At a moment when Mark Twain was down on the hustle and bustle of life at home, Bermuda was a tonic; he admired the colony's slow pace, cleanliness and orderliness and was inclined to attribute its virtues to British rule. Although he and Twichell vowed a speedy return, they did not come back together until early 1907. Mark Twain also returned in March 1908 with H. H. ROGERS—a trip that inspired his creation of the ANGELFISH Club. In November 1909, he went to Bermuda with A. B. PAINE, whose biography of Mark Twain has a firsthand account of the trip. He returned home to REDDING, Connecticut a few days before Christmas Eve, when his daughter Jean died. Disheartened and with his own health declining, he returned to Bermuda in early January. He was inclined to stay there indefinitely, but Paine grew alarmed by reports of Mark Twain's declining health and fetched him home on April 12. Mark Twain made his last landing in the United States on April 14—exactly a week before he died.

Mark Twain during one of his last visits to Bermuda. (Elizabeth Wallace, *Mark Twain and the Happy Island*, 1913)

Elizabeth Wallace (1865–1960), a friend he made in Bermuda, wrote *Mark Twain and the Happy Island* (1913) about his visits there.

Bernhardt, Sarah (October 22, 1844, Paris, France– March 26, 1923, Paris)   The most distinguished actress of her time, Bernhardt caught Mark Twain's attention in 1879, when he read stories about her having a child out of wedlock—behavior he thought typified the mor-

Dan Beard's rendering of Clarence in Connecticut Yankee *is modeled on a photograph of Sarah Bernhardt dressed as a boy.*

als of FRANCE. By contrast, his story "THE BELATED RUSSIAN PASSPORT" (1902) alludes to her as a paragon of acting ability. He first met her in December 1905, when they both appeared in a New York benefit for Russian Jews. His speech on that occasion recalled an anecdote about Bernhardt's performing in Hartford years earlier.

Dan BEARD used photographs of Bernhardt as models for two *Connecticut Yankee* illustrations. He adapted his picture of CLARENCE as a page boy from a photograph of Bernhardt dressed as a troubadour. His drawing of MORGAN LE FAY shows the queen in a jewel-encrusted dress that Bernhardt made famous on the stage.

Betsy   Minor character in *Huckleberry Finn*. Betsy appears briefly in chapter 17 as a household slave of the GRANGERFORD family.

"Bible Teaching and Religious Practice" Essay written toward the end of Mark Twain's life and first published in EUROPE AND ELSEWHERE in 1923. Arguing that religion has been responsible for the "lion's share" of changes in history, this 1,800-word piece compares changes in Christianity with those in medicine. The Christian Bible, for example, "is a drug store. Its contents remain the same; but the medical practice changes." As the world changes its views towards such matters as witchcraft and slavery, the church falls into line. It is, therefore, the world that corrects the Bible. "The Church never corrects it; and also never fails to drop in at the tail of the procession—and take the credit of the correction."

Big River Musical adaptation of *Huckleberry Finn*. With music and lyrics by Roger Miller (1936–1992), *Big River* opened in Cambridge, Massachusetts on February 22, 1984. In June, it moved to Broadway, where it won seven Tony Awards, including best musical. Daniel H. Jenkins played Huck and Ron Richardson was Jim.

Huckleberry Finn mentions the Mississippi River by name only twice, but alludes to it as the "big river" perhaps half a dozen times; the first instance is in chapter 7.

Bilgewater Nickname used in *Huckleberry Finn*. The younger of the two con men who board Huck and Jim's raft in chapter 19 claims to be the Duke of BRIDGEWATER. The older man, who styles himself "KING Looy Seventeen," occasionally calls the DUKE "Bilgewater" or "Bilge." In chapter 25, he calls him simply "Biljy."

Mark Twain gives "Bilgewater" as the name of the playwright of *Blood, Hair and the Ground Tore Up* in an 1865 newspaper sketch. Another sketch has a "Captain Bilgewater," and *Roughing It* mentions a "Colonel Bilgewater" (chapter 77). In *1601,* the Duchess of Bilgewater is a 22-year-old courtier of Queen ELIZABETH I who was "rog'red by four lords before she had a husband."

Bilgewater is the foul water that collects in the bottoms of vessels, and *bilge* has long been nautical slang for worthless talk. Mark Twain's essay "About All Kinds of Ships" defines bilgewater as a place where "only the dead can enjoy life."

Bill Name of three characters in *Huckleberry Finn*. When Huck boards the derelict steamboat WALTER SCOTT, he overhears men named Bill and Jake PACKARD planning to kill a third man (chapters 12–13). He later invents a brother named "Bill" when he tells the GRANGERFORDS where he comes from (chapter 17). Another Bill is one of the BRICKSVILLE loafers (chapter 21).

billiards Mark Twain's favorite game, billiards became increasingly important to him in his last years. While he probably started playing billiards during his Mississippi PILOTING days, his serious interest in billiards began

Mark Twain in his Stormfield billiards room in 1908. On one print of this photograph, he wrote that even John the Baptist "couldn't get a count out of an arrangement like that." (Courtesy, Library of Congress, Pictures & Prints Division)

when he was in NEVADA in the early 1860s; he also played frequently while living in SAN FRANCISCO, and *Innocents Abroad* contains many references to playing billiards in Europe in 1867. His 1868 sketch "THE FACTS CONCERNING THE RECENT RESIGNATION" cites the government's failure to give him an amanuensis with whom to play billiards as a reason for resigning his clerkship.

When Mark Twain built his Hartford house in 1874, he made an airy billiard room the outstanding feature of the top floor—thus realizing the fantasy of an attic billiard room that the narrator of *Roughing It* expresses in chapter 41. During his Hartford years, Mark Twain made long billiard sessions with friends routine, and habitually stayed up all night at the table. After leaving Hartford in 1891, he played billiards infrequently until H. H. ROGERS's wife made a new table an early Christmas present to him in November 1906. He quickly resumed his old habit of marathon billiard sessions in which A. B. PAINE became his only regular opponent; Paine later credited this billiard table with forging his personal friendship with Mark Twain. When Mark Twain had his STORMFIELD house designed in Redding, Connecticut, a large billiard room was one of his only specific requirements. He continued his intense billiards sessions there and made the room headquarters of his ANGELFISH Club for young girls.

Billings, Josh (April 21, 1818, Lanesboro, Massachusetts–October 14, 1885, Monterey, California)   Pseudonym of Henry Wheeler Shaw, a popular humorist and friend of Mark Twain. The son of a Massachusetts congressman, Billings went west at an early age and worked as a farmer, coal miner, steamboatman, auctioneer and real estate dealer. He studied the work of Artemus WARD and began publishing humorous writings at 45. In 1864, he gained national attention with "Essa on the Muel"; the following year, he published the first of many popular books, including a series of burlesque almanacs. He also wrote for the *New York Weekly* and established himself as one of the most popular humorous lecturers of his time. In 1869, he met Mark Twain on the lecture circuit, beginning a friendship that they frequently renewed.

Like many humorists of his time, Billings relied heavily upon deliberate misspellings and faulty grammar for humorous effect, but he was also regarded as a great "crackerbox" philosopher because of his facility for coining witty aphorisms. Mark Twain admired this talent in Billings, comparing him favorably to Benjamin FRANKLIN and adapting some of Billings's sayings into MAXIMS of his own; however, he found Billings's reliance on bad spelling and grammar merely tiresome. His AUTOBIOGRAPHY lists Billings among once-popular humorists who are forgotten because they relied more on verbal trickery than on substance. Nevertheless, he included six pieces by Billings in MARK TWAIN'S LIBRARY OF HUMOR (1888).

In his book titled CHRISTIAN SCIENCE, Mark Twain compares the probability of Mary Baker Eddy's having written her own autobiography to the likelihood of Josh Billings's rising up to claim that he wrote Herbert Spencer's philosophies (book 2, chapter 3).

Mark Twain died on Billings's birthday.

Billings, Mr.   Minor character in *Roughing It*. Billings is mentioned in chapters 69 and 73 as the narrator's companion on his visit to the island of Hawaii. Mark Twain's original letters to the SACRAMENTO UNION call this character "Mr. BROWN" and give him a much larger role. Jim BLAINE's tale about his grandfather's old ram in chapter 53 mentions an unrelated "widder Billings."

"CAPTAIN STORMFIELD'S VISIT TO HEAVEN" mentions Edward H. Billings as a Tennessee tailor who is the greatest poet in the universe.

birth, Mark Twain's   Mark Twain was born in FLORIDA, Missouri on November 30, 1835—a Monday—as HALLEY'S COMET passed over the Earth. The sixth of seven children of John M. and Jane Lampton Clemens, he was named Samuel Langhorne Clemens after his grandfather Samuel B. CLEMENS and a Virginia friend of his father named Langhorne. A young physician named Dr.

Guests at Mark Twain's 70th birthday banquet at Delmonico's, left to right: Kate Douglas Riggs, Mark Twain, Joseph Twichell, Bliss Carmen, Ruth Stuart, Mary E. Wilkins Freeman, Henry Mills Alden, Henry H. Rogers. (Courtesy, Library of Congress, Pictures & Prints Division)

Thomas Jefferson Chowning attended at his delivery, which was two months premature (just as the birth of Mark Twain's son Langdon Clemens would be, 35 years later). He barely survived his first winter and was considered sickly for some time.

The two-room house in which Mark Twain was born has been moved to a museum in MARK TWAIN STATE PARK near Florida; the house's original location is marked as a state historic site.

Bixby, Horace E. (May 8, 1826, Geneseo, New York–August 2, 1912, Maplewood, Missouri)   Mississippi PILOT who trained Mark Twain. One of the great STEAMBOAT pilots of his time, Bixby happened to be working on the undistinguished PAUL JONES when Mark Twain, then 21-year-old Sam Clemens, took passage on it from Cincinnati in February 1857. By the time they reached New Orleans, Mark Twain had persuaded Bixby to take him on as an apprentice. Bixby's fee was $500: $100 in advance, the rest to be paid from later wages. Decades later, Bixby hinted that he reduced the fee when he turned his cub over to another pilot.

Bixby had come to the Mississippi from upstate New York when he was 18 and started as a lowly mud clerk. He was 31 when Mark Twain met him, and was already licensed to pilot on both the OHIO and Lower Mississippi rivers. At some point he was president of the pilots' association. "OLD TIMES ON THE MISSISSIPPI" recounts Mark Twain's experience cubbing under "Mr. B." (Bixby's full name is given in the slightly revised chapters in *Life on the Mississippi*). He learned early that Bixby had an explosive temper, but cooled down quickly and was a relentless instructor. When the load of information that Bixby piled on him drove his cub to protest he did not have "brains enough to be a pilot," Bixby reputedly replied, "When I say I'll learn a man the river, I mean it. And you can depend on it, I'll learn him or kill him." To the cub's amazement, he eventually did learn the river. In later years, Bixby rated Mark Twain a fine pilot.

Although "Old Times" gives the impression that Mark Twain was an inexperienced child when he met Bixby, he was 21 years old—just nine years younger than Bixby. Within a few years, they developed a relationship of professional equality and mutual respect.

Bixby began Mark Twain's training the moment they returned upriver together on the COLONEL CROSSMAN. In St. Louis they moved to the CRESCENT CITY. They may also have worked together on the RUFUS J. LACKLAND in July and August, and on the WILLIAM M. MORRISON in October. At some point between midsummer and November of 1857, Bixby went to work on the better-paying but more demanding MISSOURI RIVER, where he qualified for a full license in a remarkably short period. He evidently invited Mark Twain to accompany him, but his cub elected to stay on the Mississippi, which he was still struggling to learn.

Bixby appears to have been back on the Mississippi by the following winter. He was on the *Crossman* when it exploded and burned near New Madrid, Missouri, on February 4, 1858, and he performed heroic rescue work. Uncertain evidence indicates that he and Mark Twain were together on the NEW FALLS CITY from the end of October into December. They definitely worked together on the ALECK SCOTT from mid-December until April 1859, when Mark Twain got his own license. Mark Twain's piloting career began and ended with Bixby: They were full partners as copilots on the *Alonzo Child*, from September 1860 until May 1861. Meanwhile, Bixby married for the first time in 1860.

At the start of the CIVIL WAR, Mark Twain abandoned piloting and went west. Bixby stayed on the river through the war and piloted the U.S.S. *Benton,* the flagship of the Union's Western Flotilla, from September 1861 to August 1862. Mark Twain recorded details of Bixby's war experiences in a NOTEBOOK that has since been published. After the war, Bixby continued to work on the Mississippi, even as steamboat commerce declined.

Mark Twain wrote to Bixby in 1870 and they met again in May 1882, in New Orleans. Chapter 48 of *Life on the Mississippi* describes Bixby as not having aged perceptibly. He was now captain of the new Anchor Line packet CITY OF BATON ROUGE, on which Mark Twain returned to St. Louis. Bixby did much of the piloting himself and Mark Twain was often with him in the pilothouse, sharing steering duties occasionally.

By the time Bixby entered his last decades, he had attained a certain celebrity as Mark Twain's "lightning pilot." During the 1890s he seemed to enjoy the attention he received, and freely granted interviews. Over the next decade, however, being an appendage of Mark Twain's fame was wearing on him and he grew more irascible in interviews. When A. B. PAINE interviewed him in the spring of 1907, he was piloting a government snag-boat out of St. Louis. He was still an active pilot until he died in a St. Louis suburb at age 86.

Bixby has been portrayed in several dramatic adaptations of Mark Twain's writings. Robert Barrat played him in the 1944 film THE ADVENTURES OF MARK TWAIN; however, the script has Mark Twain himself perform the difficult piloting maneuver attributed to Bixby in chapter 7 of *Life on the Mississippi.* Tobias Andersen played Bixby in the 1979 television drama MARK TWAIN: BENEATH THE LAUGHTER. The following year Robert Lansing played him in the PBS production of *Life on the Mississippi.*

Blab, W. Epaminondas Adrastus   PEN NAME that Mark Twain occasionally signed to sketches in his brother's HANNIBAL JOURNAL in 1852. He first used the pseudonym on September 16, 1852, a week after using the name "W. Epaminondas Adrastus PERKINS." He occasionally signed pieces "W. E. A. B." and later wrote letters to his brother's *Muscatine Journal* signed simply "W."

Black Avenger of the Spanish Main   Nickname that Tom SAWYER adopts in *The Adventures of Tom Sawyer.* In chapter 8, he fantasizes about being the "Black Avenger of the Spanish Main." He gives himself this name in chapter 13, when he plays PIRATES on JACKSON'S ISLAND. He dubs his friends "Huck Finn the Red-Handed" and "Joe Harper the Terror of the Seas." The novel's description of these names as coming from titles in Tom's "favorite literature" appears to be a minor anachronism. Ned BUNTLINE's dime novel *Black Avenger of the Spanish Main* was not published until 1847—perhaps three years after *Tom Sawyer* takes place. Another contemporary writer, B. P. SHILLABER, also used "Black Avenger" for a play-pirate name used by his character "Ike."

Black Forest   Narrow mountain district paralleling the Rhine River in southwestern GERMANY's Baden state. From late July through early August 1878, Mark Twain stayed at BADEN-BADEN and explored the region with Joseph TWICHELL. Chapter 22 of *A Tramp Abroad* contains a BURLESQUE story, "Skeleton for a Black Forest Novel," incorporating ideas that the two men worked out together while hiking in the region.

Blaine, Jim   Character in chapter 53 of *Roughing It.* A stalwart old miner—apparently in Nevada—Blaine is notorious for starting to tell a story that he never finishes about "his grandfather's old ram" (a title under which his tale has been published on its own). On the advice of "the boys" (who are never identified), the narrator watches Blaine carefully to determine when he is satisfactorily drunk—the only time to hear his story. When the moment arrives, he and the boys crowd into Blaine's cabin to listen to him. Blaine begins by telling about the bully old ram his grandfather fetched from Illinois from a man name Bill Yates . . . This is as far as Blaine ever gets about the ram. From this point, each name he mentions leads to another digression, carrying him hopelessly far from his original subject, until he falls asleep.

Blaine's monotonous 1,550-word recitation touches on a variety of unsavory and macabre themes, including drunkenness, freak accidents, physical disfigurement, gruesome death, cannibalism, and predatory undertakers. It mentions 27 different characters:

1. his grandfather;
2. Bill Yates, from whom the grandfather gets the ram;
3. Thankful Yates, Bill's father;
4. Seth Green, an acquaintance of Blaine's grandfather;
5. Sarah Wilkerson, Green's wife;
6. Sile Hawkins, whom Blaine momentarily mistakes for Sarah's former suitor;
7. Filkins, the last name of Sarah's correct suitor;
8. Nixon, apparently a political candidate;
9. Deacon Ferguson, who ejects Filkins from a prayer meeting;
10. Miss Jefferson, a glass-eyed woman on whom Filkins landed;
11. Miss Wagner, a heavy borrower, who uses Miss Jefferson's glass eye and Miss Higgins's wooden leg, neither of which fits her properly;
12. Miss Higgins, who lends Miss Wagner her wooden leg;
13. Miss Jacops, a woman who wears a wig and is married to a coffin-maker;
14. Jacops, the coffin-maker who waits for Robbins to die;
15. old Robbins, who is slow to die;
16. old Squire Hogadorn from the Indiana town to which Robbins returned;
17. the widder Billings, Hogadorn's second wife, the former Becky Martin;
18. Deacon Dunlap's first wife, the daughter of the widder Billings;
19. Maria, the daughter of Becky Martin who marries a missionary and dies in grace when she is eaten by savages;
20. the missionary who marries Maria and is also eaten by savages—who later convert, demonstrating the power of Providence;
21. Blaine's Uncle Lem, another example of Providence who has an Irishman fall on him;
22. the Irishman, a hod carrier who misses a dog when he falls on Lem;
23. Uncle Lem's dog, which is part bull and part shepherd;
24. Parson Hagar, the former owner of the dog;
25. Hagar's mother, who was formerly a Watson;
26. Hagar's sister, who married William Wheeler;
27. William Wheeler, who gets nipped by a carpet-weaving machine and is woven into 14 yards of three-ply carpet, which his widow has buried.

One of Mark Twain's best-known stories told by a narrator unconscious of his story's humor, the "old ram's tale" has become virtually synonymous with a story that goes nowhere. Mark Twain himself often recited it—in a modified form—in his public lectures.

When Mark Twain wrote this story in 1870 or 1871, Pennsylvania congressman James G. Blaine (1830–1893) was Speaker of the House. When Blaine became the Republican candidate for president in 1884, Mark Twain openly opposed him.

Blair, Walter (April 21, 1900, Spokane, Washington–June 29, 1992, Chicago, Illinois) A pioneer in the scholarly study of American humor, Blair was also an authority on Mark Twain. In 1931, he earned a doctorate in American literature at the University of Chicago, where he taught until 1968. In addition to textbooks, he wrote books on Davy Crockett, Mike Fink and James Russell Lowell and is probably best known for *Native American Humor (1800–1900)* (1937). Decades later, he coauthored *America's Humor: From "Poor Richard" to "Doonesbury"* (1980) and wrote the two-volume *Mirth of a Nation: America's Great Dialect Humor* (1983). His book *Mark Twain & Huck Finn* (1960) is a penetrating exploration of the relationship between *Huckleberry Finn* and Mark Twain's life and other writings. Blair also coedited *The Art of Huckleberry Finn* (1962) and was editor of the MARK TWAIN PAPERS volumes *Hannibal, Huck & Tom* (1969) and *Huckleberry Finn* (1988).

Blakely, Captain Ned Character in *Roughing It*. Chapter 50 describes Blakely as a San Francisco sea captain of 50 years' experience and relates a story about an incident occurring two decades earlier, when he avenged the murder of his black mate in the Chincha Islands. Having a sailor's distrust of the law, he insisted on exacting justice himself. After Bill Noakes killed his mate, Blakely personally arrested him. The next day, he invited other captains to watch him hang Noakes, but they insisted on a trial. Blakely could not understand why a trial was necessary, since it seemed impossible that anyone would judge Noakes not guilty. He was also surprised that others thought Noakes himself should attend his trial. After conceding that Noakes should be there, however, he balked at allowing someone other than himself to deliver him. Next, he was unhappy with the makeup of the jury, so he let its members know that they had better vote "right." His patience finally reached its limit after Noakes was pronounced guilty and Blakely was told that a "sheriff" would do the hanging. In the face of his boundless wrath, that suggestion was judiciously dropped.

As a gruff, simple, Bible-quoting old salt, Blakely is clearly modeled on Captain Ned WAKEMAN, whom Mark Twain met in 1866. Nothing in Wakeman's history, however, suggests that the Chincha Islands episode really occurred. Mark Twain apparently invented the story—which has no organic connection with the rest of *Roughing It*—simply to illustrate the administration of justice in frontier situations. He later re-created Blakely as Sim ROBINSON, the judge in "THOSE EXTRAORDINARY TWINS," who is determined to see justice done, regardless of the niceties of the law.

Blakely's story has been anthologized as "A Trial." *Life on the Mississippi* mentions a Union Army officer named "Captain Blakely" (chapter 31).

Blanc, Mont   Peak in the French ALPS. Western Europe's highest mountain at 15,781 feet, Mont Blanc is part of a 30-mile long massif of the same name that straddles southeastern France's borders with Switzerland and Italy. In early September 1878, Mark Twain and Joseph TWICHELL visited nearby Chamonix, which has a commanding view of the mountain. Chapters 42–45 of *A Tramp Abroad* describe the region and give a burlesque account of the narrator's attempt to earn a climbing diploma by using a telescope to ascend Mont Blanc. Chapter 45 tells the story of 11 climbers who fell to their deaths in 1870 in the mountain's worst mountaineering disaster.

Innocents Abroad mentions Mont Blanc among the sights that QUAKER CITY excursionists could expect to see (chapter 1), but Mark Twain apparently did not see the mountain himself during his 1867 visit to France. Chapter 8 of *Roughing It* alludes to "simpletons" who unnecessarily climb perilous peaks such as Mont Blanc and the MATTERHORN, and *Tom Sawyer* alludes to the mystery of why anyone would want to climb Mont Blanc for amusement (chapter 2).

Blankenship, Benson (Bence or Ben) (c. 1829–?)   Childhood acquaintance of Mark Twain. The older brother of Tom BLANKENSHIP, Bence was a rougher boy whom Mark Twain remembered as a fisherman and popular loafer in Hannibal. Bence was probably a model for Muff POTTER in *Tom Sawyer*. Mark Twain also remembered Bence's nobly looking after a fugitive slave for several weeks, passing up the chance to collect a $50 reward. The incident helped inspire the episode in chapters 8 to 11 of *Huckleberry Finn* in which Huck helps the runaway slave JIM on JACKSON'S ISLAND.

Blankenship, Tom (c. 1831 –?)   Childhood friend of Mark Twain and model for Huck Finn. In a 1906 autobiographical dictation, Mark Twain said that in creating Huck he had drawn Tom Blankenship "exactly as he was." Blankenship differed from Huck in having a large family, which lived in a run-down house near the Clemenses in Hannibal. His father, Woodson Blankenship, resembled Pap FINN in being a town drunk,

but was quite different in having a wife, Mahala, and eight children, all of whom were born in Missouri. The Blankenships were desperately poor, undisciplined and disreputable. Tom Blankenship consequently grew up badly fed, unschooled, unwashed and unsupervised. Again like Huck, Blankenship was a pariah. Boys in respectable families were forbidden to play with him—a fact that enhanced his popularity among the respectable boys. Despite his limitations, Mark Twain said that "he had as good a heart as ever any boy had."

Perhaps Blankenship's most important contribution not only to Huck Finn's makeup, but to Mark Twain's developing philosophy of life, was that he experienced and valued true freedom. Mark Twain called him "the only really independent person—boy or man—in the community, and by consequence he was tranquilly and continuously happy, and was envied by all the rest of us." Blankenship seems, however, to have had more initiative than Huck had, for it was apparently he—not the young Mark Twain—who led the local boys' GANG, and it was he who suggested hunting for treasure—an episode reenacted in *Tom Sawyer*.

Evidence for Blankenship's later years is sketchy. His family left Hannibal around 1850, but he himself later returned. There are reports of his being arrested in Hannibal for petty theft in 1858 and 1861. He may have left town again a few years later. In 1889 Mark Twain heard that Blankenship had died of cholera years earlier; a decade later, a sister of Blankenship reportedly said that both Tom and his older brother were dead. In 1902, however, Mark Twain visited Blankenship's sister Elizabeth in Hannibal and heard that Tom was then a respected justice of the peace in Montana.

Mark Twain's unfinished novel "Three Thousand Years Among the Microbes" has a character named "Bkshp" whose name evidently is a contraction of Blankenship.

blatherskite   Slang term for a boaster or talker of nonsense (blather). With roots in 17th-century *bletherskate*, the word gained popularity in America during the Revolution, thanks to the song *Maggie Lauder* ("Jog on your gait, ye bletherskate."). Around the 1890s, Mark Twain used the word frequently, usually for characters talking nonsense. Examples include chapter 12 of *Connecticut Yankee* (1889), in which Hank MORGAN calls the airheaded SANDY a "blatherskite," and chapter 9 of *Pudd'nhead Wilson* (1894), in which Tom DRISCOLL calls ROXY a "blatherskite" when she tells him that she is his mother. Tom Sawyer calls Huck and Jim "ignorant blatherskites" in chapters 3 and 8 of *Tom Sawyer Abroad* (1894). Chapters 3, 6 and 8 of *Tom Sawyer, Detective* (1896) use *blatherskite* in a different sense, to mean something more like a RAPSCALLION.

In "THE £1,000,000 BANK-NOTE" (1893), "Lord and Lady Blatherskite" are among the oddly named English aristocrats at the American ambassador's dinner party.

blind lead MINING term for an ore vein that is not exposed on the surface and thus is unlikely to be discovered except by chance. In chapters 40–41 of *Roughing It*, the narrator's partner HIGBIE discovers a "blind lead" running diagonally through the Wide West mine in Nevada's ESMERALDA district. Since this lead has its own well-defined structure and direction, it is public property. The men take in the Wide West's foreman as a partner, file a claim, then sit back to dream of future riches. Because of outside distractions that draw all three men away from Esmeralda, they fail to do the work necessary to keep their claim valid. Ten days later, it is seized by other miners, who later realize huge fortunes.

Ruing the fact that he was once "absolutely and unquestionably worth a million dollars" for 10 days, the narrator insists that "many witnesses" and "official records of Esmeralda District" will confirm his story. In March 1906, Mark Twain received a letter from Calvin Higbie that moved him to retell the blind lead story in his AUTOBIOGRAPHY in essentially the same form as in *Roughing It*. The episode appears to be based on a promising claim that Mark Twain and Higbie lost in 1862. Though the claim later proved valuable, it would not have made the men millionaires.

Bliss, Elisha (1822, Springfield, Massachusetts–September 28, 1880) Book publisher. In 1867, Bliss became secretary of the AMERICAN PUBLISHING COMPANY after having worked in the retail dry-goods trade. When Mark Twain returned from his QUAKER CITY excursion in November 1867, Bliss invited him to write a book about the cruise. The following January, Mark Twain visited Bliss in Hartford and agreed to write what became *Innocents Abroad* (1869), though he did not sign a contract until October. His stay with Bliss—who lived near Joseph TWICHELL's church—also began his infatuation with Hartford.

Recognizing the sales potential in Mark Twain's humor, Bliss stood by *Innocents Abroad* when his conservative directors grew uneasy about the book's reputedly "blasphemous" contents; he even threatened to publish the book himself if they rejected it. His skillful promotion of the book and management of the company's SUBSCRIPTION-BOOK campaign helped make *Innocents Abroad* a major best-seller. In 1870, he became president of the company; the following year he reverted to secretary, then became president again in 1873, holding that title until his death. Whatever his title, he was the driving force behind the company's expansion, and negotiated Mark Twain's contracts for *Roughing It, The Gilded Age, Sketches, New and Old, Tom Sawyer* and *A Tramp Abroad*. Bliss increased the company's list so greatly, in fact, that he incurred Mark Twain's resentment—he felt that company agents were devoting insufficient time to promoting his own books.

In October 1870, Bliss hired Mark Twain's brother Orion Clemens to edit a company magazine. During his brief tenure, Orion alerted Mark Twain to questionable aspects of Bliss's royalty-accounting procedures, making him suspect that Bliss was cheating him. Mark Twain nevertheless stayed with the American Publishing Company until Bliss died, and later published books with Bliss's son, Frank BLISS. His suspicions about Elisha Bliss continued to rankle. He may have been thinking of him when he wrote "THE FACTS CONCERNING THE RECENT CARNIVAL OF CRIME IN CONNECTICUT" (1876), which equates absence of conscience with "Bliss, unalloyed bliss." As late as 1906, he called Bliss "a tall, lean, skinny, yellow, toothless, bald-headed, rat-eyed professional liar and scoundrel" who "never did an honest thing in his life, when he had a chance to do a dishonest one."

Bliss, Frank E. (1843–1915) Book publisher. The son of Elisha BLISS, Frank Bliss was treasurer of his father's AMERICAN PUBLISHING COMPANY until early 1878, when he left to form his own SUBSCRIPTION-BOOK company to publish Buffalo Bill CODY's autobiography. Unhappy with Elisha Bliss, Mark Twain secretly contracted with Frank Bliss in March 1878 to publish the book he planned to write about his coming European trip. After returning from Europe in September 1879, however, he arranged—with Frank Bliss's approval—to have Elisha Bliss publish *A Tramp Abroad*. The younger Bliss returned to the American Publishing Company the following year and became its manager on his father's death.

Always suspicious of the American Publishing Company's integrity, Mark Twain took his next books to James R. OSGOOD, but was so disappointed with their sales that he negotiated with Bliss to publish *Huckleberry Finn* and U. S. GRANT's memoirs a few years later. When Bliss refused to meet his terms, he formed his own firm, Charles L. WEBSTER & COMPANY. After that company failed a decade later, he returned to Bliss with *Pudd'nhead Wilson* (1894) and *Following the Equator* (1897). Mark Twain was in Europe while Bliss was preparing the latter book for publication and was unaware of the substantial cuts that Bliss made in its text.

Blodgett, Reverend Elexander Alias used in *Huckleberry Finn*. In chapter 24 the KING meets a young man named Tim COLLINS and introduces himself as Blodgett, "one o' the Lord's poor servants."

Blucher (William Blucher) Character in *Innocents Abroad*. A fictional QUAKER CITY passenger, Blucher is a young man from the Far West making his first voyage. He is naive, but full of blustering self-confidence and chauvinism. Chapter 2 introduces him just before the voyage, in New York, where he is astonished to learn that not *everyone* is going to Paris that summer as he is. In chapter 5, he is confused about his new watch's failing to keep up with "ship time." In the same chapter, he treats nine people to dinner in the AZORES, but thinks himself ruined when he is billed 21,700 "reis." The next chapter establishes his ineptitude on a donkey ride; this poises him for disaster in chapter 9, when he nearly rides a mule into a TANGIER mosque. Chapter 19 describes how he wrote a note in garbled French to a Parisian landlord. At the Crimean War battlefields of SEVASTOPOL, Blucher is the ship's most enthusiastic relic collector and fills his stateroom with mislabeled bones and mementos (chapter 35). The final reference to him appears in chapter 41, in which he is mentioned as a member of the narrator's expedition through the HOLY LAND. He is also mentioned briefly in chapters 6, 19 and 37.

Mark Twain invented Blucher as a foil for his narrator in travel letters he wrote to the NEW YORK TRIBUNE, which gives his full name as "William Blucher." Blucher has a close affinity with the "Mr. BROWN" of Mark Twain's letters to the SAN FRANCISCO ALTA CALIFORNIA. Indeed, five anecdotes involving Brown in *Alta* letters (including each incident mentioned above, except the Azores dinner party) are credited to Blucher in *Innocents Abroad*. In January 1870, Mark Twain wrote a letter to Mary FAIRBANKS that identifies "Blucher" as Frederick H. Greer—a 25-year-old passenger from Boston whom Mark Twain had also identified as the "INTERROGATION POINT" in an earlier letter. More likely, Blucher is a composite of more than one real or imagined persons. For example, though Greer went to Tangier with Mark Twain, the man who nearly violated a mosque was Major James G. Barry. Also, Greer—unlike Blucher—was not with Mark Twain in the Holy Land.

Mark Twain used "Blucher" as a fictional name at least as early as 1865. His column in the July 1865 *Californian* names a "Lord Blucher" as a character in a play called *Blood, Hair and the Ground Tore Up* by BILGEWATER. Chapter 59 of *Roughing It* features a "mendicant Blucher" who finds a dime and is happy until he meets a starving beggar. Mark Twain acknowledged basing this character on his friend J. H. RILEY.

bluejay yarn Tall tale in *A Tramp Abroad*. Chapter 2 introduces Jim BAKER, a simple-hearted old California miner who has lived alone so long that he has learned the languages of the beasts and birds and come to the conclusion that bluejays are the best talkers of them all. The next chapter—subtitled "Baker's Blue-jay Yarn"—is devoted entirely to his story of a bluejay's attempt to fill a hole in the roof of a vacant cabin with acorns. Mark Twain first heard this story from Jim GILLIS at JACKASS HILL in the winter of 1864–65. Gillis evidently based his story on a jay he had seen on the roof of an abandoned cabin; he modeled Baker on his partner Dick STOKER.

Boggs Fictitious name used in *Roughing It* for Mark Twain's friendly rival Clement T. RICE of the VIRGINIA CITY UNION. In chapter 43, the narrator cannot obtain a copy of the local school report because the principal hates his newspaper. After using a pitcher of hot punch to coax Boggs into lending his copy, the narrator gets his story in on time, but Boggs gets drunk and the *Union* goes to press without the school report. When the next report is due, Boggs gets revenge by stranding the narrator in a mine shaft, causing him to miss his deadline.

Boggs Character in *Huckleberry Finn*. In chapter 21, Huck is idling in the scruffy village of BRICKSVILLE, when Boggs charges in on a horse during his monthly drunk. A red-faced man in his fifties, Boggs rides about wildly, hurling insults and threats, proclaiming that he has come to kill Colonel SHERBURN. Drunk or sober, he is known to be harmless, so people merely laugh at him. Sherburn, however, is not amused; he warns Boggs that he will endure his taunting only until one o'clock; if Boggs persists after that, it will be his end. Sherburn later shoots Boggs and has to confront a lynch party.

Details of the Boggs episode are inspired by a shooting that Mark Twain saw as a boy, when William OWSLEY shot Samuel SMARR. It is possible that Mark Twain picked up the name from Lilliburn W. Boggs (1792–1860), Missouri's governor from 1836 to 1840. He also uses Boggs for a detective's name in "THE STOLEN WHITE ELEPHANT."

Boomerang Fictional mining camp in early versions of the JUMPING FROG STORY. The story's first published version (November 1865) calls its setting "the ancient mining camp of Boomerang"; later versions call it "the decayed mining camp of ANGEL'S." Mark Twain's earliest known draft of this story reveals a great deal about Boomerang, which it describes as having just 20 "crazy houses" occupied. It suggests, however, that surrounding lodes contain enough gold to restore the "ancient magnificence of Boomerang."

Chapter 29 of *Roughing It* lists a "Boomerang" among Humboldt mining camps in Nevada. While the name may reflect an Australian influence in western mining camps, the word may also be related to "boomer," a term with several meanings in mining. For example, a "boomer" could be either a person participating in a rush to a "boom" area or the sudden discharge of water in placer-mining.

Booth's Landing Village in *Huckleberry Finn*. In chapter 13, Huck tells a FERRYBOATMAN that a woman named Miss HOOKER was visiting at Booth's Landing upriver. She was in a horse ferry crossing the river that lost its steering oar and got swept into the wreck of the steamboat WALTER SCOTT.

Boss, The Hank MORGAN's unofficial title in *Connecticut Yankee*. The novel's narrator and central character, Hank is identified three different ways. In the opening sequence, the FRAME-narrator (possibly Mark Twain himself) identifies Hank only as a stranger whom he calls "the YANKEE"—a name repeated in four chapter titles (11, 27, 34 and 39). Hank mentions his real name only twice within his narrative: In chapter 15 he imagines his 19th-century girlfriend calling him "Hank"; in chapter 39, he quotes a newspaper article referring to him as "the King's Minister, Hank Morgan, the which is surnamed The Boss." This last name originates in chapter 8, in which Hank discusses his antipathy toward ranks and titles. He claims that he has never sought a title and even declined one when it was offered—presumably by King ARTHUR. The only title he wants is one issuing "from the nation itself." After running the kingdom for several years, he receives just such a title when a village blacksmith coins a title that sweeps the nation and becomes the *only* name by which Hank is known thereafter. Translated into modern speech, this title is "the Boss." Hank relishes being a "The," since it makes him a "Unique"—like *The* King" or *The* Queen."

Although Hank is never formally knighted, five characters violate chivalric custom by calling him "Sir Boss": SANDY (chapter 19); Sir Ozana le Cure Hardy (twice in chapter 21); a telephone man named Ulfius (chapter 24); Queen GUENEVER (chapters 26 and 39) and even Arthur (chapter 27).

Despite Hank's frequent protestations of democratic sentiments, he has a strong dictatorial bent that a title such as "the Boss" satisfies. Shortly after arriving in CAMELOT, for example, he expresses confidence that he will "boss the whole country inside of three months" (chapter 2). He later expresses pride in demonstrating "what a despot could do with the resources of a kingdom" (chapter 10)—an ambition that recalls New York's corrupt political leader "Boss" Tweed (1823–1878).

"THE BELATED RUSSIAN PASSPORT" (1902) has a character named Prince Bossloffsky.

Boston Of all the towns unable to claim Mark Twain as a resident, Boston, Massachusetts may be the one in which he spent the most time. He went there often to visit James REDPATH'S LECTURE bureau and his publisher James R. OSGOOD. He also enjoyed visiting his friend W. D. HOWELLS, the ATLANTIC MONTHLY editor whom he met during his first Boston lecture engagement in November 1869. He selected Hartford, Connecticut for his home in 1871 partly because it was midway between Boston and NEW YORK CITY, with easy train connections to both. Over the next 35 years he spoke frequently in Boston and met most of New England's leading literary figures there.

He regarded the success of his first Boston lectures as an important triumph proving that the Eastern cultural world would accept him. The city was also the site of one of his greatest embarrassments—a speech honoring WHITTIER's birthday at the Hotel Brunswick on December 17, 1877. He found some consolation in a more successful speech at a breakfast honoring Oliver Wendell HOLMES in Boston two years later.

Despite Mark Twain's familiarity with Boston, he mentions it infrequently in his writings. In chapter 62

of *Roughing It*, WILLIAMS tells the Old ADMIRAL a preposterous lie about a Boston lynching that helped trigger the Civil War. In chapter 23 of *Huckleberry Finn*, Huck relates a garbled biography of England's King HENRY VIII that makes Henry personally responsible for the Boston Tea Party. The narrator of "TRAVELING WITH A REFORMER" is on his way to Boston as the 1893 story unfolds.

Bots, Stephen Dowling Figure mentioned in *Huckleberry Finn*. The subject of a sentimental ode by Emmeline GRANGERFORD that Huck admires in chapter 17, Bots was a boy who "fell down a well and was drownded." His surname is ironic; although the poem states that he suffered from neither coughing nor any other sickness, "botts" was a slang term for colic. The popularity of the ode is attested to by the English poet A. E. Housman (1859–1936), who in 1927 told Cyril CLEMENS that he knew it by heart.

Mark Twain's original draft of *Pudd'nhead Wilson* disposes of Aunt Patsy COOPER's obnoxious sons by having them fall down a well and drown.

Bourget, Paul (September 2, 1852, Amiens, France– December 25, 1935, Paris, France) French writer. Bourget gained renown with several volumes of poetry during the mid-1870s. He later published important essays exploring French pessimism and wrote a series of novels that made him one of FRANCE's leading novelists. After visiting the United States in 1893, he published a critical journal of his travels containing broad, negative generalizations about America—particularly American women—that offended Mark Twain. In January 1895, Mark Twain published "What Paul Bourget Thinks of Us" in the NORTH AMERICAN REVIEW. Objecting to Bourget's suggestion that America had blindly adopted the outstanding facets of French civilization, Mark Twain argues that the influence is in the other direction. The essay also discusses how the novel can be a medium that reveals a national culture. After the *Review* printed a reply signed by "Max O'Rell," Mark Twain responded with "A Little Note to M. Paul Bourget," implying that "O'Rell" was Bourget himself; however, it was actually another French writer, Paul Blouet (1848–1903). Mark Twain's second essay on Bourget first appeared in his anthology *How to Tell a Story and Other Essays* (1897).

Bowen, Barton W. Stone (c. 1830–c. June 1868) Childhood neighbor of Mark Twain. The second oldest brother of Will and Samuel A. BOWEN, Bart Bowen was one of several family members to work as a steamboat PILOT on the Mississippi. He piloted the ALFRED T. LACEY in July 1858 when Mark Twain took this boat to Memphis at the time his brother Henry Clemens died. Bowen and Mark Twain copiloted the same boat in May 1859. From early August until October 1, 1859, Mark Twain piloted the EDWARD J. GAY when Bowen was captain and part owner. Bowen is credited with encouraging Mark Twain to write the satire of Captain Isaiah SELLERS that he published in the *New Orleans Crescent* in May 1859. Bowen, like Mark Twain's brother Henry, died from steam burns he received in a steamboat accident.

Bowen, Samuel Adams, Jr. (c. 1838–1878) Childhood friend of Mark Twain. A younger brother of Bart and Will BOWEN, Sam Bowen grew up with Mark Twain in Hannibal and preceded him as a Mississippi steamboat PILOT. From early August to mid-October, 1858, Mark Twain cubbed under him aboard the JOHN H. DICKEY. Mark Twain may also have cubbed under Bowen aboard the WHITE CLOUD in late October 1858. The evidence is more certain that Bowen and Mark Twain served together as copilots on Mark Twain's last steamboat, the ALONZO CHILD, from late 1860 through May 1861.

When the CIVIL WAR started, Bowen and Mark Twain joined the MARION RANGERS together. Bowen remained a soldier after Mark Twain went west. He was arrested by Union troops and held prisoner in Hannibal until he swore allegiance to the Union. He became a pilot for the North, but secretly carried Confederate army mail on the river. He later died from yellow fever while working as a steamboat pilot. When floodwaters later exposed his grave on a Mississippi River island, Mark Twain is said to have helped arrange for his reburial.

According to Mark Twain's AUTOBIOGRAPHY, Bowen lived with a young woman whose wealthy father named her sole beneficiary in his will. The will identified her as "Mrs. Samuel A. Bowen," so she and Bowen quickly married and had their marriage certificate predated. Unfortunately, relatives discovered their deception and had Bowen's bride cut out of her inheritance. Chapter 49 of *Life on the Mississippi* relates this story, giving Bowen the name "George Johnson."

Bowen, Will (1836–1893) Lifelong friend of Mark Twain. In 1870, Mark Twain wrote a letter to Bowen describing him as "My First, & Oldest & Dearest Friend." That letter, which is often reprinted, recalls many experiences that the men shared as boys—experiences that Mark Twain used in his fiction, particularly *Tom Sawyer,* in which Bowen appears as Tom's "bosom friend" Joe HARPER. Certain elements of Tom Sawyer himself doubtless derived from Bowen. Will was one of seven children of Samuel Adams Bowen (1790–1853), who settled his family in Hannibal a few years before the Clemenses arrived. The senior Bowen was Mark Twain's model for Captain Harper, Joe's father in "TOM SAWYER'S CONSPIRACY."

In 1844 Will Bowen caught the measles during a local epidemic. Mark Twain later recalled that the suspense of waiting for the disease to catch up with him was so unsettling that he went to Bowen's house and climbed in bed with him in order to infect himself. He used this incident in chapter 4 of "Tom Sawyer's Conspiracy," in which Tom Sawyer tries to catch measles from Joe Harper. This should have been a tall order, as Tom already had measles in chapter 22 of *Tom Sawyer.*

Along with several of his brothers, Bowen went to work on the Mississippi River. He earned his PILOTING license in 1857. He and Mark Twain were copilots on three riverboats between 1859 and 1861: the ALFRED T. LACEY, the A. B. CHAMBERS and the ALONZO CHILD. Disagreement over a money matter, as well as political differences over the CIVIL WAR, led to a falling-out between the two men that lasted until just after the war. Bowen initially supported the Confederacy, but switched allegiance to become a pilot on a Union transport boat. In 1868 he left the river to sell insurance in St. Louis. Around 1880 he moved to Austin, Texas. He visited Mark Twain at Hartford in 1888.

Boyhood Home, Mark Twain's Hannibal, Missouri house in which Mark Twain lived from around late 1843 to mid-1853 and later used as the model for Tom Sawyer's fictional home. Located at 206 Hill Street, the modest two-story frame structure is now fully restored and preserved as a public museum by the MARK TWAIN HOME FOUNDATION.

When Mark Twain's family moved to Hannibal in November 1839, his father, John M. Clemens, purchased the Hill Street property on which the Boyhood Home now stands. It is not known exactly when he had the house built, but the family was living in it by the time Mark Twain was eight years old. The Clemenses occupied the house until 1853, except for an interval in 1846–47, when they boarded in the nearby PILASTER HOUSE. Through these years, Sam and Henry Clemens shared a second-floor bedroom from which they could see the Mississippi River and escape through a window for nocturnal adventures. At times, their sister Pamela Clemens MOFFETT used the parlor to teach piano, and their older brother Orion Clemens published a newspaper out of the house.

After 1853, the house was rented to frequently changing tenants and may have been a restaurant briefly. Mark Twain revisited it several times. In *Life on the Mississippi,* he recalls walking through Hannibal in early 1882, when he observed a black family in his former home (chapter 54). He also saw the house in 1885 and had his picture taken in front of it in May 1902. During this last visit, he remarked that each time he returned home, the house seemed to grow smaller; one more visit, he feared, would transform it into a birdhouse. Descriptions of the house are scattered through his AUTOBIOGRAPHY and various Tom Sawyer stories.

When the structure was threatened with demolition in 1911, a civic leader named George A. Mahan (1851–1936) bought it and had it restored to something resembling its original condition. The following year, he donated it to the city, which opened it as a public museum

Mark Twain's last visit to his boyhood home in 1902. (Courtesy, Library of Congress, Pictures & Prints Division)

known as the "Mark Twain Home." A fence was later erected next to the house to celebrate the FENCE WHITE-WASHING episode of *Tom Sawyer*. In 1937, the federal Works Progress Administration erected a permanent museum next to the house and did additional renovation work on the house itself.

Since 1912, the fragile structure has attracted over six million visitors, whose sheer numbers threatened to wear it out. In 1984, visitors were excluded from the interior of the house and a study was begun to determine its original appearance. It was soon discovered that Mark Twain had not simply imagined the house growing smaller; it *was* smaller than it had been during

his youth. After a major restoration project began in 1990–91, portions of the house that had been removed around the 1880s were restored under the direction of curator Henry Sweets III, and every effort was made to make it appear as it had been during Mark Twain's youth. Visitors can now inspect the inside of the house from a metal platform built between it and the museum that allows them partial entry into the house's rooms while preserving the structure from further wear.

"Boy's Manuscript"   A short story that Mark Twain wrote sometime late in 1868, "Boy's Manuscript" is his earliest known piece of fiction inspired by his Hannibal childhood and it clearly anticipates both *Tom Sawyer* and "EXTRACTS FROM ADAM'S DIARY." It takes the form of a diary spanning several weeks in the life of lovesick Billy ROGERS, who is smitten by a beautiful, blue-eyed blonde eight-year-old named Amy. Billy's efforts to impress Amy by showing off, and the heartache her fickleness causes him, parallel much of what happens between Tom SAWYER and Becky THATCHER in chapters 3 through 18 of *Tom Sawyer*. In contrast to the later novel, however, this story ends with Billy's breaking up with Amy and then falling in love with a much older girl. It is probably significant that Mark Twain wrote this story while in the midst of courting Livy; certain incidents and nuances in the story may reflect that courtship.

Although Mark Twain finished this 7,400-word story, he never published it himself. Whatever title he may have given it was lost along with its first two manuscript pages. A. B. PAINE supplied the title that has been used since the story was first published in *Mark Twain at Work* (1942) by Bernard DEVOTO—who dubbed the story the "embryo of *Tom Sawyer*."

Bradish   Figure mentioned in *Huckleberry Finn*. In chapter 8, Jim tells Huck that Bradish was the owner of a one-legged slave who started a "bank" in which Jim lost five dollars. "THE $30,000 BEQUEST" mentions a rising young lawyer named Bradish whom Aleck and Sally FOSTER consider as a possible mate for one of their daughters.

Bradish, Bat   Minor character in "TOM SAWYER'S CONSPIRACY." Bradish is the nearsighted slave trader whom Tom wishes to involve in his abolitionist hoax by fooling him into thinking that he—Tom in blackface—is a runaway slave. Before Tom's plan is carried out, Bradish is murdered by real conspirators and Jim is arrested for the crime. Near the end of the unfinished novella the KING and DUKE of *Huckleberry Finn* are shown to be the true murderers.

Bricksville   Fictional ARKANSAS town in *Huckleberry Finn*. In chapters 21–23, Huck spends four days in Bricksville. The first day, he sees Colonel SHERBURN shoot BOGGS, follows a lynch mob to Sherburn's house and sneaks into a circus. In the evening, the KING and DUKE stage a SHAKESPEARE performance in the courthouse that flops miserably. Over the next three nights, however, they pack the courthouse with the lurid ROYAL NONESUCH. Taking care to slip out of town before its third show begins, they deny the townspeople their revenge. Bricksville is not mentioned by name until chapter 28, when Huck tells Mary Jane WILKS that she can prove the King and Duke are frauds by sending to Bricksville for witnesses.

Huck describes Bricksville as a one-horse town whose streets are all mud, whose houses are elevated to escape floodwater and whose riverfront houses are buckling and falling into the river. The name "Bricksville" is ironic; its houses are frame structures that have never even been painted.

Mark Twain modeled Bricksville and its location partly on NAPOLEON, Arkansas. His description of Bricksville's sleepy main street, where loafers like Buck HARKNESS sit whittling and chewing, also recalls his description of Hannibal in chapter 4 of *Life on the Mississippi*.

Bridgeport   CONNECTICUT town that was the headquarters of showman P. T. BARNUM. The narrative of *Connecticut Yankee* begins in nearby Hartford, where Hank MORGAN is knocked unconscious in a fight. After he awakens in sixth-century England, a knight in armor takes him to CAMELOT. Believing that his captor escaped from a circus, Hank thinks he is being taken to Bridgeport when he sees the castle—doubtless because he is thinking of Barnum's famous home.

"THE BELATED RUSSIAN PASSPORT" mentions Bridgeport as the hometown of Alfred Parrish.

Bridgewater, Duke of   Name used in *Huckleberry Finn*. In chapter 19, two rogues join Huck and Jim aboard their raft. The younger man claims to be the rightful Duke of Bridgewater; throughout the balance of the narrative, he is known as the DUKE, and the name "Bridgewater" is not mentioned again. The older rogue, who is known as the KING, usually calls the Duke "BILGEWATER."

The Duke claims that his "great-grandfather, eldest son of the Duke of Bridgewater," came to America and died, leaving a son, about the same time that his own father died. The late duke's second son then seized the title and estates, while the rightful duke, the infant, was ignored. The rogue claims to be the lineal descendant of that infant.

Bridgewater was the name of a real English dukedom that died out before Mark Twain's time. The third and last Duke of Bridgewater was Frances Egerton (1736–1803). As one of the richest men of his time, he had a title to which the greedy might naturally aspire. However, he never married, shunned women after a romantic disappointment, and died childless. The title "Bridgewater" was carried over into an earldom, but in 1829 it, too, expired. The well-known wealth and eccentricities associated with the Bridgewater name assured its frequent use in 19th-century humor.

Briggs, John B. (April 18, 1837, near Hannibal, Missouri–July 17, 1907, near New London, Missouri)   Lifelong friend of Mark Twain. The son of a Hannibal businessman and civic leader, Briggs was one of Mark Twain's closest friends during his childhood. In later years Mark Twain named Briggs, John GARTH and Laura HAWKINS as the only three childhood playmates who lived in his memory. Details of his friendship with Briggs are, however, less well known than are those of his friendship with Will BOWEN. Even the fictional character that he modeled on Briggs, Ben ROGERS, is not well developed. One thing that is known is the fact that Briggs joined the CADETS OF TEMPERANCE with young Sam Clemens. Later, however, he worked in a tobacco factory. Briggs remained in the Hannibal region as a respected farmer and saw Mark Twain during the latter's last visit there in 1902. Shortly before Briggs died, he was interviewed by A. B. PAINE, who was preparing a biography of Mark Twain.

Briggs had an older brother, William Briggs Jr., who joined the GOLD RUSH TO CALIFORNIA in 1849. Mark Twain saw him in SAN FRANCISCO in the 1860s, by which time Briggs had become a professional gambler. Mark Twain was romantically interested in their sister, Artemissa Briggs, but she gently rebuffed him and married a Hannibal bricklayer in 1853.

Briggs, Scotty   Character in *Roughing It.* In chapter 47, Briggs is the VIRGINIA CITY committeeman delegated to interview a young preacher newly arrived from the East to plan his friend Buck FANSHAW's funeral. Like Fanshaw, Briggs is a stalwart rough and a member of the fire department; he shows up in his full uniform, with red fire helmet and patent leather belt with a spanner and a revolver attached. Though a marked contrast to the pale theological student (modeled on Franklin S. Rising), Briggs has a warm heart that sees him through, though he and the preacher speak such vastly different argots that every sentence each man utters mystifies the other. Briggs nearly overwhelms the preacher with a torrent of obscure slang taken from the mines, cards, games and other sources, but eventually makes himself understood. When the grand funeral finally comes off, he serves as a pallbearer. Later, he becomes the first local rough to convert to religion, and teaches a Sunday school class in which he tells children stories in language that they can understand. A month before Briggs dies, *Roughing It*'s narrator hears him recite a slang-riddled version of the story of Joseph and his brothers.

Brooks, Van Wyck (February 16, 1886, Plainfield, New Jersey–May 2, 1963, Bridgewater, Massachusetts) Literary scholar. Soon after graduating from Harvard in 1908, Brooks published the first of more than two dozen books on American literature that would make him one of the country's most popular and influential literary authorities. In 1920, he launched an ambitious exploration of the impact of the American environment on three selected writers with publication of *The Ordeal of Mark Twain* (he later wrote on Henry JAMES and EMERSON). A pioneering attempt at psychobiography, this book has had a seminal impact on Mark Twain studies. Its basic thesis is that Mark Twain's development as a writer was arrested by early childhood traumas, an emotionally overbearing mother, mid-Victorian morality and the stultifying influences of the western frontier. When Mark Twain became an author, according to Brooks, he was incapable of seeing literature as "art," instead of merely a line of activity in which he made a living.

The first major rebuttal of Brooks's thesis came in 1932, when Bernard DEVOTO published *Mark Twain's America.* Attacking Brooks's limited and often selective use of evidence—much of which came from A. B. PAINE's biography of Mark Twain—DeVoto countered that a virile, vigorous environment actually stimulated Mark Twain into responding with great creativity. Brooks softened his thesis in a revised edition of *The Ordeal of Mark Twain* the following year. By the time he published *The Times of Melville and Whitman* in 1947, he had modified his views on Mark Twain considerably, but his original arguments remain controversial even now.

Brown, Dr. John (September 22, 1810, Lancashire, England–May 11, 1882, Edinburgh, Scotland) Scottish physician and author. Mark Twain met Brown in Edinburgh in August 1873. When his wife needed medical treatment, he sought out Brown because of his reputation as the author of the children's story *Rab and His Friends* (1859). After this meeting, Brown became a close friend of the Clemens family and corresponded with Mark Twain until he died. One of Mark Twain's letters to Brown is important for identifying his personal contributions to *The Gilded Age*, which he coauthored with C. D. WARNER.

An essay by Brown on the prodigy Marjorie FLEMING inspired Mark Twain later to write his own essay on her. Mark Twain mentions *Rab and His Friends* in "THE LOVES OF ALONZO FITZ CLARENCE AND ROSANNAH ETHELTON" and "Which Was the Dream?"

Brown, Mr.   Character in several series of travel letters that Mark Twain wrote during the 1860s. "Brown" first appears in Mark Twain's letters from HAWAII to the SACRAMENTO UNION in 1866, in which he is called "a bitter enemy of sentiment." Brown does not appear in the *Roughing It* chapters drawn from the Hawaii letters, but briefly resurfaces as "Mr. Billings" in chapters 69 and 73.

"Brown" next appears in the letters to the SAN FRANCISCO ALTA CALIFORNIA that Mark Twain wrote during his journeys from California to New York and through the Midwest, from December 1866 to June 1867. These letters have been published as MARK TWAIN'S TRAVELS WITH MR. BROWN (1940).

Mark Twain used "Brown" in his early letters to the *Alta* from his QUAKER CITY cruise, which began in June 1867, but gradually lost interest in the character. Brown disappeared completely when Mark Twain revised the letters for *Innocents Abroad*. Of 22 references to "Brown" in the original *Alta* letters, 15 are cut completely, five are attributed to a character named "BLUCHER" and two are attributed to a character named "Jack" (VAN NOSTRAND). One omitted passage, for example, concerns Brown's problems identifying water closets in Paris.

Throughout all these letters, "Brown" is a foil who allows Mark Twain to say things that he might hesitate to utter in his narrators' voices. In one *Alta* letter, for example, when the narrator comments on the voluptuousness of young women in NICARAGUA, Brown tastelessly interjects that the women are "heifers." Apologizing for Brown's intrusion, the narrator explains that Brown "always unearths the disagreeable features of everything that comes under his notice."

"Brown" may have been partly inspired by William BROWN, an irascible steamboat pilot under whom Mark Twain served in 1858. This man appears as "Mr. Brown" in "OLD TIMES ON THE MISSISSIPPI" and in early chapters of *Life on the Mississippi*. Like Mark Twain's imaginary travel companion, William Brown combined total recall with an inability to discriminate between important and unimportant facts. The name may also be a playful reference to Mark Twain's friend John Ross BROWNE.

Chapter 52 of *Life on the Mississippi* also mentions another, apparently unrelated "Mr. Brown"; this man is the fictitious St. Louis benefactor of an ex-convict who writes a moving letter to Charlie WILLIAMS.

Brown, Walter Francis (January 10, 1853, Providence, Rhode Island–1929, Venice, Italy)   Illustrator. In the spring of 1879, Brown was in Paris studying art when he met Mark Twain, who recommended him to Frank BLISS to help illustrate *A Tramp Abroad*. Mark Twain was aware of Brown's work in ST. NICHOLAS and in HARPER'S WEEKLY. During May and June he inspected Brown's drawings as he submitted them to Bliss. Brown drew more than 120 illustrations for the book, signing them with both "W. F. B." and his full name. He used a variety of styles, from comic caricatures resembling the work of William Wallace DENSLOW to rough-hewn action scenes similar to the work of True WILLIAMS. Brown later retired to Venice, Italy.

Brown, William (c. 1810s–June 19, 1858, Mississippi River)   Steamboat PILOT under whom Mark Twain cubbed in 1858. When Horace BIXBY switched to the Missouri River, he left Mark Twain under Brown's tutelage on the PENNSYLVANIA in November 1857 and from early February through early June 1858—one of the most unpleasant periods in Mark Twain's early life. Chapter 18 of *Life on the Mississippi* describes Brown as a "middle-aged, horse-faced, ignorant, stingy, malicious, snarling, fault-finding, mote-magnifying tyrant." Every night, Mark Twain's alter ego, the cub, goes to bed trying to think of new ways to kill him. Meanwhile, his fellow cub, George RITCHIE, enjoys life under the amiable George EALER.

Mark Twain's tense relationship with Brown came to a head when Brown got into a dispute with the former's brother, Henry Clemens, then a lowly clerk on the *Pennsylvania*. One day, Mark Twain witnessed Brown ignoring Henry's effort to deliver a message from the captain. After Brown told the captain that Henry had not given him any message, an argument ensued. As the nearly six-foot-tall Brown jumped at Henry, Mark Twain abandoned the helm, bashed him with a stool, and pounded him. Chapter 19 of *Life on the Mississippi* recounts the affair—apparently the only documented instance of Mark Twain's brawling as an adult.

To Mark Twain's amazement, Captain KLINEFELTER applauded his attack on Brown and offered him Brown's job for the return voyage from New Orleans when he could not find a licensed replacement. Mark Twain declined, however, leaving Brown to pilot the *Pennsylvania* up the Mississippi, while he followed on the ALFRED T. LACEY. On June 19, 1858, the *Pennsylvania*'s boilers burst near MEMPHIS. Brown disappeared. Had Mark Twain remained on the boat, he might have been killed instead.

According to *Life on the Mississippi*, Brown had a prodigious memory (he is "Mr. J." in "OLD TIMES ON THE MISSISSIPPI"), but could not discriminate between interesting and uninteresting facts and was consequently a tedious storyteller (chapter 13). Brown may have been an inspiration for the imaginary traveling companion, Mr. BROWN, in some of Mark Twain's other writings. He may also have been a model for Flint BUCKNER in "A DOUBLE-BARRELLED DETECTIVE STORY."

Browne, John Ross (February 11, 1821, Dublin, Ireland–December 8 or 9, 1875, Oakland, California)   Irish-American writer, illustrator and diplomat. After coming to America in 1833, Browne lived in Kentucky, where he worked on flatboats, trained in stenography and did police reporting. He reported for the *Congressional Record*'s precursor in 1841, then shipped on a whaler to the Indian Ocean, later returning to work as a Senate reporter and to travel in the West for the federal government. In early 1868, he was named to succeed Anson BURLINGAME as American minister to China, where he served for a year. His first book was *Etchings of a Whaling Cruise* (1846), which Herman Melville reviewed before writing *Moby Dick* (1851). In 1853, Browne began publishing travel sketches in HARPER'S MAGAZINE and other magazines, often illustrating his own work. His later travel books include *Yusef, or the Journey of the Frangi* (1853) about Asia, *Crusoe's Island, with Sketches of Adventure in California and Washoe* (1864) and *An American Family in Germany* (1866).

During the early 1860s, Browne increased his magazine output while establishing himself as a lecturer in California and Nevada. He settled in Oakland, California when Mark Twain was living in San Francisco. While it is uncertain whether the two men knew each other in Nevada, they certainly met just before Mark Twain's first professional lecture in San Francisco in October 1866. A month later, Mark Twain stayed in Browne's home when he passed through Oakland on a lecture tour. He saw Browne again in WASHINGTON, D.C. in late 1867; in February 1868, he accepted Browne's invitation to join his diplomatic staff in China, but turned his attention to other matters and did not go. He last saw Browne in LONDON in October 1872.

Browne may have influenced Mark Twain's early writing career, either as a model or as an adviser on writing travel books. Like Mark Twain, he had an informal, breezy style and parodied sentimentalism. He anticipated Mark Twain in using a comic persona as his narrator, and he had a similar knack for working marginally relevant reminiscences into passages. For his part, Mark Twain's choice of "Mr. BROWN" as the name of his fictional traveling companion may have been an attempt at good-natured needling; he used the name only in letters to western newspapers that Browne saw. *Roughing It* names Browne among writers who have told the Hank MONK anecdote (chapter 20). Mark Twain's publisher pirated five pictures from Browne's *Adventures in the Apache Country* (1869) for *Roughing It* (pages 254, 260, 265, 302 and 340 of the first edition). Browne may have had this piracy in mind when he later wrote that Mark Twain "made plenty of money on his . . . books—some of it on mine."

Browning, Robert (May 7, 1812, Camberwell, England–December 12, 1889, Venice, Italy) English poet. Browning was one of Mark Twain's favorite writers. He owned many of Browning's books, read from them often and enjoyed reading aloud from them to groups. In the late 1880s, Mark Twain conducted study groups on Browning in his home. Browning's poem "Tray" probably helped inspire his "A DOG'S TALE" (1903), and Browning's monologues likely influenced his writing style in KING LEOPOLD'S SOLILOQUY (1905) and "THE CZAR'S SOLILOQUY" (1905).

Browning married the poet Elizabeth Barrett (1806–1861) in 1846 and they moved to FLORENCE, Italy the next year. After Elizabeth died, Browning returned to London, where Mark Twain met him in the summer of 1873. Like Browning's wife, Mark Twain's wife, Livy, later died in Florence. At her funeral, Joseph TWICHELL read from Browning's poetry.

Bryn Mawr Women's college founded in 1880 at Bryn Mawr, PENNSYLVANIA, 15 miles northwest of PHILADELPHIA. Mark Twain's daughter Susy Clemens entered Bryn Mawr in 1890, but dropped out before completing the academic year. She relished being on her own, but her father evidently begrudged her her independence. During her time at Bryn Mawr, Susy formed an intimate friendship with a slightly older student, Louise Brownell (1870–1961), who eventually earned a doctorate there (Charles NEIDER includes some of Susy's correspondence with Brownell in his edition of Susy's biography of her father). Susy's cousin Ida Langdon (1881–1964), a daughter of Charles LANGDON, also studied at Bryn Mawr and later taught English there.

On March 23, 1891, Mark Twain spoke at Bryn Mawr, upsetting Susy with a recitation of the "GOLDEN ARM" story that he had promised not to tell. Her class made him an honorary member.

Buchanan, James (April 23, 1791, Stony Batter, Pennsylvania–June 1, 1868, Lancaster, Pennsylvania) Fifteenth president of the United States (1857–1861). Buchanan's administration coincided almost exactly with Mark Twain's time as a steamboat PILOT on the Mississippi River. Two days before Buchanan left office, he signed the organic act creating the Territory of NEVADA, in which Orion Clemens would become territorial secretary. One of Mark Twain's few published references to Buchanan appears in chapter 11 of *Connecticut Yankee,* in which Hank MORGAN alludes to having been a boy during "Buchanan's administration."

Buckner, Flint Character in "A DOUBLE-BARRELLED DETECTIVE STORY." A silver miner in HOPE CANYON, California, Buckner is a sadistic bully who holds young Fetlock JONES in bondage until Jones blows him up. Afterward, Archy STILLMAN learns that Buckner's real name was Jacob FULLER—the father he has spent years trying to locate in order to avenge his abused mother. Buckner's habit of leaving the camp's tavern at the same time every night is an important element of Jones's murder scheme. As a bully, Buckner seems to be modeled partly on William BROWN, the steamboat pilot whom the young cub in *Life on the Mississippi* dreams of murdering.

Buckner, Lafe Minor character in *Huckleberry Finn.* Buckner is mentioned once, as one of the lazy BRICKSVILLE, Arkansas tobacco chewers Huck sees in chapter 21. "JOURNALISM IN TENNESSEE" mentions a Buckner who is the imbecilic editor of the *Daily Hurrah.*

Buckstone, John Minor character in *Pudd'nhead Wilson.* "A great politician in a small way," Buckstone is heavily involved in DAWSON'S LANDING public affairs. He appears at David WILSON's house in chapter 11 to invite the CAPELLO brothers to a Sons of Liberty meeting and is a member of a committee that asks Wilson to run for mayor in chapter 13. In chapter 20's trial scene, he testifies as one of the first persons to arrive at the scene of the murder. In "THOSE EXTRAORDINARY TWINS," Buckstone appears briefly as a confused witness at the Capellos' assault trial in chapter 5.

Bud Background figure in *Huckleberry Finn.* In chapter 18, Buck GRANGERFORD tells Huck how his 14-year-old cousin Bud was shot by Baldy SHEPHERDSON in a family feud, about three months earlier.

Buffalo Industrial center and commercial hub in western NEW YORK. Mark Twain first passed through Buffalo on August 22, 1853, while going to NEW YORK CITY. In mid-August 1869, he became a resident after buying into the BUFFALO EXPRESS. For two and a half months

During his brief stint as an editor of the Buffalo Express *Mark Twain visited Washington, D.C. in July 1870 and was photographed at Mathew Brady's studio with David Gray of the* Buffalo Courier *(at left) and George Alfred Townsend.* (Courtesy, Library of Congress, Pictures & Prints Division)

he lived in an East Swan Street boardinghouse near the newspaper, then went on a LECTURE tour through January. On February 3, 1870, the day after his MARRIAGE to Olivia Langdon in ELMIRA, he returned to Buffalo by train with Livy and members of the wedding party. Expecting a friend to have secured new boardinghouse lodgings for him, Mark Twain was surprised to be driven to an expensive, fully furnished house that was a wedding gift from his father-in-law, Jervis LANGDON.

Through the next 13 months, Mark Twain and Livy lived near the city center at 472 Delaware Avenue. With only a few close friends—such as David GRAY and his wife—they experienced a string of disasters that turned their Buffalo residence into a nightmare. In the spring, Jervis Langdon began a painful bout with stomach cancer that ended with his death in August. Worn out and pregnant, Livy then fell ill. Her houseguest Emma NYE stayed to nurse her, but Nye contracted typhoid fever and died in their house in late September. In November, Livy delivered Langdon Clemens prematurely; then both she and the baby became gravely ill. Meanwhile, Mark Twain struggled to meet burdensome writing commitments, including *Roughing It.* Exhausted after their first year in Buffalo, they put their house and *Express* interests up for sale on March 2, 1871. Two weeks later, they went to Elmira, where they stayed until renting a house in Hartford, Connecticut in October.

Their Buffalo house became a restaurant in the 20th century and was torn down in 1963.

Buffalo Express   Daily BUFFALO, New York newspaper that began in 1846. When Mark Twain became engaged, he wanted to settle down as a journalist and looked for a newspaper in which to invest. After J. R. HAWLEY rejected his bid to buy into the *Hartford Courant,* he borrowed $25,000 from Jervis LANGDON and bought a one-third interest in the *Express* from Thomas A. Kennett (1843–1911) in August 1869. His partners were George H. Selkirk, who handled most business matters, and Josephus Nelson Larned (1838–1913), the paper's political editor.

Mark Twain's editorial duties were only vaguely defined. His growing national reputation helped publicize the *Express,* to which he was expected to contribute humor. In mid-August 1869, he began working in the paper's East Swan Street offices. After two and a half months, he left on a LECTURE tour of the Northeast, but continued to send stories to the *Express.* After marrying Olivia Langdon in February 1870, he returned to Buffalo and established a new routine. Family problems, commitments to write for the GALAXY and other publications and a new book, *Roughing It,* interfered with his *Express* duties and he ceased to visit the offices regularly. In March 1871, he decided to quit journalism altogether and leave Buffalo. He sold out his interest in the *Express,* losing $10,000 of his original investment.

Mark Twain's known contributions to the *Express* include 60 features, 31 editorials and 30 brief items. Many of his *Express* sketches also appeared in the *Galaxy* and in SKETCHES, NEW AND OLD. The better-known of these include "A CURIOUS DREAM," "THE CAPITOLINE VENUS," "A GHOST STORY," "JOURNALISM IN TENNESSEE," "Last Words of Great Men," "A MEDIEVAL ROMANCE" and "RUNNING FOR GOVERNOR." He also wrote a series called "AROUND THE WORLD."

The *Express* merged with its former rival the *Courier* in 1926. The *Buffalo Courier-Express* folded on September 19, 1982.

Bunker, Hank   Figure mentioned in *Huckleberry Finn.* In chapter 10, Huck calls Bunker a person who once defied superstition by looking at a new moon over his left shoulder and bragging about it. "In less than two years he got drunk and fell off of the shot tower and spread himself out so that he was just a kind of a layer, as you may say; and they slid him edgeways between two barn doors for a coffin."

Buntline, Ned (March 20, 1823, Stamford, New York– July 16, 1886, Stamford, New York)   Pen name of Edward Zane Carroll Judson, the first and most famous "dime novelist." Buntline began writing for magazines in the mid-1840s—as Mark Twain was growing up—and eventually published more than 400 stories. Though he had many real adventures of his own, he is best known for giving "Buffalo Bill" CODY his nickname and making him famous. Mark Twain read Buntline's stories as a boy and may have met him in California in May 1868, when they traveled on the same Sacramento River steamboat.

With such titles as *The Black Avenger* (1847) and *The Red Revenger* (1848), Buntline's stories are the kind of literature that Tom SAWYER prefers. In fact, Tom appropriates Buntline's title "BLACK AVENGER OF THE SPANISH MAIN" for himself when he plays PIRATES in *Tom Sawyer.*

Bunyan, John (November 1628, Elstow, England–August 31, 1688, London, England)   Author of *The Pilgrim's Progress.* A Baptist minister of limited education, Bunyan wrote his most famous work while imprisoned for preaching against England's established church. *The Pilgrim's Progress* (1678 and 1684) is an allegory about a man named Christian who travels to the Celestial City and comes to understand God's plan for salvation. Mark Twain was familiar with this book from his childhood and owned several copies, including a facsimile of the original edition. Fascinated by Bunyan's concept of "PILGRIMS," he wanted to call his first travel book *The New Pilgrims' Progress;* however, to avoid confusion about the nature of his book, he instead called it *The Innocents Abroad.* "The New Pilgrims' Progress" appeared as a subtitle to the American edition and as the title of the second volume of the first English edition.

In chapter 17 of *Huckleberry Finn,* Huck sees *The Pilgrim's Progress* in the home of the GRANGERFORDS and says that the book is "about a man that left his family it didn't say why." After reading much of the book, he concludes that its "statements was interesting, but tough." Bunyan's influence on Mark Twain can also be seen in "CAPTAIN STORMFIELD'S VISIT TO HEAVEN."

burglary   On September 18, 1908—exactly three months after Mark Twain moved into STORMFIELD—two men entered his home and removed family silverware. Mark Twain woke up when his butler fired a pistol at the fleeing burglars, who were arrested several hours later. Mark Twain met the suspects at the police station, spoke at their arraignment and attended their trial in November. One man was sentenced to four years in prison, the other to 10 years. Clara Clemens helped pay for a mechanic's course for one of them, Henry Williams, who later published an anonymous autobiography, *In the Clutch of Circumstances* (1922), in an attempt to explain his role in the burglary.

Though deeply upset by the theft of his wife's silverware and the resignations of his entire domestic staff, Mark Twain publicly maintained a comic pose about the burglary. A month later, he had a burglar alarm installed—such as he had parodied decades earlier in "The MCWILLIAMSES and the Burglar Alarm" (1882).

burlesque   In literary terminology, a "burlesque" is a comically distorted imitation of another work, writer or genre of writing. The term comes to English, by way of French, from an old Italian word for "ridiculous." While burlesques tend to be short, they can take almost any form of prose, poetry or drama. Two types have been defined: *high burlesque,* which treats trivial subjects with exaggerated seriousness; and *low burlesque,* which treats serious subjects with exaggerated levity. Burlesque departs from SATIRE in aiming more for humorous effect than for the arousal of indignation. It becomes parody when it consciously imitates a particular work, author or school. Whatever form it takes, its essential quality is the ridiculous discrepancy between its subject matter and its style.

During the 19th century, burlesque was a popular and well-understood form in America, particularly on the frontier, where Mark Twain learned his craft. He consciously wrote burlesques, a notable early example being Mark Twain's BURLESQUE AUTOBIOGRAPHY (1871). Until he found his own voice, he was inclined to burlesque well-known writers, such as SHAKESPEARE. Burlesque permeates his whole body of writings, particularly his early sketches, such as "AURELIA'S UNFORTUNATE YOUNG MAN" and "LUCRETIA SMITH'S SOLDIER." Burlesque elements appear even in his major works, such as the "King's Camelopard" episode in *Huckleberry Finn.* An example of an extended late effort is "A DOUBLE-BARRELLED DETECTIVE STORY," which contains a savage burlesque of Conan Doyle's Sherlock HOLMES.

Many of Mark Twain's unfinished burlesques appear in the MARK TWAIN PAPERS edition, *Mark Twain's Satires & Burlesques* (1968), which includes "Burlesque *Il Trovatore,*" "A Novel: *Who Was He?,*" "The Story of Mamie Grant," "L'Homme Qui Rit," "Burlesque HAMLET," and "1002D ARABIAN NIGHT."

Burlesque Autobiography, Mark Twain's ("A Burlesque Biography") (1871)   Sketch published as a booklet. Tending more toward farce than BURLESQUE, this fictional history of Mark Twain's ancestors is an exercise in euphemism. While it describes most of his ancestors as carefree humorists, a close reading reveals them to be clever criminals who met violent ends. The sketch is also laced with historical and geographical nonsense, such as a reference to ancestors living in Aberdeen (a Scottish town) in the county of Cork (Ireland) in England. Parenthetical insertions in the synopsis that follows explain some of the sketch's references.

SYNOPSIS

In response to public demand, the author tenders his family's history. The earliest recorded Twain was an 11th-century friend of the family named Higgins in Aberdeen. It remains a mystery why the family has since gone by the maternal name rather than Higgins. During the time of William Rufus (England's William II), Arthour Twain was a noted highway solicitor who died suddenly after visiting the resort at Newgate (a prison). Augustus Twain achieved renown in the mid-

12th century by sticking passersby with his saber until he carried this joke too far. Authorities removed one end of him, and mounted it on a high place on Temple Bar (i.e., he was beheaded). Over the next two centuries, the family tree shows a succession of high-spirited soldiers.

In the early 15th century, Beau Twain had infinite sport imitating the handwriting of others until he contracted to break stone for a road. During 42 years in the stone business, he was a conspicuous member of the benevolent society known as the Chain Gang.

John Morgan TWAIN came to America in 1492 as a passenger with COLUMBUS. After he grumbled about the food and Columbus's navigating and fretted constantly about his "trunk," the crew threw him overboard, only to have him steal the ship's anchor. On the positive side, he was the first white person interested in civilizing INDIANS, for whom he built a jail and a gallows (on which he appears to have been the first white man hanged in America). His 17th-century great-grandson, known as "the old Admiral," commanded a fleet of well-armed vessels that hurried merchantmen across the ocean (i.e., he was a pirate). Eventually, he was cut down—though his widow thought that if he had been cut down 15 minutes sooner he might have lived (i.e., he was hanged).

Charles Henry Twain was a late 17th-century missionary who converted 16,000 South Sea islanders. They remembered him as a good, tender man and wished they had more of him (i.e., they ate him). In the mid-18th century, Pah-go-to-wah-wah-pukketekeewis, "Mighty-Hunter-with-a-Hog-Eye-Twain," helped General Braddock fight the oppressor Washington (Washington fought *with* Braddock in 1755).

Other ancestors are better known to history by their aliases—such as Richard Brinsley Twain, alias Guy Fawkes; John Wentworth Twain, alias Sixteen-String Jack; William Hogarth Twain, alias Jack Sheppard; Ananias Twain, alias Baron Munchausen; John George Twain, alias Captain Kydd. A collateral branch of the family includes George Francis Train, Tom Pepper, Nebuchadnezzar and Baalam's Ass, who differed from the ancient stock in going to jail instead of getting hanged.

The author points out that while RICHARD III had the advantage over him in being born with teeth, he had the advantage over Richard in being born without a humpback. The author decides to leave his own history unwritten until he is hanged like his ancestors.

PUBLICATION HISTORY

Anxious to capitalize on his post–*Innocents Abroad* fame, Mark Twain arranged with his GALAXY editor Isaac Sheldon to publish this 2,180-word sketch in a three-part booklet titled *Mark Twain's (Burlesque) Autobiography and First Romance*. The booklet included a short story better known as "A MEDIEVAL ROMANCE" and a series of cartoons drawn by Henry Louis STEPHENS titled "The

House that Jack Built"—a parody of the popular nursery rhyme, caricaturing Jay GOULD and other figures connected with the Erie Railroad scandal.

Mark Twain hoped to have the booklet ready for the 1870 Christmas market, but production problems delayed its publication until the following February. J. C. HOTTEN issued a pirate edition in London several months later, followed by ROUTLEDGE's authorized English edition in May.

Later fearing that this booklet might damage his reputation, Mark Twain bought its plates from Sheldon and destroyed them. Nevertheless, the sketch later appeared as "A Burlesque Biography" in *The $30,000 Bequest and Other Stories* (1906).

Burlingame, Anson (November 14, 1820, New Berlin, New York–February 23, 1870, St. Petersburg, Russia) American politician and diplomat. Raised and educated in the Midwest, Burlingame entered politics in Massachusetts in 1852 and served three terms in the U.S. House of Representatives (1855–61). After he failed to win a fourth term, President LINCOLN appointed him minister to AUSTRIA. Burlingame's support for Hungarian independence led to his speedy withdrawal and reassignment to China—to which he was returning when he met Mark Twain in HAWAII in 1866. In China, Burlingame gained popularity by championing stronger central government and opposing special privileges for foreigners. In late 1867, he resigned his ministerial post in order to head a Chinese mission to America and Europe, and was replaced by John Ross BROWNE. After negotiating a favorable treaty for China in Washington, D.C. in 1868, Burlingame continued his mission in Europe. He died in St. Petersburg, Russia before completing the mission.

Burlingame's brief acquaintance with Mark Twain in Hawaii in June 1866 was an important turning point in the latter's life. Burlingame and his son got Mark Twain out of a sickbed to interview the survivors of the clipper ship HORNET disaster, enabling him to write a scoop that greatly enhanced his celebrity as a journalist; Mark Twain describes the incident in "MY DÉBUT AS A LITERARY PERSON." He also mentions Burlingame in his Hawaii letters and in *Roughing It* (chapters 54 and 68). More importantly, perhaps, Burlingame may have made a strong impression on Mark Twain. He reputedly told him that he had genius and advised him to seek the "refinement of association" with persons of superior intellect and character. The effect that such advice may have had on Mark Twain has become a subject of debate among his biographers, who point to his marriage to Livy and his friendships with such people as Mary FAIRBANKS, H. H. ROGERS and Andrew CARNEGIE as evidence that he took Burlingame seriously.

Burlingame died exactly three weeks after Mark Twain and Olivia Langdon married and settled in Buffalo, New York. Mark Twain immediately wrote a eulogy for the BUFFALO EXPRESS that has been collected in anthologies as part of "Two Mark Twain Editorials."

Praising Burlingame's generosity and world view, Mark Twain calls him "a very, very great man."

The city of Burlingame in California's San Mateo County was named after Burlingame by a friend in 1868.

Burton   Minor character in *Huckleberry Finn.* Burton is a PIKESVILLE neighbor of Silas PHELPS. In chapter 33, Huck learns that Jim, whom Phelps calls "the runaway nigger," has told Phelps and Burton about the KING and DUKE's "scandalous" ROYAL NONESUCH. Burton in turn tells the rest of the townspeople, who break up the King's CAMELOPARD performance and then tar and feather the rascals.

Byron, George Gordon, Lord (January 22, 1788, London–April 19, 1824, Missolonghi, Greece)   English poet. Mark Twain enjoyed reading Byron from at least the early 1860s, when he occasionally quoted and satirized him in his journalism. *Innocents Abroad* (1869) mentions Byron several times: Chapter 23 describes a visit to Byron's VENICE home; chapter 27 makes fun of "butchered to make a Roman holyday"—a cliché from the fourth canto of Byron's *Childe Harold* (1818); and chapter 33 alludes to Byron's famous swim across the Hellespont. In "THE AGED PILOT MAN" spoof in chapter 51 of *Roughing It* (1872), "Lord Byron's works" are thrown overboard in a storm. Chapter 21 of *Tom Sawyer* (1876) includes Byron's "The Assyrian Came Down" among the school's Examination Night recitations. Mark Twain also mentions Byron in "Last Words of Great Men," "IN DEFENSE OF HARRIET SHELLEY," "SCHOOLHOUSE HILL" and other writings.

Cable, George Washington (October 12, 1844, New Orleans, Louisiana–January 31, 1925, St. Petersburg, Florida) Southern writer. A Confederate veteran of the CIVIL WAR, Cable wrote sympathetically about African Americans and is best known for short stories and novels set in LOUISIANA, particularly *Old Creole Days* (1879) and *The Grandissimes* (1880).

When Mark Twain revisited New Orleans in April 1882, Cable entertained him and Joel Chandler HARRIS. Their meeting is described in *Life on the Mississippi,* which calls Cable "the South's finest literary genius" (chapters 44 and 47). A year later, Cable visited Hartford and was laid up in Mark Twain's house with the mumps for several weeks. Afterward, Mark Twain got the idea of hiring a private train car and managing a lecture tour in which he, Cable, W. D. HOWELLS and Thomas ALDRICH would travel in style. Howells and Aldrich turned him down, but Cable joined him for a long reading and lecture tour through the East and Midwest in late 1884. Billed by their promoter James B. POND as the "Twins of Genius," they opened in New Haven, Connecticut on November 5, and made more than 100 stops before closing the tour in WASHINGTON, D.C. on February 28, 1885. Typical performances consisted of Cable and Mark Twain alternating reading selections from their writings, with Cable singing a few songs. The long tour was a success, but it strained their friendship. As the manager of the tour, Mark Twain resented Cable's cheapness and came to regard him as a pious bore. By the end of the tour, he reported to Howells that Cable had taught him to hate all religions and "abhor & detest the Sabbath-day & hunt up new & troublesome ways to dishonor it." Afterward, Cable and Mark Twain had little contact with each other.

Cadets of Temperance One of the many childhood experiences that Mark Twain used in *Tom Sawyer* was his brief membership in the Cadets of Temperance. During the late 1840s, temperance crusades swept the eastern United States, and a chapter of the Sons of Temperance formed in Hannibal around May 1847. When a cadet branch formed three years later, Mark Twain and his brother Henry Clemens were among the boys who joined. As a 14-year-old cadet, Mark Twain pledged to refrain from drinking and smoking; however, while he enjoyed the organization's regalia and processions, he could not abide its rules and restrictions and quit after just three weeks. In *Tom Sawyer,* Tom lasts just five days in ST. PETERSBURG's Cadets of Temperance (chapter 22). He looks forward to marching in Judge FRAZER's coming funeral, but quits when it appears that Frazer is getting well. Immediately after he quits, however, Frazer dies. The Cadets of Temperance are also among the civic groups that honor Senator DILWORTHY during his visit to HAWKEYE in *The Gilded Age* (chapter 20).

Caesar, Julius (c. 100 B.C.—March 15, 44 B.C., Rome) Roman general and statesman who was assassinated by noblemen at the peak of his power. His death is the subject of Mark Twain's sketch "THE KILLING OF JULIUS CAESAR 'LOCALIZED' " (1864), which burlesques SHAKESPEARE's *Julius Caesar.* When Mark Twain was in ROME in 1867, he visited the Forum where Caesar was killed, and he mentions it in chapters 26 and 28 of *Innocents Abroad* (1869). He also mentions Caesar in "SOME THOUGHTS ON THE SCIENCE OF ONANISM" (1879) and "CAPTAIN STORMFIELD'S VISIT TO HEAVEN," in which Caesar's military talent is compared to that of Absalom Jones. "THE MEMORABLE ASSASSINATION" (1898) compares the murder of Austria's empress to that of Caesar. "THE TURNING POINT OF MY LIFE" (1910) cites Caesar's decision to cross the Rubicon in 49 B.C. as an example of a seemingly small moment that becomes significant. Mark Twain admired Caesar's military writings, to which he favorably compared U. S. GRANT's *Memoirs.*

Cairo ILLINOIS town about 200 miles south of ST. LOUIS, at the southern tip of Illinois, where the OHIO RIVER enters the Mississippi. Though a St. Louis man laid out Cairo in 1818, a permanent settlement was not established until the early 1850s. A railway link followed in 1856 and heavy levees were built to protect the town from the powerful river waters washing the finger of land on which it stands. During the CIVIL WAR it became an important Union supply depot. Mark Twain first saw Cairo in early 1857, during his first long STEAMBOAT trip. Over the next four years, he must have stopped there frequently while piloting steamboats on the Lower Mississippi. After his last visit to Cairo in 1882, he described its development favorably in *Life on the Mississippi* (chapter 25).

Cairo is an important symbol in *Huckleberry Finn* as Huck and Jim's primary goal in their quest for Jim's freedom (chapter 15). Since they must know that Illinois is no haven for escaping slaves, they plan to sell their raft at Cairo and take a steamboat up the Ohio River to greater safety. This plan fails, however, when they drift past tiny Cairo during a foggy night (chapter 16). The "RAFT CHAPTER"—which is omitted in most editions of *Huckleberry Finn*—contains an important clue to where they are. In this chapter Huck learns how to tell the difference between Mississippi and Ohio river waters; this knowledge makes possible his subsequent discovery that he and Jim have passed Cairo. After they pass the town, their new plan is to paddle their canoe back up the river to reach it; however, they lose the canoe and cannot easily get back upriver. Their next plan is to continue going downriver on the raft, until they can buy another canoe in which to return to Cairo.

Cairo is discussed in Mark Twain's unfinished "TOM SAWYER'S CONSPIRACY." When it appears that the scoundrels known as the KING and DUKE may get control of Jim again and sell him down the river, Tom and Huck hit on the idea of accompanying them to Cairo, where they will buy Jim themselves so they can send him to freedom (chapter 9). Cairo is also mentioned in chapters 1 and 8 of *Pudd'nhead Wilson*.

Similarities between the Mississippi and Nile rivers prompted the naming of Cairo after EGYPT's capital city, but Illinois's town has always been pronounced *kay-ro*.

Calaveras County   Region in the foothills of CALIFORNIA's Sierra Nevada, directly east of SAN FRANCISCO Bay. From late January through late February 1865, Mark Twain prospected around the county's placer-mining center at ANGEL'S CAMP during a hiatus from his stay in TUOLUMNE COUNTY, just across the Stanislaus River to the southeast. He helped immortalize the county's name with his JUMPING FROG STORY, which was published under several titles, including "The Celebrated Jumping Frog of Calaveras County" and "The Notorious Jumping Frog of Calaveras County." Mark Twain mentions Calaveras once in *Roughing It* (chapter 61), and praises it generously in a sketch he published in the CALIFORNIAN in March 1865.

One of California's original 27 counties, Calaveras takes its name from a local river, which in turn takes its name from the Spanish word for skulls.

California   Pacific Coast state that entered the Union in 1850, two years after a GOLD RUSH launched a period of rapid growth. Mark Twain lived in northern California for a total of about two years during the mid-1860s. While in California, he continued his training as a professional newspaper writer, had his last MINING camp experiences, and won a national reputation with his publication of the JUMPING FROG story.

It is difficult to pinpoint when Mark Twain first entered California. During his first years in the West, he lived along the western border of NEVADA and may have stepped across the California border as early as September 1861, when he visited Lake TAHOE. Around the same time, he also visited AURORA, a Nevada mining camp a few miles from the border that was then mistakenly believed to be in California. Mark Twain thus *thought* he was in California when was in Aurora. He probably entered California during the months he spent prospecting around Aurora in early 1862; he definitely entered California in August, when he camped at MONO LAKE.

While working as a reporter in VIRGINIA CITY, Mark Twain vacationed in SAN FRANCISCO in May and September 1863. At the end of May 1864, he moved to California and made San Francisco his home until the end of 1866. This sojourn he interrupted with a three-month stay in TUOLUMNE and CALAVERAS counties (December 1864–February 1865) and a six-month trip to HAWAII (March–August 1866). He also spent part of late 1866 on a LECTURE tour of northern California and western Nevada. In December, he left California as a correspondent for the SAN FRANCISCO ALTA CALIFORNIA and went to NEW YORK CITY; however, he still considered himself a California resident in March 1867, when he signed on to the QUAKER CITY cruise as "Sam Clemens, Cal." His letters to the *Alta* from the cruise became the basis of *Innocents Abroad*, much of which he wrote in California, after returning to San Francisco in April 1868. During this visit, he again lectured in northern California and Nevada before leaving California for the last time on July 6, 1868. He considered returning to California to lecture in 1871 and 1895, but never came any closer to the state than a brief pass through northern Oregon in August 1895.

Aside from his mining camp stories, Mark Twain's most extensive writing about California appears in *Roughing It*. His last surviving daughter, Clara Clemens, and his only grandchild, Nina GABRILOWITSCH, both died in California during the 1960s, and the bulk of his manuscripts are held by the MARK TWAIN PAPERS project at the University of California in Berkeley.

Californian   SAN FRANCISCO literary weekly. Charles Henry WEBB launched the *Californian* on May 28, 1864—the day before Mark Twain left Nevada for San Francisco—and alternated its editorship with Bret HARTE. A month later, Mark Twain's first contribution appeared in the magazine. By September, the magazine was paying him $50 a month for one article per issue; it eventually published about 50 items under his name, many of which were reprinted from newspapers. Webb and Harte's editorial guidance was an important part of Mark Twain's early development as a writer, particularly as a satirist. His most significant *Californian* pieces include "Whereas" (October 1864; later revised as "AURELIA'S UNFORTUNATE YOUNG MAN"), "THE KILLING OF JULIUS CAESAR 'LOCALIZED' " (November 1864), "LUCRETIA SMITH'S SOLDIER" (December 1864) and "The Christmas Fireside" (December 1864; later retitled "THE STORY OF THE BAD LITTLE BOY").

After selling out most of his interests in the magazine, Webb left the Pacific Coast in early 1866. Two years later, the *Californian* ceased publication and Harte turned his attention to the new OVERLAND MONTHLY. *Roughing It* rues the *California*'s passing (chapter 50).

Webb's journal was not related to a San Francisco newspaper of the same name that was published in 1847–48 after being founded as the state's first newspaper in Monterey in 1846. Another, unrelated literary magazine called the *Californian* was published in San Francisco from 1880 to 1882 while the *Overland Monthly* temporarily suspended publication.

"The Californian's Tale" Short story written in 1892. Unusually sentimental for a Mark Twain story, this tale embellishes the story of a man whom Mark Twain met in CALIFORNIA during his MINING days. In 1882, he outlined the story in his NOTEBOOKS, but set it aside for a decade. While the real miner's wife died in a stagecoach accident, the wife of Mark Twain's fictional miner is killed by INDIANS.

The story first appeared in 1893 in *The First Book of the Authors Club, Liber Scriptorum*, edited by Arthur Stedman. Mark Twain published it in HARPER'S MAGAZINE in March 1902 and it was collected in *The $30,000 Bequest and Other Stories* a few years later.

SYNOPSIS

Set near Tuttletown, a real mining town in California's TUOLUMNE COUNTY, in the late 1850s, this story is told 35 years later by an unnamed narrator. While prospecting around the Stanislaus River, he has met many prematurely aged miners who are so worn out by 40 that they are "living dead men." One such man, named Henry, lives in an unusually neat cottage. Like most local miners, he invites the narrator in, and he shows off all the wonderful homey touches provided by his wife, whose beautiful daguerreotype the visitor admires. Henry tells his guest that his bride was 19 on her last birthday— the day that he married her.

It is a Wednesday, and the woman (who is never named) is due home on Saturday evening. As the days pass, the visitor eagerly anticipates meeting his host's wife. Other prospectors drop by as well, to ask when she will arrive and to hear Henry read her latest letter. By Saturday night, Henry, the narrator and three other prospectors prepare to greet Henry's wife, but she does not arrive on schedule. Henry grows sick with fear until a message comes reporting that his wife is delayed. After he finally passes out, his friends tenderly put him to bed and start to leave. When the visitor begs them to wait until Henry's wife arrives, they explain that the woman was killed by Indians 19 years earlier. Never completely sane since then, Henry has gone through this same ritual every year around the same time that his wife disappeared. Over the years, the number of miners who wait up with him has shrunk from 27 to three, and they have to drug him to get him through the ordeal.

Cambenet English village in *Connecticut Yankee*. In chapter 34, Earl GRIP rescues Hank MORGAN and King ARTHUR from angry peasants in ABBLASOURE and takes them about 32 miles south or southeast to Cambenet. The same day they arrive, they are sold as slaves in an auction and marched off in a caravan that eventually takes them to LONDON.

camelopard (cameleopard) Archaic term for giraffe. One of the most outrageous moments in *Huckleberry Finn* occurs in the "King's Camelopard," or "ROYAL NONESUCH," scene in chapter 23. The KING goes on stage naked and painted with multicolor stripes. He dances about wildly, to the amusement of an all-male audience. Mark Twain's use of "camelopard" may have been inspired by Edgar Allan POE's "Four Beasts in One; or the Homocameleopard" (1836). In this story, an ancient Syrian king prances on all fours in the skins of a beast. In *Innocents Abroad*, Mark Twain mentions "cameleopards" among the animals that he would have accepted for transportation in the Holy Land (chapter 41).

Camelot The legendary seat of England's King ARTHUR, Camelot is a principal setting in *Connecticut Yankee*, whose narrator, Hank MORGAN, is there through chapters 1–10 and 39–43. In common with many Arthurian legends—particularly those recorded since the 13th century—*Connecticut Yankee* depicts Camelot as a huge hilltop castle overlooking a town and a broad plain. The novel does not describe the castle in detail, but offers glimpses of a drawbridge, an arched gateway, towers, turrets and vaulted ceilings, as well as wall hangings that resemble the 11th-century Bayeux Tapestry (chapters 1–2)—all features suggesting architecture and culture of the High Middle Ages instead of the sixth century in which the story is set.

Camelot cannot be confidently linked to any historical site. Sir Thomas MALORY—Mark Twain's major source— identified Camelot with Winchester, a city in southern England about 60 miles west-southwest of LONDON. This location conforms with *Connecticut Yankee*'s vague geography. The novel's best geographical clues appear in chapter 37, when Hank communicates with Camelot by telegraph from London. He orders CLARENCE to send 500 knights from Camelot to London, then calculates that at an average gait of seven miles per hour on horseback, the men should reach London in nine hours—including time to change horses twice. If we allow one hour for changing mounts, the knights would travel just over 55 miles at this rate. Furthermore, since haste is imperative, Hank instructs the knights to enter London at its *southwest* gate—a point suggesting that Camelot itself is southwest of London.

Evidence in chapter 24 suggests that the nearest route from Camelot to the sea lies to the *north,* and that the VALLEY OF HOLINESS is about 75 miles *south* of Camelot. These details seem to rule out Camelot's being near Winchester, which is 20 miles north of the English Channel; however, *Connecticut Yankee*'s geography should probably be regarded as tolerantly as that of the Mississippi River in *Huckleberry Finn*'s latter chapters.

Camelot Weekly Hosannah and Literary Volcano Newspaper in *Connecticut Yankee.* Believing that he cannot modernize sixth-century England without a newspaper, Hank MORGAN starts planning one in chapter 9 by having a priest cover a tournament. In the next chapter, he begins training CLARENCE as an editor. Hank sees the first issue of the *Hosannah* while he is in the VALLEY OF HOLINESS in chapter 26. Though he relishes the paper's liveliness, he fears that its overall tone may be too irreverent.

Though the *Hosannah* is mentioned by name only in chapter 26, it is probably the same paper that Hank sees being peddled in London several months later (chapter 36), as well as the morning paper that he reads in Camelot in chapter 39. The next chapter jumps ahead three years, by which time there are several newspapers in the kingdom. When Hank returns from Gaul in chapter 42, he finds that Clarence has been keeping his newspaper going despite the Church's INTERDICT, while covering the civil war between King Arthur and Launcelot.

The title of the *Hosannah and Literary Volcano* resembles those of newspapers mentioned in Mark Twain's "JOURNALISM IN TENNESSEE" (1869), such as the *Avalanche, Moral Volcano, Semi-Weekly Earthquake* and *Thunderbolt and Battle Cry of Freedom.*

Canada America's northern neighbor became a dominion within the British empire in July 1867. From mid-1869 through early 1871, Mark Twain lived in BUFFALO, New York, just over a mile from Ontario, Canada. He crossed the Niagara River early on and described the Canadian side of the NIAGARA Falls in a sketch for the BUFFALO EXPRESS. Between 1881 and 1895, he entered Canada a half dozen times, visiting Quebec, Ontario, Manitoba and British Columbia.

The absence of effective international copyright laws allowed Canadian publishers to prey on Mark Twain's early books. He was hurt particularly badly in 1876, when the Toronto publisher Charles BELFORD issued *Tom Sawyer* before the American edition even appeared. To combat this problem, Mark Twain spent several weeks in Montreal in November–December 1881 with James R. OSGOOD to meet a residency requirement to protect his *The Prince and the Pauper* copyright. During this visit he was feted by literary society and befriended by Canada's poet laureate, Louis Fréchette (1839–1908). He and Osgood returned to Canada in May 1883 to protect *Life on the Mississippi*'s copyright.

In late 1884 and early 1885, Mark Twain and G. W. CABLE visited several Canadian cities during their long LECTURE tour. They spoke in Toronto in early December—a visit that Mark Twain also used to protect his *Huckleberry Finn* copyright. They returned to Ontario in mid-February and spoke again in Toronto and in Brockville, London, Ottawa and Montreal. In mid-1895, Mark Twain began his round-the-world lecture tour with a trip across North America that took him to Winnipeg in late July and British Columbia in mid-August. After a week in Vancouver and Victoria, he and his wife and daughter Clara sailed into the PACIFIC on the WARRIMOO. The first chapter of *Following the Equator* summarizes his journey across North America, to which he did not return for five years. He paid his last visit to Canada in August 1901, when he sailed to New Brunswick and Nova Scotia on the KANAWHA.

"Cannibalism in the Cars" Short story written in 1868. At Terre Haute, Indiana the narrator changes trains and meets a man in his late forties. When the stranger learns that the narrator is from WASHINGTON, D.C., he asks him many well-informed questions about government affairs, but his mood changes when he overhears the name "Harris," and he begins a story that he has never told before.

In December 1853, the stranger took a train from St. Louis to Chicago that carried 24 passengers—all men. The first night out, snowdrifts blocked the train. It carried plentiful firewood, but no provisions, and was 50 miles from help. On the seventh night without food, a passenger named Gaston proposed that it was time to decide who should die to feed the rest. Another man, named Williams, then nominated the Reverend James Sawyer to be the first meal, Wm. R. Adams nominated Daniel SLOTE, and Charles J. LANGDON nominated Samuel A. BOWEN. After Slote declined in favor of John A. VAN NOSTRAND, Van Nostrand objected, launching an argument over procedure. Eventually, Gaston was elected chairman, along with a four-man selection committee.

The passengers then caucused before submitting nominations. After a complex floor debate, a passenger named Harris was elected to become dinner. For eight days, two men a day were elected as breakfast and dinner—with the stranger commenting on their varying gastronomic qualities. The surviving passengers were finally rescued just after electing a man for breakfast.

As the stranger prepares to get off the train, he invites the narrator to visit him, assuring him that he could like him "as well as I liked Harris himself." The stunned narrator learns from the conductor that the stranger, a former member of Congress, once nearly starved while snowed in on a train. Since then, he has retold his grisly story over and over, usually carrying it to a point where everyone in the train but him is eaten. The narrator is so relieved to know he has been listening to a harmless madman, not a bloodthirsty cannibal, that he overlooks contradictions in the stranger's story—which names nearly 40 persons, including a boy, on a train supposedly carrying only 24 men.

BACKGROUND AND PUBLISHING HISTORY

"Cannibalism" was one of the first fictional pieces that Mark Twain wrote after returning from the QUAKER CITY excursion. His idea for the story may have originated in an article published in his brother's MUSCATINE, Iowa newspaper in February 1855 concerning a trainload of snowbound legislators who ate dogs to stay alive. To develop the story's intricate satire on legislative procedure, he drew on his own experience reporting on NEVADA's territorial legislature and the federal Congress. He also played with names; most of his characters have the names of real friends and acquaintances, including several connected with the QUAKER CITY excursion.

The 3,400-word story first appeared in the November 1868 issue of London's *Broadway*, a house organ of George ROUTLEDGE and Sons. It was subsequently collected in SKETCHES, NEW AND OLD (1875) and in MARK TWAIN'S LIBRARY OF HUMOR (1888). The story's notion of having "a man for breakfast" reappears in a chapter on desperadoes in *Roughing It* (chapter 57).

Canty, Gammer Minor character in *The Prince and the Pauper*. The vicious grandmother of Tom CANTY, Gammer Canty lives with Tom's family in OFFAL COURT. In chapter 3, Tom tells Prince EDWARD how Gammer beats him; the prince himself gets a sample of her treatment when John CANTY brings him home in chapter 10. At the end of that chapter, the family flees Offal Court and Gammer Canty disappears from the narrative, aside from Tom's later recollection of a nasty beating she once gave him (chapter 15).

The female equivalent of *gaffer*, "gammer" is a term for old wife that goes back to at least the mid-16th century.

Canty, John ("John Hobbs") Character in *The Prince and the Pauper*. The abusive father of Tom CANTY, John Canty is a professional thief who forces his children to beg and regularly beats them and his wife. Though he is brutal enough to kill Father ANDREW (chapter 10) and brag about it to his criminal gang (chapter 17), there are limits to his cruelty. For example, he hesitates to punish the boy he believes is his son when he claims to be EDWARD, Prince of Wales, thinking him mad. Though the boy proves worse than useless as a gang member, Canty struggles to recapture him each time he escapes—perhaps out of parental instinct. Once the boy is arrested for stealing in chapter 22, however, Canty drops out of the narrative completely. By then, he has also lost contact with his mother, wife and daughters. After Edward is restored to his throne in chapter 33, he offers to have Canty hanged—if Tom so desires and the law allows—but the final chapter reveals that Canty is never heard from again.

Canty, Mrs. Character in *The Prince and the Pauper*. The kindhearted, middle-aged mother of Tom CANTY, Mrs. Canty protects Tom from her husband and mother-in-law, though she herself is often beaten. When her husband brings Prince EDWARD home, thinking *he* is Tom, she worries about the boy's apparent madness and is beaten for her solicitousness (chapter 10). Having opposed Tom's book-learning, she sees the boy's claim to be the Prince of Wales as a delusion caused by his reading. After the prince falls asleep, however, she starts wondering if he may in fact *not* be her son. She devises a test to learn the truth; remembering that Tom habitually shields his eyes with the back of his hand when startled, she jars the prince awake several times to test his reactions, but with inconclusive results.

When the Cantys flee Offal Court at the end of chapter 10, they get separated in the crowd and Mrs. Canty apparently never sees her husband again. She reappears in chapter 31 when Tom spots her in the crowd as he rides in the coronation procession. Her sudden appearance so startles him that he instinctively shields his eyes with his hand—the old habit that proves his identity to his mother's satisfaction. Though Tom spurns his mother when she approaches him, their chance meeting prepares him to renounce his false kingship the moment the real Edward appears. At the conclusion of the narrative, Mrs. Canty and her 15-year-old twin daughters, Bet and Nan, are reunited with Tom.

Canty, Tom Character in *The Prince and the Pauper*. The "pauper" of the novel's title, Tom is born in London's OFFAL COURT on the same day as EDWARD, Prince of Wales. He appears to be about 13 years old when the main narrative begins.

As Tom grows up, he leads a tough life in the slums. Hungry, cold and regularly beaten by his father and grandmother, he is forced to beg; however, he preserves some dignity by refusing to steal. Despite his hardships, he is happy because he does not know any better. Consistent with an archaic meaning of *canty*, he is inherently cheerful and finds real pleasure in life. He plays games with other boys, swims in the THAMES and revels in reading Father ANDREW's books and hearing stories that appear to come from the ARABIAN NIGHTS. Tom Canty is a kind of composite of Huckleberry Finn and Tom Sawyer, and his shabby neighborhood resembles their hometown of ST. PETERSBURG in important ways.

As the impoverished but good-hearted son of an abusive father, Tom anticipates Huck. He also resembles Tom Sawyer in being obsessed with romantic stories and loving gaudy entertainments, such as parades, fairs and Punch and Judy shows. Like Tom Sawyer, he is an inventive and natural leader; he directs street gangs in mock wars and organizes a mock royal court, with himself as a prince. His wisdom is recognized by many in the neighborhood, including adults, who come to him for advice. When he later finds himself on the real throne of England, his good-heartedness and wisdom come to the fore. During his first days in Prince EDWARD's palace, Tom wants nothing more than to be liberated from his captivity. He initially cowers in the presence of nobles and courtiers, but gradually his confidence grows and he asserts his natural leadership. Seeing the cruelty and illogic in archaic laws, he moves to strike down brutal punishments, and pardons as many prisoners as he can. He even tells off the gloomy Princess MARY—the later queen "Bloody Mary"—for having a hard heart (chapter 30). At the same time, however, he delights in regal pomp and multiplies his servants and retainers to gratify his need for show.

By coronation day, Tom is so reconciled to being on the throne that he suppresses guilty thoughts about the fate of the real king, and even manages to put his loving mother and sisters out of his mind. It is only when he sees his mother while riding to Westminster Abbey that his purer instincts reemerge. Though he initially disavows her, he is so consumed with guilt that he is ready to renounce all the trappings of power to make amends. Indeed, the moment that the real king reappears, Tom immediately defers to him and does everything he can to have him acknowledged as the true king. After Edward is restored to his throne, he rewards Tom's loyalty and exemplary behavior by making him the "King's Ward," giving him a distinctive outfit to wear, and making him head of CHRIST'S HOSPITAL.

After Olivia Clemens dramatized *The Prince and the Pauper* for family productions, Mark Twain's daughters and neighbor girls typically played the prince and Tom Canty. Their casting anticipated that of eight-year-old Elsie Leslie Lyde in a professional production in 1889. When the first substantial film adaptation was made in 1915, 32-year-old Marguerite Clark played both roles, as Tibi Lubin (1922), Sean Scully (1962) and Mark Lester (1977) later would. Meanwhile, 13-year-old twins, Bobby and Billy Mauch, shared the leads in the 1937 film.

"The Canvasser's Tale" Short story published in 1876. A comparatively simple story of 2,340 words, this tale touches on several themes that Mark Twain develops more fully elsewhere. For example, the narrator of this tale resembles characters in "THE $30,000 BEQUEST" (1904) in being ruined by relying on receiving a rich inheritance. He also resembles a man in "THE CAPITOLINE VENUS" (1869) who must have money to win the hand of his sweetheart. The story concerns the narrator's uncle, who collected echoes. As a duplicate sound, an echo is a kind of twin—a theme Mark Twain later explored in stories such as *Pudd'nhead Wilson* (1894). That novel opens with an incident similar to one in "The Canvasser's Tale." David WILSON expresses a wish to own half a barking dog, so that he could kill his half. In "The Canvasser's Tale," a man who owns one of two hills containing the world's greatest echo wants to level his hill in order to destroy the entire echo.

"The Canvasser's Tale" is told as a FRAME-STORY in which neither the setting nor the time is specified. A tired, shabby man with a portfolio comes to the door of the anonymous narrator, who assumes him to be a canvasser (i.e., a salesman). He takes pity on the stranger and allows him to relate his own story, describing events that apparently occurred about 30 years earlier.

SYNOPSIS

Orphaned while young, the stranger was raised by his rich, generous uncle ITHURIEL. After completing college, he traveled abroad and got the idea of persuading his uncle to take up the foreign custom of collecting rarities. His uncle adopted this idea eagerly, and turned his fortune to building a cow-bell collection. Eventually, he needed a single bell to complete his collection, but the owner of the only existing specimen refused to sell. Not interested in keeping a collection he could never complete, Ithuriel sold out and began collecting brickbats, only to experience the same frustration again. After failing to complete collections of flint hatchets, Aztec inscriptions, and stuffed whales, he decided to go after something no one else collected: echoes. He purchased great specimens in Georgia, Maine, Kansas and Tennessee, and bought a masterpiece in Oregon for $216,000.

Meanwhile, the nephew courted Celestine, the daughter of an English earl, happy in the knowledge that he would be sole heir to his uncle's fortune. Trouble began, however, when his uncle went after the world's greatest echo, the "Great Koh-i-noo," or Mountain of Repetitions, in a remote New York location. This fabulous echo would talk for 15 minutes after hearing a single word. Unfortunately, the hills containing the echo were owned by two people and there was a competing collector in the field. Ithuriel bought the echo's east hill for over three million dollars; his rival bought the other hill for a similar amount. Neither man was content, but neither would sell out to the other. Finally, Ithuriel's rival decided that if he could not own the entire echo, he would destroy his half so no one could have it. After Ithuriel secured an injunction to stop the man from taking down his hill, his rival appealed the case up to the Supreme Court. The Court ruled that the two men were tenants in common in the echo; therefore, if one took down his hill, he must indemnify the other for the echo's value. Further, neither man could use the echo without the other's consent—which neither would give. The result was that the echo was useless and the properties unsalable.

A week before the nephew was to marry the earl's daughter, news of his uncle's death came, along with the will naming him sole heir. After reading this document, the earl concluded that the nephew had inherited nothing but debt and called off the wedding. Within a year, Celestine died of a broken heart, leaving the nephew wishing only for death.

Although the narrator has had his fill of canvassers, he agrees to buy two of the stranger's echoes.

BACKGROUND AND PUBLISHING HISTORY

Mark Twain wrote this story during the summer of 1876, after setting aside his *Huckleberry Finn* manuscript. He initially considered having Ithuriel collect caves, but switched to echoes. He probably got the idea of using echoes from his travels in ITALY in 1867, when he observed superb echoes in PISA and near MILAN. Chapter 19 of *Innocents Abroad* describes the latter as "the most remarkable echo in the world," asserting that it repeats words 52 times.

"The Canvasser's Tale" first appeared in the ATLANTIC MONTHLY in December 1876. It was later reprinted in PUNCH, BROTHERS, PUNCH!, THE STOLEN WHITE ELEPHANT, ETC., *Tom Sawyer Abroad; Tom Sawyer, Detective and Other Stories.*

Capello, Angelo and Luigi   Characters in *Pudd'nhead Wilson.* In "THOSE EXTRAORDINARY TWINS," Mark Twain's original version of *Pudd'nhead Wilson,* the Capellos are central characters who happen to be SIAMESE TWINS. When that story was revised to become *Pudd'nhead Wilson,* they were recast as ordinary twins with much reduced roles. Careless editing in this transformation left obvious traces of their previous conjoined condition. Although they are not physically connected, they appear always to be together.

The Capellos come from FLORENCE, Italy—where Mark Twain was living when he finished *Pudd'nhead Wilson.* Their family was "of the old Florentine nobility." When they were about 10, their father backed the losing side of a war, so the family had to flee to Germany as their estates were confiscated. Well educated, the young twins were both multilingual and musical prodigies. After a month in exile, their parents died deeply in

The Capello brothers, as ordinary twins, entertain visitors to Patsy Cooper's home in Pudd'nhead Wilson.

debt, leaving the twins to be exploited by creditors. They were exhibited in a Berlin museum for two years, then traveled "everywhere," including East Asia, and acquired adult skills early.

In chapter 5 of *Pudd'nhead Wilson,* the Capellos arrive in DAWSON'S LANDING to board in the home of Aunt Patsy COOPER, who thinks that they are the most handsome and distinguished young men the region has ever seen. Aside from the fact that one twin is slightly fairer than the other, Aunt Patsy says they are "exact duplicates." In the next chapter, she glories in introducing both twins to neighbors as "counts." Dawson's Landing takes to them quickly and everyone wants to entertain them. Their participation in a DUEL in chapter 14 makes them so "prodigiously great" that they decide to stay permanently and apply for citizenship. Both are asked to run for the new city council.

As close as the twins are to each other, they are divided by differences reflected in their given names. The blond Angelo is a pious teetotaler with "angelic" qualities, while the dark-haired Luigi (read "Lucifer") is a nonbeliever, drinker and general troublemaker. In chapter 11, David WILSON reads Luigi's palm and discovers that he once killed someone. Luigi explains that he killed a man to save Angelo's life, but rumors that he is an "assassin" later gain wide acceptance. The machinations of Tom DRISCOLL alienate Luigi from his natural ally, Judge York DRISCOLL, who turns against both twins with a vengeance. When the brothers are caught at the scene of the judge's murder in chapter 19, their case looks hopeless.

The Capellos are mentioned in less than half the chapters of the book, and in most of these they appear so briefly that they scarcely serve a purpose in the narrative. In fact, no reason for coming to Dawson's Landing is ever given. Their main function is to act as catalysts in Wilson's career. Luigi gives Wilson his first legal case (chapter 5) and elevates Wilson's new prestige even higher when he has him act as his second in a duel (chapter 14). Finally, Wilson's defense of Luigi in the climactic murder trial lifts him to heroic stature.

When Mark Twain initially created the Capellos as Siamese twins, he wanted to explore the comic possibilities of brothers with contrasting personalities sharing a single body with two heads, four arms, one torso and two legs. Just as their names symbolize their natures, so do their relative positions: Angelo is on the right, Luigi on the left. They disagree on almost everything but cannot escape each other's influence. When Angelo gets sick, Luigi is confined to bed. When Luigi drinks, the nondrinking Angelo gets drunk. As Siamese twins, they have marvelous mechanisms for coping with their physical limitations. Each brother controls the legs for exactly one week, regardless of time zone. In such routine tasks as eating, they are adept at helping each other. Despite being Siamese twins, they have remarkable physical differences. Luigi, for example, has a darker complexion and is hardier, more masculine and assertive. Angelo

The Capello brothers, as Siamese twins, in "Those Extraordinary Twins."

gets sick more easily, but "cannot abide medicines," so Luigi takes them for him.

Early editions of *Pudd'nhead Wilson* render the twins' surname inconsistently. *Capello* (Italian for "hair") appears most frequently, with *Cappello* (Italian for "hat" or "cap") appearing occasionally. Mark Twain's handwritten corrections suggest that he may have preferred the latter spelling.

Capet   Name of a medieval French dynasty. In chapters 21 and 26 of *Huckleberry Finn*, the DUKE sarcastically calls his partner the KING "Capet." Familiar with Thomas Carlyle's history of the French Revolution, Mark Twain

would have known that revolutionists called the deposed King LOUIS XVI "Citizen Louis Capet." Louis XVI was the father of Louis XVII—the person whom *Huckleberry Finn*'s King claims to be. Alternatively, "Capet" may be the Duke's garbled pronunciation of "Capulet," the name of Juliet's family in ROMEO AND JULIET. Since the Duke has the King play Juliet in his "Shaksperean Revival," "Capet" may be his way of insulting the King.

"The Capitoline Venus (Legend of)"   Short story written in 1869. Written with some of the conventions of a drama, the story is divided into six brief chapters, or "scenes," and most of its text is dialogue. As a story about an art HOAX, this piece resembles "IS HE LIVING OR IS HE DEAD?" It opens in the Rome studio of a young American sculptor, George Arnold, who is talking with a woman named Mary about the futility of their relationship. Mary's father will not let her marry George until he acquires $50,000. In the next scene, the father repeats this demand. George owns a wonderful statue he calls "America," but the father cares only about market value; he gives George six months to come up with $50,000.

Back in his studio, George explains his problem to a childhood friend, John SMITH, who scoffs at him and promises to raise the money in *five* months. He has George swear not to oppose anything he does, then takes a hammer to the America statue, disfigures it badly and carts it away, leaving George in a state of collapse. The day that George's six-month deadline is up, tradesmen appear at his studio to deliver expensive goods on credit—which his banker tells him is excellent. Mary's father then appears to tell him he can wed Mary, who arrives next. The bewildered George proclaims he is saved, but has no idea why or how.

The fifth scene cuts to a café, where several Americans are reading the weekly *Il Slangwhanger di Roma* ("The Roman Rebuker"). The newspaper tells about a "John Smithe" who bought land in the Campagna six months earlier and transferred its title to George Arnold with a promise to improve the property. Smithe later unearthed a damaged but otherwise remarkable ancient statue of a woman that the government seized. After a month of secret study and deliberation, a government commission has announced that the statue is a third-century B.C. Venus worth 10 million francs. Under Roman law, the government must pay half this sum to Arnold.

The sixth scene jumps ahead 10 years; George and Mary discuss the famous Capitoline Venus and the fact that John Smith is the author of their bliss. When a baby coughs, George chides Mary for taking inadequate care of the children. A brief afterword admonishes readers to keep their own counsel when they hear about such things as petrified men near Syracuse, New York. Moreover, "if the BARNUM that buried him there" offers to sell, "send him to the Pope!"

BACKGROUND AND PUBLISHING HISTORY

Mark Twain wrote this 2,000-word piece shortly after the so-called Cardiff Giant was discovered near Syracuse on October 15, 1869. The story appeared in the BUFFALO EXPRESS as "Legend of the Capitoline Venus" on October 23. The title was abbreviated when the story was republished in SKETCHES, NEW AND OLD five years later. The Cardiff Giant was an artificially aged gypsum sculpture of a man that someone had buried near Syracuse a year before he dug it up. Its unearthing caused a sensation; many people believed it to be a petrified giant, while others were sure it was an ancient sculpture. The episode had remarkable similarities to Mark Twain's PETRIFIED MAN HOAX, which he published in Nevada seven years earlier.

The idea of selling antiquities to the Roman government came out of Mark Twain's visit to Rome in July 1867. The city was then under papal government, which had a policy of buying all freshly discovered antiquities at half their assessed market value. Chapter 28 of *Innocents Abroad* comments that "when a man digs up an ancient statue in the Campagna, the Pope gives him a fortune in gold coin."

"Captain Stormfield's Visit to Heaven" Unfinished SATIRE, presented in the form of a first-person narrative by an old sea captain who has died and gone to heaven. Shortly before his own death, Mark Twain published two chapters of this story as "Extract from Captain Stormfield's Visit to Heaven."

SYNOPSIS

The fullest published form of this story begins with a prologue signed by Mark Twain in which the author describes Captain STORMFIELD as a person he knows well. He explains that although Stormfield has told him this story as a true experience, he himself regards it as a dream. The narrative that follows is divided into six chapters, the third and fourth parts of which correspond to chapters 1 and 2 of "Extract from Captain Stormfield's Visit to Heaven."

Chapter 1
Stormfield describes his death aboard a ship, where he overhears a doctor and other crew members planning his burial at sea. They assume that Stormfield expects to go to hell. He dies a moment later and finds himself hurtling through space. As he passes through a dark void, then through the sun, he calculates that the time it takes for him to reach the sun means that he is traveling at the speed of light.

After Stormfield passes through the sun, another man comes alongside him and joins his journey. Stormfield finds that his hunger for companionship allows him to overlook the fact that his new companion, Solomon Goldstein, is a Jew. He explains to Goldstein that they

Albert Levering's frontispiece to "Extract from Captain Stormfield's Visit to Heaven."

appear headed for hell; Goldstein accepts Stormfield's logic but later grows morose when he realizes its implication that he will never see his daughter again.

Chapter 2
As Stormfield and Goldstein continue their journey, many other travelers join them. Hearing these people pour out their tragic stories makes Stormfield realize the falsity of the notion that death brings rest. After a week, the convoy numbers 36, but Stormfield drives some of its less agreeable members away.

Chapter 3
This chapter—the first in the "Extract" portion of the story—opens with Stormfield in his 30th year of racing through space "like a comet." There is no explanation for the disappearance of the traveling companions introduced in the earlier chapters. There is also no expla-

nation of a new name, "PETERS," to whom he is now addressing his narrative.

By Stormfield's own calculations, his average velocity is roughly a fifth the speed of light. We can infer, therefore, that he has traveled about five light-years—only far enough to take him to our solar system's nearest stellar neighbor, though the story seems to suggest a far longer journey. Meanwhile, Stormfield thrills in passing slow comets, until he encounters an unimaginably huge one that tempts him into altering his course by a point in order to engage in a race. The scale of this other comet is such that 200 billion crewmen are sent aloft to alter its rigging and 100 billion passengers rush to the decks to watch the race. As Stormfield passes the comet, he thumbs his nose at it. This enrages its captain, who orders its stupendous cargo of brimstone—presumably bound for hell—jettisoned, allowing the comet to leave Stormfield far behind.

As Stormfield approaches a blazing array of lights, he assumes they are furnaces and that he has finally arrived at "the wrong place." However, the lights turn out to be the gates of Heaven. He lands and reports to a head clerk, who asks where he is from. "San Francisco" means nothing to the clerk, nor do "California" and the "United States." Only when he mentions Jupiter while trying to describe Earth's location is progress made. It turns out that he has arrived in the wrong district of Heaven because of veering off course while racing the comet. A clerk takes two days to find Earth on a map "as big as Rhode Island," and then announces that it is known as the "Wart." Stormfield, now officially admitted to Heaven, spends a day wandering the great hall, until he is told how to use a "wishing carpet" to teleport himself instantaneously to his own part of Heaven, millions of leagues away. Everything about heaven's size, he learns, is unimaginably huge.

The moment that Stormfield arrives in his proper district, he is recognized and issued all the angelic accoutrements he was disappointed not to receive when he first arrived: wings, halo, harp, hymn book and palm branch. The clerk who greets him is a PIUTE Indian whom he had known in California's Tulare County. He soon discovers, in fact, that INDIANS constitute a big majority in his district.

As Stormfield joins a multitude headed for a cloud bank to take up his duties as an angel, he is puzzled by the horde of despondent people returning from the clouds and dumping their angel gear along the way. However, after he has spent a day of monotonously trying to make music by singing and playing a harp while sitting on a cloud, his own enthusiasm for being an angel wanes. "This *ain't* just as near my idea of bliss as I thought it was going to be, when I used to go to church," he tells another angel. He then leaves the clouds himself and gratefully sheds his angel gear.

Stormfield next encounters Sam Bartlett, a man he apparently knew on Earth, who explains to him what a busy place Heaven is. His Sunday-school notion of a Heaven filled with psalm-singing, do-nothing angels is the exact opposite of the real Heaven, in which people are busy learning and fulfilling themselves in ways they could not on the worlds from which they came. Several months later he meets Sandy McWilliams, a man from New Jersey who has been in Heaven for 27 years. McWilliams teaches Stormfield about coming to terms with one's original age in Heaven. They spot an unhappy woman whose infant child had died just before McWilliams came to Heaven; McWilliams suspects that she is downcast because she has found her daughter to be a mature, highly educated adult with whom she has nothing in common. Another of Stormfield's preconceptions about the hereafter is punctured.

Chapter 4

Stormfield's difficulties in adjusting to life in Heaven include using his angel wings. McWilliams explains that most angels only wear their wings for special occasions since they have no practical value for transportation. Excitement is mounting in Stormfield's district because of the impending arrival of a New York bartender who drowned in a ferryboat accident the very night that he rediscovered religion. The heavenly host are expected to turn out in big numbers for him. Most people get whatever they want in Heaven. An example of someone who will *not* get what he wants, however, is the Brooklyn pastor Thomas De Witt Talmage, who expects heaven to be just for the elect, when in fact it is for everyone. McWilliams explains to Stormfield that one of the main charms of Heaven is that "there's all kinds here—which wouldn't be the case if you let the preachers tell it."

Stormfield also learns about the hierarchy of prophets and patriarchs in Heaven. ADAM is not at the top of this hierarchy, but he is one of the most popular figures there and the best at drawing a crowd. Ordinary Christians tend to perceive heaven as a republic, though it is ruled by a king. How, he asks, "are you going to have a republic under a king?" The answer is that Heaven is as authoritarian as RUSSIA and there is little mingling between people at different levels.

Stormfield is surprised to learn that persons such as SHAKESPEARE and Homer are regarded as "prophets" in heaven. He is even more shocked to learn that one of the highest-ranking prophets is a common tailor from TENNESSEE named Edward H. Billings, who is the greatest poet in the universe. Heaven, Stormfield learns, recognizes those who do not get their just rewards on Earth. Another such person is a Hoboken butcher named Richard Duffer, who fed and supported poor people so quietly and unobtrusively that he went to his grave unjustly scorned as a miser. One more such person is Absalom Jones, an obscure Boston bricklayer who was "the greatest military genius our world ever produced."

Heaven also proves to be a place in which humans learn how significant their own world is in the larger scheme of things. When beings from the colossal planet

Goobra, for example, learn that the Earth "is so little that a streak of lightning can flash clear around it in the eighth of a second, they have to lean up against something to laugh." Stormfield further learns that white people are such an insignificant minority in the American section of Heaven that "you can't expect us to amount to anything in heaven, and we *don't.*"

When the bartender finally arrives, Stormfield and McWilliams join millions of other angels who magically teleport themselves to his reception. Hundreds of thousands of torch-carrying angels troop by. The reception climaxes when Moses and Esau suddenly appear to welcome the bartender. Soon after they vanish, the "Extract" version of the story ends abruptly.

Chapter 5
Stormfield reflects on the time that he has spent in Heaven. He and McWilliams discuss the astronomical scale of Heaven and the meaning of a light-year. Their journeys take them to an "asterisk," or asteroid, where they encounter a race of tiny beings whom Stormfield compares to Gulliver's Lilliputians. This chapter essentially ends Stormfield's personal narrative.

Chapter 6
The final fragment relates McWilliams's narrative about a man named Slattery who had been born in Heaven, and who fell along with Satan aeons ago. Slattery was involved in a scheme by Satan to populate a region with a race of people he created in whom all positive and negative moral qualities are equally balanced—leaving them "ciphers." A second experiment was attempted, this time mixing up the moral qualities randomly in individuals, thereby creating the human race, with all its unexpected results.

Stormfield meanwhile learns from McWilliams that providence actually reacts quickly—in heavenly time—to earthly wrongs. Since a thousand years of Earth time is equivalent to only a day in Heaven, what seems a slow response to us is actually rapid. Prayers are always answered, and quickly in heavenly time. Unfortunately, in the minute that Heaven takes to answer a prayer, a entire year passes on Earth.

BACKGROUND AND PUBLISHING HISTORY

In a February 1906 autobiographical dictation, Mark Twain relates how he met Captain Edgar WAKEMAN, who in 1868 told him he had visited heaven. Drawing on Wakeman's story, Mark Twain began writing "Stormfield" that same year. By around 1873, his manuscript had grown to 40,000 words and he showed it to W. D. HOWELLS, who recommended its publication. Instead of publishing it, however, Mark Twain—by his own admission—"turned it into a BURLESQUE of *The Gates Ajar,* a book that had imagined a mean little ten-cent heaven about the size of Rhode Island." *The Gates Ajar*—which Mark Twain mentions by name in "Stormfield"—was a popular novel published in 1868 by Elizabeth Stuart Phelps (1844–1911). Though senti-

mental, Phelps's story rejects many traditional Christian notions about heaven, such as the idea that angels will find fulfillment in prayer and psalm-reading. Mark Twain claimed to burlesque her book, but he actually adopted many of her ideas. One of these was that a person's rank in heaven is measured by his intrinsic worth, not by his earthly accomplishments. This, for example, is why a bricklayer is honored as the world's greatest military genius.

Over the next three decades, Mark Twain periodically returned to this story; he occasionally added to it, but always ended up stowing it away again. He clearly had doubts about the direction the story should go. His notes indicate, for example, that he considered having Stormfield visit hell, an idea that he gave up on. At some point he worked his close friend Joseph TWICHELL into the story. Twichell is the "PETERS" to whom Stormfield is talking in the two "Extract" chapters.

Mark Twain's slowness in finishing and publishing "Stormfield" has long been taken as an indication of his ambivalence about its subject matter. His wife, Olivia Clemens, evidently admired the story, but regarded it as blasphemous, a sentiment with which Mark Twain was inclined to agree. While he was not averse to poking fun at religion, he was hesitant to offend believers. Whatever his own reservations, it may have been Livy's opposition that discouraged him from publishing the story until after she died. Meanwhile, Mark Twain enjoyed reading the story aloud to friends.

Not long after Mark Twain dictated his remarks about the writing of "Stormfield," he submitted part of it to HARPER'S MAGAZINE. Ironically, after Mark Twain had withheld the story for decades for fear of offending Christians, Harper's editor George HARVEY rejected it because it was "too damn godly." Harvey changed his mind a year later, however, and published the two "Extract" chapters in *Harper's* December 1907 and January 1908 issues. In October 1909 Harper's published *Extract from Captain Stormfield's Visit to Heaven* as a Christmas gift book, stretching the approximately 15,000 words of text out over 121 pages. Appropriately, this tale about heaven was the last book that Mark Twain published during his lifetime.

Mark Twain's surviving "Stormfield" manuscripts present special problems to scholars because of the difficulty of dating their composition. The fact that Mark Twain himself never supervised an edition of his entire manuscript has left minor inconsistencies between the "Extract" that he published in 1909 and the posthumously published fragments. For example, the first chapter from the posthumous version calls the title character "Captain Ben Stormfield," while the first "Extract" chapter calls him "Captain Eli Stormfield." And whereas he calculates his speed as at or over the speed of light in the first chapters, he estimates it at about a fifth of that in the "Extract."

In 1952 a fuller version appeared in a new edition, *Report from Paradise,* which Dixon WECTER prepared before his sudden passing. This version attached the first two "chapters" summarized here and a previously unpublished piece, "Letter from the Recording Angel." In 1970 Ray B. Browne published a still fuller version in a new book, *Mark Twain's Quarrel with Heaven: "Captain Stormfield's Visit to Heaven" and Other Sketches,* adding the last two chapters.

The 1985 claymation film THE ADVENTURES OF MARK TWAIN includes a dramatization of Stormfield's arrival at heaven.

Cardiff Hill (Holliday's Hill) Originally Mark Twain's fictional name for a prominent ST. PETERSBURG hill in *Tom Sawyer,* Cardiff is the name now used for the real Hannibal hill on which its fictional counterpart was modeled. It is mentioned in chapters 2 and 7 of *Tom Sawyer* as a place that beckons Tom away from his chores and schoolwork.

In Mark Twain's time the hill was called Holliday's Hill, after Captain Richard Holliday, who built a large house on it around 1840. Mark Twain took the hill's fictional name from a place in Cardiff, Wales that reminded him of Holliday's Hill when he visited there in the early 1870s. Rising about 300 feet above the Mississippi River, the Hannibal hill is the southern end of a long escarpment that parallels the river. It stands at the northern edge of central Hannibal, several blocks from Mark Twain's BOYHOOD HOME. Mark Twain often played on the hill as a child. Chapter 58 of *Innocents Abroad* recalls a moment during his youth when he and a friend rolled a boulder from the summit and smashed a cooper's shop in town.

Captain Holliday left Hannibal to join the GOLD RUSH to CALIFORNIA in the late 1840s and died soon afterward. His widow, Melicent Holliday, continued to live on the hill. Popular and generous, she was a good friend of Mark Twain's mother, Jane Clemens. In *Tom Sawyer,* Mark Twain used Mrs. Holliday as the model for the Widow DOUGLAS, who lives atop Cardiff Hill. The area around her house becomes the center of action in chapters 25 through 29, when Tom and Huck search for treasure in the vicinity, and INJUN JOE attempts to assault the widow in her home. At the end of *Tom Sawyer,* the widow takes Huck in. Huck is thus living in her Cardiff Hill house through the early chapters of *Huckleberry Finn.* That novel alludes to the hill several times, but does not mention it by name.

When Mark Twain paid his last visit to Hannibal in June 1902, he revisited Cardiff Hill with his childhood friend John BRIGGS. In later years, the hill became a shrine to his memory. In 1926, a bronze statue of Tom and Huck by Frederick HIBBARD was erected at its base. In late 1934, a lighthouse was erected at its top to illuminate the following year's centennial celebration of his BIRTH; using a telegraphic button, President Franklin D. ROOSEVELT switched the light on from the White House on January 15, 1935. At the end of the year, the lighthouse was strengthened to become a permanent memorial. After a windstorm knocked it down in June 1960, a new lighthouse was built. In May 1963, President John F. Kennedy duplicated Roosevelt's task by switching on the new lighthouse's beacon from the White House. President Bill Clinton participated in yet another such ceremony when the lighthouse was rededicated on July 2, 1994.

Carleton, George Washington (1832–October 1901) Publisher. In 1857 Carleton and Edward P. Rudd founded a bookstore and publishing company in New York City that became G. W. Carleton after Rudd died in 1861. A decade later, Carleton made George W. Dillingham a partner and renamed the firm G. W. Carleton and Company. Though he specialized in humorous books by such writers as Thomas Bailey Aldrich, Bret HARTE, Josh BILLINGS, John Phoenix, Q. K. Philander Doesticks and Artemus WARD, Carleton also published popular American fiction, European literature and general trade books that made his firm one of the most successful of its time. When Carleton retired in 1886, Dillingham continued the firm as G. W. Dillingham Company.

In early 1865, Artemus Ward asked Mark Twain to contribute a sketch to a collection he was assembling for Carleton. When Mark Twain finally submitted his JUMPING FROG STORY in October, Carleton gave the story to Henry Clapp, who published it in his SATURDAY PRESS in November. An ironic result of Mark Twain's late submission was that magazine publication brought his story far greater notice than a book would have. In early February 1867, Mark Twain personally approached Carleton about publishing a volume of sketches, after Charles WEBB had arranged a meeting for him. Carleton dismissed him brusquely, leaving Mark Twain bitter for years. In 1898, Carleton visited him in Switzerland and apologized, confessing that his main distinction in life was having refused a book by Mark Twain, which made him "the prize ass of the nineteenth century."

Carnegie, Andrew (November 25, 1835, Dunfermline, Scotland–August 11, 1919, Shadow Brook, Massachusetts) Scottish-American industrialist and philanthropist. Born just five days before Mark Twain, Carnegie came to America with his family in 1848 and settled near Pittsburgh, Pennsylvania. By his early twenties, he had attained a powerful position in the Pennsylvania Railroad; at 30, he started a steel company that developed into the world's largest. In 1901, he sold his consolidated holdings to J. P. MORGAN's United States Steel Company and devoted the rest of his life to dispersing over $350 million to various philanthropic causes, particularly libraries.

Mark Twain knew Carnegie in the early 1890s, when he tried to interest him in investing in the PAIGE COMPOSITOR. In later years, he spoke at several dinners in Carnegie's honor, and he devoted several long passages in his AUTOBIOGRAPHY to Carnegie that appear in MARK TWAIN IN ERUPTION.

Carpet-Bag Short-lived humor magazine in which Mark Twain's first published story, "THE DANDY FRIGHTENING THE SQUATTER," appeared in May 1852. B. P. SHILLABER, the creator of "Mrs. Partington," started the weekly magazine in Boston in late March 1851 and edited it until it expired exactly two years later. Shillaber's other contributors included Artemus WARD, who worked as a typesetter for the magazine and occasionally wrote for it as "Lieutenant Chubb." The *Carpet-Bag* took its name from a popular type of travel bag made from folded carpet material.

Carson City Capital of NEVADA and birthplace of the pen name "MARK TWAIN." Located in Eagle Valley, about eight miles east of Lake TAHOE, Carson began as a STAGECOACH stop in 1851. Seven years later a town was laid out on the site and named in honor of frontiersman Kit Carson (1809–1868). Discovery of the COMSTOCK lode a year later shifted much of Carson's business to nearby VIRGINIA CITY, but Carson remained an important stop for stagecoaches and emigrant trains and developed into a lumber center. It became the territorial capital in 1861 and the state capital three years later. It was later the site of a federal mint (1870–93).

On August 14, 1861, Mark Twain arrived in Carson by stage with his brother, Orion Clemens, who was secretary of the new territorial government. Apart from trips to Tahoe and ESMERALDA, he remained there until early December and clerked for the territorial legislature's first sessions in October and November. Most of this time he lived in a boardinghouse owned by a woman he calls Mrs. O'FLANNIGAN in *Roughing It,* which covers this period in chapters 21–25.

After going to HUMBOLDT in December 1861, Mark Twain returned to Carson in late January, staying several months before relocating to AURORA and later to VIRGINIA CITY, where he became a reporter for the TERRITORIAL ENTERPRISE. Thereafter, he stayed with his brother's family in Carson during visits to cover legislative sessions, the territory's constitutional convention and other events. During a visit to Carson in February 1863, he first signed an article "Mark Twain"—the pen name by which he would later become famous. The following year, his brother bought a house at the northwest corner of North Division and Spear streets where he often stayed; this house is still standing. After leaving Nevada in May 1864, Mark Twain revisited Carson during lecture trips in November 1866 and April 1868.

Cauchon, Pierre (1371, near Reims, France–December 18, 1442, Rouen, France) Historical figure and character in *Joan of Arc.* The bishop of Beauvais, a town near ROUEN, Cauchon acted as England's agent in ransoming Joan from the Burgundians and presiding over the trial that led to her execution. As the conscienceless villain

of Mark Twain's novel, he is first mentioned in chapter 39 of book 2 and figures prominently throughout book 3. The narrator DE CONTE describes Cauchon as a wheezing, obese brute with a splotchy complexion, cauliflower nose and malignant eyes (book 3, chapter 4). Mark Twain's personal feelings about Cauchon are revealed in a characteristic remark he attributes to his narrator de Conte, who wonders why Cauchon should want to go to heaven, when "he did not know anybody there" (book 3, chapter 18).

Cave Hollow Small valley by the entrance to the Mark Twain CAVE, several miles south of Hannibal. Chapter 3 of *Huckleberry Finn* mentions "Cave Hollow" as the place where Tom Sawyer's GANG attacks a Spanish and Arab caravan that turns out to be a Sunday-school picnic. Huck also mentions Cave Hollow in "DOUGHFACE."

Cave, Mark Twain Cave near Hannibal, Missouri. The narrative of *Tom Sawyer* climaxes when Tom and Becky THATCHER are lost in a cave near ST. PETERSBURG. Called "McDougal's Cave" in the novel, it is closely modeled on a real—but smaller—limestone cave two miles south of Hannibal, near the right bank of the Mississippi River. The cave was discovered in 1819—the year that Hannibal was settled—and was originally called Simms's Cave after its discoverer. Mark Twain played in the cave as a boy, when it was known as "McDowell's Cave," after its owner, Dr. Joseph Nash McDowell. By the 1840s, the cave was already becoming a subject of legend. *Life on the Mississippi* describes how McDowell used the cave as a mausoleum for his daughter, whose body he was trying to petrify (chapter 55). Before the CIVIL WAR, the cave was reputedly an underground railroad stop for escaping slaves; in later years, it was rumored to be a hideout of Jesse JAMES.

Mark Twain's earliest description of the cave was probably a sketch that he wrote in 1852, comparing its stalactites to the fairy palaces of the ARABIAN NIGHTS. In *Innocents Abroad* (1869), he recalls that the cave "was always in my mind, with its lofty passages, its silence and solitude, its shrouding gloom, its sepulchral echoes, its flitting lights, and more than all, its sudden revelations of branching crevices and corridors where we least expected them."

Mark Twain's best-known description of the cave is in *Tom Sawyer.* In chapter 29, picnicking children pour into the cave. Tom and Becky THATCHER get separated from the others and are lost for three days until Tom finds an opening five miles south of the main entrance, through which they escape. To keep others from getting lost, Judge THATCHER has the main entrance sealed with an iron door. Afterward, INJUN JOE is found dead, just inside the cave's new door. The novel concludes with Tom returning to the cave with Huck Finn through the new entrance he has discovered. Inside they find a chest of gold coins hidden by Injun Joe (chapter 33). In

The cave near St. Petersburg that Tom, Becky and other children explore in Tom Sawyer *closely resembles the real cave near Hannibal.*

Huckleberry Finn, Tom uses the cave as the headquarters of his robber GANG (chapters 2–3).

Tom Sawyer's description of the cave closely matches the real cave: from its narrow opening on the slope of a hill, to its "vast labyrinth of crooked aisles." Its distance from the town, however, seems somewhat greater in the novel than in real life, as does its size. The steamboat landing mentioned in the book also matches a real landing used by cave visitors during Mark Twain's time.

Publication of *Tom Sawyer* in 1876 began the cave's transformation into a tourist attraction. Within a decade, it had a part-time guide. Eventually, it became known as "Mark Twain's Cave," though it has also been called "Tom Sawyer's Cave." Since 1923 it has been owned by a local family that operates a sizeable tour business. Their guides treat the events of *Tom Sawyer* as though they actually happened, leading visitors to spots where events in the novel purportedly occurred. Mark Twain himself fed this myth by claiming in his AUTOBIOGRAPHY to have gotten lost in the cave with a girl when he was a boy. The claim seems doubtful, however, since Laura HAWKINS—the childhood sweetheart on whom he modeled Becky Thatcher—denied ever being lost in the cave herself. In 1972 the U.S. National Park Service designated the cave a natural landmark.

An unrelated cave that plays an important part in *Huckleberry Finn* and "TOM SAWYER'S CONSPIRACY" is set on JACKSON'S ISLAND.

The Celebrated Jumping Frog of Calaveras County, and Other Sketches (1867) Mark Twain's first book. On the advice of his friend Charles H. WEBB, Mark Twain assembled this collection of sketches in early 1867, only to have it rejected by George W. CARLETON and other publishers. Webb himself then published the book in May. Four months later, George ROUTLEDGE issued an unauthorized edition in London, with the same title and contents.

The book's 200 pages contain 27 items, including the JUMPING FROG STORY of the title, "AURELIA'S UNFORTUNATE YOUNG MAN," "CURING A COLD," "LUCRETIA SMITH'S SOLDIER" and "THE KILLING OF JULIUS CAESAR 'LOCALIZED.'" Aside from the frog story, virtually all the items originally appeared in the VIRGINIA CITY TERRITORIAL ENTERPRISE and the CALIFORNIAN. With Webb's help, Mark Twain assembled the collection from clippings he had saved; to avoid offending easterners, he made many minor revisions, such as removing allusions to death and drinking.

Preoccupied with a midwestern lecture tour and preparations for the QUAKER CITY excursion, Mark Twain paid little attention to the book's production and later expressed dissatisfaction with its many typographical errors and unauthorized editorial changes. The book sold poorly and soon went out of print. Mark Twain later reprinted much of its contents in other collections. In 1903, HARPER issued a new book, *The Jumping Frog. In English, Then in French, Then Clawed Back into a Civilized*

Language Once More by Patient, Unremunerated Toil. Aside from its title story, this edition has nothing to do with the earlier book.

Cellini, Benvenuto (November 1, 1500, Florence, Italy–February 13, 1571, Florence, Italy) Florentine goldsmith and sculptor. Cellini was famous for his picaresque *Autobiography,* which describes his dramatic escape from a Roman prison. Mark Twain admired Cellini's book and alluded to him in several works. In chapter 17 of *Connecticut Yankee,* for example, Hank MORGAN calls Cellini "that rough-hewn saint." In chapter 35 of *Huckleberry Finn,* Tom Sawyer mentions books by heroic escapees such as "Benvenuto Chelleeny." Tom's other heroes include Baron Frederick von Trenck (1726–1794), Giovanni Jacopo Casanova (1725–1798) and France's King Henri IV (1553–1610).

The Prince and the Pauper mentions furniture in WESTMINSTER Palace decorated with gold that is the work of "Benvenuto" (chapter 7).

Century Magazine Monthly New York magazine. Taking its name from New York's Century Club, the Century Company was created in 1881, when it bought the 11-year-old *Scribner's Monthly Magazine* and changed its name to *Century Illustrated Monthly Magazine.* Under the editorship of Richard Watson Gilder (1844–1909), *Century* developed into a leading literary magazine. During the 1880s, it published CIVIL WAR memoirs of GRANT and other veterans, while continuing *Scribner's* tradition of publishing the leading fiction writers of the time. Much of Mark Twain's most important fiction of the 1880s and early 1890s first appeared in it, and it also published extensive criticism of his work. After Gilder died in 1909, the magazine declined until it expired in 1930.

Mark Twain's first contribution to *Century* was "A CURIOUS EXPERIENCE," in November 1881. Three years later, he let Gilder publish several heavily edited extracts from his unfinished *Huckleberry Finn.* "THE PRIVATE HISTORY OF A CAMPAIGN THAT FAILED" followed in December 1885. The magazine later published four extracts from *Connecticut Yankee* (November 1889) and serialized all of *The Prince and the Pauper* (December 1893–June 1894), using Louis Loeb's illustrations. Mark Twain's other contributions to *Century* include "ENGLISH AS SHE IS TAUGHT" (April 1887), "Meisterschaft" (January 1888), "THE £1,000,000 BANK-NOTE" (January 1893), "FROM THE 'LONDON TIMES' OF 1904" (November 1898), "MY DÉBUT AS A LITERARY PERSON" (November 1899) and "TWO LITTLE TALES" (November 1901).

Cervantes, Miguel de (September 29, 1547, Alcalá, Spain–April 23, 1616, Madrid, Spain) Author of *Don Quixote of La Mancha* (1605–15), a book that many regard as the first modern novel. Though Cervantes was born into a poor Spanish family and ended his life in humble circumstances as a civil servant, he experienced incredible personal adventure. He fought at the Battle of Lepanto in 1571 and was captured and imprisoned for five years by Algerians. His novel, a SATIRE attacking romanticism, provides an interesting contrast with his life. Its hero, Don Quixote, is an old man who reads so many romances about chivalry that he cannot tell fantasy from reality. Seeing himself as a knight-errant, he goes forth to find wrongs to right, and his rich imagination transforms ordinary windmills into fearsome dragons. As Quixote experiences his imaginary adventures, he is joined by a peasant named Sancho Panza, who remains stubbornly anchored in reality.

Mark Twain called *Don Quixote*—which he read by the late 1860s and probably earlier—one of the most exquisite books ever written. He admired its satire, and credited Cervantes with sweeping away admiration for the nonsense of medieval chivalry—which he regretted to see Walter SCOTT's novels restoring (*Life on the Mississippi,* chapter 46). *Don Quixote*'s influence can be seen in much of Mark Twain's important fiction. The character Tom Sawyer, for example, has many quixotic attributes. A voracious reader of romantic stories, Tom often confuses fantasy and reality. While this trait is overt when he plays Robin Hood and PIRATE games, it also colors his entire view of life. By contrast, Huck Finn is his Sancho Panza. Where Tom sees the extraordinary, Huck sees only the ordinary. Early in *Huckleberry Finn,* for example, Huck quits Tom's GANG after concluding that its fabulous escapades are nothing but pretense. When Huck complains that the rich caravan of Spaniards and Arabs that the gang attacks in CAVE HOLLOW is merely a Sunday-school picnic, Tom tells him that he must read *Don Quixote* to understand the "enchantment" masking the caravan (chapter 3).

Though Huck himself is anything but quixotic, the novel *Huckleberry Finn* is often compared to *Don Quixote* because of picaresque elements in both. *The Prince and the Pauper,* which has similar elements, casts Miles HENDON in the role of Sancho Panza to an apparently deranged boy who thinks himself the king of England. *Connecticut Yankee* is sometimes seen as consciously imitating *Don Quixote*'s use of satire to attack medieval institutions and romanticism. For example, when SANDY leads Hank MORGAN on a mission to rescue princesses imprisoned by ogres, Hank finds that the princesses are pigs and the ogres are swineherds. Like Tom Sawyer, Sandy explains away the discrepancy as due to an enchantment (chapter 20).

Mark Twain's posthumously published "Three Thousand Years Among the Microbes," contains characters named Don Quixotte and Sancho Panza. Cervantes was a close contemporary of SHAKESPEARE, who is among the people who discuss Cervantes at Queen ELIZABETH I's court in *1601.*

Ceylon An island off the southern coast of India now called Sri Lanka, Ceylon was a British Crown Colony from 1833 until 1948. While sailing from AUSTRALIA to INDIA, Mark Twain landed at Ceylon's capital, Colombo, on the island's southwest coast, on January 13, 1896. He stayed there overnight before spending six days sailing up the western coast of India to Bombay. Mark Twain devotes chapter 37 of *Following the Equator* to Ceylon, which he regarded as the first "utterly Oriental" place he had experienced. After spending two months in India, he again stopped at Colombo. This time he spent several days and delivered two public lectures; however, *Following the Equator* dismisses this second visit in a single line at the beginning of chapter 62.

Chambers (Valet de Chambre) Name used by two characters in *Pudd'nhead Wilson*. The true "Chambers" is the son of the slave woman ROXANA (Roxy) and the white aristocrat Colonel Cecil Burleigh ESSEX. Though only 1/32 black, Chambers is considered a "Negro," and is legally the slave of Percy DRISCOLL. He is born on February 1, 1830—the same day that his master's own son, Tom DRISCOLL, is born. Tom's mother soon dies, leaving Roxy to raise both boys. When they are seven months old, she switches them to protect Chambers from ever being sold down the river. From that moment, in chapter 3, until David WILSON reveals the boys' true identities in chapter 21, the character known to the world as "Chambers" is actually Tom Driscoll. Meanwhile, the true Chambers grows up as "Tom." (However, after Roxy tells her natural son his true identity in chapter 9, she calls him Chambers in private.)

The narrative says little about the boy raised as "Chambers," except that he has a hard life from infancy. He seems to get no affection from anyone. His natural mother is dead; his foster mother, Roxy, favors her natural son; and his natural father regards him as only a slave. "Tom"—who has assumed this character's birthright—treats him miserably. While Chambers's emotional strength is a cipher, he grows up physically strong and healthy. Tom uses him as a bodyguard as he bullies other boys, and then cuffs him relentlessly, knowing that his father will not tolerate Chambers's lifting a hand against him. By the time the boys are 15, Tom's abuse becomes so outrageous that his uncle, Judge York DRISCOLL, buys Chambers to prevent Tom from persuading Percy to sell him down the river.

Except for a brief mention in chapter 8—when Chambers is working in Judge Driscoll's house—Chambers disappears from the narrative between chapters 4 and 20. After Tom is exposed as a murderer and imposter at the conclusion, Chambers finds himself rich and legally free. He is not, however, psychologically free. Aside from suddenly finding himself an orphan, he must deal with the realization that he has been horribly cheated through his entire life. Handicapped by illiteracy and a coarse slave dialect and trained to have the attitudes and mannerisms of a slave, he is petrified by the company of white people. His chances for happiness appear bleak.

"Chambers" is a familiar form of the character's full name, *Valet de Chambre* (variously spelled in the original text), a French expression that translates literally as "room servant." Roxy takes on a similar title when she works on a steamboat as a "chambermaid" after being freed in chapter 4. It is probably a mere coincidence that Mark Twain himself worked on a steamboat named A. B. CHAMBERS in 1859–60. A list of fictional names that Mark Twain entered into a NOTEBOOK around 1880–81 includes "Valet de Chambre Utterback."

chamois (gemsbok) Goatlike alpine antelope mentioned frequently in *A Tramp Abroad*. Once common in Europe's ALPS, chamois were hunted nearly to extinction for their meat and skin—which became famous as "shammy" leather. Viewing stories about hunting chamois as romantic nonsense, Mark Twain uses *A Tramp Abroad* to burlesque the mammal as if it were a flea—precisely what he calls it in his private notebooks. He may also be using "chamois" as a codeword for flea to attack the uncleanliness he found in many Swiss villages. In chapter 35, for example, the narrator's companion HARRIS is covered with chamois bites after walking through a field of "liquid fertilizer" to get to Leukerbad, whose unappealing "Chamois Hotel" the travelers shun.

Charles VII (the Dauphin) (February 22, 1403, Paris–July 22, 1461, Méhun-sur-Yèvre, France) Historical figure and character in *Joan of Arc*. The son of Isabella of Bavaria and France's King Charles VI (1368–1422), Charles VII became heir (Dauphin) to the French throne in 1417, when a brother died. By the time he succeeded to the kingship in 1422, however, his position was compromised by his suspected complicity in the murder of the Duke of Burgundy in 1419 and his father's treaty with England, which disinherited him the following year. His authority in southern France was tenuous, and England occupied most of northern France and was expanding south. JOAN OF ARC's emergence in 1429 reversed the shrinkage of Charles's domain and legitimized his authority by getting him properly crowned at Reims. Charles rewarded Joan by ennobling her family and exempting her village from taxation, but ignored her plight after she was captured by the Burgundians a year later.

Mark Twain's novel depicts Charles as a weakling dominated by disloyal advisers, particularly his chancellor, Georges de la Trémoïlle. In Mark Twain's eyes, Charles's chief crime was ingratitude. After failing to ransom Joan from her captors, he later had her reputation rehabilitated primarily in order to save his own reputation, since she was responsible for his coronation. The authority of the historical Charles grew after Trémoïlle's assassination 'n 1433 and he did much to rebuild his kingdom. During the 1440s, he campaigned against the English himself and established a regular army. He played a major role in the expulsion of the English from France in 1453.

Chatto, Andrew (c. 1840–March 13, 1913, London)
English book publisher. Chatto joined John Camden HOTTEN's firm in 1856 and eventually became its publications manager. After Hotten died in 1873, Chatto purchased his firm and reorganized it as Chatto and Windus, with a poet named W. E. Windus as a junior partner. In contrast to Hotten, Chatto made clear contracts with his authors, paid royalties faithfully, improved book production and performed many services for authors, such as procuring research materials. In late 1873, Chatto wrote to Mark Twain proposing a formal publishing relationship. Mark Twain ignored this initial approach, since he was then content to work with George A. ROUTLEDGE; however, he contracted with Chatto to publish *Tom Sawyer* two years later, after seeing strong recommendations from Ambrose Bierce, Tom Hood and Charles STODDARD, as well as Moncure D. CONWAY—who arranged the connection.

Chatto first met Mark Twain in New York in July 1877, at the opening of the play AH SIN. Working hard to cultivate his relationship with Mark Twain, Chatto became a close personal friend, earning the distinction of being the only publisher that Mark Twain never turned against. Chatto also worked out a scheme for simultaneous publication of Mark Twain's books in Britain and America that helped combat piracy before the international copyright convention was signed in 1891. Chatto published almost all of Mark Twain's books. Aside from minor differences in typesetting errors and proofing, most Chatto editions are nearly identical to their American counterparts in content. Chatto's edition of *Tom Sawyer Abroad,* however, escaped the expurgation to which most of the American edition was subjected, and Chatto's MORE TRAMPS ABROAD is a more complete book than *Following the Equator,* its American counterpart.

Windus retired from the firm in 1909 and died the following year. Chatto retired in 1911.

Chicago Mark Twain first visited Chicago in August 1853, while traveling from St. Louis to New York City, when the ILLINOIS city was on the threshold of major growth. In 1868, he wrote half a dozen travel letters to the *Chicago Daily Republican.* LECTURE tours returned him to Chicago in January 1869, December 1871 and January 1885—when he did readings with G. W. CABLE. He was also in Chicago in November 1879, when he spoke at an army reunion banquet honoring General GRANT. He again passed through Chicago in the summer of 1886, while taking his family to KEOKUK, Iowa.

In late April 1893, Mark Twain went to Chicago with Frederick HALL for the World's Fair, but illness confined him to his hotel room and he left without even glimpsing the fair. He used the incident in "TRAVELING WITH A REFORMER" later that year. The fair's world congress of religions attracted such widespread interest that when Mark Twain visited INDIA three years later, he found people who thought Chicago was some kind of holy

city. *Following the Equator* comments on the Chicago fair (chapters 41, 53 and 54), and uses a Pudd'nhead Wilson MAXIM to correct the idea that the city is holy by having Satan tell a new arrival to Hell, "The trouble with you Chicago people is, that you think you are the best people down here; whereas you are merely the most numerous" (chapter 60).

The four decades between Mark Twain's first and last visits to Chicago saw the city grow from an inconsequential town to the Midwest's greatest industrial and commercial center. *Life on the Mississippi* describes the city as changing so rapidly that "she is never the Chicago you saw when you passed through the last time" (chapter 60). A decade later Mark Twain dubbed BERLIN the "German Chicago" because of its similarly rapid modernization.

Mark Twain's investment in the PAIGE COMPOSITOR died in Chicago, where it underwent its final test at the *Chicago Herald* in late 1894. The machine's inventor, James PAIGE, is also rumored to have died in Chicago, in a poorhouse.

Child of Calamity Minor character in the "RAFT CHAPTER" of *Huckleberry Finn* (chapter 16) and *Life on the Mississippi* (chapter 3). One of the tough-talking boatmen whom Huck sees on a giant raft, the "Child of Calamity" brags about his prowess before taking on another big tough named Bob; however, a smaller man named DAVY comes along and thrashes both of them. Later, the Child of Calamity discovers Huck in his hiding place.

Choice Humorous Works of Mark Twain **(1872)** Title of a pirated collection of stories published by John Camden HOTTEN in London. Six years later, Mark Twain revised and corrected an authorized version of the book for Andrew CHATTO.

cholera Bacterial disease that caused several pandemics directly affecting Mark Twain's life. The disease might even be credited with determining the place of his BIRTH: When his family came to Missouri in 1835, they decided against settling in ST. LOUIS because of a cholera scare there and instead went upstate to FLORIDA, where he was born later that year.

"Cholera" has been loosely applied to a variety of acute, short-term diarrheal diseases. Some forms are mild—such as the "cholera morbus" that *Innocents Abroad* reports Mark Twain suffering from in DAMASCUS in 1867 (chapter 45). In modern medical terminology, "cholera" generally refers to a form that is often fatal. This disease attacks the intestine, inducing severe diarrhea that can cause terminal dehydration. Cholera spreads mainly through dirty water and unclean raw food, and tends to be endemic in severely crowded poor regions. Though the disease goes back thousands of years, world pandemics have been reported only since the early 19th century. One such pandemic struck North

America during the 1840s and raged through the Mississippi Valley. Mark Twain's AUTOBIOGRAPHY exaggerates the fear it engendered, claiming that for each person cholera killed, three more died from fright. An echo of this fear is heard in *Huckleberry Finn*'s "RAFT CHAPTER," in which a raftsman brags, "I'm the man they call Sudden Death and General Desolation! Sired by a hurricane, dam'd by an earthquake, half-brother to the cholera, nearly related to the small-pox on the mother's side!"

Since the cholera bacillus incubates within one to five days, quarantine is an effective way to control its spread. Mark Twain observed many quarantines in 1867—just as a world pandemic was winding down. In early January, he sailed from NICARAGUA to New York aboard the steamship *San Francisco*, on which cholera killed seven steerage passengers. When the ship put in at Key West, Florida, many passengers went ashore, but Mark Twain stayed with the ship to New York, where the captain avoided quarantine by attributing the deaths to "dropsy." Chapter 79 of *Roughing It* mentions this voyage, which is more thoroughly described in chapters 6–7 of MARK TWAIN'S TRAVELS WITH MR. BROWN.

Later the same year, Mark Twain's voyage on the QUAKER CITY was constantly upset by cholera epidemics and scares, though no case was ever reported aboard his ship. The disease was a major concern throughout ITALY, where travelers were "fumigated" in several towns. To avoid quarantine complications, Mark Twain and his companions left the *Quaker City* at LEGHORN and went south on their own. Meanwhile, Leghorn was declared an "infected port," costing the *Quaker City* its clean bill of health and keeping it in quarantine more than a week in the Bay of NAPLES. Later, Greek authorities would not allow it to land at ATHENS.

After the *Quaker City* left EGYPT, the balance of its scheduled itinerary was severely disrupted by cholera concerns. Maintaining a clean bill of health to make landing at SPAIN was a high priority, so the ship skipped Malta, touched at Sardinia and Algiers without landing, then skipped Majorca. Nevertheless, when it reached Malaga, its passengers were not allowed ashore unless they waited out a long quarantine, so the ship went directly to GIBRALTAR, robbing most passengers of their best chance to go through Spain. The final disappointment came at Madeira, where officials insisted on a three-day quarantine before anyone could come ashore.

Other world pandemics followed, including one during the early 1890s that killed the Russian composer Peter Tchaikovsky. Mark Twain wrote "The Cholera Epidemic in Hamburg," an essay about the impact of this pandemic in GERMANY that later appeared in EUROPE AND ELSEWHERE. It may have been the residue of this same pandemic that he encountered at Honolulu, HAWAII in August 1895. He was scheduled to lecture there, but no one was allowed ashore because of cholera. *Following the Equator* also discusses cholera's impact on BENARES (chapter 52). In "Three Thousand Years

Among the Microbes," which Mark Twain began writing shortly afterward, the narrator is a cholera microbe.

Christian Science Religion founded in 1879 by Mary Baker Eddy (1821–1910). Formally called the Church of Christ, Scientist, this sect is based on the teachings of *Science and Health* (1875), a doctrine of "divine healing" that Eddy wrote after claiming to have cured herself of several terminal maladies. Its central thesis is that Christ's mission was not merely to redeem souls, but to cure sickness; sick people may therefore cure themselves by absorbing His consciousness through His acts and sayings. The doctrine denies the reality of the physical world and teaches that physical illness and sin are illusions to be conquered by the mind.

Mark Twain had a long and deep interest in various forms of mental science. Impressed by accounts of Christian Science healings, he suspected that the religion's tenets might be sound, but found Eddy's writings largely incomprehensible. Between 1899 and 1903, he published articles about Christian Science in COSMOPOLITAN and the NORTH AMERICAN REVIEW. His first article predicts that membership in Christian Science would grow so rapidly that there would be 20 million members in America alone by 1930 and that by 1940 the church would control the republic.

In 1907, he combined his magazine articles with fresh material in *Christian Science, With Notes Containing Corrections to Date*, a book that HARPER'S reluctantly published. The 63,000-word volume is divided into "books" of 9 and 15 chapters, with 7 appendixes and a conclusion. The first book examines Christian Science tenets and practices, questioning whether divine healing is dangerous. It opens with a BURLESQUE in which the narrator breaks every bone in his body in a fall off a cliff, only to be told by a "Christian Science doctor" that there is nothing wrong with him. The second book focuses more on Eddy. On the basis of inconsistencies in writing style, it challenges her claim to have written *Science and Health* and criticizes her hunger for power and wealth.

Regarding Eddy as a dangerous power-monger, Mark Twain built an elaborate SATIRE around her in "The Secret History of Eddypus, The World-Empire." In this complex unfinished story about future history, dates are denoted "A.M.," for "Anno Matris," after her. His nearly finished novel NO. 44, THE MYSTERIOUS STRANGER reflects his interest in the Christian Science tenet that reality exists only in the mind, and it alludes directly to Christian Science in chapter 30. IS SHAKESPEARE DEAD? (1909) lists Eddy among notorious "claimants" (chapter 1).

Mark Twain's daughter Clara later joined the Christian Science church and wrote *Awake to a Perfect Day; My Experience with Christian Science* (1956), in which she tries to explain her father's views on Eddy.

Christ's Hospital ("Christ's Church") London home for orphan children mentioned in *The Prince and the*

Pauper. In 1552, England's King EDWARD VI founded Christ's Hospital as a home ("hospital") for foundlings on property that his father had seized from the Grey Friars Church. Although *The Prince and the Pauper* is set about five years before the time the historical Christ's Hospital was founded, the institution figures into its narrative and is the subject of several long appendix notes by Mark Twain. In chapter 4, Edward—still a prince—goes to Christ's Hospital (initially misnamed "Christ's Church") hoping for succor since his father had created it. After being roughly treated by the home's ignorant boys, he vows to transform the institution into a school. When he is restored to his throne in chapter 33, he makes good on his vow and names Tom CANTY the hospital's chief governor. The real institution did later become a school, which was moved to Sussex in 1902.

"The Chronicle of Young Satan" Unfinished novel written between 1897 and 1900 and published posthumously. A story about an angel who visits AUSTRIA in the early 18th century, "Chronicle" is the second of four versions of similar stories that Mark Twain never finished. These manuscripts are collectively known as "THE MYSTERIOUS STRANGER" stories—the same title that Mark Twain's literary executor A. B. PAINE gave to a condensed and bowdlerized version of "Chronicle" that he published as an authentic Mark Twain work in 1916. Until the full extent of what has been called Paine's "editorial fraud" was revealed nearly a half century later, *The Mysterious Stranger, A Romance* was the only version of "Chronicle" known to the world. In 1969, Mark Twain's original text was finally published as he wrote it, with his own title, "The Chronicle of Young Satan."

Many characters in the Mysterious Stranger stories are modeled on people Mark Twain knew during his youth. In fact, he placed the first version of these stories in a mid–19th-century Missouri setting similar to that of his Tom Sawyer and Huck Finn stories. When he wrote "Chronicle," he transplanted his earlier version's characters and settings to Austria.

Though the Mysterious Stranger stories are intertwined, each has a distinct story line and themes. "Chronicle" reflects the issues that concerned Mark Twain in the late 1890s, as well as philosophical questions that he would later explore more fully in "WHAT IS MAN?" and other writings. The fact that the story is set in Austria in 1702 is almost irrelevant, as the questions that it addresses are universal.

The structure of the story is similar to that of JOAN OF ARC, with an elderly narrator, Theodor FISCHER, recalling a time in his youth when he was close to a remarkable being—indeed, one not of this Earth. The SATAN of the story's title is an angel who is visiting the Earth on an unexplained mission. Unimaginably old by Earth standards, Satan has been everywhere and seen everything, and has godlike powers that allow him to move freely in time and space. Not constrained by the moral sense, he sees himself as being on a plane vastly higher than that of man, whom he regards as inconsequential. Seeing man as nothing more than a "machine" with no ability to create, he laughs at the idea that man's civilizations have achieved anything to be proud of. As Satan weaves in and out of the lives of the villagers, he amuses himself by tampering with the fates of persons whom he encounters.

SYNOPSIS

"Chronicle" has 11 chapters of uneven length, totalling 54,300 words. Theodor Fischer's narrative begins in AUSTRIA in the spring of 1702 and ends abruptly about a year later, when Satan takes Theodor to India and Ceylon.

Chapter 1

The story opens in the Austrian village of ESELDORF in May 1702, when its narrator, Theodor FISCHER, is a boy. The village is a paradise for Theodor and his friends, but trouble comes when a Hussite woman distributes literature that goes against Catholic beliefs. After a warning by the village's stern priest, Father Adolf, the village never admits another Hussite. Father Adolf is always on hand each December 9 when the village celebrates the Assuaging of the Devil at the bridge that villagers tricked the Devil into building 700 years earlier. Father Adolf is respected because he does not fear the Devil, but the village's best-loved priest is Father Peter, whom Adolf got the bishop to suspend for saying that God would find a way to save *all* his children. Now nearly destitute, Father Peter and his niece Marget face foreclosure on their house.

Chapter 2

Theodor spends most of his time with Nikolaus Baumann, a judge's son, and Seppi Wohlmeyer, the son of the principal innkeeper. The local castle's serving-man Felix Brandt often tells them stories, and teaches them not to fear supernatural beings. One day after Brandt tells them about seeing angels, the boys are playing on a hill when a handsome, well-dressed young stranger approaches. The stranger seems to read Theodor's mind and performs amazing tricks, such as lighting a pipe by blowing on it. After showing the boys that they can have anything they wish, he uses clay to fashion animals that spring to life, then makes hundreds of miniature people who begin building a castle.

The stranger reveals that he is an angel, and startles the boys by saying that his name is "SATAN." A nephew of the great Satan, he is 16,000 Earth years old. When Satan's tiny clay workmen quarrel, he casually crushes them—at the very moment he is explaining that angels cannot commit sin. Though disturbed by Satan's callousness, the boys feel drunk with the joy of being with him. He has been everywhere and seen everything and forgets nothing; however, his remarks about humans reveal that he considers them as inconsequential as flies. When the castle is finished, Theodor marvels at its perfection, but Satan creates a fierce storm over it and lightning sets off its magazine, causing the castle and its people to be swallowed into the earth. The boys are devastated, but Satan is indifferent.

Satan instructs the boys to call him "Philip TRAUM" in the presence of others, adding that he will prevent their tongues from revealing what they know about him.

When Father Peter approaches, he walks *through* Satan as though the angel were not there. The boys are also invisible to the priest. As Satan explains the differences between himself and man, he emphasizes that he lacks the moral sense. After he dissolves himself to go on an errand, the boys wonder if they have been dreaming. Father Peter returns, searching for his wallet, which he is astonished to discover is filled with gold coins. Despite reassurances from the boys—who correctly guess that Satan has left the money for him—the priest is perplexed about what to do with it.

Chapter 3
After Father Peter pays his mortgage the next day and deposits the rest of the gold with Solomon Isaacs, the villagers again become friendly with him and his niece. Several days later, Father Adolf returns from a trip and asks the boys about Peter's gold. Adolf pronounces that the money has been stolen from him and has Peter arrested. When Peter is set to be tried in a civil court, Marget is soon in a desperate financial plight, and Ursula her housekeeper tries to help her.

One day Theodor encounters Satan and they find Ursula comforting a stray kitten, which Satan says is a lucky cat that will provide for its owner. After Ursula leaves, Theodor wishes he could see Marget and is suddenly in her parlor with Satan, whom he introduces as Philip Traum. When Ursula arrives, she is upset to see Satan get Marget to invite him to supper, but plentiful food miraculously appears.

When Theodor thinks to himself that he would like to see the inside of a jail, he and Satan are suddenly in a torture chamber. Theodor expresses shock at a prisoner's "brutal" mistreatment, but Satan corrects his choice of words, saying that such cruelty is a *human*, not a *brute*, thing. A moment later, Satan transports him to a French village, where they see poor people working themselves to death under miserable conditions. Satan derides the human race as illogical and unreasoning. A moment later, they are back in the village, where they learn that Hans Oppert, the village loafer, has disappeared after beating his dog. Satan repairs the dog's wounds, talks with it and learns that Oppert fell over a precipice.

Chapter 4
During a dull week in which Satan does not appear, the boys occasionally see Ursula. She boasts that things are going so well that she has hired a servant, Gottfried Narr—whose family has been under a cloud since his grandmother was burned as a witch. Though suspicious about Narr, the villagers seek his company hoping to learn why Marget is suddenly so prosperous. Suspecting that witchcraft is involved, Father Adolf encourages villagers to spy on Marget and Ursula. When Marget invites 40 people to a party, Adolf arrives uninvited. The priest studies the bottle of wine he is drinking from and calls for a large bowl. He fills it from his bottle, then pronounces the house "bewitched and accursed." As guests rush out, Satan slips into the priest's body, calls for a funnel and pours the contents of the bowl back into the bottle. The guests now cry out that Father Adolf is possessed, as the priest goes to the market square, where he juggles a hundred balls at once and astounds everyone with his acrobatics. Confident that their priest is possessed by witches and devils, the villagers wail that God has forsaken them.

Theodor returns to Marget's house, where the atmosphere is funereal. When Satan enters, however, everyone brightens. They discuss music and poetry, and Satan dazzles everyone with an amazing display of chess skill against Marget's suitor, Wilhelm Meidling. Afterward Satan composes the most beautiful music on the spinet that anyone has ever heard.

Chapter 5
The next day, the villagers are anxious about the witchcommission's failure to summon Father Adolf, who has disappeared. Meanwhile, Satan, as "Traum," charms the entire village. As Theodor's parents discuss this marvelous stranger, Theodor's sister Lilly admits that she is infatuated with him—though betrothed to Joseph Fuchs. When Joseph arrives, he reports that all anyone is discussing is Traum, adding that the strange youth is doing things that might get him in trouble—such as saving a man from drowning without getting himself wet. Joseph implies that Traum—like Father Adolf—may be possessed, and adds that he has offended Wilhelm, whom he might need to get himself out of legal trouble. Wilhelm then arrives and describes another of Traum's musical miracles, adding that Marget has professed her slavish devotion to the stranger. Insinuating that his own life is ruined, Wilhelm goes to a back room for liquor. When Satan arrives, Wilhelm tries to stab him with a butcher knife, but Satan lets the knife fall to the floor harmlessly and soothes Wilhelm's feelings.

Chapter 6
That night, Theodor tries to talk Lilly into forgetting about Satan, but gets nowhere and goes to bed worrying about the misfortunes that have befallen the village since Satan's arrival. Satan rouses him with music and takes him to China. When Theodor accuses Satan of causing unhappiness by not taking into account the consequences of his actions, Satan counters that he *always* knows what the consequences will be. He explains that though the villagers are nothing to him, he likes Theodor and his friends and Father Peter. He also

explains that whereas man is simply a "machine" in which happiness and suffering are about equally divided, he himself has a mind that can *create*. He goes on to explain that the things he is doing for the villagers will actually bear good fruit some day. For example, he is changing Nikolaus's fate so that both he and a neighbor child whom he tries to save from drowning will drown, instead of enduring years of misery as cripples. He also assures Theodor that Father Peter will be exonerated and will be happy for the rest of his life. He tells Theodor that he has put Father Adolf on the far side of the moon and that he will spare the priest from his long and odious future by having him burned.

Chapter 7

Theodor and Seppi spend all their spare time with the doomed Nikolaus until Satan's grim prophecy is fulfilled. At the ensuing funeral, a carpenter seizes the body of the girl whom Nikolaus tried to save in payment of a debt. The girl's mother goes mad with grief, so the boys beg Satan to relieve her distress. He responds by arranging for her to be condemned as a witch, and the chapter ends with the boys seeing the woman burned at the stake.

Chapter 8

When Satan next appears, he shows Theodor and Seppi the history of the human race's progress. He begins by recreating the Garden of Eden at the moment that Cain clubbed Abel to death, then follows with a long series of wars, murders and massacres. Next, he shows some slaughters of the future and tells the boys about the bloody wars that are coming. He soon begins laughing and making fun of the human race, but when he sees that he is upsetting the boys, he stops and gives them wine in extraordinarily beautiful goblets.

Satan is never alone, as animals love him and follow him everywhere. Often he frees them from traps. When four gamekeepers discover him freeing a trapped rabbit, they threaten to punish him for poaching. After he starts revealing dark secrets about each man, he denounces one of the keepers, Conrad Bart, as a murderer. The man puts a gun to Satan's chest, but Satan turns him to stone, then turns himself into Father Adolf and flees. After a jury rules that Bart met his death by the visitation of God, his family prospers by exhibiting his petrified body.

Chapter 9

Theodor considers asking Satan to predict his own future, but decides that he would prefer not to know. Instead, he asks to know Seppi's future, and gets the answer in a multivolume book that he will read for the rest of his life. He also later learns that Seppi is doing the same thing with *his* life. Occasionally, Theodor and Seppi get Satan to tell them what will happen in town a day or two in advance, and use the information to win bets with other boys. The boys often travel with Satan over great distances and times. Sometimes they stay away for weeks and months, yet return within a fraction of the second when they left.

When villagers become impatient with the failure of the witch-commission to go after Father Adolf, they chase down a suspected witch themselves. Theodor suggests that only Catholics could have such courage, but Satan disagrees and takes him to Scotland to show him Protestants persecuting a witch. They return to Eseldorf in time to see the suspected witch being hanged. Though sickened by the spectacle, Theodor joins the crowd in throwing a stone at her, causing Satan to laugh aloud. When three men turn on Satan and accuse him of failing to throw a stone, he predicts that all three of them will soon die—including one who has just five minutes to live. Four and a half minutes later, one man starts gasping for breath and is soon dead. As Satan leaves with Theodor, he says that of the 68 people in the mob, 62 did not want to throw stones at the woman. He explains that the human race is made up of sheep governed by minorities. When Theodor objects, Satan cites the example of human wars; although there has never been a just or honorable war, the minority of people advocating war always prevail. Two centuries in the future, England will bear the most honorable name a nation has ever borne, yet it will spoil its good name by letting itself be drawn into a shameful war (an allusion to the South African War, 1899–1902).

Chapter 10

Many days pass with no sign of Satan. However, Father Adolf is back. Satan has stopped visiting Marget, who asks for Wilhelm to defend her uncle in his coming trial. When Father Peter's trial finally begins, he himself is too feeble to attend. Father Adolf testifies that two years earlier he found the bag of gold coins that Peter later stole from him. When the boys give their testimony, people merely laugh. Wilhelm does the best he can to represent Father Peter, but his case is hopeless. Theodor's spirits rise when Satan appears standing next to Wilhelm and melts into him. Through Wilhelm, Satan asks Father Adolf to confirm that he found his sack of coins *two* years earlier, then points out that since the dates on most of the coins are only *one* year old, the gold could not have been Adolf's. The court dismisses the case.

Theodor and the others rush to tell Father Peter the good news, but Satan visits him first and tells him that he lost the case and is forever disgraced as a thief. The shock so unsettles the old man that he goes mad; however, he is happy—as Satan predicted he would be.

When Satan later argues that the human race lives a life of continuous and uninterrupted self-deception and has hardly a single fine quality, Theodor cites the sense of humor as such a quality. Here, also, Satan disagrees, saying that humans have merely "a bastard perception of humor." Humans laugh at a thousand low-grade and trivial things, while failing to appreciate the 10,000 high-grade comicalities in religion and hereditary royalties and aristocracies. As an example, he cites the pope's infallibility. He calls laughter the race's only effective weapon against such juvenilities, but says that the race does not think to use it. When Satan realizes that Theodor feels hurt, he lets up, then flashes Theodor around the world, making quick stops in strange countries. In INDIA, they watch a juggler, then Satan transforms himself into a native. He takes a seed from the juggler, places it on the ground and causes a wonderful tree to shoot up, with its branches heavy with oranges, grapes, bananas, peaches and other fruits. As people fill their baskets with fruit, a Portuguese man arrives and commands everyone to leave his land. Satan pleads for him to let people harvest fruit for just one more hour, but he refuses. When the man strikes and kicks Satan, the tree's fruit and leaves suddenly die. In a voice that none of the Indians understands, Satan tells the man that though the tree will never again bear fruit, he must personally water it in each hour of the night or he will die. Satan and Theodor then vanish away to Ceylon.

Chapter 11
Theodor still hungers to see Satan show off some more. To accommodate him, Satan takes him to a place where a magician performs a trick for a rich rajah. As Satan starts to expose the man as a fake, the narrative ends.

BACKGROUND AND PUBLISHING HISTORY

After settling in VIENNA in September 1897, Mark Twain began writing the first version of "The Mysterious Stranger" stories, setting the narrative in the ST. PETERSBURG of his Tom Sawyer and Huck Finn stories. Between November 1897 and January 1898, he reworked this first fragment into the early 18th-century setting of "The Chronicle of Young Satan." He resumed work on the manuscript in May 1899, just before he left Vienna for London, where he continued working on it into October. He wrote the second half of the manuscript between June and August 1900, then set it aside for more than two years. After returning to it in late 1902, he revised the first chapter to set the story in the late 15th century, then shifted its direction so radically that he ended up with a fourth version, which he called NO. 44, THE MYSTERIOUS STRANGER.

After A. B. PAINE published a bowdlerized edition of "Chronicle" as THE MYSTERIOUS STRANGER, A ROMANCE in 1916, Mark Twain's original manuscript was largely forgotten until John S. TUCKEY revealed the extent of Paine's intervention in 1963. Six years later, "Chronicle" was published in the MARK TWAIN PAPERS's edition of *The Mysterious Stranger*, edited by William M. Gibson.

"Chronicle" has not yet been adapted to the screen, but the 1985 claymation film THE ADVENTURES OF MARK TWAIN includes the scene in which Satan fashions miniature people from clay.

Cincinnati   Southwestern Ohio city. Mark Twain came to Cincinnati from KEOKUK, Iowa on about October 24, 1856. Over the next four months, he worked as a printer for T. Wrightson & Co. at 167 Walnut Street while living in a boardinghouse at 76 Walnut Street. The Cincinnati period of his life is poorly documented, but while he was there, he wrote two letters to the *Keokuk Post* under the pen name "Thomas Jefferson SNODGRASS." An autobiographical passage that he wrote four decades later indicates that he got the deterministic ideas that he would later develop in WHAT IS MAN? from a fellow Cincinnati boarder named MACFARLAND. He also alludes to his Cincinnati residence in chapter 5 of *Life on the Mississippi* and in "THE TURNING POINT OF MY LIFE." On February 16, 1857, he boarded the steamboat PAUL JONES and left Cincinnati for NEW ORLEANS. He returned to Cincinnati in early January 1885, during a lecture tour with G. W. CABLE.

City of Baton Rouge   The last STEAMBOAT on which Mark Twain traveled on the Lower Mississippi River, and possibly the last true river steamboat that he ever steered. After Mark Twain revisited NEW ORLEANS in May 1882, he returned to St. Louis aboard the *Baton Rouge*, a fast new boat in the Anchor Line captained by his original master pilot, Horace BIXBY. He describes the journey in chapter 51 of *Life on the Mississippi*.

City of Memphis   STEAMBOAT on which Mark Twain worked as a PILOT. An 865-ton Railroad Line packet made in 1857, the *Memphis* was reputedly the largest and finest steamboat of its time built in St. Louis. Mark Twain piloted the boat at least twice, and possibly as many as five times, between St. Louis and New Orleans. His first trip may have been in late March 1860. More certainly, he piloted the boat from late May into July that year, when Wesley Jacobs was his copilot and J. Ed MONTGOMERY his captain. On June 22, he allowed the *Memphis* to crash into another boat while he dutifully waited for Captain Montgomery to take charge as the boat entered New Orleans harbor. Montgomery accepted full responsibility and earned Mark Twain's praise for his integrity. The account of this incident in chapter 49 of *Life on the Mississippi* incorrectly identifies the *Memphis* as the CRESCENT CITY.

The *Memphis* survived the CIVIL WAR to meet its end in a boiler explosion in 1866.

Civil War   Arguably the pivotal event in American history, the Civil War was fought between April 1861 and April 1865. This war might also fairly be called the pivotal event in Mark Twain's life. Indeed, it might even be argued that but for the war, there would never have been a "Mark Twain." Although his personal involvement in the conflict was slight, it forced a clear separation between his youth and his adulthood and ended any aspirations he might have had to remain a steamboat PILOT on the Mississippi River. On a national level, the war definitively ended slavery and accelerated western expansion. It also temporarily destroyed the South's economy and aggravated the South's long estrangement from the rest of the Union. Finally, the war increased the interest of the rest of the country in the South—a phenomenon that doubtless enhanced the popularity of Mark Twain's books set in the South.

Between late December 1860 and early February 1861, South Carolina, Mississippi, Florida, Alabama, Georgia and Louisiana seceded from the Union. In February, their delegates met in Montgomery, Alabama to form the Confederate States of America and elected Jefferson DAVIS president. Texas joined them a few weeks later. In March, Abraham LINCOLN was inaugurated president of the United States; one month after that, armed conflict began in South Carolina. Soon thereafter, Virginia, Arkansas, Tennessee and North Carolina left the Union for the Confederacy, bringing to 11 its membership. The status of slavery was a major issue in the war; however, though all Confederate states were slave states, not all slave states were Confederate. Several "border states," including Delaware, Maryland, Kentucky, and Mark Twain's own state, Missouri, never formally declared for the Confederacy. Missouri's sympathies were split between North and South, but the state was seized by the Union before it could choose sides.

The South won important battles during the first year, but the tide gradually shifted against it. Part of the North's grand strategy was to split the South, beginning with a wedge driven down the Mississippi River. An early Union priority was occupation of Missouri, which it had firmly under martial law by the end of August 1861. The conflict intensified as Union forces under General U. S. GRANT pushed the war farther south, leaving Missouri comparatively unscathed. After Admiral David Farragut took NEW ORLEANS in April 1862, another Union thrust moved north, joining Grant's force at VICKSBURG. With Louisiana and Mississippi safely under Union control, the Union moved to split the remaining Confederate states through Tennessee and Georgia. General William T. SHERMAN led his famous march through Georgia, then turned north to take South and North Carolina, as Grant fought Robert E. Lee in Virginia. The war effectively ended on April 9, 1865, when Lee surrendered to Grant at Appomattox, Virginia.

As the war approached, Mark Twain was constantly traveling up and down the Lower Mississippi. He was in New Orleans on January 26, 1861, the day that LOUISIANA seceded from the Union; he was also there on April 12, 1861, when news of the firing upon Fort Sumter indicated that the war had begun. Several weeks later, he paid his last visit there as a pilot and found himself out of work. The war was bringing commerce on the Mississippi to a standstill. Mark Twain's captain on the ALONZO CHILD took his boat over to Confederate service, and some of Mark Twain's former associates on the river, such as Horace BIXBY and J. Ed MONTGOMERY, turned their piloting skills to important military service; however, Mark Twain's piloting days were over. After securing passage on the NEBRASKA, one of the last boats back to St. Louis, he spent several weeks with the family of his sister Pamela Clemens MOFFETT, then returned to Hannibal.

While Missouri never formally declared for the Confederacy, its new governor, Claiborne Fox Jackson (1806–1862), called for militia volunteers early in 1861. In June Mark Twain joined 14 other young men in Hannibal to form the MARION RANGERS. By this time, Union forces were massing on the state's northern border. After two weeks of haphazard training and moving around under constant threat of Union attack, the unit disbanded without seeing any real military action. The circumstances of Mark Twain's leaving the Rangers have led to charges by some that he was a "deserter." Whatever the exact circumstances of his separation from the Rangers, it is clear that he was reticent to discuss his war service until many years after the war ended.

In the meantime, Mark Twain's brother Orion Clemens was appointed secretary of the recently established territorial government in NEVADA. On July 26, 1861, Mark Twain joined Orion in a cross-country trip to the Far West, where he remained until December 1866—well after the war had ended. Surrounded by both Northerners and Southerners throughout these years, he generally avoided discussing or writing about anything dealing with the war. At the moment that the war ended, in April 1865, he was in San Francisco.

Most of the Marion Rangers were men with whom Mark Twain had grown up in Hannibal. These included Ed Stevens, Sam BOWEN, Arch Fuqua and John ROBARDS. Others of his contemporaries to see service included Will BOWEN and John D. Meredith. Although the war did not devastate Missouri as it did the states to its south, it did have traumatic effects on many peoples' lives. Mark Twain's childhood sweetheart, Laura HAWKINS, for example, was married to a Kentucky physician, Dr. James W. Frazer. Union troops imprisoned Frazer in St. Louis because of his pro-Southern sympathies, but later released him to practice medicine. Mark Twain's brother-in-law, William A. MOFFETT, fared less well. He saw the war ruin his St. Louis business, and he died just four months after the war ended.

Many people with whom Mark Twain later associated were Civil War veterans: J. A. DALY, J. R. HAWLEY, James B. POND, Carl SCHURZ, Joseph TWICHELL and others. Associates who served as newspaper correspondents during the war included Whitelaw REID, James REDPATH, E. C. STEDMAN and Bayard TAYLOR. The author of *Uncle Tom's Cabin*, Harriet Beecher STOWE, was later Mark Twain's neighbor in Connecticut. Mark Twain had extensive contact with war veterans on the QUAKER CITY cruise in 1867. Among the veterans with whom he sailed were Dr. Abraham R. JACKSON, a Union doctor, and William R. Denny, a Confederate colonel.

Considering the seminal impact of the war on his life, Mark Twain wrote surprisingly little about it. None of his major fiction touches on it directly; however, it has been suggested that he replayed Civil War battles in *Connecticut Yankee*. His most important fiction set in America was placed before the war—an era he was inclined to idealize.

Through the early 1880s, Civil War themes figure into *The Gilded Age*, a novel that he coauthored, and only a few of his stories: "LUCRETIA SMITH'S SOLDIER," "A TRUE STORY," the Karl RITTER story and "A CURIOUS EXPERIENCE." Scattered anecdotes appear elsewhere, as in "SOME RAMBLING NOTES OF AN IDLE EXCURSION," which draws on an experience of Joseph Twichell. By the late 1870s Mark Twain was becoming increasingly outspoken about his own Civil War experience in occasional speeches. In 1885, Robert Underwood Johnson, an editor of CENTURY MAGAZINE, persuaded Mark Twain to write on his Civil War experience. The result was "THE PRIVATE HISTORY OF A CAMPAIGN THAT FAILED," an embellished account of the Marion Rangers. Fascinated by the idea that he might have confronted Grant if he had continued in military service, he tentatively titled the piece "My Campaign Against Grant." He also considered developing the story into a novel that would place Tom, Huck and Jim in the Missouri campaign.

Meanwhile, Johnson had persuaded Grant himself to write his Civil War memoirs. After writing several articles for *Century*, Grant was persuaded by Mark Twain to write his memoirs as a book for his publishing firm, Charles L. WEBSTER & COMPANY. Webster also published the war memoirs of McClellan, SHERIDAN and Sherman.

The few comments that Mark Twain makes about the war in his AUTOBIOGRAPHY are mostly perfunctory. In "THE TURNING POINT OF MY LIFE," he acknowledges that the war pushed him "ahead another stage or two toward the literary profession." His most extensive treatment of the war appears in *Life on the Mississippi*. After 20 chapters on his years as a cub pilot, chapter 21 summarizes the next two decades of his life in one page, with only a brief allusion to the war. The balance of the book, which describes his return to the river in 1882, compares many places along the river with their prewar condition. Occasionally, it offers vivid descriptions of wartime destruction, particularly in Vicksburg (chapter 26). Chapter 45 discusses the importance of the war in Southern consciousness, and the next chapter levels a stinging indictment against the novelist Walter SCOTT for helping to cause the war by encouraging archaic romanticism.

Elsewhere, Mark Twain was fascinated by the idea of undiscovered genius. He explored this theme in "CAPTAIN STORMFIELD'S VISIT TO HEAVEN," in which Lincoln, Grant, Sherman and Sheridan are cited as examples of men whose greatness would never have been discovered without the Civil War.

Civitavecchia City in ITALY. The chief seaport of ROME, Civitavecchia is 35 miles northwest of the capital city. The cruise ship QUAKER CITY was scheduled to land there, but bypassed the port after losing its clean bill of health at LEGHORN. Meanwhile, Mark Twain and several friends avoided quarantine problems by taking a French steamer from Leghorn to Civitavecchia on July 26, 1867, before continuing to Rome by train. Mark Twain saw just enough of Civitavecchia to call it, in chapter 25 of *Innocents Abroad*, "the finest nest of dirt, vermin and ignorance" he had yet seen. Three months after he passed through the city, French forces occupied it in the ongoing struggle for Italian unification.

Clagett, William Horace (September 21, 1838, Upper Marlboro, Maryland–August 3, 1901, Spokane, Washington) Attorney and politician. Clagett and Mark Twain became friends when Clagett was studying law in KEOKUK, Iowa, where he was admitted to the bar in 1858. He practiced law there until early 1861, when he got married. The day of his wedding, he started across the Plains with a brother and took up law in NEVADA. In December 1861 he joined Mark Twain's prospecting party to HUMBOLDT and remained in UNIONVILLE as a notary public. That same month he bought a horse from Mark Twain that may have been the "Genuine Mexican Plug" described in *Roughing It* (chapter 24). The following October his wife joined him there after coming from Iowa with Mollie CLEMENS. Clagett later served in both houses of Nevada's state legislature, then resettled in Montana, where he was elected a delegate to Congress (1871–73) before that territory became a state. *Roughing It* mentions him by name in chapters 27 and 29, but errs in calling him a Montana congressman. Clagett is also the source of the story about Henry Clay DEAN in chapter 57 of *Life on the Mississippi*.

Clarence (Amyas le Poulet) Character in *Connecticut Yankee*. The novel's most important purely invented male character—apart from the Yankee Hank MORGAN himself—Clarence is a 15-year-old court page boy when Hank meets him in chapter 2. Hank immediately dubs him "Clarence"—possibly after Edmund Clarence STEDMAN—and does not mention his real name, Amyas le Poulet, until chapter 13. Mark Twain probably takes this name from Sir Amyas Paulet (or Poulet) (c. 1536–1588), an English ambassador to France who was famous as the "keeper" of Mary Queen of Scots during the last two years of her life. Paulet was related to Lord ST. JOHN (Sir William Paulet) of *The Prince and the Pauper*. In several ways, Clarence mirrors the historical Paulet in being Hank Morgan's "keeper." He is with Hank from his arrival at Camelot until his end at Merlin's

Cave. He helps him in prison, becomes his right-hand man, rescues him from execution, and finally sees to the concealment of his body and the completion of his manuscript. Also like the historical Paulet, Clarence probably does not outlive his charge for long, as the novel ends with him in an apparently hopeless situation.

Clarence has a complex combination of traits. As an irreverent scoffer, he is a foil to Hank, much as Mark Twain's "Mr. BROWN" was in his early travel writings. Clarence is wittier than Hank and enjoys his greatest comic triumph when he proposes replacing England's ruling family with a cat dynasty (chapter 40). Although Clarence has many modern attitudes to go with his natural skepticism, he also has many of the superstitions of his times. For example, when Hank claims to be able to blot out the sun early in the narrative, Clarence collapses in fright (chapter 5).

Clarence befriends Hank at court because he is naturally outgoing and talkative. On his first appearance, he closely resembles a young American in *A Tramp Abroad* who barrages the narrator with questions without waiting to hear the answers (chapter 27). After seven years pass, Clarence is taking on characteristics of a young Mark Twain, writing irreverent articles in the CAMELOT WEEKLY HOSANNAH, which Hank has trained him to edit. By the end of the narrative, he has adopted most of Hank's views and is the only person in the kingdom older than 17 who stands by Hank during the INTERDICT.

Hank's description of Clarence gives him androgynous characteristics that inspired the illustrator Dan BEARD to model him on the actress Sarah BERNHARDT.

Since he is not a fully rounded character, Clarence has not fared well in dramatic adaptations. In most films, his character simply disappears, with some of his functions distributed among other characters. When Clarence does appear in a film, he usually bears little resemblance to Mark Twain's character. Film actors who have played him include Charles Gordon (1921), Frank Albertson (1931), Rodney Bewes (1979) and Bryce Hamnet (1989).

Clark, Charles Heber (July 11, 1847, Berlin, Maryland–August 10, 1915, Conshohocken, Pennsylvania) Journalist who wrote humorous stories as "Max Adeler." Best known for his sketches in *Out of the Hurly Burly* (1874), Clark also published a novella that treats many of the same themes as Mark Twain's *Connecticut Yankee*. Clark's 23,000-word fantasy, originally published in England as "Professor Baffin's Adventures" in *An Old Fogey and Other Stories* (1881), appeared in America as the title story in *The Fortunate Island and Other Stories* (1882).

Clark's fantasy concerns an American sociology professor, E. L. Baffin, and his daughter Matilda, who happen upon a floating island in the North Atlantic after their passenger ship sinks. The island is a remnant of King ARTHUR's England on which 100,000 people preserve ancient chivalric customs. Also an inventor, Baffin is carrying a large stock of modern apparatuses in his baggage. As an outspoken antimonarchist, he wants to modernize the island by introducing telephones, telegraphs, railroads and other improvements. Like *Connecticut Yankee*'s Hank MORGAN, he is taken for a wizard when he does such simple things as igniting matches and smoking. Baffin also resembles Hank in struggling with a suit of armor—particularly its lack of pockets; using a revolver against belligerent knights; and being drawn toward marriage with an airheaded damsel. To rescue a woman from a castle, he builds a small steamboat, then booby-traps it to blow up her abductors. The story ends when Baffin bumps his head and awakens to find that he has been dreaming.

Just before *Connecticut Yankee* was published in December 1889, Clark sent Mark Twain a telegram charging that the novel plagiarized "The Fortunate Island." Mark Twain responded to the charge early the following year in an interview he gave to the *New York World*. In a rambling discourse on the universality of plagiarism, he implied that he had not seen "The Fortunate Island" until recently. While it seems likely that Mark Twain was influenced to some extent by Clark's fantasy, Clark himself might equally have been influenced by Mark Twain's earlier sketch "THE GREAT REVOLUTION IN PITCAIRN."

Charles Heber Clark was not related to Charles Hopkins Clark (1848–1926), the *Hartford Courant* editor who helped prepare MARK TWAIN'S LIBRARY OF HUMOR. Mark Twain's early notes for this anthology indicate that he intended including a "Max Adeler" piece, but Charles Heber Clark was not represented when the book appeared in 1888.

Clay, Henry (April 12, 1777, Hanover County, Kentucky–June 29, 1852, Washington, D.C.) The most distinguished KENTUCKY politician of his time, Clay was Speaker of the U.S. House of Representatives several times, an author of the Missouri Compromise (1819), a cabinet member and senator, and a candidate for president of the United States three times. Huck finds a copy of Clay's speeches in the GRANGERFORDS' home in chapter 17 of *Huckleberry Finn*—circumstantial evidence that the Grangerfords themselves live in Kentucky.

Clemens, Benjamin (June 8, 1832, Pall Mall, Tennessee–May 12, 1842, Hannibal, Missouri) A brother to whom Mark Twain was close as a young boy, Benjamin was remembered as a sweet child who died suddenly after a brief illness. Mark Twain was just six years old at the time, but never forgot the grief Benjamin's death brought to the family—a memory made more poignant because it was the only moment he ever saw his parents kiss. The location of Benjamin's burial site in Hannibal is no longer known.

Clemens, Clara Langdon (June 8, 1874, Elmira, New York–November 19, 1962, San Diego, California) The second of Mark Twain's three daughters, Clara was the only child to survive him. Shortly after she was born, the family nicknamed her "Bay," mimicking her sister Susy's pronunciation of "baby." Clara received most of her education at home from her mother, governesses and tutors. She also spent a year at Hartford's public high school and attended a BERLIN boarding school for American girls while her family was staying in Italy (1892–93). More willing to travel than her sisters, Clara sailed to America with her father in August 1893 and returned to Italy on her own to rejoin her mother and sisters. Two years later, she was the only daughter to accompany her parents on Mark Twain's round-the-world lecture tour; *Following the Equator* alludes to her presence on the tour, but does not mention her name. Clara's desire to study piano under Theodor Leschetizky (1830–1915) was a primary reason that the family settled in VIENNA in late 1897. She met her future husband, Ossip GABRILOWITSCH, a fellow piano student there, but gave up the piano in early 1899 and turned to singing with the goal of becoming a professional contralto.

After the family returned to America in 1900, Clara continued studying singing in New York City. She went to Europe on her own in early 1902 to see Gabrilowitsch, but both her musical plans and her relationship with Gabrilowitsch were disrupted by family problems after she returned home in the fall. Over the next several years, she spent much of her time helping to nurse her invalid mother and run the household. After her mother died in 1904, Clara had a nervous breakdown and spent much of the following year under treatment in a Connecticut sanatorium. In later years, she found solace in various metaphysical beliefs and mental science and joined the CHRISTIAN SCIENCE church. Clara rejoined her father in his New York City home in November 1905 and resumed her role as his household manager. In the fall of 1906, Mark Twain let her select the site in REDDING, Connecticut on which he built his last home. Meanwhile, Clara sang occasionally in informal concerts and enjoyed her first major success in a recital at Norfolk, Massachusetts.

In addition to running her father's household and acting as his hostess, Clara advised him on his social behavior. For example, she objected to his new fondness for wearing WHITE SUITS in public and wrote instructions for his behavior when he went to England in June 1907. The following year, Clara revisited Germany to study singing. When she returned in October, she took an apartment in New York City, but continued to oversee her father's household. She disapproved of Isabel LYON and Ralph ASHCROFT's role in her father's business affairs and persuaded him to expel them in early 1909. Later that year, she renewed her relationship with Gabrilowitsch, whom she brought to Stormfield to recuperate after an operation. In September, they both performed at a benefit for the Redding library that Mark Twain established and announced their engagement. Joseph TWICHELL conducted their wedding ceremony at Stormfield on October 6, 1909. The couple then left for Europe, where they intended to settle permanently. The following April they were back in Redding, four days before Mark Twain died.

As her father's sole heir, Clara remained at Stormfield to deal with the estate. After delivering her only child, Nina GABRILOWITSCH, at Stormfield in August 1910, she went back to Europe with Ossip. World War I made it impossible for Gabrilowitsch, a Russian national, to work in Germany, so they returned to America and eventually settled in Detroit. Clara abandoned her professional singing ambitions, but occasionally sang on Ossip's concert tours. She was also active in Detroit theater groups and played Joan of Arc in productions of G. B. Shaw's *Saint Joan* and an adaptation of her father's *Joan of Arc*. On her first visit to Hannibal, Missouri in January 1924, she gave a singing recital to help raise funds for the Mark Twain Memorial Park Association. She revisited Hannibal in 1935 to help open the museum now run by the MARK TWAIN HOME FOUNDATION.

After Gabrilowitsch died in 1936, Clara moved to the Hollywood Hills in Los Angeles, where she enjoyed a comfortable living off the estates of her father and husband. She married another Russian musician, Jacques SAMOSSOUD, on May 11, 1944. Seven years later, they moved to La Jolla, near San Diego. In 1962, Clara died there at the age of 88—a year older than Mark Twain's mother had been at her death.

Clara played an important role in the development of her father's posthumous image. When Elizabeth Wallace published a book about Mark Twain's time in BERMUDA, for example, Clara made sure that it included no embarrassing pictures of her father with members of his ANGELFISH Club. Clara had a close relationship with Mark Twain's literary executor, A. B. PAINE, who complied with her desire to preserve her father's image as a sweet, wholesome humorist.

After Paine died, Clara frequently fought with his successor, Bernard DEVOTO, a professional scholar who rejected Paine's quiet censorship. She resisted DeVoto's publication of MARK TWAIN IN ERUPTION, claiming to find many passages in it that would offend relatives of people Mark Twain criticized. DeVoto published that book with minimal changes, but Clara suppressed his edition of LETTERS FROM THE EARTH until shortly before she died. Meanwhile, DeVoto quit his editorial position in frustration.

Clara herself wrote *My Father: Mark Twain* (1931), an homage whose chief value lies in its firsthand accounts of Mark Twain's world tour and last years. She also published *My Husband: Gabrilowitsch* (1938) and *Awake to a Perfect Day; My Experience with Christian Science* (1956). Her will, written in 1958, left the bulk of her father's papers to the University of California, which built the MARK TWAIN PAPERS project around them, and created the MARK TWAIN FOUNDATION.

Clemens, Cyril Coniston (July 14, 1902, St. Louis, Missouri–) President of the INTERNATIONAL MARK TWAIN SOCIETY. Born in ST. LOUIS five and a half weeks after Mark Twain's last visit there, Clemens shares a common ancestor with Mark Twain in Ezekiel Clemens (1696–c. 1778)—a connection that makes them third cousins, twice removed. Cyril's father, Dr. James Ross Clemens, knew Mark Twain when both men were in LONDON in 1897. When James Clemens became ill, a rumor arose that Mark Twain was dying and a reporter visited Mark Twain to learn if the rumor was true. Mark Twain explained that he had been confused with his relative, who was now well, adding that "the report of my death was an exaggeration."

After graduating from St. Louis's Washington University, Cyril Clemens lived off his private income and devoted his life to promoting Mark Twain by giving lectures, writing pamphlets and collecting manuscripts. In 1927, he became president of the Mark Twain Society in Kirkwood, Missouri. He soon transformed this informal body into the International Mark Twain Society by diligently inviting famous statesmen and literary figures to accept honorary offices. In 1936, he launched the *Mark Twain Quarterly,* which later became the MARK TWAIN JOURNAL. A sampling of his largely anecdotal books about Mark Twain includes *Mark Twain the Letter Writer* (1932), *Mark Twain and Mussolini* (1934), *Mark Twain Wit and Wisdom* (1935), *My Cousin, Mark Twain* (1939) and *Mark Twain's Jest Book* (1963). He also wrote brief books on Petroleum V. NASBY, B. P. SHILLABER, Dan BEARD and Harry S Truman.

Clemens, Henry (July 13, 1838, Florida, Missouri–June 21, 1858, Memphis, Tennessee) The last child of John and Jane Clemens, Henry was probably the sibling to whom Mark Twain was closest in his youth. Their closeness doubtless was reinforced by the death of their 10-year-old brother Benjamin Clemens in 1842. Despite their closeness, their relationship was occasionally tempestuous. Mark Twain tells an often-repeated anecdote about a feud he had with Henry, culminating in his dropping a watermelon rind on Henry's head from a second-story window. Their relationship is mirrored in Tom Sawyer's relationship with Sid SAWYER in *Tom Sawyer.* Mark Twain's AUTOBIOGRAPHY records that Henry "is Sid in *Tom Sawyer.* But Sid was not Henry. Henry was a very much finer and better boy than ever Sid was."

When their older brother Orion Clemens moved to MUSCATINE, Iowa in 1853, Henry followed him and worked as an apprentice printer. Henry also accompanied Orion to KEOKUK, where Orion resettled in June 1856. Mark Twain rejoined his brothers there around this same time. He and Henry worked together as printers until Mark Twain left for Cincinnati in October.

In February 1857 Mark Twain began his apprenticeship as a steamboat PILOT. A year later, Henry joined him on the PENNSYLVANIA, on which he signed as an unpaid "mud clerk." Mark Twain later left the boat after an altercation with a pilot named William BROWN, whose abuse of Henry he could not abide. Shortly afterward, the *Pennsylvania* exploded near MEMPHIS. While rushing to the scene of the disaster, Mark Twain heard contradictory reports about his brother's condition. Henry, it turned out, had severely damaged his lungs inhaling steam. Mark Twain arrived in time to be at his side when he died; there was some question as to whether Henry died from his injury or from an improperly administered dose of morphine. In any case, Mark Twain felt himself personally responsible for Henry's death, since it was he who had encouraged him to work on the river. He tells the story of Henry's death in some detail in chapter 20 of *Life on the Mississippi.* Shortly after Henry died, Orion wrote a letter eulogizing Henry in which he compared Henry's temperament to that of their sister, Pamela Clemens MOFFETT.

Henry was buried alongside John M. Clemens in Hannibal's Baptist cemetery. In 1876 Mark Twain arranged to have Henry's and his father's remains moved to MOUNT OLIVET CEMETERY. The date of Henry's death—June 21—is the date on which Hank MORGAN's scheduled burning at the stake is interrupted by an ECLIPSE in *Connecticut Yankee.*

Clemens, Jane Lampton (June 18, 1803, Lexington, Kentucky–October 27, 1890, Keokuk, Iowa) Mark Twain's mother. The daughter of Benjamin LAMPTON, Jane Lampton married John M. Clemens on May 6, 1823. She may have married out of spite, after having been spurned by a man named Richard Barrett, for her marriage was noticeably lacking in affection despite her own demonstrable personal warmth.

Of the seven children she bore, she outlived all but three, and she was widowed in 1847. By then, she had four living children and was supported by the two oldest until Mark Twain was able to contribute to her support. In 1851, her daughter Pamela Clemens MOFFETT left Hannibal; Mark Twain left two years later. When her oldest son, Orion Clemens, moved to MUSCATINE, Iowa in 1853, Jane accompanied him with her youngest son, Henry. After Orion relocated to KEOKUK the following year, she moved in with Pamela and her husband in ST. LOUIS. Mark Twain often saw her there while piloting on the Mississippi River and took her to New Orleans on a steamboat excursion in 1861.

Shortly after Mark Twain settled in Buffalo, New York in 1870, his mother moved to nearby FREDONIA, with Pamela, who by then was widowed. Around 1883, she made her final move, to Keokuk, where she lived with Orion for the rest of her life. After leaving Hannibal, Mark Twain corresponded with his mother regularly, but saw her infrequently—usually while on LECTURE tours. In January 1885, for example, he passed through Keokuk on a tour and his mother heard him and G. W. CABLE do readings at the Opera House. For her part, she visited his Hartford home at least twice. Mark Twain last saw her in August 1890, three months before she died, and he attended her funeral in Hannibal.

Jane Clemens had a prodigious influence on Mark Twain's life. He remembered her as a cheerful, courageous, and warm-hearted person who could find the good in anybody. In sharp contrast to his father, his mother was affectionate and fun-loving. She was also a master storyteller who doubtless inspired him by example. Van Wyck BROOKS and others argue that Jane Clemens exerted a repressive influence on Mark Twain's artistic development by making him pledge as a boy to be as upright and industrious as his father had been. Apart from the question of whether Jane Clemens *wanted* her son to be like her dour, unloving husband, Mark Twain's later behavior scarcely indicates that he was attempting to live by such an oath.

Traits of Jane Clemens can be seen in several of Mark Twain's fictional creations, most notably Aunt POLLY of *Tom Sawyer.* Her energetic tomboy spirit and courage can also be found in Hellfire Hotchkiss and JOAN OF ARC. Shortly after she died, Mark Twain wrote "Jane Lampton Clemens," a tribute that remained unpublished until A. B. PAINE inserted a truncated version in *Mark Twain's Autobiography* (1924); the complete text appears in Walter BLAIR's *Hannibal, Huck & Tom* (1969).

Clemens, (Jean) Jane Lampton (July 26, 1880, Elmira, New York–December 24, 1909, Redding, Connecticut)

The youngest daughter of Mark Twain was named after her paternal grandmother but was always called Jean. After contracting scarlet fever at two, she remained in delicate health and later also suffered from epilepsy. She may have suffered her first seizures in late 1890, shortly after both her grandmothers died; however, her condition was not diagnosed as epilepsy until six years later—shortly after her sister Susy died. A search for medical relief then became a constant family concern. In 1899, Mark Twain took the family to Jonas KELLGREN in SWEDEN primarily to have Jean treated.

Years of nearly constant traveling after 1891 left Jean with little opportunity to do things on her own. As she grew increasingly despondent over her lack of a vocation and her father's resistance to her developing romantic relationships with men, she channeled her energy into animal rights issues and hobbies. Her epilepsy worsened after her mother's death in 1904; she was in and out of sanitoriums over the next five years and saw little of her father. During epileptic attacks in late 1905 and early 1906, she twice tried to kill housekeeper Katy LEARY. In September 1908, she went to Germany with a friend to seek treatment. Around the following April, she moved into STORMFIELD and replaced Isabel LYON as her father's private secretary.

The day before Christmas in 1909—a few days after Mark Twain returned from BERMUDA—Jean died in her morning bath, apparently the victim of a heart attack suffered during a seizure. Too ill to attend her funeral in Elmira, Mark Twain spent the next few days writing "THE DEATH OF JEAN"—the last substantial work he ever completed.

Two television productions have focused on Mark Twain's relationship with Jean. Kay Howell played Jean in MARK TWAIN: BENEATH THE LAUGHTER (1979) and Talia Shire played her in MARK TWAIN AND ME (1991).

Clemens, John Marshall (August 11, 1798, Campbell County, Virginia–March 24, 1847, Hannibal, Missouri)

Mark Twain's father. The oldest child of Samuel B. CLEMENS and Pamelia Moorman, Clemens was named after John Marshall, the VIRGINIA politician who became chief justice of the United States in 1801. Clemens's family called him "Marshall," but he later signed his name "John M. Clemens." After his father died in 1805, his mother resettled in Adair County, KENTUCKY; in 1809 she married Simon Hancock (1774–1856), with whom she had four more children.

Clemens went to work as a clerk when his mother remarried, but managed to study law under a local attorney and was licensed to practice in 1822. After turning 21, he spent most of what he had inherited from his father's estate to reimburse his stepfather for raising him. With what was left, he married Jane Lampton on May 6, 1823. Two years later, they moved across the state line to GAINESBORO, Tennessee, where their first child, Orion, was born in July 1825. After another two years, they moved east to FENTRESS COUNTY and settled in JAMESTOWN, where they had three more children. Clemens built the town's first substantial structure and became the county's first circuit court clerk, while maintaining a law practice and occasionally serving as acting attorney general. Meanwhile, he began accumulating the thousands of acres that became the family's "TENNESSEE LAND."

Around 1831, Clemens moved his family to THREE FORKS OF WOLF RIVER for several months, then to nearby PALL MALL. In mid-1835, he followed his brother-in-law John QUARLES to FLORIDA, Missouri, where Mark Twain was born in November. There Clemens ran a store with Quarles until he opened his own dry goods store in 1837. That year saw the peak of his fortunes. The state legislature put him on a board promoting navigation on the Salt River and he headed a commission to promote a local railroad; he also became a Monroe County judge. After several years, however, he suspected that Florida would not develop as he had hoped. In 1839, he moved his family to the more promising Mississippi River town of Hannibal, where he set up a general store and practiced law.

Clemens's financial fortunes continued to decline in Hannibal. In 1841, he had to mortgage his land and sell off the last family slave. Meanwhile, he busied himself in civic affairs. He sat on a circuit court jury that sent three abolitionists to the penitentiary in September 1841 and was a justice of the peace by the following year. He supplemented his income with the meager fees from routine judicial duties, such as issuing subpoenas and taking depositions. Occasionally, he was involved in more dramatic cases. In *Innocents Abroad,* Mark Twain recalls a moment in 1843 when he sneaked into his father's office at night and discovered the corpse of a murder victim that had been left on the floor (chapter 18). Clemens also took depositions after William OWSLEY murdered Sam SMARR in 1845, an incident that inspired SHERBURN's murder of BOGGS in *Huckleberry Finn.*

After being cheated in a business deal in 1846, Clemens hoped to revive his fortunes by being elected circuit court clerk. Though considered a shoo-in for the post, he campaigned hard in cold weather, contracted pneumonia and died in March 1847. His sudden passing left his family in straitened circumstances from which they did not fully escape until Mark Twain became a success decades later.

Although Clemens failed in all his commercial ventures, he was respected as a judge. Mark Twain remembered him as stern, honest and distant; he never saw him laugh or openly display affection. After growing up with an exaggerated notion of his father's legal power, he later used him as a model for such characters as *Tom Sawyer*'s Judge THATCHER and *Pudd'nhead Wilson*'s Judge DRISCOLL—who, like Clemens, is fiercely proud of his Virginia ancestry. "VILLAGERS OF 1840–3" calls Clemens "Judge Carpenter"—the same name used in "Hellfire Hotchkiss." In addition to remembering his father in many passages of his AUTOBIOGRAPHY, Mark Twain discusses him in *Life on the Mississippi* (chapter 4) and *Following the Equator* (chapter 38).

Clemens's body, originally buried in a cemetery near Hannibal's CARDIFF HILL, was moved to MOUNT OLIVET CEMETERY in 1876. The building in which he practiced law was saved from demolition by Warner Brothers when it was making THE ADVENTURES OF MARK TWAIN during the 1940s. The studio bought the building and gave it to the city with funds to repair it. A decade later, it was moved to Hill Street, across from the Mark Twain BOYHOOD HOME, where it was restored as the "John Marshall Clemens Law Office" and opened to public viewing in 1959.

Clemens, Langdon (November 7, 1870, Buffalo, New York–June 2, 1872, Hartford, Connecticut) Mark Twain's first child and only son. Born just nine months and five days after his parents married, Langdon was—like his father—a premature baby. His mother's health had been shaky throughout 1870; her condition worsened after the deaths of her father in August and her friend Emma NYE in September. In October she nearly miscarried; when she delivered Langdon in November, he weighed four and a half pounds and was not expected to live. Through his first year, Langdon

had a constant cold and cried incessantly, unless dosed with laudanum. His development was so slow that he never learned to walk in his 19 months of life. His death in June 1872 was attributed to diphtheria, but Mark Twain later blamed himself for having allowed Langdon's blanket to slip off in cold weather. Langdon died two and a half months after his sister Susy was born. He is buried in Elmira's WOODLAWN CEMETERY; his death mask is on display in Hannibal's Mark Twain Museum.

Clemens, Margaret L. (May 31, 1830, Jamestown, Tennessee–August 17, 1839, Florida, Missouri) Mark Twain's sister. The fourth child of John M. and Jane L. Clemens, Margaret died when Mark Twain was just under four years old. Her death, attributed to "bilious fever," was the last of several misfortunes the family endured in FLORIDA before moving to Hannibal three months later.

Clemens, Mary Eleanor (Mollie) Stotts (April 4, 1834–January 15, 1904, Keokuk, Iowa) Mark Twain's sister-in-law. The daughter of a childhood friend of Jane Lampton Clemens, Mollie Stotts married Orion Clemens on December 19, 1854, when Orion was visiting KEOKUK, Iowa. After a brief residence in MUSCATINE, the couple returned to Keokuk, where Mark Twain spent considerable time with them while employed in Orion's printing office. He came to know Orion's wife as "Sister Mollie." Mollie delivered her only child, Jennie, on September 14, 1855—a moment when Mark Twain was in Keokuk.

In July 1861, Orion left for NEVADA to take up his appointment as territorial secretary. Mollie and Jennie joined him there 15 months later, after taking the route through Central America and California with the wife of W. H. CLAGETT. In CARSON CITY, Mollie relished her role as wife of a leading Nevada official and often welcomed Mark Twain as a houseguest during his visits to the capital. In May 1864, however, he embarrassed her by publishing a burlesque article in the VIRGINIA CITY TERRITORIAL ENTERPRISE suggesting that proceeds from a SANITARY COMMISSION ball that she sponsored would go to an eastern miscegenation society. Meanwhile, Jennie died of cerebrospinal meningitis ("spotted fever") on February 1, 1864.

In later years, when Orion was struggling to make a living, Mollie stood by him and encouraged many of his ill-fated schemes. Although Mark Twain liked Mollie, he regarded her as vain and ambitious and may have used her as a model for Aleck FOSTER in "THE $30,000 BEQUEST." He learned of her death while he was in Florence, Italy, in early 1904, and kept the news from his wife Livy, who died five months later.

Clemens, Olivia (Livy) Langdon (November 27, 1845, Elmira, New York–June 5, 1904, Florence, Italy) Mark Twain's wife. The second of three children of Jervis and Olivia LANGDON, Livy was born shortly after

Cameo portrait of Olivia Clemens, with whom Mark Twain purportedly fell in love when he saw this ivory miniature in 1867. (Courtesy, Mark Twain Papers, the Bancroft Library).

her parents settled in ELMIRA, New York. Thanks to her father's booming coal business, her family was soon on its way to becoming Elmira's richest—at the same moment that Mark Twain's family was sliding into poverty in Missouri. Livy's early life was quiet and comfortable. Educated at seminary schools until she was 16, she enjoyed reading but had no special training in any field.

Through the 36 years that Livy knew Mark Twain, her health was fragile at best, and often quite poor. Two years after she died, Mark Twain dictated a passage in his AUTOBIOGRAPHY attributing her frailty to a fall on ice when she was 16. Claiming that her fall left her partly paralyzed and bedridden for two years, he added that her case seemed hopeless until a notorious quack, Dr. James Rogers Newton, effected a mind-cure. A. B. PAINE's inclusion of this story in *Mark Twain, A Biography* (1912) later gave Van Wyck BROOKS fuel to argue that Livy was a neurotic whose condition drove her to exercise an essentially negative influence on Mark Twain's creative powers. Later scholars have challenged Brooks's argument, while agreeing that Livy's ailments were more mental than physical. Recent research, however, indicates not only that the story of her falling on ice is unsubstantiated, but that her disability began at least

two years before she was 16. From age 14 until she was about 20, she was treated for a medical problem that can now be tentatively diagnosed as tuberculosis of the spine, or Pott's disease. Whatever Mark Twain himself really believed about her, Livy's frailty probably had a physical basis.

The same month that Mark Twain dictated his famous story about Livy's falling on ice, he also dictated a passage about how he saw her for the first time in an ivory miniature that her brother, Charles LANGDON, carried on the QUAKER CITY in 1867. Mark Twain finally met Livy at the end of that year, when he dined with the Langdon family in NEW YORK CITY and took Livy to hear Charles DICKENS read. Over the following year, he courted her during several visits to Elmira. Both his contemporary correspondence and later memoirs show that he saw Livy as a paragon of genteel refinement and feminine delicacy. She was the opposite of how he saw himself, and he appealed to her to guide and "reform" him. After Livy rejected his first marriage proposal in September 1868, he had a genuine fall on ice of his own, which gave him an excuse to prolong his stay in Elmira. After Livy finally accepted his proposal in November, her parents approved the engagement— on the condition that it be kept secret while her father checked Mark Twain's references. In February 1869, their engagement was formally announced; their MAR-RIAGE took place on February 2, 1870.

Livy began married life in BUFFALO, New York, where Mark Twain purchased a part interest in the BUFFALO EXPRESS with money that her father had lent him. Her father also set her up comfortably in a large furnished house with servants. Nevertheless, her first year of married life was disastrous. Her health broke under the strain of seeing her father die from cancer in August and watching her friend Emma NYE die in her home a month later. After nearly suffering a miscarriage in October, she delivered her first child, Langdon Clemens, prematurely in November. By her wedding anniversary, she had typhoid fever and both she and her baby appeared on the edge of death. Soon afterward, Mark Twain pulled up stakes and took Livy and Langdon back to Elmira, where Livy's sister Susan CRANE helped tend her and Langdon until they relocated to Hartford.

By the time Langdon died in June 1872, Livy had given birth to the first of three daughters, Susy Olivia Clemens. Through the couple's first four years of marriage, Mark Twain was often away from home for long periods—on LECTURE tours and trips to ENGLAND—and he began making frequent business trips out of town. During two decades in Hartford, Livy managed a large staff of servants in a house that she helped architect E. T. POTTER design, and she oversaw the feeding and entertainment of a steady stream of guests. A substantial inheritance from her father's estate enabled the family to live lavishly, while giving her husband the freedom to write and publish at his own pace and invest in enterprises such as Charles L. WEBSTER & COMPANY and the PAIGE COMPOSITOR. When his publishing company went bankrupt in 1894, Livy was declared the primary creditor; the family's home and Mark Twain's literary copyrights were saved by being put in her name.

Meanwhile, the family closed down the Hartford house and went to Europe in 1891, expecting to return in about a year. Mark Twain crossed the Atlantic five times over the next four years, but Livy did not return to America with him until 1895. After resting in Elmira that year, she and her second daughter, Clara, joined his round-the-world lecture tour that resulted in *Following the Equator*. At the end of the tour in England in August 1896, she and Clara returned to America to check on Susy's deteriorating health, but arrived shortly after she died, then went back to England with her youngest daughter, Jean. Susy's death was a staggering blow. Livy never returned to the Hartford house. The death also put a strain on Livy's relationship with her husband and contributed to the wanderlust that prevented them from settling long in one place.

In April 1902, a year and a half after the family returned to America and settled temporarily in RIVERDALE, New York, Livy arranged to buy a house in TARRYTOWN, New York that was to become the family's first permanent home in 13 years. A precipitous decline in her health kept the family from ever occupying the house, however. They spent the summer of 1902 in YORK HARBOR, Maine, where on medical advice, Livy had long periods isolated from her husband. Over the next year, her health continued to decline, and Mark Twain was rarely allowed to see her. After doctors advised Livy to seek a warmer climate, the family moved to FLORENCE, Italy in late 1903. Livy died there on June 5, 1904. Mark Twain returned her remains to Elmira, where she was buried in WOODLAWN CEMETERY.

Mark Twain clearly loved and respected Livy, but the full nature of his feelings toward her is puzzling. He praised her character and the joy of being married so excessively that he often seems as sincere as Hank MORGAN, when the hero of *Connecticut Yankee* describes being married to the simple-minded SANDY as the "dearest and perfectest comradeship that ever was" (chapter 41). It is difficult to separate what Mark Twain really felt from what he *wanted* to feel; if he treasured Livy's comradeship as much as he often said, why did he spend so much time away from her?

From the time that Livy became engaged to Mark Twain, she helped edit his books. Much has been said about the extent to which she influenced his writing, but her contributions were confined mostly to proofreading, recommending occasional modifications of language and trying to discourage ventures into coarse or profane directions. While it is impossible to know what Mark Twain *might* have written had he never married Livy, what he *did* write shows only superficial evidence of her influence. As is often observed, he would not change anything in a manuscript that *he* did not want to change.

Under various guises, Livy herself appears occasionally within Mark Twain's writings. She is Mrs. MCWILLIAMS in three stories about domestic woes, and all Mark Twain's stories about EVE are homages to her. Portia LANGHAM of "THE £1,000,000 BANK-NOTE" is modeled on Livy, just as Henry ADAMS's courtship of Portia bears a striking resemblance to Mark Twain's own courtship of Livy. The notion of a suitor having to impress a prospective father-in-law by showing substantial income and suitable references is also a theme in "THE CANVASSER'S TALE" and "THE CAPITOLINE VENUS."

Clemens, Orion (July 17, 1825, Gainesboro, Tennessee–December 11, 1897, Keokuk, Iowa) Mark Twain's oldest brother. After John M. Clemens died in 1847, Orion became head of the family. Though intelligent, honest and hard-working, he was an unstable dreamer who inherited his father's aptitude for failure. Ten years and vast temperamental differences separated him from

Orion Clemens at 55, when he was working for Elisha Bliss in Hartford. (Courtesy, Mark Twain Papers, the Bancroft Library)

his younger brother Sam, but their lives remained intertwined and they were warm friends to the end, even though Mark Twain had to support Orion through his last decades.

Orion was nearly 15 when his family moved to Hannibal. He clerked in his father's general store, whose failure he helped assure through generous extensions of credit to people who could not pay. In the early 1840s, he apprenticed to a local newspaper, then went to ST. LOUIS to work. There he began exhibiting eccentricities that his brother would later weave into fiction. For example, Orion once took his printing career so seriously that he tried patterning his life on the austere precepts that Ben FRANKLIN describes in his autobiography. Nevertheless, he was practical enough to forge a valuable friendship with the attorney Edward BATES, in whose office he began studying the law.

Around 1849, Orion returned to Hannibal and bought a small weekly newspaper, the HANNIBAL JOURNAL, which he converted into the HANNIBAL WESTERN UNION. In January 1851, Mark Twain went to work for the paper, where he began his journalistic career by writing occasional sketches. Mark Twain also occasionally ran the paper on his own when Orion was out of town—as when he was away trying to sell the family's TENNESSEE LAND. With imagination and irreverence that Orion neither understood nor appreciated at the time, Mark Twain boosted circulation with satirical attacks on local personages. These efforts led to clashes with Orion, who never paid him anyway, so he struck out on his own in June 1853 and made his way to the East Coast. Meanwhile, Orion had so reduced his newspaper's subscription and advertising rates that he was living hand to mouth. In September, he sold out and moved to MUSCATINE, Iowa, where he started the *Muscatine Journal,* in which he published Mark Twain's letters from the East.

On December 19, 1854, Orion married Mollie Stotts of KEOKUK, Iowa, where they settled the following June. There he bought the tiny Ben Franklin Book and Job Office and concentrated on printing. Mark Twain and Henry Clemens joined him there about a month later. Once again, however, Orion was unable to pay wages, so Mark Twain went to CINCINNATI in October 1856. As unsuccessful at printing as he had been at journalism, Orion was soon reduced to living with his in-laws. His fortunes took a dramatic turn for the better after Abraham LINCOLN was elected president in 1860. Since Orion had campaigned hard for Lincoln, Edward Bates—Lincoln's new attorney general—got him appointed secretary of the new territory of NEVADA at a salary of $1,800 a year. By this time, Mark Twain had become the family's chief support, thanks to his budding career as a Mississippi steamboat PILOT. Ironically, the forces that led to Lincoln's election and Orion's opportunity in the West also brought the CIVIL WAR that ended Mark Twain's piloting career by killing off commercial steamboating on the Mississippi. The timing was fortunate, however, since Mark Twain was not only happy to go

west with his brother, but was able to pay for both their passages. On July 18, 1861, they left St. Louis together and went to ST. JOSEPH, from which they crossed the plains by STAGECOACH to Nevada.

After arriving in CARSON CITY, Mark Twain was nominally Orion's unpaid private secretary, but the job gave him little to do and he soon drifted off to explore MINING opportunities. As Orion helped organize the new government, he subsidized his brother's mining ventures in return for a share of profits that never materialized. After Orion had been in Nevada a year, his wife Mollie and daughter Jennie (who would die in February 1864) joined him and he had an expensive house built in Carson City. Around the same time, Mark Twain became a reporter in nearby VIRGINIA CITY and often visited Orion's home.

During three and a quarter years in office, Orion occasionally acted as governor during James W. NYE's absences and built a solid reputation for honesty and impartiality. His popularity was such that when Nevada was being rushed into statehood in 1864, he was considered a shoo-in to be elected its first secretary of state. Unfortunately, he had what Mark Twain later called a "spasm of virtue" and decided it would be improper to attend the Republicans' nominating convention; he also suddenly adopted an unpopular anti-whiskey stand. Consequently, he failed to win nomination and found himself unemployed when the new state government formed in November. After a futile attempt to earn a living as a lawyer, he sold his home at a loss, left Nevada with Mollie in August 1866 and returned to Keokuk. Several years later, he went to New York and worked as a newspaper proofreader for $10 a week.

Orion's economic lifeline was his brother's newly developing success. Publication of *Innocents Abroad* in 1869 launched Mark Twain on a writing career that enabled him to subsidize Orion for the rest of his life. When he wrote *Roughing It,* he gave Orion $1,000 for lending him his journal about their stagecoach journey. In late 1870, he got Elisha BLISS to hire Orion as an editor for his company's new *American Publisher* magazine. After visiting Mark Twain in BUFFALO, Orion took up his new job in Hartford in December. He was not happy working for Bliss, however, and either quit or was fired in March 1872. Before leaving, he alerted his brother to irregularities in Bliss's business procedures, leaving Mark Twain permanently suspicious of all publishers. The following summer, Orion and Mollie house-sat at Mark Twain's rented Hartford home, while his brother's family vacationed at NEW SAYBROOK.

Orion then returned to Keokuk, where his life revolved around failed attempts to practice law, raise chickens, write novels and invent gadgets while he lived on the $500 or more a year that his brother quietly provided. In the early 1880s, his mother, Jane L. Clemens, settled in Keokuk, where Mark Twain bought her a house that she shared with Orion and Mollie. Mark Twain revisited Keokuk several times and probably saw Orion for the last time just after their mother's death in 1890. Orion himself died seven years later, while Mark Twain was living in VIENNA.

Though Mark Twain had a deep affection and respect for his brother, he also regarded him as a vacillating chump who provided useful fodder for fiction. In an 1879 letter to W. D. HOWELLS, he said that no character in literature was as well developed as Orion; he described some of Orion's strangest behavior and encouraged Howells to write a novel about him. His AUTOBIOGRAPHY describes Orion as "the strangest compound that ever got mixed in a human mold." Fascinated by the volatility of Orion's religious and political beliefs, he later described him as never having "acquired a conviction that could survive a disapproving remark from a cat."

While Howells shied away from exploiting Orion's pathetic life, Mark Twain himself used his brother as a model for several characters. Orion's first significant appearance is in *Roughing It,* which depicts him simply as the majestic "SECRETARY" with whom the greenhorn narrator goes to Nevada. He appears in "SCHOOLHOUSE HILL" as the intellectually unstable Oliver Hotchkiss, and in "Hellfire Hotchkiss" he is the inept Oscar Carpenter, whom Hellfire saves from an ice floe. In 1877, Mark Twain began writing what he called "Orion's autobiography," assigning incidents from his brother's life to an apprentice printer named Bolivar. Later given the title "Autobiography of a Damned Fool" by A. B. PAINE, this unfinished story was published in Mark Twain's SATIRES & BURLESQUES (1967). Mark Twain persuaded Orion to take up his own autobiography, but his brother's manuscript (which Paine later lost) apparently showed no potential for commercial publication.

Many of Mark Twain's writings apply selected traits of Orion's to characters. Colonel SELLERS of *The American Claimant,* for example, changes religions so suddenly that even his wife cannot remember what belief he currently follows (chapter 3). *Pudd'nhead Wilson*'s Angelo CAPELLO is similarly volatile in his religions, and the same novel's title character resembles Orion in being a lawyer who goes 20 years without a case.

Though Orion was apparently named after the Orion constellation (which appears in the winter—not at the time of Orion's birth, as is often suggested), his name was pronounced with stress on the first syllable *(or'-ree-on).* Orion and his wife are buried in Hannibal's MOUNT OLIVET CEMETERY.

Clemens, Pleasant Hannibal (*fl.* c. 1828 or 1829, Jamestown, Tennessee) A brother who died before Mark Twain was born, Pleasant was the third child of John M. and Jane L. Clemens. His date and place of birth can only be estimated. He is believed to have lived just three months and his very existence is known only through a family oral history recorded by Samuel Charles Webster in *Mark Twain, Business Man* (1946). Mark Twain himself left only a bare acknowledgment that he had a brother named "Han." Pleasant was named after two uncles: Pleasant Clemens (1800–1811),

who had a popular Quaker name, and Hannibal Clemens (1803–?).

Clemens, Samuel B. (1770, Virginia–1805, Mason County, West Virginia) Paternal grandfather after whom Mark Twain was named. Clemens married Pamela Goggin (1775–1844) on October 29, 1797 in Virginia and the couple had their first child, John M. Clemens, just under a year later. They also had a daughter, Elizabeth, and two other sons, Pleasant and Hannibal. By 1804, Clemens was farming in what is now Mason County, West Virginia, where he became first commissioner of revenue when the county was organized that year. The following year he was accidentally killed when a log rolled over him during a house-raising. His widow moved to Kentucky and remarried.

Clemens died at 35—the same age at which Mark Twain would marry. His death inspired an incident mentioned in *The American Claimant.* Chapter 1 reveals that Simon Lathers and his twin brother have both been killed by a log "at a smoke-house raising" at Duffy's Corners, Arkansas—owing to carelessness "induced by overplus of sour-mash."

Clemens, Samuel Langhorne (November 30, 1835, Florida, Missouri–April 21, 1910, Redding, Connecticut) Mark Twain's real name. The sixth child of John

"Born 1835; 5 ft. 8½ inches tall; weight about 145 pounds . . . dark brown hair and red moustache, full face with very high ears and light gray beautiful beaming eyes and a damned good moral character."

Olivia, Clara, Jean, Sam and Susy Clemens on the "ombra" *(porch) of their Hartford home in 1884.* (Courtesy, Mark Twain Papers, the Bancroft Library)

M. and Jane L. CLEMENS, Mark Twain was named "Samuel" after his paternal grandfather and "Langhorne" after a family friend in Virginia (in later years, he occasionally traveled as "Samuel Langhorne" to avoid recognition). After he adopted "MARK TWAIN" as a pen name in 1862, friends knew him as "Mark," "Sam" or "Clemens," but his family always knew him as "Sam," and Clemens remained his legal name until his DEATH.

Mark Twain grew to medium height and maintained a trim physique. In 1878 he wrote a letter to Bayard TAYLOR describing himself as "5 ft. 8½ inches tall; weight about 145 pounds, sometimes a bit under, sometimes a bit over; dark brown hair and red moustache, full face with very high ears and light gray beautiful beaming eyes and a damned good moral character."

Clemens, (Susy) Olivia Susan (March 19, 1872, Elmira, New York–August 18, 1896, Hartford, Connecticut) Mark Twain's oldest daughter was called Susy (originally Susie) from birth, but began calling herself Olivia when she started college. A brilliant but often morose child, she had fragile health that restricted her physical activity. At 13, she began writing a biography of her father—much of which he later incorporated into his AUTOBIOGRAPHY, adding his own commentary. The first full edition of her book was published in 1985 as *Papa: An Intimate Biography of Mark Twain,* edited by Charles NEIDER.

Though Susy aspired to be a writer or a singer, she never progressed far in either field. In the fall of 1890, she entered BRYN MAWR, but dropped out the following spring and accompanied her family to Europe. Reasons advanced for her leaving Bryn Mawr range from her homesickness to Mark Twain's disapproval of the college. An intense relationship that she developed with another student, Louise Brownell (1870–1961), may also have had something to do with her leaving.

After four years in Europe, Susy returned to America with her family in 1895, then declined the chance to join her father's round-the-world lecture tour. Her sister Clara went with them instead, while Susy and her other sister Jean stayed in ELMIRA with their aunt Susan CRANE—after whom Susy was named. When the trip ended, Susy and Jean were to rejoin the family in London. Just as her parents were settling in England, however, Susy became seriously ill while visiting Hartford. On August 15, her condition was diagnosed as spinal meningitis; she died in the family's Hartford house three days later, with Jean, her Aunt Susan, Patrick MCALEER, Katy LEARY and Joseph TWICHELL present. A telegram carried the tragic news to Mark Twain in GUILDFORD, while Livy and Clara were sailing home to nurse Susy. Susy was buried in Elmira's WOODLAWN CEMETERY on August 23.

Susy is generally believed to have been Mark Twain's favorite child. He rued the books that she would never write and said that "this family has lost its prodigy." Neither he nor Livy ever recovered completely from Susy's death and they found it impossible to return to their Hartford home. To commemorate the first anniversary of Susy's death, Mark Twain wrote a poem that was published in HARPER'S MAGAZINE in November 1897. Susy was Mark Twain's model in at least two of his books. Even before she died, he used her as a model for JOAN OF ARC in his novel about France's national hero. Later he used Susy as the model for Cathy ALISON in "A HORSE'S TALE," though he claimed not to realize that he had done so until after he finished the story.

Cleveland, Grover (March 18, 1837, Caldwell, New Jersey–June 24, 1908, Princeton, New Jersey) Governor of New York (1883–84) and 22nd and 24th president of the United States (1885–89, 1893–97). A Democrat, Cleveland was elected president in 1884 after campaigning for civil service reform and low tariffs. Though generally a backer of Republicans, Mark Twain sided with the mugwumps in this election by openly supporting Cleveland against James Blaine. Regarding Cleveland as superior in public virtue, he dismissed as irrelevant charges that Cleveland had fathered an illegitimate child.

Cleveland had begun his legal and political career in New York's Erie County, where he was elected sheriff while Mark Twain was living in BUFFALO; however, they did not meet until December 1884—a month after Cleveland was elected president. Mark Twain visited Cleveland in Albany, New York, along with G. W. CABLE. At the end of the following February, he completed a lecture tour in WASHINGTON, D.C., where he again visited Cleveland shortly before his inauguration. During this visit, Cleveland told him the old joke that Sir DINADAN recites in chapter 9 of *Connecticut Yankee*. In November, Mark Twain discussed international copyright issues with Cleveland at the White House.

Mark Twain retained his high opinion of Cleveland for the rest of his life. In 1908, he described Cleveland as "all that a president ought to be"—in contrast to Theodore ROOSEVELT, whom he called "all that a president ought not to be."

Cody, William Frederick ("Buffalo Bill") (February 26, 1846, Scott County, Iowa–January 10, 1917, Denver, Colorado) A showman who began his career as a wrangler, prospector, pony-express rider, STAGECOACH driver, buffalo hunter and Indian fighter, Cody was a contemporary of Mark Twain, with whom he shares credit for developing an authentic western vernacular. After Ned BUNTLINE made him famous as "Buffalo Bill" in dime novels, Cody organized a "Wild West show" in 1883. With such attractions as Wild Bill Hickok, Annie Oakley and Chief Sitting Bull, he toured the eastern United States and Europe until 1913, when he retired to Wyoming—whose town of Cody is named after him.

While Mark Twain seems not to have met Cody, he was aware of his flamboyant reputation. He alludes to "Buffalo Bill" in chapter 7 of *The American Claimant* (1892) and uses him as a character in the "THE HORSE'S TALE" (1906). Like Mark Twain, Cody became famous for his flowing white hair, and Mark Twain enjoyed having children mistake him for Buffalo Bill.

Collins, Tim Minor character in *Huckleberry Finn*. In chapter 24, Huck and the KING meet Collins, "an innocent-looking young country jake," walking toward a steamboat that is loading cargo. When the King gives Collins a canoe ride to the steamboat, Collins tells him about the recent death of Peter WILKS in a nearby town. He gives details on every member of the Wilks family and on all the leading townspeople. Collins himself is on his way to Rio de Janeiro ("Ryo Janeero"), where his uncle lives—possibly to act out Mark Twain's own youthful ambition to go to SOUTH AMERICA.

After Collins boards the steamboat, the King and the DUKE devise a plan to go to Wilks's town and pose as his English brothers, Harvey and William WILKS. In chapter 29, a man named HINES challenges the King's claim to be Harvey Wilks, claiming that he saw the King with Collins in a canoe the morning the imposters arrived in town. Hine's statement is the only mention of Collins's name.

Colonel Crossman First STEAMBOAT on which Mark Twain apprenticed as a PILOT. Built at CINCINNATI, the *Crossman* began its maiden voyage there in February 1857, at almost the same moment that Mark Twain left Cincinnati on the PAUL JONES. It went directly to NEW ORLEANS, where Mark Twain joined its crew as a steersman under Horace BIXBY and returned to ST. LOUIS

between March 4–11. After a layover, he and Bixby joined the CRESCENT CITY in late April. A well-appointed, shallow-draft vessel designed for the MISSOURI RIVER's non-winter trade, the *Crossman* was 217 feet long and rated at 415 tons. Although the vessel had such advanced safety features that it was called "unsinkable," it blew its boilers on the Mississippi near New Madrid, Missouri on February 4, 1858, killing many passengers. Bixby, who was on board as the off-duty pilot, personally saved many lives.

Mark Twain did not write about his time on the *Crossman,* and *Life on the Mississippi* suggests that his piloting career began on the *Paul Jones;* however, Edgar M. Branch's research has recently corrected the record.

Colt Arms Factory Hartford manufacturing plant. Founded in 1836 by Samuel Colt (1814–1862), who invented the six-shooter, the Colt factory carried the use of interchangeable parts in mass production to new levels. During the 1880s, James PAIGE used the factory's machine shops to make parts for the typesetting machine in which Mark Twain invested heavily. Paige's connection with the factory inspired Mark Twain to make Hank MORGAN, the fictional inventor of *Connecticut Yankee*, a superintendent there. Hank's adventure starts when a Colt employee knocks him out with a crowbar, sending him back to the sixth century. Hank later dreams of hearing the Colt factory whistle in the mornings (chapter 8) and alludes to the high quality of the men who worked under him there (chapter 31).

Mark Twain also mentions Colt firearms in chapters 2 and 3 of *Roughing It* and in chapter 8 of *A Tramp Abroad*.

Columbus, Christopher (c. 1541, Genoa, Italy–May 20, 1506, Valladolid, Spain) Mark Twain had a special fascination with the discoverer of America that might be compared to his interest in ADAM. His BURLESQUE AUTOBIOGRAPHY (1871), for example, claims an ancestor named John Morgan TWAIN who sailed with Columbus. One of his many pipe dreams was to buy Columbus's bones, exhibit them, and then bury them under the Statue of Liberty. Mark Twain mentions Columbus throughout his writings, often using him as a reference point by which to measure the passage of history—as in chapter 33 of *Tom Sawyer*. Chapters 17 and 27 of *Innocents Abroad* poke fun at Columbus in several passages about a guide in GENOA who delights in showing Americans Columbus relics. The narrator and his companions befuddle the guide by pretending never to have heard of Columbus.

In chapter 5 of *Connecticut Yankee,* Hank MORGAN mentions Columbus while trying to remember which explorer awed Indians by calling up an eclipse; the passage is evidently an allusion to a story about Columbus by Washington Irving. In chapter 40, Morgan considers sending an expedition to discover America in the sixth century—a feat that would render Columbus historically inconsequential if it were carried out.

Como Resort city in the Italian Alps. Como stands at the southwestern tip of Lake Como, a slender body of water shaped like an inverted "Y," whose eastern arm is also known as Lake Lecco. On July 18, 1867, Mark Twain reached Como by train and took a steamer to Bellagio in the middle of the lake. Chapter 20 of *Innocents Abroad* describes his two-day visit to the region. Lake Como's lucid water and alpine setting have made its beauty legendary, but it did not greatly impress Mark Twain, who preferred Lake TAHOE. From Como, he made a day-trip to Chiasso in nearby SWITZERLAND, but does not mention the trip in his book.

Comstock Rich silver lode in western NEVADA. "Comstock" is historically synonymous with the region around VIRGINIA CITY, under which its long vein ran. The single richest silver strike in American history, the Comstock was discovered in June 1859 and named after Henry T. P. Comstock (1820–1870), a Canadian-born prospector who owned part of the original claim—which he sold for a few thousand dollars before its full worth was understood. By the 1880s, the Comstock had produced half of America's silver, yielding over $300 million in silver and gold ore. Its wealth not only spurred western Nevada's development, but contributed to the financial and commercial growth of SAN FRANCISCO, through which its bullion, equipment, miners and investment capital passed. In addition, its big mines stimulated major innovations in ore processing and shaft construction that later made other western mines more profitable. Mark Twain lived above the Comstock vein during his years in Virginia City; he describes it in *Roughing It* (chapters 43–45 and 52).

Connecticut Mark Twain first saw Connecticut in early 1868, while visiting his publisher in Hartford, the capital city. Business trips brought him back several times over the next few years and he spoke in six Connecticut towns during a late 1869 LECTURE tour. In October 1871, he became a resident of Hartford, which remained his home until 1891. Through these years, he spent many summers in ELMIRA, New York, and left the state for several lecture tours and European trips. While he spent most of his Connecticut time in Hartford, he also summered with his family at NEW SAYBROOK in 1872 and had a particular fondness for New Haven's YALE. Over the 15 years following his 1891 departure from Hartford, Mark Twain passed through Connecticut only occasionally. In 1906, he bought property in REDDING, where he built the "STORMFIELD" home in which he spent the two last years of his life.

After 10 years in Connecticut, Mark Twain described himself as "a border-ruffian" from Missouri and "a Connecticut YANKEE by adoption. In me, you have Missouri morals, Connecticut culture; this, gentlemen, is the combination which makes the perfect man." He explores what it means to be a Connecticut Yankee in *A Connecticut Yankee in King Arthur's Court* (1889), a novel that sends a 19th-century Hartford man to sixth-century England. Connecticut is also the setting of "THE FACTS CONCERNING THE RECENT CARNIVAL OF CRIME IN CONNECTICUT" (1876) and "A CURIOUS EXPERIENCE" (1881); a New Haven rooming house is an important element in "THE BELATED RUSSIAN PASSPORT" (1902).

***A Connecticut Yankee in King Arthur's Court* (1889)** One of Mark Twain's most complex and ambitious novels, *Connecticut Yankee* is a pioneering SCIENCE FICTION story about a 19th-century American who tries to implant modern technology and political ideas in sixth-century ENGLAND. The novel falls within a rich literary tradition of reworking Arthurian legends in modern idioms—a tradition that TENNYSON's *Idylls of the King* revitalized in the mid-19th century.

Using MALORY's *Le Morte d'Arthur* as his starting point, Mark Twain began *Connecticut Yankee* as a SATIRE on the customs and institutions of the feudal world. The book's early chapters poke fun at medieval ignorance, superstition and notions of chivalry. As the book develops, however, it evolves into a savage attack on *all* institutions and ideologies that support monarchy, privilege, slavery and established churches. The fact that the book's portrayal of sixth-century England is romantic and ahistorical is largely irrelevant, since its real target is the modern perpetuation of oppression and antidemocratic institutions. The book has as much to do with the 19th century as it does with the time in which it is set.

Despite *Connecticut Yankee*'s often heavy-handed political diatribes, it is filled with humor and invention. Mark Twain invests its hero, Hank MORGAN, with many of the traits he admired in inventors such as James PAIGE, and has great fun turning Hank loose to build a modern civilization out of nothing. When Hank first arrives in Camelot, he is anxious to invent all the "little" things he misses, such as soap, matches, paper, ink and glass. By the end of the novel, he has created workshops and factories to produce not only the little things, but batteries, telephones, electric dynamos, steamships, trains and more. Hank also sets up newspapers, insurance companies, a stock board and other enterprises. He persuades knights to wear advertising sandwich-boards and ride on bicycles, he gets kings to play baseball in armor, and he has a holy hermit power a sewing machine. Hank himself becomes history's first true fire-breathing dragon when he scares enemies into submission simply by blowing tobacco smoke out of his helmet.

Connecticut Yankee contains too many contradictions and inconsistencies to permit easy analysis. It is a sprawling mixture of satire, crude burlesque, sociological diatribes and horrifying violence, and its tone often changes abruptly. One moment, for example, Hank silently vows to hang MORGAN LE FAY for cold-bloodedly killing a page boy; the next moment, he approves her hanging her entire band simply for performing badly. Later, Hank boasts of England's dramatic gains in prosperity and education, then immediately admits to hang-

Mark Twain particularly admired Dan Beard's rendering of the helmets in this frontispiece picture depicting Hank Morgan's rude introduction to the sixth century.

ing the country's first author for publishing a stale joke. The most shocking change in tone, however, occurs at the end. Once Hank realizes that his modern civilization is doomed, he unleashes the full destructive force of late 19th-century technology on England's massed chivalry, killing more than 25,000 knights, who doubtless include many men who earlier saved him from hanging.

SYNOPSIS

Slightly longer than *Huckleberry Finn* at 119,000 words, *Connecticut Yankee* is divided into a brief preface, an untitled prelude and 44 numbered chapters. Its story is told within a FRAME set in the present (i.e., around 1889). While touring an English castle, the unidentified frame-narrator—probably Mark Twain himself—meets an American (Hank MORGAN) who tells him a fabulous story about being transported to the sixth century. After growing too tired to continue, Hank leaves the narrator a manuscript containing his story and goes to bed. The narrator then stays up all night reading the manuscript, which forms chapters 1–43 of the novel. The 44th chapter is recorded by Hank's assistant, CLARENCE. Appended to the end of this chapter is a "P.S." signed

"M. T." that returns the story to the present, with the narrator finishing his reading and going to Hank's room in time to see him die.

Hank's narrative spans roughly 10 years of the early sixth century, with most of its action unfolding within five comparatively brief episodes followed by chapters that sweep over several years. In the prelude, Hank explains that he was knocked unconscious in Connecticut in 1879 and woke up in England in A.D. 528. He is immediately captured, taken to CAMELOT and sentenced to the stake. Chapters 1–6 cover several days in which Hank befriends Clarence and uses his knowledge of a coming ECLIPSE to stop his own execution and make people think he is a powerful magician. By chapter 7, he is King ARTHUR's prime minister. In chapters 7–10 he begins a four-year period of reorganizing the kingdom's administration while gradually introducing modern civilization. Chapter 10 indicates that seven years have passed.

Once Hank's new civilization is running smoothly, he takes his first trip away from Camelot in chapters 11–21. Donning armor, he rides with a woman named SANDY to rescue damsels from ogres. Along the way, he visits Queen Morgan le Fay (chapters 16–18). After

Hank discovers the "ogre" castle to be a pigsty and its "princesses" hogs, he and Sandy join a pilgrim caravan to a religious shrine (chapter 21).

In chapters 22–26, Hank spends several weeks in the VALLEY OF HOLINESS, where he enhances his reputation by restarting a holy fountain. Later, King Arthur comes to the valley and conducts business for several days. In chapter 27, Hank and Arthur begin a new adventure together, leaving the valley disguised as freemen in order to study common people firsthand. Several weeks later, their picaresque journey ends abruptly when angry peasants turn on them. A passing nobleman carries them to safety, but then sells them into slavery in chapter 34.

Chapters 35–38 cover the months in which Hank and the king accompany the slave caravan to LONDON, where Hank's escape gets all the slaves condemned to hang. After a dramatic rescue by knights on bicycles (chapter 38), Hank returns to Camelot, where he humiliates knight-errantry on the tournament field (chapter 39). Chapter 40 hurries through the next three years, with Hank unveiling his secret schools, mines and factories in order to begin his revolution in earnest.

Chapters 41–44 take place over several months during which the legendary tragedy of Arthur's destruction unfolds in the background. Now married to Sandy, Hank takes his family to France. While he is away, a civil war erupts, resulting in Arthur's death. Hank returns to England to find that the Church's INTERDICT threatens his modern civilization. Meanwhile, Clarence has fortified a stronghold and assembled loyal boys to meet a coming assault by more than 25,000 knights. Hank's modern weapons annihilate the knights, but he and his tiny army are trapped amid the enemy dead. A spell cast by MERLIN puts Hank to sleep until the 19th century, leaving Clarence to finish writing Hank's narrative.

For the sake of simplicity, the synopsis that follows calls the narrator "Hank" throughout, although this name does not appear until late in the narrative. Text enclosed in parentheses does not come directly from the chapters in which it appears.

Preface
The laws and customs depicted in this tale are historical. If they did not exist in sixth-century England, they existed later. Furthermore, for each custom or law taken from a later time, one may be sure that the sixth century had something worse.

Word of Explanation
In WARWICK CASTLE the FRAME-narrator meets a stranger whose candid simplicity, familiarity with ancient armor and restful company are attractive. The stranger does all the talking, seemingly drifting into another time, uttering such names as Sir LAUNCELOT and Sir GALAHAD with easy familiarity. Their guide interrupts with a remark about a bullet hole in Sir SAGRAMOUR LE DESIROUS's chain-mail. He suggests it may have been made during Cromwell's time, but the stranger smiles and says he

made it himself. That night at the Warwick Arms, the narrator reads about Launcelot in MALORY. The stranger enters his room, has a few whiskeys and begins telling his story:

An American born and reared in Hartford, Connecticut, the stranger calls himself a practical and unsentimental "YANKEE of Yankees." He is the son of a blacksmith and nephew of a horse doctor, and was himself both until going to work at the (COLT) arms factory, where he learned how to make everything from guns to engines. Good at figuring out *how* to make things, he became superintendent over a thousand men. One day, he fought with a man named Hercules, who cracked him on the head with a crowbar.

The Yankee (identified as Hank MORGAN in chapter 39) woke up under a tree with a helmeted horseman staring at him. Challenging Hank to "just" (joust), the horseman charged with a spear, chasing him up the tree. Hank agreed to accompany the man, certain he must be from a circus or asylum. An hour's walk took them to a turreted fortress on a hill. Hank asked if it was BRIDGEPORT, but the man told him it was CAMELOT.

After starting to nod off, Hank gives the narrator a manuscript in which he has recorded his entire story, and retires for the night. Under dim writing on parchment pages, the narrator sees traces of old Latin. He begins reading the narrative where Hank left off.

Chapter 1
Near Camelot, a young naked girl approaches Hank and his captor. Though she is indifferent to the circus man, she is astonished by Hank. Townspeople react similarly; everyone stares at Hank but ignores his captor. Falling into the wake of a gorgeous cavalcade, he and his captor cross a drawbridge into the castle.

Chapter 2
Thinking that the castle must be some kind of asylum, Hank tries to find someone who is not a patient. He meets a good-natured page boy, with whom he quickly makes friends. The boy asks many questions without waiting for answers, then unnerves Hank by mentioning that he was born in the year 513. Hank asks him if everyone here is crazy, but the boy explains that he is at King ARTHUR's court and that the date is June 19, 528. Though unsure why, Hank tends to believe him. He then remembers that the early sixth century had only one total solar ECLIPSE—on June 21, 528 O.S. (Old Style). Since he also knows that no eclipse is due in 1879—the year from which he comes—he expects to know the truth about where he is within 48 hours.

Hank then decides that whether this is an asylum or the sixth century, he will boss the place within three months. He dubs the page "CLARENCE" and learns that his captor is Sir KAY THE SENESCHAL. Clarence tells Hank that he can expect to be imprisoned, but promises to help him. He then leads Hank into the great hall, where lofty banners hang over a company of colorfully dressed men sitting at a round table. There are also about 20 other prisoners, many maimed and caked with blood.

Chapter 3
Most of the gracious and courtly talk that Hank overhears consists of monologues about adventures—usually DUELS between strangers. Though the whole company appears nearly brainless, Hank finds something lovable about these men and sees a manliness in most faces, especially those of Galahad and Launcelot.

The crowd listens closely when several prisoners step forward, identifying themselves as captives of Kay, who rises to speak. Kay tells how Launcelot slew seven giants and helped him defeat nine foreign knights, then wore his—Kay's—armor and vanquished 50 more knights. These he ordered to report to Queen GUENEVER as Kay's prisoners. Clarence scoffs throughout Kay's narrative, then grows despondent when an old man, MERLIN, rises to recite a tale that he has told a thousand times. Merlin drones on about taking Arthur to the Lady of the Lake, soon putting everyone but Hank to sleep.

Chapter 4
The first person to wake is Sir DINADAN, who rouses the hall by tying mugs to the tail of a dog, making the crowd laugh themselves to tears. After explaining his prank repeatedly, Dinadan recites a string of stale jokes. Kay then explains how he captured Hank, calling him a "prodigious giant" whom he met in a distant land of barbarians. He concludes by ordering Hank executed at noon on June 21. When others question whether Hank's strange clothes contain enchantments that will protect him, Merlin suggests stripping him. Moments later, Hank stands naked before everyone's unembarrassed eyes, then is sent to the dungeon.

Chapter 5
When Hank wakes up the next morning, he thinks he has been dreaming; however, Clarence arrives and jolts him back to reality by telling him he is to be burned at the stake the next day. Hank begs Clarence for help, but Clarence thinks escape impossible because Merlin has cast a spell over the dungeon. Calling Merlin a humbug, Hank laughingly proclaims that he himself is a magician, and sends Clarence to tell the king that he will cause a great calamity if any harm befalls him. Hank then frets about *what* his calamity will be until he remembers the eclipse. His troubles now seem over.

When Clarence returns, he reports that the king was ready to release Hank until Merlin talked him out of it, arguing that by not naming his calamity, Hank proved his powerlessness. Assuming a dramatic posture, Hank orders Clarence to inform the king that he will blot out the sun!

Chapter 6
Though Hank realizes he is in great danger, he is heartened by the thought that the eclipse will make him the kingdom's greatest man. Suddenly, soldiers burst in and tell him that he is to be burned *immediately*. As they take Hank to a courtyard before 4,000 hushed spectators, Clarence appears. Thinking that he is helping Hank, Clarence excitedly explains that he got Hank's execution date changed by saying that his enchantment needs another day to reach full potency. Hank is too stunned to admit he is ruined.

As a monk holds a torch to Hank's feet, the crowd stares at the sky, where a dark edge is moving across the sun. The eclipse is beginning! Merlin orders the torch applied, but King Arthur forbids it. Hank then proclaims he will destroy anyone who moves. Arthur begs him to banish the darkness, offering him *anything*—even half his kingdom. Hank asks for time to consider. He cannot stop the eclipse and is also unsure *what* eclipse is happening, since he thinks the date is June 20 until the monk tells him that it is actually the 21st. Hank now dictates his terms: The king may keep his dominions, but must make him perpetual minister and executive and pay him one percent of all added revenue he raises. As the crowd applauds, the king orders Hank freed.

Still unsure of the eclipse's duration, Hank advises the king to reconsider before he agrees to turn back the darkness. Meanwhile, he struggles into the sixth-century clothes brought to him. When the eclipse becomes full, Hank proclaims that the king's silence affirms their agreement, and he orders the enchantment to end. The crowd cheers when the rim of the sun reappears.

Chapter 7
Richly rewarded, Hank is now the kingdom's second personage. Despite his new luxuries, he misses little conveniences like soap, matches, mirrors, glass, chromos, gas, candles, books, pens, paper and ink. He especially misses sugar, coffee, tea and tobacco. Seeing himself as another Robinson Crusoe (DEFOE's castaway), Hank must invent, contrive and reorganize to make life bearable.

Hank becomes the talk of the kingdom; everyone wants to see him, and the public pressures him to perform another "miracle." A lunar eclipse is coming, but not for another two years, so he must think of something else. When he learns that Merlin is plotting against him, he has the old magician imprisoned and announces that he will perform just *one* more miracle. Working secretly, he and Clarence prepare to blow up Merlin's tower, packing the ancient structure with blasting powder and erecting a lightning rod as a detonator. After warning the growing mass of spectators to keep their distance, Hanks watches the weather. When conditions appear favorable, he starts the show. He lets Merlin try his enchantments, then gestures as the tower explodes. Afterward, the king wants to banish Merlin, but Hank retains him to "work" the weather.

Chapter 8
After the tower episode solidifies Hank's position, he begins accepting that he is not living in a dream. The only threat to his colossal power is the Roman Catholic

Church. It a curious country in which he finds himself. Its simple people are like rabbits; they know no better than to love and honor the nobility and the Church, despite receiving nothing in return but blows. Hank believes that *any* kind of royalty or aristocracy is an insult. Most British subjects are slaves, in both name and fact; the rest are slaves in fact, without the name.

Inherited ideas about pedigree and inherited dignities determine how people regard Hank. They admire and fear him, but no one *reverences* him since he lacks a pedigree or inherited title. The Church has converted a nation of men to a nation of worms, inventing the "Divine Right of Kings," preaching humility, obedience and self-sacrifice to commoners, introducing heritable ranks and aristocracies and teaching people to bow down before them.

Hank's anomalous position as a giant among pygmies makes him Britain's only truly great man. He could get a title, but does not ask for one, and declines one when it is offered. The only title he wants must be conferred by the nation itself. After several years, he wins just such a title when a village blacksmith dubs him "the boss"—a name that sweeps the kingdom.

Chapter 9

Hank regards Camelot's frequent tournaments as wearisome bullfights, but attends them out of political and social necessity and looks for ways to improve them. Launcelot and others want Hank to participate in the tournaments, but he pleads that his work keeps him too busy.

During one long tournament, Hank tests his plans for starting a newspaper by having a priest from his Department of Public Morals and Agriculture cover the tournament as a journalist.

One day, as Hank sits in his box, Dinadan enters to tell him jokes. As the knight recites a particularly stale story, Hank's mind so wanders that he scarcely notices when Dinadan is called to joust. He awakens in time to see Sir GARETH knock Dinadan hard. By the time Hank mutters his wish that Dinadan be killed, Gareth is knocking Sir SAGRAMOUR LE DESIROUS off his horse. Thinking Hank's remarks meant for him, Sagramour challenges him to duel—*after* he spends three or four years searching for the HOLY GRAIL.

Chapter 10

Sagramour's challenge makes Hank the subject of court gossip, and the king pushes Hank to seek adventures to gain renown, but Hank protests that he needs three or four years to get the kingdom running smoothly. During the three years or so he has been in office, he has begun new industries, gathered the brightest minds of the kingdom, trained expert teachers, set up graded schools, established religious freedom and a variety of Protestant churches, and begun scientific mining.

As four more years pass, Hank shows what a despot can do with the resources of a kingdom behind him. However, he still waits to turn on the full light of his

new civilization because he is not ready to confront the Church. Meanwhile, he establishes a WEST POINT military academy and a naval academy.

Clarence, now 22 years old, can do anything. Hank trains him for journalism, to which he takes like a duck. Hank also has telegraph and telephone lines laid secretly. Since no one knows where any place is, he sends out a mapping expedition, but drops the idea when priests interfere. He systematizes taxes, but the condition of the kingdom as a whole is about the same as it was when he started. With everything running smoothly, however, he feels ready for a rest.

Chapter 11

The country is full of liars who occasionally appear at court with wild tales of princesses or others needing help. One day a woman shows up claiming that three ogres have been holding her mistress and 44 beautiful "young" girls in a castle for 26 years. Every knight begs permission to rescue them, but the king gives the job to Hank.

The woman calls herself the Demoiselle Alisande la Carteloise (Hank starts calling her SANDY in the next chapter). When she cannot even explain where the castle is, Hank fumes, but Clarence wonders why he even asks her for such information, since she will accompany him on his mission. Scandalized by the idea of traveling alone with a woman, Hank mentions that he is nearly engaged to someone named Puss FLANAGAN.

Much is made of Hank's coming expedition, and knights fill him with advice. Finally, he struggles into a suit of heavy armor and is hoisted onto his horse. With Sandy behind him, they depart.

Chapter 12

As they ride into the country, Hank is miserable inside his armor. He needs a handkerchief, but cannot get at it. His armor heats up, rattles noisily and grows heavier. Unable even to scratch, Hank reaches the peak of his misery when a fly invades his helmet. He dismounts and has Sandy remove his helmet, fill it with water and pour it down his armor. As they await help to get Hank back on the horse, Sandy talks constantly, but never expresses an idea—like a perfect BLATHERSKITE.

Chapter 13

When they resume their journey, Hank discovers new irritations. He longs to smoke his pipe, but has no matches. He is hungry, since he follows the knightly custom of trusting to providence instead of carrying food. The first night, he sleeps in his armor during a storm, which sends bugs and worms seeking shelter inside his outfit. In the morning, he rises crippled with rheumatism, but Sandy is fresh as a squirrel. They start off again at sunrise, with Sandy on the horse and Hank limping behind.

Soon they meet peasants repairing a road. The peasants are flattered by Hank's offer to eat with them. Though these people are "freemen," they have so many

Sandy helps Hank cool off in chapter 12.

duties to their lord, restrictions on their movements, and taxes that they resemble the French before the blessed Revolution. Nevertheless, they remain humbly reverent toward the king and the Church. Hank asks them if a nation in which *every* man could vote would ever elect a single family to reign over it and grant special privileges to another hundred families. The idea of a nation giving every man a say has never occurred to the peasants, so Hank tells them that he has seen such a nation. One man who grasps what he is saying declares that stealing the will from a nation must be the greatest crime. Sensing this man's potential, Hank sends him to be put in his "MAN FACTORY." Hank himself believes that one should be loyal to one's country, not to its institutions or office-holders. Since he now lives in a country that gives only six persons in a thousand a say, he thinks that what the other 994 persons need is a "NEW DEAL."

Chapter 14

After Hank gives his hosts three pennies, they give him a flint and steel—which he uses to light his pipe after mounting his horse. The first blast of smoke from his helmet sends everyone running.

The next day, Hank and Sandy encounter a half-dozen armed knights and their squires. When the knights charge, Hank lights his pipe and blows smoke through his helmet, causing the knights to scatter. Confident that Hank has disabled the men, Sandy secures their surrender and their promise to report to Camelot as Hank's property.

Chapter 15

When Sandy tells Hank that he has captured *seven* knights and their squires, he asks who they are, but quickly regrets giving her a chance to launch another long narrative. She describes Sir Uwaine and Sir GA-WAINE's long struggle with Sir Marhaus, with Hank interrupting occasionally to criticize her archaic speech. In the afternoon, they approach a castle.

Chapter 16

As Hank wonders who lives in the castle, a horseman approaches, wearing a sign for "Persimmon's Soap." It is Sir LA COTE MALE TAILE, one of several knights promoting soap for Hank as part of his secret plan to introduce hygiene among the nobility while making knight-errantry look foolish. His soap factory runs night and day, stinking up Camelot.

La Cote identifies the castle as the abode of Arthur's sister, Queen MORGAN LE FAY. Inside, Hank is startled to find Morgan gracious, beautiful and youthful looking, despite her reputation as an evil old woman. She looks young enough to be the granddaughter of her husband King Uriens. Hank suspects that Morgan has been mis-represented, until she casually stabs a young page for accidentally touching her. When Hank carelessly compliments Arthur, Morgan orders him and Sandy to the dungeon, but Sandy warns the guards that the Boss will destroy them. Morgan instantly becomes sweet again, and claims merely to be jesting so she can see Hank blast her guards to ashes.

Chapter 17

Morgan le Fay wants Hank to demonstrate his powers by killing someone, but the call to prayers interrupts her. Relieved, Hank expresses his admiration of the Church's ability to keep its murderous nobility religious. Later, he and Sandy dine in a great banquet hall, where a horrible band plays a tune sounding like the first draft of "The Sweet By-and-By." After dinner, the queen orders the composer hanged. Meanwhile, more than a hundred people eat everything in sight, become drunk and tell anecdotes that would embarrass even Queen ELIZABETH. At midnight, an old woman appears and calls down a curse on the queen for killing her grand-child, the page boy. When Morgan orders the woman to the stake, Sandy startles Hank by proclaiming that the Boss will dissolve the castle if Morgan does not recall her command. Morgan complies, but collapses while everyone else rushes for the exits.

Morgan is now too frightened even to hang her com-poser without Hank's permission. Looking for a way to lift her spirits, Hank has the band play "The Sweet By-and-By" again, then gives her permission to hang the *whole* band. After Hank hears a distant shriek, Morgan proudly leads him to a cell, where her executioner is racking a man named HUGO who is accused of killing a stag. In a private interview, Hugo tells Hank that he *did* kill the stag, but will not confess so that his family will not be stripped of their property. Hank orders his release and sends him to his Man Factory.

Chapter 18
When priests later denounce the executioner's crimes, Hank admits that many priests are *not* frauds and self-seekers after all—a thought that disturbs him since he dislikes anything that might reconcile people to an Established Church. He punishes the executioner by making him leader of the queen's new band.

The next day, Hank inspects Morgan's dungeons. Their inmates include a prematurely aged couple imprisoned since their wedding night for refusing a nobleman his customary rights to enjoy the bride (on her wedding night)—*le droit du seigneur*. For nine years, they have been within 50 feet of each other without knowing the other was alive. Hank frees 47 prisoners, leaving only a lord who ruined a village's well. Most of these people were imprisoned for trifling offenses. The most recent captive, for example, merely suggested that kings and commoners would look the same without clothes. Another prisoner has spent 22 years peering at his home through a crack, trying to see his wife and five children. After observing five funerals, he was tormented by not knowing which member of his family was still alive. When Hank frees him, however, he discovers that *everyone* in his family is still alive; the queen faked all the funerals simply to torture him. His crime: saying that she had "red hair," when "auburn" was the only acceptable description for one of her rank. Five persons have not seen daylight in 35 years; no one remembers their names or when or why they were incarcerated.

Chapter 19
The next morning, Hank and Sandy go back on the road. Sandy begins a new narrative about Sir Marhaus that concerns the seven knights whom Hank captured earlier. He considers what a curious country this is for people who seem never to get old, but the conversation stops abruptly when he asks Sandy her age.

Chapter 20
After riding 10 miles, they see an approaching knight—Sir Madok de la Montaine, who carries an advertisement for "Peterson's Prophylactic Toothbrush." Madok is trying to catch up with Hank's stove-polish man, Sir Ossaise of Surluse, for tricking him into chasing after potential customers—who turned out to be Morgan's toothless former prisoners.

Later, Hank and Sandy see the reunion of a family with a man who had been imprisoned for 50 years. Hank regards their failure to express outrage at their oppressors as evidence that all true revolutions must begin in blood.

Two days later, Sandy spots the ogres' "castle." All Hank sees is a pigsty, but he humors her by pretending that an enchantment hides the castle from his eyes. He promises to treat her "princesses" as ladies, even though they appear to be hogs—which he buys from the starveling swineherds who Sandy thinks are "ogres." When they reach home later, Sandy quarters the unruly hogs in the house.

Chapter 21
Hank gets little sleep that night with the hogs cavorting through the house, and ponders whether Sandy is sane. He concludes that she is, given her training, and allows that people would consider *him* insane if they knew what he was trained to believe. At breakfast, he is shocked to learn that Sandy does not know whose house they are in; however, he is relieved to learn that they can leave her "princesses" there to be collected by friends. His distress returns when Sandy says she will stay with him until a knight wins her away in fair combat.

After departing, Hank and Sandy fall in with a procession of cheerful PILGRIMS headed for the VALLEY OF HOLINESS, where they plan to cleanse themselves of sin by drinking water from the miraculous fountain. In the afternoon, they overtake a procession of slaves chained together by the neck who have tramped 300 miles in 18 days. When their master ruthlessly whips a young woman, Hank decides not to interfere, but vows to be the death of slavery.

At a village inn, Hank meets a knight who is promoting plug hats for him. Just arrived from the Valley of Holiness, Sir Ozana Le Cure Hardy reveals that the miraculous fountain stopped flowing nine days earlier and that Merlin has been trying to restart it. Hank has Ozana carry an order to Clarence in Camelot to send supplies and assistants to the valley as fast as possible.

Chapter 22
Now that the holy fountain has stopped flowing, the pilgrims' desire to see it is 40 times greater. At the valley, the overjoyed abbot begs Hank to restore the fountain immediately, but Hank refuses to act until after Merlin quits. The next day he visits the fountain inside its chapel and finds that it is an ordinary well with a leak. While Merlin works his incantations from outside, Hank spreads the idea that restarting the fountain will be difficult.

When Hank later discusses the hermits with Sandy, he chides her for not grasping his modern jargon until he notices how hard she is trying to understand him. After he apologizes, they become better friends and he realizes that he is developing a mysterious reverence for her. They tour the strange menagerie of hermits, who compete to be the most unclean and verminous. For 20 years, the valley's greatest hermit has done nothing but stand atop a 60-foot-high pillar bowing up and down continuously. Hank later harnesses the hermit to a sewing machine and gets him to turn out 18,000 tow-linen shirts over five years.

Chapter 23

On Saturday, Hank inspects Merlin's progress and finds him in a foul mood. Proclaiming that a potent Eastern spirit has laid a spell that no mortal can break, Merlin says that the water will *never* flow again, and quits. Hank tells the distressed abbot that Merlin's remarks about the spirit are true, but that it *may* be possible to break the spell. Merlin gleefully reminds Hank that in order to break the spell, he must not only know the spirit's name but *pronounce* it—an act that will kill him. Hank's cracks about Merlin's weather forecasting abilities anger the magician, who decides to remain in order to see Hank fail.

That evening two experts arrive from Camelot with tools, supplies and fireworks and help Hank patch the well. By the next afternoon, when they complete their preparations, the water is back to its normal level. The men install a pump and set up fireworks. That evening, criers announce the coming miracle and the valley fills up with people. After men chant in Latin, Hank mounts a platform, reaches to the sky and pronounces: "Constantinopolitanischserdudelsackspfeifenmachersgesellschafft!" ("The Bagpipe Manufacturers Company of Constantinople") as blue flares illuminate the area. More awful words and colored flares follow, creating a display so dazzling that even the hermit atop the pillar stops bowing to watch. Finally, Hank commands the spell to end and pronounces the dreaded spirit's name: "BGWJJILLIGKKK!" As rockets light up the sky, water gushes from the chapel and the crowd goes wild.

Chapter 24

With his influence in the valley now prodigious, Hank persuades the abbot to allow the monks to bathe again and has his men rebuild an ancient bath in the monastery's basement. Before he can leave the valley, however, he catches a bad cold. As he recuperates, he plans to tour the country alone disguised as a peasant.

One morning, Hank stumbles upon a cave with a telephone office that Camelot men have set up the previous night. He phones Clarence and learns that the king, queen and half the court are headed for the valley to see the restored waters and should arrive in two and a half days. He also learns that the king has started raising the standing army that he (Hank) has been planning and is already officering it with nobles instead of West Point cadets. Clarence connects him with the superintendent at West Point, whom he orders to send a cadet to the valley.

Back at the monastery, Hank is annoyed to find a new magician regaling monks by revealing what anyone—such as a distant emperor—is doing at the moment. Fearing that his own reputation may suffer, Hank challenges the man to reveal what he himself is doing with a hand hidden behind his back; however, the fraud claims that his magic works only with royalty. When the abbot asks what King Arthur and his court are doing, he says they are sleeping after a hunt. This remark leads to an argument with Hank, who insists that the king is *riding*. Hank stakes his reputation on his prediction that the king will arrive in the valley in two days. After the king appears on schedule, the monks carry the magician out on a rail.

Chapter 25

As he typically does while traveling, Arthur holds court in the valley. Though a wise and humane judge, he is biased toward the upper classes. In one case, he rules in favor of a bishop who claims a young bride's estate because she married privately to evade *le droit du seigneur*.

Arthur has started staffing his army before Hank has had time to prepare a plan for selecting officers through examinations that only his own cadets can pass. Three priests whom Arthur has brought with him as an examination board refuse to examine Hank's commoner candidate, Malease Webster. After Arthur permits Hank's West Point professors to examine Webster, the cadet displays dazzling expertise in the sciences of war, mathematics and astronomy. By contrast, neither of the nobles who came with Arthur can answer anything. Nevertheless, the official board awards the lieutenancy to the noble with the most impressive pedigree.

Afterward, Hank interests Arthur in staffing a "King's Own Regiment" entirely with high-ranking noble officers—most of whom will pay to get in. This regiment would do whatever it wants, while commoner regiments would do the real military work. Hank also thinks of using this regiment as a means of replacing the hated royal grants.

Chapter 26

When Hank tells Arthur about his idea of touring the country in disguise, the king wants to join him. First, however, he must attend to the "kings-evil"—a rite in which he touches scrofulous subjects, giving each a coin. Hank saves the treasury nearly a day's expenses by substituting his mint's new nickels for the gold pieces traditionally handed out. As he waits for the ceremony to end, he buys a copy of the first newspaper, the CAMELOT WEEKLY HOSANNAH AND LITERARY VOLCANO, from a newsboy.

Chapter 27

That night, Hank prepares Arthur for their journey by hacking his hair and whiskers and outfitting him in coarse garments. At dawn, they slip away and walk 10 miles before resting. When Hank sees upper-class people coming, he dashes to the king, who is slow to adopt a humble posture. A flunky raises a whip to Arthur, but Hank jumps to take the blow. Afterward, the king becomes a constant anxiety to Hank.

Arthur later asks Hank why he does not warn him *before* he (Arthur) does something foolish. After starting to admit that he cannot read minds, Hank explains that his gift of prophecy works only for distant future events—in contrast to Merlin, who can see only a few days ahead. Hank now has to satisfy the king's hunger to hear about the future.

For several days, Hank steers Arthur away from further encounters with knights. One day, Hank happens to fall down—an accident that makes him realize he should get rid of the dynamite-bomb in his knapsack. As he holds the bomb, wondering what to do with it, several knights nearly run the king down, provoking Arthur to curse at them. The knights turn on the king, but Hank gets them to chase him instead, then blows them to bits with his bomb.

Chapter 28
Hank devotes the fourth day to drilling the king's dangerous habits out of him. He tells Arthur that his bearing is all wrong—he stands too straight and looks too confident. Hank must explain everything to the king, one detail at a time.

Chapter 29
That afternoon, Hank and the king reach a darkened hut by a denuded field. Inside, Hank finds a woman warning him to flee, as God has cursed her house, but he ignores her warnings. After fetching water, he finds the king inside the hut opening shutters. When he sees that the woman has smallpox, he urges Arthur to flee, but the king insists on helping, and carries the woman's dying adolescent daughter down from a loft. To Hank, this is heroism at its greatest: challenging death without defenses. Arthur then brings down another daughter, who is already dead, and lays her by her dead father. The woman tells her story:

Her family's troubles began a year earlier, when the local lord planted fruit trees on their farm. One day her three grown sons discovered the trees cut down and reported the crime. They were thrown in a dungeon, where they remain. Only the woman, her husband and daughters remained to protect and gather their crops—which ripened at the same time as their lord's. As the woman and her daughters harvested the lord's crop, they were fined for being a man short. Meanwhile, their own crops perished. Between their fines and crop losses they ended up with nothing and then contracted smallpox. Driven mad by hunger and frustration, the woman uttered a blasphemy that brought down the Church's ban.

As the woman concludes her story, she hears her daughter's death rattle.

Chapter 30
At midnight, Hank and the king cover four corpses and leave the house. Hearing footsteps, they hide outside and listen to men excitedly calling out to their parents that they are free. Hank pushes the king to move on.

The sight of a burning house in the distance interests Hank because he is starting up a fire insurance business and a fire department. As they move through the darkness, a storm threatens and Hank walks into a man hanging from a tree. Lightning reveals more bodies hanging nearby. Finding the manor house burned to the ground, Hank and the king rush off. Several miles away, the wife of a charcoal-burner welcomes them into her house.

After rising late the next day, Hank and the king learn about the previous night's affair from the woman and her husband (identified as MARCO in the next chapter). When the manor caught fire, people swarmed to the rescue and saved everyone but the lord. After he was found bound and stabbed, suspicion fell on a family he had recently mistreated, and his retainers led the villagers in pursuit of everyone connected with the family, killing 18 people. Hank is grieved to learn that every prisoner in the manor house burned to death, but the king interjects that three men escaped, and urges they be caught. Marco agrees, but Hank senses his lack of enthusiasm. He leaves with Marco to show him which way the escapees went. Away from the house, he startles the man by asking if the escaped men are his cousins. Once Hank declares that letting the men escape would be honorable, the relieved Marco pours out his true feelings, admitting that he helped hang his neighbors the previous night only for fear of being thought disloyal to his lord.

Chapter 31
While Hank and Marco kill time to make it appear they have been searching for the escaped prisoners, Hank studies the ways in which different classes treat one another. Suddenly a mob of frightened children rush out of the woods, where Hank and Marco rescue a boy the children nearly hanged while imitating their elders.

In the hamlet of ABBLASOURE, Hank is pleased to see his new coins circulating and has a goldsmith change a $20 gold piece for him. He meets several master mechanics and invites the most interesting of them, the blacksmith DOWLEY, to Sunday dinner at Marco's. Marco's pleasure at Dowley's acceptance vanishes when Hank also suggests inviting Dickon the mason and Smug the wheelwright. However, Hank calms him by promising to pay for everything. He also buys Marco and his wife new outfits, claiming they are a gift from the king, whom he calls "JONES," describing him as a prosperous but eccentric farmer and himself as a farm bailiff. At the hamlet's best shop, he orders everything needed for the banquet—arranging for the goods to be delivered on Saturday and the bill on Sunday.

Chapter 32
The arrival of Hank's order on Saturday makes the Marcos nearly faint. Besides abundant food, there are extra staples, furniture and crockery, as well as new outfits for the Marcos, who are too excited to sleep that night. On Sunday, the guests assemble under a tree. As everyone becomes congenial, Dowley boasts about how he rose from friendless orphan to master blacksmith and describes his lavish life-style—making Hank want to humiliate him. The guests are astonished when Mrs. Marco sets out a new table and stools, followed by

sumptuous dishes. Each item outdoes the blacksmith's domestic grandeurs. When the storekeeper's son arrives to collect the bill for 39,150 milrays, Hank has him read it aloud, then casually gives the boy four dollars, telling him to keep the nine cents change. To Hank's gratification, Dowley is crushed.

Chapter 33
Hank soon has Dowley happy again. After dinner, conversation turns to business and wages, with Hank and Dowley doing most of the talking, while Arthur nods off. Under King BAGDEMAGUS, this realm has the protection system, in contrast to the free trade system Hank is promoting. Dowley boasts about high local wages, which are about double Camelot's. Hank argues that since prices here are *more* than double, his own land is actually better off, but the others cannot grasp his reasoning. So far as Dowley is concerned, the fact that local wages are higher is the only thing that matters.

Smarting at losing this argument to Dowley, Hank determines to strike back. He starts with a discussion about an unwritten law dictating that wages must steadily rise, predicting future wage levels that amaze the other men. Even more amazing is his prediction that one day workers will form trade unions and dictate their own wages. Discussion turns to the pillory, which Hank argues should be abolished. He points out that being sentenced to the pillory can mean death for someone convicted of a minor crime, particularly if that person is unpopular. When he suggests that none of the other men is unpopular for exciting his neighbors' envy, Dowley winces. After getting everyone to agree that persons failing to report a crime should be pilloried, Hank mentions the local law fixing wages and casually recalls Dowley's earlier admission that he once paid higher than legal wages. The moment the others grasp what Hank is driving at, they go to pieces. Hank has scared the men too much.

Chapter 34
After Hank calms the panicky men down, the king awakens from his nap and starts prattling about agriculture. He calls onions "berries" and plums "cereal" and makes other mistakes, causing the men to grow more restless. Crying out that one man would betray them and that the other is mad, the men suddenly attack Hank and the king, and Marco runs for help. By the time Marco returns with more men and dogs, Hank and the king are in woods, where they hide their tracks in water and climb a tree. Eventually, their pursuers find them and force them down with fire. At that moment, horsemen arrive. Their leader, Earl GRIP, drives the peasants away and lets Hank and the king ride with him about 10 or 12 miles.

The next morning Hank and the king are invited to continue with Grip's men to CAMBENET, where they see the same slave caravan that they encountered earlier. Hank fumes when he hears an orator declaiming about "glorious British liberties." Suddenly, Grip's men hand-

cuff him to the king, and Grip orders them sold as slaves. They cry out that they are freemen, but the orator reminds them that the burden of proof lies with them. The master of the slave caravan buys them at auction, paying seven dollars for the king and nine dollars for Hank, then marches them away.

Chapter 35
Brooding about having fetched only seven dollars, Arthur bores Hank by monotonously arguing that he should have brought at least $25. Gradually, the slave driver realizes that the king's regal style spoils his marketability, and tries unsuccessfully to beat it out of him.

During a month of marching, Arthur grows seriously interested in the slavery question and thrills Hank by declaring himself ready to abolish slavery. The king's new attitude sets Hank to planning their escape. Meanwhile, they have several adventures. One night, as the slaves huddle in a deadly blizzard, a woman accused of being a witch seeks their protection. When her pursuers catch up with her, the slave master makes them burn her amidst his slaves, in order to keep them warm.

Later, they see an 18-year-old girl hanged for petty theft in a LONDON suburb. A priest tells her heartrending story: She was happily married until her husband was impressed into the navy and disappeared. Never told what became of him, she gradually became mentally disordered and stole a bit of cloth to buy her baby some food. As the executioner slips the noose over her head, she hugs her child desperately, crying that it will die without a father or mother. The good priest promises to be both, allowing the girl to die happy.

Chapter 36
When the slave caravan enters LONDON, Hank sees people he knows, including Sandy, but getting their attention is hopeless. The sight of a newspaper boy and telegraph lines cheers him, but his biggest interest is finding a piece of wire with which to pick the lock on his chains. Eventually, he steals a metal pin from a prospective buyer. Hank unlocks his chains that night, but the master arrives before he can free the king. As the master leaves, Hank pounces after him. Outside, he jumps the man and struggles with him until they both are arrested. Then he discovers he has attacked the *wrong* man.

Chapter 37
Hank's concern about what is happening at the slave quarters robs him of his sleep in the noisy jail. The next morning, he tells the court he is a slave of Earl Grip, for whom he was on an important errand when the other man attacked him. Begging Hank's pardon, the court frees him and orders the other man whipped.

Hanks finds the slave quarters empty except for the master's battered corpse, and learns that his mysterious escape so angered the man that he whipped the other slaves until they rose and killed him. *All* the slaves are now condemned to be hanged tomorrow and a massive search is underway for Hank. After buying another outfit to disguise himself, Hank goes to a telegraph office and contacts Clarence, whom he orders to send help immediately.

While waiting for help to come, Hank begins upgrading his clothes in stages, in order to approach local grandees whom he knows for help. This plan soon crumbles, however, when one of the condemned slaves and an officer capture him. Hank boasts that no one will be hanged, but the officer tells him that his capture means that everyone will be hanged *today!* Hank estimates that the knights will arrive about three hours too late to rescue them.

Chapter 38

That afternoon a multitude assembles outside London's walls to witness the hangings. When Arthur proclaims himself King of Britain, the crowd merely taunts him. Hank receives the same treatment when he identifies himself as the Boss. Soon, the grim ceremony begins. After two slaves are hanged and a blindfold is put on the king, 500 fully equipped knights suddenly enter the compound on bicycles. As Launcelot sweeps in, Hank springs up and commands the assemblage to salute the king. Clarence then arrives and explains he has been training the knights for just such an occasion.

Chapter 39

Home at Camelot again, Hank reads a newspaper story about his coming combat with Sir Sagramour. Interest in the match is widespread because it will be the first tournament under a law permitting combatants to use any weapons they choose. More importantly, the battle is seen as a final struggle between the land's two mightiest magicians: Merlin, who is helping Sagramour, and the Boss. As the champion of hard, unsentimental reason, Hank wants to destroy knight-errantry.

On the day of combat, Sagramour is an imposing tower of iron mounted on a mighty steed, while Hank wears only a gymnast costume and rides a slender horse. After Merlin casts spells to make Sagramour invisible, the contest begins. The men charge each other; just as Sagramour's lance nears its target, Hank twitches his horse aside. After two more misses, Sagramour futilely tries chasing Hank down. On Sagramour's final charge, Hank ropes him off his horse. The astounded audience cheers for more. After Hank almost effortlessly lassos seven more knights, including Launcelot, Merlin steals his lasso. Sagramour then challenges Hank again—this time bent on death. Though ostensibly unarmed, Hank does not budge until Sagramour is 15 paces away. He then whips out a revolver and fires. Before anyone knows what has happened, Sagramour lies dead on the field. No one can figure out what killed him.

No other knights challenge Hank, so he dares *all* of them to come at him at once. Five hundred men scramble to their saddles and charge together. This time, Hank fires two revolvers; he is just two bullets away from disaster when the knights break rank and flee.

Chapter 40

With knight-errantry humbled, Hank uncovers all his secret schools, mines and factories to an astonished world. To keep the knights down, he issues a permanent challenge—advertising that he stands always ready to meet the world's massed chivalry with just 50 men on his side.

Over the next three years, England prospers, with schools everywhere, as well as colleges, newspapers and even authors—though Hank suppresses Sir Dinadan's stale jokebook and has him hanged. Slavery is gone, and all men are now equal before the law. The telegraph, telephone, phonograph, typewriter, sewing machine and other devices are at work throughout the land. There are STEAMBOATS on the THAMES, steam warships at sea, and Hank is preparing an expedition to discover America. A railway line connects Camelot and London and more lines are being developed.

Hank's biggest remaining plans are to replace the Catholic Church with several Protestant faiths and to introduce universal suffrage after Arthur dies—in perhaps 30 years. Looking forward to the coming republic, Hank admits to having a "base hankering" to be the first president. Clarence prefers a modified republic with a hereditary royal family, and argues convincingly for a royal family of cats, until Hank realizes he is joking.

One morning, Sandy rushes in to tell Hank that their baby, HELLO-CENTRAL, is suffering from croup (Hank explains that he is married in the next chapter). Sir Launcelot, now the stock-board president, happens by and ends up staying three days to help Hank watch the baby. Doctors recommend sea air for Hello-Central, so Hank and Sandy cruise the French coast in a warship for two weeks, then settle ashore on the doctors' recommendation. After a month in France, Hank sends the vessel home for supplies and news. He particularly wants to hear about a pet project—baseball teams comprised of kings.

Chapter 41

When the baby's croup worsens, Sandy proves again what a flawless wife and mother she is. Hank explains that when he realized he could not keep Sandy from his side, he married her. Their first year of marriage proved how fortunate he was to have her as a wife.

When Hello-Central recovers two and a half weeks later, Hank remembers that his warship has not returned and rushes to the sea, where he finds that his great oceangoing commerce has vanished. Leaving his family behind, he returns to England the next day. Dover's harbor has ships, but no activity. In Canterbury he discovers that the Church has put England under the INTERDICT. After disguising himself, he makes his way to Camelot alone. Desolate silence prevails everywhere, even in London—whose Tower shows recent war scars. When he reaches Camelot several days later, he finds the town shrouded in darkness.

Chapter 42

Clarence, drowned in melancholy, tells Hank how Launcelot's affair with Queen Guenever triggered the Interdict. Launcelot made a stock-board killing that hurt Arthur's nephews, Sir Agravaine and Sir MORDRED, badly. They got revenge by telling Arthur about Launcelot and Guenever. The king then laid a trap that caught Launcelot, who killed Agravaine and 12 other knights. This incident started a civil war. When Arthur sent Guenever to the stake, Launcelot rescued the queen, accidentally killing his faithful friends Sir Gaheris and Sir Gareth in his blind fury. After several battles, the Church patched up a peace that satisfied everyone but Sir Gawaine, who remained bitter about Launcelot's slaying his brothers. Arthur then joined Gawaine, leaving his kingdom in the hands of Mordred—who attempted a permanent takeover. After Mordred chased Guenever to the Tower of London, the Archbishop of Canterbury laid down the Interdict.

Arthur fought Mordred in southeast England, then began negotiating a peace that would give Mordred part of his kingdom. After dying in battle, Gawaine appeared to Arthur in a dream and warned him not to let anyone fight, for one month. The ensuing truce collapsed when a knight raised his sword to an adder. In the next great battle, Arthur and Mordred killed each other.

The Church, which has all the knights on its side, now controls the country and will maintain the Interdict so long as Hank remains alive. Hank scoffs until Clarence tells him that virtually all his followers have deserted to the Church and all his modern communication and transportation systems have shut down.

During Hank's absence, Clarence prepared for the coming war by assembling 52 trained teenage boys who grew up free from the Church's influence. He fortified Merlin's Cave to withstand a siege, wiring it to dynamite charges under all the modern factories, workshops and magazines. The cave itself is surrounded by wire fences connected to an electric dynamo; its approaches are guarded by Gatling guns; and a wide belt surrounding it is mined with dynamite torpedoes covered with sand.

After praising Clarence's preparations, Hank proposes to strike. The next day he issues a proclamation declaring that the death of the king has ended the monarchy, leaving executive authority vested in him until a new government is created. Meanwhile, the nobility, privileged classes and Established Church no longer exist, and a republic is proclaimed.

Chapter 43

At the cave, Hank sends out word that his factories will be blown up without warning. Through a week of waiting, he converts his diary into a narrative and writes letters to Sandy, though he cannot send them. Meanwhile, his spies report that the Church is massing the knights against him. His proclamation of the republic generates excitement for one day; then the Church takes control. With all England now marching against them, Hank's boys beg not to be asked to destroy their country, but Hank explains that their only true foes are the knights who will march in the vanguard.

After the huge enemy host arrives, its front ranks charge into the SAND BELT and are blown to bits. Hank then detonates the charges to destroy his factories and congratulates his army on their victory. Declaring that the war with the English nation—as a nation—is over, he says that they must now kill *every* knight in order to end the conflict. Explosions have dug a ditch in the sand belt, so Hank has a stream diverted for the next emergency.

That night, Hank creeps out to the perimeter and finds knights pouring into the ditch. The electric fences are so powerful that they kill before victims can cry out. Back at the cave, Hank turns on floodlights that reveal three walls of corpses surrounding them. While the lights immobilize the enemy, he turns on the remaining fences, killing another 11,000 men, then signals to turn the brook's water into the ditch, as Gatling guns spit bullets into the 10,000 knights still alive. Within 10 minutes, the enemy is annihilated. Hank and his 53 men are masters of England.

Hank's narrative now ends.

Chapter 44

Clarence closes the narrative, explaining that when the Boss went out to help the wounded, he was stabbed by the first man he met—Sir Meliagraunce. His wound was not serious, but his men's position was desperate because they were trapped by the enemy dead surrounding them. Several days later, an old woman appeared, offering to cook. One night Clarence caught her doing something over Hank—it was Merlin in disguise, gloating that Hank would now sleep for 13 centuries. As Merlin laughed, he bumped into an electric wire and was instantly killed.

Clarence ends the manuscript promising that if the Boss does not awaken, they will carry him to a remote recess and hide this manuscript with him.

A final "P.S.," signed "M. T.," returns the narrative to the present day. It is morning as the narrator lays the manuscript aside. He goes to Hank's room and finds him on his back, mumbling to Sandy about Hello-Central, Clarence, his cadets, and strange dreams of an abyss of 13 centuries that separate them. Growing incoherent, he starts to cry out, but never finishes.

BACKGROUND AND PUBLISHING HISTORY

The genesis of *Connecticut Yankee* goes back to Mark Twain's 1866 visit to HAWAII. Fascinated by elements of feudalism that he observed there, he later planned to write a novel set in the islands. Meanwhile, several visits to England gave him ideas for a medieval tale. He finally started his Hawaiian novel in 1884, but soon abandoned it. By then he was familiar with Arthurian romances, which he read to his children. In December 1884, G. W. CABLE gave him a copy of MALORY's *Le Morte d'Arthur,* which stimulated him to begin a burlesque of Arthurian romances. By early 1886, he was seriously at work on *Connecticut Yankee.* In November of that year, he gave a public reading from his draft manuscript at the Military Service Institution on New York's Governor's Island.

After four years of intermittent writing, Mark Twain completed *Connecticut Yankee* in April 1889, then spent several months revising it in typescript. CENTURY magazine published four extracts in November; Charles L. WEBSTER & COMPANY published the book on December 5, with CHATTO and Windus issuing an English edition the next day. Meanwhile, Charles Heber CLARK accused Mark Twain of plagiarizing the story from a novella he had published nearly a decade earlier.

While completing his manuscript, Mark Twain saw illustrator Dan BEARD's work in COSMOPOLITAN magazine and arranged with him to illustrate *Connecticut Yankee.* Given considerable freedom in subject matter and treatment, Beard contributed a major dimension to the book. His 220 pictures capture the author's intentions fully, while adding shadings of characterization and strengthening the book's humor and its serious political message. Beard used real people such as Sarah BERNHARDT and Alfred, Lord TENNYSON as models for characters, and drew wickedly savage caricatures of Jay GOULD, WILHELM II, EDWARD VIII and Queen VICTORIA.

Since its first publication, *Connecticut Yankee* has remained in print continuously and is still available in many editions. In 1979, the MARK TWAIN PAPERS project published the first corrected edition—which is also the first modern edition to use all of Beard's illustrations. With Mark Twain's corrected typescript no longer extant, the project drew on his original manuscript—now in the New York Public Library's Berg Collection—and on the *Century* extracts, which contain corrections not made in the Webster edition.

Connecticut Yankee, dramatic adaptations of

Connecticut Yankee has become one of the stage and screen's most frequently adapted Mark Twain stories. Most adaptations set their FRAMES in the periods in which they are made, instead of going back to the novel's 1879 starting point. While typically emphasizing humorous contrasts between past and present, they tend to expand the romantic story line and add modern-day characters who parallel people whom the Hank MORGAN character meets in the sixth-century—much like the dual characters in *The Wizard of Oz.* Most productions alter Hank MORGAN's name—possibly to avoid confusion with MORGAN LE FAY.

In the first film version of *Connecticut Yankee* in 1921, Harry Myers starred as the Boss, "Martin Cavendish," after Douglas Fairbanks turned down the role. The film opens with Cavendish reading Mark Twain's novel and dreaming about introducing 20th-century technology to Camelot. The story line from this film was adapted to Richard Rodgers and Lorenz Hart's musical *A Connecticut Yankee* six years later. William Gaxton played the Boss, "Hank Martin," in that production, which had 418 performances on Broadway in 1927–28. The same play also had 45 performances in London in 1929. This musical was revived in an updated Broadway production in 1943, with Dick Foran playing Hank as a member of the United States Navy. The 1943 version was adapted to television in 1955, with Eddie Albert as Hank.

The first sound film of *Connecticut Yankee,* in 1931, used an entirely new script and cast Will Rogers as the Boss, Hank Martin, a radio technician. This adaptation gave Rogers an opportunity to work in jokes about the Depression and display his roping skills. In 1949, the first color film of *Connecticut Yankee* starred Bing Crosby as Hank Martin, a blacksmith who turns up in Camelot after being knocked off his horse in 1905. This film's songs are unrelated to the Rodgers and Hart score. Although Edmund Beloin's script often departs radically from the original novel, it is unusual in using a FRAME similar to that of the original novel.

In 1979, Disney released a new theatrical film adaptation with the unlikely title *Unidentified Flying Oddball,* which was later changed to THE SPACEMAN AND KING ARTHUR. This loose adaptation sends an astronaut and a robot back to Camelot.

Connecticut Yankee has been adapted to television at least nine times. Boris Karloff played MERLIN against Thomas Mitchell's Boss in a 1952 *Studio One* play. Three years later, Karloff played King Arthur to Eddie Albert's Boss. Meanwhile, Edgar Bergen played the Boss in *Kraft Television Theatre*'s 1954 production. Later television productions took on increasingly unusual qualities. In 1960, for example, Tennessee Ernie Ford starred in "A Tennessee Rebel in King Arthur's Court." CBS-TV broadcast an animated *Connecticut Yankee* in 1970; in 1978, it aired "A Connecticut Rabbit in King Arthur's Court," with Bugs Bunny. That same year, PBS-TV broadcast one of the most thoughtful adaptations of the original story, with Paul Rudd as the Boss, Richard Basehart as King Arthur, and Roscoe Lee Browne as Merlin.

In December 1989, NBC-TV celebrated the 100th anniversary of the novel's publication with a major new television film. This production—which cast a 12-year-old girl, Keshia Knight Pulliam, as the Boss—alternated faithfully following Mark Twain's original dialogue with such radical departures as having the Boss leave Camelot in a hot-air balloon reminiscent of the end of *The Wizard of Oz.* Three years later, the *MacGyver* television series presented a two-part episode loosely based on *Connecticut Yankee,* having the inventive MacGyver draw on all his skills to save Merlin and King Arthur from their enemies.

Constantinople

TURKEY's largest city and most important seaport, Constantinople has been called Istanbul since 1939. It straddles the Bosporus, a strait connecting the Mediterranean and Black seas where Europe and Asia meet. When Mark Twain visited it in 1867, Constantinople had a million residents and was capital of Turkey's Ottoman Empire. He arrived on August 17, 1867 aboard the QUAKER CITY; two days later, the ship continued into the Black Sea, leaving behind eight passengers, including Emeline and Moses S. BEACH, Dan SLOTE and Jack VAN NOSTRAND. The ship returned on August 29, remaining for five days to take on coal. *Innocents Abroad* makes the second stop seem briefer than it actually was by devoting chapters 33–34 to the first stop, while giving the second stop only a single line in chapter 38. Though the book describes Constantinople as beautiful from the harbor, it adds that "its attractiveness begins and ends with its picturesqueness." The book emphasizes the city's more sordid aspects and finds Stamboul's great bazaar one of its few worthwhile sights.

In chapter 23 of *Connecticut Yankee*, Hank MORGAN pretends to cast a magical spell by uttering a German tongue twister: *"Constantinopolitanischerdudelsackspfeifenmachersgesellschafft."* This literally means "The Constantinople Bagpipe Manufacturers Company."

Constantinople Fictional Missouri town in *Tom Sawyer.* Mentioned in chapter 4 as the county seat, 12 miles from ST. PETERSBURG, that Judge THATCHER and his daughter Becky THATCHER are from. In chapter 22 Becky returns to Constantinople for the summer. The town is modeled on PALMYRA, Missouri, the seat of Missouri's MARION COUNTY. In his first draft of *Tom Sawyer,* Mark Twain called the town "Coonville."

Conway, Moncure D[aniel] (March 17, 1832, Falmouth, Virginia–November 15, 1907, Paris, France) Clergyman and author. A Southern minister who became an abolitionist, Conway went to ENGLAND in 1863 on behalf of the Unitarian Church. In September 1872, he met Mark Twain in LONDON while covering one of his speeches for a newspaper. When Mark Twain returned to England the following year, Conway arranged sightseeing tours for his family. During his own lecture tour in America, Conway stayed with Mark Twain's family in Hartford in January 1876 and returned to England with a manuscript copy of *Tom Sawyer* that he arranged for CHATTO and Windus to publish. Conway continued as Mark Twain's English agent until 1881. Mark Twain again saw Conway in Paris in March 1879, when Conway helped show his family the city and took him to several formal parties. The following summer, Conway entertained Mark Twain's family in England and accompanied them to Stratford-on-Avon.

Conway's own writings include popular books about Thomas Paine, Carlyle, EMERSON and Hawthorne, as well as an autobiography (1904) that recalls his acquaintance with Mark Twain.

Cook, Captain James (October 27, 1728, England–February 14, 1779, Hawaii) An English explorer of the Pacific Ocean, Cook is credited with discovering HAWAII in 1778 and naming the archipelago the "SANDWICH ISLANDS." When he returned the following year, Hawai-

ians killed him on the island of Hawaii—apparently because of a misunderstanding. In late May 1866, Mark Twain visited Kealakekua Bay, where Cook was killed. Drawing principally on a book by J. J. JARVES, he wrote a detailed account of Cook's death in a letter to the SACRAMENTO UNION. *Roughing It* gives a briefer account, calling Cook's murder "justifiable homicide" because Cook had repaid kindness and generosity with insult and ill-treatment (chapters 71–72). Cook is also discussed in chapters 64, 66 and 76 of *Roughing It* and in chapters 3, 9 and 10 of *Following the Equator.*

Mark Twain's original letter about Cook's death anticipates the "AMERICAN VANDAL" theme that he would develop a few years later. He has his fictional companion Mr. BROWN attempt to steal the lava on which Cook was killed, then try to remove the tree stump serving as Cook's memorial.

Coon, Ben (*fl.* 1860s) The original source for Mark Twain's JUMPING FROG STORY, Coon was a bartender at Tryon's Hotel in ANGEL'S CAMP, California when Mark Twain met him in late January 1865. As a former steamboat PILOT on the Illinois River, Coon would naturally have had a good rapport with Mark Twain. During a week-long rainstorm, they spent considerable time exchanging yarns, and Coon deeply impressed Mark Twain with a wildly humorous story about a man named Coleman with a prize jumping frog, though Coon himself was never aware that his story was funny. Mark Twain incorporated Coon's storytelling talent into the fictional Simon WHEELER and later made a similar deadpan delivery an important part of his own speaking technique.

Cooper, Aunt Patsy Character in *Pudd'nhead Wilson.* A widow with three children—Rowena Cooper and two younger sons—Aunt Patsy owns a DAWSON'S LANDING cottage and a slave, Nancy, but must rent out a spare room to boost her income above subsistence. In mid-1853, after advertising the room for more than a year, she is so thrilled to take in the CAPELLO twins that she basks in glory even before they appear. After they arrive in chapter 6, she vanishes from the narrative. She returns as the twins go on trial for murder in chapter 20, when she and David WILSON are the only townspeople to stand by them.

Aunt Patsy has a much larger role in the original story, "THOSE EXTRAORDINARY TWINS." In chapter 5 of its published version, she is called as a witness at the Capellos' assault trial. Unable to comprehend court procedures, she tries to deal with the presiding judge, Sim ROBINSON, as an acquaintance until he dismisses her and throws her evidence out.

Cooper, James Fenimore (September 15, 1789, Burlington, New Jersey–September 14, 1851, Cooperstown, New York) Perhaps the most popular American novelist of the early 19th century, Cooper is best known for his "Leatherstocking Tales," which include *The Pioneers*

James Fenimore Cooper, whose "Leatherstocking Tales" Mark Twain thought should have been called the "Broken Twig Series." (St. Nicholas Magazine, 1894)

(1823), *The Last of the Mohicans* (1826), *The Prairie* (1827), *The Pathfinder* (1840) and *The Deerslayer* (1841). Mark Twain read and reveled in Cooper's books as a boy, but grew up to despise them because of the romantic notions about American INDIANS they ingrained in him. After he arrived in NEVADA in 1861, he developed such negative stereotypes of Indians that he concluded Cooper was a liar. In *Roughing It,* his book about this period, the narrator calls himself "a disciple of Cooper and a worshipper of the Red Man" who is shocked to find himself disgusted by the local Goshoot (GOSIUTE) Indians (chapter 19). Mark Twain's first book, *Innocents Abroad* (1869), calls Cooper's Indians "an extinct tribe that never existed" (chapter 20) and compares Cooper to the travel writer GRIMES in finding beauty where it does not exist (chapter 50).

After completing *Huckleberry Finn* in 1884, Mark Twain started a new novel, "HUCK FINN AND TOM SAWYER AMONG THE INDIANS," which was to be an antidote to Cooper's Leatherstocking Tales. He abandoned this novel, but later launched a more direct assault on Cooper in the 4,900-word essay "Fenimore Cooper's Literary Offenses," published in the NORTH AMERICAN REVIEW in July 1895. Often reprinted, this essay pillories Cooper's writing style, plot contrivances and romantic notions. Around this same time, Mark Twain wrote another essay on this theme that was first published in 1946 as "Fenimore Cooper's Further Literary Offenses"; it later appeared as "Cooper's Prose Style" in LETTERS FROM THE EARTH. He also takes a dig at Cooper in chapter 22 of *Following the Equator.*

Mark Twain himself, of course, is not innocent of all the "literary offenses" he attributes to Cooper. For example, while he makes great fun of Cooper's frequent use of "broken twigs" as a plot device, he uses the same device himself at least three times—in chapter 29 of *Tom Sawyer* and in chapters 1 and 40 of *Huckleberry Finn.*

Cooper, Rowena (Roweny)   Character in *Pudd'nhead Wilson.* The 19-year-old daughter of Aunt Patsy COOPER, Rowena is "amiable, and very pretty, but otherwise of no consequence." She is a romantic in the manner of Walter SCOTT—from whose novel *Ivanhoe* she got her name—and finds herself infatuated with the CAPELLO twins even *before* they arrive. She is nominally the girlfriend of Tom DRISCOLL, but falls for Angelo Capello when she meets him in chapter 6. This infatuation leads nowhere, however, and Rowena is later mentioned only when Driscoll thinks about her.

Rowena's romance with Angelo is developed more fully in "THOSE EXTRAORDINARY TWINS," in which they become engaged. Rowena finally throws Angelo over in chapter 9, however, after she sees him get drunk when his Siamese-twin brother drinks heavily. Angelo protests that he does not drink himself, but Rowena counters, "you get drunk, and that is worse."

Cord, Mary Ann (c. 1798, Maryland–c. 1888, Elmira, New York)   The QUARRY FARM cook of Susan and Theodore CRANE, Cord had seven children and her husband taken from her when she was a slave before the CIVIL WAR. During the war, she was reunited with her youngest son, Henry (c. 1845–1927), who had escaped to the North. After she told Mark Twain her story in the summer of 1874, he adapted her simple eloquence into "A TRUE STORY," in which she appears as "Aunt Rachel."

"Corn-pone Opinions"   Posthumously published essay. This exercise of just over 2,000 words explores an idea that is central to the philosophy that Mark Twain developed in WHAT IS MAN?—namely, that man is incapable of independent thought. He wrote the essay around 1901; A. B. PAINE published a slightly abridged version in EUROPE AND ELSEWHERE (1923) and Paul Baender published a corrected version *What Is Man? and Other Philosophical Writings* (1973). It is not known whether the essay's "Jerry" existed.

SYNOPSIS

Mark Twain recalls a young black man, a slave named Jerry. Fifty years earlier, he enjoyed hearing Jerry's daily sermons and regarded him as the finest orator in the United States. One of Jerry's texts was: "You tell me whar a man gits his corn-pone, en I'll tell you what his 'pinions is." Mark Twain interprets this to mean that no man is independent enough to hold views that might interfere with his bread and butter. Since every man gets his views from others, there can be no such thing as an original opinion. He further argues that public opinion is formed by the instinct that moves individual people to conform. That instinct in turn is a product of the need for self-approval—which really means the approval of others.

Cosmopolitan Monthly magazine. Founded by Joseph N. Hallock in Rochester, New York in 1886, *Cosmopolitan* moved to New York City a year later. John Brisben Walker (1847–1931) purchased the magazine in 1889 and as its editor transformed it into a leading fiction magazine before selling it to William Randolph Hearst in 1905. Meanwhile, W. D. HOWELLS edited the magazine briefly in 1892. The following year, Walker gave Mark Twain a contract to write 12 stories for *Cosmopolitan*. Among the stories that he published in 1893 are "IS HE LIVING OR IS HE DEAD?" (September), "THE ESQUIMAU MAIDEN'S ROMANCE" (November) and "TRAVELING WITH A REFORMER" (December)—the last two of which are illustrated by Dan BEARD. *Cosmopolitan* later published Mark Twain's "At the Appetite Cure" (August 1898) and "CHRISTIAN SCIENCE and the Book of Mrs. Eddy" (October 1899).

Crane, Susan Langdon (February 18, 1836, Spencer New York–August 29, 1924) Mark Twain's sister-in-law. Born Susan Dean, Crane was adopted as an infant by Jervis and Olivia LANGDON after her natural parents died. Although nearly 10 years older than her sister Olivia Langdon Clemens, she and Livy grew up close and remained intimate friends throughout their lives. In December 1858, Susan married her father's business manager, Theodore Crane (1831–1889).

When her father died in 1870, Crane inherited QUARRY FARM, near ELMIRA, New York, where she lived the rest of her life. Over the next two decades, Mark Twain spent nearly every summer at her home with his family, and he did much of his best writing there. In 1874, Crane built a detached study for his exclusive use.

With no children of their own, Crane and her husband were close to Livy's family. She nursed Livy at Langdon Clemens's birth in Buffalo in 1870, and attended at the births of all three of Livy's daughters. She also accompanied Mark Twain's family when they went to Europe in 1891 and was with Susy Clemens when she died in Hartford in 1896. The following year she visited the Clemenses in London.

Crescent City STEAMBOAT on which Mark Twain apprenticed as a PILOT. After he completed his first voyage on the COLONEL CROSSMAN, he and Horace BIXBY joined

the *Crescent City* at ST. LOUIS in late April 1857 and made three round-trips to NEW ORLEANS over the next two months. A 688-ton side-wheeler built in 1854, the *Crescent City* took its name from a popular New Orleans nickname. *Life on the Mississippi* relates a story about an accident on the *Crescent City* that actually occurred when Mark Twain was piloting the CITY OF MEMPHIS (chapter 49).

Crimea Peninsula on the Black Sea's north coast. Now in Ukraine, the Crimea was part of RUSSIA when Mark Twain visited it in August 1867. Just over a decade earlier, it had been the scene of a major war in which Russia had fought Turkey, Britain, France and Sardinia (1853–56). Crimean War sites were among the attractions listed in the prospectus for the QUAKER CITY excursion in which Mark Twain participated; his book about the trip, *Innocents Abroad*, describes the devastation that the war left, especially at SEVASTOPOL (chapters 35–37). The book also mentions François Certain Canrobert (1809–1895), France's commander at Crimea, whom Mark Twain saw at a military review in PARIS (chapter 13).

A letter that Mark Twain wrote to the SAN FRANCISCO ALTA CALIFORNIA about Jerusalem's Church of the HOLY SEPULCHER says that the Crimean War was fought to determine which nation had the right to build a new dome over the ancient church. *Innocents Abroad* retains the allusion to a war having been fought over this issue, but omits the reference to the Crimea (chapter 53).

The Crimea is also a major setting for the short story "LUCK" (1891), about a British general who blunders his way to glory in the Crimean War.

cupbearer, queen's Narrator of *1601*. As the noble holder of a hereditary post, the cupbearer is in attendance at Queen ELIZABETH I's court. There he overhears a conversation among nobles and commoners that shocks him; however, he is so bored by the proceedings that he has trouble staying awake.

Mark Twain created this character from his research for *The Prince and the Pauper*, in which a cupbearer is among the "silk-and-velvet discomforters" who beset Tom Canty (chapters 6–7). Years after writing *1601*, Mark Twain alluded to its narrator as a "stupid old nobleman."

"Curing a Cold" Sketch first published in the GOLDEN ERA, as "How to Cure a Cold," on September 20, 1863. After catching a nasty cold when his hotel burned down in VIRGINIA CITY, Nevada, the narrator does *everything* he is advised to do to get rid of it. When told to "feed a cold and starve a fever," he does *both*. He drinks warm salt-water, a solution of molasses, aquafortis and turpentine—then gin and molasses and onions and other concoctions. He also tries applying a sheet bath and a mustard plaster and takes a steam-bath at Steamboat Springs (a spa near Virginia City). When he visits

SAN FRANCISCO, *two* friends recommend that he drink a full quart of whiskey a day—so he drinks a half gallon. He advises other sufferers to follow his course of treatment, since "if it don't cure, it can't more than kill them." Revised versions of the 1,800-word sketch appeared in THE CELEBRATED JUMPING FROG OF CALAVERAS AND OTHER SKETCHES (1867) and in SKETCHES, NEW AND OLD (1875).

"A Curious Dream"   Sketch written in 1870. Set in "no particular city," this story relates a macabre dream about a midnight procession of moth-eaten human skeletons marching past the narrator's doorstep, lugging decaying gravestones and coffins. One skeleton stops to talk. His headstone identifies him as John Baxter Copmanhurst, deceased in May 1836. Copmanhurst complains about his rags, his battered headstone and the dreadful conditions in the neglected cemetery. He no longer even takes pride in his epitaph—"Gone to His Just Reward." Passersby merely laughed at it, so he scratched it off. Fed up with the townspeople's disregard for their ancestors' graves, he and his fellow corpses are leaving to find a town that cares enough to maintain its cemetery properly. At dawn, the narrator awakens suddenly. He assures the reader that "if the cemeteries in his town are kept in good order, this Dream is not leveled at his town at all, but is leveled particularly and venomously at the *next* town."

Mark Twain wrote this 3,400-word sketch—subtitled "Containing a Moral"—to call attention to a neglected BUFFALO cemetery. It appeared twice in the local BUFFALO EXPRESS: on April 30 and May 7, 1870. According to A. B. PAINE, the sketch launched a reform movement. It was issued as a pamphlet in 1872 and reprinted in SKETCHES, NEW AND OLD three years later. In 1907, Vitagraph adapted the story to film, with Mark Twain's approval. ("A Curious Dream" is not related to "A Strange Dream," which Mark Twain published in 1866.)

"A Curious Experience"   Short story written and published in 1881. Mark Twain's longest narrative set in the CIVIL WAR, "A Curious Experience" purports to be the authentic firsthand account of an incident that a Union Army major experienced during the winter of 1862–63. Told within a FRAME signed with the initials "M. T.," the story concerns a teenage boy named Robert Wicklow who fakes a conspiracy to take a Union fort. Wicklow's elaborate scheming anticipates Tom Sawyer's "EVASION" conspiracy in *Huckleberry Finn*, as well as his abolition scare in "TOM SAWYER'S CONSPIRACY." Wicklow's account of how he was orphaned also anticipates some of Huck's elaborate lies in *Huckleberry Finn*.

The 10,660-word story first appeared in CENTURY MAGAZINE in November 1881. It was later collected in *The Stolen White Elephant* and in *The American Claimant and Other Stories and Sketches*.

SYNOPSIS

The unnamed officer recalls commanding Fort Trumbull at New London, Connecticut. One night a boy named Robert Wicklow appeared and begged permission to enlist. After Wicklow related a moving story of escaping from NEW ORLEANS—where his pro-Union father was lynched—the major enrolled him as a drummer-boy. Later, he heard disturbing stories about Wicklow's strange behavior and learned that the boy was studying the fort's armaments and manpower and sending messages to allies who intended to capture the fort. After getting authorization to administer martial law, the major rounded up suspects and got Wicklow to confess to being the center of a conspiracy. Wicklow's alleged accomplices were arrested, but none corroborated his story and Wicklow himself escaped. After he was tracked down, he was found to be a local Connecticut resident who had manufactured the whole conspiracy in his imagination.

"A Curious Pleasure Excursion"   SCIENCE FICTION story first published in 1874 and collected in SKETCHES, NEW AND OLD. The NEW YORK HERALD published this piece as a letter signed by Mark Twain on July 6, 1874—nearly 17 years after publishing Mark Twain's letter criticizing the QUAKER CITY excursion. Capitalizing on public concern about a comet recently discovered by the French astronomer Jerome Eugene Coggia, the sketch parodies the *Quaker City* excursion by proposing a luxury cruise aboard the comet—which resembles the giant comet of Mark Twain's later "CAPTAIN STORMFIELD'S VISIT TO HEAVEN." The sketch also takes subtle digs at several notorious politicians, including the Radical Republican leader Benjamin Franklin Butler (1818–1893) and Alexander Robey Shepherd (1835–1902), the corrupt territorial governor of the District of Columbia. Mark Twain may have written the sketch to generate publicity for his play about political corruption adapted from *The Gilded Age* that opened in New York two months later.

SYNOPSIS

Mark Twain announces that he has gone into partnership with BARNUM to lease the comet from Mr. Coggia and equip it with a million staterooms and many fabulous amenities. On July 20 (1874), it will begin a voyage that will include stops throughout the solar system and at stars in several constellations. Traveling up to 40 million miles a day, the comet will return to New York on December 14, 1991.

Expecting to accommodate many politicians, the excursion's promoters have issued complimentary round-trip tickets to several public servants who have earned a rest. In the interest of promoting further business,

Mark Twain informs advertisers that the comet will carry bulletin boards and paint, and he advises cremationists that they will be going straight to some very hot places.

"The Curious Republic of Gondour" Sketch published in 1875. Two years after coauthoring *The Gilded Age*—which indicts democracy's worst abuses—Mark Twain wrote "Gondour" as a serious proposal for a political antidote to universal suffrage. The public ignored the sketch, but some of its ideas find echoes in Mark Twain's later writings. For example, his central theme—that the educated should wield the most political power—finds an ironic rebuttal in *Huckleberry Finn*, in which Pap FINN drunkenly rages that he will not vote in the same country that permits a black college professor to vote (chapter 6). The sketch's description of how Gondour citizens defer to each other in public closely resembles a moment in *Connecticut Yankee* when Hank MORGAN walks through a sixth-century English village observing how a freeman behaves toward members of different classes (chapter 31).

SYNOPSIS

After learning GONDOUR's language, the unidentified narrator studies the nation's unique political institutions. When Gondour experimented with universal suffrage, its ignorant nontaxpaying classes controlled the government and corruption was rampant. *Restricting* suffrage was unacceptable, so the problem was remedied by the appealing gimmick of *enlarging* it. While every citizen retained the vote, the constitution was quietly amended to provide additional votes based on property ownership and education in a formula assuring that the most educated people would control the government. Votes based on wealth are known as "mortal" because they can be lost; those based on education are called "immortal," because they can only be lost in cases of insanity.

Now that citizens are honored primarily for the number of votes they hold, they are disinclined to gamble, speculate or do anything that might imperil their votes. One effect of this system becomes evident when the narrator walks with a friend, whose deference to passersby is determined by how many votes they own. The greatest benefit of this system is Gondour's clean, efficient government. All office holders must pass competitive examinations, and only educated candidates of high moral character have any chance to be elected. Thanks to generous salaries, officials have no need to steal. The Grand Caliph who heads the government is elected for a 20-year term. The office has twice been held by women, who also fill many offices in the cabinet that governs the country.

After listening to Gondour's proud and contented people, the narrator is relieved to return home, where people do not feel such pride in their country.

PUBLISHING HISTORY

In the hope that readers would take this sketch more seriously without his name on it, Mark Twain published "Gondour" anonymously in the October 1875 issue of ATLANTIC MONTHLY. The magazine's editor, W. D. HOWELLS, invited him to contribute more reports on Gondour, but public indifference to the first sketch stifled Mark Twain's interest.

Never included in any of Mark Twain's authorized anthologies, the sketch first saw book publication in 1919, in *The Curious Republic of Gondour and Other Whimsical Sketches* (New York: Boni and Liveright). This unauthorized anthology also includes 15 other Mark Twain sketches, mostly from the GALAXY and the BUFFALO EXPRESS.

Curry, Abraham ("Old Abe," Abram) V. Z. (1815–1873) NEVADA merchant and civic leader. A native of New York, where he worked in the shipping trade on Lake Erie, Curry came to California in 1852 and helped plot CARSON CITY, Nevada in 1858. He then championed making Carson Nevada's capital—a cause that he advanced by giving the first territorial legislature free use of his hotel at nearby Warm Springs for its inaugural session in October–November 1861. In chapter 25 of *Roughing It*, Mark Twain credits Curry with saving Nevada's new government. Curry was also a representative in the legislature's 1862 session and a councilman in its third session in 1864.

In 1863, Mark Twain made his MASSACRE HOAX seem more credible by inserting Curry's name as an informant. In chapter 24 of *Roughing It*, Curry tells the narrator that his "Genuine Mexican Plug" is worthless. The book also frequently mentions the "Gould & Curry" mine near Virginia City that Curry helped establish. According to chapter 46, he sold out his two-thirds interest for $2,500 and an old horse. The mine was later sold for $7,600,000 in gold.

Cutter, Bloodgood Haviland (August 5, 1817, Little Neck, Long Island, New York–September 26, 1906) Passenger on the QUAKER CITY excursion who gained minor fame as the "Poet Lariat" of *Innocents Abroad*. A millionaire farmer from Long Island, Cutter hoped to earn passage on the *Quaker City* by serving as its official poet; denied free passage, he did not decide to board the ship until it was leaving Brooklyn harbor. *Innocents Abroad* never mentions Cutter by name, but alludes to him simply as "the poet" in chapters 7, 10 and 37. Mark Twain's private notes describe Cutter as a simpleminded and old-fashioned farmer with a "strange proclivity" for writing rhymes, which he hands out to anyone he encounters. One of Mark Twain's letters to the SAN FRANCISCO ALTA CALIFORNIA alludes to Cutter as one of "three uncouth characters" aboard the ship and calls him a "shameless old idiot." Chapter 7 of *Innocents* dubs him the ship's self-styled "laureate"; he is called "Poet Lariat" only in chapter 10—in a remark made by the malapropist ORACLE.

On the ship's third day at sea, Cutter recited 75 stanzas of doggerel to a captive audience; he later bored fellow passengers with verses on everything he could think of. When the ship was quarantined at NAPLES, he was one of the passengers stuck aboard; he appealed to health officials to lift the quarantine with verses such as this:

Why don't your doctor come on board
And see what in our ship is stored;
Although our ship is nice and clean
On her at all he is not seen.

Other passengers hoped that when local authorities saw Cutter's verses, they would lift the ship's quarantine to spare themselves from having to read the rest. Cutter's verses were less welcome when the passengers visited Czar ALEXANDER II in Russia. According to chapter 37 of *Innocents Abroad*, Cutter had to choose between swearing not to issue a line of poetry near the czar or remaining under guard aboard the ship.

Nearly two decades after the voyage, Cutter paid to publish a 500-page book, *The Long-Island Farmer's Poems: Lines Written on the "Quaker City" Excursion* (1886). Indifferent or oblivious to his depiction in *Innocents Abroad*, he bills himself "Mark Twain's Poet Lariat" on the book's title page.

Cutter helped inspire Emmeline GRANGERFORD, the dead poetaster of *Huckleberry Finn*. Like Cutter, Emmeline "would slap down a line, and if she couldn't find anything to rhyme with it she would just scratch it out and slap down another one, and go ahead. She warn't particular."

"The Czar's Soliloquy" Sketch published in 1905. During the fortnight after RUSSIA's Czar Nicholas II (1868–1918) had troops fire on striking workers at St. Petersburg on January 22, 1905, Mark Twain wrote this polemic to express his indignation. Inspired by reports that the czar meditated regularly after his morning bath, he has the czar indict himself in his own words. About a third of the SOLILOQUY's 2,500 words concern the importance of clothes—a theme discussed in *Connecticut Yankee* (particularly in chapter 18) and "DIPLOMATIC PAY AND CLOTHES." Later the same year, Mark Twain wrote a similar attack on Belgium's king in KING LEOPOLD'S SOLILOQUY.

SYNOPSIS

As the czar contemplates his bony, naked body before a mirror, he wonders what about himself could possibly inspire awe and reverence. Without his clothes, he believes that he would be destitute of authority and no one could tell him from any common person. Who, he asks, is the real emperor of Russia? His clothes. Further, his grand titles are part of his clothes.

He muses over the passivity of his people, wondering why they allow themselves to be abused, and laughs at moralists who, by saying that it is wrong to kill a czar, thereby support his oppressions. After considering some of his latest crimes—such as destroying the Finnish constitution and his recent massacre—he starts to fear that the nation may be stirring out of its lethargy as people discover the true meaning of patriotism: loyalty to the *nation* itself, not to a family or a fiction. If Russia's 25 million mothers were to teach their children this truth, his successor would think twice before repeating his atrocities.

The czar pulls two newspaper clippings from beneath his pillow and reads them. One tells of his atrocities in Poland; the other tells how he made subjects worship him in abject servitude. He weeps over his own cruelty and pious hypocrisy. To revive his spirits, he decides to put on his clothes—his only protection against finding himself out.

PUBLISHING HISTORY

Mark Twain signed this piece on February 2, 1905—the 35th anniversary of his MARRIAGE to Livy and the first anniversary he had without her. After appearing in the NORTH AMERICAN REVIEW in March, the piece was not anthologized until Charles NEIDER's *Mark Twain: Life As I Find It* included in 1961.

D

D. A. January STEAMBOAT on which Mark Twain may have been a cub PILOT. Inconclusive evidence suggests that Mark Twain apprenticed on the *January* under J. Ed MONTGOMERY on one trip to St. Louis in December 1857, while the PENNSYLVANIA was laid up in New Orleans. The *January's* captain at that time was Patrick Yore (1814–1889), who may have been the "good old Captain Y." of chapter 14 of *Life on the Mississippi.* Strother WILEY—"Mr. W."—may also have been a pilot on that voyage.

Daggett, Rollin Mallory (February 22, 1831, Richville, New York–November 12, 1901, San Francisco, California) Journalist and politician. Daggett came to the West Coast from Ohio in 1849 and founded the literary journal GOLDEN ERA in San Francisco in 1852. Ten years later, he went to NEVADA, where he operated a brokerage house and became a reporter and editor for the VIRGINIA CITY TERRITORIAL ENTERPRISE. In this capacity, he helped influence Mark Twain's development as a writer. Daggett is the "Mr. D." of *Roughing It* who contributes a chapter to the WEEKLY OCCIDENTAL's serial novel (chapter 51). Mark Twain's AUTOBIOGRAPHY contains an appreciative account of the help that Daggett rendered him when he was preparing for a duel with a rival newspaper editor. Daggett later represented Nevada in Congress (1879–81). After serving as American minister to HAWAII (1882–85), he collaborated with King David Kalakaua on *The Legends and Myths of Hawaii,* which Charles L. WEBSTER & COMPANY published in 1888.

Daly, [John] Augustin (July 20, 1838, Plymouth, North Carolina–June 7, 1899, Paris, France) Playwright and theater impresario. Born in the South and raised in the North, Daly began his career as a drama critic for New York newspapers and began adapting popular European plays and novels to the stage. After producing his first play in 1862, he managed a theatrical troupe that toured Union-controlled Southern cities during the CIVIL WAR. During the 1870s, he developed a strong repertory company that performed in several New York theaters that he refurbished. He wrote or adapted about 90 plays, including a musical adaptation of Mark Twain's *Roughing It* that opened in February 1873. Four years later he staged Mark Twain and Bret HARTE's AH SIN.

In the mid-1880s, Mark Twain had trouble gaining admittance into Daly's theater for an appointment—an incident that he later made the subject of a speech he delivered at Daly's Theater in 1877. He also retold the story in chapter 45 of *Following the Equator.* Daly rejected Mark Twain's dramatization of *Tom Sawyer* in 1884, but later expressed interest in obtaining the stage rights to *The American Claimant.*

Damascus Ancient Syrian city. The capital of modern SYRIA, Damascus was a Turkish administrative center when Mark Twain visited it on September 14–16, 1867. Chapter 44 of *Innocents Abroad* calls Damascus the "most fanatical Mohammedan purgatory out of Arabia" and admires Muhammad's wisdom in not entering the city after admiring it from afar. The chapter also finds humor in the biblical story of St. Luke and the crooked "street which is called straight," where St. Paul was baptized. From Damascus, Mark Twain went southwest to BANIYAS.

Damrell, Sister (Mrs.) Minor character in *Huckleberry Finn.* One of the nosy PIKESVILLE neighbors who visit the Phelpses after Jim's escape attempt, Sister Damrell questions why Jim had a ladder in his hut (chapter 41). Mark Twain's family had a neighbor named Mrs. Damrell when they lived in FLORIDA, Missouri in his infancy.

Dan HOLY LAND site. Traditionally the northernmost town in ancient PALESTINE, Dan stands at the extreme northeastern corner of modern Israel. Mark Twain passed through it after leaving nearby BANIYAS on September 18, 1867 and comments on it briefly in chapter 46 of *Innocents Abroad.* In his travel letter to the SAN FRANCISCO ALTA CALIFORNIA, he calls Dan "Dutch Flat," arguing that "from Dutch Flat to Beersheba" sounds better than "from Dan to Beersheba."

"The Dandy Frightening the Squatter" Mark Twain's earliest-known publication in the East, this 425-word sketch appeared in Boston's CARPET-BAG on May 1, 1852. The sketch purports to recount an incident that occurred in Hannibal 13 years earlier. When a steamboat stops for wood, a young dandy tries showing off for two women by scaring a backwoodsman he sees loafing on shore. Armed with pistols and a bowie knife, the dandy accosts the man, threatening him as if he knows him. Without hesitation, the backwoodsman punches the dandy in the face, knocking him into the river.

Daniel, Uncle (c. 1805–?) A slave owned by John QUARLES, Daniel was a familiar figure to Mark Twain, who spent his boyhood summers at his uncle's FLORIDA, Missouri farm. Mark Twain remembered Daniel as a clearheaded, warm-hearted and guileless man who helped instill in him a life-long affection and respect for African Americans. By his own admission, he transformed Daniel into the JIM of *Huckleberry Finn.* He also used "Uncle Dan'l" as the name of a servant of Colonel SELLERS in *The Gilded Age* and *The American Claimant.* Quarles freed Daniel in November 1855, when he was 50 years old.

Dan'l Webster Title character in the JUMPING FROG STORY. Probably a bullfrog, Dan'l Webster is owned by Jim SMILEY, who has spent three months training him to become the best-jumping frog in CALAVERAS COUNTY. Despite his giftedness, Dan'l remains exceptionally modest and straightforward. Smiley carries him to town in a lattice box, on the chance of getting up a wager on him. The frog takes his name from the American statesman Daniel Webster, who was secretary of state around the time the events in this narrative occurred.

Darwin, Charles (February 12, 1809, Shrewsbury, England–April 19, 1882, Down, Kent) English naturalist who developed a theory of evolution. During a visit to England, Mark Twain traveled to the Lake District to meet Darwin at his Windermere Lake retreat on August 19, 1879—a meeting that he later recalled as having been as awkward as his first meeting with U. S. GRANT. Darwin himself later told Charles Eliot Norton (1827–1908) that he often read himself to sleep with Mark Twain's books. The year that Mark Twain met Darwin, he was involved in a semi-serious project to erect a monument to ADAM. In "A MONUMENT TO ADAM," he argues that after Darwin's publication of *Descent of Man* in 1871, the Father of Mankind stands to be replaced by a monkey and forgotten.

Mark Twain often worked references to Darwin and his ideas about evolution into his writings. In chapter 11 of *The American Claimant,* for example, Barrow argues that aristocratic titles are empty and that it would be absurd to imagine "Darwin feeling flattered by the notice of a princess." Mark Twain also mentions Darwin in "Three Thousand Years Among the Microbes" and in "SOME THOUGHTS ON THE SCIENCE OF ONANISM"—which suggests that monkey masturbation supports Darwin's theory of evolution.

dauphin French title for the heir to the royal throne. In *Huckleberry Finn,* Huck tells Jim about the "dolphin," the son of LOUIS XVI who disappeared in prison (chapter 14). Later, an old con man who joins them on their raft claims to be the missing dauphin. After presenting himself as "Looy Seventeen," he is known as the KING (chapter 19). The real Louis XVII (1785–1795) almost certainly died in prison, but many people believed that he escaped. In later years at least 35 claimants professed to be the missing dauphin; several visited the United States. If *Huckleberry Finn*'s "King" had been Louis XVII, he would have been about 60 years old at the time the story takes place. The King is clearly older than this— a fact that the DUKE is quick to point out.

FRANCE adopted *dauphin* as a title in the mid-14th century. As King CHARLES VII's official title before he was crowned in 1429, it is the only name that Joan uses for him before his coronation in Mark Twain's novel *Joan of Arc.*

Davis, Jefferson (June 3, 1808, Fairview, Kentucky–December 6, 1889, New Orleans, Louisiana) After serving as the Confederacy's only president through the CIVIL WAR, Davis was captured by Union troops in Georgia in May 1865. He spent the next two years in a Virginia prison, from which he was released on bond on May 13, 1867. Two nights later, Mark Twain saw Davis check into the same NEW YORK CITY hotel in which he himself was staying. Mark Twain's letter to the SAN FRANCISCO ALTA CALIFORNIA of May 17 describes the encounter, remarking on how little interest New Yorkers had in the man who had once been their archenemy. A later letter to the *Alta* comments on Horace GREELEY's having gone too far by signing Davis's bail bond. The federal government finally moved to try Davis for treason in December 1868, but President Andrew JOHNSON issued a general amnesty order the following February that ended the effort.

One of the few allusions to Davis in Mark Twain's books appears in chapter 19 of *Innocents Abroad,* in which Mark Twain comments on a painting he saw in Hawaii that made Davis look like a German.

Davy Minor character in the "RAFT CHAPTER" of *Huckleberry Finn* (chapter 16) and *Life on the Mississippi* (chapter 3). Davy is a small raftsman who beats up two bigger toughs, the "CHILD OF CALAMITY" and Bob. Later, he saves Huck from being painted blue and thrown overboard.

Dawson, John D. (c. 1812, Scotland–?) Mark Twain's last schoolteacher. A Scot, Dawson opened a school in Hannibal in 1847, but joined California's GOLD RUSH just two years later. Mark Twain attended Dawson's school briefly and used it and Dawson in several stories. He also remembered Dawson clearly in his autobiographical dictations. In *Tom Sawyer,* Dawson appears as Mr. DOBBINS and his school is described in some detail in chapters 6–7 and 20–21. In "SCHOOLHOUSE HILL," the teacher Archibald Ferguson is modeled on Dawson;

however, the school is modeled on that of Mark Twain's earlier teacher, Samuel Cross.

Dawson's pop-eyed son, Theodore—whose near-perfect goodness made Mark Twain want to drown him—is the model for *Tom Sawyer*'s Willie MUFFERSON.

Dawson's Landing Fictional Missouri town in *Pudd'nhead Wilson*, "THOSE EXTRAORDINARY TWINS" and "Hellfire Hotchkiss." Located a half day's steamboat journey down the Mississippi from ST. LOUIS, Dawson's Landing is a regular stop on the CAIRO and MEMPHIS steamboat lines. When *Pudd'nhead Wilson* opens in 1830, the town is 50 years old and still growing. It appears to be a model American town, with modest but attractive houses, tidy gardens, and peaceful and contented citizens. Like Mark Twain's fictional ST. PETERSBURG, Dawson's Landing closely resembles the Hannibal of Mark Twain's youth. Like the latter, Dawson's Landing has a "Main Street" paralleling the river a block inland, is enclosed by hills "in a half-moon curve" and has pork as a major industry. Dawson's Landing also resembles Hannibal and St. Petersburg in being a slaveholding town—a fact of central importance to *Pudd'nhead Wilson*. Its being closer to the Deep South makes the horror of being "sold down the river" a constant specter in everyone's consciousness. Here the true ugliness and brutality of slavery become evident; the town is like a St. Petersburg that has lost its innocence.

In chapter 7 of *Pudd'nhead Wilson*, Judge DRISCOLL gives the CAPELLO brothers a buggy-ride tour of the town that recalls Mark Twain's descriptions of the dreary tours he endured while on the lecture circuit. The tour takes in a new graveyard, a jail, a Freemason's Hall, Methodist and Presbyterian churches and a site for a new Baptist church, a town hall, slaughterhouse, firehouse and a militia company.

The main action of *Pudd'nhead Wilson* develops in mid-1853, shortly before Dawson's Landing is to be chartered as a city. Minor aspects of the plot include David WILSON's election as mayor and the Capello brothers' unsuccessful campaigns for the new city council. While the people of Dawson's Landing are generally kindhearted, their prejudices and narrowness prevent them from appreciating the qualities of a man like Wilson until he scores a spectacular success in the climactic trial scene. Meanwhile, they do not hesitate to gush over purported Italian nobles, though they invariably prove fickle when their heroes' fortunes fall.

While it is generally acknowledged that Mark Twain took the name "Dawson's Landing" from his teacher John D. DAWSON, it is not clear why.

Dead Sea Lake between Israel and Jordan. At 1,300 feet below sea level, the Dead Sea's surface is the lowest point on the surface of the Earth. The 405-square-mile lake is fed by the JORDAN RIVER from the north, but has no outlet of its own. Consequently, it has exceptionally salty water that provides great buoyancy. During a side trip from JERUSALEM, Mark Twain swam in the northern end of the Dead Sea on September 26, 1867; he even attempted to ride his horse into the water, but was upset. Chapter 55 of *Innocents Abroad* describes this visit.

Dean, Henry Clay (October 27, 1822, Fayette County, Pennsylvania–February 6, 1887, Putnam County, Missouri) Eccentric philosopher who inspired Mark Twain's "THE WAR PRAYER." After settling in southeastern IOWA in 1850, Dean was ordained by the Methodist church and became a circuit rider in VIRGINIA. There he earned renown as an orator and was elected Senate chaplain in 1856. Also a criminal lawyer, he was noted for winning over juries with his eloquence. When Dean sensed that a sectional split within the Methodist Church foreshadowed the coming split within the Union, he quit his ministry and campaigned to preserve the Union.

Henry Clay Dean, the "archangel" of Life on the Mississippi, *in middle age.* (Courtesy, State Historical Society of Iowa—Des Moines)

After the Democratic Party split at its 1860 convention, he supported Stephen A. Douglas's nomination for the presidency in a series of brilliant speeches. Throughout the CIVIL WAR he was noted as an outspoken "Copperhead"; afterward, he published *The Crimes of the Civil War*. In 1871, he moved to a Putnam County, Missouri farm that he called "Rebel's Cove."

Mark Twain saw Dean only once when he was living in KEOKUK, Iowa, but wrote that Dean "was much talked of when I lived there." Chapter 57 of *Life on the Mississippi* describes Dean as an "erratic genius" of humble origin who educated himself by reading on curbstones, dressed like a wharf-rat and oblivious to his surroundings. The chapter also relates an incident that William H. CLAGETT observed in Keokuk in 1861, when "war fever was running high." A desperate lecture agent grabbed Dean off the street when his scheduled speaker failed to show. The tattered Dean stepped onstage to a huge crowd's derisive laughter, but ignored it and spoke "like another VESUVIUS, spouting smoke and flame" until the audience cheered wildly. At first, the crowd thought him "an escaped lunatic"; when he finished, "they thought he was an escaped archangel." Mark Twain fictionalized the incident in "The War Prayer."

"The Death Disk" Short story set in mid–17th-century ENGLAND about a young officer who is saved from execution by the fortuitous intervention of his daughter. An officer under Oliver Cromwell's Commonwealth, Colonel Mayfair is waiting to die for exceeding his orders. Ordered to feign attack on a superior force, he and two fellow officers turned their feint into a glorious victory. For their disobedience the three officers have been court-martialed and sentenced to be shot.

SYNOPSIS

The story opens as Mayfair is at home saying farewell to his family. When his daughter Abby Mayfair asks him for a story, he starts explaining what is happening to him, but is not finished when soldiers come to take him away. Abby thus never realizes that the story she has heard is about her own father. According to Mayfair's story, Cromwell faces a moral dilemma. He wants to spare two of the condemned officers, so that only one must be executed as an example. He orders the condemned officers to draw lots to determine who will be executed, but all three refuse, since they regard doing so as a willful act of suicide, which their religion will not allow.

Meanwhile, Cromwell decides to resolve the moral dilemma by having an innocent child make the choice for him. He has the first child who appears on the street brought to him. He does not realize, however, that the beautiful little girl thus found is Mayfair's daughter Abby. She so wins Cromwell over that he promises to obey her commands. He then gives her one red and two white sealing-wax disks to distribute among the prisoners, without telling her what the disks are for. When Abby finds her own father among the men, she gives him the prettiest disk—the fatal red one. Cromwell is devastated when he learns that Abby has given the death disk to her own father. He finds a way out, however, when Abby reminds him of his earlier promise and demands that her father be freed. Interpreting the incident as an expression of God's will, Cromwell pardons Mayfair and allows him to go home.

BACKGROUND AND PUBLISHING HISTORY

In early 1883 Mark Twain read Thomas Carlyle's edition of *Oliver Cromwell's Letters and Speeches* (1845). Later that year he wrote W. D. HOWELLS that he was considering writing a play about an incident concerning Cromwell's use of a young girl to select rebellious soldiers to execute. He did nothing with the idea until late 1899, however, when he wrote "The Death Disk." The story appeared in HARPER'S MAGAZINE in December 1901, with three full-page illustrations by Lucius HITCHCOCK. Early the following year, Mark Twain dramatized it and had it staged at Carnegie Hall as *The Death Wafer*. In 1909 Biograph released *The Death Disk* as a silent film—probably one reel in length. Edgar S. Werner, a New York publisher, issued the story as a book, *Death-Disk*, in 1913.

"The Death of Jean" Essay written by Mark Twain immediately after the death of his daughter Jean Clemens in 1909. On the morning before Christmas, Jean died suddenly at STORMFIELD. Over the next two days, Mark Twain remained home and wrote what he called the "end of my autobiography" as Jean was taken to ELMIRA, New York for burial. Both a catharsis and a summing up of his life, the 4,200-word essay is the last substantial writing he ever completed. It takes the form of a diary, with its first entry dated 11:00 a.m., Christmas Eve. Its final entry is dated 5:00 p.m., December 26, by which time Jean's funeral was over. After finishing the piece, Mark Twain vowed never to write again. The essay is a poignant reflection on the terrible suddenness of the calamity, paying a moving tribute to Jean and recalling Mark Twain's other losses. Now he is alone, he writes. Yesterday he was 74 years old. Who can estimate his age today?

HARPER'S MAGAZINE published the essay in January 1911 and it was reprinted in *What Is Man? and Other Essays* in 1917. Mark Twain wanted the piece to be the concluding chapter to his AUTOBIOGRAPHY, but his wish was ignored until Michael J. Kiskis published *Mark Twain's Own Autobiography* in 1990. The 1979 television drama MARK TWAIN: BENEATH THE LAUGHTER uses Mark Twain's composition of the essay as its unifying structure.

death, Mark Twain's On the afternoon of Thursday, April 21, 1910, Mark Twain quietly sank into a coma at his STORMFIELD home in Redding, Connecticut. At sunset, his heart failed and he died in his own bed. He was 74 years, four months and three weeks old.

During the last year of his life, Mark Twain suffered from angina pectoris, and his health went into a further decline after the sudden death of his daughter Jean Clemens on Christmas Eve. In early January, he went to BERMUDA to recuperate; he did not expect to live much longer. On March 24, the 63rd anniversary of his father's death, he wrote to his only surviving daughter, Clara Clemens, recalling a comet he once saw and reiterating his often expressed wish to "go out with HALLEY'S COMET"—then visible in the sky. His condition then deteriorated markedly, spurring A. B. PAINE to fetch him home from Bermuda, a week before his death. Clara also soon returned home. She and her husband, Ossip GABRILOWITSCH, Charles LANGDON, Katy LEARY and two doctors were at Mark Twain's side at the end. There is some uncertainty as to whether he knew that Clara was pregnant with what would be his only grandchild, Nina GABRILOWITSCH.

Mark Twain's body was dressed in a WHITE SUIT and carried to New York City the next day. After a large funeral procession on April 23, Dr. Henry van Dyke and Joseph TWICHELL conducted a simple funeral service at the Presbyterian Brick Church (Twichell's own wife died a few hours later). The next day, Samuel Elijah Eastman conducted a second service at the Langdon family home in Elmira. Finally, Mark Twain was buried alongside his wife and children at WOODLAWN CEMETERY during a rainstorm.

Five days after Mark Twain's death, Nobel Prize–winning writer Bjornstjerne Bjornston died. Britain's King EDWARD VII followed on May 5. The year also saw the passing of O. Henry, William James, Winslow Homer, Julia Ward Howe and Leo Tolstoy.

de Conte, Sieur Louis Narrator of *Joan of Arc.* Though based on a real person from Joan of Arc's time, Mark Twain's de Conte is a mostly fictional creation. As the ostensible author of *The Personal Recollections of Joan of Arc,* he writes from the year 1492 for his relatives' descendants. Most of his narrative comes from his firsthand participation in events and from occasional eavesdropping. He also occasionally supplements his narrative with stories taken from unnamed "histories" and testimony given at Joan's rehabilitation hearings.

Born on January 6, 1410—exactly two years before Joan—de Conte is orphaned as a child and raised by a DOMREMY priest who teaches him to read and write. Though a member of the minor nobility, he grows up close to Joan and many other peasant children. After Joan gains command of France's armies in 1429, de Conte becomes her page and secretary and remains at her side throughout her campaigns. After her capture, he disguises himself and becomes a clerk to the court recorder at her trial in ROUEN, so he is close to her until she dies. In later years, de Conte and his friend Noël RAINGUESSON return to fighting for France. After the

English are expelled from the country in 1453, he retires to Domremy an honored hero.

Like the novel's ostensible translator, Jean François ALDEN, de Conte (whose surname means "tale" in French) is an alter ego of Mark Twain, who shares his uncritical worship of Joan of Arc. It is often pointed out that the "initials" of Sieur Louis de Conte are the same as those of Samuel L. Clemens. While Mark Twain might have found significance in such congruity, "Sieur" is an honorific title—much like "Sir" or "Mister"—and is not really part of de Conte's name. More telling are the modern views that de Conte occasionally voices. For example, early in the narrative, he discusses how blind men are to women's strength and endurance (book 2, chapter 4). Later, he expresses the thought that one day peasants may discover that they are "people" and rise up to demand their rights (book 2, chapter 37). De Conte also resembles Mark Twain in calling himself fond of sarcasm, though he is not overly sarcastic throughout his narrative (book 2, chapter 18). He also carries an emotional scar similar to one that Mark Twain bore after falling in love with 14-year-old Laura Wright in 1858. During his stay at ORLÉANS, De Conte falls in love with Catherine Boucher. In a scene that anticipates Cyrano's wooing of Roxanne in Edmond Rostand's *Cyrano de Bergerac* (1897), de Conte writes a love poem to Catherine that Rainguesson recites for him. He remains a bachelor and carries Catherine's image in his heart for 63 years (book 2, chapter 25). Somewhere along the way, he loses the power of laughter (book 2, chapter 12).

Defoe, Daniel (1660, London–April 24, 1731, London) Mark Twain had a lifelong interest in *Robinson Crusoe* (1719), Defoe's story about a man marooned alone on a remote island. Its influence can first be seen in *Tom Sawyer,* in which Tom and two friends live as castaways on JACKSON'S ISLAND (chapters 13–17). *Life on the Mississippi* mentions the electric shiver that Crusoe felt when he discovered a human footprint (chapter 2)—an effect that Mark Twain recreates in *Huckleberry Finn.* In that novel, Huck spends several days hiding out alone on Jackson's Island, then stumbles upon someone else's smoldering campfire (chapter 8). Early in *Connecticut Yankee* Hank MORGAN compares being trapped in sixth-century England with Robinson Crusoe's plight. He has "no society but some more or less tame animals" and to make life bearable he must do what Crusoe did, "invent, contrive, create, reorganize things" (chapter 7). Mark Twain's 1879 speech "SOME THOUGHTS ON THE SCIENCE OF ONANISM" quotes Crusoe on masturbation.

Though it is not certain that Mark Twain read Defoe's *Roxana, or the Fortunate Mistress* (1724) after W. D. HOWELLS recommended the novel to him in 1885, it may have inspired his name for ROXANA in *Pudd'nhead Wilson.*

Denslow, William Wallace (May 5, 1856, Philadelphia, Pennsylvania–March 29, 1915) Illustrator. Best known for his work in L. Frank Baum's *The Wizard*

of Oz (1900), Denslow began collaborating with Baum during the mid-1890s and eventually specialized in animals in human situations, as in Baum's *Father Goose* (1899). After breaking from Baum, he settled in BERMUDA, where he bought his own island and styled himself "King Denslow I, Monarch of Denslow Island and Protector of the Coral Reefs." Denslow contributed six illustrations to chapter 47 of *A Tramp Abroad*.

De Quille, Dan (May 9, 1829, Knox County, Ohio–March 16, 1898, West Liberty, Iowa) Pseudonym of William Wright, a Nevada journalist and friend of Mark Twain. Born into a large Quaker family in Ohio, De Quille married and had five children in Iowa before going west alone to prospect in 1857. During five years in California and Nevada, he failed as a miner, but gained some attention by publishing humorous sketches. In early 1862, Joe GOODMAN hired him onto the VIRGINIA CITY TERRITORIAL ENTERPRISE as a reporter. De Quille wrote for the paper intermittently for 31 years and became respected as both an authority on mining and a humorous writer.

When De Quille was planning a long visit to his family at the end of 1862, Goodman hired Mark Twain—another failed miner—to fill in for him. The newcomer arrived in September and immediately hit it off with De Quille, whose sense of humor and appreciation for elaborate HOAXES he shared. After helping Mark Twain get started on the paper, De Quille went to Iowa in December. He returned eight months later and became Mark Twain's roommate. The two men developed into the *Enterprise*'s most popular writers and divided their responsibilities, with De Quille specializing in mining news and Mark Twain focusing on other matters. Chapter 42 of *Roughing It* alludes to De Quille briefly but clearly as "Dan"—the name by which he was known in Nevada.

In May 1864, Mark Twain left Virginia City just as its first great boom was subsiding. De Quille remained to see the region go through an even bigger boom in the 1870s, then a slow unrelieved decline until even the *Enterprise* collapsed in 1893. Meanwhile, after more than a decade without mutual communication, Mark Twain and De Quille suddenly wrote to each other at the same time, with their letters crossing in March 1875; years later, Mark Twain wrote about the remarkable coincidence as an example of "mental telegraphy." Two months earlier, De Quille published a sketch in the *Enterprise* about Mark Twain's old piloting friend Strother WILEY, using "Samuel L. Clemens" as a character; this sketch appeared as Mark Twain was writing "OLD TIMES ON THE MISSISSIPPI." Their renewed correspondence led to De Quille's coming to Connecticut to write a book on the history of Nevada's gold and silver mines. He arrived in Hartford in June and stayed several months—apparently at Mark Twain's expense—working on what became *The Big Bonanza*. Mark Twain helped him with his book and connected him with

Elisha BLISS to publish it with the AMERICAN PUBLISHING COMPANY; however, his own enthusiasm eventually waned. He wrote a brief and perfunctory introduction to De Quille's book, whose sales fell far short of what he had predicted.

Meanwhile, De Quille returned to Nevada in time to see a fire wipe out most of Virginia City's business district in October. As he waited for his book to be published, Mark Twain pushed him for investment tips from his contacts in the mining industry. After his book appeared, communication between the two old friends virtually ceased. De Quille later published two brief books on Nevada. After the *Enterprise* folded in 1893, he stayed in Nevada several more years, eking out a living writing for San Francisco and Salt Lake City newspapers, then retired to Iowa a few months before he died. He never fulfilled his ambition to see his more purely literary work in book form. The first such collection finally appeared in 1990 as *The Fighting Horse of the Stanislaus: Stories & Essays by Dan De Quille*, edited by Lawrence I. Berkove.

"The Dervish and the Offensive Stranger" Essay written around 1900–01 and first published in EUROPE AND ELSEWHERE (1923). Taking the form of a dialogue, the 1,300-word essay anticipates Mark Twain's longer WHAT IS MAN? While the Dervish argues that good deeds exist, the Offensive Stranger contends that *no* deed is "good" or "bad." He offers examples of good intentions gone bad, such as Utah settlers building irrigation dams that desiccate Indian lands, and COLUMBUS's discovery of America, which opened the New World to Europe's poor, while simultaneously exterminating the original Indian population. He also cites examples of evil deeds with good results, such as the French Revolution, which desolated millions of families but bestowed on Europe all its great liberties. Other historical cases discussed are American intervention in the Philippines, the South African War and Western missionaries in China.

Devil's Race-track Fictional Indian Ocean region, located roughly midway between "Kerguelan's Land" (Kerguelen Island, 49° south latitude, 70° east longitude) and the Antarctic Circle—about 2,400 miles southeast of Cape Town, SOUTH AFRICA and due south of Pakistan. A ferocious maelstrom 500 miles in diameter, the Devil's Race-track makes magnetic compasses go wild and draws ships into its center—known as the EVERLASTING SUNDAY. When it sucks the brig *Adelaide* into it in "THE ENCHANTED SEA WILDERNESS," the sky grows pitch-dark, though it is near the height of the Southern Hemisphere's summer near the Antarctic Circle.

DeVoto, Bernard (January 11, 1897, Ogden, Utah–November 13, 1955, New York, New York) Second editor of the MARK TWAIN PAPERS. A versatile and energetic scholar, DeVoto taught at Northwestern (1922–

27) and Harvard (1929–36), succeeded W. D. HOWELLS as an editor of the "Easy Chair" at HARPER'S MAGAZINE (1935–55) and was chief editor of the *Saturday Review of Literature* (1935–38). His works as a historian include *The Year of Decision: 1846* (1943) and *Across the Wide Missouri* (1947). He also wrote serious and light fiction that he published under his own name and as "John August"; his novels included *The Chariot of Fire* (1926) and *Mountain Time* (1947).

DeVoto's interest in Mark Twain scholarship began with *Mark Twain's America* (1932), a book he wrote largely in reply to Van Wyck BROOKS's *The Ordeal of Mark Twain* (1920). Deliberately overstating his case, DeVoto combatively argued that the western frontier was a positive stimulus in Mark Twain's development as a creative artist. In researching this book, DeVoto was hindered by A. B. PAINE's refusal to let him inspect Mark Twain's unpublished papers. In April 1938, a year after Paine died, the MARK TWAIN COMPANY made DeVoto custodian and editor of the Mark Twain papers, largely at the insistence of its publisher, HARPER AND BROTHERS. The estate did not, however, give DeVoto the power as literary *executor* that Paine had enjoyed, leaving him dependent on the estate and Clara Clemens for permission to publish Mark Twain's manuscripts. In contrast to Paine, who feared that controversy might damage Mark Twain's market value, DeVoto understood the purely commercial value of keeping Mark Twain scholarship alive and controversial. He opened the Mark Twain papers to qualified researchers and tried to publish some of the manuscripts that reveal Mark Twain's darker side.

DeVoto invested a large part of his time and limited resources to completing Paine's unfinished cataloging of Mark Twain manuscripts. He planned to publish an additional volume of AUTOBIOGRAPHY, several more volumes of Mark Twain letters, a new collection of previously unpublished stories and an expanded edition of MARK TWAIN'S NOTEBOOK. In eight years, however, he only completed the autobiography volume—MARK TWAIN IN ERUPTION (1940)—and LETTERS FROM THE EARTH. Though he had the latter manuscript ready in 1939, it did not see publication until seven years after he died.

DeVoto's only compensation as editor was permission to quote freely from Mark Twain's papers in his own writings. He used this privilege to write *Mark Twain at Work* (1942), which contains the first analysis of how Mark Twain wrote *Tom Sawyer* and *Huckleberry Finn* based on Mark Twain's unpublished notes. DeVoto's tenure as editor was disrupted by his struggles with Clara Clemens, who resisted publication of manuscripts that she thought would hurt her father's reputation. Despite the breadth of DeVoto's interests and achievements, Clara suspected him of trying to enhance his own reputation by capitalizing on Mark Twain. She initially opposed publication of *Mark Twain in Eruption*, arguing that it contained passages that would offend relatives of people whom her father criticized. DeVoto countered that since Mark Twain had written and revised his autobiography with the intention that it would be published, what he wrote should not be edited away. In any case, he argued, little that Mark Twain wrote would still offend anyone.

In January 1946, DeVoto resigned as editor, fed up with the delays he had to face when trying to get an estate lawyer to grant him permission to publish extracts from Mark Twain's papers. After he was replaced by Dixon WECTER, he won a Pulitzer Prize for *Across the Wide Missouri*.

Dickens, Charles (February 7, 1812, Portsmouth, England–June 9, 1870, Gadshill, Kent) The most popular British novelist of his time, Dickens led a life similar in some ways to that of Mark Twain—whose own career as an author was starting just as Dickens's was ending. Like Mark Twain, Dickens was largely self-educated and entered writing as a journalist. After gaining fame with such novels as *The Pickwick Papers* (1836–37), *Oliver Twist* (1838), *Nicholas Nickleby* (1838–39), *The Old Curiosity Shop* (1840–41) and *Barnaby Rudge* (1841), he spent a considerable part of his life abroad. Also like Mark Twain, he had an important second career in LECTURING. Finally, Mark Twain's popularity in ENGLAND would eventually be as great as that of Dickens in America.

Dickens was immensely popular as both a writer and a speaker in the United States—where his problems with pirate publishers paralleled those that Mark Twain would later have with Canadian and British pirates. He gave reading tours in America twice, in 1842 and 1867–68. After his first American tour, he wrote *Martin Chuzzlewit* (1843–44), which is partly set in the Midwest. Its depiction of a visionary land development scheme along the Mississippi River anticipates a similar theme in Mark Twain's *The Gilded Age* (1873). Dickens's unsympathetic treatment of the scheme annoyed American readers, but their ire dissipated after he published *David Copperfield* (1849–50), *Bleak House* (1852–53) and other books. Dickens also published a nonfiction account of his travels, *American Notes for General Circulation* (1842), which Mark Twain mentions in *Life on the Mississippi* (chapter 25).

Dickens arrived in Boston for his second, and much more successful, American tour on November 19, 1867—the same day that Mark Twain returned to New York from the QUAKER CITY excursion. Dickens's manager, George Dolby, later organized lectures for Mark Twain in LONDON. At the end of 1867, Mark Twain heard Dickens read in New York; the occasion was his first date with his future wife, Olivia Langdon. In September 1870, several months after Dickens died, Mark Twain published "The Approaching Epidemic" in the GALAXY, predicting that the country was about to be deluged with lecturers capitalizing on the popular author's death.

Mark Twain began reading Dickens's books around the mid-1850s. In 1879, he called himself a great admirer of Dickens and said that every two years he reread *A Tale of Two Cities* (1859)—a novel with a grave-robbing scene that he borrowed for *Tom Sawyer*. He never met Dickens face to face, but visited his grave in London's Westminster Abbey in 1872. In the late fall of 1887, Charles Dickens Jr. visited him at Hartford while on a reading tour of his father's works.

Digger Indians   Name loosely applied to several unrelated INDIAN societies of western America. A pejorative term with no precise ethnological meaning, "Diggers" derives from these peoples' practice of digging for roots. Mark Twain's allusions to California Diggers in *Roughing It* (chapter 19) and *Innocents Abroad* (chapter 19) probably refer to Southern PIUTE peoples.

Dilworthy, Senator Abner   Character in *The Gilded Age*. A corrupt MISSOURI politician, Dilworthy came from an unspecified neighboring state and profited as a Unionist in the CIVIL WAR (chapter 20). A later chapter describes him as a former state legislator, governor and member of the House of Representatives, but does not say where he held these offices (chapter 53). After being discussed in chapter 19, Dilworthy first appears in the chapter when he visits HAWKEYE. There Colonel SELLERS interests him in supporting a bill to develop the river at STONE'S LANDING. When Dilworthy goes back to WASHINGTON, D.C., he takes Washington HAWKINS along as his private secretary. Later he brings Laura HAWKINS to his Washington home (chapter 30), a mansion near the White House (chapter 39). He develops an avuncular relationship with Laura, who becomes his lobbyist for a bill to get the federal government to buy her family's TENNESSEE LAND for an industrial school for freed blacks. After enjoying initial success, Dilworthy is eventually ruined by a state legislator's revelation that he has been buying votes for his reelection to the Senate (chapter 57).

Ostensibly honest and smugly pious, Dilworthy is appalled by the suggestion that he personally might profit from supporting the Columbus River scheme. He claims to have one principle in public life—never to "push a private interest if it is not justified and ennobled by some larger public good" (chapter 35). He talks sanctimoniously and often attends prayer meetings, but his true feelings are revealed when Laura enters his study unexpectedly and catches him holding his Bible upside down (chapter 35).

Though Dilworthy is introduced in C. D. WARNER's chapters, Mark Twain contributed at least equally to his development and wrote exactly half of the 27 chapters in which he appears. The authors modeled Dilworthy closely on a Kansas politician, Senator Samuel Clarke Pomeroy (1816–1891), whose own investigation by the Senate was in the headlines as they were writing. Their outlines even called the Dilworthy character "Bumroy."

Portly and bald like Dilworthy, Pomeroy was investigated on bribery charges by his own state legislature. Although he was cleared by a Senate committee in 1873, his political career was ruined. Augustus HOPPIN used Pomeroy as his model for his illustrations of Dilworthy in *The Gilded Age*.

Dimsdale, Thomas Josiah (c. 1831–1866)   An English graduate of Oxford University, Dimsdale settled in Virginia City, Montana for health reasons. There he taught music, edited a newspaper, became the territory's superintendent of public education and collected material on outlaws. Shortly before succumbing to tuberculosis in 1866, he published *The Vigilantes of Montana; or, Popular Justice in the Rocky Mountains*—the first book printed in Montana. *Roughing It*'s account of the outlaw Jack SLADE (chapters 10–11) quotes more than 2,300 words from Dimsdale's book, modifying the text slightly and citing its subtitle incorrectly.

Dinadan the Humorist, Sir   Character in *Connecticut Yankee*. The brother of LA COTE MALE TAILE and a playful joker in MALORY's *Le Morte d'Arthur*, Dinadan is the object of Hank MORGAN's scorn in *Connecticut Yankee* because all his jokes are stale. He first appears at CAMELOT's banquet hall, where he ties a mug to a dog's tail (chapter 4). Later he bores Hank with history's most tired joke—about a humorous lecturer who fails to raise a single laugh from his audience, then is told that he was so funny that it was all everyone could do "to keep from laughin' right out in meetin' " (chapter 9). Years later, Dinadan becomes England's first published author, but Hank suppresses his book because it contains the lecture joke and has him hanged (chapter 40).

"Diplomatic Pay and Clothes"   Essay that Mark Twain wrote in VIENNA in January 1899 and published in *Forum* in March. It laments the shabby pay, clothes and housing that American diplomats have traditionally received in foreign countries and expresses the hope that American policy is changing.

Opening with an allusion to the recently concluded Spanish-American War peace conference, Mark Twain applauds the news that members of the American delegation to Paris received generous compensation. He hopes that this precedent will reverse the nation's long history of "disastrous precedents," such as the "plain black-swallow-tail" suits worn by American ministers at formal diplomatic events. Arguing that plain clothes are actually "glaringly conspicuous" in the midst of gaudy foreign diplomatic occasions, Mark Twain suggests making diplomats temporary generals or admirals, so that they may wear the corresponding uniforms. The essay also discusses the inadequate pay and housing that American diplomats generally have in foreign countries, and cites Great Britain as having a particularly good record of taking care of its diplomats properly. He concludes that it is time for the United States to "come out" and change its style.

Mark Twain's interest in the country's treatment of its diplomatic corps grew out of his anger at the government's neglect of Bayard TAYLOR. The theme emerges occasionally in other writings, notably "THE BELATED RUSSIAN PASSPORT," which depicts a dismal American consulate in St. Petersburg, Russia.

Doangivadam   Character in NO. 44, THE MYSTERIOUS STRANGER. No one knows the real name of the carefree wanderer who was nicknamed "Doangivadam" because he "don't give a damn." A tough, honest, handsome, fearless and intelligent journeyman printer, Doangivadam works throughout Europe, coming and going as he pleases. In chapter 11, he arrives in ESELDORF in time to help August FELDNER and FORTY-FOUR meet a printing deadline when most of their master's men are out on strike.

The character is probably modeled on Wales McCormick, a young printer's apprentice with whom Mark Twain worked in Hannibal. He also bears a strong resemblance to Miles HENDON of *The Prince and the Pauper* and to La Hire of *Joan of Arc*. Around the time that Mark Twain wrote this story, he occasionally wore a WHITE SUIT that he called his "dontcareadamn suit."

Dobbins, Mister   Character in *Tom Sawyer*. Tom's schoolmaster, Dobbins is modeled on Mark Twain's teacher John DAWSON. Chapter 6 introduces him simply as "the master" at a school with 25 "scholars." He and his wife live with a local sign-painter's family. Wearing a wig to cover his total baldness, he is moving into middle age ungracefully. Stern and humorless, he enjoys dishing out corporal punishment. Dobbins is also a frustrated would-be doctor; he keeps an anatomy textbook locked in his desk that he studies when his pupils are busy. Becky THATCHER accidentally tears the book; her fear of punishment suggests that Dobbins is not above whipping girls (chapter 20). He makes his last appearance in chapter 21, when the boys whom he beats in preparation for the annual "Examination Day" exact a nasty revenge.

Dodge, Mary Mapes (January 26, 1831, New York, New York–August 21, 1905, Onteora, New York)   Writer and editor. Best known as the author of *Hans Brinker, or the Silver Skates* (1865), Dodge edited ST. NICHOLAS MAGAZINE from 1873 to 1905. She personally attracted contributions from most of the top writers of juvenile stories of her time. Mark Twain considered serializing *The Prince and the Pauper* (1880) in her magazine, but decided to withhold it for book publication. Finally, he sent her *Tom Sawyer Abroad* for serialization in 1894. Though they had been good friends since at least 1890—when their families summered together at ONTEORA—Dodge angered Mark Twain by altering his

text significantly without permission. She corrected Huck's grammar; deleted allusions to death, drunkenness and swearing; substituted "darky" for "NIGGER"; and even required illustrator Dan BEARD to draw shoes over the characters' bare feet.

Dodge, Nicodemus   Character in *A Tramp Abroad* modeled on Mark Twain's childhood acquaintance Jim WOLFE. During a free-flowing conversation with HARRIS in chapter 23, the narrator recalls Dodge as a country lad he knew in a Missouri printing office as a boy. Villagers saw Dodge as a foil for practical jokes, but he was actually a formidable adversary. George Jones gave Dodge an exploding cigar that barely fazed him. When Tom McElroy tied Dodge's clothes into knots while he was swimming, Dodge retaliated by burning up McElroy's clothes. For pinning a rude note on Dodge's back in church, Dodge confined another joker overnight in the cellar of a deserted house. After practical jokers grew scarce, a young doctor proposed frightening Dodge by putting Jimmy FINN's skeleton—which he had bought for $50—in Dodge's bed. When the doctor and his friends later checked in on Dodge, they found him cheerfully enjoying treasures he had purchased with three dollars he got from selling the skeleton to a passing quack.

"Does the Race of Man Love a Lord?"   Essay published in 1902. To the assertion that "an Englishman does dearly love a lord," Mark Twain responds that Americans are no different. Indeed, all humans admire power and conspicuousness, particularly the latter, and like to rub against rank. Perceptions of what constitutes rank vary, but can be found everywhere: from the 400 million Chinese who worship their emperor to the lowliest boys' gang with one member who can thrash the rest. A "lord" is "any person whose situation is higher than our own." Admitting that he himself is not free of this impulse, he recalls his immense pleasure in having a private audience in Vienna with the emperor (Franz Josef I) several years earlier (May 25, 1899); he particularly relishes the envy he can arouse in others when he relates details of the experience.

The 4,860-word essay first appeared in the NORTH AMERICAN REVIEW in April 1902 and was collected in *The $30,000 Bequest and Other Stories* (1906).

"A Dog's Tale"   Short story written and published in 1903. The dog narrating this story is struggling to understand the ways of her human masters. Trained by her mother to help others in danger, she saves her masters' baby from a fire, only to see her own puppy cruelly sacrificed in a scientific experiment. Widely reviled as Mark Twain's most brazen concession to sentimentality, "A Dog's Tale" can be read both as a parable on slavery and as a tribute to Mark Twain's mother, who—like the narrator's mother—reputedly sent Mark Twain into the world with an oath to behave properly.

SYNOPSIS

AILEEN MAVOURNEEN reflects on her life. Though her mother was vain and frivolous, she had kind and gentle ways that she passed on to her children. When Aileen was old enough to be sold away, her mother admonished her to accept her lot without complaint and never to think of herself at times of danger to others, but to "think of your mother, and do as she would do."

Aileen's new home is wonderful. Mr. and Mrs. GRAY, 10-year-old Sadie and the servants treat her with love and kindness, and she also socializes with neighbor dogs. When she has her own puppy, her happiness is complete. One winter day Aileen is sleeping in the nursery when a fireplace spark ignites material over the baby's crib. She awakens to the baby's screams, sees flames rising and starts to run until she remembers her mother's words and pulls the baby to safety. When Mr. Gray sees Aileen dragging the baby in the hall, he beats her with a cane until he hears screams from the nursery.

With one leg badly injured, Aileen limps to the attic to hide. She hears her name called, but lays low for days while her strength ebbs. Finally, Sadie finds her, begs forgiveness and returns her to the family, where she is treated royally. Everyone is proud of Aileen's heroism, especially Mr. Gray, a scientist who tells his distinguished colleagues that Aileen acted not by instinct but through the use of reason. The scientists then discuss optics and the question of whether a certain brain injury would produce blindness.

The following spring, Gray's colleagues return and take Aileen's puppy to his laboratory. Aileen does not understand what they are doing, but is proud of the attention given to her pup. The men do something to the puppy's head that makes him shriek and stagger in confusion; Gray proclaims that his theory is correct: The puppy is *blind*. As Gray's friends congratulate him for his contribution to humanity, the puppy dies. Gray orders that it be buried in the garden and Aileen follows the servant who performs this duty. As she watches the puppy being "planted," she imagines it growing out of the ground as a fine handsome dog. However, two weeks of patient waiting leave Aileen frightened that something terrible has happened. The servants' loving ministrations only heighten her fear. She is losing her strength.

BACKGROUND AND PUBLISHING HISTORY

Mark Twain wrote this 4,400-word story at Elmira during the summer of 1903 as his family was preparing to move to Italy. Evidently writing to satisfy his daughter Jean's opposition to vivisection, he was likely influenced by Robert BROWNING's poem "Tray"—narrated by someone who wants to buy a dog that saved a child from drowning in order to open its brain "by vivisection."

The incident of the baby's crib catching fire resembles an accident that occurred when Clara Clemens was a baby and her nurse saved her from a fire.

"A Dog's Tale" first appeared in the Christmas issue of HARPER'S MAGAZINE in 1903, illustrated by W. T. Smedley. Around the same time, Britain's National Anti-Vivisection Society issued the story as a pamphlet. The following September, Harper & Brothers published it as a 36-page book. It was first collected in *The $30,000 Bequest and Other Stories* in 1906 and was adapted to a film called *Science* in 1911. Around 1930, 200 copies of the British pamphlet were discovered and donated to Williams College. To preserve their market value, they were to be sold at the rate of two copies a year, with the proceeds going to a "Dog's Tale Scholarship" fund.

Dollis Hill   English estate that Mark Twain rented from early July until early October 1900. Located just northwest of LONDON, the wooded hilltop site was his family's last and favorite residence of their nine years abroad. Mark Twain called it "nearer to being a paradise than any other home I ever occupied." In May 1901, 96-acre Gladstone Park was opened to the public on the site, in honor of the statesman William E. Gladstone (1809–1898), who had often stayed there. Now well inside London, Dollis Hill is a stop on the Underground's Bakerloo Line.

Domremy   Birthplace of JOAN OF ARC. A village on the Meuse River in the Vosges department of northeastern FRANCE's historic Lorraine region, Domremy is 30 miles southwest of Nancy. After the village fell under English rule, Joan left it in 1429, never to return. The following year, she made possible CHARLES VII's coronation and he rewarded her by exempting Domremy from taxation. The exemption was intended to be perpetual, but it lapsed during the French Revolution.

Domremy is the principal setting of the first eight chapters of Mark Twain's *Joan of Arc*, whose idyllic description of the village recalls Mark Twain's ST. PETERSBURG. Domremy also resembles the villages of Mark Twain's youth in being too dull to recognize greatness in one of its own people until the outside world celebrates it (book 2, chapter 2).

"A Double-Barrelled Detective Story"   Novella written in 1901 and published in 1902. One of Mark Twain's most outrageous BURLESQUES, this story combines grotesque violence and melodrama while spoofing detective fiction in general and Sherlock HOLMES in particular. Its central story line is about revenge. A young man with extraordinary tracking abilities pursues a father he has never known in order to punish the man for mistreating his mother. A second story line (its second "barrel") concerns a young miner's murderous revenge on another cruel tormentor.

Mark Twain earlier hinted at the theme of a man tracking down his own father in *Pudd'nhead Wilson,* in which Tom DRISCOLL regrets not being able to kill his natural father. His interest in extraordinary tracking skills probably arose out of his fascination with aborigine trackers of AUSTRALIA, whom he praises in *Following the Equator*. It is probably not a coincidence that that book compares the abilities of native Australians favorably to those of Sherlock Holmes (chapter 17).

Lest there be any doubt as to Mark Twain's burlesque intentions in this story, chapter 4 contains a passage of purple prose into which he slips remarks about "a solitary oesophagus [that] slept upon motionless wing." A lengthy footnote attached to this passage adds his mock-serious reply to letters complaining about this passage.

SYNOPSIS

Containing roughly 19,000 words in 10 chapters, the story falls into three parts. The first opens in 1880, when a man named Jacob FULLER cruelly abuses his young wife in VIRGINIA. The narrative then jumps ahead six years, when this woman—who now calls herself Mrs. Stillman—lives in New England with her son Archy, who has a bloodhound's tracking powers. When Archy is 16, she tells him about his father's abuses and he agrees to track his father down and torment him. The second part falls entirely within chapter 3, in which Archy describes his quest in his letters to his mother dated from 1897 to 1900. After finding Fuller and driving him out of Colorado, Archy discovers that he has pursued the wrong man. His three-year quest to catch up with the innocent man takes him to a California mining camp. The third part comprises the final seven chapters, which are set in HOPE CANYON, where Archy solves the murder of a ruffian named Flint BUCKNER— who turns out to be the father he has sought. He also finds the innocent Jacob Fuller and helps him regain his sanity and wealth.

Chapter 1
In 1880, Jacob Fuller marries a beautiful young woman in Virginia over the objections of her proud father, who casts her out. To avenge himself, Fuller psychologically abuses his wife for three months, then ties her to a tree, strikes her and sets bloodhounds on her that tear away her clothes. After he abandons her, never to return, she proclaims that she will bear his child. The neighbors who free her want to form a lynch party, but Fuller is gone. The woman then shuts herself up with her father. After he dies of a broken heart, she sells his estate and vanishes.

Chapter 2
In 1886, a young Southern woman calling herself Stillman is living in a New England village with her five-year-old son, Archy STILLMAN. An unusual child without friends, Archy senses that he differs from other children. When he tells his mother that he once *smelled* a postman coming, she guesses that he has the gift of the bloodhound. After confirming her theory with tests, she warns Archy never to reveal his secret.

Buoyed by her son's powers, the woman makes plans to get revenge against her husband, then bides her time, resuming her neglected interests such as painting and music. When Archy turns 16, she tells him how his father abused her. The boy's Southern sense of honor is so outraged that he wants to find and kill his father immediately; however, his mother wants him to punish the man by stalking him and wearing him down with fear and guilt. Years earlier, she explains, she paid to have his hiding place discovered. The man—Jacob Fuller—is a prosperous quartz-miner in Denver, Colorado. With her preparations made, the woman makes available to Archy all the money that he will need to carry out her plan. He is to post reward notices wherever he finds Fuller, then give him enough time to sell out his interests at a loss and move on, prolonging his suffering until he is ruined.

Chapter 3
On April 3, 1897, Archy writes his first letter to his mother from Denver, where he is in Fuller's hotel. Finding Fuller to be a cheerful, likeable person makes Archy's task harder, but he vows to persevere in his mission. On May 19, he reports that he has posted warning notices that have scared Fuller into selling his mining interests at a loss and sneaking out of Denver disguised as a woman. He has now tracked Fuller to Silver Gulch, Montana, where the man nervously keeps to himself as he prospects. Archy's June 12 letter reports that Fuller is now calling himself "David WILSON."

Back in Denver on June 20, a distressed Archy reports that he has been after the *wrong* man—his father's innocent cousin who has the same name as Jacob Fuller. Anxious to set things right, Archy returns to Silver Gulch in July, but finds the man gone. He now devotes himself to finding the innocent man again and convincing him that his persecutions were a mistake. A year later, on June 28, 1898, Archy writes from SAN FRANCISCO that Fuller—who now calls himself "James Walker"—has sailed for AUSTRALIA. Archy does not write his next letter until October 3, 1900. After chasing Fuller through Australia, INDIA and CEYLON and back to North America, he thinks Fuller is somewhere near HOPE CANYON, the California mining camp from which he writes. Archy is staying with a cheerful young man named Sammy Hillyer—the only person big-hearted enough to be friendly toward the camp's black sheep, Flint Buckner.

Chapter 4
A new camp with 200 silver miners, Hope Canyon is so remote that the outside world scarcely knows that it exists. Flint Buckner lives in a cabin at the end of the village, where he holds a young English boy named Fetlock JONES in near slavery. Other miners encourage Jones to leave Buckner, but the boy is too terrified to try and draws his only pleasure from planning ways to murder Buckner. One day, as Jones helps Buckner light the fuse to blasting powder in a mine shaft, Buckner

strands him in the shaft without a ladder. Jones overcomes his panic in time to cut the fuse. Though badly shaken, he is satisfied that Buckner has shown him a way to accomplish his goal. He vows that in two days Buckner will be dead.

Chapter 5
Late the next night, miners gather in the tavern to gossip about Jones and Buckner after the latter leaves at the same time that he always does. Discussion then turns to the camp's other mysterious character, Archy Stillman. All anyone knows about him is that he can find anybody or anything that is lost. As someone starts to describe one of Archy's feats, the camp's sole white woman—Mrs. Hogan—bursts in. Crying that her child is missing, she begs for someone to fetch Archy, who is roused from bed. While pretending to look for clues, Archy picks up the missing child's scent, then leads everyone to the wickiup (hut) of Injun Billy, who found the baby wandering outside.

Chapter 6
The next day, the arrival of Sherlock Holmes electrifies the village. Jones is momentarily alarmed by his Uncle Sherlock's arrival, but takes comfort in knowing that his uncle cannot solve *any* crime unless he arranges its details beforehand. Jones again vows that tonight will be Buckner's last on Earth. Meanwhile, villagers flock to the tavern to admire their famous visitor.

Chapter 7
That night, Jones walks with his Uncle Sherlock near Buckner's cabin, where he excuses himself to get something. After returning to the tavern, they talk for several hours. Near midnight, Jones goes out to watch Buckner leave at his usual time, then joins his uncle in the billiard room. An hour later, an explosion rocks the camp. Everyone rushes down to Buckner's destroyed cabin; Buckner's remains are found 50 yards away.

After an inquest, Holmes pores over the explosion site collecting clues. Satisfied that he has what he needs, he leads the men back to camp. The miners decide that Jones is the only logical person to have killed Buckner, but recognize that he was not even near Buckner's cabin for at least an hour before the explosion.

Chapter 8
Inside the tavern, Holmes outlines his case. After dismissing his nephew as a possible suspect, he advances robbery as a motive, then argues that since Buckner had nothing worth stealing, his killer must be stupid; further, the murderer—like *all* assassins—is left-handed. Finally, he stuns everyone by naming Sammy Hillyer as the assassin. Hillyer begs for help from Archy, who pushes forward and repudiates Holmes's conclusions. Step by step, Archy explains that the murderer used a slow-burning candle to ignite a long fuse that caused the lethal explosion. After Holmes interrupts with a few questions, Archy asks everyone to pass by him so that he can examine their feet. After 82 men

pass by, he names Jones as the assassin. Holmes tries to prove Jones's innocence, but Archy examines *his* feet and says that he provided the very matches that Jones used to light the candle. After the assembly votes to arrest Jones and try him, Jones sobbingly confesses his crime and begs to be hanged immediately.

Chapter 9
In an undated letter to his mother, Archy describes Buckner's funeral, at which he found "James Walker," the innocent man he has been chasing. Now insane, Walker fears that Sherlock Holmes is after him; however, a miner reports that Holmes was recently hanged in San Bernadino. Walker then tells the story of his persecutions, eliciting the whole camp's sympathy. Thinking Holmes responsible for Walker's misfortunes, the angry miners seize Holmes—who is still alive after all—and start to burn him at the stake. After the sheriff arrives to save Holmes, it is discovered that Jones has escaped; however, there is no interest in recapturing him.

Chapter 10
In Archy's final letter to his mother, 10 days later, he says that he is about to take "James Walker"—who is almost sane again—back to Denver. He has also learned from Hillyer that Buckner's real name was Jacob Fuller. With his father dead and buried, Archy's quest is over.

BACKGROUND AND PUBLISHING HISTORY
Mark Twain wrote this story while summering at SA-RANAC LAKE in 1901 and published it in HARPER'S MAGA-ZINE in January–February 1902. HARPER'S issued it as a 179-page book in April, with illustrations by Lucius HITCHCOCK. CHATTO and Windus followed with the English edition in June. The story was also collected in *The Man That Corrupted Hadleyburg and Other Essays and Stories* (1904). In 1965, Adolfas Mekas adapted the story to film in an independent production.

"Doughface" ("Huck Finn") Posthumously published story fragment written around either 1897 or 1902. The MARK TWAIN PAPERS edition *Hannibal, Huck & Tom* calls this fragment "Doughface"; in *Huckleberry Finn and Tom Sawyer Among the Indians* it is called "Huck Finn." Narrated by Huck, the roughly 500-word piece concerns a young prankster, "Rowena Fuller" (modeled on Roberta Jones), who borrows a horrible mask that Huck has lent to Tom Sawyer. One night she uses it to sneak up on Miss Wormly, a "superstitious old maid," who is so frightened that she goes mad and never recovers. The story is based on an actual incident that Mark Twain describes in chapter 53 of *Life on the Mississippi*.

Douglas, Widow Character in *Tom Sawyer* and *Huckleberry Finn*. One of the wealthiest residents of ST. PETERS-BURG, the Widow Douglas lives with her spinster sister, Miss WATSON, in a large house on CARDIFF HILL—the fictional name for Hannibal's Holliday's Hill, which was named after the widow's real-life model, Melicent S. Holliday (1800–?). Chapter 5 of *Tom Sawyer* introduces the widow as "fair, smart and forty." She comes to the fore in chapter 29, when Huck Finn overhears INJUN JOE plotting with a partner to assault her in order to avenge a whipping that her husband inflicted on him when he was justice of the peace. Huck saves the widow, however, by alerting JONES THE WELCHMAN, who drives off the assailants with the help of his sons. Recognizing Huck's inner goodness, the widow informally adopts him and—to his consternation—attempts to "sivilize" him. In the last chapter, Huck runs off, but Tom Sawyer talks him into returning. *Huckleberry Finn* opens with Huck still chafing under the civilizing influences of the widow and her sister. He likes the widow, but the pressures on him to reform contribute to his readiness to leave St. Petersburg forever after his brutal father shows up.

In the transition from *Tom Sawyer* to *Huckleberry Finn*, Mark Twain lost track of several details about the widow. At the end of *Tom Sawyer*, she invests Huck's share of the treasure that he and Tom found, but in *Huckleberry Finn*, responsibility for this fortune has somehow passed to Judge THATCHER. The "RAFT CHAPTER" of *Huckleberry Finn*, which Mark Twain removed before finishing the novel, alludes to the slave JIM's belonging to the widow; in the finished novel, however, Jim belongs to Miss Watson. When Huck concludes his adventures at the end of *Huckleberry Finn*, he fears that Sally PHELPS will try to adopt and "sivilize" him, apparently forgetting the Widow Douglas. He threatens to light out west, but in the sequel stories, he is back to living with the widow.

The Widow Douglas has been portrayed in many screen adaptations of *Tom Sawyer* and *Huckleberry Finn*. Jane Darwell, best known as Ma Joad in 1939's *Grapes of Wrath*, played her in Paramount's productions of *Tom Sawyer* (1930) and *Huckleberry Finn* (1931). Spring Byington had the role in the 1939 version of *Huckleberry Finn* with Mickey Rooney. More recent actresses in the role include Josephine Hutchinson (1960), Lucille Benson (1973 and 1974), Jean Howard (1975), Helen Kleeb (1981) and Sada Thompson (1986).

Douglass, Frederick (c. February 1817, Tuckahoe, Maryland–February 20, 1895, Anacosta Heights, D.C.) After escaping from slavery, Douglass went north and became a journalist, eventually coming to be regarded as one of the leading abolitionists of his time. A friend of Mark Twain's father-in-law Jervis LANGDON, Douglass first met Mark Twain in 1869. Just before James Garfield was inaugurated president in 1881, Mark Twain asked him to retain Douglass as marshal of the District of Columbia. Though he called Douglass a personal friend, he based his appeal on Douglass's character and the need to elevate African Americans. Garfield instead made Douglass recorder of deeds—a post he held for

four years. After Mark Twain and G. W. CABLE finished a speaking performance in Washington, D.C. on November 25, 1884, Douglass visited them backstage at the same time President Chester Arthur called on them.

Dowley Character in *Connecticut Yankee*. An ABBLASOURE blacksmith, Dowley is a boastful self-made man who twice becomes the target of Hank MORGAN's spite. In chapter 31, Hank invites Dowley and two other men to dinner at MARCO's home, where Dowley brags about rising from orphanhood to prosperity. Hank relishes crushing Dowley by casually paying a huge bill for the banquet items. After dinner, he and Dowley argue about wage levels in their different realms. Dowley's inability to grasp the economic concept of real wages frustrates Hank, who tries to scare Dowley by hinting that he could be pilloried for overpaying workers. Instead, he throws Dowley and the others into a panic. When King ARTHUR makes things worse by babbling about agriculture, Dowley and the others attack him and Hank (chapters 32–34).

"Down the Rhône" Posthumously published essay about a trip Mark Twain made on the RHONE RIVER in 1891. A. B. PAINE abridged this 10,000-word piece from a longer manuscript of Mark Twain's unfinished book INNOCENTS ADRIFT, publishing it in EUROPE AND ELSEWHERE (1923) with minimal editorial explanation. In late September (not August, as the essay states), Mark Twain hired a French boatman (the "Admiral") to navigate his flatboat from Lake Bourget in Savoie down the Rhone to the Mediterranean. His only other companion on the 10-day trip was his courier Joseph Verey, but the manuscript adds the fictional "Mr. HARRIS" of *A Tramp Abroad*.

SYNOPSIS

After spending a night at Lake Bourget's Castle of Châtillon, the narrator crosses the lake on the Admiral's roomy flatboat to a canal that takes them to the Rhone. As the boat drifts down this swift river, he describes passing sights. Seeing a young woman with a face like the Mona Lisa reminds him of the hours he stared at that famous painting, wondering what vanished marvels others find in its serene expression. He recalls how Noel Flagg (a Hartford painter) once told him that Dr. Horace Bushnell had advised him that his talent needed training. When Flagg and his brother first saw the Mona Lisa and other Old Masters, they scoffed. After completing their training, however, they returned to gaze on these works in awe.

To avoid being overcharged at a hotel, the narrator tries posing as a deaf-and-dumb Frenchman only to find his tariff raised the next morning. Believing that he has an honest face, he recalls an incident in New York, when he went to (Francis) Hopkinson Smith's house on a cold night and persuaded the maid—who did not know him—to lend him Smith's overcoat.

When the courier asks the narrator why he lacks the nerve to walk along a crumbling precipice, the narrator observes that while some people can skirt precipices fearlessly but dread the dentist's chair, he is just the opposite. Born without prejudices against dentists, he does not mind the pain. In fact, he offers the revolutionary idea that the exquisitely sharp effect that a dental drill produces is *too* high and perfect a sensation for our human limitations even to recognize as pain. What we feel may in fact be exquisite *pleasure*. When the flatboat goes down the Rhone Falls, the narrator gets out to walk.

Shortly after this episode, the manuscript abruptly ends. Mark Twain's interest in the voyage itself faded after just four or five days—around the time he passed St. Etienne. He wrote 174 manuscript pages, but never attempted to finish his book; however, he recalls this journey with a quote from his diary in chapter 55 of *Following the Equator*. Around 1901, he wrote a brief addendum on the trip that was later published as "THE LOST NAPOLEON."

Dreyfus, Alfred (October 19, 1859, Mulhouse, France– July 12, 1935, Paris) French army officer whose conviction on false treason charges attracted worldwide interest and rocked FRANCE's Third Republic. Born into a Jewish family in France's Alsace region—which Germany annexed—Dreyfus joined the French army and rose to captain. In 1894 he was court-martialed for selling military secrets to Germany. Convicted on the basis of secret evidence, he was sentenced to life imprisonment on Devil's Island. Three years later, another officer was charged with sending Germans messages in handwriting similar to Dreyfus's, but was acquitted. The clear prejudice behind Dreyfus's case moved Emile ZOLA to publish "J'accuse," an essay calling the French authorities traitors. After another officer confessed to forging the documents used to implicate Dreyfus and committed suicide, Dreyfus received a new court martial. He was again found guilty in 1899, but accepted a pardon. In a third court martial in 1904–06, he was finally exonerated and readmitted to the army.

Mark Twain was fascinated by the Dreyfus case, which reinforced his negative opinion of France. While living in VIENNA in late 1897, he tried to persuade his London publisher, Andrew CHATTO, to commission him to write a book on the subject. This idea came to nothing, but Mark Twain cited the Dreyfus case in several essays, including "Concerning the Jews" (1899), "MY FIRST LIE AND HOW I GOT OUT OF IT" (1899) and "MY BOYHOOD DREAMS" (1900). His story "FROM THE 'LONDON TIMES' OF 1904" (1898) is a kind of parable on Dreyfus that explores the illogic of legal trials.

Driscoll, York Leicester (Judge Driscoll) Character in *Pudd'nhead Wilson*. A county judge and prosperous storekeeper, 40-year-old Driscoll is the "chief citizen" of DAWSON'S LANDING as the narrative begins in 1830.

Partly modeled on Mark Twain's father, John M. Clemens, who was a justice of the peace, Driscoll is immensely proud of his VIRGINIA ancestry. Although he is sufficiently unconventional to consider himself a freethinker in matters of religion, he is fiercely aware of his presumed aristocratic heritage and is a slave to honor.

Driscoll lives with his wife (unnamed) and his widowed sister, Rachel PRATT. They are all childless—the one thing standing between them and complete happiness. After Driscoll's brother, Percy DRISCOLL, dies in 1845, he and his wife become guardians of Percy's son, Tom DRISCOLL. They are so gratified to have a child that they tend to overlook Tom's many faults. As Tom's behavior grows worse, Driscoll periodically disinherits him, only to soften and write him back into his will.

In 1850, Driscoll retires from the bench and devotes himself to the FREE-THINKERS' SOCIETY. By chapter 5, he has been retired for three years; he is thus about 63 years old through the last three-quarters of the narrative. Driscoll is a good friend of David WILSON, whom he greatly admires. However, he cannot sway the opinions of other townspeople, who have branded Wilson a "pudd'nhead." In fact, Driscoll's solicitous enthusiasm for "PUDD'NHEAD WILSON'S CALENDAR" merely damages Wilson's reputation further.

Driscoll's conventional side emerges in chapter 7, when he is the first person to show Angelo and Luigi CAPELLO the town. He tries to impress the twins with his past "several dignities," including service in the state legislature. As much as he likes the twins, however, he feels compelled to challenge Luigi to a DUEL in chapter 13, when Tom fails to respond appropriately to Luigi's publicly kicking him. Driscoll is not concerned with *why* Luigi kicked Tom—only with the fact that the affront requires satisfaction on the "field of honor." Indeed, he regards Luigi as a splendid fellow for promptly accepting his challenge, and admires his conduct in the duel. Afterward, however, Driscoll savagely turns against Luigi when Tom tells him that Luigi is an assassin. His parental desire to believe his own child blinds Driscoll even to Wilson's explanation of Luigi's true story.

In "THOSE EXTRAORDINARY TWINS" Percy Driscoll does not appear and York Driscoll is Tom's natural father. Mark Twain's working notes indicate that he considered making Driscoll the father of both Tom and CHAMBERS, the son of the slave ROXANA.

Driscoll, Percy (Percival Northumberland Driscoll) Character in *Pudd'nhead Wilson*. The brother of Judge York DRISCOLL, 35-year-old Percy Driscoll is a leading citizen in DAWSON'S LANDING. The narrative opens with the birth of his son, Tom DRISCOLL, quickly followed by the death of his wife. The couple had several children before this, but all died. Driscoll pours his energy into business, leaving Tom in the care of his slave ROXANA, whose own son was born the same day as Tom.

Though a patient and generally humane slave master,

Driscoll eventually loses his patience in the face of a series of household thefts and threatens to sell *all* his slaves down the river unless the thief confesses. After three slaves confess, he sells them to local buyers and wins their groveling thanks. Later he congratulates himself on his "noble and gracious" act (chapter 2). Roxy is the only slave he does not sell, but his capricious power alarms her so greatly that she is eventually driven to switching the babies to save her son from ever being sold down the river. Driscoll goes to his grave 15 years later, never suspecting the switch. Indeed, it may only be the intervention of his brother that prevents him from unknowingly selling his true son down the river to satisfy the selfishness of his false son. Worn down from struggling to save his estates, Driscoll dies in the fall of 1845. On his deathbed, he frees Roxy and leaves Tom in the care of his brother (chapter 4).

Mark Twain probably had his father, John M. Clemens, in mind when he created Driscoll. An omitted portion of his original manuscript has Driscoll do something that his father once did: Driscoll travels a great distance to collect a debt, only to let the matter go when he finds the debtor hard up. Meanwhile, he sells a slave because he is inconvenient to travel with.

Driscoll, Tom (Thomas à Becket Driscoll) Name used by two characters in *Pudd'nhead Wilson.* The true "Tom Driscoll" is the son of Percy DRISCOLL. Shortly after he is born on February 1, 1830, his mother dies, leaving him to be raised by the slave woman ROXANA—who bears her own son, CHAMBERS, on the same day. Only ¹⁄₃₂ black, Chambers is almost indistinguishable from Tom. Roxy switches the babies when they are seven months old. From chapter 4 until chapter 21—when his true identity is revealed in a dramatic trial scene—the character known to the world as "Tom Driscoll" is actually Chambers. Conversely, the true Tom Driscoll is known as "Chambers." To confuse matters further, Roxy begins calling her natural son "Chambers" after telling him his true identity in chapter 9. No one else, however, calls the true Tom by his rightful name again until the final chapter.

By switching babies, Roxy transforms her own son into her legal master—a role reversal that leads her to indulge him and treat him with unnatural deference. A "bad baby" virtually from birth, "Tom" grows up lazy, selfish, vain, greedy and mean. Oblivious to his origins, he is the worst kind of slave master. He uses Chambers as his bodyguard as he bullies other boys, while treating Chambers so badly that his uncle, Judge York DRISCOLL, buys Chambers to prevent Tom from persuading his father to sell him down the river. Tom is 15 when his presumed father dies and his uncle adopts him. Thrilled to make Tom their child, the judge and his wife indulge him badly—continuing Roxy's pattern.

Like a childhood schoolmate of Mark Twain named Neil Moss, Tom goes off to YALE for two years in chapter 5. He returns with worse habits than ever. He now drinks heavily and gambles recklessly. He also dresses foppishly, until ridicule reforms him. He collects a $50-a-month allowance from his uncle and seems to have no greater interest in life than waiting for his uncle to die so he can inherit the estate. Meanwhile, he makes increasingly long trips to ST. LOUIS, where he runs up gambling debts. To pay them off, he robs homes in Dawson's Landing.

At heart, Tom is mean-spirited and vengeful. After he tactlessly goads Luigi CAPELLO into assaulting him at a public meeting, he wins a court action against Capello, only to be publicly humiliated for lacking the courage to challenge him to a DUEL as Southern honor dictates. He seeks revenge by doing everything he can to destroy the reputation of Luigi and his brother.

After eight years of working on a steamboat, Roxy returns to Dawson's Landing in chapter 8. She learns of Tom's dissolute behavior, but is still thrilled to see him again. Unaware that Roxy is his true mother, Tom rebuffs her rudely, pushing her into confronting him with the truth. Once Roxy tells Tom who he really is, she reasserts the parental authority she abdicated long ago and he never stands up to her again. In chapter 10, Tom thinks that knowing the truth about himself—that by birth he is a black slave—will cause him to improve his behavior. However, he invariably reverts to his bad habits. Incapable of redemption, he vows to reform out of expediency, not conviction. The kindest thing that can be said about him is that he develops some respect for his mother. However, even this faint impulse to filial devotion cannot overcome his self-centeredness.

When Tom's debts threaten to get him written out of the judge's will, Roxy makes the ultimate self-sacrifice to save him: letting him sell her back into slavery. She directs Tom to sell her to someone in northern Missouri, but, characteristically, he betrays her by selling her *down* the river. Eventually, she escapes and returns to confront him and make him buy her freedom back immediately. The prospect of disinheritance drives Tom to robbing his uncle, and in so doing, he kills him. However, suspicion falls on Luigi Capello. Now confident of inheriting his uncle's estate, Tom badgers David WILSON as he tries to prepare Capello's legal defense. It is, in fact, his own foolish bravado that does him in. He visits Wilson the night before the trial and leaves the FINGERPRINT evidence that leads to his own destruction.

After Tom is exposed at the trial, he confesses his crime and is sentenced to life imprisonment. Since he is now legally a slave, creditors to the old Percy Driscoll estate demand him as their property. The governor pardons him and he is sold down the river—the very fate from which his mother had wanted to save him. (In an early draft, Tom hangs himself to avoid this fate.)

In "THOSE EXTRAORDINARY TWINS," Tom is a minor character mentioned in chapter 4 as the romantic interest of Rowena COOPER.

The significance of Tom's full name, "Thomas à Beckett Driscoll" is not clear, aside from the likelihood that Mark Twain was deliberating having fun with aristocratic-sounding English names throughout *Pudd'nhead Wilson.* He was familiar with Chaucer's *Canterbury Tales,* but there is no obvious connection between his character and Thomas à Becket (1118–1170), the archbishop whose martyrdom made Canterbury a shrine to pilgrims.

Dublin   Village in southwestern New Hampshire near which Mark Twain summered from mid-May through mid-October in 1905 and 1906. The first year he rented a place called Lone Tree Hill on the south shore of Dublin Lake from artist Henry Copley Greene. There he enjoyed having such distinguished neighbors as writer Thomas Wentworth Higginson, geologist Raphael Pumpelly and past and future cabinet members Ethan A. Hitchcock and Franklin MacVeagh. His daughters and the family maid, Katy LEARY, stayed with him, and he engaged his former coachman, Patrick MCALEER. Finding the atmosphere conducive to writing, he worked on "A HORSE'S TALE," EVE'S DIARY and "Three Thousand Years Among the Microbes."

The following summer he stayed at Upton Farm on Upper Jaffrey Road, where he dictated a considerable part of his AUTOBIOGRAPHY.

dueling   A fascination with dueling in all its forms permeates Mark Twain's writings. His fiction in particular has numerous examples of people engaged in largely meaningless conflicts that custom—rather than reason—dictates must be resolved by duels or feuds. His interest goes back to his childhood in a family with inherited Southern notions of "honor." He explores ritualized dueling in *Tom Sawyer* (1876), whose hero absorbs every hoary idea about honor and nobility to which he is exposed. In the novel's first chapter, Tom challenges a stranger, Alfred TEMPLE, to fight simply because the boy is new to town and must be tested. Mark Twain later cited the same puerile code to explain the meaningless combats fought by medieval English knights in *Connecticut Yankee* (chapter 3).

Mark Twain's notions about the Southern code find their fullest expression in *Pudd'nhead Wilson* (1894), in which Judge DRISCOLL challenges Luigi CAPELLO to a duel to avenge the honor of his nephew, who has committed the unforgivable offense of failing to issue the challenge himself. The duel itself is less important than its aftermath, which elevates its participants to heroic stature (chapter 14). Mark Twain's original manuscript—part of which was published as "THOSE EXTRAORDINARY TWINS"—reduces this duel to a grotesque farce in which Capello is a Siamese twin sharing his body with a brother morally opposed to dueling. Since one brother cannot participate without involving the other, the duel becomes a fiasco in which everyone present but the duelists is wounded.

A second influence on Mark Twain was his experience on the western frontier in the early 1860s—which he recreates in *Roughing It* (1872). Nevada's rowdy towns and mining camps were places where any disagreement might be resolved in bloody combat and a man was "not respected until he has 'killed his man' " (chapter 48). In contrast to the Southern code, honor counted less than survival. Duels were deadly serious affairs in which participants paid scant attention to etiquette or fair play. Even so, Mark Twain found it difficult to take even western dueling completely seriously. *Roughing It*'s narrator claims to have made so much trouble while temporarily running a newspaper that he left the regular editor to face six duels (chapter 55). While writing *Roughing It,* Mark Twain carried this theme even further in "HOW I EDITED AN AGRICULTURAL PAPER ONCE."

When Mark Twain visited HEIDELBERG, Germany, in 1878, he saw otherwise cultivated university students slice each other to ribbons in highly formalized combats. Little motivated by the need for satisfaction or survival, they took pride in combat for its own sake, building their reputations on battle scars such as are graphically described in *A Tramp Abroad* (chapters 5–7). Mark Twain later heard about a duel between Léon GAMBETTA and another French politician that, though bloodless, left both men bathed in glory. The contrast between this tame affray and Germany's student duels moved Mark Twain to burlesque the affair in chapter 8 of *A Tramp Abroad.* He also later wrote a long passage for *Life on the Mississippi* (1883) comparing American, German and French dueling that was deleted by his publisher.

The Duke   Character in *Huckleberry Finn.* One of Huck's RAPSCALLIONS, his real name is never given. The Duke and KING appear suddenly at the beginning of chapter 19, when both are fleeing trouble in an unnamed riverside town. They do not know each other, but soon agree to work together. Huck describes the Duke as about 30 years old and dressed "ornery." He has just been selling a product that removes tartar from teeth; the product got him into trouble because it also removed the enamel.

The Duke introduces himself as a "jour printer, by trade." In the next chapter he spends a day working in a POKEVILLE print shop, proving he could probably earn a living at this trade if he were willing. He also describes himself as doing "a little in patent medicines; theatre-actor—tragedy, you know; take a turn at mesmerism and phrenology when there's a chance; teach singing-geography school for a change; sling a lecture, sometimes." His familiarity with SHAKESPEARE and the general quality of his language suggests that he has some education.

After he and the older man have described their various vocations, he sighs audibly and tearfully announces that he is "the rightful Duke of BRIDGEWATER." He pompously adds, "here am I, forlorn, torn from my high estate, hunted of men, despised by the cold world, ragged, worn, heart-broken and degraded to the companionship of felons on a raft!" Mark Twain evidently adapted this ornate language from that of his own kinsman, Jesse LEATHERS, who claimed to be the rightful Earl of Durham. The impact that the Duke's impersonation has on Huck and Jim inspires the older con man to proclaim himself the rightful King of France. The Duke must accept this fresh imposture in order not to compromise his own.

While both the Duke and King are patent frauds, they differ in important ways. The Duke, for example, is the more inventive of the two. It is he who proposes staging the "Shaksperean Revival" and its tawdrier sequel, the ROYAL NONESUCH. He also comes up with the idea of printing handbills depicting Jim as a runaway slave; this gives them an explanation for Jim's presence on the raft and enables them to run during the daylight hours.

Scoundrel though he is, the Duke is clearly more compassionate than the King. In general, he preys on the baser instincts of people, while the King preys upon their trust. His most successful scheme, the Royal Nonesuch, for example, takes advantage of the prurient interests of men and their thirst for revenge. The King's best scheme, by contrast, is his effort to swindle the nieces of Peter WILKS out their inheritance. There are limits to how far the Duke will go; in chapter 26, he proposes taking the gold that they have already have and leaving, as he does not want to steal from orphans. He agrees to the King's plan to sell off Wilks's estate only when he is convinced that the girls will get their property back after he and the King are safely away.

In chapter 30, the Duke protects Huck from the King's wrath after they escape from what likely would have become a lynch mob. When the King turns on Huck for fleeing without him, the Duke reminds the King that he did not behave any differently himself. In the next chapter, the Duke shows sympathy for Huck's plight after he and the King have sold Jim. The Duke is inclined to tell Huck where Jim is, but thinks better of it and instead sends him off on a wild-goose chase. The next time that Huck sees the Duke, the two con men have been tarred and feathered and are being ridden out of town on rails (chapter 33).

The Duke and King reappear toward the end of Mark Twain's unfinished novella "TOM SAWYER'S CONSPIRACY." Huck runs into them on a steamboat while they are coming to Missouri with phony extradition papers looking for Jim. This time they are playing a nastier game than in *Huckleberry Finn*. When they learn that Jim is in a ST. PETERSBURG jail awaiting trial for murder, the Duke proposes an ugly scheme to save him: He and the King will have new extradition papers forged to take Jim south on a bogus prior murder charge. Once they are safely away from Missouri they will sell him. Huck and Tom Sawyer (who never meets the rascals) approve the plan as the only way to save Jim's life; however, the rascals do not return until the moment a judge is pronouncing a death sentence on Jim at his trial. As soon as the King and Duke open their mouths in the courtroom, Tom jumps up and proclaims that their voices are the same ones that he overheard at the scene of the murder. He begins to produce what appears to be conclusive proof of their guilt when the manuscript abruptly ends.

The first actor to portray the Duke on screen was Orral Humphrey in the 1920 silent film *Huckleberry Finn*. William Frawley (1887–1966), later known to television audiences as Fred Mertz in *I Love Lucy*, played the Duke opposite Mickey Rooney in 1939. Other film Dukes include Mickey Shaughnessy (1960), David Wayne (1974) and Robbie Coltrane (1993). Actors who have played the Duke in television adaptations include John Carradine (1955), Jack Carson (1957), Merle Haggard (1975), Forrest Tucker (1981) and Jim Dale (1986).

Du Mond, Frank Vincent (August 20, 1865, Rochester, New York–February 6, 1951, New York, New York) Illustrator of *Joan of Arc*. Du Mond became a member of New York's *Daily Graphic* staff at an early age, while studying at the Art Students League under Caroll BECKWITH and William Sartain. He also contributed illustrations to such magazines as HARPER'S WEEKLY, *McClures* and the CENTURY. Between 1888 and 1900, he studied and taught art in France and Italy. Mark Twain met him in Etretat, France in September 1894. Pleased with Du Mond's "views and sympathies" concerning *Joan of Arc,* he arranged to have him illustrate his book for HARPERS. Du Mond's actual illustrations, however, contradict Mark Twain's depiction of Joan as a delicate beauty. Mark Twain's 1904 essay "SAINT JOAN OF ARC" may allude to Du Mond in criticizing artists who depict Joan simply as a peasant girl—"a strapping middle-aged fishwoman, with costume to match, and in her face the spirituality of a ham."

Duncan, Captain Charles C. (1821, Bath, Maine–1898) Captain of the QUAKER CITY. Duncan went to sea as a boy and had his first command when he was in his twenties. In 1853, he settled in Brooklyn—where he joined Henry Ward BEECHER's church—and established a shipping firm on Wall Street. Through the CIVIL WAR years, he conducted his business from London; when he returned to New York, he found that an associate had cleaned out his company's funds, forcing him into bankruptcy. With help from Beecher, he planned a charter cruise to Europe and the Holy Land that he hoped would pull him out of financial trouble. He leased the *Quaker City* and signed up passengers out of his Wall Street office.

Mark Twain first met Duncan at his office in late February 1867 and signed up for the *Quaker City* cruise on March 1. The ship left Brooklyn in early June with about 65 passengers, including Duncan's wife and sons, George and Henry (Harry). Duncan's responsibilities kept him close to the ship throughout the cruise. One of his few absences from the ship was a visit to GARIBALDI in Italy. As the voyage progressed, Mark Twain's opinion of Duncan declined; he came to regard him as a pious hypocrite and an incompetent commander. By the end of the voyage, Duncan's relations with many passengers were chilly at best; he overruled a vote to visit Lisbon and began laying down draconian measures.

Although Mark Twain came to despise Duncan, he treats him respectfully throughout *Innocents Abroad,* which mentions him by name in four chapters and calls him the "captain" in several others. Duncan is introduced in chapter 1 and figures prominently in anecdotes in chapters 3 and 60 that mock the narrator rather than Duncan; chapter 10 praises him for the shortness of his Fourth of July speech. The book never alludes to Duncan's disagreements with passengers and gives no hint that Daniel LEARY, one of the ship's owners, effectively demoted him midway through the cruise. Duncan himself left a logbook—now in a Bath, Maine library—that is an important record of the cruise. He also collaborated with Emily Severance on several letters about the voyage that were published in the *New York Independent.*

After the *Quaker City* cruise, Duncan became shipping commissioner for the port of New York. In early 1877, he was investigated for possible misappropriation of shipping funds. Around the same time, he was giving lectures on the *Quaker City* cruise in which he claimed that Mark Twain was drunk and pretending to be a Baptist minister when he applied for passage. In several letters to the *New York World,* Mark Twain publicly derided Duncan, calling him the cruise's "head-waiter" and a man without principle, moral sense or honor of any kind. These remarks began a feud that lasted for several years. In 1883 Duncan was publicly accused of misappropriating government funds. In a front-page interview in the June *New York Times,* Mark Twain called Duncan a "canting hypocrite" and other names. Duncan's ensuing threats to sue for libel never reached court.

Immediately after the cruise, Mark Twain began writing a play about the *Quaker City.* Its first scene features a greedy hypocrite named "Captain Dusenberry," who is obviously modeled on Duncan. Duncan may also have been Mark Twain's model for the scoundrel in *Huckleberry Finn* called the KING—a master of false piety. Chapter 21 contains what may be an intentional reference to Duncan; the King recites a garbled version of HAMLET's soliloquy containing this line from *Macbeth:* "Wake Duncan with thy knocking!" Mark Twain may have gotten the idea for using this line from the *New York World;* the newspaper published his letters about Duncan under a headline comparing him to Macbeth, who "Kills Duncan Over Again."

Duneka, Frederick A. (?–1919)   New York journalist and publishing executive. After working as city editor of the *New York World,* Duneka became general manager

of HARPER AND BROTHERS under George HARVEY in 1900. In this capacity, he negotiated the contract that made Harper's Mark Twain's exclusive book publisher three years later. He also helped edit the AUTOBIOGRAPHY chapters that Mark Twain published in the NORTH AMERICAN REVIEW (1906–07). Angry at Duneka for defeating several projects and especially for producing a new edition of MARK TWAIN'S LIBRARY OF HUMOR, Mark Twain called him his "secret enemy at Harper's" in a letter to H. H. ROGERS.

After Mark Twain died, Duneka helped A. B. PAINE revise two of Mark Twain's unfinished manuscripts into a new book that Harper's published as THE MYSTERIOUS STRANGER (1916). The fact that Duneka was a devout Roman Catholic may have influenced him and Paine to replace Mark Twain's original Catholic priest with a new character called "the astrologer."

Dunlap, Brace   Character in *Tom Sawyer, Detective.* A prosperous southern Arkansas farmer who lives about a mile from Sally and Silas PHELPS, Dunlap is a 36-year-old widower. During the three months leading up to the start of the narrative, he has pestered Silas for permission to marry his daughter, Benny PHELPS. Dunlap is mentioned in most of the chapters, but does not appear until chapter 11, when he testifies against Silas at the latter's trial for murdering his brother, Jubiter DUNLAP. The trial climaxes when Tom Sawyer proves that Jubiter has not been murdered and that Brace has paid witnesses to testify against Silas.

In the early chapters of *Tom Sawyer, Detective,* Huck indicates that he and Tom knew the Dunlap brothers well during the period covered by the last chapters of *Huckleberry Finn;* however, the only Dunlap mentioned in that earlier story is "Sister DUNLAP." In the 1938 film adaptation, Dunlap was portrayed by Edward J. Pawley.

Dunlap, Jake   Character in *Tom Sawyer, Detective.* Twenty-seven-year-old Jake is a younger brother of Brace DUNLAP and the twin of Jubiter DUNLAP—neighbors of Sally and Silas PHELPS. At 19 or 20 he became a thief and went to an Arkansas prison, from which he later escaped and fled north. As the narrative opens, he is thought to be long dead. When Huck and Tom take a steamboat to Arkansas in the next chapter, they discover that the reclusive passenger in a neighboring cabin is the missing Jake and become friendly with him. Over the next several days, Jake reveals his sordid past—which resembles the career of Jim TURNER in *Huckleberry Finn.*

Dunlap tells the boys how he and two partners, Hal Clayton and Bud Dixon, stole two diamonds worth $12,000 in St. Louis; later, he stole the diamonds from his partners. He thinks his partners are on the steamboat laying for him, so he sneaks off the boat during a rainstorm at FLAGLER'S LANDING in chapter 4. He intends to seek the protection of his brothers while disguising himself as a deaf-and-dumb stranger. In the next chapter, his partners catch up with him and kill him. Brace and Jubiter happen upon the scene and chase off the murderers. They bury Jake, but do not recognize him. Jubiter assumes Jake's deaf-and-dumb disguise and then he is regarded as missing. When Jake's body is found later, it is believed to be that of Jubiter. Meanwhile, Huck and Tom think that Jubiter is actually Jake. Jake's death is not established until the trial scene in the final chapter; up to that moment, no one besides Tom and Huck even knows that Jake returned home.

In the 1938 film adapted from *Tom Sawyer, Detective,* both Jake and Jubiter were portrayed by William Haade.

Dunlap, Jubiter   Character in *Tom Sawyer, Detective.* The 27-year-old brother of Brace DUNLAP, Jubiter is "tall and lazy and sly and sneaky and rather cowardly." He works for Tom Sawyer's uncle Silas PHELPS, who has hired him to appease Brace, who wants to marry Silas's daughter. As Brace's tool, Jubiter does everything he can to irritate the mild-mannered Phelps. Around the same moment that Tom and Huck arrive at the Phelpses' farm, Silas becomes so mad at Jubiter that he bashes him on the head with a stick. Afterward, Jubiter disappears.

In chapter 9, Huck and Tom find a buried body that is identified as Jubiter; Silas is arrested for murder in the next chapter. Stricken with guilt, the addled man confesses to the crime. At his trial, however, Tom proves that Jubiter is not dead, that he is a deaf-and-dumb stranger who, to this moment, Tom and Huck thought was Jubiter's twin brother, Jake DUNLAP. Tom then explains how Jubiter and Brace found Jake's body immediately after the latter was murdered. Not realizing that the dead man was his brother Jake, Jubiter switched clothes with the body, while Brace buried it in order to frame Phelps for Jubiter's murder. In chapter 5, Tom and Huck attempt a conversation with Jubiter, thinking him to be Jake. At the trial, Tom not only unmasks Jubiter's disguise, but calls him a thief and shows that Jubiter has unknowingly been wearing boots concealing $12,000 worth of stolen diamonds. In his only line of dialogue in the narrative, Jubiter admits to all of Tom's charges but protests that he "hain't stole no di'monds."

During the trial, Tom recognizes Jubiter by his habit of tracing "X's" on his face with a finger. The discovery recalls an experience that Mark Twain himself had in 1882, when he was trying to travel on the Mississippi River under an alias. Shortly after he embarked on the steamboat GOLD DUST, the pilot Lemuel Gray—called Robert STYLES in *Life on the Mississippi*—recognized him by his old habit of running a hand through his hair. *The Prince and the Pauper* uses a similar device when Tom CANTY's mother recognizes him by his habit of shielding his face with the back of his hand when startled.

Dunlap was nicknamed "Jubiter" as a child, when a teacher noticed that he had a big round mole on his leg, surrounded by four small moles that together resembled the planet Jupiter and its moons. Other children thought it so funny that they dubbed him "Jubiter" and his real name was eventually forgotten.

Dunlap, Sister   Minor character in *Huckleberry Finn.* Sister Dunlap is a friend of Sally PHELPS in chapter 41; her relationship to any other Dunlaps is not mentioned, although Huck evidently knows a great deal about the Dunlap family. In chapter 2 of *Tom Sawyer, Detective,* Tom tells Jake DUNLAP about their adventures of the "last summer," demonstrating that "there warn't anything about his folks,—or him either, for that matter—that we didn't know."

Dutchy   Pseudonym mentioned in *Life on the Mississippi.* Chapter 54 describes "Dutchy" as a Hannibal boy who drowned (probably in BEAR CREEK) when Mark Twain was a child. In contrast to the sinful "Lem HACKETT" (Clint Levering) who drowned three weeks earlier, Dutchy was a MODEL BOY who recited "three thousand verses of Scripture without missing a word" the day before he drowned. Apparently from one of Hannibal's many German families, Dutchy has not been identified. If he truly died three weeks after Hackett, his drowning would have occurred in early September 1847. Mark Twain originally wrote the passage about Dutchy and Hackett for *A Tramp Abroad,* but did not use it in that book.

Ealer, George (*fl.* 1850s) Steamboat PILOT. Ealer and William BROWN were copilots on the PENNSYLVANIA when Mark Twain cubbed on that boat in late 1857 and early 1858. Mark Twain worked mostly under the disagreeable Brown, while the amiable Ealer had George RITCHIE as his cub. Deeply interested in chess, literature and music, Ealer doubtless influenced Mark Twain's education. Often while Mark Twain steered during Ealer's watches, Ealer read aloud from SHAKESPEARE, Oliver GOLDSMITH and other writers. In his 1906 essay "IS SHAKESPEARE DEAD?"—which describes Ealer as "dead now, these many, many years"—he recalls arguing Shakespearean authorship theories with Ealer (chapter 1). Ealer also figures prominently in chapter 11 of *Life on the Mississippi* in a tall tale about a sleepwalking pilot (he is "George E." in "OLD TIMES ON THE MISSISSIPPI").

After Mark Twain and Brown fought in early June 1858, the *Pennsylvania*'s Captain KLINEFELTER offered to put Brown ashore in New Orleans and let Mark Twain share piloting duties with Ealer on the return trip. Ealer was willing to take all the night shifts, but Mark Twain turned the offer down. Ealer was at the wheel when the *Pennsylvania*'s boilers exploded near Memphis on June 13. Chapter 20 of *Life on the Mississippi* describes how Ealer was hurled into the air, but got back in the pilot-house, gathered his chess pieces, and escaped unharmed. In July, Ealer became a pilot on the ALFRED T. LACEY, on which Mark Twain may have served as his cub.

eclipses Mark Twain's fascination with astronomy is revealed by his use of eclipses and comets in his fiction. He himself had two chances to see solar eclipses during his Missouri childhood—on July 28, 1842 and on July 8, 1851. The first chapter of *Tom Sawyer Abroad* alludes to an eclipse starting a revival in Missouri. Since the story takes place several years after the war between the United States and Mexico, Mark Twain was probably thinking of the 1851 eclipse when he wrote the story.

A purely fictional solar eclipse over England is a pivotal event in *Connecticut Yankee*. Shortly after Hank MORGAN arrives in CAMELOT, he is told that the date is June 19, A.D. 528 (however, he later learns that the date is actually June 20). By a remarkable coincidence, he happens to know that the *only* total eclipse of the sun visible in early sixth-century England began shortly after noon on June 21, A.D. 528, O.S. (Old Style). He also knows that no total eclipse was due in 1879—the year from which he comes. Drawing on these facts, Hank concludes that if the eclipse occurs on schedule, it will prove he really is in the sixth century and is not dreaming.

Whether or not Hank's reasoning is logical, another conclusion is possible. The fact is that *no* solar eclipse of any kind occurred anywhere in the early sixth century; in fact, no full solar eclipse was visible over England until more than a century later. Since nothing about Hank's background suggests that he should have authoritative knowledge of astronomy or history, his mistaken belief that an eclipse occurred in A.D. 528 suggests that his entire experience may have been a dream. Perhaps significantly, Hank never mentions that HALLEY'S COMET—which was of special interest to Mark Twain—appeared in A.D. 530. That was a *real* event he could have used to his advantage, though perhaps not as dramatically as he used the eclipse.

Connecticut Yankee's eclipse begins as Hank is about to be burned at the stake in chapter 6. By this time, he has warned the court that he will blacken the sky if harm comes to him, so the eclipse's onset immediately establishes him as a powerful magician. King ARTHUR offers Hank anything he wants if he will turn back the darkness, but Hank stalls for time because he is unsure how long the eclipse should last. Meanwhile, the panic among the thousands of people attending his execution mounts. The scene recalls the passage quoted in *Innocents Abroad* from Pliny the Younger's description of the darkness that VESUVIUS's eruption cast over POMPEII in A.D. 79.

After Hank's triumph, the public pressures him for more "miracles." He knows the date and hour of a coming lunar eclipse, but this event cannot help him since it is more than two years off, and it is not mentioned again (chapter 7).

By his own admission, Hank gets the idea of cowing people with the eclipse from remembering that COLUMBUS or Cortez used an eclipse in a similar fashion. Mark Twain probably got this idea from a Washington Irving story about Columbus's impressing Indians with an eclipse or a similar incident in H. Rider Haggard's *King Solomon's Mines* (1885).

Mark Twain's interest in eclipses continued after he wrote *Connecticut Yankee.* On September 3, 1895, he saw a total lunar eclipse over the Pacific while sailing on the WARRIMOO. He alludes to the difficulty of calculating eclipses in his AUTOBIOGRAPHY, in *Following the Equator* (chapter 61) and in CHRISTIAN SCIENCE (book 1, chapter 9). FORTY-FOUR creates an artificial eclipse in chapter 31 of NO. 44, THE MYSTERIOUS STRANGER.

Ed (Eddy, Edwin, Edward)   Character in the "RAFT CHAPTER" of *Huckleberry Finn* (chapter 16) and *Life on the Mississippi* (chapter 3). Ed is the riverboatman who tells a long ghost story about Dick ALLBRIGHT and the haunted barrel.

Edison, Thomas Alva (February 11, 1847, Milan, Ohio–October 18, 1931, West Orange, New Jersey)
History's greatest inventor, Edison conceived and developed the electric light, the phonograph, a motion picture camera and projection system, and hundreds of other inventions. Mark Twain met Edison at least once. When he was writing *Connecticut Yankee,* he became interested in the idea of dictating his story onto a phonograph. In June 1888, he visited Edison's Orange, New Jersey lab, where Edison made several recordings of his voice on records (which were lost in a fire in 1914). Mark Twain never used a phonograph for composing *Connecticut Yankee,* but gave its hero, Hank MORGAN, many of Edison's talents and had him introduce the phonograph to sixth-century England (chapter 40). Three years later Mark Twain tried dictating *The American Claimant* into a recording machine but soon gave up the effort.

Fascinated by inventors, Mark Twain greatly admired Edison and borrowed his name for the title of his essay "THE AUSTRIAN EDISON KEEPING SCHOOL AGAIN" (1898) on Jan SZCZEPANIK. Both his 1904 essay on JOAN OF ARC and WHAT IS MAN? (1906, chapter 6) cite Edison as an example of an extraordinary mind. In 1907, OXFORD UNIVERSITY invited Edison to receive an honorary degree along with Mark Twain, but Edison declined in order to concentrate on his work. Two years later, his movie studio produced a short adaptation of *The Prince and the Pauper.* The film includes footage of Mark Twain at his STORMFIELD home that is the only known moving picture ever taken of Mark Twain. The following year, Edison's company released *A Mountain Blizzard,* a film that evidently adapted an episode from chapters 31–33 of *Roughing It.*

Edward VI (Prince Edward) (October 12, 1537, Hampton Court, England–July 6, 1553, London)   Historical figure and central character in *The Prince and the Pauper* (1881). Edward was the only legitimate son of England's King HENRY VIII, by his third wife, Jane Seymour (c. 1509–1537). Though never formally installed as the Prince of Wales, he acceded to the throne on his father's death on January 28, 1547, when he was nine years old.

He reigned for five and a half years, first under the supervision of a regency council appointed by his father, then under lord protectors: his uncle, the Earl of HERTFORD (from 1547 to 1549) and John Dudley, the Duke of Northumberland (from 1549 to 1553). Though Edward was relatively robust when he became king, his health later deteriorated and he succumbed to measles, smallpox and tuberculosis at 15. Before dying, he named his cousin Lady Jane GREY to succeed him.

In *The Prince and the Pauper,* Edward changes clothes with Tom CANTY, a beggar boy, and is mistakenly thrown out of his palace (chapter 3). Soon afterward, his father dies, elevating him from prince to king. The novel's dominant narrative thread becomes Edward's struggle to reclaim his crown. His dispossession casts him in the role of one of Mark Twain's favorite character types—a claimant. As such, he describes himself as "forlorn and friendless" (chapter 11)—a lament remarkably similar to that of the bogus DUKE in chapter 19 of *Huckleberry Finn.*

A striking difference between the fictional and historical Edwards is age. While the historical Edward became king at nine, Mark Twain deliberately obscures his story's chronology in order to depict Edward as about 13 years old—the same age as Huckleberry Finn and Tom Sawyer. It is also roughly the same age that Mark Twain himself was when his father died—a fact that may bear on the way his fictional Edward reacts to his father's death. Until recently, history has seen Edward as a sickly child; Mark Twain portrays him as healthy and robust. Edward proves his toughness by enduring hardships and beatings and by boldly standing up to his oppressors, such as HUGO—a bigger boy whom he thrashes in chapter 22. Mark Twain's Edward is resolute in his convictions almost to the point of absurdity. While never wavering from his claim to be the Prince of Wales—later the king—he is blind to the difficulty others might have in believing his fantastic claim.

In Mark Twain's reading of English history, he saw tendencies toward compassion and justice in Edward's reign that were absent under other monarchs. To a certain extent, *The Prince and the Pauper* is his attempt to explain *why* Edward's reign was different. At first, Edward is so used to having his way that he impatiently blurts out rash threats against his detractors. He softens as the narrative progresses and his picaresque adventures outside the palace expose him to poverty, cruelty and injustice that incline him toward reform. His mistreatment at the hands of children at CHRIST'S HOSPITAL, for example, moves him to provide for their education. After he regains his throne, he seeks out many of the victims of injustice he has met and tries to right the wrongs done to them. The novel's epilogue concludes that his reign "was a singularly merciful one for those harsh times."

Edward VII (November 9, 1841 London–May 6, 1910, London)   King of Britain (1901–10). Mark Twain and

Edward met twice. In June 1892, when Edward was Prince of Wales, they met at BAD NAUHEIM in Germany. Edward became king on the death of his mother, Queen VICTORIA, in January 1901. When Mark Twain visited England to accept an honorary degree at OXFORD UNIVERSITY six years later, he saw Edward at a Windsor Castle garden party, after which the *London Illustrated News* printed a full-page picture of them together. Years earlier, when Mark Twain was planning *The Prince and the Pauper* (1882), he considered setting the story in the 19th century with Edward as his boy prince, but instead used the 16th-century EDWARD VI. Dan BEARD later used Edward's face in a collage of "chuckleheads" that he drew for *Connecticut Yankee* (chapter 24).

Two weeks after Mark Twain's DEATH, King Edward died and was succeeded by his son, George V.

Edward J. Gay STEAMBOAT on which Mark Twain was a PILOT. A 823-ton side-wheeler captained by Bart BOWEN, the *Gay* had been recently built in St. Louis when Mark Twain served on it from early August to October 1859. He made three round-trips between St. Louis and New Orleans. On his second trip out of New Orleans, the *Gay* handily beat the *New Uncle Sam* in a race to St. Louis.

"Edward Mills and George Benton: A Tale" Short story written and published in 1880. An ironic moral tale, this story is a parable about cousins who grow up as foster brothers. One, George Benton, does everything wrong, but is always given a fresh start. The other, Edward Mills, strives to be good, only to be ruined by George and treated as a pariah. One of Mark Twain's archetypal town drunkards, George alternately reforms and falls; he is much like Pap FINN—the kind of RASCALLION whom charitable women favor in *Huckleberry Finn*. His career also resembles that of Charlie WILLIAMS in *Life on the Mississippi*, while the relationship between him and his foster brother anticipates themes that Mark Twain explores more fully in *Pudd'nhead Wilson*. The moral of this tale is summed up in Mark Twain's famous MAXIM: "Be good and you will be lonely."

Mark Twain wrote this 2,300-word story during the summer of 1880, as he was finishing *A Tramp Abroad*. It appeared in the August issue of the ATLANTIC MONTHLY and was reprinted in *The $30,000 Bequest and Other Stories* (1906).

SYNOPSIS

After distantly related cousins Edward Mills and George Benton are orphaned as infants, they are adopted by the Brants, a childless couple. The Brants lovingly raise the boys to believe that they will succeed if they are "pure, honest, sober, industrious and considerate of others." Edward makes this admonition his unswerving rule, but George grows up selfish and thoroughly disagreeable. Edward takes up an apprenticeship that leads to a partnership in a business, while George remains a financial drain on the Brants. When the Brants die, they leave everything to George because he needs it more than Edward; they also require him to buy out Edward's partner so that Edward can look after him.

George's drinking and gambling ruin Edward's business, leaving both men penniless. Edward diligently struggles to rebuild his life, but times are hard and the best job he finds is hod-carrying. As George continues his dissipated habits, he becomes a favorite of the Ladies' Temperance Refuge, which repeatedly rescues and reforms him. Even after he is imprisoned for embezzlement, people petition for his release and provide him with a good job and other help. Edward meanwhile quietly improves his position until he becomes a bank cashier—only to be killed by burglars when he refuses to open his employers' safe. One of his murderers proves to be George, who is sentenced to die despite a petition campaign for his pardon.

Edward's widow and children receive token relief, but the bulk of the public's sympathy goes to George and his family—especially after George discovers religion. George's grave becomes a shrine bearing the inscription, "He has fought the good fight." Edward's grave bears a more honest inscription: "Be pure, honest, sober, industrious, considerate, and you will never—."

Edwards family Characters in "THE GREAT DARK." An American family living on a ship in a dreamlike voyage, the Edwardses remember their land-life at Springport as if it were the dream. Henry Edwards begins the narrative as a healthy, energetic 35-year-old. His wife Alice is 10 years younger—just as Mark Twain's wife was 10 years younger than he was. The Edwardses begin the story with two children: eight-year-old Jessie and six-year-old Bessie, and have a third child, Harry, during the voyage. They also travel with a 28-year-old nurse called Germania, a 30-year-old black servant named George and a maid named Delia.

Mark Twain wrote "The Great Dark" in 1898, but did not set it in a specific year. Several striking parallels between its fictional Edwards family and Mark Twain's real family suggest that Mark Twain was thinking of the year 1880. On March 19 of that year, for example, his daughter Susy became eight—the age that Jessie Edwards becomes on the same date. In 1880, Mark Twain's second daughter, Clara, was six—Bessie Edwards's age. That was also the year in which Mark Twain's third daughter, Jean, was born; Jean's birth parallels that of Harry Edwards in the story—though Harry's birthday is June 8—the birthdate of both Clara and Mark Twain's brother Benjamin CLEMENS. A final parallel is that Mark Twain and his wife sailed to England on the BATAVIA in 1873—seven years before 1880. In the story, Henry Edwards remembers taking his family to Europe on the *Batavia* seven years earlier, when they met the same Dr. John BROWN in Scotland whom Mark Twain and his family met in 1873.

Egypt Northeast African country. After leaving PALES-TINE on the QUAKER CITY, Mark Twain reached Egypt's chief port at Alexandria on October 2, 1867. He spent the night there, then went by train to Cairo, about 100 miles to the southeast, with Dan SLOTE, Jack Van NOSTRAND and other passengers. From there, they rode donkeys to nearby Gizeh to explore the pyramids and the SPHINX. On October 5, they returned to Alexandria, from which they sailed two days later. Chapters 57–58 of *Innocents Abroad* describe this period, focusing on the ancient ruins. The book describes the *Quaker City*'s voyage from JAFFA to Alexandria as smooth, but the voyage was actually exceptionally rough, as was the voyage out of Egypt.

Mark Twain and his shipmates found Egypt a modern and pleasant contrast to TURKEY and the HOLY LAND, from which they had just come. They arrived at a turning point in Egypt's history. After three centuries of Turkish rule, the country had begun asserting its autonomy under the Albanian-born viceroy Muham-mad (Mehemet) Ali (1769–1849)—whom *Innocents Abroad* praises (chapter 13). The same year that Mark Twain arrived, Viceroy Ismail Pasha received the title of khedive, affirming Egypt's virtual independence. Ismail's regime worked to modernize Egypt's cities and fostered the building of the Suez Canal, which opened two years later.

More than a quarter century after visiting Egypt, Mark Twain wrote *Tom Sawyer Abroad,* in which Tom, Huck and Jim travel to Egypt by balloon. They visit the pyramids and sphinx and ride donkeys to Cairo, just as Mark Twain had done (chapters 12–13). Mark Twain considered revisiting Egypt in late 1906, but changed his mind when bronchitis wore him down.

Elexandria Town in *Tom Sawyer, Detective.* Chapters 2 and 4 mention Elexandria as the place where Jake DUNLAP boarded the steamboat on which Tom and Huck are traveling. Chapter 8 of "TOM SAWYER'S CONSPIRACY" alludes to "Elexandry" as 60 miles above St. Petersburg. "Elexandria" is probably Alexandria, a real Missouri town facing KEOKUK, Iowa across the Des Moines River.

Elizabeth I (September 7, 1533, Greenwich, England–March 24, 1603, Richmond, England) Queen of England and character in *The Prince and the Pauper* (1881) and *1601*. The daughter of King HENRY VIII by his second wife, Anne Boleyn, Elizabeth became England's queen after the death of her half-sister MARY I in 1558. *The Prince and the Pauper* mentions her several times as EDWARD VI's bright and gentle 14-year-old half-sister. Her only dialogue occurs in chapter 6, in which she saves Tom CANTY from embarrassment by replying to a statement in Greek that the Lady Jane GREY directs toward Tom.

Elizabeth is the central character of *1601*, which Mark Twain wrote while working on *The Prince and the Pauper*. Nearly 60 years old in this story, she has a randy sense

of humor and happens to be presiding over her royal court when someone flatulates loudly. To discover the culprit, she quizzes each person present, then teases several young people about their sex lives. In *Connecticut Yankee,* Hank MORGAN suggests that the language used by sixth-century women at court is so risqué that it might embarrass Elizabeth (chapter 17).

Mark Twain also mentions Elizabeth in "Last Words of Great Men," "HOW TO MAKE HISTORY DATES STICK" and his 1879 speech "SOME THOUGHTS ON THE SCIENCE OF ONANISM."

Elmira Industrial city on NEW YORK's Chemung River, near its confluence with the Susquehanna River and the Pennsylvania border. Elmira was the home of Jervis LANGDON, Mark Twain's father-in-law. Langdon built a fortune in the coal industry, which flourished thanks to several local railroad junctions. Mark Twain married Olivia Langdon in the Langdons' home at the corner of Church and Main streets—a location now at the center of Elmira's modern business district. Razed in the late 1950s, the house is commemorated by a plaque in a strip mall.

After 1871, Livy's sister, Susan Langdon CRANE, lived just outside of Elmira at QUARRY FARM, where Mark

Mark Twain relaxes at his sister-in-law's home during his last visit to Elmira in 1903. (Thomas E. Marr photograph, courtesy, Library of Congress, Pictures & Prints Division)

Twain and his family spent most of their summers for the next two decades. While the rest of his family was living in Europe in May 1893, Mark Twain visited Elmira and it was there that he brought his family when they all returned in late May 1895. He made his last visit to the city in April 1907.

Elmira College now owns the Cranes' Quarry Farm home, which is the site of the Center for Mark Twain Studies. Each summer the city stages a musical drama featuring a nearly full-sized replica of a Mississippi River steamboat and a reproduction of the original Langdon house. Most members of both the Langdon family and Mark Twain's family are buried in Elmira's WOODLAWN CEMETERY.

Emerson, Ralph Waldo (May 25, 1803, Boston, Massachusetts–April 27, 1882, Concord, Massachusetts) American philosopher and poet. After resigning his Boston pastorate in 1833, Emerson joined the Transcendentalist movement and became a widely read essayist and poet. Mark Twain admired Emerson and kept a brass fireplace plate on his family hearth that features a quote from him.

Mark Twain first met Emerson at an ATLANTIC MONTHLY dinner in BOSTON in December 1874. Three years later, at a banquet honoring John Greenleaf WHITTIER's birthday, he delivered a burlesque speech caricaturing Emerson, LONGFELLOW and Oliver Wendell HOLMES as uncouth ruffians. He afterward apologized to Emerson and the others, but Emerson's hearing was too poor for him to understand the speech and he was not offended. In April 1882, shortly before Emerson died, Mark Twain and W. D. HOWELLS visited his home to pay their respects.

A character in Mark Twain's unfinished novel "The Secret History of Eddypus" is a journalist named Ralp Waldo Edison.

"The Enchanted Sea Wilderness" Unfinished story originally written for *Following the Equator*. The first of several nightmare-voyage stories that Mark Twain wrote, "The Enchanted Sea-Wilderness" is a FRAME-STORY about a ship trapped in an eerie maelstrom near Antarctica in 1853–54. Its roughly 65-year-old narrator is a sailor whom Mark Twain met on a ship in late 1895 or early 1896. He began writing the story around late October 1896, after completing about 14 chapters of *Following the Equator*. It was first published in 1967 in *Mark Twain's Which Was the Dream*, edited by John S. TUCKEY.

The unnamed man's narrative treats a theme paralleling a recent event in Mark Twain's life. The narrator sees his ship's disaster as a judgment on his captain for having left a dog to die after it had saved everyone else. Mark Twain wrote the story while obsessed with guilt over having left his daughter Susy Clemens alone at home, where she burned up with fever while he was traveling around the world. It may have been his inabil-

ity to resolve the fate of the captain—whom he modeled on himself—that caused him to abandon the story. Seven years later, he took up a similar theme in "A DOG'S TALE," in which a master cruelly mistreats his pet dog after it saves his baby from a fire.

SYNOPSIS

Scattered about the oceans are spots in which compasses go mad, forcing sailors to steer by the heavens. The worst such spot is a huge circle in the southern Indian Ocean. Its great outer circle, tossed by eternal storms, is known as the DEVIL'S RACE-TRACK; its calm center is the EVERLASTING SUNDAY. An old sailor aboard the author's ship has been there; he tells his story.

In December 1853, the sailor was a 23-year-old crewman on the brig *Mabel Thorpe*, which carried provisions and blasting powder to the gold mines of AUSTRALIA under a hard-hearted master named Elliot Cable. Two months before sailing, the *Thorpe* took aboard a beautiful St. Bernard dog, which became a valued and beloved member of the crew. One night, when the ship was becalmed below SOUTH AFRICA, the dog detected a fire and awakened the captain in time to stop it from reaching the powder-kegs and killing everyone. The dog then helped the crew load the lifeboat as the ship burned. Before the lifeboat shoved off, however, the captain tied the dog to the ship's mainmast. When the crew pleaded to save the dog, the captain said it would only get in the way and would eat too much. As flames consumed the piteously wailing animal, the men predicted that a judgment would come on the captain.

The next morning the men spotted the *Thorpe*'s sister ship, the *Adelaide*, a slower brig that had preceded them on the same course. Since the *Adelaide*'s Captain Moseley and two mates had died from illness, Cable took command of it and continued its course to Australia. Almost immediately, however, a gale began driving the ship southeast, pushing it hundreds of miles through wild seas. Eventually, the captain calculated that they were about halfway between Kerguelan's Land and the Antarctic Circle, nearing the Devil's Race-track. On the 18th day, their ship entered a wild storm and its compass went crazy, confirming everyone's worst fears. For nine days, it was too dark to tell day from night, but on the 10th morning, they entered the calm center—the Everlasting Sunday, where they drifted helplessly.

Seven months later, they came upon a fleet of becalmed ships, on which they found the desiccated bodies of long-dead people. The first ship they examined was the *Horatio Nelson*, on which the narrator's uncle had disappeared 13 years earlier. They also found a New England whaler; an English ship, the *Eurydice*, which had been bound for Australia with convicts; a Spanish ship; and the British man-of-war *Royal Brunswick*, which was wonderfully preserved though it had been there since 1740. Unlike the merchant ships, the warship maintained its log up until the end.

"An Encounter with an Interviewer" Sketch written around 1875. The narrator befuddles a reporter from the *Daily Thunderstorm* with bizarre answers to his questions. For example, he gives his age as 19, but says that he began writing in 1836. He cannot account for this discrepancy, or for the fact that he was born on October 31, 1693—a date that should make him 180 years old. As the most remarkable person he has ever met, he names Aaron Burr (1756–1836). He happened to be at Burr's funeral, when Burr asked him to make less noise. He finds Burr remarkable because he got up to observe his own funeral and rode to his grave next to his driver. The narrator also explains that he was born a twin, but that either he or his brother died in their bath—no one was sure which. He admits, however, that it was actually *he* who drowned, and that his family buried the wrong child.

The 1,500-word sketch was published in PUNCH, BROTHERS, PUNCH! (1878), THE STOLEN WHITE ELEPHANT (1882), and other collections.

England The largest component of the United Kingdom of Great Britain and Northern Ireland, England was one of Mark Twain's favorite countries. In nine visits he spent more than three years there, mostly in LONDON. In 1867, several fellow QUAKER CITY passengers worked England into their itineraries (*Innocents Abroad*, chapter 15), but he himself did not go there until 1872. In late August that year, he sailed from New York to Liverpool on the steamer *Scotia* (mentioned in chapter 46 of *The Gilded Age*). His goals for the trip included planning a later LECTURE tour, finding a non-pirate publisher for *Innocents Abroad,* securing a copyright for *Roughing It* and collecting notes for a satirical book on the country. He established a publishing relationship with George ROUTLEDGE, but soon abandoned plans for his satirical book and concentrated on sightseeing and meeting literary figures.

The following May, he returned with his family and toured England until October, interrupting this stay with side-trips to SCOTLAND, IRELAND and BELGIUM—where he covered the Shah of Persia's visit to Europe for the NEW YORK HERALD. After lecturing in London in October, he took his family home, then returned almost immediately—this time with C. W. STODDARD as his personal secretary. Through mid-January, he lectured on "Roughing It" and the "Sandwich Islands" in London, Leicester and Liverpool. Several of his essays and sketches from these early visits appear in EUROPE AND ELSEWHERE (1923).

Though anxious to return quickly, Mark Twain did not revisit England for another five years. Meanwhile, he began studying English history in earnest. By mid-1879, when he passed through England again, his feelings for the country had cooled, largely because he resented English snobbery toward America. *A Tramp Abroad* dismisses his 1879 visit in four words (chapter 50). Through the next decade, when he stayed at home,

his resentment against English class privilege, the Anglican Church and the monarchy grew. Often focusing on Matthew ARNOLD's criticisms of America, he used his NOTEBOOKS to record such remarks as the suggestion that England's coat of arms should depict a lion's head and shoulders on a "cur's hindquarters."

Mark Twain passed through England briefly in May 1894 and April 1895, while he lived on the Continent and made business trips to the United States. After completing his world lecture tour at Southampton in July 1896, he rented houses in GUILDFORD and London's Chelsea district until July 1897, when he took his family to SWITZERLAND and later to AUSTRIA. He used that year to write *Following the Equator,* the only book he completed in England. By then his English publisher was Andrew CHATTO.

In June 1899, Mark Twain and his family returned to London, where they stayed through mid-October 1900. By this time, his feelings toward England had warmed again and he was even willing to concede that British imperialism was a good thing, despite his growing reservations about imperialism generally. His final visit to England came in the summer of 1907, when he accepted an honorary degree at OXFORD UNIVERSITY. He ended this last transatlantic trip with a poignant farewell speech in Liverpool.

Mark Twain's interest in English history began early, perhaps influenced by his reading of Charles DICKENS. He was proud of his own English ancestry, but mocked it in BURLESQUE AUTOBIOGRAPHY (1871), which is filled with ludicrous distortions of English history. During the late 1870s he wrote *The Prince and the Pauper* (1881), a historical fantasy about the mid–16th-century boy king EDWARD VI. Though presented as a children's romance, the novel can be read as an attack on monarchical institutions and hereditary privilege. A by-product of his research for this book is *1601,* a bawdy dialogue set in Queen ELIZABETH's court. Over the next few years, he developed MARK TWAIN'S MEMORY BUILDER, a history game that emphasizes dates in English history—as does his essay "HOW TO MAKE HISTORY DATES STICK." He was also sufficiently interested in SHAKESPEARE to write a short book on him in later years.

Mark Twain's strongest and most direct attack on English institutions is *A Connecticut Yankee in King Arthur's Court* (1889), a time-travel story that uses a modern American, Hank MORGAN, to compare America and England. A gentler satire is *The American Claimant* (1892), in which an English noble, Lord BERKELEY, visits America and explores the differences between English and American political ideals.

References to England are also scattered through *Huckleberry Finn* (1884), in which the DUKE and KING pose as English actors and pretend to be Peter WILKS's English brothers. They make Huck pose as "ADOLPHUS," their English servant, but he gets himself into trouble when Joanna WILKS asks him about England (chapter 26). *Tom Sawyer Abroad* (1894) begins with a balloon voyage headed for England; however, the craft ends up in North Africa.

"English As She Is Taught" Essay published in April 1887. A Brooklyn schoolteacher named Caroline B. LeRow approached Mark Twain with a manuscript she had assembled from her pupils' most outlandish answers to questions. She later published the manuscript as *English As She Is Taught;* meanwhile, Mark Twain wrote this 4,275-word essay with choice extracts from LeRow's material and brief comments on the state of education. He gave the $250 that CENTURY MAGAZINE paid him for the article to LeRow and later extracted some of its contents in chapter 61 of *Following the Equator.* A decade later, when Mark Twain's financial distress was common knowledge, LeRow begged permission to give the $250 back to him.

Extracts include definitions such as assiduity being the "state of being an acid," an equestrian "one who asks questions," and a eucharist "one who plays euchre." Under the heading of grammar, one pupil defines gender as "the distinguishing nouns without regard to sex," while another asserts that "every sentence and name of God must begin with a caterpillar." Mathematics pupils assert that "parallel lines are lines that can never meet until they run together" and that "a circle is a round straight line with a hole in the middle." One geography pupil says that Austria's principal occupation "is gathering Austrich feathers." Another explains that "Ireland is called the Emigrant Isle because it is so beautiful and green." Many pupils like to assign the year 1492 to any important historical event, such as the birth of George Washington and the Declaration of Independence. One pupil calls Edgar A. POE "a very curdling writer" and another identifies Chaucer as "the father of English pottery."

Ephesus Ruined city in Asia Minor. One of the great cities of the eastern MEDITERRANEAN during Roman times, Ephesus stood in western Anatolia (the Asian portion of present TURKEY). It contained the Temple of Diana—one of the "Wonders of the World"—and is mentioned prominently in the New Testament. On September 6, 1867, Mark Twain was among about 60 QUAKER CITY passengers and American naval officers who made a day-trip by special train from SMYRNA to Ephesus; he describes the trip in chapter 40 of *Innocents Abroad* and recalls it in chapter 39 of *A Tramp Abroad.* Chapter 41 of *Innocents* claims that local officials confiscated all the relics that *Quaker City* passengers collected at Ephesus, but this may not be true. *Innocents* also offers a burlesque version of the "Legend of the Seven Sleepers"; like Hank MORGAN in *Connecticut Yankee* (1889), these men die shortly after awakening from centuries of sleep in a cave.

Erickson, Simon Minor character in *Roughing It.* In chapter 70 Erickson is a middle-aged man on the island of Hawaii who is thought crazy because of his fixation on an alleged correspondence with Horace GREELEY. He claims that while he was a minister in Michigan, he wrote to Greeley for advice on behalf of a Kansas woman named Beazely, whose son was obsessed with turnips. Young Beazely had gone into a funk because he could not get turnips to grow on vines. Greeley's handwritten reply was so difficult to read that Erickson himself became unbalanced trying to decipher it. By the time Greeley's clerk sent a legible translation, young Beazely was dead and Erickson unhinged.

Aside from burlesquing Greeley's notorious penmanship, this fictitious anecdote is the fullest development of Mark Twain's fascination with turnips as a humorous symbol of stupidity. The idea of growing them on vines also appears in "HOW I EDITED AN AGRICULTURAL PAPER ONCE" (1870). In chapter 11 of *The Gilded Age,* Colonel SELLERS makes a dinner of nothing but raw turnips, turning them into a "banquet." In chapter 27, he talks about transforming a region into "turnip country," where fortunes will be made once a "contrivance [is] perfected for extracting olive oil out of turnips—if there's any in them."

Eseldorf Fictional village in "THE CHRONICLE OF YOUNG SATAN" and NO. 44, THE MYSTERIOUS STRANGER. Although the first story is set in 1702 and the second in 1490, both describe Eseldorf as being in the "Middle Ages" in the "middle" of AUSTRIA. Standing beside a river in a woody and hilly region, the sleepy village is just below a castle. Physically it resembles a description of WEGGIS, Switzerland that Mark Twain wrote in mid-1896, just before going to Vienna, where he began writing "Chronicle." Eseldorf's setting also resembles KALTENLEUTGEBEN, a resort town near Vienna where he stayed a year later, and it has something of Mark Twain's own Hannibal and its fictional counterpart ST. PETERSBURG. Like these American towns, it is a "paradise for boys," who roam the nearby woods, swim, boat, fish and enjoy winter sports.

Several parts of Eseldorf figure into the narrative of "Chronicle," which involves many different villagers. By contrast, most of *No. 44* takes place within a castle containing a print shop that has little contact with the village.

Mark Twain evidently chose the name "Eseldorf"—GERMAN for "assville" or "donkeytown"—to emphasize the small-mindedness of its residents, who hesitate to hold any opinion not sanctioned by the Church. His working notes show that he originally called the village Hasenfeld, or "Rabbitfield"—a similarly disparaging name. The region's hereditary prince, who remains nameless in "Chronicle," is called Rosenfeld ("Rosefield") in *No. 44.*

Esmeralda A historic MINING district in western NEVADA, about 100 miles southeast of CARSON CITY, Esmeralda enjoyed a brief boom during the 1860s. Mark Twain visited the district to secure mining claims for himself and his brother in September 1861. After a futile prospecting trip to the HUMBOLDT district, he returned to Esmeralda in April 1862 to prospect and develop his claims. For about five months, he lived in a small cabin in the district's chief town of AURORA. *Roughing It* mentions Esmeralda in chapters 26, 30, 33, 35, 37–39, 41–42 and 52.

At the time Mark Twain lived in Esmeralda, the district was thought to be inside California. When he wrote "A DOUBLE-BARRELLED DETECTIVE STORY" four decades later, he may have forgotten that a border survey in 1863 determined that the district was within Nevada. His story places HOPE CANYON in California (chapter 3), then describes it as in the Esmeralda region (chapter 4). Nevada's modern Esmeralda County is southeast of the historic mining district.

"The Esquimau Maiden's Romance"   Short story written in 1893. Using his own name as the narrator, Mark Twain describes spending a week with a young Eskimo woman named Lasca, apparently at or near the Arctic Circle—a region that he never personally visited. The bulk of the FRAME is Lasca's narrative of her tragic romance with a young man named Kalula.

Lasca explains how her father's great wealth—which comprises 22 iron fish-hooks—has ruined her life. People treat her differently, everyone is greedy, and she cannot find a suitor who loves her for herself. About two years earlier, however, Kalula came into her life. Coming from a remote community, the handsome young stranger knew nothing of her father's wealth. The couple fell in love and became engaged. Unfortunately, the morning after Lasca's father shows off his fish-hook collection to Kalula, a hook is missing. Kalula confesses to having gotten up during the night to fondle the fish-hooks admiringly, but denies taking one. Nevertheless, a trial of community elders finds him guilty and puts him to the "trial by water." Since Kalula does not sink, he is proclaimed guilty. Lasca renounces him and he is cast adrift on an iceberg.

Nine months later, on the day of the "Great Annual Sacrifice, when all the maidens of the tribe wash their faces and comb their hair," Lasca finds the missing fish-hook in her hairdo. She and her father agree that they have murdered Kalula.

The story satirizes the inverted ideas that Eskimos and westerners have about wealth. The Eskimos think nothing of wearing sables and other furs that are of immense value to westerners; their idea of wealth is metal objects such as ordinary fish-hooks that are worth little to westerners. The result is that "a hundred million dollars in New York and twenty-two fish-hooks on the border of the Arctic Circle represent the same financial supremacy."

This 6,000-word story first appeared in the November 1893 issue of *Cosmopolitan,* with illustrations by Dan

The man sitting with the heroine of "The Esquimau Maiden's Romance" looks suspiciously familiar in J. Luis Mora's illustration.

BEARD. It was later collected in *The Man That Corrupted Hadleyburg and Other Essays and Stories.*

Essex, Colonel Cecil Burleigh   Background figure in *Pudd'nhead Wilson.* A prominent citizen of DAWSON'S LANDING, Essex is the natural father of the boy who grows up as "Tom DRISCOLL" (the real CHAMBERS) by the slave ROXANA. He is identified in chapter 1 and dies in chapter 4—around the same moment as Percy DRISCOLL; he otherwise plays no role in the narrative. His relationship to Roxy is not explained, but she is immensely proud that Essex is her son's father, as he comes from one of the "First Families of VIRGINIA." In chapter 9, Roxy tells Tom that Essex was his father. She raves about Essex's "Virginia blood" in chapter 14, but Tom's interest extends only to wishing that he had had a chance to kill the man. Mark Twain's notes indicate that he considered making Tom's hunt for his father part of the plot, but he saved this idea for "A DOUBLE-BARRELLED DETECTIVE STORY" and left Tom instead to kill his foster father, York DRISCOLL.

***Europe and Elsewhere* (1923)** Collection assembled by A. B. PAINE. The book's 35 essays, sketches and travel letters are a mixture of previously published and unpublished Mark Twain materials. They include fragments from two unfinished travel books, "A MEMORABLE MIDNIGHT EXPERIENCE" (1873) and "DOWN THE RHÔNE" (1891). Aside from "THE WAR PRAYER"—which Paine previously published in his biography of Mark Twain—most of the book's previously published items are minor, such as articles on AIX-LES-BAIN and MARIENBAD written for the NEW YORK SUN and his letters on the visit of the Shah of Persia to England in 1873, printed here as "O'SHAH." Of greater importance are two anti-imperialist essays from the NORTH AMERICAN REVIEW—"To the Person Sitting in Darkness" and "To My Missionary Critics." There are three sketches on ADAM AND EVE and two on Satan.

Other essays include "AS REGARDS PATRIOTISM," "CORN-PONE OPINIONS," "THE LOST NAPOLEON," "SOME NATIONAL STUPIDITIES," "The United States of Lyncherdom" and "A Word of Encouragement for Our Blushing Exiles." The book also includes tributes to Anson BURLINGAME, Marjorie FLEMING, Dr. Louis Loeb, Samuel Erasmus Moffett and Thomas Brackett REED.

Paine supplies a brief preface and reprints a long essay on Mark Twain that Brander MATTHEWS wrote for a uniform edition in 1899.

evasion Popular shorthand expression for the last 10 chapters of *Huckleberry Finn*. In chapter 39, Tom Sawyer reveals the last details of his elaborate plans to liberate Jim, explaining that "when a prisoner of style escapes, it's called an evasion." Thereafter, "evasion" is a codeword for Tom's escape scheme.

"Eve Speaks" Sketch written around 1900 and first published in EUROPE AND ELSEWHERE. Eve narrates the first three of four brief sections of this 1,000-word ADAMIC DIARY. The time is three months after the Fall. Eve wonders why she and ADAM have been driven from the Garden of Eden, feeling it is unfair that they have been punished for their ignorance. They did not know right from wrong, because they lacked the moral sense. Adam arrives. Their son Abel sleeps. A day later, Abel still sleeps. His parents find him drenched in blood after his brother struck him. Later Eve finds that they cannot wake Abel at all. Is it death? The last paragraph is extracted from the diary of Satan, who acknowledges that Abel is dead. He says, "the product of the Moral Sense is complete. The Family think ill of death—they will change their minds."

Everlasting Sunday The calm center of the DEVIL'S RACE-TRACK—a maelstrom that sucks vessels in and then preserves them as in a museum. In "THE ENCHANTED SEA WILDERNESS," the brig *Adelaide* enters the Everlasting Sunday after nine days of being drawn through the stormy outer darkness. Within its black wall of clouds, the *Adelaide* crew finds perfect stillness under a bright cloudless sky. They drift helplessly for seven months, then come upon a fleet of becalmed ships filled with desiccated bodies. The scene resembles a passage omitted from *Life on the Mississippi* (1883) about a balloon voyage into a dead-air belt containing becalmed balloons carrying desiccated corpses.

Mark Twain associated Sundays with stillness and inactivity—a point he discusses in chapter 24 of *A Tramp Abroad*. Throughout his writings, he generally uses "everlasting" in a negative sense, as with "everlasting fire" (*Huckleberry Finn*, chapter 31; IS SHAKESPEARE DEAD?, chapter 11; *The Prince and the Pauper*, chapter 20); "everlasting hell" (*Joan of Arc*, book 3, chapter 14; "Was It Heaven or Hell?," chapter 9) or other "everlasting" punishments (*Roughing It*, chapter 65; *Life on the Mississippi*, chapter 10). "Everlasting Sunday" is thus his idea of an ultimate hell.

***Eve's Diary* (1906)** Short story written in 1905 and later slightly expanded and published as an illustrated book. Written in the form of actual diary entries, it chronicles the entire relationship of ADAM AND EVE.

SYNOPSIS

The diary begins on a Saturday, when Eve is a day old. Feeling "like an experiment," she inspects her surroundings and notes such flaws as ragged mountains, too many stars and a loose moon. She wants to put some stars in her hair, but cannot reach them with a pole and cannot hit them with clods, blaming her failure on the fact that "I am left-handed and cannot throw good."

Eve soon observes another "experiment"—whom she later learns is Adam—and follows it about. She thinks it is a man, but cannot be sure since she has never seen a man. She cannot understand why it ignores her. She chases it up a tree; when she throws clods at it, she hears language for the first time. Eve spends a week following it, trying to get acquainted. Eventually they get along, and Eve takes over Adam's task of naming everything he sees. She is lonely when Adam is not around and experiences her "first sorrow" when he avoids her. Disappointed when Adam takes no interest in her name, she spends time with her "sister"—her reflection in a pool. Eve experiments with sticks that create pink dust that burns her; she experiences pain and calls the dust "fire." Further experiments with the pink dust start a forest fire, which inspires Eve to invent such words as "smoke" and "flame." Eve works on improving her estate, but Adam takes little interest. Her discovery of fire has led to another, unwelcome discovery: fear.

A brief "Extract from Adam's Diary" is inserted in which Adam makes allowances for Eve's youth and confesses that he is starting to appreciate her beauty.

He marvels that she finds interest in *everything*. Eve even tames a brontosaurus that wanders in, but Adam does not want it around, for fear it will crush his house accidentally.

As Eve's own diary resumes, Eve goes several days without seeing Adam, so she spends more time with the animals and travels great distances. Eve is curious about everything—for example, how does the water in the stream get back up the hill at night? Why can wood swim, but not stone?

The diary then jumps ahead, to after the Fall. Eve finds that she and Adam love each other and she wonders *why* she loves him. It cannot be because he is bright, for he is not; nor can it be because he is gracious, industrious, educated or chivalrous, for he is none of those things. She concludes that she loves him, "Merely because he is *mine* and is *masculine*."

After 40 years pass, Eve prays that if one of them must die first, it be she since Adam is stronger and she could not live without him. At her grave, Adam says, "Wheresoever she was, *there* was Eden."

BACKGROUND AND PUBLISHING HISTORY

Mark Twain wrote this 6,000-word story for the 1905 Christmas issue of HARPER'S MAGAZINE. W. D. HOWELLS and Henry ALDEN reprinted it in a Harper collection, *Their Husbands' Wives*, in March 1906. It was then illustrated by Lester RALPH and stretched to fit a 106-page book by itself in June 1906, with some additional material that Mark Twain had written for "EXTRACTS FROM ADAM'S DIARY."

Mark Twain's interest in Adam and Eve continued after he published *Eve's Diary*. Several fragments later published in LETTERS FROM THE EARTH as "Papers of the Adam Family" elaborate on Eve's story. In two extracts from "Eve's Autobiography," Eve looks back to the idyllic days in Eden, when she and Adam regarded themselves as scientists. Their proudest discovery was Adam's finding that water runs *down*hill; however, when someone else later got credit for this discovery, Adam's heart was broken. Eve discovered how milk got *into* cows, viz., through their hair. This fragment also includes "Interpolated Extracts from Eve's Diary," which discuss Eve's discovery that the teeth in lions suggests that they are intended to be carnivores. She and Adam make further discoveries and invent new words.

Most of Mark Twain's ADAMIC DIARIES were written at least partly as BURLESQUES of the Bible, but he seemed to have a special reverence for "Eve's Diary." The conclusion that he intended it as an homage to his recently deceased wife, Livy, is made inescapable by Adam's comment on Eve's death: "Wheresoever she was, *there* was Eden." Scholars have suggested that the story's depiction of Adam and Eve's relationship has autobiographical undertones similar to those in the MCWILLIAMS stories.

Mark Twain wanted the illustrations to be serious instead of comic, and he was delighted with Ralph's elegant line drawings. At least one provincial library banned *Eve's Diary*, however, because the illustrations depicted Adam and Eve undressed.

In 1988 David Birney adapted Adam and Eve's diaries into a single stage play in which the characters alternate their remarks. The production was broadcast on Public Television's "American Playhouse" series as *The Diaries of Adam and Eve*.

Extracts from Adam's Diary Sketch originally published in 1893 that was later revised and reissued in several forms. Lighter and more comic in tone than the later ADAMIC DIARIES, this sketch does not mention God and generally avoids religious themes. It is written in the form of actual day-to-day diary entries by ADAM and should be compared to Mark Twain's much earlier "BOY'S MANUSCRIPT."

The diary begins when Eve arrives in Eden—which surrounds the NIAGARA FALLS—and continues, with widening chronological gaps, until Abel is 10 years old. Adam initially puzzles over "the new creature with the long hair" who gets in his way, and resents her naming "everything that comes along." For example, he had already named the estate "Garden of Eden," but she has renamed it "Niagara Falls Park." She has other faults, such as eating too much fruit. The new creature eventually identifies herself as Eve.

Eve wants Adam to quit going over the Niagara Falls; he does it anyway, in a barrel and in a tub. After he tires of Eve's research and experimentation, he moves to a more remote location. Meanwhile, Eve continues trying to get apples in the forbidden tree. When she finally eats one, death comes to the world; a tiger eats Adam's horse. Adam finds a place outside the park that Eve calls Tonawanda. Eve follows him; she is "curtained in boughs and bunches of leaves" and blushes and titters when Adam removes them. As Eve makes their clothes out of animal skins, Adam begins to find her a good companion.

A year later, a new creature appears among them who is named Cain. Adam thinks that Eve "caught it while I was up country trapping on the North Shore of the Erie." He puzzles over the new creature and Eve's curious devotion to it. As he studies it, he concludes it must be a kangaroo. When Cain is about two years old, Adam concludes he is not a kangaroo. Months later, another baby, Abel, appears. Adam cannot understand why *he* never finds one. The final paragraph jumps ahead 10 years. Adam now understands that Cain and Abel are boys; there are some girls as well. He concludes that he "was mistaken about Eve in the beginning; it is better to live outside the Garden with her than inside it without her."

BACKGROUND AND PUBLISHING HISTORY

This simple text, originally about 4,000 words in length, has had a complex publishing history that has produced multiple versions. Mark Twain wrote his original draft some time before early 1893. When he was invited to contribute a humorous piece to the *Niagara Book,* a souvenir publication for the 1893 BUFFALO World's Fair, he reworked his Adam material by placing Eden at NIAGARA FALLS and working in local Buffalo place names, such as Lake Erie and Tonawanda. The resulting piece appeared in the book as "The Earliest Authentic Mention of Niagara Falls, Extracts from Adam's Diary. Translated from the Original Ms. by Mark Twain." In 1897 the story was included in the English edition of *Tom Sawyer, Detective,* but without reference to Niagara Falls; this may have been Mark Twain's original version. Meanwhile, Mark Twain occasionally read extracts from the text during his 1895–96 worldwide lecture tour.

In April 1904 HARPER published *Extracts from Adam's Diary* as an 89-page book, using the *Niagara Book* version and adding illustrations by Fred STROTHMANN. The following year, Mark Twain rewrote the story, removing all references to Niagara so it could be merged into "EVE'S DIARY," which he was then writing for HARPER'S MAGAZINE. Harper's did not, however, publish any "Adam's Diary" material in its Christmas issue. Next, when "Extracts from Adam's Diary" was collected in *The $30,000 Bequest* anthology, it contained only minor revisions of its original text. Mark Twain's new 1905 material was finally incorporated into the book publication of EVE'S DIARY in 1906. The 1904 book edition was reprinted unchanged in Harper's 1931 book, *The Private Lives of Adam and Eve.* In 1988, actor David Birney adapted both "diaries" to a stage play, *The Diaries of Adam and Eve.* He and Meredith Baxter Birney played the title roles, wearing clothes contemporary to Mark Twain's time.

Eye Openers: Good Things, Immensely Funny Sayings & Stories (1871) Pirated collection of Mark Twain sketches, published by John Camden HOTTEN. The unauthorized book includes Mark Twain's BURLESQUE AUTOBIOGRAPHY and 26 sketches, including the first book publication of "JOURNALISM IN TENNESSEE."

"A Fable" Aesopian tale first published in 1909. Borrowing animal characters from KIPLING's *The Jungle Book* (1894), Mark Twain presents a simple allegory about the role of training in aesthetic appreciation. A human artist paints a picture, but among the animals, only his house cat can find its beauty.

Mark Twain wrote this 1,100-word tale in DUBLIN, New Hampshire, in June 1906 and published it in HARPER'S MAGAZINE in December 1909. It was later collected in *The Mysterious Stranger and Other Stories* (1922).

SYNOPSIS

After painting a picture, an artist places it to be viewed through a mirror to double the distance and soften its beauty. His cat tells the animals of the woods that the picture is the most beautiful thing he has ever seen, explaining that a "picture" is something flat and a "mirror" is a hole in the wall. Doubting that anything can be as beautiful as the cat describes, the ass goes to see for himself, but when he stands *between* the picture and the mirror, he sees only an ass in the hole and returns to denounce the cat as a liar. Hathi the elephant sends Baloo the bear to investigate. Baloo calls both the cat and the ass liars, as there is nothing in the hole but a bear. Each of the other animals also sees only its own kind in the hole. After Hathi himself finally goes, he denounces all the others as liars and says that the cat is morally and mentally blind since the hole contains nothing but an elephant.

The cat draws this moral: "You can find in a text whatever you bring, if you will stand between it and the mirror of your imagination."

***Fables of Man, Mark Twain's* (1972)** Collection of posthumously published material, edited by John S. TUCKEY for the MARK TWAIN PAPERS. Mark Twain wrote most of this material after 1895, with some pieces going back to the 1870s. Most are unfinished, but some he completed and did not publish because he or his publishers thought them too bold for publication. Several items appear in earlier books edited by A. B. PAINE and Bernard DEVOTO; however, Tuckey's volume is the first to publish critically edited texts.

Most selections reflect the growing despair of Mark Twain's last years, when he became convinced that man is the creature of a remote and uncaring god and that mankind will forever repeat its greatest follies. Each selection is a fantasy exploration of some aspect of the nature or condition of mankind. Tuckey has arranged the 36 stories under three broad headings. "The Myth of Providence" contains 16 mostly satirical explorations of ideas about man and the universe. "Little Bessie" (1908–09), for example, is about a precocious three-year-old who questions the harshness of divine justice. "The International Lightning Trust"—which Mark Twain was about to publish when he died—is about two men who get rich selling insurance, while convincing themselves that they are merely instruments of God's will.

The seven stories in "The Dream of Brotherhood" challenge the notion that there will ever be true brotherhood. Its longest selection is the unfinished novel "The Refuge of the Derelicts," in which victims of various misfortunes gather together. This section also includes "You've Been a Dam Fool, Mary. You Always Was!" and two short pieces about Jews.

"The Nightmare of History" has 13 stories exploring the possibility of new religious myths enslaving mankind. The section's longest piece, "The Secret History of Eddypus, the World-Empire," projects a nightmare future in which Mary Baker Eddy's CHRISTIAN SCIENCE religion dominates the world. Several shorter selections were previously published as part of the "Papers of the Adam Family" in LETTERS FROM THE EARTH.

Tuckey's *The Devil's Race-Track: Mark Twain's Great Writings* (1980) includes "The Refuge of the Derelicts" and 11 shorter pieces from *Fables of Man*.

"The Facts Concerning the Recent Carnival of Crime in Connecticut" First published in 1876, this short story is Mark Twain's first major exploration of the power of one's conscience. It is a theme frequently touched on in *Tom Sawyer*, which he published the same year. He carried this exploration further in *Huckleberry Finn*, in which Huck finally concludes that "it don't make no difference whether you do right or wrong, a person's conscience ain't got no sense, and just goes for him anyway" (chapter 33). While the anonymous narrator of this 6,600-word story differs from Mark Twain in having an ambulatory son and an aunt named

Mary, he resembles the author in other details, such as speaking with a drawl and being a prosperous 40-year-old writer.

SYNOPSIS

Pleased to receive a letter from his morally upright Aunt Mary announcing her imminent visit, the narrator vows that if his "most pitiless enemy" appeared, he would right any wrong he may have done him. At that moment, the door opens and a shriveled dwarf enters. About 40 years old, misshapen and covered with green mold, the dwarf seems like a dim burlesque of the narrator himself. The dwarf's rude behavior and exaggerated drawl also remind the narrator of himself.

When the narrator threatens to toss him out, the dwarf accurately describes how he recently turned away a tramp and broke a young writer's heart by refusing to read her manuscript. Everything that the small fiend says is an accusation, and every accusation a painful truth. When the dwarf admits that he is the narrator's *conscience*, the narrator joyfully springs at him, but he jumps atop a bookcase. After the man's son enters the room and is chased out, the man discovers that his conscience is invisible to all but him. He tries to lure his conscience closer, but cannot get at him.

From his pygmy visitor, the narrator learns that consciences harass people repeatedly for the same offense not only because it is their business, but because they enjoy it. He also learns that when people listen to their consciences, the consciences grow; however, when people—such as the narrator—ignore them, they go to sleep and shrivel. The conscience of one man he knows sleeps in a cigar-box; that of another man is 37 feet tall. The conscience of a thieving publisher (John Camden HOTTEN?) can be seen only with a microscope.

When Aunt Mary arrives, she berates the narrator for neglecting people whom he promised to look after and chides him for his smoking habit. As she talks, the narrator's conscience falls to the floor and weakens, allowing the man to tear him to shreds and burn the pieces. Now a free man, the narrator orders his aunt out. Since then, his life has been bliss. In settling old scores, he has killed 38 persons, burned down a house and swindled widows and orphans. He concludes by inviting medical colleges seeking tramps for research to examine the lot in his cellar.

PUBLISHING HISTORY

After delivering this story as a paper to Hartford's MONDAY EVENING CLUB on January 24, 1876, Mark Twain published it in the ATLANTIC MONTHLY in June. It was later collected in *The Stolen White Elephant, Etc.* and in *Tom Sawyer Abroad, Tom Sawyer, Detective and Other Stories.* In 1988, Richard Henzel appeared in a television adaptation of this story titled "Mark Twain's Carnival of Crime." Dressed as an elderly Mark Twain, sitting in his study recalling the incidents of the story, Henzel

recites most of the original text, while acting out its various characterizations.

"The Facts Concerning the Recent Resignation" Sketch first published in the NEW YORK TRIBUNE on February 13, 1868 and reprinted in SKETCHES, NEW AND OLD. After working in WASHINGTON, D.C. for two months as Senator William M. STEWART's private secretary, Mark Twain wrote this piece as a SATIRE on the pretensions of minor government officials. He later wrote two similar sketches, "MY LATE SENATORIAL SECRETARYSHIP" (1868) and "RUNNING FOR GOVERNOR" (1870).

SYNOPSIS

Dateline: Washington, December 2, 1867. Mark Twain announces that he has resigned as clerk of the Senate Committee on Conchology after only six days on the job because of outrages heaped on him. He has not, for example, been given an amanuensis with whom to play BILLIARDS. More importantly, he has not received due courtesies from other cabinet members. He went to the secretaries of the Navy, War Department and Treasury with trenchant advice, only to be treated rudely and ignored. When he attempted to sit in at a cabinet meeting, even the president (presumably Andrew JOHNSON) treated him brusquely, demanding to know who he was. Told that clerks are not invited to cabinet meetings, he left, only to suffer a final indignity back at his own office when a member of his Senate committee demanded that he get out some reports. Appalled that for $6 a day he was expected to *work*, he quit, crying "Give me liberty or give me death!" When he billed the Treasury Department for his services, the secretary disallowed every item but his salary for six days. The items not allowed included three $50 fees for consultations with cabinet members and a $2,800 reimbursement for 14,000 miles of travel to JERUSALEM.

Fairbanks, Mary Mason (1828, Perry, Ohio–December 8, 1898, Providence, Rhode Island) Friend of Mark Twain. A former schoolteacher, Fairbanks was married to Abel Fairbanks (c. 1817–1894), the owner and editor of the *Cleveland Herald*. In 1867, she traveled on the QUAKER CITY excursion alone and became the center of a popular shipboard coterie that included Mark Twain. She spoke French fluently and was much appreciated by other passengers for facilitating communications in many situations. Though she and Mark Twain grew close as the voyage progressed, they seem not to have made any side-trips on land together. *Innocents Abroad* neither mentions Fairbanks nor contains any clear allusions to her. Nevertheless, her influence on its author was considerable. Mark Twain enjoyed her company, sought her advice on social matters and regarded her as a mentor, whom he affectionately called "Mother Fairbanks." It has long been asserted that Fairbanks played an important role in helping Mark Twain edit his travel letters during the cruise; however, the evidence for her actually having done so is tenuous. Fairbanks herself wrote 27 letters about the cruise that were published in her husband's newspaper under the anagrammatic byline "Myra."

After the cruise, Fairbanks and Mark Twain corresponded steadily and visited each other occasionally for three decades. As Mark Twain courted Livy, his future wife, he expressed his feelings more frankly to Fairbanks than to his own family, giving his correspondence with her special interest. Before his marriage, he considered buying into the *Cleveland Herald* but instead bought into the BUFFALO EXPRESS. Fairbanks attended his marriage in Elmira, New York, in February 1870 and she visited the newlyweds in their Buffalo home the following November. For his part, Mark Twain stayed with the Fairbankses when he passed through Cleveland on several lecture tours and visited them with his wife, Livy, in May 1872.

In 1879, Abel Fairbanks declared bankruptcy after overextending his investments. The Fairbankses' fortunes declined further, until their Cleveland newspaper interests collapsed completely in the late 1880s. They moved to Omaha, Nebraska and then to Newton, Massachusetts. Mark Twain saw Mary Fairbanks for the last time in New York in late February 1894, four months before her husband died.

Fanshaw, Buck   Background character in *Roughing It.* A recently deceased VIRGINIA CITY saloon keeper and high official in the fire department, Fanshaw was found by an inquest to have become so delirious from typhoid fever that he took arsenic, shot himself, cut his throat and jumped out of a high window. After due deliberation, the jury ruled death "by the visitation of God." More than anyone else, Fanshaw brought peace to the town—by beating the daylights out of anyone who disturbed it. He never went back on a friend, never shook his mother and never wavered from his motto, "No Irish need apply!" Generally acknowledged as representing the highest stratum of the mining community's society, he truly merited a grand funeral—which his friend Scotty BRIGGS struggles to arrange in chapter 47 of *Roughing It.*

This long anecdote is occasionally published by itself as "Buck Fanshaw's Funeral." Mark Twain evidently modeled Fanshaw on a man named Tom Peasely, owner of Virginia City's Sazerac saloon, who was murdered in Carson City in 1863.

feet   MINING term for a portion of a claim. During Mark Twain's time in NEVADA, the silver mines were generally linear tunnels or shafts whose ownership was measured in "feet." The title to each foot of a mine was recorded in deeds, and mine shares were sold and traded in "feet." *Roughing It*'s chapters on Nevada use the term frequently after chapter 26, which describes the people of the HUMBOLDT district as "feet crazy."

Feldner, August   Narrator of NO. 44, THE MYSTERIOUS STRANGER." Like Theodor FISCHER of "THE CHRONICLE OF YOUNG SATAN," Feldner tells his story from the perspective of old age. Indeed, the first chapter of his narrative is virtually identical to Fischer's, although his story is set two centuries earlier. About 16 or 17 years old at that time (chapters 2 and 23 give different figures), Feldner is in his second year as an apprentice printer in the Austrian village of ESELDORF. Though timid, he risks the disapproval of his fellow printers to befriend the marvelous visitor FORTY-FOUR, who reveals to Feldner his dream-self and eventually proves that existence itself is nothing more than a dream.

The Fence Painter   Quarterly bulletin of the Mark Twain Boyhood Home Associates in Hannibal, Missouri. Published since 1981, the newsletter is written and edited by the museum's curator, Henry Sweets III. While it focuses on the BOYHOOD HOME itself and activities of the organization, it also presents fresh information on other aspects of Mark Twain's life and writings, as well as local history.

fence, whitewashing of   One of the most famous episodes in Mark Twain's fiction occurs in *Tom Sawyer* when

True Williams's version of Tom Sawyer's *fence-painting episode reveals his inattention to the book's description of the fence.*

Aunt POLLY condemns Tom to whitewash a fence 30 yards long and nine feet high (chapter 2). Overwhelmed by the size of the job before he even starts, Tom tries to bribe JIM, a young slave boy, to help. After Aunt Polly forbids this, Tom recruits an army of other boys to do the whitewashing for him. Astonishingly, Tom does not pay them—they pay *him*. Now part of American folklore, this episode is annually reenacted in a fence-painting competition during TOM SAWYER DAYS in Hannibal—where a fence erected next to Mark Twain's BOYHOOD HOME stands as a permanent monument. The episode is also commemorated on a U.S. POSTAGE STAMP using a Norman Rockwell painting.

Tom entices other boys to pay for the privilege of whitewashing by making the job appear to be fun, not work. From the catalog of loot that he amasses, it appears that as many as 20 different boys help. Only three, however, are named: Billy FISHER, Johnny MILLER and Ben ROGERS. Among the items that Tom collects are an apple, a dead rat, a key, a piece of chalk, a glass bottle-stopper, a tin soldier, a one-eyed kitten, a brass door-knob, a dog collar and a knife handle, as well as fire-crackers, 12 marbles and several tadpoles. The next day, he swaps most of these items at Sunday school, using them to accumulate enough "tickets" to claim a prize Bible.

According to Mark Twain's AUTOBIOGRAPHY, he created the fence-painting episode during a visit to England in the early 1870s. He told the story to Sir Henry Irving and the Irish playwright William Gorman Wills at a dinner, then returned to his hotel and wrote it out.

Fentress County East-central TENNESSEE county in which Mark Twain's family lived before he was born. Located just below the Kentucky border, the 498-square-mile county was organized in 1827, around the same time that the Clemens family arrived. As the family lived successively in JAMESTOWN, THREE FORKS OF WOLF RIVER and PALL MALL, John Clemens purchased around 70,000 acres of local land that became notorious in Mark Twain's life as the "TENNESSEE LAND."

Ferguson Joke name for guides in *Innocents Abroad*. A running gag throughout *Innocents* is the inability of the narrator and his companions to handle the foreign names of their guides, most of whom they call "Ferguson"—just as they give names like "JACKSONVILLE" and "JONESBOROUGH" to Arab villages. "Ferguson" appears 35 times in *Innocents,* referring to five different guides. These include a Frenchman named A. Billfinger in Paris (chapters 13–15); an Italian in Genoa (chapter 27); a French guide in Rome (chapters 27–28); a Turk dubbed "Faraway Moses" in Constantinople (chapter 35); and ABRAHAM, a Maltese dragoman in the Holy Land (chapters 45–57). The deleted chapter on SPAIN also calls a guide (Michael Benuñes) "Ferguson." The travelers' favorite "Ferguson" is the patient, trusting Frenchman in Rome, whom the Doctor (Abraham JACKSON) exasper-

ates with inane questions about a mummy. In chapter 35, the narrator says that "all guides are Fergusons to us. We cannot master their dreadful foreign names."

ferryboatman Minor character in *Huckleberry Finn*. After Huck and Jim escape from the wrecked steamboat WALTER SCOTT in chapter 13, Huck boards a steam ferry and awakens its watchman—who owns the boat. Huck blubbers out a dramatic story about his fictitious family and a Miss HOOKER being stranded on the wrecked steamboat. An evident penny-pincher, the ferryboatman is concerned about who will pay for a rescue effort. When he mentions a local rich man named Jim HORNBACK, Huck quickly says that Hornback is Miss Hooker's uncle. At the prospect of a reward, the ferryboatman jumps into action, but the steamboat apparently breaks apart before he can reach it.

Fiji Southwest PACIFIC island group. On September 10, 1895, Mark Twain interrupted his voyage from HAWAII to AUSTRALIA with a stop at Viti Levu, Fiji's largest island, where he spent the afternoon ashore. Though he had facetiously alluded to Fijians as cannibals in *A Tramp Abroad* (chapter 49) and *Pudd'nhead Wilson* (chapter 18), the Fijians he saw impressed him favorably. Disturbed by the high-handed way in which Britain annexed the islands in 1874, he began questioning his earlier views about British imperialism. *Following the Equator* describes his brief visit (chapters 7–8).

fingerprinting Fingerprinting has been used since ancient times to identify people, but Mark Twain was the first writer to employ it as a plot device in a novel when he used it in *Pudd'nhead Wilson* (1894). As this novel neared completion, he called his use of fingerprints "virgin ground—absolutely *fresh*." He seems to have forgotten, however, that he himself had already used the device a decade earlier, when he wrote the Karl RITTER story for *Life on the Mississippi* (1883). That story, set during the Civil War, has Ritter use a bloody thumbprint to track down a murderer.

The leading 19th-century innovator in scientific fingerprinting was Sir Francis Galton (1822–1911), an English anthropologist who systematized identification techniques. Mark Twain read Galton's book *Finger Prints* shortly after it was published in 1892; it changed his entire conception of the *Pudd'nhead Wilson* story that he had started writing, causing him to drop his idea of using *foot*prints to establish identity—a device used in *Huckleberry Finn*, in which Huck recognizes his father's distinctive bootprint in the snow (chapter 4).

One of the eccentricities that earns David WILSON the nickname "Pudd'nhead" is his hobby of collecting finger marks from people on glass slides. He starts collecting prints in 1830—decades before fingerprinting was scientifically applied to criminology. However, he does not use prints as forensic evidence until 1853. In a dramatic murder trial in chapter 21 of *Pudd'nhead Wilson*, he creates a sensation by using his collection of slides not only to identify a murderer who left bloody prints on a knife, but to prove that two men—one free, the other a slave—were switched as babies.

When Mark Twain wrote *Pudd'nhead Wilson,* he did not create Wilson until he wrote the climactic trial scene. He then went back and rewrote earlier chapters to establish Wilson's background and interest in finger-printing. Although Wilson's fingerprint files contain all the evidence he needs, Wilson does not suspect the truth about the murderer until Tom DRISCOLL visits him and unintentionally leaves his prints on a glass plate. Wilson instantly recognizes his prints as those of the murderer. He then studies Driscoll's childhood prints and makes a second startling discovery: that Driscoll is an imposter; born a slave, he was switched in infancy with a free child.

In court Wilson sets out a melodramatic but authentic explanation of fingerprinting evidence. He establishes that individual human prints are unique; that they do not change as one ages; that prints of the left and right hands are different; that even prints of otherwise identical twins differ; and that individuals can be positively identified by their prints. After establishing that his clients cannot be the murderers, he proves that Driscoll is the true murderer and that Driscoll was born a slave named "CHAMBERS."

Finn, Huckleberry Character in much of Mark Twain's important Mississippi fiction and arguably his most famous creation. Huck Finn appears in all the stories containing Tom SAWYER and he narrates most of them. Indeed, Huck proved an important narrative device for Mark Twain by providing him with an authentic vernacular voice through which to express himself. Huck is the central character in *Adventures of Huckleberry Finn* and a major character in *The Adventures of Tom Sawyer,* "HUCK FINN AND TOM SAWYER AMONG THE INDIANS," "TOM SAWYER'S CONSPIRACY," *Tom Sawyer Abroad* and *Tom Sawyer, Detective.* He also appears briefly in "SCHOOLHOUSE HILL" and narrates "DOUGHFACE."

Huck is introduced in chapter 6 of *Tom Sawyer* as a friend of Tom. He is "the juvenile pariah of the village," a good-hearted but socially disreputable waif. His mother is dead and his drunken father, Pap FINN, is never around, leaving Huck to fend for himself. He sleeps where he wishes, dresses as he likes, fishes when-ever he wants to, and never goes to school. Like Tom BLANKENSHIP—the boy on whom he is modeled—Huck is the freest boy in ST. PETERSBURG and the most envied by other boys. Though Blankenship is the model for Huck's character, Huck's vernacular voice has a strong black strain. Indeed, in recent years he has been shown to speak with much the same voice as Mark Twain's "SOCIABLE JIMMY"—a young midwestern black person whom Mark Twain met in the early 1870s.

As is the case with Tom Sawyer, Huck's age and physical description are vague throughout *Tom Sawyer.*

True Williams was the first artist to illustrate Huck Finn, for chapter 6 of Tom Sawyer.

Chapter 17 of *Huckleberry Finn,* however, reveals Huck to be "thirteen or fourteen or along there." His surname probably derives from Jimmy FINN. In 1895, Mark Twain said that there was "something about the name 'Finn' that suited Huck," adding that a name such as "Arthur Van de Vanter Montague" would not do.

What Huck most values in life is his freedom. He loses this freedom in *Tom Sawyer,* then struggles to regain it in *Huckleberry Finn.* What most threatens his independence is success. At the end of *Tom Sawyer,* he and Tom split a treasure worth $12,000 and he becomes a hero for helping to save the Widow DOUGLAS from INJUN JOE. He then becomes the widow's reluctant ward. He even has to pledge himself to become respectable in order to win membership in Tom Sawyer's GANG.

Huckleberry Finn begins where *Tom Sawyer* leaves off, adding several new assaults on Huck's freedom. He now attends school regularly and has a nemesis. The widow's sister, Miss WATSON, now lives in her household, and she burdens Huck with frightening talk about heaven

Mark Twain thought E. W. Kemble's early drawings of Huck for Huckleberry Finn *were "too Irishy."*

and hell. Some of these changes have their rewards, however. Throughout *Tom Sawyer,* Huck is completely illiterate; he can now read and write with some facility. Several times he will use these skills to his advantage.

Huck's new wealth creates another problem for him: It draws his father, Pap FINN, to town. Pap removes the last vestiges of Huck's independence by imprisoning him in a cabin. This final blow impels Huck to escape all his oppression.

When Huck first plans to flee from his father, he intends to tramp east through Illinois. After he finds a canoe in chapter 7, however, he decides to paddle south about 50 miles, then camp permanently near the river. His primary goal is never to be found by either Pap or the widow. Ironically, the novel ends with Huck almost precisely where he was at the beginning; this time, however, it is Tom's Aunt Sally PHELPS who wants to adopt him. He considers lighting out for INDIAN TERRI-TORY, "because Aunt Sally she's going to adopt me and sivilize me and I can't stand it. I been there before."

Although Huck and Tom Sawyer experience many adventures together, they are different kinds of charac-

ters. Where Tom is romantic and creative, Huck is realistic and practical. While Tom is often clever, his inventiveness tends towards quixotic fantasies. Huck is probably at least equally clever, but his inventiveness is always directed toward quick, practical solutions to problems. The most outstanding example of their differences comes in the "EVASION" chapters in *Huckleberry Finn,* in which they scheme to liberate Jim from captivity. To Huck, the problem is simple: Wait uncle Silas Phelps falls asleep, snatch his key to Jim's hut, then spring Jim free and flee. Tom's solution is to spend weeks laboriously reenacting the romantic aspects of famous escapes about which he has read.

Huck demonstrates his intelligence repeatedly throughout *Huckleberry Finn.* He plans and executes a complex escape from his father that does not waste a single step. As a result, he gets away with a large horde of supplies, and within a single day he has convinced everyone that he is dead and his body has disappeared in the Mississippi River. Later, as he and Jim go down the river, he must repeatedly invent fresh aliases and explanations of who he is and what he is doing to satisfy the demands of strangers, some of whom are hostile. He also saves the WILKS sisters from being robbed by the KING and DUKE and manages to locate Jim and get the raft away from the scoundrels' grasp without arousing their suspicion. His intelligence seems to fail him only when he falls under the influence of Tom Sawyer, as at the end of *Huckleberry Finn,* when he goes along with Tom's preposterous "evasion" plan.

Another of Huck's distinctive characteristics is his good-heartedness and his sensitivity toward the suffering of others. Throughout *Huckleberry Finn* he suffers under the burden of trying to reconcile conflicting demands. He commits himself to helping Jim gain his freedom, but suffers guilt pangs because he is "stealing a poor old woman's nigger that hadn't ever done me no harm." He finally concludes that standing by Jim is the greater imperative and that he is willing to go to hell to see the matter through.

Huck's sensitivity extends to all human beings. During their first days together, Huck plays several boyish tricks on Jim, but he comes to regret taking advantage of Jim's trust so greatly that he overcomes all his training as a white Southerner and humbles himself before the black man to ask forgiveness. His kindness even extends to proven criminals. In chapter 13, he and Jim strand three murderers aboard the derelict steamboat WALTER SCOTT. His conscience will not, however, let him rest, so he tricks a FERRYBOATMAN into trying to save the men. Later, he even tries to save the King and Duke from a lynching at PIKESVILLE, despite all the nasty things these scoundrels have done to him and Jim.

Huck appears in all the finished and unfinished sequels to *Huckleberry Finn,* but none of these stories significantly develops his character.

Huck's precursor, in "BOY'S MANUSCRIPT," is a character named Wart Hopkins. The latter character is similar to Huck in being somewhat disreputable, but differs in being a mean-spirited person. In his AUTOBIOGRAPHY, Mark Twain explains that Huck is his childhood friend Tom Blankenship, drawn "exactly as he was." Elements of other people can also be found in Huck, however. Blankenship's older brother, Bence, for example, is known to have helped an escaped slave. Huck also has similarities with another of Mark Twain's characters—Tom CANTY, whom Mark Twain created while interrupting his work on *Huckleberry Finn* to write *The Prince and the Pauper.*

In the first draft of *Tom Sawyer,* Mark Twain evidently intended to carry the story into Tom's adulthood. He wrote a note about his characters "fifty years later," calling Huck "Bishop Finn."

Dozens of actors have portrayed Huck on stage and screen, going back to late–19th-century efforts to dramatize *Tom Sawyer.* Robert Gordon was the first actor to play Huck in films, in two silent film adaptations made of *Tom Sawyer* in 1917–18. Junior Durkin was the first to play Huck in talking films, in 1930–31. One of the best-known portrayals was by 19-year-old Mickey Rooney in 1939. The next feature film adaptation of *Huckleberry Finn* was not made until 1960, when 13-year-old Eddie Hodges played Huck. Jeff East played Huck in musical adaptations of *Tom Sawyer* and *Huckleberry Finn* made in 1973–74. Ron Howard was 21 when he played Huck in a made-for-television film in 1975. More recent actors include Kurt Ida, Anthony Michael Hall, Patrick Day and Elijah Wood. Daniel H. Jenkins played Huck in the Broadway musical BIG RIVER in 1984.

Finn, Jimmy (?–c. November 6, 1845, Hannibal, Missouri) Neighbor of Mark Twain during his youth in Hannibal; one of Mark Twain's models for the fictional father of Huck Finn, Pap FINN. Mark Twain remembered the real Finn in his AUTOBIOGRAPHY as co-holder of the "well defined and unofficial office" of "Town Drunkard." His own father, Judge John M. Clemens, once attempted to reform Finn, just as a judge tried to reform Pap Finn in chapter 5 of *Huckleberry Finn.*

Mark Twain used Finn as a model for drunks in some of his other writings, including "Autobiography of a Damned Fool." He reported several versions of Finn's death. Chapter 56 of *Life on the Mississippi,* for example, says that "Jimmy Finn . . . died a natural death in a tan vat, of a combination of delirium tremens and spontaneous combustion. When I say natural death, I mean it was a natural death for Jimmy Finn to die." MARION COUNTY records show a disbursement of $8.25 for Finn's burial as a pauper.

Chapter 23 of *A Tramp Abroad* contains a sketch about an apprentice printer named Nicodemus DODGE (based on Jim WOLFE), on whom people loved to play practical jokes. The yarn claims that a local doctor paid Finn $50 for his skeleton—money that "had gone promptly for whisky and had considerably hurried up the change of ownership in the skeleton." After Finn was dead, the

doctor allegedly tried to play a joke on "Dodge" by putting Finn's skeleton in his bed. As in previous jokes played on Dodge, however, the tables were turned. Dodge sold Finn's skeleton "to a traveling quack for three dollars."

Finn, Pap Character in *Huckleberry Finn.* Huck's father is mentioned occasionally in *Tom Sawyer* and often throughout *Huckleberry Finn,* but he appears only in chapters 5–8 of the latter narrative. Mark Twain's working notes for *Tom Sawyer* indicate that he considered using Pap Finn as INJUN JOE's partner in that book's grave-robbing scene. In the third chapter of *Huckleberry Finn,* Huck says that Pap has not been seen around town for "more than a year." When Pap finally appears, he comes from "away down the river," but it is never revealed where he has been, or what he has been doing while away.

In chapter 3, Huck hears that the rotting body of a drowned man found upriver has been identified as Pap, but he is sure Pap is still alive. The next chapter provides

Pap Finn waits in Huck's room to surprise him in chapter 5 of Huckleberry Finn.

Pap with an eerily dramatic entrance. One winter's day, Huck finds fresh tracks made in the snow with a familiar bootprint. He visits the slave Jim, who tells his fortune with a hairball. Jim's reading contains ominous references to Huck's father. The chapter ends when Huck goes to his room that night and finds Pap awaiting him.

Notorious as a former town drunkard, Pap is a widower who has evidently long abused Huck. Chapter 5 of *Huckleberry Finn* describes Pap in some detail. About 50 years old, he has long, black, greasy hair, a long beard, and sickeningly white skin. His clothes are pure rags; his toes poke through his boots. He wears a black slouch hat with the top caved in. The moment Huck enters his room, Pap turns on him, berating him for living so well and especially for learning how to read. Since neither he himself, his deceased wife, nor any member of their family could read, he will not stand for Huck's being literate.

Pap has been in town for two days and knows about Huck's finding treasure. Indeed, Huck's money is the reason for his coming. Over the next several weeks, he cadges money from Huck that he uses to get drunk and is regularly in and out of jail. A judge attempts to reform him at the end of chapter 5, but Pap's attempt at reform fails spectacularly, and nearly kills him in the process. Frustrated in his efforts to get Huck's money, Pap eventually takes Huck to an isolated cabin in ILLINOIS, about three miles upriver. There he keeps Huck locked up while he visits the town to work on his legal case. Over about two months, his treatment of Huck grows more abusive, forcing Huck to plan his escape. Eventually, Pap returns to the cabin. Even more drunk than usual, he goes into a tirade about the injustices of the government. That night he has a delirium tremens attack and chases Huck with a knife. The next day Huck completes his escape by faking his own murder. Pap last appears in the narrative early in chapter 8, when Huck sees him among the townspeople aboard the ferryboat that is searching for his body in the river.

In chapter 11, Huck learns from Judith LOFTUS that Pap left town soon after Huck's faked murder. Many townspeople suspect that Pap murdered Huck, and there is a $200 reward out for him. People were ready to lynch Pap, but suspicion shifted to the slave Jim when it was found that he had run off. Huck further learns that a few days after his faked murder, Pap persuaded Judge Thatcher to give him money to hunt for Jim in Illinois. Pap may thus be among the men that Huck hears in the Illinois woods in chapter 8. Pap was last seen in town when he got drunk and left with hard-looking strangers.

Meanwhile, in chapter 9, Huck and Jim find the "HOUSE OF DEATH" floating in the flooded river. A naked dead man is lying on the floor of a second-story room littered with playing cards and whiskey bottles. Jim determines that the man was shot in the back and has been dead for two or three days. He warns Huck not to look at the body's face and the next day refuses to discuss the dead man with Huck. In the final chapter of the book Jim finally tells Huck that the dead man was his father, Pap.

Despite Pap's harsh treatment of Huck, it is evident that he has helped to shape Huck's character. At least five times Huck recalls things he has learned from his father. In chapter 12, for example, Huck recalls: "Pap always said, take a chicken when you get a chance, because if you don't want him yourself you can easy find somebody that does, and a good deed ain't ever forgot."

Mark Twain modeled Pap partly on the real Jimmy FINN. Though a town drunk, the real Finn lacked Pap's brutish qualities. Perhaps significantly, he died in November 1845—around the same time that the fictional Pap Finn would have died. Mark Twain drew on other models as well, such as the hard-drinking father of Tom BLANKENSHIP—his model for Huck.

Huck's father was developed into a major character in the 1902 Klaw and Erlanger musical *Huckleberry Finn*. While Pap has figured in many film adaptations of *Huckleberry Finn*, his role has generally been a limited one on the screen. Frank Lanning was the first film actor to play him, in the silent *Huckleberry Finn* (1920). Richmond Warner was the first actor to play Pap in a sound version of the novel, in 1931. Victor Kilian (1891–1979) played Pap opposite Mickey Rooney in 1939. Other film portrayals include Neville Brand (1960), Gary Merrill (1974) and Ron Perlman (1993). Actors who have played Pap in television adaptations include Rance Howard (1975), Cliff Osmond (1981) and Frederic Forrest (1986).

Fischer, Theodor Narrator of "THE CHRONICLE OF YOUNG SATAN." Like *Joan of Arc*'s Sieur Louis DE CONTE, Fischer tells his story about his youth from the vantage point of old age. At the time his story takes place, he is about the same age as Huckleberry Finn, whom he resembles in being both a narrator and a person acutely sensitive to the suffering of others. As an ordinary Austrian village boy in ESELDORF, Fischer also enjoys the same diversions as Huck, such as playing in the woods, swimming and fishing. He differs in having a conventional family, with parents named Rupert and Marie and a sister named Lilly—who is being wooed by Joseph Fuchs, the son of the prosperous brewer. Fischer's father is the church organist, village bandleader, violin teacher and tax collector and seems also to be a judge (chapters 2 and 5).

Fischer provides the focus of the narrative by befriending the angel SATAN, who confides in him and reveals countless wonders to him, such as trips to faraway places. Also a foil for Satan's diatribes about the human race, Fischer appears to be coming around to Satan's point of view when his narrative ends abruptly in Ceylon, where Satan has taken him for diversion.

Theodor Fischer does not appear in NO. 44, THE MYSTERIOUS STRANGER; however, that story has an unrelated character named Gustav Fischer who is one of the better-natured printers.

Fisher, Billy Minor character in *Tom Sawyer*. One of only three boys identified by name as paying for the privilege of whitewashing the FENCE in chapter 2, Billy gives Tom a kite for his chance.

Fitch, Thomas (January 27, 1838, New York–November 12, 1923, Decoto, California) NEVADA journalist and politician. After editing a newspaper in Milwaukee, Fitch came to California in 1860, practiced law and became a state assemblyman (1862–63). In June 1863, he moved to Nevada, where he became an editor of the VIRGINIA CITY UNION, the rival of Mark Twain's newspaper. A year later, he launched the short-lived WEEKLY OCCIDENTAL, a literary journal to which Mark Twain contributed. *Roughing It*'s description of the *Occidental* alludes to Fitch as "Mr. F." (chapter 51). Fitch later represented Nevada in Congress (1869–71).

"The Five Boons of Life" Mark Twain's first publication in HARPER'S WEEKLY (July 5, 1902), this 765-word fable takes the form of a condensed novel in five chapters. It is a pessimistic summing up of the futility of seeking any lasting joy in life, apart from release. Mark Twain would later amplify this sentiment in "THE DEATH OF JEAN" (1909), which calls his daughter's death "the most precious of all gifts."

SYNOPSIS

The good fairy offers a youth the chance to choose Fame, Love, Riches, Pleasure or Death as a gift, warning him that only one is truly valuable. The youth chooses Pleasure, but eventually discovers that each pleasure he experiences is short-lived and disappointing. When the fairy returns, the youth makes Love his second choice. Years later, he sits by a coffin; desolated by his losses, he curses Love. Next he chooses Fame. Soon his name fills the world and everything is good—until envy comes, followed by detraction, hate, persecution and, finally, pity—the funeral of fame.

His fourth choice is Wealth—which represents power. In just three years, however, he is reduced to shivering in a garret, clothed in rags. Now he curses all the gifts as nothing but temporary disguises for the lasting realities of Pain, Grief, Shame and Poverty. Finally realizing what the fairy has been trying to tell him, he calls out for the inestimable gift that will end his pain and grief. However, when the fairy returns, Death is not among the gifts she can offer, as she has given it to a child who asked the fairy to make the choice for her. When the man asks what is left for him, the fairy answers, "the wanton insult of Old Age."

Flagler's Landing Fictional ARKANSAS location in *Tom Sawyer, Detective*. In chapter 4, Jake DUNLAP sneaks ashore from a steamboat at a woodyard about 40 miles above Silas PHELPS's farm. In chapter 11, Tom Sawyer identifies the spot as "Flagler's Landing." Mark Twain may have taken this name from Henry Morrison Flagler (1830–1913), an associate of H. H. ROGERS at Standard Oil who developed Florida resorts.

Flanagan, Puss Background figure in *Connecticut Yankee*. Remarks scattered through the novel indicate that before Hank MORGAN came to sixth-century England, he had a girlfriend named Puss in Hartford who was half his age. In chapter 11, he tells CLARENCE that he is "as good as engaged to be married" to "Puss Flanagan" of "*East* Har—." Later he recalls his sweetheart as a 15-year-old telephone operator whom he used to call in the mornings just to hear her voice (chapter 15). Years later, he thinks about his "Hello-girl" from *West* Hartford at the moment of his triumph over the massed knights (chapter 39). Even after marrying SANDY, Hank dreams of Puss and cries out "Hello-Central" in his sleep. Thinking that Hank is calling out the name of a lost love, Sandy tries to please him by naming their baby "HELLO-CENTRAL" (chapter 41).

In naming Puss Flanagan, Mark Twain may have been thinking of his childhood playmate and cousin Tabitha Quarles, who was known as "Puss" during the summers that he spent at his uncle John QUARLES's farm.

Fleming, Marjorie (November 15, 1803, Kirkcaldy, Scotland–December 19, 1811, Kirkcaldy) Scottish child prodigy who wrote poems and diaries. Celebrated by Sir Walter SCOTT, who called her "Pet Marjorie," Fleming died at eight and her name fell into obscurity until Dr. John BROWN published an essay about her in 1863. A decade later, Brown brought Fleming to Mark Twain's attention. Fascinated by Fleming's precociousness and "purity"—which he treasured in young girls such as his "ANGELFISH"—Mark Twain later published "Marjorie Fleming, the Wonder Child" in HARPER'S BAZAAR (December 1909).

Florence Italian city in which Mark Twain spent about a year and a half of his life. Located in north-central ITALY on the Arno River, Florence was historically both a rich merchant state and an important center of the Renaissance. It was annexed by Sardinia in 1860 and was capital of the new kingdom of Italy from 1865 until 1870—when ROME joined the kingdom. Mark Twain visited Florence in four different periods. His first visit was his briefest. On July 23, 1867, he arrived by train from VENICE, stayed two days, then continued west to PISA. Chapters 24–25 of *Innocents Abroad* give a largely negative account of Florence, probably because Mark Twain arrived there exhausted and immediately got lost. He dismisses its "weary miles of picture galleries" and derides its mistreatment of Galileo and its veneration of the Medici family.

In later years, Florence became Mark Twain's favorite Italian city. In October 1878, he spent two weeks there with his family—a visit mentioned in chapter 50 of *A Tramp Abroad*. The Clemens family had another two-week stay there in May 1892 that proved so enjoyable that they returned in September and leased a villa through the middle of June 1893. Mark Twain often raved about the serenity and beauty of his surroundings there. During this period, he began *Joan of Arc* and wrote most of *Pudd'nhead Wilson*, whose fictional CAPELLO twins are members of the old "Florentine nobility."

In November 1903, after his wife's health declined precipitously, Mark Twain took his family back to Italy and rented a villa outside of Florence, where they stayed until Livy died in the following June. This final stay was mostly unpleasant. Aside from Livy's deteriorating health, their house was unsatisfactory and their landlady—an American turned Italian countess—was intolerable.

Florida   Northeastern Missouri village that was laid out by the Salt River in MONROE COUNTY in 1831. Mark Twain was born in Florida in November 1835—at a moment, according to his AUTOBIOGRAPHY, when its population numbered exactly 100. His family had

moved there from TENNESSEE the previous May or June, encouraged by his uncle John Adams QUARLES, who had settled there a year earlier. Mark Twain later used Florida as the model for HAWKEYE in *The Gilded Age*—a novel that fictionalizes his family's history during this period. His father, John M. Clemens, hoped that a railroad line would be extended from St. Joseph to Florida and that the Salt River would be made navigable down to the Mississippi. Either development would have given the town a potential for vast economic expansion, but neither ever occurred. After a brief growth spurt, Florida even lost out to nearby Paris in its bid to become the county seat. Even a century after Mark Twain's birth, Florida's population had barely doubled.

The Clemens family experienced several misfortunes there, culminating in the death of Mark Twain's sister Margaret CLEMENS in early 1839. Later that year, the family moved to Hannibal, about 35 miles to the northeast. Over the next eight years, Mark Twain spent his summers at the Quarleses' Florida farm. Many of the pleasant boyhood memories that later found their way into his depiction of the fictional ST. PETERSBURG doubtless derived from his Florida summers. He revisited the town in mid-July 1855, and stayed in or near it when he was with the MARION RANGERS in 1861—at a moment when U. S. GRANT was campaigning in the vicinity.

Mark Twain's father built the third house in which the Clemens family lived in Florida by joining two cabins; it was still standing in 1906. (Courtesy, Library of Congress, Pictures & Prints Division)

Since the completion of the Clarence Cannon Dam on the Salt River in 1983, Florida has stood on the shores of MARK TWAIN LAKE. The house in which Mark Twain was born—the first of two in which the family lived in Florida—was moved in 1930 to a nearby site in MARK TWAIN STATE PARK, where a modern museum has been erected around it. The original site of the Clemens family home is identified with a simple marker. Displays in the park museum include maps showing the Clemens and Quarles family land holdings around Florida. Margaret CLEMENS, John and Martha Quarles, and Benjamin LAMPTON are buried in the town cemetery.

Following the Equator: A Journey Around the World (1897)

Mark Twain's fifth and last travel book, written in 1896–97 and published in 1897. In contrast to his earlier travel writings, *Following the Equator* is a relatively straightforward narrative of the round-the-world LECTURE tour that he made between July 1895 and July 1896. Its narrative follows his itinerary faithfully, often inserting specific dates and places, and it contains few attempts at invention or embroidery. In another departure from his earlier books, Mark Twain makes no attempt to mask his identity as its narrator. In contrast

Mark Twain relaxes aboard ship during his round-the-world tour in this frontispiece to Following the Equator.

to *A Tramp Abroad,* for example, he alludes to traveling with his wife and daughter, though he never mentions either's name (chapters 1, 34, 40, 44, 48 and 65; his wife Livy can be seen in a photograph on page 66 of the early editions). He specifically mentions "Clemens" in a story about meeting General Grant (chapter 2) and in a list of horse billiards scores (chapter 4); later he discusses the "Mark Twain Club" (chapter 25) and explicitly identifies himself as "Mark Twain" (chapter 45).

While *Following the Equator* contains many humorous passages, its general tone is more serious than that of the earlier travel books. It has lengthy discussions of Australian labor recruitment, history and economic development; Indian culture; British rule in India; and South African politics. It offers only three tall tales (chapters 2, 13 and 28) and attempts BURLESQUE only rarely—as in Mark Twain's claim to have been bitten by a cobra (chapter 57) and a preposterous summation of South Africa's tangled politics (chapter 65). The book lifts many passages directly from Mark Twain's NOTEBOOKS and extracts quotes from about 30 other authors that total about 24,000 words.

Each chapter head presents at least one MAXIM attributed to "PUDD'NHEAD WILSON's New Calendar." The original American edition is a lavishly illustrated one-volume book; most later editions are sparsely illustrated sets, with 36 chapters in the first volume and 33 separately numbered chapters in the second volume. While the narrative follows Mark Twain's itinerary closely, it distributes its space unevenly. Though he spent nearly equal amounts of time in Australia, India and South Africa, 40 percent of the book is devoted to India, 27 percent to Australia and 10 percent to South Africa. The remaining space covers his Pacific voyage and his visits to New Zealand, Ceylon and Mauritius.

SYNOPSIS

Following the Equator contains 188,000 words in 69 numbered chapters and a conclusion. The first chapter summarizes Mark Twain's journey from ELMIRA, New York—which he left on July 14, 1895—across the northern United States to British Columbia. On August 23, he sailed into the PACIFIC OCEAN on the steamship WARRIMOO. The next seven chapters cover his voyage, during which he touched at HAWAII (August 30) and FIJI (September 10). This section also discusses the recruitment of South Seas islanders to plantations in Australia's Queensland colony, which Mark Twain never visited (chapters 5–6).

After reaching Sydney, AUSTRALIA on September 15, he was joined by Carlyle SMYTHE, who accompanied him on the rest of his tour as his agent. They traveled around Australia's southern periphery by train and ship until November 1 (chapters 9–25, 27–29 and 36), then sailed to NEW ZEALAND, where they also traveled by train and ship from November 6 through December 13 (chapters 26, 30–35). After returning to Australia, they spent a week in New South Wales. On December 23, Mark Twain left Sydney aboard the *Oceana,* touching at several Australian ports before making his final departure from the continent on January 4, 1896.

He reached CEYLON on January 13, 1896 (chapters 37 and 62), continuing on to INDIA the next day. After reaching BOMBAY on January 20, he spent over two months traveling through India, mostly by train (chapters 38–61). On March 28, he left CALCUTTA aboard the *Wardha,* stopping in Madras and Ceylon before continuing to MAURITIUS, where he landed on April 15 (chapters 61–63). On April 28, he sailed for SOUTH AFRICA, stopping in Mozambique on May 4 (chapter 64) before reaching Durban on May 6. Over the next two months, he traveled through South Africa by train (chapters 65–Conclusion). He considered his lecture tour ended in Cape Town, from which he sailed on July 15. After touching at Madeira, he reached Southampton, England on July 31.

The chapter numbers below are taken from the one-volume American edition of *Following the Equator,* whose first 36 chapters match the first book of two-volume editions. Chapter numbers for the second book of two-volume editions are inserted in parentheses. Information taken from outside chapters—such as names and dates—is presented within parentheses.

MORE TRAMPS ABROAD, the British edition of *Following the Equator,* has 72 numbered chapters and a conclusion. Most of its chapters have nearly identical counterparts in *Following the Equator;* however, all but the first nine are numbered differently. Both editions also have chapters that break differently, so there is no consistent numerical relationship between chapters in the two editions. In the chapter synopses that follow, numbers of *More Tramps* chapters corresponding to each *Following the Equator* chapter are given in square brackets. For example: "*Chapter 62 (2:26) [MTA–65 & 66]*" indicates *Following the Equator,* chapter 62 (chapter 26 in volume 2) [*More Tramps Abroad,* chapters 65–66]. Additional comments within brackets describe substantive differences between chapters of the two editions. These remarks ignore the minor differences in spelling, punctuation, phrasing and paragraph breaks that pervade the two editions.

Chapter 1 [*More Tramps Abroad*–1]
The LECTURE journey starts in PARIS, where Mark Twain has been living with his family. After he sails to America with his whole family, two family members (Olivia and Clara Clemens) elect to continue with him. They start west from New York (July 14, 1895) with Major POND managing the tour to the West Coast. A slow march takes them to Victoria, British Columbia, where they sail on the PACIFIC OCEAN aboard a comfortable ship (WARRIMOO) with good discipline and a pleasant crew (August 23).

The ship's brightest passenger is a young Canadian. A "remittance man," he is a dissipated ne'er-do-well who has been sent abroad to live on monthly remittances since he cannot keep pledges of abstinence. Most such pledges do not strike at a problem's root—the *desire* to drink. For his own part, Mark Twain once got relief from lumbago when he stopped smoking and drinking coffee, tea and alcohol. He later recommended a similar regimen to a woman whose health had run down; unfortunately, she could not stop doing any of these things because she no bad habits to break.

Chapter 2 [MTA–2]
Several days out, the ship encounters such hot weather that the passengers and crew begin wearing white linen. Shipboard conversation wanders to instances of extraordinary memory. One passenger who had served under India's viceroy recalls a Brahmin memory expert. Mark Twain recalls his own second meeting with General GRANT, who remembered a remark that Mark Twain had made the first time they had met, 10 years earlier.

A popular game among passengers is finishing incomplete stories. One man offers $50 to anyone who can satisfactorily end a story that he began reading 25 years earlier, when a train wreck interrupted him before he finished. None of the proposed endings satisfies a jury, so Mark Twain leaves it to readers to end the story themselves.

Chapter 3 [MTA–2 & 3]
On the seventh day out (August 30), the ship anchors off Honolulu, but no one can go ashore because of CHOLERA. Seeing HAWAII reminds Mark Twain of his earlier visit there (1866) and of KAMEHAMEHA I and his successors. The old monarchy is gone now, replaced by a republic, and the islands are modernizing. [This chapter matches the end of chapter 2 and all of chapter 3 in *More Tramps Abroad.*]

Chapter 4 [MTA–4]
The ship sails the next morning. On September 3, the passengers see a lunar ECLIPSE. Two days later, they cross the equator, but there are no "fool" ceremonies, such as are often customary during crossings. A popular shipboard diversion is "horse-billiards," or shovel-board (shuffleboard), a game demanding skill and luck [*More Tramps Abroad* has an additional half-page on horse-billiards]. In a tournament, Mark Twain wins a cheap Waterbury watch that later perplexes him when he tries to reconcile its time with that of the eccentric bells of Pretoria's parliament clock.

Deck-washing aboard the ship begins early; crew members never warn passengers when they will begin, and enjoy sloshing water through their ports. Passengers also often ruin their clothes when they brush up against freshly painted surfaces. When the ship crosses the International Dateline on September 8, it suddenly becomes September 10. A child who is born in steerage at that moment will probably go through life never knowing its correct birthday.

Chapter 5 [MTA–5]
In an argument among Scottish passengers about pronouncing Scottish words, Mark Twain annoys everyone by interjecting his own opinion; however, his timely invention of a couplet that he attributes to Robert Burns ends the argument agreeably.

As the ship proceeds, interest in the Southern Cross constellation mounts. After it enters a Milky Way of islands, it passes through the Horne (Futuna) Islands, in the region from which workers are recruited for Australia's Queensland plantations. In former times, "recruiting" was simply man-stealing, but workers must now come voluntarily. A book by Captain Wawn, a former recruiting shipmaster, says that labor recruiters are popular among the islanders, but Wawn's own evidence suggests otherwise.

Chapter 6 [MTA–6]
A pamphlet by the missionary William Gray is a strong indictment against Queensland labor recruiting. Since everyone involved in recruiting profits but the recruits themselves, one wonders why they go to Queensland willingly.

Chapter 7 [MTA–7]
After entering the FIJI islands, the ship lands at Suva on September 11. A single sailing vessel from Duluth (Minnesota) represents the American commercial marine in the harbor. As everyone goes ashore to explore, Mark Twain visits the governor's country residence. Fiji's last king ceded the islands to Britain in order to stave off American occupation.

Chapter 8 [MTA–8]
A glance at a map of the South Pacific reveals what a stupendous island wilderness the region is. Much remains unknown about it. Twenty years ago, two men speaking an unknown language drifted to Fiji on a canoe; even now, no one knows where they came from.

As the ship returns to sea, its most cultivated passenger is an English naturalist who lives in New Zealand. Owning an exhaustive knowledge of Australasia's fauna, he regards the region's most remarkable creature to be that curious combination of bird, fish, amphibian, burrower, crawler, quadruped and Christian called the Ornithorhyncus (duckbill platypus), the most grotesque of animals. His poetic tribute to the creature recalls Julia MOORE's verses.

Chapter 9 [MTA–9 & 10]
On the evening of September 15, the ship approaches Sydney, AUSTRALIA. Its harbor is enclosed by a dangerous precipice that once caused a tragedy when the *Duncan Dunbar,* loaded with schoolgirls and their mothers, broke up on its rocks (1857). The beautiful harbor and city have a fine climate, but Australia as a whole has really good climate only around its edges. Its broad interior regions are dry and forbidding, generating hot winds that blow dust storms resembling Nevada's alkali dust storms (ZEPHYRS). [*More Tramps Abroad* omits most of the final paragraph on dust storms.]

Chapter 10 [MTA–11 & 12]
Modern Australian history began in 1770 with Captain COOK's founding of a British colony. Australia and Tasmania soon became harsh penal colonies. As more respectable colonists arrived, provisions were made for their protection, but a body called the "New South Wales Corps" became exploitative and oppressive and made rum the currency of the land. Eventually, New South Wales grew rich from mines and wool ranching, and developed every kind of cultural amenity.

Chapter 11 [MTA–13]
The people of all English-speaking colonies, including New South Wales, are lavishly hospitable. Sydney is an English city with American trimmings. Its finest homes are mostly residences of "squatters"—the Australian term for great landowners. Australians resemble Americans closely in dress, general appearance and speech, though they tend toward pronunciations such as *piper* for "paper."

Chapter 12 [MTA–14]
In Sydney, Mark Twain dreams that the visible universe is the physical body of God, within which the vast worlds we see in space are corpuscles, and human beings and other creatures are mere microbes. A missionary, Mr. X., finds Mark Twain's dream similar to sacred Hindu accounts of their origins. He thinks that one reason Christianity does not catch on in India is that its miracles pale next to those of Hindu legends.

Chapter 13 [MTA–15 & 16]
Australasia spends liberally on public works, such as government buildings, hospitals and parks. The continent has four or five governors, but they are always away, leaving the lieutenant-governors to do the work; however, the country practically governs itself, limiting the governor's functions and making his ball a major event. Attending a Government House ball is the first of Sydney's great social pleasures; others include visiting Admiralty House, touring the harbor and fishing for sharks—the swiftest fish in the sea.

A previously unpublished story tells how impoverished young Cecil RHODES arrived in Sydney in 1870 and caught a great shark containing a copy of the *London Times* just 10 days old. The paper reported that since France had declared war on Prussia (July 19, 1870), wool prices were shooting up. Rhodes took the valuable news to Sydney's richest wool-broker, with whom he made a deal to corner the colony's entire crop, thereby pocketing his first fortune. [This chapter contains all of chapter 15 and the first two paragraphs of chapter 16 of *More Tramps Abroad.*]

Chapter 14 [MTA–16]
Health problems keep Mark Twain from visiting Queensland. Instead, he takes a train to Melbourne, the

capital of Victoria. Australian distances are deceiving; Victoria looks small on a map, but is actually as large as Britain. The gauges of Australian trains change at each colony's borders, requiring passengers and freight to be shifted to different trains. Mark Twain changes cars at Albury, then slides smoothly through game-less plains.

Chapter 15 [MTA–17]
Wagga-Wagga is the former home of the famous TICH-BORNE CLAIMANT, who had been a butcher there. For a quarter of a century, this impostor claimed to be "Sir Roger Tichborne," only to confess on his recent death-bed that he was Arthur Orton of Wagga-Wagga [*More Tramps Abroad* has four additional pages on Orton].

In Melbourne, Mark Twain hopes to unravel a mystery about another impostor—a man who once posed as *him*. On the day that President Garfield was shot (July 2, 1881), Mark Twain's wife received a letter from an English friend—here called "Henry Bascom"—whom he had known in England during the 1870s. Then in Melbourne, Bascom expressed condolences about Mark Twain's death during an Australian lecture tour. Bascom added that he reached Melbourne too late to see the body, but was in time to be a pallbearer. Since then, Mark Twain has been anxious to learn who the dead impostor was. The mystery has since grown larger; Bascom himself is now dead, and Sydney and Melbourne journalists never heard of the impostor. Just as the mystery appears unsolvable, it unexpectedly clears up; however, the rest of this story is saved for later *(see chapter 25).*

Chapter 16 [MTA–18]
A stately city, Melbourne covers an immense area. The Melbourne Cup, run on November 5, Guy Fawkes's Day, is Australasia's biggest annual event.

What most interests travelers to other lands are the people, novelties and local history. While novelties are rare in Australia's modern cities, the country's history is almost always picturesque; it reads like beautiful lies. [*More Tramps Abroad* adds a two-page anecdote about an escaped convict named Buckley (c. 1780–c. 1856) who lived among Aboriginals for 32 years, then spent the rest of his life in Australia's European society.]

British colonial audiences welcome Americans warmly. Although the war-cloud hanging over England and America makes Mark Twain a prospective prisoner of war, he encounters no trouble anywhere (an allusion to friction between the United States and Britain over Britain's border dispute with Venezuela).

Chapter 17 [MTA–19]
The British Empire contains about 400 million people. Against such numbers, Australia's four million are nearly nothing; however, statistics show that they command a tenth part of Britain's trade.

In the 17-hour train ride from Melbourne to Adelaide (October 11), Mark Twain meets a judge going to Broken Hill. That town in New South Wales is only 700 miles from Sydney, but to get there by train, the judge travels 2,000 miles by way of Adelaide. The route takes them through the kind of scrubby plains in which one expects to find hostile Aboriginals lurking, as in Australian novels. Aboriginals are great trackers; they may be assigned to the bottom level of human intelligence, but they can follow trails that would baffle Sherlock HOLMES.

Chapter 18 [MTA–20]
As they pass through beautiful hills, Mark Twain asks a man the difference between gorse and broom; the man cannot answer, though he has been in Australia more than 50 years. When he was 20, he came from England hoping to amass £200 within five years and go home, but he is still here. His story seems pathetic, until Mark Twain learns that the man once helped discover fabulous copper mines and is now rich enough to buy a city. Since the copper strikes saved South Australia, the province has also developed prosperous wool and grain industries.

The train also carries an American with the unique vocation of buying Australia's kangaroo-leather crop for shoes.

Chapter 19 [MTA–21]
An Australian specialty is the botanical garden. Whatever we can grow under glass will flourish outdoors in Australia. At Adelaide's zoo, Mark Twain sees a laughing jackass and a dingo. South Australia is confusingly named, as it is really *middle* Australia. As early as 1871–72, the province built a telegraph line across the continent to Port Darwin, connecting Australia with the rest of the world. To reach San Francisco, telegrams from Melbourne pass through 20 stops over 20,000 miles.

Chapter 20 [MTA–22]
Mark Twain encounters a friend, Mr. G., whom he knew at BAD NAUHEIM. While discussing mutual acquaintances, he tells G. about a fox-hunt he once saw in England, and also recalls how he once got away from Nauheim in time to avoid a CHOLERA quarantine. When he took his family into ITALY, getting through customs would have been an ordeal, had he not carried a letter from the Italian consul-general at Frankfurt.

Chapter 21 [MTA–23]
Before visiting Australia, Mark Twain had never heard of the "weet-weet"—a lightweight object that Aboriginals can throw incredible distances using a technique that no one else understands. Their reputation for low intelligence must be due to race-aversion.

Whites have used many methods to keep the native population down, and there has been a long history of distrust on both sides. One of the kindest and most gentle ways, however, was a Christmas pudding laced with arsenic that whites gave to blacks. One of the many humorous things in the world is the white man's notion that he is less savage than other savages. [*More Tramps Abroad* has two additional pages about aborigines.]

Chapter 22 [MTA–24]
Australia provides no end of materials to imaginative writers. A whole literature could be made out of the Aboriginal alone. The prize curiosity of all the races, Aboriginals have incredible athletic skills, amazing hunting and tracking ability and refined artistic skills. They also can stand immense physical pain. Australia's colorful slang contains such expressions as "Never-never country" for unpopulated plains and "new chum" for tenderfoot.

Chapter 23 [MTA–25]
From Adelaide, the travelers go to Horsham, Victoria on October 17. They visit a nearby agricultural college, where magpies are out in full force. From there, they visit Stawell in the gold-MINING country. [Chapters 23 and 24 are combined in *More Tramps Abroad*'s chapter 25.]

Chapter 24 [MTA–25]
The travelers next go to Ballarat, where the first great Australian gold strike occurred in 1851, after smaller strikes elsewhere had begun drawing immigrants to Australia. Though comparatively small, Ballarat has the amenities of a major city, and its English is the standard dialect of cultivated Australasians.

Chapter 25 [MTA–26]
On October 23, Mark Twain goes (north) from Ballarat to Bendigo—a mining center that has turned out half as much gold as CALIFORNIA. His stay is made memorable by a hospitable Irishman, "Mr. Blank," who has an amazing familiarity with Mark Twain's books. Blank had been president of the 32-member Mark Twain Club of Corrigan Castle, Ireland, with which Mark Twain once conducted a prodigious correspondence. At first, the club's attentions flattered him; gradually, however, he came to dread its long monthly reports and its voluminous questions about his work, so he stopped replying. Blank confesses that *he* was the club's sole member; he wrote every speech and report himself. He also confesses to having written the "Henry Bascom" letter about Mark Twain's death in Australia *(discussed in chapter 15).*

Chapter 26 [MTA–27]
After visiting Maryborough and other towns, Mark Twain sails for NEW ZEALAND—a country about which he knows little. Aboard the steamer, he meets Professor X. of YALE UNIVERSITY, who describes the prodigious effort that he and fellow Yale professors once made to impress a visiting New Zealander with their knowledge of his country.

Chapter 27 [MTA–28, 29 & 30]
Mark Twain's November 1 diary entry describes sailing past Tasmania, whose native peoples are now dead and gone. Years ago, the long wars between whites and blacks were finally ended by the heroic work of a bricklayer named George Augustus Robinson. Alone in his belief that the native peoples were human beings, Robinson single-handedly talked them into surrendering peacefully. [This chapter has parts of three *More Tramps Abroad* chapters. It omits a two-and-a-half-page extract from James Bonwick's *The Lost Tasmanian Race* that is in *More Tramps Abroad*'s chapter 28; it also omits a page and a half about Robinson from *More Tramps*'s chapter 29; it has all of chapter 30 except a Pudd'nhead Wilson maxim.]

Chapter 28 [MTA–31]
Robinson proves the truth behind the aphorism, "Given the Circumstances, the Man will appear." His tale recalls a pre–CIVIL WAR story about a man named Ed JACKSON, who went from Memphis, Tennessee to New York. Jackson's friends gave him a fake letter of introduction to Commodore VANDERBILT from a man whom Vanderbilt purportedly knew as a boy. His friends expected Jackson to get into trouble; instead, he won Vanderbilt's confidence and returned as the director of a vast commercial project.

Chapter 29 [MTA–32 & 33]
The travelers stop at Tasmania's remarkably clean capital, Hobart—one of many "Junior Englands" they encounter. [This chapter matches chapter 32 and the first three pages of chapter 33 of *More Tramps Abroad*, which has two additional pages on convicts from J. S. Laurie, *The Story of Australasia*.]

Chapter 30 [MTA–33]
Mark Twain's first New Zealand stop is at Bluff, where the country's rabbit plague began. On November 6, he passes Invercargill and stops at Dunedin. There he meets Dr. Hockin, whose home is a museum of Maori art and antiquities. Hockin has a ghastly curiosity—a lignified caterpillar with a plant growing out of its neck that exemplifies nature's gift for playing nasty tricks. [This chapter matches the last four pages of *More Tramps Abroad*'s chapter 33, which omits a paragraph on tapeworms.]

Chapter 31 [MTA–34]
On November 11, the travelers ride a New Zealand "express" train that goes just over 20 miles per hour. Its cars are unusually modern and pleasant, however, in contrast to those on a train they rode to Maryborough, Australia. On that trip, a stranger described what may be the world's worst hotel.

Chapter 32 [MTA–35]
The train passes through "Junior England" to Christchurch, whose museum has many interesting native artifacts and the skeleton of an extinct moa. Four days later, the travelers go to Lyttleton. From there they sail for Auckland aboard the overcrowded *Flora*—the foulest boat on which Mark Twain has ever sailed. (About 375 words criticizing the company that operates the *Flora* are omitted in *MTA*.) At their first chance, they switch to the *Mahinapua*.

New Zealand women got the vote in 1893, they have proven that women are not as indifferent to politics as many people believe.

Chapter 33 [MTA–36]
During a quiet day at Nelson, the travelers learn about the notorious "Maungatapu Murders" of 30 years earlier—Nelson's one great historical event. The confession of Burgess, one of the convicted murderers, may be without peer in the literature of murder as a succinct, cold-blooded account of grisly crimes.

On November 20, they reach Auckland, but poor health keeps Mark Twain from visiting Rotorua's geyser region. They all sail from Auckland on November 26.

Chapter 34 [MTA–37]
On November 27, they anchor at Gisborne, where they watch passengers transfer between their ship and a tug on a swinging basket-chair. They leave Napier by train on December 2 and pass through Waitukurau.

Chapter 35 [MTA–38]
They continue their journey to Wanganui, where they see many Maori, who—unlike native Australians—were not exterminated. Wanganui has some curious war monuments paying tribute to white men "who fell in defense of law and order against fanaticism and barbarism." Calling Maori patriotism "fanaticism" cannot, however, degrade it. A strangely thoughtless monument honors Maori who fought *against* their own people. While Mark Twain is in Wanganui, a lunatic bursts into his room to warn him that Jesuits plan to kill him.

On December 9, the travelers reach Wellington, from which they sail back to Australia.

Chapter 36 [MTA–39]
On December 13, they sail aboard the *Mararoa.* At sea, Mark Twain reads poems from Julia MOORE's *Sentimental Song Book,* which has the same charm as GOLDSMITH's *Vicar of Wakefield.* After reaching Sydney on December 17, they spend several days visiting nearby towns. Meanwhile, Mark Twain collects curious town names—such as Coolgardie, Mullengudgery, Murriwillumba and Woolloomooloo—from which he composes a poem on Australian weather.

Chapter 37 (volume 2: chapter 1) [MTA–40]
On December 23, the travelers sail on the steamer *Oceana.* They stop at Melbourne for Christmas and at Adelaide for New Year's, then pass Cape Leeuwin on January 5, 1896 to begin the eight-day voyage to CEYLON.

Chapter 38 (2:2) [MTA–41]
The next day they continue their journey aboard the *Rosetta* and reach INDIA on January 20. A bewitching city, Bombay is the ARABIAN NIGHTS come again. India is a land of dreams and romance, of fabulous wealth and fabulous poverty, palaces and hovels, famine and pestilence, tigers and elephants; it is a hundred nations, a thousand religions, and two million gods.

At the travelers' hotel, the German manager and three assistants take them to their rooms, followed by 14 baggage-carriers with one item each. The burly German cuffs a servant, suddenly transporting Mark Twain back to his Missouri boyhood, when he saw slaves treated similarly. Through the evening, employees scream orders through hotel passageways; shouting, crashing, bird-screeching and other sounds continue until midnight. At five the next morning, the din begins afresh when a crow begins jabbering.

Chapter 3:9 (23) [MTA–42]
Old dreams of India rise in a vague moonlight over one's opaque consciousness, illuminating a thousand forgotten boyhood visions of barbaric gorgeousness, with sumptuous princely titles such as Maharajah of Travancore, Nabob of Jubbulpore and Begum of Bhopal. One's day in India begins when a "bearer" knocks at the door to announce in his strange "Bearer English" that the bath is ready. Manuel X., the first bearer whom the travelers hire, is so slow and forgetful that he is soon replaced by a younger man whom Mark Twain dubs "Satan." The first task that Satan performs is to announce a visitor whom he calls "God"—a Mohammedan deity who is surprisingly familiar with Huck Finn.

Chapter 40 (2:4) [MTA–43]
Other strong images of India are Government House and the mansion of a young native prince. Mark Twain interests himself in ceremonies and visits the Towers of Silence, where the Parsee leave their dead to be dried and cleaned by nature—a funeral system equivalent to cremation as a sanitary measure.

Chapter 41 (2:5) [MTA–44]
A Mr. Gandhi shows the travelers a Jain temple; then they see an Indian prince receive a Jain delegation in a colorful ceremony. Compared to this, a Christian exhibition would be a hideous affair—with the added disadvantage of white complexions. Nearly all black and brown skins are beautiful, but beautiful white skin is rare.

Chapter 42 (2:6) [MTA–45]
Near midnight the travelers see the betrothal ceremony of a 12-year-old Hindu girl. As they ride back in the dark, rats scurry around dim human forms stretched everywhere on the ground, illuminated by faint lamps. As Mark Twain writes this passage a year later, he reads cables reporting that plague is now sweeping Bombay. [This chapter's final passage, 775 words from Alexander William Kinglake's *Eothen* (1844) on plague in Cairo, is not in *More Tramps Abroad.*]

Chapter 43 (2:7) [MTA–46]
A Bombay trial of a cold-blooded murderer recalls the forgotten days of Thuggee, when professional murderers and thieves roamed India. The trial's official report reads like a Thug report of 50 years earlier; the criminal

side of Indians has always been picturesque and readable.

There is only one India, and it has a monopoly of grand and imposing specialties and marvels all its own. India invented the plague, the Car of Juggernaut, and Suttee—which once moved widows to throw themselves on their husbands' funeral fires. India's specialty is famine; it has two million gods and worships them all; everything is on a giant scale—even poverty. On top of all this, India is the mother of that wonder of wonders—caste, as well as that mystery of mysteries—the satanic brotherhood of the Thugs.

Chapter 44 (2:8) [MTA–47]

On January 28, Mark Twain learns of an official Thug-book as he prepares to travel by train. Two days later, the railway station provides a great spectacle of people. Satan ruthlessly pushes a path through them; he was probably a Thug in an earlier incarnation. As Mark Twain travels, he reads about these strange Thugs and reaches the intensely Indian city of Baroda on January 31.

Chapter 45 (2:9) [MTA–48]

On a trip out of town, Mark Twain rides an elephant, then visits the Gaikwar of Baroda. During the train ride back from Baroda, he meets a man traveling with a remarkably long, low dog that reminds him of a dog that once saved him from embarrassment:

> While taking a train into New York City to visit Augustin DALY at his theater once, Mark Twain happened to read a newspaper article about "bench-shows" for dogs that listed the dimensions of a prize Saint Bernard. When he reached New York, James Lewis surprised him with the warning that he would never get into Daly's office. That evening, a giant Irishman let him in the back entrance of Daly's theater, only to tell him that he would go no farther. As the man grilled him about what business he was in, Mark Twain spotted the man's pet dog; it was a Saint Bernard identical to the one he had seen in the newspaper, so he said he was a "bench-show" operator. The Irishman challenged him to prove it by giving his dog's dimensions. Quoting what he remembered from the paper, Mark Twain won the man over with precisely correct figures and was soon in Daly's office. As the only man ever to run Daly's back-door blockade, Mark Twain won an envied reputation among theater people.

Chapter 46 (2:10) [MTA–49]

Still on the Indian train, Mark Twain reads more about Thugs and cites incidents of their murderous activities before the British government suppressed them. Thugs were remarkable in many ways; they worked together without regard for religious or caste differences. Rarely fastidious about whom they killed, they were motivated by piety, gain and the sport of killing.

Chapter 47 (2:11) [MTA–50]

There are many indications that Thugs often killed for sport. One might think that they were too callous to have human feelings; however, they had a passionate love for their own kin—a fact that a shrewd British officer used against them to help end their depredations.

Chapter 48 (2:12) [MTA–51]

The travelers leave Bombay for Allahabad by night train (February 2). On Indian trains, passengers do not pay extra for sleeping space, so they often must compete for places. The trains are manned exclusively by Indians, who are easily the world's most interesting people, but also the nearest to being incomprehensible. Their character, history, customs and religion are filled with riddles.

Chapter 49 (2:13) [MTA–52]

The journey from Bombay to Allahabad is long, but too interesting to be tiring. The day begins early in the countryside, where nine-tenths of the people are farmers. India is not beautiful, but there is an enchantment about it. Its many names describe it correctly as the land of contradictions. For example, it is both the land of splendor and the land of desolation. The land where all life is holy, it is also the land of the Thug and poisoner.

Allahabad, the "City of God," is having a great religious fair near the confluence of the sacred Ganges and Jumna rivers, from which many people carry holy water.

Chapter 50 (2:14) [MTA–53]

The train ride to Benares takes just a few hours (February 5). Midway, the travelers change cars—a dull thing in most countries, but not in India, with its huge crowds, splendid costumes and confusion. There is another wait outside Benares, where women are carried in palanquins to stay hidden from view. The long ride to the hotel passes dusty, decaying temples. Though the region aches with age and penury, Benares does not disappoint. Older than history, it is as busy as an anthill, unspeakably sacred and equally unsanitary. Religion is its business.

Chapter 51 (2:15) [MTA–54]

A great religious hive, Benares is a sort of army and navy store, theologically stocked. It offers everything for the pilgrim, from purification and protection against hunger to long life. It is a religious VESUVIUS in whose bowels theological forces have thundered and smoked for ages.

Chapter 52 (2:16) [MTA–55]

In a Benares temple, the travelers see a man shaping tiny gods from clay; every day he throws 2,000 of them into the Ganges—Benares's supreme show-place. As the travelers cruise on the river, they see nine corpses being burned, and marvel that people drink its dreadful water. They also visit the temple of the Thug goddess,

Bhowanee or Kali. With Indians, all life seems to be sacred—except human life.

Benares is also the site of an important episode in the career of Warren Hastings, who saved the Indian Empire in 1781—the best service ever done to the Indians.

Chapter 53 (2:17) [MTA–56]
In Benares, Mark Twain sees his second living god, Sri 108 Swami Bhaskarananda Saraswati. Of the many wonders he has seen in the world, none interests him as much as these gods. What makes something a wonder is not what *we* see in it, but what *others* see. After Sri 108—who has attained a Hindu state of perfection—suggests that they exchange autographs, Mark Twain gives him a copy of *Huckleberry Finn*.

Chapter 54 (2:18) [MTA–57]
A train takes the travelers to India's capital, Calcutta (February 8), a city rich in historical memories, particularly of Clive's and Hastings's achievements. Its only great monument, however, is a lofty tower to Ochterlony (Sir David Ochterlony, 1758–1825). If India built similar monuments to all who deserved them, the landscape would be monotonous with them.

England is so far from India that it knows little about the eminent deeds its servants have performed there. The average person is profoundly ignorant of remote countries. All that most Hindus know about America, for example, is George Washington and CHICAGO—the "holy city" of the recent Congress of Religions. To outsiders, "Calcutta" infallibly evokes thoughts of the Black Hole. Visitors rush to see it, but nothing remains.

Chapter 55 (2:19) [MTA–58]
On February 14, the travelers leave Calcutta for Darjeeling. As they pass countless villages, they seem to be within a single vast city—the biggest on Earth. Multitudes of men work the fields, but no women. The hymn "From Greenland's Icy Mountains" (by Reginald Heber) speaks of lifting heathen lands from "error's chain," but when Mark Twain recalls seeing elderly women doing backbreaking work in GERMANY and AUSTRIA, he thinks that we should first lift *ourselves*.

After changing to a smaller train, the travelers begin a picturesque ascent into tiger country and eventually reach Darjeeling in the Himalayas, where they admire the mighty mountains.

Chapter 56 (2:20) [MTA–59]
Over the next few days, they view the stupendous mountains. Before leaving, they ascend even higher on a regular train, then fly down a 35-mile track in a canopied hand-car the size of a sleigh as if on a toboggan, stopping occasionally to gather flowers and see the view. It is the most enjoyable day Mark Twain has spent on Earth.

Chapter 57 (2:21) [MTA–60]
Nothing is left undone to make India the most extraordinary country under the sun. For years, the government has tried to destroy murderous wildlife, but statistics still show a curious uniformity in the numbers of people annually killed by animals. Snakes alone kill 17,000 people a year, though 10 times that number of snakes are killed. Narrow escapes do occur. In the same jungle where Mark Twain killed 16 tigers and some elephants, a cobra bit him, but *it* got well.

From Calcutta, the travelers zigzag west through Muzaffurpore, Dinapore, Benares and Lucknow.

Chapter 58 (2:22) [MTA–61]
Of the many causes of India's Great Mutiny of 1857, the chief was the East India's Company's annexation of the Oudh kingdom. Though caught wholly unprepared, England crushed the Mutiny in perhaps the greatest chapter in its military history. Many moving stories of suffering and heroism are demonstrated in extracts from G. O. Trevelyan (Sir George Otto Trevelyan [1838–1928], author of *Cawnpore* [1865]).

Chapter 59 (2:23) [MTA–62]
The travelers ride over the route of Campbell's retreat from Lucknow (February 22) and visit Cawnpore. At Agra, one expects too much of the Taj Mahal to appreciate it fully in one visit. Just as he had to see NIAGARA 15 times in order to clear away his imaginary falls, Mark Twain must see the Taj many times.

Chapter 60 (2:24) [MTA–63]
The travelers wander contentedly, visiting various towns such as Lahore, where the lieutenant-governor lends Mark Twain an elephant, drifting as far as Rawal Pindi on the Afghan border. They also visit Delhi and have a long rest near the intensely Indian town of Jeypore (Jaipur) (early March). The most picturesque and outlandish show Mark Twain has ever seen develops when a rich Hindu marches a religious procession into town, drawing an immense, colorfully dressed audience.

By this time, they have lost their servant Satan, who cannot obey orders to stay sober. He is replaced by a Mohammedan, Sahadat Mohammed Khan.

Chapter 61 (2:25) [MTA–64]
India's colleges resemble our high schools in oversupplying the market for highly educated employees. A little book published in Calcutta, *Indo-Anglian Literature*, is filled with letters written by educated Indians begging for help. The authors of these letters reveal that their education consists mainly of learning *things* without their meanings. Such learning contrasts with that of Helen KELLER; though deaf, dumb and blind since infancy, she not only knows things, but understands their meanings. Proof that the education of many American students is as empty as that of their Indian brothers is found in ENGLISH AS SHE IS TAUGHT, a collection of examination answers from Brooklyn schools.

Chapter 62 (2:26) [MTA–65 & 66]
Finally, the travelers sail from Calcutta (March 28), spending a day at Madras and several days on Ceylon

before heading toward MAURITIUS. The ship's captain cannot tell the truth plausibly—the opposite of a Scottish passenger, who cannot lie in an *un*plausible way. One day, the captain tells about an Arctic voyage on which the mate's shadow froze to the deck.

No day can be more restful than one aboard a ship cruising in the calm tropics. Without mail, telegrams or newspapers to distract, the world is so far away that it seems a dream. If he could, Mark Twain would sail on forever and never live on land again. On April 15, the travelers reach Mauritius; the next day, they go ashore and take a train to Curepipe in the mountains.

Chapter 63 (2:27) [MTA–66]
In 1892, Mauritius experienced a devastating cyclone followed by a deluge of rain. It is the only place on earth where no breed of matches can stand the damp. Nevertheless, what there is of Mauritius is beautiful.

In thinking about French civilization, one wonders why the English let FRANCE have Madagascar. After all, robbing each other's territories has never been a sin among European nations. *All* territorial possessions of all nations—including America—are pilfered. AFRICA has been as coolly divided among the gang as if they had bought and paid for it; now they are beginning to steal each other's grabbings. All the world's savage lands will fall under European rule; this is good, as dreary ages of bloodshed and disorder will give way to the reign of law. When one compares what India was before to what she is now, one must concede that the most fortunate thing ever to befall her was Britain's establishment of supremacy. [This chapter matches the second half of chapter 66 in *More Tramps Abroad*.]

Chapter 64 (2:28) [MTA–67]
The finest boat that Mark Twain has seen in these seas, the *Arundel Castle* is thoroughly modern. On May 4, it lands at Mozambique's Delagoa Bay, where the travelers spend an afternoon ashore. Two days later, they reach Durban in SOUTH AFRICA. Meanwhile, a fellow passenger tells Mark Twain how P. T. BARNUM bought SHAKESPEARE's birthplace around the same time that he was trying to buy the elephant JUMBO. Mark Twain heard the story from Barnum himself.

Chapter 65 (2:29) [MTA–68]
In Durban, the travelers stay at a hotel where servants repeatedly awaken them to offer unwanted services in the early morning. Durban is a neat, clean town in which splendidly built Zulu pull rickshaws. Outside of town, the travelers visit a Trappist monastery, where every detail that makes life worth living has been placed out of reach. In the nearby Transvaal, politics has been in a confused state since Cecil RHODES and his chartered company attempted an invasion.

Chapter 66 (2:30) [MTA–69]
Information on South African politics is so conflicting that strangers cannot avoid being confused. Four

months earlier, Dr. Jameson led about 600 armed men into the Transvaal, where the Boer government quickly captured and imprisoned them. Much of the confusion about these events is cleared up by the time Mark Twain writes these pages in May 1897. He has learned that foreign—"Uitlander"—capitalists in the Transvaal had chafed under burdens imposed by the Boers, whose republican government they wanted to reform. Sensing a chance to profit from their discontent, Rhodes arranged for Jameson to lead men into the Transvaal to support an expected rising. Jameson received a letter from the Transvaal Reformers urging him to come rescue women and children, but waited two months to launch his raid. By then the Reformers no longer wanted him to come. Publication of that letter made Jameson a hero in Britain and inspired an homage from the poet laureate (Alfred Austin). [*More Tramps Abroad* has an additional half page on the laureate.]

Chapter 67 (2:31) [MTA–70]
Jameson's raid caused serious political problems for the Transvaal Reformers, but Mark Twain finds the military problems more interesting. Always fond of giving military advice, he reviews the incident and shows how Jameson should have done things differently. During the Anglo–Boer war of 1881, the British lost 1,300 men to the Boers' loss of just 30. Since the Transvaal Boers were ready to put 8,000 men against Jameson, what Jameson needed was 240,000 *men*—not the 530 boys that he actually had. Overencumbered by artillery and Maxim guns, Jameson would have done better to bring a battery of Pudd'nhead Wilson maxims—which are deadlier and easier to carry.

Chapter 68 (2:32) [MTA–71]
True to form, Rhodes got the Transvaal Reformers into trouble while staying out of it himself. He has always been judicious this way. He and his gang are also lawfully reducing the population of Rhodesia (now Zimbabwe) to a form of slavery even worse than the old American slavery.

Johannesburg has the world's richest concentration of gold mines, whose capital came from England and mining engineers from America. Mark Twain once knew everything that these people know about MINING—except how to make money at it.

Religious, ignorant, obstinate, bigoted, lazy and unclean, the typical Boer is also hospitable and honest with whites while remaining a hard master to blacks. He has good hunting skills, loves political independence and prefers the veld's seclusion. Given his nature, it is surprising that Uitlanders expected Boer government to be different than what it was.

During several train journeys in the Cape Colony, Mark Twain enjoys the veld's surpassing beauty. African women he sees in King William's Town and Bloemfontein remind him of people he had known 50 years earlier.

Chapter 69 (2:33) [MTA–72]
After Rhodes, South Africa's most interesting convulsion of nature is Kimberley's diamond crater. One of the strangest things in history is that sparkling diamonds lay there for so long unnoticed.

The travelers' arrival at Cape Town in July ends their African journey. They have now seen every great South African feature except Rhodes himself. Many reasons are advanced to explain Rhodes's formidable supremacy: his prodigious wealth, his personal magnetism and persuasive tongue, his majestic ideas, his vast schemes for England's territorial aggrandizement. Frankly admitting that he admires Rhodes, Mark Twain concludes that when the man's time comes, he will buy a piece of the rope for a keepsake.

Conclusion [MTA–Conclusion]
Before leaving Cape Town, Mark Twain visits Parliament and some old Dutch homes. In one home, he sees a portrait of Dr. James Barry, an army surgeon who came to the Cape 50 years earlier and rose to a high position. Only after Barry died (1865) was "he" discovered to be a woman.

On July 15, 1896, the travelers sail on the *Norman*, which delivers them to Southampton, England, two weeks later, after a stop at Madeira.

BACKGROUND AND PUBLISHING HISTORY

After completing his lecture tour and reaching England at the end of July 1896, Mark Twain settled in GUILDFORD with Livy and Clara. He expected his other daughters, Susy and Jean, to join him soon, and planned to begin writing as soon as he found a suitable house in London for the family. However, in mid-August Susy suddenly became ill and died in Hartford. The crushing news delayed Mark Twain's work and darkened his attitude. He finally started writing during the last week of October; six months later he completed the chapters on India and pronounced his book finished. He had set aside his notes on South Africa for another book, but in order to bring his manuscript up to the necessary size for a SUBSCRIPTION BOOK, he hastily added more chapters on South Africa and was busy with revisions through another month. An important supplement to *Following the Equator* is MARK TWAIN'S NOTEBOOK, which contains lengthy extracts from his travel journals. Three chapters in Clara's book *My Father, Mark Twain* (1931) contain her account of the tour.

Mark Twain's dark mood as he wrote *Following the Equator* is revealed in a letter to W. D. HOWELLS that he wrote two years later, saying that he wrote the book "in hell," trying to give the impression that "it was an excursion through heaven." To lighten his manuscript's tone, he deleted many passages containing self-pitying remarks and removed two long sections that have been posthumously published as "THE ENCHANTED SEA-WIL-DERNESS" and "Newhouse's Jew Story."

After finishing his revisions on May 18, 1897, he sent a copy of the manuscript to Frank BLISS's AMERICAN PUBLISHING COMPANY in Hartford. With the help of Bram STOKER, he negotiated a new contract with Andrew CHATTO, his English publisher, whom he gave a copy of the manuscript in mid-June. As his publishers prepared their different editions, he busied himself with new writing projects. He took his family to SWITZERLAND in mid-July and to VIENNA two months later.

Finding an appropriate title for the book proved difficult. As Mark Twain finished his revisions, he preferred "Imitating the Equator" or "Another Innocent Abroad." He also considered "The Latest Innocent Abroad" and "The Surviving Innocent Abroad," but finally settled on "Following the Equator" in late July, while Chatto chose "More Tramps Abroad" for the English edition.

Meanwhile, Bliss—without consulting Mark Twain—lopped the ends from many chapters and removed passages that he considered dull. Chatto made only minor cuts from his edition, which is much the closer to Mark Twain's original manuscript. In mid-November, Bliss issued *Following the Equator;* Chatto issued MORE TRAMPS ABROAD around the same time. In October, the NEW YORK HERALD published about 6,000 words from the book in an advance review without Mark Twain's permission. Mark Twain himself published just one extract from the book, as "From India to South Africa" in *McClure's Magazine* (November 1897). His original manuscript is now held by New York Public Library's Berg Collection. Since its original publication, *Following the Equator* has been reprinted only occasionally, apart from uniform editions of Mark Twain's works. The MARK TWAIN PAPERS project has tentatively scheduled a corrected edition for the year 2007.

The first edition of *Following the Equator* is Mark Twain's most elaborately decorated book. Its cover has a color picture of an African elephant framed by stamped gold arabesques repeated on the spine, and its 712 pages are printed on coated paper. It has 193 illustrations, including the first photographs published in a Mark Twain book, and original art by 11 illustrators, most of whose pictures are signed. Dan BEARD contributed about 24 drawings scattered through 14 chapters. Other illustrators include F. M. SENIOR (13 pictures), Thomas J. Fogarty (10), C. H. WARREN (9), Frederic Dielman (8), F. Berkeley SMITH (7, plus the cover), A. B. FROST (7), Charles Allan Gilbert (5), Peter NEWELL (5), Benjamin West Clinedinst (4) and A. G. Reinhart (3). By contrast, the first edition of *More Tramps Abroad* has just four illustrations.

Foo-foo the First, King of the Mooncalves   Facetious title used in *The Prince and the Pauper.* In chapter 17, King EDWARD is cast among a gang of beggars and thieves. Offended by Edward's calling himself "king of England," the gang's RUFFLER tells him that if he must call himself a "king," to choose another title. When the tinker proposes dubbing Edward "Foo-foo the First, King of the Mooncalves," the gang subjects Edward to a humiliating mock coronation. Five chapters later, however, Edward wins a cudgel-fight against HUGO and is renamed the "King of the Game-Cocks."

Early 19th-century American slang for an insignificant fool, "foo-foo" also appears in *Innocents Abroad,* which quotes a spurious future encyclopedia entry by "the learned Ah-ah Foo-foo" (chapter 31). "Mooncalf" goes back to at least the late 16th century, when it meant a false pregnancy or a monster. A later meaning—likely the one Mark Twain intends in *The Prince and the Pauper*—is "simpleton."

Forty-four (44; Quarante-quatre) Name of similar characters in "SCHOOLHOUSE HILL" and NO. 44, THE MYSTERIOUS STRANGER. In both of these unfinished novels, Forty-four is a boy who suddenly arrives in a village, where he astounds people with his marvelous powers. In "Schoolhouse Hill," he appears at the mid–19th-century Missouri school that Tom Sawyer attends. At first he speaks only French (he introduces himself as "Quarante-quatre"), but absorbs knowledge so rapidly that by midday he speaks perfect English and has mastered Latin, Greek and other subjects. The Forty-four of *No. 44* (whose name is generally rendered "44") visits the late 15th-century Austrian village of ESELDORF, where he joins the household of a print shop owner. Though utterly untutored, he proves himself incomparably knowledgeable and quickly masters the printing craft. Both stories' characters go on to demonstrate a wide range of powers as they involve themselves in village life. While the career of "Schoolhouse"'s Forty-four is truncated by Mark Twain's early abandonment of the story, the 44 of *No. 44* develops into a quite different type of character and appears to carry his mission to a conclusion when he reveals himself to his Austrian friend August FELDNER as nothing more than a creation of August's own imagination (chapter 34).

Both Forty-four characters resemble SATAN in Mark Twain's earlier story "THE CHRONICLE OF YOUNG SATAN." They differ from the latter in being slower to explain who they are and where they come from. "Schoolhouse Hill"'s Forty-four eventually reveals that he is the son of Satan and is millions of Earth-years old (chapters 4–5), while *No. 44*'s 44 admits that he is not of this world, but does not reveal that he is merely a figment of Feldner's imagination until the end of the narrative. Meanwhile, he explains that one of his reasons for coming to Earth is so that he can shut off his "prophecy-works" and enjoy being surprised (chapter 30). This 44 also differs from both of the other characters in being despised by most of the people around him.

An unanswered question about these characters is what, if anything, the name "44" meant to Mark Twain. To complicate matters, *No. 44*'s character calls himself "Number 44, New Series 864,962." Mark Twain's "Schoolhouse Hill" notes suggest that he may have chosen "44" randomly, as his character was to be one of an untold number of Satan's children, each of whom is identified by a complex number. While various explanations of "44" have been advanced, Mark Twain may have chosen the number simply because it sounded right. Perhaps, he saw it as an abbreviated form of "144." As the square of 12, 144 is the highest number in the standard multiplication table—a learning device that bedeviled Mark Twain throughout his life. Indeed, in a passage immediately preceding Forty-four's introduction to the teacher in "Schoolhouse Hill," the "multiplication class" recites "up to 'twelve times twelve.' " The number 144 is also suggestive because there are 12 feet, or 144 inches, in two fathoms—the nautical depth equivalent to "MARK TWAIN."

Foster, Electra (Aleck) Character in "THE $30,000 BEQUEST." At the beginning of the narrative, Electra has been married to Saladin FOSTER since she was 19—a period of 14 years. Shrewd and patient with money, she purchased some land after marrying and nurtured her modest investment into a solid, dividend-paying asset. The narrative starts as she and her husband learn that a relative who is about to die will leave them $30,000. She insists on investing the entire capital and not spending any of its proceeds until it grows significantly. As they wait for the bequest to come through, Aleck uses the money to make a series of imaginary investments; over five years, she works her fantasy portfolio to over $2 billion. Only then is she willing to spend the money freely. While Saladin blows imaginary millions on pleasures, Aleck fantasizes about doing good works, such as building hospitals and universities and supporting missionaries. Though generally more sensible than her husband, she finally loses all their imaginary fortune in one reckless gamble. She takes some comfort in the reminder that the *real* bequest is yet to come, but after discovering that it, too, is illusory, she has nothing left to live for.

As the vain but practical wife of a dreamer, Aleck appears to be modeled at least partly on Mark Twain's sister-in-law Mollie CLEMENS.

Foster, Gwendolen (Gwen) and Clytemnestra (Clytie) Minor characters in "THE $30,000 BEQUEST." The comely daughters of Saladin and Electra FOSTER, Gwendolen is 13 and Clytemnestra 11 at the start of the narrative. Over the next five years, their parents amass an illusory fortune and become obsessed with finding the girls worthy husbands. Toward the end of the narrative, five years later, their mother tells their father that she is arranging for "royal" marriages; in their foolish vanity, they decide to insist on "morganatic" marriages.

"Clytemnestra" is an odd name for a woman named "Electra" to give her own daughter. In Greek mythology, Clytemnestra is the wife of Agamemnon and mother of Electra; after she murders her husband, Electra and her other children kill her.

Foster, Saladin (Sally) Character in "THE $30,000 BEQUEST." When the narrative begins, Foster is 35 years old. For 14 years he has been bookkeeping for the principal store in Lakeside, a small town in the Far West. For 10 years, his $800-a-year salary has been one of the town's highest, but he and his wife, Aleck FOSTER, are not satisfied. Foster is honest, capable and hard-working, but he fantasizes about spending vast sums on dissolute pleasures. When he thinks he is about to inherit $30,000 from his only living relative, Tilbury Foster, his thoughts go first to how he will spend the money. It is only at his wife's insistence that he agrees to concentrate on protecting the capital. When their illusory fortune evaporates at the end of the story, he finally realizes that his greed has caused him to miss the true happiness that he could have found in a simple life.

frame-story Literary term for a story "framed" by— or contained within—another story. A *frame* is a story within which one or more other stories is told; a *frame-story* is a narrative told within the frame. Well-known examples include the tales of the ARABIAN NIGHTS, the *Decameron* and Chaucer's *Canterbury Tales*. Mark Twain uses this device so often that it is one of the outstanding characteristics of his fiction. Perhaps the best-known example is his JUMPING FROG STORY. Its frame is the narrative of a person who meets Simon WHEELER while trying to locate another man; Wheeler then narrates the frame-story about Jim Smiley and his frog. Almost all of *Connecticut Yankee* is a frame-story in the form of a manuscript read by Mark Twain.

Other notable examples of Mark Twain's frame-stories include "CANNIBALISM IN THE CARS," "THE CANVASSER'S TALE," "THE ESQUIMAU MAIDEN'S ROMANCE," "THE STOLEN WHITE ELEPHANT," "LUCK," the Karl RITTER story, "A TRUE STORY" and several yarns related in *A Tramp Abroad*.

France European country in which Mark Twain spent nearly two years of his life. Mark Twain's interest in France goes back to his youth. He had a lifelong admiration for the ideals of the French Revolution; as a boy he became fascinated with JOAN OF ARC, and he began studying French during his PILOTING days. By his own account—doubtless embellished—much of his enthusiasm for joining the QUAKER CITY excursion in 1867 came from his desire to visit PARIS. His interest in France and the French emerges repeatedly throughout his writings, including *Huckleberry Finn*—one of whose con men claims to be Looy Seventeen, the rightful KING of France.

Mark Twain first entered France at MARSEILLES on July 4, 1867. The next day he and two companions went by train to Paris, where they stayed nearly a week. They saw Versailles and most of Paris's main sights, and also happened to see Emperor NAPOLEON III at a time when Mark Twain had a high regard for the man. Chapters 10–16 of *Innocents Abroad* cover this visit; Mark Twain wrote most of these chapters nearly a year after leaving France.

Mark Twain's first extended visit to France came during his long 1878–79 European trip. In September 1878, he skirted the country's eastern edge while exploring the Alps from his base in SWITZERLAND. After a long sojourn in GERMANY, he took his family to Paris at the end of February 1879, remaining there through mid-June. Although this visit lasted nearly four months, it merited only one sentence in chapter 50 of *A Tramp Abroad* (1880). By then, his feelings toward France were already souring—possibly because he was ill most of the time he was there.

On his next trip to Europe, in June 1891, he and his family went first to France, passing through Paris to AIX-LES-BAINS, where they spent more than a month. After visiting Switzerland and Germany, they returned to France in the fall and visited Arles and Nimes. They next passed through the country in March 1892, when they spent three weeks in Menton, a Riviera resort. Mark Twain intended to write a book about these travels, but produced only fragments, such as "DOWN THE RHÔNE"—which were posthumously published in EUROPE AND ELSEWHERE (1923).

Mark Twain's next extended visit to France began two years later. He was in Paris from mid-March through mid-June, 1894, then in La Bourboule for a week. While he was at the latter town, an Italian anarchist assassinated the president of France in Lyons and a mob threatened to drive the Italian employees from his hotel; the experience moved him to write "A Scrap of Curious History," which later appeared in *What Is Man? and Other Essays* (1917). He returned to Paris; was in Etretat from late August through September; Rouen through October; and Paris again through May 1895. During this period, he wrote *Joan of Arc*—his only novel with a French setting, aside from an interlude in chapters 40–41 of *Connecticut Yankee* when Hank Morgan visits France. Like Morgan, Mark Twain himself left France for the last time from Calais, on May 31, 1899— while going from Vienna to London.

After the late 1870s, Mark Twain's feelings towards France became increasingly negative. His personal NOTEBOOKS from 1878–79 are filled with invective about the French and their alleged predilections for adultery, prostitution, general immorality and artificiality. He intended to vent his anti-French feelings in *A Tramp Abroad*, but that book does little more than poke fun at French dueling. He probably wrote "The French and the Comanches" for *A Tramp Abroad*, but this savagely francophobic essay was not published until LETTERS FROM THE EARTH appeared 80 years later. His antipathy to the French continued unabated through the rest of his life—though he suppressed it in *Joan of Arc*—and he developed a particular aversion to French standards of justice as he followed the case of Alfred DREYFUS through the late 1890s.

Franklin, Benjamin (January 17, 1706, Boston, Massachusetts–April 17, 1790, Philadelphia, Pennsylvania) One of America's most accomplished Founders, Franklin was a central icon in Mark Twain's life. As a man who achieved greatness through diligence and hard work, celebrating his success in a classic autobiography, Franklin became a model against whom countless boys measured themselves as they grew up. Few American schoolchildren of the early 19th century could have escaped hearing such Franklin homilies as "Early to bed, early to rise makes a man healthy, wealthy and wise," or "A penny saved is a penny earned." Mark Twain came to regard Franklin as the despoiler of boyhood happiness, summing up his feelings about the man in "The Late Benjamin Franklin," a sketch that he published in the GALAXY in July 1870.

As a boy, Mark Twain was aware that Franklin had been a printer—a fact that put added pressure on him to conform to Franklin's example (*Roughing It*, chapter 42). While working for Hannibal newspapers as a boy, he took it on himself to salt their pages with Franklin quips. His brother Orion Clemens was an even more devout Franklin disciple who periodically modeled his day-to-day life on Franklin's austere dietary and exercise regimens—behavior that Mark Twain later burlesqued in his unfinished novel about Orion, "Autobiography of a Damned Fool."

Despite Mark Twain's ostensible resentment toward Franklin, he visited Franklin sites as soon as he arrived in PHILADELPHIA in 1853. When he later returned from the East Coast, he joined Orion in KEOKUK, Iowa, where his brother had named his print shop the "Ben Franklin Book and Job Office." During this period, he delivered his first real public speech at a dinner honoring Franklin's 150th birthday. Thirty years later, he would deliver another speech honoring Franklin's birthday before a New York printers' association.

Franklin's imprint on Mark Twain's writings is diverse. One of Tom Sawyer's classmates recalls Franklin as the inventor of the lightning rod (*Tom Sawyer*, chapter 21) and Tom has a cousin named "Thomas Franklin Benjamin Jefferson Elexander Phelps" (*Huckleberry Finn*, chapter 39). In "DIPLOMATIC PAY AND CLOTHES," Mark Twain blames Franklin for establishing the precedent of having American diplomats wear plain apparel. He also mentions Franklin in WHAT IS MAN?, "Which Was It?," "Hellfire Hotchkiss," and other works. His unfinished novel "Three Thousand Years Among the Microbes" uses "Ben Franklin" as a character's name. On a more subtle level, Franklin's influence on Mark Twain is reflected in the latter's penchant for writing MAXIMS and in his desire to write an AUTOBIOGRAPHY that—like Franklin's—would serve to be "a model for all future autobiographies."

Frazer, Judge   Minor character in *Tom Sawyer*. In chapter 22, Tom anxiously awaits the death of ST. PETERSBURG's elderly justice of the peace, so that he can wear his CADETS OF TEMPERANCE sash in a funeral procession. When Frazer appears to be recovering, Tom quits the Cadets. Immediately afterward, the judge has a relapse and dies.

Fredonia   NEW YORK town on Lake Erie, about 45 miles southwest of BUFFALO. When Mark Twain settled in his new home in Buffalo after his MARRIAGE in February 1870, he encouraged his sister, Pamela MOFFETT, to visit nearby Fredonia. She and her daughter, Annie, liked the town and immediately rented a house. Mark Twain's mother, Jane Lampton Clemens, was initially reluctant to join Pamela there, but she also came to like the town and remained there until around 1883, when she moved to KEOKUK, Iowa. In October 1870, Mark Twain and his wife spent a week with Pamela and his mother in Fredonia; he is also known to have visited the town in December 1871, August 1874 and September 1881. In September 1875, Annie Moffett married a Fredonia man, Charles L. WEBSTER, who became Mark Twain's business manager.

Free-thinkers' Society   Organization in *Pudd'nhead Wilson*. The Free-thinkers' Society of DAWSON'S LANDING has two members: Judge York DRISCOLL and David WILSON. They meet for weekly discussions, which often center on Wilson's "PUDD'NHEAD WILSON'S CALENDAR." After Driscoll's retirement, the society becomes his main interest in life. In chapter 7, he takes the CAPELLO twins to a meeting. Since the essence of "freethinking" is rejection of religious authority, such a society is not likely be popular in a conservative Protestant community like Dawson's Landing. However, as the town's leading citizen, Driscoll need not answer for his behavior, while Wilson is considered too inconsequential to matter.

The society seems to be a bigger organization in "THOSE EXTRAORDINARY TWINS," in which it shares a large hall with a Baptist Bible class.

Frohman, Daniel (August 22, 1851, Sandusky, Ohio–December 26, 1940, New York, New York) Along with his brother, Charles Frohman (1860–1915), Frohman was one of the leading American theatrical impresarios of the early 20th century. In 1886, shortly after beginning his career, he produced the play *Colonel* SELLERS in Hartford. Three years later he collaborated with Abby Sage Richardson (1837–1900) to adapt *The Prince and the Pauper* to the stage. Frohman was later married to the actress Margaret Illington (1879–1934) and was a close friend of Mark Twain, whose "ANGELFISH" club listed him as its "legal staff." Frohman's autobiography is titled *Daniel Frohman Presents* (1935).

"From the 'London Times' of 1904" Short story about an American army officer executed for murder, even after a miraculous invention that anticipates modern television proves him innocent. An example of near-future SCIENCE FICTION, the story was written while Mark Twain was living in VIENNA in early 1898 and was following the Alfred DREYFUS affair. It appeared in CENTURY MAGAZINE the following November. The story takes the form of three contributions to the *London Times* that are signed "Mark Twain" and datelined Chicago, April 1, 15 and 23, 1904 (Mark Twain himself would be in Florence, Italy, on those dates). The conclusion of the story is one of many examples in Mark Twain's writings of trial scenes resulting in twisted justice.

SYNOPSIS

The narrator recalls a gathering in Vienna in March 1898, when he saw American army officer John Clayton and Polish inventor Jan SZCZEPANIK argue violently over the latter's telelectroscope invention. Three years later the two men met again in Chicago. By then, the telelectroscope was being used everywhere, enabling instant visual communication around the globe. Clayton and Szczepanik quarreled several more times, then Szczepanik disappeared. At the end of 1901, a corpse found in Clayton's basement was identified as Szczepanik and Clayton was convicted of murder.

Clayton's hanging was delayed for several years, however, as the governor—his wife's uncle—stayed his execution until public pressure finally made further delays impossible. Trying to make Clayton as comfortable as possible, the governor allowed him the use of a telelectroscope. Mark Twain stood by as the execution neared and happened to watch the czar's coronation in China on the telelectroscope. Moments before Clayton was to be hanged, Szczepanik appeared on the screen. After Szczepanik explained that he had been hiding from the attention that his fame brought him, Clayton was pardoned and freed.

Soon a new public clamor arose: Szczepanik may have been alive, but *someone* was killed, and Clayton must be the murderer. A new trial has just been held. Since an 1899 amendment to the U.S. Constitution requires all retrials to be heard by the U.S. Supreme Court, that body has convened in Chicago. The Court rules that even though Szczepanik is alive, Clayton should be executed on the basis of his original conviction. The chief justice cites a French precedent in Dreyfus's case: "Decisions of courts are permanent and cannot be revised." The fact that Clayton has already been pardoned for that conviction is dismissed: "A man cannot be pardoned for a crime that he has not committed; it would

be an absurdity." The governor issues Clayton a new pardon, but the Court annuls it and Clayton is hanged. In a pointed commentary on the Dreyfus affair, the story ends with the comment that "all America is vocal with scorn of 'French justice,' and of the malignant little soldiers who invented it and inflicted it upon the other Christian lands."

Frost, Arthur Burdett (January 17, 1851, Philadelphia, Pennsylvania–June 22, 1928, Pasadena, California) Illustrator. After beginning as an apprentice wood engraver, Frost taught himself how to draw. In 1874, he helped illustrate *Out of the Hurly Burly* by Charles Heber CLARK (Max Adeler); its success launched his career as an illustrator. Two years later, he joined the staff of HARPER'S MAGAZINE. He specialized in outdoor sports, farm animals and folk humor. While studying in London in the late 1870s, he attracted the attention of Lewis Carroll, for whom he illustrated several books. He also illustrated works by Charles DICKENS, Thomas Nelson Page, John Kendrick Bangs, Thomas B. ALDRICH and Joel Chandler HARRIS—who praised his ability to capture American character.

Around 1894, Frost communicated to Mark Twain an interest in illustrating his work. While he was on the staff of *Harper's Magazine* in 1896, he illustrated *Tom Sawyer, Detective*. Mark Twain called Frost "the best humorous artist that I know of" and asked his publisher to have Foster help illustrate *Following the Equator*. Frost drew seven pictures for this book, mostly of shipboard scenes and of MAURITIUS in chapters 62–63.

A humorist in his own right, Frost published *Stuff & Nonsense* (1884), *The Bull Calf and Other Tales* (1892) and *Carlo* (1913), as well as *A Book of Drawings by A. B. Frost* (1904).

Fuller, Frank (1827–1915) Friend of Mark Twain. A creative man of wide experience, Fuller became secretary of UTAH's territorial government after campaigning for Abraham LINCOLN. He arrived in SALT LAKE CITY in September 1861—a month after Mark Twain and his brother Orion Clemens had passed through Utah. In his AUTOBIOGRAPHY, Mark Twain incorrectly states that Fuller was Utah's acting governor when he was in Salt Lake City; however, he did not meet Fuller until the following year (the "acting governor" to whom *Roughing It* alludes was Francis H. Wootton).

After Fuller returned to the East Coast, he prospered in various ventures and headed his own health food company. By Mark Twain's own account, Fuller had boundless energy that produced "one enthusiasm per day, and it was always a storm." When Mark Twain arrived in NEW YORK CITY in early 1867, he visited Fuller almost immediately. In May, Fuller acted as his impresario for several public lectures on HAWAII. Mark Twain's autobiography has a long account of Fuller's prodigious efforts to make his appearance at the Cooper

Union a triumph that enhanced his reputation. In later years, Fuller tried to interest Mark Twain in various investments; the two men saw each other occasionally and corresponded through at least 1906. After Mark Twain's death, Fuller provided information to his biographer, A. B. PAINE.

Fuller, Jacob Name of two characters in "A DOUBLE-BARRELLED DETECTIVE STORY." The first Fuller is a 26-year-old man from an old but "unconsidered" family who resents his cavalier VIRGINIA father-in-law's opposition to him and gets revenge by brutalizing his wife and abandoning her in 1880. His wife bears his son, Archy STILLMAN, who later goes after him to avenge her mistreatment.

With information obtained by his mother, Archy finds Fuller in Denver, Colorado, where he is a prosperous, cheerful and popular miner. After tormenting this man and driving him away, Archy learns that this Fuller is a younger cousin of his father with the same name. As the innocent Fuller explains in chapter 9, he flees out of fear of being unjustly lynched for his cousin's crimes. Archy spends three years chasing Fuller around the world in order to explain his mistake and make amends. By the time he finally finds Fuller again in California, the man has changed his name to James Walker and has gone mad. The narrative ends with Fuller regaining his sanity and Archy about to take him back to Colorado to restore his original wealth. By this time, Archy has learned that a sadistic Hope Canyon miner named Flint BUCKNER who has been murdered was really his father, Jacob Fuller.

Funston, Frederick (November 9, 1865, New Carlisle, Ohio–February 19, 1917, San Antonio, Texas) American army officer. In March 1901, Funston commanded a volunteer regiment in the Philippines that used trickery to capture the nationalist leader Emilio Aguinaldo (1869–1964). Funston received the Medal of Honor and was later made a brigadier general in the regular army. Regarding the capture of Aguinaldo as treacherous and dishonorable, Mark Twain was outraged when Funston addressed New York's Lotos Club, where he suggested that Americans who had not supported American occupation of the Philippines were traitors. He responded by publishing "A Defence of General Funston" in the NORTH AMERICAN REVIEW in May 1902. This essay charged that Funston's popularity was a grotesque form of patriotism for which American military policy deserved the blame.

Funston later commanded the army troops who assisted during San Francisco's 1906 earthquake and led the American occupation of Vera Cruz in 1914. In 1911 he published *Memories of Two Wars*.

Gabrilowitsch, Nina Clemens (August 18, 1910, Redding, Connecticut–January 16, 1966, Los Angeles, California) Mark Twain's only grandchild and last direct descendant, Nina was the daughter of Clara Clemens and Ossip GABRILOWITSCH. Four months after Mark Twain's DEATH at STORMFIELD, she was born in the same house on the 14th anniversary of Susy Clemens's death. Katy LEARY assisted at her birth.

After spending her first three years in Europe, Nina grew up in Detroit, Michigan. In 1934, she graduated from New York City's Barnard College and attempted to launch an acting career. Around this same time, she may have married a man named Carl Rutgers (or Roters). After her father died in 1936, she changed her name to Clemens and moved to Los Angeles, where she took up photography.

Shortly before Clara married Jacques SAMOSSOUD in 1944, she set up a trust fund on which Nina lived for the rest of her life. Apparently at Samossoud's insistence, Clara's will excluded Nina, but Nina later settled out of court with Samossoud for a substantial share of the royalties from Mark Twain's writings. After a lonely life of failed artistic aspirations, alcoholism and drug addiction, Nina died from an overdose of barbiturates in a motel near her Hollywood penthouse. She is buried in the Clemens family plot at Elmira's WOODLAWN CEMETERY.

Gabrilowitsch, Ossip (February 7, 1878, St. Petersburg, Russia–September 14, 1936, Detroit, Michigan) Pianist, orchestra conductor and son-in-law of Mark Twain. A piano prodigy as a child, Gabrilowitsch played for Anton Rubinstein at age 10 and then studied under Rimsky-Korsakoff and Victor Tolstoff at the St. Petersburg Conservatory. At 16, he went to VIENNA to continue his studies with Theodor Leschetizky (1830–1915), through whom he met Mark Twain's family in April 1898. Over the next four years, he saw Clara Clemens intermittently in Europe and America and became engaged to her. Meanwhile, he developed a warm friendship with her parents.

After Olivia Clemens's death in 1904, Clara stopped seeing Gabrilowitsch and their engagement was forgotten. In 1909, she learned that he had undergone a dangerous mastoidectomy in New York and brought him home to recuperate at STORMFIELD. In late September, they announced their engagement, and they were married on October 6. Their honeymoon in Atlantic City was interrupted when Gabrilowitsch had an appendicitis attack and had to go to New York City for an appendectomy. Afterward, they went to Europe to live permanently. They returned briefly the following year, arriving in time to be with Mark Twain when he died.

By then having gained distinction as a conductor, Gabrilowitsch took over Munich's Konzertverein Orchestra. On the outbreak of war in 1914, the Germans arrested him as an enemy national. After Bruno Walter helped to free him, Gabrilowitsch took his family back to the United States for good, settling first in Philadelphia, where he worked with Leopold Stokowski and the Philadelphia Symphony. After turning down the Boston Symphony's conductorship because it would have limited his ability to give piano concerts, he accepted the more flexible directorship of Detroit's new Symphony Orchestra in 1918. He remained with this orchestra the rest of his life, while also performing many piano concerts. He earned enough money to support his family and allow Clara to save what she received from her father's estate.

After Gabrilowitsch died from stomach cancer at 58, he was—at his own request—buried at the foot of Mark Twain in Elmira's WOODLAWN CEMETERY, where Clara later erected a monument to both men. She also published a memoir, *My Husband, Gabrilowitsch* (1938).

Gainesboro TENNESSEE town in which Mark Twain's parents lived before he was born. Located on the Cumberland River in east-central Tennessee, about 30 miles south of the Kentucky border, Gainesboro is the seat of Jackson County. Mark Twain's parents, Jane and John Clemens, moved there sometime in 1825. In June of that year, Jane's sister Martha Ann ("Patsy") married John A. QUARLES in Gainesboro. Mark Twain's brother Orion Clemens was born there a month later. Around 1827, the Clemenses moved 40 miles east to JAMESTOWN. Orion revisited Gainesboro in March 1867.

Galahad, Sir Sir LAUNCELOT's son in Arthurian legends, Galahad was said to be so pure that he alone succeeded in finding the Holy GRAIL. He is a minor

Clara and Ossip's wedding party included Mark Twain in his Oxford gown, Jervis Langdon, Jean Clemens, Ossip Gabrilowitsch, Clara Clemens Gabrilowitsch and Joseph Twichell. (Courtesy, Library of Congress, Pictures & Prints Division)

character in *Connecticut Yankee*. Hank MORGAN first sees him in chapter 3, and lassoes him off his horse in chapter 39. Later Galahad becomes president of the stock-board, a post he sells to Launcelot (chapter 40).

In "Three Thousand Years Among the Microbes," Sir Galahad is a college student and brother of Lemuel Gulliver.

Galaxy Monthly magazine founded by William Conant Church (1836–1917) and his brother Francis P. Church in New York City in 1866. In an effort to become a major national magazine, the *Galaxy* attracted such writers as Henry JAMES, Ivan Turgenev and E. C. STEDMAN. Mark Twain contributed several sketches, including "MY LATE SENATORIAL SECRETARYSHIP," in 1868. After the sudden success of *Innocents Abroad* in 1869, the Churches invited him to write a monthly 10-page humor department for $20 a page—two and a half times their regular rate. He accepted on the condition that his department not be billed as "humorous," and he published his column under the title "Memoranda." What Mark Twain wrote was more than 80 pieces of diverse SATIRE. He

enjoyed the editorial freedom that the *Galaxy* gave him and sent it most of his best work. His contributions included whimsical pieces, such as "THE STORY OF THE GOOD LITTLE BOY" (May 1870) and "HOW I EDITED AN AGRICULTURAL PAPER ONCE" (July 1870); trenchant social satire, such as "ABOUT SMELLS" (May 1870) and "GOLDSMITH'S FRIEND ABROAD AGAIN" (October 1870); and insights into his literary background, including "My Bloody MASSACRE" (June 1870), "THE PETRIFIED MAN" (June 1870) and "My First Literary Venture" (April 1871).

The year that Mark Twain wrote for the *Galaxy* was one of the busiest and most difficult in his life. He launched his column a few months after marrying and settling in BUFFALO, New York, where he was co-owner and editor of the BUFFALO EXPRESS. He was also trying to write *Roughing It* while dealing with family problems. By March 1871, he was worn out, and vowed never to contribute regularly to any magazine again. His last "Memoranda" column appeared in *Galaxy*'s April 1871 issue—just as the magazine's circulation peaked at 22,000 issues. Afterward, its circulation began falling;

it suspended publication in 1878 and sold its subscription list to the ATLANTIC MONTHLY.

The first of Mark Twain's *Galaxy* sketches to see book publication were pirated in EYE-OPENERS (1871), SCREAMERS (1872) and other books published by John Camden HOTTEN. Authorized reprints came later. Ten *Galaxy* sketches appeared in SKETCHES, NEW AND OLD (1875). Others were collected in the unauthorized *Curious Republic of Gondour and Other Whimsical Sketches* (1919). In 1961, Bruce R. McElderry Jr. collected facsimile reproductions of all Mark Twain's *Galaxy* material in *Contributions to the Galaxy, 1868–1871*. That same year, Charles NEIDER published two dozen *Galaxy* sketches in *Mark Twain: Life As I Find It*.

Galilee, Sea of (Sea of Tiberias)   Lake in northeastern PALESTINE. Now on the Israel–SYRIA border, Galilee is a 64-square-mile lake, fed by the JORDAN RIVER, that is rich in biblical associations because Christ preached by its shores. Mark Twain reached the lake from the north on September 18, 1867. He and his companions spent several days working their way down its western shore—a journey described in chapters 47–49, 51 and 55–56 of *Innocents Abroad*. Gravely disappointed by Galilee's bleak setting, Mark Twain comments at length about how previous travel writers have exaggerated its beauty. He softens his criticisms, however, with a lyrical passage in chapter 48 about the beauty of Galilee under the night sky that he drafted for a lecture two months after the voyage was over.

"A Gallant Fireman"   Mark Twain's earliest known publication, this 150-word sketch appeared in the HANNIBAL WESTERN UNION on January 16, 1851. It reports on a fire that broke out in a neighboring grocery store a week earlier. As the staff prepared to remove equipment, its apprentice (Jim WOLFE) carried off old cleaning materials. An hour later, he returned—after the fire was extinguished—thinking himself a hero. The sketch's first book publication came in 1979 in *Early Tales & Sketches*, edited by Edgar M. Branch and Robert H. Hirst.

Gambetta, Léon (April 2, 1838, Cahors, France–December 31, 1882, near Paris)   French politician. After helping topple NAPOLEON III, Gambetta helped found FRANCE's Third Republic, and later became president of the Chamber of Deputies (1879–81). While Mark Twain was in MUNICH during the winter of 1878–79, Gambetta publicly denounced Marie François Fourtou (1836–1897), with whom he fought a duel in which neither man was hurt. Mark Twain burlesqued this bloodless encounter in "The Recent Great French Duel," published in the February 1879 ATLANTIC MONTHLY. He revised the sketch for *A Tramp Abroad*, which portrays Mark Twain himself as Gambetta's second (chapter 8). Binney Gunnison adapted this story in a play, *The French Duel*, in 1900. Mark Twain met Gambetta at a PARIS reception on March 21, 1879. Gambetta later briefly served as premier of France and died from an accidentally self-inflicted gunshot wound.

Gang, Tom Sawyer's   Tom Sawyer's formation of a "robbers' gang" links the end of *Tom Sawyer* with the beginning of *Huckleberry Finn*. In chapter 33 of the first book, Tom reveals his plans for a gang. Two chapters later, he tells Huck that he must become respectable in order to be fit for membership. Tom finally organizes the gang in the second chapter of *Huckleberry Finn*, when he, Huck, Joe HARPER, Ben ROGERS, Tommy BARNES and perhaps one or two other boys go to the CAVE south of ST. PETERSBURG. After swearing everyone to secrecy, Tom shows them the entrance to the cave that he discovered in *Tom Sawyer*. Inside, he has each boy take a terrible oath, promising to commit all kinds of bloody mayhem. At the suggestion of Ben Rogers, the gang adds the rule that it will wipe out the family of any member who reveals its secrets. This rule is soon tested and found to be flexible, when Tommy Barnes responds to the teasing of the older boys by threatening to tell the gang's secrets.

A caravan of Arabs and Spaniards rout Tom Sawyer's gang at Cave Hollow in chapter 3 of Huckleberry Finn.

Tom wants the gang to be high-toned: "We ain't burglars. That ain't no sort of style. We are highwaymen." The gang's main activities will be robbing and killing people and holding prisoners for ransom. The full launching of these plans is delayed by the boys' struggle to find a meeting day that will not conflict with the Sabbath. Tom is elected first captain, with Joe Harper as second captain.

The gang's biggest operation occurs in chapter 3, when it raids a caravan of rich Spaniards and Arabs at CAVE HOLLOW. So far as Huck can tell, however, the caravan is a Sunday-school picnic, "and only a primer-class at that." Huck does not buy Tom's explanation that magicians turned the caravan into a picnic out of spite. By the end of the chapter, Huck and the other boys have all resigned.

Gareth, Sir (Garry) Minor character in *Connecticut Yankee*. The favorite brother of Sir GAWAINE in MALORY's *Le Morte d'Arthur*, Gareth appears twice in *Connecticut Yankee*. In chapter 9, Hank MORGAN fondly calls him "Garry" and quotes a long journalistic account of a tournament in which Gareth defeats 14 other knights. As in Arthurian legend, Gareth is later accidentally killed by Sir LAUNCELOT. This so angers Gawaine that he refuses to accept a settlement of Launcelot's war with King ARTHUR, giving the Church the pretext to lay down the INTERDICT (chapter 42).

Garibaldi, Giuseppe (July 4, 1807, Nice, France–June 2, 1882, Caprera, Italy) Italian patriot leader. After beginning his military career in South America, Garibaldi returned to ITALY in 1848 and became a national hero fighting against the Austrian and French occupation of northern Italy. After another period abroad—this time in the United States, where he became a citizen—he returned to Italy in 1854 to retire on the island of Caprera, near LEGHORN. Six years later, he emerged to reconquer Sicily and Naples, allowing Sardinia's Victor Emmanuel to become Italy's first king. After several campaigns against ROME, Garibaldi retired to Caprera under the eye of Italian authorities.

A visit to Garibaldi's home was a prospective highlight in the QUAKER CITY itinerary in 1867. While the ship was at Leghorn, local authorities, suspecting it was secretly aiding Garibaldi, posted a gunboat to watch it. Nevertheless, Captain Charles DUNCAN led a handful of people to Caprera to meet Garibaldi on July 25. Mark Twain just missed this outing. Two months later, as the *Quaker City* sailed back into the Atlantic, Garibaldi began his final march on Rome. Mark Twain's publishing house, Charles L. WEBSTER & COMPANY, negotiated for the rights to Garibaldi's autobiography in 1887, but did not publish the book.

Garrett, Edmund Henry (October 19, 1853, Albany, New York–April 2, 1929) Painter and illustrator. After studying art in Paris under Henri Laurens, Gar-

rett worked for *Life* magazine and for James R. OSGOOD's publishing companies. He was a major illustrator of *Life on the Mississippi* (1883), which contains at least 40 Mississippi landscapes and street scenes with his signature or initials. He also illustrated books by Keats, Lowell, Dumas, Bulwer and others. His own books include *Romance and Reality of the Puritan Coast* (1897) and *The Pilgrim Shore* (1897).

Garrick, David (February 19, 1717, Hereford, England–January 20, 1779, London) English actor. Noted for managing London's Drury Lane Theatre, Garrick was also renowned for promoting SHAKESPEARE festivals. In chapter 20 of *Huckleberry Finn*, the DUKE opens his carpetbag and reveals a handbill describing him as the "world renowned Shaksperean tragedian, Garrick the Younger, of Drury Lane, London." He uses this name through the next two chapters, when he attempts to stage a "Shaksperean Revival" in BRICKSVILLE. Emulating one of the real Garrick's most famous roles, he plays Richard in the sword fight scene from RICHARD III. As the Duke doubtless knows, however, there was no "Garrick the Younger." Further, Garrick died in 1779; if he had left a son, this "Garrick the Younger" would have been at least 60 years old during the time in which *Huckleberry Finn* is set, and the Duke is only about 30.

Garth, John H. (March 10, 1837, Rockbridge County, Virginia–1899) Childhood friend of Mark Twain. The son of a tobacco and grain merchant, Garth moved to Hannibal with his family from Virginia in 1844. He later graduated from the University of MISSOURI and helped run the family tobacco business. In 1860, he married another childhood friend, Helen Kercheval (1838–1923). The Garths moved to New York City two years later, but returned to Hannibal in 1871. Garth prospered in several enterprises and owned a 600-acre estate when Mark Twain was his houseguest in May 1882.

Garth was one of several of Mark Twain's friends who helped inspire the character Tom SAWYER, as well as Joe HARPER. Later in his life, Mark Twain named Garth, John BRIGGS and Laura HAWKINS as the only youthful playmates who lived in his memory. Garth's brother, David J. Garth (1822–1912), was one of Mark Twain's Sunday-school teachers, and he became the head of the family tobacco business. Mark Twain recalls smoking Garth's cigars in his AUTOBIOGRAPHY.

Gawaine, Sir Minor character in *Connecticut Yankee*. A central figure in Arthurian legends, Gawaine was the nephew of King ARTHUR and brother of GARETH and Gaheris. *Connecticut Yankee* first mentions him in chapter 15, in which SANDY recites a long tale about Gawaine's exploits taken from MALORY's *Le Morte d'Arthur*. Following Malory, the novel makes Gawaine a major instigator in the civil war between Arthur and Sir LAUNCELOT, who accidentally kills Gawaine's brothers while rescuing GUENEVER. Vowing revenge, Gawaine refuses to accept Arthur and Launcelot's peace settlement and is later killed while fighting with Arthur against MORDRED.

Genoa Northwestern Italian city. ITALY's chief port, Genoa was the first Italian stop on Mark Twain's QUAKER CITY cruise. After the ship landed there on July 14, 1867, he spent two days seeing local sights before going north by train to Alessandria and MILAN. His generally favorable remarks about Genoa appear in chapter 17 of *Innocents Abroad*. The *Quaker City* itself stayed at Genoa for nine days before moving on to LEGHORN. Mark Twain also passed through Genoa with his family on the way to FLORENCE in November 1903 and sailed from there with his daughters after Livy died the following June.

Gerhardt, Karl (January 7, 1853, Boston, Massachusetts–1940) Sculptor whose career Mark Twain fostered. In early 1881, Gerhardt was a mechanic in Hartford when his wife Hattie asked Mark Twain to inspect a statue that Gerhardt had sculpted. Won over by the young couple's charm and the self-taught Gerhardt's raw talent, Mark Twain had professional artists inspect his work; one of them recommended sending Gerhardt to Paris for training. With the encouragement of his wife, Livy, Mark Twain decided to subsidize Gerhardt himself; in early March, the Gerhardts sailed to Europe at his expense. In 1883, the couple had a daughter in Paris whom they named Olivia after Livy Clemens. After three years in Paris, Gerhardt returned home in the summer of 1884; in July, he set to work sculpting a bust of Mark Twain at Elmira, New York. He accidentally spoiled his completed work four or five weeks later, but quickly redid it. Mark Twain liked the result well enough to use a photograph of it as a frontispiece in *Huckleberry Finn* (1884).

Not shy about capitalizing on his patron's name, Gerhardt aggressively sought commissions, which included a bronze statue of Nathan Hale at the capitol in Hartford. In March 1885, he showed Mark Twain a clay bust he had made of U. S. GRANT from a photograph. A. B. PAINE's edition of Mark Twain's AUTOBIOGRAPHY contains a long passage on this incident that Mark Twain dictated just two months later. Impressed by Gerhardt's bust, Mark Twain took him to New York the next day to show it to Grant's family, who let him complete it as the ailing Grant sat for him. Mark Twain thought the result was the best portrait of Grant in any medium, but he later lost money trying to mass-market reproductions.

After Grant died in July, Gerhardt made his death mask, but later got into an acrimonious dispute with Grant's family over its ownership. To settle this dispute in December, Mark Twain offered to cancel all Gerhardt's debts to him if he would simply turn the death mask over to Grant's widow.

The Clemenses socialized occasionally with the Gerhardts and kept in touch with them until at least 1895. Their household decor included a statue of Eve made by Gerhardt.

German language Of all the foreign languages that Mark Twain attempted to learn, German was the one he came closest to mastering. His interest in German began during his youth in Hannibal, where he and a friend paid a shoemaker to give them language lessons. He first traveled in Europe in 1867, but did not visit a German-speaking country until 1878, when he took his family to GERMANY and SWITZERLAND. Eventually, he spent a total of nearly three years in those countries and in AUSTRIA.

Several months before the 1878 trip, Mark Twain hired a German nurse, Rosina Hay, to tutor him and his family in German and accompany them to Europe. He had some German-speaking ability by the time he arrived in Germany, but apparently did not develop much more during the next year and a half he spent in Europe. *A Tramp Abroad*, his account of that trip, often makes German a target of humor. The book begins with its narrator stating that one of his goals is to learn the German language. Later, however, when he and his companion HARRIS are talking privately in a train filled with Germans, Harris nervously says, "Speak in German—these Germans may understand English" (chapter 11). Mark Twain's frustrations with learning the language are summed up in an appendix titled "THE AWFUL GERMAN LANGUAGE." Around the time he finished *A Tramp Abroad*, he also published a short story, "Mrs. MCWILLIAMS and the Lightning," in which a domestic crisis is complicated by a couple's comic misreading of a German book.

Though Mark Twain did not travel abroad during the 1880s, he continued studying German intermittently. He filled his notebooks with lists of German words and quotations from German poems, and he wrote random notes in German. He also often wrote German endearments in letters to Livy, for whom he translated part of *The Pied Piper of Hamelin*. During the late 1880s, he had a German class meet at his home and wrote "Meisterschaft," a play using German for the group's amusement. His interest in German also shows up in his various writings from this period, such as "TAMING THE BICYCLE" (1884), which compares learning to ride with learning German.

Hank MORGAN, the hero of *Connecticut Yankee* (1889), also knows some German. In chapter 22, he alludes to "the Mother of the German Language" and remarks on the syntax of literary Germans. In the next chapter, he climaxes a spectacular public display with several German tongue-twisters, including *Mekkamuselmannenmassenmenchenmoerdermohrenmuttermarmormonumentenmacher!* ("A marble monument manufacturer commemorating the Moorish mother of the assassins who perpetrated the general Mohammedan massacre at Mecca").

W. F. Brown's interpretation of a complete German word for A Tramp Abroad.

When Mark Twain returned to Germany in 1891, he renewed his study of the language and began reading German newspapers carefully. That same year he translated a book of children's verses that was posthumously published as SLOVENLY PETER. Always amused by mixing other languages with English to point up their differences, he occasionally spoke in public using English words in Germanic constructions. After one such speech in VIENNA in 1898, he wrote "Beauties of the German Language," a brief essay later published in his AUTOBIOGRAPHY. By the time he left German-speaking countries for the last time in 1899, he read and wrote German reasonably well, understood spoken German well and had a fair speaking ability. After Livy died in 1904, he had her tombstone inscribed with "Gott sei dir gnädig, O meine Wonne!" ("God be gracious to you, Oh my bliss!").

Mark Twain's daughters Jean and Clara attained much greater proficiency in German than he ever did. German was particularly important to Clara, who studied music in Austria and Germany and was courted by Ossip GABRILOWITSCH in German until he learned English.

Germany Mark Twain made two extended visits to Germany. When he went to Europe with his family in 1878 to collect material for what became *A Tramp Abroad,* he went first to Hamburg in late April. After spending a week there, he worked his way south to HEIDELBERG, where he stayed nearly two months. From there he went to BADEN-BADEN, explored the BLACK FOREST and traveled on the NECKAR River. In mid-August he and his friend Joseph TWICHELL began a

month in SWITZERLAND, from which he took his family to FRANCE and ITALY. In mid-November, the family returned to Germany and stayed in MUNICH through mid-February 1879. About half of *A Tramp Abroad* deals with his time in southwestern Germany; his Munich sojourn receives only scattered references.

During this first visit, the German empire was barely seven years old and Wilhelm I (1797–1888) was ruling. Mark Twain was in Heidelberg when attempts to assassinate Wilhelm were made in May and June 1878. A decade later, Wilhelm's son became Emperor WILHELM II. Mark Twain returned to Germany with his family in August 1891 and they spent most of the following year in the country. After short stays at MARIENBAD, Bayreuth, Nuremberg and Frankfurt, they lived in BERLIN from mid-October until the following March. From there they went to France and Italy, returning to Germany in June to begin a three-month stay at BAD NAUHEIM. They also passed through Germany again briefly in June–July 1893.

Mark Twain developed a great fondness for Germans and Germany, and devoted considerable effort to learning GERMAN. He particularly liked German manners, hygiene and cleanliness—traits he praises throughout *A Tramp Abroad.* Aside from this travel book, however, he wrote little about Germany.

"A Ghost Story" Story written and published in 1870. Mark Twain's interest in what he called the "petrification mania" began in 1862, when he wrote his PETRIFIED MAN HOAX in Nevada. In October 1869, while he was living in BUFFALO, New York, farmers near Syracuse unearthed a huge stone figure that became notorious as the "Cardiff Giant." Mark Twain responded to this hoax by writing "The Legend of the CAPITOLINE VENUS." Within a few months, P. T. BARNUM was compounding the hoax by exhibiting a plaster copy of the Cardiff Giant in New York City. This time Mark Twain responded with "A Ghost Story" for the BUFFALO EXPRESS (January 15, 1870). Later collected in SKETCHES, NEW AND OLD, the 2,460-word story has no relation to the "THE GOLDEN ARM" story, which was published under the same title in 1888.

SYNOPSIS

The anonymous narrator takes a big room in a building far up Broadway. On his first night in the long-unoccupied building, he is overcome by dread when he goes to his room alone as a storm rages outside. During the night, something tugs at his bedclothes. After examining the room, he is satisfied that the door is still locked, but the sight of a giant footprint on the hearth horrifies him. Eventually, he confronts a huge form in the dark. Once it takes shape, however, he is relieved to see that it is only the Cardiff Giant, whom he invites to join him in a smoke. The specter explains that he is the ghost of the giant on display across the street. Anxious to be reburied so that he can rest, he hopes that if he scares people badly enough, his body will be taken away. Since the museum is empty at night, he has crossed the street to try his luck. The narrator tells him that he is wasting his time haunting a plaster cast of himself, as the "real" Cardiff Giant is in Albany. The embarrassed giant says that the petrified Man has not only "sold" everybody else, but is selling its own ghost. He leaves, taking the narrator's robe and sitz bathtub with him.

Gibraltar Western MEDITERRANEAN enclave visited by Mark Twain in 1867 and 1903. A British naval base since the early 18th century, Gibraltar is a two-square-mile peninsula on the coast of southern SPAIN. Its 1,400-foot-high rock—one of the PILLARS OF HERCULES—dominates the entrance to the Mediterranean. Mark Twain visited Gibraltar with the cruise ship QUAKER CITY, landing there on June 29 and October 17, 1867. He spent most of the first stop on a side-trip to TANGIER. The second stop lasted a week, while the ship prepared for its return voyage across the ATLANTIC. Most passengers remained aboard, but Mark Twain and several companions spent the week touring southern Spain. Chapter 7 of *Innocents Abroad* describes the first visit in detail; chapter 59 merely mentions the second stop. Mark Twain also touched at Gibraltar on November 3, 1903, while taking his family to Italy.

Gibson, Dr. William (1813–1887) Passenger on the QUAKER CITY in 1867. A physician, banker and railroad official from Jamestown, Pennsylvania, Gibson was the self-styled "Commissioner of the United States of America to Europe, Asia, and Africa" mentioned in chapters 2 and 7 of *Innocents Abroad*. Anxious to travel in an official capacity, he persuaded someone in the federal department of agriculture to endorse him as a representative of the United States, in return for his promise to collect specimens for the Smithsonian Museum. Though his official status was flimsy, it may have helped Captain DUNCAN to arrange a meeting with GARIBALDI in Italy. In EGYPT, Gibson took his specimen-collecting chores a bit too far; an entry in Mark Twain's notes names him as the "iconoclast" whose attempt to chip off a piece of the SPHINX is described in chapter 58 of *Innocents Abroad*. When Mark Twain lectured in Sharon, Pennsylvania in March 1869, Gibson and his wife traveled 20 miles to hear him speak.

***The Gilded Age: A Tale of To-day* (1873)** Mark Twain's first novel; written in collaboration with C. D. WARNER. A sprawling epic with multiple story lines and dozens of characters, *The Gilded Age* is both a melodramatic saga of a midwestern family nearly destroyed by its faith in illusory wealth and a fierce SATIRE about post–CIVIL WAR America. The novel skewers government and politicians, big business and America's obsession with getting rich. It is now best remembered for its title, which gave its name to the era that it describes.

Senator Dilworthy addresses Hawkeye's church in chapter 20 of The Gilded Age.

While *The Gilded Age* touches on many themes as it shifts uncomfortably between melodrama and satire, occasionally verging into BURLESQUE, it always projects a powerful message about the futility and self-destructiveness of chasing after riches. This theme is personified in the character of Colonel SELLERS, who sees "millions" in countless visionary schemes, though he rarely rises above grinding poverty. Sellers, however, is primarily a creature of burlesque. The novel's dominant story line is a melodramatic one, following the saga of the Hawkins family, from its patriarch Si HAWKINS's unshakable faith that his worthless TENNESSEE LAND will eventually enrich his heirs, to the destruction of his adopted daughter Laura, who is drawn into the corruption of Washington politics, where she loses her innocence and eventually her life. Another central character is Missouri's corrupt Senator Abner DILWORTHY, who is closely modeled on a real politician of the time. Many other minor political and judicial characters in the story are also modeled on real-life people, as is Laura HAWKINS. The novel specifically deals with hypocritical politicians, vote-buying, conflicts of interest, court corruption and the jury system. It indicts political corruption during President GRANT's administration, but Grant himself is not attacked, though he makes a fleeting appearance in the story.

In addition to attacking the corruption and values of its time, *The Gilded Age* parodies then-popular sentimental and melodramatic novels. It does this by presenting many deliberately exaggerated sensational elements: the steamboat AMARANTH's disastrous explosion; Laura Hawkins as the possible heiress of unknown parents; Laura's false marriage to Colonel Selby; Clay Hawkins as a heroically self-sacrificing adopted son; Ruth Bolton as a woman hovering between life and death; long-suffering Alice Montague, who never reveals her love for Philip Sterling; and Philip's heroic search for a coal vein. Not surprisingly, these elements do not all fit together neatly.

Mark Twain and Warner contributed nearly equally to the book, with each writing mostly about the characters that he himself created. Mark Twain drew on his own family's background to launch the narrative with the story of the Hawkins family, whose move from Tennessee to Missouri resembles that of his family during the 1830s. He modeled Si Hawkins closely on his father, Washington HAWKINS on his brother Orion Clemens, and Sellers on a cousin of his mother. While the early chapters fictionalize events that the Clemens family experienced in the 1830s, the fictional events are set more than a dozen years later. A key to their chronology is Laura Hawkins: She is five years old at the beginning of the novel and 28 at its end. After chapter 40 specifies that it is "the winter of 187– and 187–," the narrative continues at least another year, but presumably not beyond 1873—the year in which it was written. Since the narrative spans 23 years in Laura's life, it must begin around the late 1840s. Chapter 18

carries the story through at least 1868 (a year in which Mark Twain lived in WASHINGTON, D.C.), and possibly a bit later. The bulk of the book is therefore set just after the CIVIL WAR.

An odd gimmick of *The Gilded Age* is the insertion of "mottoes" at the head of each chapter. Most are quotations from foreign languages, including many in non-roman alphabets and characters. Mark Twain's Hartford friend J. H. TRUMBULL selected the quotes from 42 different languages, including tongues as exotic as Arawak, Choctaw, Efik, Old English, Eskimo, Kanuri, Quiché, Sanskrit, Wolof and Yoruba. Most of the quotes relate to the content of the chapters. A Chippewa phrase at the beginning of chapter 1, for example, translates as "He owns much land"—an obvious allusion to Hawkins's Tennessee Land. Early editions of *The Gilded Age* presented the quotes untranslated, evidently as a subtle joke. In *A Tramp Abroad* (1880), Mark Twain claims to have "a prejudice against people who print things in a foreign language and add no translation" (chapter 16). Later editions of *The Gilded Age* added an appendix with Trumbull's translations of the book's quotations.

SYNOPSIS

The novel contains 161,000 words in 63 numbered chapters. Its first 11 chapters (written by Mark Twain) cover about a dozen years in the history of the Hawkins family. The story opens in eastern TENNESSEE around the late 1840s, when Si Hawkins gets a letter from his friend Beriah Sellers that persuades him to move his family to northeastern MISSOURI. Along the way, he and his wife adopt two recently orphaned children, Clay and Laura. Chapter 6 advances the narrative 10 years, by which time Hawkins and Sellers have each made and lost several fortunes and Sellers has settled in nearby HAWKEYE. Though desperately poor, Hawkins refuses to sell his Tennessee Land. As his children grow up, level-headed Clay becomes the family's main support, while Washington dreams of easy riches. After Si Hawkins dies, the revelation that he adopted Laura changes her life.

The next 12 chapters (by Warner) introduce a new story line revolving around two young easterners, Philip Sterling and Harry (Henry) Brierly, who go to Missouri to work on a railway survey. They meet Sellers, who excites Brierly's interest in developing STONE'S LANDING into a major river and railroad entrepôt. Sellers and Brierly prepare a petition to Congress to improve navigation on the village's river. Meanwhile, in a subplot unrelated to the rest of the book, Sterling conducts a tenuous long-distance romance with Ruth Bolton, a headstrong Quaker woman in Philadelphia. Chapter 18 makes it clear that the CIVIL WAR has passed. During the war, Laura Hawkins married Colonel Selby, an already married Confederate officer who abandons her. After the war, Senator Dilworthy visits Missouri and becomes interested in Sellers's river-development scheme. When he returns to Washington, D.C., he takes Washington Hawkins with him as a secretary and starts working for a congressional appropriation for the river scheme.

By chapter 24, the novel's focus is shifting to the national capital, while Sellers and Brierly remain in Missouri, directing a crew working on the river project. As they run out of money, their attention shifts east. In chapter 30, Laura Hawkins goes to Washington as Dilworthy's guest and Sellers accompanies her as a chaperon. Laura becomes the senator's lobbyist, and she, Sellers, Brierly and Dilworthy work to promote a new bill to get the government to buy the Hawkinses' Tennessee Land for the purpose of building an industrial school for freed slaves. Meanwhile, Sterling becomes a partner in the coal business of Ruth Bolton's father.

The story makes a dramatic shift in chapter 38, when Laura sees Selby again in Washington and tries to reestablish a relationship with him. From this point, she is the central character. Just as Congress moves to approve Dilworthy's bill to purchase the Tennessee Land, Laura's relationship with Selby reaches a crisis. She follows him to New York and kills him. Over the next year, she becomes a national *cause célèbre* while awaiting her murder trial. Meanwhile, as the effort to push the land bill through Congress drags on, Dilworthy's attempt to buy his reelection to the Senate is exposed. The novel reaches an ironic double climax when the land bill is unanimously voted down at the same moment that Laura is acquitted of murder. The sudden end of the Hawkins family's dream of wealth finally drives Washington Hawkins back to reality, but Laura now hopes to capitalize on her notoriety by launching a lecture tour. The vicious reception she gets at her first engagement breaks her heart, and she dies. Meanwhile, through all of these tumultuous events, Sterling stoically searches for a coal mine, which he fortuitously discovers just as his straitened circumstances are about to make him give up. In contrast to almost everyone else in the novel, Sterling gets rich through hard, honest work, and he wins Ruth's hand.

The authors wrote all but three chapters separately. In the chapter summaries that follow, the initials of each chapter's author are given in parentheses. The first 31 chapters are numbered identically in both one- and two-volume editions. The chapters numbered 32–63 in one-volume editions are numbered 1–32 in the second volume of two-volume editions; both sets of numbers are given below. For example, "Chapter 45" in one-volume editions is equivalent to "2:14" in two-volume editions. Information enclosed within parentheses in chapter synopses comes from sources outside of the chapters themselves. For example, chapter 36's summary places "Mr. Buckstone" in parentheses after his title as a committee chairman because his name is not given until the next chapter.

Chapter 1 (MT)
On June 18 in an unspecified year (probably the late 1840s; June 18 was the birthday of Mark Twain's mother), Squire Si HAWKINS, the postmaster of tiny OBEDSTOWN, Tennessee, meets the monthly mail carrier, who brings a single letter for Hawkins himself. After reading it, Hawkins tells his wife Nancy that he will go to MISSOURI, and gushes about how his 75,000 acres of TENNESSEE LAND will one day bring prosperity to their children. As he reads his letter from Beriah SELLERS aloud, Nancy recalls to herself how Sellers once nearly ruined them in Kentucky with a scheme to export slaves to Alabama. Sellers's letter advises the Hawkinses to come to Missouri as quickly as they can. Within four months, Hawkins makes the necessary arrangements and the family leaves Obedstown.

Chapter 2 (MT)
On the Hawkinses' third day on the road, they stop at a log cabin, where a 10-year-old boy named Clay is mourning the death of his mother. An old woman explains that Clay's entire family has been lost to fever, leaving him without kinfolk or friends to raise him. Hawkins immediately offers to adopt Clay, whom his wife warmly welcomes into the family.

Chapter 3 (MT)
Another week of travel takes the family to a shabby Mississippi River village, where Clay, Emily and Washington HAWKINS admire the mighty river with the family slaves Aunt JINNY AND UNCLE DAN'L. When a STEAMBOAT appears, Dan'l thinks that it is the Almighty Himself and prays frantically.

Chapter 4 (MT)
The next day, the Hawkinses take passage aboard the steamboat *Boreas*. Though initially terrified by the craft's unfamiliar sights and sounds, they soon adjust and the children frolic. Clay and Washington are in the pilothouse when a rival boat, the AMARANTH, is spotted. As the *Amaranth* closes on the *Boreas*, the latter fires up to race. After taking the *Boreas* through "Murderer's Chute," the pilot is startled to see the *Amaranth* gaining and guesses that it took on a "lightning pilot" (Wash Hastings) at NAPOLEON. Just as the *Amaranth* finally pulls even with the *Boreas*, a sudden roar and thundering crash leave it a helpless wreck, and the *Boreas* turns to save as many people as it can.

Chapter 5 (MT)
The day after the *Amaranth* accident, the *Boreas* continues upriver. Laura Van Brunt, a five-year-old girl from the wrecked boat, clings to Si Hawkins. A careful search fails to find her parents, so Hawkins and his wife add her to the family. From ST. LOUIS, they take a smaller steamboat another 130 miles upriver to a shabby Missouri town, whence they travel overland for two days to an inland village of about a dozen cabins (alluded to as "Murpheysburg" in chapter 18). After welcoming them

warmly, Sellers explains that his latest speculation is raising mules for the Southern market. Within a week or two, the Hawkinses are in a log-house of their own. Hawkins buys out the village store and reads farm reports in big-city newspapers to keep ahead of the local market. He does well enough to build a two-story house that is renowned for its magnificence and abundance of lightning rods; villagers think him lucky and eventually dub him "Judge Hawkins."

Chapter 6 (MT)
Ten years have passed. Hawkins and Sellers have made and lost two or three moderate fortunes and are again poor. Hawkins, who now has eight children, is back to his log-house, and Sellers—who also has eight children—has moved to HAWKEYE, 30 miles away. All the children have grown considerably. Though Laura Hawkins is becoming a rare beauty, no one guesses that she was not born into the family.

After each of Hawkins's first two BANKRUPTCIES, he rejected cash offers for his Tennessee Land. Now his family is so desperate that he is ready to sell. However, when an agent for an iron company offers him $10,000 for the land, he loses his head and demands $30,000 just for half the rights to the land's iron. After the man leaves, Hawkins realizes his blunder, but cannot find the man again. He then gathers the family to discuss their dire financial plight. Washington proposes to accept Sellers's invitation to join him in Hawkeye, and Laura and Emily offer to go to St. Louis. Clay arrives the next day from where he has been working for over a year, saving money that helps the family out of its immediate predicament.

Chapter 7 (MT)
When Washington Hawkins reaches Hawkeye, Sellers greets him earnestly. He dazzles Washington with talk of vast speculations, and recalls details of what led to Si Hawkins's ruin. Washington is relieved to see that Sellers lives in a substantial brick house, but its sparse furniture is threadbare and Sellers's children are shabbily clothed. As Sellers talks about a huge speculation involving London bankers, Washington—chilled to the bone—edges toward a tiny stove and accidentally knocks its door off, revealing that it contains only a candle. Unperturbed, Sellers explains that his "stove" is an invention that prevents rheumatism by giving the *appearance* of heat, rather than the heat itself.

Chapter 8 (MT)
After sharing the Sellerses' meager supper, Washington sleeps in a cold bed and awakens to notice that Sellers has sold his sofa. Over breakfast, Sellers explains his plan to help the Rothchilds buy up wildcat midwestern banks, adding that he is developing a solution to cure sore eyes that will make millions—especially in Asia. Mesmerized by Sellers's broad vision, Washington writes a glowing letter to his mother, then accompanies Sellers

to a real estate office where Sellers has arranged for him to clerk for General Boswell, one of the town's richest men.

Chapter 9 (MT)
Washington's new job includes board in his employer's home, where Boswell takes him for supper. There Washington immediately falls in love with Boswell's teenage daughter, Louise. As time passes, Washington also dines occasionally at the Sellerses', where the bill of fare is declining. When his father becomes gravely ill, Washington is called home to join the family vigil at the patriarch's bedside. Just before Judge Hawkins dies, he calls everyone together and admonishes them, "Never lose sight of the Tennessee Land!"

Chapter 10 (MT)
Shortly after Hawkins's funeral, something changes his daughter Laura's life. An inquest into the death of a corrupt politician named Major Lackland finds evidence that Laura is not the Hawkinses' natural child, setting village gossips to buzzing. Laura digs into her father's papers and finds correspondence between him and Lackland concerning her origins. Several years earlier, an unknown party discovered that her natural father survived the *Amaranth* accident and lost his memory. It appears that Hawkins was waiting until the man's mental health improved before telling him about Laura, but the man disappeared again. Intrigued by the idea that she has a mysterious father somewhere, Laura tells everything to her mother. Her revelation does not affect her family's love for her, but she is bitter about the gossips and feels that Ned Thurston—her prospective beau—has let her down badly.

Chapter 11 (MT)
The Hawkins family has now been in Hawkeye for two months. Washington Hawkins suddenly decides to drop in for dinner at the Sellerses after a long absence. Mastering his surprise, Sellers welcomes him and sits him down at the family table, where the dinner consists solely of fresh water and turnips. As Washington eats, Sellers prattles about new speculations and about how turnips and water prevent rheumatism. Miserable knowing that he is robbing the children of food, and afflicted by the turnips in his stomach, Washington excuses himself and leaves.

Chapter 12 (CDW)
In NEW YORK CITY, young Philip Sterling and Harry (Henry) Brierly discuss how to make their fortunes. A multitalented YALE graduate, Philip studied law, but hates practicing it. After turning to writing, he has not been able to find a newspaper position and is ready for any change. When Harry proposes that they both go to St. Joseph, Missouri to work as engineers on a railway survey contracted by his uncle, Philip jumps at the chance to get away.

Chapter 13 (CDW)
As Philip and Harry travel to Missouri by train and steamboat, they make friends with several men with whom they will be working. When they stop at ST. LOUIS, Philip learns of Harry's intention to work on the commercial aspects of the Salt Lick Pacific Extension, instead of as an engineer. During a long delay, they meet Sellers, who impresses them as an important businessman—although he gets Philip to pick up a big bar tab.

Chapter 14 (CDW)
Meanwhile, a letter from Philip reaches Ruth Bolton in Philadelphia, where she lives with her Quaker family. After quitting a stifling school, she wants to study medicine, although her parents worry about her fragile health. Her businessman father, Eli Bolton, admires Philip, but has reservations about his lack of capital.

Chapter 15 (CDW)
After Ruth's parents reluctantly permit her to study medicine, she is soon happy in her new undertaking. Meanwhile, many businessmen visit the Boltons' home, talking glibly with Ruth's father about their ideas for vast "schemes."

Chapter 16 (CDW)
In St. Louis, the surveying party is detained by an engineer's illness. As Philip and Harry run out of money, Philip writes to Ruth about his impatience. Meanwhile, he and Harry often see Sellers, who excites Harry with his grandiose plans for developing STONE'S LANDING into a railroad and steamboat hub. When Philip and Harry finally leave by steamboat, Sellers sees them off. After returning upriver, they go overland to the surveying camp near Magnolia—a "town" consisting of one house.

Chapter 17 (CDW)
After two weeks in camp, Harry writes to Sellers, assuring him that the railway line will go through Stone's Landing. When the surveyors finally reach this town, however, all they find is a minute village next to a crooked, sluggish stream called Goose Run. Sellers soon appears in a wagon. He welcomes Philip and Harry to "Napoleon" and the "Columbus River" and sits down with Harry to lay out the future city. When the surveying party moves on, Harry returns to Hawkeye with Sellers to prepare a petition to Congress to improve navigation on the river.

Chapter 18 (CDW)
It is now eight years since the death of Si Hawkins, and the years between 1860 and 1868 have transformed America dramatically. The conflict between the Union and the Confederacy (the "CIVIL WAR" is never named) has left its imprint on Missouri. Washington Hawkins served bravely, but without distinction, and Sellers was captain of Hawkeye's home guards. The war has also changed Laura Hawkins. After escaping from Mur-

pheysburg's gossips, she took solace in reading and developed crude notions of women's emancipation. Nevertheless, she fell in love with George Selby, a Confederate colonel posted to Hawkeye. After Selby was transferred to southwestern Missouri, Laura followed him and they were married. For three months, she was devoted to him, until he was ordered to New Orleans. After refusing to take her with him, he admitted to being married already. Laura then returned to Hawkeye, with nobody but her mother and Washington knowing about her mock marriage.

Chapter 19 (CDW)
Harry is still in Hawkeye, helping Sellers prepare their petition. Fitting into local society well, he flirts with Laura and engages her imagination by remarking how easily one can break into Washington society. When Laura later asks Sellers about visiting Washington with him, Sellers hints that Senator DILWORTHY wants him to go there to lobby for Missouri. In one of his hallucinations, Sellers remembers Dilworthy's staying at *his* home during a visit to Hawkeye. During the summer, Philip passes through Hawkeye.

Chapter 20 (CDW)
During Dilworthy's visit to Hawkeye (which Sellers remembers incorrectly in the previous chapter), the senator stays with his old friend General Boswell. After Sellers presides over a public reception at which Dilworthy speaks, he and Harry take him to "Napoleon" and outline their plans. Though little interested in the town itself, the senator favors the appropriation for the river. Afterward, he arranges for Washington Hawkins to become his private secretary in Washington. After meeting Laura, he spends much of his remaining time in her company and invites her to visit Washington, D.C. during the winter.

Chapter 21 (CDW)
Meanwhile, as Ruth Bolton tires of her medical studies, she grows more interested in her letters from Philip, who silently hopes that she will come around to wanting marriage. In the autumn, Ruth enrolls in the Fallkill Seminary in Massachusetts, where she stays with Philip's friends, the Montagues. She becomes close to Alice Montague and enjoys her new life in Fallkill.

Chapter 22 (CDW)
During the winter lull in the Missouri railroad work, Philip and Harry go east, where Harry has trouble interesting investors in Napoleon but manages to interest his uncle and some brokers in the Columbus River scheme. During a week-long side-trip to Fallkill, they visit the Montagues frequently.

Chapter 23 (CDW)
In New York City, Harry gets a letter from Sellers urging him to rush to Washington to confer with Dilworthy, who is presenting their petition to Congress. Dilworthy then introduces Harry to important people

in the capital. Meanwhile, Philip is growing dissatisfied with the railway contractors' large but indefinite promises. By now proficient as an engineer, he continues studying his new vocation and publishes some articles on the subject. When he returns to the West, he heads a division in the field.

Chapter 24 (MT)
Washington Hawkins marvels at the capital city and finds his new life an unceasing delight. The capital's major sights include the Capitol building, the unfinished Washington Monument and the president's fine white barn. The city has many boardinghouses—in which congressmen are not welcome. Everyone in the city represents some kind of political influence. As the river appropriation bill works its way through committees, Hawkins writes home to Sellers in his official capacity as Dilworthy's secretary.

Chapter 25 (MT)
Elated by news from Hawkins and Harry about the appropriation bill's progress, Sellers hires men to begin work at Stone's Landing. Hawkins also writes to Louise Boswell to report that he is about to sell the family's Tennessee Land for $40,000—a figure he vows to increase many times over in new investments.

Harry rejoins Sellers at Stone's Landing, where he directs a crew working to straighten out the river. The work stalls when money from the appropriation does not come through. Harry and Sellers pay their workers with 30-day orders, but shopkeepers eventually refuse to honor them, leaving the workers ready to rebel. After Harry goes east to get the money from the new Columbus River Slackwater Navigation Company, the workers are angry enough to hang Sellers, but he beguiles them with talk of future riches, gives them each a lot in Napoleon, and shares his own cash savings with them.

Chapter 26 (CDW)
When Ruth Bolton returns home from Fallkill, her plan to pursue a medical career seems less important, but this feeling passes. Her mother tells her that Philip will be surveying some land that her father has acquired to see if it has coal, as pressures build on Bolton's business interests. Meanwhile, Philip himself writes to Ruth, telling her about his reservations over the "Napoleon" and railway schemes.

Chapter 27 (MT)
His reputation damaged by the work stoppage, Sellers anxiously awaits the appropriation funds. He remains enthusiastic about the future, expecting that Napoleon's development will eventually cause Hawkeye to die. As he assures his wife that good news should soon come from Harry, a letter arrives.

Chapter 28 (MT)
Harry's letter recounts his experience in New York City, where he visited the president of the development company and learned that *no* money is coming from it. Furthermore, because he and Sellers owe money for the stock that they have subscribed, they are personally responsible for the $9,640 due to the workers and they each *owe* the company $4,000. Harry also learned that most of the appropriation money went to paying off congressmen and lobbyists; however, the company's president assures him that things will pick up when larger appropriations are obtained in coming sessions of Congress.

At this same time, Louise Boswell hears from Washington Hawkins, who reports that he has refused the $40,000 offer for the Tennessee Land.

The following summer, the people of Hawkeye suddenly subscribe such a large share in the railway that the railroad line is routed through their town instead of through Stone's Landing—whose development stops, dashing all Sellers's hopes.

Chapter 29 (CDW)
Philip Sterling takes a train to Ilium, Pennsylvania. Along the way, he gets into a fight with a conductor who mistreats a woman. Thrown off the train, he walks five miles to the next station and makes plans to sue the railroad. After reaching Ilium, he sets up camp five miles outside of town and spends a month carefully surveying Bolton's land. He concludes that a fine vein of coal runs through it and gets Bolton's permission to begin mining operations.

Chapter 30 (MT)
Louise learns from Washington that Dilworthy plans to sell the Hawkinses' Tennessee Land to the government. The news raises Laura's hopes of being invited to go to the capital herself. Eventually, an official invitation comes from her brother, conveying a check for $2,000 as a loan from the senator for her to buy clothes in New York. Laura also receives two "dead-head" tickets for railway passage and invites Sellers to accompany her. They arrive in Washington in late November.

Chapter 31 (CDW)
Meanwhile, Harry Brierly leaves New York for Washington, where Sellers wants him to help lobby for a benevolent scheme for black people. He lingers in Philadelphia, where Philip—now Bolton's coal business partner—is also staying. Philip shares his concerns about Ruth with Alice Montague, who is also visiting there. One night, all four young people go to a concert. A false fire alarm starts a panic, and Philip is seriously injured when he tries to protect the women.

Chapter 32 (volume 2: chapter 1) (MT)
Delighted that his beautiful sister is in town, Washington Hawkins spends two weeks showing Laura the sights—including sessions of Congress, which is just opening. Invitations pour in, and Laura is soon "in society." Dilworthy is so pleased with the attention Laura receives that he adds new clothes and jewelry to her wardrobe—as loans against the future sale of her family land. The

first formal reception that Laura attends is at a cabinet secretary's home, where she is the center of attention. Harry Brierly is also there. Unable to get near Laura, he overhears guests describing her as a landed heiress from a distinguished western family who wants to sacrifice her estates to help uplift the downtrodden negro.

Pleased with Laura's debut, Dilworthy begins calling her "daughter" the next morning. He gives her more money and unfolds the plans in which he wishes her to assist him.

Chapter 33 (2:2) (MT)

Laura learns about Washington's three aristocracies: the old families known as the "Antiques"; the wealthy parvenus; and the families of powerful public figures. She also learns how to deal with the tiresome customs of exchanging social visits. One of her callers is the wife of the Honorable Patrique Oreillé (Patrick O'Reilly)—a contractor who helped Wm. M. Weed steal $20 million from New York City before becoming respectable.

Chapter 34 (2:3) (MT)

Three months in Washington make Laura confident in her beauty and social skills. She is also now used to large sums of money, which she spends freely and shares with her mother, brother and Sellers—who insists on giving her notes for "loans." Laura is on good terms with many members of Congress. Generally believed to be very wealthy and soon to be become more so, she is much courted and envied. Her brother Washington is also adjusting to a celebrity of his own.

Chapter 35 (2:4) (MT & CDW)

Laura and Dilworthy discuss Laura's progress in persuading Senator Hopperson and other members of Congress to support the Tennessee Land bill. By this time, Laura is well acquainted with many journalists, with whom she exchanges gossip. Sellers also enjoys talking with these men, and discusses Senator Balloon's checkered career with them.

Chapter 36 (2:5) (MT)

While waiting for the chairman of the House Committee on Benevolent Appropriations (Mr. Buckstone) to appear, Laura enters a bookshop. When she asks for copies of (Hippolyte) Taine's *Notes on England* and *Autocrat of the Breakfast-Table* (by Oliver Wendell HOLMES), the smug, ignorant clerk does not know what she is talking about. He tries to interest her in other books, only to receive a blast of her sarcasm.

Chapter 37 (2:6) (MT)

When Buckstone does not appear outside the shop as Laura expects, she sends him a note inviting him to call on her. That evening, she flirts with the chairman for two hours, emerging confident that she can get him to vote for the land bill. Though aware of Laura's coquettish designs, Buckstone is confident that he will triumph in the end.

Chapter 38 (2:7) (CDW)

At a day reception given by Representative Schoonmaker's wife, Laura spots Colonel Selby and rushes away with her brother. Seeing her former lover so unnerves Laura that she skips the president's reception and stays in her room for two days. When she finally emerges, she borrows a revolver from Washington. After visiting Mrs. Schoonmaker to learn where Selby is staying, she sends him an anonymous note asking him to call at Dilworthy's house about cotton claims.

Chapter 39 (2:8) (CDW)

When Selby arrives, seeing Laura staggers him. Recognizing danger in her calm, icy tone, he tries to temporize, but admits that his wife is alive and with him in Washington. When Laura moves toward him, he grasps her hands. Pleading that he may still love her, he claims to be helpless since the war has ruined him. Laura collapses into a chair, Selby kisses her and falsely swears his love. For the moment, Laura is happy, but she presses Selby to commit himself to some course of action. When Selby leaves, Laura is confident that he belongs to her, but Selby merely curses to himself.

Chapter 40 (2:9) (CDW)

The narrative is now explicitly in the 1870s. Sellers is one of the best-known men in Washington. Always in the midst of gigantic schemes, speculations, and gossip, he thrives in the capital's bustle and confusion. He knows President GRANT, as well as all the senators and representatives and people in every department. He is a favorite on newspaper row, which feeds on his confidential revelations. Aided by Harry Brierly, he meanwhile advances his own affairs, particularly the Columbus River navigation scheme and the Tennessee Land plan. He is responsible for a dispatch to a New York paper concerning Dilworthy's support for creating an industrial school for colored people on the Hawkinses' Tennessee Land. This story excites Washington Hawkins's interest, and Sellers assures him that there are millions in the plan.

Meanwhile, Laura's life rushes on in intrigues. She sees Selby publicly and privately, and grows impatient with his failure to take steps to free himself from his wife.

Chapter 41 (2:10) (CDW)

Hopelessly in love with Laura, Harry spends much time at the Dilworthys' in order to be near her, but she barely notices him. He confronts her about rumors concerning her and Selby, and surprises her with the news that Selby plans to take his family to Europe soon. He then writes her a long, passionate letter, but she merely sighs and burns it.

Meanwhile, Philip Sterling has spent a pleasant winter being nursed by Ruth and Alice. When he learns about Harry's obsession with Laura, he decides to go to Washington to check on him. He is also concerned that a man named Pennybacker is doing something to harm Eli Bolton's business interests.

Chapter 42 (2:11) (MT)
Congressman Buckstone's "campaign" is brief, but it is he, not Laura, who is conquered, and he becomes champion of her "Knobs University Bill." After learning that Mr. Trollop is the bill's greatest enemy, Laura devises a scheme to blackmail him. First she has Buckstone persuade Trollop to deliver a major speech on a pension bill that he supports. As the chapter later reveals, Buckstone writes Trollop's speech, but Laura copies it in her own hand and has her version delivered to Trollop at the last minute—with a crucial page missing. Trollop later visits Laura to discuss the university bill, which he calls a fraud on the government. Laura convinces him that *she* wrote his pension speech and shows evidence of his support for other frauds. Her threat to expose her authorship of his speech induces him to promise to support her bill.

Chapter 43 (2:12) (MT)
The next day, Buckstone gives notice of the Knobs Industrial University Bill to the House. All the newspapers except the *Washington Daily Love-Feast* immediately attack the bill. The vicious opposition of New York papers disturbs Laura, but Dilworthy assures her that journalistic persecution will actually help them by eliciting public sympathy. Buckstone later formally presents the bill to the House, where it is referred to the Committee on Benevolent Appropriations. Over the next 10 days, a storm develops in the press over the "Negro University Swindle." A tide of congressional defections is reversed when Trollop announces his support.

Chapter 44 (2:13) (CDW)
After talking with Harry about his obsession with Laura, Philip wants time to adjust to Washington before deciding what to do. He sees Sellers, who is still filled with grandiose ideas. Although Sellers dismisses the ugly rumors about Laura, Philip realizes that he should steer Harry away from the woman.

Meanwhile, Laura confronts Selby, who denies that he is going to Europe and promises to run away with her after her bill passes. Unable to trust him, Laura vows that if he betrays her again, it will be his last time. When Philip visits Laura, she admits that Harry means nothing to her and promises to leave him alone. Harry meekly accepts this bad news from Philip, but inwardly thinks that Philip simply does not understand women.

Chapter 45 (2:14) (MT)
There is much anticipation in the air on the day that Buckstone presents the university bill to the House of Representatives. Outlining the bill's provisions, he argues that colored people should be trained to become productive workers and that the Hawkins land in Tennessee is an ideal site for a training institution. After a motion to suspend the rules is carried, the bill's supporters allow no recesses in order to let the opposition wear itself out. By dawn, the bill is carried.

Chapter 46 (2:15) (CDW)
The next morning, Philip Sterling accompanies Dilworthy to the latter's home. They are surprised to find that Laura is gone and that her room shows evidence of a hasty departure. At Harry's lodging, Philip finds a note from Laura asking Harry to escort her to New York. Philip immediately goes there. At Jersey City, he sees a newspaper reporting that Laura has shot Selby in a hotel parlor. Before dying an hour later, Selby issued a deposition claiming that Laura was a lobbyist who had hounded him to leave his wife and had threatened to kill him. Both Laura and Harry—who was with her when she shot Selby—are in jail. The sensational story sweeps the nation.

Chapter 47 (2:16) (CDW)
The next day, Philip gets Harry out of jail with the help of Harry's uncle. Sellers and Washington Hawkins visit Laura and pledge to support her. Dilworthy also promises to stand by her, and her mother soon arrives from Missouri. By the following day, newspapers are beginning to treat Laura more sympathetically. After she is indicted for first-degree murder, the city's two most distinguished criminal lawyers are retained to defend her. Laura's land bill fails to pass in the Senate and must await the next session. Meanwhile, Philip takes Harry to Pennsylvania to help in his coal-mining operation.

Chapter 48 (2:17) (CDW)
In Pennsylvania, the contracting firm of Pennybacker, Bigler and Small is doing badly, and Eli Bolton reluctantly allows them to borrow money on his name. Meanwhile, Philip Sterling opens the coal mine and works through the summer, with few signs of success. Harry is recalled to New York for Laura's trial, but it is delayed.

Chapter 49 (2:18) (MT & CDW)
After finally striking coal, Philip cautiously reports to Bolton, whose business interests are at a low ebb. This news buoys Bolton's position, until Philip reports that his initial find was worthless. Bolton then arranges to sell his house. In the fall, news of his business failures stops work at the mine. Philip later buys the Ilium tract cheaply and goes home.

Chapter 50 (2:19) (CDW)
At his mother's home, Philip still thinks about finding coal at Ilium. He visits Fallkill, where Squire Montague approves of his plan to study law in his office; however, Montague has such confidence in Philip's coal mine that he lends him money to reopen it in the spring. When Philip passes through Philadelphia again, he sees Ruth and hears from Harry that Laura's trial is about to begin.

Chapter 51 (2:20) (MT)
In December, Washington Hawkins and Sellers are still looking after the University Bill. Hawkins frets over Laura's trial, but Sellers remains optimistic. As they discuss the cost of getting a bill passed in Congress, a telegram arrives reporting that Laura's trial is postponed until February. Sellers is confident that before the trial ends, the bill will be passed and they will have a million dollars to send to the jury.

Chapter 52 (2:21) (MT)
Weeks drag by monotonously as Sellers and Hawkins await developments in Congress and occasionally visit Laura in New York. Spending more time with Dilworthy than with Sellers, Hawkins behaves as if he were in mourning. To help the bill, Dilworthy promotes a public image of Hawkins as a meditative man concerned only with benevolent enterprises benefiting the downtrodden.

Chapter 53 (2:22) (MT)
As Congress nears its close, Dilworthy goes home to solicit support for his reelection to the Senate in his state legislature. He meets with his biggest opponent, Mr. Noble, attends prayer meetings and goes out of his way to speak to a Sunday school in Cattleville. Before Dilworthy leaves the state capital, Noble assures him of his support in the legislature.

Chapter 54 (2:23) (CDW)
Laura's trial finally opens on February 15. It is less than a year after the shooting, and public sympathy has swung in her favor. When she enters Judge O'Shaunnessy's courtroom, her simple, dignified appearance elicits admiration. During the jury selection process, any prospective juror who appears to know anything is dismissed. When the jury is impaneled four days later, it has only two members who can read. District Attorney McFlinn opens the case for the state and calls Harry Brierly to the stand.

Chapter 55 (2:24) (CDW)
After taking the stand, Harry describes his trip to New York with Laura. The defense attorney, Braham, cross-examines him, doing what he can to imply that Harry himself had an interest in eliminating Selby. Over the next week, other witnesses testify and evidence is given that Selby started to retract his deposition when he realized that he was dying, admitting that he once wronged Laura. After the prosecution finishes, Braham opens the case for the defense, emphasizing aspects of Laura's background that might have contributed to her becoming insane. He calls Harry the "spark" that finally set her off.

Chapter 56 (2:25) (MT & CDW)
Two days later, Mrs. Hawkins and her son both testify about Laura's origins and her mock marriage to Selby, and Sellers testifies about the search for Laura's natural father. Medical experts then testify that there were

sufficient causes for Laura to become insane; later it is learned that the chief expert was paid $1,000. Two weeks later, the lawyers sum up their cases. Braham's summary moves half the courtroom to tears. By the time the jury goes out, Washington Hawkins and Sellers have returned to Washington, feeling dispirited.

Chapter 57 (2:26) (MT)
Congress's decision on the University Bill, a verdict in Laura's trial and Dilworthy's reelection are all imminent. Sellers and Washington Hawkins arise early in their excitement. Impatient for news, they go out and see a newspaper bulletin posted reporting that Dilworthy was *not* reelected after Noble told the state legislature that Dilworthy had bribed him. Hawkins and Sellers then rush to the Capitol, arriving in time to see the Senate vote their bill down unanimously. Hawkins is in a state of collapse; Sellers helps him home, where they find a telegram reporting that Laura has been found *not* guilty.

Chapter 58 (2:27) (CDW)
The moment the jury foreman announces that Laura is not guilty, the courtroom erupts into cheers, and women throw themselves on the defense attorney. The judge then orders that Laura be sent to the State Hospital for Insane Criminals and she is taken away; however, the authors immediately explain that since "this is history and not fiction," Laura is actually freed. Her mother wants to take her home, but she refuses. Laura then receives a telegram from her brother reporting the bad news about the bill and Dilworthy. A LECTURE agent named Griller appears and offers her $12,000 to give 30 lectures on whatever subject she chooses.

Harry goes to the West Coast on an unspecified new venture and Philip rushes back to Philadelphia.

Chapter 59 (2:28) (MT)
Reacting calmly to his public disgrace, Dilworthy returns to the Senate and demands "an investigation." Eventually, the full Senate accepts the report of a committee that exonerates Dilworthy, who returns home to a warm reception.

Chapter 60 (2:29) (MT)
While adjusting to her restored freedom, Laura considers six or seven letters from former lovers proposing marriage, but burns each letter and decides to take up lecturing. At her first engagement, she steps onto the stage before a mostly empty hall, in which a handful of coarse people laugh at her and begin to throw things. She flees outside, where an angry mob assaults her. After making her way home, she sinks into a torpor. The next morning, she is found dead. An inquest rules the cause to be heart disease.

Chapter 61 (2:30) (MT)
Clay Hawkins, who has prospered in AUSTRALIA, rushes back to America when he belatedly hears about Laura's trial. After learning of her acquittal in San Francisco, he goes directly to Hawkeye, arriving in time to comfort his mother when news of Laura's death comes.

Meanwhile, Sellers and a prematurely aged Washington Hawkins are preparing to leave their cheap Washington boardinghouse. Hawkins receives a telegram from Louise saying that her father—who is now poor—consents to their marriage. Swearing that he is forever done with the family's Tennessee Land, Hawkins vows to turn to real work. At this moment a telegram arrives from Obedstown demanding $180 for current taxes on the land. After hesitating, Hawkins shreds the letter and pronounces the spell broken.

Chapter 62 (2:31) (MT)
Back at his Pennsylvania mine, Philip Sterling is growing discouraged. His tunnel has passed the place where he calculates the main coal vein should be. When he runs out of money, he discharges his workers and sells most of his tools and materials. One man stays on for a week to help him; then Philip continues working by himself until his last hope is gone. After one final blast, he does not even check the results; however, his fortuitous discovery of a stream of water indicates that he has struck a rich vein. He returns to his cabin and finds a telegram reporting that Ruth is very ill.

Chapter 63 (2:32) (CDW)
At Ilium, news of Philip's strike is already lifting his reputation, but he rushes to Philadelphia to be at the side of Ruth, who is delirious with a fever. His presence helps her to rally and she finally professes her love to him. Afterward, Eli Bolton goes to Ilium to arrange for developing the coal mine, which Philip has reconveyed to him under the terms of their original partnership. The mine proves even richer than Philip originally suspects. After Ruth fully recovers, she and Philip plan a happy future together. Alice Montague wishes them both well, never revealing her own feelings for Philip.

Appendix
The authors apologize for failing to find Laura's lost father.

BACKGROUND AND PUBLISHING HISTORY

According to Mark Twain's biographer A. B. PAINE, Mark Twain and Warner got the idea of writing *The Gilded Age* together during a dinner-table conversation in early 1873. After they had heartily criticized modern novels, their wives suggested that they write something better and they accepted the challenge immediately. Since Mark Twain already had a story idea, he began writing first. After completing 11 chapters, he turned the manuscript over to Warner, who added the next 12. Thereafter, they swapped the manuscript back and forth frequently as each man grew bored with it. In several instances, both purportedly wrote key chapters, then had their wives select which to use. Mark Twain's version of Laura's fate in chapter 60 is a prime example.

While Mark Twain's most personal contribution was adapting his family's history to the Hawkinses, Warner used his experience from surveying a Missouri railway survey in the early 1850s and his study of law to write the chapters on railroad surveying and on Laura's murder trial. Each author contributed a share of characters and plot elements. Mark Twain created the Hawkins family, Sellers, Dilworthy (whom Warner introduces in chapter 19), Washington society people, and congressmen. His chapters concentrate on Hawkins family history, the fate of the Tennessee land, Sellers's speculations, and the investigation of Dilworthy. Warner's main characters are Sterling, Brierly, the Bolton and Montague families, Selby, and the New York legal figures. His chapters center around these characters and around Laura's murder trial. In general, Warner uses Mark Twain's characters more than Mark Twain uses Warner's. A copy of the book that Mark Twain personally annotated indicates the passages that each author wrote. While most chapters were written primarily by one man or the other, his notes show that both contributed at least something to nearly every chapter. Warner wrote chapter 18, for example, but it follows Mark Twain's plan. Another example is Warner's chapter 29, in which the episode of Sterling being thrown off a train is based on an incident that Mark Twain once personally witnessed.

Although it is not possible to determine the full extent of each author's influence on his partner's chapters, it seems likely that Mark Twain influenced how Warner treated his characters—particularly Sellers. For example, it is in one of Warner's chapters that Sellers reveals that he was born in VIRGINIA—a point probably suggested by Mark Twain (chapter 13). By contrast, Mark Twain says little about Warner's most important characters. Of the 18 chapters in which Ruth Bolton is mentioned, for example, he wrote only one, and it mentions her just once (chapter 62).

After finishing the book in April 1873, the authors copyrighted it and the AMERICAN PUBLISHING COMPANY issued it as a SUBSCRIPTION BOOK the following December, with illustrations by Henry Louis STEPHENS, True WILLIAMS and Augustus HOPPIN. Its initial sales were even better than those of *Innocents Abroad* and *Roughing It*, but they tapered off within a few months. *The Gilded Age* was the most widely reviewed of Mark Twain's early books, and the American reviews were generally favorable. While *The Gilded Age* has never been regarded as one of Mark Twain's most significant works, it has generally remained in print since its original publication. In 1961, Charles NEIDER published an abridgement of the book called THE ADVENTURES OF COLONEL SELLERS, which reduces Warner's chapters to synopses, while leaving Mark Twain's chapters intact. The MARK TWAIN PAPERS project is tentatively planning to issue a corrected and annotated edition of *The Gilded Age* around the year 2003.

Several months after the book was published, a San Francisco journalist named Gilbert B. Densmore dramatized it. In April 1874, he put his play on stage with John T. RAYMOND in the role of Colonel Sellers. After

Warner and Mark Twain learned about this unauthorized production, they agreed that each would relinquish to his partner dramatic rights in the characters he created. Mark Twain then bought out Densmore's play and revised it for a successful New York production that was soon renamed *Colonel Sellers*. With Raymond continuing in the lead role, this play toured for a decade and made Mark Twain more money than he got from the novel. Later he tried to write another play about Sellers that he eventually transformed in a short novel, *The American Claimant* (1892), which is a sequel to *The Gilded Age*.

Gillette, Francis (December 14, 1807, Bloomfield, Connecticut–September 30, 1879, Hartford, Connecticut) A Connecticut politician, abolitionist and insurance company executive, Gillette represented his state in the U.S. Senate (1854–55). In 1853, he and his brother-in-law John Hooker bought NOOK FARM, which they developed into a prestigious Hartford residential community where Mark Twain later became his neighbor. Gillette also helped found Joseph TWICHELL's Asylum Hill Church. Gillette's daughter Elisabeth (1838–1915) married George H. Warner (1833–1919), C. D. WARNER's brother. His youngest child, William Hooker Gillette (1855–1937), became an actor noted for portraying Sherlock HOLMES. Mark Twain helped pay for his early training and helped him get parts, including a role in a Hartford production of *The Gilded Age* in 1875.

Gillis, James Norman (Jim) (c. May 2, 1830, Georgia–1907) Mark Twain's "Sage of Jackass Hill," Gillis was a gold prospector in California's TUOLUMNE COUNTY. After studying medicine in Tennessee, Gillis came to California with his father, Angus Gillis, in 1849. He ranched briefly in Sacramento County, then went to Tuolumne County, where he spent the rest of his life prospecting. In 1864, he met Mark Twain in San Francisco, where his parents and brother Steve GILLIS lived. Mark Twain left San Francisco in December and spent nearly three months with Gillis, his brother William and their partner Dick STOKER at JACKASS HILL. During this period, Mark Twain accompanied Gillis to his claim at nearby ANGEL'S CAMP, where he first heard the JUMPING FROG STORY. Chapter 60 of *Roughing It* describes this interlude, alluding to Gillis only as an "old friend."

Gillis was a natural humorist and master storyteller with whom Mark Twain spent much time swapping tall tales. Many of Gillis's yarns featured Stoker as a character. The brief interlude proved a long-term stimulus to Mark Twain's writing career. He later developed several of Gillis's tales, as well as his storytelling techniques, into the stories about Dick BAKER and his cat TOM QUARTZ in *Roughing It*, Jim Baker's BLUEJAY YARN in *A Tramp Abroad*, and the ROYAL NONESUCH episode in *Huckleberry Finn*.

Gillis, Steve (July 17, 1838, Wyatt, Mississippi–April 13, 1918, Jackass Hill, California) Friend of Mark Twain. Gillis came to San Francisco with his family in the early 1850s and was a compositor at the VIRGINIA CITY TERRITORIAL ENTERPRISE when Mark Twain joined its staff in 1862. The two men became close friends, and Gillis purportedly acted as Mark Twain's second at an alleged "duel"—an episode Mark Twain describes in his AUTOBIOGRAPHY. At the end of May 1864, Gillis and Mark Twain went to San Francisco, where they roomed together in a series of boardinghouses while working for the SAN FRANCISCO CALL. In December, the feisty Gillis got into trouble over a brawl and left the town at the same moment Mark Twain did. While Mark Twain joined Steve's brothers Jim and William GILLIS in TUOLUMNE COUNTY, Steve returned to Virginia City and became foreman of the *Enterprise*'s print shop. Three years later he married a niece of Joe GOODMAN's wife and returned to San Francisco. In 1871, he came back to Virginia City, where he worked as a news editor for the *Enterprise* and later for the local *Chronicle*. In 1894, he left Nevada for the last time and spent the rest of his life quartz-mining with his son at JACKASS HILL in Tuolumne.

William Gillis later published *Memories of Mark Twain and Steve Gillis* (1924), a collection of fanciful anecdotes that went through several revisions and was also issued as *Gold Rush Days with Mark Twain*.

Glover, Samuel Taylor (March 9, 1813–January 22, 1884) Missouri lawyer. Originally from Kentucky, Glover came to Missouri in 1837, practiced law in PALMYRA and became well-known in Hannibal. John M. Clemens sat on the jury when Glover defended three abolitionists in 1841. Two years later, Glover represented Clemens in a successful suit against William B. Beebe. Glover also defended William Perry OWSLEY on a murder charge in 1846. In another celebrated murder trial three years later, he defended a slave. That same year he moved to ST. LOUIS, where he gained statewide prominence in the emancipation movement. He was active in Whig politics and knew Orion Clemens during the 1850s. Glover also played a leading part in keeping Missouri in the Union during the CIVIL WAR. Afterward, he was considered the West's leading constitutional lawyer of his time.

Despite Glover's courtroom brilliance and legal reputation, residents of Hannibal apparently thought little of him. Noted for lisping, Glover is probably the "perfect chucklehead" described in *Life on the Mississippi* who went to St. Louis and became "the first lawyer in the State" (chapter 53). He may also have been Mark Twain's model for the title character in *Pudd'nhead Wilson*.

Gold Dust STEAMBOAT on which Mark Twain traveled. When Mark Twain returned to the Mississippi River in April 1882, he went from St. Louis to VICKSBURG, Mississippi aboard the Anchor Line packet *Gold Dust,* completing his voyage to New Orleans aboard the *Charles Morgan.* He found the *Gold Dust* a pleasant and companionable vessel that gave him several opportunities to relive his piloting days as a steersman. He describes the trip in chapters 23–36 of *Life on the Mississippi,* which uses the fictitious names "Uncle" MUMFORD for the mate and Robert STYLES for the pilot, as well as the captain's real name, McCord. While he was writing about this trip later, he learned that the *Gold Dust* blew up on August 7, 1882, near Hickman, Kentucky, killing 17 people, including the pilot.

Gold Hill Western NEVADA mining town. Founded in 1859 after a gold strike was made just south of Mount Davidson, Gold Hill was separated from VIRGINIA CITY by a ridge known as the "Divide." During the 1860s, it developed into one of the COMSTOCK's most prosperous towns while Mark Twain was living in Virginia City. With a population of about 3,000 people, it supported most urban amenities, including a daily newspaper. *Roughing It* mentions Gold Hill several times and describes its mines in chapters 26 and 52. Chapter 45 tells how Reuel GRIDLEY took his SANITARY COMMISSION flour sack there. Mark Twain revisited Gold Hill in November 1866 during a lecture tour. *Roughing It* recounts how his old Comstock friends held him up as he returned to Virginia City from his Gold Hill lecture (chapter 79).

The Comstock's silver boom of the early 1870s pushed Gold Hill's population toward 10,000 people, an increase that led to its physically merging with Virginia City. Afterward, however, it declined rapidly and is now little more than a ghost town.

gold rush America's greatest gold rush began in CALIFORNIA soon after James W. Marshall found gold near SACRAMENTO in January 1848. Almost all other activities stopped as thousands of Californians poured into the region. The real rush, however, began a year later, as people began flooding in from all over the world, giving rise to the nickname "forty-niners." In one year, the state's non-Indian population grew from just 15,000 to 100,000—a figure that rose to 250,000 when the rush crested three years later. The rush then settled down, but gold mining continued to feed California's growth and remained the state's primary industry into the 20th century.

The gold rush developed in three distinct districts, the most important of which, the "Mother Lode," extended south from the Sacramento area to Mariposa County. The first wave of prospectors concentrated on placer-mining in streams, whose easily exploitable ore they quickly exhausted. Attention then necessarily turned to more capital-intensive methods of extraction, forcing individual prospectors either to work for wages, turn to other trades, go home, or find new fields elsewhere.

The impact of the gold rush on the West is difficult to exaggerate. It not only accelerated California's development by decades; it stimulated the entire region, including NEVADA, whose silver mining industry was begun by men originally drawn to California's gold fields. The gold rush also spurred the development of transcontinental communications and transport, including STAGECOACH lines, the pony express, the telegraph and the railroads, as well as transportation routes across Central America.

Even in distant Missouri it was impossible for Mark Twain to escape the contagion of gold rush fever. Many of those it drew west passed through his state when he was learning the printing trade on local newspapers. As many as 80 residents of his hometown, Hannibal—including a newspaper editor—may have gone to California. When Mark Twain finally went west in 1861, California's gold rush had long since played itself out; however, its fever remained alive in Nevada, where he first settled. During most of his first year there, he channeled his energy into prospecting and MINING, but without success. Three years later, he tried his luck in California's Mother Lode, when he prospected with friends in TUOLUMNE and CALAVERAS counties. Again, he was unsuccessful.

Roughing It, which recounts Mark Twain's western years, is not about the gold rush. It does, however, convey the spirit of that era throughout its pages and discusses the impact of the gold rush itself in chapter 57, though the book does not use this term.

"The Golden Arm" Folk story that Mark Twain often recited on the LECTURE platform. A fright story popular among African Americans whom Mark Twain knew as a boy, "The Golden Arm" originated in European folklore. In later years, Mark Twain enjoyed reciting a version of the story in black dialect. The simple tale concerns a man whose dead wife has been buried with her solid-gold arm. Avarice soon drives him back to the graveyard to steal the golden arm. As he carries the arm home through an eerie night, a disembodied voice follows him, moaning, "W-h-o g-o-t m-y g-o-l-d-e-n arm?"

Mark Twain's 1895 essay "HOW TO TELL A STORY" relates the story in its entirety, adding parenthetical instructions on sounds to make and when to pause. When Mark Twain told the story, he always focused his attention on a remote member of his audience—preferably a girl. As his spooky voice closed continued moaning, "W-h-o — g-o-t —- m-y —- g-o-l-d-e-n arm?" he would pause until the audience hushed, then spring at his target and yell, *"You've* got it!" If his timing were right, he could count on the person jumping violently.

Mark Twain was probably telling the story regularly by 1881, when he wrote to Joel Chandler HARRIS to encourage him to work it into his Uncle Remus stories. Eventually, the story wore out its welcome in Mark

Twain's own home, however. When he spoke at BRYN MAWR in 1891, he apparently offended his daughter Susy by reciting the story against her express wishes.

Golden Era SAN FRANCISCO literary journal. Founded in December 1852 by Rollin M. DAGGETT and J. Macdonough Foard, the *Golden Era* was the Pacific Coast's leading literary magazine for a dozen years. It published local fiction and poetry, translated literature, and local news, helping to develop such writers as Artemus WARD, Adah Isaacs MENKEN, Joaquin MILLER and Charles Warren STODDARD. When Mark Twain first visited San Francisco in May 1863, the *Era* published his sketch "Stories for Good Little Boys and Girls"; it published "CURING A COLD" in September. Meanwhile, Mark Twain began working as a reporter for the SAN FRANCISCO CALL, which operated out of the same building as the *Era.* He often visited the *Era* offices, but by this time, Charles Henry WEBB was publishing a higher quality journal, the CALIFORNIAN. Mark Twain soon shifted his literary efforts to it. Over the next three years, several dozen pieces by Mark Twain appeared in the *Era,* but most were reprinted from other publications, particularly the VIRGINIA CITY TERRITORIAL ENTERPRISE. After the 1860s, the *Era* declined until it ceased publication in 1893.

Goldsmith, Oliver (November 10, 1728, Pallas, Ireland–April 4, 1774, London) Irish-born English playwright and novelist. Mark Twain was first exposed to Goldsmith's works while apprenticing as a steamboat PILOT on the Mississippi, when he listened to George EALER read aloud from Goldsmith and SHAKESPEARE during watches (*Life on the Mississippi,* chapter 19). In an 1860 letter to his brother, Mark Twain praised Goldsmith's *The Citizen of the World* (1762) as "fine writing." This book, an epistolary novel in which a Chinese philosopher writes letters home from London, inspired him to write "GOLDSMITH'S FRIEND ABROAD AGAIN" a decade later. Goldsmith's pastoral novel *The Vicar of Wakefield* (1766) contains a spurious debate about Greek cosmogony (chapter 14) that may have influenced the passage in *Huckleberry Finn* in which the King tries to explain the word ORGY (chapter 25). Mark Twain eventually came to detest Goldsmith's writing. *Following the Equator* compares *The Vicar of Wakefield* to the sentimental doggerel of Julia MOORE (chapter 36) and calls it a wastepipe of goody-goody puerility and dreary morality (chapter 62).

"Goldsmith's Friend Abroad Again" (1870) Story told in seven letters to Ching-Foo by the fictional Ah Song Hi, a Chinese immigrant to the United States. Ah Song Hi indentures himself to an American labor broker and leaves China for America believing that it is a land where "all are free all equal, and none reviled or abused." Soon, however, he experiences a different reality. The American consul in Shanghai cheats him and 1,300 other immigrants out of a fee that they should not have to pay. Ah Song Hi crosses the ocean in a ship's steerage. He patiently endures it when the captain uses scalding steam to control the crowded Chinese passengers because he believes that the same system is used on American passengers.

The moment that Ah Song Hi steps ashore in SAN FRANCISCO, he is assaulted by a policeman. His luggage is taken from him and he is made to spend the last of his money on a smallpox vaccination he does not need, since he has already had the disease. Through everything, he remains optimistic.

A month later Ah Song Hi writes his fourth letter. By now he has been set free by his employer, who cannot hire him out. A white man sics his dogs on Ah Song Hi. Another man persuades a policeman to stop the attack, but the dogs' owners abuse Ah Song Hi verbally and the policeman arrests him for disorderly conduct. He is beaten yet again and tossed in jail. Within his crowded cell he is beaten by other prisoners. That night a badly beaten prisoner is thrown into the cell. This man dies the next day.

Only when Ah Song Hi reaches the courtroom does his optimism begin to fade. He observes the strong correlation between a defendant's ethnicity and his chance of acquittal. He also discovers that Chinese people cannot testify against whites in court. His white benefactor arrives to testify in his behalf, but loses his nerve and slips out of the courtroom. Ah Song Hi is convicted. As he is being remanded to prison, he learns that the local newspaper's court reporter will inevitably write a report that will "praise all the policemen indiscriminately and abuse the Chinamen and dead people."

BACKGROUND AND PUBLISHING HISTORY

Mark Twain worked as a newspaper reporter in San Francisco during the early to mid-1860s, at a time when tens of thousands of Chinese immigrants were coming into California through San Francisco. He developed a high regard for these immigrants and was inclined to report honestly on the mistreatment that he witnessed. His paper, the SAN FRANCISCO CALL, did not welcome criticism of the police, so Mark Twain saved his pen for articles and books to be written later. He found his inspiration for the form of this story in Oliver GOLDSMITH's *The Citizen of the World* (1762), which purports to contain letters from a Chinese philosopher exposing the hypocrisies and shams of 18th-century English society.

Mark Twain published "Goldsmith" in GALAXY in October–November 1870. Neither he nor A. B. PAINE included the story in any of their standard anthologies. It did appear, however, in the unauthorized edition, THE CURIOUS REPUBLIC OF GONDOUR AND OTHER WHIMSICAL TALES, in 1919, and has since been reprinted occasionally in special collections. The story was possibly omitted from early collections because of its stridency and its raw subject matter. It touches on police brutality, diplomatic corruption, anti-Chinese violence, pornography, prostitution, alcoholism, journalistic lack of integrity, greed and hypocrisy.

Gondour   Fictitious nation visited by the anonymous narrator of "THE CURIOUS REPUBLIC OF GONDOUR." Gondour's contented people, who speak a language other than the narrator's, have lived at least several generations under a democratic government that awards extra votes to people on the basis of their wealth and education. The nation's unit of currency is the *saco*—a name possibly deriving from a Greek word for shield.

Goodman, Joseph T. (September 18, 1838, Masonville, New York–October 1, 1917, San Francisco, California) Nevada newspaper proprietor and poet. A pivotal influence in Mark Twain's literary career, Goodman went west in 1854. Like Mark Twain, he started as a compositor and was self-educated. He wrote and set type for San Francisco publications, including the GOLDEN ERA, where he met Rollin M. DAGGETT and Denis MCCARTHY. After a stab at prospecting, he and McCarthy bought into the VIRGINIA CITY TERRITORIAL ENTERPRISE in March 1861. Two and a half years later, they were sole proprietors, with Goodman directing the editorial side and McCarthy the print shop. Aided by the influx of money that the region's mining boom brought in, they built the *Enterprise* into a prosperous daily noted for lively writing and courageous editorial independence. Goodman had a particular knack for hiring gifted writers, such as Dan DE QUILLE and Mark Twain, whom he gave free rein to develop their talent. Goodman himself was a fine writer; under his enlightened editorship, Mark Twain developed much of the imagination and writing skill on which he would draw throughout his career. Goodman became a lifelong friend of Mark Twain and watched his later career with a steadfast notion of what Mark Twain's true calling was; he objected strongly to Mark Twain's squandering his talent in works such as *The Prince and the Pauper*.

In September 1865, well over a year after Mark Twain left Nevada, Goodman bought out McCarthy, and ran the *Enterprise* alone until February 1874, when he sold out and returned to San Francisco. With $600,000 earned in a mine deal, he went into the brokerage business. Never a great businessman, he lost everything and went back to work for local newspapers. In 1884, he founded a short-lived weekly, the *San Franciscan,* and later borrowed money to grow grapes near Fresno. After selling out this enterprise at a small profit around 1886–87, he devoted 12 years to studying Maya hieroglyphs—a subject on which he published a book in 1902.

After Mark Twain left Nevada, he and Goodman never lost touch. Goodman ran into him in New York in the late 1860s and spent several months with him while Mark Twain was writing *Roughing It* in early 1871—a visit that provided invaluable encouragement when Mark Twain's spirits were low. Goodman is one of the few people whose real surnames appear in *Roughing It* (chapters 42, 45 and 55), although the narrator suggests that the name "Mr. Goodman" is invented. In 1890, Goodman traveled from California to the East Coast three times in an unsuccessful effort to help Mark Twain organize Nevada mining investors into a stock company that would capitalize the PAIGE COMPOSITOR. Four years later, Mark Twain devoted several passages of his AUTOBIOGRAPHY to Goodman, whom he last saw in New York in 1906. He wrote his last letter to Goodman the month that he died. Goodman later helped Mark Twain's biographer, A. B. PAINE, gather information.

Gorky, Maxim (March 14, 1868, Novgorod [now Gorki], Russia–June 18, 1936, Moscow) Russian writer regarded as the founder of Soviet "proletarian" literature. In April 1906, Gorky visited the United States seeking financial support for RUSSIA's anti-czarist movement. Prepared to support this cause, Mark Twain introduced Gorky at a dinner in New York City on April 11. A few days later, Gorky's campaign unraveled when the *New York World* revealed that the traveling companion he had introduced as his wife was actually his mistress. Hotels refused to accommodate him, and Mark Twain and W. D. HOWELLS withdrew their support. In a brief note that was later published as "The Gorky Incident" in LETTERS FROM THE EARTH, Mark Twain argued that Gorky had blundered unforgivably by failing to learn American customs in order to avoid offending against them.

Goshen   Town mentioned in *Huckleberry Finn.* In chapter 11, Huck—disguised as a girl—tells Judith LOFTUS that he is trying to reach an uncle named Abner Moore in Goshen. Loftus says that Goshen is 10 miles upriver from ST. PETERSBURG. Goshen is modeled on the tiny historical village of MARION CITY. *Goshen* is the Old Testament name for a land of plenty through which MOSES led the Israelites out of EGYPT.

Gosiute (Goshute)   INDIAN society of the western plains. A small branch of Shoshone-speaking peoples distantly related to the Ute and Comanche, the Gosiute live in and around a reservation straddling UTAH's border with NEVADA near the Deep Creek Mountains. In August 1861, Mark Twain traveled by STAGECOACH through this region and got his first close look at American Indians. Appalled by the squalor in which the Gosiute lived, he shed the romantic stereotypes of Indians he had gleaned from James Fenimore COOPER novels and began substituting negative stereotypes. He devotes chapter 19 of *Roughing It* to the Gosiute, describing them as the "wretchedest type of mankind" he had ever seen. Mark Twain's description of the Gosiute overlooks the harsh environment in which they lived. Traditionally, they inhabited the southern fringes of Utah's Great Salt Lake Desert, an arid, barren region that supported little more than bare subsistence living. They necessarily devoted most of their energy to foraging for edible plants, supplementing their diet with small animals and insects that whites found repulsive. At the time Mark Twain passed through their region, they were under unprecedented pressure from expanding white settlements and displaced Ute communities.

Gould, Jay (May 27, 1836, Roxbury, New York–December 2, 1892, New York, New York) America's most notorious "robber baron," Gould used illegal stock deals, political bribery and other tricks to make himself one of the nation's most powerful railroad executives. After he and James Fisk (1834–1872) precipitated a financial panic in 1869 by trying to corner the gold market, he was forced out of the Erie Railroad, but later controlled other major companies. Mark Twain regarded Gould as the greatest corrupter ever of American commercial morals. He had Henry Louis STEPHENS caricature Gould, Fisk and other Erie Railroad figures

in his BURLESQUE AUTOBIOGRAPHY (1871) and was inspired by their careers to write *The Gilded Age* (1873). Dan BEARD later used Gould's face on his picture of *Connecticut Yankee*'s cruel slave driver.

Grail, Holy A Christian talisman associated with the cup Christ used at the Last Supper, the Holy Grail has been legendary since early medieval times. In the late 12th century, Arthurian romances began incorporating tales of knights searching for the Grail, which only knights who were free of sin—such as Sir GALAHAD—had a chance to find. Such quests figure prominently in MALORY's *Le Morte d'Arthur* and TENNYSON's *Idylls of the King*.

In *Connecticut Yankee,* Sir SAGRAMOUR challenges Hank MORGAN to fight, but immediately excuses himself since he is about to go "grailing" (chapter 9). Hank scoffs at the idea of expeditions spending years seeking the Grail, only to have other expeditions spend more years searching for them, and calls the Grail "the Northwest Passage of that day."

Grand Mogul Fictional STEAMBOAT in *Pudd'nhead Wilson.* After being freed from slavery in 1845, ROXANA goes to work as a chambermaid on the *Grand Mogul,* a steamboat that runs between CINCINNATI and NEW ORLEANS. During the winters, she works on a packet out of VICKSBURG on the Lower Mississippi. After eight years, she leaves the *Grand Mogul* in New Orleans, planning to retire on her savings. When she discovers that her bank has failed, she returns to the boat, whose crew takes up a collection in her behalf (chapter 8). Later, Roxy escapes from slavery on an ARKANSAS farm and finds the *Grand Mogul* laid up nearby; the boat is now on a run to St. Louis—exactly where she wants to go. Her former crewmates give her $20 and take her there (chapter 18).

Pudd'nhead Wilson omits a long description of the *Grand Mogul* from Mark Twain's original manuscript that indicates that the ornately decorated steamboat is 250 feet long. The published version of "THOSE EXTRAORDINARY TWINS" does not mention the boat.

The name "*Grand Mogul*" reflects the popularity of romantic Oriental names for steamboats, such as the *Grand Turk* and the *Sultana,* that are mentioned in *Life on the Mississippi* (chapters 14, 16 and 17). *Roughing It* describes the office of STAGECOACH agent as a "grand mogul" (chapter 6) and its list of HUMBOLDT mines includes "Grand Mogul" and "Sultana" (chapter 29). The term "grand mogul" also appears in *Tom Sawyer Abroad* (chapter 11).

Grangerford Fictional family in *Huckleberry Finn.* At the end of chapter 16, Huck and Jim are separated when a steamboat runs down their raft a few days south of CAIRO, Illinois. Huck swims to the left bank of the river. In the next chapter, he stumbles onto the farm of a family named Grangerford. The precise location

Dan Beard used Jay Gould as his model for the Slave Driver in Connecticut Yankee.

of their farm is vague; circumstantial evidence—such as a book of Henry CLAY's speeches in their parlor—suggests that they live in KENTUCKY, near the TENNESSEE border. Huck stays with the family through chapters 17 and 18—a period lasting perhaps two weeks, possibly longer.

The family comprises Colonel Saul GRANGERFORD, his wife Rachel, three sons and two daughters. Bob Grangerford, the oldest child, is in his early thirties; his brother Tom is slightly younger. Both are "tall, beautiful men with very broad shoulders and brown faces, and long black hair and black eyes." Charlotte Grangerford is 25, a tall, imperious woman with the bearing of her father. The youngest children are Sophia and Buck GRANGERFORD.

Originally there were at least nine Grangerford children. Three unnamed sons were killed—apparently in the feud with the SHEPHERDSON family. A daughter, Emmeline GRANGERFORD, died at 15. The family has numerous other relatives in the region, but it is not specified which, if any, of them are surnamed Grangerford. These relatives include a 14-year-old cousin, Bud, killed by a Shepherdson about three months earlier, and Buck's cousin Joe, who is killed in chapter 18.

The Grangerfords own more than a hundred slaves. Each family member has a personal slave; even Huck has one while he lives with the family. Only two slaves are named: Huck's servant, JACK, and BETSY, a household servant.

Like the farm of the PHELPS family that Huck meets later in the narrative, the Grangerfords' farm is modeled on that of Mark Twain's uncle John QUARLES. Huck describes its decor in some detail in chapter 17—a passage that closely resembles the description of "The House Beautiful" in chapter 38 of *Life on the Mississippi*. The Grangerfords seem to personify Mark Twain's idea of the shallowness of Southern civilization. They live in a large, ornately decorated house, wear fine clothes, are pious and have impeccable manners. Beneath their refined veneer, however, they are savages, ready to destroy themselves in a senseless feud. Huck admires the family and comes to love some of its members, but cannot make sense of their ideals.

Huck's time with the Grangerford family is a turning point in the novel, separating the chapters in which Huck and Jim are alone on the raft from those in which they travel with two con men, the KING and the DUKE. After Mark Twain wrote the earlier chapters, his story stalled so badly that he wrote a scene in which the RAFT is destroyed and put his manuscript aside. After an interval of several years, he resumed the novel with the Grangerford episode, which ends with Huck and Jim's reunion and Huck's discovery that the raft is not really destroyed after all. After Huck witnesses the horrifying events of the Grangerford–Shepherdson feud, he resumes his raft journey with enormous relief. His painful memories stay with him, however, magnifying his already strongly compassionate nature.

The Grangerford episode was the first part of *Huckleberry Finn* to be published. A slightly modified version of chapters 17 and 18 appeared as "An Adventure of Huckleberry Finn" in the CENTURY magazine in December 1884.

Grangerford, Buck   Character in *Huckleberry Finn*. The youngest member of the GRANGERFORD family, Buck befriends Huck in chapters 17–18. He shares his clothes and bedroom with Huck and looks forward to a long friendship. He and Huck are about the same age—13 or 14. Buck is so anxious to kill a Shepherdson in the family feud that he ambushes Harney SHEPHERDSON in chapter 17. One of the most poignant passages of *Huckleberry Finn* is Huck's description of Buck's being killed in chapter 18.

Grangerford, Emmeline   Background figure in *Huckleberry Finn*. Deceased at 15, Emmeline was the youngest daughter of the GRANGERFORD family, which preserves her room as an apt memorial to her fascination with death. She was obsessed with painting funerary tributes and writing obituary poems. Huck describes her work in chapter 17, in which he recites her finest poem, an ode to Stephen Dowling BOTS. Huck particularly admires Emmeline's ability to "slap down" lines without even having to think about them. According to a neighbor, she was so quick to compose verses on a person's death, "it was the doctor first, then Emmeline, then the undertaker." What killed her, apparently, was her inability to find a rhyme for "WHISTLER"—a demise recalling that of ANDREW JACKSON in the JUMPING FROG STORY. Huck regrets that no one has written a verse about Emmeline herself. He attempts to fill the gap himself, but soon gives up.

Mark Twain modeled Emmeline's literary inclinations on those of his *Quaker City* shipmate Bloodgood H. CUTTER and the popular contemporary versifier Julia A. MOORE.

Grangerford, Saul (Colonel Grangerford)   Character in *Huckleberry Finn*. The first member of the GRANGERFORD family to confront Huck in chapter 17, the "colonel" is distinguished-looking, approximately 60 years old, tall and slim, with "a darkish-paly complexion." He has a thin face, thin lips and nostrils, a high nose, heavy eyebrows, piercing black eyes and a high forehead. His hair is black (or gray), straight and long. An immaculate dresser, he is never frivolous and never loud. Though stern, he is kind and, according to Huck, "everybody loved to have him around." Grangerford's description closely resembles that of Judge Griswold in "Simon Wheeler, Detective." Both characters borrow features from Mark Twain's father, John M. Clemens.

In many ways, Grangerford is an archetypal Southern gentleman, from his white linen suits to his honorific title "colonel." As the owner of several farms and a hundred slaves, he is wealthy and aristocratic. Despite his kindness, however, he seems to value honor so highly that he is willing to risk destroying his family in a meaningless feud with the SHEPHERDSONS. When Huck meets him, he has already lost three sons to the feud. By the end of chapter 18, the feud kills him, his remaining three sons and other relatives.

Grangerford, Sophia Character in *Huckleberry Finn.* The beautiful and gentle 20-year-old daughter of the GRANGERFORD family, Sophia elopes with Harney SHEPHERDSON, precipitating the final confrontation in the feud between the two families. The couple's relationship as lovers separated by a family feud recalls ROMEO AND JULIET. In contrast to the Shakespearean tragedy, however, Sophia and Harney escape alive, leaving their families to kill each other off. Sophia's story also bears a striking resemblance to the yarn that Huck tells her family about himself in chapter 17. He invents an imaginary Arkansas family, explaining that it was destroyed when a sister named MARY ANN eloped.

Grant, Ulysses S. (April 27, 1822, Point Pleasant, Ohio–July 23, 1885, Mount McGregor, New York) Commander of the Union Army during the CIVIL WAR and 18th president of the United States (1869–77). An 1843 graduate of WEST POINT, Grant served with some distinction in the Mexican War (1846–48). Afterward, his regiment was garrisoned in Missouri, where he married a St. Louis woman. His career languished as the army moved him around the country until he resigned in 1854. After rejoining his wife in St. Louis, he struggled at various trades until the Civil War started in 1861. In June, he was appointed colonel of an Illinois regiment based in PALMYRA, Missouri—near the area in which Mark Twain was then serving in an irregular Confederate unit called the MARION RANGERS. Grant's promotion to brigadier general in August shifted his operations to southeastern Missouri and began his steady rise. He was promoted to major general in early 1862 and campaigned in Tennessee through the rest of the year. In early 1863, he began a successful campaign to take VICKSBURG, Mississippi. Further successes caught the attention of President LINCOLN, who named him commander over all Union armies in March 1864. Over the next 13 months, the Union completed the defeat of the Confederacy, and Grant personally accepted Robert E. Lee's surrender at Appomattox in April 1865.

After the war, Grant became a full general and was chief of the army. In August 1867, President Andrew JOHNSON made him interim secretary of war. After Johnson's impeachment struggle in early 1868, Grant emerged as one of the most popular men in the country. Siding with the Radical Republicans on Reconstruction issues, he was nominated for president unanimously by the Republican Party in May and was elected in November, with Schuyler Colfax (1823–1885) as his vice president. His two terms as president were undistinguished; members of his administration were charged

Ulysses S. Grant during the Civil War. (Courtesy, National Archives, Still Picture Branch)

with graft and corruption, but his personal integrity remained untainted.

After leaving office, Grant toured the world for two years. He returned home to find his personal popularity unabated, but his bid for a third presidential term in 1880 failed. The following year, he settled in New York City, where he entered the brokerage business. A dishonest partner caused this business to fail in May 1884, leaving Grant broke. As Grant tried working his way out of debt by writing about the Civil War for CENTURY MAGAZINE, he learned that he had throat cancer. Later that year, Mark Twain offered to publish his memoirs as a SUBSCRIPTION BOOK through his own firm, Charles L. WEBSTER & COMPANY.

The question of when Mark Twain first met Grant is confused by conflicting accounts in his AUTOBIOGRAPHY and *Following the Equator* (chapter 2). It appears, however, that Senator William STEWART introduced him to Grant in late 1867. Mark Twain again saw Grant in November 1879, when he spoke at an army reunion in Chicago honoring Grant's return from abroad; he also spoke at meetings when Grant visited Hartford in October 1880 and June 1881.

Mark Twain's relationship with Grant became close during the last year of Grant's life. In late 1884, he offered Grant generous terms to publish his Civil War memoirs through his own company. They signed a contract in February 1885 and saw each other frequently through the ensuing months, during which Mark Twain involved himself deeply in the book's production and promotion. He also had to squelch rumors that it was Grant's former aide, General Adam Badeau, who was actually writing Grant's memoirs. Grant died shortly after completing his book—the first volume of which Webster issued in December. Initial sales of *Personal Memoirs of U. S. Grant* enabled Mark Twain to present Grant's widow with a royalty check for $200,000 three months later; it was the largest single royalty payment ever made up to that time. The second volume of the *Memoirs* was issued in March, and Grant's widow eventually received over $400,000 for the book, which is considered a classic of modern military history.

The summer that Grant died, Mark Twain considered writing a Huck Finn and Tom Sawyer story set in the Civil War involving Grant during his period of campaigning in northeastern Missouri. He never undertook this story, but later that year did write "THE PRIVATE HISTORY OF A CAMPAIGN THAT FAILED" about his own experience as a Confederate irregular, when he come close to encountering Grant's regiment in 1861. *Innocents Abroad* speculates on how the distant future will remember Grant's great military deeds (chapter 31). Much of *The Gilded Age* is set in Washington during Grant's administration and has Colonel SELLERS brag about advising President Grant on foreign policy (chapter 40). In *The American Claimant,* Sellers's wife names Grant among the Civil War luminaries who used to visit their home (chapter 3). The unfinished novel "Which Was the Dream?" uses one of Grant's early nicknames, "Lt. Useless Grant," for a character. Like the historical Grant, this man could find no function after the Mexican War. The same story's central figure, Major General X, resembles Grant in being a great war hero whose trusting nature and business naïveté lead to his being financially ruined by a dishonest partner.

Gray Fictional family in "THE DOG'S TALE" (1903). The story's narrator, AILEEN MAVOURNEEN, is owned by 38-year-old Mr. Gray; his gentle 30-year-old wife, Mrs. Gray; and their 10- and one-year-old daughters. Mr. Gray is a renowned scientist interested in neural systems; his prosperous family lives on an estate with many servants. The Grays love Aileen and treat her wonderfully, until the day that she saves their baby from a fire. When Mr. Gray sees Aileen dragging the baby in a hallway, he beats her severely, breaking her leg. After Aileen's heroism is discovered, however, the Grays treat her better than ever. Mr. Gray appreciates her gallantry and admires her intelligence, but later kills her puppy in an experiment.

Gray, David (November 8, 1836, Edinburgh, Scotland– March 18, 1888, Binghamton, New York) BUFFALO newspaper editor. Gray came to America with his family in 1848. In 1859, he joined the staff of the *Buffalo Daily Courier* as a reporter, and became an editor in 1868. Though working for a rival of the BUFFALO EXPRESS, Gray began a close friendship with Mark Twain in 1870 that lasted the rest of his life. He became the *Courier's* editor-in-chief in 1876, but a stroke forced him to retire six years later.

"The Great Dark" Unfinished novel written in 1898 and published posthumously. "The Great Dark" is one of several stories that Mark Twain began about prosperous, happy family men who suddenly find themselves in nightmare worlds so real that they wonder if their "normal" lives are the dreams. Filled with allusions to details from Mark Twain's own life, these stories may reflect his struggle to cope with the disasters that his family experienced in the 1890s, when his publishing firm failed, his investment in the PAIGE COMPOSITOR evaporated, his daughter Susy died and his daughter Jean suffered from epilepsy. "The Great Dark" begins at a moment that corresponds to the year 1880 in his own life, when Susy was eight and Clara was six; seven years earlier his family had sailed to Europe on the BATAVIA—an event alluded to in the story.

As an exploration of human beings being reduced to microscopic size, "The Great Dark" anticipates another unfinished SCIENCE FICTION story, "Three Thousand Years Among the Microbes." The story's unnamed ship sails in perpetual darkness—a condition that recalls Mark Twain's fascination with fear of the dark, as he describes it in "A MEMORABLE MIDNIGHT EXPERIENCE," *A Tramp Abroad* (chapter 13), *The Prince and the Pauper* (chapter 18), *Connecticut Yankee* (chapter 30) and elsewhere.

SYNOPSIS

The narrative begins on the birthday of eight-year-old Jessie EDWARDS. Alice EDWARDS describes her husband Henry and two daughters as they use a microscope to study tiny animal life in a drop of water. Mr. Edwards then writes a statement that continues the narrative. In explaining his experiments, he thinks how much what he sees in the water drop resembles an uncharted ocean. As he contemplates these wonders, the Superintendent of Dreams appears and promises to give him a comfortable ship and crew with which to explore his microscopic ocean with his family.

A moment later, Edwards is on a ship at sea on a blustery night, listening to a mate named Turner complain that he has never been more puzzled about *where* he is; even the captain does not know. Their unnamed ship has just sailed over the spot where an island should be and they are now in the middle of where Greenland should be. Turner also admits seeing a whale with hairy spider legs, but Edwards does not reveal that his description matches something he saw under his microscope. Turner mentions occasionally seeing a human specter—who turns out to be the Superintendent of Dreams. In Edwards's cabin, Turner elaborates on the strange voyage: All the water through which they have sailed is the same temperature, and both days and nights are dark, with no sign of sun, moon or stars in the sky. As Turner explains why he thinks the world has come to an end, the invisible Superintendent of Dreams playfully drinks Turner's coffee. Afterward, Edwards reproaches the superintendent for playing such tricks.

The superintendent reveals that the ship has sailed 2,350 miles across the drop of water, which is 6,000 miles wide. He does not tell Edwards how much longer the voyage will last, but assures him that the ship will never run out of provisions. He explains that it is always night because the drop of water is mostly outside the microscope's luminous circle. When Edwards proposes ending this dream, the superintendent startles him by saying that he (Edwards) has spent his whole life on this ship, and that his *other* life is the dream. Quickly accepting this idea, Edwards decides to tell his wife the truth immediately. He is surprised to discover that Alice has vastly different memories of their past experiences. For example, he remembers their sailing to Europe together seven years earlier on the BATAVIA with Captain Moreland (in October 1873 Mark Twain's family sailed to Europe on the *Batavia* with Captain John E. Mouland), but Alice insists that he has dreamed the trip, just as he has dreamed meeting Dr. John BROWN. Not able to remember living anywhere other than on the ship— except in "dream homes"—Alice remembers things that Edwards does not, such the captain's son being eaten by a spider squid. As they talk, Edwards begins remembering other incidents. After Alice asks him how long it has been since he boxed or fenced with George (George

GRIFFIN?), their black servant, he is soon boxing with George and remembering having often done it before.

Before dinner, Henry asks his daughters if they remember living anywhere else, but Jessie remembers only dream homes. At dinner, everything seems real, and Edwards finds that he seems to know everyone well, except a stranger sitting next to him. After an argument between Captain Davis and his mate breaks up the dinner party, Edwards struggles to remember things from his lives on the ship and on land, but as his memories of events on the ship sharpen, those of his life on land dim.

The narrative jumps to "Book 2, Chapter 1," and the narrator admits having lost "Book 1." Several years have now passed, and the Edwardses have a new son named Harry. The puzzled crew, who now think that they are headed for the South Pole, have mutinied several times over the years. Growing increasingly restless as huge animals are sighted, the crew wants the captain to turn the ship back. One day, a giant squid seizes the ship, throwing the crew into a panic until the captain turns Gatling guns on the beast. Meanwhile, Edwards and his wife search for their children, who are found hiding in the ship's hold.

With the ship in a dead calm and unable to escape the squid's domain, mutineers confront the captain and demand to know where they are. When they try to shoot him, however, they discover that their guns are unloaded. The captain admits not knowing where they are, but insists that since they are in the hands of God, it is safe to go ahead. The manuscript then ends.

PUBLISHING HISTORY

While living in Austria in the fall of 1898, Mark Twain wrote most of "The Great Dark" at the same time he worked on "MY DÉBUT AS A LITERARY PERSON," which deals with the sinking of the HORNET. He left his roughly 24,500-word story untitled; his literary executor A. B. PAINE called it "Statement of the Edwardses." Paine's successor, Bernard DEVOTO, gave it the name "The Great Dark" and included it in LETTERS FROM THE EARTH. After publication of that book was delayed, DeVoto included an extract from the story in his own book, *Mark Twain at Work* (1942). The complete story was finally published in *Letters from the Earth* in 1962. Five years later, John S. TUCKEY included a corrected text in WHICH WAS THE DREAM? AND OTHER SYMBOLIC WRITINGS (1967).

"The Great Revolution in Pitcairn" Sketch written in 1878. While in Europe, Mark Twain evidently heard news concerning Pitcairn. A British admiral who had recently visited the South Pacific island reported on nearly idyllic conditions among its 90 inhabitants: Their sole occupations were farming and fishing and their sole recreation was religious services; money did not exist on the island, and everyone over 17 could vote.

The admiral's report casually added that a "doubtful acquisition"—an American stranger—had settled on the island.

From that presumably factual premise, Mark Twain invents a second report—made four months later by a Captain Ormbsy of the American ship *Hornet.* The resulting sketch speculates on what impact an aggressive modern American might have on a simple, isolated society, and plays with themes that Mark Twain would later develop more fully in *Connecticut Yankee.* A special aspect of Pitcairn that must have appealed to him is the confused relationships among its inhabitants, all of whom were descended from the same handful of H.M.S. *Bounty* mutineers. His fictional stranger gains power by trading on the fact that he alone on the island is not motivated by nepotism—since he is the only person not related to everyone else.

The American, Butterworth STAVELY, quickly ingratiates himself on Pitcairn by throwing all his energy into religion. He then fosters discontent by calling attention to such matters as overly short Sunday services, the limited voice of women in prayer meetings and the insufficient amount of children's Sunday school. After engineering the ouster of the chief magistrate, he turns the population against English overrule. Citing ITALY and GERMANY as nations to emulate, he calls for unification, and persuades the islanders to proclaim independence and create an empire—with him as emperor.

Stavely sets up orders of nobility, using HOLY LAND names for titles, and establishes an army and a navy. Staffing these services proves problematic, and discontent with the new regime begins. It accelerates after Stavely raises a woman named Nancy Peters to the peerage and marries her; she angers a third of the women on the island by inviting the other two-thirds to be her maids of honor. More trouble follows when Stavely levies taxes to pay for the military. He finally goes too far by taking up a collection at church to pay off the national debt. After a Social Democrat tries to assassinate him, he is overthrown in a general revolt. He is punished with banishment from church services, and the nation reverts to its old ways.

Mark Twain originally wrote this 4,350-word sketch as a chapter for *A Tramp Abroad,* but instead published it in the ATLANTIC MONTHLY in March 1879. Its first book publication was in THE STOLEN WHITE ELEPHANT, ETC. (1882), whose contents were later incorporated into *Tom Sawyer Abroad* and TOM SAWYER, DETECTIVE.

Greece From about August 13–17, 1867, the cruise ship QUAKER CITY sailed through the Greek Islands, stopping only at the harbor of ATHENS (August 14–15). While returning from Constantinople several weeks later, it passed through Greece's eastern islands. Chapter 32 of *Innocents Abroad* describes Mark Twain's illicit visit to Athens; the next chapter comments on Greece's poverty. His posthumously published NOTEBOOKS contain additional notes on the country.

Greeley, Horace (February 3, 1811, Amherst, New Hampshire–November 29, 1872, Pleasantville, New York) One of the most influential Americans of his time, Greeley founded the NEW YORK TRIBUNE in 1841 and edited it until he died. During his long career, he crusaded for liberal reforms, often taking contradictory positions. He helped create the Republican Party, opposed slavery, advocated a general amnesty for the South after the CIVIL WAR and made himself unpopular by signing Jefferson DAVIS's bail bond—an action that Mark Twain criticized—and died shortly after an unsuccessful presidential campaign against U. S. GRANT. Whitelaw REID then succeeded him as the *Tribune*'s editor. While building the *Tribune* into one of the nation's most respected and widely read newspapers, Greeley himself became the object of insults and satire—to which Mark Twain contributed a share. In November 1868, for example, he wrote "Private Habits of Horace Greeley" for the humor magazine *Spirit of the Times.* Mark Twain wrote occasionally for the *Tribune,* but met Greeley just once, around 1871, when he accidentally entered Greeley's office only to be chased out.

Horace Greeley some years after Hank Monk made a fool of him. (Greeley, Recollections of a Busy Life, *1868)*

When Greeley crossed the country by stagecoach in 1859, he included a lecture stop in Placerville, California on July 30 in his itinerary. Anxious to make the 60-mile trip from Nevada on time, he told his driver Hank MONK to hurry. Monk drove his coach down a mountain road so fast that Greeley pitched about inside until he begged Monk to slow down. Monk's reply—"Keep your seat, Horace, I'll get you there on time!"—became legendary, much to Greeley's embarrassment. Mark Twain used the story in chapter 20 of *Roughing It,* in which four successive passengers on the narrator's stagecoach repeat the anecdote. While finishing *Roughing It* in August 1871, Mark Twain wrote to Greeley to ask if Monk's story was true. Greeley did not reply, so Mark Twain appended a footnote to his chapter saying that the incident never happened.

Mark Twain takes another crack at Greeley in chapter 70 of *Roughing It,* which has a long anecdote about a man named Simon ERICKSON who goes crazy trying to decipher a letter about turnips from Greeley, whose handwriting was notoriously illegible. Mark Twain evidently got the idea of connecting Greeley with turnips from Greeley's tract *What I Know of Farming* (1871), which Greeley sent to him in his capacity as an editor at the BUFFALO EXPRESS.

Grey, Lady Jane (October 1537, Broadgate, England–February 12, 1554, London, England) Historical figure and character in *The Prince and the Pauper* (1881). A great-granddaughter of England's King Henry VII, Jane Grey was a cousin of EDWARD VI. After Edward died in 1553, the Duke of Northumberland led a faction that made Jane queen. Nine days later, MARY I replaced her and had her beheaded.

Jane appears several times in *The Prince and the Pauper* as the frivolous companion of Princess ELIZABETH and the playmate of Tom CANTY—who takes Edward's place. When Tom first meets her, he trembles in her presence—causing her to start the palace rumor that Prince Edward is mad (chapter 5).

In *Huckleberry Finn,* Tom Sawyer mentions Lady Jane Grey as an example of a state prisoner with a coat of arms (chapter 38).

Gridley, Reuel Colt (January 23, 1829, Hannibal, Missouri–November 24, 1870, Paradise, California) Childhood friend of Mark Twain, whom he later met in NEVADA. Though nearly seven years older than Mark Twain, Gridley attended school with him in Hannibal before volunteering to serve in the Mexican War. In 1852, he went to California and ran a newspaper in Oroville. A decade later, he settled in central Nevada's Austin, where he ran a general store. Mark Twain's AUTOBIOGRAPHY recalls how Gridley recognized him by his voice in CARSON CITY, although they had not met since the 1840s.

Roughing It tells a colorful but substantially true story about Gridley's raising money for the United States SANITARY COMMISSION by repeatedly auctioning off an ordinary sack of flour in Nevada mining towns (chapter 45). Gridley's campaign began when he lost an election bet and had to carry the sack through town. After a crowd urged him to auction the sack off to raise money for the Sanitary Fund, he ended up selling it repeatedly, raising several thousand dollars. According to *Roughing It,* news of this event excited VIRGINIA CITY, which invited Gridley to bring the sack there. In two days, he raised over $40,000 in COMSTOCK mining towns, while Mark Twain covered his auctions for his newspaper. Gridley then went to California and the East Coast, eventually raising $150,000 for the fund.

Mark Twain's correspondence from the period shows that *Roughing It* errs in calling Gridley a candidate in the Austin election, and that the book exaggerates how much money Gridley raised. After leaving Nevada, Gridley spent more than a year carrying his flour sack through California and eastern towns, and eventually raised at least $175,000, while traveling at his own expense and neglecting his Austin business.

In 1866, Gridley resettled in Stockton, California, and later moved to Paradise in Butte County. He died in late 1870, as Mark Twain was writing *Roughing It.* Mark Twain wrote an obituary letter about Gridley for the NEW YORK TRIBUNE. Gridley's flour sack was later incorporated into Austin's official town seal, and his original sack was exhibited in a Reno museum.

Griffin, George (?–1897) Mark Twain's butler. A former slave and one of several models for *Huckleberry Finn*'s Jim, Griffin came to Mark Twain's Hartford home to wash windows in the late 1870s and was hired onto the household staff. In 1878, he accompanied the family to Europe, but apparently left their employ when they returned to Europe in 1891. Mark Twain had great respect for Griffin, and admired him even more after seeing him in NEW YORK CITY in September 1893. Despite the current financial panic, Griffin had been working as a Union League Club waiter and was prospering as a private banker for other waiters.

Grimes, William C. Fictitious name in *Innocents Abroad.* The author of *Nomadic Life in Palestine,* "Grimes" is a thinly veiled pseudonym for William Cowper PRIME, the author of *Tent Life in the Holy Land* (1857). Mark Twain also uses the name "Grimes" for characters in several stories, including "CANNIBALISM IN THE CARS" and "TOM SAWYER'S CONSPIRACY."

Grip, Earl Minor character in *Connecticut Yankee.* An important noble who lives near CAMBERNET, Grip rescues Hank MORGAN and King ARTHUR from angry peasants and conveys them to Cambenet, where he sells them in a slave auction (chapter 34). Hank later escapes in LONDON and is arrested in a scuffle; the court frees him when he claims to be a slave of Grip (chapter 37).

Guenever, Queen Minor character in *Connecticut Yankee.* In Arthurian legends, Guenever is the beautiful Roman wife of King ARTHUR and is coveted by the king's nephew MORDRED. Thomas MALORY began the enlargement of her role in the legends by making her the tragic lover of Sir LAUNCELOT. Guenever rarely appears in *Connecticut Yankee,* but betrays her interest in Launcelot as early as chapter 3. Later, Arthur wistfully remarks that Guenever is unlikely to notice his absence when Launcelot is around (chapter 26). Guenever speaks only once in the novel—when she remarks on Hank's not wearing armor before his combat with Sir SAGRAMOUR in chapter 39.

Three years later, Guenever's affair with Launcelot is revealed to Arthur while Hank is out of the country. Arthur orders her burned at the stake, starting a civil war. After Launcelot rescues Guenever, Mordred tries to make her marry him, but she eventually becomes a nun in Almesbury (chapters 41–42).

Guildford Town in Surrey, ENGLAND, 25 miles southwest of LONDON. After completing his round-the-world lecture tour in late July 1896, Mark Twain rented a house on Guildford's Portsmouth Road. In mid-August, he received a telegram there reporting the death of his daughter Susy. After his wife and other daughters rejoined him in Guildford in early September, they relocated to London.

Lewis Carroll, who often stayed with his sisters in Guildford, died there in January 1898.

Guildhall LONDON building that is a setting in *The Prince and the Pauper.* Originally built in the early 15th century, Guildhall is the historic town hall of the City of London, as well as the site of such historic trials as those of Anne Askew and Lady Jane GREY. It is famed for its immense banquet hall, in which Tom CANTY dines in chapter 11 of *The Prince and the Pauper.* While Tom is inside, the real Prince EDWARD is outside, where he meets Miles HENDON. Mark Twain's description of the hall mentions its great carved figures of Gog and Magog, which were actually not placed there until 1708. Guildhall was largely destroyed by London's fire of 1666. After being rebuilt and renovated several times, it was again badly damaged by fire in 1940 during the blitz. Mark Twain also mentions Guildhall in his "o'SHAH" letters, in which he reported on the Shah of Persia's visit there in 1873.

Gunn, Dr. John C. (*fl.* 1830s) Author of a home medical manual popular during the mid-19th century. In chapter 17 of *Huckleberry Finn,* Huck finds a copy of *Dr. Gunn's Family Medicine* in the home of the GRANGERFORDS. Mark Twain doubtless was thinking of a real book called *Gunn's Domestic Medicine, or Poor Man's Friend, in the Hours of Affliction, Pain and Sickness.* First published in 1832, this popular book was a home medical guide that specialized in describing medicinal roots and herbs available in the South and West.

H

Hackett, Lem Character in *Life on the Mississippi*. Chapter 54 describes "Lem Hackett" as the "fictitious name" of a childhood friend of the narrator who drowned on a *Sunday*. "Being loaded with sin, he went to the bottom like an anvil." That night, the rest of Hannibal's boys lay awake repenting as a wild storm whipped up their fears of divine punishment. The narrator prayed, trying to divert God's attention from his own sins to the more wicked acts of his friends, only to make himself feel even more guilty. Three weeks later, the children's ideas about divine retribution were shaken when a MODEL BOY named "DUTCHY" drowned.

Hackett is a pseudonym for Clint Levering, a childhood friend of Mark Twain, who drowned on August 13, 1847—a *Friday*, not a Sunday.

Hadleyburg Fictional town in "THE MAN THAT CORRUPTED HADLEYBURG" whose residents take pride in their incorruptibility. After a stranger's vengeful scheme destroys the town's reputation, the residents adopt a new name that is not revealed. Aside from the fact that Hadleyburg is near a town called "Brixton," its location is not specified. Real-life models that have been suggested for the arrogant town include FREDONIA, New York. The story equates "Hadleyburg" with "hell"; it is possibly a play on HEIDELBERG, Germany, which Mark Twain also called hell. Alternatively, it may be have been inspired by Hannibal, which Mark Twain once called "H—l."

Whatever "Hadleyburg's" origin, it in turn clearly inspired the name of the town in the 1952 Western film *High Noon*, in which Gary Cooper plays a lawman who single-handedly defends a smugly arrogant town against outlaws when its leading citizens abandon him. An early scene shows a sign revealing the town's name to be "Hadleyville."

Hagan, Sowberry Name mentioned in *Huckleberry Finn*. In chapter 6, Pap FINN alludes to Hagan as an accomplished cusser whom he once heard "in his best days."

Hall, Frederick J. (*fl.* 1880s–90s) Business partner of Mark Twain. Hall joined Mark Twain's publishing firm, Charles WEBSTER & COMPANY, during the mid-1880s and assisted in the preparation of U. S. GRANT's *Memoirs*. He became a partner in the firm in April 1886, replaced Webster as manager in February 1888 and bought out Webster's interest for $12,000 when Webster retired at the end of the same year. Over the next six years, Hall struggled to keep the company afloat as Mark Twain's investments in the PAIGE COMPOSITOR ate up its resources.

During the early 1890s Mark Twain moved his family to Europe, but returned to New York frequently to attend to his business interests and consult with Hall. In April 1893, they went to CHICAGO together to see the World's Fair. A year later, Webster and Company declared BANKRUPTCY and Hall lost his investment. Though Mark Twain initially praised Hall's business management, he later described him as incompetent. Meanwhile, Hall cooperated with A. B. PAINE when the latter was researching his biography of Mark Twain, which Hall later praised for treating the story of Webster's failure honestly.

Halley's Comet Periodic comet with an approximately 75-year orbit that passed by the Earth around the times of Mark Twain's BIRTH and DEATH. The comet reached perihelion (its nearest approach to the sun) on November 15, 1835. Its appearance that year was unimpressive, but it was clearly visible 15 days later, when Mark Twain was born in Missouri. Throughout his life Mark Twain knew that he had been born under Halley's Comet. Aware of the length of the comet's period—which Edmund Halley (1656–1720) had determined—he occasionally predicted that he would "go out with the comet," and he spent decades working on "CAPTAIN STORMFIELD'S VISIT TO HEAVEN," a story that treats a comet as a kind of doppelgänger. Shortly before Mark Twain died, he wrote to his daughter Clara, recalling the passage of Donati's comet, which he had seen in 1858. When Halley's Comet returned in 1910, its transit was one of the most spectacular on record. Mark Twain died on April 21, 1910—the day before the comet reached perihelion—a coincidence noted in many obituaries. The comet reached its most spectacular appearance in the sky two weeks later.

An early transit of Halley's Comet has an ironic relevance to *Connecticut Yankee*, in which a solar ECLIPSE set in A.D. 528 is a plot device. No such eclipse was visible over England during or near that year; however, Halley's Comet passed over the Earth two years later.

In anticipation of the comet's return in 1986, the U.S. Postal Service issued an aerogramme commemorating Mark Twain's unique relationship with its history. First-day-of-issue forms were postmarked in Hannibal on December 4, 1985. David Carkeet's modern SCIENCE FICTION novel *I Been There Before* (1985) uses the return of Halley's Comet as the occasion for Mark Twain's return to Earth.

Hamlet   Play by SHAKESPEARE whose title character is the crown prince of Denmark. After Hamlet's uncle murders his father and usurps the throne, Hamlet's father appears to Hamlet as a ghost and commands him to avenge his murder. Hamlet's agonizing over what he should do is the central theme of the play, as well as the subject of his famous SOLILOQUY (Act 3, Sc. 1). *Huckleberry Finn* BURLESQUES this soliloquy when the DUKE organizes a "Shaksperean Revival" in which the KING recites the soliloquy. Since the Duke has no copy of the 35-line monologue, he pieces it out from memory. The resulting 24-line version mixes lines from the original text with random lines from other parts of *Hamlet,* RICHARD III and *Macbeth.* One line from *Macbeth*—"Wake Duncan with thy knocking!"—might possibly be a sly reference to Captain Charles DUNCAN, a likely model for *Huckleberry Finn*'s King. After hearing the two scoundrels rehearse the soliloquy on the raft, Huck recalls it from memory in chapter 21; the king's actual performance is not described.

In an unpublished portion of *Life on the Mississippi,* Mark Twain recalls seeing an English actor deliver a fractured version of *Hamlet*'s soliloquy when he was a child. A hint of this survives in the published book; a passage in chapter 28 lists things that one formerly saw floating down the river, such as "a random scow bearing a humble Hamlet and Co. on an itinerant dramatic trip" (chapter 28). Mark Twain was familiar with *Hamlet* at least as early as 1866, when he burlesqued Polonius's advice to his son in his 18th letter to the SACRAMENTO UNION from Hawaii. In 1881, he wrote a 14,000-word burlesque of the play. This manuscript, first published in 1968, adds a character named Basil Stockmar, a SUBSCRIPTION-BOOK canvasser who observes events from a fresh perspective. Other allusions to *Hamlet* appear in chapter 39 of *Connecticut Yankee* and chapter 26 of *Innocents Abroad.*

Hannibal   Northeastern Missouri town in which Mark Twain grew up from 1839 to 1853. Located on the Mississippi River, Hannibal is roughly 150 miles by water, or 117 miles by road, above ST. LOUIS. It stands in a valley through which BEAR CREEK flows into the Mississippi, cutting a gap between two prominent hills. On the north, a long scarp ends at CARDIFF HILL; a precipitous hill known as LOVER'S LEAP rises on the south. The location was well suited for STEAMBOAT

landings, as well as for overland connections to the West.

Like many other midwestern towns, Hannibal takes its name from classical history. Named after the Carthaginian general famous for trying to invade Rome by crossing the Alps, it was founded in 1819, two years before Missouri became a state. Though it had only 30 residents a decade later, it was poised for rapid growth because of its favorable position in the middle of the river's developing steamboat traffic. MARION CITY briefly threatened to eclipse Hannibal as a navigation center, but its tendency to flood hampered its development. When Hannibal was incorporated as a "town" in March 1839, it had nearly a thousand residents. That same year, Mark Twain's father, John M. Clemens, concluded that nearby FLORIDA was unlikely to develop as he had hoped. In November, he sold off most of his Florida property, bought land in Hannibal and moved his family there.

The Clemenses moved around within Hannibal several times, but always lived on or near Main and Hill streets, several hundred yards west of the river and a similar distance south of Cardiff Hill. By 1844, they occupied a modest house at 206 Hill Street—a building now known as the Mark Twain BOYHOOD HOME.

Mark Twain grew up in Hannibal during the period of its most rapid development. In February 1845, the state legislature chartered Hannibal as a "city." By the late 1840s, Hannibal's commerce supported a variety of stores, a brothel or two, and various professional people. Its industries included sawmills, tobacco and hemp factories, a tanyard and a distillery. Especially important were its slaughterhouses and pork-processing plants. Its tradesmen included blacksmiths, coopers, tinners and tailors. In addition to two churches and two schools, the town boasted book dealers, a substantial library, several newspapers, two hotels and a complement of saloons. Its position as a transportation hub made it modestly cosmopolitan for its size. Steamboats landed there three times a day and emigrant wagons passed through constantly. Lecturers, circuses, actors, minstrels, mesmerizers and other entertainers also visited regularly, especially during the summer months.

The discovery of gold in CALIFORNIA in 1848 brought a new surge of migrants through Missouri, and Hannibal saw more than 200 of its own people join the GOLD RUSH. Mark Twain caught the fever himself, though it would not be until 1861 that he went west. Meanwhile, he harbored the common boyhood dream of becoming a steamboatman and was one of several Hannibal youths who became PILOTS. Ironically, the basis for Hannibal's future growth would prove to be its favorable location as a railroad terminus.

As a child, Mark Twain attended Protestant Sunday schools and small private schools taught by Sam Cross, John DAWSON and Mary Ann NEWCOMB. He worked summer jobs as a delivery boy, grocery clerk and blacksmith's helper. Around 1848, he began apprenticing as

Six boyhood friends of Mark Twain's who still lived in Hannibal in 1922. (Courtesy, Library of Congress, Pictures & Prints Division)

a printer, working for Joseph AMENT and for his own brother Orion Clemens. By the end of the decade, Hannibal's population was nearing 3,000—triple what it had been when the Clemenses arrived.

After Hartford, Connecticut, Hannibal is the place where Mark Twain lived the longest, and it is certainly the place that made the deepest imprint on his writing. His memoirs of living in Hannibal are scattered through his AUTOBIOGRAPHY, *Life on the Mississippi* and other works—such as chapter 18 of *Innocents Abroad*. Under such fictional guises as ST. PETERSBURG, DAWSON'S LANDING and ESELDORF, Hannibal appears in much of his fiction. Elements of the town can also be found in other fictional creations such as *Huckleberry Finn*'s BRICKSVILLE and PIKESVILLE. In these fictional guises, Hannibal projects Mark Twain's idealization of boyhood and of the innocence of the time before the gold rush, railroads, war and modern industrialism changed the face of the frontier. The St. Petersburg of *Tom Sawyer*—Hannibal's most famous fictional counterpart—is almost a never-never land compared to the real Hannibal, which was larger and far more complex.

The Clemens family exodus from Hannibal began in late 1851 when Mark Twain's sister married to become Pamela Clemens MOFFETT and moved to St. Louis. Mark Twain left in mid-1853; his brothers and mother left a few months later. None of his immediate family ever lived in Hannibal again, but four members were later buried in its MOUNT OLIVET cemetery.

After Mark Twain left Hannibal, the town's growth continued. Its first railroad line, to PALMYRA, was built in 1856; soon, three separate railroad lines met at the town, assuring its place as a transportation center. By the start of the CIVIL WAR, its population exceeded 6,000—a figure that more than doubled by the end of the century. During the war, most Hannibal residents sympathized with the Confederacy, but Union troops occupied the town so quickly that its active participation in the war was minimal. After the war, the town resumed its development. Lumbering became a major industry during the 1870s and 1880s.

Mark Twain revisited Hannibal at least seven times, spending a total of perhaps 10 days there. He first returned in mid-July 1855, shortly after settling in KEOKUK, Iowa. He paid another quick visit in 1861, when he joined the MARION RANGERS. In April 1867, he returned during a LECTURE tour that he describes in letter 14 of MARK TWAIN'S TRAVELS WITH MR. BROWN and mentions at the end of *Roughing It* (chapter 79). These visits he called mere "glimpses," compared with his May 1882 stop, when he spent three days in the town during his month on the Mississippi River. Chapters 53–56 of *Life on the Mississippi* describe this stay and include nostalgic passages that are significant additions to his AUTOBIOGRAPHY.

During a lecture tour with G. W. CABLE, Mark Twain spoke in Hannibal on January 13, 1885 and stayed overnight with friends. In late 1890, he returned for his mother's funeral. His final visit lasted from May 29 to June 3, 1902, when he made an unannounced stop during a trip to the University of MISSOURI to accept an honorary degree. During this visit, he saw such childhood friends as Tom NASH, John BRIGGS, John L. ROBARDS and Laura HAWKINS and was photographed in front of his Boyhood Home. Although Mark Twain revisited Hannibal four times after marrying Olivia Langdon in 1870, he never took his wife or children any closer to Missouri than Keokuk, Iowa. His daughter Clara became the first member of his family to see Hannibal when she sang at a benefit concert on January 1, 1924. In April 1935, she participated in the opening of a Mark Twain Museum.

Since George A. Mahan (1851–1936) donated the Boyhood Home to the city in 1912, Hannibal's name and that of its most famous resident have become inextricably linked. Literally millions of tourists have visited Mark Twain sites. In 1935, the city mounted an elaborate centennial celebration of Mark Twain's BIRTH that launched a permanent museum, and erected a lighthouse as a memorial atop Cardiff Hill. The following year, President Franklin D. ROOSEVELT visited the town and personally dedicated the new MARK TWAIN MEMORIAL BRIDGE. Efforts to mount a major sesquicentennial

Mark Twain's heritage in Hannibal is indelibly imprinted on the town's businesses. (Photograph by author)

birthday celebration in 1985 had only a modest success, however.

Hannibal's population leveled off at around 19,000 residents in the late 20th century. The city still bears Mark Twain's indelible imprint, and tourism continues to buttress the local economy. Most of the thousands of tourists who visit annually converge on the town's "historic district" around Hill Street. In addition to the Boyhood Home, the district contains the PILASTER and BECKY THATCHER houses and the John M. Clemens law office. Nearby are Frederick HIBBARD's statues of Mark Twain and of Tom and Huck. The Mark Twain CAVE south of town and a "Mark Twain" steamboat ride are also popular attractions. Throughout Hannibal, one finds streets with names such as Huckleberry Drive and Mark Twain Avenue. Commercial enterprises abound with such names as the "Tom 'n Huck Motel," "Huck Finn Shopping Center," "Aunt Polly's Handicrafts," "Pudd'nheads," "Injun Joe Campground and Water Slide" and "Mark Twain Family Restaurant."

Hannibal is also noted for producing the painter Carroll BECKWITH; Navy admiral Robert Coontz (1864–1935), a son of Mark Twain's childhood friend, Benton Coontz (1838–1892); and Margaret Tobin Brown (1867–1932)—better known to the world as "The Unsinkable Molly Brown."

Hannibal Courier First newspaper for which Mark Twain is known to have worked. The *Courier* began as the *Missouri Courier* in PALMYRA in 1832. Joseph AMENT bought it in 1844 and moved it to nearby Hannibal in May 1848, when he merged it with the two-year-old *Hannibal Gazette* that he bought from Henry D. LaCositt. Some time after Ament's arrival, he took on Mark Twain as an apprentice printer. In 1851, Mark Twain switched to his brother's HANNIBAL WESTERN UNION. When Ament returned to Palmyra in 1855, he took the *Courier* with him.

Hannibal Journal One of several newspapers founded in Hannibal by J. S. Buchanan, the *Journal* began as the *Pacific Monitor* in May 1840. After several name changes over the next two years, it was called the *Journal*. Around 1850, Orion Clemens bought the paper from the Buchanan family and merged it with his own HANNIBAL WESTERN UNION. Mark Twain set type for the paper and occasionally wrote sketches for it until he went to the East Coast in June 1853. Many of his letters home appeared in the *Journal*, beginning his career as a travel writer. Orion published the combined paper under several names until September 1853, when he moved to Iowa and started the MUSCATINE JOURNAL.

Hannibal Western Union Newspaper started by Orion Clemens in Hannibal in September 1850. Shortly afterward, he bought the local *Journal*, which he merged with the *Western Union* and put through several name

This earliest known photograph of Mark Twain captures him as a 15-year-old printer's apprentice. A tintype, it presents a mirror image of him holding metal type of the letters "MAS." (Courtesy, Mark Twain Papers, the Bancroft Library)

changes. For several years, Mark Twain worked for his brother on the *Western Union*, apparently without pay. His earliest-known sketch, "A GALLANT FIREMAN," appeared in the paper on January 16, 1851.

Harkness, Buck Minor character in *Huckleberry Finn*. In chapter 22, Harkness leads the BRICKSVILLE mob that goes after Colonel SHERBURN for shooting BOGGS. Sherburn calls the mob cowardly, lacking a single "real man." However, he singles out Harkness as a "part of a man," or "half a man." In the previous chapter, Huck mentions a "Buck" as one of the loafers he seeks in town; this person could well be Buck Harkness.

Harley, John J. (*fl.* 1870s–1880s) Illustrator. A staff artist for James R. OSGOOD, Harley split the main illustrating chores of *The Prince and the Pauper* (1882) with Frank MERRILL. While Merrill concentrated on refined palace scenes, Harley used his more rugged style for scenes away from the palace. He was also the major illustrator of Osgood's edition of *Life on the Mississippi* (1883). At least 85 of its pictures are signed "Harley" or "H," and Harley may also have been responsible for a similar number of unsigned pictures. The MARK TWAIN

PAPERS project editions of *Huckleberry Finn* use Harley's pictures from *Mississippi* for the "RAFT CHAPTER."

Harper, Joe Character in *Tom Sawyer* and other stories. Tom's "bosom friend," Joe first appears in chapter 3 of *Tom Sawyer*, when he and Tom oppose each other as generals in a mock war. Four chapters later, Joe sits next to Tom in school and joins him in playing with a tick on Tom's slate. In chapter 8, both boys play hookey and meet on CARDIFF HILL, where they act out Robin Hood games.

Unlike Tom and Huck Finn, Joe has two living parents. His mother, Sereny Harper, appears several times in *Tom Sawyer*. His father, Captain Harper, is mentioned but is never seen on his own. Joe, like Tom, gets into mischief readily, and he shares Tom's feelings of being put upon by the world. In chapter 13, he joins Tom and Huck in running off to JACKSON'S ISLAND to become a PIRATE. While the boys are on the island, Joe's mother meets with Aunt POLLY in chapter 15 to agonize over the boys' disappearance. After the Jackson's Island episode, Joe ceases to be a central character. In chapter 18 Becky THATCHER invites him and his sister, Susy, to a picnic. In chapter 22, he is mentioned as one of the boys who got religion during a revival while Tom Sawyer was laid up with the measles.

Joe plays no visible role at Becky's picnic in chapter 29, but his family has a part in the events that follow. Before leaving for the picnic at McDougal's CAVE, Becky Thatcher tells her mother that she will spend the night at the Harpers' instead of returning home. Becky and Tom get lost in the cave and do not return, however. Mrs. Thatcher and Aunt POLLY are not aware that they are missing until the next day, when Mrs. Harper tells them that Becky never came to her house.

The final mention of Joe in *Tom Sawyer* is in chapter 33, in which Tom names him as one of the boys he will invite to join his robber band. Joe returns as a member of Tom's Gang in chapters 2, 3 and 8 of *Huckleberry Finn*, in which he is called "Jo Harper." He also makes a mute appearance in "TOM SAWYER'S CONSPIRACY." In that story, he is bedridden with the measles. Tom gets in bed with him to contract the disease himself—even though he already had the measles in *Tom Sawyer*. It turns out, however, that what Joe has is scarlet fever. Tom contracts that disease and nearly dies. Joe's fate is not mentioned.

The childhood friend of Mark Twain generally regarded as the primary model for Joe Harper is John B. BRIGGS. Mark Twain also drew on other friends, however, notably John GARTH and Will BOWEN.

Harper and Brothers (Harper's) New York publishing firm founded in 1817 by James and John Harper, brothers in the printing business. After two older brothers joined their firm, it became "Harper and Brothers" in 1833 and later launched HARPER'S MAGAZINE, HARPER'S WEEKLY and other magazines.

In May 1895, H. H. ROGERS helped Mark Twain negotiate a contract with Harper's; the firm published *Joan of Arc* and *Tom Sawyer Abroad; Tom Sawyer, Detective and Other Stories* the following year. In October 1903, Rogers negotiated a new agreement making Harper's Mark Twain's exclusive American publisher and ending his connections with the AMERICAN PUBLISHING COMPANY. The new agreement guaranteed him $25,000 a year, but his income from the company generally exceeded this amount.

After Mark Twain died in 1910, his literary executor A. B. PAINE maintained his relationship with Harper's, which published all Paine's own books relating to Mark Twain as well. Harper's remained the exclusive American publisher of Mark Twain until his copyrights ran out. In 1899, Harper's began issuing uniform editions of Mark Twain's books. It later offered various combinations of titles in 24- and 37-volume sets, some of which included Paine's biography of Mark Twain.

Harper's Bazaar (Bazar) Originally founded as a women's weekly in 1867, this New York magazine became a monthly in 1901. While Elizabeth Jordan was its editor (1900–1913), Mark Twain published "A Helpless Situation" (November 1905), "Marjorie FLEMING: Wonder Child" (December 1909) and "THE TURNING POINT OF MY LIFE" (February 1910) in the magazine.

Harper's Magazine New York monthly founded by Fletcher Harper of HARPER AND BROTHERS in 1850. Called *Harper's New Monthly Magazine* until it became *Harper's Monthly* in 1900, the magazine initially filled its pages with serials pirated from English writers such as Charles DICKENS. It enjoyed unprecedented success and reached a circulation of 200,000 in its first decade. In 1869, Henry Mills ALDEN began a 50-year tenure as chief editor during which he built *Harper's* into a forum for American writers and illustrators. Under his editorship, W. D. HOWELLS and C. D. WARNER contributed regular columns.

Mark Twain published more than 30 essays, stories and serialized novels in *Harper's*. An article about the clipper ship HORNET in the December 1866 issue was his first publication in a major eastern magazine. Exactly 16 years later, *Harper's* published his "The MCWILLIAMSES and the Burglar Alarm." In the early 1890s, *Harper's* published "A MAJESTIC LITERARY FOSSIL," "LUCK," "Mental Telegraphy" and a few other short pieces. In 1895–96, it serialized *Joan of Arc* and *Tom Sawyer, Detective*. After that, *Harper's* became Mark Twain's most important publishing outlet. Among the pieces he later published in it are "Concerning the Jews," "THE MAN THAT CORRUPTED HADLEYBURG," "THE DEATH DISK," "A DOUBLE-BARRELED DETECTIVE STORY," "A DOG'S TALE," "EVE'S DIARY," "A HORSE'S TALE" and "Extract from CAPTAIN STORMFIELD'S VISIT TO HEAVEN." After Mark Twain's death, A. B. PAINE published several of his manuscripts in *Harper's,* including "THE DEATH OF JEAN" (1911) and his own version of "THE MYSTERIOUS STRANGER" (1916).

Harper's Weekly New York magazine founded by Fletcher Harper of HARPER AND BROTHERS in 1857. Printed on good paper and noted for its illustrators—especially Thomas NAST—*Harper's Weekly* was a prestigious magazine that emphasized current issues. An indicator of its popularity is *Roughing It*'s reference to boardinghouse residents decorating their rooms with Harper's illustrations (chapter 21). Mark Twain himself began publishing in *Harper's Weekly* in 1902 with "THE FIVE BOONS OF LIFE," "Amended Obituaries," "THE BELATED RUSSIAN PASSPORT" and a eulogy to Thomas Brackett REED. Over the next several years, *Harper's Weekly* published a dozen more contributions from him, including "THE $30,000 BEQUEST," "A MONUMENT TO ADAM," "THE NEW PLANET" and eulogies to John HAY and Carl SCHURZ.

Among the magazine's chief editors were George William Curtis (editor, 1863–92), Carl Schurz (1892–94), Henry Loomis Nelson (1894–98), John Kendrick Bangs (1898–1901) and George HARVEY (1901–13). In December 1905, Harvey staged a birthday banquet for Mark Twain at New York's Delmonico's Restaurant. The Christmas issue of *Harper's* covered the banquet in a 32-page supplement.

The McClure syndicate bought the magazine in 1913 and merged it with the *Independent* three years later.

Harris (Mr. Harris; the Agent) Character in *A Tramp Abroad.* A fictional traveling companion through most of the narrative, Harris is loosely modeled on Joseph TWICHELL, who traveled with Mark Twain in GERMANY's BLACK FOREST and SWITZERLAND. Mark Twain found his time with Twichell so stimulating that he expanded Harris's role to provide a coherent thematic structure for his entire narrative. After the book was published, he wrote Twichell an appreciative note specifying many "Harris" anecdotes that actually happened.

Harris is introduced at the beginning of chapter 1 as an "agent" whom the narrator hires to accompany him on a walking tour through Europe. Nothing is said about his background or physical appearance. The balance of *A Tramp Abroad* refers to him as either "Harris" or the "agent." In some chapters, neither Harris nor the agent is mentioned, but the narrator's use of the first-person plural makes it clear that Harris is with him.

Harris's duties as "agent" are not completely clear, especially since the narrator also hires a professional courier in chapter 24 before proceeding south. As a narrative device, however, Harris's role as agent relates closely to the book's primary running joke—namely, that while the narrator boasts about making a "walking" tour, he does most of his traveling on boats, trains and carriages. He extends this joke by using Harris as his proxy, particularly for disagreeable tasks—such as at-

tending an opera (chapter 10), practicing bowing at tables (chapter 18), attending church (chapter 24) and running after driftwood in a river when the narrator needs exercise (chapter 33). Harris balks, however, when the narrator suggests that he jump 1,200 feet from the RIFFELBERG to a glacier using an umbrella as a parachute (chapter 39). When the narrator orders Harris to climb a perilous ladder in chapter 35, Harris accomplishes the job through a sub-agent of his own.

Harris's biggest assignment is visiting and reporting on Switzerland's Furka region in chapter 30 (he signs his report "H. Harris"; the "H." may stand for *Herr,* German for "mister"). This incident was probably inspired by a three-day trip that Twichell made in the Alps on his own while Mark Twain and his family rested from climbing the RIGI-KULM.

When Mark Twain began writing *A Tramp Abroad* in HEIDELBERG, before Twichell joined him, he experimented with a fictional companion called the "Grumbler" (a pseudonym he had used 25 years earlier as a counterpoint to the "RAMBLER") and then with someone named "John." In each case, he was evidently trying to create a character similar to the "Mr. BROWN" and "BLUCHER" that had worked for him during the 1860s. After finally settling on "Harris," he found himself constrained by this fictional companion's clear relationship to the very real Twichell—whose feelings and reputation concerned him. As a result, he left Harris a bland and rather flat character who rarely expresses a strong opinion—in sharp contrast to the earlier Mr. Brown. Harris comes to life only briefly, when he rails against Catholic cantons in Switzerland in chapter 36, finding almost everything within Protestant Swiss cantons to be superior—including "Protestant glaciers."

Mark Twain later worked "Harris" into an unfinished book about his boat trip on the RHONE in 1891—part of which has been published as "DOWN THE RHÔNE."

Harris, Joel Chandler (December 8, 1848, near Eatonton, Georgia–July 3, 1908, Atlanta, Georgia) Writer and friend of Mark Twain. Harris grew up on a Georgia plantation and developed a keen ear for black dialect and folk tales that he adapted into his "Uncle Remus" stories. Like Mark Twain, he worked as a printer as a teenager and went on to become a journalist. He joined the staff of the *Atlanta Constitution* in 1876 and published his first Uncle Remus stories in that paper three years later. *Uncle Remus, His Songs and His Sayings,* the first of several books, appeared in 1880.

Mark Twain greatly admired Harris's work; he regularly read Uncle Remus stories to his daughters and occasionally read from Harris's work in public. In the writing of black dialect, he called Harris "the only master the country has produced." In 1881, he wrote to Harris about joining him on a lecturing tour. Although Harris had no public speaking experience, he was attracted by Mark Twain's confident predictions of money to be made, as he hoped to escape the grind of a full-time job in order to concentrate on creative writing. In May 1882 Harris went to NEW ORLEANS to meet Mark Twain, G. W. CABLE and James R. OSGOOD—who published his next book—in a meeting described in chapter 47 of *Life on the Mississippi*. To Mark Twain's disappointment, Harris proved to be "the bashfulest grown person" he had ever met; he was too shy even to read to children from his own work. His joining Mark Twain and Cable on a speaking tour was out of the question, but he visited the Clemens family in Hartford a year later and corresponded with Mark Twain through at least 1885.

Mark Twain maintained his affection for Harris until the end of his life. In 1905 he nominated him for membership in the American Academy of Arts and Letters. Chapter 49 of *Following the Equator* adapts a line ("Brer fox he lay low") from Uncle Remus to comment on the commercial canniness of India's Brahmin caste. Mark Twain also mentions Harris in "MY BOYHOOD DREAMS."

Harte, [Francis] Bret[t] (August 25, 1836, Albany, New York–May 5, 1902, London, England) Short-story writer. Harte's early life paralleled that of Mark Twain in several ways. Harte grew up in a poor family, his

Bret Harte in 1871, shortly after leaving California. (Courtesy, National Archives, Still Picture Branch)

father died when he was nine and his formal education ended when he was 13. In 1853, Harte's mother moved to California, where he joined her the following year, beginning a 17-year residence that would provide story material for the rest of his life. Although his activities during the 1850s are poorly documented, he appears to have spent time in mining camps such as JACKASS HILL and ANGEL'S CAMP around late 1855.

By 1860, Harte was setting type in SAN FRANCISCO and writing poems and short stories for the GOLDEN ERA. A year or two later, he went to work for the federal mint, continuing to make a name for himself as a writer along the West Coast. In 1864, he helped Charles WEBB start the CALIFORNIAN; four years later, he became editor of the OVERLAND MONTHLY. In that magazine he published his most famous stories, such as "The Luck of Roaring Camp" (1868), "Outcasts of Poker Flat" (1869) and "The Heathen Chinee" (1870). When he returned to the East Coast in 1871, he had a national reputation and a one-year contract with the ATLANTIC MONTHLY to write 12 stories for $10,000. The quality of his work soon declined, however, and he later lived largely on his early reputation. Always in financial trouble, he accepted a consular post in Germany in 1878; from 1880 to 1885, he was the American consul at Glasgow, Scotland. He spent his last years in London and never returned to the United States.

When Mark Twain first came to San Francisco in the mid-1860s, Harte befriended him and helped him write and publish his work. Later Mark Twain told Thomas Bailey ALDRICH that Harte was responsible for transforming him into a real writer. When Mark Twain revisited San Francisco in the spring of 1868, Harte helped him edit his *Innocents Abroad* manuscript. In return, he let Harte print four excerpts in the *Overland Monthly*, in which Harte later favorably reviewed the published book.

In late 1876, Harte stayed at Mark Twain's Hartford home, where he wrote a popular story, "Thankful Blossom," and collaborated with Mark Twain on the dramatization of his "Heathen Chinee" story, which they produced the following year as AH SIN. During this visit, Harte offended Mark Twain deeply enough to incur his lasting enmity. Mark Twain's opinion of Harte sank even further after Harte left his family behind when he went to Europe. His letters and memoirs of later years are filled with descriptions of Harte as a liar and a fraud. While he acknowledged signs of Harte's genius as a writer, he regarded the substance of Harte's work as false and accused him of imitating Charles DICKENS—Harte's favorite writer during his youth. Despite his criticisms, he included four pieces by Harte in MARK TWAIN'S LIBRARY OF HUMOR (1888).

Mark Twain mentions Harte by name in a number of works, including chapter 7 of IS SHAKESPEARE DEAD? (1909), in which he criticizes Harte's MINING jargon. In chapter 59 of *Roughing It*, he acknowledges Harte's help in getting his material published in the *Californian*.

The Hartford home that many called "Steamboat Gothic" in 1905. (Courtesy, Library of Congress, Pictures & Prints Division)

Hartford   Capital city of CONNECTICUT. Hartford was Mark Twain's home for two decades (1871–91)—a period longer than he lived anywhere else. However, nearly a third of this time he spent away from the city, on LECTURE tours, European trips and summers in ELMIRA, New York. America's insurance capital and home to the COLT ARMS FACTORY, Hartford was also a book-publishing center. Mark Twain first visited the city in January 1868 to meet publisher Elisha BLISS. He was immediately taken with the city's beauty and intellectual climate, and doubtless noticed that it occupied a convenient position midway between BOSTON and NEW YORK. While staying with Isabella HOOKER's family, he began a lifelong friendship with Joseph TWICHELL. Over the next three years, he returned to Hartford frequently to consult with Bliss about his books.

Before marrying Olivia Langdon in early 1870, Mark Twain tried to buy into the *Hartford Courant.* Its pub-

lisher, J. R. HAWLEY, turned him down, so he instead settled in BUFFALO, New York. When he and his wife decided to leave Buffalo a year later, his thoughts returned to Hartford. After a sojourn in Elmira, he rented the Hookers' Forest Street house in west Hartford's NOOK FARM area in October 1871. Their infant son, Langdon Clemens, died there the following June.

Encouraged by the success of his early books, Mark Twain and his wife bought Nook Farm property of their own in early 1873 and built a large house, where they lived from 1874 to 1891. In June 1891, they shut down the house and went to Europe. Until mid-1896, they expected to return to Hartford, but after Susy Clemens died in the family house no family member ever lived in Hartford again. Mark Twain himself revisited Hartford during business trips from Europe in 1893, 1894 and 1895. He next returned in October 1900 for his friend C. D. WARNER's funeral—an occasion that apparently ended any thoughts he may still have had about living in Hartford again. After finally selling his Hartford house in 1903, he visited the city for the last time in June 1906. His former home is now maintained by the MARK TWAIN MEMORIAL.

During his Hartford years, Mark Twain enjoyed the greatest personal happiness and professional success of his life. He raised three daughters (all born in Elmira), enjoyed warm friendships with neighbors and fellow members of organizations such as the MONDAY EVENING CLUB and entertained a steady stream of famous and distinguished guests. Through these years he published *Roughing It, The Gilded Age, Tom Sawyer, A Tramp Abroad, The Prince and the Pauper, Life on the Mississippi, Huckleberry Finn* and *Connecticut Yankee*—whose title character is a native of Hartford—and he enjoyed extraordinary early success with his publishing firm, Charles L. WEBSTER & COMPANY.

Harvey, Colonel George Brinton McClellan (February 16, 1864, Peacham, Vermont–August 20, 1928, Dublin, New Hampshire)   Political journalist. Harvey bought the NORTH AMERICAN REVIEW in 1899 and edited it until 1926. As president of HARPER and Brothers (1900–15), he also edited HARPER'S WEEKLY (1901–13). In this latter capacity, he sponsored Mark Twain's 70th birthday banquet in 1905. Over the next two years, he published 25 installments of Mark Twain's AUTOBIOGRAPHY in the *Review.*

In a speech to New York's Lotos Club in February 1906, Harvey was the first person publicly to suggest Woodrow Wilson as a presidential candidate, and he later helped to get Wilson elected. He also supported the election of President Warren G. Harding, who made him ambassador to Great Britain (1921–23).

haunted houses   Locations in several stories. In chapter 25 of *Tom Sawyer*, Tom and Huck Finn search for PIRATE treasure near "the old ha'nted house up the STILL-HOUSE BRANCH," behind CARDIFF HILL. After vainly digging near a tree, they venture closer to the house. In the next chapter they nerve themselves to go inside. As they explore upstairs, INJUN JOE and his partner enter. The boys see Joe find gold under the floorboards; by the end of the novel, they own the gold themselves. When word of where it was found gets out, townspeople tear up every "haunted" house in the vicinity (chapter 35).

In *Pudd'nhead Wilson*, David WILSON lives at the western edge of DAWSON'S LANDING. Three hundred yards of vacant land separate his property from a decaying two-story log-house that townspeople know as *"the haunted house."* After ROXANA returns to the town in chapter 8, she arranges with her son Tom DRISCOLL to meet regularly at this house, and she sleeps in it while visiting the town. She watches from the house as Judge York DRISCOLL and Luigi CAPELLO fight a DUEL in chapter 14.

Huckleberry Finn's "HOUSE OF DEATH" also has certain elements of a haunted house.

Hawaii (Sandwich Islands)   Located in the middle of the north PACIFIC OCEAN, just below the Tropic of Cancer, Hawaii is a chain of 20 volcanic and coral islands that Mark Twain visited in 1866. Two-thirds of the archipelago's land area is concentrated on one island, which is also called Hawaii. When Mark Twain visited the islands, they were an independent kingdom that King KAMEHAMEHA I had built at the beginning of the 19th century. In 1866, the last member of his dynasty, KAMEHAMEHA V, ruled under a two-year-old constitution that provided for a Western-style legislature and judiciary. The government included several influential American and European officers; American missionaries were a powerful presence on the islands, and the United States and several European nations kept ministers at Honolulu, the capital city on Oahu. Hawaii was then developing important trade links with the United States—particularly in sugarcane—and Honolulu was a vital base for American whaling ships. The closest port on a major landmass was SAN FRANCISCO, 2,400 miles to the northeast.

The native Hawaiian islanders (KANAKAS) were a Polynesian-speaking people who migrated from Tahiti and the Marquesas a millennium earlier. By the 1860s, about 60,000 Hawaiians remained—perhaps a fifth the number still alive in the 1770s, when Captain James COOK visited the islands and opened European contacts that brought devastating contagious diseases. Cook's name for the archipelago, the "SANDWICH ISLANDS," was the name by which Mark Twain knew it.

In February 1866, Mark Twain arranged to write travel letters from Hawaii to the SACRAMENTO UNION. He sailed from San Francisco aboard the steamer AJAX on March 7, arriving at Honolulu 11 days later. He intended to stay one month, but remained exactly four months and a day. The last fifth of *Roughing It* covers his Hawaiian experiences, but rearranges the sequence of his travels, adds invented anecdotes and condenses or omits several important episodes (chapters 62–77).

Mark Twain spent most of his first month around Honolulu, then went to the island of Maui on April 14. Over the next five weeks, he explored Maui and studied its sugar plantations. After returning to Oahu on May 22, he spent four days in Honolulu, during which he attended a session of the legislature. On May 26, he sailed for the big island of Hawaii aboard the *Emeline*, an inter-island schooner that he calls the *Boomerang* in *Roughing It.* He landed at Kailua on the western Kona Coast two days later and sailed down the coast to Kealakekua Bay, where Cook was killed, the next day. On May 29, the *Emeline* left him at Kau on the southeastern coast, from which he traveled by foot to KILAUEA volcano and Hilo, which he reached on June 8. From there he continued on foot and horseback to Kawaihae on the northwest coast, from which he returned to Oahu on about June 15. During his remaining month on Oahu, he met Anson BURLINGAME, the American minister to China, and wrote a scoop on the sinking of the clipper ship HORNET, whose survivors he met. He also attended funeral rites for the royal princess VICTORIA KAMAMALU. On July 19, he sailed from Honolulu aboard the clipper ship *Smyrniote*, which arrived in San Francisco on August 13.

Mark Twain eventually wrote 25 letters to the *Union,* totaling about 90,000 words. He wanted to rework this material into a book the following year, but failed to find an interested publisher and set the project aside. Five years after leaving Hawaii, he returned to his *Union* letters, reworking about a third of their material and adding about 5,000 new words to make chapters 62–77 of *Roughing It.* The deleted material includes statistics and other notes on the sugarcane and whaling industries, a description of Honolulu's prison, the account of the *Hornet* disaster and details on Hawaiian history, politics and daily life. The book says little about his time on Maui—when he stopped writing letters for a month—and drops "Mr. BROWN," a fictional companion he used in the letters. The new material includes extended coverage of his visit to Kilauea and invented anecdotes about WILLIAMS and the "ADMIRAL" and about Simon ERICKSON and Horace GREELEY. The original *Union* letters were republished in Walter Francis Frear, *Mark Twain and Hawaii* (1937) and in A. Grove Day, *Mark Twain's Letters from Hawaii* (1966). Both books employ the same individual letter numbers used in the *Union.*

After returning to San Francisco, Mark Twain discovered that his Hawaiian letters—which had been extensively reprinted on the Pacific Coast—had greatly enhanced his reputation, and that many Americans were interested in Hawaii. On October 2, 1866, he launched his professional LECTURING career at Maguire's Opera House, speaking on "Our Fellow Savages of the Sandwich Islands." The success that he enjoyed encouraged him to take his Sandwich Islands lecture on a quick tour through northern California and western Nevada. Over the next seven years, he lectured on Hawaii more than a hundred times in the United States and England.

Retaining fond memories of Hawaii through the rest of his life, Mark Twain had mixed feelings about what was best for its future. On January 9, 1873 he published a widely quoted letter in the NEW YORK TRIBUNE advocating American annexation of the islands—an opinion he soon revised. He wanted to revisit the islands, but only got close enough for a tantalizing look during his round-the-world lecture tour in 1895–96, when he scheduled a stop in Honolulu. On the night of August 30, 1895, his ship, the WARRIMOO, anchored off Honolulu, where 500 people had bought tickets to hear him lecture. Because of a CHOLERA epidemic, however, no one could go ashore. Chapter 3 of *Following the Equator* describes that moment; it also recalls Mark Twain's earlier time in Hawaii and summarizes the history of the islands, whose monarchy had been toppled two and a half years earlier. By 1895, Hawaii was a provisional republic with an American president. Three years later the United States annexed the islands.

Fascinated by the similarities between Hawaii's traditional social and political system and medieval European feudalism, Mark Twain started writing a novel about Hawaii in 1884. He abandoned this effort fairly quickly, but later took up similar themes in *Connecticut Yankee,* which reflects his mid–19th-century views of Hawaii. Indeed, it has been suggested that Kamehameha V was one of his models for King ARTHUR.

Hawkeye   Fictional town in *The Gilded Age.* When Si HAWKINS brings his family to MISSOURI, he settles them in a small village later alluded to as Murpheysburg (chapter 18). Hawkeye is first mentioned in chapter 6 as the place to which Colonel SELLERS has relocated. It is 30 miles from Murpheysburg, which in turn is five miles from Swansea, to which Hawkeye is linked by stagecoach. When Washington HAWKINS moves to Hawkeye in chapter 7, he finds it a "pretty large town for interior Missouri." The rest of his family moves there shortly after his father dies (chapters 10–11). Hawkeye is 10 miles from STONE'S LANDING (chapter 17), which Sellers wants to develop into a major railroad and river transportation hub. This dream is dashed when the people of Hawkeye subscribe enough shares in the railroad to ensure that it will pass through their town instead of Stone's Landing (chapter 28).

Loosely modeled on FLORIDA, Missouri, Hawkeye also has elements of the river town Hannibal—the second Missouri home of Mark Twain's family.

Hawkins, [Anna] Laura (December 1, 1837, Georgetown, Kentucky–December 26, 1928, Hannibal, Missouri)   Childhood friend of Mark Twain and the model for Becky THATCHER. Hawkins came to Hannibal with her 12-member family around the same time that Mark Twain's family arrived in 1839, and her father, Elijah Hawkins—like Mark Twain's—ran a general store. In the mid-1840s, the Hawkinses moved into a Hill Street house directly opposite the Clemens family home.

Late in life, Mark Twain said that Hawkins had been his "first sweetheart" when he was seven—a time that would have been before the families lived on the same street. He also recalled Hawkins as one of only three childhood friends who lived on in his memory; the others were John BRIGGS and John GARTH. The fact that Mark Twain and Hawkins had birthdays a day apart may have helped them to feel a special closeness. Mark Twain's Becky Thatcher is modeled almost entirely on Hawkins and several incidents involving Tom and Becky in *Tom Sawyer* actually happened to Mark Twain and Hawkins. In 1899, Hawkins herself recalled how Mark Twain showed off in front of her house the first time she saw him—just as Tom shows off for Becky. Hawkins

Laura Hawkins admires Mark Twain's portrait at a Hannibal theater playing the silent film adaptation of Connecticut Yankee *in 1922.* (Courtesy, Library of Congress, Pictures & Prints Division)

denied, however, ever having been lost in the CAVE with Mark Twain.

Mark Twain's childhood romance with Hawkins did not extend into adulthood. He left Hannibal in 1853; five years later, Hawkins married James W. Frazer, a Kentucky physician, and moved west. During the CIVIL WAR, Union troops jailed Dr. Frazer in St. Louis for his Confederate sympathies, but released him to practice medicine. After her husband died in 1875, Hawkins and her two sons returned to MARION COUNTY. In June 1896 she became matron of a Hannibal home for orphans and indigent adults. Mark Twain saw her when he visited Hannibal in May 1902. The last time that they were together was in October 1908, when Hawkins and her granddaughter were guests for two days at STORMFIELD. Around this same time, Hawkins corresponded with Mark Twain's biographer A. B. PAINE about Mark Twain's childhood and she visited Paine in Connecticut. She spent her last years living with a son in Hannibal, where she died at 91.

Although Hawkins achieved some fame as "Becky Thatcher" late in life, she did little to encourage it. Nevertheless the building in which she grew up is now preserved as the BECKY THATCHER HOUSE.

Mark Twain also used Hawkins as the model for a character in "BOY'S MANUSCRIPT," one of his earliest pieces of fiction, in which she appears as the Becky Thatcher–like Amy—the object of Billy ROGERS's affections. Curiously, when Billy gives up on Amy, his interest switches to a 19-year-old girl whose name is *Laura* Miller. A few years after writing this story, Mark Twain used the name Laura HAWKINS for an older character in *The Gilded Age.* Little beside this character's name resembles his childhood friend, however.

Hawkins, Laura (the "Duchess") Character in *The Gilded Age.* Laura first appears as five-year-old Laura Van Brunt, whom Nancy and Si HAWKINS adopt when the AMARANTH disaster orphans her (chapter 5). By the end of the novel, she is 28 years old (chapter 60). Her natural parents are believed to have been prosperous easterners, who came to New Orleans by way of Cuba before taking passage on the *Amaranth.* By the time Laura is 12, everyone but her new parents forgets that she is adopted, despite the fact that she is developing into an exquisite beauty quite unlike her foster sister Emily. At 15, she is "willful, generous, forgiving, imperious, affectionate, improvident [and] bewitching" (chapter 6) and her family later calls her the "Duchess" (chapter 9).

After Si Hawkins dies, Laura discovers that he had learned that her natural father was still alive (chapter 10). This man, said to be mentally unbalanced, again disappears without a trace, however. Insensitive villagers gossip about Laura's mysterious background, making her distrustful of people. Nevertheless, she falls deeply in love with a Confederate colonel, George Selby, during the Civil War; she follows him to another town and marries him (in a chapter written by C. D. WARNER); three months later, Selby tells her that he already has a wife and abandons her (chapter 18). Thereafter, Laura never fully trusts men and rejects countless suitors. Later she becomes a ruthlessly effective lobbyist for Senator DILWORTHY in Washington, D.C., where she again becomes involved with Selby. When Selby betrays her a second time, she follows him to New York and kills him. By the time she is tried, public sentiment has swung in her favor and she is acquitted. At the same time, however, Dilworthy's career is ruined and a congressional bill on which Laura pins her hopes of profiting from her family's TENNESSEE LAND collapses. She tries to start a new life as a lecturer, but public hostility is so devastating that she dies of heart failure.

Although Mark Twain gave this character the name of his childhood friend Laura HAWKINS, he appears to have modeled her—as a youth—on Laura Wright, a 14-year-old girl with whom he became infatuated on a STEAMBOAT in 1858. The character's adult career is partly modeled on the experiences of a San Francisco woman named Laura D. Fair who gained notoriety in the early 1870s during two sensational trials for killing her lover. Fair's case received national attention because of her dependence on an "emotional insanity" plea. Fair was never a lobbyist, but like the fictional Laura, she saw her attempt to launch a lecture career quickly ruined by an angry mob.

Hawkins, Si (Silas)   Character in *The Gilded Age*. The patriarch of his family, Hawkins is an honest, well-meaning man who is easily lured by get-rich schemes—particularly those advocated by his friend Colonel SELLERS, who lures him to MISSOURI. When introduced in chapter 1, Hawkins is about 35 years old and is known as "Squire Hawkins" because he is postmaster of tiny OBEDSTOWN, where he runs a general store out of his house. After resettling in Murpheysburg, Missouri, he buys another small store and makes it a success by studying market trends in big-city newspapers. He gets a reputation for being lucky and gradually becomes known as "Judge Hawkins" out of respect. He and Sellers make a fortune raising mules to sell in New Orleans, but lose it on a sugar speculation. Three BANKRUPTCIES in 10 years eventually break his spirit, leaving him with eight children in desperate poverty. Despite being hard-up, he has avoided accumulating serious debts.

Many aspects of Hawkins's life are taken from that of Mark Twain's father, John M. Clemens: from his deep-rooted sense of Southern honor to his naive faith that the future welfare of his children is assured by his "TENNESSEE LAND." The narrative's chronological clues suggest that Hawkins dies in his late forties—also like Clemens. Further, both men die condemning their children to lifetimes of false hopes in the land. And just as Clemens died kissing his daughter Pamela, Hawkins dies kissing his daughter Laura. Unlike Clemens, however, Hawkins is generally warmer and more demonstrative.

Jim BLAINE's old ram's tale in *Roughing It* mentions an unrelated character named "Sile Hawkins" (chapter 53).

Hawkins, (George) Washington   Character in *The Gilded Age* and *The American Claimant*. Introduced early in *The Gilded Age* as the 10-year-old son of Si HAWKINS, Washington is the family's dreamer—much like Orion Clemens in Mark Twain's own family. His thoughts are always on impractical inventions, vast speculations and the riches he hopes to reap from the family's TENNESSEE LAND. At some point, he is educated in ST. LOUIS (chapter 6), but he avoids steady employment. When the family's fortunes decline, he goes to HAWKEYE hoping that Colonel SELLERS will steer him to riches. Instead, Sellers gets him a bookkeeping job with General Boswell, with whose daughter Louise he falls in love (chapter 8). After years of getting nowhere, he serves briefly in a Confederate unit during the CIVIL WAR (chapter 18). Several years after the war, Senator DILWORTHY is so impressed by Hawkins's guilelessness and adaptability that he takes him to WASHINGTON, D.C. as his unpaid private secretary—a post similar to the one that Mark Twain held under William M. STEWART (chapter 20). Hawkins flourishes in the capital; he makes good money clerking for two congressional committees and throws himself into working for Dilworthy's bill to get the government to buy his family's land. The arrival of his beautiful foster sister, Laura HAWKINS, even transforms him into a society favorite. By the end of the narrative, however, all his pipe-dreams are smashed and he renounces the Tennessee Land in favor of solid work. Now about 33 years old, he looks forward to returning to HAWKEYE to marry Louise (chapter 61).

When *The American Claimant* opens about 15 years later, Hawkins is still poor. He is now stout and about 50, but looks much older. He is married to Louise, has children and is living in the Cherokee Strip in what is now Oklahoma (chapter 2). Returning to Washington as an unofficial congressional delegate, he again falls under Sellers's influence. He is practical enough to investigate having one of Sellers's inventions marketed, but otherwise accepts Sellers's wild schemes without question—from materializing the dead to manipulating sunspots to alter Earth's weather. Sellers appreciates Washington's loyalty and steadily magnifies his importance by referring to him with increasingly exalted titles, such as major, senator and admiral (much as the baggage-car man in "THE INVALID'S STORY" shows his growing respect for a presumed corpse with increasingly exalted titles) Hawkins is referred to as "George Washington Hawkins" just once, in chapter 5 of *The Gilded Age.*

Hawley, Joseph Roswell (October 31, 1826, Stewartsville, North Carolina–March 17, 1905, Washington, D.C.) CONNECTICUT journalist and politician. Trained as a lawyer, Hawley became the editor of the Hartford *Evening Press* in 1857 and invited his old college classmate C. D. WARNER to become his assistant editor three years later. When the CIVIL WAR began, he joined the Union army, leaving Warner to run the newspaper. He concluded his war service a brevet major general and was elected governor of Connecticut (1866–67). In 1867, he oversaw the consolidation of the *Press* with the *Hartford Courant,* of which he became editor. He later served in the U.S. House of Representatives (1872–1875, 1879–81) and the U.S. Senate (1881–1905). In 1869, Hawley turned down Mark Twain's offer to buy into the *Courant,* but they later became good friends and fellow members of the MONDAY EVENING CLUB. In 1879, Hawley agreed to present Mark Twain's petition to build a monument to ADAM before Congress, but backed out, fearing ridicule.

Hay, John (October 8, 1838, Salem, Indiana–July 1, 1905, Newburg, New Hampshire) American statesman, diplomat and writer. After growing up on the Mississippi River in Warsaw, Illinois, Hay studied at Brown University. He later became a private secretary to President LINCOLN (1861–65) and held several diplomatic posts in Europe. During the 1870s, he was an editorial writer on the NEW YORK TRIBUNE and then became assistant secretary of state (1878–81). Through these years he published poetry and fiction, and he later coauthored a 10-volume biography of Lincoln (1890). President McKinley appointed Hay ambassador to Great Britain and made him secretary of state the following year. Holding this post until his death in 1905, Hay helped conclude the Spanish-American War, formulate America's Open Door policy in China and secure American control of the Panama Canal Zone.

After meeting Hay at the *Tribune* in 1871, Mark Twain remained his warm friend for the rest of his life. Hay was a great admirer of Mark Twain's writing and helped to get *1601* printed in 1880. Mark Twain mentions Hay in "MY BOYHOOD DREAMS" (1900) and devotes a long passage in his AUTOBIOGRAPHY to praising him as a man worthy to be president. "A HORSE'S TALE" (1906) adapts its bullfight descriptions from *Castilian Days* (1871), a book that Hay wrote after serving as a diplomat in Madrid.

Heidelberg City in southwestern GERMANY. The site of a 14th-century university, Heidelberg is on the south bank of the NECKAR River, 12 miles above the Rhine.

From May 6 to July 23, 1878, Mark Twain and his family stayed at Heidelberg in its famous Hotel Schloss, which commanded a panoramic view of the city and its medieval castle. Meanwhile, Mark Twain began writing *A Tramp Abroad* in a rented cottage room. From Heidelberg, he took his family south to BADEN-BADEN. *A Tramp Abroad* discusses Heidelberg in chapters 2, 4–7 and 11 and Appendix B, giving special attention to student DUELING. The family returned to Heidelberg for a week from late August to early September 1891, before moving on to Switzerland.

Heilbronn City in southwestern GERMANY. The commercial center of Baden-Wurttemberg, Heilbronn is on the right bank of the NECKAR River, 27 miles north of Stuttgart. Mark Twain and Joseph TWICHELL visited Heilbronn on August 8, 1878, after passing through HEIDELBERG. An account of their trip is the first of *A Tramp Abroad*'s many BURLESQUE travel stories (chapters 11–12).

Hello-Central Minor character in *Connecticut Yankee.* Hank MORGAN's daughter, Hello-Central first appears in chapter 40, when she has a croup attack—similar to those that Clara Clemens suffered as a baby. It is not until the next chapter, however, that Hank explains that he married the baby's mother SANDY some time during the previous three years. This chapter also recalls how Sandy chose "Hello-Central" for the baby's name—thinking it meant something dear to Hank, since he mumbles the words in his sleep. The phrase is actually one he used when calling his former fiancée, Puss FLANAGAN, on the telephone in Hartford. When *Connecticut Yankee* ends, Sandy and Hello-Central are evidently stranded in France.

Hendon, Edith Character in *The Prince and the Pauper.* The wife of Hugh HENDON, her cousin, Edith is the orphaned daughter of an earl who has left her a lapsed title. Like other female characters created by Mark Twain—as well as his own wife—Edith is not only beautiful, gentle and good, but is an heiress to a fortune. Formerly, she was a ward of her father-in-law, Sir Richard Hendon, who originally wanted her to marry his oldest son, Arthur. She, however, has always loved the middle brother, Miles HENDON, who is four years her senior. Arthur hoped to arrange for her to wed Miles, but Miles went off to war when Edith was 16 and did not return for 10 years. Meanwhile, Sir Richard and Arthur died, leaving Hugh to trick Edith into marrying him.

Miles describes Edith in chapter 12; she first appears in chapter 25, when she denies knowing him. It is not revealed until the final chapter that she has disavowed Miles in order to save his life. After Hugh dies, she marries Miles.

Hendon, Hugh Character in *The Prince and the Pauper.* Hugh is the younger brother of Miles HENDON, who describes him as having always been "a mean spirit, covetous, treacherous, vicious, underhanded—a reptile" (chapter 12). Like Mark Twain's Tom DRISCOLL and other bad boy characters, Hugh was his father's pet. When Miles returns to HENDON HALL after a 10-year absence, he finds Hugh—who pretends not to recognize him—the master of the estate (chapter 25). Miles later learns that Hugh forged a letter reporting his death and forced Miles's own sweetheart, Edith, to marry him. In chapter 33, Hugh is in London for King EDWARD's coronation, hoping for a peerage. Instead, the new king has him arrested and stripped of his estates. Afterward, neither Edith nor Miles will testify against Hugh, who goes to the Continent and soon dies.

Hendon, Miles (Earl of Kent)   Character in *The Prince and the Pauper*. A member of a Kentish family of the lesser nobility, 30-year-old Hendon is in England after three years of fighting in "continental wars" and seven in foreign captivity. He explains in chapter 12 that he was so wild as a youth that his treacherous brother Hugh HENDON persuaded their father that Miles intended to run off with Edith HENDON, whom their father intended for the oldest brother, Arthur. To prevent this, the father banished Miles to Europe for three years to help mature him.

Hendon first appears in the narrative in chapter 11, when he rescues Prince EDWARD from ruffians. Similar in dress, aspect, and bearing to Don Caesar de Bazan (a character in Victor Hugo's *Gil Blas*), Hendon is tall, trim and muscular and has the swaggering carriage of a "RUFFLER of the camp." Hendon admires Edward's noble spirit. Determined to make the boy his ward, he puts up with his royal pretensions, not believing Edward's claims until he sees him on the throne in chapter 33. Meanwhile, he never expresses his doubts aloud, for fear of causing the lad's diseased mind further harm. His devotion to Edward is complete. He twice puts off returning home to HENDON HALL in order to find Edward after John CANTY abducts him, and he takes a lashing in Edward's place in chapter 28.

For his part, Edward repays Hendon by allowing him to sit in his royal presence. He also makes Hendon a knight and later Earl of Kent—titles that he confirms after he is safely on his throne. According to the concluding chapter, Hendon's earldom endures until the 17th-century civil wars, in which the last Earl of Kent dies fighting for the king.

When Hendon finally reaches home, his brother disavows him and he finds himself in the same position as Edward as a claimant. Mark Twain identified closely with Hendon, whose struggle to prove that he is not an impostor has been compared to Mark Twain's choosing to write *The Prince and the Pauper* in order to prove himself respectable as a writer. Appropriately, Mark Twain played Hendon in family dramatic productions of *The Prince and the Pauper*. As a broadly conceived, swashbuckling character, Hendon has also been portrayed by several flamboyant film actors, including Errol Flynn (1937); Guy Williams, television's "Zorro" (1962); and Oliver Reed (1977).

Hendon Hall   Fictitious place in *The Prince and the Pauper*. Located near Monk's Holm (also apparently fictitious) in Kent, Hendon Hall is the ancestral home of Miles HENDON. The estate has a 72-room house maintained by 27 servants. Hendon tells King EDWARD about Hendon Hall in chapter 12 and they spend about three days riding to get there from LONDON in chapter 25.

Henry VIII (June 28, 1491, Greenwich, England–January 28, 1547, Hampton Court, England)   Historical figure and minor character in *The Prince and the Pauper*. England's king from 1509 to 1547, Henry is remembered for detaching England's national church from the Roman Catholic Church in order to divorce the first of his six wives. He then dissolved England's monasteries and nunneries and confiscated their property. He left three children who succeeded him on the throne, beginning with EDWARD VI, the nine-year-old son of his third wife, Jane Seymour (c. 1509–1537). Edward was followed by MARY I and ELIZABETH I.

Henry is also remembered for having two of his wives executed for infidelity. In chapter 3 of *The Prince and the Pauper*, the prince describes his father as having a sharp temper and a heavy hand, but being gentle with him; he recalls his warm feelings for his father in chapters 12 and 17. Henry himself first appears in chapter 5, in which Tom CANTY meets him face to face. Tom expects to be summarily hanged for unintentionally usurping the prince's place; however, the king accepts Tom as his own son and forbids him to say otherwise—a command that accounts for Tom's acquiescence in his new role. In chapter 8, Henry presses his lord chancellor (Thomas Wriothesley, who is not named) to expedite the execution of the Duke of NORFOLK. Tom learns of the king's death in chapter 11, while banqueting at GUILDHALL; the real prince—who is outside the hall at that moment—learns of his father's death in the next chapter while he and Miles Hendon are fleeing a mob.

King Henry's dissolution of the monasteries has important ramifications in *The Prince and the Pauper*. One dispossessed priest is Father ANDREW, whose consequent poverty forces him to live in OFFAL COURT, where he educates Tom Canty. Another dispossessed priest is the murderous HERMIT whom Edward meets in chapter 20.

Mark Twain also mentions Henry VIII in other writings, such as "HOW TO MAKE HISTORY DATES STICK." In chapter 23 of *Huckleberry Finn*, Huck tells Jim about Henry. Confusing the English king with Shahriyar of the ARABIAN NIGHTS, he says that Henry "used to marry a new wife every day, and chop off her head next morning," while making his wives tell him tales that he collected in the Domesday Book. Huck also mistakenly credits Henry with initiating the Boston Tea Party, writing the Declaration of Independence and drowning his father, the Duke of Wellington. "CAPTAIN STORMFIELD'S VISIT TO HEAVEN" describes Henry as a resident of heaven who has made a reputation as a tragedian who is particularly good in scenes in which he kills people.

Herbert, Sir William (Earl of Pembroke) (c. 1501–March 17, 1570, Hampton Court, England) Historical figure and minor character in *The Prince and the Pauper*. An English soldier and courtier, Herbert was the brother-in-law of King HENRY VIII's last wife, Catherine Parr, and became a member of EDWARD VI's privy council. After Edward died, Herbert supported MARY I's succession and helped end Lady Jane GREY's short reign. Herbert appears briefly in chapter 6 of *The Prince and the Pauper* as the privy chamber officer who takes Tom Canty to a room to rest. In chapter 10, the real prince awakens in Canty's house; thinking that he has been dreaming, he calls out Herbert's name.

The historical Herbert was made Earl of Pembroke—the given name of Pembroke HOWARD in *Pudd'nhead Wilson*.

hermit, holy Character in *The Prince and the Pauper*. While wandering alone in the woods, EDWARD VI stumbles upon the house of an old man whom he joyfully calls a "holy hermit" (chapter 20). The white-haired man quietly accepts Edward's claim to be a "king," then reveals that he is an archangel who would have been pope, had not "the king" dissolved his religious house and cast him out into the world. When Edward further identifies himself as king of "England," the hermit deduces that he is the son of his despoiler, HENRY VIII, and determines to kill him. He is about to stab Edward when Miles HENDON arrives. When he leads Hendon off on a wild goose chase, John CANTY arrives and spirits the prince away.

Mark Twain also uses the expression "holy hermit" in chapter 14 of *Connecticut Yankee* and in the table of contents of *Innocents Abroad,* for chapter 55. *The Prince and the Pauper*'s description of the hermit as an "archangel" recalls *Roughing It*'s description of a Mormon "Destroying Angel" in chapter 12; both characters are filthy, impoverished men bent on killing to do the Lord's work.

Hertford, Earl of (Edward Seymour; Duke of Somerset) (c. 1501-1506–January 22, 1552, London, England) Historical figure and character in *The Prince and the Pauper*. The brother of King HENRY VIII's third wife, Jane Seymour (c. 1509–1537), Hertford became an earl after his sister gave birth to EDWARD VI in 1537. Henry's will called for a 16-member council of regency to rule England after he died in 1547, but Hertford quickly established himself as lord protector over nine-year-old King Edward, made himself the Duke of Somerset and ruled England as a virtual dictator for two years. In 1549, his enemies replaced him with the Duke of Northumberland and later had him beheaded for treason.

An important character in *The Prince and the Pauper*, Hertford first appears in chapter 5, when Tom CANTY meets the king. After Tom accidentally takes Prince Edward's place, Hertford dismisses the boy's claim not to be the true prince and becomes his steadfast and loyal adviser. He even fails to recognize his true nephew when he sees both boys side by side at the coronation in chapter 32. As "a man of merciful and generous impulses," Hertford approves Tom's desire to outlaw cruel punishments (chapter 15); however, once his real nephew establishes his identity at the coronation, he turns against Tom, ordering that he be "stripped and flung into the Tower."

Among the actors who have portrayed Hertford in films are Claude Rains (1937), Donald Houston (1962) and Harry Andrews (1977). The 1937 adaptation has Hertford learn early that Tom Canty is not the real prince, then plot to murder him.

Hibbard, Frederick (June 15, 1881, Canton, Ohio–December 12, 1950, Chicago, Illinois) Sculptor of the Mark Twain statue in Hannibal's Riverview Park. Hibbard was young and inexperienced in 1912, when he was chosen from among 12 sculptors competing to de-

Frederick's Hibbard's recently restored sculpture of Huck and Tom. (Photograph by author)

sign a larger-than-life statue of Mark Twain to overlook the Mississippi River. He was the only competitor to visit Hannibal to study the site. Several years later, he was commissioned to sculpt the bronze statue of Tom Sawyer and Huckleberry Finn at the base of CARDIFF HILL. This statue, financed by George A. Mahan, was dedicated in 1926.

Hicksville Ohio town mentioned in *Huckleberry Finn.* When Tom Sawyer arrives at the PHELPSES' house in chapter 33, he calls himself "William THOMPSON" and claims to be from "Hicksville, Ohio." Hicksville is the name of a real Ohio town in the state's northwestern Defiance County. Aside from the obvious allusion to the slang term for a country bumpkin, Mark Twain may have chosen the name as a wordplay on "BRICKSVILLE."

Higbie, Calvin H. (1831?–1914) A MINING partner of Mark Twain in NEVADA, Higbie is the person to whom the dedication of *Roughing It* is addressed. Trained as a civil engineer, Higbie lived for a period in California's TUOLUMNE COUNTY before going to AURORA, Nevada, in the spring of 1861. The following year, he and Mark Twain shared a cabin and worked claims together there. *Roughing It* mentions Higbie several times by his last name and describes him leading the narrator to MONO LAKE in pursuit of the mysterious WHITEMAN (chapter 39). Later, through Higbie's ingenuity, he and the narrator stake a claim to a rich "BLIND LEAD," only to lose it when Higbie again chases off after Whiteman (chapters 40–41).

Mark Twain never saw Higbie again after he left Aurora; however, a postscript to *Roughing It*'s chapter 41 alludes to hearing from him around 1870. During the mid-1870s, Higbie went to Greenville in northern California's Plumas County, where he spent the rest of his life. In March 1906, he wrote to Mark Twain seeking advice on selling his memoir about their mutual mining experiences to the NEW YORK HERALD. Mark Twain wanted to help, but found Higbie's manuscript so inaccurate that he discouraged its publication. Part of Higbie's memoir appeared in the *Saturday Evening Post* in 1920.

Hightower, Brer Minor character in *Huckleberry Finn.* Hightower is one of the nosy PIKESVILLE neighbors who visit the Phelpses after Jim's escape attempt in chapter 41. He enumerates all the jobs done in Jim's hut and says that 40 people could not have done that much work.

Hines Minor character in *Huckleberry Finn.* Hines lives several miles upriver from the town in which the WILKSES live. He appears only in chapter 29, in which he challenges the KING's claim to be Harvey WILKS. He wants to know why, if the King's claim to have come to town in a steamboat is true, he saw the King and Huck a few miles upriver, sitting in a canoe with a local man, Tim COLLINS. Hines's accusation leads to a quick inquest

at the inn. Afterward, he holds onto Huck when everyone goes to the graveyard to exhume Peter Wilks. When Wilks's coffin is opened, a sack of gold is found; Hines lets out a whoop and inadvertently releases Huck.

Hirst, Robert H. (August 11, 1941, New York, New York–) General editor of the MARK TWAIN PAPERS project (1980–). While doing postgraduate work in literature at the University of California at Berkeley, Hirst began working as an editor on the Mark Twain Papers project under Frederick ANDERSON in 1966. Ten years later, he received his doctorate after completing a dissertation on Mark Twain's *Innocents Abroad* and he started teaching English at UCLA. In January 1980—a year after Anderson died—Hirst returned to Berkeley to assume general editorship of the Mark Twain Papers.

As the first head of the Mark Twain project trained in literary editing, Hirst tightened the project's professional standards and combined the various facets of its complex publication program into a single definitive edition. Under his direction, the project launched its first systematic effort to locate and identify all known Mark Twain documents in order to publish a comprehensive edition of Mark Twain's correspondence. Hirst's plan to arrange *all* the letters in strict chronological order requires republication of the contents of several earlier volumes. Hirst has also implemented the policy of publishing all of Mark Twain's works with their original illustrations. As pressures have mounted to cut costs and accelerate the project's publication schedule, Hirst has remained committed to producing volumes that will meet the standards of future scholars, even if it means leaving some of the project's publication goals unmet.

Hitchcock, Lucius Wolcott (December 2, 1868, West Williamsfield, Ohio–June 18, 1942) Illustrator of the first book editions of Mark Twain's "A DOUBLE-BAR-RELLED DETECTIVE STORY" (1902) and "A HORSE'S TALE" (1907). Mark Twain owned several books that Hitchcock illustrated for Margaret Wade Deland, Basil King and Booth Tarkington.

hoax As a kind of subliterary genre, a hoax is a deliberate attempt to fool readers into accepting as fact something that has not happened. Long a staple of American folklore and humor, hoaxing enjoyed a new vogue in the 19th century with the spread of newspapers, which allowed news to travel more rapidly than it could be verified. Influenced by the example of P. T. BARNUM and such famous hoaxes as the Cardiff Giant (1869), Mark Twain himself became one of the great hoaxers of his time. The VIRGINIA CITY TERRITORIAL ENTERPRISE, for which he worked in the early 1860s, tolerated its writers' inventing of news where none existed. His friend Dan DE QUILLE, for example, fooled many readers with a story about a man freezing to death while crossing a torrid desert in a refrigerator suit.

While Mark Twain was at the *Enterprise,* he wrote stories about the discovery of a PETRIFIED MAN and about a gory MASSACRE. He later demonstrated how any wary reader should have seen these hoaxes as the impossibilities that they were. Another of his hoaxes of that period is "The Great Landslide Case," which he later modified to create chapter 34 of *Roughing It.* Many years later, he used "A DOUBLE-BARRELLED DETECTIVE STORY" (1902) to insert a hoax about how "far into the empty sky a solitary oesophagus slept upon the motionless wing." He also wrote stories about art hoaxes, including "Legend of the CAPITOLINE VENUS" and "IS HE LIVING OR IS HE DEAD?"

Hobson, Reverend Minor character in *Huckleberry Finn.* A Baptist minister, Hobson appears in chapters 24–25 and 27 to conduct the funeral service for Peter WILKS. He and his wife are among the townspeople taken in by the KING and DUKE's claim to be Wilks's brothers.

Hodges, Jimmy Figure mentioned in *Tom Sawyer.* An acquaintance of Tom, Hodges has died just before the novel begins (chapter 8). Tom feels sorry for himself and envies Hodges because he has been released from worldly cares.

Holbrook, Hal (February 17, 1925, Cleveland, Ohio–) ACTOR who has helped to define American perceptions of Mark Twain through four decades of performing as a 70-year-old Mark Twain. Holbrook's connection with Mark Twain began when he was a college drama student in Ohio. In 1947, he began touring the country performing two-person shows at schools—first with his wife and later with another actress. An early routine featured Holbrook as Mark Twain being interviewed by a reporter. After performing this sketch for several years, Holbrook met James B. POND's son, James B. Pond Jr., who had known Mark Twain during his own childhood. Pond coached Holbrook's vocal impersonation and helped him develop a one-man show, incorporating Jim BLAINE's old ram's tale, "THE AWFUL GERMAN LANGUAGE," "THE GOLDEN ARM" and other material. Holbrook studied Mark Twain's speaking career and learned as much as he could from Isabel LYON, Samuel C. Webster, Dorothy QUICK and other people who had known him. He settled on presenting Mark Twain as a 70-year-old man and adopted a cigar as a prop, though Mark Twain never smoked while speaking publicly. In March 1954, he launched *Mark Twain Tonight!* at a Pennsylvania college. He nearly abandoned this show when he got a regular acting job on daytime television in New York, but kept it going as a nightclub routine for several years. After appearances on national television shows and a tour with *Mark Twain Tonight!,* Holbrook opened his show off-Broadway in January 1958 and moved it to Broadway a year later. Over the next decade, he won a Tony Award for his Broadway show, released two rec-

ord albums of Mark Twain material and presented the show on network television (March 6, 1967). Since then, he has maintained a busy career in television and films and has continued to perform *Mark Twain Tonight!* on regular tours around the country, while helping to build the perception of Mark Twain as an elderly cigar-smoking curmudgeon in a WHITE SUIT.

Holland (Netherlands) Mark Twain visited Holland briefly in 1879. After several months in PARIS, he took his family through BELGIUM to Rotterdam in mid-July. They spent several days at Amsterdam, Haarlem and the Hague before leaving for England from Flushing on July 19. *A Tramp Abroad,* Mark Twain's book about this European trip, dismisses the country in one line; however, his NOTEBOOKS indicate that he was favorably impressed by Holland's beauty and cleanliness.

Hollis, Jim Minor character in *Tom Sawyer.* A friend of Tom, Jim is briefly mentioned in chapters 4, 6 and 22. In the latter chapter, he is one of the boys who gets religion during a revival while Tom has the measles.

Holmes, Oliver Wendell (August 29, 1809, Cambridge, Massachusetts–October 7, 1894, Boston, Massachusetts) New England writer. After studying medicine, Holmes became a professor of anatomy at Harvard (1847–82) and pioneered in the application of anesthetics. He was also a prolific poet noted for his humor, as well as a novelist and an essayist. In 1857, he helped launch the ATLANTIC MONTHLY with essays that he published the next year as *The Autocrat of the Breakfast-Table.* A strong admirer of Holmes's writing, Mark Twain especially liked this book, which he mentions in *The Gilded Age* (chapter 36).

Mark Twain saw Holmes occasionally in BOSTON. In 1869, he gave him a copy of *Innocents Abroad,* a book whose dedication he later believed that he had unconsciously plagiarized from Holmes's dedication in *Songs in Many Keys* (1862). He made "unconscious plagiarism" his topic when he spoke at a dinner celebrating Holmes's 70th birthday. Meanwhile, he embarrassed himself at a banquet commemorating J. G. WHITTIER's 70th birthday by giving a speech in which he caricatured Holmes, EMERSON and LONGFELLOW as ruffians, describing Holmes as being "fat as a balloon" with "double chins all the way down to his stomach." Holmes took no offense, however, and later published a poem in the *Critic* celebrating Mark Twain's 50th birthday.

Holmes, Sherlock Character in "A DOUBLE-BARRELLED DETECTIVE STORY." One of the most famous characters in literature, Sherlock Holmes was introduced by Sir Arthur Conan Doyle (1859–1930) in *A Study in Scarlet* in 1887. Mark Twain enjoyed the stories, but had a low regard for detectives. In *Following the Equator* (1897), he compares Sherlock Holmes's tracking talents unfavorably to those of native Australians (chapter 17). In addition to his brilliant deductive powers, Holmes was famous for bouncing back to life after dying. In Mark Twain's own detective story, Holmes visits the remote mining camp of HOPE CANYON—apparently to see his nephew Fetlock JONES. After he arrives, a man named Flint BUCKNER is murdered. Holmes investigates the crime, impressing everyone with his brilliant analysis of clues until the moment that he names Sammy Hillyer the murderer. Archy STILLMAN then steps forward and embarrasses Holmes by proving not only that Holmes's nephew is the real murderer, but that Holmes himself was Jones's unknowing accomplice. Holmes's humiliation is complete when Jones explains that he involved him in his crime because he was confident that his uncle would never be able to solve it.

In chapter 9, Holmes is reported to have been mistakenly hanged in San Bernardino; however, he is still alive in Hope Canyon. When a deranged man appears in camp claiming that Holmes has been unjustly persecuting him, a lynch mob forms. Aware of Holmes's reputation for not staying dead, the mob tries burning him at the stake until a sheriff stops them.

Holsatia   Steamship on which Mark Twain sailed from New York to Hamburg, GERMANY with his family in April 1878. Other passengers whom Mark Twain knew included Bayard TAYLOR and journalist Murat Halstead (1829–1908). *A Tramp Abroad* mentions the *Holsatia* and says that its two-week voyage was a pleasant one (chapters 1 and 27); however, the passage was actually stormy. Mark Twain was fascinated with the ship's ability to aim for a spot 3,000 miles away and hit it dead center, even in fog. The problem of hitting a distant landfall is central to "CAPTAIN STORMFIELD'S VISIT TO HEAVEN"—a story on which Mark Twain worked during the voyage.

Holy Land   To Jews and Christians, the Near Eastern region historically known as PALESTINE is the "Holy Land." A more narrow definition goes back to the Old Testament, which calls ancient Judea the "holy land" in the book of Zechariah (2:12). In any case, "Holy Land" is more a concept more than a precise term. In 11th-century Europe, for example, "holy land" became synonymous with the land in which Christ himself lived. When Mark Twain visited the Near East with the cruise ship QUAKER CITY in 1867, he traveled through LEBANON, western SYRIA and northern Palestine—all of which were then under the rule of TURKEY. *Innocents Abroad* frequently refers to the "Holy Land"—usually as a synonym for Palestine. Chapter 45 is explicit; it mentions "stepping over the border and entering the long-sought Holy Land" near BANIYAS. The next chapter comments on the Holy Land's size.

Though the Holy Land was to be the highlight of the *Quaker City* excursion, it disappointed most participants. *Innocents Abroad* attributes this to the high expectations that the excursionists brought with them after a lifetime of Protestant Bible training; their expectations were raised even higher by dishonest travel books, such as the works of William PRIME.

Mark Twain's interest in the Holy Land occasionally resurfaces in his fiction. In "THE GREAT REVOLUTION IN PITCAIRN" (1879), for example, a self-styled emperor creates a peerage filled with nobles taking their titles from Holy Land places: the Duke of Bethany, Archbishop of Bethlehem, Viscount Canaan, Grand Duke of Galilee and Countess of Jericho. *Tom Sawyer Abroad* defines "Holy Land": When Tom tells Huck that crusades are wars to "recover the Holy Land from the paynim," Huck wants to know "*which* Holy Land?" Tom answers that "there ain't but one" and explains that Christians have a duty to get it because it "was our folks, our Jews and Christians, that made it holy."

Holy Sepulcher, Church of the   Christian shrine in JERUSALEM. Built in the third century, the Church of the Holy Sepulcher covers most of the sites relating to

Innocents Abroad's sentimental narrator weeps over the tomb of his ancestor Adam at the Church of the Holy Sepulchre.

Christ's crucifixion, as well as such dubious sites as the tomb of ADAM and a column marking the "center of the Earth." Representatives of most Orthodox churches and of the Roman Catholic Church maintain separate chapels within the structure. Mark Twain visited the church around September 23, 1867. Chapters 53–55 of *Innocents Abroad* devote more space to it than to any other structure mentioned in the book; however, while they imply that Mark Twain visited the church several times, his private notes suggest that he was there for just one day. The church's general atmosphere struck him as gloomy; he found it spiritually unmoving and was fascinated by the latent hostility among the Christian sects sharing this most holy of Christian shrines.

In *Joan of Arc*, Joan invites her English enemies to join her on a crusade to rescue the Holy Sepulcher (book 2, chapter 14). Mark Twain also mentions the shrine in CHRISTIAN SCIENCE (book 2, chapter 8).

Holy Speculators, Church of the   Nickname that Mark Twain coined for Joseph TWICHELL's Asylum Hill Congregational Church during his first visit to Hartford, Connecticut in early 1868. An obvious wordplay on Jerusalem's Church of the HOLY SEPULCHER—which Mark Twain had recently visited—the nickname poked fun at the prosperity of the congregation's members.

Honey Lake Smith's   Historic STAGECOACH station on the Carson River, about 36 miles northeast of CARSON CITY, Nevada. When Mark Twain and several companions were returning from HUMBOLDT in mid-1862, a sudden flooding of the river stranded them at the station's inn for nine days. *Roughing It* offers an exaggerated account of their ordeal there, adding an invented ruffian named "ARKANSAS," who terrorizes the crowded inn (chapters 30–31). The station was named after its owner, who had come from Honey Lake, California. Its original buildings are now beneath the surface of artificial Lake Lahontan.

Hooker, Isabella Beecher (February 22, 1822, Litchfield, Connecticut–January 25, 1907, Hartford, Connecticut)   Suffragist leader. An eccentric spiritualist who hoped to head a matriarchal government, Hooker called a women's rights convention in Hartford in 1869 and helped pass a state law giving women the legal right to own property. She was a sister of Henry Ward BEECHER and Harriet Beecher STOWE, and married John Hooker (1816–1901). As a close friend of Mark Twain's future mother-in-law, she made Mark Twain a guest in her NOOK FARM home during his first visit to Hartford in early 1868. During the early 1870s, she rented her house to him.

Hooker, Miss   Name mentioned in *Huckleberry Finn*. In chapter 13, Huck and Jim leave several criminals stranded on the wreck of the derelict steamboat WALTER SCOTT. Huck then tries to get help for them ashore. To win the sympathy of a FERRYBOATMAN, he says that someone named "Miss Hooker" is stranded on the wreck along with his family and implies that she is related to Jim HORNBACK, a wealthy local man.

Hookerville   Fictional town mentioned in *Huckleberry Finn*. In chapter 11, Huck—disguised as a girl—tells Judith LOFTUS that he is from Hookerville, seven miles below ST. PETERSBURG. The town is also mentioned in "TOM SAWYER'S CONSPIRACY." Mark Twain's working notes for the latter story indicate that Hookerville is modeled on Saverton, a real Missouri town seven miles below Hannibal.

Hooper, Johnson Jones (June 9, 1815, Wilmington, North Carolina–June 7, 1862, Richmond, Virginia)   Southern journalist and humorist. After settling in Alabama, Hooper wrote widely reprinted stories about a comic character named Simon Suggs, an unprincipled rascal whose motto is "It is good to be shifty in a new country." Mark Twain was familiar with Hooper's *Some Adventures of Captain Simon Suggs, Late of the Tallapoosa Volunteers* (1846); he included a Suggs story in MARK TWAIN'S LIBRARY OF HUMOR. Another Suggs story, "The Captain Attends a Camp-Meeting," may have helped inspire the episode of the KING at the POKEVILLE camp meeting in chapter 20 of *Huckleberry Finn*.

Hope Canyon   Fictional CALIFORNIA mining camp in "A DOUBLE-BARRELLED DETECTIVE STORY." The scene of the novella's last seven chapters, Hope Canyon is in a deep gorge in a remote part of the ESMERALDA district (actually part of NEVADA). The two-year-old silver-mining camp has yet to prove itself and is unknown to the outside world. Its residents include about 200 miners, one white woman and child, several Chinese washermen and some INDIANS.

Hopkins, Aleck James   Alias used by Huck in *Huckleberry Finn*'s "RAFT CHAPTER" when he sneaks aboard a large raft. Immediately after he is discovered, he gives his name as Charles William ALLBRIGHT. On further questioning, he invents the name "Aleck James Hopkins" and says he lives on his father's trading scow.

Hopkins, Mother   Figure mentioned in *Tom Sawyer*. In chapter 6, Huck Finn alludes to Mother Hopkins as a reputed witch and tells Tom that his father, Pap FINN, once drove her off when she was "a-witching him." Although Mother Hopkins does not actually appear in the narrative, True WILLIAMS includes her portrait in his illustrations. In the play that Mark Twain adapted from the novel, Mother Hopkins is developed into a real witch.

Mark Twain used the name "Hopkins" for many characters, particularly in his posthumously published writings. In view of the fact that Huck cites Mother Hopkins as an expert on curing warts in *Tom Sawyer*, it may be significant that Mark Twain used the name "Wart Hopkins" for a character who foreshadowed Huck in "boy's manuscript."

Hopkins, P. (Philip?) Name of the alleged murderer in Mark Twain's MASSACRE HOAX (1863). Said to be a 42-year-old native of western Pennsylvania, Hopkins supposedly lived near CARSON CITY, Nevada with a wife and nine children. Though regarded as affable and nonviolent, he went mad after losing his fortune in San Francisco water company stock and brutally murdered most of his family. He then slit his own throat and rode into Carson City, dropping dead in front of the Magnolia Saloon.

In an article published in 1870, Mark Twain says that the person whose name he used for the alleged murderer in his hoax "was perfectly well known to every creature in the land as a *bachelor*." This remark almost certainly alludes to Peter Hopkins, the real owner of the saloon in front of which the fictional murderer dies. The original hoax lends a note of verisimilitude by feigning confusion over the murderer's name, which is rendered "P. Hopkins, or Philip Hopkins."

Hoppin, Augustus (July 13, 1828, Providence, Rhode Island–April 1, 1896, Flushing, New York) An illustrator of *The Gilded Age*. After beginning a legal career, Hoppin began drawing for magazines in the late 1840s and became a successful book illustrator. His work includes W. D. HOWELLS, *Their Wedding Journey* (1872) and C. D. WARNER, *Backlog Studies* (1873). A satirist and caricaturist of manners in his own right, he wrote *Ups and Downs on Land and Water* (1871), *Crossing the Atlantic* (1872) and other books. After Thomas NAST and William Thomas Smedley turned down offers to illustrate *The Gilded Age*, Hoppin was offered the job. To save money, he was asked to do only full-page prints, leaving the mass of smaller pictures to True WILLIAMS. Hoppin drew 16 pictures for the book, concentrating on the primary characters; each picture bears his clear signature.

Hornback, Jim Figure mentioned in *Huckleberry Finn*. In chapter 13, Huck meets a FERRYBOATMAN near BOOTH'S LANDING who mentions that Hornback is a wealthy local resident. Huck wants the ferryboatman to go to the wrecked steamboat WALTER SCOTT. He says that his family and a Miss HOOKER are stranded on the wreck, implying that Miss Hooker is related to Hornback. Hoping to be rewarded by Hornback, the ferryboatman takes his boat out.

Hornet Clipper ship whose 1866 sinking in the Pacific Mark Twain wrote about in several stories. The *Hornet* left New York City in January 1866 under Captain Josiah Mitchell (c. 1812–?). On May 3, 1866, it caught fire—apparently accidentally—during a dead calm in the Pacific, about 1,300 miles west of the Galapagos Islands and 3,000 miles east–southeast of HAWAII. Its 31 passengers and crew members crowded into two lifeboats with only 10 days' rations. All 15 men on Mitchell's boat reached Hawaii in late June.

Mark Twain was bedridden with a fever in Honolulu when the *Hornet* survivors arrived, but with the help of Anson BURLINGAME, he recorded their accounts and put a dispatch to the SACRAMENTO UNION aboard a ship leaving the next morning. His resulting scoop, which appeared in the *Union* on July 19, was a sensation that was being reprinted across the country by the time he returned to San Francisco himself. Citing the story's success, he persuaded the *Union* to pay him 10 times his normal rate for it. By then, he had gathered more information from Mitchell and other survivors with whom he had returned from Hawaii. He used this material to write "Forty-three Days in an Open Boat," which he published in HARPER'S MAGAZINE in December. He returned to the subject a final time in a 1899 essay, "MY DÉBUT AS A LITERARY PERSON."

"THE GREAT REVOLUTION IN PITCAIRN" (1879) mentions an apparently fictional ship named *Hornet* that supposedly visited Pitcairn during the late 1870s under a captain named Ormsby.

Horr, Elizabeth (c. 1790, New York, New York–1873) First schoolteacher of Mark Twain. The wife of a Hannibal cooper, Benjamin W. Horr (c. 1789–1870), Elizabeth Horr ran a small private school that Mark Twain began attending before he was five. She was assisted by daughter Lizzie and others, including Mary Ann NEWCOMB. Mark Twain had fond memories of Horr. In 1870 he sent her a copy of *Innocents Abroad*. In a 1906 autobiographical dictation, he recalled her half-accurate prediction that he would become president of the United States and would "stand in the presence of kings unabashed."

"A Horse's Tale" Novella written in 1905 and published in 1906. One of the last major pieces of fiction that Mark Twain published in his lifetime, "A Horse's Tale" ranks with "A DOG'S TALE" among his most melodramatic and sentimental works. Its primary setting is the fictional Fort Paxton, which seems to be in the Rocky Mountains of Montana or Wyoming. No time period is specified, but allusions to historical persons and events suggest that it takes place in the late 1860s—after the Civil War and before the completion of the transcontinental railroad in 1869. The story uses the historical Seventh Cavalry, but not George Armstrong Custer, its only commander. One of its characters is a "young" Buffalo Bill, who is clearly based on the historical Buffalo Bill CODY, though he scouted for the Fifth Cavalry during the late 1860s and early 1870s, not for the Seventh Cavalry as the story states. The narrative concludes in Spain, taking its bullfight descriptions from John HAY's *Castillian Days*. Mark Twain also used the story to pillory Henry A. Butters (?–1908), an officer of

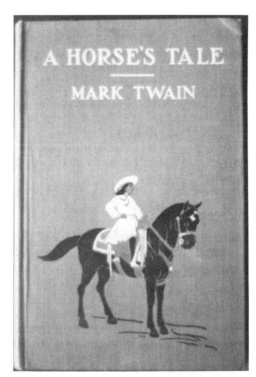

The first edition of A Horse's Tale, *illustrated by Lucius Hitchcock.* (Courtesy, Kevin Bochynski)

the PLASMON company, who appears as the horse thief "Hank Butters" in chapter 6.

SYNOPSIS

Containing about 19,750 words, "A Horse's Tale" is divided into 15 numbered chapters. The narrative opens at the fictional Fort Paxton headquarters of the Seventh Cavalry, with SOLDIER BOY introducing himself as Buffalo Bill's favorite scout horse. Shortly afterward, Cathy ALISON, the orphaned niece of Brigadier General Thomas Alison, arrives from France. She quickly becomes a favorite among both soldiers and local Indians and is the special pet of Buffalo Bill, who teaches her to ride. After Soldier Boy saves Cathy from wolves, Buffalo Bill gives him to her. When General Alison retires, he takes Cathy and Soldier Boy to SPAIN, where Cathy elects to remain with her Aunt Mercedes. Shortly after they arrive, Soldier Boy is stolen. About six months later, Cathy sees a bull gore Soldier Boy in a bullfight ring. When she rushes to her horse's side, she too is fatally gored.

Information not given within the chapters—such as Buffalo Bill's last name—generally appears below within parentheses. However, for the sake of simplicity, the synopsis occasionally mentions personal names where they do not appear within the chapters. For example, chapter 8 is subtitled, "The Scout-Start. BB and Lieuten-ant-General Alison," but does not mention Buffalo Bill or Cathy by name within its text.

Chapter 1
Introducing himself as the favorite horse of Buffalo Bill (CODY), Soldier Boy boasts about his pedigree, strength and speed as a scout horse. Just returned from a 40-day scouting expedition up the Big Horn, he is at Fort Paxton, where the Seventh Cavalry is garrisoned. The fort awaits the arrival of the orphaned niece of its commander, Brigadier General (Thomas) Alison.

Chapter 2
Mercedes, the Spanish sister-in-law of the general's deceased brother, writes to Alison from ROUEN, France. She explains that Catherine's parents wanted their daughter to go to him because he is about to retire and because her own health is broken. Mercedes says that Cathy is exceptionally high-minded and good-hearted, has an acute sense of justice and loves animals.

Chapter 3
General Alison writes to his mother in San Bernardino (California) about the arrival of Cathy, who has quickly conquered everyone with her winning ways. The Indians have already nicknamed her "firebug." The general describes Cathy's first meeting with Buffalo Bill and Soldier Boy.

Chapter 4
Cathy writes to her Aunt Mercedes about her wonderful life at the fort. She loves the plains, the animals and the Indians, and tells how Buffalo Bill took her on Soldier Boy to Chief Thunder-Bird's and Chief White Cloud's camps. She is learning to ride and shoot a bow.

Chapter 5
Alison writes to Mercedes, describing Cathy's great popularity. Both the Seventh Cavalry and the Ninth Dragoons have adopted her and made her an officer. Despite her special treatment, Cathy is popular with other children, whose lives she has made more exciting. Under Buffalo Bill's tutelage, she has become an extraordinary rider. To help care for her, Alison's mother has sent Mammy Dorcas, a servant who has been with the family since she was a slave. Dorcas and Cathy are already as devoted to each other as mother and daughter.

Chapter 6
Soldier Boy meets another horse, a Mexican Plug (called "Mongrel" in the next chapter), who is the property of a horse thief named Hank Butters, the partner of Blake Haskins. Familiar with Soldier Boy's reputation, the Plug is impressed by his claim of descent from fossils. Soldier Boy also boasts about Cathy's riding skill and mentions that she refused to ride him in a steeplechase in order to give the other children a chance to win. The only person who has ridden Soldier Boy for over two months, Cathy has been training her own army unit, "the 16th," or "1st Battalion Rocky Mountain Rangers,"

which has elected her lieutenant-general and bugler. Soldier Boy also talks about the cavalry's dog Shekels.

Chapter 7
Soldier Boy tells Shekels about Mongrel, the Mexican Plug, who overheard the horse thieves planning to get Buffalo Bill.

Chapter 8
Buffalo Bill compliments Cathy on her army unit, the Rangers, and she offers to have this unit serve as his guard of honor when he goes to Fort Clayton.

Chapter 9
Soldier Boy tells Shekels that after Cathy escorted Buffalo Bill to Fort Clayton, she learned that he had been shot in an ambush, then immediately rode to his rescue. After four hours in the saddle, she went to sleep, fell and broke her arm. Soldier Boy stood by through the night, fighting off hungry wolves. The next morning Buffalo Bill arrived on a litter pulled by Mongrel and another horse that he and the scout Thorndike got when they killed Blake Haskins and his fellow tough (Butters). When Buffalo Bill saw the wolves that Soldier Boy killed, he gave the horse to Cathy in return for a kiss.

Chapter 10
While Cathy convalesces, Dorcas tells Alison that Cathy is having too much company and is too busy trying to supervise her army unit. She also tries to persuade Alison that animals talk to each other, citing Shekels as an example. When Dorcas says that Cathy wants the general to stand in for her at the court-martial of one of her child officers, Alison makes up an excuse to delay the proceeding, hoping that Cathy will get well soon enough to preside herself.

Chapter 11
Several months later, Thorndike—who now rides Mongrel—talks with Antonio, an Andalusian. Antonio reminisces about Spain and bullfighting, which he considers the grandest sport.

Chapter 12
Mongrel and another horse named Sage Brush discuss man's cruelty to dumb animals. They wonder if bullfighting is a religious service.

Chapter 13
General Alison has taken Cathy, Dorcas and Soldier Boy to Spain. He describes their travels in a letter to his mother, reporting that Cathy has decided to stay with her Aunt Mercedes. Alison himself is not sure if he and Dorcas will ever return home. When Cathy left the post, she was given a grand military send-off, complete with the bands playing and escorts. In a postscript, Alison mentions that Soldier Boy was stolen the previous night.

Chapter 14
Soldier Boy talks to himself. Since being stolen five or six months earlier, he has traveled almost constantly and is worn down. He has changed hands perhaps a

dozen times, each time going to a lower-level master. Now a bony scarecrow, he thinks that his end may be near and wants only to see *her* again.

Chapter 15
General Alison writes to Mrs. Drake, the wife of the Seventh Cavalry's colonel. He reports that Cathy has been on the lookout for her horse. He also describes how a bull has ripped open a horse in the ring; as the animal drags its bowels on the ground, Cathy issues a bugle call and rushes into the ring, where the horse falls at her feet—just before the bull gets her. She is carried away unconscious. Before she dies at home, she asks for "Taps" to be blown.

BACKGROUND AND PUBLISHING HISTORY

According to A. B. PAINE, actress Minnie Maddern Fiske (1865–1932) wrote to Mark Twain in September 1905, asking him to help her campaign against bullfighting in Spain. She hoped that he might write something similar to "A DOG'S TALE," which had been used by antivivisectionists. That same month Mark Twain began writing "A Horse's Tale." HARPER'S MAGAZINE published the story in two installments in August–September 1906, with five illustrations by Lucius Wolcott HITCHCOCK. In October 1907, Harper's published *A Horse's Tale* as a 153-page book, using Hitchcock's illustrations. Paine later included the story in *The Mysterious Stranger and Other Stories* (1922).

Hotchkiss, Oliver   One of several fictional characters that Mark Twain modeled on his brother Orion Clemens, Hotchkiss is the head of the household in which the marvelous stranger FORTY-FOUR is rooming in "SCHOOLHOUSE HILL." The description of Hotchkiss fits Orion in almost every particular: He is kind, patient, generous, unenvious, eager to learn, and constantly changing his beliefs. His wife, Hannah, however, is just the opposite in this last regard. Typical of his dreamy nature, Hotchkiss is so engrossed in a book on spiritualism the night that a great blizzard rages outside his door that he fails to notice it until it is brought forcefully to his attention. When he sees Forty-four go out into the storm against his orders, he concludes that the boy will die and calls everyone together to hold a seance. After Forty-four returns safely, he identifies himself as the son of Satan and tells Hotchkiss that he wants to work to alleviate the burden mankind has been carrying as a result of Adam's fall. Hotchkiss eagerly accepts his invitation to help him in the task just as the manuscript ends.

Hotchkiss, Sister   Minor character in *Huckleberry Finn*. The most gossipy neighbor of the Phelpses in chapter 41.

Hotten, John Camden (September 12, 1832, London–June 14, 1873, London)   English book publisher. After spending seven years in America, Hotten opened a LONDON bookshop in 1855 that he built into a publishing firm. In 1866, he signed his first major author, poet Algernon Charles Swinburne, with whom he set his future standard of shady dealing. Taking advantage of the lack of international copyright protection for American authors, Hotten began pirating Mark Twain's books in 1870, beginning with *Innocents Abroad*. Over the next three years, he published several additional volumes, including EYE OPENERS, SCREAMERS and CHOICE HUMOROUS WORKS. Mark Twain countered by authorizing George A. ROUTLEDGE to publish his books in England. When he visited England in 1872, he published a letter in the *Spectator* denouncing Hotten as a pirate, dubbing him "John Camden Hottentot."

Also an antiquarian and an amateur scholar, Hotten wrote a slang dictionary and books on Macaulay, Thackeray and DICKENS, and on other subjects. He reputedly choked to death when Ambrose Bierce angrily confronted him about a bad check. His widow sold his firm to Andrew CHATTO.

House, Edward H. (Ned) (September 5, 1836, Boston, Massachusetts–December 17, 1901, Tokyo, Japan) Journalist, musician and dramatist. Mark Twain met House while the latter was writing for the NEW YORK TRIBUNE in early 1867; House accompanied him on his first visit to Charles DUNCAN when he inquired about the QUAKER CITY cruise. Three years later, House went to Japan, a country with which he would develop a long association. Meanwhile, he read Mark Twain's *The Prince and the Pauper* manuscript in 1880 and gave him several helpful suggestions. A decade later, he claimed that Mark Twain had given him sole rights to dramatize this novel and filed an injunction to stop Daniel FROHMAN's New York production of *The Prince and the Pauper*. The ensuing bad publicity led to House's estrangement from Mark Twain, who felt that House had betrayed him.

"House of Death" Derelict house in *Huckleberry Finn*. In chapter 9, while Huck and Jim are living on JACKSON's ISLAND, they find a two-story frame house brought down the river by the floods. They enter a second-story room at night, but find it too dark to explore. At daybreak, they reenter the room and discover a man who has been shot to death, evidently in the midst of a drunken card game. Jim will not allow Huck to look at the dead man's face. They carry off candles, kitchen utensils, tools and other practical supplies. In chapter 11, Huck uses a dress taken from the house to disguise himself as a girl when he visits Judith LOFTUS. In chapter 43, Jim finally tells Huck that the dead man he saw in the house was his father, Pap FINN.

The term "House of Death" is frequently used in modern Mark Twain criticism; however, it does not appear within *Huckleberry Finn*. The original heading to chapter 9 uses "The Floating House."

Hovey, Deacon Lot Minor character in *Huckleberry Finn*. A friend of Peter WILKS who, along with his wife, is taken in by the KING and DUKE in chapters 24–25.

"How I Edited an Agricultural Paper Once" Sketch written for the GALAXY (July 1870) and later republished in SKETCHES, NEW AND OLD and in MARK TWAIN'S LIBRARY OF HUMOR. Similar in tone to "JOURNALISM IN TENNESSEE," this 2,225-word sketch parodies the notion that newspaper editors must know anything. It recalls two moments in Mark Twain's life when he temporarily took over a newspaper. As a youth in Hannibal, he ran his brother Orion's paper and boosted circulation with facetious attacks on a rival. After his unhappy brother returned, he left town permanently. A decade later, he left NEVADA under similar circumstances—according to *Roughing It* (chapter 55). The sketch also anticipates Mark Twain's later playful writings on agriculture. Chapter 70 of *Roughing It*, for example, is built around a joke about turnips growing on vines. In *Connecticut Yankee*, Hank Morgan creates a "Department of Public

The temporary editor of the agricultural paper fancies that one of his readers is displeased.

Morals and Agriculture" in Camelot (chapter 9); when King ARTHUR later pretends to be a farmer he makes remarks about agriculture as outrageous as those of this sketch's narrator (chapter 34).

SYNOPSIS

The narrator, an editor of 14 years' experience, temporarily takes over an agricultural paper during its editor's vacation. After he publishes his first issue, an agitated old gentleman reads his editorial about shaking turnips from trees and angrily protests that turnips do not grow on trees. When the editor amends his statement to say that turnips grow on vines, the man shreds the paper and stomps out. The next caller tells the editor to read aloud his remarks about the "guano bird" and other nonsense, then leaves satisfied that he is not the one who is crazy.

The regular editor returns outraged that his paper's reputation has been injured. Acknowledging that the narrator's issue has had a record sale, he says he prefers not to be famous for lunacy and cites some of the paper's most bizarre statements—about a molting season for cows and other matters. When he complains that the narrator never told him he knew nothing about agriculture, the narrator protests that this is the first time he has ever heard of a man's having to know anything to edit a newspaper. To prove his point, he asks who writes drama critiques, book reviews, and editorials on finance and Indian campaigns? The answer is people who know nothing about these subjects. He then resigns.

"How to Make History Dates Stick" Posthumously published essay written in SWEDEN in 1899. Aimed at helping to teach children historical dates, this 5,425-word essay explains two systems based on visual clues. The first is one that Mark Twain used in 1883 to teach his own children the dates of ENGLAND's monarchs. While his family was at QUARRY FARM, he staked out 817 feet along a carriage-road to represent the 817 years that had elapsed since William the Conqueror (1066), adding signposts to mark each reign. As his children mastered these dates, they added more signs to represent other historical events.

His second system uses a technique that he developed in his LECTURING days, when he drew pictures to help remember his lecture topics. This system requires only a pen and small squares of colored paper. Though he thinks it essential that each person draw his own pictures, he suggests specific images to get readers started and provides his own crude drawings as samples. For example, he recommends drawing pictures of a whale and the appropriate dates on 21 slips of white paper to represent each year of William the Conqueror's reign. Like "William," "whale" starts with a "W" and the huge animal symbolizes the magnitude of William's reign. For succeeding monarchs, he suggests such images as a hen

for Henry, a lion for Richard, an editor for Edward and a burning martyr for Bloody Mary. From there, readers are trusted to continue on their own.

The essay first appeared in HARPER'S MAGAZINE in December 1914. A. B. PAINE later included it in *What Is Man? and Other Essays of Mark Twain* (1917).

"How to Tell a Story" Essay written and published in 1895. This often-reprinted 2,070-word essay sums up Mark Twain's views on the proper recitation of "humorous" stories, which he defines as an American invention differing from French and English "witty" or "comic" stories in that they depend for effect on the *manner* of their telling, not their *matter*. Unlike the telling of a comic story, telling a humorous story properly is a difficult art. It requires stringing together incongruities and absurdities of which the teller is seemingly unaware. Its other ingredients include "slurring" its main point, dropping in studied or incongruous remarks, and pausing at the right moment—all techniques that Artemus WARD had mastered.

"The Wounded Soldier" is an example of a witty story that relies on its "nub": A soldier carrying a wounded comrade does not realize that his friend's head has been shot off until someone tells him. When he sees the decapitated body, he exclaims, "But he told me it was his *leg!*" As an example of a humorous story, Mark Twain retells the "GOLDEN ARM" story in full, while explaining the crucial importance of the pause.

This essay does not mention the JUMPING FROG STORY, although it is precisely the kind of humorous story that Mark Twain has in mind. Mark Twain wrote this essay shortly after publishing *Joan of Arc*, which contains another yarn that fits his humorous story definition perfectly—even though it is told by a Frenchman, Joan's uncle Laxart, who "drone[s] out the most tedious and empty tale one ever heard," without suspecting that it is "anything but dignified and valuable history." Like Simon Wheeler's frog story, Laxart's tale concerns remarkable animals—a bull that he rides to a funeral, and a swarm of bees that sting him so badly that his face looks like a raisin pudding. Joan nearly dies laughing at the ridiculous story, but her uncle has no idea *what* she is laughing at (book 2, chapter 36).

After appearing in the October 3, 1895 issue of *Youth's Companion*, this essay was collected in two different anthologies titled *How to Tell a Story and Other Essays*, one of which was later reissued as LITERARY ESSAYS.

Howard, Pembroke Minor character in *Pudd'nhead Wilson*. A middle-aged bachelor, Howard ranks as DAWSON'S LANDING's "recognized second citizen" after Judge York DRISCOLL, with whom he grew up in VIRGINIA. Like Driscoll, he is first and foremost a gentleman, always ready to defend what he believes on the field of honor. Although Howard contrasts with the freethinking Driscoll in being a determined Presbyterian, the two men are fast friends. In chapter 12, they are fishing together when Driscoll learns of his nephew Tom DRIS-COLL's failure to challenge Luigi CAPELLO to a DUEL. When the judge takes on Capello himself, Howard acts as his second (chapter 14). Considered the town's "great lawyer," Howard is the public prosecutor at Capello brothers' murder trial in chapter 20.

Howells, John Mead (August 14, 1868, Cambridge, Massachusetts–September 11, 1959, Kittery Point, Maine) Architect who designed "STORMFIELD," Mark Twain's house in REDDING, Connecticut. The son of W. D. HOWELLS, John Howells knew Mark Twain from his early childhood. After studying at Harvard and Paris's Ecole des Beaux-Arts, he practiced architecture with I. N. Phelps Stokes in New York City. In mid-1906, Mark Twain commissioned him to design and build an Italianate house at Redding, then paid little attention as Howells and his own secretary, Isabel LYON, supervised construction. After World War I, Howells achieved fame by overseeing the rebuilding of the University of Brussels with Raymond Hood (1881–1934). In 1922, he, Hood and J. André Fouilhoux won a competition to design and build Chicago's Tribune Tower.

Howells, William Dean (March 1, 1837, Martin's Ferry, Ohio–May 11, 1920, New York, New York) Novelist, critic and editor. In six decades as an author, Howells wrote more than 100 volumes of poetry, travel, essays, criticism, biography, drama, sketches, stories and novels. In a long parallel career as an editor, he knew the leading literary figures of his time and worked to introduce new writers. He ended his career as the first president of the American Academy of Arts and Letters (1908–20).

Howells was also an intimate friend of Mark Twain, whose position in American literature he helped to secure. Their early lives had much in common. Both grew up in the Midwest, worked as printers as boys, became journalists and educated themselves through reading. While their adult careers took different paths, they also shared similar personal problems that brought them closer. Both had semi-invalid wives and lost daughters at an early age. During four decades of friendship, they corresponded voluminously and often exchanged visits.

While working for Columbus's *Ohio State Journal* in 1860, Howells wrote a campaign biography of Abraham LINCOLN, who rewarded him with a consulship in VENICE, Italy (1861–65). After using his Italian sojourn to begin writing seriously, Howells returned to the United States when the CIVIL WAR ended and became assistant editor of New York City's new *Nation* magazine. Early the next year, he became James T. Fields's assistant editor at Boston's ATLANTIC MONTHLY and he succeeded Fields as editor in 1871. As arbiter of what went into the nation's leading literary magazine, as a frequent book reviewer and as an increasingly respected author in his own right,

William Dean Howells, who later called Mark Twain the "Lincoln of our literature," around 1908. (Courtesy, Library of Congress, Pictures & Prints Division)

Howells became one of the most influential figures in American literature. He used his influence to broaden the *Atlantic*'s selection of writers, while encouraging realism over sentimentalism in fiction.

While he was assistant editor at the *Atlantic*, Howells had a free hand in choosing books to review. In 1869, he used his freedom in an unlikely way by giving a lengthy notice to a SUBSCRIPTION BOOK—Mark Twain's *Innocents Abroad*. Mark Twain so appreciated the favorable review that he made an unannounced visit to the *Atlantic*'s office to thank the anonymous reviewer personally at the end of the year. Howells vividly recalls the meeting in *My Mark Twain*.

Howells helped Mark Twain's literary career in several ways. Mark Twain bounced ideas off him and had him read and correct his manuscripts. Howells encouraged Mark Twain to move his work along and occasionally discouraged him from publishing manuscripts that might prove embarrassing—such as the "1,002D ARABIAN NIGHT." Howells also reviewed most of Mark Twain's books, assuring them serious and favorable notice. Finally, as an editor, Howells drew Mark

Twain into the pages of the *Atlantic*, giving him the literary respectability that he craved. The two writers also collaborated on several projects, but only MARK TWAIN'S LIBRARY OF HUMOR came to anything.

After leaving the *Atlantic* in 1881, Howells concentrated on writing novels. Among his books, he regarded *The Rise of Silas Lapham* (1885), *Indian Summer* (1886) and *A Hazard of New Fortunes* (1890) as his best work. *Silas Lapham* shows curious parallels with Mark Twain's life. Like Mark Twain, Lapham has a wife more refined than he who acts as his conscience. Though he hungers for acceptance into polite Eastern society, Lapham embarrasses himself with an inappropriate speech at a Boston society dinner—much as Mark Twain did at WHITTIER's 70th birthday banquet. Perhaps prophetically, Lapham experiences much of the same bad luck that was to afflict Mark Twain's later business career. The novel also contains a direct quote from Mark Twain's JUMPING FROG STORY; one of Lapham's daughters says of her sister's suitor, "I don't see any p'ints about that frog that's any better than any other frog" (chapter 7).

Howells returned to magazine work in 1886, when he began writing the "Editor's Study" for HARPER'S MAGAZINE (1886–92). In 1888, he relocated to New York City and spent his last 20 years writing the "Easy Chair" for *Harper's*. In 1906, Mark Twain repaid part of his debt to Howells with an essay in *Harper's* praising him as one of the finest writers in the English language. Shortly after Mark Twain's death four years later, Howells published *My Mark Twain*, an affectionate memoir that ends: "Emerson, Longfellow, Lowell, Holmes—I knew them all and all the rest of our sages, poets, seers, critics, humorists; they were like one another and like other literary men; but Clemens was sole, incomparable, the Lincoln of our literature."

Huck and Tom; or, The Further Adventures of Tom Sawyer (1918)   Film starring Jack Pickford (1896–1933) as Tom Sawyer and Robert Gordon as Huck Finn. A sequel to the previous year's film *Tom Sawyer*, this five-reel silent film completes the story of Mark Twain's original *Tom Sawyer*. Its highlights include the grave-robbing scene, INJUN JOE's trial, and Tom and Becky's adventure in the CAVE.

"Huck Finn and Tom Sawyer among the Indians" Unfinished novel. A direct sequel to *Huckleberry Finn*, this roughly 18,000-word fragment begins a story that Mark Twain started writing in July 1884. While hoping to cash in on the popularity of Western stories, Mark Twain evidently intended to attack romantic notions about INDIANS and life in the West. Once he started, however, the story took him in a direction that he could not easily go, and he abruptly abandoned it.

As the narrator, Huck Finn picks up exactly where he left off in *Huckleberry Finn*—which ends with him afraid that Aunt Sally PHELPS will try to adopt and civilize him. His suggestion that he may have "to light out for the Territory" appears to anticipate the new story, which takes him, Tom and JIM deep into the Central Plains region that later became NEBRASKA.

SYNOPSIS

Chapter 1
Tom and Huck are growing bored at the Phelpses' farm when Aunt POLLY calls them back to Missouri. Immediately after they get home, Polly takes Tom, his brother Sid and his cousin Mary to the western side of the state to visit relatives on a hemp farm. Huck goes along to keep Tom company and Jim joins them, fearing that he might be put back into slavery by crooked white men if he remains behind. At the hemp farm, Tom again grows bored and proposes to go west to travel among INDIANS. Huck and Jim are content where they are, but by extolling Indian virtues, Tom wins Jim over, and Huck agrees to go along to avoid being left alone.

Chapter 2
The adventurers quietly make their preparations, buying provisions, barter goods and mules that they stash in an abandoned house. When a full moon arrives, they slip away with their pack train. After leaving Aunt Polly a note telling her that they will be gone, but not where they are going, they head west into the Plains, traveling by night for four days to avoid detection. About six days out, they encounter a family emigrating from southern Missouri to Oregon who invite them to join their party. The MILLS family has three grown sons and two daughters—seven-year-old Flaxy and beautiful 17-year-old Peggy, on whom everyone dotes. Tom and Huck learn how to ride, rope and shoot from the brothers during a week of traveling. At the Platte River they find a small Indian camp.

Chapter 3
The emigrants camp by the river, letting their horses rest while awaiting Peggy's sweetheart, Brace JOHNSON, an experienced frontiersman. Everyone becomes friendly with the five Indian men (later identified as Oglala Sioux), who satisfy all of Tom's romantic ideas about Indians. They are manly, friendly, gallant and entertaining. Peggy baffles Huck by showing him a knife that Brace gave her for killing herself if she is ever captured by Indians.

After several days, Tom and Huck ask the Indians if they can visit their community and are thrilled to learn that they plan a buffalo hunt for the next day. When the Indians notice Peggy staring off into the distance, they ask what she is looking for and seem perturbed when Huck says that *seven* friends are expected. That evening the Indians come to eat with the emigrants in war dress; Tom suspects that something is amiss when the Indians do not smoke. As he goes to warn the Millses, the Indians suddenly kill everyone but the girls and Jim, whom they take prisoner, and Huck and Tom, who escape into the woods. The next morning, the boys are left alone. With all the food and pack animals gone, they are in a desperate situation.

Chapter 4

Accepting responsibility for getting Jim into his predicament, Tom pledges not to turn back until he rescues him, and Huck insists on helping. For several days, the boys forage for food while awaiting Brace Johnson. When Brace finally arrives, hearing that Indians have captured Peggy makes him frantic, but Huck calms him down by assuring him that Peggy has her knife, though he is not really sure about this. Huck asks Brace *why* he wishes Peggy were dead and is satisfied by the answer—which we do not hear. When he later finds Peggy's knife, he hides it from Brace.

Chapter 5

After burying the massacre victims, Brace and the boys discuss the disaster. Details about the Indians' behavior convince Brace—who grew up among Indians—that the massacre was probably a private vendetta avenging the murder of someone by a white person. After he locates the Indians' trail, he and boys strike off in pursuit of the killers. Several days later, they find an abandoned camp; Brace sends Huck and Tom ahead without him, asking them to find and bury Peggy's body. After Huck tells Tom why Peggy's death is so important to Brace, Tom agrees to join Huck in pretending to find and bury her. They let four hours pass, then return and tell Brace that they have followed his instructions.

Chapter 6

Four more days on the trail bring Brace, Huck and Tom closer to the Indians and teach the boys more about Brace's background and his respect for Indian religion. When Brace realizes that he has accidentally eaten antelope meat on a Friday, violating an Indian superstition, he becomes angry with himself for the bad luck that this carelessness will bring. The next morning, Tom gets lost in a heavy fog.

Chapter 7

Brace searches for Tom while Huck tends a fire that serves as a beacon. After a while, Brace returns with a dehydrated white man whom he has found wandering in a delirium. He leaves the stranger with Huck, telling him not to let the man eat or drink more than an occasional spoonful of soup, and goes back to look for Tom. During the night, Huck leaves the tent to tend the mules and ends up spending hours looking for a missing animal as a storm kicks up. He returns to find that his fire is out and it is raining too hard to restart it. When he enters the tent, a sudden flash of lightning illuminates the grinning face of the stranger, who has gorged himself to death on food. At dawn, Brace returns with Tom. After they bury the stranger, they rest for a day or two to allow the exhausted Tom to recuperate.

Chapter 8

Brace and the boys continue their quest, which takes them up the North Fork of the Platte River, approaching Wyoming, where they find signs of a large party of horsemen. While Huck is alone tending mules, two white men chasing an antelope stop when they see him. Sensing that the men are thieves after his mules, Huck leads them directly to Brace. The men shoot at Huck, then Brace overtakes and kills both of them. Farther up the river, Brace, Huck and Tom stumble upon the rustlers' camp. When they go back down the river, a flash flood roars down the valley. Avoiding its path, they watch the rustlers' camp wash past and scramble up a hill to save themselves.

Chapter 9

Floodwaters turn the hill into an island, where Brace and the boys spend eight days waiting for the water to recede. When they return to the trail, they come upon the remains of a large, recently occupied Indian camp, in which Huck and Tom find traces of the Indians who killed the Millses. Brace finds a white woman's shoe-print, but does not suspect it could be Peggy's. By now thoroughly disenchanted with Indians, Tom finally admits that "book Injuns and real Injuns is different." In order to convince Indians that he is crazy, Brace sews small dried animals all over his clothes. As he and the boys pick up the Indians' trail again, the manuscript ends.

BACKGROUND AND PUBLISHING HISTORY

Mark Twain began writing this story while correcting proofs for *Huckleberry Finn* in July 1884. His abrupt abandonment of the story—in which he invested considerable research—remains puzzling. Walter BLAIR, who edited the MARK TWAIN PAPERS project edition of the story, suggests that Mark Twain set an impossible task for himself. Trying to write a realistic story about Indians abducting a white woman was leading him toward a frank treatment of rape—a subject about which he was incapable of writing. On the other hand, Mark Twain had a history of setting aside manuscripts for years before finishing them. In 1889 or 1890 he had the entire manuscript of this story typeset on the PAIGE COMPOSITOR and printed—a possible indication that he still intended to complete it.

For unknown reasons, the pages of Mark Twain's original manuscript were dispersed among six locations, with most of the surviving pages held by the Detroit Public Library. The story was first published in the December 20, 1968 issue of *Life* magazine, with illustrations by James McMullan. The following year Universal Studios bought its film rights. Meanwhile, the story appeared in its first book edition, *Hannibal, Huck & Tom* (1969), edited by Walter Blair. The story is also in the popular edition, *Huck Finn and Tom Sawyer among the Indians and Other Unfinished Stories* (1989), edited by Blair and Dahlia Armon.

huckleberry   Nineteenth-century slang for an inconsequential person, "huckleberry" is the name of a variety of deep-blue edible berry (genus *Gaylussacia*) native to North America. Huckleberries are often confused with blueberries, which are softer in texture and are filled with tiny seeds. The common wild huckleberry (*G. resinosa*) flourishes in eastern states, but is not native to the Missouri region, where Huckleberry Finn got his name. Like blueberries, huckleberries are eaten both raw and baked in muffins, breads, or pies. Huckleberry pie is often called "fly pie." At the end of the 1960 MGM film *The Adventures of Huckleberry Finn*, an Arkansas sheriff invites Huck (Eddie Hodges) back to his house for freshly baked "huckleberry pie"—unlikely fare for that region in the 1840s. Huck responds sensibly by snorting at the invitation. Mark Twain himself did not discover huckleberries until 1868. In "Morality and Huckleberries," a piece he wrote for the SAN FRANCISCO ALTA CALIFORNIA from Hartford in September 1868, he mentioned that huckleberries were in season and that this was his "first acquaintance with them."

In the novel *Huckleberry Finn*, only two characters call Huck by his full name, "Huckleberry." Miss WATSON uses the name four times when she admonishes him to behave in chapters 1 and 4. The KING uses it once in chapter 24.

In *Connecticut Yankee*, an article in the CAMELOT WEEKLY HOSANNAH alludes to Sir Palamides the Saracen as "no huckleberry himself" (chapter 26).

Huckleberry Finn, Adventures of (1884)

Generally regarded as Mark Twain's major work, his third novel commands about as much attention from students and scholars as all his other works combined. It is certified as an American "classic" and is often called a "masterpiece"—even *the* great American novel. Despite its elevation to such eminence, however, Mark Twain himself did not regard it as exceptional. Even as late as 1908, he ranked it below *Joan of Arc* and *The Prince and the Pauper* among his favorite books. In creating *Huckleberry Finn*, he was as unaware of its significance as his youthful narrator Huck was of his own virtue.

Huckleberry Finn's importance lies in both its content and its construction. Essentially the coming-of-age story of a young white boy helping a slave to escape servitude in the pre–CIVIL WAR South, the novel is simultaneously a children's story, a humorous adult novel and a profound sociological document. In this latter regard, it explores such universal themes as freedom and bondage, race relations, conscience, greed and vice. Mark Twain invested considerable humor in the book, but one of its overriding themes is human cruelty and callousness. Huck begins his journey by escaping from a brutal captivity imposed by his father, then travels down the river and witnesses brawls, murders, lynch mobs, a pointless bloody feud, and greedy chicanery. With such horrors as a backdrop, Huck is consumed with guilt over his promise to help Jim escape—a promise that has led him to steal the property of Jim's owner, Miss

Mark Twain at the time Huckleberry Finn *was published.* (Courtesy, Library of Congress, Pictures & Prints Division)

Watson, thereby flouting the legal and social conventions of his society. Sure that he will go to hell for this sin, he writes a letter to Miss Watson revealing where Jim is, but suddenly decides he would rather go to hell than betray his friend. Few novels have more poignant moments.

As is the case with most of Mark Twain's books, the structure of *Huckleberry Finn* is flawed. Its problems reflect Mark Twain's uncertainties about what kind of book he was writing. He begins it in the same light spirit as *Tom Sawyer,* whose sequel he initially intended it to be. Then he shifts to a more sober tone as he sends Huck and Jim got down the Mississippi River. Finally, he returns to the light mood of the beginning with a long—and now much reviled—concluding sequence. The novel's greatest strengths lie in its central chapters, set on the river. Despite its structural inconsistencies, the book achieves greatness through Mark Twain's decision to tell its story through the voice of a simple, uneducated boy. It is the first major American novel written entirely in an authentic vernacular. School officials and librarians regarded the book's language as

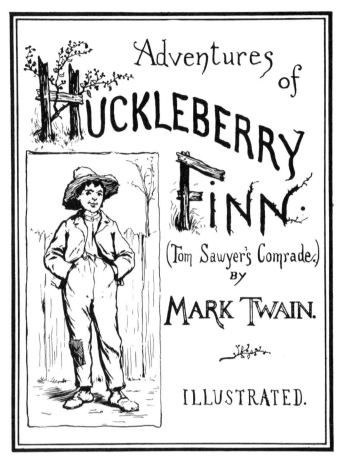

Cover of the first edition of Huckleberry Finn.

town of ST. PETERSBURG and ends in PIKESVILLE, 1,100 miles down the Mississippi River, nearly a year later. The narrative divides into three distinct sections.

Its first 11 chapters are set in or near St. Petersburg. The earliest chapters continue the action of *The Adventures of Tom Sawyer* and are very much in the same vein. The narrative makes a sharp change when Huck's father, Pap FINN, appears. Pap takes Huck upriver and keeps him in a cabin in ILLINOIS. In chapter 7, Huck fakes his own death and goes to JACKSON'S ISLAND. There he finds the slave Jim, who has run away to avoid being sold down the river. They remain on the island through chapter 11.

The second part of the narrative constitutes almost precisely half the entire text. In chapters 12 through 30, Huck and Jim go down the Mississippi River on a RAFT, interrupting their journey several times with episodes on shore. Nevertheless, this section of the novel contains virtually the entire story of the journey. In chapter 19, two con men—the KING and the DUKE—board the raft and take control of the voyage.

The final part comprises chapters 31 through 43. All the action takes place in and around Pikesville, where Huck finally rids himself of the King and the Duke. Meanwhile, Jim is captured and held prisoner at the nearby farm of Silas and Sally PHELPS. Huck goes to the Phelpses to help Jim escape and is mistaken for their nephew Tom Sawyer. When Tom himself arrives, he pretends to be his own brother, Sid, and offers to help free Jim. Most of the action in these chapters concerns Tom's elaborate "EVASION" plans for Jim's escape. Huck, Jim and Tom are still in Pikesville at the conclusion.

Chapter 1

Huck Finn introduces himself as narrator and summarizes the most important events concluding *The Adventures of Tom Sawyer*, in which he and Tom find and split a pirate treasure worth $12,000. Judge THATCHER now manages their money, which earns each boy a dollar a day in interest. The Widow DOUGLAS has taken Huck for her son, and she and her spinster sister, Miss WATSON, are trying to "sivilize" Huck. Huck chafes under the confinements of his new life. Such things as clean clothes, shoes, his own room, regular meals, prayers and so on hold few attractions for him. He tries fleeing, but Tom persuades him to return so that he can be respectable enough to join Tom's new robbers' gang.

When Huck returns, the widow cries over him, but life soon returns to its previous pattern. After supper, the widow tells Huck about Moses and the "Bulrushers," but his interest soon fades. Miss Watson wears him down with talk about the "good place" that only makes him hope that he will not go there if she does.

After Huck goes to his room, Tom Sawyer calls for him at midnight.

Chapter 2

As Tom and Huck sneak out through the widow's backyard, Huck trips and Miss Watson's slave Jim comes out to investigate. Unable to see anyone, Jim sits under a

unnecessarily coarse and banned it for this reason, as well as for its presumably objectional morals; however, the book's language has come to be appreciated as the core of its realism, and as a feature that makes the book a valuable document of its time. It was probably for this reason that Ernest Hemingway issued his famous dictum that "all modern American literature comes from one book by Mark Twain called *Huckleberry Finn.* . . . It's the best book we've had. All American writing comes from that. There was nothing before. There has been nothing as good since" (*The Green Hills of Africa,* 1935).

It should be noted that the full title appearing on the title page and cover of the first edition of this book is *Adventures of Huckleberry Finn (Tom Sawyer's Comrade).* E. W. KEMBLE's illustration for the half-title page that opens the first chapter reads "The Adventures of Huckleberry Finn"; however, *"The"* is not properly part of the book's title, though it has been used more often than not in reprint editions.

SYNOPSIS

The novel has about 112,000 words in 43 chapters of uneven length. The narrative begins in Huck's home-tree and falls asleep. Not able to resist playing a joke, Tom puts Jim's hat on a limb over his head. Later, Jim makes a reputation among other slaves with stories about the night he was bewitched.

Joe HARPER, Ben ROGERS and two or three other boys join Huck and Tom and they all boat down the river. After the others swear an oath of secrecy, Tom leads them to a hidden entrance to the CAVE that he found in *Tom Sawyer*. Inside, they agree to form a robber's band to be called "Tom Sawyer's GANG." They draw up an oath that each boy signs in blood. One boy suggests that the family of any member who tells gang secrets should be killed. The others like the rule; however, it seems to exclude Huck, who has no real family to kill. His offer of Miss Watson is satisfactory, so he is allowed to join. At the end of the meeting, the boys tease young Tommy BARNES for having fallen asleep. Tommy churlishly threatens to reveal the gang's secrets, but Tom buys his silence for five cents. Huck returns home shortly before dawn.

Chapter 3

The next morning, Miss Watson scolds Huck for soiling his clothes. The widow, however, merely looks sorry, making Huck feel guilty. Miss Watson prays with Huck in a closet and encourages him to pray daily, telling him that he will get whatever he prays for. When he gets a fishline, but no hooks, he is confused as to the efficacy of prayer. Occasionally, the widow talks to Huck about Providence and gets his hopes up, but Miss Watson typically dashes them the next day.

Huck has not seen his father, Pap FINN, for over a year. A man found drowned in the river above town is reported to be his father, but Huck senses that the drowned person is someone else.

After about a month in Tom's gang, Huck and the others quit. Huck is bored because they have not really robbed or killed anyone, but merely pretended; he cannot share Tom's belief that enchantments are at work. On one occasion, the gang gathered at CAVE HOLLOW to attack Spanish merchants and rich Arabs, who turned out to be a Sunday-school picnic. The gang scattered the picnickers and collected loot that included a hymnal and a religious tract, but the Sunday-school teacher routed them. Afterward, Tom explained that the caravan was enchanted, as in (CERVANTES's) *Don Quixote*. Though skeptical, Huck tries Tom's suggestion of rubbing an old lamp to call up a genie but eventually concludes that magic lamps and genies are just another of Tom's lies.

Chapter 4

Three or four months carry the narrative into winter. Huck attends school regularly, though he occasionally plays hookey and gets whipped. At first he hates school, but comes to tolerate it. He even finds things to like about the new ways of living with the Widow Douglas.

One day Huck spots ominously familiar bootprints in the snow near the widow's house. He flies off to Judge Thatcher and tries to persuade him to take his entire fortune of $6,000, plus interest. The judge senses that something is wrong, but Huck will not explain. He calms Huck by offering to buy his fortune for a "consideration" of one dollar. Huck next visits Jim, who uses an ox's hairball to tell his fortune. Jim's reading contains cryptic references to Huck's father and warns him to keep away from water.

Huck feels troubled that night as he goes up to bed. He enters his room and finds his father sitting on a chair.

Chapter 5

Seeing his father scares Huck momentarily. A history of beatings has made Huck afraid of him, but once he sees how bedraggled his father is, his fears melt away. Pap immediately turns on Huck, berating him for wearing starchy clothes and being educated. He makes Huck read aloud, then smacks the book away and demands that Huck quit school. In town for two days, Pap has come from downriver, where he heard about Huck's money; he knows that Judge Thatcher controls the money and wants Huck to get it for him. Claiming that he does not really have any money, Huck challenges Pap to ask Thatcher for himself. The next day Pap calls on Thatcher while he is drunk and tries bullyragging him.

Judge Thatcher and the Widow Douglas go to court to have one of them appointed Huck's legal guardian, but a new judge rules in Pap's favor. Pap celebrates by getting drunk and lands in jail for a week. The new judge tries to reform him by taking him into his own home, where he and his wife clean him up and give him new clothes and a nice room. Pap repays them by sneaking out at night, swapping his new coat for booze, then returning to get drunk. He wrecks the room, crawls out the window, breaks his arm in two places and nearly freezes in the snow.

Chapter 6

After recovering, Pap goes to court seeking control of Huck's money. He continues to torment Huck for staying in school, occasionally beating him. Huck now wants to stay in school to spite his father. Huck gets small amounts of money from the judge to give to Pap, who repeatedly gets drunk and lands in jail.

Pap finally spirits Huck away to a spot three miles up-river, on the Illinois side. He puts Huck in a secluded old log cabin in the woods, where they live off fish and game. When the widow sends a man to get Huck, Pap chases him off with his gun. Pap keeps a close eye on Huck, locking him in the cabin when he goes out. Apart from Pap's occasional thrashings, Huck mostly enjoys this life. He can cuss, smoke and fish, and he does not have to go to school. After two months, his clothes are rags and he cannot imagine returning to the widow.

Huck's pleasure wanes as Pap grows more abusive. As his father spends longer periods away, Huck begins planning his escape. He finds an old saw blade and starts cutting through a log at the rear of the cabin, hiding his work with a blanket when he hears Pap coming.

One day Pap returns to the cabin in an especially foul mood. His lawsuit against the judge is going poorly and there is talk of another trial to get Huck away from him and make the widow his guardian. This news alarms Huck. He does not want to return to the widow's any more than he wants to stay with Pap. He plans to tramp overland to get away. That night Pap gets drunker than usual and rages about how the government keeps him from having his rights and even allows black men to vote. He drinks until he has delirium tremens, rages incoherently through the night and chases Huck with a knife, calling him the "Angel of Death." To protect himself, Huck sits in a corner with the gun.

Chapter 7

The next morning, Pap awakens Huck demanding to know why he has the gun. Huck explains that someone tried to break into the cabin during the night. Satisfied by the explanation, Pap sends Huck out to check fishlines. It is now June, and the river is rising rapidly. A big canoe drifts by, and Huck seizes it. This unexpected booty gives him a new idea. He hides the canoe and now plans to go 50 miles downriver and find a permanent place to camp. He begins figuring out how to keep both Pap and the Widow Douglas from coming after him.

Later that day, Huck and Pap capture a big piece of drifting raft that Pap later tows across the river to sell. Huck launches his escape plans by cutting the rest of the way through the log wall and getting out of the cabin. He packs all the cabin's supplies into the canoe and then covers his tracks and the hole he cut in the wall. To make people think that he has been killed, he smashes the cabin door with an ax and spreads a wild pig's blood around inside. To make it appear that his body has been dumped in the river, he drags a sack full of rocks from the cabin to the shore. He then leaves a trail of cornmeal from the cabin to a nearby pond so it will appear that his killers escaped inland. He even pulls out some of his own hair and sticks it to the ax with pig blood. Finally, he goes a short distance down the river in the canoe and waits for the moon to rise. He falls asleep in the canoe, but awakens when he hears Pap rowing toward him. After Pap passes him, Huck heads downriver. Eventually, he reaches the Illinois side of uninhabited JACKSON'S ISLAND, where he goes ashore and sleeps in the woods.

Chapter 8

The next morning Huck awakens to booming noises and sees a crowded ferryboat cruising by the island. The boat is firing a cannon across the water, evidently to bring Huck's carcass to the surface. Huck clearly sees the people aboard, who include Pap, Judge Thatcher, Becky THATCHER, Joe Harper, Tom Sawyer, Aunt POLLY, Sid SAWYER and Mary (SAWYER). The boat rounds the island, leaving Huck confident that no one else will come looking for him.

After three days on the island, Huck stumbles upon fresh campfire ashes. Frightened, he climbs a tree to spy around and nervously stays aloft for hours. He crosses to Illinois to be safe, but the sounds of horses and human voices scare him back to the island. Now determined to learn who built the fire, he scouts around until he finds Miss Watson's slave Jim. Huck is immensely relieved, but Jim is terrified because he thinks Huck must be a ghost. After Huck persuades him otherwise, Huck learns that Jim has been on the island as long as he has. Huck explains how he escaped from his father. Before Jim admits that he has run off, he gets Huck to promise not to tell on him. Jim then explains that he overheard Miss Watson talking about selling him to someone in NEW ORLEANS for $800. That possibility was enough to make him leave immediately. He sneaked aboard a big commercial raft with the intention of going down the river some distance, but slipped off to avoid detection and swam to the island. In a long conversation, Jim impresses Huck with his vast knowledge of folk superstitions.

Chapter 9

Huck shows Jim a rugged ridge in the center of the island in which they find a spacious cave. At Jim's insistence, they move all their gear into the cave. Huck thinks that the cave's location is inconvenient, but Jim argues that it would provide both a good hiding place and protection against the rain he thinks is coming. Soon after they settle in, a heavy storm begins.

Over the next 10 or 12 days, the river rises rapidly, inundating much of the island. The floodwater brings with it more debris, which Huck and Jim venture out at night to explore. One night they catch a section of a well-constructed lumber RAFT. Another night, they find a two-story frame house (the "HOUSE OF DEATH") floating down the river that they investigate at daybreak. In an upstairs room they discover the naked body of a man shot in the back, but Jim will not let Huck look at the man's face. After they load their canoe with clothes, utensils and other supplies they find in this floating house they return to the island.

Chapter 10

Huck asks about the dead man, but Jim refuses to discuss him because it would be bad luck (Jim finally identifies the dead man in the last chapter). When they rummage through clothes taken from the house, they find eight dollars sewn inside a coat. Huck reminds Jim of his recent prediction that they would encounter bad luck because Huck had handled a snakeskin two days earlier. Jim insists that the bad luck is still coming.

Three days later Huck kills a rattlesnake in the cave and puts its body on Jim's bedding. That night another rattler bites Jim as he goes to bed. Huck kills the snake and follows Jim's instructions for disposing of it, but is careful not to tell him he was responsible for the first snake. The snakebite keeps Jim laid up for four days. Huck ponders on the dangers of defying superstition and recalls the disastrous example of Hank BUNKER.

As days pass, the river falls. Jim and Huck catch a catfish more than six feet long. Feeling restless, Huck proposes slipping into town to learn the news. Jim approves and suggests that Huck use a dress they found in the house to disguise himself as a girl to avoid recognition. Huck paddles the canoe up the Illinois shore, crosses the river near the ferry landing, and drifts down the opposite side before going ashore. He sees a light in a shanty that had long been unoccupied before he left town. Through its window he sees a woman he does not know.

Chapter 11
When the woman invites Huck in, he introduces himself as Sarah WILLIAMS from HOOKERVILLE. The woman chats idly and drifts to the subject of Huck's "murder." She tells Huck that many people think the murderer is Pap Finn, while others think it is the runaway slave Jim. There are rewards out for both. Pap left town with some toughs shortly after Huck was presumed killed and many people think that he killed his son so he could get at Huck's money without a lawsuit.

The woman also tells Huck that she has seen smoke rise from Jackson's Island and that her husband is going there that very night to hunt for Jim. Huck nervously picks up a needle and tries to thread it. The woman asks him his name again. This time he gives "Mary Williams." She notices the contradiction and tries several tricks that prove Huck is a boy. Huck invents a new story about having been apprenticed to a mean farmer when his parents died. He says that his name is really George PETERS and that he has run away to find his uncle Abner MOORE in GOSHEN. As the woman prepares food for Huck and sends him off, she identifies herself as Mrs. Judith LOFTUS.

Huck rushes back to the island, stops at its north end to build a fire as a diversion, then continues to the camp. He awakens Jim and tells him, "They're after us!" Without a word, Jim helps pack everything onto the raft, and he and Huck leave the island.

Chapter 12
After a long night drifting downriver, Huck and Jim establish a routine of hiding by day and rafting by night. They tie up among cottonwood trees on an Illinois sandbar and camouflage the raft. The next evening, Jim pulls up some of the raft's planks and builds a wigwam shelter elevated above the main deck.

The second night they run between seven and eight hours in a current that Huck estimates at over four miles an hour. They talk and fish and occasionally swim to keep themselves awake. On the fifth uneventful night, they pass ST. LOUIS. Occasionally, Huck slips ashore to buy or borrow food. After discussing the morality of "borrowing," Huck and Jim decide that it would be

better if they were to quit borrowing, so they resolve to quit taking crabapples and persimmons.

Five nights south of St. Louis, a lightning storm comes up. The raft drifts into a wrecked steamboat precariously perched on rocks. Huck wants to board it to explore, but Jim wants to leave well enough alone and ignore it. Huck prevails. They fasten the raft to the steamboat's starboard derrick and go aboard. Huck cautiously works his way toward the captain's cabin on the texas deck.

Huck hears voices in a cabin and sees two men—Jake PACKARD and BILL—who have tied up a third, Jim TURNER. The first two men are arguing about killing Turner. They finally agree to go ashore and wait for the steamboat to break up, so that Turner will be drowned. Huck rushes back to Jim and proposes they cut the murderers' skiff loose so the sheriff can catch them. Jim tells Huck that their raft has broken loose. Now *they* are marooned on the doomed steamboat.

Chapter 13
As Huck recovers from his initial shock, he realizes that he and Jim must now find the murderers' skiff in order to save themselves. Just as they locate it, the murderers appear and board it themselves. Before these men shove off, however, they remember that they have failed to take Turner's share of loot from him. They go back to get it, allowing Huck and Jim to escape on their skiff.

As Huck and Jim search for their raft, Huck worries about the men aboard the doomed steamboat. He dislikes the idea of leaving even murderers in such a fix—especially since he might one day be a murderer himself. He tells Jim to land near the next light they see, so he can go ashore and find someone to rescue the murderers.

The storm worsens, but Huck and Jim find their raft. They also see a light. Huck rows the skiff ashore, as Jim takes the raft farther downstream. Huck boards a steam ferry and awakens its watchman. The FERRYBOATMAN turns out to be the boat's owner. Huck tearfully tells him a story about his family and a Miss HOOKER being stranded on the wrecked steamboat—which the startled ferryboatman identifies as the WALTER SCOTT. The man happens to mention a rich local person named Jim HORNBACK. He is concerned about who will pay for the rescue effort. When Huck mentions that Hornback is the uncle of the fictitious Miss Hooker, the ferryboatman jumps to begin organizing his rescue effort.

Before the ferryboat reaches the *Walter Scott*, the steamboat breaks up and washes downstream. Huck rows his skiff around the drifting wreck and calls out, but no one answers. Eventually, he rejoins Jim farther down the river. They go to an island, hide the raft, sink the skiff and sleep soundly.

Chapter 14
The next morning Huck and Jim sort out the goods from the steamboat that the murderers left in the skiff

and find boots, blankets, books, clothes, cigars and other things. After they rest, Huck crows about their adventure aboard the steamboat. Jim, however, says he does not want any more adventures, explaining that when he discovered the raft was missing, he thought that he would either die or be sold down the river. Huck concedes that Jim is right and has "an uncommon level head for a nigger."

As Huck reads to Jim, they take up the subject of kings and royalty. They debate whether King SOLOMON was truly a wise man and then discuss King LOUIS XVI and his son the DAUPHIN. Finally, they argue about why some people speak French. Though Jim applies superior logic in each argument, Huck fails to see that he has been bested and concludes that "you can't learn a nigger to argue."

Chapter 15
Huck and Jim plan go as far as CAIRO, Illinois, where they will sell the raft and take a steamboat up the OHIO RIVER to the free states. They calculate that three more nights will get them to Cairo. On the second night, however, heavy fog forces them to tie up on a sandbar. Huck takes the canoe out to find something to fasten the raft to. The swift current separates him from the raft; then he and Jim spend the night trying to find each other in the fog. The situation worsens when they drift in among small islands and swirling currents. Both of them fall asleep from exhaustion.

When Huck awakens under a clear night sky hours later, he finds the raft. Jim is worn out and asleep, and the deck is littered with dirt and leaves. Huck boards the raft and lies down, as if he has been sleeping. When Jim awakens, he is immensely relieved to find Huck alive and safe, but Huck tries to convince him that he has merely dreamt the night's misadventures. As Jim tries to explain the meaning of each detail in his dream, he realizes he has been fooled when Huck asks him to explain what the litter strewn on the raft means. Jim then shames Huck by contrasting his own concern for Huck's safety with Huck's effort to make a fool of him, and goes to the wigwam without a further word.

After spending 15 minutes preparing to "humble myself before a nigger," Huck finally does it, then admits that he has not been sorry since then. He plays no more tricks on Jim.

Chapter 16
After sleeping through the day, Huck and Jim set out again and find themselves behind a huge raft with about 30 men in its crew. They discuss the difficult problem of finding the tiny village of Cairo.

(Some editions of *Huckleberry Finn* insert the "RAFT CHAPTER" here.)

Huck and Jim continue watching for Cairo. As Jim's prospects of being truly free grow, Huck feels guilty about helping him to escape. It grieves him to think that he is stealing from Jim's owner, Miss Watson. Jim talks enthusiastically about saving money to buy the freedom of his wife and children, adding that if he cannot buy his children, he will find an abolitionist to steal them. Huck is so shocked by Jim's plans that he decides to report Jim as a runaway.

Huck takes the canoe to scout out where they are. As he paddles off, Jim calls after him, thanking him for being such a good friend. Two slave hunters then approach him in a skiff. Huck now has his chance to turn Jim in, but cannot bring himself to do it. Instead, he concocts a story that makes the slave hunters think that he has relatives with smallpox aboard the raft. The men feel guilty about not helping Huck, so each gives him a $20 gold piece. Jim, who has been hiding underwater, is more grateful than ever to Huck.

As Huck and Jim drift downriver, their faith in finding Cairo erodes. One morning, they notice *two* channels in the river. One is the unclouded water of the Ohio; the other, the muddy water of the Mississippi. There is now no doubt; they have passed Cairo. They guess that they missed the town in the fog a few nights earlier and blame their bad luck on the snakeskin that Huck handled on Jackson's Island. They now plan to return upriver in the canoe; however, they awaken that night to find their canoe missing. They decide to continue downriver instead until they can buy another canoe in which to return.

After dark, they shove off again on their raft. The night is particularly dark. A steamboat coming up the river ignores their signal lantern and plows into them. Jim dives off one side of the raft, Huck off the other. After swimming under the boat's paddle-wheel, Huck surfaces and calls out for Jim, but gets no reply. He grabs hold of a plank and drifts with the current to the left bank and goes ashore. About a quarter of a mile inland, he stumbles upon a big log house. When barking dogs corner him, he freezes.

Chapter 17
A voice calling from a window orders Huck to identify himself. He gives his name as "George JACKSON" and says that he fell off the steamboat. The voice asks if he knows the SHEPHERDSONS, then orders him to enter the house slowly. Inside, Huck finds three tall men pointing guns at him. There are also an old woman and two young women. As he soon learns, he is in the home of the GRANGERFORDS.

The older man, Colonel GRANGERFORD, is satisfied that Huck is not a threat, and the old woman instructs her slave Betsy to fetch Huck food. The youngest son, Buck GRANGERFORD, takes Huck to his room for dry clothes. As Huck eats, he answers questions and invents a biography. He claims to come from southern Arkansas. After his sister MARY ANN ran off to marry, his family disintegrated until only he remained. He was coming up the river as a deck passenger when he fell off the steamboat. The Grangerfords invite Huck to stay indefinitely. When Huck awakens the next morning, he finds that he has forgotten his new name. He challenges Buck to spell it for him, then writes it down so he can remember it.

Everything about the Grangerford house impresses Huck. It is full of touches usually found only in houses in towns, such as brass doorknobs and a parlor without a bed. He describes its decor and sees such books as John BUNYAN's *Pilgrim's Progress*, Henry CLAY's speeches and Dr. GUNN's *Family Medicine*. He also describes the melancholy artwork and poetry of the family's deceased daughter, Emmeline GRANGERFORD.

Chapter 18
Huck takes quickly to the Grangerfords, who have many kinfolk living in the region. Another big aristocratic family, the Shepherdsons, also live nearby. One day as Huck and Buck hunt in the woods, a rider whom Buck recognizes as Harney SHEPHERDSON comes along. They duck into the brush. Buck shoots at Harney, knocking his hat off. Harney rides up and aims his rifle at Buck, but leaves without firing. Later, Buck tells Huck about the long-standing feud between the Grangerfords and the Shepherdsons.

The following Sunday the Grangerfords and the Shepherdsons attend the same church. All the men carry guns, and Huck feels the tension. Afterward, Sophia GRANGERFORD has Huck go back to fetch a Testament she forgot. Inside her Testament, he finds a note: "Half-past two." It means nothing to him, but thrills Sophia.

Later that day, the slave JACK leads Huck to a swamp on the pretext of showing him water moccasins. Jack slips away, leaving Huck to find Jim, who has been hiding there since the raft was smashed. Jim explains that he followed Huck ashore that night, keeping silent for fear of capture. Since then, he has been repairing and restocking the raft, which is not as badly damaged as Huck had thought.

The next day, Huck awakens at the Grangerfords' to find almost everyone gone. Jack reports that Sophia has run off with Harney Shepherdson and that the Grangerford men are trying to catch them as the women round up relatives. Huck hurries to the timber yard by the steamboat landing, where he sees Buck and his cousin JOE shooting at horsemen. Huck climbs a tree to watch. When Buck and Joe move closer to his tree, Huck shouts to them. Buck says that the Shepherdsons have killed his father and brothers in an ambush. Two or three Shepherdsons are also dead. Sophia and Harney have escaped across the river.

The Shepherdsons surprise Buck and Joe by attacking from behind, on foot. The boys run to the river. The Shepherdsons shoot them as they try to swim away. These sights are so horrifying to Huck that he later still dreams about the awful experience. When darkness falls, Huck climbs out of the tree, pulls the boys' bodies

ashore, then rushes back to the swamp. He and Jim board their raft and leave immediately.

Chapter 19
Huck and Jim continue their cruise down the river, enjoying two or three of the most idyllic days of their journey. By day, they hide in the cottonwood; by night, they drift on the raft. One morning, Huck finds a canoe and paddles up a creek to hunt for berries. Two ragged men tear along a path toward him, begging for help to escape their pursuers. Huck has them go upstream first, so they can wade down the creek, to throw the dogs off their scent. He then takes the men back to the raft.

The two men are strangers to each other. Each explains the various scams he specializes in. The younger man suggests they "double-team it together." After a long silence, the younger man grows somber and begins moaning about being "degraded." He alludes to the "secret of his birth" and suddenly blurts out: "By rights I am a DUKE!" He explains that he is the rightful Duke of BRIDGEWATER and asks to be treated with the respect due his rank. Huck and Jim agree to wait on him.

After dinner, the older man makes an announcement of his own. He is the "late DAUPHIN," the son of LOUIS XVI and "Marry Antonette." This makes him "Looy the Seventeen," the "rightful KING of France." Jim and Huck agree to serve him as well. After a frosty moment, the men agree to be friends. Though Huck knows that both men are frauds, he is content to avert trouble and says nothing.

Chapter 20
The King and the Duke suspect that Jim is a runaway slave, but Huck protests that no runaway slave would be going *south*. He also invents another biography for himself, claiming to be from Missouri's PIKE COUNTY. When hard times hit, he, his father, younger brother IKE, and Jim began rafting downriver in order to live with his Uncle BEN, near NEW ORLEANS. A steamboat hit their raft, drowning his father and Ike. He and Jim are continuing the journey, traveling by night to avoid troublesome encounters with people by day.

The King and Duke appropriate the wigwam as their own sleeping quarters, leaving Jim and Huck to sleep in the rain. As he often does, Jim stands Huck's watch on top of his own. The next morning, the King and Duke begin scheming. The Duke has a carpetbag filled with handbills, mostly for dramatic productions. He persuades the King to perform with him in scenes from ROMEO AND JULIET and RICHARD III in the towns they will visit.

Eventually they land the raft below a town called POKEVILLE and go ashore. Most townspeople are at a religious camp meeting outside of town. The Duke takes over an untended print shop as Huck and the King go the camp meeting, where they join a lively group. The King gets up and tearfully tells the crowd that he was a PIRATE for 30 years on the Indian Ocean, but now he wants to devote the rest of his life to working as a missionary among the pirates. The enthusiastic crowd has him pass the hat. He collects $87.75 and manages to cadge a jug of whiskey as he leaves.

Meanwhile, the Duke has been busy in the print shop, where he has taken in $9.50 doing small jobs and selling newspaper subscriptions. He has also printed handbills advertising a $200 reward for a runaway slave whose description matches Jim's. The bills give the address as "ST. JACQUES PLANTATION," below New Orleans. The Duke explains that they can now run the raft by day. If anyone challenges Jim's presence, they can simply show a handbill and say they are going south to collect the reward. In order to make this scheme work, however, they will have to tie Jim up when anyone approaches, or when they leave him alone on the raft.

Early the next morning, Jim tells Huck that he has had his fill of kings.

Chapter 21
As the raft continues downstream, the Duke and King rehearse the balcony scene from *Romeo and Juliet* and the sword fight from *Richard III*. The Duke also teaches the King to recite HAMLET's SOLILOQUY, giving him a version reconstructed from memory. Huck is impressed by the King's recitation. During a stopover at a village, the Duke has handbills printed to announce the coming production.

Two or three days later, they stop above another town (BRICKSVILLE), which appears promising because a circus is performing there that very day. The Duke hires the courthouse and posts bills for their "Shaksperean Revival," featuring "David GARRICK, the Younger" and "Edmund KEAN, the Elder." As Huck idles about the town, he comments on its tumble-down condition and its loafers such as Ben THOMPSON. A rowdy drunk named BOGGS rides into town yelling threats aimed mostly at a man named Colonel SHERBURN, who warns him to stop his abuse after one o'clock. When that hour arrives, Sherburn shoots Boggs and the crowd cries for a lynch party.

Chapter 22
After collecting rope, a mob swarms to Sherburn's house, where they knock down the fence. Sherburn steps out on the roof over his porch. Holding a double-barreled gun, he stares the crowd into uncomfortable silence. He then dresses them down for their cowardice, calling Buck HARKNESS, their leader, a "half a man." Huck leaves as the mob disperses, then sneaks into the circus, where he gushes over every wonder he sees.

That night the King and Duke stage their "Shaksperean Revival" to 12 unappreciative people. The only person who does not leave before it ends is a boy who has fallen asleep. The angry Duke declares that what these "Arkansaw lunkheads" really want is "low comedy." The next day, he makes up new handbills advertis-

ing "The King's CAMELOPARD or The ROYAL NONESUCH . . . Ladies and Children Not Admitted."

Chapter 23
The King and Duke rig a stage at the courthouse, which they pack that night. The Duke introduces the "Royal Nonesuch" with a provocative speech. When the curtain rises, the King comes out on all fours. Naked and painted with multicolored stripes, he delights the crowd by prancing about wildly. After two encores, the Duke ends the show. The audience rises angrily, but one man persuades the others to give the rest of the town a chance to be taken in by the frauds to spare those present from becoming laughingstocks.

The second performance goes as on the first night. Afterward, the King and Duke have Jim and Huck move the raft to a point below the town. On the third night, Huck recognizes men who attended the previous performances. The crowd is armed with rotten fruit and eggs, as well as dead cats. Once the house is packed, Huck and the Duke slip out, run to the raft and take off downstream. Huck is concerned about leaving the King behind, but is surprised to find him already aboard the raft. The con men find that their three-night take adds up to $465.

After the King and Duke are asleep, Jim and Huck discuss what RAPSCALLIONS kings are. Huck talks about kings such as HENRY VIII. Jim again stands Huck's watch during the night. Toward daybreak, Huck overhears Jim moaning about his wife and children and gets him to talk a little about them. Jim relates a painful story about a time when he smacked his daughter 'Lizabeth for disobeying him before he realized that the scarlet fever had left her deaf and dumb.

Chapter 24
The next day, the King and Duke scout new villages to exploit. When Jim asks for some relief from being tied up all day, the Duke dresses him up as King Lear, paints him blue and posts a sign on the raft saying that he is a "sick Arab," telling Jim to howl and carry on if anyone approaches.

The rascals want to try their "Royal Nonesuch" show again, but figure that they are not far enough from the last place where they performed it for it to be safe. The Duke goes off to inspect a village, while Huck stays with the King to check out another village downriver. After Huck and the King put on recently bought store clothes, the improvement in the King's appearance astounds Huck. The King suggests boarding a steamboat that is loading freight nearby, so they can arrive in the next village in style. As they canoe downriver, they see a "young country jake" (Tim COLLINS), whom the King offers a ride to the steamboat. He introduces himself as the Reverend Elexander BLODGETT and calls Huck "ADOLPHUS," as if he were a servant. The man initially takes the King for a Mr. Wilks, explaining that someone named Peter WILKS in the next town has just died, while he was expecting his English brothers to arrive. The King pumps the man for every detail about Wilks, his family and neighbors.

After the man boards the steamboat, Huck and the King return for the Duke. The King tells the Duke everything he has learned about the Wilkses. His plan is to impersonate Harvey WILKS and have the Duke impersonate Harvey's deaf and dumb younger brother, William WILKS. They hail a big steamboat (the SUSAN POWELL), which they ride to the village, where they are immediately received as Peter Wilks's brothers.

Chapter 25
Most of the town turns out to greet the impostors and lead them to Wilks's house, where Peter Wilks's nieces, Mary Jane, Susan and Joanna WILKS, greet their supposed uncles. The King and Duke pay sobbing tribute over the coffin, disgusting Huck with their exaggerated grief. The King impresses everyone by rattling off the names of all of Peter Wilks's special friends.

Mary Jane presents a letter from her deceased uncle that the King reads. Wilks has left his house and $3,000 in gold to his nieces and has left his successful tanyard, other houses and land, and $3,000 in gold to his brothers Harvey and William. The letter tells where the gold is hidden in the basement. Huck accompanies the King and Duke downstairs to find it. When the impostors count the gold, they find that it is $415 short of $6,000. To avoid suspicion of dishonesty, the Duke suggests they make up the "deffisit" by contributing their own money. He then suggests giving *all* the money to the girls—an idea that wins everyone's approval upstairs.

The King prattles on, upsetting the Duke with talk about the funeral "ORGIES." Dr. ROBINSON arrives and quickly denounces the scoundrels as frauds, calling the King's English accent the worst he has ever heard. He appeals to the girls to shun the frauds, but Mary Jane hands the King the bag of gold and asks him to invest the money for them and not to bother with a receipt.

Chapter 26
That night, the Wilks girls put on a big dinner at which Huck acts as the King's servant. Afterward, he eats in the kitchen with Joanna, who asks him about ENGLAND. Skeptical of Huck's unlikely answers, Joanna asks him to swear he is telling the truth. Mary Jane and Susan arrive at this moment and take her to task for not treating Huck properly as a guest. The sisters' sensitivity and Joanna's beautiful apology make Huck feel so bad about his role in the King and Duke's swindle that he decides to steal the girls' gold back from the impostors.

Huck searches the Duke's and King's rooms, and he hides in the King's room when the scoundrels arrive. He then hears the Duke say that he wants to take the money that he and the King already have and leave immediately. The King insists on staying so they can auction off Wilks's properties. The Duke is concerned about Dr. Robinson, but the King laughs him off. Huck

sees the King hide the money in his bed and grabs it after the men leave the room.

Chapter 27
After waiting a bit, Huck takes the gold downstairs. He wants to hide it outside the house, but the doors are locked. When he hears someone else coming, he stuffs the money inside Wilks's coffin and hides as Mary Jane enters the parlor. He agonizes over leaving the money in the coffin, but cannot retrieve it without being seen.

The next morning, Huck finds the parlor shut. He watches people carefully to detect whether anything unusual has happened. In the afternoon, as the Reverend HOBSON conducts the funeral in the parlor, Huck is not sure if the gold is still in the coffin.

After Wilks is buried, the King says that he must return to his congregation in England. Saying that he is anxious to settle the estate as soon as possible and take the girls back to England, he immediately puts Wilks's property up for auction. The next day everyone is shocked to learn that the King has already sold the family slaves, sending the two boys upriver and their mother downriver. On the morning of the auction, the King and Duke awaken Huck and grill him about the missing gold, but Huck shifts suspicion onto the slaves who have just been sent away.

Chapter 28
Later that morning, Huck sees Mary Jane in her room crying about the slave family being separated. Momentarily forgetting himself, he assures her that the slaves will soon be reunited. He now feels compelled to tell her the whole truth. After making Mary Jane promise to leave town for a few days, he confesses that her supposed "uncles" are frauds. He adds that prematurely exposing the frauds could mean trouble for someone whom he cannot name.

Huck finally settles on a plan for Mary Jane to spend just one day with the LOTHROP family outside of town—long enough for him to make his getaway. He tells her that if proof that the King and Duke are frauds becomes necessary, she can write to Bricksville and mention the "Royal Nonesuch." He insists that she leave immediately, to avoid accidentally betraying that she knows something is wrong. He also gives her a slip of paper telling her where he hid the money. After Mary Jane leaves, Huck tells Susan and Joanna that Mary Jane has gone across the river to visit Hanner PROCTOR.

At the auction that same day, virtually all the Wilks property is sold off. Later that day, a steamboat lands and townspeople are delighted that two more men claiming to be Harvey and William Wilks have arrived.

Chapter 29
The arrival of more claimants excites the town, but does not faze the King and Duke. The distinguished-looking newcomer who calls himself Harvey Wilks says that since their luggage went ashore at the wrong town, he

and his brother cannot prove who they are. They will therefore retire to a hotel to await their luggage, which contains their proof. The King jokes about them, but several people do not laugh, including Dr. Robinson and Levi BELL, newly returned to town. Another man (HINES) steps forward and says he saw the King and Huck in a canoe upriver the morning of the day they came to town.

Robinson proposes taking Huck, the King and the Duke to the hotel to confront them and the newcomers together. He also demands that the townspeople take charge of Wilks's gold until his true brothers are identified; this forces the King to reveal that the gold is missing. The resulting investigation at the hotel lasts over an hour. Huck thinks it should be obvious to anyone that the King is lying and that his freshly arrived counterpart is telling the truth. When Huck testifies about life in England, Robinson merely laughs and tells him he is not much of a liar.

Bell has the King and Duke write something down, then surprises them by comparing their handwriting with letters written by the real Harvey and William Wilks. This test appears to prove them impostors; however, the new "Harvey" fails as well. He claims that William transcribes all his letters for him, but his brother cannot write anything with his arm in a cast. At the least, Bell concludes, the test proves the King and the Duke *not* to be Harvey and William Wilks. The King tries to talk his way out of this by suggesting that the Duke deliberately altered his own handwriting as a joke.

The man that Huck thinks is the real Harvey asks if anyone there helped prepare Peter's body for burial. Ab TURNER and another man present themselves. The man then asks the King what was tattooed on Peter's chest. The King calmly answers, a "small blue arrow." The other Harvey says the tattoo was the letters "P-B-W"; however, neither Turner nor the other man remembers seeing any mark on Peter's chest. A voice rises suggesting that all four claimants be lynched, but Bell proposes opening Peter Wilks's grave to examine his body. Dr. Robinson makes sure that Huck and the four claimants are kept under restraint.

As the crowd marches to the cemetery, the sky darkens ominously. Huck now regrets sending Mary Jane out of town, fearing that he is about to be hanged. Just as the lid to Wilks's coffin is removed, a flash of lightning reveals the bag of gold. The excited mob surges forward, allowing Huck to escape. He runs to the river, grabs a canoe and paddles to the raft. Thinking himself finally free of the scoundrels, he calls to Jim to set the raft loose. Just as they start to drift off, however, the King and Duke row up to the raft. Huck almost cries.

Chapter 30
When the King and Duke board the raft, the King turns on Huck for trying to run out on them. Huck protests that he thought that the King and Duke must be dead,
so he was merely trying to save his life. The Duke makes the King leave Huck alone, reminding him that he had not looked out for anyone but himself. He then blames the King for doing everything wrong from the start—except for his remark about the blue-arrow tattoo, which saved their lives.

The realization that they have not only lost their chance at the Wilks fortune, but their "Royal Nonesuch" money, causes the King and Duke to argue over who is responsible for the disaster. Each accuses the other of having hidden the money in the coffin with the idea of coming back later to dig it up for himself. The argument ends when the Duke throttles the King, forcing him to confess that he stole the money. Eventually, both get drunk and become friends again. Once they are asleep, Huck tells Jim what has happened.

Chapter 31
The raft drifts south for "days and days" without stopping at any settlements. When the King and Duke feel safe again they start working towns, but everything they try fails: temperance lecturing, a dancing school, elocution lectures, "missionarying," "mesmerizering," doctoring, telling fortunes and other things. Their money runs out and they grow morose and talk secretly with each other.

Eventually, the band lands the raft about two miles below a town named PIKESVILLE. The King goes into town alone, leaving instructions for the Duke and Huck to follow at noon if he does not return. By now, Huck is determined to escape the con men at the first opportunity. At noon, he and the Duke go into town and find the King drunk in a saloon. As the Duke and King argue, Huck runs back to the raft, but Jim has disappeared. Huck returns to the road and finds a boy who tells him that a runaway slave fitting Jim's description has been caught and taken to the farm of Silas PHELPS, two miles farther downstream. He explains that an "old fellow" with a handbill offering a reward for the slave has sold the runaway for $40.

Huck's guilt over helping a slave escape resurfaces. He is ashamed of his sinfulness, but cannot bring himself to pray. Instead, he writes a letter to Miss Watson, telling her where Jim is. After he completes the letter, he feels washed clean of sin for the first time, but trembles to think how close he has come to consigning himself to hell. Second thoughts creep in, however. He recalls all the ways in which Jim has become a friend. Finally, he decides, "All right, then, I'll go to hell" and tears up the letter. He is now determined to win back Jim's freedom.

Huck shifts the raft to an island (SPANISH ISLAND), where he spends the night. The next day he puts on his store-bought clothes and paddles the canoe ashore. When he reaches the town, the first person he sees is the Duke, who is pasting up handbills for a new "Royal Nonesuch" performance. Huck invents a story to account for his absence the day before and tells the Duke that the raft has disappeared. The Duke reveals that the King has sold Jim for $40—money that he quickly blew on whiskey and gambling.

When the Duke accuses Huck of trying to give them the shake, Huck points out that it would not make sense for him to leave without his slave, and blubbers about losing the only property he owns. Taking pity on Huck, the Duke offers to tell him where Jim is—provided that he not give away the secret of their "Royal Nonesuch." The Duke starts to tell the truth, but abruptly switches to a lie, telling Huck that a man named Abram G. Foster—40 miles inland—has Jim, and he insists that Huck start walking immediately. Huck walks about a mile, then doubles back and heads for the Phelps farm.

Chapter 32

Huck arrives at the Phelps farm on a hot, quiet afternoon. As he approaches the house, barking hounds surround him. A slave woman named LIZE chases the dogs away; then a white woman and several children come out to greet him. The woman puzzles Huck by acting as if she expects him. She tells her children that he is their cousin Tom and insists that he call her "Aunt Sally." Not knowing which direction she thinks he has come from, Huck invents a noncommittal story about his steamboat's blowing out a cylinder-head, and adds that he has hidden his luggage near the town.

Aunt Sally's detailed questions make Huck almost ready to give up his unintentional masquerade. However, she sees her husband coming home and tells Huck to hide so they can play a joke on him. When Mr. Phelps comes in, Aunt Sally springs Huck on him and asks who he thinks it is. The man has no idea, so she proclaims: "It's *Tom Sawyer!*" Immensely relieved, Huck confidently answers a flock of questions about "the Sawyer family." The sound of a steamboat whistle reminds him that the real Tom Sawyer may arrive soon, so he insists on returning to town alone to fetch his luggage, hoping to find Tom before he reaches the Phelpses.

Chapter 33

Huck takes the Phelpses' wagon to town and meets Tom along the road. After convincing his friend that he is not a ghost, Huck fills him in on his situation. Tom proposes that Huck return to the house alone with his luggage and that he arrive later. When Huck adds that he plans to free Jim from captivity, Tom eagerly offers to help. It shocks Huck that the respectable Tom would stoop to the level of a "nigger stealer." Huck gets back to the house sooner than he should, but innocent old Uncle Silas suspects nothing.

Later, Tom appears at the door and asks for Mr. Archibald NICHOLS, a neighbor. When Aunt Sally invites Tom in, he introduces himself as William THOMPSON. He prattles on about where he is from, then stuns Aunt Sally by suddenly kissing her on the mouth. Eventually, he identifies himself as his own brother, Sid SAWYER, explaining that he begged to come along on this trip.

(From this point through chapter 42, Huck goes by the name Tom, and Tom goes by the name Sid.)

At supper, Huck learns that the townspeople are planning violence at the King and Duke's Royal Nonesuch. Jim has told Uncle Silas and a man named BURTON all about their show. That night Huck and Tom slip out and go to town. Huck wants to warn the rascals of the danger they are in, but as the boys reach town, they see the two con men covered with tar and feathers and being carried out on rails. The sight sickens Huck.

Chapter 34

As the boys return home, Tom guesses that Jim is being kept prisoner in a cabin where he has observed a slave (NAT) entering through a locked door with food. Tom proposes to Huck that they each devise a plan for freeing Jim. Huck's plan is to steal the key to the cabin off Uncle Silas while he sleeps, then spring Jim free and break for the raft, but Tom insists on something vastly more elaborate. At the farm, they examine the cabin from outside and inspect the surrounding area.

The next morning, Huck and Tom accompany Nat when he takes food to Jim. They find Jim chained to his bed inside the dark cabin. When Jim sees them, he cries aloud; however, Huck and Tom pretend that they have heard nothing and convince Nat that he only imagines having heard Jim. Tom whispers to Jim not to let on that he knows them and that they are going to get him free.

Chapter 35

Under Tom's direction the next day, the boys begin gathering supplies for Tom's elaborate escape plans. It soon becomes clear that he wants to do everything in the most complicated and time-consuming manner possible. For example, instead of having Jim free his leg chain from his bed by simply lifting up the bed to slip it off, he wants Jim to saw the bed's leg off. All his ideas come from books he has read about famous escapes by people such as "Baron Trenck . . . Casanova . . . Benvenuto Chelleeny [CELLINI] . . . Henri IV" and others.

Chapter 36

That night Huck and Tom begin digging at Jim's cabin with case-knives. They work for hours until their hands are blistered, but barely make an impression. Tom reluctantly concedes that they should use real digging tools and "*let on* it's case-knives." When they resume with picks and shovels, they make rapid progress. When they quit, Tom's hands are so raw he cannot climb the lightning rod to their room. He follows Huck's suggestion to come up the stairs, "and let on it's a lightning rod."

The next day Tom and Huck steal more supplies, such as tin plates, for Jim. That night they dig all the way into Jim's cabin and gently awaken him. He is tearfully grateful and wants them to find a chisel to break his chain so he can leave immediately. However,

Tom explains his escape plan, assuring Jim that they will spring him loose immediately if an emergency arises. Jim agrees to go along. During a long chat, the boys learn that the Phelpses have been treating Jim very kindly.

The next morning the boys begin smuggling supplies to Jim on his food plate. They accompany the slave Nat to the cabin. While they are there, dogs begin pouring into the cabin through the hole dug the previous night. After chasing the dogs out and covering the openings, Tom persuades Nat that he has only imagined seeing the dogs in the cabin.

Chapter 37
Huck and Tom smuggle implements to Jim for scribbling messages. Aunt Sally begins noticing things missing from around the house, such as candles, a shirt, a sheet, a spoon and a candlestick. The spoon turns up in Uncle Silas's pocket; then Tom and Huck confuse Aunt Sally by making it impossible for her to count her spoon collection accurately. To add to her confusion, they replace the missing sheet, and then steal and replace it repeatedly until she no longer pays attention to its absence. Finally, they shred the sheet to make a rope for Jim and smuggle as much of it to Jim as they can fit inside a pie that they bake in a bed-warming pan. They also smuggle tin plates in to Jim. He scratches marks on them and throws them out his window.

Chapter 38
Tom insists that Jim scratch on the wall a coat of arms that he designs for him. He also wants Jim to inscribe "mournful" messages on his wall. However, Tom is not satisfied with log walls, so he and Huck steal a big grindstone from a nearby mill. Since they cannot handle the grindstone by themselves, Jim leaves his cabin to help. Tom enlarges the hole in the ground in order to get the grindstone into the cabin.

Tom's next idea is to collect spiders, snakes and rats for the cabin, but Jim draws the line at rattlesnakes. Tom's final idea is for Jim to grow a flower in the corner of his cell watered by his tears. When Jim protests that he does not cry enough to keep a flower alive, Tom promises to smuggle an onion to him to help produce tears.

Chapter 39
The next morning the boys fill a wire trap with rats and hide it under Aunt Sally's bed. While they are off catching spiders, Sally's children open the cage. Sally whips the boys, but they simply capture more rats. They also add spiders, insects and dozens of harmless snakes to the menagerie they are collecting for Jim. The snakes escape from a bag in their room, and for some time afterward are found throughout the house, making Aunt Sally a nervous wreck.

After three weeks of preparation, everything is ready for the escape, which Tom calls an "EVASION." Both boys and especially Jim are exhausted. Meanwhile, Silas

Phelps has been writing to the nonexistent St. Jacques plantation near New Orleans. Since no reply has come, he talks about advertising in St. Louis and New Orleans newspapers to find Jim's owner. Huck's anxiousness to free Jim mounts.

Tom now wants to send anonymous letters to make sure that the actual escape does not go unnoticed. He has Huck borrow the frock of a servant girl to wear while delivering a letter that warns of brewing trouble. Over the next several nights, Tom posts ominous pictures on the Phelpses' door, causing Aunt Sally to grow increasingly anxious. Finally, Tom writes a long letter warning that a cutthroat gang of abolitionists is planning to steal the runaway slave the next night and spirit him away to INDIAN TERRITORY.

Chapter 40
The next day, Huck and Tom relax by fishing and examining the raft. At home they find everyone in a sweat over Tom's anonymous letter. Aunt Sally hustles the boys to their room, where they sleep until nearly midnight. When they arise, Tom puts on a dress he has stolen from Aunt Sally in order to play the role of Jim's mother in the escape. Tom sends Huck downstairs to get butter for their provisions. There, Huck bumps into Aunt Sally, but manages to hide a slab of corn pone and the butter under his hat. Not satisfied with Huck's reasons for being in the cellar, Aunt Sally takes him into the sitting room, where he finds 15 farmers armed with guns. As she questions Huck in the hot room, streaks of butter begin oozing down his face, making Aunt Sally think Huck has "brain fever." Relieved to find only butter under his hat, she sends him back to his room.

The moment Huck is upstairs, he and Tom go out the window and head for Jim's cabin. Tom is pleased about the armed men in the house. After he and Huck enter the cabin, armed men pour inside. Nevertheless, Tom, Huck and Jim quietly slip out through the hole dug under Jim's bed. As they go over a fence, the men shoot at them and set dogs on them. The dogs know the boys, however, and lose interest in the chase when they catch up with them.

Once they seem safe on the raft, Jim and Huck are happy. However, Tom is the happiest—because he has a bullet in his calf. This news takes all the pleasure out of the escape for Jim and Huck, who insist on fetching a doctor immediately. Huck takes the canoe to go find a doctor.

Chapter 41
Huck finds a kindly old doctor and tells him that his brother has shot himself on SPANISH ISLAND. The doctor heads for the island with Huck, but he will not ride in the flimsy canoe with a second person, so he leaves Huck behind and paddles to the island by himself.

That night, Huck sleeps in a lumber pile and awakens in broad daylight. Before he can start back to the island, he runs into Uncle Silas, who makes him accompany him home. The house is full of farmers and their wives talking about the crazy runaway slave who has left all manner of strange things in the cabin, such as the giant grindstone. No one can explain who did all the work that must have been done in the cabin.

As the day wears into night and Tom does not appear, Aunt Sally and Uncle Silas grow increasingly worried. Huck tries to reassure Aunt Sally, who makes him promise not to leave the house again. Three times he slides down the lightning rod, but changes his mind about leaving when he sees Aunt Sally patiently sitting on the front porch with a candle.

Chapter 42

The next morning, Uncle Silas fails to learn anything in town about Tom's whereabouts. When he returns, he gives Aunt Sally a letter he collected at the post office the day before. It is from her sister, Aunt Polly. Sensing what trouble that message must contain, Huck starts to leave, but at that moment, Tom appears. He is carried to the house on a mattress. The old doctor is with him, as is Jim, with his hands tied behind him.

Jim's captors are treating him roughly and some want to hang him as an example for other would-be runaways. Others are opposed because they do not want to be responsible for paying Jim's owner. The men take Jim back to the cabin and chain him up tightly, but the doctor suggests that Jim be treated more kindly. He explains how when he found Tom on the island and needed help badly, Jim emerged from hiding and gave him all the help he could, risking his own freedom to provide it. The men agree that Jim has acted well, but no one moves to lighten his load of chains.

As Aunt Sally nurses Tom through the night, Huck dodges Uncle Silas in order to avoid embarrassing questions. The next morning Huck visits Tom, who astounds Aunt Sally by confessing that he and Huck are behind Jim's escape. His ecstasy is spoiled, however, when he learns that Jim is again a prisoner. He now stuns both Huck and Aunt Sally by saying that Jim is a free man. Miss Watson died two months earlier, he reveals, freeing Jim in her will. Tom explains that he engineered the entire escape for the "adventure of it" and demands that Jim be set free immediately.

At that moment, Aunt Sally's sister Polly enters the room. Aunt Sally gets her third thunderbolt when Polly explains that "Sid" is really Tom and "Tom" is really Huck Finn. Her confusion is tame, however, compared to what Uncle Silas experiences when everything is explained to him. Aunt Polly verifies that Jim is free. It emerges that Tom has been intercepting all the letters she has sent to Sally.

Chapter the Last

When Huck finally speaks privately with Tom, he asks what Tom intended to do with Jim if the "evasion" worked. Tom explains that he had hoped to continue rafting down the river, having adventures. Then, when

Tom and Huck share Jim's pleasure in being free.

they reached the mouth of the river, he would tell Jim that he was free and take him home on a steamboat, "in style, and pay him for his lost time," and have a big reception for him on his arrival at home.

Jim is freed soon after Aunt Polly's arrival. Tom gives him $40 for having been a patient prisoner and suggests that some time he, Huck and Jim make a trip into Indian Territory. Huck says he could not afford to pay for the outfit, because he reckons that his Pap has all his money by now. Now it is Jim's turn for a revelation. He tells Huck that the murdered man they saw in the floating house (chapter 9) was his father.

After Tom gets well, he wears his bullet around his neck on a watch-guard. Huck says that Aunt Sally wants to adopt him. He cannot stand that idea and reckons that he must "light out for the Territory ahead of the rest."

BACKGROUND AND PUBLISHING HISTORY

Few of Mark Twain's books had a more fitful start and painful development than *Huckleberry Finn*. Thanks to the research of Walter BLAIR, the history of the book's composition is now reasonably firmly established. Mark Twain worked on it intermittently over eight years, during which his conceptions of what he was writing changed radically.

The quick success of *Tom Sawyer* in 1876 moved Mark Twain to begin a sequel immediately. Determined to use a boy as his narrator in the new book, he thought Tom would be unsuitable and selected Huck—a decision that probably sent his narrative in directions that he never expected it to go. By the end of the summer of 1876, he had written at least as far as chapter 16, in which a steamboat smashes Huck and Jim's raft. This incident evidently left Mark Twain baffled as to where next to take his story. Three years later he resumed the story, carrying it to around chapter 21. After another interval, he wrote the book's second half around late 1882 and early 1883, adding significant passages to chapters 12–14. By this time, he had already extracted a passage known as the "RAFT CHAPTER" for another book, *Life on the Mississippi,* in which he alludes to having worked on his novel "by fits and starts, during the past five or six years" (chapter 3). Though *Life on the Mississippi* also says that he might finish his novel "in the course of five or six more [years]," he pronounced *Huckleberry Finn* done in the summer of 1883, shortly after *Mississippi* was published. Through the following year, he edited the book with the help of his friend W. D. HOWELLS.

To illustrate the book, Mark Twain commissioned E. W. KEMBLE, who drew about 175 pictures for it. In later years, he was uncertain how well he liked Kemble's work. Meanwhile, he had a photograph of the bust that Karl GERHARDT sculpted of him inserted as a second frontispiece to *Huckleberry Finn.*

To publicize his forthcoming book, Mark Twain published extracts in CENTURY MAGAZINE in December 1884 and January and February 1885. The novel was published as a book in England and Canada on December 10, 1884. On February 18, 1885, Mark Twain's own firm, Charles L. WEBSTER & COMPANY, issued the first American edition of the novel as its own inaugural publication. Since then, *Huckleberry Finn* has remained in print continuously, selling an estimated 20 million copies in more than 50 different languages.

The typeset pages of the first American edition of *Huckleberry Finn* were comparatively faithful to his manuscript, but Mark Twain was unhappy with them and lacked the time to correct proofs thoroughly. One of the most glaring errors that slipped through was the name "Bessie" for Becky Thatcher—a mistake in chapter 8 that he himself had corrected. The first fully corrected edition was published on the 100th anniversary of the novel's original American publication. In 1985, the editors of the MARK TWAIN PAPERS project published a meticulously corrected and annotated edition, making every effort to follow Mark Twain's original intentions for the book. They worked from Mark Twain's handwritten manuscript of the last 60 percent of the book—the only portion then known to exist; from the book's first American edition; from the *Century Magazine* excerpts; from an incomplete set of first edition page proofs; and from chapter 3 of *Life on the Mississippi,* in which the "Raft Chapter" was first pub-

lished. Two typescripts used in intermediate editing phases are not known to survive.

One of the most dramatic events relating to modern Mark Twain scholarship occurred in February 1991, when the rediscovery of the long-lost portion of Mark Twain's handwritten manuscript was announced. Missing from the BUFFALO and Erie County Public Library since the turn of the century, the pages were found among the papers of the Buffalo civic leader who originally persuaded Mark Twain to donate the manuscript to the library. It is thought that this man borrowed the manuscript to read shortly before he died, and that it then became mixed up with own papers, which were stored away and forgotten. When the legal status of these pages is resolved, the Mark Twain Papers project plans to use the manuscript to issue a new edition of *Huckleberry Finn* around 1997.

***Huckleberry Finn*, dramatizations of** Since *Huckleberry Finn*'s publication in 1884, its story has inspired numerous stage plays and musicals, more than a half-dozen feature films and a like number of television productions, as well as cartoons and an opera. While many of these adaptations have treated certain episodes of the novel faithfully, none has attempted to adapt all the book's major episodes. Ironically, the very first dramatic production to be called "Huckleberry Finn" had almost nothing to do with the novel. In November 1902, a Klaw and Erlanger musical titled *Huckleberry Finn* ran briefly in Hartford. This production used Jim and several other *Huckleberry Finn* characters, but was actually based mostly on episodes from *Tom Sawyer.*

The first film adaptation, in 1920, was a silent movie titled *Huckleberry Finn,* featuring Lewis Sargent (1904–?) as Huck and George Reed (1867–1952) as Jim. Shot on Mississippi River locations, the film was designed to resemble E. W. KEMBLE's original book illustrations. Paramount produced the first sound film adaptation in 1931. This production was actually a sequel to Paramount's 1930 *Tom Sawyer,* with Junior Durkin (1915–1935) returning as Huck and Jackie Coogan (1914–1984) as Tom; Clarence Muse (1889–1979) played Jim. In order to capitalize on *Tom Sawyer*'s success, the film gave Becky Thatcher a major role and had Tom accompany Huck and Jim on their raft journey. Eight years later, MGM released a more orthodox adaptation, with Mickey Rooney (1920–) as Huck and Rex Ingram (1895–1969)—who was born on a steamboat near CAIRO, Illinois—as Jim. William Frawley (1887–1966), later known as Fred Mertz in "I Love Lucy," played the Duke. In contrast to the Paramount production, this film did not use Tom Sawyer at all.

It was not until two decades later that another feature film was made from *Huckleberry Finn.* Meanwhile, several adaptations appeared on television in the mid-1950s, and Josh Logan announced in 1951 that a Broadway musical, *Huck and Jim,* with book by Maxwell Anderson and music by Kurt Weill, was under production. This play was never produced, however, possibly because MGM announced the following year that it planned to produce a musical version of *Huckleberry Finn* that would star Dean Stockwell as Huck, Gene Kelly as the King and Danny Kaye as the Duke. This film was not produced, either, but MGM released the first color film adaptation of the novel in 1960 as *The Adventures of Huckleberry Finn*, a big-budget production with several songs by Alan Jay Lerner and Burton Lane. Eddie Hodges (1947–) played Huck, and boxing champion Archie Moore (1913–) was Jim. An example of the condensation that typifies adaptations is the film's reduction of the entire Grangerford–Shepherdson feud to a two-minute description.

In 1974 Reader's Digest and United Artists combined to release *Huckleberry Finn* as a musical sequel to their previous year's *Tom Sawyer*. Jeff East returned as Huck, and Paul Winfield (1941–) played Jim. The following year, a new television film of *Huckleberry Finn* aired on ABC-TV, with 21-year-old Ron Howard (1954–) as Huck and his "Happy Days" costar Donny Most (1953–) as Tom Sawyer. Antonio Fargas (1946–), soon to be a regular on "Starsky and Hutch," played Jim, and Royal Dano (1922–1994) appeared as Mark Twain to introduce the story. The 1979 television play MARK TWAIN: BENEATH THE LAUGHTER dramatized two poignant scenes from *Huckleberry Finn* that rarely appear in full-length productions. Another television film, *The Adventures of Huckleberry Finn*, aired on NBC-TV in July 1981, though it was made two years earlier. In this production, Kurt Ida played Huck and Brock Peters (1927–) played Jim; Larry Storch (1923–) and Forrest Tucker (1919–1986) were the King and Duke.

In 1984, a Broadway production of *Huckleberry Finn* was finally launched as BIG RIVER, winning a Tony Award for best musical. In early 1986, the most ambitious adaptation of the novel to date aired on public television as a miniseries, with Patrick Day as Huck and Samm-Art Williams (1946–) as Jim. Although this four-hour production was faithful enough to the original story to incorporate the "Raft Chapter," it omitted the Wilks episode. Seven years later, Disney contributed its own adaptation as *The Adventures of Huck Finn*, a feature film with Elijah Wood (1982–) as Huck and Courtney Vance as Jim. This film gave extended treatment to the Grangerford and Wilks episodes, while omitting Tom Sawyer and the "EVASION" episode altogether. It also greatly expanded Jim's role by having him captured by the Grangerfords and having him go ashore with Huck and the con men in the Wilkses' village.

Mark Twain's novel has also inspired several prose adaptations. The most interesting of these is John SEELYE's *The True Adventures of Huckleberry Finn* (1970 and 1987), which retains most of Mark Twain's original text, while reducing Tom Sawyer's role significantly, eliminating the evasion sequence and rewriting many passages in stronger language.

Hugo   Character in *The Prince and the Pauper*. Somewhat older and bigger than King EDWARD VI, Hugo is a member of the RUFFLER's criminal gang. In chapter 13, he helps John CANTY spirit the king away from LONDON BRIDGE, but is not identified by name until chapter 17, when the Ruffler assigns him to supervise the king. The king refuses to cooperate, however, forcing Hugo to struggle to keep him from escaping. At first, Hugo is reasonably cheerful and agreeable, but the king's rebelliousness eventually brings out his cruelest impulses. After the king humiliates him in a fight, Hugo tricks him into being arrested for theft, and he himself disappears from the story (chapter 22).

Hugo   Minor character in *Connecticut Yankee*. An approximately 30-year-old man whom MORGAN LE FAY's executioner is torturing in chapter 17, Hugo tells Hank MORGAN that he killed a stag that was ravaging his fields, then dumped it in a forest to avoid detection. Though nominally guilty, he refuses to confess in order that his family not be stripped of everything they own. His wife, however, begs him to confess to end his suffering on the rack. Impressed by the couple's courage, Hank has Hugo freed and sends him to his MAN FACTORY.

Humboldt   Historic MINING district in northern NEVADA. The region called "Humboldt" in *Roughing It* centered on the Humboldt Mountains and the lower Humboldt River, just over 100 miles northeast of Lake TAHOE. Interstate Highway 80 now follows the river from northeastern Nevada to the Humboldt Sink, where it disappears near the southwestern foothills of the mountain range; this same route was a major entryway to CARSON CITY and the Sierra Nevada for wagon trains in the mid-19th century. The region encompassing the sink and mountains is now in Pershing County, *south* of modern Humboldt County. After a major silver strike was made in the mountains in June 1861, prospectors flocked to the region and founded UNIONVILLE. In December, Mark Twain and three companions left Carson City with a large load of mining supplies and walked to Unionville to try their luck prospecting. After two weeks of frustration, Mark Twain gave up and returned to Carson City with three other men in mid-January. His return trip took 15 days, during nine of which he was stranded at HONEY LAKE SMITH's inn. *Roughing It* offers a colorfully embroidered account of this episode, calling his various fictionalized travel companions OLIPHANT, BALLOU, CLAGETT and OLLENDORFF (chapters 26–33). The Humboldt district enjoyed a minor silver boom in 1868, but by 1880 all production was finished.

Ike Name mentioned in *Huckleberry Finn.* In chapter 20, Huck invents a story to explain to the KING and DUKE why he and Jim are rafting down the Mississippi River. Huck tells the con men that he, his father and his four-year-old brother Ike were heading to a relative's home near New Orleans when a steamboat struck their raft. Ike and the father drowned.

Illinois Mark Twain grew up in Hannibal, Missouri, from which he could daily see the heavily forested shoreline of Illinois across the Mississippi River—a view that remains little changed today. In summer he could—and probably occasionally did—swim the mile width of the river, though taking a boat or a raft must have been more common. In the winter he could skate or walk across the river when it froze over. While only a mile separated his "slave state" from the "free state" of Illinois, the cultural chasm between the two states was enormous, contributing to feelings of hostility and even occasional armed animosity, as during the 1840s, when Illinois towns supported the MORMON communities driven out of Missouri. The looming presence of free Illinois across almost the entire Mississippi River frontage of Missouri made it difficult for Missouri to feel itself entirely a part of the slave South. However, despite Illinois's "free" status, it was never a haven for escaped slaves. Under the terms of the country's fugitive slave laws, Illinois citizens stood to earn generous rewards for capturing and returning any blacks unable to produce documentation proving they were not slaves.

Mark Twain's first significant trip into Illinois occurred in 1853 when he passed through the state to CHICAGO, on his way to New York. In later years he made several extended visits to Chicago. He also passed through many Illinois towns on lecture tours in 1869, late 1871 and early 1885.

Illinois's presence can be felt through much of Mark Twain's Mississippi fiction. In *Huckleberry Finn,* Pap FINN takes Huck to a cabin on the Illinois side of the river; this puts him beyond the jurisdiction of Missouri authorities, making it difficult for Judge THATCHER and the Widow DOUGLAS to get him back (chapter 6). JACKSON'S ISLAND, to which Huck and Jim later flee, is in or near Illinois, and CAIRO, Illinois is the first place to which they want to go when they begin their raft journey down the Mississippi.

"In Defense of Harriet Shelley" Essay published in 1894. One of Mark Twain's longest forays into serious literary criticism, this essay analyzes a biography of Percy Bysshe Shelley (1792–1822) published in 1886 by the Irish Shakespearean scholar Edward Dowden (1843–1913). Rejecting Dowden's claim that Shelley had no responsibility for the suicide of his first wife, he calls Dowden's work "perhaps the strangest book that has seen the light since Frankenstein."

In 1811, Shelley eloped with 16-year-old Harriet Westbrook. He treated her with indifference for three years, then abandoned her and the two children she had borne and went to Switzerland with Mary Wollstonecraft (1797–1851). In early 1816, Harriet's body was found in a London park lake. Just three weeks later, Shelley married Wollstonecraft—who as Mary Shelley wrote *Frankenstein* in 1818.

In the face of Shelley's callous treatment of Harriet, Mark Twain asks rhetorically why someone would try to write biography when simple facts mean nothing to him. He also attacks Dowden's writing style as a "literary cake-walk" in which artificial elegance substitutes for substance.

This 15,000-word essay first appeared in the July–September 1894 issues of NORTH AMERICAN REVIEW. It was collected in HOW TO TELL A STORY AND OTHER ESSAYS and in LITERARY ESSAYS—which was also issued as *In Defense of Harriet Shelley and Other Essays.*

India In 1896, Mark Twain spent more than two months in India on the third major leg of his round-the-world LECTURE tour. Between late January and late March, he delivered about 20 lectures in 12 Indian cities, mostly within the triangular region between Bombay, Calcutta and Delhi. After leaving AUSTRALIA, he reached CEYLON with his wife and daughter Clara on January 13, 1896. The next day, they sailed up India's west coast, landing at Bombay on January 20. At the end of the month, they went north to Baroda, returned to Bombay, then made a two-day train trip northeast to Allahabad. After several days there and in the nearby Hindu religious center Benares (Varanasi), they went southeast to Calcutta for a week. On February 14, they traveled north to Darjeeling, where they were within viewing range of Mount Everest for several days. After returning to Calcutta, they passed through Benares

Mark Twain leads a procession of baggage carriers into his Bombay hotel in Dan Beard's illustration for chapter 38 of Following the Equator.

again, stopping at Muzaffurpore (Mirzapur), Lucknow, Agra and Jaipur (Jeypore). In late March, they continued northwest into what is now Pakistan, then returned to Calcutta. On March 28, they sailed for MAURITIUS on the *Wardha,* stopping at Madras for a day and at Ceylon for several days before entering the open sea.

Mark Twain's lecture audiences in India typically comprised local American residents and British civil servants and soldiers, with a minority of Indians. Throughout India, he was treated almost royally. High colonial officials entertained him and Indians invited him to attend ceremonies that few Western tourists witnessed. Despite the warmth of his reception, his stay in India was an uncomfortable one. Heat, insects, dirt, long train trips and general discomforts wore him down. Sick almost half the time he was there, he had to cancel or reschedule many lecture appearances.

Despite Mark Twain's weakened condition and his dismay at seeing India's overwhelming poverty and disease, he managed to inject a great deal of energy into his chapters on India in *Following the Equator*—about 40 percent of which is devoted to the country (chapters 12, 38–61). In contrast to his other travel writings, his chapters on India say more about India's people and history than about his own experiences there. He gives considerable space to Thuggee (chapters 43, 46–48), Suttee (chapters 43, 48, 52) and religion in Benares (chapters 50–51, 57). Several chapters offer almost purely historical accounts of such subjects as the Black Hole of Calcutta (chapter 54) and India's 1857 Mutiny (chapter 58).

In the novella "A DOUBLE-BARRELLED DETECTIVE STORY" (1902), Archy STILLMAN retraces Mark Twain's route through India while pursuing a man (chapter 3). In other writings, Mark Twain often invokes the name of India's ruined city of Golconda as a symbol of fabulous wealth.

Indian Territory Region congruous with modern Oklahoma—except the Panhandle—during the 19th century. The federal government designated the region a home for the Five Civilized Tribes who were being removed from eastern states. Indians governed most of the eastern part of the territory. The rest of the territory had no organized government, but was closed to white settlement until the 1890s. By the end of that decade, the territory was split in half: Oklahoma Territory in the west, and Indian Territory in the east. The original territory was reunited and made the state of Oklahoma in 1907.

Before the 1890s, the ungoverned part of the territory was a haven for outlaws. The border separating ARKANSAS from Indian Territory was only about 200 miles from PIKESVILLE, where the last chapters of *Huckleberry Finn* are set. At the end of chapter 39 of *Huckleberry Finn,* Tom Sawyer posts an anonymous letter warning that abolitionists are about to steal the runaway slave Jim and take him to "Ingean Territory." In the final chapter, Tom Sawyer proposes that Huck and Jim join him on an expedition "amongst the Injuns, over in the Territory." The penultimate line of the novel is famous: Huck says that he wants to "light out for the Territory ahead of the rest, because Aunt Sally she's going to adopt me and sivilize me and I can't stand it." Huck is so anxious to escape Sally PHELPS's attention that he apparently wants to go to the Indian Territory without waiting for Tom and Jim to join him. When Tom, Huck and Jim finally make their trip in Mark Twain's unfinished "HUCK FINN AND TOM SAWYER AMONG THE INDIANS," they pass through western Missouri and NE-BRASKA, without going near Indian Territory proper.

Indians, American Although Mark Twain prided himself on being free of ethnic and racial prejudice, he had a blind spot that long prevented him from seeing anything positive in American Indians. By his own admission, he absorbed a distorted, romantically idealized notion of Indians from the novels of James Fenimore COOPER. Until he went west as an adult, his closest exposure to real Indians may have been limited to the occasional "civilized" person such as Hannibal's town drunk "Injun Joe"—the real-life model for the INJUN JOE of *Tom Sawyer*. He first saw Indians in their own environment when he crossed the Plains to NEVADA in 1861. Along the STAGECOACH trail he heard worrisome rumors about "hostiles," but did not encounter any Indians until he reached the desperately poor GOSIUTE of the Utah–Nevada border area. What he saw of them not only cured him of romantic ideas about "noble savages," but turned him into a fierce critic, and he immediately wrote home to report his conversion. Over the next five years, most of the Indians whom he saw were poor hunter-gatherers regarded as dangerous nuisances by white settlers. An early short story, "AURELIA'S UNFORTUNATE YOUNG MAN" (1864), reflects this attitude in having a character who is scalped by Owens River Indians. In 1870, Mark Twain summed up his prejudices in "The Noble Red Man," a sketch for the GALAXY.

A statement that Mark Twain makes in *Roughing It* (1872) epitomizes his attitude toward Indians in later years: "Wherever one finds an Indian tribe he has only found Goshoots more or less modified by circumstances and surroundings" (chapter 19). *Roughing It* is full of references to Indians, few of which are not negative. The narrator relishes describing unsavory aspects of Indian diet and hygiene, as well as examples of their cunning and treachery. *Innocents Abroad* contains an even more sweeping statement of Mark Twain's prejudice. After dismissing Cooper's Indians as nonexistent, he states, "I know the Noble Red Man. I have camped with the Indians; I have been on the war-path with them, taken part in the chase with them—for grasshoppers; helped them steal cattle; I have roamed with them, scalped them, had them for breakfast. I would gladly eat the whole race if I had a chance" (chapter 20).

When Mark Twain visited Europe in 1878–79, he noted—apparently with some regret—that many Germans feared migrating to America because of the danger of hostile Indians, who they thought were everywhere. He mentions this in chapter 21 of *A Tramp Abroad*.

Life on the Mississippi (1883) says a great deal about Indians, particularly in its final chapters on Mark Twain's trip up the Upper Mississippi. The book relates several lengthy Indian legends; on the whole, they are presented neutrally, but there is an underlying disrespect for the cultures behind them. Chapter 60, for example, presents "a most idiotic Indian legend" about White Bear Lake.

There are no Indian characters in *Huckleberry Finn* but the novel contains many allusions to stereotyped behavior, such as "whooping and yelling" like "Injuns" (chapters 16, 21 and 22). While correcting proofs of *Huckleberry Finn*, Mark Twain began a sequel hinted at toward the end of that novel, in which Tom suggests that he and Huck "go for howling adventures amongst the Injuns, over in the Territory"—likely a reference to INDIAN TERRITORY. Mark Twain then wrote nine chapters of "HUCK FINN AND TOM SAWYER AMONG THE INDI-ANS" in a deliberate effort to debunk Cooper's "noble savage." The story begins with Tom raving about Indians being "the most gigantic magnificent creatures in the whole world." He persuades Huck and Jim to join him on an expedition to find Indians. Once they are on the Plains, they join up with the emigrant MILLS family, who are visited by a band of Oglala Sioux. Everything about these Indians confirms Tom's romantic notions, until one day when the Indian men suddenly appear in warpaint and massacre everyone in the Mills family but the daughters, whom they kidnap, along with Jim. In the aftermath of this disaster, Huck asks Tom where he got the idea that Indians were "noble." Tom reluctantly answers, "Cooper's novels." After Brace JOHNSON, the rugged fiancé of Peggy, one of the kidnapped daughters, arrives, he is obsessed with fear that Peggy may not have killed herself with a knife he gave her. Mark Twain never explains *why* Johnson wants her dead; however, from whispered asides and from the nature of the sources on which he drew in researching his story, it is clear that he saw Peggy's fate as gang rape and sexual torture. To make his point about Indians, he would have had to lead the story to this ignoble conclusion; his inability to write frankly about such a theme probably was the reason he abandoned the story.

Connecticut Yankee (1889) occasionally uses Indians as models of savagery against whom Hank MORGAN measures sixth-century Englishmen. In chapter 2, he calls the bloodthirsty knights "white Indians." Later, he compares them to Comanches (chapter 15)—just as Mark Twain compares the French with Comanches in a posthumously published essay.

There are indications that Mark Twain's attitude toward Indians mellowed in later years. A passage of his AUTOBIOGRAPHY recorded in 1906 discusses the irony of

Americans celebrating "Thanksgiving" after the original reason for being thankful was gone—namely the extermination of all the Indians. He suggests that the success of white men in this regard indicates that God was on their side, not that of the Indians. That passage is obviously meant to be ironic. Something he published several years later, however, is more straightforward. In his extract from "CAPTAIN STORMFIELD'S VISIT TO HEAVEN" (1909), the clerk who greets Stormfield in heaven is a PIUTE Indian whom Stormfield had known in California's Tulare County. Stormfield discovers, in fact, that Indians are a vast majority in heaven—perhaps Mark Twain's concession that God regards Indians at least as highly as He does anyone else.

Injun Joe   Character in *Tom Sawyer*. Described by Huck Finn as a "murderin' half-breed" (chapter 9), the cruel and vengeful Injun Joe is the novel's one truly villainous character; he has been a disreputable resident of ST. PETERSBURG for at least five years. He appears only a few times in the narrative, but usually unexpectedly. Even when he is not present, his specter looms.

Tom Sawyer dreams that Injun Joe is after him in chapter 14 of Tom Sawyer.

In chapter 9, Huck and Tom stumble upon Injun Joe, Muff POTTER and Dr. ROBINSON opening a grave in the town cemetery. Injun Joe argues with Robinson over a past slight, and then kills him while Potter is momentarily knocked out. When Potter awakens, Injun Joe convinces him that *he* (Potter) is the killer. The next day, when Tom and Huck see Injun Joe give his version of what happened, they are so dumbfounded that he is not struck dead that they conclude he is in league with Satan. Some townspeople want to run Injun Joe out of town for body-snatching, but no one has the nerve to take him on. He reappears at the murder trial in chapter 23, when he testifies convincingly against Potter. Just as Potter's situation looks hopeless, Tom is called as a surprise witness. As Tom starts to declare Injun Joe the murderer, Injun Joe bolts from the building and disappears, leaving Tom more scared than ever.

In chapter 26 Tom and Huck again happen on Injun Joe, at the HAUNTED HOUSE. He has been living in town, unrecognized, as a "deef and dumb Spaniard." He has a new partner—who is never identified—with whom he is planning a new crime. After he satisfies his need for vengeance against an unnamed party, he intends to flee permanently to TEXAS. Purely by chance, he finds a box of gold coins in the house. Huck and Tom are determined to get hold of the treasure, so they stalk Injun Joe and his partner.

As Tom goes off to McDougal's CAVE on Becky THATCHER's picnic in chapter 29, Huck follows Injun Joe and his partner to CARDIFF HILL. He eavesdrops and learns that Injun Joe intends to mutilate the Widow DOUGLAS. Injun Joe wants revenge for a public horse-whipping that the widow's husband gave him when he was justice of the peace. His partner resists the idea, but Injun Joe threatens to kill him. Huck alerts JONES THE WELCHMAN, who, with his sons, chases the villains off. Injun Joe again disappears.

Meanwhile, Tom and Becky get lost in the cave. While searching for a way out a day or two later, Tom sees Injun Joe in the cave. Tom escapes detection and eventually finds a way out of the cave. Correctly guessing that Injun Joe has hidden the gold in the cave, Tom does not tell anyone that he has seen him there. After spending two weeks recuperating from his ordeal, Tom learns that Judge THATCHER has had the cave's entrance sealed shut with an iron door. Tom finally reveals that Injun Joe is still in the cave. People rush to the cave and they find Injun Joe dead. His body is just beyond the new door. He has died of starvation after eating candle stumps and bats while trying to dig out with his Bowie knife. Injun Joe is buried just outside the cave. The anonymous narrator reveals that there had been a popular movement to petition the governor to pardon Injun Joe, even though the man is believed to have murdered five people in the town.

Mark Twain took Injun Joe's name from a Hannibal resident about two years older than himself whose real name may have been Joe Douglas. This man was an

Osage INDIAN who had been scalped by Pawnees as a child and brought to Hannibal by cattlemen as a teenager. Mark Twain's AUTOBIOGRAPHY claims that the real Injun Joe once subsisted on bats while lost in the cave. He died a respected citizen in 1925. Injun Joe does not appear in any other stories, but Mark Twain mentions him in IS SHAKESPEARE DEAD?

Innocence at Home Nickname that Mark Twain chose for his new REDDING, Connecticut home in June 1908 to replace "AUTOBIOGRAPHY HOUSE." The new name reflected his growing interest in his ANGELFISH Club for girls. Club rules called the name especially appropriate, since a primary purpose of the house was to accommodate club members. After Clara Clemens returned from Europe in September, she objected to the house's name and persuaded her father to change it to "STORMFIELD."

The Innocents Abroad, or The New Pilgrims' Progress; Being Some Account of the Steamship Quaker City's Pleasure Excursion to Europe and the Holy Land (1869) Mark Twain's first book, aside from a small collection of republished sketches, *Innocents Abroad* is an embroidered account of his five-month cruise through the MEDITERRANEAN in 1867 aboard the steamship QUAKER CITY. Most of it is adapted from letters he wrote to the SAN FRANCISCO ALTA CALIFORNIA and other newspapers during the cruise, but he heavily revised many of his letters after the cruise and added a considerable amount of new material.

If the book has a central theme, it is the need for modern Americans not to be awed by the Old World. Almost everywhere the narrator goes, he refuses to be impressed by the sights he has been trained to reverence. BURLESQUE permeates the book, which pokes fun at local legends, dubious relics, paintings of the Old Masters, annoying guides and romantic travel books—especially those about the Holy Land. Patriotic, often almost chauvinistic, *Innocents* never hesitates to describe foreign government incompetence and corruption, poverty, filth and disease—all of which it finds almost everywhere the travelers go. The book's tone is often inconsistent, however. Some chapters shift between ridicule and praise. To some extent, these inconsistencies are a function of *when* Mark Twain originally wrote each passage. While most chapters are revisions of his travel letters, some—such as those on France—were written mostly after the cruise was over.

The line between fact and fiction in *Innocents* is not always sharp. While the book clearly builds itself around Mark Twain's own experiences, its narrator does not necessarily speak in Mark Twain's voice at all times. In the earliest chapters, the narrator is naive and stumbles into comic situations, but as the book progresses he becomes increasingly worldly and more critical of what he sees.

A major part of the interest and humor in *Innocents Abroad* derives from its remarks about the other Americans with whom Mark Twain traveled. The book is as much about them as it is about Europe and the Holy Land, and it treats them at least equally savagely. *Innocents* mentions only a few *Quaker City* passengers and crew members by their full names, and then only when they do something praiseworthy—as when Moses S. BEACH is named in chapter 58. For the most part, the book treats other passengers with varying levels of good-natured fun or fierce ridicule. It assigns nicknames or abbreviations to many persons, such as "Dan" (Dan SLOTE), "Jack" (Jack VAN NOSTRAND), the "Doctor" (Abraham JACKSON), the "ORACLE" (Dr. Edward Andrews) and "Dr. B." (Dr. George Bright Birch). Though the real identities of most characters can be determined, anecdotes attributed to them are not necessarily all true. Some characters are composites. For example, while Mark Twain himself identified the blundering "BLUCHER" as a passenger named Frederick H. Greer, several Blucher anecdotes draw on mishaps to other men, as well as the author's imagination.

Innocents does not attempt to account for every passenger involved in the *Quaker City* cruise. Several people who became close friends of Mark Twain—such as Mary Mason FAIRBANKS and Emily Severance—make no discernible appearance in the book. Likewise, the book does not account for every trip and adventure that Mark Twain experienced during the cruise. For example, it neglects to mention his brief visit to SWITZERLAND, and it reduces his week-long trip through SPAIN to a single sentence. By contrast, it devotes two chapters to TANGIER, where he spent just one day.

Mark Twain's struggle to give the book coherent thematic unity is reflected in his struggle to find a satisfactory title. His working titles included "The New Pilgrim's Progress," "The Exodus of the Innocents," "The Crusade of the Innocents," and "The Irruption of the Jonathans." He was inclined to go with "The New Pilgrims' Progress," but feared it might cause the book to be confused with John BUNYAN's classic religious work. He compromised by using that phrase as a subtitle, while settling on "The Innocents Abroad" for the book's main title.

SYNOPSIS

A book of 191,720 words, *Innocents Abroad* contains a brief preface, 61 numbered chapters (only 60 of which are in most tables of contents) and an unnumbered conclusion chapter. While *Innocents* mixes fact and fiction, its narrative structure generally follows the actual journey that Mark Twain made. Between June 8 and November 19, 1867, he was a passenger on the steamship *Quaker City*, which took him from New York City to the Mediterranean and back. Along the way, he visited the Azores, Gibraltar, Tangier, France, Italy, Greece, Russia, Turkey, Syria, Palestine, Egypt, Spain and Bermuda, with brief stops at other ports. *Innocents Abroad* mentions few specific dates—and some of those it does mention are inaccurate. In the synopsis that follows here, wherever the narrator's arrivals and departures can be confidently linked to Mark Twain's movements, his actual dates of travel are inserted within parentheses. In some instances, these dates differ from the apparent chronology given in *Innocents Abroad.*

The book's first two chapters discuss preparations for the trip. Chapters 3–6 cover the two weeks that the *Quaker City* spent sailing to the AZORES (June 10–23, 1867). Chapters 7–9 continue the voyage to GIBRALTAR, including a side trip to TANGIER (June 23–July 1). Chapters 10–16 cover ten days in France, beginning with the July 4 landing at MARSEILLES, from which Mark Twain went to PARIS and back. The ship left Marseilles on July 13 and landed at GENOA the next day. Chapters 17–31 are set entirely in ITALY, which the *Quaker City* and all its passengers left on August 11.

Through chapters 32–40, the ship moves about frequently. It enters the Greek islands, stops at ATHENS (August 14–15), CONSTANTINOPLE (August 17–19), SEVASTOPOL (August 21), ODESSA (August 22–24) and YALTA (August 25–28). A second stop is made at Constantinople (August 30–September 3), followed by a landing at SMYRNA (September 5–6), from which most passengers take a train to EPHESUS.

Chapters 41–56 cover Mark Twain's overland journey with seven other men from BEIRUT to the HOLY LAND, culminating in his rejoining the ship at JAFFA (September 11–October 1). His five-day stop in EGYPT is described in chapters 57–58 (October 2–7). Chapters 59–60 summarize the voyage home (October 7–November 19). During this long stretch, the *Quaker City* made extended stops only at Gibraltar, from which Mark Twain made a side trip through SPAIN (October 17–25), and BERMUDA (November 11–15); each of these episodes receives just a paragraph in the book.

Through the first 27 chapters of both one- and two-volume editions, chapter numbers match. Chapters in the second volume of two-volume editions are numbered from 1 through 33; this synopsis gives both sets of chapter numbers. Information not in parentheses comes directly from the chapters; parenthesized information comes from other sources.

Chapter 1
For months, the great pleasure excursion to Europe and the Holy Land is discussed everywhere. It is to be a novelty—a picnic on a gigantic scale. Participants will sail over the breezy Atlantic and the sunny Mediterranean, scampering about the decks, shouting and laughing, dancing, smoking, singing and making love. They will hobnob with nobility and converse with kings. The brave conception is well advertised, but hardly needs to be. Who can read its program without longing to participate? Not only will the company be selected by a pitiless "Committee on Applications"; a similarly pitiless committee will select the vessel.

The narrator submits his application, rejoicing to learn that staterooms are still vacant. To get past the committee's scrutiny, his references are all the people of high standing *un*likely to know him. Regrettably, none of the cruise's celebrities—Henry Ward BEECHER, General SHERMAN, a popular actress (Maggie Mitchell) and the Drummer Boy of the Potomac (Robert Henry Hendershot)—can go.

Chapter 2
The impressive passenger roster includes three ministers, eight doctors, 16 or 18 ladies, several titled military men, professors and—most impressive—a man styling himself "Commissioner of the United States of America to Europe, Asia, and Africa" (Dr. William GIBSON). Thrilled to be headed for Paris, the narrator spends a happy month hanging about in New York with a fellow passenger, Mr. BLUCHER, who is convinced that *everybody* is going to Paris. Blucher astounds a shopkeeper by offering to pay the balance of what he owes him in Paris during the summer. The ship departs on a June Saturday (June 8, 1867), only to anchor farther down the harbor to wait out an approaching storm. Soon, a gong sounds for prayer meeting.

Chapter 3
On Monday morning (June 10), the ship finally goes to sea. One of the few passengers not to get seasick, the narrator takes smug satisfaction in observing the distress of others. The ship is loaded with "captains": Captain DUNCAN is chief of the expedition, Captain (Ira) Bursley is the executive officer, "Captain L****" (Daniel LEARY) is the ship's owner and Captain (William) Jones is chief mate.

Chapter 4
Over the next week or so, the ship plows through the Atlantic without incident as passengers enjoy such amusements as horse billiards. Many gather for evening prayer meetings in a saloon that the unregenerate call the "Synagogue." Numerous passengers diligently begin journals, but most soon lose interest. One young journal keeper, Jack (VAN NOSTRAND) reports daily on his progress; however, by the time he reaches Paris, he reckons he is 4,000 pages behind. Other entertainments include music from an asthmatic melodeon and dancing—an activity impeded by the rolling of the ship. The passengers also celebrate a birthday (Captain Duncan's wife) and stage a mock trial.

Chapter 5
Early on the morning of June 21, passengers are awakened to the news that the AZORES are in sight. Because of rough weather, the ship anchors at the nearest island, where swarthy, noisy, lying, shoulder-shrugging, gesticulating Portuguese boatmen carry the passengers ashore. Happy to be on solid land, Blucher celebrates by treating nine shipmates to a feast at Horta's principal hotel. When he is billed 21,700 reis, he thinks himself

ruined. The day is saved when he learns that the amount is equivalent to only $21.70 in American money.

Chapter 6
Since none of the passengers knows anything about the Azores, the narrator supplies dry facts and details on local history. The community is eminently Portuguese—slow, poor and shiftless—and Jesuit humbuggery flourishes. An old cathedral has the first of many religious relics the travelers will encounter, including a piece of the true cross.

Chapter 7
The next week's voyage is rough, curtailing activities and making passengers seasick again until the ship reaches GIBRALTAR (June 29). Many passengers buzz about going through SPAIN to Paris, but the narrator stays behind. As he enjoys the magnificent view from atop the Rock of Gibraltar, an officious guide bores him with a local legend about the "Queen's Chair." A few passengers are also proving annoying. A man dubbed "the ORACLE," for example, insists that *both* PILLARS OF HERCULES are in Africa. He is tolerable enough, but two others are less so: the ship's self-anointed Poet Laureate (Bloodgood H. CUTTER) and a young idiot dubbed the "INTERROGATION POINT." A small party of passengers crosses the strait to TANGIER.

Chapter 8
Tangier gives the sightseers exactly what they have been seeking: something thoroughly and uncompromisingly foreign. It is right out of the ARABIAN NIGHTS.

Chapter 9
The travelers experience their first real adventure in Tangier when the heedless Blucher nearly rides his mule into a mosque. Later they visit a jail and learn how severe punishments for crimes can be. They also learn about contracted marriages and polygamy; Morocco's ruler (Mohammed IV, 1803–1873) reputedly has 500 wives. Tangier is full of interest for one day, but after that it becomes a weary prison. The American consul (Jesse H. McMath) has been here for five years; his post would be an apt punishment for perpetrators of particularly heinous crimes.

Chapter 10
The Fourth of July is celebrated aboard the *Quaker City* on a characteristically beautiful Mediterranean day. After decorating the ship, holding meetings and setting committees to work, the passengers spend the evening toasting, speaking and dancing on deck. The ship then reaches MARSEILLES, where the narrator and his friends rush ashore (still July 4). After clearing customs with little fuss, they dash to the nearest café, only to find communication in French nearly impossible.

Chapter 11
The eager travelers are adjusting well to all manner of strange customs. One thing they cannot easily adjust to, however, is providing their own soap in hotels. During a dinner, another American embarrasses them with his boisterous talk and laughter and his pitiful bragging about never dining without wine. The travelers visit the local Prado and take a boat to Castle d'If, whose notorious dungeon is famed as the prison of the Count of Monte Cristo and the Man in the Iron Mask. At the zoo, they study a tall, ungainly bird whose tranquil self-righteousness wins him the nickname "The PILGRIM."

Chapter 12
A train carries the narrator and two companions (Dan SLOTE and Abraham JACKSON) 500 miles through the heart of France. French railroads offer much to admire: their trains are spacious and comfortable and they run like clockwork. In PARIS (July 5), the travelers speed through the streets, find a hotel, then look for a place that will satisfy the narrator's wish for a shave in a palatial Parisian barbershop. He settles, however, for a wigmaker's shop, where he endures a dreary and painful shave.

Chapter 13
The next morning the travelers engage a dignified-looking guide, who appears to be quiet and unobtrusive. Hoping for a guide with a romantic French name, they are distressed to learn that his name is "Billfinger," so they call him "FERGUSON" instead. At breakfast they make the mistake of having Ferguson join them; his appetite is insatiable. He also has the annoying habit of stopping at shops to buy things; his delays keep the travelers from the Louvre until shortly before it closes. On their third day in Paris, the travelers visit the International Exposition. Overwhelmed by its size, they leave after just two hours when they hear that Emperor NAPOLEON III and Turkey's Sultan ABDUL AZIZ will appear in a military review.

Chapter 14
The next day the travelers inspect Paris's Notre Dame Cathedral, a brown old Gothic pile whose relics include nails from the true cross, a fragment of the cross itself and part of the crown of thorns. They also visit the morgue, Jardin Mabille and Jardin Asnières—where they see the high-wire act of Blondin (Charles Blondin, 1824–1897) and cancan dancers—and they study miles of paintings in the Louvre.

Chapter 15
A pleasant visit to Père la Chaise, France's national burying-ground, recalls the tragic story of ABELARD AND HÉLOISE. Meanwhile, the travelers still struggle to communicate in Paris. Many shops advertise "English Spoken Here," but their English-speaking attendants are never on the premises. Other frustrations include the difficulty of finding bartenders who can mix American drinks.

Chapter 16
The travelers spend a day at Versailles (July 10), the beautiful old palace outside of Paris that compares favorably with the Garden of Eden. Everything about it stupefies—especially its gigantic scale. Back in Paris, the travelers tour the "antipodes" of Versailles—the Faubourg St. Antoine, a crowded slum.

Chapter 17
When the travelers return to Marseilles (July 12), they learn that the ship's crew has been warring with British sailors; however, no great harm has been done. Many passengers are still on their own overland journeys. The ship next sails to GENOA (July 14), where they find the prettiest women in Europe. The narrator and his friends hire a guide who delights in showing off everything connected with Christopher COLUMBUS. The vast Cathedral of San Lorenzo has a Madonna painted by St. Luke, as well as religious relics. The homes of wealthy Genoese are palatial, and massive architecture is everywhere in view.

Chapter 18
A train takes the travelers through mountains to MILAN (July 17), where their greatest desire is to see the renowned cathedral. That night and the next day, they admire the marble colossus, which they explore thoroughly. Their guide shows them a hideous natural-looking sculpture of a skinless man, which reminds the narrator how hard it is to forget repulsive things. He recalls a childhood experience that left an indelible mark on him. One night, instead of going home late, he sneaked into his father's office to sleep. Gradually, he became aware of the presence of a corpse on the floor (James McFarland, a man killed in Hannibal, Missouri in September 1843).

In the cathedral's crypt, the travelers stand among treasures worth 50 million francs. They also see the usual holy relics—including Christ's crown of thorns, though it is not as complete as the one at Notre Dame.

Chapter 19
Outside Milan's cathedral, the travelers are harried by their guide, who speaks execrable English and never pauses to let a person appreciate what he shows them. They visit La Scala, the Ambrosian Library and other sights and stroll Milan's streets. At a public bathhouse, they object to being put in one tub, and they find that no soap is provided. They are, however, learning to emulate the English, who carry soap with them. Later they see Leonardo da Vinci's badly ravaged *The Last Supper* in a tumble-down ruin of a church.

Chapter 20
After taking a train from Milan to COMO (July 18), the travelers lodge at a Bellagio hotel on Lake Como. On their arrival, they are fumigated by local authorities concerned about CHOLERA.

In 1843 Mark Twain found the corpse of a murdered man in his father's law office. Visitors to the restored building now hear a recording of Hal Holbrook reading the Innocents Abroad *passage recalling the incident.* (Photograph by author)

Chapter 21
A steamer carries the travelers down Lake Lecco, from which they go by carriage to Bergamo (July 20). Now well into interior Italy, they see solid stone houses, idle peasants, slow-moving carts and innumerable shrines to saints. They pass through strange old towns, which are unaffected by the changes in the modern world. As they speed past a medieval castle, their guide tells them the legend of the noble Count Luigi Gennaro Guido Alphonso di Genova, who fought in the Crusades and returned 30 years later to rescue his wife and daughter from his brother. The travelers reach Bergamo shortly before their train is to leave for Venice.

Chapter 22
At night, the travelers enter VENICE (July 20), a once-great city that has fallen prey to poverty, neglect and melancholy decay. Even the romantic gondola disappoints; it is nothing but a rusty old canoe with a sable hearse-body clapped on. Just as all the romance of Venice seems about to disappear, 2,000 gondolas illuminated by lanterns cross the Grand Canal in a festival that lasts all night. Venice is like an overflowed Arkansas

town, with still waters lapping at doorsteps and boats clustered under windows. By day, it has little poetry; only under moonlight does it become the princeliest among the nations of the Earth.

Chapter 23

Over time, Venetian gondolas grow more interesting; it is quaint to see people conduct routine errands aboard these graceful boats. The travelers themselves go almost everywhere in their gondola—including St. Mark's Square. It is difficult to adjust to the local custom of staring at the faces of pretty young Venetian women, though they seem to like it. However, the travelers enjoy learning curious customs, so they can show off back at home. Some tourists, however, carry this too far—even forgetting their own language.

Visiting a long list of churches and art galleries, the travelers see pictures of enough martyrs and saints to regenerate the world. The narrator regrets lacking the appreciation for the Old Masters that the other passengers have. In Venice, the travelers find their first guide who actually knows anything—a man born into slavery in South Carolina who came here as an infant.

Chapter 24

As fellow *Quaker City* passengers converge on Venice from the north, the travelers go by train to FLORENCE (July 22–23). There they try to traverse its weary miles of picture galleries, but their enthusiasm is gone. One night, the narrator gets lost and walks miles to find his hotel.

The travelers next visit PISA, where they climb the Leaning Tower. Later the same day, they rejoin their ship at LEGHORN. Back in the company of none but fellow countrymen, they exult in speaking and hearing only their own language. Meanwhile, local authorities question why a steamer would cross the Atlantic merely for a pleasure excursion; they suspect that its people are incendiary, bloodthirsty Garibaldians in disguise. Some passengers visit General GARIBALDI, reinforcing the authorities' suspicions. To avoid the risk of being quarantined on the ship at Naples, the narrator and his friends take a French steamer to CIVITAVECCHIA.

Chapter 25

Italy has many things not easily understood, such as why its bankrupt government builds palatial railroad depots and marvelous turnpikes. The new national government is squandering its resources; its problems are compounded by having to compete with the Church, which owns the richest lands, while paying no taxes. Despite its wealth, even the Church is surrounded by poverty and squalor, with wretched beggars at its very doors. For 1,500 years, Italy has poured its energy, finances and industry into building churches, while starving half its people. Italy is a vast museum of magnificence and misery. Florence's grand mausoleum is an example. It was built to bury the Savior back when

Crusaders hoped to bring the HOLY SEPULCHER to Italy; instead, it holds the Medicis, who cruelly tyrannized Florence.

Chapter 26

Nothing confers more delight than discovery. The narrator imagines being a Roman who visits America and reports to ROME on what he discovers there: a country with no overshadowing church, a government not protected by foreign soldiers, common people who can read and write, thousands of schools and books, and newspapers everywhere. It is a place where common men own the land they till, where Jews are treated as human beings, and where no mendicant priests beg for the Church.

The travelers spend considerable time at Rome's great Church of St. Peter, which is so vast one scarcely knows what to compare it with. They also explore the ancient Forum and the Coliseum—where the narrator finds a copy of an ancient playbill advertising an extravaganza that includes a "General Slaughter" in which lions and barbarian prisoners will war until all are exterminated. He also finds a copy of the *Roman Daily Battle-Ax* that reviews this same performance.

Chapter 27

Proud of avoiding BYRON's old saw "butchered to make a Roman holyday," the narrator recalls Judge (Augustus W.) Oliver, with whom he once trudged across Nevada's Great American Desert in winter. No matter how bad things got, Oliver never complained. Later he lived in rude houses built into the sides of hills, but after large animals fell through his roof three times, he said, "this thing is growing monotonous." Byron's oft-repeated quote is similarly monotonous.

It is also so monotonous to hear about Michelangelo—who seems to have designed *everything* in Italy—that it is a relief to learn he is dead. The travelers enjoy asking unsuspecting guides inane questions about him. Whatever a guide has to show—even an Egyptian obelisk—they ask if Michelangelo made it. When the travelers discover how much guides enjoy arousing admiration, they cease to admire anything, even the sublimest wonders.

Chapter 28 (volume 2: chapter 1)

The picturesque horrors of the Vatican's Capuchin Convent are fascinating. Arches made of human thighbones, pyramids of skulls and other works of art assembled from monks' bones decorate its underground vault. A monk tells stories about the men who left these bones, using their fragments to illustrate his points in as grotesque a performance as one could ever witness.

The Vatican's wilderness of statues, paintings and curiosities is dizzying. Where one old master in a palace might be moving, acres of them leave one numb. Why are there so many paintings of Virgins and popes, while Rome's own history remains unpainted? Without wishing to be irreverent, the narrator suggests that Rome ranks Holy Personages in this order:

1. the Virgin Mary;
2. the Deity;
3. Peter;
4. some 12 or 15 canonized popes and martyrs;
5. Jesus Christ—but always as an infant in arms.

Chapter 29 (2:2)
When the travelers reach NAPLES by train (c. August 1), they find their ship quarantined in the harbor. While their ship is now a prison, they are free to move about, and they comfort their quarantined shipmates by boating out to them daily to tell them about what they are missing ashore. A trip to Mt. VESUVIUS is memorable, but before the narrator gets around to describing it, he tells about a trip to the Isle of Ischia, a concert at which the audience taunts an aging singer, and a wretched religious imposture—the miraculous liquefaction of the blood of St. Januarius.

Chapter 30 (2:3)
Merely *seeing* Naples may not make one die—as the ancient adage suggests—however, *living* there may produce a different result. In any case, the best way to see Naples is from high up on Vesuvius at dawn. Within the city itself, the filth and smells are intolerable; Naples has 625,000 inhabitants in a space that would hold an American city of 150,000. Nowhere are contrasts between magnificence and misery greater.

Chapter 31 (2:4)
POMPEII dispels one's old ideas about descending dark stairways and gloomy tunnels. Half the city is excavated and open to sunlight. It is now a city of hundreds of roofless houses and tangled mazes of streets. Though its houses seem much alike, they are admirably decorated; many of its ancient pictures are more pleasing than the celebrated rubbish of the Renaissance. What were people doing the night that Pompeii was destroyed? Evidence of Pompeii's customs and history is everywhere, but one wonders what traces an American city buried by a volcano would leave.

Italy's many stately ruins make one reflect on the transitory nature of fame. After just 20 centuries flutter away, what mark is left by those thinking they have made history? Little more than undecipherable inscriptions in stone. Forty centuries from now, perhaps all that will be left of General GRANT's great name will be a garbled encyclopedia entry: "URIAH S. [or Z.] GRAUNT—popular poet of ancient times in the Aztec provinces of the United States of British America."

Chapter 32 (2:5)
For the first time in weeks, all the passengers are together, and the ship leaves Naples with everyone cheerful (August 11). They sail past Stromboli and through the Strait of Messina. After a pleasant cruise through the Greek islands, they anchor at Piraeus, from which

they can just make out the Parthenon in ATHENS (August 14). In no previous land has everyone been so eager to rush ashore; however, local authorities tell them to accept an 11-day quarantine or leave. That night, the narrator and three other men (William Denny, George Bright Birch and Abraham JACKSON) sneak ashore to visit the Acropolis.

Chapter 33 (2:6)
As the ship moves north (August 15), views of barren landscapes make one wonder what supports Greece. Amidst such poverty, even its throne went begging until a Danish prince (George I) accepted it. At the Dardanelles, the ship enters another land rich in history—and poor as the Sahara in everything else—and anchors at CONSTANTINOPLE (August 17). From the anchorage, the Turkish capital is the handsomest city the travelers have seen. Ashore, it is a different matter—an eternal circus, with shops that are mere coops and people thicker than bees.

The chief interest of the famed Mosque of St. Sophia is that it was transformed from a Christian church with little alteration. The travelers also visit the Dancing Dervishes, the Thousand and One Columns, the marble mausoleum of Sultan Mahmoud and the great Bazaar in Stamboul—one of the few sights worth seeing, but a place where the only thing one cannot smell is something that smells good.

Chapter 34 (2:7)
While Constantinople has many mosques, churches and graveyards, morals and whiskey are scarce. Parents still sell girls, though not publicly as in the past, and the market for them is up, for various reasons—including the recent return of the sultan (Abdul Aziz) from Europe. If American newspapers were published in Constantinople, they probably would present a "Slave Girl Market Report," such as a sample that follows. Commercial morals are uniformly bad. Constantinople's official scavengers, its celebrated dogs, have been misrepresented. The wretched curs are everywhere, but seem too weak even to cross a street. It is surprising to see newspapers hawked in streets where giants and genii of the Arabian Nights once dwelt. However, the papers are unpopular with the government, which regards them as a mild form of pestilence.

Chapter 35 (2:8)
The ship sails for the Black Sea (August 19), while a dozen passengers remain in Constantinople in the clutches of "Far-away Moses," a famous rascally guide. The first port is SEVASTOPOL (August 21), a town horribly battered by the recent (Crimean) war. Though warned in Constantinople to be careful about passports in Russia, the narrator has lost his and is carrying that of his roommate (Dan Slote), who has stayed in Constantinople. Happily, the American flag is all the passport the travelers need, for Sevastopol is the most hospitable stop yet. As plans to visit the emperor of

Russia develop, the travelers comb the nearby battle-fields for relics.

Chapter 36 (2:9)

To take on coal, the ship sails to ODESSA (August 21–22), which reminds the narrator of a typical American city and makes him feel at home. Happy to learn that Odessa has no sights to see, the travelers celebrate with idling and an ice-cream debauch.

Chapter 37 (2:10)

At YALTA (August 25), the American consul (Timothy C. Smith) advises how to behave before the emperor, explaining that he should be greeted with a smile signifying love, gratification and admiration. Everyone practices this complicated smile, and the narrator helps draft a formal address to the emperor. The next day the emperor (Czar ALEXANDER II) receives the travelers warmly at his summer palace.

The travelers accept invitations to visit the nearby homes of the crown prince and the czar's younger brother, Grand Duke Michael (Michael Nicholaevitch, 1832–1909). The czar rejoins them at the grand duke's home—prompting the narrator to revise his old ideas about emperors, who behind the scenes are strangely like common mortals.

Chapter 38 (2:11)

After another stop in Constantinople (August 30–September 3), the ship turns toward Asia. Crew members torment the travelers by repeatedly burlesquing their introduction to the czar and the narrator hears his little speech so many times that its words become intolerable. Meanwhile, the first Asian port the travelers visit is SMYRNA (September 6)—a typical Oriental city, with dark, comfortless houses, crooked streets, confusing bazaars, dirt, fleas, broken-hearted dogs and awful stenches. Such is Oriental splendor.

Chapter 39 (2:12)

From Smyrna, the travelers ride donkeys to a lofty citadel where one of Asia's Seven Apocalyptic Churches stood 18 centuries earlier. As they ascend, veins of oyster shells unexpectedly appear in the mountain. The narrator wonders if the oysters climbed up themselves. A guide tells them that followers of Miller (William Miller, 1782–1849) gathered on this mountain three years earlier to await the ascension.

Chapter 40 (2:13)

The travelers go by train and donkey to EPHESUS (September 7), the site of the fabulous ancient Temple of Diana. The city's former greatness brings to mind the "Legend of the Seven Sleepers":

> About 1,500 years ago, seven young Christians left Ephesus to avoid persecution. They took along bottles of curious liquors, but forgot them in a cave. Five years later, they returned to the cave, found the bottles, drank them and fell asleep. When they awak-

ened, they were naked and their coins lay on the ground, corroded with age. Everything in Ephesus had changed. When the men realized that they had slept for 200 years, they lay down and died. Their names still appear on their tombs: "Johannes Smithianus, Trumps, Gift, High, and Low, Jack, and The Game." Their bottles are inscribed with the names of ancient heathen gods: "Rumpunch, Jinsling, Egnog."

Chapter 41 (2:14)

The travelers leave Ephesus without their usual haul of relics after an official confiscates their plunder, and they sail from Smyrna (September 8). Their excitement grows as they make plans for the Holy Land and divide into small traveling parties. The narrator joins seven others (Dr. George Birch, William F. Church, Joshua William Davis, Colonel William R. Denny, Abraham Jackson, Jack Van Nostrand and Dan Slote) who will go to Damascus and down the length of Palestine. Others plan less ambitious journeys. At Beirut (September 10), the narrator's party engages a dragoman (guide) named ABRAHAM to organize their expedition and they leave Beirut in astonishing style (September 11).

Chapter 42 (2:15)

The travelers' first camp is near a place called Temnin-el-Foka (September 12), which they dub "JACKSONVILLE." The next day, they pass through historically rich country and pay their respects at Noah's tomb. Its authenticity is beyond doubt: Noah's son Shem showed it to his descendants, who showed it to theirs, and so on.

Chapter 43 (2:16)

Five tedious hours take the travelers across the torrid Valley of Lebanon, where farmers still plow with sharp sticks and winnow wheat as the prophet Abraham did. At BAALBEK (September 13), the travelers admire the great ancient temples, some of whose stones are larger than a steamboat hull. It seems inconceivable that these blocks were quarried and raised to such heights. Gods or giants must have built Baalbek.

Refusing to travel on the Sabbath, the party's pious "PILGRIMS" insist on completing a three-day journey to Damascus in two days, ignoring the other men's pleas to show compassion for their tired horses.

Chapter 44 (2:17)

The next day brings another 13-hour ride, through hot, barren terrain. At twilight, the travelers look down on DAMASCUS, which is beautiful from the mountain. If the narrator visited Damascus again, he would camp above the city as there is no need to go inside. A tradition claims that Damascus stands on the site of the Garden of Eden. True or not, it is no paradise now. At sundown (September 14), they reach the gates of Damascus, Syria's only walled city, to which even BAKSHEESH cannot buy entry after dark. The city has no street lamps; people go out at night with lanterns, as in the days of the Arabian Nights. After making their way through the narrow streets, the travelers find their hotel through a hole in the wall. The next day, they again fight their way through the streets to see St. Luke's famous crooked "street which is called Straight."

Chapter 45 (2:18)
During his last 24 hours in Damascus, the narrator lies gravely ill, but leaves with his companions in the middle of the hottest day thus far (September 16). The motley horsemen present a ludicrous sight as they bounce along single-file: Each man wears green glasses and carries a bobbing umbrella. After passing the spot where Saul was converted, they camp near a place they call "JONES-BOROUGH." The next morning takes them to BANIYAS and the sources of the River JORDAN (September 17). It is curious to stand on ground on which the Savior walked—it seems to contradict the mystery one attaches to a god. The travelers are shocked by the sight of young children whose eyes are covered with flies. People flock to be treated by Dr. B. (Birch), whom they see as a mighty healer.

Chapter 46 (2:19)
The next stop is DAN in the HOLY LAND (September 18). After days of riding over rocks, the travelers find a smooth, open plain and spur their horses on. Fearing Bedouins, their guide wants to halt; his anxiety brings to mind Wm. C. GRIMES's purported hairbreadth escapes from Bedouins. The richly historic region also recalls stories of Joshua and untold numbers of kings. The very name "PALESTINE" seems to suggest a country as large as the United States, but the reality is much different. At daybreak, one expects grass to sparkle with dew, fragrant flowers to enrich the air and birds to sing in trees. Alas, there is no dew, no flowers, no birds, no trees.

Chapter 47 (2:20)
The travelers stop Jack from clodding a turtle. After hearing the pilgrims talk about this land of milk and honey, where the "voice of the turtle" is heard, he resents the turtle's refusal to sing. Later, the travelers visit the pit into which Joseph was cast by his brothers.

The travelers relish swimming in the Sea of GALILEE, but find its beauty wildly exaggerated. Even so, they are eager to sail on it and say they will pay *anything* for a boat ride. However, they miss their only chance for a boat by dickering over its price, and then become upset with each other. As they pass the shapeless ruin of Capernaum, where Christ gained fame healing the sick, they reflect on how small was the portion of Earth from which Christianity sprang.

Chapter 48 (2:21)
Like all Syrian villages, Magdala is not beautiful; it is cramped, squalid and ringing with cries for baksheesh. The travelers examine Mary Magdalene's dwelling, remove bits of the wall for specimens, then go to Tiberias (September 19), where they see only poor and uncomely people. The celebrated Sea of Galilee is neither as large

nor as beautiful as Lake Tahoe. Silence and solitude brood over both, but the solitude of the latter is as cheerful and fascinating as the solitude of the former is dismal and repellent. Writers rave about the beauty of Galilee and its surroundings; typical examples appear in books by Grimes and "C. W. E." (Charles Wyllys Elliott). Many visitors here must be Presbyterians; they come for evidences to support their creed and find a Presbyterian Palestine. Likewise, Baptists find a Baptist Palestine, and so on.

Chapter 49 (2:22)
The travelers again swim in the Sea of Galilee, but bypass the warm baths near Tiberias. In the morning a fantastically outfitted Arab appears, heavily armed with antiquated weapons. The dragoman (Abraham) explains that the man is to be their guard through Bedouin country. In actuality, the man is simply a source of revenue for the local sheikh. The travelers ascend to a site where Saladin fought a great battle against the Crusaders 700 years earlier.

Chapter 50 (2:23)
From Tabor, it is two hours to Nazareth (September 20), where the travelers visit the grotto where the Annunciation occurred. Thousands of miles away, one can imagine the angel appearing here before the Virgin; but *here*, few can do it. They also inspect the places where Jesus worked as a carpenter and the ruins of the synagogue from which He was driven by a mob. Only fragments of its ancient walls remain, but the pilgrims—whose chief sin is lust for "specimens"—break off pieces.

Chapter 51 (2:24)
Nazareth is interesting because it seems to be precisely as Jesus left it. Its sights make the narrator think of passages he has copied from the "Apocryphal New Testament"—such as chapter 19, which tells how Jesus was charged with throwing a boy off a roof, then miraculously caused the dead boy to speak and acquit Him. Meanwhile, it seems likely that some members of the party will eventually be shot. Its pilgrims read Grimes's *Nomadic Life* and keep their hands always on their pistols—which they often draw and aim at imaginary Bedouins.

At Endor, the travelers find more dirt, degradation and savagery than at any place they have seen yet. Their journey then takes them through Nain, Shunem and the Plain of Jezreel before they camp at Jenin (September 21). The next morning they visit Samaria (September 22).

Chapter 52 (2:25)
At Shechem, the travelers see one of the patriarch Jacob's residences and a manuscript said to be the oldest document on Earth. The narrator, however, has purchased one even older—which he will publish when he finishes translating it (an allusion to EVE's DIARY?). Near Shechem they visit Joseph's tomb and Jacob's well. Early

the next day, they pass Shiloh and a shapeless mass of ruins still called Beth-el—from which angels lifted Jacob to Heaven. After the pilgrims take what is left of the ruin, they continue on. No more tiresome landscape exists than that bounding the approaches to JERUSALEM. They halt above the city and marvel at its smallness: it is no larger than an American village of 4,000, or a Syrian city of 30,000. Just after noon they enter through the famed Damascus Gate (September 23).

Chapter 53 (2:26)
Jerusalem is small enough for a person to walk around in an hour. Its streets are badly paved, crooked and so narrow that cats jump across them, from roof to roof. Lepers, cripples and idiots beg for baksheesh everywhere. Jerusalem is mournful, dreary and lifeless. The travelers' first stop is the Church of the HOLY SEPULCHER—a vast structure housing Christ's tomb and the main Crucifixion sites. It also has the tomb of ADAM. Touched by unexpectedly finding the grave of a blood relation in so distant a land, the narrator weeps unashamedly.

Chapter 54 (2:27)
Other holy sites in Jerusalem that the travelers see include the Sorrowful Way, Ecce Homo Arch, St. Veronica's home and the house of the Wandering Jew—who must be amused to see blockheads such as these calling what they are doing "traveling." After visiting the Mosque of Omar and other places, they are surfeited with sights; only the Church of the Holy Sepulcher holds their interest. Outside the walled city, they cross the Valley of Hinnom and visit the Garden of Gethsemane and other sites.

Chapter 55 (2:28)
As other shipmates converge on Jerusalem, the travelers organize an expedition to the DEAD SEA. Though war rumors are flying, no one backs out; instead, each person struggles to maintain an unostentatious position at the rear of the caravan. Ancient Jericho (September 25) proves not much to look at; Joshua hardly left enough of the city to cast a shadow. In order to best a rival guide, the dragoman rushes the party to the River Jordan before dawn. At daybreak, they disrobe and enter the river singing, but not for long in the frigid water. Eventually, they wade across and continue to the Dead Sea, where they swim.

After a hideous ride across a torrid plain, the party spends the night in Marsaba's convent. Its ascetic monks seem dead to the outside world, but are kind and generous hosts. Though raised to hate everything Catholic, the narrator cannot help feeling grateful to the Catholic convents that make Holy Land travel tolerable. Refreshed, the travelers proceed to Bethlehem (September 26), where they visit the grotto where Christ was born. Even here, it is impossible to meditate; the tumult of

beggars, cripples and monks permits one to think only of baksheesh. It is a relief to get away.

Chapter 56 (2:29)
After visiting all the holy places around Jerusalem that they had missed earlier, the travelers head for the coast (September 29). They spend their first night at the convent of Ramla and then ride hard for JAFFA, where they see the ship (September 30). So ends the pilgrimage.

Chapter 57 (2:30)
Relieved to be at sea again (October 1), free of anxiety about where to go and other questions, the travelers find being back aboard the *Quaker City* incomparably satisfying after their wearisome pilgrimage. A pleasant voyage takes them to EGYPT. The moment they anchor at Alexandria (October 2), Jack and the narrator go ashore. Their shipmates follow the next morning. At Jaffa the ship took on 40 members of a failed religious commune led by George J. ADAMS.

Alexandria is too European to be novel, so the travelers take a train to Cairo (October 4), a satisfactorily Oriental city. Their hotel is the world's worst, apart from one in which the narrator once stayed in America. He quotes from an old notebook about the "Benton House" (actually the Heming House, in KEOKUK, Iowa), where he was grudgingly allowed a reading lamp that served merely to illuminate the grimness of his surroundings.

Chapter 58 (2:31)
By donkey and boat, a party of excursionists go up the Nile to Gizeh (October 5), passing the place where Pharaoh's daughter found Moses in the bulrushes. At the Pyramid of Cheops, muscular men besiege them, demanding to pull them up the pyramid for money. The great pyramid compares favorably in size with both Washington's Capitol and Rome's St. Peter's Cathedral. Its prodigious height reminds the narrator of a time when he thought that a bluff by the Mississippi River must be the highest mountain in the world. Earlier still, he thought Holliday's Hill (CARDIFF HILL) near his hometown a noble mountain, but it was nothing compared to the pyramid.

The nearby SPHINX has a sad face and a dignity not of Earth. Though stone, it seems sentient as it gazes out over the ocean of Time. It is Memory—Retrospection—wrought into visible, tangible form. As the travelers reflect on its grand loneliness and impressive mystery, they hear a familiar clink—a fellow passenger (Dr. William GIBSON) is trying to break off a specimen. Little is said about the great mosque of Mehemet Ali, Joseph's well, Cairo and others sights along the return route to Alexandria (October 7).

Chapter 59 (2:32)
As the ship recrosses the Mediterranean and the Atlantic, its passengers relish the chance to rest. Along the

way, they pass Malta and touch at Sardinia (October 13), Algiers (October 15) and Malaga, Spain (October 17), but because of cholera fears, no one goes ashore at any of these places and the days grow monotonous. While the ship recoals at Gibraltar (October 17–24), the narrator and three companions (Abraham Jackson, Julius MOULTON and Julia NEWELL) spend a delightful week in southern SPAIN. Their experiences are too numerous for a short chapter and there is not enough room for a long one, so they are left out.

Chapter 60 (2:33)
Immediately after the excursionists rejoin the ship at Cadiz, it sails (October 25). One passenger takes his complaints about the ship's coffee directly to the captain, only to make an egregious ass of himself before everyone when the coffee he denounces proves to be tea. That ass is the narrator.

Several pleasant days at sea carry the ship to Madeira (October 28). Told they must wait out a quarantine before going ashore, the passengers vote to sail on. Next, they reach BERMUDA, where they enjoy one of the most pleasant stops of the entire cruise (November 11–15). The ship's final run returns them to New York, so they busy themselves with separating group purchases, packing, and preparing for customs. Some passengers want to enter New York harbor dressed as Turks; however, when the ship finally lands, everyone is dressed in Christian garb (November 19). The long, strange cruise is over.

Chapter 61 (2: unnumbered)
An article written by Mark Twain for the NEW YORK HERALD of November 20, 1867 is reprinted, with his signature, to sum up the cruise.

Though advertised as a "pleasure excursion," the cruise did not look or act like one. Parties to a pleasure excursion should be young and giddy; they should dance and sing and make love, but sermonize very little. By contrast, three-fourths of the *Quaker City* passengers were between 40 and 70. They were not gay and frisky, they never romped, they talked little and they never sang—except at prayer-meetings. The pleasure ship was a synagogue, the pleasure trip a funeral excursion without a corpse.

After mentioning the trip's highlights, Mark Twain says that he bears no malice or ill will toward anyone connected with the cruise. Things he did not like yesterday, he likes very well today.

Conclusion
Nearly a year after the pilgrimage is over, the author records his thoughts as he writes in SAN FRANCISCO. He finds that his memories of the trip have grown more pleasant. If the *Quaker City* were to embark on the same voyage again, he would gladly join it—even with the same captain, same pilgrims and same sinners. He made eight or nine good friends among the passengers and was even on speaking terms with the rest—a good average at sea. Indeed, he would rather travel with an excursion party of Methuselahs than have to change ships and comrades constantly. He finds no fault with the manner in which the excursion was conducted. Its program was faithfully carried out, leaving him with good thoughts about the many places he visited.

BACKGROUND AND PUBLISHING HISTORY

Soon after Mark Twain first left the Midwest in 1853, he began writing travel letters for newspapers. By early 1867, his letters to California papers, such as the SACRAMENTO UNION and the SAN FRANCISCO ALTA CALIFORNIA, were winning him real celebrity; as a result, he began thinking about extending his travels to encompass the whole world. In February 1867, he was writing regular letters to the *Alta* from New York City when he learned of plans for the coming summer's *Quaker City* excursion. Bored with writing about one place, he persuaded the *Alta* to buy him passage on the *Quaker City* and pay him $20 each for 50 letters that he would write on the voyage. He also arranged to write additional letters for the NEW YORK HERALD and NEW YORK TRIBUNE. As early as March, he was discussing the coming cruise in letters to the *Alta* that provide a commentary on the preparations for the voyage up the eve of its departure.

When Mark Twain contracted to write letters about the cruise, he was already thinking about getting a book out of the trip; he thus composed his letters with the idea of revision in mind. Within two weeks of his return from the voyage in November, Elisha BLISS approached him about writing a book for the AMERICAN PUBLISHING COMPANY. After visiting Bliss in Hartford in January, Mark Twain began working on his book in WASHINGTON, D.C., drawing upon clippings of his travel letters assembled in a scrapbook by his sister, Pamela MOFFETT. A firsthand description by a journalist friend depicts him furiously cutting and pasting from these clippings, adding revisions in the margins of the pages. He soon discovered, however, that these letters alone would not provide enough material to fill the kind of book that Bliss needed for his SUBSCRIPTION-BOOK market.

By March, Mark Twain had completed 10 chapters of his book when he learned that the proprietors of the *Alta* objected to his using the letters for which they had paid. He sailed for San Francisco, where he persuaded the *Alta* people to give him all the rights to his letters. He then remained in California for several months. After a brief lecture tour that took in western Nevada, he returned to work on his book in San Francisco in May. While he was there, Bret HARTE helped him with the manuscript, in return for which Harte was invited to extract whatever he wanted for his new magazine, the OVERLAND MONTHLY. Harte seems to have limited his advice to suggesting the deletion of passages he thought improper, irrelevant or overly irreverent. Mark Twain accepted Harte's recommended cuts, the most substantial of which was a full chapter on Spain. Harte, in turn, published extracts from the manuscript on France and Italy in four issues of his magazine.

On June 23, 1868, Mark Twain pronounced his manuscript done; two weeks later he left San Francisco for good. He delivered his manuscript to Bliss in Hartford on August 4, 1868 and finally signed a publishing contract with him two and a half months later. In mid-November, he began a lecture tour in the Midwest and East with "THE AMERICAN VANDAL ABROAD" as his topic, generating valuable publicity for his coming book. After completing his tour in March, he turned his attention to correcting proofs of the book with the help of his new fiancée, Olivia Langdon.

The American Publishing Company issued the book as *Innocents Abroad* in late July 1869. The first edition contains 234 line drawings. Most of these pictures are unsigned, but True WILLIAMS and Rosswell Shurtleff (1838–1915) are among the known contributors. In the summer of 1870, the London publisher John Camden HOTTEN issued *The Innocents Abroad: The Voyage Out,* the first volume of an unauthorized two-volume edition. Six weeks later, the second volume, *The New Pilgrims' Progress: The Journey Home,* appeared. The following year, Hotten issued a one-volume edition as *Mark Twain's Pleasure Trip on the Continent.* In 1872, George ROUTLEDGE published an authorized edition in London, with minor revisions, but pirated editions continued to appear in England.

Although *Innocents* was published in the United States by a subscription house, it was widely and favorably reviewed; it received especially important notices from W. D. HOWELLS in the ATLANTIC MONTHLY and Bret Harte in the *Overland Monthly.* Critics praised the book for both its humor and its eloquence, but generally preferred the former. Though the book's reviews were almost uniformly positive, Mark Twain himself later regretted what he came to regard as the crudity of its writing.

Mark Twain's original 1866-to-early-1867 letters to the *Alta* were republished in MARK TWAIN'S TRAVELS WITH MR. BROWN (1940), edited by Franklin Walker and G. Ezra Dane; his letters from the *Quaker City* excursion itself were collected in 1958 as *Traveling with the Innocents Abroad: Mark Twain's Original Reports from Europe and the Holy Land,* edited by Daniel Morley McKeithan. Since the original publication of *Innocents Abroad,* however, no substantially revised edition has ever been issued. In 1984, the Library of America published the first edition with scholarly annotations in a combined volume with *Roughing It* edited by Guy Cardwell. The MARK TWAIN PAPERS project at the University of California has tentatively scheduled publication of a fully corrected edition of *Innocents Abroad* for 1996.

While the 50 letters that Mark Twain wrote for the *Alta* form the core of *Innocents Abroad,* the book contains considerable material from other sources. Many passages, including some entire chapters, derive from his letters to the *Herald* and the *Tribune;* others he wrote from scratch after the voyage, drawing on his own NOTEBOOKS—which have since been published—and the writings of fellow passengers, many of whom published travel letters of their own. In combining all these materials, he often rewrote episodes with new casts of characters or added passages to change the tone, as when he softened his criticisms of the Sea of Galilee by adding a lyrical description of the lake at night.

The original manuscript of *Innocents Abroad* is not known still to exist. The Mark Twain Papers project holds the remnants of the original scrapbook from which Mark Twain worked, and the library at Vassar College has the original manuscripts of the fragments that Mark Twain deleted before delivering the manuscript to Bliss.

A television dramatization of *Innocents Abroad* that first aired on PBS on May 9, 1983 featured Craig Wasson as Mark Twain, David Ogden Stiers as Dr. Jackson and Brooke Adams as Julia Newell.

The Innocents Adrift Title of an unfinished book. In September 1891, Mark Twain made an 11-day boat trip down the RHONE RIVER. Afterward, he began writing a narrative of the trip, hoping to combine this material and travel letters he was writing to the NEW YORK SUN into a book similar to *A Tramp Abroad.* After working on his manuscript in 1894 and 1904, he had 174 pages, but never made a serious attempt to complete the book. In 1923, A. B. PAINE published a 10,000-word abridgement in EUROPE AND ELSEWHERE as "DOWN THE RHÔNE."

The Innocents at Home Title of volume 2 of the English edition of *Roughing It,* published by George ROUTLEDGE & Sons in 1872. Labeled a "sequel" to *Roughing It,* this volume includes chapters 46–79 of the one-volume editions. It omits the book's three appendixes, but includes Mark Twain's previously published BURLESQUE AUTOBIOGRAPHY.

Interdict Ecclesiastical weapon that churches use to control communities by restricting their sacraments. During the Middle Ages, the Roman Catholic Church made especially effective use of the Interdict at a time when most western Europeans were Roman Catholics. In chapter 41 of *Connecticut Yankee,* Hank MORGAN returns to England from France to learn that the Archbishop of Canterbury has put the country under an Interdict. Though the Church aims the Interdict at King Arthur and Sir Launcelot's civil war, its real target is Hank, whose worst fears concerning an Established Church are confirmed. The Interdict wins back all but a handful of the thousands of people he trained in modern technology and politics, bringing his civilization to a sudden end.

Interlaken Health resort on SWITZERLAND's Aare River, between the lakes of Thun and Brienz. Interlaken is particularly noted for its commanding view of the

JUNGFRAU in the Bernese Alps. Mark Twain visited the town on August 21, 1878 and made it and the Jungfrau the subjects of chapters 31–32 of *A Tramp Abroad*. When he returned to Switzerland in the summer of 1891, he wrote his essay "Switzerland, the Cradle of Liberty" at Interlaken.

International Mark Twain Society Organization devoted to promoting Mark Twain. Based in Kirkwood, Missouri, where it was founded as a local discussion group in 1923, the society changed dramatically when Cyril CLEMENS became its president in 1927. After ending the society's meetings, he built up a nominal international membership of over a thousand people—mostly prominent literary figures and statesmen. With Clemens as its only active member, the "society" held no meetings and had no constitution, bylaws or dues.

Clemens tirelessly wrote to prominent personages to inform them of their "unanimous election" to such distinctions as honorary vice-president, or "knight" or "daughter" of Mark Twain. Most recipients of the honors Clemens offered accepted, but some turned him down because he made the Italian dictator Benito Mussolini honorary president in 1927. Those accepting society honors included Ethiopia's Emperor Haile Selassie, Czechoslovakia's President Tomas Masaryk, Britain's Prime Minister Ramsay MacDonald, Belgium's King Leopold III, President Franklin D. ROOSEVELT, Somerset Maugham, H. G. Wells, Aldous Huxley, and many others. In 1936, Clemens launched the *Mark Twain Quarterly* (later renamed MARK TWAIN JOURNAL), in which he often published his correspondence with the society's famous members.

The Interrogation Point Minor character in *Innocents Abroad*. Chapter 7 mentions an irritating young passenger on the QUAKER CITY known as the "Interrogation Point" who constantly asks questions but is too dense to recognize contradictions in the answers he gets. In a March 1869 letter to Mary Mason FAIRBANKS, Mark Twain identifies the Interrogation Point as Frederick H. Greer, a young passenger from Boston whom he also identifies as "BLUCHER" in a later letter.

"The Invalid's Story" ("Limburger Cheese Story") Short story published in 1882. The "invalid" is the unnamed narrator, a 41-year-old bachelor who feels like a married 60-year-old. He recalls an experience from two years earlier, when his boyhood friend John B. Hackett died, leaving a request for him to return Hackett's body to his parents in Bethlehem, Wisconsin.

SYNOPSIS

Although the narrative that follows describes the horror that the narrator and another man experience when they are overwhelmed by a putrid stench in the railway

Even fire cannot defeat limburger cheese in "The Invalid's Story."

car carrying Hackett's coffin, the narrator explains immediately that Hackett's corpse was *not* in the car with them; the odor came from limburger cheese. It was only afterward, he explains, that he learned that Hackett's pine coffin was accidentally switched with a box of rifles when the train left Cleveland. As the train pulled out, someone put a package of limburger cheese on the box.

Knowing nothing about limburger's pungency, the narrator assumes that the foul stench in the baggage car comes from his friend's "coffin." As this foul smell grows more powerful, the narrator and the baggage man Thompson do everything they can to find relief. They smoke cigars, push the box into a corner, spread carbolic acid around it and even set fire to a pile of garbage. All this only makes the stench worse, finally forcing them to ride outside the car in a snowstorm. When the train stops, they are removed frozen and insensible. The narrator has a violent fever for three weeks and is now going home to die.

BACKGROUND AND PUBLISHING HISTORY

Several sources have been suggested as Mark Twain's inspiration for this story. The humorist J. M. Field (1810–1856) published a similar sketch in 1846, and Artemus WARD used a version of the story in a lecture that Mark Twain heard in Nevada in 1863. Joseph TWICHELL has also been suggested as a source of the story. When Mark Twain wrote the 2,600-word story around 1877, he intended to work it into "SOME RAMBLING NOTES OF AN IDLE EXCURSION" until W. D. HOWELLS persuaded him to leave it out. Howells apparently also talked him into leaving the story out of *A Tramp Abroad* (1880). Later, however, Mark Twain did work it into "Rambling Notes" for his *Stolen White Elephant* (1882) anthology. The story later appeared by itself in LITERARY ESSAYS and other collections.

Iowa Mark Twain lived in the southeast corner of Iowa for over a year during the mid-1850s and visited the state at least five times in later years. Shortly after Mark Twain left Missouri in mid-1853, his brother Orion Clemens moved to MUSCATINE and started a newspaper there. Mark Twain lived with Orion in Muscatine in mid-1854, then went to St. Louis. After Orion moved to KEOKUK in 1855, Mark Twain joined him there and remained in Iowa through the fall of 1856. Orion left the state in 1861, but returned in early 1872; his mother, Jane Lampton Clemens, joined him in Keokuk in 1886. Meanwhile, Mark Twain returned to Iowa on lecture tours and visits to his family. He was in Keokuk in 1867 and in Iowa City and Davenport in 1869. During his first steamboat trip on the Upper Mississippi River in May 1882, he passed several Iowa towns that he describes in *Life on the Mississippi* (chapters 57–58). Three years later his lecture tour with G. W. CABLE took him to Keokuk and Burlington in mid-January 1885. He paid his final visit to the state in August 1890 to see his mother.

Ipsen, L. S. (*fl.* 1880s) Illustrator. A staff illustrator for James R. OSGOOD's publishing companies, Ipsen drew the ornate half-title pages for chapters in *The Prince and the Pauper* (1881).

Typical L. S. Ipsen half-title page in The Prince and the Pauper.

Ireland Mark Twain visited Ireland just once, spending two weeks there with his family from late August to early September 1873. Little is known about this trip beyond the fact that his stops included Belfast and Dublin.

"Is He Living or Is He Dead?" Story about an art HOAX that Mark Twain wrote while visiting New York in 1893. The unidentified narrator recalls an incident in March 1892, at Menton, on FRANCE's Riviera coast—where Mark Twain actually was on that date. The narrator meets a man, whom he calls Smith, who one day calls his attention to a prosperous retired silk manufacturer from Lyons named Théophile Magnan. That evening, Smith tells him an incredible story that becomes the narrative for most of the rest of the story.

When Smith was young, he was struggling as an artist in France, where he joined with three young French painters, Claude Frère, Carl Boulanger and François MILLET—a name instantly recognizable to the narrator as "the *great* François Millet." After they had been starving together for two years, Boulanger suggested a bold way out of their poverty. He pointed out "that the merit of many a great artist has never been acknowledged until after he was starved and dead. This has happened so often that I make bold to found a law upon it." He therefore proposed that they cast lots for one of their number to "die." The man thus elected was to start as many paintings as possible for several months—leaving the canvases for his comrades to finish. Once sufficient pictures were ready, his comrades would announce his death, as he changed his name and disappeared. Millet is the artist elected, and the comrades carry out the scheme to perfection. Millet even serves as a pallbearer at his own funeral. Smith concludes his tale by revealing that Théophile Magnan is Millet himself.

This FRAME-STORY was part of Mark Twain's 12-submission deal with COSMOPOLITAN magazine, in which it appeared in September 1893, with eight illustrations by Alice Barber Stephenes (1858–1932). It was later reprinted in *The Man That Corrupted Hadleyburg and Other Essays and Stories* (1900). Mark Twain used it as the basis for a play, *Is He Dead?*, that he wrote in 1898 but failed to have produced.

Is Shakespeare Dead? **(1909)** Extended essay published as a book. Ostensibly an essay arguing that William SHAKESPEARE could not have written the plays attributed to him, this 21,350-word book originated in Mark Twain's autobiographical dictations. With many passages that are important parts of Mark Twain's AUTOBIOGRAPHY, the book is of greater interest for what it says about him than for what it contributes to theories about Shakespearean authorship.

HARPER AND BROTHERS published *Is Shakespeare Dead?* a year before Mark Twain died; it was the next-to-last book he published within his lifetime. A. B. PAINE later included its text in *What Is Man? and Other Essays* (1917).

SYNOPSIS

Chapter 1
The author's autobiography contains many passages about claimants, such as Satan, Louis XVII, Arthur Orton (the TICHBORNE CLAIMANT), Mary Baker G. Eddy and William Shakespeare. Never has there been a claimant who failed to get a hearing and accumulate a rapturous following, no matter how flimsy his claim may be. A new book, *The Shakespeare Problem Restated* (by George Greenwood, 1908), rekindles the author's interest in the theory that (Francis) BACON wrote Shakespeare's plays. He recalls Delia Bacon's earlier book (*The Philosophy of the Plays of Shakespeare Unfolded*, 1857), which appeared during his steamboat PILOTING days. As an apprentice, he spent hours listening to George EALER quote Shakespeare and rebut Baconian theories. To satisfy Ealer's need for an argument, he took up the Baconian position that Shakespeare lacked the background in law that the plays' author must have had.

Chapter 2
The author recalls his interest in Satan as a child, when his desire to write Satan's biography was frustrated by the fact that everything "known" about him was conjectural.

Chapter 3
As with Satan, pitifully few facts are known about Shakespeare's life. There is no evidence that he ever wrote anything, that anyone thought him remarkable during his lifetime or that he was connected with the plays attributed to his name. So far as anybody knows, he never wrote a play, he received just one letter during his entire life and he wrote only one short poem. Anything else said about him is conjectured.

Chapter 4
A detailed examination of conjectures about Shakespeare's life does not support the idea that he somehow got legal training. William Shakespeare's biography is like a reconstructed brontosaur: nine bones and 600 barrels of plaster of Paris.

Chapter 5
There are three Shakespeare "cults": Shakespearites, who *know* that Shakespeare wrote the plays; Baconians, who *know* that Bacon wrote them; and Brontosaurians, who know that Shakespeare did *not* write the plays, but merely *suspect* that Bacon did. The author is a Brontosaurian.

Chapter 6
Shakespeare's death attracted little attention because he did nothing to merit celebrity. What is known about the author's life in Hannibal provides an interesting contrast with what is known about Shakespeare's life in Stratford. Although the author lived in Hannibal for just 15 years more than 50 years earlier, 16 childhood schoolmates still remember him. By contrast, years after Shakespeare died *in* Stratford—where he lived for 26 years—virtually no one could be found who remembered him.

Chapter 7
The issue of Shakespeare's authorship of the plays can be reduced to a single question: Did *he* ever practice law? To write about any occupation convincingly, one must be trained in it. The author's own expertise in MINING, for example, sets his writing about miners apart from that of Bret HARTE—whose lack of experience is instantly revealed in his unauthentic dialogue.

Chapter 8
A summary of Greenwood's work finds ample evidence in Shakespeare's plays and poems that their author not only had extensive knowledge of law, but knew the workings of the courts and legal life generally. Since Shakespeare clearly had no such experience, he could not possibly have written the plays.

Chapter 9
No one can be sure whether Bacon wrote the plays. He *could* have written them, but conclusive proof is missing.

Chapter 10
The author of Shakespeare's plays must also have had "wisdom, erudition, imagination, capaciousness of mind, grace, and majesty of expression"—none of which Shakespeare is known to have possessed.

Chapter 11
Denying that he expects people to change their minds about Shakespeare, the author says that he is not so foolish as to believe that people will abandon cherished superstitions.

Chapter 12
The author also denies expressing any irreverent ideas—in contrast to the irreverence of the "Stratfordolaters" and "Shakesperiods."

Chapter 13
If one compiled a list of the 500 most celebrated figures in British history back to Tudor times, biographical particulars could be found about every one of them *except* the most illustrious by far—Shakespeare. Nothing that is known about him indicates that he was anything other than a commonplace person. Almost nothing is known about him because he had no history to record.

A postscript to this chapter cites a recent newspaper clipping from Hannibal that attests to the fame that Mark Twain still enjoys in his hometown. He also cites a recent obituary of a Hannibal woman as an example of a person who certainly would have remembered him in Hannibal, but would not have remembered Shakespeare, had she lived in Stratford. Even Hannibal's town drunkards have left behind more lasting memories than Shakespeare did in his own town.

Italy Country in which Mark Twain spent more than a year and a half of his life during five extended visits.

He first visited Italy in 1867, before its political unification was complete. At the beginning of the 19th century, most of Italy was under foreign domination; after the Napoleonic wars, movements for independence and unification began in earnest. The first wave of unification—led by GARIBALDI and others—created the kingdom of Italy in 1861. Venetia was added in 1866 and Rome in 1870.

After the cruise ship QUAKER CITY landed at GENOA on July 14, 1867, Mark Twain spent nearly a month traveling through Italy, mostly by train. He visited MILAN, COMO, VENICE, FLORENCE, PISA, LEGHORN, ROME and NAPLES. Chapters 17–31 of *Innocents Abroad*—nearly a quarter of the book—cover this period. Most of these chapters derive from his original letters to the SAN FRANCISCO ALTA CALIFORNIA, but some—notably those on Rome—he wrote after the voyage. The book's remarks about Italy become increasingly negative as they reflect his progress through the country. Some of his most general criticism is in chapter 26, which condemns what he regarded as the pernicious influence of the Roman Catholic Church, government mismanagement, and the filth, ignorance and poverty that he saw everywhere. The strong feelings he developed about the danger of an established church later found expression in *Connecticut Yankee* (1889).

In mid-September 1878, Mark Twain returned to Italy with his family for a two-month visit that took in most of northern Italy's major cities, including Turin, which he had not visited in 1867. The last four chapters of *A Tramp Abroad* focus on Turin, Milan and Venice, with briefer remarks about Florence. Their tone is much more positive than that in the Italian chapters of *Innocents Abroad*. From this time, Mark Twain's opinion of Italy steadily improved. He returned to Italy with his family in late March 1892. Over the next two months, they visited Pisa, Rome, Venice and Florence. After a sojourn in GERMANY, they came back to Florence in September and rented a villa until the following June. This long visit was pleasant enough to persuade them to return to Italy in late 1903, when the health of Mark Twain's wife Livy was failing. After she died in June 1904, Mark Twain left the country for the last time.

Ithuriel, Uncle Character in "THE CANVASSER'S TALE." The rich uncle of the story's narrator—whom he raised as a son—Ithuriel amassed $5 million in the pork business. At his nephew's suggestion, he took up collecting hobbies, but ended up blowing his entire fortune on echoes, leaving his nephew only mortgages.

A rabbinical name meaning "discovery of God," Ithuriel is the name of an angel in Milton's *Paradise Lost* whom Gabriel commissions to search for Satan. As a near homophone of *ethereal*, it is also an apt name for a man who collects things without material substance.

J. C. Swon (John C. Swon) STEAMBOAT on which Mark Twain PILOTED. A fast and well-known boat named after a famous riverman, the *Swon* was a Railroad Line packet. It appears that Mark Twain worked on this boat on two round-trips between St. Louis and New Orleans, between late June and late July 1859, when its captain was Isaac H. Jones.

Jack Minor character in *Huckleberry Finn*. After Huck settles into the home of the GRANGERFORDS in chapter 17, a personal slave is assigned to him. Chapter 18 identifies the man as Jack. Unbeknownst to Huck, Jack is looking after Jim, who is hiding near the plantation. Eventually, Jack takes Huck to Jim, being careful not to implicate himself, if trouble arises.

Jack is also the name of one of the lazy tobacco chewers whom Huck sees in BRICKSVILLE in chapter 21.

Jackass Hill Mining camp in California's TUOLUMNE COUNTY. Located near Tuttletown, about 100 miles east of San Francisco and 16 miles west of Sonora on modern Highway 49, Jackass Hill takes its name from mules that clustered around it when it was a pack-train stop. Around 1848, a placer-mining boom began that quickly attracted about 3,000 gold miners. By the time Mark Twain arrived there in early December 1864, the camp was a pale shadow of its former glory. A log-and-slab cabin that Dick STOKER had built in 1850 was one of its few remaining habitations (Bret HARTE reputedly spent a night or two at Stoker's cabin in 1855).

In order to avoid trouble with SAN FRANCISCO authorities because of stories he had written about police corruption, Mark Twain spent nearly three months at Jackass Hill with Stoker and Jim and William GILLIS and their cat, TOM QUARTZ. In the midst of this period—from January 22 to February 20, 1865—he and Jim Gillis, his "Sage of Jackass Hill," prospected at ANGEL'S CAMP, seven miles to the northwest in CALAVERAS COUNTY. After returning to Jackass Hill, Mark Twain left for San Francisco on February 23. *Roughing It*'s brief description of this period mentions Tuolumne, but not Jackass Hill (chapters 60–61).

Stoker's original cabin burned down during the 1890s. A replica erected on the same site in 1922 has become a tourist attraction as "Mark Twain's Cabin." There is some doubt about whether the rebuilt cabin's chimney and fireplace actually belonged to the original structure.

Jackson, Abraham Reeves ("the Doctor") (June 17, 1827, Philadelphia, Pennsylvania–November 12, 1892, Chicago, Illinois) Ship's doctor on the QUAKER CITY excursion. A CIVIL WAR veteran, Jackson had a general practice in Stroudsburg, Pennsylvania when he joined the *Quaker City* cruise in 1867. He soon became a friend of Mark Twain, whom he accompanied to TANGIER and PARIS and through ITALY and southern SPAIN. They did not, however, travel together in the HOLY LAND. Jackson shared Mark Twain's irreverent and unconventional sense of humor. He appears frequently in *Innocents Abroad* as "the Doctor"—a character whose dialogue often borrowed Jackson's actual words. Chapter 27 describes the Doctor as having a gift for maintaining his composure while looking like "an inspired idiot." In Genoa, for example, he exasperates a guide who raves over Christopher COLUMBUS by pretending never to have heard of the great discoverer. In the deleted chapter on Spain, the Doctor pretends to take every uniformed official for a high-ranking government dignitary. Jackson recorded his own account of the voyage in 18 letters published in the Monroe County, Pennsylvania *Democrat* and one in the NEW YORK HERALD.

In 1869, Jackson's first wife died; two years later, he married Julia NEWELL, another *Quaker City* passenger, and moved to Chicago, where he founded the Woman's Hospital of Illinois. He later became president of the American Gynecology Society (1891). In the 1983 television adaptation of *Innocents Abroad*, David Ogden Stiers played Jackson.

Jackson, Ed Character in *Following the Equator*. Chapter 28, titled "When the Moment Comes the Man Appears," presents a tale inspired by the previous chapter's true story about a man in Tasmania who emerged from obscurity to stop the settlers' wars against the native population. The fictional Jackson is a guileless young man who leaves MEMPHIS, Tennessee before the CIVIL WAR to visit New York City. As a joke, his friends give him a phony letter of introduction to Commodore VANDERBILT purporting to be from a man who grew up with Vanderbilt. The joke backfires with happy consequences, however, when Vanderbilt accepts the letter as genuine, makes Jackson his houseguest and returns him to Memphis as the director of a vast scheme to control the local tobacco commerce. Jackson's friends expect him to be in a vengeful mood, and they avoid him, until he reveals his wonderful news and promises them all jobs.

Jackson, George Alias that Huck uses in *Huckleberry Finn*. In chapter 17, Huck stumbles onto the farm of the GRANGERFORDS. Asked to identify himself, he gives his name as "George Jackson" and claims to have fallen off a steamboat. He invents an autobiography, telling the family that he comes from southern ARKANSAS. His sister MARY ANN eloped; other family members died or left, until he and his father were the only ones who remained. When his father died, he decided to go upriver and took deck passage on the steamboat from which he claims to have fallen. Since he has no family, and no place to go, the Grangerfords invite him to stay with them. That first night Huck shares a bedroom with Buck GRANGERFORD. He awakens the next morning to find that he has forgotten his new alias. He gets Buck to remember it for him by challenging him to spell it.

In what most likely is a coincidence, the FERRYBOATMAN whom Huck meets in chapter 13 utters "My George!" and "By Jackson" in consecutive remarks.

Jackson's Island Fictional island in *Tom Sawyer* and *Huckleberry Finn*. Jackson's Island is on the Mississippi River, about three miles below ST. PETERSBURG, where the river is a mile wide. In chapters 13 to 16 of *Tom Sawyer*, Tom, Huck and Joe HARPER spend a week on the uninhabited island playing PIRATES. When they explore the island, they determine that it is about three miles long and a quarter mile wide (chapter 14). A 200-yard-wide channel separates the island from the ILLINOIS shore, leaving it about 1,100 yards from the Missouri shore. It has a large sandbar on its northern end, where the boys land, and is heavily forested.

In *Huckleberry Finn*, Huck flees to Jackson's Island to escape from his brutal father and joins forces with the runaway slave Jim there. Chapter 7 describes the island as "standing up out of the middle of the river"; however, a fuller description in chapter 9 matches that of *Tom Sawyer*. This chapter also adds a new feature: a 40-foot-high rocky ridge near the center of the island in which Huck and Jim find a huge cave that they use as a hideout until they begin their raft journey. Tom, Huck and Jim use the same cave for their headquarters in "TOM SAWYER'S CONSPIRACY."

Mark Twain reputedly modeled Jackson's Island on a real island near Hannibal that was known as Glasscock's Island in his time. That island's subsequent erosion by the river, however, makes it a poor model for a place with a rocky cavern. There are still several other islands near Hannibal that resemble Mark Twain's Jackson's Island—a name given to one of them on modern tourist maps.

Jacksonville Facetious nickname for a village in LEBANON. On the first night of his overland journey into the Holy Land (September 12–13, 1867), Mark Twain camped at Temmin el Foka, a village near Zahlah, about 25 miles east of BEIRUT. Chapter 42 of *Innocents Abroad* calls the village "Jacksonville" because it is "easier to remember." There is also a Jacksonville in Missouri, about 50 miles west of Mark Twain's hometown of Hannibal.

Jaffa (Joppa) Long PALESTINE's main MEDITERRANEAN port, Jaffa was absorbed by modern Israel's Tel Aviv in 1949. The QUAKER CITY anchored there from September 16–30, 1867, waiting for passengers to complete their overland expeditions. After Mark Twain rejoined the ship there on September 30, it sailed for EGYPT the next day. Before leaving, it took aboard 41 followers of George J. ADAMS. Chapter 56 of *Innocents Abroad* offers a brief description of Jaffa.

Jake, Uncle Figure mentioned in *Tom Sawyer*. A slave belonging to the family of Ben ROGERS, Jake occasionally allows Huck Finn to sleep in a hayloft and gives him food. Huck tells Tom Sawyer that Jake likes him because he (Huck) never acts as if he were above him and occasionally even eats with him (chapter 28). Huck's friendship with Jake anticipates his relationship with Jim in *Huckleberry Finn*.

James, Henry (April 15, 1843, New York, New York– February 28, 1916, London, England) American novelist. A close contemporary of Mark Twain who wrote about many similar themes, James was temperamentally and artistically a much different kind of writer, whose work Mark Twain did not like to read. The two writers met several times. In the summer of 1879, they dined together in LONDON, where James later settled permanently. They also met there in May 1900 and saw each other twice at George HARVEY's home in late 1904. The character Waymarsh in James's *The Ambassadors* (1903) may be based on Mark Twain.

Mark Twain also met James's brother, psychologist William James (1842–1910), in FLORENCE in 1892 and in New York in February 1907.

James, Jesse (September 5, 1847, Kearney, Missouri– April 3, 1882, St. Joseph, Missouri) Legendary outlaw. After fighting with William Quantrill's Confederate guerrillas in the CIVIL WAR, James became a fugitive with his brother Frank, leading gangs on a crime spree throughout the Midwest. By 1880, he was living quietly in St. Joseph, while there was a large price on his head. In a famous act of treachery, a fellow gang member shot James in the back. James's legend, already strong, mushroomed. Eventually, it would even encompass Hannibal, whose nearby CAVE James was said to have used as a hideout. Meanwhile, news of James's murder in April 1882 spread just as Mark Twain was preparing to return to the Mississippi River. In chapter 29 of *Life on the Mississippi* he alludes to hearing "no end of Jesse James and his stirring history" as he traveled overland to St. Louis. He goes on to compare James's criminal career unfavorably with that of the earlier river pirate, John MURRELL.

Jamestown   Tennessee town in which Mark Twain's family lived before he was born. Now standing on east-central Tennessee's Highway 127, 13 miles south of the Kentucky border, Jamestown is the seat of FENTRESS COUNTY. Mark Twain's parents, John and Jane Clemens, moved there from GAINESBORO around 1827, just before the county was organized; they are believed to have built the town's first substantial structure. Three of their children were born in Jamestown: Pamela Clemens MOFFETT (1827), Pleasant CLEMENS (1829) and Margaret CLEMENS (1830). Around 1831, the family moved nine miles farther north, to THREE FORKS OF WOLF RIVER. Mark Twain later apparently used Jamestown as the model for *The Gilded Age*'s fictional OBEDSTOWN.

Jarves, James Jackson (August 20, 1818, Boston, Massachusetts–June 28, 1888)   The founder and editor of HAWAII's first newspaper, the *Polynesian* (1840–48), Jarves also wrote *History of the Hawaiian or Sandwich Islands* (1843) and other works. Mark Twain drew heavily on Jarves's book in passages on Hawaiian history that he wrote for his letters to the SACRAMENTO UNION and in several chapters of *Roughing It,* though only chapter 65 mentions Jarves by name.

Jasper   Minor character in *Pudd'nhead Wilson*. A young black slave "of magnificent build" in chapter 2, Jasper flirts with Roxy (ROXANA), who hints that Jasper has a relationship with the Coopers' slave Nancy. When Roxy leaves DAWSON'S LANDING in chapter 4, she says good-bye to Jasper as he chops wood for David WILSON.

The original manuscript of *Pudd'nhead Wilson* gives Jasper a more important role. A passage deleted from chapter 2 has Jasper stop a runaway horse-and-buggy, saving his young mistress and her baby and nurse—an incident inspired by a rescue performed by Mark Twain's acquaintance John T. LEWIS. Jasper's grateful master liberates him, allowing him to approach Roxy as a free man.

Mark Twain's long unfinished story, "Which Was It?," has a strong slave character named Jasper who earns his freedom and eventually dominates his former master through blackmail.

Jerusalem   A Near Eastern city holy to Judaism, Christianity and Islam, Jerusalem is in the Judaean Hills, 35 miles from the MEDITERRANEAN SEA. Mark Twain arrived there on September 23, 1867; over the next week, he explored the city and used it as a base for side-trips to Bethlehem and the DEAD SEA. Chapters 52–56 of *Innocents Abroad* describe his stay there. His general impression of Jerusalem was negative; whatever grandeur ancient Jerusalem had had was lost; it had become a "pauper village." The city had about 14,000 residents when he was there and he estimated that a person could walk entirely around it in an hour. Of the city's many religious sights, he was most interested in the Church of the HOLY SEPULCHER.

Jim   Character in *Tom Sawyer*. Described in chapter 1 as "a small colored boy," Jim works for Aunt POLLY. In the next chapter, Tom tries to persuade him to help him whitewash the FENCE until Aunt Polly intervenes. Mark Twain probably modeled this character on a young boy named Sandy who worked for his family briefly when he was a child. In an essay on his mother, Mark Twain recalls being driven to distraction by Sandy's constant singing, until his mother reminded him that Sandy sang to keep his mind off having lost all his family. The fictional Jim is singing "Buffalo Gals" when Tom accosts him by the fence.

This character is not related to the Jim of *Huckleberry Finn*, who never appears in *Tom Sawyer*.

Jim   Character in *Huckleberry Finn* and other stories. A slave of indeterminate age, Jim first appears in the "RAFT CHAPTER" (chapter 3 of *Life on the Mississippi*), which Mark Twain excerpted from his unfinished *Huckleberry Finn* manuscript. This chapter alludes to Jim's being owned by the Widow DOUGLAS. In the completed *Huckleberry Finn*, Jim belongs to the widow's sister and housemate, Miss WATSON.

Chapter 1 of *Huckleberry Finn* describes Miss Watson as newly arrived in ST. PETERSBURG. It is not clear, however, whether Jim also is newly arrived. Miss Watson may have bought him after joining her sister, though her apparently straitened circumstances make this seem unlikely. Chapter 16 mentions that Jim's wife is a slave "on a farm close to where Miss Watson lived." It seems logical that Jim was once on this same farm with his wife, for chapter 23 makes it clear that he enjoyed a time when he shared a house with his children. Less clear, however, is *where* the farm is. It could be near either Miss Watson's current home in St. Petersburg or some previous residence.

Jim is not a character in *Tom Sawyer* (a slave child named JIM in that novel is a different character), so there is no record of his being in St. Petersburg before the events of *Huckleberry Finn*. On the other hand, in chapter 42 of *Huckleberry Finn*, Tom says that he and Huck "have knowed [Jim] all his life." Earlier, in chapter 23, Huck says that Jim is "low and homesick; because he hadn't ever been away from home before in his life." These two remarks suggest that Jim has lived in or near St. Petersburg for a long time.

Jim's age is also uncertain. Huck occasionally calls him "old Jim." In chapter 35, Huck is concerned with the slowness of Tom's escape plan for Jim and complains that Jim is "too old" to wait. "He won't last."

Jim rests after spending the night fighting the Mississippi's strong currents alone in chapter 15 of Huckleberry Finn.

Despite these remarks, it seems doubtful that Jim could be much over 40. In chapter 8, a slave trader offers to buy him for $800—a high price for any but a comparatively young man.

Chapters 16 and 23 offer clues about Jim's family. In chapter 23, Jim talks about his children, 'Lizabeth and Johnny, and tells a story about 'Lizabeth's contracting scarlet fever at four. The tone of his remarks suggests that both children are still very young. None of Jim's family appears in any story; however, fragmentary notes in Mark Twain's papers indicate that he once considered writing a story in which Huck and Tom buy Jim's wife and (one) child and present them to him as a Christmas gift.

Some writers on *Huckleberry Finn* have called Jim "Jim Watson," but this is not a name that Mark Twain himself uses. Indeed, such would not have been the naming practice of the time, although emancipated slaves often took the surnames of their masters. Another misconception about the novel is that Jim is called "the Nigger Jim." Jim is frequently called a "NIGGER" in the book, but the phrase "Nigger Jim" never appears there.

Huckleberry Finn introduces Jim as a friend of Tom and Huck, who enjoy testing his superstitions. When Jim overhears that Miss Watson intends to sell him down the river to raise money, he sneaks onto a large raft floating down the Mississippi. He intends to go some distance downriver, but swims to JACKSON'S ISLAND to avoid discovery on the raft. He wants to make his way to free territory, where he can earn money to buy the freedom of his wife and children. Huck, also hiding out on the island, stumbles on Jim and agrees go with him to free territory. As their journey develops, Huck feels increasingly guilty about his complicity in helping Jim to escape from slavery.

It happens that Jim leaves St. Petersburg the same night that Huck Finn is reported murdered. The coincidence makes Jim a prime suspect. He is thus a doubly wanted man. Huck learns this news from Judith LOFTUS when he goes back to town. He also learns that her husband and another man intend to search Jackson's Island for Jim. He rushes back to the island, and he and Jim gather their possessions together and leave as fast as they can.

Their plan is to raft down the Mississippi to CAIRO, Illinois, from which Jim can go up the OHIO RIVER to a safe free state. They go past Cairo during a foggy night, however, so they decide to continue downriver until they can buy a canoe in which to paddle back to Cairo. Each mile they go deeper into the South increases Jim's peril of remaining a slave. The journey builds a strong bond between Jim and Huck, who gradually comes to appreciate Jim's great dignity. Huck learns of Jim's love for his family and becomes his surrogate son. Jim's innate intelligence and common sense constantly shine through his surface ignorance. Many critics and scholars have called Jim the most noble character that Mark Twain created, but it seems to be his lot perpetually to face perils from which Huck and Tom must save him.

In *Huckleberry Finn*, Jim's constant fear of recapture dominates the middle chapters. Much of the narrative follows Huck, however, while Jim hides, away from the action. Jim's peril increases greatly after the KING and DUKE join them on the raft; these con men, who would sell their own mothers for a profit, stand ready to sell Jim at the first opportunity. Jim's worst nightmare comes true in PIKESVILLE, where the King sells him for $40. Jim is then held prisoner at the farm of Sally and Silas PHELPS, who happen to be Tom Sawyer's aunt and uncle.

When Huck learns where Jim is, he goes to the farm. Tom Sawyer appears shortly afterward and offers to help free Jim, although he privately knows that Miss Watson has recently died, freeing Jim in her will. Instead of revealing this fact and sparing Jim further suffering, Tom concocts an elaborate plan to bust Jim out of his makeshift jail. His complex "EVASION" scheme succeeds, but at the cost of risking his, Huck's and Jim's lives. After Tom himself is shot in the leg, Jim sacrifices his freshly won freedom to help a doctor treat him. Jim is thus back in custody again and is nearly lynched by irate townspeople. Only after Jim endures all this does Tom reveal that Jim has been legally free for two months.

Jim next appears in the unfinished novel "HUCK FINN AND TOM SAWYER AMONG THE INDIANS." As the story opens, Jim is back in St. Petersburg. When Aunt POLLY takes Huck and her own family to western Missouri, Jim accompanies them so he will be safe from men who might try to put him back into slavery while his friends are gone. Jim then accompanies Huck and Tom on an extended outing on the western plains, where he is captured by a band of INDIANS. Blaming himself for getting Jim into this new fix, Tom vows to rescue him, but the manuscript ends abruptly before Jim is seen again.

Tom Sawyer Abroad places Jim, Huck and Tom in a balloon journey across North AFRICA. Jim has little to do beyond serving as a foil for Tom's arguments about everything from the Crusades and Catholic bishops to fleas and sand. Jim is again placed in peril briefly when the boys strand him atop the SPHINX, from which they rescue him from an angry mob. This novella ends with Jim's piloting the balloon from Mount Sinai to Missouri and back in order to fetch Tom a corncob pipe.

Jim does not appear in *Tom Sawyer, Detective,* but returns in the unfinished novella "TOM SAWYER'S CONSPIRACY." Now a paid employee of the Widow Douglas, Jim is finally saving money to buy his wife and children. Nevertheless, he has enough idle time to join Huck and Tom in an abolitionist hoax as a summertime diversion. The "conspiracy" backfires when real conspirators murder the local slave trader and Jim is charged with the murder. Tom, confident that he and Huck will help apprehend the real culprits, makes things even worse for Jim by suggesting a plausible motive for his killing the slaver. Eventually, Jim goes on trial for the murder. Just as the judge is pronouncing a death sentence on him, the Duke and King enter the courtroom and ask for the judge's attention. Tom—who until now has never met the con men—cries out that their voices are those of the true murderers. He begins to present incontrovertible proof of their guilt but is cut off when Mark Twain's manuscript ends abruptly.

In his AUTOBIOGRAPHY, Mark Twain confessed to modeling Jim partly on Uncle Dan'l, a middle-aged slave on the FLORIDA, Missouri farm of his uncle John QUARLES. Mark Twain admired Daniel's levelheadedness, guilelessness and warmth. It was while spending his youthful summers at the Quarles farm that Mark Twain developed an affection for black people that emerges in his characterization of Jim. Other models for Jim include John T. LEWIS, a tenant farmer at QUARRY FARM, and George GRIFFIN, Mark Twain's longtime butler.

Since George Reed (1867–1952) played Jim in the first film adaptations of *Huckleberry Finn* in 1920 and 1931, Jim has become an important role for black actors. The ages of actors playing him have ranged from 29-year-old Antonio Fargas in a 1975 television film and 33-year-old Paul Winfield in a 1974 film, to 64-year-old George Reed in 1931 and 54-year-old Brock Peters in a 1981 television film. Other actors who have portrayed Jim include Rex Ingram (1939), Archie Moore (1960), Samm-Art Williams (1986) and Courtney Vance in the 1993 Disney adaptation. Jim's wife never appears in *Huckleberry Finn;* however, Odessa Cleveland played her in a role written into the 1974 film.

Jinny, Aunt, and Uncle Dan'l Characters in *The Gilded Age* and *The American Claimant.* In the first novel, 30-year-old Jinny and her 40-year-old husband Dan'l are the family slaves of Si HAWKINS who accompany his family from Tennessee to Missouri (chapter 3). After one of Hawkins's bankruptcies about 10 years later, they are sold at auction and taken downriver (chapter 7). In *Claimant,* they reappear as elderly household servants in the Washington, D.C. home of Colonel SELLERS (chapter 3). Described as "old wrecks," they not only do no housework, they require another, younger servant to take care of them. They often quarrel loudly about religion; Dan'l is a "Dunker Baptist" and Jinny a "shouting Methodist."

Joan of Arc, Saint (c. January 6, 1412, Domremy, France–May 30, 1431, Rouen, France) Patron saint and national hero of FRANCE and the subject of Mark Twain's last finished novel. An illiterate peasant born in the village of DOMREMY, Joan took command of the armies of France when she was 17. Within 13 months, she had led them to victories that turned the tide of the Hundred Years' War, paving the way for France's complete liberation from England two decades later. After being captured by the Burgundians in May 1430, she was ransomed by the English and tried for heresy in ROUEN by a French ecclesiastical court headed by Bishop Pierre CAUCHON that sentenced her to be burned at the stake. Two decades later, France's King CHARLES VII had the Vatican retry her case, and she was officially rehabilitated in 1456. In 1920, the Roman Catholic Church canonized her.

Joan of Arc was Mark Twain's favorite historical figure. According to A. B. PAINE's biography, when Mark Twain was a youth in Hannibal, a stray leaf from a history book containing a moving passage about Joan's captivity in Rouen blew into his hands. Paine sees this moment as a turning point in Mark Twain's life—it not only launched his lifelong fascination with Joan, but gave him an appetite for history generally. While scholars disagree over whether this romantic incident actually occurred, it is clear that Mark Twain became fascinated with Joan early in life. By at least 1868, he was citing her name in speeches. By the early 1890s, he decided to tell her story in the form of the novel that became *Personal Recollections of Joan of Arc.* Following the outlines of Joan's life closely, he took little license in interpreting her career. For example, though he was skeptical about the "voices" that Joan claimed were guiding her, his novel simply accepts them as given, with no attempt to explain them. On the other hand, while he considered her an "ideally perfect" character, he gave her a robust sense of humor. He also exaggerated her physical attractiveness. At 16, she is "shapely and graceful, and of a beauty so extraordinary that I might allow myself any extravagance of language in describing it" (book 1, chapter 5). He later acknowledged modeling Joan's description on that of his own daughter, Susy, whom he also idealized. Nearly a decade after writing JOAN OF ARC, Mark Twain again praised her extravagantly in an essay for the December 1904 HARPER'S MAGAZINE, "Saint Joan of Arc," which calls her career "beyond fiction." In 1919, HARPER AND BROTHERS MAGAZINE, published

The execution of Joan of Arc, from a mural by J. E. Lenepveu (1819–1898) used in Harper's edition of Joan of Arc.

Mark Twain's "Saint Joan of Arc" as a book, with some of the introductory passages from *Joan of Arc* and new color illustrations by Howard Nye.

Joan of Arc, Personal Recollections of (1896) The last novel that Mark Twain published in his lifetime, *Joan of Arc* occupies a unique place among his major works. Mark Twain regarded the book as his best and most important work, but modern opinion holds just the opposite view—a discrepancy that awaits full explanation.

Though *Joan of Arc* naturally falls among Mark Twain's historical novels, it differs markedly from the others. Unlike *The Prince and the Pauper* (1881), which alters the recorded history of mid–16th-century England, or *A Connecticut Yankee in King Arthur's Court* (1889), which revises a myth, *Joan of Arc* follows its subject's known history closely. Indeed, it often reads

as history, with frequent insertions of dates and other historical facts—including a summary of FRANCE and England's Hundred Years' War (book 2, chapter 31). Despite its historical faithfulness, the novel avoids the central issue in Joan's life—her religious calling. It never tries to explain where her "voices" come from or why she is so devoted to God. Likewise, it does not consider whether the Roman Catholic Church had reasons other than vindictiveness for prosecuting her. Since Joan's story unfolds in a void in which she is an innocent champion of virtue fighting inexplicable evil, the novel's main purpose seems to be to extol her nobility.

The extent to which *Joan of Arc* is a "novel" can be measured by the range of Mark Twain's creative contributions. His most obvious inventions are characters such as the PALADIN and Noël RAINGUESSON, who offer comic relief without seriously disturbing Joan's known history. Otherwise, Mark Twain distances himself from the story through two levels of fictional narrators. He presents his book as Jean François ALDEN's modern translation of an authentic narrative by Sieur Louis DE CONTE, a contemporary of Joan's. De Conte supposedly recorded his story in 1492 for his relatives' descendants to read. His narrative voice shifts between the immediacy of his participation in events with Joan and the distance of an old man reflecting on the past. Mark Twain's voice intrudes occasionally when de Conte slips out of his own era to explain things that modern readers might not understand—such as the nature of French village life in the 15th century and the recent history of France.

Joan of Arc contains Mark Twain's most extensive depiction of war. Like the narrator of "THE PRIVATE HISTORY OF A CAMPAIGN THAT FAILED" and Mark Twain himself, both the narrator and the chief protagonist of *Joan of Arc* are unfitted for war and are appalled by its brutality. De Conte's descriptions of actual fighting tend to be distant and superficial, reflecting his anxiousness to move on to more agreeable matters.

SYNOPSIS

Joan of Arc contains just over 150,000 words of text. Both one- and two-volume editions contain 73 numbered chapters that are divided among three "books." The first book, with eight chapters, constitutes about 14 percent of the novel; the second, with 41 chapters, about 55 percent; and the third, with 24 chapters, about 31 percent. There is also an unnumbered conclusion.

Information given below in parentheses comes from outside the chapters. For example, the mileages given, the most direct distances between towns, are taken from *The Times Atlas of the World*. Most dates in the chapter summaries are taken from Mark Twain's own text and are thus not in parentheses.

Translator's preface
A person's character can typically be judged only by the standards of the person's time. Joan of Arc's character,

however, is unique in that the standards of *all* time would find it ideally perfect. She may be the only entirely unselfish person in profane history. Her biography is also unique in being the only story of a human life that comes to us under oath—from the official records of her two trials. De Conte's account of Joan's life is unimpeachable, but the particulars that he adds must be judged on his own word alone.

De Conte's note
It is 1492 and the author is 82 years old. He relates things that he saw as a youth. His name is mentioned in all the histories of Joan of Arc because he was with her from the time they were children, through the wars, to her end. To this day, he remembers her clearly, and his hand was the last that she touched in life. After all these years have passed, he now recognizes her for what she was—the most noble life that was ever born into this world save only One (presumably Jesus Christ).

Book 1, chapter 1
The author was born in Neufchâteau on January 6, 1410—exactly two years before Joan of Arc was born in nearby DOMREMY. Orphaned after the English shattered France at Agincourt (1415), de Conte was raised in the home of a priest in Domremy, where Joan and her brothers were among his many childhood friends.

Book 1, chapter 2
Like all village children, those of Domremy live in humble dirt-floored houses and tend flocks. They particularly enjoy dancing around a majestic beech tree, which is the home of fairies until the village priest banishes them. The children are heartbroken, but Joan alone confronts the priest to plead the fairies' case. So effectively does she argue that the priest asks for forgiveness.

Book 1, chapter 3
De Conte also recalls a stormy winter night when a ragged stranger came to the house of Joan, who admitted him before her father could stop her. The stranger proved to be a good man who showed his gratitude for the porridge Joan gave him with a noble recitation of the Song of Roland.

Book 1, chapter 4
Domremy's children, like all others, have nicknames; Joan has several. On one terrible day, they learn that their mad king Charles VI has given France to England in a treaty (1420). The boys laugh when the girls say they would like to fight for France, but are interrupted when a madman charges at them with an ax. Everyone scatters but Joan, who gently leads the man back to the village—a deed for which she is nicknamed "the Brave."

Book 1, chapter 5
France's next year is dismal. On a day when Domremy's boys are trounced in a fight with Maxey's Burgundian boys, they hear that their king is dead and that English armies are sweeping the land. Several years of false alarms and scares follow, until war reaches Domremy

in 1428. Marauders ravage the village, wreaking violence that appalls Joan. One day, when the lad known as the PALADIN ridicules France's generals, Joan defends them as the pillars of the nation. When the children discuss what they would do if they became heroes, Joan quietly predicts their futures.

Book 1, chapter 6
Over the next year and a half, Joan grows melancholy, but when de Conte says that France's situation is hopeless, she confidently predicts that France will win its freedom. Wondering where Joan draws such confidence, de Conte watches her. On May 15, 1428, he sees her at the enchanted beech tree, where she converses with an invisible presence.

Book 1, chapter 7
After mysterious voices leave, Joan tells de Conte that for three years these "voices" have told her that within a year she is destined to lead the armies that will begin freeing France and that *she* will crown the DAUPHIN to make him king (CHARLES VII). Further, de Conte is to help her. First, she must ask Robert de Baudricourt, the governor at Vaucouleurs (11 miles north of Domremy), for an armed escort to take her to the king. With her uncle Laxart, she visits Vaucouleurs, but the governor rebuffs her.

Book 1, chapter 8
In Domremy, Joan's family and neighbors think that she has disgraced their village and they shun her, but she remains steadfast through the summer. When the Paladin claims that Joan promised to marry him, she is called before a court at Toul (20 miles northeast of Domremy), where she defends so herself eloquently that she wins back her parents' affection. Meanwhile, England's siege of ORLÉANS begins.

Book 2, chapter 1
On January 5, 1429, Joan reveals that her "voices" have finally given her clear instructions: within two months she will be with the Dauphin. Joan's uncle now believes in her wholeheartedly. The next day—her birthday—she bids her village a tearful farewell. She is now 17.

Book 2, chapter 2
At Vaucouleurs, Joan lodges with a wheelwright's wife and gradually wins the respect of the common people. When MERLIN's ancient prophecy that a woman would one day save France is recalled, Joan's reputation soars. Eventually, the governor visits her and decides to have bishops test whether she is a saint or a witch. Joan's impatience mounts, however. She tells the governor that the Dauphin is suffering a military defeat that will be known in nine days. Meanwhile, she assembles a tiny force, including two knights, and prepares to march to the king. Just as she sets off, the governor arrives. He confirms her report of the king's defeat and gives her his sword and an armed escort.

Book 2, chapter 3

Joan now leaves with about 25 men, including her brothers Jacques and Jean D'Arc, and is soon in enemy territory. The next morning, de Conte discovers that the Paladin and their mutual friend Noël RAINGUESSON are among the men whom the governor gave to Joan the night before—thus fulfilling another of Joan's prophecies.

Book 2, chapter 4

After inspecting her men and instructing them on how to behave, Joan leads horsemanship drills, then continues the march. For five nights, they fight off ambuscades. As the men grow fatigued, Joan remains so strong that some of them suspect that she is a witch and plot to kill her. She confronts the plotters, however, telling them that their scheme cannot work, and she predicts that their ringleader will soon die. After his horse stumbles in a river and he drowns, the conspiracies end.

On a stormy night, Joan rides straight into an enemy force and has a long interview with its commander, who thinks that she is one of his own lieutenants. Without lying, she answers his questions, then leads her band safely away. After 10 days, her band crosses the Loire and reaches Gien (38 miles east–southeast of Orléans).

Book 2, chapter 5

After resting at Gien, the band pushes on and Joan has her knights carry a message to the king at Chinon. Near Chinon, the knights return and report that the king's minister Georges de la Tremouille and the Archbishop of Rheims (Reims) have kept them away from the king. Joan's only ally at court is the king's mother-in-law, Queen Yolande of Sicily, who eventually helps Joan's knights reach the king. When the king's priests come to interview Joan, she insists on speaking directly to the king. The next day, the king arranges for her band to stay at the Castle of Courdray, where Joan charms people from the court.

Book 2, chapter 6

After further delays, the king sends priests to Lorraine to investigate Joan's background. Eventually, she is invited to meet him. Dressed simply, she enters a splendid court. A dazzling crowned and bejeweled figure sits on a throne, but Joan ignores him and amazes everyone by finding the true Dauphin among the courtiers. After she kneels before him, they talk privately and she whispers something that visibly bolsters him. De Conte later learns that Joan has assured the Dauphin that his birth is lawful.

Book 2, chapter 7

As Joan awaits further developments at Courdray, the Paladin buys a gaudy cavalier outfit and regales people at the local inn with his shameless bragging.

Book 2, chapter 8

Though Joan's secret message has reassured the king, his advisers suggest that her inspiration may come from Satan, not God. The king sends bishops to test her daily, but they cannot decide about her, so he sends her to Poitiers to be examined by theology professors. After three wasted weeks, Joan's inquisitors conclude that she is indeed sent by God.

Book 2, chapter 9

Meanwhile the king's priests return from Lorraine with favorable reports on Joan, and good luck begins flooding in. Since Joan is to be a soldier, the Church permits her to wear male attire; the king names her "General-in-chief of the Armies of France" and makes his cousin, the royal Duke of Alençon, her chief of staff.

Book 2, chapter 10

Joan's first official act is to dictate a letter to the English commanders at Orléans, ordering them to leave France. The king has armor made for Joan, who sends a knight to Fierbois to fetch an ancient sword that her "voices" have described to her. As she prepares her army, she assigns important posts to each childhood friend: She makes de Conte her page and secretary, Rainguesson her messenger and the Paladin her standard bearer.

Book 2, chapter 11

As de Conte and Rainguesson discuss the amazing honor that Joan has bestowed on the boastful Paladin, they realize that she has the "seeing eye." Meanwhile, Joan sends for the swashbuckling old commander La Hire to take charge of training the new recruits at Blois (midway between Tours and Orléans) and she starts on her first war-march.

Book 2, chapter 12

At Blois, Joan hits it off well with La Hire and shocks the profane old veteran by insisting that he and all the troops attend mass voluntarily. Within three days, all the women and other camp followers are gone and the troops are attending mass. Joan's biggest victory is getting La Hire to say a prayer—one that makes her laugh heartily.

Book 2, chapter 13

Under the command of La Hire and four other seasoned generals, Joan's army marches from Blois to Orléans. Ignoring her order to approach the city from the north, the generals try to fool her by crossing the Loire to the south side of the city. When she detects their trick, she asks Dunois, the Bastard of Orléans, to explain the generals' blunder. When he cannot, she sends the bulk of the army back upriver to advance on Orléans from the north. She, La Hire and Dunois then lead a thousand troops into Orléans, where she and her friends put up in the house of Dunois's treasurer, Boucher.

Book 2, chapter 14

On April 30, Joan sends a message asking the English to reply to her earlier letter, in which she invited them to join her in a crusade to recapture the HOLY SEPULCHER. They respond by threatening to capture and burn her. She orders Dunois to fetch the rest of her army from Blois.

Book 2, chapter 15
As they await the army, de Conte, Rainguesson, the Paladin and Joan's brothers all fall in love with beautiful Catherine Boucher. The most smitten is de Conte, who writes a poem in her honor. He lets Rainguesson recite it to Catherine in company; between Rainguesson's recitation and the Paladin's excessive weeping, de Conte himself is overlooked.

Book 2, chapter 16
The next night, the Paladin learns through a deserter that the English plan to assault Orléans. The news spurs Joan to prepare for battle. As she meets La Hire's troops the next morning, she sees a huge soldier who is being held for desertion; she inquires about his case and learns that he is a good soldier who returned voluntarily after running off to see his dying wife. Joan pardons the man—who is called the "Dwarf"—and makes him her personal guard.

When Joan leads her army past the English strongholds, not a shot is fired. When she learns that the English have weakened their forts on the south side of the river, she wants to attack them there, but her generals delay her for four days.

Book 2, chapter 17
Back at the Bouchers' house, the Paladin taunts de Conte for having fallen off his horse during the march and de Conte wins a knight's praise by frankly admitting his fear.

Book 2, chapter 18
At midday, Joan suddenly senses that a battle is raging and rushes off to join it. The people of Orléans have spontaneously attacked the Burgundy Gate, where Talbot's more numerous English troops are routing them. Joan's arrival turns the tide and the French capture the English fort at St. Loup. It is Joan's first real battle and the first significant French victory since the siege began seven months earlier.

Book 2, chapter 19
As everyone rests from the battle, de Conte and his friends try to solve a mystery about a ghost in the Bouchers' house.

Book 2, chapter 20
When Joan learns that her irresolute generals plan a long siege against the English troops, she promises to oust the enemy in three days and begins by ordering an assault on the English forts guarding bridges at Augustins and Tourelles. Under her leadership, her army takes the first English position the next day and she is wounded in the foot.

Book 2, chapter 21
That evening, Joan dictates a letter, telling her parents not to worry when they learn that she is wounded.

Catherine Boucher grows upset when she learns that Joan is referring not to her foot wound, but to a terrible wound that she expects to receive the next day.

Book 2, chapter 22
The next morning, Joan leads the assault on Tourelles and is struck between her neck and shoulder by a bolt from a crossbow. When she hears a retreat being sounded, she rises to countermand the order and leads a successful assault on Tourelles. As she has predicted, she lifts the siege of Orléans. The city has ever since celebrated Joan's victory on May 8.

Book 2, chapter 23
By dawn, Talbot has evacuated Orléans and the French can scarcely believe that they are again free. Joan marches to report to the Dauphin, whom she finds at Tours. She encourages him to go immediately to Rheims (135 miles northeast of Orléans) for his coronation, but Tremouille's cautious advice makes him hesitate to act. When the Dauphin offers Joan whatever she wants in reward for relieving Orléans, she simply blushes. He ennobles her and her family, dubbing her "Joan of Arc," surnamed "Du Lis."

Book 2, chapter 24
Joan's ennoblement excites the whole country, but dismays the Paladin and Rainguesson because Joan's brothers now greatly outrank them.

Book 2, chapter 25
As the king causes further delays, Joan's army begins disintegrating. To induce the king to go to Rheims, Joan proposes raising a new army to clear a path for him between Tours and Rheims. After assembling 8,000 soldiers, she begins her march on June 6.

Book 2, chapter 26
As Joan leaves Tours, the king orders her generals to do nothing without her sanction; however, they still resist her aggressive tactics. She promises to take Jargeau (10 miles east of Orléans) by direct assault—a plan that La Hire enthusiastically endorses.

Book 2, chapter 27
The next day, the army finally moves on Jargeau. After driving its English defenders within its walls, Joan gives them an hour to leave. They fail to comply, so she resumes the assault the next day until they surrender.

Book 2, chapter 28
As Joan dictates to de Conte, Catherine Boucher drops in to express her concern about Joan's safety. Joan predicts that she will achieve a major victory within four days, then goes into a trance and says that she will die a cruel death within two years. Catherine thinks that Joan is merely dreaming, but de Conte knows that Joan's remarks are prophetic.

Book 2, chapter 29
No one wants to believe Joan's prophecy that she must complete her work within a single year, but de Conte

keeps her prophecy about her death to himself. At dawn, Joan leads her army to Meung and Beaugency. After taking the latter town without a fight, she bombards its castle till night. When Richemont, the Constable of France, approaches, D'Alençon opposes letting him join her forces because the king is estranged from him; however, Joan gets D'Alençon to relent. On the morning of June 17, the French learn that Talbot and Fastolfe's forces are coming. Joan decides to take up the battle the next day. Meanwhile, maneuvering among the English leads to the surrender of Beaugency.

Book 2, chapter 30
On June 18, Joan's army cautiously advances through the plains of La Beauce toward Patay (15 miles northwest of Orléans). After stumbling on the English position, they take up battle. In three hours of fierce fighting, the French prevail, and Joan predicts that the English power in France is broken for a thousand years. Later, de Conte finds her crying over a dying English prisoner.

Book 2, chapter 31
It is now 91 years since the Hundred Years' War began, and its English side is looking sick. The Battle of Patay is one of the truly great battles in history, as it has lifted France from convalescence to perfect health.

Book 2, chapter 32
News of Patay spreads through France in 24 hours. When Joan's army returns to Orléans, the overjoyed town welcomes her as the "Saviour of France."

Book 2, chapter 33
In looking back from the future, de Conte lists Joan's five "great deeds" as raising the siege of Orléans; the victory at Patay; the reconciliation at Sully-sur-Loire; the king's coronation; and the bloodless march. The reconciliation was between the king and Richemont, who later transformed the king into a man and a determined soldier. De Conte likens Joan's moves to a chess game whose "checkmate" came when Richemont and the king joined forces after her death.

Book 2, chapter 34
After the Loire campaign, Joan is anxious to take the king to Rheims to be crowned. The king fears crossing English-held territory, but the march to Rheims proves to be a holiday excursion. On June 29, Joan rides out of Gien at the side of the king and d'Alençon, with 12,000 men. After Troyes surrenders without a fight, she permits its English and Burgundian soldiers to carry away their goods, but her men are outraged when each enemy soldier marches out with a French prisoner on his back. The Dwarf gets into an argument with a Burgundian, whom he kills for insulting Joan. Conceding that the enemy are within their rights to take their prisoners with them, Joan solves the problem by having the king ransom all the Frenchmen.

Book 2, chapter 35
As Joan's army marches on, Châlon (35 miles northeast of Troyes) surrenders to her army. On July 16, they reach Rheims, where they receive an enthusiastic welcome. The next day, Joan is at the king's side during his coronation. Afterward, when she requests permission to go home, Charles asks what grace he can bestow upon her for her services. She asks only that her village have its taxes remitted, so Charles decrees that Domremy will be freed from taxation forever.

Book 2, chapter 36
As Joan rides from the coronation, she sees her father and uncle Laxart in the crowd. The king orders that they be honored and offers them fine quarters, but they prefer to stay at the humble Zebra's Inn. When the city gives the king a grand banquet, D'Arc and Laxart eat in a gallery to avoid attention. Afterward, Joan and her Domremy friends join the men at their inn, where Joan tries to put them at ease. She says that her military work is done and that she will soon be home. Their talk covers many things, and Joan nearly suffocates with laughter when her uncle tells a tedious story about getting entangled with beehives while trying to ride a bull to a funeral.

Book 2, chapter 37
Joan asks her father why he came to town without telling her. His admission that he feared being snubbed gives de Conte the idea that peasants might actually be "people" who one day will rise up and demand their rights. Joan comforts her father and shows him her pike and sword. As they gossip about Domremy, a messenger summons Joan to a council of war.

Book 2, chapter 38
De Conte follows Joan to the council, where she mocks the notion that a "council of war" is even needed. Asserting that only *one* rational course of action is open—to march on PARIS—she boldly confronts the king's chief minister, Tremouille, and the chancellor, who want to treat with the Duke of Burgundy and wait before moving against Paris. Joan warns that if they hesitate now, the half-year's work now facing them will take another 20 years to complete. Buoyed by his generals' enthusiasm, the king gives Joan his sword to carry to Paris.

Book 2, chapter 39
Joan issues orders to her generals and dictates a letter inviting the Duke of Burgundy to make peace. The next morning, she bids farewell to her father and uncle and leads her army out. Again, her march is a holiday excursion, with English strongholds surrendering along the way; nevertheless, the king loses his nerve. He goes back to Gien and makes a truce with Burgundy. Joan can handle the English and the Burgundians, but is no match for French conspirators. On August 26, 1429, she camps at St. Denis, near Paris.

Book 2, chapter 40

Joan sends messages trying to get the king to join her at St. Denis. After nine wasted days, she begins an artillery barrage on the gate of St. Honoré. As her troops enter, she is wounded and carried off. She wants to resume the assault the next day, but the king forbids it. Heartbroken, she asks permission to retire and go home, but the king will not let her go, and her "voices" tell her to stay at St. Denis. At Tremouille's insistence, the king orders Joan to return her army to the Loire, where he disbands it. France's disgrace is complete, and the unconquerable Joan of Arc is conquered.

Book 2, chapter 41

Eight months of drifting follow as Joan accompanies the king and his council from place to place. The king occasionally lets her lead sorties—in one of which de Conte is wounded. While campaigning near Compiègne (40 miles north–northeast of Paris), which the Duke of Burgundy is besieging, Joan leads the last march of her life on May 24, 1430. She is captured by the Dwarf and Paladin are killed, and her brothers and Rainguesson are wounded trying to defend her.

Book 3, chapter 1

De Conte hopes to hear that Joan is ransomed, but the king remains silent. Over the next five months, Joan twice tries to escape and is moved to Beaurevoir. Meanwhile, the Duke of Burgundy—desperate for money—ransoms Joan to the English through Bishop CAUCHON, who is promised the archbishopric of ROUEN. Since Joan's military record is spotless, she is to be tried for religious crimes at Rouen.

Book 3, chapter 2

Though still suffering from his wound, de Conte goes out on a sortie in October and is wounded again at Compiègne. There he encounters Rainguesson, who has been a prisoner all this time. Heartbroken to learn that Joan has been sold to the English, they go to Rouen to be near her in January (1431).

Book 3, chapter 3

De Conte gets a job clerking for a good priest named Manchon, who will be chief recorder in Joan's trial. Manchon reveals that Cauchon has packed Joan's jury with 50 distinguished men sympathetic to England. Although an inquisitor from Paris refuses to hear Joan's case because she was already tried at Poitiers, Cauchon gets around all the jurisdictional difficulties. Not only does he not allow Joan to have legal help, he eavesdrops on her when she confesses to his confederate Nicolas Loyseleur, a great University of Paris personage who pretends to be a priest from Joan's region.

Book 3, chapter 4

Joan's trial finally starts on February 21. De Conte distrusts the formidable court set against Joan, who is brought in chains.

Book 3, chapter 5

Before continuing his narrative, de Conte promises to stick faithfully to the official trial record—something that his translator affirms he has done. Attending as Manchon's aide, de Conte rejoices to see that Joan's spirit is not broken. The judge summarizes the particulars against Joan, he tells her to kneel and swear that she will truthfully answer all questions. She refuses, however, saying that she cannot tell what her "voices" have revealed. The judges rail at her for three hours, then allow her to swear her own oath. When the first day ends after five hours, only Joan is not exhausted. During the trial, she often looks at de Conte and Rainguesson—who is in the audience—but does not betray that she knows them.

Book 3, chapter 6

That night, de Conte learns that Cauchon has tried to make clerks twist Joan's testimony in a special record but failed. The next day, the trial moves to larger chambers and the number of judges is increased to 62. Cauchon again presses Joan to take an oath, but she refuses. He then turns her over to Beaupere, a wily theologian who asks her about her "voices" and presses her on the matter of her male attire. Despite hours of questioning, he fails to trap her.

Book 3, chapter 7

During the court's third session, on February 24, Beaupere springs his biggest trap: asking Joan if she is in a "state of grace." Since the question is unanswerable, even some of Cauchon's judges object to it. However, Joan replies calmly, "If I be not in a state of Grace, I pray God place me in it; if I be in it, I pray God keep me so." Her brilliant answer takes the heart out of Beaupere's interrogation.

Book 3, chapter 8

When the court meets on the 27th, Joan is again asked about her "voices," whom she identifies as St. Catherine and St. Marguerite. Weary of hearing the same questions repeatedly, she suggests that the court send to Poitiers for the record of her earlier trial.

Book 3, chapter 9

On March 1, the judge tries to trick Joan into naming which of the several men who claim to be pope is the true one. It is a dangerous topic, so when she innocently asks, "Are there *two*?," the matter is dropped. De Conte is mortified when a letter that Joan once dictated to him is read aloud and Joan points out its transcription errors. Gradually, Joan grows impatient and rises to predict future French military successes against the English—which de Conte confirms later happened. Her predictions agitate the court and raise further questions about her "voices." De Conte suspects that many in the courtroom are starting to think that Joan really is sent by God and that they themselves may be the ones in peril.

Book 3, chapter 10
In one of the court's stormiest sessions, on March 3, the judges lose their patience. Aside from keeping them from other duties, the trial is making them laughing-stocks. They all try to go at Joan at once, with questions about her wanting to be worshipped, trying to commit suicide in prison and blaspheming.

Book 3, chapter 11
Eventually, Cauchon halts the trial because he is losing ground. After letting all but the toughest judges leave, he spends five days sifting testimony. When the trial resumes on March 10, it is closed to the public. Joan now looks tired and weak, but by the third day she is looking less worn. The questions turn to her use of her own standard in battle.

Book 3, chapter 12
When the judge begins asking about the Paladin's old claim that Joan once promised to marry him, Joan loses her temper. Cauchon then questions her more about her male attire and her efforts to escape from prison. The session on March 17, the last day of this trial, begins with a new trap. Joan is asked if she will submit her words and deeds to the determination of the Church; however, she replies that she will submit them only to God. When she is carelessly asked if she would give fuller answers to the pope, she suggests they take her to him. Cauchon blanches, since he realizes—as Joan does not—that she has that right, and that if she were to reach Rome, she would receive a fair trial that would free her. He changes the subject.

Book 3, chapter 13
Before the second trial ends without result, Cauchon asks a lawyer for his opinion and is outraged when the man lists four reasons why the trial should be ruled null and void. The third trial begins on March 27. The reading of 66 articles takes days. They charge Joan with being a sorceress, false prophet, companion of evil spirits, dealer in magic, schismatic, idolater, apostate, blasphemer, disturber and more. This third trial also ends without result, so Cauchon reduces the 66 charges to 12 for a new trial.

Book 3, chapter 14
Joan falls ill on March 29, after her third trial ends. Calling the new charges against her "the 12 lies," de Conte explains why each is false. These charges include such accusations as Joan's claiming to have found her salvation; refusing to submit to the Church; threatening death to those who would not obey her; and claiming never to have committed a sin. When the 12 articles are sent to doctors of theology in Paris, Manchon boldly writes in the margins that many of the statements attributed to Joan are the *opposite* of what she actually said.

Meanwhile, concern over Joan's health grows. The English party does not want her to die before the Church formally condemns her. After doctors bleed her, she improves until one of Cauchon's men storms at her. When de Conte accompanies Manchon and Cauchon to Joan's cell, Joan asks to confess, but Cauchon insists that she submit to the Church and threatens her with damnation.

Book 3, chapter 15
The court opens again on May 2, with Cauchon and 62 judges. Joan is again brought in chains. An orator reads the 12 charges against her and threatens her with the stake unless she submits, but she remains steadfast and again baffles the court.

Book 3, chapter 16
As news of Cauchon's latest defeat spreads, people laugh at him and make puns on his name, which resembles *cochon,* a word for "hog." On May 9, de Conte and Manchon are with Cauchon when he summons Joan to a torture chamber and threatens to rack her. She remains calm, however, and says that if forced to confess, she will later recant. The bishops eventually send her back to her cell, and Cauchon again becomes a target of laughter in Rouen.

Book 3, chapter 17
As 10 more days pass, de Conte and Rainguesson rue Joan's plight. While admitting that Joan was always great, de Conte thinks that she was at her greatest during these trials.

Book 3, chapter 18
A report finally arrives from the Paris theologians, who find Joan guilty on all 12 articles, asserting that her "voices" belong to fiends. On May 19, 50 judges sit to determine her fate. Four days later, she is again called to court. When a canon of Rouen calls on her to renounce her errors, she refuses.

Book 3, chapter 19
Still anxious for Joan to condemn herself publicly, Cauchon considers his devious options. He has Loyseleur visit Joan disguised as a pro-French priest. Meanwhile, de Conte and Rainguesson hope for a last-minute rescue by La Hire.

Book 3, chapter 20
Cauchon leads Joan to a stake over burning coals and has an ecclesiastic preach at her. This fails to move her, however, until he denounces King Charles as a heretic. Meanwhile, the crowd—expecting a burning—grows impatient. When the preacher shows Joan a written form and asks her to abjure, she starts to weaken before the fire. Finally, when Cauchon reads the sentence of death, Joan agrees to submit. A priest reads a form that she is to sign, but she is helped to sign a *different* paper that is substituted, in which she admits to being a sorceress and other things. Cauchon then shocks Joan by pronouncing a sentence of perpetual imprisonment. Joan expects to be taken to a church prison, but is instead returned to her harsh English prison.

Book 3, chapter 21

As Joan is led away, the angry crowd hurls stones at the ecclesiastics. After Joan is returned to her cell, Cauchon keeps trying to wear her down. He allows her to wear female attire, but is confident that she will relapse.

Book 3, chapter 22

Unaware of Cauchon's machinations, de Conte and Rainguesson are excited about the prospect of Joan's becoming free. A few days later, however, they hear a report that Joan has relapsed. When de Conte later visits her cell with Manchon, he sees her in male attire because a guard has switched her clothes. Cauchon is triumphant.

Book 3, chapter 23

That night, de Conte learns that Joan wants him to write a letter to her family. Since de Conte cannot go to her cell, Manchon passes on her message, which says that she has seen the "Vision of the Tree" and that there will be no rescue. The next day, May 29, Cauchon's court meets to pronounce Joan a relapsed heretic and turn her over to secular authority for punishment. De Conte and Manchon go with the priests who prepare Joan for her execution. When she hears that she is to burn, she becomes so upset that de Conte throws himself at her feet; however, she touches his hand and whispers that he should not imperil himself. Cauchon allows Joan to have communion and she goes to her death serenely.

Book 3, chapter 24

As Joan rides to her execution in a cart, Loyseleur rushes forward from the crowd and begs forgiveness, which she grants. On a platform in the market square, a priest delivers a sermon and pronounces Joan excommunicated. She kneels and prays for the king of France. Everyone, including the secular judge, is so moved that Joan goes to her death without being officially sentenced. After she is chained to the stake, she asks for a cross. An English soldier fashions one of sticks for her. Her last words are to Cauchon: "I die through you."

Book 3, Conclusion

The narrator looks back on these events from a time many years later. As Joan had prophesied, her brother Jacques died in Domremy while she was tried in Rouen. Shortly after her martyrdom, her father died of a broken heart. Her mother lived for many more years and was granted a pension by Orléans. Meanwhile, de Conte and Orléans returned to Domremy until Richemont replaced Tremouille as King Charles's chief minister; then they returned to war. De Conte was with Rainguesson when he died in the last great battle (1453) and he is now the sole survivor of those who fought with Joan.

Charles was indifferent to Joan's fate until after the English were finally expelled from France. They began calling attention to the fact that he had received his crown from someone in league with Satan, so he appealed to the pope, who appointed a commission to investigate Joan. The result was that she was rehabilitated.

BACKGROUND AND PUBLISHING HISTORY

Mark Twain boasted of spending 12 years researching *Joan of Arc*, but his actual research work was slight. He began compiling a reading list in the early 1880s. By 1891, he had read several books on Joan, including Janet Tuckey's popular *Joan of Arc, The Maid* (1880). In September of that year, he asked Andrew CHATTO to send him additional books. In a letter to H. H. ROGERS, he admitted to lifting the framework of the first two-thirds of his story from just two standard histories. His final section, on Joan's trial, he based on another five or six books—all of which are listed at the beginning of the novel as "authorities" examined to verify de Conte's narrative. Much of *Joan of Arc* he wrote by simply redrafting the historical outline of Joan's life, adding dialogue and occasional fictional glosses.

Mark Twain began the actual writing of the novel on August 1, 1892, while he was living in FLORENCE, Italy. He wrote rapidly until the following March, by which time he had 22 chapters and had reached the part in which Joan had raised the siege of Orléans. He was ready to end the narrative there, but during a trip to New York in which he negotiated serial publication of the story in HARPER'S MAGAZINE, its editor H. M. ALDEN persuaded him to carry Joan's story to the end of her life. After returning to Europe, Mark Twain continued writing at a more leisurely pace until he pronounced himself finished on February 8, 1895. (He describes his reaction to this moment in "The Finished Book," a brief essay posthumously published in *Europe and Elsewhere*.)

Mark Twain feared that people would not take his book seriously with his name attached to it, so he arranged for *Harper's Magazine* to publish it anonymously. When HARPER AND BROTHERS issued *Joan of Arc* as a book in May 1896, Mark Twain's name appeared on its spine and cover, but not on its title page (the English edition listed him as "editor," however).

Since the book's original publication, it has seen comparatively few editions. The book comprised two volumes in Harper's various uniform editions and has occasionally been reprinted in small editions. The MARK TWAIN PAPERS project has tentatively scheduled *Joan of Arc* so far down its list of future publications that it is doubtful that the project will ever publish a corrected edition. The book was, however, saved from oblivion in 1994 when the Library of America included it in *Mark Twain: Historical Romances*, which is lightly annotated by Susan K. Harris.

While he was staying in Paris, Mark Twain commissioned Frank Vincent DU MOND to illustrate *Joan of Arc*. Later, he complained that Du Mond's pictures made Joan look too much like an ordinary peasant girl (which was probably historically accurate). When he wrote "Saint Joan of Arc" in 1904, he may have been thinking of Du Mond in decrying artists who remember only that Joan was a peasant girl and forget everything else, painting her "as a strapping middle-aged fishwoman, with costume to match," forgetting that "supremely great souls are never lodged in gross bodies."

Joe Name of two minor characters in *Huckleberry Finn*. A 19-year-old cousin of Buck GRANGERFORD named Joe is killed by the SHEPHERDSONS in chapter 18. An unrelated "Joe" is among the BRICKSVILLE loafers whom Huck sees in chapter 21.

John H. Dickey STEAMBOAT on which Mark Twain was an apprentice PILOT, from early August through mid-October 1858. The *Dickey* was a St. Louis–Memphis packet, on which he made between seven and 11 round-trips while cubbing under Sam BOWEN (whose copilot may have been Strother WILEY). At the end of October, he followed Captain Daniel Able, an old Hannibal acquaintance, to the WHITE CLOUD.

John J. Roe (Jonathan J. Roe) STEAMBOAT on which Mark Twain was an apprentice PILOT in 1857. A 691-ton side-wheeler built in 1856, the *Roe* was a slow freight carrier that Mark Twain remembered as friendly and fun. While Horace BIXBY was on the Missouri River, Mark Twain cubbed for Zeb Leavenworth (1830–1877) and Beck Jolly under Zeb's brother, Captain Mark Leavenworth. Between August 5 and September 24, 1857, he probably made two round-trips between St. Louis and New Orleans before shifting to the PENNSYLVANIA. The *Roe* blew up in 1864. Chapter 16 of *Life on the Mississippi* describes the boat as "so slow that when she finally sunk in Madrid Bend, it was five years before the owners heard of it."

Johnson, Andrew (December 29, 1808, Raleigh, North Carolina–July 31, 1875, Carter's Station, Tennessee) Seventeenth president of the United States (1865–1869). A former tailor who became a governor, senator and Abraham LINCOLN's vice-president, Johnson acceded to the presidency when Lincoln was killed. Faced with the complex problems of post–CIVIL WAR Reconstruction, he ran afoul of radical members of his own party who attempted to force him out of office. From late November 1867 through late February 1868, Mark Twain was in WASHINGTON, D.C. as the House of Representatives brought articles of impeachment against Johnson. Three months later, Mark Twain was in California as the U.S. Senate fell one vote short of convicting Johnson, who then finished his term, to be succeeded by U. S. GRANT.

Mark Twain's published writings contain scattered allusions to Johnson. A few weeks before the president's impeachment, he published a satire on federal government, "THE FACTS CONCERNING THE RECENT RESIGNATION," with an unnamed president as a character. He mocked Johnson's pride in being a self-made man in his sketch "Last Words of Great Men" (1869). An appendix in *Roughing It* (1872) reiterates this ridicule by calling the Mormon leader Brigham YOUNG "a second Andrew Johnson in the small beginning and steady progress of his official grandeur." Mark Twain's most extensive attack on Johnson comes in his posthumously published burlesque of Victor Hugo's novel *L'Homme Qui Rit*, which he wrote in 1869.

Johnson, Brace Character in "HUCK FINN AND TOM SAWYER AMONG THE INDIANS." A 26-year-old archetypal frontier he-man, Johnson draws on skills that he learned from growing up among Indians to lead Huck and Tom after Oglala Sioux who have massacred his fiancée's family, the MILLSES. Mark Twain's physical description of Johnson closely matches a description that Buffalo Bill CODY wrote of Wild Bill Hickok.

Jones Pseudonym used in *Connecticut Yankee*. In chapter 31, Hank MORGAN tells the charcoal-burner MARCO that King ARTHUR, his traveling companion, is a prosperous farmer named "Jones." Earlier, Hank pretends to CLARENCE that he is a magician who has known MERLIN through centuries under many different names, including several of Mark Twain's favorite stock names: Jones, Smith, Robinson and Jackson (chapter 5).

Jones, Captain Hurricane Name given to a caricature of Captain Edgar WAKEMAN in "SOME RAMBLING NOTES OF AN IDLE EXCURSION," Mark Twain's account of a 1877 trip to Bermuda with Joseph TWICHELL. Aside from the fact that Twichell had struck up a chance acquaintance with Wakeman three years earlier, "Jones" has nothing to do with the rest of the travel account. Mark Twain justifies his inclusion in the sketch by suggesting that he was the object of gossip on the Bermuda cruise.

Mark Twain's description of Jones resembles that of Captain Eli STORMFIELD, whom he called "Hurricane Jones" in an early draft of "Captain Stormfield's Visit to Heaven." Like Stormfield, Jones is a sea captain, a formidable swearer and a "profound biblical scholar— that is, he thought he was." A long anecdote that follows is largely an account of Wakeman's efforts to convert Twichell, here called Reverend Mr. PETERS, to his views on Old Testament miracles in 1874. Several pages are given over to Jones's explanation of Isaac's struggle against the prophets of Baal. The anecdote ends with Jones remarking that "there ain't a thing in the Bible but what is true; all you want is to go prayerfully to work and cipher out how 'twas done." A character similar to Jones reappears in *The American Claimant* as Captain Saltmarsh, a hard-swearing Bible-misquoter who has become a painter.

Jones, Fetlock Character in "A DOUBLE-BARRELLED DETECTIVE STORY." A 16- or 17-year-old English nephew of Sherlock HOLMES, Jones is virtually a slave to Flint BUCKNER when Archy STILLMAN arrives in HOPE CANYON mining camp in 1900. Too terrified of Buckner to accept the offers of help that he receives, the likeable young Jones finds solace in spending his nights inventing ways to kill Buckner—a goal that he achieves in chapter 7. After Stillman proves him guilty, Jones escapes, but no one tries to recapture him.

Jones's obsession with planning ways to kill Buckner recalls the cub pilot of *Life on the Mississippi* who spends his nights planning ways to kill his tormentor, William BROWN (chapter 18). Unlike the cub, Jones actually kills Buckner by blowing him up—a fate similar to the accidental death of the real Brown.

Jones's given name, "Fetlock," is an old English word for the tuft of hair above the hoof behind a horse's leg. Mark Twain probably uses it as a play on the name of Jones's uncle "Sherlock."

Jones the Welchman Character in *Tom Sawyer*. Jones lives on CARDIFF HILL, below the Widow DOUGLAS. In chapter 29, he is introduced simply as "the Welchman" (a name that the original illustrator True WILLIAMS renders as "Welshman"). After Huck Finn warns him that INJUN JOE and his partner are about to attack the widow, Jones and his two sons chase the assailants away. Afterward, Jones welcomes Huck back and gives him food and a bed. In chapter 33 he is finally identified as "Jones." Mark Twain modeled the character on a Hannibal bookseller named John Davies (c. 1810–1885), who married Mark Twain's schoolteacher, Mary Ann NEWCOMB, in the late 1840s.

Jonesborough Syrian village. Halfway between DAMASCUS and BANIYAS, Mark Twain and his companions passed through a village called Kefr Hauwar—notable for claiming to have Nimrod's tomb. One of Mark Twain's travel letters to the SAN FRANCISCO ALTA CALIFORNIA renders the village's name correctly; however, he pretends to forget it in a later letter and in *Innocents Abroad*—instead calling it "Jonesborough," since his companions "refuse to recognize the Arab names or try to pronounce them" (chapter 45).

Jonson, Ben (c. June 11, 1572, London–August 6, 1637, London) English dramatist and poet. A contemporary and friend of SHAKESPEARE, Jonson is best known for his satirical plays, including *Volpone* (1606), *The Alchemist* (1610) and *The Devil Is an Ass* (1616). Quotes from these works head five chapters (1, 7, 8, 17 and 42) of *The Gilded Age*. Jonson appears in Mark Twain's *1601* as a character at Queen ELIZABETH's court and is mentioned in "IS SHAKESPEARE DEAD?" (chapters 3, 6 and 10).

Jordan River Near Eastern river. The largest river of modern Israel and Jordan, the Jordan rises in eastern LEBANON and western SYRIA and flows south about 223 miles, through the Sea of GALILEE, to the DEAD SEA. In biblical times, the river defined the eastern boundary of

PALESTINE. Mark Twain saw the river several times during his trip through the HOLY LAND in September 1867; he mentions it frequently in chapters 45–47 and 55–56 of *Innocents Abroad*.

Josh Early PEN NAME. While prospecting in Nevada's ESMERALDA district in early 1862, Mark Twain began sending humorous letters signed "Josh" to the VIRGINIA CITY TERRITORIAL ENTERPRISE. Though the *Enterprise* did not pay him for these contributions, its editor thought enough of them to offer him a staff position. When he began at the *Enterprise* in September, he dropped "Josh" as a pen name—five months before adopting "MARK TWAIN" as his pen name.

Since complete files of the *Enterprise* no longer exist, none of Mark Twain's original Josh letters has survived. *Roughing It* alludes to these letters (chapter 42), but does not mention the name "Josh" (unless its reference to *joss* lights as "Josh-lights" in chapter 54 is a deliberate play on the name). Mark Twain's use of "Josh" preceded that of humorist Henry Wheeler Shaw, who gained fame as "Josh BILLINGS" several years later.

"Journalism in Tennessee" Sketch published in the BUFFALO EXPRESS on September 4, 1869 and later collected in SKETCHES, NEW AND OLD. Possibly inspired by an incident in which a MEMPHIS editor assaulted a journalist for calling him a Radical, this sketch is set in TENNESSEE's opposite corner. Its parody of Southern journalism anticipates *Roughing It*'s depiction of frontier journalism in NEVADA, where fights among editors were common. It also anticipates *Connecticut Yankee*'s comparison of the CAMELOT WEEKLY HOSANNAH AND LITERARY VOLCANO with Southern newspapers, and it parodies DUELS that are more hazardous to bystanders than to combatants.

SYNOPSIS

After moving to the South for health reasons, the unnamed narrator becomes associate editor of the *Morning Glory and Johnson County War-Whoop*. Assigned to write on the "Spirit of the Tennessee Press," he drafts a dignified summary of the positions taken on controversial issues by the *Semi-Weekly Earthquake*, *Higginsville Thunderbolt and Battle Cry of Freedom*, *Mud Springs Morning Howl* and *Daily Hurrah*. Calling his article "gruel," the chief editor immediately starts rewriting it. As he works, Smith, the *Moral Volcano*'s editor, shoots at him through a window; he fires back, wounding Smith, who then shoots off the narrator's finger. Next, the explosion of a grenade tumbling down the stove-pipe knocks out some of the narrator's teeth.

As the editor admires his revised article—calling rival editors liars and scoundrels—a brick thrown through the window hits the narrator. Colonel BLATHERSKITE Tecumseh then bursts in with a pistol. He and the editor exchange six shots; one mortally wounds Tecumseh, the others hit the narrator.

When the editor goes out, he tells the narrator what to do with Jones, Gillespie and Ferguson when they show up; however, these men later turn the tables, throwing him out the window and whipping and scalping him. When the editor returns with friends, a general riot begins. Finding Southern hospitality "too lavish," the narrator resigns and checks into a hospital.

Julesburg (Overland City)   Historic town on the South Platte River in northeastern Colorado. On July 30, 1861, Mark Twain and his brother spent about an hour in Julesburg while their STAGECOACH changed rigs. After describing the brief stop in chapter 7, *Roughing It* mentions the town variously as "Julesburg" and "Overland City" (chapters 6, 9, 10, 17 and 20). Then an important station on the Overland stagecoach line, Julesburg took its name from Jules Beni (or Reni), an agent for the line whom Jack SLADE reportedly killed earlier in 1861. Modern Julesburg was founded in 1884 on a site several miles north of the site visited by Mark Twain.

Jumbo (Hassan Ben Ali Ben Selim Abdallah Mohammed Moisé Alhammal Jamsetjejeebhoy Dhuleep Sultan Ebu Bhudpooris)   Name of the missing animal in "THE STOLEN WHITE ELEPHANT" (1882). Jumbo is a sacred "royal white elephant" that the narrator is conveying to England as a gift from the king of Siam. During a layover at Jersey City, Jumbo disappears and is believed stolen. Several weeks later, Inspector Blunt finds Jumbo dead from cannon-shot wounds he received during his escape.

The narrator's formal deposition describes Jumbo as dull white, 19 feet tall, 26 feet long from forehead to rump, with tusks over nine feet long. At the time of his disappearance, he is wearing a castle with seats for 15 persons. Jumbo likes squirting people with his trunk and will eat *anything;* he is capable of downing five men or 500 Bibles in one meal. The night he escapes, he reportedly kills 60 persons and injures 240 others.

With some comic exaggeration, the fictional Jumbo's description matches that of a real "Jumbo," an African elephant that was a major London ZOO attraction at the same time that Mark Twain wrote his story. By a remarkable coincidence, P. T. BARNUM brought the real Jumbo to New York in April 1882—just two months before *The Stolen White Elephant, Etc.* was published as a book. A long anecdote about Barnum's acquisition of Jumbo appears in chapter 64 of *Following the Equator,* in which Mark Twain claims to have gotten the story from Barnum himself. Jumbo's removal from England to the United States received great publicity in both countries, and the elephant entertained millions until it was accidentally killed by a train in Ontario. Canada in September 1885. Meanwhile, Barnum imported a reputedly genuine "white elephant" from Siam in March

1884. Since this animal was mostly gray, it was overshadowed by a truly white elephant exhibited by one of Barnum's rivals—until the latter beast was found to be painted.

In colloquial English, a "white elephant" is an expensive possession of no value to its owner. The expression derives from the alleged practice of Siamese kings who bankrupted their enemies by giving them sacred white elephants, whose upkeep was ruinously expensive. In "The Stolen White Elephant," the king of Siam gives such an elephant to the queen of England to atone for being wrong in a frontier dispute. Perhaps the king actually wants to avenge himself against the queen; in any case, his gift has the effect of ruining the queen's civil servant who narrates the story.

jumping frog story   Mark Twain wrote and published this story in 1865. It first appeared as "Jim Smiley and His Jumping Frog" and was subsequently revised and published under a variety of titles, including "The Notorious Jumping Frog of Calaveras County" and "The Celebrated Jumping Frog of Calaveras County." (Modern scholars often refer to it as simply the "jumping frog story.")

Told within the classic structure of a FRAME-STORY, the 2,600-word narrative recounts the career of a wily gambler who meets his match when a stranger passes through the camp. While the story builds to several comic climaxes, the essence of its humor is the deadpan delivery of its simple narrator, Simon WHEELER. In the story's earliest published version, Mark Twain himself narrates the frame in the form of a letter to Artemus WARD about his visit to a fictitious mining camp called BOOMERANG. Subsequent versions of the story alter the frame, dropping the structure of a letter and making the narrator anonymous. Further, Boomerang's name is changed to ANGEL'S CAMP—a real place in California's CALAVERAS COUNTY.

SYNOPSIS

The narrator describes visiting an old mining camp in behalf of a friend seeking news of a man named Leonidas W. SMILEY. In a dilapidated tavern, he meets garrulous old Simon Wheeler. Wheeler cannot recall a *Leonidas* Smiley, but does recall a *Jim* SMILEY who lived in the camp around 1849 or 1850. Most of the balance of the story is Wheeler's narrative about Jim Smiley.

Notorious for betting on anything that he could, Smiley was uncommonly lucky. He would bet on horse races, dog fights, chicken fights—even which of two birds on a fence would fly away first. He owned a mare known as the "fifteen-minute nag"; the horse looked broken-down, but always rallied to win its races. Another of his animals was a bull-pup named ANDREW JACKSON that won fights by seizing hold of its opponents' hind legs. He also had rat-terriers, chicken cocks, tomcats and other things on which he was always ready to wager. Once he caught a frog he named DAN'L WEBSTER and spent three months training him to jump.

One day a stranger in camp saw Dan'l Webster and said that he could not see any points about him that were any better than any other frog, but Smiley offered to put up $40 that Dan'l could out-jump any frog in the county. The stranger was willing to take the bet, but had no frog, so Smiley laid down $40 and went off to find one for him. While Smiley was gone, the stranger pried open Dan'l Webster's mouth and filled him with quail-shot. After Smiley returned with another frog, the new frog hopped off smartly, but Dan'l Webster merely shrugged. The stranger scooped up the money to leave, pausing to repeat his remark about Smiley's frog having no special points about it. After he was gone, Smiley picked up Dan'l Webster and discovered that he was full of shot. He took off after the stranger, but never caught him.

Wheeler's narrative is interrupted when he is called outside. He returns to start up a fresh story about Jim Smiley's tail-less one-eyed cow, but the narrator slips away.

BACKGROUND AND PUBLISHING HISTORY

An incident on which the jumping frog story is based actually occurred at or near Angel's Camp and was reported in a Sonora newspaper in 1853. Mark Twain heard the story from an old bartender named Ben COON in Angel's Camp in early 1865. His brief notes indicate that the frog's owner was called Coleman and that the amount of money wagered was $50. Shortly after leaving Angel's Camp, Mark Twain began writing his own version of the story, but it took him half a year and several false starts to find a satisfactory framework. In October, he sent his manuscript to George W. CARLETON in New York for a book that Artemus Ward was editing, but Carleton turned it down—probably because his book was nearly ready to print. Carleton passed the manuscript to Henry Clapp at the SATURDAY PRESS, which published it on November 18, 1865.

An immediate sensation, the story was reprinted in newspapers and magazines throughout the country. Meanwhile, Mark Twain published a revised version in San Francisco's CALIFORNIAN magazine. In May 1867, it became the title story of Mark Twain's first book, THE CELEBRATED JUMPING FROG STORY OF CALAVERAS COUNTY, AND OTHER SKETCHES. Eight years later, it reappeared in SKETCHES, NEW AND OLD as "The Jumping Frog in English, Then in French, Then Clawed Back into a Civilized Language Once More by Patient, Unremunerated Toil." This version adds a poor French translation of the story, along with the original text and Mark Twain's own literal retranslation. Mark Twain published a further elaboration of the story in the April 1894 issue of the NORTH AMERICAN REVIEW, as "The Private History of the Jumping Frog Story." This version adds an anecdote about Henry van Dyke's telling him that the story's roots go back to ancient Greece. Unbeknownst to either man at the time, another scholar had adapted Mark Twain's story into a Greek tale for a textbook. In November 1903, HARPER collected all these materials in a single volume, *The Jumping Frog in English, Then in French, Then Clawed Back into a Civilized Language Once More by Patient, Unremunerated Toil,* freshly illustrated by Fred STROTHMANN.

The jumping frog story has been adapted to the screen in a variety of forms. Both the 1944 and 1985 films titled THE ADVENTURES OF MARK TWAIN, for example, contain versions of the jumping competition. The 1948 feature film *Best Man Wins* is loosely adapted from the original story, with Edgar Buchanan (1903–1979) as Jim Smiley. Television dramatizations of the story followed in 1949 and 1981 and an animated adaptation aired in 1982.

Jungfrau Peak in SWITZERLAND's Bernese ALPS. Taking its name from a German word for "virgin," the 13,642-foot high Jungfrau is the southernmost peak in a group including the Eiger ("Ogre") and the Mönch ("Monk"). It rises about 10 miles south–southwest of INTERLAKEN, which Mark Twain visited in late August 1878. Interlaken gave Mark Twain a dramatic view of the pure-white Jungfrau framed between two closer peaks. Moved by this view and by the aptness of the mountain's name, he drew a sexually suggestive picture of the scene in his NOTEBOOK. Many editions of *A Tramp Abroad* contain a toned-down version of this drawing in chapter 32, which is devoted to the mountain. "Switzerland the Cradle of Liberty," an essay that he wrote at Interlaken in 1891, has several long passages on the Jungfrau, calling it "the most impressive mountain mass that the globe can show."

Kaltenleutgeben Austrian town in which Mark Twain stayed from late May to mid-October 1898. He and his family lived in a villa next to a pine forest about 15 miles southwest of central VIENNA, which was 40 minutes away by train.

Kamehameha I (c. November 1758, Kohala, Hawaii–May 8, 1819, Kailua, Hawaii) Warrior king who unified HAWAII. After inheriting the kingship of the big island of Hawaii in 1782, Kamehameha consolidated his control and devoted three decades to bringing the other Hawaiian Islands under his rule. Meanwhile, he organized an efficient government and began allowing foreign traders in. Though remembered as a great warrior, he was also revered for bringing peace and prosperity to the islands. After he died in 1819, his son Liholiho, or Kamehameha II (1797–1824), abolished the tabu system and invited American missionaries in, beginning Hawaii's modern era.

Mark Twain read and heard a great deal about Kamehameha I during his visit to the islands in 1866 and he mentions him frequently in his letters to the SACRAMENTO UNION. The Hawaii chapters of *Roughing It* also mention Kamehameha frequently, emphasizing his military exploits and comparing him to Napoleon as a military genius (chapter 64); they also present a long description of his funeral (chapter 68). Chapter 3 of *Following the Equator* summarizes Kamehameha's entire career.

Kamehameha V (Lot) (December 11, 1830, Honolulu, Hawaii–December 11, 1872, Honolulu) King of HAWAII during Mark Twain's 1866 visit to the islands. Kamehameha V ascended to Hawaii's throne after the death of his brother Kamehameha IV on November 30, 1863. The next year, he replaced his brother's constitution with one restricting suffrage and increasing royal power at the legislature's expense. He also founded the leper colony on Molokai. He died without an heir, ending the dynasty founded by KAMEHAMEHA I and leaving Hawaii's legislature to choose a successor.

Impressed by Kamehameha's down-to-earth nature, Mark Twain praised him in several letters to the SACRAMENTO UNION. *Roughing It* describes the king and his court, but does not mention his name (chapter 68). It has been speculated that Mark Twain used Kamehameha as a model for King ARTHUR in *Connecticut Yankee*, a novel that grew out of his original idea for a book on feudal Hawaii.

kanaka Polynesian word for "person" or "human being" applied to all South Pacific islanders during the 19th century. A respectful term in HAWAII, "kanaka" was a pejorative term for imported laborers in AUSTRALIA. Mark Twain uses the word throughout his Hawaii writings and in *Following the Equator*'s discussion of labor conditions in Queensland, Australia (chapter 6).

Kanawha Yacht on which Mark Twain cruised several times. When H. H. ROGERS bought the two-year-old, 227-foot-long steam yacht *Kanawha* in April 1901, he become the owner of one of the country's largest and fastest private yachts. Mark Twain acknowledged Rogers's status by nicknaming him the "Admiral" and cruised with him the following August. From mid-March into April 1902, Mark Twain and other friends joined Rogers on a three-week cruise of the western Caribbean. Sailing from Key West, Florida, they visited the Bahamas, sailed around Cuba, and returned up the East Coast to New York. Later that year, Rogers had the *Kanawha* stand by at YORK HARBOR, Maine, where Mark Twain was summering, in case his gravely ill wife, Livy, needed to be moved. Livy finally returned home by train, however.

In late August 1906, Mark Twain spent 10 days on the *Kanawha* cruising the coast with Rogers. In September 1907, Rogers lent him the ship to sail to Hampton Roads, Virginia, as honorary head of a centennial exposition honoring Robert Fulton's invention of the STEAMBOAT.

In April 1920, the *Kanawha* was purchased by the Black Star Line, a shipping company run by Marcus Garvey's black nationalist organization, which planned to use it for passenger service. The yacht's badly corroded boilers burst during a harbor excursion, killing a crew member. After two disastrously expensive cruises to the Caribbean—including one on which Garvey himself sailed—the *Kanawha* was abandoned at Antilla, Cuba in August 1921.

Kaolatype Process for making engraved printing plates. In February 1880, Dan SLOTE, whose company produced Mark Twain's self-pasting SCRAPBOOK, sold Mark Twain a patent that he had acquired for a new engraving process. Predicting that this invention, Kaolatype, would revolutionize engraving in the printing industry, Mark Twain formed the Kaolatype Engraving Company in NEW YORK CITY with himself as president and principal stockholder. Slote and Charles Perkins, his Hartford lawyer, were minor partners and officers.

Also known as the "chalk-plate" process, Kaolatype involved coating a steel plate with a layer of kaolin (china clay) in which an image was cut to the metal surface. Molten metal poured into the resulting matrix created a die for printing. Though ingenious, the process was soon outmoded by new photographic etching techniques that produced cheaper and better results.

Not satisfied with using Kaolatype to make printing plates, Mark Twain thought of adapting it to make brass molds for stamping book covers. He hired Charles Sneider, an associate of Slote, to develop his idea into a patentable process and invested considerable money in the company over the next year. Sneider's apparently promising start encouraged Mark Twain to invest in enlarging his Hartford property and undertaking expensive remodeling work. Meanwhile, other engravers began infringing on the Kaolatype process and Mark Twain grew dissatisfied with Slote's management of the company. In March 1881, he brought Charles L. WEBSTER in to investigate the company and soon put him in charge. Webster discovered that Sneider was a fraud and tried to straighten out the company, but Kaolatype was doomed. Even the illustrators of Mark Twain's own *Life on the Mississippi* refused to have their work engraved by that process. Mark Twain eventually lost about $50,000 in the scheme.

Kay the Seneschal, Sir Character in *Connecticut Yankee.* As the foster brother of King Arthur, Kay is a pervasive figure in Arthurian legends. In the prelude to *Connecticut Yankee,* Kay captures Hank MORGAN the moment that Hank awakens in the sixth century. He takes Hank to CAMELOT in chapter 1, in which Hank calls Kay the "circus man" before learning his name in the next chapter. Kay then regales the court with a long story about Sir LAUNCELOT's wearing his armor while capturing other knights (chapter 3). In chapter 4, Kay tells how he captured Hank, then suppresses a yawn as he orders Hank to be burned at the stake. Chapter 4 of *Pudd'nhead Wilson* alludes to the story of Launcelot and Kay, but reverses the knights' roles.

Seneschal is an Old French word for the household steward of a feudal lord.

Kean, Edmund (March 17, 1787, London–May 15, 1833, Richmond, England) English Shakespearean actor. The leading tragedian of his time, Kean was known as "Kean the Elder" to differentiate him from his son, Charles John Kean (c. 1811–1868). The younger Kean toured America in 1830 and 1845–47 and was an acclaimed HAMLET. He was even better known for his lavish "Shakespearean Revivals"—a fact of which the DUKE seems to be aware in *Huckleberry Finn.* In chapters 21–23, the Duke makes up handbills advertising a "Shaksperean Revival" in which he bills his partner, the KING, as "Edmund Kean the Elder" and himself as "David GARRICK the Younger."

Keller, Helen Adams (June 27, 1880, Tuscumbia, Alabama–June 1, 1968, Westport, Connecticut) Though deaf and blind from the age of 19 months, Keller became famous as an author and lecturer. She was born a month earlier than Mark Twain's daughter Jean Clemens and first met Mark Twain in March 1895, beginning a warm friendship that lasted through the rest of Mark Twain's life. Already an admirer of Mark Twain's writings, Keller was impressed by his uncondescending sensitivity to her disabilities—which she later recalled in *Midstream: My Later Life* (1929). For his part, Mark Twain regarded Keller as an extraordinary spirit and intellect, and he paid tribute to her in *Following the Equator* (chapter 61). In late 1896, he appealed to his friend H. H. ROGERS to support Keller's education; Rogers then quietly paid her way through Radcliffe, where she graduated in 1904. Four years later, Mark

Helen Keller, whom Mark Twain called "the most marvelous person of her sex that has existed on this earth since Joan of Arc," in 1893. (St. Nicholas Magazine, December 1893)

Twain had her as a guest at his STORMFIELD home and hosted a party to promote her book, *The World I Live In* (1908).

Kellgren, Jonas Henrik (1837–1916) Swedish practitioner of a form of osteopathy variously known as "Swedish movements," "mechano-therapeutics" and the "Kellgren Treatment." Kellgren, who disdained drugs, used massage and exercise to stimulate patients' nerve endings. In search of a cure for their daughter Jean's epilepsy, Mark Twain and his wife went to Kellgren's summer institute at Sanna, SWEDEN in July 1899. During two and a half months of treatment, Jean improved markedly. Mark Twain himself underwent the therapy for his chronic bronchitis and experienced such relief that he became an enthusiastic supporter of Kellgren and osteopathy—a subject on which he wrote several unpublished essays. Livy, meanwhile, was treated for her rheumatic hip. When the family resettled in London in October, they chose a place near one of Kellgren's institutes. In February 1901, Mark Twain spoke favorably about Kellgren before a committee of the New York State Assembly considering a bill to legalize osteopathy.

Kemble, Edward Windsor (January 18, 1861, Sacramento, California–September 19, 1933, Ridgefield, Connecticut) Illustrator of *Huckleberry Finn* and other works. Kemble was born in CALIFORNIA, where Mark Twain may have been acquainted with his father, Edward Cleveland Kemble, the founder of the SAN FRANCISCO ALTA CALIFORNIA. Kemble studied art in New York briefly, but was otherwise self-taught. He became a staff cartoonist on New York's *Daily Graphic* in 1881 and began contributing to *Life* when that magazine started two years later. One of his *Life* cartoons moved Mark Twain to ask him to illustrate *Huckleberry Finn* in 1884. This was Kemble's first book-illustrating job. He received $1,200 and attention that helped make his career.

Although he worked with many distractions and never had a complete manuscript of *Huckleberry Finn* in his hands, Kemble completed more than 175 drawings within a few weeks. He used a 14-year-old New York boy named Cort Morris as his model for virtually all the characters. Kemble had almost free rein to select what to illustrate and how to treat each subject. Mark Twain evidently expected him to follow the flavor of True WILLIAMS's *Tom Sawyer* drawings, but Kemble's work was less idealized and less pretty, reflecting the more somber mood of *Huckleberry Finn*. Mark Twain never discussed individual pictures with him, but inspected his work as it arrived and occasionally complained about certain tendencies, such as making Huck look "too Irishy." His initial reaction to Kemble's work was lukewarm; later he decided that Kemble's pictures pleased him, only to change his mind again still later.

Despite Mark Twain's inspections, several mistakes slipped through. On the first page of chapter 1, for example, Kemble printed the novel's title as "*The* Adven-

tures of Huckleberry Finn." Also, he made Huck look too small for his age—a fact especially evident in several pictures showing Huck and the identically aged Joanna WILKS together. More important, while Kemble invested many of his drawings with a gritty realism, his pictures of black characters—particularly Jim—tended toward stereotyped caricatures.

In his later career, Kemble treated a wide range of subjects but became most famous for illustrating black people. He illustrated books by Harriet Beecher STOWE and by G. W. CABLE and other Southern writers, and wrote illustrated books of his own, inlcuding *Kemble's Coons, Comical Coons* and *Kemble's Sketch Book*.

Kemble also illustrated Mark Twain's "THE PRIVATE HISTORY OF A CAMPAIGN THAT FAILED" for CENTURY MAGAZINE in 1885. A few years later, Mark Twain had him draw nearly 200 original illustrations for MARK TWAIN'S LIBRARY OF HUMOR, hoping that Kemble's reputation would help the book's sales. He found Kemble's work for this book monotonous, however, and afterward turned to other illustrators, such as Daniel BEARD. Nevertheless, Kemble illustrated *Huckleberry Finn* and *Pudd'nhead Wilson* for new standard editions in 1899. One of his last projects was reillustrating *Huckleberry Finn,* for the Limited Editions Club in 1933.

Kentucky Mark Twain's mother, Jane Lampton Clemens, was born in south-central Kentucky's Adair County, where she married his father. Mark Twain claimed that his parents began their married life in Lexington, in north-central Kentucky; however, there is no record of their having lived there. They apparently moved to GAINESBORO, Tennessee soon after marrying. A house in which they did live in Columbia, Kentucky has been preserved as "the Clemens house." Many other members of the Lampton family also lived in Kentucky during the early 19th century, and Mark Twain's sister Pamela Clemens MOFFETT married William A. Moffett in Green County in 1851.

Mark Twain lived in CINCINNATI, Ohio, across the river from Kentucky, in 1856–57, and he probably landed in Kentucky frequently during his PILOTING days on the Mississippi River in 1857–61. He and G. W. CABLE did readings in Paris and Louisville during their 1884–85 lecture tour.

Kentucky is not mentioned by name in *Huckleberry Finn,* but the state's southwest corner is probably the location of the feud between the GRANGERFORDS and SHEPHERDSONS in chapters 17–18. The probability that the Grangerfords live in Kentucky is enhanced by the fact that they keep a copy of Henry CLAY's speeches in their parlor. The town of Louisville is mentioned in chapter 25, in which the Arkansas lawyer Levi BELL is said to be there on business.

Keokuk Town in the extreme southeastern corner of IOWA, where the Des Moines River enters the Mississippi, about 45 miles due north of Hannibal, Missouri.

With a population of around 6,500 people, Keokuk was a comparatively large frontier town when Mark Twain's brother Orion Clemens settled there in June 1855 with his wife, Mollie Stotts, a Keokuk native. After Orion bought a small printing company, Mark Twain and his brother Henry joined him in July and helped him to publish the *Keokuk Journal* out of a building located at the current site of 202 Main Street. During this period, Mark Twain lived at First and Johnson streets.

In late 1855, Mark Twain may have worked for a newspaper in Warsaw, Illinois, across the river. In any case, he was in Keokuk by mid-January 1856, when he gave his first public speech—at a dinner honoring Benjamin FRANKLIN's sesquicentennial birthday. By the fall of 1856, Mark Twain had left Keokuk. In his AUTOBIOGRAPHY, he recalls finding a $50 bill blowing along a snow-covered Keokuk street in the "midwinter of 1856 or 1857" and using the literal windfall to buy a ticket to CINCINNATI. In actuality, he went to Cincinnati around late October 1856—*after* he visited St. Louis and briefly returned to Keokuk. It was while he was in these other towns that he wrote letters under the name "Thomas Jefferson SNODGRASS" to George Rees's *Keokuk Post* and earned his first money as a writer.

Mark Twain never lived in Keokuk again, but revisited it several times, including July 1860. A year later, Orion left Iowa to take up a government job in NEVADA, to which he and Mark Twain traveled together. Several letters that Mark Twain wrote home were published in the *Keokuk Gate City*. Mark Twain revisited Keokuk in April 1867 and wrote about it at length in letters to the SAN FRANCISCO ALTA CALIFORNIA that were later published in MARK TWAIN'S TRAVELS WITH MR. BROWN. One letter describes Keokuk's Heming House as a horrible hotel—this is the "Benton Hotel" which *Innocents Abroad* calls the world's worst (chapter 57).

Orion resettled in Keokuk permanently in 1872. Mark Twain visited him there in May 1882, by which time Keokuk had 15,000 residents. This visit is described in *Life on the Mississippi*, which also tells an anecdote about Henry Clay DEAN speaking in Keokuk in 1861 (chapter 57). Mark Twain stayed overnight with Orion in mid-January 1885, while he and G. W. CABLE were on a lecture tour. By then, his mother, Jane Lampton Clemens, was living there in a house that is still standing at 628 High Street. In the summer of 1886, Mark Twain brought his family to Keokuk for a reunion. He made his last visit in August 1890, shortly before his mother died. Orion and Mollie spent the rest of their lives operating a boarding house in Keokuk.

Kilauea A volcano on the island of HAWAII, Kilauea is in Hawaii Volcanoes National Park. Its 4,100-foot summit is dwarfed by nearby Mauna Loa's 13,680-foot altitude; however, its four-square-mile crater is the world's largest among active volcanoes. Kilauea has long attracted tourists to the easily accessible molten lava lakes, fountains and rivers on its crater floor, 500 feet below its rim. The volcano is often active, but its eruptions are relatively harmless because they release lava through fissures in the mountain's flanks. Visitors can safely stay at a hotel near Kilauea's summit and climb down to the crater floor.

In early June 1866, Mark Twain spent about five days around Kilauea when its crater, then 500 feet deeper, was more active than it is currently. On a night when volcanic activity made his guides unwilling to enter the crater, he spent several hours crossing Kilauea's floor to examine its lava lakes. (The trepidation that he felt standing on the crater's thin crust is recalled in a remark made by Henry ADAMS in "THE £1,000,000 BANK-NOTE.") Mark Twain wrote his last Hawaii letter to the SACRAMENTO UNION *before* seeing Kilauea, but describes his visit in chapter 75 of *Roughing It*. The next chapter describes his visit to the even-larger crater of extinct Haleakala on Maui, which Mark Twain visited earlier—in contrast to *Roughing It*'s account. He never saw Kilauea erupt, but used a description of such an eruption as a popular part of his "SANDWICH ISLANDS" lectures. He also mentions Kilauea in *Innocents Abroad*, comparing it favorably to Italy's VESUVIUS, which he visited a year later (chapter 30).

"The Killing of Julius Caesar 'Localized' " Sketch published in San Francisco's CALIFORNIAN on November 12, 1864. Described by Mark Twain as a "travesty" of what he calls minutely detailed reporting on sensational items, the sketch describes Julius CAESAR's assassination as it might be treated by a modern newspaper covering a political murder during an election. Its core is a translation of a purported article in the *Roman Daily Evening Fasces* that closely follows the characters, events and even some of the dialogue of the third act of SHAKESPEARE's *Julius Caesar*, salted with modern political jargon. The conspirator "George W. Cassius," for example, is described as the "Nobby Boy of the Third Ward." The sketch concludes with the suggestion that Caesar's mantle will be a key piece of evidence at the coroner's inquest. Meanwhile, as Brutus and Mark Antony speak at the Forum, the chief of police prepares for a riot.

Mark Twain wrote this 3,000-word sketch after covering the 1864 presidential election for the SAN FRANCISCO CALL. He published it four days after Abraham LINCOLN was reelected. The sketch anticipates chapter 26 of *Innocents Abroad*, in which the narrator translates a review from another ancient newspaper, *The Roman Daily Battle-Ax*. It was reprinted in THE CELEBRATED JUMPING FROG OF CALAVERAS COUNTY (1867) and in SKETCHES, NEW AND OLD (1875).

The King (Dauphin) Character in *Huckleberry Finn*. One of Huck's RAPSCALLIONS, the "King" is a con artist who allies with a younger man known as the DUKE when both join Huck and Jim on the RAFT in chapter 19 after being chased out of a town. His real name is never given. At least 70 years old, he is bald, heavily whiskered, foul-

The King (left) and the Duke agree to "double-team it" in Huckleberry Finn.

maintains his composure so well that he and the Duke get a fresh chance to escape lynching.

Where the King fails to match the Duke in inventiveness, he makes up for it in greater ruthlessness. While the Duke tends to prey upon people's base instincts, the King preys on their generosity and trust. For example, the King induces a pious camp meeting at POKEVILLE to give him money to become a missionary, and he convinces the trusting Wilks girls that he is their uncle. What dooms the King in almost every venture is his careless cockiness and his inability to control his greed. If he were to follow the Duke's advice in chapter 26, he could easily pocket nearly $3,000 in gold. His insistence in going for the entire Wilks estate not only costs him this gain, but also the money he made on the ROYAL NONESUCH; it also nearly costs him his life.

The King's negative characteristics are many. He is alcoholic, he has a violent temper and he has no scruples whatever. But for the Duke's intervention, he appears ready to throttle Huck after they all escape from the Wilks fiasco. Later, he sells Jim for $40, then gets drunk and blows the entire sum on gambling. The King is also a lecher. At the camp meeting, pretty girls—taken in by his false piousness—ask to kiss him, "and some of them he hugged and kissed as many as five or six times." Mark Twain's manuscript revisions show that he toned down the King's lecherous behavior when he meets the Wilks girls in chapter 25; however, he overlooked a passage in chapter 28 alluding to the King's kissing Mary Jane "sixteen or seventeen times" when they met. (John SEELYE restores and magnifies the King's lecherous nature in *The True Adventures of Huckleberry Finn*.) The King returns in "TOM SAWYER'S CONSPIRACY" to attempt stealing Jim again, and may even be a murderer.

Mark Twain had a fascination with claimants to royal titles and doubtless took elements of the King from many charlatans. One person in particular who may have influenced him was Charles C. DUNCAN, captain of the QUAKER CITY. A possible allusion to Duncan appears in the King's bogus *Hamlet* soliloquy. Another possible model from the *Quaker City* voyage was George J. ADAMS, a phony prophet described in chapter 57 of *Innocents Abroad*. The King may have elements of San Francisco's Emperor Norton, who also claimed royal French descent. A purely fictional model may have been Johnson Jones HOOPER's comic character, Simon Suggs. An ironic coda to Mark Twain's life is the fact that A. B. PAINE later dubbed *him* the "King."

As is the case with the Duke, the King has provided a rich character role for many actors. Film actors who have portrayed him include Tom D. Bates (1920), Walter Connolly (1939), Tony Randall (1960), Harvey Korman (1974) and Jason Robards (1993). Actors who have played the King in television adaptations include Thomas Mitchell (1955), Basil Rathbone (1957), Jack Elam (1975), Larry Storch (1981) and Barnard Hughes (1986).

smelling and shabbily dressed and possesses only a ratty carpetbag. Huck calls the man "baldhead" until he establishes his identity. The old man tells the younger man that he was running "a little temperance revival," making "five or six dollars a night" until word got out that he was drinking on the sly and he was run out of town. His background also includes "doctoring," "layin' on o' hands," telling fortunes and preaching.

After both con men list their credentials, the younger man suddenly announces that he is the true Duke of BRIDGEWATER. The old man sees how this ploy wins Huck and Jim's deference. He tops the Duke by tearfully confessing that he is the DAUPHIN, the true King of France, Louis XVII. Although Huck knows the man is a fraud, he refers to him as "the King" thereafter.

The King and Duke soon control the raft, giving the story a plausible reason for continuing the voyage *down* the river, away from Jim's chance for freedom. The two charlatans plan to work riverfront towns and use the raft for quick getaways.

The King is coarser and less educated than the Duke, but is at least the latter's equal in intelligence. He thinks quickly on his feet and has a prodigious memory. He easily learns the Duke's SOLILOQUY from HAMLET and masters every detail about the WILKS family and their neighbors that he can squeeze out of Tim COLLINS in chapter 24. He also has steely nerves. Even when his imposture as Harvey WILKS is exposed in chapter 29, he

Theo. C. Marceau made this portrait in 1905, around the time Mark Twain wrote King Leopold's Soliloquy. *(Courtesy, Library of Congress, Pictures & Prints Division)*

King Leopold's Soliloquy: A Defense of His Congo Rule (1905) Polemic tract. In late 1904, E. D. Morel asked Mark Twain to support the Congo Reform Association, which was focusing international attention on King LEO-POLD II's brutally exploitative regime in what is now Zaïre. After joining the American branch of the association, Mark Twain wrote this rambling "soliloquy" as a satirical attack on Leopold, who condemns himself with hypocritically pious responses to the charges brought against him. Writing primarily for American readers, Mark Twain did not realize that the United States was not a signatory to the 1884 Berlin Conference that legitimized Leopold's Congo rule. After he discovered his error, his interest in the reform movement waned, but his tract nevertheless may have helped to bring down Leopold's Congo regime.

SYNOPSIS

Alone, apparently in his palace, King Leopold angrily throws down pamphlets that he has been reading, and curses and rages about the charges leveled against him in the press. He sees himself as an agent committed to bringing Christianity to the Congo and rooting out slavery. He knows this is true because he has the blessing of 13 European nations that met in Berlin. Periodically, he interrupts his raging to kiss his crucifix.

As he details the charges brought against him, he wonders why people are so anxious to denounce atrocities and so slow to approve the good things that he has done. He takes some solace in getting America's official approval of the humane and benevolent purposes of his Congo scheme—especially since he knows that America will not confess its blunder by withdrawing its endorsement. He chuckles as he reads from a missionary's suggestion that the United States did not realize it was endorsing Leopold's *personal* rule when it recognized his Congo government.

As he grumbles about meddlesome missionaries who spy and write about what they see, he reads passages from articles and pamphlets by missionaries and others. One of his detractors is the British consul (Roger) Casement—who has the effrontery to publish excerpts from a *private* diary kept by a Congo official. A passage about mutilations of Africans points up the difficulty of arguing with critics. His own people point out that the mutilations they inflict merely follow native customs, but critics ask how *inventing* a barbarity differs from *imitating* one from savages.

A pamphlet complaining about the practice of ransoming prisoners to collect debts fails to acknowledge how hard it is to collect debts without ransom. Ordinary punishments are useless against ignorant savages. Leopold is especially irritated by the charge that he provides nothing in return for the taxes that he extracts. Does he not, after all, furnish the gospel to Africans?

Leopold's most powerful enemy is the kodak (camera)—the only witness he cannot bribe. When he reads a pamphleteer's admission that people shudder and turn away when they hear particulars of his atrocities, Leopold concludes that *that* is his protection. He knows the human race well enough to be confident that people will continue to ignore him.

PUBLISHING HISTORY

After the NORTH AMERICAN REVIEW, which had just published "THE CZAR'S SOLILOQUY," rejected the Leopold piece, P. R. Warren of Boston published it as a 50-page soft-covered book in September 1905. The Congo Reform Association added illustrations—including photographs of Africans with severed hands—and sold the book for 25 cents. Later printings added supplemental documentation and a notice confirming Mark Twain's instruction that all profits go to the association's work.

Kipling, Rudyard (December 30, 1865, Bombay, India–January 18, 1936, London) English writer. Born in INDIA and educated in England, Kipling began writing fiction while working for Indian newspapers during the 1880s. In 1889, he returned to England, where his novel *The Light That Failed* (1890) and other works quickly won him renown. Before reaching England, however, he stopped in the United States to meet his literary hero, Mark Twain—whom he visited unannounced at ELMIRA in the summer of 1889. He later recalled how pleased he was not to be disillusioned when "brought face to face with a revered writer." For his part, Mark Twain remembered Kipling's visit in his AUTOBIOGRAPHY. He recalls being impressed by Kipling, but had no idea who he was until a year later, when C. D. WARNER showed him Kipling's *Plain Tales from the Hills* (1888) and predicted that Kipling would become famous. Around this same time, Kipling published his informal interview with Mark Twain in the NEW YORK HERALD (August 17, 1890).

After marrying an American woman, Caroline Balestier, in 1892, Kipling lived in Brattleboro, Vermont for four years. Mark Twain was in Europe most of this time, but saw Kipling during return visits in April 1893 and January 1894. By then, he was a great admirer of Kipling's writing—which he later said he knew better than anybody else's. Through the rest of his life, he read Kipling's books—often aloud to family and friends. *Following the Equator* mentions Kipling several times (chapters 46, 54 and 62). In 1907, both men received honorary degrees at OXFORD UNIVERSITY. That same year, Kipling also received the Nobel Prize for literature.

Kipling is best known for his writings on India, such as *The Jungle Book* (1894), *Kim* (1901), and *Just So Stories* (1902). Mark Twain borrowed several animal names from *The Jungle Book* for "A FABLE" (1909) and "Refuge of the Derelicts." Kipling, who referred to Mark Twain as "the great and godlike Clemens" in 1903, mentions Mark Twain frequently in his nonfiction writings. Mark Twain's influence can also be seen in some of Kipling's fiction. *Kim*, for example—a story about an Irish orphan who searches India for the River of Immortality with a Tibetan lama—has strong thematic parallels with *Huckleberry Finn*.

Klinefelter, Captain John S. (1810–1885) STEAMBOAT captain. Chapters 19–20 of *Life on the Mississippi* recall the months when Mark Twain apprenticed as a PILOT on the PENNSYLVANIA, when Klinefelter was captain in late 1857 and early 1858. After fighting with the pilot William BROWN, Mark Twain expected the captain to have him put in irons. Instead, Klinefelter was delighted that Brown had been pummeled, and—according to *Life on the Mississippi*—even told Mark Twain to lay for Brown ashore. He offered Mark Twain Brown's place as a regular pilot, but the young cub pilot did not feel ready for the responsibility, so he instead got off the boat in New Orleans. Klinefelter wrote him a chit allowing him to return up the Mississippi as a passenger on the ALFRED T. LACEY. On June 13, the *Pennsylvania* blew up, killing Brown and Mark Twain's brother, Henry Clemens. Klinefelter was unhurt.

Kruger, Private   Character in *Life on the Mississippi*. In a tale told in chapter 31, Kruger is a German-American soldier who allies with his cousin Franz ADLER to rob Karl RITTER's family in NAPOLEON, Arkansas. Against Kruger's wishes, Adler murders Ritter's wife and daughter. Ritter tracks Kruger down, identifying him by his missing thumb. After ingratiating himself with Kruger in order to learn the identity of his accomplice, Ritter finally confronts Kruger with the truth about his crime. Kruger is sincerely remorseful and offers Ritter the $10,000 in gold that he and Adler have accumulated. Ritter is grateful to Kruger for having tried to save his family, but he later kills him when he mistakes him for Adler. Ritter discovers his mistake years later, when he finds Adler alive in Munich. Determined to make amends to Kruger's surviving son, Ritter tells the book's narrator where Kruger's gold is stashed in Napoleon and asks him to retrieve it and send it to Kruger's son in MANNHEIM, Germany.

L

La Cote Male Taile Minor character in *Connecticut Yankee.* The brother of Sir DINADAN, La Cote is the "missionary knight" promoting soap whom Hank MORGAN and SANDY encounter near MORGAN LE FAY's castle in chapter 16. In a tale taken from MALORY, La Cote's chief fame rests on an excursion similar to Hank and Sandy's that he once made with a foulmouthed damsel aptly named Maledisant.

Lally Rook STEAMBOAT mentioned in *Huckleberry Finn.* In chapter 32, Sally PHELPS tells Huck that her husband Silas PHELPS once traveled from New Orleans to Arkansas on "the old Lally Rook," which blew a cylinder head during his voyage. A real side-wheeler, the *Lallah Rookh* operated on the Mississippi from 1838 through 1847. Its name derives from an epic poem written by Thomas MOORE in 1817.

Lampton, Benjamin (May 24, 1770–March 18, 1837, Florida, Missouri) Mark Twain's maternal grandfather, Lampton was a successful farmer and storekeeper in KENTUCKY's Adair County in the early 19th century and he served as a lieutenant colonel in the militia (1812–15). In 1801, he married Margaret Montgomery Casey (1783–1818), the daughter of Revolutionary War hero Colonel William Casey (1754–1816)—after whom Kentucky's Casey County is named. Margaret gave birth to Mark Twain's mother, Jane L. Clemens, in 1803 and she died 15 years later. In 1819, Lampton married Mary Margaret Hays (1788–1842). By this time, his business interests were waning and he was thinking about moving west. He visited Missouri in the late 1820s and returned with such enthusiastic reports that his son-in-law John QUARLES settled in FLORIDA, Missouri. Lampton followed Quarles there in the mid-1830s—just before Jane and her family arrived. Lampton was in Florida when Mark Twain was born, but did not live long enough for his grandson to know him.

Lampton, James J. (1817–March 2, 1887) A favorite cousin of Mark Twain's mother, Lampton followed the Clemens family from Kentucky to Missouri, where he practiced law. Lampton was an eternally optimistic visionary who inspired the fictional Colonel SELLERS. Mark Twain's AUTOBIOGRAPHY describes Lampton as spending his life floating "in a tinted mist of magnificent dreams," none of which he ever saw realized. Mark Twain also claims that many of the incidents in his Sellers stories actually happened—including the turnip-banquet of *The Gilded Age* (chapter 11). Mark Twain last saw Lampton in St. Louis in January 1885, while he and G. W. CABLE were on a reading tour. Cable overheard Lampton gushing over a fanciful scheme and immediately recognized him as "Colonel Sellers."

Mark Twain's mother also had a half-brother named James Andrew Hays Lampton (1824–1879).

Langdon, Charles Jervis (August 13, 1849–November 19, 1916) Brother-in-law of Mark Twain. The only son of Jervis and Olivia LANGDON, Charley Langdon was 17 when his parents sent him abroad on the QUAKER CITY in 1867. He had recently graduated from ELMIRA's Gunnery School and was being groomed to take over the family coal business. Aboard the *Quaker City,* he fell into Mary FAIRBANKS's circle and became a fawning admirer of Mark Twain, who initially seems to have regarded him as a pest. Langdon may well have been the "INTERROGATION POINT" of *Innocents Abroad.*

Nearly four decades after the *Quaker City* cruise, Mark Twain recalled a moment when the ship was in the bay of SMYRNA, when Langdon showed him an ivory miniature with a picture of his sister Olivia, launching a love affair that was to lead to his marriage to her. Whether or not this incident occurred, Langdon introduced Mark Twain to his sister at a reunion of *Quaker City* passengers in New York City in December 1867. Shortly thereafter, he invited him to Elmira as a houseguest, thereby facilitating the couple's budding romance.

In October 1869, Langdon's parents sent him off on a trip around the world with a tutor from Elmira College named Darius Ford (1824–1904). Mark Twain and Ford arranged to collaborate on a series of travel letters that Ford would send to Mark Twain for revision and publication as the "AROUND THE WORLD" series. Meanwhile, Langdon missed attending Livy's MARRIAGE to Mark Twain in February 1870, but returned when his father's health abruptly deteriorated the following summer. After his father died in August, he took over the family business. In October, he married Ida B. Clark (1849–1934), with whom he had three children: Julia

Olivia (1871–1948), Jervis (1875–1952) and Ida (1880–1964).

As Langdon's responsibilities grew, he looked upon his brother-in-law's use of Livy's money with increasing disapproval. When Mark Twain asked him to invest in the PAIGE COMPOSITOR in 1889, Langdon turned him down. Nevertheless, they remained cordial with each other, corresponding regularly and seeing each other occasionally through their remaining years—usually in Elmira. Langdon was with Susy Clemens when she died in Hartford in August 1896; he visited Mark Twain in VIENNA in 1898 and was at his side when he died in 1910.

Mark Twain's story "CANNIBALISM IN THE CARS" (1868) uses Langdon's full name for a character. The 1944 film THE ADVENTURES OF MARK TWAIN has Langdon (William Heary) meet Mark Twain aboard a Mississippi steamboat, instead of on the *Quaker City.*

Langdon, Jervis (January 11, 1809, Vernon, New York–August 6, 1870, Elmira, New York) Mark Twain's father-in-law. After marrying Olivia Lewis (1810–1890) in 1832, Langdon worked as storekeeper in upstate New York and did well in the lumber business. In 1845, he settled in ELMIRA, where he prospered in the coal industry. By the mid-1860s, he controlled several mines and a shipping network and was one of Elmira's leading citizens. Also a noted abolitionist, he was a friend of Frederick DOUGLASS and helped found Elmira's antislavery Park Congregational Church, whose pastor was Thomas K. BEECHER.

Langdon and his wife had three children: Susan Langdon CRANE, Olivia Langdon Clemens and Charles LANGDON. After Mark Twain began courting his daughter Livy in 1868, Langdon grew sufficiently fond of him to approve their engagement, despite Mark Twain's failure to provide satisfactory references. He encouraged Mark Twain to pursue a stable career in journalism and lent him $25,000 with which to buy into the BUFFALO EXPRESS. As a wedding present, he bought the couple an expensive house in BUFFALO.

In the spring of 1870, Langdon's health declined rapidly. His long and painful bout with stomach cancer was one of several disasters marring the first year of Mark Twain's marriage and hampering his writing of *Roughing It.* On his death in August 1870, Langdon left his wife and children bequests worth a million dollars, and his son Charles took over the family business. Livy's inheritance enabled Mark Twain to maintain a comparatively lavish life-style through the ups and downs of his income from writing and his usually unsuccessful investments.

Olivia L. Langdon lived until November 28, 1890—a month longer than Mark Twain's own mother—and was a frequent visitor to Mark Twain's household.

Langham, Portia Character in "THE £1,000,000 BANK-NOTE." Portia is the 22-year-old stepdaughter of Brother B, a wealthy Englishman who lends Henry ADAMS a million-pound bank-note while conducting a wager with his brother. Portia meets Henry at a dinner party at the home of the American minister she is staying with. She and Henry immediately fall in love, but Henry does not learn who her stepfather is until the end of the story, which concludes with their marriage.

In naming Portia, Mark Twain may have been thinking of Shakespeare's *Merchant of Venice,* in which Portia is a wealthy heiress in love with Bassanio, who borrows money in order to court her in style. Portia's surname probably derives from Langham Place, a London street connecting Regent Street to Portland Place—where Adams meets Portia's stepfather and uncle. Mark Twain stayed at the street's Langham Hotel in 1873. The name "Langham" also bears a striking resemblance to "LANGDON," the maiden name of Mark Twain's wife, Olivia. Beautiful, cheerful and understanding, Portia matches Mark Twain's descriptions of Olivia—with whom he fell in love as quickly as Henry does with Portia. And just as Portia's wealthy stepfather overlooks Adams's inability to provide satisfactory references, so did Jervis LANGDON when Mark Twain could not come up with any.

Lathers, Simon Figure mentioned in *The American Claimant.* A relative of Colonel SELLERS, Lathers is the latest claimant to the ROSSMORE earldom in England at the beginning of the novel. Almost immediately, however, he and his unnamed twin brother are reported to have been killed by a log at Duffy's Corners, ARKANSAS "at a smoke-house raising, owing to the carelessness on the part of all present . . . induced by overplus of sour-mash." Sellers becomes Lathers's heir-presumptive and has the remains of the Lathers brothers shipped to England for burial in the Rossmore family plot.

Mark Twain modeled Lathers on a distant cousin, Jesse M. LEATHERS, who claimed to be the rightful Earl of Durham. Unlike the fictional Lathers, Leathers died from tuberculosis and alcoholism in a New York City hospital. Lathers's bizarre death, however, closely resembles that of Mark Twain's grandfather, Samuel B. CLEMENS.

Launcelot of the Lake, Sir Character in *Connecticut Yankee.* In medieval Arthurian legends, Launcelot is a central figure as King ARTHUR's bravest knight. Later retellings of these legends—notably those of MALORY and TENNYSON—emphasize how Launcelot's adulterous affair with Queen GUENEVER leads to a civil war that destroys the kingdom. This same event brings down Hank MORGAN's civilization in *Connecticut Yankee.* Nevertheless, of all the traditional Arthurian characters who appear in this novel, Launcelot is treated with the most respect.

Connecticut Yankee mentions Launcelot frequently, but gives him no significant role until chapter 38, when he leads 500 knights mounted on bicycles from CAMELOT to London to rescue Hank and the king. In the next chapter, Launcelot is among the knights whom Hank unhorses with his lasso. Filled with admiration for Hank's courage, Launcelot then offers to fight Sir SAG-RAMOUR in his place after Merlin steals Hank's lasso. Three years later, Hank sees Launcelot for the last time when both men sit up all night watching croup-afflicted HELLO-CENTRAL (chapter 40).

After Hank leaves England, Launcelot becomes president of the stock-board and makes a killing that provokes MORDRED and Agravaine to tell Arthur about his affair with Guenever, thus touching off the destructive civil war (chapter 42).

Lawrence, Amy Minor character in *Tom Sawyer*. Amy is Tom's girlfriend until he sees Becky THATCHER in chapter 3. As Tom showers attention on Becky, Amy simpers in the background. Later, Tom flirts with Amy to make Becky jealous (chapter 18), but after he and Becky make up, Amy disappears from the story. In "BOY'S MANUSCRIPT," an earlier story that anticipates *Tom Sawyer*, "Amy" is the name of a character who is Becky's prototype.

Lear, King Title character of a SHAKESPEARE tragedy. In chapter 24 of *Huckleberry Finn*, the DUKE dresses Jim up in a Lear outfit, "a long curtain-calico gown, and a white horse-hair wig and whiskers," paints his face blue, and posts a sign on the raft: "Sick Arab—but harmless when not out of his head." In *A Tramp Abroad*, Mark Twain mentions seeing *King Lear* performed in Germany (chapters 9–10).

Leary, Daniel D. (*fl.* 1860s) One of the owners of the QUAKER CITY, Leary was also a passenger on the ship's 1867 excursion. Chapter 3 of *Innocents Abroad* calls him "Capt. L****." Hoping to sell the ship for £50,000, Leary was a prime instigator behind the meeting with Czar ALEXANDER II in Russia. The czar was not interested, so Leary tried selling the ship to the viceroy of Egypt. Never popular with other passengers, Leary enhanced his disrepute in Italy, where he delayed the ship's departure from LEGHORN just before that port was declared a CHOLERA zone; as a result, the *Quaker City* was certified a health risk and had to endure a long quarantine in NAPLES Bay. After the voyage, Mark Twain wrote that while Leary had "unpleasant traits," his generous instincts made up for them.

Leary, Katy (Catherine) (March 17, 1856, Elmira, New York–October 5, 1934, Elmira) Family servant. The second of four children of Irish immigrants, Leary was born and raised in Elmira, where her sister Mary Leary (1862–1928) was a live-in maid in Charles J. LANGDON's home. After summering in Elmira in 1880, Mark Twain's wife Livy hired Katy Leary as a maid and brought her back to Hartford in October. Leary remained in the family's service until October 1910, serving as a nursemaid, seamstress and nanny. Through these years, she traveled with the family, except in 1895–96, when she looked after Susy and Jean Clemens in Elmira while Mark Twain went around the world with Livy and Clara. She was with Susy at her death in Hartford in 1896, then returned with the family to Europe. She later nursed Livy, who died in her arms in FLORENCE in 1904. After Livy's death, Leary was Mark Twain's housekeeper. She found Jean when she died at STORMFIELD in 1909 and was present at Mark Twain's death the following year. Afterward, she helped Clara at Stormfield and attended her when she gave birth to Nina GABRILOWITSCH. After Clara and her husband returned to Europe, Leary ran a small boardinghouse on New York City's West 97th Street while living on a $10,000 bequest from Mark Twain and a monthly pension from Clara.

In 1922, Leary returned to Elmira, where she had inherited her parents' Connelly Avenue house. A few years later, Mary Lawton, a friend of Clara Clemens, spent two weeks interviewing Leary and wrote her memoirs as *A Lifetime with Mark Twain* (1925)—a book that portrays Leary as less articulate than she actually was. Mark Twain's dialogue WHAT IS MAN? alludes to Leary when the "Young Man" describes an "old servant" of 22 years who has become absentminded.

Leathers, Jesse Madison (c. 1846–1887) A distant relation of Mark Twain on his mother's side, Leathers was an impoverished newspaper ad salesman and collections agent from Kentucky who considered himself the rightful Earl of Durham. From mid-1875 until the year before he died of tuberculosis in New York City, Leathers wrote to Mark Twain regularly, soliciting financial help to press his claim to the earldom. Though Mark Twain himself evidently fantasized occasionally about becoming the Earl of Durham, he regarded Leathers's claim as "inconceivably slender." He enjoyed hearing from Leathers, gave him small amounts of money and encouraged him to publish his autobiography to press his claim, but otherwise avoided closer involvement. Samuel Webster's book *Mark Twain, Business Man* (1946) claims that Leathers occasionally visited Mark Twain; however, it is not certain that the two men ever met.

Clearly fascinated by Leathers's story, Mark Twain made claimants a major theme of his 1892 novel *The American Claimant*, in which he fictionalized Leathers as Simon LATHERS. Leathers also probably helped inspire the claimant in *Huckleberry Finn* who calls himself the DUKE of BRIDGEWATER; like Leathers, the Duke has an ornate and cliché-ridden style of speech. In his autobiographical writings, Mark Twain does not mention Leathers by name, but alludes to him while discussing the LAMPTON family and the Durham earldom.

Lebanon Mark Twain visited what is now the Republic of Lebanon in 1867, six years after the region had become an autonomous province within TURKEY's Ottoman Empire. *Innocents Abroad* mentions the Mountains of Lebanon and the Valley of Lebanon (chapters 41–44, 49–50), but alludes to the region itself as part of SYRIA. The *Quaker City* landed at BEIRUT on September 9, 1867. From there Mark Twain went to a village he nicknamed "JACKSONVILLE" and to the ruins at BAALBEK before entering what is now Syria.

Lecky, William Edward Hartpole (March 26, 1838, Dublin, Ireland–October 22, 1903, London)   British historian specializing in moral and religious issues. Trained at Dublin's Trinity College, Lecky wrote *History of the Rise and Influence of the Spirit of Rationalism in Europe* (1865) and other works examining the struggle between religious dogmatism and toleration. In *History of European Morals from Augustus to Charlemagne* (1869), he explores how changing notions of virtue have affected human happiness. His major work was an eight-volume history of 18th-century England (1878–90) focusing on political ideas and institutions. From 1895 to 1902, he represented Dublin University in Parliament.

Mark Twain met Lecky at least once, when he dined at Lecky's London home in March 1900. He owned and carefully read most of Lecky's books and was profoundly influenced by Lecky's views in his own historical novels and philosophical writings such as WHAT IS MAN? He was particularly interested in Lecky's evidence of the Roman Catholic Church's pernicious role in Western history. Lecky's influence is especially evident in *Connecticut Yankee*, in which Hank MORGAN campaigns against the Church; a footnote to chapter 22 credits Lecky for information about hermits in the VALLEY OF HOLINESS. Other episodes drawing on Lecky include the kings-evil rite (chapter 25), discussion of the pillory (chapter 33), a witch burning and the story of a young woman hanged for stealing (chapter 35).

lecturing   One of the great public speakers of his era, Mark Twain delivered nearly a thousand lectures and speeches. His career happened to blossom as the post–CIVIL WAR years fostered the development of lyceum lecture circuits. People across America hungered for edification and entertainment from traveling lecturers, and Mark Twain had a rare talent for supplying both. One of his hour-and-a-half lectures on the SANDWICH ISLANDS, the HOLY LAND or the western frontier could shake an audience with laughter, yet send it home satisfied that it had learned something useful.

Before he ever earned a dollar from a book, Mark Twain discovered that he could make good money from lecturing, almost for the asking. Between 1866 and 1874—his peak lecturing years—he earned a reputation as a lecturer that would have made him famous even if he had never written books. However, his writing and speaking careers were closely intertwined. Just as his writing successes drove him to the lecture platform, lecturing helped shape him as a writer and helped advertise his books.

True Williams captured Mark Twain's first-lecture stage fright so well that the publisher used this picture to promote Roughing It.

Mark Twain's bent for public speaking may have begun in his boyhood, when the only school routine that he enjoyed was the weekly spelling bee. A star performer, he relished being a center of public attention and began learning how to play before audiences. He later gave his spelling talent to Tom Sawyer, whose own fictional career may provide clues about Mark Twain's youth. Though Tom speaks well enough in settings such as courtroom trials, public speaking does not come naturally to him. When he recites Patrick Henry's famous oration at school Examination Night in *Tom Sawyer*, "ghastly stage-fright" reduces him to a quivering jelly (chapter 21). Does his disaster reflect an experience from Mark Twain's youth?

Mark Twain gave his first true speech at a dinner of KEOKUK, Iowa printers on Benjamin FRANKLIN's birthday in January 1856. Eight years later, he spoke several times before Nevada's burlesque "THIRD HOUSE" in CARSON CITY. By then familiar with professional lecturers who passed through Nevada, he was confident enough to compare himself with the likes of Artemus WARD—the most popular humorous lecturer of that time. In 1866, Mark Twain returned from HAWAII to SAN FRANCISCO to discover that his newspaper letters from the islands had made him so famous that he might earn money by lecturing on the "Sandwich Islands." On October 2, 1866, he spoke for the first time before an audience that had paid solely for the privilege of hearing *him*. According to a story he often retold, he arrived at the lecture hall convinced it would be empty and instead found it packed. Stage fright paralyzed him at first, but after a few minutes, he overcame it and never experienced it again. *Roughing It* offers a colorful account of that evening (chapter 78).

The success of his San Francisco lecture prompted Mark Twain to undertake his first tour. Between October 11 and December 10, 1866, he delivered 16 lectures throughout northern CALIFORNIA and western NEVADA, helped by Denis E. MCCARTHY. The following spring, he returned to Missouri and IOWA on a brief lecture tour. He then settled in NEW YORK CITY, where he reluctantly took his friend Frank FULLER's advice to give a lecture at the great Cooper Union—the city's biggest hall—on May 6. The critical success of his first major lecture before an Eastern audience helped embolden him to speak anywhere; he recalls it vividly in his AUTOBIOGRAPHY.

Over the next year, when he was not busy cruising on the QUAKER CITY and writing *Innocents Abroad*, Mark Twain spoke occasionally in and around New York City and WASHINGTON, D.C. In early 1868, he returned to the West Coast, where he retraced the route of his first lecture tour, this time speaking on the Holy Land. In the middle of the following November, he launched his first major tour, beginning in Cleveland, Ohio. From then through late March 1869, he had 42 engagements in Ohio, Pennsylvania, NEW YORK, Michigan, Indiana, ILLINOIS and Iowa. This tour wore him down so much that afterward he wrote to his family saying that he hated lecturing and shuddered to think that he might never escape it. Around this same time, however, he was approached by James REDPATH, then organizing the Boston Lyceum Bureau. Under Redpath's management, Mark Twain began a new tour in November. This time he went through Pennsylvania, MASSACHUSETTS, Rhode Island, CONNECTICUT, New Jersey and New York. He finished in late January 1870—a week and a half before his MARRIAGE. His next tour for Redpath ran from mid-October 1871 until February 1, 1872, taking him on a circuitous route through Pennsylvania, Delaware, Vermont, Massachusetts, New York, MAINE, Michigan, Ohio and Illinois.

Mark Twain at the time of his 1884–85 lecture tour with George Washington Cable. (Courtesy, Library of Congress, Pictures & Prints Division)

Redpath wanted to book Mark Twain on a tour every year, but Mark Twain now had enough income from writing to spurn the lecture platform in America until 1884. Through the intervening years, his speaking engagements were irregular and mostly informal. George Dolby, who managed Charles DICKENS's American tours, managed two short lecture tours for Mark Twain in ENGLAND during late 1873 and early 1874. In the early 1880s, Mark Twain got an idea for a grand tour that he would manage himself, with his friends W. D. HOWELLS, Thomas ALDRICH and G. W. CABLE accompanying him on salary. While the others turned him down, Cable joined him for what became his busiest American tour. James B. POND organized 104 engagements that took the two writers from Connecticut in early November 1884 to Washington, D.C. in late February 1885. Along the way, they passed through New York, Pennsylvania, parts of CANADA, Michigan, Ohio, KENTUCKY, Indiana, Missouri, Iowa, Illinois, Minnesota, Wisconsin and New Jersey. In contrast to his earlier tours, Mark Twain concentrated on reading from his published writings—including *Huckleberry Finn*—which was published in the United States just as the tour ended.

Over the next decade, most of Mark Twain's public addresses were unpaid speeches at banquets and club meetings and occasional informal readings. The BANKRUPTCY of his publishing company in 1894 forced him back to lecturing to pay his debts. He considered returning to California for a tour the following year, but Pond talked him out of it. Though he was approaching 60 and not in good health, he then arranged the most ambitious tour of his life: 140 engagements that took him around the world. With Pond managing the North American part of his tour, Mark Twain left ELMIRA, New York with his wife and daughter Clara on July 14, 1895 and gave his first lecture in Cleveland, Ohio the next day. Over the next five weeks, he passed through Michigan, Canada, North Dakota, Montana, Idaho, Washington and Oregon, giving lectures in most of these states before sailing across the PACIFIC OCEAN from British Columbia.

In Sydney, AUSTRALIA, Mark Twain was joined by his Australian manager, Carlyle SMYTHE, who stayed with him for the balance of his tour. He spent two and a half months touring Australia and NEW ZEALAND, and similar periods in INDIA and SOUTH AFRICA. After officially concluding his tour in Cape Town on July 15, 1896, he returned to England. This tour and *Following the Equator*—his book about the trip—earned him enough to pay his debts. The following year, Pond offered him $50,000 and expenses to give another 125 lectures in America, but Mark Twain turned him down. The round-the-world trip closed his career as a paid lecturer, but he was still gaining momentum as a public speaker. Over his remaining years, he gave more than 200 speeches. The last was an address at the graduation ceremonies of a Baltimore girls' school on June 9, 1909.

Aside from the chapter in *Roughing It*, Mark Twain says little about his lecturing in his published writings. Even *Following the Equator* barely mentions the lecturing that he did on his tour. There are, however, many accounts of lecturing in his posthumously published AUTOBIOGRAPHY and letters. Whatever Mark Twain's real feelings were toward lecturers, his fictional lecturers are mostly a sorry lot. His coauthor of *The Gilded Age*, C. D. WARNER, places Laura HAWKINS on the threshold of prosperity and respectability as a lecturer after she is acquitted in her trial (chapter 58). Two chapters later, however, Mark Twain dashes Laura's hopes at her first lecture by giving her a nearly empty house populated by hostile drunks (chapter 60). The KING and DUKE of *Huckleberry Finn* fail at lecturing on temperance because they drink too much (chapter 31), while Colonel SELLERS of *The American Claimant* fails at temperance lecturing because he drinks too little (chapter 24). On the other hand, George Benton, the dissolute drunkard of "EDWARD MILLS AND GEORGE BENTON: A TALE," finds just the right balance. More subtle allusions to Mark Twain's lecturing experiences can be found in other works. In *Connecticut Yankee*, for example, Hank MORGAN's preparations for restarting the fountain in the VALLEY OF

HOLINESS reflect Mark Twain's ideas about "working" an audience (chapter 23). When Judge Driscoll shows the Capello brothers the sights of Dawson's Landing in *Pudd'nhead Wilson* (chapter 7), one recalls Mark Twain's boredom on the lecture circuit when the mayor of every one-horse town insisted on showing him the firehouse and the town hall.

Lee   Western MASSACHUSETTS town. In July 1904, a month after his wife died in Italy, Mark Twain returned to the United States with his daughters and spent a few days in NEW YORK CITY. He and Jean Clemens then went to Tyringham, near Lee, where they stayed in a cottage on the farm of CENTURY MAGAZINE editor Richard Watson Gilder. At the end of the month, Jean was seriously injured when her horse ran into a trolley car in Lee. In September, Mark Twain took up more permanent quarters in New York City.

Leghorn (Livorno)   A major seaport in central Italy's Tuscany region, Leghorn was the port at which Mark Twain rejoined the QUAKER CITY after traveling from GENOA through northern Italy. The ship reached Leghorn on July 24; Mark Twain and his companions arrived the next night—just missing an opportunity to join a group visiting Giuseppe GARIBALDI on a nearby island. Tired of sightseeing, Mark Twain paid scant attention to Leghorn and left for CIVITAVECCHIA the next day; the episode is briefly described in chapter 24 of *Innocents Abroad*. Meanwhile, the *Quaker City* stayed at Leghorn until the end of July. The ship's owner, Daniel LEARY, accidentally delayed its departure long enough to cost it its clean bill of health when Leghorn was declared a CHOLERA port.

Leo XIII, Pope (March 2, 1810, Carpenito, Italy–July 20, 1903, Vatican)   Soon after succeeding Pius IX as head of the Roman Catholic Church on February 21, 1878, Leo XIII opened the Vatican archives to researchers. Leo went on to write important encyclicals, become an effective statesman and establish himself as one of the most respected modern pontiffs. Mark Twain's interest in him grew out of the success that his publishing firm, Charles L. WEBSTER & COMPANY, had enjoyed with U. S. GRANT's *Memoirs* in 1885. Mark Twain reasoned that every Catholic family in the world would want an authorized biography of the pope. Early the next year, his company secured the pope's sanction for a biography and signed Bernard O'Reilly (1823–1907), a Catholic priest, to write it. In June, Charles WEBSTER himself had a private audience with the pope, who gave the project his official blessing and later awarded Webster a papal knighthood.

Webster's promotional copy billed the biography as "The Greatest Book of the Age!" and claimed that its prices were kept low to enable everyone to own a copy. The company issued editions in six languages, but Mark Twain expected eventually to publish editions in every language spoken by Catholics around the world. His confident projections of sales made even W. D. HOWELLS a believer, but as Howells later admitted in *My Mark Twain,* they failed to consider how many Catholics could read, and of those that could, how many would really want to read the book. O'Reilly's *Life of Pope Leo XIII* (1887) was profitable, but its earnings fell so far short of expectations that Mark Twain regarded it as a colossal failure.

Leopold II (April 9, 1835, Brussels, Belgium–December 17, 1909, Laeken, Belgium) King of BELGIUM. A close contemporary of Mark Twain and the brother of Mexico's "empress" Carlotta, Leopold became Belgium's king in December 1865. In the 1870s, H. M. STANLEY's crossing of equatorial AFRICA revealed the commercial potential of the Congo Basin to the world, prompting Leopold to form the International African Association in 1876 to explore it. Drawing on his own resources, he hired Stanley to survey the Congo region and begin creating an administration. Stanley and other agents eventually acquired treaties over nearly a million square miles of territory, spurring European nations to gather in Berlin in 1884 to formulate rules for partitioning Africa amongst themselves.

After getting other nations to recognize his rights over the Congo, Leopold created the Congo Free State as his own private domain; he then turned it into a ruthless commercial empire by selling commercial leases to mining and rubber companies that forced Africans to work and punished them brutally when they failed to meet quotas. Atrocities perpetrated by these companies and Leopold's administration caught the attention of the outside world when Roger Casement, a British consular official, delivered a graphic report on Congo abuses to his government in 1903. Among those outraged by this evidence, Mark Twain joined the Congo Reform Association the following year. In 1905, he wrote KING LEOPOLD'S SOLILOQUY, a satirical attack that attracted attention to Leopold's abuses and indirectly helped bring down his private empire. In August 1908, the Belgian government took the Congo Free State away from Leopold—who never visited his African domain—and reorganized it as the Belgian Congo, which is now the independent republic of Zaïre.

"Letters from the Earth" Treatise on mankind and religion written in 1909 and first published within a book of the same title in 1962. The last substantial manuscript that Mark Twain wrote, "Letters" played an important role in reinvigorating popular interest in his work a half century after he wrote it. Its publication occurred during the same year that the MARK TWAIN PAPERS signed a publishing agreement with the University of California Press that helped launch it as a professional editing project. The death of Clara Clemens later that year left the editors of her father's papers with unprecedented freedom to select and edit material.

Meanwhile, publication of *Letters from the Earth* garnered national attention and alerted the public to a serious side of Mark Twain that hitherto had not been generally known.

Not easy to assign to a genre, "Letters" begins with an omniscient narrator describing a scene in heaven in which the archangels Satan, Gabriel and Michael are characters. Its focus then shifts to Satan. Temporarily banished from heaven, he visits Earth and writes his observations about mankind in a series of letters to Gabriel and Michael. Initially, his tone is personal, with frequent use of first- and second-person pronouns. Gradually, however, his letters become less personal and increasingly vitriolic. By its end, the document is essentially a polemic.

Apparently sincere in saying that he expected "Letters from the Earth" never to be published, Mark Twain used it to express his frank opinions about Christianity, moral beliefs and human sexuality. "Letters" expands on themes that he explored as early as *Huckleberry Finn* (1884), which opens with Huck considering the nature of heaven (chapter 1) and often has him ponder the efficacy of prayer (especially in chapters 3, 8, 28 and 31). The passages about prayer in "Letters" also bear an affinity to "THE WAR PRAYER," and Satan's mocking remarks about man's concepts of heaven recall CAPTAIN STORMFIELD'S VISIT TO HEAVEN. Satan's discussion of man's moral sense also develops ideas that Mark Twain explores fully in WHAT IS MAN?, his ADAM AND EVE writings and elsewhere. "Letters" has also raised questions about Mark Twain's personal life. Satan's discussion of human sexual intercourse, for example, has led to speculation that Mark Twain may have been impotent in middle age.

Bernard DEVOTO prepared the first edition of "Letters from the Earth" by combining two separately paginated manuscript fragments that Mark Twain probably intended to connect. The first fragment—which Mark Twain left untitled—is a roughly 1,500-word narrative setting the stage for Satan's banishment. The second fragment, which Mark Twain titled "Letters from the Earth," contains about 17,500 words of "letters." Mark Twain left most of Satan's letters unnumbered; DeVoto gave them 11 sequential roman numerals. Paul Baender's corrected text for the Mark Twain Papers edition (discussed below) ignores DeVoto's numbers but follows the same sequence. For the sake of clear identification of passages, the synopsis that follows employs DeVoto's letter numbers. Parenthetical notes are inserted where his numbers differ from the original manuscript.

SYNOPSIS

Seated on His throne, with Satan, Gabriel and Michael at his feet, the Creator lifts His hand and a million suns burst forth and scatter in the blackness of space. After leaving the Grand Council, the archangels discuss what they have just seen. Suggesting that the new feature in the universe that the Creator has established is automatic and self-regulating law, Satan gives it a name: the Law of Nature, or the Law of God.

After three centuries of celestial time—100 million Earth years—a messenger invites the archangels to watch the Creator make animals. The Creator explains that the animals are an experiment in morals and conduct. Each animal has its own temperament. For example, while the tiger's nature is ferocity, that of the rabbit is lack of courage. Though the animals constantly kill each other, they are blameless because they are merely following their nature. The Creator then displays His masterpiece—man, as millions of humans pour into view. He explains that He is putting into each man different measures of moral qualities, such as courage and cowardice, ferocity and gentleness and so on, and is sending them to Earth.

Several celestial days later, Satan is heard uttering sarcastic remarks about the Creator's industries and is banished from heaven for a celestial day. Instead of going into the empty void of space, as he usually does when banished, he visits Earth to see how the human-race experiment is faring. Later, he writes about it to Gabriel and Michael in private letters.

Satan's Letter (unnumbered)
Finding Earth to be an extraordinarily strange place, Satan thinks that it, its people and its animals are all insane. He finds man a marvelous curiosity because man thinks that he is the "noblest work of God" and the Creator's pet, though his prayers are never answered. Equally incredible, man thinks that he is going to heaven.

Letter 2 (manuscript letter 4)
Nothing about man is not strange to immortals. For example, man imagines a heaven that leaves out his chief delight—sexual intercourse. He fills his heaven entirely with diversions that he cares nothing for on Earth. In his imagined heaven, prayer is substituted for sexual intercourse, everybody sings and everybody plays the harp. Further, man imagines a heaven in which all the nations are jumbled together, even though they all hate each other on Earth. Finally, there is not a rag of intellectuality in heaven, though every man on Earth possesses some share of intellect. In short, heaven contains everything repulsive to man, and nothing that he likes.

Letter 3 (manuscript letter 5)
Satan discusses Christianity, as it is set forth in the Testaments, which Christians believe are dictated by God. The Bible is actually made from fragments of older Bibles. It has only two new things in it: hell and its singular heaven. Though man has invented both, he credits them to God.

According to the biblical account of Creation, God spent five days making the Earth, then created the rest of the universe in one day. And the purpose of all the other suns and planets? Simply to illuminate the Earth! The Bible says that the universe is 6,000 years old, but inquiring minds now know that its age is 100 million years.

God put ADAM AND EVE in the Garden, telling them not to eat the forbidden fruit, but made them curious, so naturally they ate it. This gave them the moral sense and led to their discovery of sexual intercourse and immodesty. The latter is a strange convention on Earth, since it has no standard. For example, Indian women cover their faces and breasts and expose their legs, while European women cover their legs and expose their faces and breasts.

God expelled Adam and Eve from the Garden for disobeying a command that He had no right to utter. He made one code of morals for Himself, another for His children. Despite His manifest unfairness, He is daily praised for being just and righteous.

Letter 4
After leaving the Garden under a curse, the first pair constantly practiced the "Supreme Act." Cain and Abel and their sisters followed and the work of populating the Earth proceeded. Eventually, God was dissatisfied with the world's morals. Concluding that people were bad, He decided to abolish them by drowning all but a sample on Noah's Ark. Despite being farsighted, however, He failed to foresee that people would go rotten again.

Letter 5
Records of how many animals Noah collected, or how long he spent collecting them, are lost. Further, the Bible suppresses the fact that Noah deliberately sailed before many large animals arrived because he did not have enough room to carry them.

Letter 6 (manuscript letter 7)
On Noah's third day out, a fly was found to have been accidentally left behind, so he spent 16 days going back for it. By saving the fly, he also saved typhoid fever.

The Bible's contradictions are hard to understand. For example, jealousy is a weakness, yet God is a "jealous God." At first He commanded that no *other* Gods should be put before Him; later He said that He was the *only* God. Jealousy is the key. Since Adam and Eve ate the forbidden fruit in order to be as Gods, God still seeks revenge. A human being is a machine and the Creator has planned an enemy to oppose each of its mechanisms. Man equips the Creator with every trait that makes a fiend, then calls him "Our Father."

Letter 7
Noah and his family were saved, but were full of microbes; the most important part of his cargo was disease germs. Most animals are distributed to various regions, but not the fly. He is everywhere and is the Creator's special representative. Houseflies destroy more lives than all the rest of the Creator's death-agents combined. The Creator's affliction-inventions are specially de-

signed to persecute the poor. In fact, the worst enemy of the poor is their Father in Heaven. All of the Creator's specially deadly disease-producers are invisible—making it impossible for man to understand his maladies for thousands of years.

Letter 8

Man is the most interesting fool there is. He has not a single written law—in or out of the Bible—with any purpose other than to limit or defeat a law of God. Temperament is a law of God, written in the heart of every creature, and must be obeyed. The Bible does not allow adultery at all, but makes no distinction between temperaments. The commandment against adultery does not distribute its burden equally. It is easy on the very young and very old, but hard on others—especially women.

Letter 9

Although God chose Noah from all the Earth's peoples, and although He could see ahead, the first thing that Noah did after his Ark landed on Ararat was to plant a vineyard, drink the wine and be overcome. Did the Creator see how badly things would go? When it comes to intellect, the Deity is the head pauper in the universe.

Letter 10

The two testaments are interesting. The Old Testament gives a picture of the Deity before He got religion; the other gives a picture of Him afterward. The Old Testament is interested mainly in blood and sensuality, the New Testament in salvation—by force. The first time that the Deity came to Earth, He brought life and death; the next time, He brought hell. After the Deity realized that death was a mistake because it freed man from his suffering, He invented hell. And it was as Jesus Christ that He invented hell. (In the original manuscript, a new letter begins immediately after this passage.)

The Bible is filled with examples of God's cruel justice (verses are quoted from Num. 31 and Deut. 20). Biblical law says "Thou shalt not kill," but God plants in the heart of man another law: "Thou shalt kill." God cannot keep His own commandments.

Letter 11

Human history is red with blood and bitter hate—but only God in biblical times goes to war with no limits. Totally without mercy, He slew everyone—the innocent along with the guilty. The worst punishment He ever dealt, however, was to put 32,000 Midianite women into prostitution. Even Indians did not carry tortures this far. The sarcasms and hypocrisies of the Beatitudes should be read from the pulpit along with the passages from Numbers and Deuteronomy in order to get an all-around view of the Father in Heaven.

BACKGROUND AND PUBLISHING HISTORY

Mark Twain wrote "Letters from the Earth" between early October 1909—when his daughter Clara married

and left his home—and late November, when he went to BERMUDA. This was also the same moment that HARPER'S published *Extract from Captain Stormfield's Visit to Heaven*, which explores similar themes.

When Bernard DeVoto became literary editor of the Mark Twain Estate in 1938, one of his first tasks was to select the previously unpublished manuscripts that he thought most merited publication in a new book. A year later, he presented *Letters from the Earth* to the trustees of the estate. In addition to "Letters"—which fills about a fifth of the book's pages—the volume includes the thematically similar "Papers of the ADAM Family" and "Letter to the Earth" (later published as "Letter from the Recording Angel"). The rest of the book is unrelated material, including the whimsical "A Cat Tale," "COOPER's Prose Style," "Official Report to the I.I.A.S. [Indianapolis Institute of Applied Science]," "The GORKY Incident," "Simplified Spelling," "Something about Repentance," "From an English Notebook," "The French and the Comanches," "From an Unfinished Burlesque of Books on Etiquette," "The Damned Human Race" and "THE GREAT DARK." Publication of *Letters from the Earth* was stalled when Clara Clemens objected to its contents, fearing that it misrepresented her father's views on religion. The manuscript was set aside until Clara withdrew her objections in 1962, by which time DeVoto had died. Henry Nash SMITH, then editor of the Mark Twain Papers, wrote a new preface to the book, explaining that aside from a few editorial remarks, it was as DeVoto prepared it in 1939, though several of its pieces had been published between then and 1962. Harper & Row issued the book in September 1962 and *Life* magazine published excerpts in its September 28 issue. An immediate critical success, *Letters from the Earth* made the *New York Times* best-seller list and has remained in print ever since.

In 1973, the Mark Twain Papers project published *What Is Man? and Other Philosophical Writings* in the Works of Mark Twain edition. This volume, edited by Paul Baender, includes corrected and annotated texts of "Letters from the Earth" and several other fragments on religion from *Letters from the Earth*. The Library of America's *Collected Tales, Sketches, Speeches, & Essays* (1992), edited by Louis J. Budd, uses Baender's version of "Letters" and several other pieces from his volume.

Levering, Albert (1869, Hope, Indiana–April 12 or 14, 1929) Illustrator. After practicing for several years as an architect in San Antonio, Texas, Levering became a magazine illustrator in New York. He had a regular full-page feature in HARPER'S WEEKLY, for which he drew, for the February 7, 1903 issue, a cartoon story about CHRISTIAN SCIENTISTS refusing to sell *Science and Health* to Mark Twain, who is disguised as various characters from his books. Six years later, Levering drew the cover and frontispiece for Harper's edition of *Extract from* CAPTAIN STORMFIELD'S VISIT TO HEAVEN. Levering's illustrations, which depict Stormfield piloting a comet,

John T. Lewis chats with Mark Twain during the author's last visit to Elmira in 1903. (Courtesy, Library of Congress, Pictures & Prints Division)

are somewhat misleading. Within the story, Stormfield is not riding a comet; if anything, he *is* a comet.

Lewis, John T. (1835, Carroll County, Maryland–July 1906, Elmira, New York)

A free-born African American, Lewis moved to New York in 1862 and began farming as a tenant on Susan and Theodore CRANE'S QUARRY FARM around 1870. In August 1877, Mark Twain saw Lewis risk his life to stop a runaway carriage, saving Charles LANGDON's wife Ida, their daughter Julia and a nursemaid from nearly certain death. Generously rewarded, Lewis stayed at Quarry Farm into his retirement, to which Mark Twain contributed. Though averse to publicizing Lewis's heroism, Mark Twain adapted his heroic feat in several fictional works. A passage omitted from *Pudd'nhead Wilson*, for example, describes JASPER performing an almost identical rescue. In chapter 52 of *Life on the Mississippi*, Charlie WILLIAMS fakes a letter from a nonexistent ex-convict describing a similar rescue.

Mark Twain greatly respected Lewis's character and used him as one of his models for Jim in *Huckleberry Finn*. Mark Twain was also interested in Lewis's Dunkard Baptist beliefs. Lewis often argued religion with the Cranes' cook Mary Ann CORD—whom Mark Twain described as a "violent Methodist." Their theological spats inspired the "Dunker Baptist" Uncle Dan'l and the "shouting Methodist" Aunt JINNY of *The American Claimant*.

Life on the Mississippi (1883)

Though generally classified as a travel book, *Life on the Mississippi* does not lend itself readily to simple categorization. The book

combines an embroidered memoir of the author's apprentice steamboat PILOT days with a narrative of his return to the Mississippi River 20 years later, as well as history and statistics and a hodgepodge of unrelated sketches. If the book lacks focus, it is because Mark Twain himself was unsure what it was he was assembling. Nevertheless, its strengths are many; it is widely regarded as both one of Mark Twain's major works and a classic on the Mississippi itself. Its early chapters especially are unrivaled in evoking the excitement of their time. The balance of the book presents a powerful portrait of how much both the river and its commerce could change in a few decades, as well as a savage depiction of the postwar South.

As with much of Mark Twain's other travel writing, these later chapters are often discursive, mixing physical descriptions, economic statistics and travel anecdotes—with occasional tall tales of little or no relevance to

"TELL ME WHERE IT IS — I'LL FETCH IT!"

A rag-picker offering to do a diplomatic service for the emperor of Russia could not have been more astounding than the narrator's offer to help the mate of the Paul Jones *in chapter 5.*

"I WAS GRATIFIED TO BE ABLE TO ANSWER PROMPTLY, AND I DID. I SAID I DIDN'T KNOW."
—Life on the Mississippi, Ch. 6

Courtesy of the *Mark Twain Journal*.

anything else. The book is narrated in the first person, but we cannot take for granted that the anonymous narrator is always Mark Twain himself. The best assurance we have that it is comes in chapter 50, when he recalls how he adopted his pen name. Otherwise, his narrative voice shifts unpredictably.

The text mentions many real people, such as Horace BIXBY, G. W. CABLE, George RITCHIE and others, by name, while disguising others with pseudonyms, such as "Uncle" MUMFORD, Robert STYLES and THOMPSON AND ROGERS. There are also figures of pure invention, such as Karl RITTER, Charlie WILLIAMS and John Backus.

SYNOPSIS

With over 147,500 words—including 12,800 words in appendixes quoted from other sources—*Life on the Mississippi* has 60 chapters, which fall into three distinct groups. The first three chapters form a historical prelude to the rest. Chapters 4–21 are a memoir of Mark Twain's early piloting years. The first 14 of these chapters originally appeared in seven magazine installments in 1875 as "OLD TIMES ON THE MISSISSIPPI."

Chapters 22–60 cover Mark Twain's return to the river in 1882. He happened to arrive when the Mississippi was experiencing a record flood—a subject on which he comments frequently. Chapters 22–33 take him from St. Louis through Arkansas; chapters 34–40 continue the journey to Baton Rouge, Louisiana; chapters 41–50 pertain to NEW ORLEANS—the longest stop on the trip. Chapter 51 summarizes the return trip to St. Louis; chapters 53–56 cover his stay in Hannibal and offer significant insights into Mark Twain's early AUTOBIOGRAPHY. The remaining chapters complete the journey to St. Paul, Minnesota.

Information inserted within parentheses in the synopsis below does not appear in the original chapters.

Chapter 1
A passage from an 1863 issue of HARPER'S MAGAZINE describes the Mississippi River and compares it to the other great river systems of the world. The first chapter emphasizes that the Mississippi "is not a commonplace river, but on the contrary is in all ways remarkable." It is extraordinarily long, it drains a vast region, it carries a huge volume of water, it is remarkably crooked, it is constantly reshaping itself, and it is always shifting its channels.

A capsule history of early exploration drawn from the writings of Francis Parkman (1823–1893) remarks that De Soto's discovery of the river in 1542 gives America's national history "a most respectable outside aspect and rustiness and antiquity."

Chapter 2
Remarks about La Salle and about Joliet and Marquette's 1673 expedition continue the capsule history. La Salle returned in 1681 to prove that the river empties into the Gulf of Mexico. By a remarkable coincidence, three of the first four great explorers converged on the future location of NAPOLEON, Arkansas.

Chapter 3
During the 70 years after La Salle proved where the Mississippi emptied, European settlements arose slowly along the river. It took another 50 years for serious commerce to develop. The earliest river commerce was on barges and keelboats. As STEAMBOATS killed off this traffic, a new era of giant coal and timber rafts began. To illustrate this era, a long excerpt from an unfinished manuscript (*Huckleberry Finn*'d "RAFT CHAPTER") is included.

Chapter 4
The narrator remembers that when he was a boy, the only permanent ambition among his comrades was to be a steamboatman. The mere arrival of steamboats pumped life into the "white town drowsing in the sunshine of a summer's morning." Within minutes, the town awakened to a frenzy of activity as a steamboat landed. Immediately after the boat left, the town sank back into its previous torpor. Once, a boy who had earlier disappeared showed up as an apprentice steamboat engineer to become the object of envy and hate. Other boys were later thrilled to hear that his steamboat had blown up; however, he not only did not die, but he returned home a bigger hero than ever. Of all the positions on a steamboat, PILOT is the grandest. Eventually, the narrator ran off to ST. LOUIS to become a pilot, only to be rudely ignored.

Chapter 5
Later, the narrator goes to CINCINNATI, from which he intends to travel to SOUTH AMERICA's Amazon to become an explorer. He buys passage to NEW ORLEANS on the steamboat PAUL JONES. As he goes down the OHIO RIVER, he imagines himself a member of the crew and hangs around the big mate. When the boat gets stuck on rocks near Louisville, he offers to fetch a tool for the mate, only to be humiliated by the man's reaction to his amazing presumption. He then plays up to the boat's most

humble person, the night watchman—a talkative fellow who claims to be the son of an English nobleman.

Chapter 6
During the *Paul Jones*'s two-week voyage, the narrator gets to know one of its pilots (later identified as Horace BIXBY). After reaching New Orleans, he discovers that there is no prospect of any vessel ever shipping to the Amazon, so he looks for an alternative career. Bixby agrees to teach him the river between New Orleans and St. Louis for $500.

The new cub pilot begins by steering the steamboat out of New Orleans. (The narrator calls this boat the *Paul Jones;* Mark Twain actually began his apprenticeship on the COLONEL CROSSMAN.) As it goes north, Bixby rattles off names of nondescript features along the river. The young cub has a rude awakening when he is turned out for his first middle-of-the-night watch and is equally amazed that Bixby expects to find a plantation in the blackness of night. When Bixby asks the cub the names of points they passed earlier, he impresses on him that he *must* learn these things and tells him to get a NOTE-BOOK in which to record information. Bixby finds the plantation in the darkness, but the cub attributes it to luck.

After traveling 700 or 800 miles up the river, the cub's notebook is filling up, but his head remains empty. The chapter ends with the cub following Bixby to another steamboat.

Chapter 7
Aboard their new boat (the CRESCENT CITY), the cub returns to New Orleans and discovers that *down*stream navigation differs greatly from *up*stream navigation. The boat's big pilot house typically has eight to 10 veteran pilots who are studying the river—which happens to be low on this voyage. Their cryptic discussion about the river discourages the cub. The boat is delayed when a pilot runs it aground. Afterward, Bixby tries to make up lost time by taking it through a dangerous crossing to reach water deep enough for safe night sailing. The other pilots think the feat impossible, but Bixby pulls it off.

Chapter 8
Each time the cub thinks he has mastered piloting, Bixby adds something new to learn. After the cub has learned the names of features along the river, Bixby tells him that he must also learn the river's *shape*—which changes constantly.

One night, when the second pilot, "Mr. W." (Strother WILEY), arrives late, Bixby angrily turns over the wheel without, as is customary, telling him where they are. Thinking Bixby insanely irresponsible, the cub stays in the pilot house to give the other pilot this important information himself, but falls asleep. The next morning, Bixby chastises him for even thinking that the other pilot *needed* to be told where he was.

The cub learns how difficult it is to perceive the river's shape in the night but eventually masters this

knowledge, only to have Bixby ask him about the river's *depth* at various points. He despairs that he does not have enough brains to be a pilot, but Bixby promises that when he says he will "learn a man the river," he means it. Further, he will "learn him or kill him."

Chapter 9
As the cub masters the river's soundings, Bixby tells him he must next learn to "read" the river as a book. He explains "bluff reefs" and how to maneuver past them. The next day, Bixby leaves the cub alone at the wheel, while secretly watching him. Proud of his new responsibility, the cub gaily whistles until a bluff reef looms ahead. He starts to run the boat ashore, just as Bixby reappears. When he explains that he was dodging a "bluff reef," Bixby scoffs and tells him to run over the next one he sees. The cub does as ordered, but the next hazard turns out to be a harmless "wind reef." As the face of the water gradually becomes "a wonderful book," all the romance goes from the river.

Chapter 10
After mastering the river's *visible* features, the cub thinks his education is complete. Bixby now tells him, however, that he must learn to read the river's depth from its banks and other clues, and how to know whether the river is rising or falling. The cub's education begins anew.

Chapter 11
The cub learns about the difficulties of navigating a rising river, with rapidly changing conditions and small craft constantly drifting downstream. He recalls a story about George EALER, who was once piloting a big boat through a treacherous stretch of low water near Helena, Arkansas when he felt he needed help. His fellow pilot, Mr. X., who had navigated the stretch recently, suddenly appeared and took the wheel. He did the sweetest bit of piloting Ealer ever saw, but Ealer later learned that the man had been sleepwalking.

Chapter 12
Occasionally, when the river is low, steamboats send out small craft to take soundings—work that cubs particularly enjoy. The narrator recalls a voyage on which he and another cub competed for the attentions of a pretty 16-year-old girl. When it was time for him to board the sounding boat, his rival tricked him into running an unnecessary errand and took his place in the boat—impressing the girl with his courage. In the foggy gloom, the steamboat accidentally ran the small boat down. After dramatically disappearing, the other cub was rescued and became a hero.

Chapter 13
Pilots need exceptional memories, and Bixby is a prime example. When higher wages drew him to work on the difficult MISSOURI RIVER, he needed just a few trips to master over a thousand miles of the river and earn his full license. Meanwhile, the narrator was under the tutelage of a pilot named (William) BROWN.

Pilots also need cool courage and the intelligence to make quick decisions. Every cub's master tests him with tricks to develop his confidence. Bixby, for example, once left the narrator alone at the wheel as their boat entered a safe deep-water crossing, but then tested the cub's confidence about how deep the crossing was. Unbeknownst to the cub, Bixby conspired with the leadsmen and was watching him from a hiding place. As a crowd gathered on the hurricane deck, the captain added to the cub's uneasiness by acting concerned about Bixby's absence. Soon, the nervous cub rang for the leadsmen, who called out such alarmingly shallow readings that he begged the engineer to reverse the engines. When Bixby reentered the pilot house, a roar of laughter rose from the crew, and Bixby counseled the cub to have more confidence in what he knew to be true.

Chapter 14

The narrator explains the minutiae of piloting because he loves the profession better than any other, and because he took measureless pride in it. In the old days, he explains, a pilot was the "only unfettered and entirely independent human being that lived in the earth." The pride of steamboating extended down to even the lowliest crew members, especially on such stately boats as the ALECK SCOTT and the *Grand Turk*.

Once a pilot named "Stephen W." (Strother Wiley) was so desperate for a job that he agreed to pilot a boat out of New Orleans for half wages. His captain promised not to tell anyone what he was paying him, but nevertheless boasted about his bargain-rate pilot. When word got back to Stephen, he steered the boat up the middle of the river so slowly that the captain agreed to pay him full wages in order to get the boat moving faster.

Chapter 15

Before the CIVIL WAR, a rapid increase of licensed pilots cut wages in half. To reverse the trend, a dozen bold veterans chartered a benevolent association to fix wages at $250 a month. In return for a nominal initiation fee, any pilot could join and receive $25 a month in benefits while unemployed. Owners, captains and employed pilots derided the association—but as increased river traffic gradually created a pilot shortage, owners began hiring association members. Association pilots could work only with fellow association pilots, however, further increasing demand for their services. As association pilots returned to work, they built a network to exchange information on the river among members. Eventually, their superior safety record moved underwriters to insist that owners hire only association pilots. As the remaining non-association pilots applied for membership, they found that they had to pay stiff initiation fees to cover their past earnings.

Once the association firmly established itself, it acted to restrict licensing of new pilots. The association was set to have wages doubled in September 1861, but by then, the war halted commercial steamboat traffic. After the war ended, new competition from railroads and huge tow barges reduced steamboat traffic to a fraction of its former size. The glory days of piloting were over.

Chapter 16

Although the public always thought steamboat racing was dangerous, the opposite was true—at least after laws restricted boiler-pressure levels—because engineers were more alert and attentive during races. A description of a typical New Orleans–St. Louis race shows that races were generally won by the better pilots. The narrator recalls serving on a particularly slow boat, the JOHN J. ROE, and lists the best speed records the top boats achieved.

Chapter 17

One of the Mississippi's remarkable features is its tendency to shorten itself by cutting off bends—especially in the alluvial-banked lower stretches. During the 175-year period after 1700, for example, the length of the channel between New Orleans and CAIRO, Illinois decreased from 1,215 miles to 973 miles. At that rate—1.3 miles per year—the river must have been 1.3 million miles long a million years ago. In another 742 years, the river should be just 1.75 miles long.

The chapter concludes with another anecdote about Stephen W.—a notorious borrower. Once he borrowed $250 from a newcomer to the river, "Young Yates." After tormenting Yates for weeks with false promises of repayment, he lined up his creditors and promised to settle his debts in *alphabetical* order.

Chapter 18

In summing up his apprenticeship years, the narrator recalls working with many pilots on many steamboats. Now, whenever he finds a well-drawn character in fiction or biography, he generally takes a warm personal interest in him, because he has already met him on the river. An example is Mr. Brown (William Brown), under whom the narrator cubbed on the PENNSYLVANIA during one of Bixby's absences. Brown tormented the narrator for months, while another cub, George RITCHIE, was having good times under the mild-mannered George Ealer. Each night when the narrator went to bed, he fantasized about murdering Brown.

Chapter 19

While the narrator was cubbing on the *Pennsylvania*, his brother Henry (Henry Clemens) was a mud clerk on the boat. One day Henry relayed the captain's instruction to make a certain stop to the partly deaf Brown, who ignored him. When Captain KLINEFELTER asked Brown why he failed to stop, Brown said that Henry had not given him the message. After the captain left, Brown moved to strike Henry, but the cub knocked him down with a stool and pummeled him. Meanwhile, the steamboat plowed down the river with no one at the wheel. Brown finally seized the wheel and ordered the cub out, but the cub stayed to unload pent-up verbal abuse on him. When the cub went to account for himself before the captain, he figured that his piloting career was finished and that a prison term might even await him; however, the captain laughed at the thought of Brown's being beaten and advised the cub to lay for him ashore. When Brown demanded that either the cub went or he would leave, the captain invited *him* to leave.

Chapter 20
During a layover in New Orleans, Klinefelter could not find a pilot to replace Brown, so he asked the cub to stand daylight watches, while Ealer took the night watches. The narrator felt unready for that responsibility, so Brown piloted the *Pennsylvania* upriver while the narrator followed two days later as a passenger on the ALFRED T. LACEY. When the *Lacey* reached Greenville, Mississippi, he learned that the *Pennsylvania* had exploded near MEMPHIS, Tennessee. At Memphis, he learned that at least 150 people had died; Henry was fatally injured and Brown had disappeared, but Klinefelter and Ealer were unhurt.

Chapter 21
A half-page summary of the narrator's life over the next 23 years recalls how he got his piloting license only to have his career interrupted by the Civil War. He then became a silver miner and reporter in NEVADA, a gold miner and reporter in CALIFORNIA, a special correspondent to HAWAII, a roving correspondent in Europe, a LECTURER, and finally, "a scribbler of books, and an immovable fixture among the other rocks of New England."

Chapter 22
After 21 years away from working on the Mississippi, the narrator wants to see it again. He enlists "a poet (James R. OSGOOD) for company and a stenographer (Roswell H. PHELPS)." To avoid attracting attention, he adopts aliases, but has trouble remembering them. The travelers go by train to St. Louis, which the narrator compares with the smaller city that he knew two decades earlier. Dismayed by the virtual disappearance of steamboats from the wharves, he reflects on what a strangely short life the steamboat trade has had.

Chapter 23
The travelers want to go downriver stopping at each interesting town, but the infrequency of steamboat departures makes this impractical. After inspecting a filthy packet, they decide to take the GOLD DUST, a well-maintained VICKSBURG packet. The night the *Gold Dust* leaves port, the narrator begins discovering startling technological changes on steamboats—such as electric floodlights. He also soon learns how much the river has changed its shape.

Chapter 24
The first night out, the narrator visits the pilot house. Not recognizing the man at the wheel, he sits down to observe quietly. When he eventually asks about a new piece of equipment, the pilot offers to explain every-

thing and reels off a "tranquil pool of lies." He reaches his finest form when he calls a passing coal-shuttle an "alligator boat," explaining that "alligator reefs" were once the river's most serious hazard. As he talks, he drops his own name, "Robert STYLES"—whom the narrator recognizes as a former fellow cub. After telling another alligator yarn, Styles begins an anecdote about Captain Tom Ballou of the *Cyclone*, but the narrator interrupts to point out contradictions. Finally, Styles addresses his visitor by his name and suggests that *he* take the wheel, claiming that he recognized him immediately.

Chapter 25
As the *Gold Dust* continues toward Cairo, the narrator comments on sights along the river, such as Cape Girardeau, Missouri. The steamboat's second mate, Uncle MUMFORD, fills in details for him. Mumford recalls how the old *Paul Jones* sank nearby. About 200 steamboat wrecks are scattered over the 200 miles separating St. Louis from Cairo. The narrator recognizes many changes in the river and compares modern Cairo with the town that Charles DICKENS described 40 years earlier. By the end of the chapter, the boat is nearing Hickman, Kentucky.

Chapter 26
The narrator and his companions discuss the Civil War. A *Gold Dust* pilot who served in the Confederate river fleet recounts how scared he was when his boat got caught in middle of the Battle of Belmont (November 7, 1861)—U. S. GRANT's first battle. A passenger tells the narrator about a terrible feud in this region between the Darnells and the Watsons years earlier. As the boat approaches New Madrid, Missouri, the narrator describes changes along the KENTUCKY shores, as well as the effects of the current floodwater.

Chapter 27
Near New Madrid, the narrator describes the flood conditions. He also comments on the many foreigners who have written about the river and quotes from books by Basil Hall, Frances Trollope, Charles Augustus Murray, Frederick MARRYAT and Alexander Mackay.

Chapter 28
Further down the Mississippi, the narrator sees a steamboat at the mouth of Kentucky's Obion River that is named for him (presumably the "MARK TWAIN"). The romance has been knocked out of the river by such things as beacon lights, efficient snag removal, floodlights, and scientific charts developed by Bixby and Ritchie. Worse, the Anchor Line has raised captains above pilots and decreed that pilots must always be at their posts, even when their boats are tied up.

The United States River Commission works to control the river with dams and dikes. Reshaping the river is a hot topic of debate along the Lower Mississippi. The narrator and Uncle Mumford doubt strongly that the Mississippi can be tamed; however, the narrator recognizes the value of improving navigation. He cites the example of a single towboat taking two weeks to move 32 bargeloads of coal—an amount that 1,800 railroad cars would need an entire summer to move.

Chapter 29
The *Gold Dust* passes Fort Pillow, Tennessee—the site of the worst massacre in American history (after the Union's Fort Pillow surrendered on April 12, 1864, Confederate troops killed several hundred prisoners, most of whom were black). The narrator notes further changes in the river as the boat approaches Memphis. Half the chapter contains a long extract on the river pirate John MURRELL from a now forgotten book (by Marryat). The chapter concludes with a brief description of a stopover in Memphis.

Chapter 30
After leaving Memphis, the boat passes the site of the *Pennsylvania's* wreck, entering a region in which many itinerant black workers move between jobs by steamboat. The narrator then recalls an incident that occurred shortly after he left St. Louis. A young passenger from Wisconsin approached him; he claimed to have learned all about the steamboat and insisted on explaining everything. After the man unloaded his cargo of lies, the narrator spotted him laughing. The narrator has the last laugh, when he is alone at the wheel at a moment when the young prankster looks into the pilot house and recognizes him.

The narrator has himself called early each morning in order to watch the incomparable river sunrises. The boat makes a short stop at Helena.

Chapter 31
As they near Napoleon, Arkansas, the narrator wants to get off the boat to perform an important errand, but his companions want to stay aboard. He explains his errand by relating "A Dying Man's Confession," the story of Karl RITTER, who told him where he had hidden $10,000 in the wall of a building in Napoleon. The narrator wants to recover the money and send it to the German son of a man whom Ritter mistakenly killed.

Chapter 32
Ritter's story stuns THOMPSON AND ROGERS, who protest sending that much money to a simple German shoemaker. All three men agree that $10,000 would hurt the German, so they decide to send him just $5,000. As their discussion heats up, they work the figure down to $500. Finally, they decide that instead of money, they will send the shoemaker a "chromo." When the narrator discovers that his companions expect to split the $10,000 with him, they get into a fight. When he finally tells Captain McCord that he wants to go ashore at Napoleon, the captain is amazed. Uncle Mumford explains that a flood washed Napoleon away completely.

Chapter 33
Examples are given of the strange things that the river does to islands as it cuts and shifts. The town of Napo-

leon may be gone, but its old rival Greenville is flourishing. The Calhoun Land Co. is a new scheme to grow cotton in Chicot, Arkansas, which promises to treat black workers fairly.

Chapter 34
At Lake Providence, Louisiana, an ARKANSAS passenger named "Mr. H." (Harvey) claims that his state has been held back because of exaggerated accounts of its mosquitoes, which are actually small and diffident. He and a companion claim that the really tough mosquitoes are to be found in LOUISIANA's Lake Providence.

Chapter 35
The packet reaches Vicksburg, Mississippi, which suffered greatly during a long siege in the Civil War. Details of the terrible conditions during the war are given and the city's postwar recovery is described.

Chapter 36
The previous chapter ended by introducing this chapter as "THE PROFESSOR'S YARN," which is narrated by a college professor who went to California years earlier. Aboard his ship, he befriended John Backus, an Ohio cattleman carrying his life savings in gold to California to take up ranching. As the ship neared SAN FRANCISCO, Backus got drawn into a card game with professional gamblers and wagered his entire fortune on one hand. The professor thought that Backus was ruined, but Backus triumphed as the ship entered the Golden Gate and he turned out to be a professional gambler himself.

This chapter ends with the travelers leaving the *Gold Dust.*

Chapter 37
While writing these chapters much later, the narrator learns that the *Gold Dust* has blown up near Hickman, Kentucky (August 7, 1882), killing 17 people and scalding dozens. The captain and other crew members recovered from their injuries, but the pilot Lem Gray ("Robert Styles") died.

Chapter 38
Aboard a Cincinnati–New Orleans boat (the *Charles Morgan*), the travelers continue their journey south. Decades earlier, Dickens declined to call Mississippi steamboats either "magnificent" or "floating palaces," but the narrator suggests they *were* magnificent to most passengers—who never saw anything approaching their opulence ashore. To make his point, he describes the "house beautiful"—the typical finest home in every river town between St. Louis and New Orleans. Each house has the same white fence, grassy yard, parlor furnishings and decor, with certain books and certain patriotic and sentimental pictures. Against such dreary finery, even a town's principal citizens would think steamboats magnificent.

Chapter 39
Near Vicksburg the river has straightened itself out, leaving the old river port of Delta inland. The narrator

describes Natchez, Mississippi, which is divided into a prosperous hilltop section and a rowdy, depressed lowland, and quotes Frances Trollope on its charms. A striking change in Natchez is its development into a railroad center and manufacturing stronghold, with a modern ice factory and a yarn mill.

In an overheard conversation, two "drummers" (traveling salesmen) discuss oleomargarine and the versatility of cottonseed oil. The chapter ends as the boat passes Port Hudson, Louisiana.

Chapter 40
At Baton Rouge, the travelers arrive in the "absolute South." From here to New Orleans is a pilot's paradise— wide, deep water without snags or other perils. The state capitol building is modeled on a medieval castle— a subject that opens the narrator's attack on Sir Walter SCOTT, whom he charges with having had a debilitating influence on the South. The chapter ends with a description of the region between Baton Rouge and New Orleans that includes quotations from Frances Trollope and Basil Hall.

Chapter 41
At New Orleans the narrator finds that the city has grown since his last visit, but has not changed fundamentally—except in being cleaner and healthier and having better newspapers. Aside from cemeteries, the city has no real public architecture, but does have attractive domestic architecture.

Chapter 42
A description of above-ground vaults in New Orleans cemeteries spurs an argument on cremation as a hygienic and economic alternative to burial.

Chapter 43
A New Orleans undertaker who has found undertaking to be the dead-surest business in Christendom points out that one thing that is never cheap is a coffin. Contrary to popular belief, undertakers do not prosper during epidemics—since people rush to bury bodies and cut back on profitable extras, such as embalming and ice. The narrator recalls that when he expressed his own wish to be cremated to his pastor (presumably Joseph TWICHELL), the man told him, "I shouldn't worry about that, if I had your chances."

Chapter 44
G. W. CABLE leads the travelers on a tour of New Orleans, beginning with the French Quarter. Other sights include the filthy old St. Louis Hotel, which is now a municipal office building; a women's broom brigade; and the West End—where they eat pompano.

Chapter 45
A rambling discussion of the Civil War and Southern sports pays particular attention to a cockfight and a mule race. The war is such a dominant topic of conversation in the South that it is what "A.D." is elsewhere— they date from it. Although New Orleans newspaper editors are strong and direct, their reporters tend to be gushy and romantic. They become unsettled when they write about women.

Chapter 46
The travelers have missed Mardi Gras, but the narrator recalls seeing one 24 years earlier. Because the soul of such a festival is romantic, it could not exist in the North. The South, however, is afflicted by the "Walter Scott disease." While CERVANTES's *Don Quixote* swept away admiration for the silliness of medieval chivalry, Scott restored it. Scott had so large a hand in molding the South's prewar character that he is, in great measure, responsible for the war.

Chapter 47
Joel Chandler HARRIS meets the travelers in New Orleans. They all gather at G. W. Cable's house, where Harris proves too shy to read aloud from his own work. Cable's problems in giving fictional characters unusual French names that turn out to be used by real people reminds the narrator of the problem that he and C. D. WARNER had with the name "Eschol Sellers," which they changed to (Colonel) "Mulberry" SELLERS.

Chapter 48
The narrator encounters Horace Bixby on a New Orleans street. Now the captain of the new CITY OF BATON ROUGE, Bixby has scarcely changed in 21 years. The travelers join him on a harbor trip. Discussions with veteran steamboatmen tell the narrator what has become of some "former river friends." One pilot became a spiritualist and was bilked for years by a New York medium named Manchester, whom the narrator once visited with a friend.

Chapter 49
Most former pilots have become farmers. The narrator recalls piloting under Captain (J. Ed) MONTGOMERY on the *Crescent City* (actually the CITY OF MEMPHIS), which he once allowed to crash when Montgomery failed to give orders to stop the boat. Anecdotes about heroic pilots include the story of a man who died at the wheel while steering his burning boat to shore. There is no example in the history of Mississippi piloting of a pilot leaving his post to save his own life while he still had a chance to save others.

The chapter concludes with the story of "George Johnson" (Samuel Adams BOWEN Jr.), a steamboat clerk whose greed and foolishness got him drawn into an unwanted marriage.

Chapter 50
Conversations with other steamboatmen recall the name of Captain Isaiah SELLERS, whom the narrator once pilloried in a newspaper sketch. It was from Sellers that he appropriated his pen name "MARK TWAIN."

Chapter 51
As Bixby's *City of Baton Rouge* leaves New Orleans, the narrator vicariously relives his first experience as a cub

when he observes an apprentice steering under Bixby's watchful eye. The boat reaches Natchez in just 22½ hours. Along the way, George Ritchie runs a half dozen difficult crossings in the fog, using a chart that he and Bixby devised. When they land at St. Louis, the narrator regrets how quickly the delightful trip has passed. He recalls an apprentice blacksmith he knew as a child who was so stagestruck after seeing two Englishmen perform the swordfight scene from RICHARD III that he ran off to St. Louis to become an actor and spent the rest of his life performing bit parts.

A chance meeting with an old acquaintance recalls an experience the narrator had in St. Louis nearly 30 years earlier. During a period of civil unrest, he joined a volunteer militia to quell riots. As his unit marched into action, he handed his gun to this acquaintance so that he could step out to get something to drink. He never returned.

Chapter 52
Under the chapter title "A Burning Brand," the narrator remembers wanting to find a St. Louis grain-merchant named Brown. Nine years earlier his clergyman read a letter from an ex-convict named "Jack Hunt" to a prisoner named "Charlie WILLIAMS." Hunt's letter—printed here—tells the heartrending story of struggling to go straight, and of his good fortune in winning the trust of Brown, who gave him a job. Hunt owed everything to what he had learned from Williams while in prison. His letter was read from many pulpits, causing a sensation. The narrator was about to write an article about it, when C. D. Warner questioned its genuineness. Investigation proved that Williams had faked the letter, hoping that it would win his release.

Chapter 53
A fast boat (the *Gem City*) takes the narrator to Hannibal—his first real visit to his boyhood home since 1853. He enters the town on a quiet Sunday morning, remembering it as it was three decades earlier. As he climbs Holliday's Hill (CARDIFF HILL) to look over the rooftops, he has the dreamy feeling of still being a boy. He asks an old man, who came to Hannibal a year after he left, about people he once knew. A man long regarded as a perfect chucklehead (Samuel Taylor GLOVER?) went to St. Louis and became a great lawyer. A woman who had been scared out of her wits (an incident Mark Twain fictionalizes in "DOUGHFACE") died insane 36 years later.

When the narrator mentions his own name, the stranger candidly calls him "another d—d fool" who surprised everyone by succeeding. He is glad that he introduced himself as "Smith."

Chapter 54
From atop Holliday's Hill, the narrator gazes at houses and remembers families from his youth. One family had a son named Lem HACKETT (Clint Levering) who drowned as a child. Village boys saw Lem's death as punishment for his sins, but were thrown into confusion

three weeks later when a "MODEL BOY" named "DUTCHY" drowned. The narrator descends the hill passing his BOYHOOD HOME and is corralled into speaking to a Sunday-school group.

Chapter 55
During his three days in Hannibal, the narrator discovers that many old acquaintances—especially women—have changed considerably. He recalls a saddler named John Stavely who never met a passenger or collected a cargo, but greeted every steamboat arrival so enthusiastically that outsiders dubbed the town "Stavely's Landing." He also recalls a childhood hero—a carpenter who claimed to have murdered 60 people, earning the nickname the "MYSTERIOUS AVENGER."

Now a "city" with 15,000 people, Hannibal has a mayor and even a waterworks. BEAR CREEK has nearly disappeared. The CAVE below the town is mentioned in an anecdote.

Chapter 56
When the narrator was 10, he once gave matches to Jimmy FINN, a town drunk. The same day, Finn went to jail, where he used the matches to set fire to his cell and was burned to death before he could be freed. As a child, the narrator agonized over murdering Finn and feared that his brother would hear him confess in his sleep.

Chapter 57
As the journey continues north (aboard the *Minneapolis*), the narrator praises industrious communities such as Quincy, Illinois and KEOKUK, Iowa—whose "erratic genius," Henry Clay DEAN, delivered a stunning speech in 1861. The narrator also comments on MARION CITY, Missouri, and on IOWA's MUSCATINE and Burlington.

Chapter 58
As the voyage continues upriver, towns such as Davenport, Iowa and Rock Island, Illinois are described, and economic statistics on the region are given. Particularly impressive is the rapid growth of St. Paul and Minneapolis in Minnesota. There are also comments on local Indian legends and on the devastating impact that railroads have had on steamboat commerce. The chapter ends as the boat passes Prairie du Chien, Wisconsin.

Chapter 59
Among the passengers who board at La Crosse, Wisconsin is one of the region's early settlers. He rattles off colorful stories about Indian legends. The tale of Winona and Maiden's Rock is one of many stories along the river about an Indian maiden throwing herself from a LOVER'S LEAP. The chapter concludes with the legend of "Peboan and Seegwun," taken from a book by Henry Rowe Schoolcraft (1793–1864).

Chapter 60
The journey ends at St. Paul, 2,000 miles from New Orleans. Local snowfall moves the narrator to deride tired newspaper banalities about differences between

Northern and Southern weather. St. Paul's history includes a legend about the original postmaster, who took the first letter his office received to Washington, D.C. to ask what should be done with it. The chapter concludes with an idiotic Indian legend about White-Bear Lake, whose inconsistencies the narrator derides.

Appendixes

Appendix "A," which pertains to chapter 26, is an article from the March 29, 1882 *New Orleans Times-Democrat* about a relief boat the newspaper sent to help flood victims. Appendix "B" is an article by Edward Atkinson (1827–1905) on Mississippi River improvements. Appendix "C" is a defense by Frances Trollope of Basil Hall's book on America. Appendix "D" is Henry Rowe Schoolcraft's version of the Indian legend about the "Undying Head."

BACKGROUND AND PUBLISHING HISTORY

Mark Twain began thinking about writing a book on the Mississippi at least as early as 1866. When he visited the Midwest in early 1872, he was struck by the great diminution of steamboat traffic on the OHIO RIVER and became anxious to document the steamboat era before it vanished altogether. It was, however, only after W. D. HOWELLS pushed him to contribute something to the ATLANTIC MONTHLY in late 1874 that he finally acted. With the additional prodding of Joseph TWICHELL, he started writing about piloting on the Mississippi. The result was "OLD TIMES ON THE MISSISSIPPI," a serial published in the *Atlantic* in 1875.

After using the "Old Times" articles to reveal the little-known profession of piloting, Mark Twain set aside the idea of a more general book about the Mississippi and turned his attention to other projects. Before returning to his Mississippi book seven years later, he would complete *Tom Sawyer, A Tramp Abroad* and *The Prince and the Pauper* and begin *Huckleberry Finn*—a novel whose genesis owed much to his writing of *Life on the Mississippi*. He did not want to pursue the Mississippi book project until he found a friend—preferably Howells—to accompany him on a return trip to the river. Howells professed interest as late as mid-1881, but he could not make time for such a trip. By the end of the year, however, Mark Twain's new publisher, James R. OSGOOD, agreed to go; Osgood also arranged for Roswell H. PHELPS to come along as Mark Twain's stenographer. Osgood and Phelps would become *Life on the Mississippi*'s "poet" and "stenographer"—THOMPSON AND ROGERS.

On April 10, 1882, Mark Twain signed with Osgood to publish his book; his unusual contract effectively made him the publisher and Osgood his agent and distributor. A week later, he, Osgood and Phelps went overland from New York City to St. Louis, where they boarded the steamboat GOLD DUST to go downriver. Mark Twain began traveling under an alias, "C. L. Samuel," but was recognized almost immediately and gave it up. In Vicksburg the travelers switched to a

boat to New Orleans, where they spent a week. They returned to St. Louis on Bixby's *City of Baton Rouge* and then used other boats to continue farther north. By the end of May, Mark Twain was back in Hartford, where he immediately settled down to write his book for Osgood.

One of the first things that he did was incorporate the "Old Times" articles, which he rounded out with three new chapters on his apprenticeship days. He wanted to write not about his piloting days, but about the Mississippi River itself; however, the "Old Times" pieces were too handy to pass up. His disdain for writing more about his years as a pilot is revealed in the single paragraph of chapter 22 that sums up his years as a licensed pilot and ends abruptly with the remark that "the war came, commerce was suspended, my occupation was gone."

From July through September, Mark Twain wrote new material while staying in ELMIRA, New York. He returned to Hartford with drafts of chapters 1–44, 50 and 54 and then spent the rest of the year finishing the book. Its completion proved far more difficult than he had expected. Although he had returned from the river with both his own notes and a set recorded by Phelps, he found that he had much less material than he needed. As his writing bogged down, he looked increasingly to other sources for material and drew heavily on books by such writers as Frances Trollope, Frederic MARRYAT and Basil Hall. Aside from appendixes, he incorporated about 11,000 words from other sources. He even worked in a portion of his unfinished *Huckleberry Finn* manuscript—the so-called "RAFT CHAPTER," as well as several chapters left over from *A Tramp Abroad*.

When it came time to select a title for the book, Mark Twain was inclined to use a variation of his previous travel titles—such as *Abroad on the Great River, Abroad on the Father of Waters* or *Abroad on the Mississippi*. After he settled on "Life on the Mississippi," Osgood published his book on May 17, 1883—one year to the day after he left Hannibal. CHATTO and Windus soon followed with an English edition. Since then, *Life on the Mississippi* has remained in print almost continuously, with little alteration in its original text. The first edition has about 310 original illustrations drawn by Edmund H. GARRETT, John HARLEY and A. B. Shute.

After he had struggled mightily to flesh out his book, Mark Twain found that his manuscript was much longer than it needed to be, so he invited Osgood and his editors to cut whatever they wanted. As a result, more than 15,000 words were deleted. Most cuts were made to conserve space, but Osgood omitted one chapter to avoid offending Southerners. This chapter—which would have been "48" if it had been retained—criticized Southern laws and regional chauvinism, portrayed Southerners as lacking independent thought, and attacked the cowardice of mobs. Thirty years later, the chapter was published as a four-page pamphlet titled *The Suppressed Chapter of "Life on the Mississippi."*

Other substantial deletions included two whole chapters on foreign travel writers, and substantial passages on the siege of VICKSBURG, government corruption, DUELING and other subjects. Most of the deleted material would have added little that was fresh to the book; however, a wild tale about a balloon voyage into a "dead-air belt" was also among the casualties. Fortunately, Mark Twain's original manuscript has been preserved, in New York's J. Pierpont MORGAN Library. Most of the omitted passages were finally published in an edition of *Life on the Mississippi* issued in 1944 by the Limited Editions Club and Heritage Press. The restored passages in this edition appear in appendixes, keyed to the chapters or pages from which they were removed. The Penguin American Library later reissued this edition, adding a previously unpublished chapter on Hannibal.

According to Howells, Mark Twain regarded *Life on the Mississippi* as his greatest book. His regard for it is attested to by the fact that it is the only book that he attempted to rewrite after publication. He began revising it in May 1908, but never finished the task.

***Life on the Mississippi*, dramatizations of** Material from *Life on the Mississippi* (1883) was loosely adapted into the 1944 film THE ADVENTURES OF MARK TWAIN, in which Jackie Brown played Sam Clemens as an adolescent and Fredric March played him as an adult. In November 1980, the Public Broadcasting System aired a television dramatization titled *Life on the Mississippi* that was based mostly on the book's early chapters. David Knell played the young cub, Sam, with Robert Lansing as his mentor, Mr. Bixby. The script simplifies the narrative by confining the action to two steamboats, the PAUL JONES and the ALECK SCOTT (one stern-wheeler evidently portrayed both). Its many liberties include placing Captain KLINEFELTER and William BROWN on the *Scott* and having the *Jones* blow up, killing George RITCHIE. The production concludes with Bixby reciting Mark Twain's own famous remark about growing up with the "one permanent ambition" of becoming a steamboatman—a surprising ambition for a boy (Bixby) raised in Geneseo, New York.

Lincoln, Abraham (February 11, 1809, Hardin County, Kentucky–April 15, 1865, Washington, D.C.) Sixteenth president of the United States (1861–65). Though Mark Twain was away from the eastern United States through most of Lincoln's presidency, Lincoln's impact on his life was profound. When Lincoln was inaugurated in March 1861, Mark Twain was renewing his license as a steamboat PILOT, expecting a long career on the Mississippi River. Lincoln's election, however, provided the final stimulus to the CIVIL WAR, which erupted a month later. By the end of April, Mark Twain's piloting career was over. Meanwhile, Lincoln followed the advice of Attorney General Edward BATES by naming Mark Twain's brother, Orion Clemens, secretary of NEVADA's new territorial government. Just three months after leaving the river, Mark Twain was on his way to Nevada with Orion.

Another Lincoln decision that affected Mark Twain's life was to push for early Nevada statehood in order to increase the number of Republican-controlled states. On March 21, 1864, Lincoln signed the enabling act to admit Nevada to the Union. Two months later, Mark Twain left Nevada, partly because he expected statehood to depress its mining industry. During Lincoln's 1864 reelection bid, Mark Twain covered the local campaign for the SAN FRANCISCO CALL, which supported Lincoln, until he left the paper in October. Lincoln was reelected in November, while Orion Clemens saw his chances for a Nevada political career disappear in the first state elections.

References to Lincoln in Mark Twain's books are rare. *Roughing It* mentions Lincoln just once—when he appointed James W. NYE governor of Nevada (chapter 25). *The Gilded Age* describes a statue of Lincoln in Washington, D.C. (chapter 24). Mark Twain also left few recorded opinions of Lincoln. His NOTEBOOKS show that he greatly admired the language of the "Gettysburg Address" and that he evidently wanted to find something written by Lincoln to include in MARK TWAIN's LIBRARY OF HUMOR. At a Lincoln birthday celebration in New York's Carnegie Hall in 1901, he praised Lincoln not only for emancipating black slaves, but for setting white men free. His AUTOBIOGRAPHY names Lincoln among the geniuses "discovered" by the Civil War. His best-known connection with Lincoln, however, is found in W. D. HOWELLS's tribute in *My Mark Twain* (1910), which calls Mark Twain "the Lincoln of our literature."

Literary Essays (In Defense of Harriet Shelley and Other Essays) Collection of previously published essays. Harper's first issued the volume in 1899 and later included it in all its uniform Mark Twain editions. It contains "IN DEFENSE OF HARRIET SHELLEY" (1894), "Fenimore COOPER's Literary Offenses" (1895), "TRAVELING WITH A REFORMER" (1893), "Private History of the JUMPING FROG STORY" (1894), "Mental Telegraphy" (1891), "Mental Telegraphy Again" (1895), "What Paul BOURGET Thinks of Us" (1895), "A Little Note to M. Paul Bourget" (1896), "THE INVALID'S STORY" (1882), "Stirring Times in Austria" (1898), "The German Chicago [BERLIN]" (1892), "Concerning the Jews" (1899), "About All Kinds of Ships" (1893), "FROM THE 'LONDON TIMES' OF 1904" (1898), "A MAJESTIC LITERARY FOSSIL" (1890), "At the Appetite Cure" (1898), "Saint JOAN OF ARC" (1904), a memorial poem to Susy Clemens (1897) and a biographical sketch by Mark Twain's nephew Samuel E. Moffett. Seven of the first eight items were also in the earlier Harper's anthology, *How to Tell a Story and Other Essays* (1897). In 1900, the AMERICAN PUBLISHING COMPANY issued its own edition of *How to Tell a Story and Other Essays*, which is almost identical to *Literary Essays*.

Livin' the Life Off-Broadway musical based on Mark Twain's Mississippi writings, with particular emphasis on *Tom Sawyer*. With book and lyrics by Dale Wasserman and Bruce Geller, the play had 25 performances at the Phoenix Theatre in April–May 1957. Alice Ghostley played Aunt POLLY.

Lize Minor character in *Huckleberry Finn*. A household slave of the PHELPSES, Lize is the first person Huck sees when he reaches the Phelps plantation in chapter 32. 'Lizabeth is the name of Jim's daughter, who is described in chapter 23.

Loftus, Mrs. Judith Character in *Huckleberry Finn*. Mrs. Loftus and her husband have recently settled in a long-unoccupied "shanty" near ST. PETERSBURG. At the end of chapter 10, Huck visits the town disguised as a girl, hoping to gather some news. When he sees Loftus knitting through her parlor window, he calculates that as a newcomer to town, she would not know him, but should know the latest gossip. In the next chapter, the woman invites Huck in. He introduces himself as Sarah Mary WILLIAMS. In one of the novel's most famous scenes, Loftus uses several ruses to get Huck to reveal that he is a boy. These include tossing an object on his lap—that he catches with his knees—as a boy would, instead of with his dress, as a girl would. Mark Twain evidently borrowed this "lap-test" from chapter 63 of Charles Reade's *The Cloister and the Hearth* (1861).

Mrs. Loftus finally gets Huck to confess that he is a boy, but does not totally accept his revised alias of "George PETERS." Even so, she provides him with a snack before he leaves and tells him to send word if he needs help.

This meeting is significant in two ways. It tests Huck's ability to think quickly under pressure and it provides Huck with crucial information. He learns from Mrs. Loftus that the townspeople think that Jim is his murderer. He also learns that her husband intends to hunt for Jim on JACKSON'S ISLAND that same night, so he rushes back to the island in order to flee with Jim.

Mrs. Loftus is about 40 years old in the novel, but her most famous screen portrayer, Lilian Gish, was 90 when she played her in the 1986 PBS adaptation of *Huckleberry Finn*.

London Capital of Great Britain. During most of the three-plus years that Mark Twain spent in ENGLAND he was in London—including two periods of residence of about a year each. He first visited the city in late 1872; he returned for long visits twice in 1873–74 and for short visits in 1879, 1894 and 1895. After completing his world LECTURE tour in July 1896, he stayed in GUILDFORD until October, then rented a house at 23 Tedworth Square in London's Chelsea district, near the River THAMES. Over the next ten months, he worked on *Following the Equator*. It was during this period that he

advised a journalist who called on him to describe reports of his death as "exaggerated." After finishing his book, he took his family to SWITZERLAND in July 1897. Two years later, he returned to London and rented an apartment at 30 Wellington Court in Knightsbridge. In July 1900, he relocated to DOLLIS HILL for three months. Through this period he often spoke at banquets and public meetings and met many cultural figures. He last visited London in 1907, when he returned to England to accept an honorary degree from OXFORD UNIVERSITY.

Mark Twain wrote two novels and several short stories with important London settings. *The Prince and the Pauper* (1881) is set mostly within London shortly after the death of King HENRY VIII in 1547. It includes scenes in such historic sites as WESTMINSTER, GUILDHALL and LONDON BRIDGE, as well as the fictional OFFAL COURT. In *Connecticut Yankee* (1889), which is set in sixth-century Arthurian England, King Arthur and Hank MORGAN are pressed into a slave caravan and taken to London, where knights from CAMELOT rescue them (chapters 35–38). London was founded well before the sixth century, but the novel anachronistically refers to the Tower of London, which was not begun until the 11th century (chapters 7 and 42). "THE DEATH DISK" (1901) is set in mid–17th-century London, and "THE £1,000,000 BANK-NOTE" (1893) is set almost entirely within contemporary London.

Mark Twain's remarks about London in his other published writings are comparatively scarce. *Huckleberry Finn* contains many allusions to London theaters (chapters 20–23). *A Tramp Abroad* contains several allusions to his time in London (18, 24 and 47), as do *Following the Equator* (chapters 10, 15, 20 and 59) and his AUTOBIOGRAPHY.

London Bridge LONDON's oldest bridge goes back to Roman times. The name properly applies to the *location*—not a specific structure—where the City of London is joined with Southwark. It was the city's only bridge across the River THAMES until 1750. A stone span built in the late 12th century figures prominently in *The Prince and the Pauper*. During the 16th century, this bridge was a village unto itself, crowded with shops and houses; its history and teeming life are described in chapter 12 of the novel. Tom CANTY's family lives several hundred yards from the bridge's north end, off PUDDING LANE. When Tom's father, John CANTY, flees justice in chapter 10, he tells his family to meet on the bridge—a rendezvous apparently not kept. Meanwhile, Prince EDWARD escapes from Canty's grasp when the latter is accosted by drunken revelers on the bridge. In the next chapter, Edward returns to the bridge with Miles HENDON, who has a room in one of its inns. After Canty confronts Hendon at the inn, he sends a boy named HUGO to fetch the prince away while Hendon is away shopping the next morning. When Edward and Hendon return about two weeks later, they get separated by a drunken crowd while recrossing the bridge (chapter 29).

In the mid-18th century, London Bridge's wooden buildings were removed; the bridge itself was replaced by another stone structure in 1831. This bridge was dismantled and moved to Arizona's Lake Havasu in the early 1970s.

Longfellow, Henry Wadsworth (February 27, 1807, Portland, Maine–March 24, 1882, Cambridge, Massachusetts) A revered American poet, Longfellow is known for metrically precise romantic works, including *Evangeline* (1847), *The Song of Hiawatha* (1855) and *The Courtship of Miles Standish* (1858). Mark Twain owned many of his books and read from them often.

When the *New York Times* interviewed Mark Twain on the occasion of Longfellow's 100th birthday in 1907, he recalled first meeting Longfellow around 1870, but no encounter stood out in his memory except the birthday banquet for WHITTIER in 1877. On that occasion, he delivered a speech burlesquing Longfellow, EMERSON and HOLMES as drunken ruffians, describing Longfellow himself as built like a prize-fighter with hair that looked like a wig made out of brushes. Thinking that he had offended the Boston literati horribly, Mark Twain formally apologized afterward; however, Longfellow assured him that no offense had been taken. They had a happier meeting at a breakfast honoring Holmes two years later.

Mark Twain's writings occasionally quote Longfellow. Chapter 42 of *Innocents Abroad,* for example, paraphrases the latter's "Psalm of Life." Other Longfellow poems are quoted in chapter 45 of *The Gilded Age* and chapter 28 of *Life on the Mississippi.*

Lorelei The subject of a modern German legend, the Lorelei is a rock cliff jutting into the Rhine River over a dangerous reef between Koblenz and Bingen. In 1801, the German poet Clemens Maria Brentano (1778–1842) published a ballad in an authentic folk idiom associating a woman named "Lore Lay" with the rock. Soon accepted as a genuine folk legend, his ballad was amplified in 1827 by Heinrich Heine (1797–1856), whose song *Die Lorelei* introduced the notion of a beautiful siren sitting atop the Lorelei, luring sailors to their death with her singing. Mark Twain first learned about the Lorelei in 1878 while sailing to Germany with Bayard TAYLOR, who sang Heine's song. *A Tramp Abroad* devotes chapter 16 to the song, including the original lyrics and score and a humorously bad English translation alongside Mark Twain's own translation of the GERMAN.

"The Lost Napoleon" Posthumously published essay. Around the eighth day of his RHONE RIVER boat trip in southern FRANCE in September 1891, Mark Twain spotted a mountain range whose profile resembled Napoleon Bonaparte lying on his back. After failing to note the range's precise location, he wrote this essay about a decade later, calling the vista the "lost Napoleon" because he forgot exactly where it was. He expresses confidence, however, that if his great discovery were found again and promoted, it would become a major tourist attraction.

A. B. PAINE found this essay among Mark Twain's unpublished papers and included it in EUROPE AND ELSEWHERE (1923), noting that in 1913 he himself found the lost range—east of the Rhone, visible from near the village of Beauchastel, a few miles south of Valence. Paine offers a fuller description and painting of the view in chapter 12 of *The Car That Went Abroad: Motoring Through the Golden Age* (1921).

Lothrop, Mister Figure mentioned in *Huckleberry Finn.* In chapter 28 Huck persuades Mary Jane WILKS to leave town to avoid inadvertently revealing that she knows the KING and DUKE to be frauds. She agrees to go to the home of Mr. Lothrop, about four miles inland. After she leaves, Huck tells her sisters that she has gone across the river to help tend Hanner PROCTOR.

Louis XVI (August 23, 1754, Versailles, France–January 21, 1793, Paris) King of FRANCE. Overthrown during the Revolution of 1789, Louis was later executed along with his wife, Marie Antoinette. In *Huckleberry Finn,* Huck tells Jim about Louis's beheading and mentions that his son, the DAUPHIN, was believed to have died in prison (chapter 14). Later, a con man claiming to be the missing dauphin boards their raft and becomes known as the KING (chapter 19). Still later, Tom Sawyer discusses Louis XVI's botched attempt to escape before his execution (chapters 39–40).

In *A Tramp Abroad,* Mark Twain discusses how Louis XVI's martyrdom has caused history to treat him kindly (chapter 26).

Louisiana Mark Twain first visited Louisiana in February 1857, as a passenger aboard the steamboat PAUL JONES. At New Orleans he signed on as an apprentice PILOT on the COLONEL CROSSMAN and he spent the next four years going between New Orleans and St. Louis, Missouri. Through this period he spent so much time in New Orleans during layovers that it might be fair to regard Louisiana as one of his homes.

Mark Twain was in Louisiana when it seceded from the Union on January 16, 1861 and he made his last visit to the state as a pilot in May of that year—a month after the CIVIL WAR began. The war's onset ended commercial steamboat traffic on the river; Mark Twain left piloting in mid-May, returning north on the NEBRASKA—possibly the last commercial steamboat out of Louisiana. The conquest of Louisiana was a prime Union objective during the war. As Union troops advanced from the north, Admiral David Farragut occupied New Orleans on April 25, 1862. Almost exactly two decades later, Mark Twain paid his last visit to

Louisiana, when he returned to the river to gather material for *Life on the Mississippi.* Chapters 34–50 of this work include a description of his week-long visit to the state.

Among Mark Twain's fictional works, *Huckleberry Finn* and *Pudd'nhead Wilson* both contain many references to New Orleans, but neither mentions Louisiana by name. Mark Twain seems, however, to have been thinking about the state when he created the fictional town of PIKESVILLE. Just before Huck and Jim reach Pikesville in chapter 31 of *Huckleberry Finn,* they "come to trees with Spanish moss on them, hanging down from the limbs like long gray beards." Chapter 34 of *Life on the Mississippi* describes entering Louisiana at Lake Providence, the "first distinctly Southern looking town you come to, downward bound . . . shade-trees hung with venerable gray beards of Spanish moss." Passages such as this make it appear that Louisiana—or a site across the river in Mississippi—could be the setting of the last chapters of *Huckleberry Finn.* Other evidence, however, indicates that Mark Twain meant to place Pikesville in southern Arkansas. In the short story "A CURIOUS EXPERIENCE," the narrator warmly recalls details of his experience in Louisiana before the Civil War.

Lover's Leap Natural landmark in Hannibal, Missouri. A rugged 225-foot-high precipice at the south end of central Hannibal, Lover's Leap stands a quarter mile west of the Mississippi River. It combines with CARDIFF HILL on the north side of town to frame a valley that opens to the river. *Life on the Mississippi* estimates that there must be 50 "Lover's Leaps" along the river from which lovesick Indian girls have jumped (chapter 59). Hannibal's own hill takes its name from a similar legend current during Mark Twain's youth; it was reputedly named by his brother, Orion Clemens. In October 1844, the hill was one of many sites throughout the eastern United States on which followers of William Miller (1782–1849) gathered to meet the end of the world—an event discussed in chapter 39 of *Innocents Abroad.*

Mark Twain's working notes for his unfinished novel "SCHOOLHOUSE HILL" indicate that he was considering a scene in which Tom and Huck perform a witches' Sabbath atop Lover's Leap.

"The Loves of Alonzo Fitz Clarence and Rosannah Ethelton" Story written in 1877 and published in the ATLANTIC MONTHLY in March 1878. A condensed novel in four chapters, "Loves" is about a couple who conduct their romance entirely through transcontinental telephone conversations—a form of long-distance communication that did not actually exist until 1915. Early action in this BURLESQUE love story is obscure, since the fact that the lovers are speaking by telephone is not clarified until the third chapter. They never meet face-to-face within the story.

SYNOPSIS

Chapter 1
On a winter day in Eastport, MAINE, Alonzo Fitz Clarence sits in his parlor. Uncertain about the time his clock is keeping, he tries getting the attention of a servant and his mother, then speaks to his Aunt Susan from his desk. When she tells him that the time is 9:05, he adjusts his clock to 12:35. As they talk, Alonzo hears a voice singing "The Sweet By-and-By" and is introduced to his aunt's ward, Rosannah Ethelton. Alonzo and Rosannah talk for two hours, after which Alonzo realizes that his heart is now in SAN FRANCISCO. Rosannah is equally smitten with Alonzo—compared to whom a man named (Sidney Algernon) Burley, whose sole talent is mimicry, suddenly seems shallow.

Chapter 2
Four weeks later, Burley calls on Rosannah to learn why she is avoiding him. He happens to overhear her talking to Alonzo and is distressed by her obvious affection for this rival suitor. When Burley overhears Alonzo's Eastport address, he leaves. Meanwhile, Alonzo's mother and Aunt Susan are thrilled to learn that Alonzo and Rosannah are betrothed; they dismiss the young couple and begin planning the wedding.

Chapter 3
Two weeks later, a man calling himself the Reverend Melton Hargrave of Cincinnati is visiting Alonzo regularly, claiming to have invented a device that prevents telephone eavesdropping; Alonzo is keen to have the device. On one of his visits, the man finds Alonzo's parlor vacant and hears "The Sweet By-and-By" coming from the telephone. Imitating Alonzo's voice, he interrupts Rosannah and asks her to sing something else. When Alonzo returns, the man hides. Rosannah angrily turns on the bewildered Alonzo and calls off their engagement. Alonzo leaves to find his mother so she can plead his case with Rosannah, giving the intruder the chance to seize the phone in his absence and reject Rosannah's attempt to retract her harsh words.

After Alonzo returns, he spends hours trying to reestablish contact with Rosannah. His Aunt Susan reports that Rosannah has packed and left. Alonzo is stunned, but when he finds a card on his floor with Burley's name, he guesses what his rival has done.

Chapter 4
For two months, Alonzo searches for Rosannah with a carpet-sack and portable telephone poles in the hope of hearing a signal carrying her voice. When his spirit and body are nearly broken, he is taken to a madhouse in New York. One March morning, he hears Rosannah's singing and finds a telephone, which he uses to tell her of Burley's trickery. The couple make up and agree to wed on April 1—giving Aunt Susan time to get from San Francisco to Honolulu, where

Rosannah now is. Burley happens to call on Rosannah as she is talking with Alonzo; she tells him that she will yield to his importunities on April 1—intending to repay him for his villainy.

On April 2, the *Honolulu Advertiser* carries a notice of Rosannah's marriage to Alonzo; similar notices appear in New York newspapers the same day. Later, Aunt Susan takes Rosannah across the continent to meet Alonzo for the first time. Burley, who has vowed revenge, dies while trying to do violence to a crippled artisan.

Lucerne City in central SWITZERLAND. Standing at the northwestern tip of the Lake of Lucerne, Lucerne has long attracted tourists who use it as a base for boat trips to admire the surrounding mountains. After Mark Twain toured southern Switzerland with Joseph TWICHELL, he joined his family at Lucerne on August 12, 1878 and stayed in its Schweitzerhof Hotel. Before moving on to INTERLAKEN on August 21, he visited nearby towns and ascended the RIGI-KULM. The region around Lucerne is the subject of chapters 25–31 of *A Tramp Abroad*. Chapter 26 discusses the town's "Lion of Lucerne," a monument that Danish sculptor A. B. Thorvaldsen (1770–1844) carved into a rock cliff in 1820–21. It commemorates the massacre of the Swiss Guard, who defended France's King LOUIS XVI in Paris in August 1792. Mark Twain revisited Lucerne in August 1897, when he wrote a poem to commemorate the first anniversary of his daughter Susy's death.

"Luck" Story first published in 1891. A FRAME-STORY, "Luck" opens as the narrator attends a LONDON banquet honoring one of Britain's most illustrious military heroes—a lieutenant general whom he assigns the fictitious name Lord Arthur Scoresby. Thirty years earlier, "Scoresby" won immortality at the CRIMEA. As the narrator admires this demigod's unassuming nobility, his clergyman friend mutters, "Privately—he's an absolute fool." His friend's honesty and judgment are beyond reproach, so the narrator burns to hear an explanation. The clergyman later relates how he was Scoresby's instructor at Woolwich 40 years earlier. The young cadet was "good, sweet and lovable," but a hopelessly ignorant dunce whom the clergyman tutored out of pity. Amazingly, Scoresby earned top marks in every examination; by pure luck, he was tested only in the few things he knew. The clergyman thought himself a Frankenstein for helping qualify this "wooden-head" for promotion.

When Scoresby became a captain in the Crimean War (1854–56), the clergyman joined his unit in order to keep an eye on him. Scoresby never did anything during the war but blunder; however, every blunder had such a good result that he was deemed a genius. As Scoresby's reputation grew, he gained greater responsibility and more potential for disaster. After he became a colonel, Scoresby's finest moment came when he routed an entire Russian army with his lone regiment. When the Russians saw his men advancing on their position, they assumed his regiment was the vanguard of the *entire* British army, since no regiment would be foolish enough to attack them alone. The Russians turned and were routed. Dizzy with astonishment and admiration, Marshal Canrobert (François Certain Canrobert, 1809–1895) decorated Scoresby on the spot. Scoresby's success arose from his not knowing his right hand from his left. Ordered to fall back to his *right*, he had mistakenly gone forward to his *left*. Every medal on his chest records some similar stupidity—proof that the best thing that can befall a man is to be born lucky.

Mark Twain initialed a footnote to the story claiming that he heard it from a clergyman who had been at Woolwich. He also claimed to have been told by two Englishmen that Scoresby was really Lord Garnet Joseph Wolseley (1833–1913), who lost an eye at Crimea and later became commander-in-chief of the British army.

Mark Twain wrote this 1,800-word story around early 1886—a date consistent with the narrator's allusion to Scoresby's being at Crimea 30 years earlier. Mark Twain evidently thought little of the story, as he set it aside until 1891. Feeling pressed for money that year, he sent it to HARPER'S MAGAZINE, which published it in its August issue. The following year the story was collected in MERRY TALES—all of which was later incorporated into *The American Claimant and Other Stories and Sketches*.

"Lucretia Smith's Soldier" Sketch first published in the CALIFORNIAN on December 3, 1864. Taking the form of a BURLESQUE condensed novel, this 1,800-word tale targets the sentimentalism of romantic war stories that were popular at the time. It opens with a pompous prefatory note, signed "M. T.," in which the author affirms that the story is true because its facts were compiled from official War Department records. He also acknowledges various sources of help and inspiration, including a local San Francisco beer.

In the first miniature chapter, it is May 1861. Reginald de Whittaker, a clerk in Bluemass, Massachusetts (a fictional place named after a pharmacological powder used to make blue pills), is anxious to tell his sweetheart, Lucretia SMITH, that he has enlisted in the army. In the next chapter, however, she turns him away before he can even speak. His newfound pride as a soldier prevents him from staying to explain. The next morning (chapter 3), Lucretia learns that Reginald has enlisted; she upbraids herself for treating him unfairly and then suffers silently for weeks while hoping for a letter from him. Finally, she sees a report from the war mentioning that "R. D. Whittaker, private soldier" is desperately wounded. In chapter 4, she goes to Washington to nurse Whittaker, whose head is completely wrapped in bandages. When doctors remove the dressings three weeks later, Lucretia angrily discovers that she has wasted her time on the wrong man.

A hit throughout the country, "Lucretia Smith's Soldier" was frequently reprinted—often without attribution. Its first appearance in book form was in THE CELEBRATED JUMPING FROG OF CALAVERAS COUNTY (1867), in which the prefatory paragraph is severely truncated.

Lyon, Isabel Van Kleek (1863–1958) Mark Twain's secretary. In November 1902, Lyon entered the Clemens family's service after working as a governess in the home of F. G. WHITMORE. She was hired as a secretary to Livy, but soon had wider duties as a general family assistant. After accompanying the family to ITALY, where Livy died in 1904, she became Mark Twain's private secretary, bookkeeper and household manager, as well as occasional nurse to his epileptic daughter Jean Clemens. A fawning admirer of Mark Twain, she also became a valued, if uncritical, commentator on his writing.

At the beginning of 1908, Lyon vacationed in BERMUDA with Mark Twain and Joseph TWICHELL. Afterward, she worked closely with architect J. M. HOWELLS to plan Mark Twain's new REDDING home and set up housekeeping. In November, Mark Twain gave Lyon and Ralph ASHCROFT power of attorney over his business affairs and later deeded Lyon a cottage on the estate, known as the "Lobster Pot." Despite Lyon's loyal service, Mark Twain's daughters distrusted her. Clara Clemens,

in particular, resented Lyon's assumption of many of her mother's former roles and feared that Lyon had marital designs on her father. In an apparent effort to defuse that fear, Lyon married Ashcroft in March 1909. Under Clara's prodding, Mark Twain began distrusting both of them. Convinced that Lyon was dishonest, he fired her in mid-April, evicted her from her cottage and turned her secretarial duties over to his daughter Jean. In September, he arranged a legal settlement that broke all his ties to Lyon and Ashcroft. Even after Lyon was out of the picture, Clara remained vindictive. She persuaded A. B. PAINE to expunge virtually all records of Lyon from his biography of Mark Twain, and she got Elizabeth Wallace to omit Lyon from her book about Mark Twain in Bermuda.

There is no evidence that Lyon ever abused her trust. Although she was poorly paid by Mark Twain and badly treated at the end of her service to him, she never spoke or acted against him or Clara. She later gave the detailed diary she had kept of her years with Mark Twain to the MARK TWAIN PAPERS project, with the condition that it not be opened to scholars until after Clara's death.

Lyon remained married to Ashcroft until the 1920s and later worked for a Brooklyn title insurance company until dying in her mid-90s.

M

McAleer, Patrick (1846, County Tyrone, Ireland–February 1906, Hartford, Connecticut) Mark Twain's coachman. McAleer came to America from Ireland at age 16 and went to work for Mark Twain in 1870, when Jervis LANGDON hired him to his new son-in-law's household staff in BUFFALO. McAleer stayed with the Clemens family until they went to Europe in 1891, living on their property in a detached coach-house. Meanwhile, he married and raised eight children of his own. He returned temporarily to Mark Twain's employ in 1905 at DUBLIN, New Hampshire. Mark Twain remembered McAleer fondly as a faultless employee and a gentleman.

McCarthy, Denis E. (February 22, 1840, Melbourne, Australia–1885) Nevada newspaperman. McCarthy began his career in SAN FRANCISCO, where he learned the printing trade at local newspapers and became a friend of Joe GOODMAN at the GOLDEN ERA. In early 1861, he and Goodman went to Nevada and bought into the impoverished VIRGINIA CITY TERRITORIAL ENTERPRISE. With Goodman directing the editorial department and McCarthy the print shop, the paper prospered. McCarthy and Goodman became the paper's sole owners in October 1863; two years later, McCarthy sold out to Goodman and returned to San Francisco. After losing his new fortune in stocks, he went back to Virginia City to run the *Enterprise* print shop—this time as an employee.

In the fall of 1866, McCarthy managed Mark Twain's lecture tour through northern California and western Nevada. When they reached Virginia City, several old friends played a joke on Mark Twain by holding up him and McCarthy at gunpoint. When Mark Twain learned that McCarthy was in on the joke, he fired him. *Roughing It*'s account of the incident calls McCarthy "Mike" (chapter 79).

McCarthy later made another fortune in mining stocks when Nevada boomed again, and used it to buy the Virginia City *Evening Chronicle* in 1875. This paper flourished for several years, only to decline along with the mining industry, driving McCarthy increasingly to alcohol before he died at 44.

Macfarlane (fl. 1856–57?) Around 1898, Mark Twain wrote a thousand-word portrait of a fellow CINCINNATI boardinghouse resident from four decades earlier named Macfarlane. This sketch, which A. B. PAINE later inserted in his edition of Mark Twain's AUTOBIOGRAPHY, is the only known record that Macfarlane existed. Mark Twain may have invented "Macfarlane" as a vehicle to express his own negative philosophy about mankind. He portrays Macfarlane as a humorless, self-educated Scot about 40 years old. Though he says that he conversed with Macfarlane in the latter's room every evening for half a year, he knew almost nothing about the man's life away from the boardinghouse.

Immensely proud of his mastery of the dictionary, Macfarlane also knew the Bible intimately. His conversation always dealt with heavy matters, such as concepts of human evolution similar to those later expressed by DARWIN. Macfarlane's views of mankind were essentially negative; he saw man as the only creature that felt malice, envy or hate, as well as the only creature that robbed, enslaved and killed its own kind. He also believed that man's intellect degraded him below other animals, as there was never a man who did not use his intellect solely to help himself at the expense of others. Similar ideas appear in many of Mark Twain's MAXIMS and in such writings as WHAT IS MAN?

McWilliams family Characters in three FRAME-STORIES published between 1875 and 1882. The stories are told by Mortimer McWilliams, a pleasant New York man with a wife and two children whom the frame narrator meets on what appears to be a commuter train. Each story details a crisis in McWilliams's household. Although McWilliams explicitly addresses "Mr. Twain" in two of the stories, the stories themselves reflect incidents in Mark Twain's own domestic life in Hartford. For example, his daughter Clara had croup as a baby, and his wife Livy greatly feared lightning. As a trilogy, the stories combine to form a subtle joke: the first two concern gross overreactions to false alarms; the third is about an elaborate alarm system that is ignored when real emergencies occur.

"McWilliams" was the name of a real family with whom Mark Twain boarded when he first lived in BUFFALO in 1869. He later used the name Sandy McWilliams for a character in "CAPTAIN STORMFIELD'S VISIT TO HEAVEN" (1909).

"Experience of the McWilliamses with Membranous Croup" (1875) relates how McWilliams got into a mild argument with his wife Caroline (called Evangeline in the next story) over her giving their baby Penelope a pine stick to chew. When McWilliams returned home that evening, his wife reported that a baby named Georgie Gordon had contracted the croup and had little hope of survival. When Penelope coughed, Mrs. McWilliams panicked and launched an extraordinary night of shifting sleeping arrangements around in order to watch over Penelope and protect their infant son (not named) from the croup. When a doctor finally came, he diagnosed Penelope's cough as due to pine slivers in her throat. Since then, McWilliams and his wife have never discussed the incident. The frame-narrator (not identified in this story) adds that readers might find McWilliams's experience an interesting novelty, since very few married men have similar experiences

This 2,440-word story first appeared in SKETCHES, NEW AND OLD (1875) and was reprinted in MARK TWAIN'S LIBRARY OF HUMOR (1888). *Connecticut Yankee* (1889) details the lengths to which Hank and Sandy Morgan go to protect their daughter HELLO-CENTRAL from membranous croup (chapter 40).

"Mrs. McWilliams and the Lightning" (1880) expands the BURLESQUE of exaggerated fear of lightning begun in "POLITICAL ECONOMY" (1870). During his train ride with the frame-narrator, Mr. Twain, McWilliams describes a night at their "summer establishment" (presumably Elmira) when Evangeline awakened him during a storm, demanding that he protect his family against lightning. Evangeline believed that during a lightning storm it is dangerous to lie in bed, stand near a window or a wall, open a door, sing a song or run water. She also thought that lighted matches, woolen clothes and open chimneys attract lightning; that it is vital to say one's prayers before a storm; and that cats are full of electricity. After struggling to decipher a GERMAN book, she made McWilliams stand on a chair set on glass tumblers, while wearing a metal fireman's helmet, saber, and spurs, and ringing a bell to ward off lightning. Passersby who shone a lantern through their window to learn what the racket was about revealed that what the McWilliamses thought was a storm was actually distant fireworks celebrating (President James) GARFIELD's nomination (June 8, 1880).

This 2,555-word story was first published in the ATLANTIC MONTHLY in September 1880 and was later collected in *The Stolen White Elephant, Etc.* and in *The American Claimant and Other Stories and Sketches*.

The final story, "The McWilliamses and the Burglar Alarm" (1882), is inspired by Mark Twain's experience with an unreliable electric alarm system in his own home. His AUTOBIOGRAPHY contains a passage written by his daughter Susy about this system. His autobiography also relates the problems of a neighbor, Francis Goodwin, with his burglar alarm. Many details, such as Goodwin's cook setting off the alarm early in the morning, closely match details in the McWilliams story. In contrast to the first two stories, the crises in "Burglar Alarm" are real and are partly due to McWilliams's own incompetence.

With money left over from building their house (which physically resembles Mark Twain's Hartford house), Mrs. McWilliams insisted on installing a burglar alarm. After a New York electrician installed a system on the house's first floor, McWilliams met a burglar who entered through the *second* floor. He had the system extended to the second floor, only to meet a burglar who entered through the third-floor BILLIARD room. After the system covered the entire house, the family and domestic staff were often confused about turning it on and off and they experienced a rash of false alarms. As McWilliams pumped ever more money into improving the system, burglars gradually cleaned out his house and then stole the burglar alarm itself. After nine years of suffering, McWilliams gave up.

This 2,350-word story first appeared in the 1882 Christmas issue of HARPER'S MAGAZINE. It was first collected in the posthumous *The Mysterious Stranger and Other Stories* (1922).

Maine Mark Twain first visited this New England state during brief lecture stops at Portland in December 1869 and November 1871. He apparently did not return to Maine again until August 1901, when he spoke at Bar Harbor. The following year, he spent the summer at YORK HARBOR with his family.

In 1877, Mark Twain wrote "THE LOVES OF ALONZO FITZ CLARENCE AND ROSANNAH ETHELTON," a short story in which the title characters conduct a telephone romance between San Francisco, California and Eastport, Maine—two of the most distantly separated cities in the continental United States.

"A Majestic Literary Fossil" Essay published in 1890. The literary relic to which the title alludes is *A Medicinal Dictionary* (which Mark Twain mistitles *Dictionary of Medicine*), published in 1743 by Robert James (1705–1776), a fashionable English physician later famous for his nostrums. He was a friend of Dr. Samuel Johnson, who contributed biographies to James's book.

Mixing quotes with his own commentary, Mark Twain shows how little the medical thinking in James's book differs from that of ancient times. Further, the book reflects the state of medical knowledge current during Mark Twain's youth—a time when the ancient Greek physician Galen could have practiced medicine proficiently. Over the next 50 years, however, medical thinking advanced so much that Galen would be hanged if he tried to practice. The dramatic change reflects a general revolution in intellectual thought made possible by the belated recognition that *new* ideas have value.

This essay's theme is echoed in *Pudd'nhead Wilson*, in which Percy DRISCOLL loses all his children to the "antediluvian methods" of early 19th-century doctors (chapter 1). "THOSE EXTRAORDINARY TWINS" devotes chapter 7 to the ignorance of doctors and calls Galen "the only medical authority recognized in Missouri." The 5,140-word essay first appeared in the February 1890 issue of HARPER'S MAGAZINE and was collected in LITERARY ESSAYS.

Malory, Thomas (1416?–March 14, 1471, London) English author of *Le Morte d'Arthur* (1485), the first major English version of Arthurian legends and the source of many popular modern ideas about King ARTHUR and the knights of the Round Table. The book became a literary classic during the 16th century and enjoyed new popularity in the 19th century with TENNYSON's publication of *Idylls of the King*. In a great literary irony, details about Malory's life are as shadowy as those of the historical Arthur. Little is known about him beyond what he reveals in his book, such as his admission that he was in prison around 1469–70. Malory is now generally believed to have been Sir Thomas Malory, a once respectable Warwickshire landowner and member of Parliament who was imprisoned several times for criminal activities and died in Newgate in 1471.

Mark Twain reportedly learned about Malory in December 1884, when G. W. CABLE gave him a copy of *Le Morte d'Arthur* during their joint lecture tour. He came to regard Malory as one of the finest writers in English and drew on him heavily to write his own Arthurian romance, *A Connecticut Yankee in King Arthur's Court* (1889), which borrows many of Malory's characters and spellings. Mark Twain's book mentions Malory by name in the prelude, in which the FRAME-narrator spends an evening reading *Le Morte d'Arthur*. It also paraphrases several Malory tales—particularly those which SANDY recites to Hank MORGAN.

"The Mammoth Cod" Sketch about male sex organs attributed to Mark Twain. This scatological sketch was first ascribed to Petroleum V. NASBY in a book privately published in the early 20th century. It has since been credited to Mark Twain—who some scholars believe to have written it in early 1902. In 1976, the Maledicta Society published *The Mammoth Cod* under his name in a booklet edited by Gershon Legman.

The sketch is ostensibly a letter from a man deriding the "Mammoth Cod Club"—an organization of men proud of their prodigious sexual organs. Its central feature is a four-stanza poem praising bulls, rams and boars for providing meat, thanks to their efficient use of their mighty cods. It concludes that man is the only beast that "plays with his mammoth cod" merely for fun. A postscript claims that the author wrote the poem to instruct children by showing how "animals do better by instinct than man does by reason." The author suggests that the poem be sung in Sunday schools.

Though the subject matter of "The Mammoth Cod" has superficial similarities with that of Mark Twain's "SOME THOUGHTS ON THE SCIENCE OF ONANISM" and

1601, its flat style does not resemble his writing, and his authorship of it remains unproven.

Man Factory Training center in *Connecticut Yankee*. A central theme running through this novel is the idea that a person's beliefs and reasoning powers are solely the product of training. Recognizing that he cannot achieve the political and social revolution he desires without fundamentally retraining people, Hank MORGAN creates an academy to which he alludes occasionally as a "Man Factory" whose mission is to "turn groping and grubbing automata into *men*" (chapter 17). He first mentions the factory in chapter 13, when he sends a spirited peasant to report to CLARENCE there for training. Aside from promising the man that he will learn to read and that no priests are connected with his factory, Hank says nothing about who runs it, where it is, or what else it teaches.

"The Man That Corrupted Hadleyburg" Novella written by Mark Twain while he was in VIENNA in December 1898. It is about a stranger who repays an arrogantly pious town for mistreating him by drawing all its leading citizens into a hoax that destroys the town's reputation for honesty.

SYNOPSIS

Hadleyburg is so vainly proud of its reputation as the region's "most honest and upright town" that no one notices when it deeply offends a passing stranger. The bitter man spends over a year plotting revenge to attack what the town values most—its pride. One night he returns to Hadleyburg and leaves a heavy sealed bag at the home of Edward Richards. A note identifies him as a foreigner who visited the town "a year or two ago," when a local man gave him $20 along with advice that turned his life around. According to the note, the bag contains $40,000 in gold to be given to his benefactor, whom he is confident that Hadleyburg's honest citizens will find. All the stranger's unknown benefactor must do to identify himself is give the Reverend Burgess a sealed envelope containing the advice that he rendered to the stranger. At a public meeting Burgess is to open the envelope and compare it with a copy of the correct statement that the stranger has sealed in his bag of gold.

Richards jokes about how easy it would be simply to keep the stranger's gold and deny everything, but his wife rebukes him. He delivers the stranger's note to Cox, the local newspaperman, for publication. When he returns, he and his wife agree that the only person in town who could have given the stranger $20 is the recently deceased Barclay Goodson, who was hated by the townspeople for publicly belittling its self-righteousness. The only person the town hates more is the Reverend Burgess, who is reviled for an offense he committed years earlier. Richards, however, has always known that Burgess was innocent, but he was too cowardly to speak up to save Burgess's reputation, though he did secretly save him from being run out of town on a rail.

As it dawns on the Richardses that the deceased Goodson is probably the man for whom the gold is intended, they regret their hastiness in giving the stranger's note to Cox. Richards rushes out to find Cox, but newspapers are already publishing the news. The next morning Hadleyburg awakens to find itself famous. The town's 19 principal citizens are especially proud, but soon their thoughts turn to wondering what Goodson told the stranger.

Three weeks later, Richards receives a letter from a "Howard L. Stephenson," who says he saw Goodson give a stranger $20 and heard what he told him. Stephenson adds that Goodson once mentioned feeling indebted to Richards for some "very great service." For this reason, Stephenson feels that Richards is the legitimate heir to Goodson's fortune, and he reveals the crucial message: *"You are far from being a bad man; go, and reform."* Though thrilled by the prospect of riches, Richards struggles to remember what service he might have performed for Goodson. Meanwhile, Hadleyburg's 18 other leading citizens receive similar letters; they also struggle to recall their services to Goodson. With 19 families expecting sudden wealth, the town goes on a spending binge. Meanwhile, 19 people slip sealed envelopes to Reverend Burgess.

At the end of a month, 480 people pack the town hall to see Burgess present the sack of gold to the Hadleyburg "incorruptible." After Burgess reads the first sealed message, the crowd is amazed to learn it was written by Deacon Billson—a notorious cheapskate who would never give money away to anyone. Bewilderment turns to astonishment when both Billson and a man named Wilson rise to take credit for the message. Wilson is found to have submitted a nearly identical statement, but neither precisely matches the message that Burgess takes from the sealed bag. Wilson nevertheless appears to carry the day with a glib explanation that wins over the crowd, but before he can claim his prize, Burgess opens a third envelope that contains the same message.

The crowd's amusement reaches a fever pitch as Burgess reads submission after submission with the same message—all signed by leading citizens. Meanwhile, Richards squirms in anticipation of his own coming humiliation; he rises to confess, but is shouted down. To his astonishment, Burgess quits after the 18th message, and Richards himself is hailed as the town's only true "incorruptible."

Burgess then reads the balance of the note removed from the bag, in which the stranger reveals that the whole scheme is a hoax. The stranger chides the town for its pride and naivete, pointing out that by long insulating itself against temptation, it has created "the weakest of all weak things . . . a virtue which has not been tested in the fire." The bag itself, which is filled with gilded lead slugs, is auctioned off to raise money for Hadleyburg's "one clean man," Richards. Unbe-

knownst to the crowd, the bag goes to the perpetrator of the hoax, who winds up reselling it to Dr. Harkness for $40,000, which he gives to Richards. Harkness later uses the notorious lead coins to win election to the state legislature by having the image of his opponent, Pinkerton, stamped on them with a humiliating reminder of Pinkerton's shameful connection with the fraud.

The Richardses, confused and exhausted by the attention they are receiving, receive a note from Burgess explaining that he saved them at the town meeting to repay the time that Richards had "saved" him. Fearing that Burgess actually intends to expose their hypocrisy for having earlier failed to clear his name when his reputation was unjustly ruined, the Richardses become gravely ill. In his delirium, Richards thinks that Burgess has exposed him. On his deathbed, he confesses that he alone knew of Burgess's innocence in his old scandal, and publicly forgives Burgess for exposing him. He dies without realizing that he has once again wronged Burgess. Mrs. Richards dies the same night.

To hide their shame, the people of Hadleyburg petition to change the name of their town, and they drop the "not" from their original motto, "Lead Us Not into Temptation."

PUBLISHING HISTORY

HARPER'S MAGAZINE published the 17,500-word story in December 1899, and it first appeared in book form in *The Man That Corrupted Hadleyburg and Other Essays and Stories* in June 1900. The story has since been reprinted in numerous collections of 19th-century short stories, as well as most collections of Mark Twain's best short works. It was dramatized on television's *American Short Story* series in 1980, with Robert Preston playing the stranger.

"The Man Who Put Up at Gadsby's" FRAME-STORY told within chapter 26 of *A Tramp Abroad*. Watching people patiently fish at LUCERNE prompts the narrator to recall an incident he witnessed in WASHINGTON, D.C. in the winter of 1867. He was walking on Pennsylvania Avenue with (John H.) RILEY on a stormy night when a man named Lykins rushed up to ask Riley for help pushing through his application for San Francisco's vacant postmaster position. Armed with a 200-signature petition, Lykins expected to wrap up the whole matter in one day. Riley, however, cornered him and told him about the man who put up at Gadsby's:

Back in (President Andrew) Jackson's time, when Gadsby's was Washington's principal hotel, a Tennessee man came to Washington expecting to collect a small claim against the government. He arrived with a coachman, a splendid four-horse carriage and an elegant dog. At Gadsby's, he told his coachman merely to wait for him, since his claim would not take long. Late that evening, however, he ordered a bed. It was January 3, 1834. On February 5, he sold his carriage and bought a cheaper one. On August 11, he sold two horses. On December 13, he sold another horse. On February 17, 1835, he replaced the carriage with a buggy. On August 1, he swapped the buggy for an old sulky and on August 29, he sold his coachman. On February 15, 1837, he sold the sulky and got a saddle. On April 9, he sold the saddle, saying that bareback riding was safer. On April 24, he sold his horse, saying that at 57 he was better off walking. On June 22, he sold his dog.

When Lykins pressed Riley to know what happened next, Riley replied that the Tennessean still saw him daily and still expected to get his claim through soon. When Lykins failed to grasp the story's point, Riley advised him to consider putting up at Gadsby's himself, then turned on his heel and disappeared.

Mark Twain originally wrote this story for the VIR-GINIA CITY TERRITORIAL ENTERPRISE in February 1868, when he was working in Washington, D.C. and was beginning to appreciate the slowness with which the federal government operated. Around the same time, he also published "THE FACTS CONCERNING THE RECENT RESIGNATION," a thematically similar story. Mark Twain revised the Gadsby story as a last-minute addition to *A Tramp Abroad*. He later introduced the "New Gadsby" hotel as the Washington hotel in which Lord BERKELEY and One-Armed Pete stay in *The American Claimant*. The hotel burns down in chapter 7.

Mannheim City in southwestern GERMANY. Located at the confluence of the Rhine and NECKAR rivers, 13 miles northwest of HEIDELBERG, Mannheim is its region's principal commercial center. Mark Twain visited Mannheim several times while staying at Heidelberg in 1878. In late May, he attended performances of Shakespeare's *King Lear* and Richard WAGNER's *Lohengrin* there and describes them in chapters 9–10 of *A Tramp Abroad*. During this period he became a friend of the American consul at Mannheim, Edward M. Smith, who appears in *A Tramp Abroad* as "Mr. X."

In *Life on the Mississippi*'s Karl RITTER story, the son of Private KRUGER lives at No. 14 Königstrasse in Mannheim (chapter 31).

Marco, the son of Marco Character in *Connecticut Yankee*. A charcoal-burner living near the village of ABBLA-SOURE, Marco figures prominently in chapters 30–34, in which Hank MORGAN and King ARTHUR stay with him and his wife after visiting his cousins' "SMALL-POX HUT." The night before Hank meets him, Marco is out helping to hang neighbors suspected of burning down the manor house and killing the local lord. Hank nevertheless regards Marco as an essentially good-hearted man drawn into mob actions out of fear. Marco himself is immensely relieved to learn that Hank shares his dislike

for the nobility. Later, Marco basks in glory at the banquet that Hank stages for DOWLEY and other leading village artisans at his home. However, Marco is quick to join the others in turning against Hank and the king when they appear to be dangerous.

Marco first appears in chapter 30, but is not named until the next chapter, in which Hank calls him "Marco," or "Marco, the son of Marco." Hank calls Marco's good-natured wife "Dame Phyllis" (chapter 31) and "Mrs. Marco" (chapter 33) and refers to the couple as "the Marcos" (chapters 31–32).

"Marienbad—A Health Factory" Essay published in the NEW YORK SUN on February 7, 1892. In late August 1891, Mark Twain spent about two weeks in the Bohemian health resort Mariánské Lázne (Marienbad in German), near the western tip of what is now the Czech Republic. His essay describes the scenic splendor of the western approach to the town, but finds little else about Marienbad to praise. Put off by cold and wet weather, rude residents, and visitors who talk only about their ailments, Mark Twain rues the fact that the town's springs, which are famous for curing gout, rheumatism, leanness, fatness, dyspepsia and other ailments, cannot cure poor manners. The essay is collected in EUROPE AND ELSEWHERE, in which A. B. PAINE omitted a paasage containing a burlesque love poem about a liver ailment. Charles NEIDER restores the missing passage in *The Complete Essays of Mark Twain* (1963).

Marion City Town in northeastern Missouri, 12 miles up the Mississippi River from Hannibal. During the 1830s, Marion City threatened to rival Hannibal as a transportation hub, but flooding problems so limited its potential that it never grew substantially. It may be the stagnating midwestern town that inspired "Eden" in Charles DICKENS's *Martin Chuzzlewit* (1844). Mark Twain wrote about Marion City in a letter to the SAN FRANCISCO ALTA CALIFORNIA in April 1867. After seeing the town again in 1882, he described it as having gone backward since he had first seen it 35 years earlier (*Life on the Mississippi*, chapter 57). He later used Marion City as the model for GOSHEN in *Huckleberry Finn* (chapter 11).

Mark Twain was in FRANCE when an Italian anarchist assassinated French president Marie Sadi-Carnot (1837–1894) in June 1894. Afterward, he wrote "A Scrap of Curious History," comparing the mob psychology of angry French people with Missourians he had seen hang an abolitionist named Robert Hardy at Marion City in 1845 (an incident not confirmed by other sources). This essay was first published in HARPER'S MAGAZINE in October 1914 and was later collected in *What Is Man? and Other Essays*.

Marion County Located in northeastern Missouri, Marion County is on the Mississippi River, between Ralls County on the south and Lewis County on the north. Hannibal stands at the 438-square-mile county's southeast corner. From 1839 to 1853, when Mark Twain lived in Hannibal, the county grew from about 5,000 to 13,000 residents. Its modern population is about 29,000 people, two-thirds of whom live in Hannibal. PALMYRA is the county seat.

Marion Rangers Name of the irregular Confederate unit that Mark Twain helped to form in Hannibal in June 1861. Twenty-five years later, he published an embellished account of the episode, "THE PRIVATE HISTORY OF A CAMPAIGN THAT FAILED." According to this story, he and his fellows named their unit after their home county, on the suggestion of a member he described as "given to reading chivalric novels" (presumably those written by Sir Walter SCOTT). This is an apparent allusion to his friend John L. ROBARDS, whom he calls "Dunlap" in the article. After two weeks of alternately skylarking and fleeing phantom Union troops, the unit disbanded. About half the men saw further service with the Confederacy; the rest—including Mark Twain—scattered. Though nominally under the command of Brigadier General Thomas H. Harris, the unit never had any trained military leadership during its brief existence.

"Mark Twain" PEN NAME used by Samuel L. Clemens from early 1863. *Mark twain* is a nautical expression for a depth of water; it literally means "two marks," which stands for two fathoms, or 12 feet. During Clemens's years as a PILOT, he frequently heard leadsmen call out this and other terms for soundings as they cast their knotted lead-lines into the river. On February 3, 1863— a date that some have dubbed the "birth of Mark Twain"—the VIRGINIA CITY TERRITORIAL ENTERPRISE published a letter from Carson City, Nevada that Clemens signed "Mark Twain".

In 1874, Clemens wrote a letter claiming to have borrowed the pseudonym from the veteran pilot Isaiah SELLERS, whom he had once pilloried in a newspaper sketch. He explained that Sellers signed "Mark Twain" to items he published in New Orleans papers during the 1850s, but stopped writing after Clemens's lampoon appeared. When Clemens heard about Sellers's death in 1863, he took the pseudonym "Mark Twain" for himself, partly in homage to Sellers. Chapter 50 of *Life on the Mississippi* tells essentially the same story.

The problem with this story is that while Sellers did write newspaper items, there is no evidence of his ever having signed them "Mark Twain." Furthermore, Sellers died on March 6, 1864—more than a year after Clemens began using the pen name "Mark Twain" himself. Clemens's account of how he became "Mark Twain" thus appears to be an invention, though it is possible that he saw a false report of Sellers's death before he adopted the name. If so, it would not be the only time that a death of "Mark Twain" was exaggerated.

Scholars have also debated what the words *mark twain* meant to Clemens himself. Aside from their vigor and their appearance of being a real name, they convey at least two possible symbolic meanings. *Twain* derives from an Old English word for "two," and may thus have appealed to Clemens's fascination with duality. He occasionally used the word by itself, as in chapters 26 and 53 of *Innocents Abroad,* in which he alludes to cleaving bodies "in twain."

In steamboating jargon, the two-fathom depth for which "mark twain" stands happened to be the dividing line between safe and dangerously shallow water for STEAMBOATS. It has often been said that Clemens found comfort in hearing the words *"mark twain"* because they meant "safe water." However, while these words meant safe water to boats leaving shoal water, they meant just the opposite to boats leaving deep water. This distinction is made clear in chapter 13 of *Life on the Mississippi,* which recalls a moment when Horace BIXBY tricks his cub pilot (Clemens) into thinking that a deep-water crossing was dangerously shallow. As the cub steers the ALECK SCOTT into the crossing, its leadsmen give him false soundings, calling out shallower and shallower depths, until he panics and signals to stop the engines. By his own admission, he becomes "helpless" when he hears them cry *"Mark* twain!" This instance is hardly an example of the phrase *"mark twain"* meaning "safe water."

After 1863, Clemens published almost all his work under the name "Mark Twain," though he generally inserted "Samuel L. Clemens" in parentheses on the title pages of his books. The pen name was certainly not intended to hide his identity. He was known as "Mark" to some of his friends, and occasionally signed letters as "Mark" or "Mark Twain." In 1908, he incorporated the MARK TWAIN COMPANY in New York. Since that date, the Mark Twain Estate has maintained that "Mark Twain" is a *trademark,* not a pseudonym, and thus not affected by copyright rules. After Mark Twain's books started falling into the public domain, many publishers issued them with the name "Samuel L. Clemens" as author in order to avoid trademark problems.

Mark Twain Name of several STEAMBOATS. Between the widespread use of *mark twain* as a nautical term and Mark Twain's fame as a writer, it is not surprising that many boats have been dubbed the *"Mark Twain."* Mark Twain apparently saw a steamboat with this name in April 1882, when he was going down the Mississippi. Chapter 28 of *Life on the Mississippi* recalls passing the mouth of Kentucky's Obion River, where he used a telescope to see a steamboat that "was named for me." This boat was presumably the *Mark Twain,* not the *"Samuel L. Clemens."*

When Mark Twain was in ST. LOUIS 20 years later helping to dedicate the grounds for the coming world's fair, he attended the rechristening of the 30-year-old harbor steamboat *St. Louis* as the *Mark Twain.* In a brief cruise around the harbor on this boat, he had his last turn at the wheel of a Mississippi steamboat. A year later, HARPER'S WEEKLY reported that St. Louis newspapers were printing headlines with such embarrassing remarks as "Mark Twain in Need of Repairs" and "Mark Twain's Boilers Explode."

Mark Twain is also the name of the replica steamboat that has circled "Tom Sawyer Island" in southern California's Disneyland since 1955. There are also modern tourist boats based at Hannibal and St. Louis named *Mark Twain.*

***Mark Twain and Me* (1991)**   Television movie about Dorothy QUICK's friendship with Mark Twain. The narrative begins with Mark Twain (Jason Robards) in London with A. B. PAINE (R. H. Thomson) just before he receives an honorary degree from OXFORD UNIVERSITY in 1907. On the return voyage, he meets 11-year-old Dorothy (Amy Stewart), whom he sees frequently through the remainder of his life. Talia Shire plays his daughter Jean Clemens. This Disney production, which first aired in November 1991, was directed by Daniel Petrie from a script by Cynthia Whitcomb. Robards also played the KING in Disney's *The Adventures of Huck Finn* (1993).

Mark Twain: Beneath the Laughter   Television drama made in 1979. Irish actor Dan O'Herlihy (1919–) plays Mark Twain reflecting on the meaning of his life. The script was written by Gill Dennis and Larry Yust, who also directed it. The 60-minute production first aired on PBS on December 15, 1979.

The story begins as Mark Twain returns from BERMUDA aboard a ship with his biographer, A. B. PAINE (Lyn Seibel), as reporters ask him about his AUTOBIOGRAPHY. At home, he finds his daughter Jean Clemens (Kay Howell) preparing for Christmas. One night he dreams he is in his nightclothes in a vast hall filled with formally dressed people who do not believe he is Mark Twain. Early the next morning, his maid awakens him with the terrible news that Jean is dead. He rushes to the bathroom, where Jean lies still on the floor.

That same morning, he begins writing "THE DEATH OF JEAN," reading portions aloud to himself. He talks of the dream that goes on and on, sometimes seeming "so real I almost believe it *is* real." Moments from his life and writings come alive. He visualizes the painful moment from "THE PRIVATE HISTORY OF A CAMPAIGN THAT FAILED," when, as a young man (Gavan O'Herlihy), he participated with his comrades in shooting down an innocent rider during the CIVIL WAR. He also recalls being a cub PILOT under Horace BIXBY (Tobias Andersen), lecturing on public platforms, and seeing his boyhood chum Tom NASH as a deaf old man on his last visit to Hannibal (1902). *Huckleberry Finn* comes alive as he pictures Colonel SHERBURN (Peter Henry Schroeder) shooting BOGGS (Sam Edwards) and facing down a lynch mob.

He also recalls a day he lay abed, reading "THE WAR PRAYER" to a disapproving Jean; the scene cuts back and forth to the story itself, in which a robed stranger (Richard Moll) stuns a Protestant congregation with a message "from the Throne." While reflecting on the power of laughter, Mark Twain imagines another moment from *Huckleberry Finn,* when the drunken Pap FINN rails about what the country is coming to when a black man can vote. The following morning, Mark Twain looks out a window as Jean's coffin is carried away. He remembers the moments when he received an OXFORD degree and delivered his "Begum of Bengal" speech in Liverpool (1907). The drama ends with Mark Twain at home, uttering the speech's final words: He is "homeward bound."

Mark Twain Circle of America   Founded at the December 1986 Modern Language Association (MLA) convention, the Circle serves mainly to disseminate information about Mark Twain studies and activities among several hundred members who pay nominal dues. Its primary organ is the *Mark Twain Circular,* a quarterly newsletter published in association with the MARK TWAIN JOURNAL in Charleston, South Carolina. The organization meets annually at conventions of the MLA, with which it established formal ties in 1991. Though most Circle members are college instructors, membership is open to all people interested in Mark Twain.

Mark Twain Company   Legal entity created by Mark Twain in 1908. Motivated by the need to control the use of his pen name and protect his literary copyrights, Mark Twain registered the "Mark Twain Company" in the state of New York on December 23, 1908. A few days later, he assigned all his copyrights and his pen name to the company. The idea of forming the company came from his business adviser Ralph ASHCROFT, whom he named a director—along with himself, his daughters and Isabel LYON. A falling-out with Ashcroft and Lyon led to their removal from the board a few months later. By the end of the summer, the company was organized on a more professional basis, with a board made up of Mark Twain, Zoeth Freeman (member, 1909–10), Jervis Langdon (1909–43), Charles Tressler Lark (1910–43), Edward E. Loomis (1909–37) and A. B. PAINE (1909–13). After Lark and Langdon resigned in 1943, Thomas Chamberlain (1943–78) and the Manufacturers Hanover Trust Company of New York replaced them.

After Mark Twain's DEATH in 1910, the company's directors also usually served as his executors. In July 1911, his estate was appraised at $471,136—including 50 shares of the Mark Twain Company worth $200,000. The estate also included stock in various industrial companies worth nearly $182,000 and "STORMFIELD," Mark Twain's Redding, Connecticut house. His unpublished personal and literary manuscripts were not valuated.

Mark Twain's will instructed that his estate be held in trust. His daughter Clara Clemens was sole beneficiary; she received an income from the estate but could not dispose of its assets until her own death. Meanwhile, the company's directors invested the estate's fiscal assets and controlled its literary properties, which evolved into the MARK TWAIN PAPERS. In February 1964, 15 months after Clara died, assets of Mark Twain's estate—then worth more than $928,000—were transferred to a trust created by her will. She bequeathed her father's literary properties to the University of California, the home of the Mark Twain Papers. Income from the trust went to her second husband, Jacques SAMOSSOUD, then to his friend W. E. Seiler. Seiler's death in November 1978 closed Clara's will, which created the MARK TWAIN FOUNDATION, which in turn absorbed the Mark Twain Company.

Mark Twain Forum Electronic-mail discussion group. In electronic communications parlance, the Mark Twain Forum is a "list server" through which computer users exchange information over modems. Members of the informal group swap news, ask questions and share papers and book reviews. Taylor Roberts launched the Forum in Toronto in March 1992 in order to bring Mark Twain scholars together electronically. Over the next two years, he cast the Forum's net more widely, welcoming anyone seriously interested in Mark Twain. By 1995, over 300 members were on the Forum's list. (Anyone on Internet can join the Forum without charge by sending the message "subscribe Twain-L *username*" to either LISTSERV@VM1.BITNET on Bitnet.)

Mark Twain Foundation Charitable trust created in 1978. The will of Mark Twain's last surviving daughter, Clara Clemens, directed that after the financial residue of her estate passed through her husband, Jacques SA-MOSSOUD, and Dr. William E. Seiler (1909–1978), it be used to create a new foundation. On Seiler's death in November 1978, the Mark Twain Foundation was set up and assumed control of the older MARK TWAIN COMPANY. Administered by Manufacturers Hanover Trust Company of New York and a board of directors, the foundation controls copyright of all Mark Twain works not in the public domain, assigning permissions for their use through the general editor of the MARK TWAIN PAPERS project.

Mark Twain Home Foundation Nonprofit body that administers the Mark Twain Museum, Mark Twain BOY-HOOD HOME, PILASTER HOUSE and other sites in Hannibal, Missouri. The organization traces its roots back to Hannibal's 1935 celebration of Mark Twain's 100th birthday, for which the city created a temporary museum. At the end of the year, Hannibal's Chamber of Commerce raised funds for a permanent museum, which the federal Works Projects Administration built adjacent to the Boyhood Home. A city ordinance established the "Mark Twain Home Board" to administer its various Mark Twain sites and the new museum, which formally opened on Mark Twain's birthday in 1937.

The foundation was created later as a nonprofit branch; since 1990 it has administered the board's properties autonomously. An affiliate of the foundation, the Mark Twain Boyhood Home Associates, oversees the activities of about 300 dues-paying members and publishes a quarterly bulletin, THE FENCE PAINTER.

The collection of the Mark Twain Museum contains many of Mark Twain's personal effects and furniture. Of particular interest are his OXFORD UNIVERSITY academic robes, a death mask of his son Langdon Clemens and his Aeolian Orchestrelle. The museum also houses Norman Rockwell's 15 original paintings for modern editions of *Tom Sawyer* and *Huckleberry Finn*. The museum's research collection includes first editions of Mark Twain's works, as well as hundreds of foreign-language editions.

***Mark Twain in Eruption: Hitherto Unpublished Pages About Men and Events* (1940)** Extracts from Mark Twain's AUTOBIOGRAPHY. Acting on instructions from the Mark Twain Estate and HARPER'S, Bernard DEVOTO reviewed the typescripts from which A. B. PAINE had extracted *Mark Twain's Autobiography* (1924) in order to determine what omitted materials merited publication. After calculating that Paine had used only about half of the original typescript text, DeVoto selected about half from what remained to assemble *Mark Twain in Eruption*.

Since he was commissioned to construct a book for general readers, not scholars, DeVoto selected what he regarded as the most interesting passages in Mark Twain's unpublished typescripts, as well as material that Mark Twain had published in the NORTH AMERICAN REVIEW. He omitted portions he regarded as "irrelevant or uninteresting" and excluded some of Mark Twain's most excessive personal tirades against individual people.

In contrast to Paine's edition of the *Autobiography,* DeVoto arranged the text of *Mark Twain in Eruption* topically, joining passages on related subjects without regard to their original dates of dictation—which governed Paine's organization. He then divided the material into nine sections, titled "Theodore Roosevelt," "Andrew Carnegie," "The Plutocracy," "Hannibal Days," "Two Halos," "In a Writer's Workshop," "Various Literary People," "The Last Visit to England," and "Miscellany." These sections he broke into numbered subsections.

While the subject matter of *Mark Twain's Autobiography* and *Mark Twain in Eruption* often overlaps, the latter book tends to discuss more recent events and people whom Mark Twain knew in his later years—especially politicians, businessmen and publishers. Among the people receiving the most attention are Thomas Bailey ALDRICH and his wife, Elisha BLISS, Andrew CARNEGIE, Montana's Senator William A. Clark, Jim GILLIS, novelist Elinor Glyn, Jay GOULD, U. S. GRANT, Bret HARTE, John D. Rockefeller, Theodore ROOSEVELT, Dick STOKER, Bayard TAYLOR, Joseph TWICHELL, Ned WAKEMAN, Charles

H. WEBB, Charles L. WEBSTER and Jim WOLFE. The volume also includes illuminating remarks about the composition of "CAPTAIN STORMFIELD'S VISIT TO HEAVEN," *1601* and *Connecticut Yankee*.

After DeVoto prepared his manuscript in early 1940, Clara Clemens objected to passages that she feared would offend relatives of people whom Mark Twain criticized severely. DeVoto resisted her objections, arguing that Mark Twain himself wrote the passages with the intention that they would eventually be published. An occasionally acrimonious dispute ensued (parts of which are documented in Wallace Stegner's 1975 edition of *The Letters of Bernard DeVoto*), but Harper's published DeVoto's manuscript with few substantive changes.

Mark Twain Journal   The oldest American journal devoted to a single author, this publication began in 1936 as the *Mark Twain Quarterly*, the official periodical of the INTERNATIONAL MARK TWAIN SOCIETY. Cyril CLEMENS edited the journal for nearly 50 years, mixing substantive scholarship with antiquarian articles, newly discovered Mark Twain letters, and testimonials from famous people to whom Clemens awarded society honors.

Though founded as a quarterly, the journal never published more than two issues in a year and eventually got into trouble with federal postal authorities for this reason. In 1954, its name was changed to *Mark Twain Journal*. By 1983, it had still issued only 21 volumes of four numbers each. That year, the journal moved to Charleston, South Carolina, where Thomas A. Tenney became editor. In 1984, it officially became a semiannual with one numbered volume per calendar year. Under Tenney's editorship, the journal became more professional, emphasizing factual rather than interpretive articles, while continuing to publish original documents and pictures.

Mark Twain Lake   An 18,600-acre body of water at the confluence of the North and Middle forks of Missouri's Salt River, Mark Twain Lake nearly surrounds the town of FLORIDA, in which Mark Twain was born. Artificial, like all of Missouri's large lakes, it was created when Clarence Cannon Dam was built eight miles east of Florida between 1966 and 1983. The dam serves to control flooding and generate power as its lake develops into a major recreational area. The lake reached full capacity for the first time during the great floods of July 1993.

Mark Twain Memorial   Nonprofit body that maintains Mark Twain's Hartford, Connecticut home at 351 Farmington Avenue as a public museum and research center. Founded in 1929, the organization is supported by foundation grants, private contributions, dues-paying members, admission fees and profits from a museum shop. It publishes a quarterly newsletter, organizes lectures, symposia, concerts and other events and maintains a collection of books, pictures and documents relating to Mark Twain, as well as the sole surviving PAIGE COMPOSITOR. Immediately east of the house is Harriet Beecher STOWE's house, which is maintained by the Stowe-Day Foundation. The Mark Twain House is open to visitors throughout the year.

The name "Mark Twain Memorial" was long perceived as synonymous with the house itself. To remove possible confusion about the nature of its trust, the organization began calling the building *"The* Mark Twain House" in 1993. This new name replaced "Mark Twain Memorial" on publications, but the organization's institutional name remains unchanged.

The Memorial's history begins with the house itself. After living for several years in a rented house in Hartford's NOOK FARM community, Mark Twain and his wife Livy purchased more than five acres above a nearby stream in early 1873 and engaged Edward T. POTTER to design a house for them. The family moved into the new house on September 19, 1874, before it was completed. Following a plan drafted by Livy, Potter designed a mainly brick structure three stories high with 19 rooms, five balconies, steeply gabled roofs and prominent wooden structural members and railings. The basically rectangular ground floor is on a north–south axis, with the dining and drawing rooms facing Farmington Avenue on the north. The main entrance opens to a curved driveway on the east. The southwest corner contains a large library with a semicircular solarium facing south. The kitchen area—enlarged in 1881—is an annex off the northwest corner. The second floor contains family bedrooms, a schoolroom and a servants' wing over the kitchen. The main feature of the third floor is a large BILLIARD room, where Mark Twain wrote when he worked at home. A stairwell connecting the three levels begins in the ornately carved ground-level entrance hall. The house's east exterior has a long covered porch known as the "Ombra," which extends south of the house. In 1881, the house underwent a major redecoration in which Louis Comfort Tiffany's firm incorporated American Indian textile motifs into wallpaper and stenciling throughout the interiors.

Mark Twain lived in the house with his family and a staff averaging seven servants for 17 years. In June 1891, the high cost of maintaining the household led him to close it down and go to Europe in the hope of reducing expenses. Though his family planned to return after a year or so, they never again lived in the house as a family. During the family's residence abroad, Mark Twain visited the house several times while on business trips to the United States. In 1896, as Mark Twain was completing a world lecture, the family was still intending to return to the house. When he, his wife and daughter Clara reached England in August, his oldest daughter, Susy—who had not accompanied him—became seriously ill while visiting friends in Hartford. She was taken to the family house, where she died.

Afterward, her parents could not face living there again, but did not put the house on the market until April 1902.

In May 1903, the president of the Hartford Fire Insurance Company, Richard M. Bissell, bought the house for $28,000—a fraction of what the Clemenses had invested in it. Bissell's family lived there until 1917, when they rented the house to Kingswood School for boys. After the school relocated in 1922, the house was sold. It was later used as a warehouse and still later was converted to a public library downstairs and a rooming house upstairs—a period evoked in *Murder Stalks the Circle* (1947), a mystery novel by Lee Thayer (1874–1973).

Civic concern over the fate of Mark Twain's house led to the formation of the Mark Twain Memorial Committee, which raised funds to buy it in 1929. Major restoration began in 1954 with a study of the house's physical condition. After funds were raised, structural repairs were made and new studies were undertaken to determine the original decor of the house. Since the major work was completed in 1974, there has been a continuing effort to perfect the restoration.

Mark Twain Memorial Bridge   Bridge connecting Hannibal, Missouri with Illinois on Highway 36 across the Mississippi River. During Mark Twain's time, people crossing the river at Hannibal used ferryboats. As a reflection of the town's growing importance as a railroad center, a railroad-and-wagon bridge was erected in 1871, and the Mark Twain Memorial Bridge was built 65 years later. On September 4, 1936, President Franklin Delano ROOSEVELT personally dedicated the bridge. At the same moment, Clara Clemens pressed a telegraph key in Los Angeles to light the bridge's traffic signals. Other dignitaries attending the dedication at Hannibal included Missouri's Senator Harry S Truman.

In July 1993, rising floodwaters forced the temporary closing of this bridge and all others between St. Louis and Burlington, Iowa.

Mark Twain National Forest   A wooded region of the Ozark Mountains, Mark Twain National Forest covers about 2,345 square miles of southeastern Missouri in eight noncontiguous blocks—mostly south of Interstate Highway 44.

Mark Twain Papers (Mark Twain Project)   Based at the Bancroft Library of the University of California at Berkeley, the Mark Twain Project is a literary and documentary publishing project dedicated to preparing a comprehensive and authoritative edition of Mark Twain's writings. Since 1967, when it began issuing volumes through the University of California Press, it has completed two dozen different volumes. These fall into two major groups: "Papers," which are previously unpublished documents and manuscripts; and "Works,"

which are meticulously reedited editions of previously published writings. The project's comprehensive schedule calls for about 28 additional Papers volumes (including 20 more volumes of letters) and about 26 additional Works volumes. If it meets its long-range goals, the project will eventually issue nearly 80 volumes of Mark Twain writings—about half of which will not have seen print in any other form.

The project owes its existence to Mark Twain's habit of saving manuscripts and correspondence. In 1906, he invited A. B. PAINE to join his household as his official biographer. Paine used this opportunity to begin organizing Mark Twain's huge and chaotic collection of papers—which remain the core of the manuscript collection now housed in Berkeley. On Mark Twain's death in 1910, Paine became his literary executor, making him, in effect, the first editor of the Mark Twain Papers. Through the rest of his own life, Paine maintained the collection, drawing on it occasionally to publish new anthologies, collections of letters and speeches, AUTOBIOGRAPHY volumes and a selection of Mark Twain's NOTEBOOKS. By the time Paine died in 1937, the bulk of the papers were stored at Harvard University.

In 1938, Bernard DEVOTO succeeded Paine as editor of the Mark Twain Estate. For the first time, he opened the collection to other scholars for inspection, inaugurating a new era in Mark Twain scholarship and setting a precedent that has been followed ever since. During eight years as editor, he drew on the papers to assemble MARK TWAIN IN ERUPTION (1940) and LETTERS FROM THE EARTH (which was not published until 1962). On DeVoto's resignation in 1946, Dixon WECTER took over and moved the collection to southern California's Huntington Library. Three years later, Wecter moved the papers to the Bancroft Library (to which Clara Clemens later willed them). Wecter published several new volumes of Mark Twain letters and wrote the first volume of what was to be a major new biography of Mark Twain before he died in 1950. His letters volumes set a new standard for scholarship in what was then the infant field of document publishing, but they also established a principle that would later be abandoned of building letter collections around limited topics.

After a hiatus, Henry Nash SMITH was named editor of the papers when he came to Berkeley to teach in 1953. Under his editorship, the first long-term plans were made. In 1962, the "Mark Twain Papers" project was formally organized at Berkeley to publish material in the project's collection. Meanwhile, an affiliated project, the "Works of Mark Twain," was organized at the University of Iowa to publish definitive new editions of Mark Twain's books. Both the "Papers" and "Works" projects contracted with the University of California Press to issue their editions. Since then, the work of the two projects has gradually merged.

After Smith resigned in 1964, Frederick ANDERSON became editor of the Mark Twain Papers. He began building a permanent staff of assistant editors—many of whom are still with the project. He oversaw publication of the project's first books, which included volumes of previously unpublished stories, business correspondence and early notebooks. In 1976, Anderson suspended work on a new volume of Mark Twain's family correspondence to launch the first systematic search for letters outside of the project. This effort accelerated the project's accumulation of photocopied material from other repositories and would lead to a reorientation of the project's publishing scheme. After Anderson died in 1979, Smith served as interim editor until Robert HIRST, a former project assistant, became general editor the following year. Under Hirst, the project set publication of a truly comprehensive edition of Mark Twain's writings as its primary goal and combined both the "Papers" and "Works" editions under a single general editor for the first time. In 1980, it officially became the "Mark Twain Project."

Mark Twain State Park Northeastern Missouri state park established in 1924, next to FLORIDA, the town in which Mark Twain was born. Completion of the Clarence Cannon Dam on the Salt River in 1983 created MARK TWAIN LAKE, which now divides the park's land into three sections. In addition to recreational camping, boating, fishing and swimming facilities, the state park system maintains the Mark Twain Birthplace State Historic Site (also known as the Mark Twain Memorial Shrine) in the park's central section, adjacent to Florida. The house in which Mark Twain was born has been relocated and preserved inside the site's modern Mark Twain Museum.

Mark Twain's Library of Humor (1888) Anthology of American writers. After Mark Twain got the idea of compiling a humor anthology from a book dealer in the early 1880s, he arranged with James R. OSGOOD to publish such a volume and began assembling it with the paid help of W. D. HOWELLS. A Hartford newspaper editor named Charles Hopkins Clark (1848–1926) compiled preliminary lists of material from which Howells made selections. Mark Twain then made the final selections and set the overall organization. Meanwhile, Osgood's company collapsed, so Mark Twain's own firm, Charles L. WEBSTER & COMPANY, published the anthology, with nearly 200 original illustrations by E. W. KEMBLE. Because Howells had an exclusive contract with HARPER'S, his name did not appear in the book.

The volume contains a cross section of America's best humorists, with more than 50 writers represented. They include Thomas Bailey ALDRICH (2 selections), Ambrose Bierce (7), Josh BILLINGS (6), Eugene Field (2), Joel Chandler HARRIS (2), Bret HARTE (4), Oliver Wendell HOLMES (2), Howells (6), Washington Irving (1), John HAY (1), John Phoenix (8), Harriet Beecher STOWE (1), Artemus WARD (9) and C. D. WARNER (7). Mark Twain himself is represented in 20 selections, including "CANNIBALISM IN THE CARS," "Experience of the MCWILLIAMSES with Membranous Croup," "HOW I EDITED AN AGRICULTURAL PAPER," the JUMPING FROG story and "The SIAMESE TWINS," and extracts from *The Gilded Age* (chapter 7), *Tom Sawyer* (chapters 2, 5 and 12), *Innocents Abroad* (chapters 15, 27 and 53), *Roughing It* (chapters 5, 24, 31, 46 and 61) and *A Tramp Abroad* (chapters 2–3, 13 and 49).

In 1906, Harper's published a different multivolume work titled *Mark Twain's Library of Humor*. Under Frederick A. DUNEKA's direction, a humorist named Burges Johnson (1877–1963) compiled a much larger collection of material, keeping about a quarter of the original book's selections. Duneka left Mark Twain's original foreword in the new edition, thereby implying that Mark Twain himself had endorsed the volumes. Outraged by Harper's violation of its promise to reissue his original book in a cheaper format, Mark Twain tried to suppress the new edition's publication.

Mark Twain's Memory Builder Board game patented by Mark Twain. During the early 1880s, Mark Twain devoted considerable time to developing a memory-training game built around dates in English history. The complex game awarded points for correctly remembering dates and kept score with pins on a board similar to a cribbage board. His family enjoyed playing the game, but after he patented it on August 18, 1885, his interest waned until 1891, when he had several models manufactured for test-marketing. Too complicated to have broad appeal, the game failed to catch on and Mark Twain gave up on it entirely the following year.

Mark Twain's Notebook (1935) Condensation of Mark Twain's NOTEBOOKS AND JOURNALS published by HARPER'S. Drawing selectively on Mark Twain's notebooks, A. B. PAINE rearranged the material into 35 roughly chronological chapters. His brief introduction states that the notebooks "are now offered in full," but the 120,000-word volume actually contains less than a quarter of Mark Twain's original notebook text. After Bernard DEVOTO succeeded Paine as the Mark Twain Estate's editor, he intended to publish an expanded edition, but never got around to it. In 1975, the MARK TWAIN PAPERS project began issuing an uncut edition that supersedes Paine's. Since the new edition's first three volumes cover only 1855–1891, *Mark Twain's Notebook* retains some value, as it includes material recorded through 1906. Chapters 22–27 cover Mark Twain's round-the-world lecture tour of 1895–96 that led to *Following the Equator*, and chapters 27–32 and 34 cover his last years in Europe.

Mark Twain's Own Autobiography **(1990)**   First book publication of Mark Twain's AUTOBIOGRAPHY to follow the original arrangement of chapters he published in the NORTH AMERICAN REVIEW in 1906–07. Published by the University of Wisconsin Press in 1990, this new edition contains an introduction and notes by Michael J. Kiskis, as well as appendixes summarizing the content of the various editions of the autobiography and a thorough index. Its title reflects the fact that its 25 chapters are the only parts of Mark Twain's autobiography that he himself prepared for publication.

Mark Twain's Travels with Mr. Brown **(1940)**   Collection of 26 travel letters that Mark Twain wrote to the SAN FRANCISCO ALTA CALIFORNIA between December 20, 1866 and June 6, 1867. The letters cover his voyage from California to the East Coast, residence in NEW YORK CITY and LECTURE tour in the Midwest. Franklin Walker and G. Ezra Dane edited and lightly annotated the volume, which was published in 1940. The "Mr. BROWN" of the title is a fictitious companion whom Mark Twain created in his earlier letters from HAWAII.

These dispatches, also known as Mark Twain's "American Travel Letters," originally appeared in the *Alta* between January 18 and August 18, 1867. They link the period immediately after his Hawaii letters with that of his QUAKER CITY letters. Most of them he wrote from New York, which he was visiting for the first time since 1853. Highlights include his first meeting with Captain Ned WAKEMAN ("Waxman" in the letters); crossing NICARAGUA; observing CHOLERA aboard the steamship *San Francisco;* and his return to Missouri after five years. They also comment on his preparation of THE CELEBRATED JUMPING FROG OF CALAVERAS COUNTY for publication; his lecture at New York's Cooper Union; a chance encounter with Jefferson DAVIS; and preparations for the *Quaker City* voyage.

Marlow, Humphrey   Character in *The Prince and the Pauper*. The 12-year-old whipping boy of EDWARD VI, Humphrey is an orphan son of Sir Humphrey Marlow, a former palace official and friend of Miles HENDON's father. When Tom CANTY meets Humphrey, he is amazed to learn that the boy is flogged whenever the prince performs badly in his studies (chapter 14). Humphrey dislikes being flogged, but needs the job to support himself and his sisters, so he is thrilled when Tom dubs him "Hereditary Grand Whipping-Boy." Tom discovers that Humphrey is a mine of information on the court and the real prince's life, so he arranges to meet with him regularly. In chapter 29, Miles Hendon heads for London, hoping to find Sir Humphrey Marlow in order to gain an audience with the new king. By chance, the first person he meets at the Palace of Westminster is the younger Marlow (chapter 33).

Mark Twain's original manuscript of *The Prince and the Pauper* contained a long anecdote that Humphrey recited to Tom Canty. He removed it from the novel, but published it as "A Boy's Adventure" in a Hartford newspaper in June 1880. This narrative supplies additional background about Humphrey's father and tells about a wild adventure he had when he put on a gaudy outfit belonging to his father and tried to ride a bull. His adventure proved a disaster when the bull kicked in a beehive. A modified version of Humphrey's bull-and-bees anecdote appears in *Joan of Arc* (book 2, chapter 36).

Marples, Brother   Minor character in *Huckleberry Finn*. Marples is one of the nosy PIKESVILLE neighbors who visit the Phelpses after Jim's escape in chapter 41. He marvels at how many things were done in Jim's hut, suggesting that "they must a ben a house-full o' niggers in there every night for four weeks, to a done all that work."

marriage, Mark Twain's   Mark Twain married Olivia Langdon on Wednesday, February 2, 1870 in ELMIRA, New York. Two Congregational ministers, Joseph TWICHELL and Thomas K. BEECHER, performed the ceremony in the parlor of the Langdon family home. The hundred guests included Mark Twain's brother Orion Clemens and sister Pamela MOFFETT, but not his mother, Jane L. Clemens—who had missed his siblings' weddings and did not want to show favoritism to him. Other guests included Isabella HOOKER, Mary FAIRBANKS and their husbands. After an evening ceremony, an alcohol-free supper was served and the guests danced. The newlyweds spent their first night together in Elmira. The next day, many guests accompanied them in a private train car to BUFFALO, where the couple took up residence in a house given them by Jervis LANGDON.

Marryat, Captain Frederick (July 10, 1792, London–August 9, 1848, Langham, England)   English novelist and travel writer. Marryat had a long career in the Royal Navy. After retiring in 1830, he began writing adventure novels such as *Peter Simple* (1834) and *Mr. Midshipman Easy* (1836), whose popularity extended as far as Hannibal during Mark Twain's boyhood. Marryat toured the United States in the late 1830s and published his *Diary in America* in two volumes (1839–40). *Life on the Mississippi* quotes Marryat's description of the river as the "great sewer" (chapters 1 and 27) and attributes a long extract on John MURRELL to an unnamed and "now forgotten book" that is actually Marryat's second American diary (chapter 29). Marryat's second diary also has a description of a religious camp meeting near Cincinnati that may have helped inspire the POKEVILLE camp meeting in *Huckleberry Finn* (chapter 20). *Innocents Abroad* opens with quotes from the prospectus for the QUAKER CITY excursion that include remarks by Marryat on Madeira (chapter 1).

Marseilles   Major French seaport on the MEDITERRA-
NEAN. Apart from GIBRALTAR, Marseilles was the first
continental European city that Mark Twain ever visited.
The QUAKER CITY landed there on July 4, 1867; the next
day, he and two companions left for PARIS by train.
They returned to Marseilles on July 13, spent the night
ashore, and left with the ship the next day. Nearly a
year later, Mark Twain wrote the account of Marseilles
that appears in chapters 10–11 of *Innocents Abroad*.
These chapters find humor in the travelers' difficulties
in communicating in French while in Marseilles, the
absence of soap in hotels, and a remarkable bird at the
local zoo that they nicknamed "The PILGRIM." Chapter
19 also makes fun of the Marseillaises' ignorance of
soap. In September 1891, Mark Twain began a boat
trip down the RHONE RIVER to Marseilles but turned
back at Arles.

While he was at Marseilles, Mark Twain boated out
to Castle d'If, where he saw the dungeon cells of prisoners who had scratched pitiful messages onto the walls.
He later recalled these images in the EVASION chapters
of *Huckleberry Finn*. In chapter 35 of that novel, Tom
explains his plans to Huck and cites the "Castle Deef"
of Marseilles, where a prisoner spent 37 years trying to
dig out of his cell with a case-knife. In chapter 18 of
Connecticut Yankee, Hank Morgan compares the dungeon of MORGAN LE FAY with Castle d'If.

**Mary I (February 18, 1516, Greenwich, England–No-
vember 17, 1558, London)**   Queen of England (1553–
58) and minor character in *The Prince and the Pauper*
(1881). The daughter of HENRY VIII by his first wife,
Catherine of Aragon, Mary was a half-sister of King
EDWARD VI. Her brief appearances in *The Prince and the
Pauper* reflect the secluded life she led during Edward's
reign. In chapter 3, Edward alludes to her as having a
"gloomy mien." Tom CANTY meets with her briefly in
chapter 14 and later rebukes her for having a heart of
stone (chapter 30). After the historical Edward's death
in 1553, Mary defeated efforts to make Lady Jane GREY
queen and seized the monarchy herself. In working to
restore Roman Catholicism as England's official religion,
her violent excesses earned her the nickname "Bloody
Mary." After she died, her half-sister ELIZABETH I became queen.

Queen Mary is also briefly mentioned in *1601* and in
"HOW TO MAKE HISTORY DATES STICK."

Mary Ann   Fictitious name mentioned twice in *Huckleberry Finn*. In chapter 16 Huck tells a slave catcher
named PARKER and his partner that his father is sick,
"and so is mam and Mary Ann." In the next chapter,
Huck tells the GRANGERFORD family that he was living
in southern Arkansas, where his family disintegrated
after a sister named Mary Ann eloped. A brother named
Bill went after her, but he never returned either. Then
three more members of the family died, leaving Huck

alone. Huck's second Mary Ann story is closely paralleled by what actually happens to Sophia GRANGERFORD
and her family in chapter 18.

Massachusetts   Mark Twain visited this New England
state almost every year between 1869 and 1890 and
lived in it briefly in 1904. He first came to Massachusetts
in early November 1869 on a LECTURE tour that took
him to BOSTON, Worcester, Charlestown, Clinton, Hol-
yoke, Danvers, Jamaica Plain, Newtonville, Warren,
Waltham, Canton, Hudson and Rockport before the
end of the year. Another lecture tour in late 1871 added
Haverhill and Milford to his list of stops. Through the
1870s, he visited Boston regularly to see W. D. HOWELLS,
James OSGOOD, and James REDPATH, and he spoke there
often. Other Massachusetts towns at which he spoke
include Springfield (1884), Northampton (1889), Pitts-
field (1889) and H. H. ROGERS's hometown, Fairhaven
(1894). After returning to the United States from Italy
in July 1904, he and his daughters spent several months
in LEE before settling in NEW YORK CITY.

massacre hoax   On October 28, 1863, Mark Twain
published a 750-word article in the VIRGINIA CITY TERRI-
TORIAL ENTERPRISE titled "A Bloody Massacre near Carson." A complete hoax about a man brutally murdering
most of his large family, it was later reprinted under a
variety of titles, including "The Dutch Nick Massacre,"
"The Empire City Massacre" and "The Latest Sensation."

SYNOPSIS

According to Abram CURRY (a real person), a man
named P. or Philip HOPKINS, who lived on the edge of
the pine forest between Empire City and Dutch Nick's,
rode into Carson with a bloody scalp in his hand and
his own throat slit from ear to ear. After five minutes
without speaking, he dropped dead in front of the
Magnolia Saloon. Sheriff Gasherie (a real person) immediately led a party out to Hopkins's house, where they
found the butchered remains of his wife and seven of
his children. Two daughters survive to explain what
happened.

Hopkins was known to be affable and nonviolent, but
his temperament began changing when his investments
went bad. He sold off his shares in local mines after
reading in San Francisco papers about dividend-cooking
games played by their managers, then invested heavily
in San Francisco's Spring Valley Water Company on the
advice of a SAN FRANCISCO BULLETIN editor. Over the
previous two months, his wife had expressed fears concerning his sanity, but no one paid her any heed. It is
presumed that he went mad when his stocks failed. The
tragedy was thus a product of the newspapers' failure
to report on the company's dishonest management.

BACKGROUND

Although deliberate hoaxes—such as Mark Twain's PET-RIFIED MAN hoax of the previous year—often appeared in the *Enterprise,* reactions to the massacre hoax were swift and negative. Even as other papers in northern California were reprinting the story as fact, Mark Twain published a retraction; however, it satisfied few, leaving his reputation as a reporter seriously damaged. He offered to resign from the *Enterprise,* but was turned down by his editor, Joseph GOODMAN. Seven years later, Mark Twain published "My Bloody Massacre" in GAL-AXY, explaining the original hoax. He claimed that his only purpose was to trick San Francisco papers into printing a criticism of the city's largest water company. Indeed, he argued that the hoax was meant to be a SATIRE showing that Hopkins was driven mad by the losses he suffered in the stock-cooking schemes. "My Bloody Massacre" lists the original article's inherent absurdities. First, the murderer had the name of a man (P. Hopkins) who was widely known to be a bachelor who had no wife or children to murder. Further, not only did the pine forest "between Empire City and Dutch Nick's" not exist; Empire City and Dutch Nick's were one place. Finally, no one with a slashed throat could possibly ride a horse four miles, not to mention survive an additional five minutes.

Matterhorn (Mont Cervin)   Alpine peak located six miles southwest of ZERMATT, on SWITZERLAND's border with Italy. The third-highest mountain in the ALPS at 14,700 feet, the Matterhorn is famous for its spectacular, sharply rising cliffs that make climbing exceptionally dangerous. After seven men became the first climbers to reach its summit on July 14, 1865, four fell to their deaths during the descent. The sole British survivor, Edward WHYMPER, wrote an account of the catastrophe that enhanced the mountain's fame. Mark Twain saw the Matterhorn from Zermatt and the RIFFELBERG in late August 1879 and discusses it in *A Tramp Abroad* (chapters 34, 36–38 and 41). He also uses "Matterhorn" as a metaphor for something large or great in *Following the Equator* (chapter 59), *Connecticut Yankee* (chapter 16) and *Life on the Mississippi* (chapter 38).

Matthews, [James] Brander (February 21, 1852, New Orleans, Louisiana–March 31, 1929, New York, New York)   Teacher and writer who was among the earliest scholars to recognize Mark Twain's writings as serious literature. In 1899, he wrote a long introduction to HARPER's first uniform edition of Mark Twain's books, summing up his opinions and placing Mark Twain in the same class as Chaucer, CERVANTES, Fielding and Moliere. Arguing that Mark Twain's greatness as a humorist has worked to obscure the depth of his work, he says that no other writer has given as full a spectrum of America, none commands such a varied style, and few have achieved the brilliance of his best passages.

Matthews and Mark Twain were friends from the mid-1870s and saw each other frequently at literary and social events. In 1887–88, they publicly debated the merits of British copyright law in the *New Princeton Review.* They both summered at the ONTEORA CLUB in 1890. At a New York dinner honoring Matthews three years later, Mark Twain delivered a well-received speech, playfully repeating "Brander Matthews," as if the name were a curse. His 1895 essay "Fenimore COO-PER's Literary Offenses" quotes Matthews, and "MY BOY-HOOD DREAMS" (1900) says that Matthews wanted to be a cowboy. Matthews visited Mark Twain in London in the summer of 1900. The next year, he dedicated *The Historical Novel and Other Essays* to him. His autobiography, *These Many Years,* appeared in 1917.

Mauritius   Now an independent country, Mauritius is a 790-square-mile island in the Indian Ocean, about 500 miles east of Madagascar. After sailing from INDIA on the *Wardha,* Mark Twain reached Mauritius's Port Louis on April 15, 1896. He went ashore with his family the next morning and took a train to Curepipe, a resort town in the central highlands. After resting there for nearly two weeks, he sailed for SOUTH AFRICA on April 28 aboard the *Arundel Castle.* At the time of his visit, the island's population was about 375,000.

FOLLOWING THE EQUATOR's chapters on Mauritius comment mostly on its weather and landscape, which Mark Twain thought charming, but not up to HAWAII's standard as a tropical island (chapters 62–63).

maxim   A synonym for aphorism, a maxim is a concise statement expressing a truth, often in the form of pointed advice. Mark Twain enjoyed expressing his fascination with language by reducing complex thoughts to a maxim's few carefully chosen words. In 1897 he summed this up: "The proper proportions of a maxim: a minimum of sound to a maximum of sense." In general, the themes and subject matter of his maxims reflect his interests and thinking, which became increasingly bitter and pessimistic toward the end of his life. He recorded hundreds of maxims in his NOTEBOOKS, particularly during the 1890s. Many are innocent foolery: "Clothes make the man. Naked people have little or no influence in society" and "Do not tell fish stories where the people know you; but particularly, don't tell them where they know the fish." Later maxims include such pessimistic thoughts as "The human race consists of the damned and the ought-to-be damned" and "At 50 a man can be an ass without being an optimist but not an optimist without being an ass." He published many of his best maxims as excerpts from "PUDD'NHEAD WILSON's CALENDAR," most of which appeared in *Pudd'nhead Wilson* and *Following the Equator.* The latter book also compares these maxims with the Maxim machine guns, suggesting that Pudd'nhead Wilson maxims "are much more deadly than those others, and they are easily carried, because they have no weight" (chapter 67).

Mayo, Frank (April 19, 1839, Boston, Massachusetts– June 8, 1896, Grand Island, Nebraska) Stage name of Frank McGuire, a popular actor who began his career in SAN FRANCISCO in 1856. After meeting Mark Twain in Nevada during the early 1860s, Mayo made his stage debut in New York in 1865 and became famous for robust character roles, notably *Davy Crockett*, which he toured in America and England after 1872. He dramatized *Pudd'nhead Wilson* himself and performed the lead role with his own touring company after opening the play in Hartford on April 8, 1895. A week later he opened it in New York, where Mark Twain gave a curtain speech at a late May performance. Mayo was still touring when he died in Nebraska. His *Pudd'nhead Wilson* play paid royalties to Mark Twain's estate for at least a decade and was the basis for a silent film in 1916.

"A Medieval Romance" ("An Awful Terrible Medieval Romance") Written in 1869 and published in 1870, this story is a condensed novel of 2,640 words in five chapters. It burlesques romance novels by piling on improbabilities that build to a bizarre dilemma, only to end suddenly as a literary hoax that refuses to resolve itself. Its central theme is confused sexual identities, which Mark Twain explored again in "1002D ARABIAN NIGHT" 14 years later.

The story first appeared as "An Awful Terrible Medieval Romance" in the BUFFALO EXPRESS on January 1, 1870. The following year Mark Twain republished it in his BURLESQUE AUTOBIOGRAPHY. It was later collected in SKETCHES, NEW AND OLD.

SYNOPSIS

Chapter 1
In the year 1222, the old German Baron Klugenstein secretly consults with his 28-year-old daughter, "Conrad," whom he has raised as a son. Klugenstein tells Conrad that his own father decreed that the ducal succession would pass to his house if he had a son and his brother Ulrich, the great Duke of Brandenburgh, did not. However, if both men had only daughters, the succession would pass to Ulrich's daughter—provided that she proved stainless. Klugenstein explains that when Conrad was born, he hanged every servant who witnessed her birth, then proclaimed that she was his *son*. Ten years later, Ulrich finally had a daughter named Constance.

Now aged and feeble, Ulrich wants his "nephew" Conrad to come and govern his duchy until "he" can succeed. Klugenstein warns Conrad not to sit in the great ducal chair before she is crowned, since any uncrowned female who sits there must die. Though Conrad objects to cheating her cousin out of her birthright,

she reluctantly goes. Afterward, Klugenstein tells his wife that he sent the handsome Count Detzin on a devilish mission to Constance three months earlier. If Detzin has succeeded, Conrad will become *duchess;* if he has failed, Conrad should still become *duke.*

Chapter 2
Six days later, Brandenburgh celebrates Conrad's coming—at the same moment that a distraught Constance curses Detzin for leaving her ruined.

Chapter 3
As months drift by, everyone praises Conrad's wise and merciful government, but Conrad is dismayed by Constance's romantic attentions. When Constance professes her love, Conrad spurns her.

Chapter 4
As more time passes, Conrad and Constance are no longer seen together and Conrad brightens. Meanwhile, rumors sweep the palace that Constance has had a baby. When Klugenstein hears this, he rejoices and praises Detzin.

Chapter 5
Conrad must reluctantly sit in judgment when Constance goes on trial for having a child out of wedlock—for which death is the penalty. Conrad stands up to pass sentence, but the justice insists that he speak from the ducal throne, which Conrad reluctantly ascends. When Conrad asks Constance to name her child's father, she points at Conrad, saying "Thou art the man!" Conrad is helpless. To disprove the charge, Conrad must reveal that he is a woman, then be condemned for sitting on the throne. His father swoons. Unable to get Conrad out of this dilemma, the narrator abandons the story.

Mediterranean Sea From the end of June through late October of 1867, Mark Twain toured the Mediterranean on the cruise ship QUAKER CITY. Aside from a three-week period in the Aegean and Black seas, the ship sailed only to Mediterranean ports. A little more than half of this four-month voyage Mark Twain spent ashore, making overland trips through FRANCE, ITALY, the HOLY LAND, EGYPT and SPAIN.

"The Memorable Assassination" Posthumously published essay. On September 10, 1898, while Mark Twain was in KALTENLEUTGEBEN, an Italian anarchist named Luigi Lucheni fatally stabbed AUSTRIA's Empress Elizabeth (1837–1898) in Geneva, Switzerland. Deeply moved by the incident, Mark Twain wrote this 4,000-word essay after seeing the empress's funeral in VIENNA a week later. After several American magazines rejected the essay, it was set aside until A. B. PAINE included it in *What Is Man? and Other Essays* in 1917. Paine's edition of MARK TWAIN'S NOTEBOOK has additional notes on the empress's funeral (chapter 31).

SYNOPSIS

Calling the murder of an empress the "largest of all events," Mark Twain says that one must go back to Julius CAESAR to find an instance of similar magnitude. Even Caesar's death, however, is not comparable, since the world has grown so much larger and the telegraph now spreads news so quickly. Indeed, this is the first time in history that the entire world has instantaneously learned of so gigantic an event.

A common form of madness is the desire to be noticed—which helps explain why a mangy Italian tramp committed this murder. In one instant he lifted himself from obscurity to immortality by striking down a woman who led a blameless and noble life.

The essay concludes with a detailed description of the empress's state funeral.

"A Memorable Midnight Experience" Sketch first published in *Number One: Mark Twain's Sketches* (1874). In mid-1873, Mark Twain visited ENGLAND intending to collect material for a travel book along the lines of *Innocents Abroad*. The only substantial segment that he wrote, however, is this 3,400-word gothic sketch. The novelist Charles Kingsley (1819–1875), a canon of WESTMINSTER Abbey, arranged for Mark Twain to have a special tour of the abbey in June. The resulting sketch's fascination with graves recalls themes that Mark Twain explores in writings such as "A CURIOUS DREAM." (1870)

SYNOPSIS

Late one night, a Mr. Wright leads the narrator and his friend through Westminster Abbey, "the tomb of the great dead of England." They examine the graves of such people as DICKENS, GARRICK, Thomas Parr, Ben JONSON, William Pitt and various royal figures. The narrator gets separated from the others and stumbles in the dark. He touches the cold hand of a reposing queen and is startled by a cat that brushes up against him. As a bell tolls midnight, he sees an illuminated clock through a window.

Memphis Mississippi River city in the southwest corner of TENNESSEE. Founded in 1819—the same year as Hannibal, Missouri—Memphis used its favorable position as a river landing to grow rapidly. Mark Twain visited the town frequently during his PILOTING days, from 1857 to 1861—especially in mid-1858, when he cubbed on the St. Louis–Memphis packet JOHN H. DICKEY. In June 1858, he spent about a week in Memphis, while his brother Henry Clemens was being nursed after being severely injured in the steamboat PENNSYLVANIA's explosion 70 miles downriver. Henry's temporary hospital was located at Main and Madison streets. Chapter 20 of *Life on the Mississippi* recalls the episode. There, and in chapter 29, Mark Twain calls Memphis the "Good Samaritan City" because of its care for disaster

victims. He also evokes this memory of Memphis in *The Gilded Age*'s account of the fictional AMARANTH disaster (chapter 6).

At the start of the CIVIL WAR, Memphis was an important Confederate military center and it was temporarily Tennessee's state capital. Union forces occupied the city on June 6, 1862, in a battle in which J. Ed MONTGOMERY commanded the South's steamboat flotilla. This battle proved a major turning point in opening the river to the Union. Mark Twain revisited Memphis twice in early 1882, by which time its population was 40,000. Twelve chapters of *Life on the Mississippi* mention Memphis. *Huckleberry Finn* mentions it just once—as the place to which the KING and DUKE sell two of the WILKS family's slave children (chapter 27).

Menken, Adah Isaacs (June 15, 1835?, New Orleans, Louisiana–August 10, 1868, Paris, France) Actress and poet. An average but popular actress, Menken had a flair for scandal and self-promotion that made her an international sensation during the 1860s. She became notorious for performing in *Mazeppa*—a play based on a BYRON poem—in which she wore a body stocking that made her look nude, earning her the nickname the "Great Unadorned." She also published poetry occasionally in the GOLDEN ERA and other journals. When she toured California in late 1863, Mark Twain saw her perform in San Francisco and wrote about her for the VIRGINIA CITY TERRITORIAL ENTERPRISE. The following February, Menken began a month-long stay in VIRGINIA CITY. She tried to draw Mark Twain into her crowd, but failed to impress him favorably. At that time, she was married to the third of at least four husbands, humorist Orpheus C. Kerr (1836–1901), whom Mark Twain already knew. In May 1867, Mark Twain wrote about Menken in a letter to the SAN FRANCISCO ALTA CALIFORNIA, criticizing published photographs of her with Alexander Dumas *père* and her propensity for using and abandoning famous people. Just over a year later, Menken died in Paris after neglecting an abscess.

Merlin Character in *Connecticut Yankee*. Since the mid-12th century, Merlin has been a central figure in Arthurian legends, usually as a powerful sorcerer and benevolent counselor to King ARTHUR, whom he helped to put in power. Nineteenth-century writers depicted Merlin as a simpler but often menacing wizard—a trend to which Mark Twain's *Connecticut Yankee* contributed. His novel makes Merlin both the primary adversary and comic foil of Hank MORGAN, who regards him as an old numskull handicapped by belief in his own magic (chapter 22).

Merlin first appears in CAMELOT's banquet hall, where he puts everyone *but* Hank to sleep with his weary tale about taking LAUNCELOT to the Lady of the Lake (chapter 3). The scene is the antithesis of the final chapter, in which Merlin puts *Hank* to sleep for 13 centuries. After Hank is put in the dungeon, he determines to

Merlin has more than an accidental resemblance to Alfred Lord Tennyson in Dan Beard's Connecticut Yankee *illustration.*

prove himself a greater magician than Merlin by threatening to blot out the sun (chapter 5). Merlin ridicules Hank's threat and is the person most eager to burn him at the stake; however, he fails to turn back the ECLIPSE, leaving Hank his vanquisher (chapter 6). Hank later gives Merlin another chance to demonstrate his power before he blows up Merlin's tower, lowering Merlin's reputation even more. Even Arthur suggests banishing Merlin, but Hank keeps him on the payroll as a weatherman, refusing to take him seriously (chapter 7).

Hank and Merlin meet again in the VALLEY OF HOLINESS, where Merlin's incantations fail to restart a holy fountain. Merlin declares that the spell over the fountain is unbreakable, giving Hank yet another opportunity to embarrass him (chapters 22–26). Merlin's next humiliation occurs in chapter 39, in which he fails to help Sir SAGRAMOUR defeat Hank in a tournament. Seeing the encounter as the "final struggle for supremacy between the two master enchanters of the age,"

Hank gains another spectacular triumph, leaving Merlin's reputation flatter than ever.

Merlin plays no role in the monumental confrontation between Hank and the Roman Catholic Church several years later, but Hank and his tiny army convert Merlin's cave into the headquarters of their coming war against the massed chivalry of England. After they annihilate thousands of knights, they are trapped inside the cave by the corpses encircling them. Disguised as an old woman, Merlin enters the cave and casts the spell that makes Hank sleep until the late 19th century. Merlin then runs into an electrified fence and dies with a triumphant laugh frozen on his face.

Joan of Arc mentions Merlin as having prophesied Joan's coming 800 years earlier (book 2, chapter 2). This allusion contrasts sharply with *Connecticut Yankee*, in which Hank belittles Merlin for being unable to prophesy more than a few years into the future (chapter 27).

The many character actors who have played Merlin in screen adaptations of *Connecticut Yankee* include Brandon Hurst (1931); Murvyn Vye (1949); Boris Karloff (1952), who also played Arthur on television two years later; Victor Jory (1954), who played INJUN JOE in the 1938 adaptation of *Tom Sawyer;* Roscoe Lee Browne (1978); Ron Moody (1979) and Rene Auberjonois (1989).

Merrill, Frank Thayer (December 14, 1848, Boston, Massachusetts–?) Illustrator. Merrill shared the illustrating of the first edition of *The Prince and the Pauper* (1881) with John HARLEY, who concentrated on scenes away from the palace, while Merrill drew the more delicate court scenes. Mark Twain was pleased with both men's work, which matched his vision of his characters. He later considered having Merrill illustrate *Connecticut Yankee*, but the assignment instead went to Dan BEARD. Merrill meanwhile illustrated new editions of other authors' classics, such as Washington Irving's *Rip van Winkle* and Louisa May Alcott's *Little Women.*

***Merry Tales* (1892)** Collection of Mark Twain's short stories published by Charles L. WEBSTER & COMPANY in March 1892. This edition contains "THE PRIVATE HISTORY OF A CAMPAIGN THAT FAILED," "LUCK," "A CURIOUS EXPERIENCE," "THE INVALID'S STORY," "The Captain's Story," "Mrs. MCWILLIAMS and the Lightning," and "Meisterschaft." All the items except "Captain's Story" were later published as the second half of the HARPER'S edition, *The American Claimant and Other Stories and Sketches*, which retains "Merry Tales" as a section title.

Milan Northern Italian city. The capital of Lombardy, Milan united with ITALY in 1861, just six years before Mark Twain's first visit. He arrived there by train from GENOA and Alessandria on July 16, 1867 and spent two days sightseeing before continuing to COMO. Most of chapter 18 of *Innocents Abroad* is about Milan's cathedral, to which the book gives more space than any structure but Jerusalem's Church of the HOLY SEPULCHER. Everything about the huge edifice impressed Mark Twain, but the chapter's most poignant passage is his largely irrelevant recollection of finding a corpse in his father's law office when he was a boy. The next chapter offers conventional descriptions of Milan's Ambrosia Library, La Scala and other sights, as well as a sarcastic description of Leonardo da Vinci's battered painting of *The Last Supper*. Mark Twain returned to Milan with his family for a week-long visit in September 1878. Chapter 48 of *A Tramp Abroad* records his modified views on the works of the old masters.

Miller, Joaquin (Cincinnatus Heine [or Hiner] Miller) (September 8, 1837?, Liberty, Indiana–February 17, 1913, Oakland, California) Western poet noted for self-promotion and embellished accounts of his life. A few years after settling in Oregon with his family in 1852, Miller ran off to California's gold fields, where he lived among Indians and had a daughter by a Modoc woman. He later studied law in Oregon, helped establish a pony express route, edited a newspaper and was a judge (1866–69). Meanwhile, he published poems about the West that were collected in *Specimens* (1868), *Joaquin et al.* (1869), *Songs of the Sierras* (1871) and other volumes. Disappointed with his critical reception in America, he went to England in 1870 and found unexpected popularity as an authentic westerner. After traveling widely in Europe, he returned to California and settled in Oakland.

Mark Twain met Miller in San Francisco during the 1860s when both were contributing to the GOLDEN ERA. In 1873, they renewed their acquaintance in London. Mark Twain saw Miller frequently that summer and interceded to get the AMERICAN PUBLISHING COMPANY to issue Miller's autobiographical *Unwritten History: Life Amongst the Modocs*. In 1875, Miller visited Mark Twain in Hartford. While Miller was being lionized in London, he wore flamboyant western clothes that stuck in Mark Twain's mind for decades. Mark Twain may have been thinking of Miller when he put Lord BERKELEY in similar clothes in *The American Claimant*.

Miller, Johnny Minor character in *Tom Sawyer*. In the FENCE WHITEWASHING episode of chapter 2, Johnny is one of only three boys to paint the fence who are identified by name. He gives Tom a dead rat on a string for the privilege. He is also mentioned in chapter 16 as a boy likely to be jealous that Tom and Joe are learning how to smoke. In chapter 18, Becky THATCHER invites Johnny's sister Grace to her picnic.

Millet, François Character to whom the title of "IS HE LIVING OR IS HE DEAD?" (1893) alludes. As a young man, Millet is one of several struggling painters who scheme to enrich themselves by faking the death of one of

their own number in order to increase the value of his paintings. Millet then serves as a pallbearer at his own funeral, then shares the rewards of the successful scheme. By 1892, he is living as a retired silk manufacturer named Théophile Magnan. Mark Twain takes the character's name from the American painter and illustrator Francis (Frank) Davis Millet (1846–1912), who had been a family friend since painting Mark Twain's portrait in 1876. The real Millet died even more dramatically than his fictional counterpart; he went down with the *Titanic*.

"The £1,000,000 Bank-Note" Short story published in early 1893. The narrator recalls an episode from his earlier life when an accident delivered him to LONDON, where he fell in love and became rich while serving as the guinea pig in a bet between two wealthy eccentrics. As a wish-fulfillment fantasy about the acquisition of sudden wealth, the story has a kind of mirror-image relationship to "THE MAN THAT CORRUPTED HADLEYBURG" (1899) and "THE $30,000 BEQUEST" (1904). It touches on a variety of themes relating to capitalism, gambling, claimants, love at first sight and the importance of clothes. Although it is generally good-natured and has a happy ending, the story has an anglophobic undertone that is especially evident in a dinner party scene.

Among Mark Twain's writings, this story is unusually playful with characters' names. The protagonist, Henry ADAMS, for example, sees his surname as evidence of his direct descent from ADAM. His fiancée, Portia LANGHAM, takes her surname from a street near her London home. All the aristocratic guests at the American minister's dinner party have odd names. By contrast, the eccentric brothers who start Adams on his adventure are initially identified only as Brother A and Brother B. At the end, A's name is revealed as Abel.

SYNOPSIS

A young mining-broker clerk (later identified as Henry ADAMS) goes sailing on SAN FRANCISCO Bay and is swept out to sea. A brig rescues him, then forces him to work without pay on a long, stormy voyage to London, where he arrives ragged and broke. As Adams wanders the streets hungry, he is invited into a fine house on Portland Place, where he meets two elderly men. As Adams later learns, these men are brothers who disagree about what would become of an intelligent and honest stranger set adrift in London with nothing but a million-pound bank-note and no way to explain how he got it. Brother A thinks that the man would starve, since he could not offer the note to a bank without being arrested; Brother B thinks that a man could survive 30 days without being jailed. After making a £20,000 bet on the question, they have purchased the only £1,000,000 bank-note in England and have been waiting for a likely stranger to appear. Adams meets their qualifications, so they make him their guinea pig.

Explaining nothing to Adams, the brothers give him an envelope containing instructions and say good-bye. After he leaves, he opens the envelope, sees money and hurries to the nearest cheap restaurant. Only after dining does he realize that he has been given a bill worth $5 million in American money. He proffers the note to the restaurant proprietor (later identified as Harris) and asks for change. The astonished man not only tells him not to worry about payment, he invites him to order anything he wants. Adams rushes back to Portland Place to correct what he is sure is a monumental mistake, but the butler tells him not to worry and that the brothers will return in a month.

Adams now reads the note in the envelope, which explains that he is being lent the money for 30 days without interest. At the end of that time, he is to report back. If the note's author wins his bet, Adams will receive "any situation" he can fill. The note is not signed, addressed or dated. Adams recognizes that the immense note is worthless to him since he cannot cash it, but determines to get through the month in order to win the promised situation, which he is confident will be a well-salaried job. At a tailor shop, he tries on a ratty, ill-fitting suit and asks he if can pay for it later. The disdainful clerk sniffs at this suggestion, but Adams freezes him with his bank-note. The equally shocked manager immediately becomes obsequious and insists on fitting Adams with a first-class wardrobe, assuring him that he can take forever to pay.

Within a week, Adams is sumptuously equipped with everything he needs and is housed in a fine hotel in Hanover Square (near Portland Place). He gets everything he wants on credit simply by showing the bank-note, and he is becoming celebrated as the "vest-pocket monster"—a foreign crank who carries million-pound notes in his pocket. He breakfasts at Harris's humble restaurant, which his patronage makes so famous that its grateful owner even forces loans on him. Despite all his borrowing, Adams figures he is remaining within the means of what his future salary should bring; however, he frets about impending disaster. Meanwhile, he receives the ultimate badge of fame: He is caricatured in PUNCH.

After 10 days, Adams visits the American minister, who invites him to a dinner party. It happens that Adams's father and the minister were boyhood friends and classmates at YALE. Among the people he meets at the dinner party are the Duke and Duchess of Shoreditch, the Earl and Countess of Newgate, Viscount Cheapside, Lord and Lady BLATHERSKITE, the minister's family, and Portia LANGHAM, a visiting friend of the minister's daughter. Adams and Portia instantly fall in love. A latecomer to the party is Lloyd Hastings—a good friend of Adams from San Francisco who is in London to sell shares in a California mine.

The dinner itself fails to come off when the matter of precedence in seating cannot be settled—a common English problem. The duke insists on sitting at the head of the table, but Adams protests on two counts. First, he ranks higher in newspaper gossip columns; second, his family name, Adams, establishes his direct descent from Adam, while Shoreditch only belongs to a collateral branch of the family. When the dinner guests retreat to play cribbage, Adams has a delightful time joking and bantering with Portia, who laughs when he reveals his incredible story. By the end of the evening, they have an understanding.

After the party, Adams walks home with Hastings, who explains his difficulties in selling shares in his mine option and asks for help. Adams offers to permit Hastings to use his own name to endorse his scheme; in return the friends will split the proceeds. Within days, investors begin buying shares. Meanwhile, Adams spends his evenings with Portia, alternating love talk with speculation about what salary Adams should expect from his unknown benefactor.

By the end of the month, Adams and Hastings have each banked a million dollars from Hastings's scheme. Adams goes to Portland Place with Portia to report on the million-pound note, which he presents to Brother B. He also shows the brothers a certificate of deposit for the £200,000 he has banked. Even Portia is surprised. "B"—who has won his bet—wants to give Adams the situation he promised him, but Adams respectfully declines. Portia climbs into the old man's lap, kisses him, then explains that the man is her stepfather. The startled Adams tells the man that there is, after all, a "situation" that he wants, namely "son-in-law." The older man starts to ask Adams about furnishing recommendations, but quickly gives in to Adams's importuning.

Since these adventures have occurred, the narrator has become truly happy. His father-in-law has had the million-pound note canceled and framed as a gift. Though the note is a million-pounder, Adams considers its value only a tenth the worth of what it has bought him.

BACKGROUND AND PUBLISHING HISTORY

Mark Twain recorded a NOTEBOOK entry containing the essence of this story's plot in early 1879. Another seed of the story appears in *Connecticut Yankee* (1889); when Hank MORGAN astonishes a sixth-century shopkeeper with a $20 gold piece, he compares the situation with the effect that a $2,000 bill would have in a 19th-century village store (chapter 31). Mark Twain finally wrote this 7,500-word story in late 1892 while he was living in Florence, Italy, and published it in CENTURY in January 1893. A month later, Charles L. WEBSTER & COMPANY made it the title piece of a new collection, *The £1,000,000 Bank-Note and Other New Stories*. CHATTO and Windus followed with an English edition in April. The collection also includes "A Cure for the Blues," "About All Kinds of Ships," "The German Chicago," "Mental Telegraphy," "The Enemy Conquered," "PLAYING COURIER," "A

Petition to the Queen of England" and "A MAJESTIC LITERARY FOSSIL." HARPER'S later incorporated the volume into *The American Claimant, etc.*

Around 1920, the Hungarian director Alexander Korda adapted this story into a silent film, *The Thousand Pound Bank Note.* A half-hour adaptation of the story aired on television's short-lived series *Your Show Time* in May 1949. Five years later, Gregory Peck starred as Adams in the first sound film adaptation, a British production titled *The Million Pound Note,* which was briefly released in America as *Man with a Million.* The popular 1983 film *Trading Places* doubtless owes something to Mark Twain's story. In that film two wealthy commodities dealers make a wager and pull an indigent (Eddie Murphy) off the street to replace a broker (Dan Aykroyd). In May 1994, *A Million to Juan,* a new film loosely adapted from "The £1,000,000 Bank-Note" was released. Directed by Paul Rodriguez, this film is set in modern Los Angeles.

Mills family Characters in "HUCK FINN AND TOM SAWYER AMONG THE INDIANS." A family migrating from southern Missouri to Oregon, the Millses invite Tom, Huck and Jim to accompany them across the Central Plains. The family consists of a 55-year-old man; his wife; adult sons Buck, Bill and Sam; and daughters 17-year-old Peggy and seven-year-old Flaxy. After INDIANS kill everyone in the family except Peggy and Flaxy, whom they carry off, Tom and Huck join Peggy's fiancé Brace JOHNSON in pursuit. When the rescuers reach an abandoned Indian camp, they find indications that Peggy is still alive just as the story ends abruptly.

mining One of the trades with which Mark Twain is most closely identified is mining. In *Life on the Mississippi,* he lists it among the "livelihoods" he pursued after ending his career as a steamboat PILOT (chapter 21). All his firsthand experience in mining occurred in NEVADA and CALIFORNIA between 1861 and 1865. One of the reasons he went west was his hope of striking it rich in Nevada's silver rush, after missing out on California's GOLD RUSH. *Roughing It* presents a highly embellished account of these years, mixing his real experiences with exaggeration and fabrication. Nevertheless, it presents accurate technical information on western mining, as well as an honest portrayal of the hopes and beliefs that motivated men to squander their lives in pursuit of elusive riches. The book is particularly honest in depicting its young narrator's growing disillusionment in his own quest for easy wealth. The outline it presents of the narrator's mining experiences corresponds reasonably well with Mark Twain's actual experiences, which fall into three distinct periods.

From late December 1861 to mid-January 1862, Mark Twain prospected unsuccessfully with several companions in northern Nevada's HUMBOLDT district. Smitten with "silver fever," the naive narrator of *Roughing It* arrives there expecting to scoop up ore in the open. He is disillusioned when he instead confronts the sweaty reality of quartz-mining, which he and his companions soon abandon in favor of the only sure way to make money from claims—*selling* them to someone else (chapters 28–33).

After returning to Carson City from Humboldt, Mark Twain went south to the ESMERALDA district, remaining there from February to September 1862 to work claims that he had acquired for himself and his brother during a brief visit in September 1861. Over the next seven months, he lived in AURORA and had several partners, including Calvin HIGBIE. None of his claims paid enough to support him, however, and he ended up working in a quartz mill for low wages—an experience that permanently soured him on quartz-mining. He enjoyed one moment of excitement when he staked a claim to a particularly promising area, but it turned out to be worthless. He magnified the episode enormously in chapters 40–41 of *Roughing It* to make it appear that he and Higbie had nearly made millions on a "BLIND LEAD."

After quitting Esmeralda, Mark Twain became a reporter for the VIRGINIA CITY TERRITORIAL ENTERPRISE in the heart of the COMSTOCK, one of the world's richest mining areas. Though surrounded by tangible evidence of mining wealth, he restricted his involvement to collecting shares ("FEET")—which he hoped would make him rich—and reported mining news occasionally. Most such reporting, however, he left to his better-qualified colleague, Dan DE QUILLE.

Mark Twain left Nevada for San Francisco in May 1864 and was away from mining activity for half a year. In December, he began his third and last mining venture when he belatedly joined the gold rush by going to TUOLUMNE COUNTY to stay with friends at JACKASS HILL. Though his reasons for going there had more to do with getting away from San Francisco than with taking up prospecting again, he spent much of the next two and a half months dabbling in "pocket mining," a method of panning surface scrapings described in chapter 60 of *Roughing It.* As before, he enjoyed no mineral success; however, he came away with a rich haul in anecdotes, stories and mining argot that he later used in his JUMPING FROG STORY, Dick BAKER tales and other writings that permanently linked his name with that of Bret HARTE and California mining camps.

After leaving Tuolumne at the end of February 1865, Mark Twain probably never handled a mining pick or pan again. By then, however, he had acquired considerable knowledge of both the techniques and the psychology of mining, and he remained fiercely proud of it to the end of his life. In chapter 7 of IS SHAKESPEARE DEAD?, for example, he discusses the importance of an author's knowing the language of the trades about which he writes. To make his point, he summarizes his personal expertise in all the phases and terminology of quartz-mining for silver, surface-mining for gold, and pocket-mining.

Aside from *Roughing It*, the main literary use that Mark Twain makes of his knowledge of mining comes in the novel he coauthored with C. D. WARNER, *The Gilded Age* (especially chapters 45, 47–49 and 50). In chapter 22 of *A Tramp Abroad*, he outlines a BLACK FOREST novel whose hero strikes a rich "manure mine." Mark Twain also concocted a scheme for a book on SOUTH AFRICA's fledgling diamond industry that remained unwritten. In January 1871, he paid John Henry RILEY to go to the South African diamond fields to collect material that he would write after Riley returned. Riley made it there and collected notes (but no diamonds), but died before Mark Twain got around to starting the book. When Mark Twain visited South Africa himself 25 years later, he retraced part of Riley's route and examined Kimberley's diamond workings. He also visited and described the gold fields of South Africa and AUSTRALIA. *Following the Equator* aptly sums up his mining career: "I had been a gold miner myself, in my day, and knew substantially everything that those people knew about it, except how to make money at it" (chapter 68).

Mississippi River   One of the world's great river systems, the Mississippi drains an area encompassing over 1,250,000 square miles in 31 states between the Rocky and Allegheny mountains. Taking its name from a Chippewa term for "big river," the Mississippi rises in northern Minnesota's Lake Itasca, from which it flows almost due south about 2,350 miles until it empties into the Gulf of Mexico below NEW ORLEANS, Louisiana. The river is traditionally divided into the "upper" and "lower" sections separated by its confluence with the OHIO RIVER. Virtually the entire river is navigable, as are major stretches of most of its tributaries.

Mark Twain was born in FLORIDA, Missouri, on the banks of the Salt River, a minor tributary of the Mississippi that his father dreamed of making navigable. When that dream faded, John M. Clemens moved his family to the banks of the Mississippi itself, in Hannibal, where Mark Twain grew up. Aside from periods on the East Coast (1853–54) and in CINCINNATI, Ohio (1856–57), Mark Twain lived on or within sight of the Mississippi from the time he was four until he was 25. After leaving Hannibal in 1853, he worked in such river towns as ST. LOUIS, Missouri and KEOKUK and MUSCATINE, Iowa. In 1857, he became an apprentice steamboat PILOT and spent four years on the river itself. After the CIVIL WAR stopped commercial steamboat traffic on the lower Mississippi in 1861, he returned briefly to Missouri, then went west—never to live on the river again.

After 1861, Mark Twain revisited the river at least eight times. He paid quick visits during lecture tours in 1867, 1869 and 1885, and family visits in 1886, 1890 and 1895. His longest visit was in April–May 1882, when he spent a month on a steamboat journey from St. Louis to New Orleans and back to St. Paul. He saw the river for the last time in June 1902, when he went to the University of MISSOURI to receive an honorary

degree. During that trip, he and a childhood friend, John BRIGGS, climbed atop Hannibal's CARDIFF HILL and gazed out over the river. In a birthday speech that he gave later that year, he recalled this moment, saying that he "was seeing now the most enchanting river view the planet could furnish. I never knew it when I was a boy; it took an educated eye that had traveled over the globe to know and appreciate it." That same view remains largely unspoiled today.

The modern Mississippi, however, is not the river that Mark Twain knew in the mid-19th century. As *Life on the Mississippi* emphasizes, the river constantly shifts its course, trading new channels for old, turning peninsulas into islands and leaving river ports high and dry—especially on the Lower Mississippi. The river never stops trying to shorten its crooked path to the sea. Even now, it threatens to cut a new exit to the Gulf through southern Louisiana, despite the efforts of the Army Corps of Engineers to tame it. As late as the summer of 1993, its waters rose to unprecedented heights, severely taxing the vast system of levees built to contain it.

Mark Twain's interest in the Mississippi revived in the mid-1870s, as he searched for a fresh subject about which to write. With the encouragement of W. D. HOWELLS, he wrote "OLD TIMES ON THE MISSISSIPPI," a memoir of his apprentice pilot days serialized in the ATLANTIC MONTHLY. These memoirs reappeared in *Life on the Mississippi*, which expands them and adds background material on the river and a long account of his 1882 trip. This book and the novels *Tom Sawyer, Huckleberry Finn* and *Pudd'nhead Wilson* have been dubbed his "Mississippi writings." Other long fictional works in which the river figures prominently include *The Gilded Age, Tom Sawyer Abroad, Tom Sawyer, Detective* and "TOM SAWYER'S CONSPIRACY." Mark Twain also mentions the river frequently in his other travel books, as well as in many short stories, sketches and essays. Chapter 58 of *Innocents Abroad*, and chapter 10 of *A Tramp Abroad*, for example, both recall his first journey on the Mississippi as a child.

The Mississippi's presence is felt throughout *Tom Sawyer*, from a moment in which Tom sits on a raft contemplating drowning (chapter 3), through his PIRATE expedition with friends on JACKSON'S ISLAND (chapters 13–16) and Tom and Huck's boating downriver to retrieve treasure from the cave (chapter 33). These and other episodes establish the importance of the river and the boys' familiarity with it. Although it is clear that people can and do drown in the river, Tom thinks nothing of making his way from Jackson's Island to his village and back in the dead of night alone.

The Mississippi is even more central to *Huckleberry Finn*. Though Huck and Jim are *on* the river aboard their RAFT in only about a fifth of its chapters, the river is at least mentioned or alluded to in almost every chapter. Remarkably, however, the name "Mississippi" appears just twice in the novel (chapters 10 and 18)—the same number of times as in *Tom Sawyer* (chapters 13 and 32) and even in *Connecticut Yankee* (in chapters

27 and 39 Hank MORGAN alludes to seeing steamboat explosions on the river and visiting the Upper Mississippi). "Mississippi" is, however, mentioned five times in the "RAFT CHAPTER," whose characters discuss the mixing of Mississippi and Ohio waters—a point that becomes important in chapter 16 of *Huckleberry Finn* when Huck notices the clear water channel, signifying that they have passed Cairo.

The Mississippi takes Jim and Huck on a one-way voyage south, from which there is no easy turning back. Along the way, it proves both bountiful and terrible. It furnishes Huck and Jim with food and supplies not easily available on land. Just before their voyage, Huck and Jim find a valuable canoe and a raft; they reap rich harvests from the HOUSE OF DEATH and the derelict WALTER SCOTT and are even given gold by slave-catchers. The river is full of terrors, as well. Aside from the horrors of the HOUSE OF DEATH and the WALTER SCOTT, Huck and Jim experience a frightening separation during a foggy night in chapter 16, which ends with their being run down by a steamboat.

Mississippi (state) Mark Twain visited the river ports of Mississippi frequently during the late 1850s, when he was a steamboat PILOT. *Life on the Mississippi* describes his return to the river in 1882, when he revisited such Mississippi towns as Greenville (chapter 33) and VICKSBURG and Natchez (chapter 39).

The geography of the second half of *Huckleberry Finn* is so vague that there is room to argue that several important episodes are set *in* Mississippi. PIKESVILLE, for example, might be in the state. When Aunt POLLY arrives there from ST. PETERSBURG, she says that she has traveled 1,100 miles (chapter 42); this same distance from Hannibal, Missouri—St. Petersburg's real-life counterpart—would place Pikesville near Natchez. Mark Twain seems, however, to have intended Pikesville to be in southern ARKANSAS—much of which faces Mississippi across the river.

Missouri River The longest river in the United States, the Missouri rises in southwestern Montana and flows about 2,715 miles generally southeast until it joins the Mississippi River just above ST. LOUIS. After Lewis and Clark explored the Louisiana Territory in 1804–06, the Missouri became an important transportation route into the northwest. Through much of the 19th century, its lower reaches were a major STEAMBOAT route and its upper reaches were navigable into Montana during high water periods. Known as the "Big Muddy" because of its massive discharge of sediment, the Missouri was notoriously difficult to navigate. It shifted channels constantly, was filled with SAWYERS, snags and other hazards, and usually iced over during the winters.

Mark Twain first saw the Missouri during a visit to St. Louis when he was about 10 years old—a trip he recalls in *Life on the Mississippi* (chapter 53). He traveled up the river at least once: in July 1861, when he and his brother Orion spent six days riding the steamboat *Sioux City* from St. Louis to St. Joseph, from which they left for Nevada by STAGECOACH. *Roughing It* vividly describes the river's navigational problems (chapter 1). As early as 1866, Mark Twain considered writing a book about the Mississippi for which he would travel overland from California to the upper Missouri and boat down to the Mississippi; however, he never made the trip. He probably last saw the river in mid-1895, during his trip across the northern states.

Missouri (state) Located near the geographical center of the continental United States, Missouri gained statehood in August 1821 under terms of the Missouri Compromise, which permitted it to become a slave-holding state, while Maine was admitted to the Union as a free state. By the 1830s, growing numbers of settlers were entering Missouri from Tennessee and Kentucky, following the example of Daniel Boone, who settled near St. Louis around 1798. Mark Twain's Quarles and Lampton relatives joined this migration in the early 1830s and his own family followed in 1834.

Much of who Mark Twain was and what he became can be attributed to the complex forces that developed Missouri. When he was born in 1835, the state stood at the physical and psychological edge of the western frontier. From the time that Lewis and Clark began exploring the Louisiana Purchase territories in 1804 until the completion of the first transcontinental railway in the 1860s, Missouri was the gateway to the West. Although slavery was legal in Missouri, there was considerable opposition to it, particularly in the northern counties. Indeed, it was Missouri's ambivalence toward slavery that led to the Dred Scott case, which resulted in the U.S. Supreme Court's 1857 decision that the Missouri Compromise was unconstitutional. Missouri's latent split over slavery became overt on the outbreak of the CIVIL WAR. Though many Missourians supported the Confederacy, the state legislature voted against secession. After the war started, the state was quickly brought under Union administration, but guerrilla warfare continued. Given Missouri's ambivalence towards the war, it becomes easier to understand the ambivalence that Mark Twain later expressed in "THE PRIVATE HISTORY OF A CAMPAIGN THAT FAILED."

Mark Twain's permanent residence in Missouri ended in 1853. After leaving Hannibal in June, he lived briefly with the family of his sister Pamela Clemens MOFFETT in St. Louis before continuing on to the East Coast. The rest of his family left Hannibal shortly afterward, leaving Pamela the only family member living in Missouri. St. Louis might be regarded as Mark Twain's last Missouri residence, as he generally stayed with Pamela's family when he passed through the town, especially during his PILOTING years, from 1857 to 1861. Pamela remained in St. Louis until 1870, when she moved to FREDONIA, New York.

In July 1861, Mark Twain and his brother Orion Clemens took a steamboat up the Missouri River to St. Joseph, from which they traveled overland to NEVADA.

Mark Twain paid his longest return visit to Missouri in 1867, during a brief lecture tour. He arrived in St. Louis in early March, stayed with his sister's family for several weeks, visited Hannibal briefly, and then went back to St. Louis before returning to New York City, from which he went to Europe aboard the QUAKER CITY. The travel letters he wrote during this visit to the Midwest appear in MARK TWAIN'S TRAVELS WITH MR. BROWN.

Eastern Missouri figures prominently in much of Mark Twain's fiction. All the Huck Finn–Tom Sawyer stories are set, in full or in part, in and around the fictional ST. PETERSBURG, and most have episodes in St. Louis and other Mississippi riverfront locations. After a brief interlude in St. Petersburg (not mentioned by name, however), "HUCK FINN AND TOM SAWYER AMONG THE INDIANS" takes Jim and the boys to a hemp farm along Missouri's western border. Though Missouri is clearly the setting of *Tom Sawyer* and the early chapters of *Huckleberry Finn,* the evidence for placing these stories in Missouri is circumstantial (such as passages pertaining to JACKSON'S ISLAND's location). The first story explicitly to place Tom and Huck in Missouri is *Tom Sawyer Abroad,* which calls Huck and Jim "a couple of sapheaded country yahoos out in the backwoods of Missouri" (chapter 1) and alludes to Tom as a "backwoods Missouri boy" (chapter 13). By contrast, *Pudd'nhead Wilson* immediately names Missouri as the location of DAWSON'S LANDING (chapter 1) and makes St. Louis an important setting in several chapters.

Mark Twain enjoyed remarking that his birth increased the population of Florida by one percent. Doubtless he would be pleased to know that about three percent of the surface of modern Missouri is now named after him, thanks to tracts of land covered by the MARK TWAIN NATIONAL FOREST, MARK TWAIN LAKE and other sites.

Missouri, University of   The first state university built west of the Mississippi River, the University of Missouri was founded at Columbia in 1839—the same year that Mark Twain's family settled in Hannibal, 65 miles to the northeast. In June 1902, Mark Twain visited the university to accept an honorary doctorate, stopping in Hannibal for the last time. On his way back, he participated in ground-breaking ceremonies for the world's fair at ST. LOUIS.

Model Boy   Character type. During the early and mid-19th century, many boys' stories were moralistic tales featuring heroes who were "model boys"—characters who avoid trouble and try to do only good. The best-known writer of such stories was Horatio Alger, Jr. (1832–1899), the author of *Ragged Dick* (1867) and many similar books. Mark Twain disliked such stories as much as he despised "model boys." In *Life on the Mississippi* he describes the "Model Boy" of his time as perfect in manners, dress, conduct, filial piety and exterior godliness, but a prig at heart; his "reproachlessness was a standing reproach to every lad in the village. He was the admiration of all the mothers, and the detestation of all their sons" (chapter 54).

By the time Mark Twain started writing fiction, a new trend was emerging in children's literature. Authors such as P. B. SHILLABER and Thomas Bailey ALDRICH were writing successful "bad boy" stories. Mark Twain himself attacked the "model boy" theme at least as early as 1865 with "THE STORY OF THE BAD LITTLE BOY," making the point that normal boys can misbehave and still become respectable adults. His major assault on Model Boy literature came in *Tom Sawyer* (1876), whose first chapter immediately establishes that Tom is "not the Model Boy of the village." The model boy is Willie MUFFERSON, whom Tom loathes. In "SCHOOLHOUSE HILL," Tom's brother, Sid SAWYER, is the model boy.

Moffett, Pamela Clemens (September 13, 1827, Jamestown, Tennessee–August 31, 1904, Greenwich, Connecticut)   Sister of Mark Twain. The second child of John M. and Jane L. Clemens, Pamela was the only sister of Mark Twain to survive to adulthood. Although eight years separated them, they had a close childhood

Mark Twain shortly after receiving an honorary degree from the University of Missouri in June 1902. (Courtesy, Library of Congress, Pictures & Prints Division)

relationship that they sustained through lifelong correspondence.

A sweet and pious child of delicate health whom Mark Twain called a lifelong invalid, Pamela was clearly the model for Tom Sawyer's fictional cousin Mary SAWYER. In 1858 his brother Orion Clemens wrote a letter comparing her temperament with that of their young brother, Henry Clemens. Pamela was a good student, interested in reading and music. Her musical skills were good enough for her to earn money giving guitar and piano lessons by the mid-1840s. On September 20, 1851, she married William A. Moffett (1816–1865), a former Hannibal resident who had become a successful merchant in Green County, Kentucky. They settled in ST. LOUIS, where they had two children, Annie E. Moffett (1852–1950) and Samuel Erasmus Moffett (1860–1908). When Mark Twain left Hannibal in 1853, he went straight to their home and stayed with them for several months while working as a printer. He also stayed with them after a sojourn on the East Coast and after visiting Orion in Iowa.

During the CIVIL WAR, Pamela worked for the United States SANITARY COMMISSION in St. Louis. The war ruined her husband's business and he died in August 1865. Afterward, Pamela's mother moved in with her. When Pamela attended Mark Twain's MARRIAGE in Buffalo, New York in February 1870, he encouraged her to consider living in FREDONIA, New York. After the wedding, she visited Fredonia and rented a house there.

Named after her paternal grandmother, Pamela, or Pamelia Moorman, Pamela pronounced her name *pah-MEE-lah'*. Her family nicknamed her "Mela."

Monday Evening Club Hartford discussion group formed in 1869. With a membership limited to 20 people, the club counted many of Hartford's most distinguished men among its members—Dr. Horace Bushnell, Charles H. Clark, J. R. HAWLEY, Calvin E. Stowe, J. H. TRUMBULL, Joseph TWICHELL, C. D. WARNER and others. From October to May, its members rotated fortnightly meetings among their homes, where they discussed papers read by fellow members. Elected to membership in February 1873, Mark Twain made "License of the Press" his first presentation a month later. From then through 1890, he presented about one paper a year on topics such as "Universal Suffrage" (February 15, 1875), "THE FACTS CONCERNING THE RECENT CARNIVAL OF CRIME IN CONNECTICUT" (January 24, 1876), "On the Decay of the Art of Lying" (April 5, 1880), "Phrenography" (November 21, 1881), "Southern Literature" (February 4, 1884) and "Machine Culture" (February 26, 1887). His February 1883 paper, "What Is Happiness?," became the basis for WHAT IS MAN?

Monk, Hank (1826–1883) Legendary STAGECOACH driver. Born in New York, Monk went west in 1852 and spent the rest of his life driving stagecoaches in California and Nevada. On July 30, 1859, he drove

Horace GREELEY from an inn near Genoa, Nevada to Placerville, California. Afraid of being late to a lecture engagement, Greeley asked Monk to rush; he was then driven over 40 miles of rough road at such a speed that he begged Monk to slow down. Monk's response became immortal: "Keep your seat, Horace, and I'll get you there on time." Monk enjoyed telling this story afterward and it became a familiar anecdote on the West Coast that Greeley tried to disavow.

In December 1863, Mark Twain reported on a ceremony at which Monk received a gold watch commemorating Greeley's ride. He later used the anecdote in *Roughing It,* in which four different men bore the narrator with identical recitations of the story (chapter 20). The narrator claims that during seven years on the coast, he has heard the same anecdote at least 481 times and suggests that it is so old it may even be in the Talmud.

Mono Lake Located near Highway 395 in the desert slopes of CALIFORNIA's eastern Sierra Nevada, Mono is a large alkaline lake standing nearly 6,400 feet above sea level. The surrounding county of the same name was created in 1861; its first seat was at AURORA, 15 miles to the north, until a survey revealed that the town was actually inside Nevada. Mark Twain spent about a week idling at Mono Lake with Calvin HIGBIE in August 1862. Chapters 37–39 of *Roughing It* describe the visit.

Notorious for the dense fly belt that encircles it, Mono is named after a local Shoshone people whose Indian neighbors dubbed them *monachi*, "fly people," because of the importance of the lake's fly pupae in their diet.

Chapter 20 of *Roughing It* accurately describes Mono as a sink whose natural level never varies. The lake's condition, however, changed radically after the 1940s, when the city of Los Angeles began diverting water from its tributaries. By 1989, the lake's level had dropped more than 40 feet, imperiling its fragile ecology—particularly the abundant bird life described in *Roughing It.* By court order, Los Angeles stopped diverting Mono's water that year; in late 1993, the city agreed drastically to cut back its diversion of Mono water in order to allow its level to rise. Mark Twain merits some credit for helping to save the lake. *Roughing It*'s colorful description, especially its humorous exaggeration of the strength of Mono's alkaline water, has played a major role in calling attention to Mono's uniqueness.

Montgomery, J[ames] Ed[ward] (c. 1817–1880s?) STEAMBOAT officer under whom Mark Twain served several times. Mark Twain may have cubbed under Montgomery when the latter was a pilot on the D. A. JANUARY in mid-December 1857 and on the NEW FALLS CITY when Montgomery was captain in mid-January 1858. It is more definite that he served under Montgomery from late March to early July 1860, when the latter captained the CITY OF MEMPHIS—mistakenly called the CRESCENT CITY in chapter 49 of *Life on the Mississippi.*

Mark Twain ran the *Memphis* into another boat at New Orleans, but Montgomery impressed him greatly by accepting full responsibility.

During the CIVIL WAR, Montgomery served as commodore of the Confederacy's river fleet. He persuaded the Confederate Congress to convert 14 steamboats into armored gunboats commanded by rivermen, not naval officers—a plan that the regular navy opposed. The result was disastrous. After he commanded a partial victory against a Union flotilla in May 1862, Montgomery's military career ended in June, when his entire flotilla was destroyed at MEMPHIS.

When Mark Twain revisited the Mississippi in early 1882, he recorded in his notebook that Montgomery was going blind.

"A Monument to Adam" Article first published in HARPER'S WEEKLY in July 1905. In October 1879, while Mark Twain was in ELMIRA, New York, he and Thomas K. BEECHER half-jokingly took up a mutual friend's suggestion to build a monument to ADAM. The idea grew out of the indignation raised by Charles DARWIN's book, *The Descent of Man* (1871), which was popularly regarded as tracing man back to the monkeys. Mark Twain and Beecher argued that since Adam was left out of Darwin's theories, something should be done to keep him from being forgotten.

Years later, Mark Twain wrote this article in response to a NEW YORK TRIBUNE item that recalled his old Adam monument project. He happened to be using the same theme in a story which he was then writing, "The Refuge of the Derelicts," or "Adam Monument." According to the article, during the earlier episode, several Elmira businessmen proposed investing $25,000 to build a memorial, and Mark Twain had tentative designs for the monument drawn in Paris. He also got up a petition to Congress to build such a monument "as a testimony of the Great Republic's gratitude to the Father of the Human Race and as a token of her loyalty to him in this dark day of his humiliation when his older children were doubting him and deserting him." Mark Twain was not among the 92 signers of the petition; he wanted to keep his participation anonymous so that the petition could be taken seriously. When his own Conecticut congressman, Joseph R. HAWLEY, happened to pass through Elmira, he persuaded him to take the petition to Congress. Hawley never mustered the nerve to present it, however.

The original "Monument to Adam Petition" is an appendix in A. B. PAINE's *Mark Twain: A Biography*.

Moore, Abner Fictitious name mentioned in *Huckleberry Finn*. When Huck meets Judith LOFTUS in chapter 11, he invents "Abner Moore" as an uncle whom he is on his way to visit in GOSHEN.

Moore, Julia A. (December 1, 1847, Plainfield, Michigan–June 5, 1920, near Manton, Michigan) Nick-named the "Sweet Singer of Michigan," Moore was a popular writer of sentimental and banal verses, particularly obituary poetry—a subject that Mark Twain celebrated in "POST-MORTEM POETRY." Her *Sentimental Song Book* (1876) was the most popular book of its genre. Mark Twain bought a copy soon after it was first published and seems to have enjoyed dipping into it through the rest of his life. Moore clearly inspired his deceased poetaster and painter Emmeline GRANGERFORD in *Huckleberry Finn*. Indeed, E. W. KEMBLE's rendering of Emmeline's "spidery" woman painting bears an uncanny resemblance to Moore herself. Most of Moore's funerary poems were about children, a tendency parodied in Emmeline's "Ode to Stephen Dowling BOTS." A similar parody (attributed to Moore herself) appears in chapter 8 of *Following the Equator* and excerpts from Moore's own verses appear in chapters 36 and 44 of the same book. In chapter 36, Mark Twain credits her with having a "subtle touch . . . that makes an intentionally humorous episode pathetic and an intentionally pathetic one funny." In 1906 he called her the "Sweet Singer of Michigan, Queen & Empress of the Hogwash Guild."

Moore, Thomas (May 28, 1779, Dublin, Ireland–February 25, 1852, Wiltshire, England) Irish poet. Mark Twain may have been familiar with Moore's poetry as early as 1853, when he published verses in a Hannibal newspaper that reveal Moore's romantic influence. One of Moore's best-known poems is *Lalla Rookh* (1817), an epic romance about an Indian princess. A STEAMBOAT that operated on the Mississippi from 1838 through 1847 took its name from this poem; Mark Twain alludes to it as the LALLY ROOK in *Huckleberry Finn* (chapter 32). SKETCHES, NEW AND OLD contains a selection entitled "A Couple of Poems by Thomas Moore and Mark Twain." It includes Moore's "Those Evening Bells" followed by Mark Twain's parody, "Those Annual Bills."

Mordred, Sir Character in *Connecticut Yankee*. A complex figure in Arthurian legends, Mordred is usually depicted as the son of MORGAN LE FAY—in some accounts he is her son by King ARTHUR's unintentional incest with his sister. In *Connecticut Yankee*, Mordred appears only in chapter 42, which identifies him as a nephew of Arthur's who triggers the civil war by revealing to the king GUENEVER's adulterous affair with LAUNCELOT. As in the legends, Mordred then tries to seize both the kingdom and Guenever for himself, until he and Arthur kill each other in battle. The novel's newspaper account of this final confrontation remarks that Mordred "smote his father Arthur."

More Tramps Abroad (1897) British edition of *Following the Equator*. Mark Twain wrote this book while living in LONDON and had Bram STOKER negotiate his contract with CHATTO and Windus. By November 1897, when Chatto issued *More Tramps*, Mark Twain was in VIENNA. As with the American edition, he paid little attention to

More Tramps's production and did not even know that it was missing most of *Following the Equator*'s illustrations until he gave a copy to someone later.

More Tramps differs from its American counterpart more than any of Mark Twain's other authorized British editions. Aside from the fact that its first edition has only four illustrations, however, these differences are not as significant as sometimes suggested. *More Tramps* has roughly 6,000 words that were cut from *Following the Equator* and it omits another 1,400 words that appear in the latter. Much of the text cut from *Following the Equator* consists of extracts from other authors. The most significant passage cut from *More Tramps* is the harsh indictment of a shipping line that appears in chapter 32 of *Following the Equator*. *More Tramps* also has a slightly different mix of PUDD'NHEAD WILSON maxims as chapter heads.

More Tramps's 72 numbered chapters follow the same order as the 69 chapters in *Following the Equator*, but they break differently in several places. The most substantial differences occur in chapters 18–33 of *More Tramps*, which have about 12 additional pages on Australian subjects (equivalent to chapters 16–30 in *Following the Equator*). Chapters 34–72 of *More Tramps* are almost identical to *Following the Equator*'s chapters 31–69.

Morgan, Hank (The Boss)   Narrator and title character of *Connecticut Yankee*. One of Mark Twain's most complex creations, Hank Morgan embodies many of the contradictions of Mark Twain himself, as well as traits of characters as diverse as Tom SAWYER, Huckleberry FINN and Colonel SELLERS. Possible models for Hank are numerous; in addition to Mark Twain, they range from Charles Heber CLARK's fictional Professor Baffin to the Hartford inventor James PAIGE. In the novel's prelude, set around 1889, the FRAME-narrator introduces Hank as a stranger he meets in WARWICK. Hank begins a fantastic story about going back to sixth-century England, then retires to bed, leaving the frame-narrator to read the rest of his story from his first-person manuscript—which becomes the core of the novel. The book concludes with the narrator finishing his reading and revisiting Hank just before he dies (chapter 44).

Clues scattered throughout *Connecticut Yankee* reveal Hank's background. When he arrives in CAMELOT in chapter 2, he gives 1879 as the year from which he has come; later developments indicate that about 10 years pass before MERLIN returns him to his own time by putting him to sleep. Not long before this happens, Hank gives his age as 40 (chapter 40); he therefore must be about 30 when he comes to Camelot, putting his birth date around 1849—a date that supports his remark about being a boy during President BUCHANAN's administration (chapter 11).

Born and raised in Hartford, Connecticut, Hank calls himself a practical and unsentimental YANKEE. His father was a blacksmith and his uncle a horse doctor; he himself was both before going to the COLT ARMS FAC-

Hank Morgan as the Boss in Connecticut Yankee.

TORY. There he supervised several thousand men and learned to make everything from guns, boilers and engines to diverse labor-saving devices—an inventive talent that he uses to modernize sixth-century England.

Though Hank presents himself as a man without formal education, he reveals a wide knowledge of history and literature. He knows exactly when two sixth-century eclipses occurred (chapters 2 and 7); he confidently discusses history from the 19th century back to the sixth century and even earlier (chapters 27 and 33); and he has a special interest in the French Revolution (chapters 13 and 20). An admirer of history's greatest inventors, he is familiar with the work of Gutenberg, Watt, Arkwright, Whitney, Morse, Stephenson and Bell (chapter 33). His reading includes Fielding's *Tom Jones*, Smollett's *Roderick Random*, SCOTT (chapter 4); Dumas (chapter 18); DEFOE's *Robinson Crusoe* (chapter 7), CELLINI (chapter 17); Casanova (chapter 18); Chaucer's *Canterbury Tales* (chapter 21); and HAMLET (chapter 39). His comments on early GERMAN and his use of German tongue twisters suggest that he speaks that language (chapter 22). Despite his literacy, however, he retains certain vulgar tastes, such as liking tacky 19th-century chromos (chapter 7).

Hank's early travels probably took him to the Midwest, the South and possibly the West. He knows what STEAMBOAT explosions look like (chapter 27), as well as sunsets over the Upper MISSISSIPPI (chapter 39). He is familiar with etiquette in ARKANSAS (chapter 3) and with journalism there and in Alabama (chapters 10 and 26). And somewhere, he learned western horsemanship and roping skills that he uses in a tournament (chapter 39). He has also picked up an INDIAN trick of making fake tobacco from willow bark (chapter 12).

Although Hank seems to shun vigorous physical activity, his background and several incidents in the narrative indicate that he must be strong and robust. In describing his arms factory job, he implies that he fought with his men frequently. He also demonstrates his toughness in episodes in which he and King ARTHUR take on an angry mob (chapter 34), he escapes from a slave caravan (chapter 36), and he faces ironclad knights on the tournament field (chapter 39). In general, his health seems good, though he has a bad cold and rheumatism in chapter 24 and once had smallpox (chapter 30).

Like Tom Sawyer, Hank loves impressing people with gaudy effects—from spectacular public displays such as blowing up Merlin's tower (chapter 7) and restarting the fountain in the VALLEY OF HOLINESS (chapter 23) to such simple things as hosting a banquet for commoners (chapter 32). He also has Tom's eye for showy details; he enjoys the theatricality of having 500 knights on bicycles rescue him and Arthur from the gallows, but regrets not pulling off the stunt at high noon (chapters 37–38).

Hank shares Colonel Sellers's entrepreneurial zeal. Appointed the king's prime minister, he immediately acts to increase revenues by putting everything possible on a paying basis—including the tournaments (chapter 9) and knight-errantry itself (chapter 19). He runs a successful insurance business (chapter 30), converts a holy hermit into a money-making sewing machine (chapter 22) and has knights scour the country promoting soap, toothbrushes, stove polish and other products.

Although Mark Twain establishes *why* Hank can do what he does, he has him accomplish far more than one man—however gifted—could possibly do in such a short period of time. Hank not only organizes factories to make everything from soap, toothbrushes, paper and matches to bicycles, steam engines, telephones and electric dynamos, he must also must personally develop *every* scrap of technology, from mining and processing raw materials to making parts for his machines. Not satisfied with doing all this and administering the kingdom, he also organizes a patent office, an insurance company, newspapers and a stock-board, and somehow sets up schools and training institutions as his "MAN FACTORY" and his WEST POINT. Meanwhile, he still finds time to attend tournaments and to travel. He gets excellent help from CLARENCE, but his right-hand man cannot know anything about modern technology beyond what Hank teaches him.

As a voice for Mark Twain's political and social ideas, Hank talks constantly about free will and democratic principles, while maintaining a stubborn belief in a mechanistic philosophy that contradicts these same sentiments. For all his expressed idealism, he ultimately regards human beings as little more than machines. One moment, for example, he praises MARCO for demonstrating his manhood by denouncing his manor lord (chapter 30). Only moments later, however, he sees Marco sniff at a slave and disgustedly suggests that "there are times when one would like to hang the whole human race and finish the farce" (chapter 31). By the end of the novel, Hank nearly does just that, when he and his few remaining followers annihilate nearly 30,000 knights—who presumably include many men he has earlier described as friends (chapter 43).

Hank's attitude toward women is puritanical. His first known contact with a woman does not occur until after he has been in Camelot for several years, when Arthur assigns him to rescue damsels from ogres. When Hank realizes that he must travel alone with a young woman whom he calls SANDY, he is scandalized, and protests that he is practically engaged to a certain PUSS FLANAGAN (chapter 11). Sandy bores Hank, but he cannot get rid of her, even after several years. He finally marries her, largely to avoid compromising her further (chapter 41). After a year of marriage, however, he unaccountably finds her the perfect mate and extols her virtues in terms that Mark Twain customarily saved for his own wife. Nevertheless, Hank cannot put his former sweetheart entirely out of his mind.

After calling this character "Sir Robert Smith" in his earliest draft of *Connecticut Yankee*, Mark Twain renamed him "Hank Morgan." A common nickname for "Henry," "Hank" is a near-homophone of "Yank." Industrialist J. P. MORGAN has been suggested as Mark Twain's inspiration for Hank's surname. Another candidate is the 17th-century PIRATE Henry Morgan, whom England rewarded with high offices and a knighthood. Some scholars see a meaningful similarity between Hank Morgan's name and that of the Queen MORGAN LE FAY of legend; however, Hank's account of his visit to the evil queen curiously fails to comment on this similarity. Hank's name, in fact, appears just twice in the novel. In chapter 15, he dreams of telephoning Puss Flanagan and hearing her say "Hello, Hank!" In chapter 39, he reads a Camelot newspaper story about his coming tournament combat that calls him "Hank Morgan." Meanwhile, Hank is known as "THE BOSS" from chapter 8 until the end.

Connecticut Yankee's illustrator Daniel BEARD modeled his drawings of Hank on a Connecticut man named George Morrison, a photoengraver who worked next to his studio.

As the central character in *Connecticut Yankee,* Hank Morgan has appeared in every dramatic adaptation of the novel, but often in different guises and under different names. Since the 1927 musical adaptation, he has most often been called "Hank Martin"—possibly to avoid confusion with Morgan le Fay. In most cases, however, he is also called "the Boss" or "Sir Boss." Actors who have played the Boss include Harry C. Myers (1921), William Gaxton (1927), Will Rogers (1931), Dick Foran (1943), Bing Crosby (1949), Edgar Bergen (1954), Eddie Albert (1955), Paul Rudd (1978) and 10-year-old Keshia Knight Pulliam (1989).

Morgan, John Pierpont (April 7, 1837, Hartford, Connecticut–March 31, 1913, Rome, Italy) The leading American industrialist of his time, Morgan headed the nation's most prosperous private bank, owned and organized several railroads and founded the United States Steel Corporation, International Harvester and other enterprises. Also a noted philanthropist, he left a large art collection to New York's Metropolitan Museum of Art. His book and manuscript collection became New York's J. Pierpont Morgan Library, which houses manuscripts of Mark Twain's *Life on the Mississippi* and *Pudd'nhead Wilson.* Because of his great organizational talent and his Hartford origins, Morgan is generally considered a possible source for Hank MORGAN's name in *Connecticut Yankee.*

Morgan le Fay, Queen (Mrs. le Fay) Character in *Connecticut Yankee.* Morgan is the wife of King Uriens, with whom she rules a realm the size of the District of Columbia that is tributary to her brother King ARTHUR. In Arthurian legends, Morgan is typically vested with magical powers. In some versions she is the mother of MORDRED—often by her brother Arthur, whom she hates. Descended from Celtic deities, she was originally a "fay," or fairy, untouched by time who has degenerated into a mortal who must use magic to keep from aging.

Morgan appears in chapters 16–18 of *Connecticut Yankee,* when Hank MORGAN and SANDY stay at her castle. Hank describes her as the sister of Arthur, but only hints at her possessing magical powers. Knowing of her evil reputation, Hank expects her to be old and repulsive, but is surprised to find her beautiful and youthful-looking enough to pass for her husband's granddaughter. He does not say how old she is, but his description of prisoners in her dungeon suggests that she and her husband have occupied their castle at least 22 years and no more than 35 years.

Aside from her unaccountable youthfulness, Morgan reveals no real magical powers in *Connecticut Yankee;* in fact, she has a terrible dread of Hank's purported powers. Her most conspicuous trait is heartless and mindless vindictiveness. For example, she kills a page boy for a trivial offense (chapter 16) and she has psychologically tortured a prisoner for 22 years because he said that she has "red" hair—which she has. After Hank releases 47 prisoners from her dungeon, Morgan wants to go after them with an ax (chapter 18).

Dan BEARD's illustration of Morgan dresses her in a jewel-adorned costume made famous by Sarah BERNHARDT on the stage.

Mormons Followers of the Church of Jesus Christ of Latter-day Saints, which Joseph Smith (1805–1844) founded in 1830. A year later, Smith moved his headquarters from New York to Ohio and launched an aggressive international missionary campaign that has continued to the present. Mormons believe that theirs is the *only* true church of Jesus Christ, that Smith's *Book of Mormon* is a factual history of early America containing a unique witness of Christ, and that their presidents are prophets who speak directly with God.

During the 1830s, Smith tried establishing a new base in western Missouri, but met fierce local opposition and instead settled in western ILLINOIS, where his followers built Nauvoo into Illinois's biggest city. Neighbors resenting the Mormons' aloofness and strange ways continued to harass them. In 1844, a mob killed Smith in nearby Carthage, and Brigham YOUNG assumed control of the church. Three years later, he led a mass migration to UTAH. Through these early Mormon struggles, Mark Twain was living only 60 miles from Nauvoo and Carthage, in Hannibal, Missouri, where he was surrounded by anti-Mormon feeling. He had his first direct encounter with Mormons while passing through Utah during his cross-country STAGECOACH trip in 1861. He was fascinated with everything connected with Mormonism, especially polygamy—a doctrine that Young had proclaimed only in 1852, though Smith had advocated it secretly earlier. *Roughing It* pokes fun at the Mormons in its Utah chapters, but maintains an essential respect for them.

Young's assumption of church leadership was opposed by a minority of Mormons who believed that the presidency should pass to Smith's son. In April 1867, Mark Twain passed through KEOKUK, Iowa, where supporters of Joseph Smith Jr. were plotting Young's overthrow—a conspiracy he reported on for the SAN FRANCISCO ALTA CALIFORNIA. Later that year, he visited Palestine on the QUAKER CITY, which evacuated followers of the former Mormon leader George J. ADAMS from Jaffa—an episode he mentions in chapter 56 of *Innocents Abroad.*

Moulton, Julius ("Moult") (1843?–c. February 16, 1916) Passenger on the QUAKER CITY excursion. A railroad man from St. Louis, Moulton was on Mark Twain's list of passengers whom he wished to keep as friends, but after the cruise they lost touch with each other. Moulton is mentioned briefly in chapters 4, 17, 56 and 58 of *Innocents Abroad* as "Moult." He was one of the "sinners" in Mark Twain's expedition through the HOLY LAND and he traveled with Mark Twain through southern SPAIN. Moulton published at least five letters about the cruise in St. Louis's *Missouri Republican*.

Mount Olivet Cemetery   Cemetery located several miles south of Hannibal, Missouri. Four members of Mark Twain's immediate family are buried in Mount Olivet: his parents, John M. and Jane L. Clemens, and his brothers Henry and Orion Clemens. Orion's wife, Mollie Stotts Clemens, is also buried there. John and Henry Clemens were originally buried in a Baptist cemetery within Hannibal; they were reinterred at Mount Olivet in 1876, shortly after it opened. Mark Twain attended his mother's funeral at Mount Olivet in late 1890 and revisited the cemetery during his last trip to Hannibal in 1902. Another brother, Benjamin Clemens, died in Hannibal in 1842, but the location of his grave has been forgotten. Mark Twain and his own family are buried in WOODLAWN CEMETERY in Elmira, New York.

Mountain Meadows Massacre   On September 11, 1857, a band of MORMONS and PIUTE Indians killed 120 members of an emigrant train from Arkansas in a valley in UTAH's southwestern corner. Under Charles Fancher's leadership, the emigrants were following a southern route to California after passing through SALT LAKE CITY. While reasons for the massacre remain controversial, it appears that some emigrants behaved insultingly and boasted about having committed anti-Mormon atrocities years earlier. For their part, the Piute believed that the emigrants had poisoned their water holes. The emigrants also happened to be passing through at a moment when Utah nervously expected an invading federal army, for which the emigrants were rumored to be spies. Without waiting for instructions from Brigham YOUNG, local Mormon militiamen tricked the emigrants into surrendering their arms in return for safe passage through hostile Indian territory. After the emigrants disarmed themselves, the Mormons and their Piute allies killed everyone in the party but infants.

The massacre became a national issue, with the question of who was responsible hotly debated. Mormon leaders tried shifting blame to the Piute, but inquiries proved that local Mormons had primary responsibility. When Mark Twain visited Utah four years later, the massacre was still controversial. *Roughing It* mentions the massacre, summarizes the contradictory explanations heard in Utah, then cites a book published by Catherine Waite in 1866 as authority for concluding that "the Mormons were the assassins" (chapter 17). An appendix in the book contains a 1,550-word paraphrase of Waite's account.

Mufferson, Willie   Minor character in *Tom Sawyer*. ST. PETERSBURG'S "MODEL BOY," Mufferson appears only in chapter 5. He is "the pride of all the mothers," and an object of loathing to his peers. Mark Twain modeled him on Theodore Dawson, the son of John D. DAWSON, his last schoolteacher.

Mumford, "Uncle"   Character in *Life on the Mississippi*. Mumford is the fictional name for the "second officer" of the GOLD DUST, on which Mark Twain traveled down the Mississippi in early 1882. He appears to be a composite character, based mostly on the real second mate of the *Gold Dust*, "Dad" Dunham. "Mumford" is a 30-year veteran on the river (chapter 25). As an outspoken travel companion, Mumford is similar to Mark Twain's imaginary Mr. BROWN. He figures in several anecdotes in chapters 25 and 28 and is also mentioned in chapters 26, 32 and 34. A drawing of Mumford in the original edition of *Life on the Mississippi* was apparently made from a photograph of Dunham.

Munich   German city. Midway through the long European trip that Mark Twain undertook in order to write *A Tramp Abroad*, he and his family stayed in this Bavarian capital from November 15, 1878 through February 27, 1879. Members of the family regarded the Munich months as a pleasant winter rest, during which they busied themselves with studying GERMAN and art instruction and enjoyed a Bavarian Christmas, while Mark Twain worked on his book. He did write at least one chapter about Munich, but omitted it from the final manuscript. *A Tramp Abroad* dismisses his Munich stay in a single line (chapter 50), even though he was in Munich three times longer than he was in SWITZERLAND—to which the book devotes 18 chapters. What remains of his comments on Munich are scattered references: discussing WAGNER with a Munich woman (chapter 10), an allusion to seeing Prince Ludwig in Munich (chapter 18) and an offhand reference in chapter 31.

Mark Twain's family lived at a pension at No. 1a Karlstrasse, where the family was well looked after by Fraulein Dahlweiner, while Mark Twain worked in a room at 45 Nymphenstrasse. He pays tribute to Dahlweiner in *Life on Mississippi*, in which the narrator tells how he met Karl RITTER while he was living in the same pension (chapter 31).

Mark Twain's son-in-law, Ossip GABRILOWITSCH, conducted Munich's Konzertverein Orchestra from 1910–14.

"A Murder, a Mystery, and a Marriage"   Unfinished story. In 1876, Mark Twain interested W. D. HOWELLS in starting an ATLANTIC MONTHLY series that would invite 12 writers to contribute a story based on the same outline, which he would provide. None of the writers would see the others' work, and the magazine would publish their stories in consecutive issues. Mark Twain's 8,500-word "A Murder, a Mystery, and a Marriage" is the only piece written for the abortive series. It has never been formally published, but an unauthorized edition was privately printed in 1945.

A BURLESQUE tale of intrigue, the story begins when a midwestern farmer finds an emaciated man lying in a snowfield. The man looks as though he had been thrown from a wagon or horse, but the snow around him is undisturbed. The farmer takes the man home, where his family nurses him back to health. They learn that he is a Frenchman named Jean Pierre Marteau, who was imprisoned for a murder he did not commit. A week earlier, he was in Paris with a prison work-party helping with a gas balloon. His tale ends abruptly at the point where he jumped into the balloon and cut it loose.

Mark Twain's interest in balloons goes back to 1868, when publication of Jules Verne's *Five Weeks in a Balloon* caused him to drop his own balloon-travel story. He himself enjoyed a brief balloon ascent in PARIS in February 1879. A few years later, he wrote a story that was omitted from *Life on the Mississippi* about balloonists getting stuck in "a stratum of dead air." In 1894, he finally developed the balloon-travel theme in *Tom Sawyer Abroad*.

Murrell, John A. (c. 1806, central Tennessee–c. 1844 / 46, Pikesville, Tennessee) Notorious early 19th-century criminal. Murrell (whose name was variously spelled) headed a thousand-member gang that terrorized a region that included Missouri from 1826 until 1834, when he was captured and imprisoned for stealing slaves. He was thought to have been planning a slave uprising in the Southwest. Murrell's reputation on the Mississippi River was still great during Mark Twain's piloting years, when he must have heard many chilling Murrell stories. Chapter 29 of *Life on the Mississippi* describes Murrell's gang as "a colossal combination of robbers, horse-thieves, Negro-stealers and counterfeiters" and compares Murrell's criminal career favorably with that of Jesse JAMES, whose April 1882 murder was news when Mark Twain went across the Plains after leaving the river. The chapter includes a long extract on Murrell from "a now forgotten book" by Frederick MARRYAT.

The tradition of Murrell's gang pillaging Mississippi River settlements and hiding their loot in secret caches forms part of the atmospheric background of Mark Twain's boys' stories, in which Tom Sawyer and Huck Finn often fantasize about finding PIRATE treasures. Indeed, Huck and Tom even overhear INJUN JOE and his partner evoke Murrell's name in chapter 26 of *Tom Sawyer,* raising the possibility that the gold treasure the two criminals find was left by the great Murrell himself. Murrell's memory is evoked indirectly in the seventh chapter of "TOM SAWYER'S CONSPIRACY," when Huck suggests that the unknown perpetrators of a local murder might belong to "Burrell's Gang."

Muscatine Southeastern IOWA town on the Mississippi River, about 30 miles west–southwest of Davenport and 75 miles north–northwest of KEOKUK. In late September 1853, when Muscatine had a population of about 5,500,

Mark Twain's brother Orion Clemens moved there and ran the MUSCATINE JOURNAL, which later became the *Tri-Weekly Journal*. Mark Twain joined him some time after April 1854. It is uncertain exactly how long he remained in Muscatine, but by early August he was back in St. Louis. He wrote nine travel letters that Orion published in the *Journal* from October 1853 through March 1855. Orion himself left Muscatine in early June 1855, selling out his interest in the *Journal* in order to move to Keokuk. The house in which he lived, at 109 Walnut Street, was razed during the 1940s.

Mark Twain stopped at Muscatine briefly in mid-May 1882, while going up the Mississippi River. He mentions the town briefly in chapters 57–58 of *Life on the Mississippi*. Chapter 57 recalls an incident when he was accosted by a knife-wielding lunatic. His posthumously published notes identify the man as Bill Israeel [sic], who drew a butcher knife "gaumed with red ink" on him and made him apologize for "some imaginary affront."

Muscatine Journal Newspaper founded by Orion Clemens. After selling the HANNIBAL JOURNAL, Orion moved to MUSCATINE, Iowa in September 1853 and launched a new *Journal*. Mark Twain was then living on the East Coast, from which he wrote letters to his family that Orion published in the *Journal*. Around mid-1854, Mark Twain came to Muscatine and worked on the paper with Orion for several months. In June 1855, Orion sold out his interest and moved to KEOKUK.

"My Boyhood Dreams" Article written by Mark Twain while in Sanna, SWEDEN in mid-September, 1899. It was first published in *McClure's* magazine in January 1900 and it was collected in *The Man That Corrupted Hadleyburg and Other Stories and Essays* the same year. The facetious 2,300-word piece recalls an evening in Boston years earlier, when a dozen friends revealed their most cherished boyhood ambitions.

In an opening that appears to be a response to a query, Mark Twain states that the only possible answer to the question of whether an old person's boyhood dreams have been realized is disappointment—a disappointment that can only be measured by the person disappointed. He asks rhetorically why anyone would want to join the French army—and says that this is a question that only Alfred DREYFUS can answer.

He then recalls an evening long ago in BOSTON, when he and 11 friends gathered and revealed to each other their boyhood dreams. The dreams of several long-lost friends, James T. Fields, James R. OSGOOD, Ralph Keeler and Boyle O'Reilly, are not revealed. The survivors include W. D. HOWELLS, who wanted to be an auctioneer but gave up when he settled for being editor of the ATLANTIC MONTHLY in 1830 (sic), and John Jay, who almost achieved his ambition of becoming a steamboat mate before falling as far as private secretary to the president, ambassador and secretary of state. The others were Thomas Bailey ALDRICH, would-be horse doctor;

Brander MATTHEWS, cowboy; Frank Richard Stockton, barkeeper; G. W. CABLE, circus ring-master; and "Remus" (Joel Chandler HARRIS), buccaneer.

The article ends with a 20-stanza verse, "To the Above Old People," celebrating the infirmities of age. A final editorial postscript (probably written by Mark Twain himself) says that when the editors submitted proofs of this article to the men named in it, they responded that "they have no recollection of any such night in Boston, nor elsewhere; and in their opinion there was never any such night. They have *met* Mr. Twain, but have had the prudence not to intrust any privacies to him. . . ." In fact, the ambitions named look suspiciously like Mark Twain's own childhood ambitions.

"My Début as a Literary Person" Essay written in 1899 recalling Mark Twain's first magazine publication. In June 1866 Mark Twain was in HAWAII when crew members of the clipper ship HORNET reached the islands six weeks after their ship had gone down in the southern Pacific. With the help of Anson BURLINGAME, Mark Twain interviewed the survivors and delivered a story to California in time to have a major scoop. Later that year he redrafted the story for HARPER'S MAGAZINE, which published "Forty-three Days in an Open Boat" in its December 1866 issue. "My Début" is a 9,000-word essay recounting how he wrote the original stories and got them published; it also provides considerable details from diaries that *Hornet* crew members composed during their voyage of survival.

Although Mark Twain had earlier scored a major success with the publication of his JUMPING FROG STORY in newspapers across the country, he could not, he explains, regard himself as a properly published author until he had something in a *magazine*. Ironically, when *Harper's* printed his *Hornet* article, it misspelled his pen name as "Mark Swain." He wrote "My Début" at a moment when he was obsessed with writing long stories, such as "THE GREAT DARK," based on dreams of being adrift at sea. He used the essay as the title piece in his 1903 collection, *My Début as a Literary Person and Essays Other and Stories*. It has also appeared in *The Man That Corrupted Hadleyburg and Other Stories and Essays* and in many modern anthologies.

"My First Lie and How I Got Out of It" Essay first published in the *New York World* on December 10, 1899. A rambling exploration of lies and how they are told, this essay has an ironic title. Confessing that he cannot remember his *first* lie, Mark Twain actually discusses his *second*. When nine days old, he recalls, he discovered that if he pretended to be stuck by a diaper pin, he received pleasant attention. Like all babies, he used this ploy regularly, learning the universal human technique of the *unspoken lie*. This leads him to the observation that "almost all lies are acts, and speech has no part in them. . . . All people are liars from the cradle onward, without exception, and . . . they begin to lie as soon as

they wake in the morning, and keep it up, without rest or refreshment, until they go to sleep at night."

The essay then develops into a serious examination of what Mark Twain calls the *lie of silent assertion*, which we tell "without saying a word." Such lies support some of the worst forms of human oppression. "It would not be possible," he argues, "for a humane and intelligent person to invent a rational excuse for slavery." As a specific example of such a lie on a grand scale, he cites France's failure to own up to Alfred DREYFUS's innocence. He then goes on to examine people in England, who "have the oddest ways. They won't tell a spoken lie . . . Except in a large moral interest, like politics or religion."

He concludes that "there is a prejudice against the spoken lie, but none against any other, and by examination and mathematical computation I find that the proportion of the spoken lie to the other varieties is as 1 to 22,894. Therefore the spoken lie is of no consequence, and it is not worth while to go around fussing about it and trying to make believe that it is an important matter. The silent colossal National Lie that is the support and confederate of all the tyrannies and shams and inequalities and unfairnesses that afflict the peoples— that is the one to throw bricks and sermons at."

"My Late Senatorial Secretaryship" Sketch first published in the GALAXY in May 1868 as "Facts Concerning the Late Senatorial Secretaryship." After returning from the QUAKER CITY excursion in November 1867, Mark Twain took up a position as Nevada senator William M. STEWART's private secretary. About two months later they had a falling-out and he quit. Around this same time, he published "THE FACTS CONCERNING THE RECENT RESIGNATION," a sketch satirizing minor government functionaries. A similar piece, "My Late Senatorial Secretaryship," burlesques his own experience as Stewart's secretary, while making fun of the tendency of legislators to dodge issues. He uses his pen name within the sketch, but is careful not to mention Stewart's name. Instead, he uses the abbreviated name "James W. N—," suggesting that he was working for Nevada's *other* senator, James W. NYE.

SYNOPSIS

Mark Twain announces that after two months he is no longer a private secretary to a senator. One morning the senator called him in after the Pacific mail had arrived. Reminding his secretary that he had believed him worthy of his confidence, the senator asked about four letters the secretary wrote on his behalf. The first was to people at Baldwin's Ranch who wanted to establish a new post office. In order to persuade the people that such a post office was unnecessary, the senator had instructed Mark Twain to answer ingeniously. What Mark Twain actually wrote, however, was a disrespectful reply telling the people that what they really wanted was a jail. Now, the senator says, he can no longer enter that district.

Mark Twain's second letter was to constituents who wanted a bill to incorporate their Methodist church in Nevada. The senator asked Mark Twain to explain to them that this was an issue for their state legislature. Instead, Mark Twain told them that Congress knew nothing about religion and that their idea was ridiculous since they could never issue stock on a corporation such as they proposed. Now the senator feels that he is finished with the religious element.

Mark Twain's third offensive letter was to a San Francisco alderman asking about water-lots. The senator wanted a noncommittal reply that would avoid real consideration of the issue. What Mark Twain wrote was atrocious nonsense. Finally, residents of Nevada's HUMBOLDT district asked about changing a post route. The senator wanted to dodge the issue by having Mark Twain write a delicate and dubious reply. Instead, Mark Twain wrote a complex tangle harping on Indian atrocities along the routes. The outraged senator orders Mark Twain to leave the house. Convinced that people like the senator cannot be pleased, Mark Twain resigns.

"My Watch" Sketch first published in the BUFFALO EXPRESS on November 26, 1870. Mark Twain describes a watch that kept excellent time until he made the mistake of letting repairmen fix it. Similar tales about watches appear in *Innocents Abroad,* in which BLUCHER struggles to keep his watch synchronized with "ship time" (chapter 5) and in *Following the Equator,* in which Mark Twain tries to synchronize a cheap watch with clock bells (chapter 4). The sketch was first collected in SKETCHES, NEW AND OLD.

Mysterious Avenger Character in *Life on the Mississippi.* Chapter 55 recalls an anecdote about the narrator's youth, when he knew a carpenter in Hannibal who styled himself the "Mysterious Avenger." This man deeply impressed the young boy by claiming to have murdered more than 60 persons named Lynch. He had sworn vengeance after his bride was murdered on their wedding day by a man named Archibald Lynch and he intended to go on killing Lynches. When the boy alerted a local resident named Lynch to his terrible peril, this man confronted the carpenter and proved that he was a humbug. The narrator later discovered that the carpenter had plagiarized his story from a book by Robert Montgomery Bird (1806–1854), *Nick of the Woods, or the Jibbenainosay, A Tale of Kentucky* (1837). Bird's book, which was popular in its time, is about a mild-mannered Quaker who leads a double life as "Nick of the Woods," a fearsome slayer of Indians.

The Mysterious Stranger, A Romance **(1916)** Novella written by A. B. PAINE and Frederick DUNEKA from an unfinished manuscript by Mark Twain, under whose name it was published posthumously. As Mark Twain's literary executor, Paine presented this story as an au-

thentic Mark Twain work, giving no hint of the editorial changes that he and Duneka made. In 1916 HARPER'S MAGAZINE serialized the story (May–November) and HARPER AND BROTHERS published it as a book in October, with illustrations by N. C. Wyeth (1882–1945). The volume's falseness is embodied in its cover illustration— Wyeth's painting of the "astrologer," a character added by Paine and Duneka. Paine later collected the story in *The Mysterious Stranger and Other Stories* (1922)—a book that is still being published under Mark Twain's name.

The title "The Mysterious Stranger" has been used in several different ways. Mark Twain himself used it only once, as the subtitle of his unfinished novel NO. 44, THE MYSTERIOUS STRANGER. Paine and Duneka made it the main title of their revised version of another unfinished Mark Twain novel, "THE CHRONICLE OF YOUNG SATAN." Finally, the title has become a generic description for both of these original Mark Twain stories, as well as for his "SCHOOLHOUSE HILL," and it was used as the title of the MARK TWAIN PAPERS project edition of all the authentic Mark Twain versions in 1969.

It was not generally known until well after Mark Twain's death that he had written more than one "Mysterious Stranger" story. Paine and Duneka knew that several versions existed, but suppressed that knowledge when they published their own version. The text published in 1916 as *The Mysterious Stranger, A Romance* is essentially a revision of "The Chronicle of Young Satan." Paine and Duneka deleted about 35 percent of the original text, rewrote many passages, added the astrologer character, and replaced "Chronicle's" final chapter with the conclusion from the *No. 44* manuscript.

Many of Paine and Duneka's changes pertain to religion. For example, while they retained Mark Twain's Father Adolf character, they gave most of his negative attributes to the nonsectarian astrologer. "Chronicle" contains about seven direct references to "Catholics," but *The Mysterious Stranger* has none. Other significant deletions include about 7,000 words describing Wilhelm Meidling's and Joseph Fuchs's romantic rivalries with Philip TRAUM and about 4,000 words concerning Traum's affection for animals. Theodor FISCHER's sister Lilly disappears, as do Traum's chess games with Meidling.

In 1963, John S. TUCKEY revealed the full extent of Paine's editorial intervention in Mark Twain's original manuscript and established the correct sequence of Mark Twain's various versions of the story. In 1968, he published *Mark Twain's The Mysterious Stranger and the Critics,* presenting Paine and Duneka's 1916 text, with annotations indicating their changes, and essays on the work. The following year, the MARK TWAIN PAPERS project published the first edition of Mark Twain's original texts as *Mark Twain's Mysterious Stranger* manuscripts, edited by William M. Gibson. Paine and Duneka's text is no longer considered part of Mark Twain's works, but since it has passed into the public domain, it is still occasionally republished under Mark Twain's name.

nabob A term for a person of great wealth or consequence, *nabob* entered English from India, where it is a Hindi and Urdu word for a mogul or provincial governor. The word appears several times in *Roughing It;* chapter 46, for example, describes NEVADA nabobs— men who have risen from poverty and obscurity to wealth and influence overnight. In chapter 6 of *Huckleberry Finn,* Huck's father, Pap FINN, denounces a free black man as "the awfulest old gray-headed nabob in the State." When Mark Twain visited INDIA in 1896, he encountered real nabobs, whom he mentions in chapters 39 and 54 of *Following the Equator.*

Naples City in southern ITALY. Naples was the last Italian port visited by the QUAKER CITY, which anchored in its harbor on August 1, 1867. Since the ship had just left LEGHORN—which was declared an "infected" CHOLERA port—it was quarantined for 10 days at Naples. Meanwhile, Mark Twain, Dan SLOTE and Dr. Abraham JACKSON arrived at about the same time by an overland route. Able to go wherever he wanted because he had not arrived on the ship, Mark Twain made side-trips to nearby Ischia, Capri, Mt. VESUVIUS and POMPEII. On August 11, all the *Quaker City* passengers were reunited for the first time since landing at GIBRALTAR, and the ship sailed to GREECE. Chapters 29–30 of *Innocents Abroad* describe the Naples visit.

Naples was also the last Italian city that Mark Twain saw when he left Italy for the last time at the end of June 1904.

Napoleon III (Louis Napoleon) (April 20, 1808, Paris, France–January 9, 1873, Chislehurst, England) Emperor of FRANCE (1852–70). A nephew of Napoleon Bonaparte, Louis Napoleon was elected president of France's Second Republic in 1849. Two years later, he assumed dictatorial powers, then proclaimed himself emperor. After a decade of autocratic rule, he gradually returned power to the national assembly. By the time Mark Twain visited France in July 1867, the country was a functioning parliamentary democracy.

Mark Twain saw Napoleon with Turkey's Sultan ABDUL AZIZ in Paris—a moment described in chapter 13 of *Innocents Abroad.* Here and in chapters 16 and 25, Mark Twain lavishes praise on Napoleon, whom he regarded as the world's greatest statesman. His opinion of Napoleon would, however, soon fall, along with the emperor's fortunes. He disliked Napoleon's abandonment of his puppet in Mexico, Maximilian, and he later deplored Napoleon's disastrous handling of the Franco-Prussian War. After losing that war in 1870, Napoleon abdicated and retired to England.

Although Napoleon did not come into power until after the time in which *Huckleberry Finn* takes place, Huck seems to have been aware of him. In chapter 14 he tells Jim that some kings who cannot find jobs "gets on the police." The remark probably alludes to Napoleon's working as a London policeman during his early exile—a story that *Innocents Abroad* mentions.

Napoleon Historic ARKANSAS town on the Mississippi River, just below its confluence with the Arkansas River. Mark Twain occasionally visited Napoleon during his PILOTING years when it was a bustling community. It was there that he saw the first printed reports of the PENNSYLVANIA steamboat disaster that killed his brother Henry Clemens. His description of Napoleon in the late 1850s as "a good big self-complacent town" in *Life on the Mississippi* is drawn from memory (chapter 32). During the CIVIL WAR the town was nearly destroyed by fire; in 1874 it was washed away by the shifting Arkansas River. The town's disappearance figures prominently in the Karl RITTER tale, and Mark Twain used it as a model for *Huckleberry Finn*'s fictional BRICKSVILLE.

Napoleon is mentioned in *The Gilded Age* as a hailing stop that the *Boreas* passes (chapter 4). Later, Colonel Sellers proposes to rename STONE'S LANDING "Napoleon" in Missouri.

Nasby, Petroleum Vesuvius (September 20, 1833, Vestal, New York–February 15, 1888, Toledo, Ohio) Pseudonym of political satirist David Ross Locke. After starting as a printer at 10, Locke worked his way into journalism and drifted to Findlay, Ohio, where he became an editor of the *Jeffersonian.* On the eve of the CIVIL WAR in March 1861, he published a powerful satiric attack on local racists that he signed "Petroleum V. Nasby." During the war, Locke made Nasby famous as an ignorant, dissolute preacher who spoke out on everything that Locke himself opposed: white supremacy, states' rights, the Democratic Party, and Copperheads (northern sympathizers of the Confederacy).

Nasby's misspellings, malapropisms, ludicrous exaggeration and absurd reasoning served to ridicule Locke's targets, making him an important anti-Confederacy voice. Touring as "Nasby," Locke became one of the most popular lecturers of his time. After the war, he became an editor and part owner of Ohio's Toledo *Blade* (1865–87) and worked for the *New York Evening Mail* (1871–79). He continued writing Nasby letters until his retirement and republished them in several collections.

Mark Twain admired Locke and devotes several passages to him in his AUTOBIOGRAPHY, including a description of one of Locke's Nasby lectures at Hartford in 1868 or 1869, when they first met. They were photographed along with Josh BILLINGS in Boston in November 1869.

Nash, Thomas S. (c. 1835–?) Childhood friend of Mark Twain in Hannibal. In his AUTOBIOGRAPHY, Mark Twain recalls skating with Nash on the frozen Mississippi one night in about 1849, when the ice began breaking up and Nash fell into the water. Nash con-

tracted scarlet fever and emerged deaf and barely able to speak. When Mark Twain saw Nash at Hannibal's train station in 1902, Nash stepped up to him and yelled, "Same damned fools, Sam!"—a moment depicted in MARK TWAIN: BENEATH THE LAUGHTER.

Nash's postmaster father, Abner O. Nash (c. 1804–1859), was the model for the down-on-his-luck postmaster in *Tom Sawyer,* and Nash himself inspired Theodor FISCHER's friend Nikolaus Baumann in "THE CHRONICLE OF YOUNG SATAN." Baumann is destined to fall in icy water and suffer the same cruel fate that Nash suffered, until SATAN arranges for him to drown instead. In NO. 44, THE MYSTERIOUS STRANGER, however, the character Johann Brinker is crippled for three decades after saving a priest from drowning in freezing water. Mark Twain's unfinished novel "Three Thousand Years Among the Microbes" mentions Tom Nash by name as an early friend of the narrator.

Nast, Thomas (September 27, 1840, Landau, Germany–December 7, 1902, Guayaquil, Ecuador) Editorial cartoonist. After coming to America as a child, Nast studied

Thomas Nast lampoons Mark Twain's going to Canada to secure the copyright for The Prince and the Pauper. *(Harper's Weekly, January 1882)*

One of Thomas Nast's strongest attacks on Tweed in Harper's Weekly. (Courtesy, Library of Congress, Pictures & Prints Division)

art and became an illustrator for the new *Frank Leslie's Illustrated Newspaper* in 1855. Several years later he began drawing cartoons for HARPER'S WEEKLY, which made him a staff artist in 1862. Nast became the most famous editorial cartoonist of his time; he made the elephant and the donkey political party symbols, invented the now-traditional "Santa Claus" costume, and used his drawings to bring down William "Boss" Tweed and New York City's corrupt political machine in the 1870s. Changing art reproduction techniques made Nast's wood-plate cartoons less popular in the 1880s, and he left *Harper's* in 1886. In 1902 he was appointed an American consul to Ecuador, where he died from yellow fever.

Mark Twain and Nast knew each other from the mid-1860s and several times tried unsuccessfully to collaborate. In early 1867, Nast proposed a joint lecture tour in which he would draw pictures while Mark Twain spoke, but Mark Twain was just about to sail on the QUAKER CITY. Six years later, Mark Twain asked Nast to accompany him to ENGLAND to illustrate a book he planned to write; in 1877, he tried to revive the joint-lecture tour that Nast had proposed a decade earlier.

During their 1884 lecture tour, Mark Twain and G. W. CABLE spent Thanksgiving at Nast's Morristown, New Jersey home. During the night, Mark Twain got up and stopped every clock in the house in order to sleep—an incident that Nast commemorated in a cartoon. A. B. PAINE later wrote a biography of Nast that Mark Twain admired so much that he agreed to allow Paine to write his biography.

Nat   Minor character in *Huckleberry Finn*. A slave of Silas PHELPS, Nat is assigned to looking after Jim, who is imprisoned on the farm. After being introduced in chapter 34, Nat is first identified by name in chapter 36.

Nebraska   At the end of July 1861, Mark Twain and his brother Orion spent four days traveling through what is now southern Nebraska. Their STAGECOACH followed the Little Blue River from Kansas into Nebraska, then passed through Fort Kearney, following the Platte River to Cottonwood before cutting through the northeast corner of Colorado, reentering Nebraska at its panhandle and passing through Scott's Bluff. *Roughing It* describes the journey in chapters 4–7.

Much of Mark Twain's unfinished novel "HUCK FINN AND TOM SAWYER AMONG THE INDIANS" takes place in Nebraska's Platte River valley at least a few years before Nebraska was organized as a territory in 1854. After present Colorado and the Dakotas were split off to form their own territories, Nebraska became a state in 1867.

Nebraska   Last STEAMBOAT on which Mark Twain traveled when he was a licensed PILOT. Mark Twain arrived in NEW ORLEANS shortly after the CIVIL WAR began and found that there would be no more piloting work on commercial steamboats. On May 14, 1861, he took passage on the *Nebraska*, the last steamboat to pass the Union blockade above Memphis. Near St. Louis, the pilot ignored a warning shot from a Union stronghold and the boat was fired upon. According to an unsubstantiated story, another shot shattered the pilothouse, removing any lingering doubts Mark Twain may have had about the wisdom of serving on a steamboat during a war.

Neither *Life on the Mississippi* nor "THE PRIVATE HISTORY OF A CAMPAIGN THAT FAILED" mentions the *Nebraska*, though both allude to Mark Twain's leaving New Orleans.

Neckar   River in southwestern GERMANY. Rising in the south end of the BLACK FOREST, the Neckar flows generally north 250 miles, through Stuttgart, HEILBRONN and HEIDELBERG until it joins the Rhine at MANNHEIM. During the 19th century, parts of the slow-moving Neckar were engineered to make it practical as a shipping canal. Mark Twain saw much of the Neckar in 1878; after spending two months in Heidelberg, he returned there in August with Joseph TWICHELL, with whom he went up the Neckar's shore by train and cart to Heilbronn. They then spent two days returning down the river on a steamer to Hirschhorn, from which they went by train and carriage to Heidelberg. *A Tramp Abroad* converts their voyage into a fictitious raft trip, in which the narrator, his companion HARRIS, and two Englishmen, "Mr. X" and "Mr. Z," spend several days going all the way from Heilbronn to Heidelberg on a big log raft (chapters 14–19). Along the way, they make several stops and hear such German legends as that of the LORELEI.

Recognizing that the Neckar was essentially a canal, Mark Twain compares it to the Erie Canal in *A Tramp Abroad*, remarking that it is narrow enough in many places to throw a dog across and that a raftsman must do some snug piloting to negotiate its turns (chapter 14). When the book's fictional rafters encounter a storm, their voyage resembles the Erie Canal boat trip of *Roughing It*'s "THE AGED PILOT MAN"—particularly when the raft springs a leak (chapter 17). *A Tramp Abroad*'s description of the sunrise over the Neckar (chapter 14) anticipates Huck's description of a Mississippi sunrise in *Huckleberry Finn* (chapter 19).

Neider, Charles (January 18, 1915, Odessa, Russia–)   Mark Twain anthologizer. Born in what was then part of Russia, Neider came to the United States in 1920. After graduating from City University of New York in 1938, he became a freelance writer and editor. He grew interested in Mark Twain in the mid-1950s, when he read *Roughing It* while researching a Western novel, *The Authentic Death of Hendry Jones* (1956). With the experience of compiling a half-dozen anthologies behind him, he assembled a one-volume collection that he confidently titled *The Complete Short Stories of Mark Twain* (1957). The book's 60 selections come directly from earlier standard editions, including several travel books from which Neider extracted a dozen stories. The collection also includes the discredited version of THE MYSTERIOUS STRANGER. As with most of his anthologies, Neider added a personal introduction, but only minimal notes on the sources and content of the stories.

In 1961, Neider published both *The Complete Humorous Sketches and Tales of Mark Twain* and *Mark Twain: Life As I Find It: Essays, Sketches, Tales and Other Material*. The material in this volume—none of which appears in the "complete" sketch book—comes directly from the GALAXY, the BUFFALO EXPRESS and other 19th-century sources. Neider's *Complete Essays of Mark Twain* followed in 1963. His other anthologies include *The Travels of Mark Twain* (1961), *The Complete Travel Books of Mark Twain* (2 volumes, 1966), *The Comic Mark Twain Reader* (1977), *The Selected Letters of Mark Twain* (1982), *Plymouth Rock and the Pilgrims and Other Salutary Platform Opinions* (1984), *Mark Twain at His Best: A Comprehensive Sampler* (1986) and *The Outrageous Mark Twain* (1987). Neider's introductions to many of these volumes are collected in *Mark Twain* (1967). He also edited *Papa: An Intimate Biography of Mark Twain by Susy Clemens* (1985).

Neider follows A. B. PAINE in editing Mark Twain's AUTOBIOGRAPHY to fit his own design. His edition of *The Autobiography of Mark Twain* (1959) rearranges Mark Twain's original text into an approximately chronological narrative. Neider has also abridged several of Mark Twain's books. *The Adventures of Colonel Sellers* (1965) is his edition of *The Gilded Age*, shorn of C. D. WARNER's chapters. He also published a new edition of *A Tramp Abroad* in 1977, deleting what he considers the book's most tedious passages. His 1985 edition of *Huckleberry Finn* condenses the "EVASION" chapters.

Nevada Mark Twain lived in Nevada for nearly three years—all within the state's brief history as a federal territory. When he arrived there in August 1861, Nevada was a rapidly growing but still sparsely settled territory whose history of white settlement was barely a dozen years old. Although *Roughing It*, Mark Twain's only extended work relating to Nevada, is partly fictionalized, it accurately captures the excitement of western frontier life, as well as the get-rich-quick atmosphere that hung over Nevada through those years.

Nevada came under American control in 1848, after the Mexican War. A year later, MORMONS established the first non-Indian settlement, Genoa, near where CARSON CITY was later founded. Over the ensuing decade, the region was administered as part of the territory of UTAH and saw little change, apart from the development of wagon-train trails and stations. Nevada's INDIAN population was comparatively sparse, with small communities of Northern PIUTE the most numerous peoples living around the western areas that would later be developed

by white settlers. The Washo people of the Lake TAHOE region contributed their name to several natural features, and "WASHOE" became the settlers' preferred name for the territory as a whole.

Nevada's real development began after mid-1858, when gold and silver were discovered in the COMSTOCK Lode—one of the world's greatest precious metal deposits. As prospectors poured in, VIRGINIA CITY and other towns arose, and several attempts were made to organize a government independent of Utah. The coming of the CIVIL WAR enhanced the importance of Nevada as a mineral producer and accelerated its constitutional development. One of James BUCHANAN's last acts as president was to sign the organic act making Nevada an autonomous territory in March 1861. After President Abraham LINCOLN took office, he appointed James W. NYE Nevada's first governor and gave the second-highest post, that of SECRETARY, to Mark Twain's brother, Orion Clemens. On August 14, Mark Twain and his brother arrived by STAGECOACH in Carson City. Chapter 21 of *Roughing It* describes the primitive administrative conditions they found there, with most top government officials working out of boardinghouse rooms. Orion busied himself helping to organize the new government and later built a substantial house for his family in Carson City.

Mark Twain's 34 months in Nevada fall into several distinct phases. After about a month in and around Carson City, he went south to the ESMERALDA mining district to buy claims for himself and his brother. On returning to Carson City, he clerked for the territorial legislature's first session in October and November. In December he began a prospecting expedition to the HUMBOLDT district to the north. At the end of January 1862, he returned to Carson City, where he remained until April, when he went back to Esmeralda and lived at AURORA until September. During this period, he made his most serious efforts at MINING and began writing his "JOSH" letters to the VIRGINIA CITY TERRITORIAL ENTERPRISE. After this newspaper offered him a position, he walked 130 miles to Virginia City to join the *Enterprise* staff in late September. About four months later, he began using "MARK TWAIN" as his pen name. He remained based in Virginia City until the end of May 1864, when he moved to SAN FRANCISCO.

As an *Enterprise* reporter, Mark Twain spent considerable time in Carson City covering legislative sessions and other events, including a state constitutional convention running from October to mid-December 1863. After the convention, fellow journalists elected him president of the burlesque "THIRD HOUSE." Meanwhile, his official and unofficial connections in the government, along with his clout as a respected *Enterprise* reporter, gave him considerable influence in the territory. By spring 1864, however, he was outgrowing Nevada, and he seems to have been wary of his own prospects for prosperity if Nevada became a state. After getting himself into trouble by publishing several injudicious articles, he resigned from the *Enterprise* at the end of May and abruptly left for San Francisco with his friend Steve GILLIS. Almost exactly five months later, Nevada became a state. Meanwhile, Orion Clemens neglected to pursue an excellent opportunity to win the Republican nomination for secretary of state and was suddenly unemployed.

During Mark Twain's residence in Nevada, he came to know most of the territory's leading journalists, businessmen and political leaders, building friendships that would help him later. After he returned from the QUAKER CITY voyage in late 1867, for example, he briefly worked as private secretary to Senator William M. STEWART, an old Nevada acquaintance who introduced him to WASHINGTON politics. His *Enterprise* editor Joe GOODMAN remained an important friend in later years. Mark Twain revisited western Nevada during lecture tours in October 1866 and April–May 1868.

"New Deal" When Franklin D. ROOSEVELT accepted the Democratic nomination for president in 1932, he pledged himself to "a new deal for the American people"—a phrase that he made a campaign slogan. According to Cyril CLEMENS, Roosevelt admitted adapting his slogan from *Connecticut Yankee*, in which the phrase "new deal" appears once. In chapter 13, Hank MORGAN compares sixth-century England to a corporation in which 994 people out of every 1,000 furnish all the money and do all the work, while the other six make all the decisions and collect all the dividends; he concludes: "It seemed to me that what the nine hundred and ninety-four dupes needed was a new deal." Throughout his narrative, Hank uses card-playing imagery often enough to suggest that he regards life as a game. His terminology includes "saving trump" (chapter 5), "rake in the chips" (chapter 39) and variations of "playing one's hand" (chapters 3, 5, 6, 32 and 39). It may also be significant that the number of trained boys with whom he fights against the massed chivalry of England is exactly 52—the number of cards in a standard deck (chapters 42–43).

Mark Twain occasionally uses "new deal" elsewhere. For example, he wrote a letter from CONSTANTINOPLE describing a horrible lunch in which he and his companions "pass" on each dish and finally call for "a new deal." In *Roughing It*, Scotty BRIGGS's conversation with a young minister becomes so opaque that he eventually suggests, "Let's have a new deal" (chapter 47).

New Falls City STEAMBOAT on which Mark Twain probably cubbed as a PILOT in 1858. An 880-ton side-wheeler completed in Paducah, Kentucky in January 1858, the *New Falls City* was the largest steamboat on which Mark Twain may have served. He apparently made a one-way trip from St. Louis to New Orleans on the boat's maiden voyage in late January 1858, when Isaac

Chauncy Cable and Zeb Leavenworth were the licensed pilots and J. Ed MONTGOMERY was captain. He also may have cubbed on the boat under Horace BIXBY on two round-trips between St. Louis and New Orleans between late October and early December the same year, when James B. Woods was captain. After the CIVIL WAR began, the *New Falls City* was commandeered by the Confederacy.

New Orleans LOUISIANA port city in which Mark Twain began and ended his career as a steamboat PILOT. Standing near the mouth of the Mississippi River on the Gulf of Mexico, New Orleans has occupied an important place in American commerce since steamboats began moving passengers and goods along the Mississippi in the early 19th century. By midcentury, it was one of the busiest ports in the entire country—a position that it retains today.

Mark Twain first visited New Orleans on February 28, 1857. He came hoping to catch a ship to SOUTH AMERICA; instead, he persuaded the pilot Horace BIXBY to take him on as an apprentice. Over the next four years he visited New Orleans perhaps 50 times while working on packets connecting it with St. Louis. His boats typically laid over several days between trips, giving him plenty of opportunity to see the city. He also occasionally stayed ashore for longer periods when he was between jobs. Although he had many reservations about the city, he thought enough of it to take his mother there for a holiday after he got his piloting license.

Mark Twain was in New Orleans with the ALONZO CHILD when Louisiana seceded from the Union on January 26, 1861. He was also on the *Child* there in May, shortly after the CIVIL WAR began. He soon returned to St. Louis aboard the NEBRASKA. Almost exactly twenty years later, he returned and toured the city with G. W. CABLE, one of the city's best-known writers. Chapters 41 to 50 of *Life on the Mississippi* describe this visit in detail, with attention to the city's architecture, cemeteries and cuisine. New Orleans is also mentioned in more than half of the book's other chapters.

Although New Orleans does not provide a setting for any of Mark Twain's novels, it is mentioned in several—usually as a far-off place to which slaves fear to be sent. Its name appears 15 times in *Huckleberry Finn* alone. In chapter 2, for example, the slave Jim claims that witches have taken him to New Orleans. When he later learns that Miss WATSON intends to sell him, he flees to avoid being sold "down to Orleans." After the KING and DUKE board the raft in chapter 20, Huck tells them that he and Jim are going downriver to find a relative living near New Orleans. Later in that chapter, the Duke prints a phony reward handbill, describing Jim as a runaway slave "from ST. JACQUES PLANTATION, forty mile below New Orleans." In chapter 27, the King sells a slave belonging to the WILKSES to a New Orleans buyer.

Finally, after Jim is taken captive in southern Arkansas, Silas PHELPS writes to New Orleans to locate his supposed owner (chapters 35 and 39).

In *Pudd'nhead Wilson,* the former slave ROXY works on the GRAND MOGUL, a steamboat packet that works the same route as the *Paul Jones*—between Cincinnati and New Orleans.

"The New Planet"   Sketch published in 1909. Noting that astronomers have recently observed "perturbations" in Neptune's orbit that suggest the presence of an unknown nearby planet, Mark Twain recalls how the perturbations in Uranus's orbit that led to the discovery of Neptune in 1846 affected him. Claiming to be so sensitive that he "perturbate[s] when any other planet is disturbed," he argues that his present perturbations prove that a new planet does exist and hopes it will be named after him. The existence of the new planet was not confirmed until 21 years later, however, when it was named Pluto.

Originally published in HARPER'S WEEKLY (January 30, 1909) and reprinted in EUROPE AND ELSEWHERE, this brief sketch reflects Mark Twain's interest in astronomy. Both *Tom Sawyer* (chapter 1) and *Innocents Abroad* (chapter 26) comment on the delight astronomers feel when they discover a new planet. WHAT IS MAN? alludes to the clues astronomers follow to find invisible planets (chapter 5).

New Saybrook (Saybrook Point)   Coastal CONNECTICUT town on Long Island Sound, just west of the mouth of the Connecticut River. Mark Twain took his family there to escape Hartford's heat from early July through late August 1872. While he was there, he worked on his self-pasting SCRAPBOOK.

New York   Mark Twain spent well over 10 years of his life in the state of New York and visited the state every year between 1867 and 1910—except 1896-99, when he was continuously out of the country. He first entered New York in August 1853, when he passed through BUFFALO, Syracuse and Albany to reach NEW YORK CITY, where he stayed for more than two months. After another sojourn of uncertain duration in early 1854, he was next in the state in 1867—a year in which he made New York City his principal residence.

Mark Twain's attachment to New York grew stronger in early 1869, when he became engaged to marry Olivia Langdon of ELMIRA. Later that year, he bought an interest in the BUFFALO EXPRESS and made Buffalo his home. Meanwhile, he persuaded his sister and mother to settle in FREDONIA. He relocated to Hartford, Connecticut in mid-1871, but from 1870 through 1889 he and his family spent almost every summer in Elmira, where he did much of his most important writing. In 1890, his family summered at ONTEORA in the Catskills. During the 1870s and 1880s, he went on several LEC-

TURE tours that took him through most of New York's major towns. He also visited New York City frequently on business.

After a long sojourn in Europe, Mark Twain returned to the United States in October 1900 and settled in New York City. Until moving to his final home in Connecticut in 1908, New York was his principal residence. During these years, he lived in New York City and nearby RIVERDALE and summered at SARANAC LAKE and TUXEDO PARK. He and his wife bought a house in TARRYTOWN in 1902, but never lived in it.

New York City   New York City was one of Mark Twain's principal residences. He lived in or near the city in 1853–54, 1867, 1900–03 and 1904–08, and visited it well over a hundred other times. He first came there on August 24, 1853 (a letter that he wrote home that day is his earliest surviving piece of correspondence). Though he came primarily to see the Crystal Palace Exposition, which had opened six weeks earlier, he liked the city so much that he stayed for two months, while working as a printer for John A. Gray and Green on 97 Cliff Street and lodging on Manhattan's Duane Street. After leaving around October 20, he returned early the following March for a stay of unknown length

Mark Twain in 1901, when he lived in New York City. (Courtesy, Library of Congress, Pictures & Prints Division)

during one of the most poorly documented periods of his life. Several major publishing firms had recently burned down, making printing work difficult to find; it may have been unemployment that drove him back to the Midwest some time between April and August 1854.

Mark Twain next came to New York on January 12, 1867 after spending more than five years in the Far West. Aside from a Midwest LECTURE tour in March–April, he was in the city until June 8, when he joined the QUAKER CITY excursion to the MEDITERRANEAN. Meanwhile, he gave his inaugural East Coast lectures and wrote letters to the SAN FRANCISCO ALTA CALIFORNIA about New York's architecture, politics, theater and people. After returning from abroad in November, he was in New York again briefly before relocating to WASHINGTON, D.C. In late December, he revisited New York City, where he met his future wife, Olivia Langdon.

Over the next 25 years, Mark Twain passed through New York City scores of times. He visited newspaper and magazine publishers, businessmen and friends and spoke before clubs and public audiences. He also used New York harbor as his main point of embarkation and landing for ATLANTIC voyages. In 1884, he established the publishing firm of Charles L. WEBSTER & COMPANY in New York City. During the first few years after he took his family to Europe in 1891, he made five return visits to the United States, spending most of his time during these visits in New York City. He was in New York for extended periods in late 1893 and early 1894 and made so many public appearances that he was dubbed the "Belle of New York."

Mark Twain brought his family back to America in October 1900 and settled at 14 West Tenth Street in Manhattan. The following October they moved to RIVERDALE, then a suburb just north of New York's city limits; it remained his principal residence until he took his family to Italy in late October 1903. After his wife died the following year, he returned to New York City in July 1904. A month later, he leased a house (no longer standing) at 21 Fifth Avenue in which he lived until moving to REDDING, Connecticut in June 1908. He continued to visit New York occasionally, last passing through the city a week before his DEATH in April 1910. A large funeral service was held for him at New York's Presbyterian Brick Church.

New York Herald   Daily newspaper founded by James Gordon Bennett (1795–1872) in 1835. On November 20, 1867, the day after Mark Twain returned from the QUAKER CITY excursion, he published a long critical letter about the cruise in the *Herald;* a slightly abridged version forms chapter 61 of *Innocents Abroad.* Bennett's son, also named James Gordon Bennett (1841–1918), took over the paper in 1872 and later courted Mark Twain to write for it. During the summer of 1897, Bennett launched a drive to raise money for Mark Twain, but the latter quickly stopped the effort and

threatened to sue the *Herald* for printing extensive extracts from *Following the Equator* without authorization. In 1924, the *Herald* and the NEW YORK TRIBUNE merged to become the *New York Herald Tribune.*

New York Sun   Daily newspaper founded in 1833 by Benjamin H. Day (1810–1889), who sold it to his brother-in-law Moses Yale Beach (1800–1868) five years later. The latter's son, Moses S. BEACH, owned the paper from 1852 until 1868, when he sold it to Charles A. Dana (1819–1897), who ran it until he died. Dana increased the *Sun's* circulation by engaging popular writers, including Mark Twain, who wrote six travel letters for the *Sun* during his 1891 European trip. These letters appeared in the *Sun* (and in other newspapers) as "AIX: The Paradise of the Rheumatics" (November 8, 1891); "At the Shrine of St. WAGNER" (December 6, 1891); "PLAYING COURIER" (January 8, 1892); "MARIENBAD—A HEALTH FACTORY" (February 7, 1892); "SWITZERLAND: The Cradle of Liberty" (March 13, 1892); and "The German Chicago [BERLIN]." The *Sun* also serialized *The American Claimant* from January through March 1892. In 1950, the *Sun* merged with the *New York World-Telegram.*

New York Tribune   One of the nation's most influential newspapers during the 19th century, the *Tribune* was founded in 1841 by Horace GREELEY, who ran it until his death in 1872. Whitelaw REID then took over until 1905. In 1867, Mark Twain published six letters in the *Tribune* about the QUAKER CITY trip; afterward, he became a regular *Tribune* correspondent in WASHINGTON, D.C., where he simultaneously served as Senator William M. STEWART's private secretary. From late November 1867 into March 1868, he used the *Tribune's* Washington office as his personal headquarters. During this period, he published "THE FACTS CONCERNING THE RECENT RESIGNATION" and several other short pieces in the *Tribune.*

In later years, Mark Twain had little direct connection with the *Tribune.* In 1886, the *Tribune* became the first newspaper to use linotype for typesetting—a development that had disastrous implications for Mark Twain's investment in the rival PAIGE COMPOSITOR. In 1924, the *Tribune* and the NEW YORK HERALD merged to create the *Herald Tribune.*

New Zealand   Island group in the southwest PACIFIC OCEAN that was a self-governing British Crown Colony in 1895, when Mark Twain spent six weeks lecturing there during his around-the-world tour. After sailing from AUSTRALIA aboard the *Mararoa* on November 1, 1895, he reached the tip of New Zealand's South Island on November 6. From there, he went up the east coast to Christchurch, lecturing in many small towns along the way. On November 17, he sailed on the *Flora* from Lyttleton to Nelson and then through Cook Strait to New Plymouth on the southwest coast of North Island.

He reached Auckland on November 20 and remained a week before continuing his voyage around North Island. After spending two weeks in Napier and Wanganui on the east coast, he made his final stop at Wellington on December 9. Four days later he returned to Australia on the *Mararoa*.

New Zealand impressed Mark Twain favorably—particularly because of its enfranchisement of women and its comparatively benign subjugation of the Maori people—but it did not capture his imagination in the way that Australia did. Much of his time there he spent bedridden with a carbuncle and he missed some of New Zealand's most spectacular scenery. *Following the Equator* describes his visit there (chapters 26, 29–35).

Newcomb, Mary Ann (1809–1894) Early schoolteacher of Mark Twain and model for several characters. Born in Vermont and trained as a teacher in the East, Newcomb came to Missouri and settled in FLORIDA, where she apparently knew the Clemens family. Around 1839, she moved to Hannibal, at about the same time that the Clemens family moved there. Initially, she taught at Elizabeth HORR's school; later she had her own. She apparently taught Mark Twain at both schools and occasionally boarded at the Clemens house. During the late 1840s, Newcomb married John Davis, who was Mark Twain's model for JONES THE WELCHMAN.

When Mark Twain revisited Hannibal in 1902, he credited Newcomb with forcing him to learn how to read. Newcomb was Mark Twain's model for Miss WATSON, the spinster who originally owned the slave Jim in *Huckleberry Finn*. Mark Twain's notes indicate that she was also his model for Miss Pomeroy in "SCHOOLHOUSE HILL" and Mrs. Bangs in his unfinished "Autobiography of a Damned Fool."

Newell, Julia (*fl.* 1860s) Passenger on the 1867 QUAKER CITY cruise. A single woman in whom Mark Twain may have been romantically interested, Newell was one of the cruise's most liberated women. Willing to endure any hardship in order to travel, she was with Mark Twain in an arduous week-long trip through southern SPAIN toward the end of the voyage. Four years after the cruise, she married another passenger, Dr. Abraham R. JACKSON. Her hometown newspaper in Janesville, Wisconsin published 14 of her letters about the voyage.

Newell, Peter (March 5, 1862, near Bushnell, Illinois–January 15, 1924, Little Neck, New York) Illustrator. Trained at New York's Art Students League, Newell did most of his work for children's books and magazines, especially HARPER publications. He illustrated several Lewis Carroll books, including a special edition of *Alice in Wonderland* (1901). His own books included *Topsys and Turveys* (1893). He also contributed to *Following the Equator* (1897), in which all five of his pictures appear in chapter 64. They include several South African

scenes and a caricature of P. T. BARNUM. He also illustrated several of Harper's standardized editions of books such as *Innocents Abroad* and occasional magazine stories, including "At the Appetite Cure" (1898) and "THE $30,000 BEQUEST" (1904).

Niagara North America's Great Lakes empty through the Niagara River, which connects Lake Erie with Lake Ontario and forms a border between CANADA and the United States. Niagara Falls, a 160-foot drop in the middle of the river, has long been one of the continent's most popular tourist sights; Mark Twain's sister Pamela Clemens MOFFETT honeymooned there in 1851. Mark Twain himself probably first saw the falls two years later, while passing through nearby BUFFALO, New York; in 1869–71, he lived in Buffalo, just 15 miles from the falls. Shortly after he settled there, the BUFFALO EXPRESS published his sketch "A Day at Niagara" (August 21, 1869), which was collected in SKETCHES, NEW AND OLD as "Niagara." In 1893, Mark Twain made Niagara the site of Eden in "EXTRACTS FROM ADAM'S DIARY," which he wrote for the *Niagara Book*, a souvenir publication for Buffalo's World's Fair. The story has Adam go over the falls in a barrel—a feat not actually accomplished until a woman did it in 1901. Some later editions of this story—which has been published under various titles—omit all references to Niagara.

Allusions to Niagara's size and beauty appear throughout Mark Twain's writings, such as *Innocents Abroad* (chapters 26 and 54), *Roughing It* (chapter 73), *Tom Sawyer* (chapter 31), *A Tramp Abroad* (chapter 22), *Connecticut Yankee* (chapter 18) and *Following the Equator* (chapter 59).

Nicaragua After leaving CALIFORNIA on the steamship *America*, Mark Twain reached San Juan del Sur, Nicaragua, near the Costa Rica border, on December 29, 1866. The next day he and about 400 other passengers began the overland journey to San Juan de Norte, or Greytown, on the Caribbean coast, following a route developed by Cornelius VANDERBILT in the 1850s to accommodate traffic generated by California's GOLD RUSH. He rode a mule-drawn wagon to Lake Nicaragua, where he boarded an overnight steamer. The next morning, at Fort San Carlos, he switched to a smaller stern-wheeler that went down the San Juan River, about a hundred miles, to Greytown. After sleeping there overnight, he boarded the steamer *San Francisco* on New Year's Day to continue his journey to New York. He describes his passage through Nicaragua in two letters to the SAN FRANCISCO ALTA CALIFORNIA (reprinted in MARK TWAIN'S TRAVELS WITH MR. BROWN), commenting mostly on the scenery, which he thought beautiful. In 1868, he crossed Central America twice through PANAMA.

Nichols, Archibald Name mentioned in *Huckleberry Finn*. In chapter 33, Tom Sawyer arrives at the PHELPS farm and pretends to be William THOMPSON. When Uncle Silas answers the door, Tom says, "Mr. Archibald Nichols, I presume?"—a subtle allusion to Henry Morton STANLEY's meeting with David Livingstone. Nichols is a neighbor who lives several miles from the Phelpses.

nigger A pejorative slang term for a nonwhite person, "nigger" goes back to mid–18th-century English, which adapted it from Spanish *negro* for "black." In America the word has been applied almost exclusively to persons of African descent. Mark Twain grew up in a white slave-holding society in which he probably heard the word more often than any other term for African American. His use of it in fictional dialogue reflects the Southern usage with which he grew up. It appears so often in *Huckleberry Finn* (211 times) that it has fueled an unending debate over the question of whether Mark Twain was a racist. During the 1950s, the National Association for the Advancement of Colored People (NAACP) called for the book's banning from schools and libraries. Film adaptations typically omit the word completely.

A minor misconception about *Huckleberry Finn* is that the book refers to the runaway slave Jim as "the nigger Jim." This expression does not appear in the novel, though two passages approximate it. In one, Huck writes a letter to Miss Watson, telling her, "your runaway nigger Jim is down here" (chapter 31); Huck later refers to another man as "the nigger NAT" (chapter 36). The notion that *Huckleberry Finn* uses "nigger" as an adjective was popularized by A. B. PAINE's *Mark Twain, A Biography* (1912), which routinely refers to Jim as "Nigger Jim" (e.g., chapters 8, 12, 23 and 153). Mark Twain himself does, however, use the phrase in the opening paragraph of "HUCK AND TOM AMONG THE INDIANS," which he began immediately after finishing *Huckleberry Finn*. This story was not published, however, until 1968.

Among Mark Twain's other works, "nigger" appears 75 times in *Pudd'nhead Wilson*, 12 times in *Roughing It*, nine times each in *Tom Sawyer* and *Life on the Mississippi* and once in *Innocents Abroad* (chapter 10). It also appears frequently in other Tom and Huck stories, including *Tom Sawyer Abroad*—which a magazine editor altered without Mark Twain's permission by changing "nigger" to "darkie" in dialogue spoken by white characters.

Nook Farm Residential community in Hartford, Connecticut. A 140-acre region along the left bank of North Park River in West Hartford, Nook Farm was created as part of a 17th-century land grant to the first governor. In 1853, John Hooker (1816–1901) and his brother-in-law Francis GILLETTE purchased the land and subdivided it. Over the next 20 years, the community gradually filled with relatives and business associates, who included Joseph HAWLEY, Harriet Beecher STOWE, C. D. WARNER and other prominent figures. In October 1871, Mark Twain rented a Nook Farm house from Hooker's wife, Isabella Beecher HOOKER. The following year, he and his wife bought property at 351 Farmington Avenue, along Nook Farm's northern boundary. There they built a new house in which they lived from September 1874 until June 1891. That structure is now maintained by the MARK TWAIN MEMORIAL.

Norfolk, Duke of (Thomas Howard II) (1473–August 25, 1554, Keminghall, England) Historical figure mentioned in *The Prince and the Pauper*. The uncle of King HENRY VIII's wives Anne Boleyn and Catherine Howard, the Duke of Norfolk was one of the most powerful figures of his time in England's government. In 1546, however, he and his son, the Earl of Surrey, were charged with treason and sentenced to death. Surrey was beheaded on January 21, 1547, but Norfolk's execution, scheduled for January 28, was canceled because King Henry had died the previous day and the ruling council thought it unwise to begin a new king's reign with an execution.

Norfolk is not a character in *The Prince and the Pauper*, but his name figures prominently in the story. Chapter 5 mentions the recent arrest of Norfolk and Surrey. In the same chapter, Tom CANTY (who everyone thinks is Prince Edward) expresses concern over Norfolk's impending death when he meets King Henry; however, the king says that Norfolk is unworthy of his concern and implies that Norfolk has delayed Edward's formal installation as the Prince of Wales. Meanwhile, Norfolk's execution is delayed because the king's Great Seal cannot be found. In chapter 8, the king commands that Norfolk be beheaded the next day; however, the king dies that night and Tom Canty is proclaimed king at GUILDHALL. Tom's first official act is to spare Norfolk—a decision that wins him immediate favor in the court (chapter 11) and later in the country at large (chapter 27).

Several film adaptations of *The Prince and the Pauper* have made Norfolk a character. At the conclusion of the 1937 film, for example, Norfolk (Henry Stephenson) replaces HERTFORD as lord protector (Hertford's actual successor was Lord Northumberland). Rex Harrison played Norfolk in the 1977 film.

North American Review A magazine founded in Boston in 1815, the *Review* was long a leading forum of political and social debate. It went through many changes in ownership and in frequency of publication, and relocated to New York City in 1878. Its editors included James Russell Lowell (editor, 1863–72), Henry Adams (1872–76), Lloyd S. Brice (1889–96) and David A. Munro (1896–99). George HARVEY bought the *Review* in 1899, editing it himself until 1926. The magazine expired 14 years later.

During the 1890s, the *Review* published a dozen of Mark Twain's essays, including some of his strongest writings on imperialism. These contributions included "Private History of the JUMPING FROG Story" (April 1894), "IN DEFENSE OF HARRIET SHELLEY" (1894), "What

Paul BOURGET Thinks of Us" (1895), "Fenimore COOPER's Literary Offenses" (1895), "To the Person Sitting in Darkness" (1901), "To My Missionary Critics" (1901), "DOES THE RACE OF MAN LOVE A LORD?" (1902), "A Defence of General FUNSTON" (1902), "CHRISTIAN SCIENCE" (1902–1903), "Concerning Copyright" (1905) and "THE CZAR'S SOLILOQUY" (1905). From September 1906 through December 1907, the *Review* published 25 installments of his "Chapters from My AUTOBIOGRAPHY." He used the money that he made from these memoirs to build his STORMFIELD home, which he originally called "Autobiography House."

notebooks and journals In June 1855, Mark Twain began a habit of keeping notebooks that he would sustain until the year he died. His 49 surviving books provide a unique record of his adult life with only a few notable gaps in their sequence: the middle years of his steamboat PILOTING period, his residence in NEVADA, and the entire period from July 1868 to May 1877—except for June–July 1873.

The content of the notebooks varies: from mundane French vocabulary lists and exercises in the first journal to ideas for his books, preliminary story drafts, MAXIMS, projections of profits to be made from investments such as the PAIGE COMPOSITOR, and other subjects. Scattered throughout are comments on persons, places and events directly and indirectly relevant to Mark Twain's life. The notebooks are most like true journals, with dated daily entries, during periods that Mark Twain spent abroad, and are particularly valuable as supplements to his travel books.

In 1935, A. B. PAINE published MARK TWAIN'S NOTEBOOK, a selection containing about a quarter of the material in the original 49 notebooks. Four decades later, the MARK TWAIN PAPERS project began publishing the complete text of the notebooks in *Mark Twain's Notebooks & Journals*. By 1979, the project had published the first 30 notebooks, covering 1855–91, in three volumes. Publication of the final two volumes in the series is tentatively scheduled for 2005–6. In addition to thorough annotations, the project's editions include detailed summaries of what Mark Twain was doing during the periods that he was writing each notebook.

Mark Twain began his second notebook shortly after becoming an apprentice steamboat pilot—a moment alluded to in chapter 6 of *Life on the Mississippi*, in which Horace BIXBY tells the cub to get a memorandum book in which to record the river's features—precisely the kind of information that Mark Twain's second notebook contains. Mark Twain's faithfulness in keeping notebooks contrasts with remarks about journal-keeping that he makes in his published writings. *Innocents Abroad,* for example, suggests that anyone who commits himself to keeping a journal is so likely to fail that a particularly cruel punishment to inflict upon a young person would be to make him pledge to keep a journal for a year (chapter 4). *Life on the Mississippi* tells the story of a man

who started a diary during the siege of VICKSBURG; he wrote prodigiously for several days, but stopped altogether within a week (chapter 35). Mark Twain's more successful fictional journal-keepers include *The American Claimant's* Lord BERKELEY, whose diary is one of the few objects that he saves when his hotel burns down (chapter 7). Hank MORGAN writes the narrative that constitutes most of *Connecticut Yankee* from a diary that he has kept during his years in sixth-century England (chapter 43).

No. 44, The Mysterious Stranger Posthumously published novel. Also known as the "Print Shop" version of THE MYSTERIOUS STRANGER stories, *No. 44* is the final version that Mark Twain wrote in this cycle and it may be considered his last novel. Set in late medieval AUSTRIA, the story concerns the unexplained appearance of a remarkable boy with extraordinary powers. Less didactic than "THE CHRONICLE OF YOUNG SATAN," *No. 44* delivers its message more through action than talk. In this version the stranger character, who calls himself "44" (FORTY-FOUR), is ostensibly a naive and sensitive boy who struggles to fit into the rough community of printers who share quarters in an old castle. Though 44 works hard, never hurts anyone and never complains, he is so despised by the other printers that they conspire to get rid of him. Unfazed by their persecution, however, 44 plods along contentedly, while surreptitiously performing miracles designed to enhance the reputation of the local astrologer so that the man will be burned by the church.

Forty-four befriends the narrator of the story, August FELDNER, an apprentice about his own apparent age. Through observing how people treat 44 and each other, August gradually realizes that man is a cruel, vain creature, whose religious beliefs are empty. After 44 teaches August that everyone is divided into a real and a dream self, the novel ends with a powerful solipsistic message in which 44 tells August that there is no other life than that which he is living now and that *nothing*—including 44—exists outside of August's dreams except August himself and empty space. This final theme reflects Mark Twain's growing interest in CHRISTIAN SCIENCE, a religion that ostensibly denies the reality of a physical world.

Though the story is far removed in time and space from his own youth, Mark Twain uses it to recreate his own experience as an apprentice printer. *No. 44* offers his fullest exposition of how men worked in print shops, which were almost the same in August Feldner's era as they were in his own. His notes make it clear that he personally suffered many of the same humiliations as an apprentice that August experiences.

SYNOPSIS

A story containing about 71,000 words in 34 chapters, *No. 44* takes place over at least several months beginning in 1490. Narrating from his old age, August Feldner is an apprentice in a print shop in an old castle overlooking the village of ESELDORF. After the arrival of a remarkable boy named "44" upsets the relationship between the shop's master and the employees, 44 uses his extraordinary powers to save the master from ruin and to humble his striking workers. He also confuses the village priest and shows August many of the wonders of life.

Chapter 1

The story opens in the Austrian village of Eseldorf in 1490, when its narrator, August Feldner, is a boy. Trouble comes when a Hussite woman distributes literature that goes against Catholic beliefs. But after the village's stern priest, Father Adolf, issues a warning, the village never admits another Hussite. Father Adolf is famous for having fearlessly faced the Devil.

Chapter 2

August is an apprentice in a print shop run by Heinrich Stein in an old castle that belongs to the local (unnamed) prince. The shop works quietly, ignored by the village and the Church. August lives in the castle with Stein's family and other employees. Another resident is Balthasar Hoffman, an astrologer whom Frau Stein, the master's stern wife, retains in the hope that he will find treasure.

Chapter 3

One winter day, a boy about August's age appears at the dining hall pleading hunger. Frau Stein wants to turn him away, but the old cook Katrina feeds him, then tells Stein that the boy will work in return for food and shelter. Over his wife's protests, Stein takes him on. When the boy gives his name as "Number 44, New Series 864,962," someone mutters that he must be a "jailbird"—a nickname that sticks. After 44 hauls in several loads of firewood, Frau Stein orders him to walk her dog. Everyone rises to protest because the dog is notoriously vicious, but 44 astonishes them by leading the dog out calmly.

Chapter 4

Resentment against 44 builds among the printers. When the apprentice Ernest Wasserman challenges him to fight, the bewildered newcomer simply grips Wasserman's wrists until he gives in.

Chapter 5

August privately sympathizes with 44, but hesitates to befriend him for fear of being ridiculed. Meanwhile, Katrina takes 44 under her care. As the days pass, people watch 44 closely, but he goes about his business quietly and proves himself the castle's hardest worker. Often he does remarkable things, for which Balthasar the magician is credited. Longing to share in 44's reputation, August visits 44 in his room one night.

Chapter 6

Forty-four receives August warmly and says how much he needs a friend, making August feel guilty about his selfish motives for coming. However, 44 seems to read his mind and forgives him. To help August not be afraid, 44 gives him mulled claret, which he seems to pull out of the air.

Chapter 7

The next morning, August thinks that the previous night's events were a dream until he meets 44, who assures him that they were not. August senses that 44 can read his mind. After breakfast, Stein praises 44 generously and promotes him to apprentice printer—an announcement coolly received by the other printers. Everyone laughs at 44 when Stein asks him if he has studied classical languages or sciences and he answers every question no, but Stein promises to be his teacher. Though pleased for 44, August knows that his friend will pay a heavy price for this favoritism. Later Ernest Wasserman confronts August and promises to reveal that August is 44's friend, until August threatens him with a dirk.

During 44's first day in the shop, the printers make things difficult for him, but he reads August's mind for instructions and performs every task perfectly. The printers now suspect that 44 is an experienced apprentice who has run away, so they cross-examine him about languages and science. His ready answers only anger them more. After 44 gets through the rest of the day by following August's instructions, Wasserman tells on August.

Chapter 8

That night August hides out in a remote corner of the castle. Before dawn, he goes to the kitchen, where Katrina feeds him and rages about the way the men persecute 44. August decides to use his entire savings to pay nuns to pray for 44. In the shop that day, the printers viciously abuse August and 44, but they cannot make 44 respond. The next day, they work even harder to upset him. Stein cannot protect 44 because he needs the other men to finish a big job for him. Nevertheless, the printers go on strike the next day, demanding that Stein get rid of 44.

Chapters 9–11

With a critical delivery date looming, Stein's situation grows desperate until the journeyman printer DOANGIVADAM arrives and joins with 44 against the strikers. After besting the other printers in a sword fight, Doangivadam tries to negotiate a settlement when word comes that invisible beings are working in the shop.

Chapter 12

Forty-four inspects the shop and reports that the printing job has been completed satisfactorily, so Stein's contract is saved. The angry printers accuse the magician Balthasar of engineering this unwelcome miracle.

Chapter 13

With the printers still uncooperative, Stein's next problem is loading the heavy crates from the job onto a wagon. Doangivadam promises to load the wagon, but several striking workers unexpectedly help. Stein's contract is now completely fulfilled.

Chapter 14

The next day, the strikers deny having helped load the wagon and discover that the empty wagon they have been watching is only a specter. Again they blame Balthasar, who in turn blames 44 and promises to burn the boy if he performs more tricks.

Chapter 15

When August offers to pray for 44, he learns that 44 has no interest in religion, so he vows to devote his own life to saving 44's soul. After performing some astonishing feats, 44 shows August how to make himself invisible.

Chapter 16

Pretending to be acting for Balthasar, 44 irritates the printers by strutting in outrageous finery just before exact Duplicates of all the men start appearing. After the "Originals" realize that the Duplicates intend to work in the shop without pay, they attack them, but the fight ends in a draw. The men now demand that Balthasar destroy 44, who reappears and suddenly explodes into flames.

Chapter 17

Distraught by 44's death, August makes himself invisible and goes through the castle. Everyone is subdued by 44's destruction except the Duplicates, who concentrate on their work. When the magician is called to account for himself before the Holy Office, he cannot be found. Forty-four's ashes are buried without ceremony in unhallowed ground, but when August returns to his room, he finds the "corpse" waiting for him.

Chapter 18

Alive again, 44 laughs and cheerfully says that he really did die. He has assembled an exotic meal, with food from America, which he has visited many times in the past, present and future. After eating, he smokes a pipe and explains that each person has a "workaday-self" that tends to business and a "dream-self" that cares only for romance and fun. He has created the Duplicates by putting fictitious flesh and bone on the dream-selves of the Originals and he hopes to stir up trouble among them.

Chapter 19

Over the ensuing days, Father Adolf pursues the magician. He declares the Duplicates are evil spirits and tries to burn them, but they vanish each time he chains one to the stake. His failures make him a laughingstock. Soon the Duplicates begin courting the young women, leaving the Originals madder than ever. August's efforts to interest 44 in religion get nowhere. When August sarcastically says it is a pity that 44 must belong to the human race, 44 reveals that he is *not* human and explains some of his views on mankind, for which he has a sympathetic pity.

Chapter 20

A week later 44 takes August to a distant town where a promising young artist named Johann Brinker saved Father Adolf from drowning in icy water 30 years earlier. The priest recovered quickly, but Brinker himself was permanently crippled, and his four sisters have sacrificed their own lives in order to tend him.

Chapter 21

The next morning, 44 appears to August in the guise of an old peasant and takes him to a woman who is waiting to be burned at the stake for witchcraft. Cold and tired, she begs 44 for someone to light her fire and end her suffering. As 44 gathers faggots, he is arrested and imprisoned, but escapes easily. However, after Father Adolf arrives to burn the woman, 44 appears again as the magician and allows himself to be captured and chained to a stake. As the priest pronounces judgment on him, 44 vanishes, leaving his empty robes in the chains.

Chapter 22

Back in August's room, 44 provides a sumptuous meal from faraway lands and explains the nature of time and the differences between man and the gods.

Chapter 23

After 44 leaves, August wants to express his affection for Stein's lovely niece, Marget Regen. After making himself invisible, he follows her through the castle and has a confusing encounter with her in which her dream-self seems to emerge, until his own Duplicate appears and interferes.

Chapter 24

August returns to his room to reflect on what has happened. He realizes that he cannot compete for Marget with his Duplicate—who calls himself Emil Schwartz. After mass the next morning, he makes himself invisible, follows Marget and Emil and spies on them.

Chapter 25

That night, August drinks heavily with Doangivadam, then visits Marget's boudoir, where three women spot him and scream. After he flees, he is relieved to learn that Stein thinks it was Emil who entered his niece's bedchamber, but August is distressed to hear Stein say that Emil must now marry Marget.

Chapter 26

Forty-four reappears before the distraught August in blackface, singing "Buffalo Gals," "Swanee River" and other songs that drive August to distraction. After 44 settles down, he offers to kill Emil and Marget's maid, but August objects, so 44 instead turns the maid into a cat.

Chapter 27–29

After napping, August talks with Emil, who does not want to marry Marget but to return to his nonphysical state so that he can wander freely in time and space.

When 44 returns in the form of Balthasar the magician, Emil pleads to be released from being a Duplicate and his wish is granted.

Chapter 30
As August and 44 eat another exotic breakfast, 44 discusses "dream-sprites," which once carried important secret messages. While commenting on the importance of accurate interpreting in messages, he cites the "CHRISTIAN SCIENCE dialect" as a particularly difficult one to understand and gives an example of a message from Mary Baker Eddy. When he starts to allude to *where* he comes from, August tries to draw him out but learns only that 44 likes visiting Earth because he can shut off his prophecy power and enjoy being surprised. Suddenly, the cat enters to warn 44—who she thinks is Balthasar—that everyone is after him and that the Originals are planning to kill the Duplicates. The news pleases 44 immensely. August becomes invisible and follows 44 and the cat out of the room.

Chapter 31
To improve an already dark and gloomy morning, 44 arranges an artificial ECLIPSE. He announces that he is inviting ghosts from all times and places to join his celebration. In the great hall, they find many armed people waiting for them, including Katrina, who comes at the supposed magician with a knife. Before she can stab him, 44 reveals who he really is by rising up in a glorious white light. His spectacular appearance and his eclipse leave everyone numb.

Chapter 32–33
As he plans a great Assembly of the Dead, 44 amuses himself by making time go backward. Eventually, his assembly gathers and skeletons start trooping by. Suddenly, he and August are alone in an empty world.

Chapter 34
Forty-four explains that he is about to leave forever. When August asks if they will meet in another life, 44 says that there is no other. Life itself is a vision and everything is a dream: "Nothing exists save empty space—and you!" Forty-four vanishes, leaving August appalled, but certain that 44's words are true.

BACKGROUND AND PUBLISHING HISTORY

In 1902, five years after he started writing "The Chronicle of Young Satan," Mark Twain began a fresh revision of that unfinished manuscript. After rewriting "Chronicle" 's first chapter and pushing its story two centuries further back in time, he shifted directions radically by making a print shop the focus of a new plot. Over the next several years, he worked on the manuscript as his family traveled around. After his wife died in Italy in June 1904, he set the story aside for another year, then worked on it again intermittently until 1908, when he set it aside for good. The long interruptions in his work and the traumas in his personal life are reflected in the manuscript's uneven tone and incompletely integrated story lines. Although his overall story line appears to be complete, he clearly left the final integration of its complex final chapters unfinished.

After Mark Twain's death in 1910, few people knew that his *No. 44* manuscript existed. When his literary executor A. B. PAINE published a heavily edited version of "The Chronicle of Young Satan" as THE MYSTERIOUS STRANGER, A ROMANCE in 1916, he grafted the final chapter of *No. 44* onto it (changing "August" to "Theodor" and "44" to "Satan" to make it fit), implying that it was a conclusion that Mark Twain had forgotten that he had written. John S. TUCKEY revealed Paine's deception in 1963, and "No. 44" itself was finally published six years later in the MARK TWAIN PAPERS project edition of *Mark Twain's Mysterious Stranger* manuscripts. In 1982, *No. 44* was published as a separate book in a popular edition. That same year, an Austrian television company produced a 90-minute adaptation of *No. 44*, with Chris Makepeace as August, Lance Kerwin as 44, Fred Gwynne as Balthasar and Bernd Stephan as Doangivadam.

Nunnally, Frances (February 27, 1891–March 1981) Atlanta schoolgirl whom Mark Twain met aboard the S.S. *Minneapolis* during his last trip to ENGLAND in 1907. Nunnally was his constant companion throughout the voyage and during his first days in London; she became one of his "ANGELFISH" after returning home. On June 9, 1909, Mark Twain spoke at her school graduation in Baltimore; it was the last public speech that he ever delivered.

Nye, Emma (January 1846, Elmira, New York–September 29, 1870, Buffalo, New York) Childhood friend of Olivia Clemens. In late August 1870, Nye was going to Detroit to teach school when she stopped at BUFFALO to help cheer up Livy after the death of her father, Jervis LANGDON. Livy, then pregnant, was exhausted and ill. Nye soon contracted typhoid fever and died in the Clemenses' house after a month-long illness. Five and a half weeks later, Livy prematurely delivered her first child, Langdon Clemens. Through all these troubles, Mark Twain struggled to write *Roughing It*.

Nye, James Warren (June 10, 1815, De Ruyter, New York–December 25, 1876, White Plains, New York) NEVADA politician. The first president of New York City's metropolitan police board (1857–60), Nye was appointed the first governor of Nevada Territory after campaigning for Abraham LINCOLN. He arrived in CARSON CITY about a month ahead of Mark Twain and his brother Orion Clemens, who would serve as secretary of Nye's government and as acting governor during Nye's frequent long absences from the territory. *Roughing It* mentions Nye's name in chapters 20, 21, 25 and 35, but says little about his administration. Chapter

21 contains a facetious account of his efforts to get rid of the camp followers known as the "Irish Brigade."

After Nevada became a state in October 1864, Nye and William M. STEWART were elected its first senators. Nye began with a two-year term; in 1866 he was re-elected for a full term, after which he retired from politics. Nye was in New York when Frank FULLER was arranging Mark Twain's first major lecture there in May 1867; he agreed to introduce Mark Twain at the lecture, but failed to appear. Forced to introduce himself, Mark Twain made jokes at Nye's expense. Years later Fuller said that Nye claimed he had never intended to intro-

duce Mark Twain because he had been a "damned secessionist." Meanwhile, Mark Twain had further fun at Nye's expense when he published "MY LATE SENATORIAL SECRETARYSHIP" in 1868. He wrote this political BURLESQUE after resigning as Senator Stewart's private secretary, but used the name "James W. N—" throughout.

Mark Twain's AUTOBIOGRAPHY describes Nye as a consummate politician, and claims that the only reason Nye accepted Nevada's governorship was to become a senator when it became a state. Like Mark Twain, Nye is buried in Elmira's WOODLAWN CEMETERY.

O

Obedstown Fictional town in *The Gilded Age*. Located in the Knobs of East TENNESSEE, Obedstown is modeled on JAMESTOWN, Tennessee, where Mark Twain's parents lived before moving to Missouri. Its 15 homes are so scattered in the woods that it is difficult for visitors to realize that they are in a "town." Nearby villages include the Forks and Shelby. Si HAWKINS and his family leave the town at the end of chapter 1. The town is mentioned again in chapter 61, when Washington HAWKINS receives a tax bill from the town on the family's TENNESSEE LAND.

Obedstown takes its name from the real Obed (or Obeds) River, a minor tributary of the Tennessee River, about 22 miles south of Jamestown. Obed was the name of several biblical figures, the best known of whom was the son of Ruth and Boaz.

Odessa City on the northwest coast of the Black Sea. Now within Ukraine, Odessa was a thriving Russian port with 133,000 residents when Mark Twain arrived there aboard the QUAKER CITY on August 22, 1867. Chapter 36 of *Innocents Abroad* describes his two-day stay; he found the city remarkably like an American town and was particularly pleased to enjoy an "ice-cream debauch." According to chapter 47 of *A Tramp Abroad,* he "robbed" an old and blind beggar woman in an Odessa church after mistakenly giving her a gold coin instead of a penny.

Offal Court Fictional LONDON street in *The Prince and the Pauper*. A "foul little pocket" packed with poor families, Offal Court is a rowdy, drunken hive off PUDDING LANE in which Tom CANTY's family lives in a third-story room (chapter 2). In chapter 3, Tom describes life in Offal Court to Prince EDWARD; the neighborhood's proximity to the THAMES RIVER, and the rugged sports in which Tom and his friends engage, recall Hannibal, Missouri, in which Mark Twain grew up.

A homophone of "awful," *offal* is a word of Middle English origin describing the viscera and trimmings that butchers remove from animals. Tom's "Offal *Court*" thus provides an apt counterpoint to Edward's royal *court*.

O'Flannigan, Mrs. Bridget Minor character in *Roughing It*. "O'Flannigan" is the proprietor of the CARSON CITY boardinghouse in which the narrator lives (chapter 21). Tired of being paid in "notes" by her "Irish Brigade" boarders, O'Flannigan appeals to Governor NYE to put his·camp followers to work. The real name of Mark Twain's Carson City landlady was Margret Murphy.

Ohio River A major tributary of the Mississippi River, the Ohio begins at the confluence of the Allegheny and Monongahela rivers near Pittsburgh, Pennsylvania, whence it flows generally southwest for nearly a thousand miles, joining the Mississippi at the junction of Kentucky, Illinois and Missouri. During heavy flood periods—as in July 1993—the Ohio can contribute as much as 65 percent of the Mississippi's flow below Cairo.

Mark Twain probably first saw the Ohio in late 1856, while he lived in CINCINNATI. In February 1857, he boarded the steamboat PAUL JONES and went down the river to the Mississippi and New Orleans.

Before the CIVIL WAR the Ohio River was a major avenue to freedom for people escaping slavery in the South. When Huck and Jim flee Missouri in *Huckleberry Finn,* their goal is to reach CAIRO, Illinois, and from there to go up the river to a place where a black person has a real chance to evade the Fugitive Slave Act. Their raft, however, floats by the Ohio in a heavy fog and they never find their way back to it. In the novel's omitted "RAFT CHAPTER" Huck learns that the Ohio's waters leave a clear channel in the Mississippi for some distance. When Huck sees this channel in chapter 16, he realizes that the raft has passed Cairo.

"Old Times on the Mississippi" Series of articles published in the ATLANTIC MONTHLY in 1875 and later incorporated into *Life on the Mississippi*. In 1874, 13 years after he left the Mississippi River, Mark Twain responded to W. D. HOWELLS's request for an *Atlantic* article by writing a memoir of his days as an apprentice steamboat PILOT. He was anxious to record a way of life that had been altered almost beyond recognition since the CIVIL WAR. Although these articles are generally acknowledged to be among his masterpieces, they cannot be read as either history or biography. Their portrayal of river life overlooks most of its sordid aspects, focusing instead on the romanticism and heroism of steamboating. Further, they depict the narrator as a much younger and more naive apprentice than the real Samuel L. Clemens was when he began cubbing at the age of twenty-one.

Containing just over 35,000 words, the seven articles appeared in the January–June and August issues of the *Atlantic* in 1875. As quickly as the original installments appeared in the *Atlantic,* they were pirated in newspapers throughout the country. Afterward, BELFORD Brothers, a Canadian publisher, collected all the articles in an unauthorized book, *Old Times on the Mississippi* (1876).

In 1882, Mark Twain revisited the river to gather fresh material for a book. When he returned home, he split his *Atlantic* articles into 14 chapters, which became chapters 4–17 in *Life on the Mississippi.* Satisfied with the editing done on the original articles and not anxious to make additional work for himself, he made only about 45 minor changes in wording, and spelled out many of the names rendered only as initials in "Old Times." "Mr. B." becomes Horace BIXBY, "Mr. J." is [William] BROWN, "George E." is George EALER and "Mr. T." is Ben Thornburg. Initials not spelled out in *Life on the Mississippi* include "Mr. W." (Strother WILEY), "Tom G.," "Mr. X." and "Captain Y." (possibly Captain Patrick Yore).

Three new chapters in *Life on the Mississippi* (18–20) completed the story of his cub piloting days. Chapter 21 covers his years as a licensed pilot in one paragraph. The balance of the book relates to his 1882 trip.

While the "Old Times" articles and the book *Life on the Mississippi* are closely related, they are not synonymous—a fact that Mark Twain himself had trouble remembering in later years. In his autobiographical dictations, for example, he incorrectly called the *book* "Old Times on the Mississippi"—a mistake corrected by A. B. PAINE when he prepared the first edition of the AUTOBIOGRAPHY for publication. "Old Times" has been reprinted only infrequently since publication of *Life on the Mississippi.*

Oliphant Character in *Roughing It.* One of the men with whom the narrator goes to HUMBOLDT (chapters 27–29), Oliphant is based on Augustus W. Oliver (1835–1918?), a probate judge for the newly formed Humboldt County with whom Mark Twain traveled in December 1861. Oliver's real name is mentioned in *Innocents Abroad*'s account of the same journey (chapter 27).

Ollendorff Character in *Roughing It* who accompanies the narrator from HUMBOLDT to CARSON CITY and back (chapters 30–33). Ollendorff is based on Mark Twain's real companion on the first leg of that journey, Captain Hugo Pfersdorff, one of the founders of UNIONVILLE. Chapter 30 of *Roughing It* identifies Ollendorff simply as a Prussian, but *not* the man "who has inflicted so much suffering on the world with his wretched foreign grammars." This remark alludes to German grammarian Heinrich Gottfried Ollendorff (1803–1865), whom "CAPTAIN STORMFIELD'S VISIT TO HEAVEN" mentions by name. *Roughing It*'s Ollendorff figures prominently in chapter 31, in which he upsets a canoe filled with travel-ers escaping from HONEY LAKE SMITH's inn, then gets the group lost in a blizzard. In the next chapter, he fails to start a fire with his pistol; when it appears that everyone will die, he asks to be forgiven for his blunders and swears off liquor, throwing his bottle away. When the travelers are saved in chapter 33, he retrieves his bottle.

Onteora Club Catskills retreat near Tannersville, New York. Founded by Candace Thurber Wheeler (1828–1923), Onteora attracted literary and artistic guests. Mark Twain visited Onteora with Livy in August 1885 and stayed there with his family from early July through mid-September 1890. Other guests that summer included C. D. WARNER, Brander MATTHEWS, Elizabeth Bacon Custer, Mary Mapes DODGE—who later died there—and Laurence Hutton (1843–1904), an editor at HARPER'S MAGAZINE. Another guest, Carroll BECKWITH, spent the summer painting Mark Twain's portrait. Mark Twain interrupted his stay with several visits to New York City and a trip to KEOKUK, Iowa to see his ailing mother. After this visit, Mark Twain apparently considered buying into the retreat but was distracted by the family's long absence abroad.

The Oracle Character in *Innocents Abroad.* A pompous old bore on the QUAKER CITY, the "Oracle" is based loosely on Dr. Edward Andrews, a passenger from Albany, New York. Chapter 7 of *Innocents* establishes the character as "an innocent old ass who eats for four," uses long words that he never understands, spouts misinformation on all subjects, quotes authors who never existed, and generally tangles up every argument in which he engages. In his first appearance, he calls the PILLARS OF HERCULES the "Pillows of Herkewls." In chapter 10, he explains how Mediterranean sunsets are related to the planet Jupiter and he dubs Bloodgood CUTTER the "Poet Lariat." He pompously discusses wine in Marseilles in chapter 17 and confuses Sodom and Gomorrah with Scylla and Charybdis when the ship passes through the Strait of Messina in chapter 32.

orgy Word discussed in *Huckleberry Finn.* "Orgy" comes to English from a Latin word for secret rites honoring a god. Since such rites often had frenzied singing and dancing, "orgy" came to mean drunken or sexual revelry. In modern English, it has taken on the more general meaning of any uncontrolled crowd behavior. Mark Twain uses the word in this latter sense in his 14th letter from HAWAII to the SACRAMENTO UNION in 1866. In discussing preparations for Princess VICTORIA KAMAMALU's funeral, he describes ceremonies that had preceded an earlier royal funeral as "funeral orgies"—a phrase that became "frightful orgies" in *Roughing It* (chapter 68).

On the eve of Peter WILKS's funeral in chapter 25 of *Huckleberry Finn,* the KING calls the rites "funeral orgies," prompting the DUKE to remind him that the correct

Mark Twain and his daughter Susy frolic on the porch of their Onteora cabin in 1890. (Courtesy, Mark Twain Papers, the Bancroft Library)

term is "obsequies." The King then invents a nonsense etymology, explaining that *orgies* combines Greek *orgo*, for "outside" or "open," with Hebrew *jeesum*, for "to plant" or "cover up." Hence, "funeral orgies is an open, er, public funeral."

Kanakas dissipate at a Hawaiian "funeral orgy" in True Williams's illustration for chapter 68 of Roughing It.

Orléans City on the Loire River in the center of FRANCE. When JOAN OF ARC began her military campaigns, Orléans was under siege by the English, who already controlled northern France. In order to stop England's southward advance, Joan made lifting the siege her first priority. After achieving this goal on May 8, 1429, she won the nickname "Maid of Orléans." Her Orléans campaign is the subject of chapters 13–22 of book 2 of *Joan of Arc*. One of her most important lieutenants during this episode is the "Bastard of Orléans," a historical figure named Jean Dunois (1402–1868), who was the son of the Duke of Orléans and cousin of King CHARLES VII. Dunois also played a major role in the later expulsion of the English from France.

Osgood, James Ripley (February 22, 1836, Fryeburg, Maine–1892, London) Publisher and friend of Mark Twain. Osgood started in publishing in 1855 in the Boston firm of Ticknor and Fields. By 1868, he was a senior partner and the firm was called Fields, Osgood and Company. During this period, he introduced Bret HARTE to a national audience and published Harte's first book. In 1871, another reorganization transformed the firm into James R. Osgood and Company.

Osgood inherited a prestigious list that included such leading American writers as ALDRICH, EMERSON, HOLMES,

James R. Osgood, the poet "Thompson" of Life on the Mississippi. *(W. D. Howells,* Literary Friends and Acquaintance, *1902)*

HOWELLS, LONGFELLOW, STOWE and WHITTIER, as well the British writers BROWNING, DICKENS, SCOTT and TENNYSON. He also published the first books by Henry JAMES and Sarah Orne Jewett. In 1872, Osgood approached Mark Twain about publishing a volume of sketches, but the latter was still contractually obligated to Elisha BLISS. In 1877, Osgood finally published a small Mark Twain collection, *A True Story, and the Recent Carnival of Crime.*

Osgood's authors liked him personally, but he ran his business poorly and was badly hurt by several disasters. The Boston fire of November 1872, for example, burned down his warehouse, forcing him to auction off his stock and sell the publishing rights to many of his authors. The Panic of 1873 made things even worse; he eventually sold off his magazines, which included the ATLANTIC MONTHLY and the NORTH AMERICAN REVIEW. In 1878 Osgood merged his debt-ridden firm with another to form Houghton, Osgood and Company. Two years later Osgood himself was forced out and the firm became Houghton, Mifflin and Company.

In 1880 Osgood launched a new James R. Osgood and Company, with Benjamin H. Ticknor as a junior partner. He began building a new stable of authors; Howells returned to him and he also signed up G. W. CABLE and Walt Whitman.

Meanwhile, Osgood encouraged Mark Twain to return to the Mississippi River to gather material for a book. In early 1882, he accompanied Mark Twain through most of his ensuing steamboat trip. In New Orleans, he met Joel Chandler HARRIS, whose first book he later published. That same year, he also published Mark Twain's *The Prince and the Pauper* and *The Stolen White Elephant.* The following year he published *Life on the Mississippi*, in which he himself is depicted as the narrator's "poet" traveling companion "THOMPSON." Mark Twain had a high personal regard for Osgood, but sales of *Mississippi* so disappointed him that he never published with Osgood again.

Although Osgood's new firm maintained a high-quality list, he went bankrupt in 1885, leaving Ticknor to run the remnant of the firm for another four years, until it, too, was absorbed by Houghton, Mifflin. Osgood, meanwhile, went to work for HARPER'S, first in New York, then in London as their agent. In 1891, he started his last firm, Osgood, McIlvaine and Company, which published Thomas Hardy's *Tess of the D'Urbervilles.* Osgood died the following year. Mark Twain remembered him in "MY BOYHOOD DREAMS" (1900).

"O'Shah" ("The Shah Letters")   Letters to the NEW YORK HERALD about the 1873 visit to ENGLAND of Nasred-Din (1831–1896), the Shah of Persia (ruled 1848–96). While Mark Twain was in England, the *Herald*'s LONDON office invited him to cover the Shah's state visit. On June 17 or 18, he went to BELGIUM with a private secretary, S. C. Thompson, who took notes for him. They watched the Royal Navy collect the Shah and carry him back to England, where they observed several state receptions honoring the Persian ruler.

Between June 18 and June 30, Mark Twain wrote about 14,500 words in five letters to the *Herald.* The assignment bored him, so he declined to cover the Shah's subsequent visit to Paris. He had a low regard for Nasr-ed-Din, whom he ranked with Turkey's ABDUL AZIZ. The tone of his letters is ironic. His narrator assumes an ingenuous persona, writing as though he personally were responsible for taking the Shah to London and "impressing" him. His letters include descriptions of Ostend and Dover, as well as English landmarks that the Shah visits in London, such as Buckingham Palace, Albert Memorial, Windsor Castle and the GUILDHALL.

The Shah letters first appeared in book form under the title "O'Shah" in EUROPE AND ELSEWHERE (1923).

Overland Monthly   SAN FRANCISCO literary magazine founded by bookseller Anton Roman in July 1868, when Roman made Bret HARTE its first editor. Using the ATLANTIC MONTHLY as a model, Harte quickly built the *Overland* into the West's leading literary journal and began attracting many promising writers. Harte used its pages to publish some of his own stories, such as "The Luck of Roaring Camp"—stories that made him famous. In 1870, he accepted a lucrative offer to write for the *Atlantic* and left the magazine to go east.

Mark Twain happened to be in San Francisco finishing *Innocents Abroad* in mid-1868, when Harte was starting the *Overland*. In return for helping Mark Twain with his manuscript, Harte published four chapters from the book in the *Overland*'s July to October issues under the title "A Californian Abroad."

A new magazine called the *Californian* replaced the *Overland Monthly* in 1880. After it expired two years later, the *Overland* was revived. In 1923 it merged with another publication to become the *Overland Monthly and Out West Magazine,* which moved to Los Angeles in 1931 and ceased publication five years later.

Owsley, William Perry (1813–?) Merchant and neighbor of Mark Twain in Hannibal. In January 1845 Owsley shot a local cattleman, Samuel SMARR, who had insulted and threatened him. Mark Twain saw Smarr die and his father, John M. Clemens, took depositions from witnesses. A year later Owsley was tried and exonerated, when he was defended by Samuel Taylor GLOVER. Mark Twain adapted this incident in chapter 21 of *Huckleberry Finn,* in which Huck sees an Arkansas merchant, Colonel SHERBURN, shoot a man named BOGGS.

Owsley went to CALIFORNIA in 1849, but returned to Hannibal after a few years. Two of his six children were Mark Twain's classmates. Mark Twain dined with one of them during his last visit to Hannibal in 1902. A distant cousin of Owsley, also named William Owsley (1782–1862), was governor of KENTUCKY from 1844–48.

Oxford University A crowning event in Mark Twain's life occurred on June 26, 1907, when ENGLAND's Oxford University conferred upon him an honorary doctorate of laws degree. Several months earlier, he had met C. F. Moberly Bell (1847–1911), the editor of the *London Times,* who asked him when he would again visit England. Having previously decided never again to travel abroad, Mark Twain reportedly replied, "When Oxford bestows its degree upon me!" In May, he received a cable from Lord Curzon (1859–1925), Oxford's new chancellor, offering him an honorary degree. Other honorees that year included Rudyard KIPLING, Auguste Rodin, Camille Saint-Saëns and the Salvation Army's General William Booth. Thomas A. EDISON declined the honor.

Mark Twain sailed for England aboard the S.S. *Minneapolis* with Ralph ASHCROFT on June 8—exactly 40 years after beginning the QUAKER CITY voyage that had made him world famous. This last visit to England became a triumphal progress during which he received an overwhelming number of requests for appearances, including a garden party given by King EDWARD VII and the even rarer honor—for foreigners—of a luncheon with the staff of PUNCH. After returning home, Mark Twain wore his Oxford gown at every possible opportunity—including his daughter Clara's wedding. The gown is now on display at the MARK TWAIN HOME FOUNDATION museum in Hannibal.

P

Pacific Ocean Mark Twain made six long voyages on the Pacific, which he first saw while visiting SAN FRANCISCO in May 1863. In March 1866 he sailed from San Francisco to HAWAII on the steamer AJAX—a voyage described in chapter 62 of *Roughing It.* After sailing among the archipelago's major islands, he returned to San Francisco in July aboard the clipper ship *Smyrniote* (*Roughing It,* chapter 78). At the end of the year, he took the steamer *America* from San Francisco to NICARAGUA, from which he continued to New York (letters 1–4 in MARK TWAIN'S TRAVELS WITH MR. BROWN). He returned to San Francisco in March 1868 by a similar route aboard the steamer *Sacramento,* this time crossing Central America through PANAMA, returning in July aboard the steamer *Montana.* He next saw the Pacific in August 1895, while passing through Washington State and British Columbia at the beginning of his around-the-world lecture tour. On August 23, he sailed from Vancouver aboard the WARRIMOO with his wife and daughter Clara. After touching at Honolulu, the ship crossed the Equator on September 9 and stopped at FIJI, NEW ZEALAND and AUSTRALIA, where it entered the INDIAN OCEAN. This voyage is the subject of the first half of *Following the Equator.*

Packard, Jake Minor character in *Huckleberry Finn.* Packard is one of three criminals whom Huck sees inside the derelict steamboat WALTER SCOTT in chapter 12. He has a partner named Bill who is itching to kill Jim TURNER, whom they have tied up. Packard suggests that instead of shooting Turner, they leave him aboard the steamboat to drown when the boat breaks up. He argues, "I'm unfavorable to killin' a man as long as you can git around it; it ain't good sense, it ain't good morals." Packard and Bill are about to row away from the steamboat in the next chapter, but remember to go back to get Turner's money, leaving Huck and Jim to take their skiff. All three criminals presumably drown when the steamboat later sinks.

Paige compositor Automatic typesetting machine. After Gutenberg invented movable type in the 15th century, typesetting technology changed little until the late 19th century, when James W. PAIGE joined a growing number of inventors seeking a practical way to set type automatically. From the early 1870s through 1894, he developed the most complex compositor ever made. His 1887 patent application had 275 sheets of drawings and 123 pages of specifications. With more than 18,000 parts—including 800 shaft bearings—his 5,000-pound compositor was too complicated to compete with the more reliable linotype machine devised by the German-American inventor Ottmar Mergenthaler (1854–1899).

The Paige compositor ultimately failed because it tried to emulate manual typesetting. With an operator working at a 109-key keyboard, the machine dropped individual pieces of type from upright channels (holding 200 characters each) into a raceway in which lines were assembled. After measuring the lines, it sent them to a justifier that inserted spaces. Meanwhile, "dead matter" was sorted underneath the machine and sent up the rear for distribution into the type channels. At its peak performance level, the machine set 12,000 ems per hour—a rate six times faster than a skilled hand compositor and a third faster than a contemporary linotype machine. In practice, however, the machine often broke down, negating its speed advantage. Its unreliability made it impractical for daily newspapers—which were to be its main market—and its ability to handle only one type size (agate) severely limited its applications.

Mark Twain's background in printing naturally drew him to Paige's invention. Between 1880 and 1894, he poured a fortune into its development. In 1886, he formed a company to perfect, manufacture and distribute the machine, and encouraged friends to invest. Optimistic projections of the huge numbers of machines that he expected to sell filled his correspondence and private NOTEBOOKS, attesting to his faith that the machine would make him rich. Had Paige developed the machine a generation earlier, it might have succeeded; however, the advent of linotype guaranteed its failure. Mergenthaler avoided the trap Paige fell into by not trying to emulate manual procedures. By pouring hot lead into brass molds to cast whole lines of type, his machine cut out the complications of handling individual pieces of type and solved the problem of distributing dead matter by simply melting it down. Though slower than Paige's compositor, linotype was simpler, more reliable and more versatile. Mark Twain and Paige scoffed when the *Chicago Tribune* began testing the linotype machine in 1886, but linotype was to set the standard for automatic typesetting over the next century.

After the first working model of the Paige compositor was built in 1887; it underwent several trials. It met its final failure when a second model was tested in October 1894 at the *Chicago Herald*—where 32 linotype machines were already working smoothly. After observing the trial, H. H. ROGERS, Mark Twain's adviser, concluded that the compositor had no commercial potential. The invention then died, dashing Mark Twain's dreams of riches and making his investment a dead loss. By this time, the money that he had put into it had helped drive his publishing firm, Charles L. WEBSTER & COMPANY, to BANKRUPTCY.

Paige assembled two working compositors. His 1887 model is preserved in the basement of the house maintained by the MARK TWAIN MEMORIAL in Hartford. His 1894 model went to Cornell University, which donated it to a scrap-metal drive during World War II.

Paige, James W[illiam] (January 1842–?) Inventor of the PAIGE COMPOSITOR. Born somewhere in New York, Paige became a machinist in Rochester and applied for his first typesetting machine patent in 1872. Three years later, he moved to Hartford, Connecticut, where he joined with the Farnham Type-Setting Company and used its rented workshop space in the COLT ARMS FACTORY to work on his compositor.

Mark Twain, also a Hartford resident, met Paige in 1880 and began investing modestly in his invention. As Paige's compositor became more elaborate, Mark Twain's enthusiasm grew. In early 1886, he bought a half interest in the invention and became Paige's partner, supporting Paige's work at the rate of $3,000 a month. After the compositor first set justified type (aligned at both margins) in 1889, he became even more enthusiastic and negotiated a new agreement with Paige. Over the next several years, as he sought additional investors, he grew increasingly impatient with Paige's drive for perfection and constant redesigning of the compositor. Whenever he confronted Paige, however, the inventor's glib arguments won him over. "When he is present," he said of Paige, "I always believe him; I can't help it." He was probably thinking about Paige when he created the mad PROFESSOR of *Tom Sawyer Abroad*, and much of Paige can be seen in *Connecticut Yankee*'s Hank MORGAN.

After many complex business shufflings—in which H. H. ROGERS participated as Mark Twain's adviser and as a compositor investor in his own right—Mark Twain finally abandoned the Paige compositor in early 1895. Paige later patented other inventions, including a multichambered pneumatic tire, but never invented anything commercially successful. He is rumored to have changed his name and ended his days in a poorhouse—possibly in Chicago, where he relocated his compositor operations in the early 1890s.

Paine, Albert Bigelow (July 10, 1861, New Bedford, Massachusetts–April 9, 1937, New Smyrna, Florida)

Albert Bigelow Paine at Mark Twain's 70th birthday banquet, shortly before becoming the author's official biographer. (Courtesy, Mark Twain Papers, the Bancroft Library)

Mark Twain's biographer and literary executor, and the first editor of the MARK TWAIN PAPERS. The single most influential person in Mark Twain scholarship, Paine wrote the first important Mark Twain biography; he controlled Mark Twain's unpublished papers for more than a quarter of a century; and he added a dozen volumes (including his biography) to the Mark Twain canon. In collaboration with Clara Clemens, he crafted a public image of Mark Twain that still weathers challenges.

Born in Massachusetts just as Mark Twain was preparing to leave Missouri, Paine came to the Midwest himself when he was a year old. His family moved to Iowa when he was one and resettled in Illinois after the Civil War. After receiving limited formal schooling, Paine went to

ST. LOUIS to learn photography when he was 20 and later spent 10 years in eastern Kansas dealing in photographic supplies. Through these years, he dabbled in writing poetry and prose. His first book, *Rhymes by Two Friends* (1893), collected verses that he and Kansas journalist William Allen White (1868–1944) composed. Eventually, HARPER'S WEEKLY began accepting his stories. Thus encouraged, he went to New York City in 1895 and got an editorial position on ST. NICHOLAS MAGAZINE. By this time, he was steadily publishing children's books and occasional adult novels.

Paine's first literary success was a biography of Thomas NAST that he published in 1904. While researching this book, he corresponded with Mark Twain, whom he first met at a club dinner in NEW YORK CITY in 1901. Paine also attended Mark Twain's 70th birthday banquet in December 1905 and saw him at another dinner a month later. An ardent admirer of Mark Twain, he asked permission to call on him to discuss writing his biography. Mark Twain responded enthusiastically. By January 10, 1906, Paine was installed in Mark Twain's home, where he immediately busied himself sorting manuscripts. From that moment until Mark Twain died, Paine was his nearly constant companion. He consulted with him about his life and papers, helped him with his AUTOBIOGRAPHY, played BILLIARDS with him frequently, traveled with him and helped manage his business affairs.

Paine began his association with Mark Twain around the same time that he bought property in REDDING, Connecticut—where he later retired. With his encouragement, Mark Twain bought property nearby on which he later built his last home, STORMFIELD. Drawn ever closer into Mark Twain's life, Paine became virtually a member of his family. Five days after Jean Clemens died in late 1909, Paine moved into Stormfield with his wife and children. When Mark Twain appeared to be near death while vacationing in BERMUDA several months later, it was Paine who went there to fetch him home.

In addition to consulting with Mark Twain and studying his papers through these years, Paine corresponded widely with Mark Twain's past acquaintances and visited sites of Mark Twain's earlier life. One by-product of this research was *The Ship-Dwellers* (1910), an account of his own trip retracing the QUAKER CITY's route.

On Mark Twain's death in April 1910, Paine became his literary executor, and the MARK TWAIN COMPANY gave him almost complete control over Mark Twain's unpublished papers. He developed close working relationships with Clara Clemens and HARPER'S, with whom he shared a proprietary interest in controlling future Mark Twain studies. Until Bernard DEVOTO succeeded him as editor of the Mark Twain Estate, no outside researchers examined Mark Twain's papers.

In 1912, Paine published *Mark Twain, A Biography: The Personal and Literary Life of Samuel Langhorne Clemens.* A work of nearly a half-million words in three volumes, Paine's monumental study remains the most ambitious biography of Mark Twain yet written. Its value is limited, however, by its paucity of source notes, its indifference to providing dates, and its reluctance to tackle any aspect of Mark Twain's life that might seriously challenge his image. Nevertheless, the biography has immense value because of its broad scope and because of Paine's unique access both to manuscript sources and to Mark Twain himself and his acquaintances. Paine drew, for example, on a manuscript autobiography by Orion Clemens that he later lost. The last third of the biography is of additional interest because it is also Paine's firsthand account of Mark Twain's last years.

Paine dedicated the biography to Clara with what might be regarded as an ironic tribute, saying that she "steadily upheld the author's purpose to write history rather than eulogy as the story of her father's life." Much of the biography, however, *is* eulogistic. A clear example of Paine's suppression of the truth is his relegation of Isabel LYON to a single inconsequential mention, though as Mark Twain's secretary Lyon had been a central figure in his last years.

Paine's personal devotion to Mark Twain extended to his handling of Mark Twain's papers. With Clara's approval, he selected which manuscripts to publish and did not hesitate to edit out passages that he thought the world unready to see. Since Paine rarely indicated his textual interventions and allowed no one else to examine the original manuscripts, it was decades before scholars determined the extent of his editorial manipulations. Clara Clemens later acknowledged his devotion to preserving her father's image by dedicating *My Father, Mark Twain* (1931) to Paine, "who understood my father and faithfully demonstrated his love for him."

Among the new Mark Twain books that Paine published, four works in particular reveal his influence. In 1916, Harper's published THE MYSTERIOUS STRANGER, which Paine represented as a work that Mark Twain had completed himself. The book is actually a bowdlerization constructed by Paine and Harper's editor Frederick A. DUNEKA. The following year, Paine published two volumes of Mark Twain's letters. Without explaining how he selected or edited the set's 450 letters, he implied that they constituted a "reasonably complete" collection. It has since been shown that Paine abridged many of the letters, which represent just five per cent of Mark Twain's surviving correspondence. Seven years later, Paine published *Mark Twain's Autobiography*, two volumes containing about 30 percent of Mark Twain's autobiographical writings and dictations. Although Mark Twain intended that the chapters of his autobiography be presented in the order in which they were created, Paine imposed his own arrangement on the volumes. Paine's final significant edition was MARK TWAIN'S NOTEBOOK (1935)—a selection of about a quarter of Mark Twain's original NOTEBOOKS.

Paine's other Mark Twain publications include *What Is Man? and Other Essays* (1917), *The Mysterious Stranger and Other Stories* (1922), EUROPE AND ELSEWHERE (1923) and a volume of speeches (1910 and 1917). He edited several uniform sets for Harper's, including a 37-volume "Definitive Edition" that incorporates his biography. He also published two condensed versions of his biography. His "Boys' Life of Mark Twain" was serialized in *St. Nicholas Magazine* (November 1915 to October 1916) and later published in book form; he wrote *A Short Life of Mark Twain* (1920) for adult readers. His many other writings include a biography of JOAN OF ARC (1925) and *The Car That Went Abroad* (1921), a narrative of his 1913 motor trip through France, where he visited sites important in the lives of Joan of Arc and Mark Twain.

The Paladin (Edmond Aubrey)   Character in *Joan of Arc*. An entirely fictional creation, the Paladin is one of Mark Twain's finest comic liars and is *Joan of Arc*'s main comic relief through its first two books. Like Markiss in chapter 77 of *Roughing It*, the Paladin is such a notorious liar that people automatically assume that anything he says is untrue (book 2, chapter 3). The joke on the Paladin is amplified by his claim that he is not "the talking sort" and will let his deeds speak for him (book 2, chapter 7).

The Paladin's real name is Edmond Aubrey, which is not mentioned after the fourth chapter. The name "Paladin" is an old French term for knight, associated with the 12 peers of Charlemagne in French legends. The son of DOMREMY's mayor—a man noted for liking to argue—Edmond is dubbed the "Paladin" as a boy because he always boasts about the armies that he will "eat up" some day (book 1, chapter 4). Though he grows into a big and powerful young man, he remains a vain windbag and often delivers comic speeches. Joan sees through his boasting, however, and surprises everyone by naming him her standard-bearer (book 2, chapter 11). Though the Paladin continues to boast, he proves unflinching in battle and dies defending Joan at Compiègne just before she is captured (book 2, chapter 41). Noël RAINGUESSON—who always enjoys twitting the Paladin—considers him supremely lucky to die this way and concedes that the Paladin has truly earned his name (book 3, chapter 2).

Palestine   Traditionally synonymous with the HOLY LAND, Palestine was a province of TURKEY's Ottoman Empire when Mark Twain spent two weeks there in 1867. After World War I, it was made a British Mandated Territory, most of which later became modern Israel. Mark Twain entered Palestine from SYRIA on September 18, 1867. He and his companions stopped first at DAN, then went south to the Sea of GALILEE, Magdala, Tiberias, Nazareth, Janin, Lubban and JERUSALEM. From there, he made side-trips to Bethlehem, the DEAD SEA and the JORDAN RIVER. After returning to Jerusalem, he rejoined his ship the QUAKER CITY at JAFFA on September 30.

Mark Twain's account of Palestine fills chapters 46–56 of *Innocents Abroad*. His posthumously published NOTEBOOKS contain additional notes on places that he expected to visit but missed. Like most of the *Quaker City* travelers, Mark Twain was disgusted by the filth, poverty, phony religious shrines and dreary landscapes that he encountered almost everywhere. Chapter 56 of *Innocents* sums up his feelings: "Of all the lands there are for dismal scenery, I think Palestine must be the prince. . . . It is a hopeless, dreary, heart-broken land."

Pall Mall   TENNESSEE village in which Mark Twain's family lived shortly before he was born. Pall Mall stands on the north bank of the Wolf River, a tributary of the Cumberland, five miles south of the Kentucky border in FENTRESS COUNTY. John and Jane Clemens moved there from THREE FORKS OF WOLF RIVER around 1831. Their second son, Benjamin Clemens, was born in Pall Mall in June 1832. Three years later, they moved to FLORIDA, Missouri.

Palmyra   Northeastern Missouri town, located 12 miles northwest of Hannibal. As the seat of MARION COUNTY, Palmyra was the town in which Mark Twain's family conducted much of its legal business. His father, John M. Clemens, died after contracting pneumonia and pleurisy while riding there in a sleet storm. Palmyra is the model for the fictional CONSTANTINOPLE in *Tom Sawyer*.

Panama   Mark Twain passed through the isthmus of Panama twice—both times in 1868. His only other crossing of Central America was through NICARAGUA in late 1866. On March 19, 1868, he arrived at Aspinwall (now Colón), on Panama's north coast, aboard the *Henry Chauncey*. He crossed the isthmus in one day, traveling mostly by train. The same evening he sailed for SAN FRANCISCO from Panama City aboard the *Sacramento*. He returned from California to Panama City aboard the *Montana*, and sailed from Aspinwall aboard the *Henry Chauncey* on July 20th. Aside from writing about a chance meeting with Captain Edgar WAKEMAN in Panama City on this return trip, he seems not to have written anything about Panama, as he had about Nicaragua.

Paris   Capital of FRANCE. Paris was the first European capital city that Mark Twain ever visited. After arriving by train from MARSEILLES on July 6, 1867, he spent five days there. He and his companions were in Paris as it was staging an international exhibition that drew many American tourists; they visited the exhibition, but Mark Twain quickly lost interest and had little to say about it. His account of Paris in *Innocents Abroad* was written mostly in 1868; its depiction of Paris is curiously distant (chapters 12–15). Aside from pedestrian descriptions of famous sights, the chapters are padded with a long burlesque about ABELARD AND HÉLOISE, as well as invented episodes about a guide called "FERGUSON," a terrible barber and the problems of communicating in French.

In late February 1879, Mark Twain returned to Paris with his family and stayed until July. The weather was miserably cold; he suffered from rheumatism and dysentery and spent most of his time in bed. This bad experience may have contributed to the negative feelings about France that he carried with him after this visit. *A Tramp Abroad* (1880), his book about this trip, says almost nothing about Paris.

Mark Twain next passed through Paris when he returned with his family to Europe in June 1891. Three years later, they were in Paris from March until June 1894; they passed through the city again in the fall, and lived there from October 1894 through May 1895. In all, Mark Twain spent well over a year of his life in Paris.

Parker and John Minor characters in *Huckleberry Finn.* In chapter 16, Huck keeps two slave catchers, identified only as Parker and John, away from the raft by begging for their help to make them think that his family has smallpox. Business has evidently been good for these men; each gives Huck a 20-dollar gold piece to ease his conscience for not helping him.

Paul Jones STEAMBOAT. On February 16, 1857, Mark Twain took passage on the *Paul Jones* in CINCINNATI, landing in NEW ORLEANS 12 days later. After this journey, he persuaded the boat's pilot, Horace BIXBY, to take him on as an apprentice. He and Bixby then returned upriver on the COLONEL CROSSMAN to St. Louis. *Life on the Mississippi* recounts this period, but misleadingly suggests that they returned together on the *Jones* (chapters 5–6)—an error recently corrected by Edgar M. Branch.

The *Jones* was a 353-ton side-wheeler captained by Hiram K. Hazlett. Mark Twain called it "an ancient tub," but it was only two years old when he was on it. It was seized by the Confederacy during the CIVIL WAR and it sank some time afterward. Chapter 25 of *Mississippi* reports that the *Jones* "knocked her bottom out, and went down like a pot" below Cape Girardeau, Missouri. "Uncle" MUMFORD attributed the disaster to the captain's foolhardiness in allowing a preacher and a gray mare to come aboard.

pen names "Mark Twain" was merely one of many pen names that Samuel L. Clemens used in his writing career. His earlier pen names included W. Epaminondas Adrastus PERKINS, W. Epaminondas Adrastus BLAB, RAMBLER, JOSH and Thomas Jefferson SNODGRASS.

Pennsylvania Mark Twain passed through Pennsylvania frequently. He first came to the state in 1853–54, when he lived in PHILADELPHIA for nearly five months.

In later years, he visited many of the state's major towns on lecture tours. Between November 1868 and March 1869, for example, he lectured in Pittsburgh, Scranton, Titusville, Franklin and Sharon. During November–December 1869, he visited several of those towns as well as Johnstown, Germantown, Wilkes-Barre and Williamsport. In October 1871, he began a long tour in Bethlehem that took him to Allentown, Wilkes-Barre, Norristown, Philadelphia and Erie by December. He and G. W. CABLE also did readings in Philadelphia and Pittsburgh in late 1884 and early 1885. His daughter Susy Clemens attended BRYN MAWR, where Mark Twain spoke in March 1891.

Pennsylvania STEAMBOAT built in 1854 that blew up in 1858. Mark Twain twice cubbed as a PILOT on this 486-ton side-wheeler. In November 1857, he joined the boat in St. Louis and went to New Orleans under the tutelage of the pilot William BROWN, with George G. EALER as the copilot and John S. KLINEFELTER as captain. When the boat began its return voyage on December 7, it was struck by the *Vicksburg* and lost its starboard wheel house. After the boat was laid up for repairs in New Orleans, Mark Twain rejoined it in early February 1858 and made six round-trips to St. Louis with the same crew. During this period his younger brother, Henry Clemens, came aboard as an unpaid "mud clerk."

In June, Brown got into an altercation with Henry that provoked Mark Twain to abandon the *Pennsylvania*'s helm in order to attack Brown. Despite this breach in discipline and safety, Captain Klinefelter offered to put Brown ashore and give Mark Twain his place until another licensed pilot could be found. Feeling unready for such responsibility, Mark Twain declined the offer and left the boat in New Orleans on June 5 with the understanding that he would rejoin it after Brown was replaced. On June 13, however, the boat's boilers exploded 70 miles south of MEMPHIS, killing about 150 people, including Brown, and fatally injuring Henry Clemens. Mark Twain's fortuitous escape from this disaster contributed to his being dubbed "Lucky"—a nickname that he resented because of the guilt he felt over his brother's death. Twenty-four years later, he recalled the episode in *Life on the Mississippi* (chapter 20).

Penrod, Brer Minor character in *Huckleberry Finn.* Penrod is mentioned once in chapter 41 as a neighbor of the Phelpses who wonders how a grindstone got into the hut in which Jim is a prisoner. A "Penrod" is also among the passengers eaten in "CANNIBALISM IN THE CARS" (1868).

Perkins, W. Epaminondas Adrastus The first PEN NAME Mark Twain is known to have used, this name was signed to "A Family Muss," a sketch published in his brother's HANNIBAL JOURNAL on September 9, 1852. He took the name "Adrastus" from the mythological

Greek king of Argos; Epaminondas was a great Theban military leader of the fourth century B.C. He possibly took "Perkins" from William M. Thackeray's then-popular *Mrs. Perkins's Ball, The Book of Snobs* (1846–47). After using this name once, Mark Twain changed "Perkins" to "BLAB" in later issues of the *Journal*.

Peters, George Alias used in *Huckleberry Finn*. In chapter 11, Huck's claim to be a girl named "Sarah Mary WILLIAMS" fails to fool Judith LOFTUS, so he instead claims to be "George Peters." In chapter 17, he adopts "George JACKSON" as an alias.

Peters, Reverend George H. Name mentioned in "CAPTAIN STORMFIELD'S VISIT TO HEAVEN." In the chapters of this narrative published as *Extract from Captain Stormfield's Visit to Heaven*, STORMFIELD addresses himself to someone named "Peters," who is not identified within the story. Peters's full name and identity can, however, be reconstructed from other sources. Mark Twain's working notes describe him as the "Reverend George H. Peters," a pastor from Marysville, California, near SACRAMENTO. Other writings leave no doubt that Mark Twain based Peters on his friend Joseph TWICHELL—whom he calls "Peters" in "SOME RAMBLING NOTES OF AN IDLE EXCURSION."

After having heard a great deal about Captain Edgar WAKEMAN—the man on whom Stormfield is modeled—Twichell happened to meet Wakeman on a ship in mid-1874 and spent considerable time in his company. Not realizing that Twichell was a Protestant minister, Wakeman lectured him at length on the Bible. Twichell's account of his meeting with Wakeman later gave Mark Twain additional material with which to build the fictional Stormfield—whose monologue to "Peters" seems to be an adaptation of Wakeman's lecturing to Twichell.

petrified man hoax On October 4, 1862, Mark Twain published a brief, apparently unsigned article in the VIRGINIA CITY TERRITORIAL ENTERPRISE soberly describing a "petrified man" recently discovered at Gravelly Ford—a spot on the Humboldt River near present Palisade, Nevada. The article states that "Justice Sewell or Sowell" went to the site to hold an inquest, concluding that the man had died from exposure. When people tried removing the body for burial, it was found to be cemented to bedrock by limestone sediment; however, the judge refused to let it be blasted free.

Over the next month, at least a dozen other California and Nevada papers reprinted the article, but only a third of them recognized it as a hoax. In June 1870, Mark Twain discussed the hoax in a GALAXY article, which was later republished in SKETCHES, NEW AND OLD (1875) as "The Petrified Man." This piece gives two reasons for his original hoax. First, he wanted to destroy what he called the growing "petrification mania" with a "very delicate satire." He also wanted to embarrass a judge (A. T. Sewall) with whom he had had a falling-out. The *Galaxy* article analyzes the original *Enterprise* piece, demonstrating how, from beginning to end, it is "a string of roaring absurdities." As proof that he never intended to deceive anyone, he shows how a careful reading of his petrified man description reveals that the body was in a nose-thumbing position—a posture graphically illustrated by True WILLIAMS's illustration in *Sketches, New and Old*.

While Mark Twain's claim that there was a "petrification mania" in the mid-19th century may be exaggerated, stories similar to his were routinely accepted during that era. When he was a child in Hannibal, Missouri, the owner of a large limestone CAVE near the town kept the body of a girl—reputedly his own daughter—in a copper tank in an experiment to see if it would petrify. The most famous "petrification" hoax of all began in October 1869, when the "Cardiff Giant" was dug up in central New York. Mark Twain quickly responded to that story with two new sketches, "The Legend of the CAPITOLINE VENUS" and "A GHOST STORY."

Phelps, Benny Character in *Tom Sawyer, Detective*. The daughter of Sally and Silas PHELPS, Benny is described in chapter 1 as "half as old as" Brace DUNLAP, the unpleasant 36-year-old neighbor who wants to marry her. Though Benny is mentioned throughout the narrative, she plays no role other than to comfort her upset father. She is not among the Phelps children named in *Huckleberry Finn*—who include Matilda, Jimmy and Thomas.

Phelps, Roswell (c. 1845, East Granby, Connecticut–1907) A Hartford insurance company stenographer, Phelps was a former schoolteacher and journalist when James R. OSGOOD recruited him to assist Mark Twain as a paid stenographer on his 1882 trip on the Mississippi River. After accompanying Mark Twain from Hartford to New Orleans and back upriver to Hannibal, Missouri, Phelps returned home to Hartford where he was later elected probate judge. The dictations he recorded along the way became part of Mark Twain's NOTEBOOKS and were an important source for the latter's writing of *Life on the Mississippi*. This book mentions neither Phelps nor Osgood by name, but occasionally alludes to them as the narrator's travel companions. In chapter 32, they emerge as the fictionalized THOMPSON AND ROGERS.

Phelps, Sally (Aunt Sally) Character in *Huckleberry Finn* and *Tom Sawyer, Detective*. The sister of Tom Sawyer's Aunt POLLY, Sally is married to Silas PHELPS, with whom she lives near PIKESVILLE, Arkansas. The Phelpses' farm and local community are closely modeled on the FLORIDA, Missouri farm of Mark Twain's uncle John Adams QUARLES where Mark Twain spent his boyhood summers. In *Huckleberry Finn*, Huck goes to the Phelpses' farm—where Jim is being held as a runaway slave—and is stunned to be warmly greeted by Aunt Sally (chapter 32). It soon emerges that she thinks he is

The Phelpses welcome Huck (Lewis Sargent), thinking that he is Tom Sawyer, in the 1920 film adaptation of Huckleberry Finn.

Tom, whom she expects momentarily. Having apparently never seen Tom before, she does not recognize him when he arrives a few hours later and pretends to be his brother Sid SAWYER. During several weeks at the Phelpses, Huck and Tom try Sally's patience with their preparations for Jim's escape. When Sally finally learns the boys' true identities, she wants to adopt Huck herself.

Sally is also a character in *Tom Sawyer, Detective,* but the story gives her little to do beyond wringing her hands in distress when her husband is charged with murder.

Huckleberry Finn describes Sally as being in her late forties. She has at least three children. When Huck arrives, an unspecified number of young children come out with her. Huck alludes to one child as Jimmy (chapter 33); he calls another Matilda Angelina Araminta Phelps (chapter 37); and a third child he calls Thomas Franklin Benjamin Jefferson Elexander Phelps (chapter 39). Sally's much older daughter, Benny PHELPS, is mentioned only in *Tom Sawyer, Detective.*

Many film and television adaptations of *Huckleberry Finn* exclude or severely truncate the episode with the Phelpses. Among the actresses who have played Sally in adaptations of *Huckleberry Finn* are Elvia Allman, in a 1981 television movie, and Geraldine Page, in the 1986 PBS television miniseries. Elisabeth Risbon played her in the 1938 film adaptation of *Tom Sawyer, Detective.*

Phelps, Silas   Character in *Huckleberry Finn* and *Tom Sawyer, Detective.* The husband of Tom Sawyer's Aunt Sally PHELPS, Silas first appears in chapter 32 of *Huckleberry Finn,* when Huck and Tom arrive at his farm. For reasons not made fully clear, the runaway slave Jim has become Silas's prisoner after being sold by the

treacherous KING. A farmer and part-time preacher, Silas is a harmless, somewhat addled person who trusts everyone and is easily bewildered. Mark Twain's notes indicate that Silas struggles with his conscience over Jim and wants to free him; in the novel, he prays with Jim daily.

Silas is a central character in *Tom Sawyer, Detective* (1896), in which he is tormented by a wealthy neighbor, Brace DUNLAP, whom he will not allow to marry his daughter, Benny PHELPS. Eventually driven to distraction by Brace's brother Jubiter DUNLAP, Silas uncharacteristically strikes Jubiter on the head with a stick. The blow does no real damage, but Jubiter is later found dead and Silas is arrested for his murder. Though Silas hysterically confesses, Tom Sawyer proves him innocent.

Tom Sawyer, Detective's characterization of Silas is partly modeled on a 17th-century Danish pastor in a novel by Steen Steensen Blicher (1782–1848). Silas has only rarely been written into film adaptations of *Huckleberry Finn.* James Almanzar played him in a 1975 television adaptation of the novel, and James Griffith played him in the 1981 television film. Porter Hall played Silas in the 1938 adaptation of *Tom Sawyer, Detective.*

A curious incident occurring before *Huckleberry Finn* was first published in the United States involved Silas. After the first copies of the book were bound, E. W. KEMBLE's illustration of the meeting between Silas and Huck was discovered to have been maliciously altered. The drawing shows Silas standing next to his wife facing Huck, with his pelvis thrust slightly forward; its caption reads, "Who do you reckon 'tis!" The altered picture shows what appears to be an erection emerging from Silas's groin. After this alteration was discovered, printed copies of the book had to be recalled, but the person responsible for the apparent obscenity was never identified.

Uncle Silas learns of Jubiter Dunlap's disappearance in chapter 8 of Tom Sawyer, Detective.

Philadelphia Mark Twain lived in Philadelphia for nearly five months in the early 1850s, when the southeastern PENNSYLVANIA city had about 400,000 residents. After working as a printer in NEW YORK CITY, he went to Philadelphia around October 20, 1853 and was soon setting type as a "sub" for the city's largest morning newspaper, the *Pennsylvania Inquirer and National Gazette*. His letters home record his fondness for Philadelphia, where he made a point of seeking out historic sites—especially those connected with Benjamin FRANKLIN. In February 1854 he visited WASHINGTON, D.C., then returned to Philadelphia to work on the *Ledger* and *North American* before going back to New York in early March. His familiarity with Philadelphia newspapers is reflected in "POST-MORTEM POETRY" (1870), a sketch making fun of the "obituary poems" they often published.

In later years, Mark Twain passed through Philadelphia frequently. He spoke there in December 1869, November 1871 and March 1895 and did readings there with G. W. CABLE in November 1884 and February 1885.

Philadelphia is an important setting in *The Gilded Age* as the home of Ruth Bolton. It is described or mentioned in 15 chapters, all but one of which (chapter 36) were written by C. D. WARNER.

Pike County Missouri county on the Mississippi River, about 15 miles south of Hannibal. The county was renowned in pre–Civil War folklore as the birthplace of worthless frontier characters. In chapter 20 of *Huckleberry Finn*, Huck claims to be from Pike himself when he tells the KING and DUKE a long story explaining his background. In an explanatory note at the beginning of the novel, Mark Twain identifies Pike County as the source of one of the main dialects that he uses in the novel.

Pikesville Fictional town in *Huckleberry Finn*. Huck and his raftmates land about two miles below this "little bit of a shabby village" in chapter 31; the remainder of the novel is set in or near the town. The novel does not specify the state in which Pikesville is located, but it is probably ARKANSAS. When Aunt POLLY arrives from ST. PETERSBURG, Missouri, in chapter 42, she says that she has traveled 1,100 miles. This same distance from Hannibal, Missouri—on which St. Petersburg is modeled—would reach Natchez, Mississippi, or Ferriday, Louisiana, well below Arkansas. Other writings, however, indicate that Mark Twain meant to put Pikesville somewhere in southern Arkansas, just above the farm of Sally and Silas PHELPS. *Tom Sawyer, Detective* does not mention Pikesville by name, but explicitly places the same Phelps farm in Arkansas. Chapter 2 of that story puts Tom and Huck's steamboat journey from their home—presumably St. Petersburg—to the Phelpses at "not so very much short of a thousand miles."

In *Huckleberry Finn*, Pikesville is the place where the KING and DUKE steal Jim from Huck and sell him as a runaway slave, and it is there that Tom and Huck see the rascals tarred and feathered.

Pilaster House (House of Pilasters) Hannibal, Missouri building standing at the southwest corner of Main and Hill streets. Pilaster House takes its name from wooden Greek Revival pilasters on its facade; it has also been known as Grant's Drug Store, after the Dr. Grant with whom Mark Twain's family shared the house in 1846–47, in return for cooking and housekeeping chores. A large two-story structure, the house was built in sections in Cincinnati and carried by steamboat to Hannibal, where James Brady—the father of Mark Twain's childhood friend Norval Brady (1839–1929)—assembled it during the 1830s.

Samuel SMARR died in the building's drugstore after being shot in January 1845. Two years later, Mark Twain's father, John M. Clemens, died more peacefully upstairs. Shortly afterward, the Clemens family returned to the house known as the Mark Twain BOYHOOD HOME, a block up Hill Street. Now fully restored, Pilaster House is a public museum maintained by the MARK TWAIN HOME FOUNDATION.

pilgrim A word whose roots go back to a Latin term for foreigner, *pilgrim* has several distinct meanings. In its broadest sense, a pilgrim is a traveler in a foreign land; more narrowly, a pilgrim is a devotee visiting a holy shrine. *Innocents Abroad* uses "pilgrim" in both senses, but the distinction is not always sharp—as in the book's subtitle, "The New Pilgrims' Progress," which adapts John BUNYAN's classic title. Through the book's early chapters "pilgrim" is a friendly nickname for *all* the passengers on the QUAKER CITY cruise. As late as chapter 41—when the narrator and seven companions begin their HOLY LAND journey—the narrator counts himself fortunate "to be a pilgrim." From there, however, he restricts the term to the most pious members of his party; as the journey progresses, he criticizes their hypocrisy, their lust for "specimens" and their eager acceptance of the nonsense in books by writers such as GRIMES. By chapter 52, the party is clearly divided between "pilgrims" and "sinners." Once they rejoin other *Quaker City* passengers in chapter 55, however, the narrator goes back to calling all the excursionists "pilgrims."

Chapter 11 of *Innocents* contains a comical passage written long after the cruise ended that reveals Mark Twain's feelings about his pious traveling companions. At the MARSEILLES ZOO, the narrator and his friends see a stoop-shouldered, awkward, ugly and ungainly bird that strikes them as serene and unspeakably satisfied. When they try to stir him up, he seems to say, "Defile not Heaven's anointed with unsanctified hands." Not knowing his name, they call him "The Pilgrim," adding that he lacks only a PLYMOUTH COLLECTION.

In *Connecticut Yankee*, Hank MORGAN travels with pilgrims going to the VALLEY OF HOLINESS, where they hope

The restored Pilaster House, in which Mark Twain's family lived briefly during the 1840s. (Photograph by author)

to cleanse themselves of sin. While this group of pilgrims is as jolly as Chaucer's, they share the insensitivity of *Innocents Abroad*'s pious hypocrites. When they see a slave driver whip a young woman, for example, their only interest is in his expert handling of the whip (chapter 21).

Pillars of Hercules Peaks that have historically marked the entrance to the MEDITERRANEAN SEA, the pillars stand at the eastern end of the Strait of Gibraltar. They consist of the Rock of GIBRALTAR on the Spanish coast and Mount Abila, directly to the south in Morocco. In *Innocents Abroad*, the ORACLE argues that both "Pillows of Herkewls" are on the African side of the strait (chapter 7).

piloting Piloting is an ancient profession whose very name has roots in early Greek. In the broadest sense of the term, pilots are helmsmen—people who steer vessels. More narrowly, pilots are persons specially qualified to steer vessels through confined or difficult waters whose safe navigation requires precise knowledge of local conditions. Oceangoing vessels normally take on pilots as they enter or leave harbor areas or pass through canals. By contrast, large vessels sailing on rivers may require pilots for their entire voyages.

During the 19th century, skilled pilots were regular members of STEAMBOAT crews, and their critical profession was well paid and prestigious. When steamboats were under way, their pilots—not their captains—were the masters. This power appealed to Mark Twain, who reckoned a pilot to be "the only unfettered and entirely independent human being that lived in the earth" (*Life on the Mississippi*, chapter 14).

Mark Twain grew up along the banks of the Mississippi River and watched steamboats passing by almost constantly. The opening lines of "OLD TIMES ON THE MISSISSIPPI" recall how when he was a boy, "there was but one permanent ambition among my comrades in our village . . . to be a steamboatman. We had transient ambitions of other sorts, but they were only transient. . . . The ambition to be a steamboatman always remained." His first career was as a printer, but the river continued to exercise a powerful pull on him. When he was a child, the prospect of actually becoming a steamboatman must have seem dizzyingly remote; however, as the years passed, he saw neighbors and friends go off to work on the river. Some, such as the BOWEN brothers, even became pilots, proving that his childhood dream need not remain a mere fantasy.

Mark Twain made a half-hearted attempt to become an apprentice pilot in July 1855. Two years later, he decided to chuck printing altogether while he was working in CINCINNATI; he wanted to make his way to SOUTH AMERICA's Amazon to become an explorer. He bought passage on the packet PAUL JONES to New Orleans, but by the time he arrived there, he had persuaded the *Jones*'s pilot, Horace BIXBY, to take him on as a cub. In late February 1857, he began his new career when he returned upriver with Bixby on the COLONEL CROSSMAN. From then until May 1861—a period coinciding with James BUCHANAN's presidency—Mark Twain worked on the river, going mostly between St. Louis and New Orleans. He was immensely satisfied with this new career and might have remained on the river indefinitely, but for the disruption caused by the CIVIL WAR.

Mark Twain's fullest account of his piloting years is given in "Old Times on the Mississippi," a series of articles that he published in the *Atlantic Monthly* in 1875. He incorporated these articles, and three additional chapters on his piloting experiences, in *Life on the Mississippi*. All these chapters focus on his two years as a cub, with his two years as a full pilot reduced to a single page. The chapters are colorful and nostalgic, but provide only a sketchy account of even his apprenticeship years. They make him seem younger than he was actually was and make his apprenticeship seem longer than it was. He earned his pilot's license on April 9, 1859—just under two years after he started as a cub. He was a licensed pilot for another two years, leaving his last boat, the ALONZO CHILD, in New Orleans on May 8, 1861.

If Mark Twain had illusions about the easy life of steamboat pilots when he started his apprenticeship, they were swiftly washed away by the flood of information that Bixby poured on him. "Old Times" catalogs the vast amount of knowledge that pilots had to master during the heyday of steamboating on the Mississippi. The value of a pilot was to a large extent a function of the difficulty of the waterways that he navigated. The MISSOURI RIVER, for example, was particularly unstable and demanded especially skilled pilots—which is why a pilot like Bixby could command premium wages there. Bixby invited Mark Twain to join him on the Missouri, but his cub elected to continue learning the thousand miles of the Lower Mississippi under other pilots.

While pilots were amply rewarded with money, respect and independence, they often had long periods of inactivity between jobs, and steamboating itself was inherently dangerous. The average boat lasted just four or five years before disemboweling itself on rocks or snags, colliding with another boat or blowing its boilers.

Many of Mark Twain's associates died on the river, and he himself just missed being aboard boats during several disasters.

Mark Twain left piloting just as the great age of steamboating was about to end. In the post–Civil War decline of steamboat traffic, pilots lost much of their exalted status. Improvements in channel maintenance, snag removal, beacon lights and other navigational aids made piloting significantly easier. When Mark Twain returned to the Mississippi in 1882, he was appalled by the decline of the pilots' status. Chapter 28 of *Life on the Mississippi* bemoans the fact that one steamboat line was paying its captains more than its pilots; worse, the line was actually requiring pilots to stand watches whether their boats were under way or tied up. "The Government has taken away the romance of our calling," he complained.

Decades after leaving the profession, Mark Twain had several more opportunities to steer steamboats. He took turns at the wheel on the GOLD DUST while going down the Mississippi in April 1882, and on Bixby's CITY OF BATON ROUGE during the return journey. His last turn at piloting a Mississippi steamboat occurred in June 1902, when he briefly steered St. Louis's newly rechristened MARK TWAIN harbor boat.

Mark Twain's years as a pilot made an indelible impact on his life. In contrast to the decade that he spent working as a printer, earning just enough to pay his keep, his piloting years earned him substantial professional success. After his hopes of becoming a successful prospector in Nevada failed a few years later, he looked back on his piloting days ruefully. In chapter 42 of *Roughing It*, he recalls, "I was a good average St. Louis and New Orleans pilot and by no means ashamed of my abilities in that line; wages were two hundred and fifty dollars a month and no board to pay, and I did long to stand behind a wheel again and never roam any more."

By many accounts, Mark Twain was much better than an "average" pilot. After he was licensed, he worked almost continuously, while many other pilots were idle, and he never had a major accident. In later years, Bixby and others who knew him on the river praised his piloting ability. In any case, by the time the Civil War started, he had saved enough money to buy passage for himself and his brother to Nevada and to help buffer his start in his next career.

His piloting years also vastly increased his stock of experiences. According to chapter 18 of *Life on the Mississippi*, he "got personally and familiarly acquainted with about all the different types of human nature that are to be found in fiction, biography, or history." Further, he discovered that when he found "a well-drawn character in fiction or biography, I generally take a warm personal interest in him, for the reason that I have known him before—met him on the river." He also brought from the river a small but defining thing in his life: his pen name, "MARK TWAIN."

The language and imagery of piloting remained fresh in Mark Twain's mind years after he left the river, and it often made vivid imprints in his writing. In chapter 6 of *Prince and the Pauper,* for example, the pauper boy Tom CANTY struggles to get through a conversation with two royal princesses. Gradually, "snags and sandbars grew less and less frequent," leaving Tom more at ease. Two of the real prince's great courtiers are less comfortable, however. "They felt much as if they were piloting a great ship through a dangerous channel; they were on the alert, constantly, and found their office no child's play."

One of the most striking examples of Mark Twain's usage of nautical language occurs in "CAPTAIN STORMFIELD'S VISIT TO HEAVEN." This story, which he began writing in 1868, is also notable as one of his earliest attempts at vernacular narration. It is told by an old sailor who tends to describe everything he sees and experiences in navigational terms.

pirates Allusions to "pirates," "freebooters," and "robbers" pervade Mark Twain's writings. His AUTOBIOGRAPHY claims ancestors who were pirates in Queen ELIZABETH's time, adding that he himself had wanted to be a pirate—a boyhood fantasy also recalled in the opening paragraph of "OLD TIMES ON THE MISSISSIPPI" (also, chapter 4 of *Life on the Mississippi*). This fantasy is central to *Tom Sawyer,* in which Tom chooses piracy as his ideal career, imagining himself the "BLACK AVENGER OF THE SPANISH MAIN" (chapter 8). Tom later tries living out this fantasy by spending a week playing pirates on JACKSON'S ISLAND with Huck Finn and Joe HARPER (chapters 13–16). In chapter 25, Tom and Huck search for buried pirate treasure, guided by local folklore and superstitions. When INJUN JOE and his partner turn up a real treasure, they assume it was left by the historical river pirate John MURRELL (chapter 26).

Tom Sawyer renews his pirate fantasy in *Huckleberry Finn,* in which he organizes a GANG whose oath he develops from pirate stories (chapters 2–3). In chapter 20, piracy becomes a somewhat more serious issue, when the KING tells a camp meeting that he has spent 30 years as a pirate in the Indian Ocean and now needs money in order to go back to convert other pirates. Another exploration of Tom Sawyer's pirate fantasy may be *Connecticut Yankee,* whose hero Hank MORGAN might be viewed as a grown-up Tom Sawyer. Though this novel never calls Hank a "pirate," he may well take his name from the 17th-century Welsh pirate Henry Morgan.

Elsewhere, Mark Twain often uses pirate terminology to describe fictional characters and real men who profited through less than honorable means. Chapter 17 of *The American Claimant,* for example, calls Captain Saltmarsh and his ally "pirates," "freebooters," and "buccaneers." Mark Twain also called men such as King LEOPOLD II and Cecil RHODES's confederate L. S. Jameson pirates and was not above applying the same term to his friend H. H. ROGERS. He also followed popular usage in calling foreign publishers such as BELFORD and HOTTEN "pirates" for issuing his books without paying him royalties.

Pisa City in northern ITALY. Around July 25, 1867, Mark Twain interrupted his journey from FLORENCE to LEGHORN to spend several hours in Pisa—long enough to climb the Leaning Tower and visit the Duomo and the Baptistery. He describes the visit in chapter 24 of *Innocents Abroad.* In early 1892, he revisited Pisa with his family.

The Baptistery's famous echo may have helped inspire "THE CANVASSER'S TALE" (1876). Pisa also contributed a vivid image to *Connecticut Yankee* (1889). In chapter 27, King Arthur dresses as a peasant in order to travel incognito; however, he manages to look only "as humble as the leaning tower of Pisa."

Piute (Paiute) Name applied to two distantly related branches of Shoshone-speaking INDIAN peoples of the western United States. The Northern Piute ranged over central and eastern CALIFORNIA, western NEVADA and eastern Oregon. The distantly related Southern Piute, who lived throughout southeastern California, southern Nevada and southern Utah, are among the peoples dubbed "DIGGER INDIANS" because they subsisted on roots. Chapter 20 of *Innocents Abroad* mentions Piute and Digger Indians in connection with the naming of Lake TAHOE. In "CAPTAIN STORMFIELD'S VISIT TO HEAVEN," the clerk who greets Stormfield in heaven is a (Southern) Piute whom Stormfield once knew in California's Tulare County.

Plasmon Trade name for a skim milk derivative used as a powdered food supplement. Around 1898–99, a German company headed by A. H. Goertz began forming a British syndicate to market Plasmon, which Mark Twain learned about while living in VIENNA. Seeing the nutritive food supplement as a panacea for world starvation and for many health problems, he invested £5,000 in the new syndicate, which made him a director after he relocated to LONDON. Because he received a £350 dividend every quarter, he returned to America in 1900 full of enthusiasm for Plasmon—which replaced the PAIGE COMPOSITOR in his fortune-making dreams.

In early 1902, Mark Twain invested another $25,000 in the new American Plasmon Company, headed by Henry A. Butters, with the financial backing of John Hays Hammond. Though the British company remained profitable, its American counterpart failed to develop, causing Mark Twain to threaten litigation against it a year later. The American company's secretary, Ralph ASHCROFT, helped in this effort, but the company's problems were never satisfactorily resolved. By the end of 1909, all the Plasmon ventures had collapsed, wiping out Mark Twain's entire investment.

"Playing Courier" Lighthearted narrative of Mark Twain's misadventures while taking his family from AIX-LES-BAINS in eastern FRANCE to Bayreuth, Germany during the summer of 1891. Mark Twain wrote the 5,500-word story as the fourth of six letters that he was committed to write for the McClure Syndicate. It appeared in the December 19 and 26 issues of the *Illustrated London News* and in the January 8, 1892 NEW YORK SUN.

Plymouth Collection Protestant hymnal compiled by Henry Ward BEECHER in 1855. The *Plymouth Collection* was the recommended hymnal for passengers on the QUAKER CITY excursion. When Mark Twain returned home, he wrote a long letter to the NEW YORK HERALD summing up the voyage; the letter includes a sarcastic paragraph about the *Plymouth Collection* and the ship's prayer meetings. This passage does not appear in the later version of the letter printed in *Innocents Abroad* (chapter 61), but the book mentions the hymnal elsewhere (chapters 1, 4 and 11) and paraphrases its hymn about the JORDAN RIVER in chapter 55. In Mark Twain's unfinished burlesque "Cap'n Simon Wheeler, The Amateur Detective," the suspected murder weapon is a copy of the *Plymouth Collection.*

Poe, Edgar Allan (January 19, 1809, Boston, Massachusetts–October 17, 1849, Baltimore, Maryland) As the writer primarily responsible for developing the short story as a literary form and as the creator of detective stories, Poe had both a direct and an indirect impact on Mark Twain. Though late in life Mark Twain regarded Poe's prose as unreadable, as a young man he read and admired Poe's work—particularly his "Murders in the Rue Morgue" (1841). Around 1864, he wrote a parody of Poe's "The Raven" that he called "The Mysterious Chinaman." The influence of Poe's psychological thrillers on Mark Twain can be seen in *Life on the Mississippi*'s Karl RITTER story (chapter 31). Poe's "The Gold Bug" probably helped inspire the treasure-hunting episode of *Tom Sawyer* (chapters 25–26). The CAMELOPARD of *Huckleberry Finn*'s "ROYAL NONESUCH" episode (chapters 22–23) may have been partly inspired by a story that Poe wrote on the "Homocameleopard." *A Tramp Abroad* mentions Poe's "The Bells" (chapter 36).

Pokeville Fictional town in *Huckleberry Finn.* In chapter 20, Huck alludes to Pokeville as a "one-horse town" on the Mississippi River. Analysis of the raft's progress suggests that Pokeville is south of Compromise, Kentucky, and north of NAPOLEON, Arkansas. It is not clear, however, on which side of the river it stands. After landing at Pokeville, Huck attends a camp meeting outside of town at which the KING claims to be a reformed PIRATE and collects money so he can become a missionary. Meanwhile, the DUKE takes over an empty printing shop in the town and sells print jobs and newspaper subscriptions for discounted cash prices.

"Political Economy" Story written and published in 1870. A parody on pompous editorial writers, "Political Economy" also anticipates Mark Twain's MCWILLIAMS stories about the joys of home ownership. Its depiction of a man overloading his house with lightning rods is repeated in chapter 5 of *The Gilded Age,* and "THE STOLEN WHITE ELEPHANT" alludes to a criminal's killing a lightning-rod agent.

The story's harassed narrator—presumably a newspaper publisher—is at home struggling to finish an essay on his favorite subject, political economy. A sentence and a half into his essay, he is interrupted by the arrival of a glib lightning-rod salesman. To minimize the interruption and not appear ignorant, he accepts all the man's installation suggestions and goes back to his writing. Throughout the day, however, the man repeatedly interrupts him with new suggestions; each interruption leads to additional installations and leaves the narrator less able to write. By the end of the day, 1,631 expensive lightning rods cover his house, which a crowd gathers to gawk at. After lightning strikes the house 764 times several days later, the narrator removes most of the rods, but is still too unsettled to resume his essay. The 285 words that he does write string together clichés such as "political economy is the basis of all good government"—and ludicrous quotations attributed to Confucius, GREELEY, BYRON, Homer and others.

First published in the GALAXY in September 1870, the 2,390-word sketch was collected in SKETCHES, NEW AND OLD.

Polly, Aunt Character in *Tom Sawyer* and other stories. Tom's kindhearted and loving guardian, Aunt Polly utters the very first word in *Tom Sawyer,* when she calls out Tom's name. Immediately described as "old," she wears glasses for appearance rather than for function. Tom, who is Polly's "own dead sister's boy," presumably takes his surname from a father, so Aunt Polly and his mother most likely shared a different surname. While Mark Twain does not assign Polly a surname in any of his novels, he calls her "Polly Sawyer" in the play he adapted from *Tom Sawyer.* However, he often erred in remembering the names and relationships of his characters.

Aunt Polly is also the guardian of Tom's half-brother, Sid SAWYER, and his cousin Mary (SAWYER?). Polly's exact relationship to these two children is not explained. As Tom's cousin, Mary could be Aunt Polly's daughter. However, there is no hint that Aunt Polly has ever been married or that she has ever had children of her own.

Aunt Polly is a nearly constant presence throughout *Tom Sawyer.* She hovers over Tom to get him to whitewash the FENCE, she sees him off to school in the mornings and she is upset on the nights that he stays out late. Although she disciplines Tom without hesitation, she agonizes when she thinks she may have gone too far. Recognizing that though Tom is mischievous, he is

Aunt Polly looks suspiciously like B. P. Shillaber's Mrs. Partington in the final chapter of Tom Sawyer.

basically not bad, she is satisfied to know that he cares for her.

Aunt Polly also appears in later stories, but as little more than a background figure. She is mentioned in chapters 1 and 8 of *Huckleberry Finn,* but does not appear until chapter 42, when she goes to the Arkansas home of her sister, Sally PHELPS, to investigate what has become of Tom. In "HUCK FINN AND TOM SAWYER AMONG THE INDIANS," the immediate sequel to *Huckleberry Finn,* Aunt Polly calls the boys home from her sister's Arkansas farm, then takes them to visit other (unnamed) relatives in western Missouri.

At the end of TOM SAWYER ABROAD, JIM goes home from Egypt to fetch Tom's pipe and returns with Aunt Polly's order for Tom and Huck to come home immediately, thus ending the story abruptly. Aunt Polly also appears briefly at the beginning of *Tom Sawyer, Detective,* and she makes her final appearance in "TOM SAWYER'S CONSPIRACY."

In his AUTOBIOGRAPHY Mark Twain admits that he modeled Aunt Polly closely on his mother, Jane L. Clemens. Like Aunt Polly, Jane Clemens was kind-hearted and loving, but differed in having a sharp tongue, an inventive mind and a lively sense of humor—none of which Aunt Polly shares. Another model for Aunt Polly can be found in B. P. SHILLABER's character,

Mrs. Partington. True WILLIAMS's illustration of Aunt Polly in chapter 22 of the first edition of *Tom Sawyer* is taken directly from Shillaber's *Life and Sayings of Mrs. Partington* (1854). Mark Twain could also have taken elements from his aunt, Martha Ann Quarles, the wife of John QUARLES—a woman whom everyone knew as "Aunt Patsy."

Pompeii   Ancient Roman city buried by an eruption of Mt. VESUVIUS on August 24, A.D. 79. During his stay at nearby NAPLES, Mark Twain visited Pompeii on August 10, 1867—more than a century after archaeologists had rediscovered its ruins. By then, half the city was excavated and open to view. Chapter 31 of *Innocents Abroad* records the deep impression that Pompeii made on him. The intimate remnants of daily life 19 centuries old moved him to reflect on the impermanence of mankind's mark on the world, as well as the unlasting character of fame. He speculates on what traces a buried American city might leave, and on how a great man like U. S. GRANT will be remembered in the distant future. These thoughts doubtless influenced *Connecticut Yankee* (1889), in which Hank MORGAN's radical transformation of sixth-century England leaves no trace 13 centuries later. The *Innocents* chapter ends with the narrator—like Morgan—awakening to find that he belongs in the 19th century, not the dusty past. A passage quoted from Pliny the Younger's firsthand description of Vesuvius's eruption anticipates Morgan's description of the eclipse in chapter 6 of *Connecticut Yankee.*

The notion of man's impermanence reappears in chapters 71 and 75 of *Roughing It,* which rue the fact that Hawaii had no Pompeii to make the story of KILAUEA's eruptions immortal.

Pond, James Burton (June 11, 1838, Cuba, New York–June 21, 1903)   LECTURE manager. After working as a printer in Wisconsin and serving as a Union cavalry major during the CIVIL WAR, Pond became a journalist in SALT LAKE CITY, Utah. He began his career as a lecture manager by joining James REDPATH's Lyceum Bureau in 1874 and handling a tour for Brigham YOUNG's ex-wife Ann Eliza. He and a partner bought out Redpath the following year, then separated to form their own agencies. In 1884–85, Pond managed the business side of Mark Twain's long tour with G. W. CABLE. He also managed the first leg of Mark Twain's around-the-world tour and accompanied him through 22 stops between New York and British Columbia in mid-1895 (his photographs from this trip have been published by Alan Gribben and Nick Karanovich). After Mark Twain completed his world tour, Pond offered him $50,000 and expenses for a new 125-lecture tour in America, but Mark Twain turned him down. He also rejected Pond's offer of $10,000 for a 10-lecture tour in 1900. Pond's memoir, *Eccentricities of Genius* (1900), includes a chapter on Mark Twain.

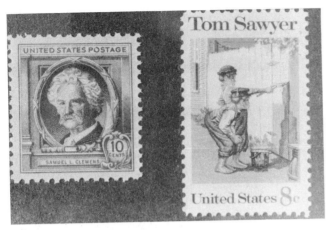

Mark Twain in the 1940 Famous Americans Authors Series of postage stamps.

postage stamps Mark Twain first appeared on an American postage stamp in February 1940, when he was depicted on the 10¢ denomination of the "Famous Americans" series' "Authors" set, which also featured Washington Irving (1¢), James Fenimore COOPER (2¢), Ralph Waldo EMERSON (3¢), and Louisa May Alcott (5¢). In October 1972 the Post Office honored Mark Twain again with an 8¢ "Tom Sawyer" stamp using Norman Rockwell's painting of the FENCE WHITEWASHING episode. To commemorate Mark Twain's sesquicentennial birthday in 1985, he was depicted on an aerogramme form featuring HALLEY'S COMET. In October 1993, the United States Postal Service released a *Huckleberry Finn* stamp in its "Youth Classics" series. Other nations, notably the former Soviet Union, have also honored Mark Twain on stamps from time to time.

"Post-mortem Poetry" Sketch written in 1870. Mark Twain facetiously praises a custom in Philadelphia newspapers of attaching sentimental verses to obituaries. He quotes examples from the Philadelphia *Ledger*, emphasizing verses about children. He calls particular attention to a "transcendent obituary poem" that concerns four children named Belknap burning to death in their home in 1863 as their neglectful mother is out and their father is being slain in war. The sketch first appeared in GALAXY in June 1870. It was collected in THE $30,000 BEQUEST AND OTHER STORIES. Mark Twain later invented the ultimate post-mortem poet, Emmeline GRANGERFORD, as a background figure for *Huckleberry Finn*.

Potter, Edward Tuckerman (1831, Schenectady, New York–October 24, 1904, Schenectady, New York) Architect of Mark Twain's Hartford house. The son of an Episcopal bishop, Potter studied architecture under the noted church architect Richard Upjohn (1802–1878) in New York and later opened his own office in Schenectady. He specialized in churches, college buildings and houses and was noted for his originality. In early 1873,

the Clemenses engaged him to design their home in Hartford's NOOK FARM, where Potter had just designed a house for George Warner (whose brother, C. D. WARNER, later bought the house). Working closely with Mark Twain's wife, Livy, Potter designed a three-story, 19-room structure of an unconventional "Steamboat Gothic" design that gained it renown as one of the state's most unusual houses. Potter personally supervised construction, which was not completed until after the family occupied the house in September 1874.

Three years later, Potter retired to Newport, Rhode Island, where he wrote poetry and music and dabbled in inventions. The only private house he designed after this date was Hartford's Colt Parish House. He also designed a system of tenement houses for New York that helped lead to the city's 1901 Tenement House Law.

Potter, Muff Character in *Tom Sawyer*. ST. PETERSBURG's amiable town drunkard, Potter is a key figure in a central story line. Tom and Huck happen to see Potter and INJUN JOE robbing a grave for Dr. ROBINSON late one night, when Injun Joe kills Robinson after Potter is knocked unconscious. When Potter awakens, Injun Joe convinces him that *he* killed the doctor (chapter 9). After Potter goes to jail, Tom and Huck—who know him to be innocent—agonize over what to do. Their mortal fear of Injun Joe prevents them from speaking out, so they ease their guilt by taking tobacco and matches to the tearfully grateful Potter. After Potter finally goes on trial in chapter 23, Tom denounces Injun Joe as the true murderer and Potter drops out of the story.

Mark Twain's inspiration for Muff Potter came from at least two sources. The character was partly modeled on Ben BLANKENSHIP, one of Hannibal's amiable loafers. Also, around 1853 there was a drunk in the town jail named Dennis McDavid, or McDermid, to whom Mark Twain recalled passing matches through a cell window.

Muff Potter has provided a colorful screen role for character actors of widely varying ages including Tully Marshall (1930), Walter Brennan (1938), Warren Oates (1973) and Buddy Ebsen (TV, 1973).

Pratt, Mrs. Rachel Minor character in *Pudd'nhead Wilson*. The childless widowed sister of Judge York DRISCOLL, in whose house she lives, Pratt helps to raise their mutual nephew Tom DRISCOLL, on whom she dotes. After her brother is murdered in chapter 19, she finds the CAPELLO twins standing by his body and testifies against them at their trial in the next chapter.

Most of the novel's 17 references to Pratt call her "Mrs. Pratt"; she is called "Mrs. Rachel Pratt" once, in the first chapter. In chapter 13, Tom alludes to receiving a gift from "Aunt Mary Pratt"—who is evidently the same character.

Prime, William Cowper (October 31, 1825, Cambridge, New York–February 13, 1905) Author of travel books, including *Boat Life in Egypt and Nubia* (1868). When Mark Twain signed onto the QUAKER CITY excursion in 1867, Prime's *Tent Life in the Holy Land* (1857) was one of the books that passengers were advised to bring with them. Rebelling against this advice, Mark Twain found the discrepancies between what he read in books such as Prime's and what he saw in the HOLY LAND so great that he was moved to campaign against them. Only one of Mark Twain's original travel letters to the SAN FRANCISCO ALTA CALIFORNIA alludes to Prime, and it uses his real name. Aside from a footnote in chapter 53, *Innocents Abroad* calls Prime "William C. GRIMES" and titles his books *Nomadic Life in Palestine* and *Scow Life in Egypt* (chapters 46, 48, 50, 51, 53 and 55). Several chapters quote sentimental and romantic passages from "Grimes," taking their texts from Prime's *Tent Life.*

A lawyer as well as a writer, Prime was also editor of the *New York Journal of Commerce* (1861–69) and became an art history professor at Princeton in 1884. The following year, Mark Twain wrote a letter calling Prime his enemy "of long standing." Nevertheless, Mark Twain once gave his wife Livy a book on pottery by Prime, who later acted as intermediary between General George Brinton McClellan and Mark Twain's firm Charles L. WEBSTER & COMPANY when it published McClellan's memoirs. Even so, as late as 1908, Mark Twain dictated a sarcastic passage about Prime that appears in MARK TWAIN IN ERUPTION.

The Prince and the Pauper: A Tale for Young People of All Ages (1881) Novel set in ENGLAND in 1547—the

year King HENRY VIII died and was succeeded by his young son EDWARD VI. The first of Mark Twain's historical novels, *The Prince and the Pauper* begins with the "what if" premise of having Prince Edward accidentally change places with a look-alike commoner named Tom CANTY just before his father dies. Canty then becomes king, while Edward—now the true king—has adventures among the poor while striving to regain his throne. Once he is restored to his proper place, he becomes a far more compassionate ruler than he might otherwise have been, permitting Mark Twain to conclude that Edward's reign was a "singularly merciful one for those harsh times."

Though outwardly a major departure from Mark Twain's other early novels, *The Prince and the Pauper* has strong parallels with *Tom Sawyer* (1876) and *Huckleberry Finn* (1884). Its lead characters, for example, are similar in age to Tom Sawyer and Huckleberry Finn and share traits of both. Tom Canty's OFFAL COURT home resembles Tom Sawyer's hometown, ST. PETERSBURG, and Canty's sudden elevation to the kingship is an acting out of what might be Sawyer's most grandiose fantasy. Meanwhile, Edward's adventures away from the court anticipate Huck's picaresque journey down the Mississippi. Along the way, he experiences the same kind of abuse from Tom Canty's father that Huck receives from Pap FINN.

The heart of *The Prince and the Pauper* is an exploration of one of Mark Twain's favorite themes: claimants. The moment that Edward is cast out of the royal palace, he becomes a "forlorn and friendless prince" who is

Tom Canty meets Prince Edward in chapter 3.

ridiculed by everyone he meets except Miles HENDON— himself a kind of claimant who merely humors Edward until the moment that he actually sees Edward on the throne. There is even a school of thought that suggests that Mark Twain himself was a claimant who wrote this genteel story in order to win respectability.

SYNOPSIS

The 73,000-word novel is divided into a brief preface, 33 numbered chapters, an unnumbered conclusion and notes by the author. The "prince" and "pauper" of the title are boys born on the same day in the 16th century. When they are about 13 years old, Prince EDWARD invites the pauper Tom CANTY into his palace, where they swap clothes for fun and discover that they look alike. An accident casts the prince out of the palace in Tom's rags. Tom remains inside, where everyone, including King HENRY VIII, thinks him to be the prince gone slightly mad. Though each boy proclaims his true identity, no one believes either of them. The next day, King Henry dies and Tom is acclaimed King Edward VI. Over the next three weeks, Tom adapts to being king as Edward struggles to win his way back to his rightful throne. On Edward's second day outside the palace, Miles HENDON, a colorful adventurer who has been out of the country for 10 years, rescues him from a mob and determines to take him to his own family home in Kent. Along the way, Edward is twice kidnapped by Tom Canty's father and endures other adventures. When they finally reach Hendon's home, Hendon discovers that his younger brother has usurped the family estate and married his own sweetheart. Hendon and Edward spend a week in prison, then return to London, where they get separated in a crowd the night before Tom Canty is to be crowned king. The next morning, Edward sneaks into Westminster Abbey, where he interrupts the coronation ceremony. Tom immediately acknowledges Edward to be the rightful king; after some confusion is resolved, Edward is crowned. The next day, Edward rewards Tom and Hendon for their loyal service.

Chapters of uneven length alternate the narrative between the palace and the countryside. Each chapter from 4 through 31 focuses on either Tom or Edward, except chapter 11, which divides its attention between Tom inside the GUILDHALL and the prince, who is outside. Both boys appear in five chapters; 17 chapters follow Edward's activities; 11 follow Tom.

[Preface]
The tale that follows has been passed down from father to son. "It may have happened, it may not have happened: but it *could* have happened."

Chapter 1
On an autumn day in the second quarter of the 16th century, two boys are born in LONDON. One is Tom CANTY, the unwanted son of the Canty family. The other is EDWARD, Prince of Wales, the much wanted and celebrated son of the Tudor family.

Chapter 2
Tom Canty grows up in London's OFFAL COURT, near LONDON BRIDGE, where he lives with his mother and father, two sisters and grandmother. His thieving father, John CANTY, and mean-spirited beggarly Gammer CANTY treat him cruelly, but Mrs. CANTY and his sisters Bet and Nan Canty are kind. He also lives near a kindly priest, Father ANDREW, who teaches him to read and instructs him in Latin. Despite his family's poverty and the brawling nature of Offal Court, Tom's life is not altogether unpleasant—especially in the summers. He often plays with other children and swims in the THAMES, and occasionally observes such spectacles as the execution of Anne Askew (c. 1521–1546).

Tom reads Father Andrew's books and grows up daydreaming about kings and princes; his main ambition is to see a real prince. Often pretending to be a prince himself, he cultivates courtly language, organizes a mock royal court and becomes known as a wise and gifted leader. His regal dreams and games are interrupted, however, by the daily real-life necessity of begging.

Chapter 3
One day, Tom wanders far from home and finds himself outside the royal palace in WESTMINSTER. Through a gate, he sees a real prince—Edward. When he moves closer, a guard cuffs him roughly. Edward sees Tom mistreated and invites him inside to his chambers and orders him food. Edward asks Tom about his life outside the palace and tells about his own family. Tom's tales of rugged outdoor sports excite Edward, who suggests that he and Tom exchange their clothes for fun. After putting on each other's outfits, they stand before a mirror and marvel at their mutual resemblance. Edward then notices that Tom's arm was bruised by a guard. As he rushes out to reprimand the man, he hides "an article of national importance" (later identified as the Great Seal). He starts to berate the guard at the gate, only to be tossed out of the palace as a common pauper and ridiculed by the crowd outside.

Chapter 4
For several hours, Edward tries to talk his way back into the palace, as the crowd taunts him. Finally, he seeks help at CHRIST'S HOSPITAL, a children's home established by his father. Instead of giving him a royal welcome, the orphans treat him roughly and chase him away. As he wanders about, a drunken ruffian seizes him; it is John Canty, who thinks Edward is his son, Tom. Canty takes him home; Edward's claims to be the Prince of Wales merely convince Canty that his son is mad.

Chapter 5
Back at the palace, Tom Canty eagerly explores the prince's chambers, but a half hour later begins worrying about Edward's failure to return. When he steps outside

the room, servants bow to him. Lady Jane GREY enters the room and Tom embarrasses her by kneeling down. After she leaves, rumors spread through the palace that the prince is mad until the king (HENRY VIII) orders the rumors to cease.

Finally, Tom is taken to the king, who chides him for jesting. Tom prostrates himself and begs to be spared. The befuddled king assures him that no harm will come to him and tests him with a question in Latin. Tom's lame Latin reply pleases the king, but Tom fails completely when the king tries French on him. The king orders that none may speak of the prince's "distemper" and orders Lord HERTFORD to see that the boy is confirmed as the Prince of Wales the next day. As Tom is led away by Hertford, his heart sinks at the realization that he is a captive.

Another noble irritates the king by reminding him about the Duke of NORFOLK, whom the king is anxious to see executed.

Chapter 6
Hertford and Lord ST. JOHN relay to Tom the king's command not to insist he is not the prince. Tom agrees, and Hertford adds that the king has commanded he be relieved of his studies for the time being. When the princesses ELIZABETH and Jane Grey arrive, Hertford tells them to ignore the prince's "humors"; St. John tells Tom to remember everything he can and to pretend to remember the rest. Conversation is strained, but Elizabeth helps Tom through rough patches. When the princesses leave, Tom asks to rest and is led to an inner apartment. St. John suspects that Tom may in fact not be the true prince, but Hertford discourages such speculation as potentially treasonous.

Chapter 7
In the afternoon, Tom suffers through being dressed for dinner, then endures a meal in which every step is a mystery. He has trouble with the utensils, does not recognize turnips or lettuce, orders his napkin removed so it will not be soiled, fills his pockets with nuts, and drinks from the finger bowl; however, no one expresses surprise. Back in the prince's private rooms, Tom tries on a suit of armor and finds a useful book on court etiquette.

Chapter 8
At five o'clock, King Henry awakens; he is anxious to see Norfolk executed, but needs the Great Seal to certify his order. He last saw the seal when he entrusted it to Edward, but the Lord Chancellor reports that the prince cannot remember where it is.

Chapter 9
At nine o'clock, a great pageant begins on the river and a gorgeously dressed Tom Canty follows Hertford to a barge (*continued in chapter 11*).

Chapter 10
Back in Offal Court, John Canty is dragging Edward home when someone steps forward to plead in the boy's behalf. Canty smashes the man's head with his cudgel. At Canty's home, Edward insists that he is the Prince of Wales. Thinking the boy to be Tom, Canty's wife and daughters rush to console Edward, but Canty and Canty's mother beat him.

As everyone goes to sleep, the girls cover Edward with straw and try to comfort him. Suspecting that there is something different about this boy, Mrs. Canty tests whether he has a certain reflex of Tom's, but the results are inconclusive. Just as Edward awakens—thinking that he has been dreaming—someone knocks at the door and warns Canty that the man he killed with his cudgel is Father Andrew. Canty rouses the family to flee, leading Edward by the hand. At LONDON BRIDGE, the prince escapes in the confusion.

Chapter 11
Meanwhile, Tom Canty rides a royal barge to GUILD-HALL, where the Lord Mayor welcomes him to a banquet. As Tom gapes at the hall's splendor, the real prince is outside, loudly proclaiming his identity. A derisive crowd assails him, but a fantastically dressed man calling himself Miles HENDON hustles him away from danger. Inside Guildhall, it is announced that the king is dead and everyone renders obeisance to Tom Canty. Assured that *his* word is now law, Tom proclaims that the Duke of Norfolk shall not die—an announcement that is joyfully received.

Chapter 12
Hendon takes Edward to London Bridge, where the boy learns that his father is dead. Near Hendon's inn, John Canty tries to seize Edward, but Hendon drives him away. Edward then stuns Hendon by usurping the bed in his room and by ordering Hendon to wash him when a servant brings them food. Thinking the boy temporarily mad, Hendon acquiesces, but Edward—

Miles Hendon asks King Edward for permission to sit down in chapter 12.

aware that he is now *king*—stretches Hendon's patience by forbidding him to sit in his presence. Hendon tells Edward about his family and relates how he has spent the last 10 years on the Continent as a soldier and prisoner of war. Grateful to Hendon for his help, Edward asks him to name a reward. Citing a precedent from the time of King John (1167–1216), Hendon requests permission merely to sit in the king's presence. Edward grants this request and dubs Hendon a knight.

Chapter 13
After supper, Hendon plays along with the boy's claim to be king by helping prepare him for bed and then sleeping on the floor. The next day, he goes out to buy a second-hand outfit for Edward. When he returns, he begins repairing the outfit and considers his plan to take Edward to HENDON HALL. Only belatedly, he discovers that Edward is gone. From a servant he learns that another boy has fetched Edward away and he goes after him (continued in chapter 17).

Chapter 14
Tom Canty meanwhile awakens in Westminster palace, thinking he has been dreaming. When he discovers that he has *not* been dreaming, he returns to sleep. A real dream conveys him to a meadow called Goodman's Fields, where a dwarf enriches him with 12 pennies every week. He reawakens to find an army of titled servants standing by to dress him for breakfast. Afterward, he puts in a weary day in the throne room conducting state business under Hertford's guidance. He is appalled to learn that £20,000 are owing on household expenses. A secretary mentions the late king's intention to raise Hertford to a duke and Thomas Seymour to the peerage.

After spending part of the afternoon with the royal princesses, Tom meets the royal whipping boy, Humphrey MARLOW, who he discovers will be a valuable source of information on court people and etiquette. Having Marlow as an ally lightens Tom's burdens, but his spirit sags again when Hertford tells him that in two days he must dine in public to quell rumors that he is mad. Hertford tests Tom's memory in subtle ways, but cannot crack the puzzle of the Great Seal's disappearance.

Chapter 15
Tom spends the next day receiving foreign ambassadors and soon wearies of holding audiences. After three days as king, however, he is adjusting; on the fourth day he is coping, but still dreading his public dinner that night. From his audience chamber, he hears a noisy mob following three people to their execution. He has the prisoners brought to him and recognizes among them a man who once saved someone from drowning in the Thames. The man is charged with poisoning someone; as Tom inquires about the evidence, he realizes that the supposed crime occurred far from the Thames at the very moment he knows that the man was saving another

person's life. Tom sets him free and elicits the admiration of his courtiers for his decisiveness. Next, Tom interviews a woman and her daughter accused of using witchcraft to start a devastating storm. After cleverly getting the woman to show that she lacks occult powers, he frees her and her daughter.

Chapter 16
By the dinner hour, Tom is more relaxed. He relishes his grand entrance into the banquet hall and gets through the dinner without a mistake (continued in chapter 30).

Chapter 17 (continued from chapter 13)
Desperate to find Edward, Miles Hendon crosses London Bridge, thinking that the boy will head for Hendon Hall in Kent. Earlier, however, Edward was led across the bridge by a boy (later identified as HUGO), who told him that Hendon sent for him. A ruffian following the boys proves to be John Canty in disguise; Canty now calls himself "John Hobbs" and he tells Edward that his new name is "Jack."

They stop at an old barn. After falling asleep, Edward awakens to find the barn filled with a rabble who have just finished feasting. Canty—who is evidently a former gang member—announces that he has killed a priest and is welcomed by the gang's RUFFLER. Several people tell their sad stories, including a man named YOKEL who explains how English law destroyed his family and forced him into slavery. Outraged by what he hears, Edward cries out that the law that made the man a slave is henceforth abolished. In the face of the gang's ridicule, he insists that he is King Edward. The Ruffler tells him, however, that if he must be a king, he should not claim to be king of England. Someone else dubs him "FOO-FOO THE FIRST, THE KING OF THE MOONCALVES" and he is subjected to a humiliating mock coronation.

Chapter 18
At the next dawn, the vagabonds march off with Edward in Hugo's charge. They help themselves to provisions as they go, while taunting people and threatening worse depredations if anyone complains. At a village, Hugo tells Edward to help him beg; while he fakes a fit, Edward is to wail and pretend that he is his grieving brother. Hugo begins his act when a kindly-looking man approaches, but Edward denounces him as a fraud and the stranger chases Hugo off. Edward escapes in the opposite direction and wanders into the woods. At nightfall, he sneaks into a barn while workmen lock the door from the outside. He tries to sleep in the pitch-black building, but feels something alive touching him. Nearly paralyzed by fright, he eventually discovers that his companion is a harmless calf, with which he peacefully goes to sleep.

Chapter 19
Edward awakens in the morning with a rat sleeping on him and concludes that he cannot sink any lower. Two young girls enter the barn and ask him who he is; they

accept his claim to be king so readily that he gratefully pours out his woes as they take him to the house for breakfast. Their kindly mother thinks Edward slightly crazed and tries various ruses to figure out where he is from. Convinced that he comes from a royal kitchen, she puts him in charge of the cooking, but he nearly lets the meal burn. Ashamed of his failure, he later washes dishes without demur, but is about to rebel against his chores when he spots John Canty and Hugo coming and slips away.

Chapter 20

Edward again wanders in the woods. As night falls, he peeks through the window of a shabby hut and sees an old man praying. Thinking himself fortunate to find a holy HERMIT, he knocks on the door and introduces himself as the king. The hermit gushes over this king who has discarded his crown and wealth, and reveals his own secret—that he is an archangel. He grows angry when he recalls that he would be pope, had the king not dissolved his religious house and cast him out into the world. Edward fears that he is in the clutches of a madman, but the hermit calms down, feeds him and puts him to bed in a back room. When the hermit asks *what* king he is, Edward answers "of England." The hermit's anger returns when he realizes that Edward is the son of the same King Henry who ruined him. After Edward falls asleep, the hermit sharpens a butcher knife and ties him up.

Chapter 21

When Edward awakens, he sees the hermit looming over him with a knife; the old man tells him to pray and calls him the "Seed of the Church's spoiler." As the man is about to stab Edward, someone knocks at his door and he goes to answer it. Edward is overjoyed to hear Miles Hendon's voice, but Hendon never looks in the back room. Instead, he rides off with the hermit, who claims to have sent the boy on an errand. After they leave, John Canty and Hugo burst in; they untie Edward and return to the forest.

Chapter 22

Over the next several days, Hugo tries to make Edward's life miserable until Edward bests him in a cudgel fight that delights the gang, which now proclaims Edward "King of the Game-cocks." Despite winning the gang's respect, Edward keeps trying to escape.

As days pass, Hugo plots his revenge. He and the tinker start to burn a sore on Edward's leg with a "clime," but Yokel saves the king from this humiliation. When the Ruffler decrees that Edward should steal instead of beg, Hugo concocts a new scheme. He leads Edward into a village where he snatches a package from a woman, dumps it on Edward and runs off. Edward is trapped by an angry crowd as Miles Hendon reappears.

Chapter 23

As a constable leads Edward off to court, Hendon tells him to be patient and trust in the justice of his own laws. In court, the stolen parcel is opened and found to contain a dressed pig; Hendon gasps, but Edward is oblivious to his peril. After the robbery victim testifies that her pig is worth three shillings and eight pence, the judge clears the court and reminds her that the punishment for stealing anything worth more than 13 pence is death. Horrified, the woman revises the pig's value to eight pence. As she leaves, the constable accompanies her; Hendon follows and overhears him pressuring the woman to sell him the pig for eight pence. Back in the courtroom, Hendon finds the judge sentencing Edward to a short jail term and a flogging.

Chapter 24

As the constable leads Edward to jail, Hendon asks him to let Edward escape. Hendon tells the man that he overheard him tricking the woman into selling him her pig—a crime he claims is punishable by death. Petrified with fear, the man lets Edward escape.

Chapter 25

After paying for his lodgings and fetching a donkey and a mule that he has purchased, Hendon gives Edward the second-hand outfit he bought earlier, and the two ride east. Over the next two days, they ride and swap adventures. As they approach Hendon Hall, Hendon talks excitedly about his family and the warm reception awaiting him. When they arrive, however, his brother Hugh HENDON claims not to recognize him and says that the family received a letter years earlier reporting Miles's death in battle. Hendon's father and other brother, Arthur, are now dead; of the 27 servants whom Hendon knew, only five remain—all of whom claim not to recognize him. Hendon suffers his worst blow, however, when his former sweetheart Edith enters and denies knowing him. Told that Edith is now Hugh's wife, Hendon turns savagely on his brother.

Chapter 26

While Hugh's servants run for help, Edward remarks how odd it is that no royal couriers are scouring the country searching for him. To establish his identity, he writes a message in English, Latin and Greek and instructs Hendon to deliver it to his uncle Hertford. Hendon, absorbed with his own problems, pockets the note without looking at it, assuming that it contains meaningless scrawls. Edith then returns and begs Hendon to flee from her wrathful husband. At Hendon's insistence, she swears that she does not know him. Officers burst into the room and seize Hendon and Edward.

Chapter 27

Hendon and Edward are put in a prison cell with 20 other men and women of various ages. Over the next week, people visit the cell to taunt Hendon. One visitor is his family's faithful old servant Blake Andrews, who first loudly denounces Hendon, then whispers an apology and offers to affirm Hendon's true identity. Hendon declines the offer. Andrews returns regularly, smuggling in food and news, while gradually filling in the history of Hendon's family during his absence. He says that Hugh is rumored to have forged the letter announcing Miles's death. Andrews also remarks that the new king is rumored to be mad and that Hugh plans to attend his coronation on the 16th (of February), hoping for a peerage from the Lord Protector (Hertford), who is now the Duke of Somerset. For the first time, Edward realizes that someone else is in his place on the throne.

Meanwhile, Edward is comforted by two gentlewomen imprisoned for being Baptists. When he finds them gone one morning, he rejoices that they are free, but is sorry to lose their company. He and Hendon are then taken into the jail-yard, where Edward is horrified to see the women tied to stakes. He does not realize, however, how grave their situation is until a torch is put to the wood piled below them. Two girls rush in and try to throw themselves on the flames, begging to die with their mothers. As they are restrained, Edward vows never to forget this awful moment.

As new prisoners pass through the jail, Edward talks with them, hoping to learn all he can about conditions in his kingdom. Their woeful tales deeply move him. One prisoner is an old lawyer who wrote a pamphlet criticizing the lord chancellor; for that, he lost his ears, was debarred, fined £3,000 and sentenced to prison for life. After a repeat offense, he was to lose the remainder of his ears, be branded on the face, fined an additional £5,000 and remain in prison.

Chapter 28

Eventually, Miles Hendon is tried, declared a "sturdy vagabond" and sentenced to two hours in the pillory; Edward is merely reprimanded and released. When Hendon is put in the stocks, a crowd begins hurling things at him, outraging Edward, who commands the officer in charge to free Hendon. Instead, the officer proposes giving Edward a lash or two; Hugh Hendon then arrives and suggests giving him *six* strokes. When Miles Hendon insists on taking the boy's lashings himself, Hugh orders that their number be doubled. Edward silently watches Hendon being whipped, vowing to himself to reward the man who has saved him from shame. He whispers to Hendon to tell him that he is now an earl. Hendon's courage causes the mob to stop abusing him.

Chapter 29

After Hendon is freed, he and Edward ride for London. Hendon hopes to reach the ear of the new king through an old friend of his father, Sir Humphrey Marlow. On the eve of the coronation they reach London, but at London Bridge they are separated in a crowd of drunken revelers.

Chapter 30

Meanwhile, Tom Canty is finally enjoying being king. Now taking his privileges for granted, he is comfortable ordering his royal "sisters" to come and go, and he gives nobles disapproving looks when they offend him. He so enjoys pomp and attention that he doubles his gentlemen-at-arms and triples his servants. He also works hard to remove unjust laws. When the stern princess Mary (later Queen MARY I) accuses him of being too lenient, he dresses her down and advises her to pray for a real heart. As time passes, he rarely thinks about the fate of the real king or of his own mother and sisters.

The night before the coronation, Edward sneaks into Westminster Abbey.

Chapter 31

On coronation morning, Tom rides a barge down the Thames to the Tower of London, from which he rides a splendid horse to the abbey in the "recognition procession." Along the way, he spots old Offal Court comrades and tosses coins to the admiring crowd. When he sees his mother, however, he instinctively raises the back of his hand to his eyes. This gesture identifies him to his mother, who rushes forward to embrace his leg. As guards push her away, Tom utters, "I do not know you woman!" Tom's disloyalty to his mother destroys all the pleasure of being king, leaving Tom in a funk. As lord protector, Somerset twice reminds him that he must appear cheerful. When Tom says that the woman in the crowd is his mother, Somerset thinks he has gone mad again.

Chapter 32

The narrative returns to early coronation morning, as Westminster Abbey begins filling up with eager spectators. Several hours pass, then the royal procession arrives and Tom Canty enters in regal splendor. At the climax of the coronation ceremony (which is briefly summarized), a hush prevails as the Archbishop of Canterbury prepares to place the crown on Tom's head. Suddenly, another boy appears and commands him to stop. The newcomer is seized, but Tom Canty orders his release, proclaiming *him* to be the true king. Only confusion reigns now.

Somerset quizzes the newcomer about the court; Edward answers correctly, but Somerset concludes that his answers do not prove his identity. He then asks Edward something that even Tom cannot answer—where the Great Seal is. Edward directs Lord St. John to go to a secret cabinet in his chambers, and Tom confirms the order. The crowd begins shifting in Edward's favor. The moment that St. John returns without the seal, however, the crowd swings back to Tom. Somerset happens to mention the seal's appearance, however, causing Tom finally to understand *what* the seal is; he prompts Edward to recall where he hid it the night they switched places. With Tom's help, Edward remembers slipping the seal into a suit of armor. St. John again goes after it; this time he returns with the seal. Everyone now acknowledges Edward to be the rightful king. Somerset orders that Tom Canty be flung into the Tower, but Edward overrules him, pointing out his uncle's ingrati-

The Prince and the Pauper: A Tale for Young People of All Ages

tude to the person who made him a duke. Edward then asks Tom how he could know *where* the seal was without knowing *what* it was. Tom nervously admits to having used it to crack nuts. The coronation is resumed and Edward is crowned king.

Chapter 33
Back at London Bridge earlier the same day, Miles Hendon emerges from the riot with his pockets picked and sets about to find Edward again. He works his way toward Westminster and goes to sleep near the river as cannons signal the king's coronation. The next morning he goes to the palace hoping to find his father's old friend Sir Humphrey Marlow. By chance, the first person whom he approaches is the whipping boy (the deceased Marlow's son), who recognizes him as the outlandish vagabond who is being sought by the king. The boy has Hendon wait inside the palace, but guards then arrest him as a suspicious character. When an officer searches him, he finds Edward's undelivered note and makes a sarcastic remark about more claimants to the throne as he leaves. Hendon figures that he is doomed; however, the officer returns hastily, shows him unexpected courtesy and leads him to the royal court.

There Hendon is left alone at the center of a vast room in which the young king is seated on his throne. In his fantastic rags, Hendon draws scornful looks and derisive remarks. Suddenly he recognizes the king as the very same boy he has been regarding as a pitiable tramp. For a moment, he wonders if he is dreaming; then he takes a chair and sits down before the king. Rough hands seize him, but Edward cries out that he is not to be touched and publicly proclaims Hendon to be his faithful servant and savior, whom he intends richly to reward. Hendon soon comes to his senses and kneels to swear allegiance to the king. At the same moment, his brother Hugh and Lady Edith enter the room. Edward has Hugh arrested.

Tom Canty then enters in an unusual but splendid costume. He kneels before the king, who announces that he is pleased with Tom's conduct during the time he occupied the throne. Edward promises to have Tom's mother and sisters provided for, proclaims Tom chief governor of Christ's Hospital and declares that Tom is forever to be known as the "King's Ward."

Conclusion
Hugh Hendon confesses that he forced Edith to repudiate Miles by threatening to kill his brother if she acknowledged him. Hugh is not prosecuted, however, because his wife and brother refuse to testify against him. He flees to the Continent, where he soon dies. Later, Miles and Edith are married amid much rejoicing. John Canty is never heard from again.

Determined to redress the evils he observed in his travels, Edward seeks to right the wrongs suffered by Yokel in the Ruffler's gang, the lawyer he met in prison, the daughters of the Baptist women burned at the stake,

and others. In the few years remaining to him, Edward frequently tells the story of his adventures in order to keep such injustices fresh in his memory, and he works to remove oppression from his kingdom. Tom Canty lives to be a very old and well-respected man.

BACKGROUND AND PUBLISHING HISTORY

Mark Twain probably began gathering the seeds of *The Prince and the Pauper* as a boy fantasizing about being a prince. The contrast between being a "prince" and being a "pauper" struck him at least as early as 1864, when he wrote a letter to his family describing his life in Nevada with the phrase, "the old California motto is applicable here: 'We have lived like paupers that we might give like princes.'"

Mark Twain began thinking about writing *The Prince and the Pauper* sometime during the 1870s. After reading Charlotte YONGE's *The Little Duke* (1854), he got the idea of writing his own story about a king becoming a more humane ruler as a result of switching places with a commoner. He initially planned to use the contemporary Prince of Wales (EDWARD VII) as his hero, but became uncomfortable with placing the living prince in compromising fictional situations, so he looked deeper into the past for a more appropriate subject. By the summer of 1876, he settled on Edward Tudor (EDWARD VI) and began researching 16th-century English history. In addition to collecting notes on history, he collected word lists from SHAKESPEARE's *King Henry IV, Part 1* and several Sir Walter SCOTT novels. The main literary product of that summer's work, however, was *1601*. He renewed his research the following summer, by which time he already had the novel's title, and he began writing the early chapters. He set the project aside in early 1878, when he left for Europe with his family on the trip that would lead to *A Tramp Abroad*.

Mark Twain resumed work on *The Prince and the Pauper* as he finished *A Tramp Abroad* in early 1880. Stimulated by his new story and relieved to escape the drudgery that writing his travel book had become, he completed his first draft in mid-September. Two months later, he arranged with James R. OSGOOD to publish the novel. After W. D. HOWELLS read the manuscript and offered suggestions, Mark Twain finished his final draft in February 1881. He then delivered the manuscript to Osgood and signed a formal contract to publish the novel as a SUBSCRIPTION BOOK. During the fall, he proofed the book with the help of Howells. In late November, he went to Montreal hoping to ensure protection of his copyright in CANADA. Osgood meanwhile arranged for Frank T. MERRILL and John J. HARLEY to illustrate the book, with L. S. IPSEN designing the half-title pages. Mark Twain limited his involvement in the illustrations to requiring that the title characters be drawn as 13- or 14-year-old boys, and he was very pleased with the results—especially's Merrill's pictures of court scenes.

CHATTO and Windus issued the novel's English edition on December 1, with Osgood issuing the first American edition 11 days later. Despite Mark Twain's arranging for a limited Canadian edition, two pirate publishers later issued editions there. Initial sales of the American edition were good, but not outstanding. Of the first 25,000 copies of the book that Osgood had made, nearly 5,000 copies remained unsold when Mark Twain's own publishing firm, Charles L. WEBSTER & COMPANY, took over the rights to the book in February 1884.

Over the century following its initial publication, *The Prince and the Pauper* went through scores of editions. The first corrected edition was issued by the MARK TWAIN PAPERS project in 1979. The project used Mark Twain's original handwritten manuscript—now held by California's Huntington Library—and the first American edition, which was made from a copy text that no longer survives. This new edition differs from earlier editions in restoring Mark Twain's original punctuation and eliminating numerous minor changes made without his permission. It also incorporates all the original illustrations. An appendix also includes a chapter on the whipping-boy Hugh MARLOW that Mark Twain removed from the original edition at Howells's suggestion.

The Prince and the Pauper, dramatic adaptations of

This story has been one of the most frequently dramatized of Mark Twain's works. Shortly after he wrote it, his wife Livy adapted a play from it that family members performed at home during the 1880s. Mark Twain himself usually played Miles Hendon, with his older daughters playing the title roles. Daniel FROHMAN and Abby Sage Richardson mounted the first professional production in Philadelphia in 1889 and other adaptations soon followed. Mark Twain attended a production performed by an educational group in New York City in 1907. Two years later, he made a brief appearance in a short silent film adaptation produced by Thomas A. EDISON's company. A British film company also filmed the story the same year.

The first feature-length film adaptation was made by the Famous Players company in 1915. Thirty-two-year-old Marguerite Clark (1883–1940) played both title roles in one of the earliest films to use split-screen shooting techniques. In 1920, the Hungarian director Alexander Korda filmed the story in Vienna, with Tibi Lubin as Tom and the prince, Francis Herter as John Canty and Francis Everth as Miles Hendon. After Korda settled a copyright dispute with the Mark Twain Estate, his film was distributed in the United States two years later.

William Keighley directed the first major sound film for Warner Brothers in 1937. Identical twins Bobby and Billy Mauch (1924–) played the title roles opposite Errol Flynn's Miles Hendon. Laird Doyle's script departed from the original story significantly by having Hertford (Claude Rains) discover Tom Canty's real identity, then send the captain of the palace guard (Alan Hale) to find and kill the true prince.

A Soviet film of *The Prince and the Pauper* was made in 1943. Other adaptations have since been made in China (1966), India (1968) and Ireland (1969). The next major adaptation was a joint British-American production released in the United States as *Crossed Swords* in 1977. Its cast included Mark Lester (Edward / Tom Canty), Oliver Reed (Miles Hendon), Harry Andrews (Hertford), Charlton Heston (Henry VIII), George C. Scott (Ruffler), Raquel Welch (Edith), Ernest Borgnine (John Canty) and Rex Harrison (Norfolk).

The story has also been animated several times. An Australian film was made in 1970 and the Disney Company made a 24-minute cartoon with Mickey Mouse 20 years later.

The Prince and the Pauper has also inspired several television adaptations. The Dumont network aired a one-hour play in October 1957, and a one-hour play was broadcast on the *Shirley Temple Theatre* two years later. In March 1962, *Walt Disney Presents* aired a three-part production that was later packaged as a feature film. Sean Scully played the title roles, with Guy Williams as Miles Hendon. In a major departure from the original story, Hendon accepts Edward's claim to be king and tries to help him get into the royal palace.

Mark Twain's work has also inspired a parallel female story—Gwen Davis's novel *The Princess and the Pauper: An Erotic Fairy Tale* (1989), set in the fictional kingdom of Perq in the Irish Sea.

"The Private History of a Campaign That Failed"

Embellished account of Mark Twain's military service as a Confederate irregular. Writing in 1885 for a magazine series about "leaders" in the CIVIL WAR, Mark Twain prefaced the piece with the remark that he was someone "who started out to do something in it but didn't." While the story is an important link in his AUTOBIOGRAPHY between *Life on the Mississippi* and *Roughing It*, the specific incidents it relates cannot all be taken literally. The story is at once a comic apologia for a former Confederate irregular who is daring to publish General U. S. GRANT's Civil War memoirs and a satiric indictment of the stupidity of the military and of war generally. In this latter regard, it ranks beside "THE WAR PRAYER."

The story begins when the unnamed narrator learns of South Carolina's secession from the Union while he is a PILOT on the Mississippi River. A month later, he is in NEW ORLEANS as LOUISIANA is seceding. A few months later, he is home in Missouri as it is being invaded by Union forces. In Hannibal he and 14 other young men respond to the governor's call for militia by spontaneously forming a unit that they call the "MARION RANGERS." Aside from Ed Stevens, most of the recruits are given fictitious names.

None of the men has any military experience. Tom Lyman is made captain; the narrator, second lieutenant.

By the time all the commissioned and noncommissioned ranks are distributed, only three privates remain. They soon learn, however, that rank counts for little, as none of them is willing to take orders from another.

The unit's first mission is to march 10 miles to New London, when an old veteran named Colonel Ralls takes out a Bible and has them swear fealty to the State of Missouri. They then move on to a spot in the forest they call Camp Ralls, where farmers bring them mules and horses for their use. Over the next few days the young soldiers drill themselves on horsemanship, mainly by riding to visit local girls. When rumors of an enemy advance reach them, they panic, wondering which way to retreat. During a dark, wet night, they get lost, until dogs set upon them and a farmer named Mason calls the dogs off. The farmer shames the men with questions about what they are doing.

The next night another rumor of Union troops sends the Rangers fleeing into the woods, where they nearly drown in mud. In the morning they again learn that the rumor has been a false alarm. They spend several days at the Masons' farm, until a new rumor of approaching Union troops scares them back to into the woods. Their officers attempt to place pickets, but no one cooperates.

As the days pass, the unit tires of reacting to false alarms, until they are ready to take whatever comes. Finally, they emerge one moonlit night to confront what may be a real threat. When a man approaches on a horse, the narrator joins his comrades in shooting him down. Once it is clear that the rider is alone, they inspect their victim and find that he is neither in uniform nor armed. Calling the incident an epitome of war, which requires the killing of strangers against whom one feels no personal animosity, the narrator concludes that he is not equipped for this awful business. He resolves to retire while he can save his self-respect.

The Rangers continue retreating until they arrive near FLORIDA, in Monroe County. When they hear word that a Union colonel (later identified as U. S. GRANT) is about to sweep in, they vote to disband. Half of them leave immediately; the rest remain in service throughout the war. As the former soldiers head home, they encounter General Harris, who futilely orders them to return to duty. The narrator concludes that "I knew more about retreating than the man that invented retreating."

PUBLISHING HISTORY

In May 1885, Robert Underwood Johnson (1853–1937), the editor of CENTURY magazine, persuaded Mark Twain to write about his Civil War experiences for his "Battles and Leaders of the Civil War" series. Johnson wanted a piece depicting conditions in Missouri at the start of the war and was very pleased with the 7,000-word manuscript that Mark Twain sent him in Novem-

ber. The article appeared in the following month's issue of *Century*, illustrated by Edward Windsor KEMBLE, with several maps drawn by Mark Twain himself. The story was first collected in MERRY TALES in 1892 and was subsequently reprinted in *The American Claimant and Other Stories and Sketches*. Mark Twain also alludes to this Civil War episode in chapter 67 of *Following the Equator*.

In April 1981, the Public Broadcasting System aired a dramatization directed by Peter H. Hunt. Gary McCleery played the second lieutenant (who is not named) and Joseph Adams played Tom Lyman. Pat Hingle played a flamboyant Colonel Ralls, and Edward Herrmann is the stranger whom the Rangers shoot. The production includes an epilogue, dramatizing "THE WAR PRAYER." Herrmann reappears as the stranger, delivering the prayer to a shocked Connecticut congregation in 1899.

Proctor, Hanner Figure mentioned in *Huckleberry Finn*. In chapter 28, Huck tells Mary Jane WILKS that the KING and DUKE are frauds and asks her to leave town so she will not inadvertently give this secret away. She goes to the home of the LOTHROP family; however, Huck tells her sisters that she has gone across the river to "set" with her gravely ill friend Hanner Proctor, who has the "pluribus-unum mumps."

Professor Character in *Tom Sawyer Abroad*. The Professor is the inventor of the balloon craft that carries Huck, Tom and Jim to AFRICA. In the first chapter, he allows people to board his craft at ST. LOUIS. Their derisive comments so anger him that he sets sail without giving Tom, Huck and Jim a chance to get off. He forces them to accompany him across the Atlantic and frightens them with his sullen and erratic behavior. In chapter 4 he gets drunk, attacks Tom during a storm and disappears after falling out of the balloon.

When Mark Twain created the Professor, he may have had in mind James W. PAIGE, a silver-tongued inventor whose typesetting machine helped push Mark Twain's publishing company to declare BANKRUPTCY on the same day that it published *Tom Sawyer Abroad* as a book.

"The Professor's Yarn" Tale told in *Life on the Mississippi*. Most of chapter 36 is related by a college professor who is identified only as a passenger on the steamboat GOLD DUST. Years earlier, the professor explains, he went to California to work as a surveyor. Aboard his ship, he befriended John Backus, an Ohio cattleman carrying his life savings to take up ranching on the coast. As they neared San Francisco, Backus was lured into a game (poker?) with professional gamblers. After drinking too much, he wagered his entire fortune on one hand. However, he emerged triumphant as the ship entered the Golden Gate and he announced that he was not a cattleman, but a professional gambler himself.

The end of chapter 35 introduces this story, pointing out that it is inserted "merely because it is a good story, not because it belongs here—for it doesn't." The disclaimer is accurate, as Mark Twain originally intended the piece for *A Tramp Abroad*. A deleted portion of chapter 35 indicates that the professor is from YALE.

publishers Through his writing career, Mark Twain had formal contractual relations with at least nine publishers, and several others issued his books without authorization. His first book, THE CELEBRATED JUMPING FROG OF CALAVERAS COUNTY AND OTHER SKETCHES, was published by Charles H. WEBB in 1867. The following year, he signed a contract to publish *Innocents Abroad* with the AMERICAN PUBLISHING COMPANY, a SUBSCRIPTION-BOOK publisher with whom he stayed through 1880. He then published several books with James R. OSGOOD. Meanwhile, he published minor works with firms not ordinarily in the book publishing business. Sheldon and Company, publishers of GALAXY magazine, issued his BURLESQUE AUTOBIOGRAPHY in 1871; Dan SLOTE's business firm published *Punch, Brothers, Punch!* in 1878.

Unhappy with Osgood's sales performance and unable to get satisfactory terms from the American Publishing Company, Mark Twain formed Charles L. WEBSTER & COMPANY in early 1884 and used it to publish *Huckleberry Finn* and other books until the company went BANKRUPT a decade later. He returned to the American Publishing Company for *Pudd'nhead Wilson* and *Following the Equator*, while negotiating a new contract with HARPER AND BROTHERS, which published all of his remaining books.

Lack of international copyright protection left Mark Twain's early works vulnerable to foreign pirate publishers such as the BELFORD brothers in Canada. After John Camden HOTTEN began publishing unauthorized editions of his books in England, Mark Twain contracted with George ROUTLEDGE to publish *Innocents Abroad* and *Roughing It* there. In 1876, he made Andrew CHATTO his British publisher for *Tom Sawyer* and stayed with Chatto for the rest of his life. Though Mark Twain never had a formal contract with Christian Bernhard von TAUCHNITZ, the German publisher issued cheap English-language editions of his most popular books and paid him royalties.

Pudding Lane Historic LONDON road on the north shore of the THAMES, about 150 yards northeast of LONDON BRIDGE. Chapters 2 and 3 of *The Prince and the Pauper* mention Pudding Lane in connection with a fictional side street, OFFAL COURT, in which Tom CANTY's family lives. Pudding Lane takes its name from the "puddings," or animal entrails, of the district's many butcher shops. In 1666, the Great Fire of London began in Pudding Lane; it is commemorated by Christopher Wren's Monument at the intersection of Pudding Lane and Monument Street. Pudding Lane is also mentioned in *Huckleberry Finn*. The DUKE's handbill advertising the "Shaksperean Revival" describes Edmund KEAN the elder as being "of the Royal Haymarket Theatre, Whitechapel, Pudding Lane, Piccadilly, London, and the Royal Continental Theatres" (chapter 21).

puddinghead Slang term for a fool. Modern etymological dictionaries tend to credit *Pudd'nhead Wilson* (1894) with coining this term. In that novel's first chapter, David WILSON makes a remark that strikes people as so odd that they immediately call him a "lummox," "a labrick," "a dam fool" and "a perfect jackass." Finally, however, they settle on "pudd'nhead"—a name that sticks for 20 years.

Mark Twain used "puddinghead" as much as five years earlier, in *Connecticut Yankee*. When Hank MORGAN and King ARTHUR are treed by an angry mob, Morgan calls a man who climbs up after them "a near-sighted, cross-eyed, pudding-headed clown" (chapter 34). In *Tom Sawyer, Detective* (1896), Jake DUNLAP calls himself and a partner "a couple of pudd'nheads" (chapter 3) and Huck describes Silas PHELPS as "simple hearted and pudd'n-headed" (chapter 8).

Pudd'nhead Wilson, The Tragedy of **(1894)** Mark Twain's last American novel, *Pudd'nhead Wilson* is regarded as a major part of his Mississippi writings. It resembles *Tom Sawyer* and *Huckleberry Finn* in being set before the CIVIL WAR in a small Missouri town modeled on Hannibal. However, it has a much more somber tone. While it contains humor, it deals frankly with small-town prejudice, slavery, miscegenation, lost birthright, degenerate aristocratic values and distorted parental love. One of its strongest themes is the effect of training on character, demonstrated by the switching of slave and free babies in infancy.

There is some uncertainty about the full title that Mark Twain intended for *Pudd'nhead Wilson*. The novel has typically been published as *The Tragedy of Pudd'nhead Wilson;* however, the phrase "The Tragedy of" on the first edition's title page might be read as a description—instead of as part of the title. Typographically, the phrase is treated the same as the phrase "And the Comedy" before *Those Extraordinary Twins* on the same page. Mark Twain himself wrote "Pudd'nhead Wilson, A Tale" on the first page of his manuscript. In any case, while the novel is clearly a tragedy, Wilson himself is not its central tragic figure.

SYNOPSIS

Pudd'nhead Wilson contains 53,000 words, divided into 22 chapters. As is discussed in the background section below, the story is a truncated revision of a longer work originally titled "THOSE EXTRAORDINARY TWINS." Mark Twain began the book as a wild BURLESQUE about SIAMESE TWINS. As the story developed, however, he found that new characters were moving his narrative toward a tragedy unrelated to his original premise. He extracted most of the Siamese twins farce and revised the remainder into its published form as *Pudd'nhead Wilson.* Some familiarity with the "Those Extraordinary Twins" story is thus essential to understanding *Pudd'nhead Wilson's* complex structure.

The narrative spans 23 years in DAWSON'S LANDING, a Missouri village on the Mississippi River. Among Mark Twain's novels, *Pudd'nhead Wilson* is unusual in assigning specific dates to events. The narrative opens in February 1830. By chapter 5, it is June 1853—a moment coinciding with the date that Mark Twain left Hannibal. The balance of the story unfolds over four or perhaps five more months, with about three-quarters of the story set in 1853. Most of the action takes place in Dawson's Landing, with several episodes in ST. LOUIS and ARKANSAS.

As in *The Prince and the Pauper, Pudd'nhead Wilson* opens with unrelated boys—one advantaged, the other disadvantaged—born on the same day. The narrative then follows three distinct story lines. The first concerns ROXANA (Roxy), a slave woman who switches her baby son, CHAMBERS, with the son of her master. Her son grows up as "Tom DRISCOLL," murders his presumed uncle for money, and is finally exposed. The second story line follows David WILSON, a brilliant young eastern lawyer whose legal career is ruined by a remark that he makes on arriving in Dawson's Landing. The final story line concerns Angelo and Luigi CAPELLO, Italian twins who come to Dawson's Landing in chapter 5.

It is 1845 when Roxy is freed in chapter 4. From that point, the narrative follows Tom Driscoll up to 1853. In chapter 8, the narrative resumes Roxy's story, with both threads converging in chapter 11. From there, the dominant story is Tom's struggle to pay off his mounting gambling debts, while staying in his uncle's good graces. The climax comes when Tom grows so desperate for money that he kills his uncle while trying to rob him. Tom appears to triumph when the Capello twins are charged with his crime, leaving him to inherit his uncle's estate. However, Wilson defends the Capellos using FINGERPRINT evidence that proves not only that Tom is the true murderer, but that he is also rightfully a slave.

Preface
Mark Twain signs his brief introduction, titled "A Whisper to the Reader," on January 2, 1893, at "Villa Viviani, village of Settignano, three miles back of FLORENCE." It explains that he has subjected the novel's "law chapters" to the scrutiny of William Hicks, who trained in law in Missouri 35 years earlier. The discursive sentence describing Hicks rambles on for 176 words (recalling Jim BLAINE's old ram's tale in *Roughing It*).

Chapter 1
The narrative opens in February 1830 in the quiet Missouri village of DAWSON'S LANDING, half a day below ST. LOUIS by Mississippi steamboat. The town's chief citizens are Judge York DRISCOLL, his friend Pembroke HOWARD, Colonel Cecil Burleigh ESSEX and Percy DRISCOLL. On the first day of the month two boys are born, one to Percy Driscoll's wife, the other to his slave ROXANA. Mrs. Driscoll dies within a week, leaving Roxana to raise both babies while Mr. Driscoll loses himself in his business speculations.

During this same month, newly qualified lawyer David WILSON arrives from the east. On his first day in the village, he is heard to remark that he wished he owned half of a yelping dog so that he could kill his half. From that moment, he is branded a fool and dubbed "Pudd'nhead Wilson."

Chapter 2
Wilson buys a house on the edge of town and sets up an office in town, advertising himself as "Attorney and Counselor-at-Law, Surveying, Conveyancing, etc." No clients come, so he soon sets law aside and works at surveying and accounting. He uses his considerable idle time to experiment with palmistry and FINGERPRINTING.

In July, Wilson overhears Roxy flirting and joking with a slave named Jasper, whose skin is very dark. Roxy herself is physically indistinguishable from a "white" person, but "the one sixteenth of her which was black outvoted the other fifteen parts and made her a Negro." Though her son, CHAMBERS, is only $1/32$ black, and is blue-eyed and blond, he, too, is a slave, and by fiction of law and custom a Negro. Chambers and Driscoll's son look so much alike that Driscoll can only tell them apart by their clothes. Wilson wonders how Roxy can tell them apart. He collects their fingerprints on glass plates—something that he does again on September 3.

On September 4, Percy Driscoll confronts Roxy and three other household slaves about thefts in the house. He is generally a humane slave owner, but his patience is exhausted. He first vows to sell the guilty slave, and then threatens to sell *all* of them *down* the river, unless the thief confesses. Roxy is innocent, but the other three confess immediately.

Chapter 3
The idea of being "sold down the river" shakes Roxy badly, and the thought of her son's suffering that fate frightens her even more. To ensure that this never happens, she decides to drown him and herself. After donning her finest dress, she puts Chambers in one of Tom's expensive gowns. When she examines her work, she remembers that Driscoll cannot recognize his own naked son, so she switches the babies by swapping their clothes and cradles. Then she practices calling each by its new name. The only person she fears is Wilson, whom she regards as the smartest man in town. Driscoll and his brother leave town on business for seven weeks. On the first of October, Wilson fingerprints the babies again, but even he suspects nothing. Roxy now feels safe.

Chapter 4

(From this point in the narrative, the boys are known by their false names.) "Tom" is a bad boy from the start. He cries without reason, bites, scratches and whines constantly, but Roxy is a "doting fool of a mother." Her relationship with Tom becomes warped. To the world, she is not his mother, but his slave. She grows increasingly obsequious and forgets "who she was and what he had been."

While the pampered Tom grows up sickly, the neglected Chambers is healthy and robust. Tom mistreats Chambers badly, but Percy Driscoll makes it clear that if Chambers ever lifts a hand against Tom, he will be thrashed. Tom uses Chambers as his personal bodyguard and plays nasty tricks on him. When the boys are about 15, Chambers saves Tom from drowning, but this only makes Tom spiteful; he even attempts to stab Chambers.

By adolescence, Tom's relationship with Roxy is strictly that of master to slave. He insults and abuses her to the point that she fantasizes about exposing his true identity for revenge. However, any trace of kindness he shows her lifts her spirits.

In the fall of 1845, the boys' natural fathers, Colonel ESSEX and Percy Driscoll, die. On his deathbed, Driscoll frees Roxy and gives Tom over to the care of his brother, Judge York DRISCOLL, who has recently bought Chambers to prevent his being sold down the river as Tom has urged. Shortly after Percy's death, "his great speculative landed estate" collapses, leaving Tom a pauper. However, Judge Driscoll promises to leave his own estate to Tom.

The newly freed Roxy becomes a chambermaid on a steamboat.

Chapter 5

Two years later, Judge Driscoll's wife dies, leaving the judge and his sister, Rachel PRATT, to raise Tom. They continue spoiling him. When Tom is 19, he goes off to YALE. He returns two years later with improved manners, but with new drinking and gambling habits. Bored with Dawson's Landing, he begins frequenting St. Louis. Meanwhile, Judge Driscoll retires from the bench. His greatest interest in life now is the FREE-THINKER'S SOCIETY. He has a high regard for his fellow member, Wilson, whose whimsical (PUDD'NHEAD WILSON'S CALENDAR) he admires. Other people like Wilson personally, but regard him as inconsequential.

The widow Aunt Patsy COOPER lives with her daughter Rowena COOPER and two younger sons. For a year she has been trying to rent out her spare room. It is now June 1853, and she gets a letter from Angelo and Luigi CAPELLO, Italian brothers who want the room. Rowena is thrilled by the prospect of Italian boarders, as the town has never known travelers. Her neighbors quickly learn about the coming visitors. Judge Driscoll arrives to congratulate Aunt Patsy. Judge Sim ROBINSON and others soon follow. The chapter ends as the Capellos arrive during a late-night storm.

Chapter 6

The next morning, the charming brothers are soon on familiar terms with everyone. They awe the Coopers with a frank history of their background. After their family—originally of the Florentine nobility—became refugees, the brothers were orphaned and had to travel constantly. The Coopers' slave Nancy interrupts them to announce that the house is filling up with people who want to meet the Italians. A reception line forms spontaneously and the occasion becomes a levee. Patsy introduces the twins to her admiring neighbors as "Count Angelo" and "Count Luigi." The Capellos win over everyone with their charm and manners. Rowena now knows for the first time the real meaning of that great word "Glory." Her ecstasy is complete when the twins entertain masterfully on the piano.

Chapter 7

By the time the crowd reluctantly leaves, the twins have collected many social invitations. Judge Driscoll shows them the town and invites them to a meeting of the Free-thinkers' Society. There they establish a warm rapport with Wilson, who invites them to visit him later that evening. As Wilson awaits the twins' arrival, he puzzles over something he observed that morning, when he saw an unfamiliar woman through the window of Tom Driscoll's room next door. Since then, Wilson has visited the house and learned that Tom is due back in town that evening, but he gets no hint that there are guests in Driscoll's home. *(This story line resumes in chapter 11.)*

Chapter 8

After leaving Dawson's Landing eight years earlier, Roxy became a chambermaid on the steamboat GRAND MOGUL. Forced by rheumatism to retire, she goes to the New Orleans bank where she has amassed $400 in savings, only to learn that the bank has gone bust. She returns to the *Grand Mogul* and goes back to Dawson's Landing. She wants badly to see Tom again, but he is in St. Louis when she reaches Dawson's Landing, where Judge Driscoll's slaves receive her warmly and load her with supplies. Over the next several days, Chambers tells Roxy that Tom has been blowing his allowance gambling in St. Louis and that the judge threatens to disinherit him because of his gambling debts. Chambers wonders why his mother is so interested in Tom.

After Tom returns, Chambers tells him that Roxy wants to see him and is beaten for his trouble. Tom reluctantly admits Roxy and receives her servile greetings indifferently. Unsettled by Tom's coolness, Roxy appeals to his charity by asking him for a dollar. He merely tells her to get out, so she appeals to him as the woman who raised him. Another rude rebuff so angers her that she turns on Tom, predicting that she will have him on his knees begging for mercy. She threatens to go to his uncle "en tell him every las' thing I knows 'bout you." Tom's guilty reaction bolsters Roxy's confidence. She makes vague threats about telling the judge things that will make him bust his will. Soon Tom is on his knees. He gives Roxy five dollars, but she tells him to meet her at the HAUNTED HOUSE.

Chapter 9
After Roxy leaves, the humiliation of abasing himself to a black woman causes Tom to collapse. Late that evening, he meets Roxy in the haunted house. When she tells Tom that he is really *her* son, he starts toward her with a piece of wood, but fails to faze her. She checks him with the lie that her proofs are written on a document that will be disclosed if anything happens to her.

Roxy makes Tom call her "mammy" and tells him that if he fails, even once, to obey her, she will ruin him. Tom's whimpering acknowledgment satisfies Roxy that her triumph is complete. She now lays down the law: He must split his $50-a-month allowance with her. Under pressure, Tom confesses that he is nearly $300 in debt and that his only plan for paying off this debt has been to raise money by stealing. He has recently staged a "raid" in town when he was supposed to be in St. Louis. Roxy approves of his stealing and promises to stay out of town, except when she calls to collect her money. Tom asks who his true father was. To his surprise, Roxy answers proudly, identifying Colonel Essex.

Chapter 10
Over the next several days, Tom adjusts to the idea of being black. He fears discovery and finds himself becoming more empathetic toward other people. People notice his behavior changing. He thinks that his character is changing, but his nature remains unaltered and his old ways gradually return.

The loot from Tom's most recent raid pays off his gambling debts. Over the next few months, he finds himself warming toward his mother, but her strong personality frightens him. Renewed visits to St. Louis soon put him in debt again. He returns to Dawson's Landing for another raid. Disguised as a young woman, he goes to his uncle's house, where he notices Wilson watching him through the window (*the incident noted in chapter 7*). He puts on "some airs and graces and attitudes" for Wilson, then changes his disguise to look like an old woman and visits Roxy at the haunted house. Tom loses his nerve and wants to call off his "raid," but after Roxy tells him about the reception for the twins going on at the Cooper house, he loots many of the neighbors' empty homes.

Chapter 11
(*Continued from chapter 7.*) The Capello brothers arrive at Wilson's house and establish a cordial friendship. Wilson reads from his calendar for them. Tom Driscoll unexpectedly drops in; he tries to embarrass Wilson about his frustrated law career. Wilson replies that while not having a chance to pursue his career has been disappointing, he keeps up his law studies. Tom then teases Wilson about his fingerprinting hobby. As Wilson takes prints from Tom and the twins, Tom teases him

about his interest in palmistry as well. This jibe misfires when the Capellos express deep respect for the art. Under coaxing, Wilson reads Luigi's palm and reluctantly reveals that Luigi has killed someone. Luigi confirms this, explaining that he once killed a man to save Angelo's life when a thief tried to steal a knife given them by an Indian prince. Tom declines Wilson's offer to read his palm.

As Tom tries to force the twins to argue with each other, John BUCKSTONE arrives to invite the Italians to an anti-temperance meeting of the Sons of Liberty. Accompanied by the uninvited Tom, the twins leave with Buckstone. The meeting elects them to membership and serves them glasses of whiskey. Luigi downs his, but Angelo says that he is a teetotaler and asks that his membership be reconsidered. After another round of drinks is served, Tom gets cheerfully loud and makes a rude pun at the twins' expense, moving Luigi to kick him off the stage into the crowd. The drunken assemblage passes Tom around until someone yells "fire" and the local firefighters arrive and wreck the hall.

Chapter 12
Early the next morning, Judge Driscoll and Pembroke Howard are fishing when another man informs them that one of the Italians kicked Tom at the previous night's meeting. As a member of one of the "First Families of VIRGINIA," the judge assumes that Tom is managing "the affair" on his own; however, he is shocked to learn that Tom has settled "an affair of honor" in court.

At home, Tom tells his uncle that he has beaten Luigi Capello—Wilson's first legal client—on assault charges in court. The stunned judge insists that Tom challenge Luigi to a DUEL that night. When Tom meekly refuses, the judge calls him a coward and promises to disinherit him. Determined to challenge Luigi himself, he asks Howard to be his second. Tom leaves the house vowing to reform in order to prove himself to his uncle.

Chapter 13
Looking for sympathetic company, Tom wanders to Wilson's house, but even Wilson berates him for taking a personal assault case to court without even consulting his uncle. Still puzzled by the mysterious woman he saw through Tom's bedroom window, Wilson wonders whether the judge is upset with Tom for any reason beyond his failure to challenge Luigi. Tom mentions that some valuables are missing from Driscoll's house, moving Wilson to suggest that a raid has been made on the town.

Just then, Robinson, Buckstone and Constable Jim Blake enter. Wilson tells them about the new thefts and Robinson rattles off the names of other townspeople who have reported robberies—mostly around the Cooper house. Blake says that his prime suspect is an old woman who was seen leaving several houses. Among the thefts was the twins' valuable dagger. Tom pales as he hears about the plans being made to capture the thief, especially when Wilson mentions that he and the twins have set their own trap.

On behalf of the Democratic Party, Robinson and the others ask Wilson to run for mayor, as Dawson's Landing is about to be incorporated as a city. Wilson accepts, gratified finally to be making his debut into the town's affairs.

Chapter 14

Meanwhile, Pembroke Howard reports to Judge Driscoll that Luigi Capello has accepted his challenge and will duel with him that very night. Both men think Luigi a splendid fellow. As Howard leaves, Driscoll reconsiders disinheriting Tom; Howard returns and witnesses Driscoll's revised will. When both leave, Tom examines the new will with quiet satisfaction. He again vows to reform, but the specter of unpaid gambling debts deflates his joy. As he goes to seek solace from Roxy, he hears distant gunshots.

Roxy is surprised to learn that Tom was not in the duel. When he laughs at the idea of dueling, he earns his mother's contempt. Disgusted by his cowardice, she suggests that his father would turn over in his grave and adds some remarks about her own proud ancestry. Tom notices that Roxy's nose is skinned. A stray bullet from the duel hit her while she was watching through a window.

When Tom tells Roxy about his latest gambling debts, she agrees that the judge is not likely to give him another chance if he misbehaves again. She outlines a plan. First, Tom must behave himself perfectly. Next, he must go to his St. Louis creditors, explain his situation, tell them that his uncle will not live much longer, and offer to pay interest on his debt until his inheritance comes through. Meanwhile, he should sell off his stolen swag to pay the interest. Roxy impresses upon Tom that he *must* behave and promises to follow him to St. Louis to watch him. One slip, and she will reveal the secret of his birth to ruin him. Much sobered, Tom again vows to reform.

Chapter 15

The next day, everyone connected with the duel basks in glory. As Luigi's second, Wilson is a "made man." The twins, now "prodigiously great," take out papers for citizenship and decide to end their days in Dawson's Landing. Both accept nomination to the city council.

Tom Driscoll chafes over these developments, especially the twins' popularity. When he encounters Wilson and Constable Blake, he taunts Blake about his investigation of the robberies. He also correctly guesses the scheme Wilson has devised to capture the thief of the twins' knife—namely, *publicly* advertising a reward for the knife, while *privately* advertising a reward for the thief. He needles Wilson by suggesting that the knife has not been found because it never existed. Or, if the knife does exist, the twins still have it. Tom leaves, satisfied that he has planted seeds of doubt.

Over the next week, Tom's uncle and aunt notice his impeccable behavior. He wins back his uncle's confidence by explaining that he could not meet Luigi on a field of honor knowing him to be an assassin—a fact he says he swore not to reveal. Never questioning Tom's story, the judge denounces Luigi as a villain for drawing him into a gentleman's combat, and vows to prevent both twins from being elected to the city council.

Tom's behavior even pleases Roxy, who is beginning to feel that she loves him. She tells him to go to St. Louis, and that she will follow shortly. That night, Tom carries his swag aboard a big steamer, but awakens to find that another thief has robbed him during the night.

Chapter 16

Roxy arrives in St. Louis to find Tom in despair. Her heart goes out to him, making her realize that she truly loves him. Her motherly endearments repulse him, but he is afraid to ask her to stop. In any case, she has a plan to save him. She says that she is worth $600 and offers to let him sell her to cover his debts. Tom is dazed.

Roxy wants Tom to forge ownership papers, take her upcountry and sell her cheap to someone not likely to ask questions. Tom does as he is told, but instead of going *up*state, he sells her to an ARKANSAS cotton farmer, rationalizing his treachery by thinking that the farmer will treat her so well that she will not mind being sold *down* the river. He even convinces himself that he is doing her a splendid service. He pays off his debts and resolves to behave himself so as not to jeopardize his uncle's will, while saving money to buy Roxy's freedom again in a year.

Meanwhile, Roxy is carried away in a steamboat. She is not supposed to know which direction the boat is taking her, but her steamboat experience allows her quickly to realize that she has been "sole down de river!"

Chapter 17

Back in Dawson's Landing, the twins campaign hard for city council, but their popularity has declined. Suspicious remarks are made about their missing knife. Judge Driscoll exhausts himself campaigning against them. For two months, Tom's behavior is so good that his uncle even gives him access to his safe. In the final speech of the campaign, the judge ridicules the twins as cheap frauds and implies that they are assassins.

The next day, Wilson is elected mayor, but the twins lose their elections badly. Tom returns happily to St. Louis. The twins withdraw from society amid rumors that Luigi will challenge Judge Driscoll to a new duel when the latter regains his strength.

Chapter 18

A week later, Tom Driscoll returns to his St. Louis lodgings shadowed by a strange, shabby man, who turns out to be his mother. As Tom blubbers self-recriminations, Roxy tells her story. The planter who bought her was not a bad man, but his wife forced her to work in the fields, conspiring with the Yankee overseer to make her life hell. One day, when the overseer beat a young girl whom Roxy had befriended, Roxy seized his stick and "laid him flat." She then fled to the river, found a canoe and paddled downstream until she found a steamboat tied up. It happened to be the *Grand Mogul.* She told her old crewmates that she had been kidnapped and sold down the river. They collected money for her and let her ride back to St. Louis.

While searching for Tom, Roxy has seen her master distributing handbills. Tom already has seen the man. He knows that Roxy was on the *Grand Mogul;* suspecting that there is something wrong with Roxy's sale, he is pressuring Tom to find her. Reading the truth in Tom's face, Roxy makes him confess what he knows, and he shows her a handbill advertising a reward for her return. He reads her everything on the bill—except his own name, which is listed as a contact for the reward. Roxy senses that he is lying and makes him admit that he has set a trap for her.

Roxy orders Tom to secure her freedom by giving the planter all the money he has and getting his uncle to give him the rest by confessing that he sold her to pay gambling debts. Tom protests that this will guarantee his being disinherited, but Roxy tells him that the alternative is to have his true identity disclosed, then "he'll sell *you* down de river, en you kin see how you like it!" She leaves the building with Tom, keeping a knife at his back. After parting from Roxy, Tom resolves to follow her plan in all details but one. Instead of asking his uncle for the money, he will *rob* him.

Chapter 19
Dawson's Landing buzzes in anticipation of a new duel; however, Judge Driscoll declines Luigi's challenge. He refuses to meet an "assassin" on the field of honor, though he is willing to meet him elsewhere. Driscoll ignores Wilson's attempt to explain Luigi's story, so Wilson warns Luigi to be ready for an attack by the judge at any time.

That night the Capellos are out for a walk as Tom Driscoll slips into town unnoticed. Tom sneaks home and prepares to rob his uncle by blacking his face and laying out a woman's dress for his getaway. To boost his courage, he carries the Capellos' Indian knife when he goes downstairs to his uncle's office. There he finds banknotes stacked on a table next to a sofa on which his uncle is asleep. As he snatches the money, his uncle grabs him and cries out for help. Tom stabs the old man and flees upstairs, leaving the knife behind. In his own room, he pulls the dress over his male clothes and then sneaks to the haunted house. There he cleans blood off himself, burns his outfits and puts on a tramp disguise. He finds a canoe at the river and paddles to the next village to take a steamer back to St. Louis.

Meanwhile, the Capellos have heard the judge's cries and rushed to his aid, only to become the prime murder suspects when Mrs. PRATT finds them standing next to the judge's dead body. Wilson then arrives and orders that nothing be touched until Judge Robinson arrives as coroner. As the sheriff takes the twins away, Wilson promises to defend them; then he and Constable Blake find the murder weapon. The next day, Tom Driscoll reads about the twins' arrest in a St. Louis newspaper. He arranges to buy Roxy back from the Arkansas planter and wires his aunt that he is coming home.

The coroner's jury finds that Luigi has committed homicide, with Angelo as an accessory. The twins are in danger of being lynched until they are transferred to the county prison. Wilson's examination of the bloody fingerprints on the knife leads him to conclude that neither twin made the marks. Since it is not known that money was taken during the murder, revenge appears to be the only possible motive. As Luigi is the only person known to have a grudge against Driscoll, the twins' case appears desperate. The only thing that Wilson can imagine saving them would be discovery of a murderer who could not have been their accomplice.

Tom returns to town and wins everyone's pity with his sorrowful demeanor.

Chapter 20
During the weeks that the twins await their trial, only Wilson and Patsy Cooper visit them. The courthouse is packed when the trial opens. Roxy and Chambers are among the spectators. Roxy, who carries her bill of sale with her everywhere, now receives a $35-a-month allowance from Tom.

Prosecutor Pembroke Howard lays out the state's case against the twins. The best that Wilson can do is to call witnesses who testify that the Capellos were not stained by blood when they were arrested. He promises to call witnesses who observed "a veiled young woman" leaving Driscoll's premises after the murder occurred. When the court recesses, Wilson and the twins feel hopeless, but Tom is so jubilant that he feels "sarcastically sorry for Wilson." He plans to torment Wilson for the rest of his life about his mystery woman.

That night Wilson studies his collection of female fingerprints, hoping to find a match with those on murder weapon. Tom drops in to taunt him; he examines a glass plate with Roxy's prints and hands it to Wilson. Wilson idly glances at the plate and is stunned by what he sees. After Tom leaves, he goes to work in earnest. He pulls out plates containing Tom's childhood prints for careful inspection. A new puzzle confronts him: Tom's earliest infant prints do not match his later prints. After a nap, Wilson awakens with a new inspiration. He checks his "records" and discovers a startling truth that has been hidden for 23 years.

Chapter 21
Through the night Wilson prepares enlarged copies of fingerprints on cardboard. In court he surprises everyone by announcing that he will not call the witnesses he

promised. Instead, he proposes to present new evidence. He begins by granting the prosecution's claim that the bloody fingerprints on the murder weapon are indeed those of the murderer and outlines a new theory for the crime. He points out that the Capellos' failure to flee the scene of the crime indicates that they are not the likely murderers. He hypothesizes why the person who stole the Capellos' Indian knife kept it, why robbery was the true motive for Judge Driscoll's murder, and why the mysterious woman seen leaving Driscoll's house was actually a man.

As Wilson prepares materials to prove his theory, the audience laughs at the familiar sight of his glass fingerprint plates. Unperturbed, he explains that human fingerprints are unique and immutable. His explanation gradually captures the audience's attention; dramatically, he raises the knife and promises to produce the murderer whose prints it bears by 12 noon.

To demonstrate how fingerprint identification works, Wilson proposes to identify several people—including the defendants—by prints they will make on window panes while he is not watching. His success electrifies the crowd. He now displays enlarged copies of the prints of the Capellos and of two children, whom he calls "A and B." The jury verifies that (1) his copies of the Capellos' prints match those the Capellos have made on the window; (2) the Capellos' prints do *not* match those on the murder weapon; and (3) the prints of one of the unnamed children do match those on the weapon. Tom Driscoll grows panicky as Wilson exhibits additional prints proving that the unnamed children were switched in their cradles. Building his argument in logical stages, Wilson pronounces: "Valet de Chambre, Negro and slave—falsely called Thomas à Becket Driscoll—make upon the window the fingerprints that will hang you!" Tom slides to the floor in a faint.

Roxy drops to her knees and begs God for mercy as the clock strikes noon. Tom is handcuffed and taken away.

Conclusion
After pondering the day's amazing events, the townspeople decide to withdraw Wilson's title of "pudd'nhead," electing themselves to replace him. The twins are once again heroes, but "weary of Western adventure," they retire to Europe. Restored to his birthright, the real "Tom Driscoll" continues Roxy's pension, but she cannot fully enjoy it. Her spirit broken, she turns to her church for solace. Though the former "Chambers" now finds himself rich and free, he is handicapped by illiteracy, his slave dialect, and the attitudes and mannerisms of a slave.

The false Tom confesses his crimes and is given a life sentence. A complication arises, however, when creditors of Percy Driscoll's estate come forward to claim Tom as their property, since legally he was Driscoll's slave when he died. When the governor understands the case, he pardons Tom at once and the creditors sell him down the river.

BACKGROUND AND PUBLISHING HISTORY

Mark Twain wrote *Pudd'nhead Wilson* while living in various locations in Europe during the early 1890s. His initial inspiration came from seeing SIAMESE TWINS on tour in 1891. His plan was to write a "howling farce" about the problems of brothers who disagreed on almost everything having to share a single body. He first discussed his plans for the book with Fred J. HALL, during a visit to New York in the summer of 1892. In September, he put *Tom Sawyer Abroad* aside to begin the new book, which he called "THOSE EXTRAORDINARY TWINS." By the end of the year, he had completed 60,000 words and was starting to assign maxims from "PUDD'NHEAD WILSON'S CALENDAR" to individual chapters.

Mark Twain signed his preface to the book in January 1893, while he was staying in Florence, Italy. In February, he shipped an 81,500-word typescript to Hall. He was now calling the novel "Pudd'nhead Wilson—A Tale." A few months later, while visiting New York again, he discussed the book with Hall, who discouraged him from publishing it as it was. He now realized that while he had started intending to write a farce, other characters had intruded and begun transforming his story. What he had now had was a hybrid monster. He decided to solve the problem by extracting the story concerning the Siamese twins.

After returning to Italy, Mark Twain did a massive scissors-and-paste revision. By the end of July, he had trimmed the manuscript to 58,000 words. He then wrote to Hall, reporting—not quite accurately—"I have knocked out everything that delayed the march of the story. . . . There ain't any weather in, and there ain't any scenery—the story is stripped for flight!" His revisions entailed fundamental changes in the story lines. The result was uneven, with some obvious internal inconsistencies. He made the twins physically separate characters and reduced their role, while giving greater roles to Roxy, Tom Driscoll and David Wilson. He now regarded his original idea merely as "an extravagant sort of a tale" that "had no purpose but to exhibit that monstrous 'freak' in all sorts of grotesque lights." In a revealing and self-deprecating preface to "Those Extraordinary Twins," he called these changes "a kind of literary Caesarean operation."

During another visit to New York in September, Mark Twain arranged for serialization of *Pudd'nhead Wilson* in CENTURY MAGAZINE and he read proofs. The serial ran in seven installments, from December 1893 to June 1894, with illustrations by Louis Loeb (1866–1909). Mark Twain hoped to publish the book with his own company, Charles L. WEBSTER & COMPANY, but it declared BANKRUPTCY in April 1894. He went back to the AMERICAN PUBLISHING COMPANY, which issued the book in late November 1894. To bulk up the book, he appended about 20,000 words of material from his original "Those Extraordinary Twins" manuscript, adding transitional passages and comments, as well as a six-page introduction explaining the relationship between this story and *Pudd'nhead Wilson*. CHATTO and Windus issued the first British edition around the same time, but did not include "Those Extraordinary Twins." Both books took their texts directly from the *Century* serialization—the only published version that Mark Twain personally corrected.

The American Publishing Co. edition was lavishly illustrated with whimsical cartoons along the margins of almost every page. F. M. SENIOR illustrated *Pudd'nhead Wilson's* chapters 1–10, 12–15 and 17–19 and all of "Those Extraordinary Twins." C. H. WARREN illustrated the remaining *Pudd'nhead Wilson* chapters. In 1899 HARPER'S reissued the book in a new standard edition of Mark Twain's works, adding a table of contents with chapter titles that do not appear in the original book. Harper also dropped all the original marginal illustrations, retaining only Senior's frontispiece to "Those Extraordinary Twins" and adding two new *Pudd'nhead Wilson* illustrations by E. W. KEMBLE.

San Francisco's Chandler Publishing Company issued a facsimile reprint of the first edition in 1968, adding a substantial new introduction by Frederick ANDERSON. Sidney E. Berger edited the first corrected version of both stories for W. W. Norton's "Critical Edition" series in 1980, drawing mainly on the *Century* magazine text, with corrections based on extant manuscripts. The Norton edition adds an extensive editorial apparatus, reviews and essays and a bibliography. A more substantially reedited edition will eventually be prepared by the MARK TWAIN PAPERS project.

MANUSCRIPTS

The earliest known surviving manuscript is a handwritten draft of about 10,000 words in the Berg Collection of the New York Public Library. These pages, which appear to be a fragment of a larger manuscript, bear the title "Those Extraordinary Twins." The long manuscript that Mark Twain sent to Hall in February 1893 is in New York's J. Pierpont MORGAN Library. The typescript version that he submitted to *Century* apparently has not survived. Since he personally corrected proofs for the magazine, its text is regarded as the most authoritative version of *Pudd'nhead Wilson*. The text used for the published version of "Those Extraordinary Twins" appears to have been taken from fragments extracted from the Morgan manuscript.

Pudd'nhead Wilson, dramatic adaptations of Frank MAYO adapted *Pudd'nhead Wilson* to the stage in 1896. A silent film was made in 1916, evidently with Alan Hale playing Wilson. In 1983, PBS television aired an adaptation with Ken Howard as Wilson and Lise Hilboldt as Roxy. Its script glosses over Wilson's reputation as a "pudd'nhead" by making it appear that he has an active law practice. While it follows the original story reasonably faithfully, it includes some odd changes. For example, Roxy does not bother telling Tom that she is his true mother until *after* he has sold her down the river. Toward the end, it is proven that the Capellos' Indian knife is a fake and that they themselves are frauds.

Pudd'nhead Wilson's Calendar Manuscript jottings of David WILSON in *Pudd'nhead Wilson*. Chapter 5 reveals that Wilson has "for some years" been privately writing a "whimsical almanac," or "calendar," containing ironic MAXIMS. His friend Judge York DRISCOLL so admires these writings that he shows samples to other townspeople. Unable to appreciate irony, they decide "that if there had ever been any doubt that Dave Wilson was a pudd'nhead . . . this revelation removed that doubt for good and all."

Each installment of CENTURY MAGAZINE's serialization of *Pudd'nhead Wilson* contained small calendars incorporating Wilson's maxims. The maxims appeared as chapter headings when *Pudd'nhead Wilson* was published as a book. Mark Twain wanted to match these maxims with chapter contents, but soon abandoned the effort. The resulting relationship between the maxims and their chapters is thus mixed. Maxims heading chapter 5, for example, aptly allude to the upbringing of characters discussed within the chapter. One reads: "Training is everything. The peach was once a bitter almond; cauliflower is nothing but cabbage with a college education." In chapter 11, Wilson reads sample maxims to the CAPELLO brothers, who tactfully ask to borrow his manuscript. A maxim heading this chapter comments on how to please an author by asking to read his manuscript. Others are less obviously connected to the chapters.

While Mark Twain's biographer A. B. PAINE is not alone in regarding the "Calendar" as *Pudd'nhead Wilson*'s most memorable feature, some critics point out that the maxims expose Mark Twain's inconsistent characterization of Wilson. Many maxims express a cynical pessimism about life that is at odds with Wilson's often conventional behavior. Why, one wonders, would Wilson write such thoughts as: " 'How hard it is that we have to die'—a strange complaint to come from the mouths of people who have had to live" (chapter 10) and "Why is it that we rejoice at a birth and grieve at a funeral? It is because we are not the person involved" (chapter 9). Neither sentiment seems consistent with Wilson's character.

Mark Twain repeated the calendar experiment three years later by inserting maxims at the heads of chapters in *Following the Equator*, crediting them to "Pudd'nhead Wilson's *New* Calendar." MORE TRAMPS ABROAD, the En-

Mr. Punch toasts Mark Twain, a "Master of His Art," in 1907, wishing him long life, happiness and perpetual youth.

glish edition of this book, contains several maxims not appearing in the American edition. "Pudd'nhead Wilson's Calendar" maxims occasionally appear elsewhere; for example, at the beginning of "THE BELATED RUSSIAN PASSPORT."

Punch British humor magazine. A London weekly founded in 1841, *Punch* originated as a radical political journal spiced with humorous writing and cartoons and it evolved into a more conservative magazine that poked fun at British social and political stereotypes. Mark Twain admired *Punch*'s trenchant humor, which he thought strong enough to kill off institutions such as the South's Mardi Gras (*Life on the Mississippi*, chapter 46). Such is the magazine's power that Henry ADAMS becomes a "made man" in "THE £1,000,000 BANK-NOTE" when *Punch* caricatures him. In June 1907, *Punch* caricatured Mark Twain himself on its cover when he visited England to receive an honorary degree from OXFORD

UNIVERSITY. The magazine also honored him with a dinner—reportedly the first it ever gave for a foreigner.

"Punch, Brothers, Punch!" Sketch that originally appeared in the February 1876 ATLANTIC MONTHLY as "A Literary Nightmare." Inspired by a jingle published in a newspaper, Mark Twain has his narrator—also named Mark—read this apparently harmless jingle:

> Conductor, when you receive a fare,
> Punch in the presence of the passenjare!
> A blue trip slip for an eight-cent fare,
> A buff trip slip for a six-cent fare,
> A pink trip slip for a three-cent fare,
> Punch in the presence of the passenjare!
>
> Punch, brothers! punch with care!
> Punch in the presence of the passenjare!

The catchy lines immediately possess Mark. For two days, their sing-song rhythms echo in his head, leaving him unable to function. When he goes walking with a clerical friend (inspired by Reverend Joseph TWICHELL), he mumbles the verses constantly, oblivious to conversation. Intrigued by the musical rhymes, the friend masters them himself, lifting the burden from Mark—who is soon back to normal. His friend, however, is now helpless. Several days later, the friend returns from Boston, where he conducted a funeral. Unable to clear the rhymes from his head, he was almost a lunatic by the time he got there. To save him from madness, Mark takes him to a local university to discharge his burden on unsuspecting students. He warns readers who encounter the merciless rhymes to avoid them like the pestilence.

In September 1875, Noah Brooks (1830–1903) and Isaac Hill Bromley (1833–1898) published a version of the streetcar jingle in the NEW YORK TRIBUNE, parodying printed instructions given to streetcar conductors. Mark Twain's version adapts theirs. His *Atlantic* sketch was so popular that he copyrighted "Punch in the Presence of the Passenjare" on sheet music the same year, with additional lyrics and music by A. O. Hand. He changed the title of the sketch in 1878, when Dan SLOTE's company published *Punch, Brothers, Punch! and Other Sketches*, a 142-page book with prominent advertisements for Mark Twain's self-pasting SCRAPBOOK. CHATTO and Windus simultaneously published an English edition under the title *An Idle Excursion. Punch, Brothers, Punch!* was also the first book to reprint "SOME RAMBLING NOTES OF AN IDLE EXCURSION," "THE LOVES OF ALONZO FITZ CLARENCE AND ROSANNAH ETHELTON" and "THE CANVASSER'S TALE." Its entire contents were reprinted in THE STOLEN WHITE ELEPHANT, ETC. (1882).

Q

Quaker City Steamship on which Mark Twain sailed from New York to the MEDITERRANEAN and back on an organized excursion between June 8 and November 19, 1867. He traveled as a working journalist, writing travel letters for the SAN FRANCISCO ALTA CALIFORNIA, which paid his fare. After the excursion, he used these letters to write *Innocents Abroad.*

The *Quaker City* excursion caught the fancy of many Americans. Interest in European travel had grown rapidly after the CIVIL WAR and a huge international exhibition in Paris made 1867 a notable travel year. The cruise itself also attracted interest because it was the first such American cruise to the Old World undertaken purely for pleasure. The original impetus behind it is not fully known; the idea started in Henry Ward BEECHER's church in Brooklyn, New York. One of his parishioners, Charles DUNCAN, organized the cruise, arranged to lease the ship and captained it.

A comparatively early oceangoing paddle-wheeler, the *Quaker City* was built in Philadelphia in 1854. Rated at 1,428 tons, it had a white-oak hull, steam boilers and side-wheel paddles. Under steam, it could cruise at 10 knots, but occasionally relied on fore and aft sails in open seas. After carrying passengers between New York and Liverpool for the Collins Line, it was converted to a Union supply ship during the Civil War. Afterward, Charles C. LEARY and several partners bought it and had it refitted as a passenger ship. When Duncan leased it, it was running between New York and Charleston, South Carolina. Leary himself joined the excursion, evidently hoping to sell the vessel. In his letter to the NEW YORK HERALD summing up the voyage, Mark Twain alludes to Leary's failure to sell the ship—suggesting that if it had been sold, the passengers would have had to walk home. This is a passage deleted from *Innocents Abroad*'s version of the letter in chapter 61.

While members of Beecher's church may have viewed the *Quaker City* voyage primarily as an educational outing, Duncan himself hoped to profit from the excursion. Passage cost a hefty $1,250 per person, but he expected enough applicants to necessitate screening procedures; however, no applicant is known to have been rejected—a fact that Mark Twain satirizes in *Innocents Abroad* (chapter 1). The ship could carry about 150 passengers; Duncan himself hoped for 110. As many as 85 may have signed up during the months before the voyage

began; however, this number dropped after Beecher announced that he definitely would not go. Mark Twain himself signed up for the cruise on March 1, 1867. The previous year he had spent nearly 60 days at sea on voyages to HAWAII, NICARAGUA and New York. Discovering that he enjoyed ocean travel, he had longed for more.

Between 65 and 70 passengers sailed on the cruise. Almost all were comparatively wealthy; most, perhaps all, were Protestants; and most were middle-aged. Of 17 women passengers, only four were unmarried. Shipboard entertainments included shuffleboard, card-playing, occasional dances and prayer meetings. Mark Twain had his own cabin; as the voyage progressed, he spent long periods sequestered there, writing his travel letters.

Mark Twain's own itinerary and that of the *Quaker City* were not identical. During about half of the four months that the ship was in the Mediterranean, he was on land. Consequently, he was not with the ship during several short voyages. He was, of course, with it when it pulled out of its Manhattan Island berth on June 8, 1867. The ship then anchored near Brooklyn for two days while waiting for the weather to improve. On June 10, it entered the ATLANTIC OCEAN. After touching at BERMUDA on the 12th, it continued to the AZORES in a crossing that many passengers found rough. It landed at Fayal Island on June 21 and left two days later. Another rough crossing—in which almost every passenger but Mark Twain became seasick—took the ship to GIBRALTAR on June 29. As the ship took on coal, Mark Twain nearly joined a group that went through SPAIN to PARIS. Instead, however, he went by local steamer with another group to TANGIER. When they returned to Gibraltar on July 1, the *Quaker City* departed for FRANCE.

The same night the ship celebrated the Fourth of July, it landed at MARSEILLES, from which most passengers went inland. Mark Twain, Dan SLOTE and Dr. Abraham JACKSON left by train for Paris the next day, returning to Marseilles on July 12. When the ship sailed the next day, Mark Twain was among just 22 passengers still aboard; it reached GENOA on July 14. Although Mark Twain and his companions would revisit the ship at LEGHORN nine days later, they would not sail on it again until it left NAPLES almost a month later, after they traveled through ITALY. Meanwhile, the ship went

The frontispiece of Innocents Abroad *makes it easy to understand why many* Quaker City *passengers got seasick.*

from Genoa to Leghorn on July 23–24 and left Leghorn for Naples on the 31st. The ship was quarantined in the Bay of Naples until just before it sailed on August 11, by which time all its original passengers were back aboard. Chapter 32 of *Innocents Abroad* records that everyone was so cheerful that for once the name *Quaker City* "was a misnomer."

The *Quaker City*'s next scheduled stop was at ATHENS, whose harbor it reached on August 14. Greek authorities would not clear the ship for landing, but Mark Twain was one of a handful of passengers who sneaked ashore to visit the Parthenon. The next day, the *Quaker City* sailed away. On August 17, it reached CONSTANTINOPLE; two days later it entered the Black Sea, touching at SEVASTOPOL on the 21st and at ODESSA the next day. On the 24th, it sailed for YALTA, where it landed at noon the next day. On August 28, the ship left Yalta; it returned to Constantinople on August 30, staying there until September 3 while recoaling. The ship then sailed down the coast of Asia Minor, landing at SMYRNA on September 5. During a two-day stop, most passengers made a day trip to EPHESUS.

From Smyrna, the ship sailed a route taking it between Turkey and Cyprus before turning south to BEIRUT, where it landed on September 10. Mark Twain and many other passengers began overland journeys to the HOLY LAND from Beirut, which the *Quaker City* itself

left on September 15. The next day, it touched at Mt. Carmel, then landed at JAFFA, where it had its longest layover of the entire voyage. Mark Twain and his companions rejoined the ship at Jaffa and sailed for EGYPT on October 1. After a rough voyage, the ship reached Alexandria at sundown the next day; it remained there for five days while most passengers traveled inland. On October 7, it began its return voyage in exceptionally rough weather. After bypassing Malta, it anchored at Cagliari, Sardinia on October 13, but was denied permission to land. Two days later, it touched at Algiers.

After a brief stop at Malaga, Spain, on October 17, the *Quaker City* landed at Gibraltar the same night. Over the next week, it took on coal, as Mark Twain and three other passengers traveled through southern Spain. On October 25, they rejoined the ship at Cadiz, where it landed the same morning. A half hour later, the ship sailed into the Atlantic. On October 28, the *Quaker City* anchored at Funchal in the Madeira Islands. Faced with enduring a quarantine, the passengers voted to sail the same night. On November 11, they reached Bermuda, where they stayed until the 15th. The *Quaker City* ended its journey at New York City on November 19.

The *Quaker City* voyage lasted 164 days, of which 46 were spent on the Atlantic and 118 on the Mediterranean and Black seas. While the ship was in the Mediterranean, Mark Twain spent roughly 66 days ashore. It is not known whether he stayed aboard or ashore at certain ports, though he told his family that he generally slept ashore when the ship was in port.

After this voyage, the *Quaker City*'s career was checkered. Its owners sold it and it briefly served as a Cuban gunrunner. In 1869 Haiti's provisional government bought it and transformed it into a warship renamed the *Republic*. It was next sold to a company that had it refitted to carry commercial cargoes between New York and Haiti. On February 22, 1871, it blew a boiler and sank off the coast of Bermuda.

More than four decades after the *Quaker City* voyage, A. B. PAINE retraced its original route and described his own travels in *The Ship-Dwellers: A Story of a Happy Cruise* (1910), which provides a kind of running commentary on *Innocents Abroad*.

The Quaker City Holy Land Excursion Unfinished play. Soon after Mark Twain returned to New York on the QUAKER CITY in November 1867, he began writing a satirical play about the voyage, encouraged by Charles Henry WEBB. After drafting just two scenes, he abandoned the effort. Elements of the play—notably the name of the ship—are closely based on aspects of the actual excursion.

The play opens in the Wall Street office of the cruise's organizer, Captain Dusenberry (modeled on Charles DUNCAN), who unctuously accepts applications for passage from a group of "old maids." His sarcastic asides indicate that his only interest is taking their money. The next scene is aboard the steamship. Two reporters— one of whom is Mark Twain himself, the other a BLUCHER-like character named Stiggers—discuss how old the other passengers are and joke about why the cruise's promised celebrities did not come. Dan Sproat (modeled on Dan SLOTE), joins them and they discuss the wearisome PILGRIMS aboard the ship until the manuscript abruptly ends.

Mark Twain's manuscript is held at Indiana University Library. It was printed privately in 1927 and published in 1968 in Dewey Ganzel's *Mark Twain Abroad: The Cruise of the "Quaker City,"* which also incorporates a related fragment from Mark Twain's NOTEBOOKS.

Quarles, John Adams (1802–1876) A favorite uncle of Mark Twain, John Quarles was married to Martha Ann (Patsy) Lampton, the sister of Jane L. Clemens. The couple had 10 children. In the mid-1830s, Quarles moved from Tennessee to FLORIDA, Missouri, where he was a successful shopkeeper and farmer. He wrote Mark

On his last visit to Quarry Farm in 1903, Mark Twain revisited the study where he did much of his best writing. (Courtesy, Library of Congress, Pictures & Prints Division)

Twain's father, John M. Clemens, a letter persuading him to bring his family to Florida and to become his partner in his store. Mark Twain recreated this incident in *The Gilded Age,* in which Colonel Sellers writes a similar letter to Si HAWKINS.

Even after the Clemens family moved to Hannibal in 1839, Mark Twain spent long summers at the Quarles farm through about 1848. Martha died in 1850; Quarles sold his farm two years later, but continued to live in the region. Mark Twain visited his uncle there in June 1855, while moving from St. Louis to Keokuk, Iowa. Although he never used Quarles as a model for a fictional character, he used his uncle's farm as the model for the Arkansas farm of Sally and Silas PHELPS in *Huckleberry Finn* and *Tom Sawyer, Detective.* He regarded his summers at the Quarles farm as the most glorious part of his youth. It was there that he had his closest acquaintanceships with black people, such as the slave Uncle Daniel who was a model for Jim in *Huckleberry Finn.* He celebrated the farm by using it as the model for the GRANGERFORD home in *Huckleberry Finn.* His notes indicate that the "Uncle Fletcher's farm" mentioned in chapter 3 of "TOM SAWYER'S CONSPIRACY" is actually Quarles's Florida farm.

Quarry Farm The home of Mark Twain's sister-in-law Susan Langdon CRANE, Quarry Farm overlooks ELMIRA, New York, and the Chemung River Valley, and takes its name from an abandoned rock quarry on the property. Jervis LANGDON bought the land in 1869 and left it to Crane when he died the following year. Crane and her husband made it their permanent home and gradually increased its size.

From 1871 to 1889, Mark Twain spent most of his summers at Quarry Farm with his family. In 1874, Crane had a small octagonal building erected on an isolated promontory for him to use as a private study. Each summer, Mark Twain spent his days there, writing such works as *Tom Sawyer, Huckleberry Finn, The Prince and the Pauper, A Tramp Abroad, Life on the Mississippi* and *Connecticut Yankee.* He last visited the farm in the summers of 1895 and 1903. His AUTOBIOGRAPHY contains several long reminiscences of his time there.

The octagonal study was moved to the Elmira College campus in 1952. In 1983, the Langdon family donated the Crane family house and 6.7 acres of the farm to the college, which created the Center for Mark Twain Studies on the site.

Quick, Dorothy (September 1, 1896–March 15, 1962) One of the first and most faithful of Mark Twain's "ANGELFISH," Quick was not quite 11 when she met him aboard the S.S. *Minnetonka,* on which they both returned home from England in July 1907. Throughout the voyage, she was Mark Twain's constant companion. Several weeks later, she and her mother visited Mark Twain at TUXEDO PARK—the first of many visits they made to his various residences from their Plainfield, New Jersey home. Quick also corresponded with Mark Twain to the day he died, receiving at least 70 letters from him or his scribes.

In addition to being a member of Mark Twain's "Aquarium Club for Angelfish," Quick belonged to his even more exclusive "Author's League." In later life she became a professional writer. Her many books include volumes of poetry and murder mysteries. She also published articles about Mark Twain in the NORTH AMERICAN REVIEW in 1935 and 1938 and a memoir, *Enchantment: A Little Girl's Friendship with Mark Twain* (1961). This book was the basis for the 1991 television film MARK TWAIN AND ME, in which Amy Stewart played Quick.

R

raft Mark Twain's first major literary use of a raft occurs in *Tom Sawyer* when Tom, Huck Finn and Joe HARPER raft downriver to JACKSON'S ISLAND to play PIRATES (chapter 13). A raft is the central focus of much of *Huckleberry Finn*, even though it figures directly into only about a fifth of the novel's chapters. In chapter 9, Jim and Huck capture a section of a lumber raft brought to Jackson's Island by the flooding Mississippi River. It is about 15 or 16 feet long and 12 feet wide, with a pine-plank deck about 6 or 7 inches above the water. When Jim and Huck leave the island in chapter 12, they tie their possessions to the raft, build a plank "wigwam" on it for shelter, and put on a mound of dirt for building fires. They also prepare an extra steering oar and a forked stick on which to hang a lantern as a running light for night travel. When they begin, they are towing a canoe that they use for trips ashore.

The fact that the raft is Huck and Jim's primary means of conveyance plays a determinative role in the development of the story, especially after they lose their canoe in chapter 16. Their original plan is to drift to CAIRO, Illinois, sell the raft and buy steamboat passage up the OHIO RIVER. After they accidentally drift past Cairo, they cannot return *up*stream on the raft, so they decide to keep drifting south until they can buy another canoe in which to return upriver. Almost immediately, however, a steamboat hits their raft, separating Jim and Huck and apparently ending their voyage. Mark Twain's working notes indicate that he was through using the raft in the narrative, and this seems to have been the point at which he set his manuscript aside for several years.

When Mark Twain resumed writing, he had Huck spend time ashore with the GRANGERFORD family. Huck then discovers that Jim is hiding nearby; the raft not only is not destroyed, Jim has repaired it and has collected fresh supplies. The moment that the Grangerford family is shattered by its feud with the SHEPHERDSONS, Huck rejoins Jim on the raft and they resume their voyage downriver as fast as they can (chapter 18). Several days later, two con men known as the KING and DUKE board the raft and take control, providing a new impetus for continuing south. After two further episodes ashore interrupt the raft journey, the voyage ends in chapter 31, when Huck hides the raft on SPANISH ISLAND and spends the remainder of the narrative with the PHELPS family near PIKESVILLE.

"Raft Chapter" Originally written for *Huckleberry Finn*, this 5,100-word chapter was omitted from the novel after it appeared in *Life on the Mississippi*. It was first restored to its originally intended place in *Huckleberry Finn* in a 1944 edition of the book. Also called the "Raft Episode" (and other things), the chapter is *not* about Jim and Huck's RAFT.

Mark Twain seems to have written most of the "Raft Chapter" along with the rest of *Huckleberry Finn*'s first 16 chapters around 1876. Several years later, when he was writing *Life on the Mississippi*, he inserted the "Raft Chapter" into that book's third chapter, titled "Frescoes of the Past," in order to illustrate life on the giant flatboats that once clogged the Mississippi. His prelude to this story recalls how he saw miles of such rafts drifting down the river during the 1840s, when he and other boys would occasionally swim out to hitch rides—exactly what Huck does in the "Raft Chapter."

When Charles L. WEBSTER prepared *Huckleberry Finn* for publication, he persuaded Mark Twain to omit the "Raft Chapter" from the novel to save space. Mark Twain agreed, since the chapter had already been published and because he thought that it contained nothing essential to the rest of the novel. Succeeding editions of *Huckleberry Finn* omitted this chapter until Bernard DEVOTO restored it in a Limited Editions Club volume in 1944. Modern MARK TWAIN PAPERS project editions of *Huckleberry Finn* also include the chapter—inserting it within chapter 16, following that chapter's second paragraph. Some other editions have printed the chapter as an appendix. The 1986 PBS television adaptation of *Huckleberry Finn* dramatized the episode, but staged it on land instead of on a raft—presumably to minimize production costs.

The "Raft Chapter"'s importance to *Huckleberry Finn* is subtle but crucial. Huck swims out to a giant raft hoping to learn how far he and Jim are from their destination, CAIRO, Illinois. He does not get an answer to this question, but does learn something else that enables him to answer the question later, at the end of chapter 16. He overhears men on the raft discussing how the clear water of the OHIO RIVER forms a visible channel in the muddy Mississippi below Cairo, where the rivers meet. When Huck later recognizes that the water on which they are floating is clear at the end of chapter 16, he concludes that "it was all up with Cairo." Without the "Raft Chapter"'s explanation of this phenomenon, his remark makes no sense.

SYNOPSIS

Impatient to learn where he and Jim are, Huck decides to visit the big raft floating near them to pick up information. He strips, swims to the raft and sneaks aboard. Thirteen tough-looking men are sitting around an open fire, passing around a jug as one man sings a ribald song. They tire of the song and tease the singer. The biggest man, Bob, claims the right to thrash the singer and boasts outrageously about his prowess, claiming, for example, to be "half-brother to the CHOLERA." Another man, who calls himself the "CHILD OF CALAMITY," counters with equally outrageous boasts. They face off, but a smaller man named DAVY gets up and thrashes both of them.

Huck meanwhile hides in the dark, smoking a pipe he finds, as another man plays a fiddle while the men dance. The men then sit down to spin yarns and get to comparing the waters of the Mississippi and Ohio rivers.

A raftsman named ED tells a ghost story about a former partner named Dick ALLBRIGHT who was pursued on the river by a haunted barrel. The climax comes when Allbright's baby, Charles William ALLBRIGHT, is found in the barrel. After Ed finishes his yarn, the other raftsmen tease him mercilessly. As Ed skulks off, the Child of Calamity finds Huck. Some men want to paint Huck blue and toss him overboard, but Davy rescues him. When asked his name, Huck fetches a big laugh by answering "Charles William Allbright." Then he calls himself "Aleck James Hopkins" and explains that he swam to the raft from his father's trading scow just for the fun of it. The men let him go, and he swims back to rejoin Jim.

Rainguesson, Noël Character in *Joan of Arc*. A purely fictional creation, Rainguesson is one of the DOMREMY boys who go to war with Joan. Free of pretension and ambition and cynical about the horrors of war, he plays the jester throughout the narrative. He especially enjoys twitting the PALADIN's vanity and considers himself the braggart's creator. His special gifts include recitation and mimicry. In ORLÉANS, he recites Louis DE CONTE's love poem to Catherine Boucher and flawlessly imitates the Paladin's boasting about imaginary battle experiences (book 2, chapter 15).

Wounded while protecting Joan during her last assault on Compiègne, Rainguesson disappears in May 1430 (book 2, chapter 41). Five months later, he escapes from his captors and rejoins de Conte at Compiègne (book 3, chapter 2). With his former lightheartedness now lost, he goes to ROUEN with de Conte and attends the public sessions of Joan's trial. De Conte's concluding chapter reveals that Rainguesson dies in the last battle against the English, which occurred in 1453.

Raleigh, Sir Walter (c. 1552, Devon, England–October 29, 1618, London) Historical English explorer and character in *1601*. A favorite of Queen ELIZABETH I, Raleigh explored the Americas during her reign and was later beheaded by King James I for insubordination. In *1601*, Raleigh is the expert gas-passer whom the CUPBEARER describes as a bloody swashbuckler and—particularly aptly—a "damned windmill." The cupbearer also alludes to Raleigh as the queen's former lover and quotes Raleigh's description of a place in the "uttermost reaches of America" where people are celibate until age 35 (the age at which Mark Twain himself married).

"IS SHAKESPEARE DEAD?" and "A MAJESTIC LITERARY FOSSIL" also mention Raleigh.

Ralph, Lester (July 19 or 29, 1877, New York, New York–April 5 or 6, 1927) Illustrator. A product of New York's Art Students League, Ralph also studied in Europe and worked as an artistic correspondent in the Turko-Greek (1897) and South African (1898–1902) wars. In 1906, HARPER's arranged for Fred STROTHMANN, who had illustrated *Extracts from Adam's Diary*, to do EVE's DIARY; however, Mark Twain wanted a more dignified treatment, so Ralph was commissioned instead. Ralph prepared more than 50 delicately ornate drawings for the new book, which has a full-page illustration at each opening. Most of the pictures depict ADAM AND EVE naked—a fact that got the book banned from at least one library.

Rambler PEN NAME that Mark Twain used in his brother's HANNIBAL JOURNAL in May 1853. He signed "Rambler" to several romantic poems, then published letters complaining about them that he signed "Grumbler." Taking advantage of Orion's absence from town, he used both pseudonyms simultaneously to carry on an acrimonious debate in the paper.

rapscallion Slang term for rascally or worthless person. Under various spellings, *rapscallion* goes back to the early 17th century; it can be found in the writings of Butler, Fielding, Smollet, Byron and others. The first book in which Mark Twain uses the term is *Innocents Abroad* (1869); chapter 54 alludes to "the rapscallions in the infernal regions down below." Chapter 58 of *Life on the Mississippi* (1883) describes the crewmen of lumber rafts as "fiddling, song-singing, whisky-drinking, breakdown-dancing rapscallions." *Huckleberry Finn* uses the word 10 times. In chapter 13, for example, Huck calls "rapscallions and dead beats" the kind of people that

Eve on a dinosaur, one of Lester Ralph's 50 drawings for Eve's Diary.

Colonel SELLERS in the first dramatic adaptation of *The Gilded Age* in 1874. After Mark Twain had Densmore's unauthorized San Francisco production stopped, he adapted Densmore's script to his own play, COLONEL SELLERS, which opened in New York City in September, with Raymond continuing as Sellers. The play ran in New York into January and Raymond toured with it for 12 years. Despite Raymond's success, Mark Twain thought his performance slighted Sellers's nobler side. Nevertheless, when he and W. D. HOWELLS wrote the play *Colonel Sellers as a Scientist* in 1884, they offered the lead to Raymond, who disliked the script and turned it down. No other actor dared take a role so closely identified with Raymond, so the play was abandoned and Mark Twain later reworked it into the novel *The American Claimant.*

One of the first AUTOBIOGRAPHY chapters that Mark Twain published in the NORTH AMERICAN REVIEW in 1906 claimed that Raymond could never play Sellers properly because he was dishonest, selfish, vulgar, ignorant, silly and heartless—an attack that Raymond's son called cowardly. A. B. PAINE omitted most of Mark Twain's attack on Raymond in his 1924 edition of *Mark Twain's Autobiography.*

Redding Town in southwestern Connecticut, located 20 miles northwest of BRIDGEPORT. In the spring of 1906, Mark Twain purchased about 248 acres of land about three miles outside the town, on Redding Road. Anxious to invest in an apparent bargain, he bought the land sight unseen after A. B. PAINE had purchased property nearby. A year later, he arranged to build a summer home on this estate and hired John Mead HOWELLS to design the house that he later called "STORMFIELD." When he went to Redding for the first time to occupy his new home on June 18, 1908, a procession of townspeople accompanied him from the train station to his house. He found the estate so peaceful and the community so congenial that he soon decided to make Redding his year-round home and gave up his NEW YORK CITY apartment. Until his DEATH in April 1910, he lived relatively quietly in Redding, entertaining his ANGELFISH friends and other guests, working on his AUTOBIOGRAPHY and playing BILLIARDS. In addition to Paine, his neighbors included Dan BEARD, biographer Ida Tarbell (1857–1944) and two of Nathaniel Hawthorne's granddaughters.

Shortly after his arrival, Mark Twain invited all his neighbors to his house. He interested himself in community affairs and helped create what became the "Mark Twain Library of Redding." He launched this project by donating his own surplus books, soliciting publishers to contribute books and helping to raise funds. After he died, his daughter Clara donated much of his personal library to the library, now located at the junction of Diamond Hill Road and Route 53.

Paine lived in Redding until 1920, returning later to

the "widow [Douglas] and good people takes the most interest in." Later, he repeatedly calls the KING and DUKE "rapscallions." When Jim says "dese kings o' ourn is regular rapscallions" in chapter 23, Huck replies that "all kings is mostly rapscallions, as fur as I can make out." In chapter 42, Aunt Sally calls Tom and Huck "little rapscallions" when she learns that they are responsible for Jim's escape. When Hank Morgan is in a London jail in chapter 37 of *Connecticut Yankee* (1889), he calls his cellmates "drunken, quarrelsome, and song-singing rapscallions." In chapter 6 of *Tom Sawyer, Detective,* Tom alludes to murderers as "rapscallions."

Raymond, John T. (April 5, 1836, Buffalo, New York– April 10, 1887, Evansville, Indiana) Stage name of comic actor John O'Brien. In a role that Gilbert B. Densmore wrote specifically for him, Raymond played spend the last two years of his life there. After he died in Florida, he was buried in Redding's Umpawaug Hill.

Redpath, James (August 24, 1833, Berwick-upon-Tweed, Scotland–February 10, 1891, New York, New York) LECTURE promoter. Soon after coming to Michigan with his family at 17, Redpath took up journalism in Detroit and was noticed by Horace GREELEY, who invited him to write for the NEW YORK TRIBUNE. Intermittently connected with the *Tribune* for three decades, Redpath became an ardent abolitionist, a supporter of Haiti, a CIVIL WAR correspondent and a postwar school superintendent in Charleston, South Carolina. He also wrote books on slavery, John Brown, Haiti and the South.

In early 1869, Redpath established the Boston Lyceum Bureau to take advantage of the growing national interest in lecturers. By standardizing fees and putting lecture-tour organization on a professional basis, he attracted such popular speakers as Henry Ward BEECHER, Josh BILLINGS, Ralph Waldo EMERSON, Greeley, Julia Ward Howe, Petroleum V. NASBY, Bayard TAYLOR and Henry David Thoreau. He also signed Mark Twain to two long tours (November 1869–January 1870 and October 1871–February 1872). Although he could not persuade Mark Twain to tour again, the two men remained friends. In 1885, Redpath took shorthand notes for Mark Twain's AUTOBIOGRAPHY while he was working with U. S. GRANT on the latter's memoirs. Meanwhile, Redpath sold his lecture bureau to James B. POND in 1875 and turned his attention to promoting Irish self-rule and other interests. He became editor of the NORTH AMERICAN REVIEW in 1886, but resigned the following year after suffering a paralyzing stroke. Mark Twain's AUTOBIOGRAPHY fondly recalls the congenial atmosphere at Redpath's BOSTON offices on School Street.

Reed, Thomas Brackett (October 18, 1839, Portland, Maine–December 7, 1902, Washington, D.C.) A Republican politician, Reed started a law career in California during the early 1860s, then had a long career in Maine politics. During two decades in Congress (1877–99), he rose to become Speaker of the House (1889–91). Mark Twain and Reed became friends through H. H. ROGERS after Reed retired from politics. They both cruised together aboard Rogers's yacht, the KANAWHA, in August 1901 and March–April 1902 and saw each other in Maine in August 1902. At a banquet for Mark Twain's birthday the following November, Reed honored Mark Twain with what proved to be his own last public speech. He died less than two weeks later, on December 7—the same day that Thomas NAST died. A eulogy that Mark Twain wrote for Reed in HARPER'S WEEKLY was later reprinted in EUROPE AND ELSEWHERE (1923).

Reid, Whitelaw (October 27, 1837, Xenia, Ohio–December 15, 1912, London) Journalist and statesman. Reid began his career as a journalist in Ohio, where he also got involved in political campaigns. He gained a national reputation as a correspondent during the early years of the CIVIL WAR and joined Horace GREELEY's staff at the NEW YORK TRIBUNE in 1868. After Greeley died in 1872, Reid became the paper's editor-in-chief—a post he held until President Theodore ROOSEVELT named him ambassador to Great Britain in 1905. Meanwhile, he served as President Benjamin Harrison's ambassador to France (1889–92) and he ran for vice-president on Harrison's unsuccessful ticket in 1892. President William McKinley made Reid a peace commissioner at the end of the Spanish-American War and Roosevelt sent him to England as special ambassador to King EDWARD VII's coronation in 1902.

Under Reid's editorship, the *Tribune* increased its circulation and rose from near bankruptcy, thanks partly to his recruitment of contributors such as Mark Twain and Bret HARTE. In late 1881 Mark Twain heard rumors that Reid was regularly slandering him in his newspaper. Infuriated, he determined to write a sensational biography of Reid that would ruin him. For several weeks in early 1882 he furiously collected material on Reid, whom he dubbed "Outlaw Reid," and planned his new book. After Mark Twain's wife insisted that he check up on the rumors, he spent several months scrutinizing Reid's *Tribune* and concluded that the rumors were false, so he abandoned his plan to write Reid's biography.

When Mark Twain went to OXFORD UNIVERSITY in 1907, Reid officially honored him in London. Early the next year Mark Twain returned the favor by speaking at a dinner in Reid's honor in New York City.

Rhodes, Cecil (July 5, 1853, Hertfordshire, England–March 26, 1902, Cape Town, South Africa) Anglo–South African industrialist. After coming to SOUTH AFRICA for his health in 1870, Rhodes soon dominated its newly discovered diamond fields and began to develop his lifelong ambition to expand British rule to the north. His election to the Cape parliament in 1880 gave him political influence and in 1890 he became the colony's prime minister. By then, his interests in the new Transvaal gold fields were increasing his financial power, and he headed a British chartered company that took control of present Zimbabwe and Zambia.

Mark Twain arrived in South Africa in May 1896, just after Rhodes's influence had peaked. On January 2, Rhodes's ally Dr. Leander Starr Jameson (1853–1917) had been captured while leading a filibustering force into the Transvaal's independent Boer republic. Exposure of Rhodes's complicity in the affair brought down his own government and took the chartered company out of his control. Mark Twain visited Jameson's men in Pretoria's prison and struggled to make sense of

South African politics. *Following the Equator* is filled with jabs at Rhodes, whom it calls a marsupial (chapter 29). Chapter 13 contains a tall tale about Rhodes going to AUSTRALIA—a place that Rhodes never visited—in 1870 and making his fortune by cornering the wool market. The book also discusses Rhodes seriously and levels heavy charges against Rhodes's chartered company for its harsh enslavement of the Africans it has conquered (chapters 65–69).

Rhone River (Rhône)   Rising in the central Swiss ALPS, the Rhone flows west through Lake Geneva into France, turning south at Lyons—where the Saône joins it—passing through St. Etienne, Valence, Avignon and Arles before emptying into the Gulf of Lions near MARSEILLES. Mark Twain first saw the Rhone in July 1867 when he took a train from Marseilles to Paris; he mentions it in chapter 12 of *Innocents Abroad*. In late September 1891, he spent 10 days boating down the river from the canal connecting it to Lake Bourget in Savoie, to Arles, returning by train. He began a manuscript about this trip that he hoped to develop into a book to be called THE INNOCENTS ADRIFT, but described just half the journey and left it unfinished. In 1923, A. B. PAINE published an abridgement as "DOWN THE RHÔNE." Mark Twain also mentions his Rhone trip in "THE LOST NAPOLEON" and in chapter 55 of *Following the Equator*.

Rice, Clement T. (*fl.* 1860s–80s)   A reporter for the VIRGINIA CITY UNION during the early 1860s, Rice became a close friend of Mark Twain, who worked for the rival VIRGINIA CITY TERRITORIAL ENTERPRISE. They conducted a playful rivalry in print, with Mark Twain calling Rice the "Unreliable," while Rice called him the "Reliable." Rice also appears in fictional guise in chapter 43 of *Roughing It* as BOGGS. In May 1863, Mark Twain went with Rice on his first visit to SAN FRANCISCO.

Rice also served as registrar of the United States Land Office in Carson City (1862–64) and dabbled in prospecting. He reportedly struck it rich and went into business in New York City, where Mark Twain saw him in March 1867. By the 1880s, however, he was appealing to Mark Twain for help in getting a job after their friendship ended.

Richard III   Tragedy by SHAKESPEARE based on the life of England's King Richard III (1452–1485). The play's climax comes when Richmond kills Richard in a sword fight (act 5, scene 5). In chapters 20–21 of *Huckleberry Finn,* the KING and DUKE practice this scene for a "Shaksperean Revival" that they stage in BRICKSVILLE in chapter 22. The King plays Richmond, while the Duke plays Richard. The HAMLET soliloquy that the Duke prepares for the King also contains several lines from *Richard III.*

Richard III was a popular vehicle for companies touring America in the early 19th century. *Life on the Missis-sippi* recalls two English actors whom Mark Twain saw perform the sword fight scene when he was a boy in Hannibal. Their performance moved a young apprentice blacksmith to run off to St. Louis to become an actor (chapter 51).

Richardson, Albert Deane (October 6, 1833, Franklin, Massachusetts–December 2, 1869, New York, New York)   Journalist. One of the first authors signed by the AMERICAN PUBLISHING COMPANY, Richardson is best known for *The Secret Service* (1865), about his experiences as a CIVIL WAR correspondent, and *Beyond the Mississippi* (1867), a collection of his earlier writings about the Far West. After both works enjoyed large sales as SUBSCRIPTION BOOKS, Richardson helped persuade Mark Twain to let his publisher handle *Innocents Abroad*. Several illustrations from Richardson's *Beyond the Mississippi* were later reused in Mark Twain's *Roughing It.*

Ridgeway, Sister   Minor character in *Huckleberry Finn.* One of the nosy PIKESVILLE neighbors who visit the Phelpses after Jim's escape attempt in chapter 41.

Riffelberg   Mountain in southern SWITZERLAND between the MATTERHORN and the town of ZERMATT. In late August 1878, Mark Twain and Joseph TWICHELL spent four hours hiking to the Riffelberg's 8,480-foot summit, spent the night at an inn, then ascended to the Gorner Grat, a ridge 2,000 feet higher, and visited the mountain's Gorner Glacier. *A Tramp Abroad* stretches this gentle mountaineering experience into its most extended BURLESQUE. Chapters 37–40 recount a massive week-long expedition to climb the Riffelberg in which the narrator and HARRIS employ 154 men, 51 animals and tons of equipment. After reaching the summit, they attempt to return by riding the slow-moving glacier down to Zermatt.

Rigi-Kulm   Mountain overlooking SWITZERLAND's Lake LUCERNE, near WEGGIS. The highest peak of Rigi, Rigi-Kulm (5,905 feet) is a famous spot from which tourists watch alpine sunrises. In mid-August 1878, Mark Twain walked to the top of Rigi-Kulm with Joseph TWICHELL while his wife and another friend ascended in an open car. After one night in a summit hotel, they descended in a train. *A Tramp Abroad* expands this incident into a BURLESQUE in which the narrator and HARRIS climb Rigi solely to see an alpine sunrise, but miss it on four consecutive days (chapters 28–29).

Riley, John Henry (1830?–September 17, 1872)   Journalist and prospector. Originally from Philadelphia, Riley joined the GOLD RUSH to CALIFORNIA during the 1850s and became a friend and drinking companion of Mark Twain in SAN FRANCISCO during the mid-1860s when both were newspaper reporters. He appears in

The narrator of A Tramp Abroad *never saw a finer sight than the entire Riffelberg expedition roped together in a procession 3,122 feet long.*

Roughing It as the witty "mendicant Blucher" of chapter 59. Riley later roomed with Mark Twain in WASHINGTON, D.C., where he was a correspondent for the SAN FRANCISCO ALTA CALIFORNIA and clerk for a congressional committee on mining. Mark Twain later praised Riley's conversation, wit and bravado in a sketch published in the BUFFALO EXPRESS (October 1870) and used Riley as a character in *A Tramp Abroad*'s tale "THE MAN WHO PUT UP AT GADSBY'S."

When Mark Twain heard about SOUTH AFRICA's diamond strikes in 1870, he invited Riley to go there as his proxy to collect notes for a book that he would write himself in the same style as *Innocents Abroad*. Since the only wealth Riley had ever gotten from mining was experience, he accepted the offer of transportation and a three-month stake. The possibility of also finding some diamonds appealed to him, as did the prospect of working the lecture circuit after he returned. On January 7, 1871, he sailed for South Africa, by way of England. He worked at Kimberley's diamond fields for three months without finding a single gem, then returned to the United States the following fall. By then,

Mark Twain was too distracted with other matters to discuss South Africa with him, and Riley was suffering from cancer. He went to Philadelphia, where he acted as consul for South Africa's Orange Free State republic until he died in September 1872. Mark Twain never used Riley's notes—about 19 pages of which are held by the MARK TWAIN PAPERS project.

When Mark Twain visited South Africa himself in 1896, he retraced part of Riley's earlier route and made a point of seeing the diamond fields. In his South African lectures, he got laughs by suggesting that Riley had purchased mining claims on his behalf that might make him the rightful owner of the diamond fields.

Ritchie, George (*fl.* 1850s–1880s) Steamboat PILOT with whom Mark Twain apprenticed. *Life on the Mississippi* introduces Ritchie as George EALER's cub on the PENNSYLVANIA in chapter 18 and mentions him in chapters 28, 49 and 51. Occasionally, Mark Twain steered during Ealer's watches, while Ritchie impersonated the tyrannical William BROWN. In 1858, Ritchie survived the explosion of the *Pennsylvania*. In later years, he also survived another steamboat explosion near Memphis in which he was so badly injured that he had to cling to a cotton bale with his teeth while awaiting rescue. Mark Twain saw Ritchie again in 1882, when the latter was piloting under Horace BIXBY on the CITY OF BATON ROUGE. By then, Ritchie and Bixby had patented a chart system for making river crossings.

Ritter, Karl   Character in *Life on the Mississippi*. Ritter is the central figure in a FRAME-STORY within a tale that spans chapters 31 and 32. In chapter 31—which Mark Twain evidently began writing in 1881—the narrator explains to his companions why he wants to get off the steamboat in NAPOLEON, Arkansas. He recalls a recent visit to MUNICH, in which he met an old consumptive named Karl Ritter. Ritter then narrates his own story, which is subtitled "A Dying Man's Confession."

A German, Ritter once lived in Arkansas, where his wife and daughter were murdered by a housebreaker during the CIVIL WAR. Vowing revenge, he tracked down the murderer, Franz ADLER, using FINGERPRINT evidence. He then disguised himself as a fortune teller in order to ingratiate himself with Adler and his partner, Private KRUGER—to whom he was grateful for trying to stop Adler from murdering his family. During a midnight meeting, he stabbed Adler to death in the dark. Over the next 15 or 16 years, Ritter wandered the Earth, until settling in Munich, where he got work in a "dead house." There he watched over corpses, in case any were still alive. One day, a body did come to life; it proved to be Adler, who gloated over Ritter's horrified realization that it was actually Kruger whom he had killed years before. Ritter then sat and savored Adler's slow, painful death. Afterward, he searched Adler's things and learned that Kruger had a son living in MANNHEIM. He secretly sent the son conscience money, while tracking down a watch containing a note revealing where Kruger hid $10,000 in Napoleon, Arkansas. Since Ritter is nearing death, he gives the note to the narrator, asking him to retrieve the money and forward it to Kruger's son.

In chapter 32, the narrator's companions, THOMPSON AND ROGERS, suggest that Kruger's son—a humble shoemaker—not only has no need for $10,000, but that such a fortune would actually harm him. They argue the amount down to just $500 and then decide simply to send him "a chromo." After the three men fight over how they will divide the money among themselves, the narrator asks the startled captain of the GOLD DUST to let him off at Napoleon. Uncle MUMFORD informs him that the Arkansas River has washed the town away.

Riverdale-on-the-Hudson   NEW YORK town. Now a part of the Bronx, NEW YORK CITY's northernmost borough, Riverdale was a separate residential community when Mark Twain rented a house there in 1901. Formerly the home of publisher William Henry Appleton (1814–1899), the three-story house was built on a spacious

Mark Twain while living in Riverdale in early 1903. (Courtesy, Library of Congress, Pictures & Prints Division)

property fronting the eastern bank of the Hudson River on West 252nd Street; it is now a New York City landmark known as Wave Hill. Mark Twain's family lived there from October 1901 through July 1903. Despite Mark Twain's professed desire to economize, he entertained lavishly at Riverdale and especially liked the house's huge dining room. He interrupted his Riverdale residence by spending the summer of 1902 at YORK HARBOR, Maine. Afterward, his wife Livy's deteriorating health frequently required her to be isolated from him. In July 1903, the family left Riverdale for ELMIRA before going to ITALY for Livy's health.

Robards, John Lewis (1838–1925)   Boyhood friend of Mark Twain. The son of a Hannibal miller, Robards attended school with Mark Twain and distinguished himself by regularly capturing Mr. DAWSON's weekly "amicability" medal, as Mark Twain took honors in the spelling bees. In 1849, Robards and his father joined the GOLD RUSH to CALIFORNIA for two years. In 1853, his father's flour won prizes at the Crystal Palace Exposition in NEW YORK CITY; the news generated by this event possibly helped stimulate Mark Twain's trip to New York later that year. As Mark Twain worked as a *jour* printer and PILOT, Robards attended the University of MISSOURI and earned a law degree at the University of Louisville. He returned to Hannibal in 1860 to practice law, but the CIVIL WAR soon brought him and Mark Twain together again in the MARION RANGERS. "THE PRIVATE HISTORY OF A CAMPAIGN THAT FAILED" depicts Robards—who changed the spelling of his name to "RoBards"—as "Dunlap," the foolish romantic who changes his name to "d'Unlap."

After the war, Robards became a civic leader in Hannibal, where he helped found MOUNT OLIVET CEMETERY and personally supervised the reinterment of Mark Twain's father and younger brother from another cemetery in 1876. He was later a director of Hannibal's Home for the Friendless, an institution with which Laura HAWKINS was also involved. Mark Twain saw Robards during each of his visits to Hannibal and corresponded with him until at least 1908. In 1913 Robards was one of the commissioners named by the state who arranged for Frederick HIBBARD to sculpt a statue of Mark Twain as a monument.

Robinson, Doctor   Minor character in *Tom Sawyer*. Robinson appears only in the grave-robbing scene in chapter 9, in which he, INJUN JOE and Muff POTTER dig up the recently buried body of Hoss WILLIAMS. When Injun Joe accuses Robinson of having treated him badly five years earlier and threatens him with his fist, Robinson knocks him down. Potter then jumps Robinson, only to get himself knocked out; at that moment, Injun Joe stabs Robinson to death with Potter's knife. Tom Sawyer and Huck Finn happen to witness the murder, and they return to the site the next day along with most of the townspeople, who see Robinson's body lying on the ground. Muff Potter is arrested for his murder.

Mark Twain's own dramatization of *Tom Sawyer* depicts the doctor as an unpleasant and pushy man who forces Potter into grave-robbing.

Robinson, Doctor   Character in *Huckleberry Finn*. A "big iron-jawed man," Robinson is introduced in chapter 24 as a friend of the late Peter WILKS. The first person to dispute the KING and DUKE's claim to be Wilks's brothers, Robinson belittles the King's English accent and laughs at his bogus explanation of "ORGIES." In chapter 29, Robinson heads an inquiry that exposes the frauds.

Robinson, Judge (Sim)   Character in *Pudd'nhead Wilson* and "THOSE EXTRAORDINARY TWINS." A DAWSON'S LANDING judge, Robinson makes several brief appearances. In chapter 5, he congratulates Patsy COOPER when the CAPELLO twins arrive as her boarders. He is mentioned in chapter 12 as the presiding judge at Luigi Capello's assault trial, but does not actually appear in the chapter. In the next chapter, he is among the town leaders who ask David WILSON to run for mayor. He is later mentioned as the coroner who attends to York DRIS-COLL's murder (chapter 19). He is *at* the ensuing murder trial, in which he appears to have some official role, but he is not named as the presiding judge—who is identified only as a "veteran" (chapter 21).

Robinson has a larger role in the published excerpts of "Those Extraordinary Twins," Mark Twain's earlier version of the story. In chapter 5, he presides over the comical assault trial of the Capellos, who are SIAMESE TWINS in this version. As a *new* judge without legal training, Robinson knows little about trial procedure and takes pride in running a court that disregards legal precedent. When he senses that the trial is headed toward a not-guilty verdict, he insists that *someone* must be found guilty. His inexperience is particularly evident in his failure to get Patsy Cooper to behave properly when she testifies. Despite his unorthodox conduct, Robinson is a popular judge because his decisions are regarded as impartial and just. His blustering behavior recalls *Roughing It*'s Ned BLAKELY, whom Mark Twain modeled on Captain Ned WAKEMAN. Indeed, it may be significant that one of the witnesses whom Robinson hears testify in "Those Extraordinary Twins" is named Wakeman.

Rogers, Ben   Minor character in *Tom Sawyer* and *Huckleberry Finn*. A friend of Tom Sawyer, Ben is one of only three boys identified by name as helping to whitewash the FENCE in chapter 2 of *Tom Sawyer*. He pays an apple for the privilege. Though he is apparently Tom's close friend, he is mentioned only in passing in later chapters. Toward the end of *Tom Sawyer*, Tom names Ben as one of the boys he wants to ask to join his new GANG; Ben appears briefly as a gang member in the early chapters of *Huckleberry Finn*. Ben has a sister, Sally, whom Becky THATCHER invites to her picnic in chapter 18 of *Tom Sawyer*.

Rogers, Billy   The prototype of Tom SAWYER, Billy is the diarist of one of Mark Twain's earliest attempts at straight fiction, a story posthumously published as "BOY'S MANUSCRIPT." Billy, whose age is not clear, is obsessed with the ups and downs of courting eight-year-old AMY—the prototype of Becky THATCHER. Many of his thoughts and actions anticipate those of Tom in *Tom Sawyer*. Billy also has in him some of the adult Mark Twain, who was courting his future wife Livy at the time he wrote this story. Billy fantasizes about falling down outside Amy's house so that he will be taken inside for loving care; Mark Twain actually had such an experience at Livy's house. Billy, however, seems more fickle than either Tom Sawyer or Mark Twain; by the end of the story, he has forgotten Amy and is obsessed with 19-year-old Laura Miller.

Rogers, Henry Huttleston (January 29, 1840, Mattapoisett, Massachusetts–May 19, 1909, New York, New York)   Standard Oil Company executive. Rogers was regarded as one of the most powerful and ruthless industrialists in America when Mark Twain first met him in the fall of 1893. A self-made man who grew up in Fairhaven, Massachusetts, Rogers began his career in Pennsylvania's oil fields and helped found Standard Oil in 1874. He became an expert in oil production and a power in distribution. By 1890, he was vice-president and director of Standard Oil and one of the wealthiest industrialists in America, with assets later valued at $100 million.

Rogers admired Mark Twain's writing and quickly indicated his willingness to help him with business problems when they met in the fall of 1893. Later that year, he went to CHICAGO to inspect the PAIGE COMPOSITOR in which Mark Twain had invested heavily. Rogers helped Mark Twain renegotiate his Paige contracts, but later concluded that the machine had no commercial value. Rogers was also on hand in early 1894, when Mark Twain's publishing firm, Charles L. WEBSTER & COMPANY, failed. After Mark Twain assigned power of attorney to him in March, Rogers used it to assign all of Mark Twain's copyrights to his wife Livy. When Webster declared BANKRUPTCY, Rogers had Livy declared the company's primary creditor and arranged the plan that enabled Mark Twain to pay off his debts in full. As Mark Twain spent most of the next seven years abroad, Rogers and his secretary Katharine I. Harrison (c. 1867–1935) managed his business affairs in America. Rogers personally negotiated with Mark Twain's publishers and arranged a major new book contract with HARPER'S in 1895.

In addition to managing Mark Twain's business affairs, Rogers became an intimate friend, with whom Mark Twain drank, played poker and BILLIARDS, yachted and attended events such as boxing matches. Mark Twain often stayed at Rogers's East 78th Street mansion in NEW YORK CITY and at his Fairhaven home. Their friendship strengthened after Mark Twain resettled in New York in 1900, especially as Livy's declining health left him more on his own. After Livy died in 1904, Mark Twain drew even closer to Rogers. He spent considerable time yachting with Rogers and his friends on the KANAWHA and went with Rogers to BERMUDA in early 1908. Rogers died in May 1909, hours before Mark Twain arrived in New York City to visit him. Mark Twain was a pallbearer at Rogers's New York funeral, but did not attend his burial in Fairhaven.

Mark Twain's relationship with Rogers is recorded in *Mark Twain's Correspondence with Henry Huttleston Rogers, 1893–1909* (1969), a collection of 462 letters edited by Lewis Leary. Mark Twain was also close to other members of Rogers's family, especially his son Harry Rogers (1879–1935), to whom he dedicated *Following the Equator*. His correspondence with Harry's wife, Mary Rogers (1879–1956), was published in 1961 in a small volume edited by Lewis Leary.

Rome Capital of ITALY. When Mark Twain first visited Rome in 1867, the city was a papal state protected by France; to enter it he had his passport visaed at FLORENCE. After the fall of NAPOLEON III in 1870, Italian troops occupied Rome and made it the capital of the whole country. Mark Twain reached Rome around July 27, 1867; about five days later he left for NAPLES by train. Chapters 26–28 of *Innocents Abroad*, which describe this period, draw heavily on a guidebook by William H. Neligan and on Mark Twain's imagination. The result mixes descriptions of standard sights, such as the catacombs, the Forum and St. Peter's Cathedral, with irrelevant anecdotes and playful burlesques. An example is chapter 26's ancient playbill of an extravaganza at the Coliseum, followed by a review from the *Roman Daily Battle-Ax*. This burlesque is reminiscent of "THE KILLING OF JULIUS CAESAR 'LOCALIZED,' " a newspaper sketch that he wrote in 1865. Chapter 28 of *Innocents Abroad* discusses the Vatican's patronage of the arts, in particular its policy of buying up antiquities found within its domains—a subject that inspired Mark Twain's short story "The Legend of the CAPITOLINE VENUS" (1869).

Mark Twain returned to Rome with his family on October 28, 1878 for a two-week visit that *A Tramp Abroad* reduces to a single sentence in chapter 50. He and his family were also there from late March through late April 1892.

Romeo and Juliet Tragedy by SHAKESPEARE. A play about lovers belonging to feuding families, *Romeo and Juliet* ends with the lovers killing themselves—thereby moving their families to end the feud. *Huckleberry Finn* has both indirect and direct references to the play. In chapter 18, Harney SHEPHERDSON and Sophia GRANGERFORD elope to get away from their feuding families. Unlike Shakespeare's lovers, they successfully escape and their families use their elopement as an excuse to destroy each other. In chapters 20–21, the KING and DUKE rehearse the balcony scene from act 2, scene 2 of *Romeo and Juliet* for a "Shaksperean Revival" staged in BRICKSVILLE in chapter 22. The elderly King protests that if he plays the youthful Juliet, his bald head and whiskers will "look oncommon odd." The Duke assures him that "these country jakes won't ever think of that."

Roosevelt, Franklin Delano (January 30, 1882, Hyde Park, New York–April 12, 1945, Warm Springs, Georgia) Thirty-second president of the United States (1933–45). According to Cyril CLEMENS, Roosevelt said that he met Mark Twain as a child and that he borrowed his 1932 campaign phrase "NEW DEAL" from *Connecticut Yankee*. On January 15, 1935, Roosevelt launched the year-long celebration of Mark Twain's centennial birthday by giving a radio speech from Washington, D.C., where he pressed a telegraph key to illuminate the new lighthouse on CARDIFF HILL. On September 4, 1936, he visited Hannibal and dedicated the MARK TWAIN MEMORIAL BRIDGE. An avid stamp collector, Roosevelt may have been instrumental in having Mark Twain put on a POSTAGE STAMP in 1940. According to Cyril Clemens, Roosevelt even considered having Mark Twain's image put on the 50¢ piece—an honor that went instead to another former printer, Benjamin FRANKLIN, in 1948.

Roosevelt, Theodore (October 17, 1858, Hyde Park, New York–January 6, 1919, Sagamore Hill, New York) Twenty-sixth president of the United States (1901–09). After gaining fame in a Spanish-American War battle in 1898, Roosevelt was elected governor of NEW YORK. Two years later he was elected vice-president under William McKinley, whose assassination in July 1901 made Roosevelt the youngest president in American history.

Mark Twain evidently met Roosevelt around 1886, when the latter was seeking the Republican nomination for mayor of New York City. In 1887 or 1888, Mark Twain considered inviting Roosevelt to publish a book about his life in the West with Charles L. WEBSTER & COMPANY, but nothing came of this idea. They saw each other occasionally over the next two decades and were probably last together when Mark Twain dined at the White House in November 1905. Mark Twain enjoyed Roosevelt's company and liked him as a man, but disliked his political impulsiveness and his tendency to switch positions on issues. Roosevelt's flamboyance and success in international affairs earned him popularity, but Mark Twain thought him an immature showoff— "the Tom Sawyer of the political world"—and eventually rated him the worst president in American history. His AUTOBIOGRAPHY describes Roosevelt as having large, fine and generous impulses, but an inability to stick to one impulse long enough to see how it will turn out.

Rossmore, Earl of Character in *The American Claimant*, which opens in his Cholmondeley Castle. A direct descendant of William the Conqueror and the father of Lord BERKELEY, Rossmore is 70 years old, tall, erect and "stern-browed." With large estates and a huge income, he is more than slightly miffed that his position is challenged by Simon LATHERS, an impoverished American relation. He is also appalled by his son's determination to go to America to trade places with the new American claimant, Colonel SELLERS. Eventually, however, he approves of his son's marriage to Sellers's daughter and finds that he even likes Sellers himself.

After Colonel Sellers declares himself the Earl of Rossmore, he gives the name "Rossmore Towers" to his shabby two-story house at 14,042 Sixteenth Street, WASHINGTON, D.C. (chapter 4).

Rouen French city in which JOAN OF ARC was executed. Located on the Seine River, 70 miles northwest of PARIS, Rouen was occupied by England in 1419. Eleven years later, the English ransomed Joan of Arc from her Burgundian captors, through Bishop Pierre CAUCHON. They imprisoned her in Rouen in December 1430 and tried her there for heresy the following spring. On May 30,

1431, she was burned at the stake in Rouen. The French recaptured the city in 1449.

Mark Twain spent most of October 1894 in Rouen and made the city the principal setting for book 3 of his novel, *Joan of Arc*, which he later finished in Paris. Rouen is evidently also the place where Cathy ALISON lived with her parents before they died in "A HORSE'S TALE."

Roughing It (1872) Mark Twain's second major book, *Roughing It* is a loose account of the five and a half years that he spent in the Far West during the early 1860s. It begins with the journey that he and his brother Orion Clemens made in July 1861, when they traveled by steamboat and STAGECOACH from Missouri to NEVADA, where Orion became SECRETARY in the new territorial government. After a brief stint as Orion's private secretary, Mark Twain dabbled in MINING and began contributing sketches to the VIRGINIA CITY TERRITORIAL ENTERPRISE and other western papers. In the fall of 1862, he gave up prospecting and joined the *Enterprise* staff until he moved to SAN FRANCISCO in May 1864. From then until the end of 1866, San Francisco was his base. Through these western years, Mark Twain became a professional writer and adopted his famous pen name; he also formed important lifelong friendships and acquired a longing to become wealthy.

While *Roughing It* is based on Mark Twain's real experiences in 1861–66, it is neither straight AUTOBIOGRAPHY nor a travel book in the same sense as *Innocents Abroad* (1869). It differs from *Innocents* in covering a much longer period and in being written much longer after its events took place. Further, while Mark Twain

Roughing It*'s young narrator dreams about Indians, deserts and silver mining the night before taking passage on a Missouri River steamboat.*

built *Innocents* around travel letters written on his journey, he wrote most of *Roughing It* from memory, supplemented by his brother's notes and by articles that he wrote for western newspapers. The book's 16 chapters on Hawaii resemble *Innocents* in construction and tone, but are so different from the rest of *Roughing It* that they hardly seem an integral part of the book.

Roughing It embroiders many episodes, invents others and overlooks some of the most important things that Mark Twain did during his years in the West. It does not, for example, mention how he became "MARK TWAIN" or tell about the HOAXES and the JUMPING FROG STORY that helped make him famous. Many real episodes that it does describe are presented out of sequence, and most are exaggerated or otherwise embellished. However, while *Roughing It* may be dubious as biography, it is an invaluable historical document that contains some of Mark Twain's best humorous writing. Mark Twain was in NEVADA during its first silver boom, he was in CALIFORNIA during the immediate aftermath of its GOLD RUSH and he was in HAWAII when American interest in the islands was rising. *Roughing It*'s descriptions of these and other developments vividly capture the authentic flavor of the times.

A prime reason for not regarding *Roughing It* as autobiography is that its unnamed narrator is younger and more naive than Mark Twain himself actually was during the early 1860s. In the first chapter, the narrator describes himself as "young and ignorant." He later implies that he is so young that Brigham YOUNG is not even sure whether he is a boy or a girl (chapter 13). A dominant theme of early chapters is the tenderfoot narrator's disillusionments. His romantic image of INDIANS is shattered when he encounters the GOSIUTE (chapter 19). His first prospecting trip in Nevada teaches him that *nothing* that glitters is gold (chapter 28). When he and several companions are later lost in a blizzard, he discovers other long-cherished western myths to be false, such as the possibility of starting a fire with a pistol and the notion that horses stay with their masters in a crisis (chapter 32).

SYNOPSIS

One of Mark Twain's longest books at 172,473 words, *Roughing It* is divided into 79 chapters and three appendixes. The first 21 chapters cover the narrator's journey from St. Louis to St. Joseph, Missouri by steamboat followed by a three-week stagecoach trip from St. Joseph to Carson City, Nevada, during which he crosses the Great Plains and the Rocky Mountains. Chapter 21 begins his stay in Carson City, where he drifts from one money-making scheme to another. In chapter 26, he begins a brief prospecting career that takes him to the HUMBOLDT and ESMERALDA mining districts. By chapter 42, he has given up on mining and settles down in VIRGINIA CITY as a newspaper reporter. Two years later,

he goes to SAN FRANCISCO (chapters 56–59). His time there is interrupted by a sojourn in a California gold-mining district (chapters 60–61). After returning to San Francisco, he takes a reportorial assignment to go the Sandwich (Hawaiian) Islands (chapters 62–77). On his next return to San Francisco, he takes up LECTURING and makes a brief tour of northern California and western Nevada before leaving the Pacific Coast (chapters 78–79). The book ends with brief comments on his return to the East Coast and an allusion to visiting his boyhood home.

While the synopsis that follows is not strictly a condensation of *Roughing It*, it occasionally uses Mark Twain's own words and spellings. Parenthetical insertions, such as dates and names, are taken from sources outside of the chapters in which they appear.

Chapter 1
The narrator recalls a moment 10 or 12 years earlier when his brother (Orion Clemens) is appointed SECRETARY of the new NEVADA Territory. He envies his brother—especially the long, strange journey he will undertake. When invited to accompany him as a "private secretary," he jumps at the chance and looks forward to spending about three months in Nevada. They begin their journey with a six-day STEAMBOAT voyage up the MISSOURI RIVER to St. Joseph.

Chapter 2
At a St. Joseph stage office the brothers pay $150 each for passage to CARSON CITY on an overland STAGECOACH. Early the next day (July 26), they learn that they can only take 25 pounds of luggage each. After shipping their surplus back to St. Louis, they have only minimal clothing, four pounds of United States statutes, a six-pound unabridged dictionary, guns, blankets and tobacco. The narrator carries a Smith and Wesson seven-shooter; George BEMIS, their only fellow passenger, carries an Allen revolver. They begin their journey by riding into the Great Plains of Kansas, sharing their coach with 2,700 pounds of mailbags. Every 10 miles they change horses. Later a woman passenger boards the coach for a 50-mile leg. She is as silent as the SPHINX until the narrator makes the mistake of speaking to her—then she never stops talking.

Chapter 3
Early the next morning the coach stops abruptly when its thoroughbrace breaks under the heavy load of mail. The passengers turn out and help remove the mailbags. After the coach is repaired, its conductor reloads only half of the bags inside the passenger compartment, where the travelers find they make excellent seats. As the journey continues, the narrator occasionally sleeps atop the coach and learns that drivers and conductors also often sleep while their coaches are moving.

They pass through Marysville, over Big Blue and Little Sandy and enter NEBRASKA at Big Sandy, about

180 miles out from St. Joseph. When they see their first "jackass rabbit," they entertain themselves by shooting at it. They also encounter SAGEBRUSH, whose inedible nature recalls a moment in SYRIA when a camel ate the narrator's overcoat.

Chapter 4

After the passengers adapt to sleeping on the mailbags, they awaken only when the horses are changed; otherwise, they tumble about happily with the unabridged dictionary inside the coach. On the third morning, they stop at a station where the driver ignores the admiring hostler, innkeeper and others. The station consists of squalid, sparsely furnished adobe buildings in which they are served an inedible meal with slumgullion. After exchanging their horses for six mules, they continue their journey to the North Platte River and Fort Kearney, 300 miles and 56 hours out from St. Joseph.

Chapter 5

On their fourth morning, the travelers see their first prairie dog villages, antelope, and coyote. An allegory of want, the coyote is always poor, luckless, friendless and despised, yet is capable of unimaginable speed and endurance.

Chapter 6

The great system of stagecoach stations between St. Joseph and SACRAMENTO, California employs numerous people. At the top are about eight agents, or superintendents, each of whom is responsible for 250 miles of the line. Under them are conductors who are responsible for seeing individual coaches through their routes. Next come the drivers, who are changed on the coaches every day. At the bottom are station-keepers and hostlers—low, rough characters, many of whom are fugitives from the law. The whole system is run by Ben Holliday (Ben Holladay, 1819–1887). The narrator recounts an incident during his travels in PALESTINE, when a young man named Jack (VAN NOSTRAND) naively compared Holliday to Moses.

At noon on the fifth day, they reach Overland City (JULESBURG), 470 miles from St. Joseph.

Chapter 7

After an hour in Overland City, the travelers continue to the South Platte River. Their new vehicle, a "mud-wagon," breaks down on the sixth morning, when they are about 550 miles out from St. Joseph. During this delay, they join a buffalo hunt in which a wounded bull chases Bemis up a tree. Bemis's description of shooting the buffalo reminds the narrator of a liar named Eckert he once met in Siam (which Mark Twain never visited) who owned a coconut-eating cat.

Chapter 8

After keeping a sharp lookout, the passengers finally see a pony express rider zoom by; then they pass through Scott's Bluffs Pass and see alkali water in the road. They also pass the site of the Indian mail robbery and massacre of 1856.

Chapter 9

That night, they go through Fort Laramie, reaching the Black Hills (now the Laramie Mountains) on the seventh morning. They breakfast at Horseshoe Station, 676 miles from St. Joseph. Now they are in hostile INDIAN country—with Indians lurking behind nearly every tree. The previous night, Indians shot up a pony rider, so the nervous passengers now sleep on their arms. That night they hear a shriek outside the coach and their driver's call for help, but the coach speeds off in the dark, and no explanation is ever provided.

Chapter 10

To show eastern readers what a Rocky Mountain desperado is like, the narrator describes SLADE. A man who established a fearsome reputation for ruthless lawlessness, Slade became an overland division-agent, cleaned up his division, got his coaches running on schedule and repeated his success at the rough Rocky Ridge division. At the next breakfast stop, the passengers meet the most gentlemanly, quiet and affable officer yet encountered—who turns out to be Slade himself! The narrator nervously sits next to him at breakfast; when Slade insists on pouring him the last cup of coffee, the narrator fears that Slade may later regret his generosity and kill him.

Chapter 11

Two or three years after the events described here, Slade was hanged in Montana. A long passage from DIMSDALE's book describes Slade's pitiful end.

Chapter 12

From the breakfast station, the stagecoach overtakes a MORMON emigrant train. The coach has covered 798 miles in eight days and three hours, while the emigrants' 33 wagons have taken eight *weeks* to travel the same distance. Now well into the heart of the Rocky Mountains, the coach passes Alkali, or Soda, Lake, where Mormons collect saleratus (a natural bicarbonate used as a leavening agent) to sell in SALT LAKE CITY. When the travelers pass a natural ice house near the pinnacle of the Rockies, they are amazed to see banks of snow in the summer. In another emigrant train, the narrator encounters a man named John whom he alienated as a boy by dropping a watermelon on his head. The coach now begins its descent.

On the tenth morning, the stagecoach crosses Green River; at five o'clock it reaches Fort Bridger, 1,025 miles from St. Joseph. Near Echo Canyon, the travelers meet army troops fresh from skirmishing with Indians. They sup with a Mormon "Destroying Angel" just outside Salt Lake, which they reach at nightfall.

Chapter 13

In Salt Lake City the travelers enjoy their first fine supper and stare at Mormons, fascinated by what they regard as a land of enchantment and awful mystery. The next day they inspect the remarkably clean, orderly and healthy city of 15,000 residents by a broad plain.

Though they are anxious to visit the Great Salt Lake, they instead have a long talk with the Mormon leader Heber C. Kimball and see the city's sights. The second day, they visit the "king," Brigham YOUNG.

Chapter 14
A Mr. (James) Street, who is responsible for laying telegraph lines across Utah, had problems with Mormon subcontractors who would not fulfill contracts with "gentiles" (non-Mormons) until Street went to Young, who ordered them to fulfill their contracts to the letter. Street is now convinced that federal officials are a sham, since Utah is an absolute monarchy in which Young is king.

The narrator's attitude towards polygamy changes when he sees Mormon women. He concludes that a man who marries one has done an act of Christian charity, and that a man who marries 60 has done a sublime deed of generosity.

Chapter 15
In a "Gentile Den," the narrator hears harrowing tales about Mormons assassinating gentiles (non-Mormons), and learns about polygamy. A young gentile named Johnson (an invented character) once breakfasted with Young. While they conversed privately, one of Young's wives entered and demanded a breast-pin like that Young had given to wife number six. Eventually, 25 wives stream through Young's office with the same demand.

Young's family is reputedly so vast that he once accepted the claim of a woman to be married to him, even though he did not know her. The child she passed off as his turned out to be an Indian painted white. Groaning under the expenses of his huge household, Young tried saving money on beds by having a single bedstead made to accommodate all 72 wives at once.

Chapter 16
A long examination of the "Mormon Bible" (The Book of Mormon) finds that it is a prosy bore with incomprehensible histories of wars among peoples whom one has never heard of in places unknown to geography. Though tiresome to read, it teaches nothing vicious and its moral code is unobjectionable.

Chapter 17
After two days in Salt Lake City, the travelers leave feeling little better informed about the "Mormon question" than when they arrived. They have gathered considerable information, but cannot tell what parts of it are reliable. The dreadful "MOUNTAIN MEADOWS MASSACRE" is an example of an issue for which their information has three sides. They return to the familiar stagecoach routine fortified with extra provisions.

Chapter 18
At 8:00 the next morning, they reach the ruins of Camp Floyd, 45 to 50 miles from Salt Lake. By 4:00 they have traveled another 45 to 50 miles and enter an alkali desert. During the night, it takes them 12 hours to cover

45 miles to the only watering spot, and 10 hours more to cross the remaining 25 miles.

Chapter 19
On the 16th day out from St. Joseph, the stagecoach is 250 miles from Salt Lake City. At Rocky Canyon, the travelers encounter Goshoot (GOSIUTE) Indians, perhaps the most degraded race in the world. Though a disciple of (James Fenimore) COOPER and a worshipper of the Noble Red Man, the narrator finds that whenever one gets close to *real* Indians, he merely finds Goshoots.

Chapter 20
The 17th day takes the coach past the highest mountain peaks yet seen. The next day, the travelers encounter telegraph-builders and send a message to Governor (James W.) NYE at Carson City, which is now 156 miles distant. On the 19th day, they cross the Great American Desert—a prodigious graveyard of bones. Across its border is Carson Lake, a typically mysterious "sink" that maintains its level though water flows in but never out. At the edge of the desert, they halt at Ragtown, an unmapped spot where the narrator recalls an anecdote that a driver told him near Julesburg. It concerns a coach ride that Horace GREELEY once made to Placerville, California. Anxious to get there quickly, he asked the driver, Hank MONK, to hurry. Monk went so fast, however, that Greeley bounced around until his head poked through the roof. A day or two later, another passenger boards the narrator's coach and tells exactly the same anecdote. A cavalry officer joins them and repeats the anecdote, as does a Mormon preacher. Finally, a derelict wanderer whom they have saved from death starts to tell the anecdote; however, they stop him and he dies.

Chapter 21
On the 20th day, the coach reaches dusty Carson City, where the narrator witnesses a man named Harris settling an argument with guns. That afternoon, WASHOE's powerful daily ZEPHYR blows through, making it impossible to see. Afterward, the new arrivals take in the governor's state palace—a two-room house. Other high officials live in boardinghouses, using their bedrooms as offices. The Secretary and the narrator board at Bridget O'FLANNIGAN's place, where their "walls" are partitions made from flour sacks. The narrator soon moves upstairs, where he takes one of 14 beds in a room shared by the "Irish Brigade"—camp followers of the governor, who tries to get rid of them by telling them to survey a railroad from Carson City over the Sierra Nevada. They balk at this, so he instead sends them east. As the men work, they bring tarantulas home, keeping them in glass tumblers on shelves. One night, a zephyr blows a roof into the boardinghouse, starting a panic when the tarantulas break free in the dark.

Chapter 22
Two or three weeks in this curious new country convince the narrator to prolong his stay. His duties as the Secre-

tary's "private secretary" are light, so he joins Johnny K. (John D. Kinney) on a hike to Lake TAHOE, which they explore in a skiff. Life at Tahoe is glorious; its pure air would invigorate even a mummy. The men claim 300 acres of forest land and undertake the work necessary to secure their legal title. After posting notices, they begin felling trees for a fence. The heavy work required proves so discouraging, however, that they abandon the effort. The next day they start building a log-house. After trimming just one log, they gradually scale their plans down until they settle on a rude house made of brush.

Chapter 23
During two or three weeks of solitude, the men idle away time at their "timber ranch," sleeping in the open and spending days drifting in the boat over Tahoe's crystal-clear water. One night, the narrator starts a fire for dinner. As he goes to the boat, the fire gallops out of control. The men watch helplessly as the conflagration destroys their ranch. They go back to Carson City, but later return to the lake for further adventures that will never be recorded.

Chapter 24
Resolved to own a horse, the narrator attends a Carson City auction at which a stranger—who turns out to be the auctioneer's brother—talks him into bidding on a "Genuine Mexican Plug." After buying it for $27, he mounts it and is bucked off instantly. After the narrator is bucked three times, a California youth tries the horse; he manages to stay on, but the animal disappears with him over the horizon. Meanwhile, an older man introduces himself as Abe CURRY and explains that the plug is a swindle. Hoping to get the horse crippled or killed so that someone else will have to pay for it, the narrator lends it out to various people, but without success. Finally, he gives it to a passing Arkansas emigrant.

Chapter 25
Formerly part of Utah, Nevada was under Mormon rule until the silver strikes of 1858 brought in a majority of outsiders who renounced allegiance to Utah. Nevada's residents appreciate having a legitimately constituted American government, but resent having strangers in authority over them. Getting legislators to serve in the territory's new government is easy; however, finding a hall in which they can meet is a different matter. Abe Curry has rescued the new government by lending it a building rent-free.

Chapter 26
By and by, the narrator catches "silver fever" from the many prospecting parties going out daily and the rapidly rising value of mining stocks. The latest cry is "HUMBOLDT"—as evidenced by lengthy extracts from an article in the VIRGINIA CITY TERRITORIAL ENTERPRISE. The narrator and three friends decide to try their luck

Roughing It's tenderfoot narrator discovers one of the drawbacks to genuine Mexican plugs.

in Humboldt, but he worries that the district's riches may be gone before he gets there.

Chapter 27
The Humboldt prospecting party consists of the narrator, a 60-year-old blacksmith named BALLOU, and two younger men named CLAGETT and OLIPHANT. They leave Carson City in December with a wagon, two horses and 1,800 pounds of provisions and tools. Their horses prove so weak that the men end up pushing the wagon themselves and require 15 days to complete the 200-mile trip—including a two-day rest stop.

Chapter 28
When the prospectors reach UNIONVILLE during a rainstorm, they erect a rude cabin on the side of a crevice. Expecting to find silver lying in the open, the narrator sneaks off to begin searching. With growing excitement, he collects bright stones, then finds a deposit of shining yellow scales that convinces him he has found gold. Excitedly, he returns to the cabin, his head filled with

dreams of wealth, but Ballou identifies his finds as granite rubbish with glittering mica.

Chapter 29
Under Ballou's guidance, the prospectors spend weary days searching for promising spots. Finally, Ballou finds a quartz ledge with enough silver and gold traces to warrant mining. Calling their new mine "Monarch of the Mountains," the men file claims and go to work. They begin sinking a shaft, but after a week of hard work it is only 12 feet deep, so the narrator, Clagett and Oliphant resign. Next, they try tunneling from the side of the mountain; however, another week of hard work produces such poor results that they all stop working. Caught up in local prospecting fever, they instead swap shares in their mine with others. After accumulating 30,000 "FEET" of the richest mines on earth, however, they cannot even get credit from the grocer.

Chapter 30
In the midst of Humboldt's boom, everyone owns thousands of feet of undeveloped silver mines, but few have any cash. Much of the frenzy is a product of misleading assays. The narrator and his partners never touch their mine after learning the *real* secret of success in silver mining: *selling* ledges to other people.

Meanwhile, mounting "assessments" on feet that the narrator and the Secretary purchased earlier in ESMERALDA mines become so burdensome that the narrator decides to investigate. After buying a horse, he starts off for Carson City and Esmeralda with Ballou and a Prussian named OLLENDORFF. For two or three days they ride through a snowstorm until they reach HONEY LAKE SMITH's inn on the Carson River. Predicting that a flood is coming, local Indians pack up and leave, but no one else can imagine the tiny river to be a threat with no rain in sight. That night, however, the river fills rapidly, marooning everyone on the inn's higher ground. Swearing, drinking, cards and occasional fights prevail among the people crowded into the inn for the next eight days.

Chapter 31
Two men at the inn unsettle the narrator—a young Swede who constantly sings the same song and a ruffian named ARKANSAS, who goads the landlord Johnson to fight. Johnson tries to back off, but Arkansas presses him until Johnson's wife cows him into submission with scissors. By the eighth day, the water is still too high to cross safely, but the narrator and his companions try to leave in a canoe. Ollendorff's incompetence causes it to overturn, sending the soaked men back to the inn. The next morning, they get away on their horses, only to discover that the road is invisible in the snowstorm. Ollendorff promises to lead them directly to Carson. After an hour, they find tracks, but as they follow them, the tracks multiply until Ballou realizes that they are following their *own* tracks in a circle. They try to follow a stagecoach that rushes past them, but cannot keep up

with it. When its tracks disappear in the snow, they realize they have no idea what direction they are going.

Chapter 32
Hopelessly lost in the blizzard, the men stop to build a fire. Ollendorff tries igniting it with his pistol, but only blows everything away. Meanwhile, the narrator accidentally releases the horses, which disappear in the storm. Hope rises when Ballou discovers four matches in his pocket, but each effort to light a fire fails. Finally, each man acknowledges that this night will be his last. Ollendorff asks forgiveness for his blunders and forgives the others for their mistakes. Wishing that he could reform and dedicate himself to good works, he swears off drinking and casts his whiskey bottle away. Ballou, in turn, swears off gambling and throws away his cards; the narrator swears off smoking and discards his pipe. Embracing as oblivion overcomes them, the men await death.

Chapter 33
When consciousness returns, the narrator thinks himself dead; however, when he gets up, he sees a stage building and a shed containing their horses just 15 steps away. Feeling humiliated, the men are angry and pettish; their joy at being delivered from death is poisoned. After breakfast, their spirits revive. Itching to smoke, the narrator sneaks off to retrieve his pipe. He fears discovery until he finds Ollendorff with his bottle and Ballou with his cards. Shaking hands, they agree to speak no more of "reform." Eventually, they reach Carson, where they remain a week during the trial of the "great landslide case."

Chapter 34
The steep mountains surrounding Carson City often unleash disastrous landslides during spring thaws, occasionally moving an entire side of a mountain. General Buncombe, who came to Nevada as a United States attorney, was once the victim of the kind of practical joke that established residents of new territories like to play on newcomers. One morning, Dick Hyde rushed into his office, asking him to conduct a legal suit in his behalf. His problem was that a landslide had slid the entire ranch of his neighbor, Tom Morgan, onto his own ranch, covering his property completely. He wanted to sue Morgan to make him leave. Outraged by Morgan's presumption in occupying Hyde's land, Buncombe assured Hyde that Morgan had no case.

That afternoon, former governor Roop (provisional governor Isaac Roop) opened a special court to hear Hyde's case. He was so solemn that some conspirators feared that he might not appreciate that the whole business was a joke. Every witness supported Hyde's position, and Morgan's attorney presented a weak case, contending that Morgan owned the land that his farm has slid over. Buncombe then delivered a powerful speech, confident that Hyde's case was won. When Roop delivered his decision, he acknowledged that the evidence favored Hyde and that Buncombe's oration was persuasive; however, he ruled that since heaven had moved Morgan's property for reasons that mere men cannot question, Hyde could not appeal its decision. He added that Hyde still owned his ranch *under* Morgan's property and was therefore entitled to dig it out. Reeling under the preposterous decision, Buncombe needed two months to realize that a joke had been played on him.

Chapter 35
The narrator and his friends continue their journey to Esmeralda with a new companion, Captain John Nye—an incomparable traveling comrade. He can do anything, solve any problem and find food and lodging anywhere. On their second day out, a poor desert inn turns them away, but Nye insists on stopping, then wins over everyone at the inn, gaining the travelers first-class treatment.

Esmeralda is a slightly more advanced version of Humboldt. The narrator's mining claims are worthless, so he discards them. For several days, he and his party take up claims and *begin* shafts and tunnels, but never finish them. Instead, they wait for buyers—who never come—and live austerely. Eventually, the narrator abandons mining and goes to work in a quartz mill for $10 a week.

Chapter 36
At the quartz mill, the narrator discovers what it means to earn one's bread by the sweat of one's brow. There is never an idle moment in the mill's many tasks. As the mill produces silver bricks, corners are chipped off for fire-assays to determine the proportions of precious metals. The desire of speculative miners for favorable assays makes some assayers less than strictly scrupulous. One man, for example, always got such rich results that he began monopolizing the business. Competitors exposed him by sending a stranger to him with a fragment of a carpenter's millstone, which he assayed at $1,284.40 a ton in silver and $366.36 a ton in gold.

The narrator's milling job lasts just one week. Afterward, he joins the frenzy over the mysterious and wonderful "cement mine."

Chapter 37
The marvelous WHITEMAN cement mine is rumored to be near MONO LAKE. Whenever Whiteman is spotted passing through Esmeralda, everyone chases after him. Local traditions claim that 20 years earlier, three German brothers survived an Indian massacre, then wandered through the desert and found an exposed cement vein containing nearly pure gold. Each took a large sample, but two brothers died during their wanderings. The third brother was so relieved to survive that he wanted nothing more to do with the mine, so he gave Whiteman his map and instructions for finding the

cement vein. For 12 or 13 years, Whiteman has searched for the lost mine. One night the narrator's new partner, HIGBIE, sights Whiteman passing through the town (AURORA). The narrator, Higbie and their friends sneak out to follow him, agreeing to meet near Mono Lake. At the rendezvous, other men pour in. Since the secret is out, the hunt ends and the treasure hunters stay to holiday at the lake.

Chapter 38
A silent, solemn and lifeless place, Mono Lake lies at the loneliest spot on earth. Its water is so alkaline that one can do laundry in it. The water is also hard on wounds, as a raw-skinned dog discovers when he dives in to escape the flies. Sea gulls lay eggs on the lake's islands; one island has a spring hot enough to cook the eggs. Providing board and laundry, the island is like a hotel. Although a half-dozen brooks feed the lake and none exits it, its water level mysteriously remains constant.

Chapter 39
One morning, the narrator and Higbie row 12 miles to explore an island. Finding that their drinking water has spoiled, they search for a stream until rising winds remind them that they have failed to secure their boat. They return to the shore to find the boat gone, making their situation frightful. However, when the boat drifts nearby, Higbie jumps in and they row back to the mainland in a storm. Just as they reach port, the boat overturns, dumping them in the alkaline water. They then spend a week fishing and camping in the Sierra Nevada, revisit the lake and return to Esmeralda.

Around this time, the narrator and his companions hire an Indian to do their laundry. Not knowing that gunpowder is hidden in the oven of a discarded stove, the man builds a fire in it to heat water. The stove blows up, taking part of the shed's roof with it.

Chapter 40
The narrator now relates the most curious episode in his slothful career. Outside of town is a rich silver-bearing ledge with an exposed comb owned by the Wide West mine. Its rich ore samples excite everyone, but Higbie suspects that they are not from the Wide West. He sneaks into its mine shaft and discovers a BLIND LEAD—a rich ledge running diagonally through the Wide West. It is public property, so he and the narrator plan to claim it. They make the Wide West foreman (identified as A. D. Allen in the next chapter) a partner to strengthen their position and they post their notices. That night they cannot sleep as they excitedly discuss how they will spend their wealth. The next day, the whole town is excited and the narrator relishes "being rich." However, the men must work on their claim within 10 days or forfeit it. Called away to help nurse Captain John Nye, the narrator leaves Higbie a note reminding him to do the necessary work.

Chapter 41

For nine days, the narrator nurses Nye through his spasmodic rheumatism. Meanwhile, he daydreams about future prosperity and sends instructions to friends and relatives concerning his spending plans and his willingness to forfeit his share of the family's "TENNESSEE LAND." After a falling-out with Nye, he walks home, reaching Esmeralda, where a crowd is gathered at the Wide West mine. Instead of investigating, he assumes that another strike has been made and helps a woman with her sick husband. Back at his cabin, he finds Higbie reading his note. Higbie left town when the narrator did—in order to chase after Whiteman again—and he left a note of his own. Their third partner, Allen, also left town on an emergency. Since *none* of them worked their claim, they have lost it to the new claimants.

Glad to leave the place of their sufferings, the narrator and Higbie spend a month or two away from Esmeralda. They return to learn that the Wide West and their former mine have merged.

Chapter 42

Pondering what to do next, the narrator reviews his past careers: one day grocery clerking; a week studying law; a stab at blacksmithery; a stint as a bookseller's clerk; part of a summer clerking in a drug store; becoming a tolerable printer and a good average steamboat PILOT. He has also been a private secretary, silver miner, and mill operative—amounting to less than nothing in each. After writing grandiloquent letters about his blind lead, he cannot stand the thought of returning home to be pitied, so he briefly yields to Higbie's appeal to try mining again.

It happens that he has occasionally sent articles to the VIRGINIA CITY TERRITORIAL ENTERPRISE. When he returns to town, he is thrilled to find a letter from the *Enterprise* offering to make him city editor at $25 a week. Afraid of being unable to support himself where he is, he accepts and goes to VIRGINIA CITY. The paper's editor, Mr. (Joseph) GOODMAN, tells him to cover the town, but he fails to find any news. Goodman suggests that he try what always works for Dan (DE QUILLE)— covering hay wagons. The narrator draws on his powers of invention to make this advice work, then gets good mileage in fanciful accounts about a murder and about emigrants coming through Indian territory.

Chapter 43

As the narrator learns about reporting, he relies more on facts and less on fancy, and swaps "regulars" with reporters from other papers, including his rival BOGGS of the VIRGINIA CITY UNION. Anxious to see the monthly school report—to which the *Union* but not the *Enterprise* has access—he uses hot punch to get Boggs to lend his copy. As he writes up his story on the report, Boggs gets drunk and fails to file his own story. When the next school report is due, Boggs gets revenge by stranding the narrator in a mine shaft. After the narrator has been in town six months, the "flush times" begin and it is easier than ever to fill columns with real news. With the COMSTOCK lode running through the town, money is as plentiful as dust.

Chapter 44

The narrator's salary rises to $40 a week, but he seldom draws it since every man in town is lavish with cash and "feet." Although only a few mines are not worthless "wild cat," speculation runs rampant. When miners file new claims, they give reporters 40 to 50 feet to inspect their mines and write about them. The narrator fills half a trunk with mining stock acquired this way. Everyone's pockets are full of stock, which they give away freely. Mr. (William Morris) STEWART, for example, offers the narrator 20 feet in a mine just for walking to his office. The narrator declines because it is dinner time, but later learns that the stock's value has risen to $150 a foot. To raise the value of wild cat mines, some schemers "salt" them with more valuable ore from elsewhere.

Chapter 45

Two years earlier, Goodman and his partner bought the *Territorial Enterprise* when it was a poverty-stricken weekly. Now the paper is a great and prosperous daily. Another evidence of the continuation of flush times is the Gould and Curry mine's investing nearly a million dollars to erect a hundred-stamp mill. Money is so plentiful that the problem is not getting it but *spending* it. By happy coincidence, the United States SANITARY COMMISSION is formed around this time. Before Virginia City can even finish organizing a committee to support it, money pours in. Donations accelerate when Reuel GRIDLEY brings his "Sanitary Flour Sack" from Austin, where he raised $8,000 for the Sanitary fund by repeatedly auctioning it off. When Gridley arrives in Virginia City, however, his first auction nets only $5,000. Disappointed civic leaders plan a new campaign for the next day. A cavalcade to nearby GOLD HILL, Silver City and Dayton returns covered in glory, and the second Virginia City auction raises $40,000. Gridley then goes on to sell the sack in Carson City, California and the East.

Chapter 46

Nevada's flush times produce countless NABOBS, such as two teamsters who in lieu of $300 cash for a hauling job took a piece of a silver mine that later made them $100,000 a year—each. John SMITH traded part of his ranch for an undeveloped mine that later earned him as much as $60,000 a month. Four years after the original owners of the Gould and Curry mine sold out cheaply, it was worth $7.6 million. In the early days, a poor Mexican traded a tiny stream on his property for a section of a mine later worth $1.5 million. Stories like these go on and on, but most nabobs drift back into poverty and obscurity.

A story about two nabobs was once current in Nevada. Blessed with sudden wealth, Colonel Jim and Colonel Jack went to New York City, where Jack wanted to indulge his lifelong desire to ride in a carriage. Unfamiliar with big cities, he boarded an omnibus, gave the driver a $20 gold piece and treated friendly New Yorkers to free rides.

Chapter 47

A philosopher has said that one way to know a community is to observe the style of its funerals. In Virginia City, it is not clear who receives more éclat—the distinguished public benefactor or the distinguished rough. In any case, Buck FANSHAW had a grand funeral. After he died, a committee sent Scotty BRIGGS to call on the town's new minister—a fledgling from the East (modeled on Franklin S. Rising). Briggs was a stalwart rough with a big heart, but as a product of Nevada's rich and varied slang, he had trouble making himself understood. Gradually, he got his message across and Virginia City put on one of its greatest funerals ever.

Chapter 48

Virginia City's first 26 graves belong to *murdered* men. The rough element always predominates in new mining districts, where no one is respected until he has "killed his man." The highest level of Nevada society was once made up of the lawyer, the editor, the banker, the chief desperado, the chief gambler and, especially, the saloon-keeper. The murderers of the men in those first 26 graves were never punished because of the imbecilic jury system—which bans intelligence and honesty and prizes ignorance, stupidity and perjury. The best-known names in Nevada Territory belonged to desperadoes such as Sam Brown, Farmer Pease, El Dorado Johnny, Sugarfoot Mike, Pock-marked Jake, Six-fingered Pete and others. While these desperadoes killed each other with little provocation, they had contempt for killing small-fry citizens.

Chapter 49

Extracts from Virginia City newspapers of 1862 reveal the temper of the times. The first tells how Deputy Marshal Jack Williams killed William Brown in a shoot-out. The second, from four months later, tells how the same Jack Williams assaulted and robbed a German engineer. An efficient city officer, Williams, was also a notorious desperado who was assassinated five months later. The third extract tells how Tom Reeder, a friend of Williams, argued about Williams's killing with George Gumbert, who stabbed him. After Reeder was treated, he went after Gumbert and was shot. He died two days later, but nothing happened to Gumbert. Trial by jury is the palladium of our liberties. There have been more than a hundred murders in Nevada, yet only two people have suffered the death penalty.

Chapter 50

Murder and jury statistics evoke memories of an extraordinary trial and execution of 20 years earlier, when

Captain Ned BLAKELY commanded a guano ship in the Chincha Islands. Bill Noakes, a bully from another ship, killed Blakely's favorite mate before many witnesses, but in the absence of local authority, no one even thought of arresting him. Furious for justice, Blakely himself arrested Noakes. When he announced he would hang Noakes the next day, other captains demanded a trial. Though exasperated by the legal obstacles they raised, Blakely let them try Noakes, *then* hanged him.

Chapter 51

Vice always flourishes during "flush times." Two unfailing signs signify when money is plentiful: a crowded police docket, and the birth of a literary paper. Virginia City has its paper, the WEEKLY OCCIDENTAL, edited by Mr. F. (Thomas FITCH). Since the paper needs an original novel, everyone pitches in. Mrs. F. (Anna M. Fitch) writes the opening chapter, introducing as characters a lovely blonde simpleton and a French duke who loves her. In the next chapter, Mr. F. adds a brilliant lawyer who gets the duke's estates into trouble and a young society lady to distract the duke. In the third chapter, Mr. D. (Rollin M. DAGGETT) adds a mysterious Rosicrucian, a masked miscreant and an Irish coachman. At this point, a dissolute stranger arrives in town who happens to be a writer; he agrees to write chapter 4, with the narrator's chapter to follow.

The stranger gets drunk and writes pure chaos that destroys every character: The coachman marries the society lady, the duke marries the blonde's stepmother, the lawyer commits suicide, the coachman breaks his neck, the blonde drowns herself and the duke kills himself after learning that he has married his own mother. Stunned by the fury of the other novelists, the stranger offers to rewrite his chapter. Unfortunately, he gets drunk again and writes something even crazier. This time the lawyer is big-hearted and the blonde falls in love with him; however, her parents insist that she marry the duke within a year. Chance puts everyone on the same ship, which burns up on the Atlantic. The survivors are rescued by two whaling vessels, but a storm separates them and neither can interrupt its voyage. One whaler carries the lawyer to the Bering Straits; the other takes everyone else to the North Atlantic. A year later, the blonde and the duke are about to be married aboard the vessel near Greenland. Meanwhile, a whale swallows the lawyer in the Bering Straits, then swims to the North Atlantic, where it is cut open by the other whaler. The lawyer pops out and stops the wedding.

The reaction to this chapter is even fiercer. The *Occidental* is issued without a novel and soon dies. Nevertheless, the narrator is proud to have been connected with a literary paper. Since he wrote poetry for it that never got published, he herein publishes a piece called "THE AGED PILOT MAN."

Chapter 52

The flush times peak in 1863, when Nevada claims to have produced $25 million in bullion. Speculation is riotous and freight charges to and from San Francisco run as high as $200 a ton. While Virginia City is a busy city above ground, another busy city exists below ground, where a vast network of timbers supports 30 miles of tunnels in which more than 5,000 men work.

Chapter 53

At the urging of the boys, the narrator is anxious to hear Jim BLAINE tell the story of his grandfather's old ram. It is necessary to catch Blaine when he is satisfactorily drunk, however, and it is a while before they find him in that condition. They settle down to hear his story, but he falls asleep before finishing.

Chapter 54

A harmless, industrious race, the Chinese are never disorderly, drunk or lazy, and prosper when left alone. Unfortunately, low-class whites abuse them. As the narrator writes this chapter, he reads about San Francisco boys stoning a Chinaman to death (June 1871). About 70,000 Chinese live on the Pacific Coast, including about 1,000 in Virginia City, where they work mainly in laundry and domestic service. All Chinese read, write and cipher; they waste nothing and can even make abandoned mines pay. Unfortunately, they are subjected to such swindles as a "foreign" mining tax. Holding their dead in reverence, the Chinese believe it critical to be buried in their homeland. For this reason, immigrant workers arrange in advance for their bodies to be shipped home if they die in America. With an ingenious refinement of Christian cruelty, California's legislature has worked to outlaw shipping corpses as a way to deter Chinese immigration.

Chapter 55

Tired of staying in one place, the narrator wants to see SAN FRANCISCO. A Nevada convention has just framed a constitution for a state government, which he fears will end the flush times. About this time a schoolmate of his boyhood appears. An allegory of poverty, he needs $46, which the narrator steps into a bank to borrow for him—never guessing that it will take two years to repay. Goodman leaves town for a week, making the narrator chief editor of the *Enterprise*. Writing the paper's daily editorials proves unbearably burdensome. After Goodman returns, the narrator does not want to go back to serving in the ranks after having been a general, so he decides to leave. At this juncture, Dan (De Quille) tells him about two men who invited him to accompany them to New York to help sell a rich silver mine, in return for a third share in the profits. Dan declined and suggested they invite a reporter from the other paper. The narrator wants to kill Dan for not telling him about this opportunity sooner, but relents, since he himself may still have a chance to go. His hopes up, he boards a stagecoach the next day, when he sees someone accidentally drop a brick on the foot of a seedy passenger. The vagabond screams in pain, but declines medical help, asking only for brandy. Once the coach is under way, he confesses to having a wooden leg.

Chapter 56

While rumbling through California's plains and valleys, the narrator wonders why people rave about California's loveliness, since *no* land with an unvarying climate can be truly beautiful. San Francisco proves a fascinating city in which to live, but its kindly climate becomes predictable and boring; it has eight months of pure sunshine, followed by four months of pure rain. While Mono has endless winter and San Francisco has eternal spring, SACRAMENTO has eternal summer. It *is* hot. Fort Yuma (Arizona), however, is even hotter. A story attributed to John Phoenix tells about a Fort Yuma soldier sent to the hottest corner of perdition, from which he telegraphed home for his blankets.

Chapter 57

As the site of much of the lucrative early gold mining, Sacramento Valley still shows its scars. Similar disfigurements are visible throughout California; it is hard to believe that flourishing little cities once stood where only meadows and forests are now visible. No other modern land has seen towns die and disappear so absolutely. California attracted a curious and unique population consisting of 200,000 vigorous young men, with women so scarce that the mere *sight* of one was a notable event. Children were equally scarce. A true story recalls how a huge, rough miner was so moved by the sight of a young child that he offered $150 in gold just to kiss it.

Chapter 58

During several months of "butterfly idleness," the narrator stays at San Francisco's best hotel and lives in the style of a man worth $100,000 and soon to become richer. While spending freely, he watches the stock market. Since Nevada has just approved a state constitution, it looks bad for mining stocks, but he holds off selling his shares while speculation goes mad. Suddenly, the bottom drops out. He loses everything and must move to a private boardinghouse and take a reporting job (for the SAN FRANCISCO CALL). Then he learns that he has missed his chance to participate in the silver mine sale. On a bright October afternoon, the narrator enjoys his first earthquake (an anachronistic allusion to the October 8, 1865 earthquake). Later he sees a copy of the *Territorial Enterprise* announcing that his rival, Marshal, has made a killing on the silver mine sale in New York. It is the "blind lead" all over again. Despondent, the narrator neglects his duties and takes the advice to resign from the newspaper before he is dismissed.

Chapter 59

For a time, the narrator writes literary screeds for the GOLDEN ERA. Then Charles WEBB and Bret HARTE engage him to write an article a week for their CALIFORNIAN. For two months his sole occupation is avoiding acquaintances. He becomes adept at "slinking" and holds on to his last 10-cent piece to avoid feeling penniless. Meanwhile, he often entertains a collector from the Virginia City bank from which he borrowed the $46. He also happens upon another child of misfortune—another former reporter—whom he calls the mendicant BLU-CHER, who once found a dime at a time when he had not eaten for 48 hours. While Blucher planned how he would dine on this dime, yet another unfortunate accosted him and pleaded for 25 cents for food. Blucher took the man to the city's best restaurant and let him run up a $6.50 tab on his own account, then feasted by himself at French Pete's on his dime.

Chapter 60
By and by, the narrator goes to a decayed mining camp (JACKASS HILL) in TUOLUMNE with an old friend (Jim GILLIS) and spends two or three months living in a hillside cabin. Where a city of 3,000 once stood, only a handful of miners remain in a melancholy exile. This part of California has a little-known and fascinating species of mining called pocket-mining, pursued by only 20 miners. The ingenious process involves washing earth in tin pans. If you find gold, you wash more pans, while working your way toward the richest deposit.

Tuolumne had two poor miners who spent 13 years hiking to a village every day for supplies. Along the way, they always rested on the same boulder. One day, two Mexicans sat on the boulder and found $800 worth of gold in it; later they explored the nearby hill, where they eventually took out $120,000 in gold. The two Americans now take turns getting up early to curse the Mexicans.

Chapter 61
One of the narrator's comrades is another victim of 18 years of blighted hopes—a gentle spirit named Dick BAKER, a pocket-miner of Dead-Horse Gulch (Jackass Gulch). Whenever he feels down, he mourns the loss of his wonderful cat TOM QUARTZ, which never cared for anything but mining. When the miners first attempted quartz-mining, they laid a charge, forgetting that Tom Quartz was asleep on a gunny sack in the shaft. The explosion sent the cat about a mile and a half into the sky, permanently prejudicing him against quartz-mining.

After two months without striking a pocket, the narrator and his friends go to ANGEL'S CAMP in Calaveras County, but have no luck there, either. Meanwhile, they keep their door open to passing miners and wander as far as the Big Trees and Yosemite.

Chapter 62
After a three-month absence, the narrator returns to San Francisco penniless and becomes the local corre-spondent for the *Virginia City Territorial Enterprise*. Within five months he is out of debt. With his vagabond instinct again strong, he gets a berth as the SACRAMENTO UNION's correspondent to the Sandwich Islands (HAWAII) and sails on the AJAX (March 7, 1866). The ship's 30 passengers include a cheerful soul named WILLIAMS, three old whaleship captains and a retired whaleman known as the "old ADMIRAL." Though beloved, the Ad-miral wears out other passengers with heated political arguments based on invented facts until he meets his match in Williams.

Chapter 63
As the islands come into sight, the narrator sees Dia-mond Head and Honolulu. The more he sees of Hono-lulu, the better he likes it. A delightfully colorful contrast to the drabness of San Francisco, it has bright-colored houses, flowers, huge trees, comely women and millions of cats.

Chapter 64
At the end of his third day in Honolulu, the narrator can barely sit down because he has ridden 15 or 20 miles on horses. After a fascinating visit to a prison, he rushed back to the American Hotel to hire a horse on which to catch up with an excursion to Diamond Head. He asked for an excessively gentle horse and got one that fell asleep on him. Eventually, he reached a place known as the "King's Grove" near interesting ruins of an ancient temple (at Wakiki) at which it is said that thousands of humans were slaughtered in old times. The missionaries deserve full credit for breaking the old tyranny and bringing the people freedom and le-gal protections.

Chapter 65
After a rugged climb, the excursionists halt on the summit of a hill with a commanding view of Honolulu. They then visit an old battleground littered with bleached bones. No one knows who fought here; some think it is where KAMEHAMEHA I fought the Oahuans. However, JARVES's excellent history tells a different story.

Honolulu has no regular livery stable, so one must hire wretched horses from KANAKAS—who are unprinci-pled horse traders. A friend named J. Smith hired a horse with a blanket glued to its hide by raw spots. Another friend bought a horse that he thought he had examined carefully, only to discover that it was blind in one eye. Mr. L. (Lewis Leland) thought that he was buying perfectly matched horses that he had to examine through windows on the opposite sides of a stable; it turned out that he had bought *one* horse that he had seen from two sides.

Chapter 66
Saturday afternoon is a festive day at Honolulu's mar-ketplace, where native girls in gaudy habits ride horses. Occasionally one sees a tattooed heathen who looks like a Washoe mendicant who was blown up in a mine. Poi merchants peddle their unseductive but nutritious mixture, and natives buy the intoxicating *awa* (kava) root. In old times, Saturday was a truly grand gala day with feasts, hula dancing and revelry, but now it has lost its gala features and the hula is largely forbidden. Missionaries have transformed natives into inveterate churchgoers, and cultivation has given women pro-found respect for chastity—in other people. Contact

with white civilization has reduced the native population from 400,000 in Cook's time to 55,000 in just over 80 years. Local society is a queer medley; a stranger is likely to be either a missionary, a whaling captain or a high government official.

Chapter 67
The national legislature contains a half-dozen white men and 30 or 40 natives. Its nobles and ministers include David Kalakaua, the king's chamberlain; Prince William (Lunalilo); and the assembly's president, His Royal Highness M. Kekuanaoa, the king's father. In former times, women were taught to know their place, but missionaries have made them the equal of men. Although Christianized, natives retain some barbaric superstitions, such as believing that enemies can *pray* them to death. They also still have the ability to lie down and die at will. Natives remain oblivious of nakedness and one often finds women bathing naked. Missionaries beg natives not to attend church naked and give them clothes, but the natives merely show up in just one odd garment or another.

Grown folk here play "empire," from the king (KAMEHAMEHA V) and his royal family down. Offices include a Royal Chamberlain, Commander-in-Chief of Household Troops, Royal Steward, Grand Equerry, First Gentleman of the Bed Chamber, Prime Minister—a renegade American (Charles Coffin Harris), Imperial Minister of Finance, Minister of War, Minister of the Navy, Lord Bishop of Honolulu (T. N. Staley), Minister of Public Instruction, governors of the islands, plus High Sheriffs and other small fry too numerous to count, as well as envoys extraordinary and ministers plenipotentiary from foreign governments. All this grandeur in a playhouse "kingdom" with less than 60,000 souls!

Chapter 68
In Honolulu the narrator witnesses the funeral of the king's sister, Her Royal Highness Princess VICTORIA. The funeral's printed program (reproduced in the book) lists so many dignitaries that one wonders where the procession will find enough people to serve as its "Hawaiian population generally." Princess Victoria's funeral ceremonies contrast with those of Kamehameha I five decades earlier. Accounts of Kamehameha's death are filled with details about former customs, such as tabus against eating and sleeping in the same house. After the king died, frightful ORGIES followed.

Chapter 69
On a Saturday afternoon, the narrator sails with Mr. BILLINGS from Honolulu to the island of Hawaii to see the great volcano and other sights. The schooner *Boomerang* is too cramped, noisy and verminous to permit sleep, so the narrator quits his miserable cabin and enjoys one of the most beautiful scenes he has ever seen: the glittering moonlit sea and broad sails straining under an angry gale. On Monday morning, they see the

snow-capped peaks of Mauna Loa and Hualaiai. They go ashore at Kailua on the western Kona coast, where they ride horses a thousand feet above sea level and pass through sugar plantations.

Chapter 70
At a plantation they meet a man said to be crazy, Simon ERICKSON, who is obsessed with talking about his correspondence with Horace Greeley. He once wrote to Greeley on behalf a woman named Beazely whose son was wasting away while trying to grow turnips on vines. Greeley replied, but his handwritten letter seemed to contain a different message every time Erickson tried to read it. At first it seemed to be about polygamy. Later it seemed to be about Bolivia and mackerel and poultices and swine. When Erickson finally deciphered "turnips," he wrote Greeley again asking to clarify the meaning of "turnips restrain passion." Greeley's clerk sent a clear translation that read "turnips remain passive." It was too late, however, as young Beazely was already dead.

Chapter 71
In the afternoon, the narrator goes down to the sea on a lava flow so old that no one remembers when it was created. At Kealakekua Bay, he sees the coconut tree stump marking the spot where Hawaiians killed Captain Cook. The narrator spends the night on the schooner anchored in the bay.

Chapter 72
In the morning, the narrator visits the ruined temple of the last god, Lono. Its chief priest was the uncle of Obookia (Henry Obookia, d. 1818), who was educated and converted in New England and became famous for wanting to bring the Bible to Hawaii. Lono, a favorite god on the islands, sailed away and never returned; many islanders later believed Cook to be Lono. Kealakekua Bay is also near the site of the last battle fought for idolatry. After Kamehameha I died, his son Liholiho attacked the old tabu system, triggering a mass revolt against the old gods.

Chapter 73
The narrator goes with a kanaka by canoe to Honaunau, where naked natives of all ages are surfing. He then visits the City of Refuge, a sanctuary of the old days; any hunted criminal or refugee who reached it and confessed to a priest obtained absolution and could leave without being harmed. Its massive walls cut from lava pose mysteries about who built it. Nearby is a well engineered road of flat stones.

Chapter 74
The schooner takes the narrator to Kau on the southwestern coast, where he bids his ship farewell. The next day he buys a horse, and a two-day ride takes him to the great KILAUEA volcano. After taking in the dimensions of its enormous crater, he settles in at the Volcano House hotel. At night, he returns to admire the crater's fiery magnificence in the dark. A colossal column of fire-

illuminated clouds towers above what looks like the infernal regions. The foreground of the crater's floor is wonderfully illuminated. Most of the floor is as black as ink, but a large area is streaked with streams of liquid fire that look like a colossal railroad map done in chain lightning on a midnight sky. Here and there are gleaming, gaping holes in the dark crust in which dazzling white lava boils furiously. The smell of sulphur is strong, but not unpleasant to a sinner.

Chapter 75

The next night, the narrator joins a dozen people who descend to the crater's floor with lanterns and native guides. A cauldron threatens to overflow, so the guides refuse to continue, but the narrator and a stranger named Marlette—who has explored the crater a dozen times during the day—proceed alone. They run across the crater's floor until Marlette loses the path and starts to fall through the crust. He finds the path again, by using his feet instead of his eyes. The spectacle at North Lake is worth twice the distance they have come to see it. A heaving sea of molten fire, the "lake" is as blinding as the noonday sun. White-hot chimneys of lava surround its shores, spouting gorgeous sprays of lava. When part of the shelf on which the men are sitting falls in the lake, jarring the surroundings like an earthquake, they take a hint and leave.

Chapter 76

The narrator rides horseback 200 miles around the island of Hawaii. The pleasant trip takes a week because the horses are used to carrying kanakas, who never pass a house without stopping to gossip. The experience reminds the narrator of a painful experience. He once took an aristocratic young lady driving with a retired milk-wagon horse that he told her he had always owned. After the horse stopped at 162 houses and delivered them to the dairy depot, his humiliation was complete.

After his journey ends at Kawaehae (a bay in the island's northwest corner), he returns to Honolulu, then spends several pleasant weeks on Maui. There he enjoys a picnic excursion to Iao Valley and a visit to the dead Haleakala volcano, whose crater dwarfs even Kilauea. Atop its 10,000-foot high rim he sees the most sublime spectacle of his life when clouds bank together a thousand feet below him, leaving only the rim of the crater visible.

Chapter 77

On Maui the narrator meets a curious man named Markiss (F. A. Ouidnot). Whatever anyone else says, Markiss tops it. The narrator meets the man everywhere and stays indoors to avoid him. One night Markiss makes a point about a truly "mean" employer with a story about a man named John James Godfrey who worked for a California mining company. One day, an accidental blast sent Godfrey so high that he was 16 minutes returning to Earth—and then the company docked him for lost time. Worn out by Markiss's stories,

the narrator leaves the island the next day, convinced that Markiss is a liar. Several years later, his verdict is vindicated. He hears that Markiss has been found dead, hanging from a beam inside his locked room. Although Markiss had a suicide note pinned on him, the jury concluded that he was killed by someone else, reasoning that Markiss was such a consistent liar for 30 years that *any* statement he made must be a lie. Furthermore, they concluded that he was *not* dead—instancing the strong circumstantial evidence of his own word that he was dead. Only after his coffin stood open in Lahaina's tropical climate for seven days did the jury change their verdict. They now ruled "suicide induced by mental aberration"—Markiss said he was dead, and *was* dead. Would he have told the truth if he had been in his right mind? No.

Chapter 78

After half a year on the islands (actually, four months), the narrator sails back to San Francisco (on the clipper ship *Smyrniote*, July 17–August 18, 1866). Once again penniless, he accepts someone's suggestion to stage a public LECTURE. After engaging a large hall and advertising—all on credit—the humorous material that he has prepared seems hopelessly dreary. Panic-stricken, he asks friends to sit near the stage and laugh when he signals for help. He even gives a stranger named Sawyer (William M. Slason, 1831?–1872) a ticket because he has a hair-trigger laugh. During the three days leading up to the event, he eats nothing and only suffers. The afternoon of the lecture, he creeps to the box office and is distressed to find it closed. At 6:00, he enters the theater from the back. After sampling the gloomy solitude of the empty hall, he waits amid the scenery. Eventually, he hears noises. Suddenly, he is onstage, staring at a sea of faces and quaking in terror. The house is full! Gradually his fright melts away and the evening develops into an unqualified triumph.

Chapter 79

The narrator boldly launches out as a lecturer by engaging his old friend Mike (Denis MCCARTHY) to be his agent on a tour of Nevada and California. Shortly before he reaches Virginia City, stagecoach robberies near the town become the subject of all conversation. The same night that he lectures there (October 31, 1866), he also lectures in Gold Hill. When he and Mike walk back to Virginia City that night, six masked men with revolvers accost them and take their valuables. The whole thing is actually a practical joke staged by friends, with 20 others watching from hiding places; even Mike is in on it.

When he returns to San Francisco, he plans a pleasure trip to Japan and around the world, but changes his mind when he decides to go home. He sails off for the isthmus (on the steamer *America*, December 15, 1866) and New York (on the steamer *San Francisco*). He revisits his home (Hannibal) and later joins the famous QUAKER CITY cruise.

The moral of the book is this: If you are of any account, stay home and make your way by faithful diligence. If you are "no account," leave home; then you must work, whether you want to or not, and become a blessing to your friends by ceasing to be a nuisance to them.

Appendixes
The first of three appendixes, "Brief Sketch of Mormon History," is an 1,840-word condensation of *The Mormon Prophet and His Harem; or, An Authentic History of Brigham Young, His Numerous Wives and Children* (1866) by Catharine Waite (1829–1913).

Appendix B, "The Mountain Meadows Massacre," also draws heavily on Waite's book and accepts her conclusion that Mormons were primarily responsible for the massacre.

Appendix C, "Concerning a Frightful Assassination that was never Consummated," contains a long letter from a small-time journalist named Conrad Wiegand to the *Territorial Enterprise* written in January 1870. Wiegand was an eccentric reformer who began publishing a newspaper in Gold Hill after Mark Twain left Nevada. When he published unsubstantiated charges against a local miner, he was beaten and threatened by the miner. His letter presents a dramatic account of his peril, along with Mark Twain's sarcastic asides.

BACKGROUND AND PUBLISHING HISTORY

Mark Twain gave little thought to writing a book about his western experiences until well after leaving the Pacific Coast. The great success of *Innocents Abroad* (1869), however, later prompted him to seek a subject for a similar travel book, and his thoughts naturally went back to his western years. Initially he thought that his time in HAWAII was the most promising subject on which to write a book—probably because he assumed that too many books had already been written on the West. While Mark Twain had 25 letters from his Hawaii trip that he could use in the way he had used his QUAKER CITY letters to write *Innocents Abroad*, writing about his mainland experiences posed a different kind of challenge. He began by gathering all the relevant material he could find. In March 1870, he asked Orion to send him the journal he (Orion) had kept of their overland stagecoach journey, as well as the scrapbook of his own western newspaper and magazine articles. Mark Twain had also recently written articles for the BUFFALO EXPRESS about his western experiences.

In July 1870, during Mark Twain's first summer sojourn in Elmira, Elisha BLISS visited him on behalf of the AMERICAN PUBLISHING COMPANY to negotiate a book contract, which he signed on July 15. By late August, he was busy writing, but family problems and such responsibilities as writing for the GALAXY soon hampered his progress. His father-in-law, Jervis LANGDON, died in August; then his wife Livy became seriously ill,

and her friend Emma NYE contracted typhoid fever and died in their Buffalo home in late September. In November, Livy delivered her first child prematurely; then both she and the baby became dangerously ill.

Mark Twain had promised to deliver his manuscript by the end of 1870, but did not begin submitting pages until mid-March 1871. Two months later, he proclaimed himself "half done." By early July, he was up to the Hawaiian phase of his narrative. He had wanted to limit this section of the book to a few chapters, but found himself so short of pages for the long book he had contracted to write that he eventually devoted nearly a fifth of the entire book to Hawaii. In August, he delivered his final pages to Bliss and began reading proofs.

In early August, Bliss copyrighted "THE INNOCENTS AT HOME" as the book's working title, changing it to "Roughing It" four months later when he copyrighted the book. Meanwhile, Mark Twain launched a LECTURE tour in mid-October, taking him through the Northeast and Midwest into early February 1872. By December he was using extracts from his new book in a lecture titled "Roughing It." The American Publishing Company began canvasing for *Roughing It* the same month and had the first printed copies from the bindery at the end of January 1872.

The first edition of *Roughing It* had 304 illustrations, about 15 percent of which contain recognizable caricatures of Mark Twain. Many of the illustrations are unsigned, but most were drawn by Edward F. Mullen and True WILLIAMS. When Williams went on a drinking binge, Bliss engaged Roswell Morse SHURTLEFF, who drew 19 pictures, including the frontispiece. Bliss also borrowed engravings from Albert Deane RICHARDSON's *Beyond the Mississippi* and adapted pictures from several other books, including John Ross BROWNE's *Adventures in the Apache Country*. Unhappiness with the quality of his book's illustrations and distrust of Bliss's cost-accounting methods eventually led Mark Twain to break from Bliss.

The American Publishing Company officially published *Roughing It* on February 19, 1872—a week after George ROUTLEDGE published a two-volume edition in England. Routledge's edition omitted the illustrations and appendixes of the American edition, substituting the text of Mark Twain's BURLESQUE AUTOBIOGRAPHY. Initial sales of the book rivaled those of *Innocents Abroad*, but tapered off more quickly. Nevertheless, the book sold 73,000 copies during the first two years. Since then, it has stayed in print almost continuously and has ranked as one of Mark Twain's most popular books.

A century after *Roughing It*'s original publication, the MARK TWAIN PAPERS project published the first corrected edition of the book. In 1993, the project issued a substantially expanded edition, with new maps and annotation materials and all the original illustrations.

Roughing It, dramatizations of While Mark Twain was writing *Roughing It*, or shortly afterward, he began to dramatize the incident in which the bully ARKANSAS terrorizes HONEY LAKE SMITH's inn in chapter 31. He abandoned this effort, however, possibly because Augustin DALY staged a musical play of *Roughing It* in New York City in February–March 1873. Daly claimed to have adapted his production from an unspecified French play about a Manhattan couple eloping to the Rocky Mountains. However, his play not only used Mark Twain's title, but incorporated scenes from his book—such as the episodes with Arkansas and SLADE. In 1910, Thomas A. EDISON's film company produced *A Mountain Blizzard,* a short silent film that evidently adapted the blizzard episode from chapter 32 of *Roughing It.* Another silent film, *The Pony Express* (1925), featured a brief episode with Charles Gerson portraying Mark Twain as a western tenderfoot—a character likely inspired by *Roughing It.*

The fifth episode of television's "Bonanza" series in 1959 had Howard Duff playing Mark Twain when he first came to Virginia City. In May 1960, NBC-TV broadcast an hour-long adaption of *Roughing It* with Andrew Prine as the young Mark Twain and James Daly as an older Mark Twain.

Routledge, George A. (September 23, 1812, Brampton, England–December 13, 1888, London) English book publisher. Routledge founded the firm that eventually became Routledge and Sons in 1843. Specializing in cheap editions of established literature, he published such American authors as Washington Irving, James Fenimore COOPER, Henry Wadsworth LONGFELLOW and Harriet Beecher STOWE. In 1867, he added Mark Twain to his list with an unauthorized edition of THE CELEBRATED JUMPING FROG OF CALAVERAS COUNTY. A year later, he published "CANNIBALISM IN THE CARS" in his *Broadway* magazine.

In the absence of international copyright protection, Mark Twain could not stop another English publisher, John Camden HOTTEN, from pirating his work, so he authorized Routledge to publish his books in the early 1870s. Routledge then issued cheap editions of BURLESQUE AUTOBIOGRAPHY, *Innocents Abroad, Roughing It, The Gilded Age* and two collections of sketches. When Mark Twain first visited England in 1872, Routledge and his brother helped introduce him to local literary society. Mark Twain's formal relationship with Routledge ended in 1876, when Andrew CHATTO offered him better terms to publish *Tom Sawyer.* Routledge's firm later sold most of its Mark Twain titles to Chatto, but continued to issue *Innocents* until 1902—apparently without paying Mark Twain additional royalties.

Roxana (Roxy) Central character in *Pudd'nhead Wilson.* When the narrative begins in 1830, Roxy is a 20-year-old domestic slave in the household of Percy DRISCOLL, in DAWSON'S LANDING, Missouri. Only 1/16th African in descent, she could easily pass for white, were it

Roxy forces her son, Tom Driscoll, to his knees in chapter 8 of Pudd'nhead Wilson.

not for her thick slave dialect. In chapter 1, she bears a son, CHAMBERS, on the same day that her master's wife bears a son named Tom. Mrs. Driscoll soon dies, leaving Roxy to raise both boys. Chambers's father is Colonel Cecil Burleigh ESSEX, whose relationship with Roxy is never explained.

After Driscoll threatens to sell his slaves down the river for stealing, Roxy becomes obsessed with the fear of having her son sold away. At first, she decides to drown herself and her son, but changes her mind after realizing that she can protect her son by switching him with Driscoll's son. By transforming Chambers into "Tom DRISCOLL," she becomes her own son's slave. Suppressing her natural maternal instincts, she badly overindulges him. As "Tom" moves into adolescence, he treats Roxy so badly, insulting and abusing her, that she fantasizes about exposing his identity for revenge. Lacking proof, however, she is helpless before the monster she has created.

Fifteen years later, the death of Driscoll leaves Roxy free, but the collapse of his investments leaves her without a home. She goes "chambermaiding" on a steamboat in chapter 4 and reappears four chapters later, after having worked for eight years on the steamboat GRAND MOGUL. Now about 43, she suffers from rheumatism that forces her to retire on $400 that she has saved in a New Orleans bank. When she discovers that her bank has gone bust, she returns to Dawson's Landing. Although Tom has never treated her well, she is desperately anxious to see him. He receives her so rudely, however, that she turns on him savagely, threatening to reveal dark secrets about him to his guardian, Judge York DRISCOLL. When Tom meets with her secretly, she overwhelms him by force of personality and begins directing his life.

Much of Roxy's motivation is true affection for her son. Her love for him is so great, in fact, that she is willing to be sold back into slavery in order to raise money to clear his gambling debts. Even after he betrays her by selling her down the river—where she becomes a common field hand—she still looks for reasons to love him. On the other hand, she demonstrates no noticeable affection for the boy she has raised as "Chambers," though she is the only parent that he knows.

Roxy's intelligence allows her to devise intricate schemes to solve problems. She anticipates contingencies, sees through duplicity and double-dealing and adapts quickly to changing circumstances. Her most glaring lapse is failing to control the terms of her sale back into slavery. She does not even know that Tom has sold her *down* the river until she travels to her new home. Ever resilient, however, she escapes, finds Tom in St. Louis and forces the truth out of him in chapter 18. Angry though she is, even now she does not renounce him. Instead, she puts him to work to regain her legal freedom.

Like many of the white characters in *Pudd'nhead Wilson*, Roxy has her own stereotyped ideas about race and honor. In chapter 14, she shames Tom for failing to fight Luigi CAPELLO in a DUEL, telling him, "It's de NIGGER in you." She thinks Tom should behave in a way befitting his Essex "blood." She is as proud of Essex's aristocratic VIRGINIA background as she is of her own descent from John Smith and Pocahontas, as well as an African king.

Roxy's role in the published fragment of "THOSE EXTRAORDINARY TWINS" is minor; however, her powerful emergence in that original story helped force Mark Twain to abandon his original plot. He developed her belatedly as he transformed "Those Extraordinary Twins" into *Pudd'nhead Wilson*. There are, consequently, major inconsistencies in her character. For example, the feminine physical features he gives her at the beginning of the narrative seem to be lost by its middle.

Generally regarded as the strongest and most fully rounded female character that Mark Twain ever created, Roxy is resilient and indomitable, taking many initiatives that drive the narrative forward. No clear models for Roxy in Mark Twain's experience are known. Two decades before he created Roxy, however, he wrote about another strong black woman, Rachel Cord, in "A TRUE STORY."

It is possible that Mark Twain took Roxy's name from Daniel DEFOE's novel, *Roxana, or the Fortunate Mistress* (1724), which W. D. HOWELLS advised him to read in 1885. Defoe's picaresque heroine is a member of upper-class English society, but like Mark Twain's Roxana, she is forced by circumstances into shady behavior.

In the 1983 PBS television adaptation *Pudd'nhead Wilson*, Lise Hilboldt played Roxy.

"Royal Nonesuch" Ribald entertainment staged in *Huckleberry Finn*. In chapter 22, the DUKE and KING distribute handbills around BRICKSVILLE, Arkansas advertising "The Thrilling Tragedy of the King's CAMELOPARD or the Royal Nonesuch!!!" The line "Ladies and Children Not Admitted" fills the house. After a solemn introduction by the Duke, the performance consists solely of the King prancing about on all fours, naked, with stripes painted all over him. After members of the audience demand two encores, they are outraged to realize that his cavorting comprises the entire performance. One man persuades the others to defer their revenge until other townspeople are duped at the next performance. On the third night, men from the first two nights return with violence in mind. The Duke pockets the gate, however, and slips out with Huck to escape on the raft with the others.

As they drift downstream, the King and Duke look for another town in which to repeat their Royal Nonesuch success. When they attempt it again in PIKESVILLE, however, the audience is ready for them. Before the show, Jim—whom the King has sold for reward money—tells a man named BURTON about their scam. The moment that the King begins his camelopard routine, the audience turns on him and the Duke. Tom and Huck reach town as the two frauds are carried out on rails, tarred and feathered (chapter 33).

In his AUTOBIOGRAPHY, Mark Twain acknowledges getting the idea for the Nonesuch episode from Jim GILLIS. He used Gillis's title, "The Tragedy of the Burn-

The Duke (Orral Humphrey) introduces the King (Tom D. Bates) in the Royal Nonesuch, in the 1920 silent film adaptation of Huckleberry Finn.

ing Shame," in his draft manuscript, but thought it too vulgar to keep in the book, though he later mentioned its name in "TOM SAWYER'S CONSPIRACY" (chapter 9). Mark Twain called his own version "mild" and "pale" compared to Gillis's "outrageously funny" and "unprintable" story. Gillis's version may have drawn on an older folk story, featuring a naked man romping on stage with a lighted candle in his rectum. Similar stories were widely told in early–19th-century America. It is even possible that the King's cavorting involved sexual pantomime and that he wore a giant smoking phallus. Huck only says, "never mind the rest of his outfit, it was just wild, but it was awful funny."

Rucker, Ben Minor character in *Huckleberry Finn.* Chapters 24–25 mention Rucker and his wife among the friends of the late Peter WILKS who are duped by the KING and DUKE.

Ruffler, The Character in *The Prince and the Pauper.* The Ruffler leads the criminal gang that John CANTY forces King EDWARD to join in chapter 17. Though exercising nearly dictatorial powers, he has a soft heart; several times he shields Edward from abuse by other gang members. Actors who have portrayed him in films include Lionel Braham (1937) and George C. Scott (1977).

The word *ruffler* appears in mid–16th-century English law as a term for a phony soldier or swaggering vagabond. When Miles HENDON first appears in *The Prince and the Pauper,* he is described as having a "swaggering carriage [that] marked him at once as a ruffler of the camp" (chapter 11). Mark Twain also uses the word in chapter 14 of *Connecticut Yankee.*

Rufus J. Lackland STEAMBOAT on which Mark Twain apprenticed as a PILOT. Launched in Cincinnati in March 1857, the *Lackland* was a 710-ton freighter captained by William B. Miller. Mark Twain made one round-trip between St. Louis and New Orleans on the boat, from July 11 to August 3, 1857. It is not known who his pilot was.

"Running for Governor" Sketch written shortly after NEW YORK'S November 1870 gubernatorial election. Using his own pen name, Mark Twain describes his entirely invented experiences since being nominated several months earlier to run for governor of New York as an independent against Mr. John T. SMITH and Mr. Blank J. Blank (based on John T. Hoffman, 1828–1888). He thought that his good character gave him an advantage over his opponents, but soon found the press ready to level unsubstantiated charges against him. One newspaper, for example, called on him to explain why he was convicted of perjury in Wakawak, Cochin China (Vietnam), in 1863. Since he has never been in Cochin China, he does not know how to reply. As a result of his silence, the paper labels him "the infamous perjurer Twain."

Next, the *Gazette* demands that he explain why he was tarred and feathered in Montana for theft. Since he was never in Montana, he again does not reply and is branded "Twain the Montana Thief." As similarly unanswerable accusations appear, his growing list of sobriquets includes "Twain the Body-Snatcher," "Mr. Delirium Tremens Twain," "Twain the Filthy Corruptionist" and "Twain the Loathsome Embracer." Urged by supporters to answer these charges, he starts preparing a reply, only to be driven to distraction by new accusations. He is now charged with burning down a lunatic asylum, poisoning his uncle and other crimes. He gives up and withdraws his candidacy.

Mark Twain first published this 1,820-word sketch in the BUFFALO EXPRESS on November 19, 1870. The GALAXY reprinted it a month later and it was collected in SKETCHES, NEW AND OLD (1875).

Russia Mark Twain visited southern Russia in 1867. All the Russian cities that he saw on the Black Sea are now part of independent Ukraine. While CRIMEA war sites were featured attractions on the itinerary of the cruise ship QUAKER CITY, the real reason the ship's owners wanted to visit Russia was their hope of selling the ship to Czar ALEXANDER II. The *Quaker City* stopped first at SEVASTOPOL on August 21, then visited ODESSA and YALTA before sailing back to TURKEY a week later. Meanwhile, Mark Twain and most of his fellow passengers visited the czar near Yalta.

Chapters 35–37 of *Innocents Abroad* cover these visits, giving a generally favorable portrayal of Russia. While Mark Twain was impressed by the cordiality of Russians in 1867, he later came to detest Russia as a backward autocracy. Unfavorable allusions to Russia appear frequently in his late fiction. In chapter 30 of *Connecticut Yankee* (1889), for example, Hank MORGAN alludes to Russians as the most degraded of peoples. Russia provides an interesting link between that novel and *The American Claimant* (1892). In chapter 2 of the latter book, Colonel SELLERS keeps a map labeled "Future Siberia," with fancifully named cities, such as "Libertyorloffskoizalinski" and "Fredomolovnaivanovichapter." In chapter 18, he outlines a plan to liberate Russia by creating an internal revolution; his ideas are similar to Morgan's plans for revolutionizing sixth-century England in *Connecticut Yankee.* Sellers wants first to buy Siberia and start a republic, drawing upon the region's many noble and capable prisoners. He explains that Russia's system of sending anyone with intelligence to Siberia "keeps the general level of Russian intellect and education down to that of the Czar."

During the early 1890s, Mark Twain began supporting American anti-czarist movements. In 1890, he wrote a long letter advocating the czar's overthrow, but did not publish it. A second such manuscript, "The Answer," anticipated "THE CZAR'S SOLILOQUY," which he published in 1905. This polemic expresses impatience at the reluctance of Russians to rise against their rulers. Meanwhile, he wrote "THE BELATED RUSSIAN PASSPORT" (1902), a short story satirizing Russian bureaucracy and repression. The tale rests on the premise that anyone caught without a passport in Russia would be sent to Siberia for 10 years. The idea may have grown out of his own nerve-racking experience of visiting Russia with a borrowed passport in 1867.

William Lyon Phelps, who visited the Clemenses in Florence in 1904, noted Mark Twain's interest in the current Russo-Japanese War, in which he favored the Japanese. "CAPTAIN STORMFIELD'S VISIT TO HEAVEN," part of which Mark Twain published in 1907, describes heaven as an authoritarian state: "Russia—only more so."

Sacramento State capital of CALIFORNIA. Founded as a Swiss colony in 1839, Sacramento is in California's central valley, 80 miles northeast of SAN FRANCISCO, from which it could be reached by steamboat in the mid-19th century. The discovery of gold nearby in 1848 launched a GOLD RUSH that swelled Sacramento's population and led to its being made the state's capital six years later. Sacramento's permanent development was assured when it became a terminus for overland STAGECOACH lines, the pony express and the state's earliest railroad. Mark Twain visited Sacramento in late February 1866, when he arranged to become the SACRAMENTO UNION's correspondent in Hawaii. In August he returned to collect his money and in October he made his final visit during a LECTURE tour.

After his first visit to Sacramento, Mark Twain described it as the "City of Saloons" and wrote about the imbecility of its state legislators. A year later, he wrote a letter from Italy comparing VENICE with "an overflowed Sacramento"—a reference that readers of the SAN FRANCISCO ALTA CALIFORNIA would appreciate. *Innocents Abroad* revises this passage to compare Venice instead with "an overflowed Arkansas town" (chapter 22). *Roughing It* comments on Sacramento's fiery summer heat and discusses its growth during the GOLD RUSH (chapters 56–57).

Sacramento (Daily) Union One of the few survivors of scores of SACRAMENTO newspapers that sprang up during the GOLD RUSH, the *Union* began in 1851 and developed into one of the Pacific Coast's most prosperous and influential newspapers over the next decade. In 1862, Mark Twain tried to get the *Union* to make him its Nevada correspondent just before the VIRGINIA CITY TERRITORIAL ENTERPRISE gave him a staff position. Nearly four years later, in late February 1866, he went to Sacramento and persuaded the *Union* editors to send him to HAWAII as a correspondent. Details of his arrangements with the paper are uncertain. "MY DÉBUT AS A LITERARY PERSON" (1899) recalls the *Union* paying him $20 a letter; however, he may have received much more. In any case, he was sufficiently satisfied to comment on the *Union*'s generosity in *Roughing It* (chapter 62).

In March, Mark Twain sailed for the islands aboard the steamer AJAX, on which he began writing letters to the *Union*. Though he planned to spend just a month in Hawaii, his trip lasted over five months, during which he wrote about 90,000 words in 25 letters that the *Union* published between April 16 and September 26, 1866. Other West Coast papers reprinted these letters, helping to build Mark Twain's reputation in the region. The highlight of his correspondence was his scoop on the sinking of the clipper ship HORNET, for which he claimed the *Union* paid him 10 times its normal rate. He later wanted to turn his Hawaii letters into a book, but instead drew on half of them to write chapters 62 to 77 of *Roughing It*. His original *Union* letters have been reprinted in several later books.

sagebrush Common name for several hardy deciduous shrubs of the genus *Artemesia*. Called *sage*brush because its odor resembles that of sage, the shrub is the dominant vegetation across the great alkaline plains of the western United States. Three years in NEVADA wearied Mark Twain of the shrub, but he admired its toughness and its practical uses. *Roughing It* mentions sagebrush (or "sagebush") dozens of times, and chapter 3 devotes several pages to it. By the time Mark Twain resettled in California, he was so closely identified with Nevada (which has since made sagebrush its state flower) that the literary journal GOLDEN ERA nicknamed him the "Sage-Brush Humorist from Silver-Land"—presumably as a pun on his sagacity.

Sagramour le Desirous, Sir Character in *Connecticut Yankee*. A short-tempered knight, Sagramour overhears something Hank MORGAN says about another knight and takes it as an insult directed at him. He challenges Hank to a duel, but sets a date three or four years in the future to give himself time to seek the HOLY GRAIL (chapter 9). Several years later, Hank reads in the CAMELOT WEEKLY HOSANNAH that Sagramour is lost and that a new expedition is about to search for him (chapter 26).

When Sagramour finally fights Hank in chapter 39, MERLIN casts an enchantment intended to make him invisible to Hank, who nevertheless rides circles around him and ropes him off his horse to win the combat. After Hank defeats seven more knights, Merlin steals his lasso and Sagramour challenges Hank again. This time Hank shoots Sagramour dead with a revolver; he then defeats all the knights at once.

The bullet hole that Hank makes in Sagramour's chain-mail is the only physical evidence that survives from the sixth century to prove that Hank was actually there. In the 19th-century prelude to *Connecticut Yankee,* Hank tours WARWICK Castle's armor collection with the FRAME-narrator and laughs when their guide points out the bullet hole, suggesting that it was made by Cromwell's soldiers. The narrative of *Connecticut Yankee* thus begins as an explanation of how Hank came to shoot Sagramour.

Mark Twain's use of the bullet hole as a plot device may go back to his visit to PARIS's Bois de Boulogne in 1867, when a guide showed him a tree with a bullet hole made by a would-be assassin of Czar ALEXANDER II. In *Innocents Abroad* he predicts that guides will point out that hole to visitors until the tree falls down in 800 years, then put up another one and keep telling the same story (chapter 14).

Saint Jacques plantation   Fictitious place mentioned in *Huckleberry Finn.* In chapter 20, the DUKE prints a hand-bill advertising a reward for a slave who has run away from a "St. Jacques Plantation," 40 miles below NEW ORLEANS. The phony bill provides an explanation for Jim's presence on the raft. In chapter 31, Silas PHELPS gets custody of Jim and writes to the nonexistent plantation to claim the reward. By chapter 39, he is giving up on getting a reply.

Saint John, Lord (William Paulet; Marquis of Winchester) (c. 1485–March 10, 1572, Basing House, Hampshire, England)   Historical figure and minor character in *The Prince and the Pauper.* The lord steward of England's royal household, Baron St. John was also president of the privy council under King EDWARD VI. In chapter 6 of *The Prince and the Pauper,* he relays King Henry's command to Tom CANTY that he not deny he is Prince Edward. When St. John expresses his doubts about the prince's genuineness, HERTFORD cautions him against treasonous remarks. After the real Edward appears at the coronation, St. John twice goes to the royal palaces to fetch the Great Seal (chapter 32).

The historical St. John was distantly related to Sir Amyas Paulet, who had the same name as *Connecticut Yankee*'s CLARENCE.

Saint Louis   Missouri's largest city during the 19th century, St. Louis was, and is, a major river port below the junction of the MISSOURI and Mississippi rivers at the center of eastern Missouri. Mark Twain spent the first 17 years of his life in FLORIDA and Hannibal, just over a hundred miles northwest of St. Louis, and later visited the city many times. At the time of his birth, St. Louis had a population of around 10,000, a number that quadrupled over the next decade.

As a child, Mark Twain regarded St. Louis as a distant wonderland. *Life on the Mississippi* recalls that any neighbor boy who had been there was regarded as a person of consideration (chapter 4). When Huck and Jim drift past the city at night in *Huckleberry Finn,* Huck describes seeing "the whole world lit up"; he has heard that St. Louis has 20 or 30 thousand people, but does not believe it until seeing the city at night (chapter 12).

Mark Twain's brother Orion Clemens worked as a printer in St. Louis through much of the 1840s and established an important connection with Edward BATES there. Mark Twain himself first visited the city, with his father, around 1845, when he was about 10 years old. His sister, Pamela Clemens MOFFETT, settled there with her husband in late 1851. After Mark Twain left Hannibal in June 1853, he stopped first at St. Louis and stayed with Pamela and her husband. By this time, the city's population was well over 60,000. While there he worked as a printer on the *Evening News* and other newspapers before moving east. He returned there around the spring of 1854, visited his sister, and then joined Orion in MUSCATINE, Iowa. By August 7 he was in St. Louis again, in time to witness the Know-Nothing election riots—an episode described in chapter 51 of *Life on the Mississippi.* This time he boarded with another family from Hannibal, the Paveys, staying through the middle of June 1855, when he left for KEOKUK, Iowa. He next visited St. Louis around mid-October 1856.

In 1857 Mark Twain started working on the Mississippi River as an apprentice steamboat PILOT, beginning a four-year period when he passed through St. Louis regularly. Between February 1857 and May 1861—when the CIVIL WAR ended commercial river traffic—he landed at St. Louis perhaps 60 times. During prolonged periods between steamboat jobs, he generally stayed with his sister's family. He paid his last visit to St. Louis in June 1902, after accepting an honorary degree at the University of MISSOURI in Columbia. During this visit he attended ground-breaking ceremonies for the 1904 world's fair commemorating Lewis and Clark's expedition and he helped rededicate a steamboat as the "MARK TWAIN."

Mark Twain mentions St. Louis frequently in his fiction, but the only novel in which the city figures prominently is *Pudd'nhead Wilson.* This story places St. Louis about a half-day's steamboat journey upriver from the novel's main setting, DAWSON'S LANDING. Tom DRISCOLL visits St. Louis frequently to gamble, and uses the city to hide out after committing crimes in Dawson's Landing. In chapter 16, he sells his mother, ROXANA, back into slavery in St. Louis; and it is there that she confronts him after escaping from her Arkansas owner in chapter 18.

Tom Sawyer mentions St. Louis twice—both times disrespectfully. Chapter 18 describes Alfred TEMPLE, a new boy in St. Petersburg, as "that Saint Louis smarty that thinks he dresses so fine and is aristocracy!" Chapter 24 alludes to a pompous St. Louis detective who comes to town to investigate Injun Joe's disappearance. A similarly sarcastic allusion to St. Louis detectives appears in chapter 15 of *Pudd'nhead Wilson.*

The action of *Tom Sawyer Abroad* begins in chapter 2, when Tom insists on going to St. Louis to look at a fabulous balloon that is on display. While he, Huck and Jim inspect the balloon, they are carried off by a mad PROFESSOR. St. Louis figures into the background to *Tom Sawyer, Detective* as the place where Jake DUNLAP and his confederates pull off a diamond heist. Huck and Tom spend four days in St. Louis in "TOM SAWYER'S CONSPIRACY," but Huck, the story's narrator, says little about the city itself (chapter 9).

Saint Nicholas Magazine Children's magazine. Founded in November 1873, *St. Nicholas* was published by Scribner until 1880, when the Century Company took it over. Under the editorship of Mary Mapes DODGE (editor, 1873–1905) and William Fayal Clarke (1905–27), the magazine attracted many major writers of juvenile literature, including Robert Louis Stevenson, Louisa May Alcott, Howard Pyle and others. It was the original publisher of such classics as Frances Hodgson Burnett's *Little Lord Fauntleroy* (1886), Rudyard KIPLING's *The Jungle Book* (1894) and Mark Twain's *Tom Sawyer Abroad* (1894).

A. B. PAINE was a member of the magazine's editorial staff from 1888 through 1900. The magazine later serialized his *Boys' Life of Mark Twain* (1915–16). *St. Nicholas* ceased publication in 1940.

Saint Petersburg Fictional town in *Tom Sawyer, Huckleberry Finn* and other stories. Clearly modeled on Mark Twain's hometown of Hannibal in northeastern Missouri, St. Petersburg appears to be at the same location, on the west bank of the Mississippi. It also matches Hannibal in having a wooded promontory, CARDIFF HILL, on the north side of town. Several miles downriver, toward the ILLINOIS shore, there is a large uninhabited island, JACKSON'S ISLAND. A few miles south of the center of town is a large limestone CAVE. Tom Sawyer lives in the center of town in a two-story house that closely resembles Mark Twain's BOYHOOD HOME of the 1840s.

Virtually all the events in *Tom Sawyer* occur in or near St. Petersburg. The town is also the setting of the first six chapters of *Huckleberry Finn*, which mentions St. Petersburg by name only in chapters 11, 12 and 42. Among the other stories about Tom and Huck, St. Petersburg is the principal setting for "TOM SAWYER'S CONSPIRACY"—which does not mention its name—and "SCHOOLHOUSE HILL"—which calls it simply "Petersburg."

While St. Petersburg physically resembles Hannibal, it differs from the real town in being smaller and less diverse. It appears to have fewer people, fewer industries and fewer activities. Incidents and characters in *Tom Sawyer* indicate that the town has a mayor, a postmaster, at least one church and one school, a newspaper, a printer, two taverns, an abandoned slaughterhouse and an abandoned tannery. An indication of the town's smallness is the fact that its graveyard has only wooden

head markers. In general, the town feels more rural than Hannibal; in this regard it resembles the nearby village of FLORIDA, where Mark Twain spent most of his summers during the 1840s. Many of the events in *Tom Sawyer* occur during a long summer vacation; it is natural that Mark Twain's depiction of life in St. Petersburg would reflect the summertime experiences of his youth.

The literal meaning of "St. Petersburg" is "Saint Peter's town," or heaven. If Mark Twain consciously intended the name to stand for "heaven," it represents an interesting contrast with "Hannibal." At least once, he wrote the latter name as "H——l," possibly implying that Hannibal was synonymous with "Hell." To call the fictional counterpart of such a place "heaven" suggests that he intended to satirize Hannibal's small-town hypocrisy—just as he did with the name HADLEYBURG in another story. Alternatively, equating St. Petersburg with heaven might simply reflect Mark Twain's idealization of his summers in Florida. In his AUTOBIOGRAPHY, he recalls the Florida farm of his uncle John QUARLES as a heavenly place for boys.

Mark Twain was also aware of St. Petersburg, RUSSIA. Anson BURLINGAME, whom he greatly admired, died there in 1870. Years later Mark Twain used Russia's capital as a principal setting in "THE BELATED RUSSIAN PASSPORT." In the meantime, his future son-in-law, Ossip GABRILOWITSCH, was born there in 1878.

Salt Lake City Capital of UTAH. Named after the Great Salt Lake to its northwest, Salt Lake City was founded in 1847 by MORMON settlers, who quickly built it into the Rocky Mountains' biggest commercial and transportation center. Mark Twain spent two days there, August 5–6, 1861, when it had at least 15,000 residents. *Roughing It* devotes most of chapters 13 to 17 to the city, comparing it to something out of the ARABIAN NIGHTS.

Samossoud, Jacques (September 8, 1894–June 13, 1966) Second husband of Clara Clemens and heir to the Mark Twain estate. Like his friend Ossip GABRILOWITSCH, Clara's first husband, who died in 1936, Samossoud was a Russian musician. He married Clara on May 11, 1944 (a week after the film THE ADVENTURES OF MARK TWAIN opened). Samossoud was then directing a Los Angeles opera company, but he did not work regularly in later years. A handsome man 20 years younger than Clara, he gambled frequently and spent her money freely. In 1951, the couple auctioned off Clara's Hollywood home and possessions—including many of Mark Twain manuscripts—and moved to San Diego, near a race track.

After Clara died in 1962, Samossoud's lawyers settled with Clara's daughter Nina GABRILOWITSCH to adjust Clara's will, which left the income of her father's estate to Samossoud. Four years later, Samossoud died, leaving the income from the original family trust to his friend Dr. William E. Seiler. On Seiler's death in 1978, the residue of the estate passed to the MARK TWAIN FOUNDATION.

Samossoud is buried in an unmarked grave in the Clemens family plot at Elmira's WOODLAWN CEMETERY.

San Francisco CALIFORNIA city in which Mark Twain lived during the mid-1860s. Built on a peninsula protecting a large enclosed bay, San Francisco was founded as a Spanish military base in 1776. When California became an American territory in 1848, the city still had less than a thousand residents. Its population exploded, however, after California's GOLD RUSH began that same year. By the early 1860s, it had well over 100,000 people and its port was one of the busiest in America. With numerous daily newspapers, opera houses, fine hotels and restaurants and other amenities, San Francisco grew from nearly nothing to became the Pacific Coast's leading city.

Mark Twain first visited San Francisco in May 1863, while on vacation from the VIRGINIA CITY TERRITORIAL ENTERPRISE in Nevada. In a visit lasting over two months, he began writing for the GOLDEN ERA, a local literary weekly, and arranged to become Nevada correspondent for the daily SAN FRANCISCO CALL. He enjoyed the city enough to make another long visit in September. At the end of May 1864, he and his friend Steve GILLIS moved to San Francisco and both went to work for the *Call*. Over the next four months, they roomed together, changing residences often. Mark Twain remained in San Francisco almost every day through 1866, with the exceptions of a two-and-a-half-month visit to TUOLUMNE and CALAVERAS counties that began in December 1864, a voyage to HAWAII in mid-1866 and a lecture tour in October–November 1866 that followed his first professional lecture in Maguire's Opera House on October 2. Through these years, Mark Twain became a member of the city's lively literary and artistic community, which included Bret HARTE, Charles Henry WEBB, Charles Warren STODDARD, Joaquin MILLER and others. He wrote for the monthly CALIFORNIAN and the SAN FRANCISCO DRAMATIC CHRONICLE and became the *Territorial Enterprise*'s Pacific Coast correspondent after just four months on the *Call*.

When Mark Twain departed from California at the end of 1866, he left as a roving correspondent for the SAN FRANCISCO ALTA CALIFORNIA newspaper, which sent him to the Mediterranean on the QUAKER CITY excursion the following year. This cruise led to his first major book, *Innocents Abroad*. On April 2, 1868, he returned to San Francisco, largely in order to get the *Alta* to release copyright to the letters he was revising for the book. Except for a quick lecture tour in late April, he remained there working on his manuscript until July 6, when he left for the last time. He wanted to come back, but the closest he came to returning was in 1895, when he tried unsuccessfully to schedule a San Francisco stop at the beginning of his round-the-world lecture tour.

Although Mark Twain spent about 22 months in San Francisco between 1863 and 1866, *Roughing It*—his book about that period—says relatively little about the city, glossing over the first two years in chapters 56–59 and the first paragraph of chapter 62. Chapter 78 focuses on his first lecture in the city in 1866. Mark Twain also makes limited use of San Francisco in his fiction. "GOLDSMITH'S FRIEND ABROAD AGAIN" (1870) is about a Chinese immigrant to San Francisco. In the "PROFESSOR'S YARN" of *Life on the Mississippi*, the narrator's ship arrives in San Francisco just as a crooked poker game is ending. San Francisco is also the place that Captain STORMFIELD announces he is from when he arrives in heaven.

During the 20th century, Mark Twain's association with San Francisco has been made famous by his alleged quip that "the coldest winter I ever spent was a summer in San Francisco." There is no evidence that Mark Twain ever uttered or wrote this remark, which flatly contradicts his recorded opinions of the city's weather, which he regarded as monotonously pleasant.

San Francisco Alta California California's first daily newspaper, the *Alta* began in late 1848 as the *Star and Californian*, which merged the San Francisco *Star* with the *Californian*, the state's first newspaper. Soon renamed the *Alta California*—from Spanish for "Upper California"—the paper flourished under the direction of Edward Cleveland Kemble (the father of E. W. KEMBLE), becoming a daily in 1850. When Mark Twain lived in San Francisco during the mid-1860s, the *Alta* competed for circulation with the SAN FRANCISCO BULLETIN and the SAN FRANCISCO CALL—for which he worked. Before returning to the East Coast in December 1866, he arranged with the *Alta*'s editor John McComb (1829–1896) to write travel letters, 26 of which appeared in the *Alta* between January 18 and August 18, 1867 (these letters were later collected in MARK TWAIN'S TRAVELS WITH MR. BROWN).

In early 1867, Mark Twain learned about the QUAKER CITY's June cruise to the Mediterranean and persuaded the *Alta* to pay his $1,250 passage on the cruise in return for at least 50 letters that he would write to the paper at $20 each. Of 58 letters about the trip that he eventually published in American papers, 50 appeared in the *Alta* between August 25, 1867 and May 17, 1868. All these letters are collected in *Traveling with the Innocents Abroad*, edited by Daniel Morley McKeithan (1958).

After the *Quaker City* voyage ended in November, Mark Twain began writing a book about it which he published as *Innocents Abroad* (1869). In January 1868, his friend Joe GOODMAN warned him that the *Alta* had copyrighted his letters and planned to publish them in a book of its own. Mark Twain returned to San Francisco in March to persuade the *Alta*'s proprietors to release their rights to him. After an apparently rancorous argument, they agreed. Decades later, he still rankled over the paper's reluctance to turn over what he regarded as rightfully his. Meanwhile, he remained in San Francisco long enough to finish *Innocents Abroad,* into which he incorporated substantial portions of his *Alta* letters. Many of these letters he revised considerably, making a particular effort to edit out references and language originally aimed at western readers—such as a comparison of Venice, Italy with SACRAMENTO, California. Aside from the prefatory acknowledgment, the book does not mention the *Alta.*

During 1868–1869, Mark Twain wrote 12 more letters from the East Coast to the *Alta.* He had no further dealings with the paper, which expired in 1891.

San Francisco Bulletin   Founded in 1855, the evening *Bulletin* soon ranked with the ALTA CALIFORNIA as a leading SAN FRANCISCO daily newspaper. In October 1862, the *Bulletin* was quick to recognize Mark Twain's PETRIFIED MAN HOAX for what it was, dubbing it "A Washoe Joke." A year later, however, its editors were not so savvy. In October 1863, the VIRGINIA CITY TERRITORIAL ENTERPRISE published Mark Twain's MASSACRE HOAX, a subtle SATIRE designed to embarrass the *Bulletin* for its complicity in "dividend-cooking" schemes in Nevada's mining industry. A careful reading of his article reveals that its murderer went crazy after losing all his money when he followed the dishonest investment advice of a *Bulletin* editor—in other words, the *Bulletin* itself was responsible for the massacre. Missing this point entirely, the *Bulletin* guilelessly reprinted the *Enterprise* piece as "The Latest Sensation." When its editors later learned that it was a hoax, they were furious.

San Francisco Call   Newspaper for which Mark Twain wrote. Founded by five printers in December 1856, the morning *Call* was long the cheapest of five daily SAN FRANCISCO newspapers. By the early 1860s, it led the others in circulation while appearing every morning but Mondays. When Mark Twain visited San Francisco in June 1863, the *Call* made him its NEVADA correspondent and published his occasional letters from August through December that year. The following May, Mark Twain moved to San Francisco with Steve GILLIS. On about June 6, 1864, the *Call*'s co-proprietor, George E. BARNES, hired Mark Twain as the paper's only full-time reporter at about $40 a week. For four months, Mark Twain put in long days covering local news, cranking out hundreds of brief articles, while Gillis worked as a *Call* compositor. Compared to Mark Twain's job on the VIRGINIA CITY TERRITORIAL ENTERPRISE, the *Call* hardly tapped his creative talents, making his routine unbearably tedious.

At that time, the *Call* shared a building at 612 Commercial Street with the GOLDEN ERA—a local literary journal in which Mark Twain found a welcome creative outlet. Meanwhile, he neglected his reporting duties until Barnes fired him (around October 10). *Roughing It*'s account of this period alludes to Mark Twain's working for a newspaper—without naming the *Call*—and implies that he was merely invited to resign (chapter 58). Mark Twain recorded a more forthright account of his dismissal 35 years later in his AUTOBIOGRAPHY. In April 1906, news reports of the great San Francisco earthquake reminded him of his time at the *Call,* prompting his painful admission that he was "discharged." A news photograph showing the *Call* building flattened by the earthquake inspired him to remark on the wisdom of Providence in settling his 40-year-old account with the paper.

Another reason that Mark Twain was unhappy at the *Call* was Barnes's cautious editorial policy. Reluctant to publish anything that might ruffle white working-class readers, Barnes often censored or suppressed Mark Twain's articles on social problems and police misconduct. After leaving the *Call,* Mark Twain became the *Enterprise*'s Pacific Coast correspondent. The *Call* itself prospered without him; it lasted until 1929, when it merged with the SAN FRANCISCO BULLETIN. Three decades later, the *Call-Bulletin* merged with another paper to become the *News Call-Bulletin,* which in turn was absorbed by the *San Francisco Examiner* in 1965. Edgar M. Branch has collected hundreds of Mark Twain's *Call* articles in *Clemens of the Call* (1969).

San Francisco Dramatic Chronicle   The only SAN FRANCISCO newspaper from Mark Twain's time that still exists, the *Dramatic Chronicle* was founded as an entertainment sheet by teenage brothers, Charles and Michael De Young, in March 1865. Mark Twain joined Bret HARTE as an early contributor to the paper and was a salaried staff member from late October through mid-December, when the paper published dozens of his brief, unsigned articles. His only *Chronicle* piece that saw book publication during his lifetime is "Earthquake Almanac," a brief BURLESQUE of weather reporting inspired by San Francisco's October 8, 1865 earthquake that he collected in THE CELEBRATED JUMPING FROG OF CALAVERAS COUNTY. The *Chronicle* dropped "Dramatic" from its masthead in September 1868.

Sand Belt   Fictional battle site in *Connecticut Yankee.* The "sand belt" is a defense perimeter that CLARENCE sets up around MERLIN's Cave, where Hank MORGAN and his tiny army take on the massed chivalry of England. Forty feet wide, the belt lies 100 yards beyond the last of a series of electrified fences that surround the cave. It is laced with explosive torpedoes covered with a thin layer of sand (chapter 42). When the first wave of knights enters the belt, they are blown to bits, leaving a deep ditch in its place (chapter 43). Afterward, Hank congratulates his men on winning the "Battle of the Sand-Belt," then puts them to work diverting the course of a nearby stream. When the next wave of attackers fills the ditch, he floods it with the stream's waters, drowning thousands of knights. The scenario resembles an incident in America's CIVIL WAR, when Union troops besieging Petersburg, Virginia were trapped and killed in a crater formed by a mine blast.

Sandwich Islands   When Captain James COOK found HAWAII in 1778, he dubbed it the "Sandwich Islands" after the chief of the British admiralty, the Earl of Sandwich. The archipelago's name officially reverted to "Hawaii" when the United States annexed the islands in 1898. After visiting Hawaii in 1866, Mark Twain delivered what he called his "Sandwich Islands" lecture more than a hundred times, often under the title, "Our Fellow Savages of the Sandwich Islands." *Roughing It* chides Cook for not having the taste to call Hawaii the "Rainbow Islands" after its omnipresent rainbows (chapter 71).

Sandy (Demoiselle Alisande la Carteloise)   Character in *Connecticut Yankee*. The novel's most important female character, Sandy first appears at CAMELOT in chapter 11, when she relates a tale about three ogres' holding 44 beautiful princesses captive for 26 years. Every knight begs permission to rescue the women, but King ARTHUR assigns the mission to Hank MORGAN. Hank then interviews the Demoiselle Alisande—whom he nicknames "Sandy" in the next chapter. The only solid information that he gets out of her is that she is from the land of Moder, has no family and is new to Camelot. He then takes her with him on his mission, remaining constantly uncomfortable with what he regards as the impropriety of traveling unchaperoned with a woman.

Throughout his mission, Hank regards Sandy as an airheaded BLATHERSKITE who relates interminable tales and disgraces the human race by abasing herself before hogs that she thinks are princesses (chapter 20). Hank is anxious to get rid of her, but discovers that she is unshakably committed to staying with him. Meanwhile, Sandy repeatedly proves herself more decisive than Hank. She secures the surrender of seven knights whom Hank frightens by blowing tobacco smoke through his helmet (chapter 14) and twice cows MORGAN LE FAY into backing down (chapters 16–17).

Hank's relationship with Sandy changes in the VALLEY OF HOLINESS, where she nurses him through an illness. One day, after he belittles her failure to grasp his modern slang, he realizes how hard she tries to please him, and he apologizes. As their friendship improves, Hank senses that he is developing "a mysterious and shuddery reverence" for Sandy (chapter 22). In chapter 27, he leaves her behind when he and Arthur tramp off disguised as peasants. Sandy reappears momentarily in chapter 36, when Hank spots her looking for him in London.

In chapter 40, the narrative jumps ahead three years, by which time Hank and Sandy have a daughter named HELLO-CENTRAL. In the next chapter, Hank explains that he has married Sandy because he could not get rid of

Dan Beard's picture of the Demoiselle Alisande la Carteloise is modeled on the actress Annie Russell.

her and did not want to compromise her. Nevertheless, he has become Sandy's worshipper after a year of marriage and calls her a "flawless wife and mother." His description of their relationship as the "dearest and perfectest comradeship that ever was" mirrors Mark Twain's description of his own marriage. Despite Hank's lavish praise of Sandy, however, he is still thinking about his old girlfriend, Hartford telephone operator Puss FLANAGAN, as late as chapter 39. He seems to be dreaming about Puss even after marrying Sandy, who overhears him call out "Hello, Central!" in his sleep.

Hank and Sandy last see each other in Gaul, where they go for Hello-Central's health. After Hank returns to England to confront the massed chivalry of the country at Merlin's Cave, he writes to Sandy daily, though there is no way for him to post letters to her (chapter 43). After he returns to the 19th century, he dies calling out Sandy's name. Daniel BEARD, whose illustrations model Sandy on the actress Annie Russell (1869–1936), suggests a happier ending for the book. His final picture shows Hank, Sandy and the baby reunited over a supine Father Time.

Actresses who have portrayed Sandy on screen include Pauline Starke (1921), Maureen O'Sullivan (1931), Rhonda Fleming (1949), Sally Gracie (1954), Janet Blair (1955) and Sheila White (1979). Constance Carpenter (1927) and Julie Warren (1943) played Sandy in Broadway musical adaptations.

Sanitary Commission, United States (Sanitary Fund) CIVIL WAR relief organization that helped care for sick and wounded Union soldiers and their families. Founded by Unitarian clergyman Henry Whitney Bellows (1814–1882) in June 1861, it was supported mainly by private contributions, especially "Sanitary Fairs." Mark Twain took a particular interest in the fund because his sister, Pamela MOFFETT, was a leader of its St. Louis branch, which organized a Mississippi Valley Sanitary Fair in February 1864. At her request, he tried to raise money for the fair in Nevada's COMSTOCK region, but had little success until Reuel GRIDLEY showed up in May with his famous "Sanitary Flour Sack." *Roughing It* recounts how Gridley's arrival stimulated fund-raising (chapter 45), somewhat exaggerating the amounts that he raised. Gridley spent over a year traveling with his flour sack, ending his tour at the St. Louis fair. Meanwhile, Mark Twain made trouble for himself in Nevada by publishing an article in the VIRGINIA CITY TERRITORIAL ENTERPRISE facetiously suggesting that money raised by Carson City women for the Sanitary Fund went to an Eastern miscegenation society and that the VIRGINIA CITY UNION was not meeting its pledges to the fund. After leaving Nevada for California, he continued to promote the fund while writing for the SAN FRANCISCO CALL and became friendly with Dr. Bellows when the latter toured the West Coast.

Saranac Lake Town near Lake Placid in northeastern NEW YORK's Adirondack Mountains. Taking its name from three nearby lakes, Saranac became noted as a health resort after 1884, when Dr. Edward Livingston Trudeau founded America's first tuberculosis sanatorium nearby; Robert Louis Stevenson convalesced there in the winter of 1887–88.

From June 21 through September 19, 1901, Mark Twain and his family lived in a rustic cottage they nicknamed the "Lair" on the shore of Lower Saranac Lake (where they used "Ampersand" for a mailing address). In August, Mark Twain interrupted his stay there to cruise on H. H. ROGERS's KANAWHA. While at Saranac, he wrote "The United States of Lyncherdom" and "A DOUBLE-BARRELLED DETECTIVE STORY." In October, the family took up residence in RIVERDALE-ON-THE-HUDSON.

Satan Character in "THE CHRONICLE OF YOUNG SATAN." A favorite nephew of the fallen archangel Satan (the narrator of LETTERS FROM THE EARTH), the young Satan is 16,000 earth-years old. He has been everywhere and seen everything (chapter 2). He is a spirit in a body that looks and feels real to the touch and can make himself invisible, merge into other bodies and move instantaneously through space and time. He has godlike powers and uses them freely.

Satan resembles the characters called "FORTY-FOUR" in Mark Twain's other "MYSTERIOUS STRANGER" stories, "SCHOOLHOUSE HILL" and NO. 44, THE MYSTERIOUS STRANGER in being a boy with marvelous powers who visits an isolated village. He differs from these other characters, however, in distancing himself more from humans, while being more forthcoming about his identity. Though he never explicitly states why he is visiting earth or what he hopes to accomplish, he explains who he is and where he comes from.

Satan first appears in "Chronicle" when he joins Theodor FISCHER and his friends, who are playing on a hill near ESELDORF (chapter 2). In the form of a boy about the same age as the others, he is so handsome, graceful and personable that the boys are instinctively drawn to him. Communication is easy, as he reads their minds and anticipates their questions and desires. After identifying himself as an angel, he tells the boys to call him "Philip TRAUM" when other people are around. As the narrative unfolds, Satan astounds the boys with his powers and increasingly intervenes in the lives of villagers. Despite his ageless wisdom, he shares the boyishness of Tom Sawyer, Hank MORGAN and other Mark Twain characters in liking to show off.

satire Literary term for a work that uses ridicule to attack ideas, institutions, people, or other objects taken from real life. In order to arouse disdain for its targets, satire belittles human weaknesses, using humor as its weapon. Throughout his career, Mark Twain consciously wrote satire, recognizing the power of humor in an ideological battle. Philip TRAUM, the title character in "THE CHRONICLE OF YOUNG SATAN," makes this point explicitly when he points up the impotence of weapons such as power, money, persuasion and persecution against the colossal humbug of "papal infallibility." By contrast, he says that "against the assault of Laughter nothing can stand."

Mark Twain also recognized the need for dispassion in writing effective satire. In an 1879 letter to W. D. HOWELLS, he wrote that a person "can't write successful satire except he be in a calm judicial good-humor"—a mood that he was having difficulty maintaining in the midst of his constant raging against all the world's great irritations.

Mark Twain uses satire throughout his major writings. *Huckleberry Finn* employs it repeatedly, as in the GRANGERFORD episode, when two otherwise admirable and intelligent families destroy each other because of a feud so old that they do not even know why they are fighting. A more sustained satire is his first novel, *The Gilded Age*, which he wrote in collaboration with C. D. WARNER. This sprawling novel satirizes almost every aspect of 19th-century America's political and social mores. Its sequel, *The American Claimant*, tends toward BURLESQUE and farce, but nevertheless contains some sharp satire, such as the story line about a democratically motivated young English noble. Lord BERKELEY comes to America prepared to give up his inherited aristocratic privileges for republican equality, only to find a society obsessed with grasping for what he wants to cast off.

Another example of a satire that is recognized as one of Mark Twain's most successful is "CAPTAIN STORMFIELD'S VISIT TO HEAVEN." This novelette has clear targets and sticks to them. One of these is its attack on human vanity: Stormfield discovers that Earth counts for so little in the cosmic scheme of things that a clerk in heaven needs two days just to find it on a map.

Satires & Burlesques, Mark Twain's Collection of previously unpublished material edited by Franklin R. Rogers for the MARK TWAIN PAPERS project in 1967. Most of the items in this collection are writings that Mark Twain left unfinished, such as "Autobiography of a Damned Fool," a story based on the life of Orion Clemens. The volume also has several stories that Mark Twain completed and intended to publish, such as "1,002D ARABIAN NIGHT." Other notable items include "Hellfire Hotchkiss," several pieces about Simon Wheeler, and BURLESQUES of Verdi's opera *Il Trovatore*, Shakespeare's HAMLET and Victor Hugo's *L'Homme Qui Rit*.

Saturday Morning Club Hartford discussion group. In October 1876, Mark Twain helped organize an informal group of 20–25 late-teenage girls for regular Saturday morning essay and debate meetings. He drafted the group's rules and often led discussions and read from his own work. Invited speakers included local Trinity College professors and such writers as W. D. HOWELLS, Bret HARTE and C. D. WARNER. The group continued to meet well after Mark Twain left Hartford in 1891.

Saturday Press Weekly magazine founded in New York in October 1858 by the noted Bohemian humorist Henry Clapp (1814–1875) and Edward Howland. After suspending publication during the CIVIL WAR, the paper resumed in 1865. Highly regarded by writers, it published important early work by William Winter, Walt Whitman and Josh BILLINGS. It is best known, however, for publishing Mark Twain's JUMPING FROG STORY. After George CARLETON gave the story to Clapp, the *Press* published it as "Jim Smiley and his Jumping Frog" on November 18, 1865. The story was widely noticed and often reprinted, but the *Press* itself folded the following year, moving Mark Twain later to write that his story killed the paper "with a suddenness that was beyond praise."

sawyer Term for a tree that has slid into a river that has eroded its banks. Still attached to solid ground below water, sawyers often bob up and down wildly and pose serious hazards to boats. During the 19th century they wrecked many STEAMBOATS, particularly on the MISSOURI RIVER. The word—whose meaning goes back to late 18th-century American usage—appears just once in *Life on the Mississippi*, at the beginning of chapter 40.

Mark Twain used "Sawyer" as a surname for several characters, most notably Tom SAWYER—whose name some scholars believe Mark Twain chose to symbolize the boy's unpredictability. Mark Twain first used the name for a minor character in "BOY'S MANUSCRIPT" (1868)—*Bob* Sawyer, who spies on Billy ROGERS—the literary predecessor of Tom Sawyer. The narrator of *Roughing It* invites a stranger named Sawyer to attend his first lecture because the man is certain to laugh at every joke (chapter 78). Mark Twain modeled this character on a hard-drinking Wells, Fargo driver named William M. Slason (1831?–1872), who was noted for his love of a good joke.

Sawyer (?), Mary Character in *Tom Sawyer*. A cousin of Tom Sawyer, Mary lives with Tom, Tom's half-brother Sid SAWYER and Tom's Aunt POLLY. Mary is a steady presence in Tom's life, but several questions about her are unanswered. For example, neither her last name nor her relationship to Aunt Polly is ever specified. Her name may be *Sawyer*, but the evidence is thin. In chapter 32 of *Huckleberry Finn*, Huck talks about Mary and the "Sawyer family" together. Does this mean she is a Sawyer? If so, what is her relationship to Aunt Polly, who is the sister of Tom's *mother*? Uncertainty about Mary's family ties confused even W. D. HOWELLS. When he reviewed the novel, he mistakenly alluded to Mary as Tom's sister.

Another question is how old Mary is. Her age is not given, but she is clearly more mature than Tom. When she first appears, in chapter 3 of *Tom Sawyer*, she is returning from a week in the country at a moment when Tom and other children are still in school. It thus appears that Mary herself is not in school. In chapter 18, however, Sid and Tom leave for school and Mary seems to be going with them. One clue to Mary's age is the fact that she is clearly modeled on Pamela Clemens MOFFETT, Mark Twain's sister, who was eight years his senior. Like Pamela, Mary is gentle and helpful. In chapter 4, she helps Tom learn his verses for Sunday school, giving him a pocketknife as encouragement. The gift is enough of an extravagance to suggest that Mary—like Pamela—has income of her own. Later, Mary stays home from Becky THATCHER's picnic to tend Tom's sick brother Sid.

Mary also appears briefly in TOM SAWYER, DETECTIVE and in "TOM SAWYER'S CONSPIRACY." In the latter story, Aunt POLLY sends Mary and Sid out of town when Tom appears to have measles.

Sawyer, Sid Character in *Tom Sawyer* and other stories. Tom's priggish younger half-brother, Sid lives with Tom, Aunt POLLY and Tom's cousin Mary (SAWYER?). He first appears in chapter 1 of *Tom Sawyer*, but is not clearly identified as a "Sawyer" until chapter 33 of *Huckleberry Finn*. As half-brothers surnamed *Sawyer*, Sid and Tom presumably had the same father and different mothers. Since Aunt Polly is identified as the sister of Tom's *mother*, Sid's relationship to Polly is unclear.

Throughout *Tom Sawyer*, Sid is a constant irritant to Tom. He spies on Tom and reports to Aunt Polly. The brothers share a bedroom, making it difficult for Tom to come and go without being observed. In the unfinished story "TOM SAWYER'S CONSPIRACY," Sid poses such a threat to Tom's scheming that Tom tries to contract measles in order to give Aunt Polly a reason to send Sid out of town.

Sid appears for just a moment in *Huckleberry Finn*. In chapter 8, Huck sees him on the boat that is searching the river for his body. Later in the novel, Tom Sawyer poses as Sid at the Arkansas farm of his aunt Sally PHELPS (chapter 33).

Sid also appears briefly in the first chapter of "SCHOOLHOUSE HILL," in which he is described as "the MODEL BOY." Mark Twain based Sid on his own younger brother, Henry Clemens.

Sawyer, Tom Arguably Mark Twain's most famous fictional creation, Tom Sawyer has come to symbolize Mark Twain's work as a whole to many. Tom and his friend Huck Finn are usually viewed as a team, as neither appears in any story without the other. Nevertheless, they are very different kinds of characters.

Mark Twain provides little physical description of Tom. When Tom first appears in *Tom Sawyer*, he is described simply as "a small boy." Little else about him is revealed, except that he has curly hair and generally goes barefoot. Also, he is tough enough to lick most boys his age and athletic enough to swim considerable distances. Mark Twain is especially vague about Tom's age, which seems to rise significantly between the beginning and end of *Tom Sawyer*. In the early chapters, Tom appears to be about nine years old. This is the age that Mark Twain himself was in 1844—the approximate year in which the novel is set. By the last chapters—and in *Huckleberry Finn* and other stories—Tom seems to be at least 13. Uncertainty about Tom's age is reflected in the illustrations of Tom that have adorned Mark Twain's books and in the casting of films adapted from these stories.

One of the changes in Tom that occur over the course of *Tom Sawyer* is his growing maturity regarding girls. Early in the narrative he has a purely boyish infatuation

True Williams's frontispiece showing Tom fishing in his Sunday best depicts a moment that never happens in Tom Sawyer.

with Becky THATCHER, a girl who clearly is about eight or nine years old. Tom expresses his emotions by showing off to Becky to get her attention, flirting with Amy LAWRENCE to make Becky jealous, and sulking when things go badly. As the narrative progresses, he proves his worth by performing real deeds. By its end, he seems to be on the threshold of becoming an adult, while Becky is still nine years old.

From the start of *Tom Sawyer*, Mark Twain makes it is clear that Tom is *not* a "MODEL BOY." He is inattentive at school and church, he plays hookey frequently, he often sneaks out at night and he is willing to lie to protect himself. These qualities make Tom an average, normal boy; however, he also has qualities that set him apart. What makes Tom special is his imagination. He is restless, often scheming and always looking for glory. Despite his lack of interest in school, he is evidently an avid reader of romantic classics, as well as contemporary pulp fiction. He likes to play games based on heroes he reads about, such as Robin Hood and characters in the works of James Fenimore COOPER. He also finds inspiration in less noble literary creations such as the BLACK AVENGER OF THE SPANISH MAIN. His impulse to manufacture adventure and to romanticize the ordinary casts him in the mold of CERVANTES's Don Quixote. In this regard, he is almost the opposite of Huck Finn, the realist who has often been called Tom's Sancho Panza.

Tom sees opportunities where others would not, and seizes them. Faced with the daunting task of whitewashing a FENCE, for example, he gets his friends to pay him for the privilege of doing his work. The next day he swaps his freshly accumulated wealth for "tickets" that net him a prize of a Bible that most Sunday-school students spend years working to earn.

Tom is both an initiator and a leader. In *Tom Sawyer*, he is a general in the boys' mock wars and he generally takes charge in make-believe games. He initiates the PIRATE expedition to JACKSON'S ISLAND and he holds the little band together when the enthusiasm of Huck and Joe HARPER fades. Later, it is his idea to search for pirate treasure, and he formulates the plan that leads to INJUN JOE's downfall. In virtually all the episodes that involve boys undertaking something together, Tom is in charge. Not all his schemes are successful, however. Indeed, some are nearly disastrous.

Several of Tom's schemes have particularly unfortunate results for the ex-slave Jim. In the last chapters of *Huckleberry Finn*, Tom puts Jim through an elaborate ordeal in order to "escape," though he alone knows that Jim is already legally free. The escape plan is a fiasco, leaving Tom with a bullet in the leg in chapter 40. Always ready to turn defeat into victory, Tom relishes the wound as a badge of honor. In "HUCK FINN AND TOM SAWYER AMONG THE INDIANS," Tom's romantic infatuation with "Cooper INDIANS" results in Jim's being taken captive by the Sioux. In "TOM SAWYER'S CONSPIRACY," Tom's elaborate attempt to organize an abolitionist hoax gets Jim arrested for murder.

Matched against Tom's tendency to create trouble for his friends are his loyalty, courage and innate tendency to do the right thing in the end. In *Tom Sawyer* he and Huck take a blood oath never to reveal to anyone that they have seen Injun Joe commit murder in the grave-robbing scene. With good reason, Tom has a mortal fear of Injun Joe. Yet, when the life of the innocent Muff POTTER is on the line, Tom steps forward to testify against Injun Joe, fully knowing the terror that awaits him. Likewise, he is willing to risk everything to rectify the mistakes that he makes. In "Indians," he commits himself to rescuing Jim or dying. To right the wrong he accidentally creates in "Conspiracy," he stands ready to spend his entire personal fortune—which is considerable, thanks to the treasure he finds in *Tom Sawyer*— and risk his own life to help free Jim.

A final trait that makes Tom special is his inventiveness. He is both intelligent and indomitable. Perhaps the most impressive demonstration of his resourcefulness is the episode in *Tom Sawyer* when he and Becky Thatcher get lost in McDougal's CAVE. By stretching their resources and strength to the limit over three days in utter darkness, he keeps Becky's hopes alive and finds a way out. Then, despite his exhaustion, he has the presence of mind not to reveal that he saw Injun Joe in the cave. He surmises, correctly, that the gold that Injun Joe found earlier is in the cave. Withholding this information gives him the chance to return to the cave later with Huck to claim the treasure. In *Tom Sawyer, Detective*, Tom's uncle Silas PHELPS is being tried for murder. The case seems so hopeless that Phelps's lawyer virtually gives up. Tom takes charge of the case, and saves his uncle with a brilliant piece of deduction.

Mark Twain's preface to *Tom Sawyer* states that Tom Sawyer "is drawn from life . . . but not from an individual—he is a combination of the characteristics of three boys whom I knew, and therefore belongs to the composite school of architecture." It is generally conceded that just as *Tom Sawyer* is Mark Twain's most autobiographical novel, Tom Sawyer is the character that reveals the most about him as a boy. His memoirs and the testimony of childhood friends, such as Laura HAWKINS, confirm that he did many of the things that he attributed to Tom Sawyer, especially in the early chapters of *Tom Sawyer*.

Between film and television adaptations of *Tom Sawyer* and *Huckleberry Finn*, dozens of actors have played Tom. They have ranged in age from 10-year-old Tommy Kelly (1938) to 22-year-old Jack Pickford (1917 and 1918). Other actors who have played Tom include Jackie Coogan (1930 and 1931), Johnnie Whitaker (1973 and 1974) and Donny Most (1975) of "Happy Days" fame.

"Schoolhouse Hill" An unfinished novel of about 15,000 words that Mark Twain wrote in November–December 1898, this story is the third of his four unfinished tales built around the "MYSTERIOUS STRANGER" theme. It is set in Huck Finn and Tom Sawyer's Missouri village around the 1840s. Here, however, the town is called simply "Petersburg," not "ST. PETERSBURG." A few familiar characters, including Tom and Huck, appear only in the first two chapters, but Mark Twain's notes suggest that they were to play a larger part in the chapters remaining to be written. The story is of special interest for an additional reason, as members of Mark Twain's own family were to appear as the fictional Hotchkiss family. The mercurial Oliver Hotchkiss, who does appear, is modeled on Orion Clemens. Although Mark Twain abandoned the story abruptly midway through its sixth chapter, the depth of his initial commitment to it is demonstrated by the polish of what he finished, as well as the detailed working notes he left for what remained to be written.

SYNOPSIS

Chapter 1

On a winter morning 30 children assemble outside Archibald Ferguson's school on Schoolhouse Hill. The scholars include Tom Sawyer, his brother Sid, and

Becky Thatcher. Huck Finn, though not a scholar, is also there with Tom. When a new boy, about 15 years old, arrives, he immediately attracts attention. His surpassing handsomeness, fine clothes and dignified and tranquil manner set him apart from the others.

After Ferguson puts the class through several lessons, he notices the new boy and asks his name. The boy speaks only French, but Ferguson can converse well enough with him in that language to explain how he must learn English. The boy astounds him by claiming to have learned the rules of English grammar merely from overhearing the class recite earlier. He proves it by reciting the rules flawlessly, then adds to Ferguson's astonishment by repeating every word, mannerism and intonation uttered by everyone in the room during the mathematics lesson. The teacher next gives him an English–French dictionary to study; 20 minutes later the boy shows that he has not only memorized every detail, he can comment intelligently on the book's inconsistencies and flaws. Ferguson recognizes that the marvelous boy is no idiot savant and treats him with great deference and respect.

The boy spends the balance of the morning mastering Latin, Greek, mathematics and "phonography" and then demonstrates remarkable computational powers. After Ferguson notices that the lunch hour has slipped by, he dismisses school early. But first the new boy gives his name as "Quarante-quatre," or FORTY-FOUR, and explains that he came to town the previous night.

Chapter 2
As the children leave the school, Tom Sawyer warns Forty-four that he will have to fight Henry Bascom, the school bully, and shows him some boxing moves. Forty-four seems merely puzzled when Henry tries to box with him, but defeats the bully effortlessly. When Henry picks on someone else, Forty-four knocks him out with a single slap. At that moment Henry's father, the local slave trader, appears and tries to whip Forty-four, who dodges the blow and crushes the man's wrist in his hand.

Chapter 3
That afternoon at the Hotchkiss home, where Forty-four has taken a room, neighbors pour in hoping to see the now-famous boy. Though hospitable, the Hotchkisses are miffed that everyone else seems to know more about their wonderful guest than they, until their visitors start marveling at little observations they have made—such as Forty-four's having found a candle in complete darkness. This miracle looms even larger when Aunt Rachel, a household slave, notes that the candle is genuine wax. Rachel also remarks that though Forty-four has no luggage, he has been seen in different outfits. Moreover, she has also seen him conversing with a cat and a mouse in their own languages.

Anxious to see Forty-four's clothes, the visitors persuade Mrs. Hotchkiss to let them look in his room. When she picks up his coat, gold and silver coins flood out of its pockets. Everyone scrambles to put the coins back, but even after the coat's pockets are stuffed, a heap of coins remain. The visitors finally leave, convinced that Forty-four is indeed "an extraordinary person."

Chapter 4
That night a severe blizzard rages, reducing visibility to inches and making outdoor travel suicidal. Oliver Hotchkiss is too engrossed in a book on spiritualism to notice the storm until Rachel alerts him to Forty-four's failure to come home. A line is tied around old Uncle Jeff, another family slave, who is sent into the storm to look for Forty-four. The line slips loose, apparently condemning Jeff to certain death. Meanwhile, Forty-four enters the house from the back door. Ignoring Hotchkiss's order to stay inside, he goes out to rescue Jeff and returns with the news that another man is huddled in a nearby shed. When he realizes that the family cares about the man's plight, he rescues him. This man, Crazy Meadows, is nearly frozen. Forty-four again leaves, in order to round up others he has seen in the storm.

Convinced that Forty-four is dying in the storm, Hotchkiss calls together everyone, including the servants, to conduct a seance. After messages are received from BYRON, Napoleon, SHAKESPEARE and other ancient notables, Forty-four himself appears in the middle of the circle. He dismisses Crazy Meadows and the servants and then discusses spiritualism with Hotchkiss, who is astonished to discover that Forty-four is actually alive. Forty-four tells Hotchkiss that he has managed to save 13 people in the storm, but that 28 have perished under the snow. Hotchkiss and Forty-four settle down to whiskey and corncob pipes by the fire.

Forty-four explains that he was raised "partly in heaven, partly in hell," and shows Hotchkiss a book that he has borrowed from London's British Museum just minutes earlier. Before the conversation proceeds further, Forty-four has invisible servants bring a steaming feast to the table. At Hotchkiss's request he makes his servants visible; they are little red horned men with spiked tails. Hotchkiss's astonishment reaches its fullest level when Forty-four tells him that his father is Satan.

Chapter 5
Forty-four continues explaining to Hotchkiss who he is and why he has come to Earth. He was born before ADAM's fall. A thousand Earth years are only a day by his reckoning, making him 15 by his measure and nearly five million years old by Earth measurement. He blames his father for Adam's fall from grace, and blames him for giving mankind the "passionate and eager and hungry *disposition to* DO *evil*." Forty-four's own reason for coming to Earth is to help alleviate the burden of evil consequences bequeathed by his father. He asks for help in this from Hotchkiss, who eagerly accepts. Before formulating a specific plan to carry out this mission, Forty-four intends to spend the night traveling the world to study its peoples. He leaves a servant to wait

on Hotchkiss while he is gone. Hotchkiss names the servant "Edward Nicholson Hotchkiss" after a deceased brother.

Chapter 6
The next morning Rachel and Jeff panic when they see the new devilish servant, but reconcile themselves to his presence when they learn that he, like them, is a slave. The supernatural servant astounds the others with his ability to perform impossible errands; at this point the manuscript abruptly ends.

UNWRITTEN CHAPTERS

Extensive working notes that Mark Twain left indicate the direction that the rest of the story was to go. Forty-four was to found a new church on Earth that would help human beings shed their "moral sense" and eliminate hypocrisy. To this end he would publish his own Bible—which Mark Twain intended to make an appendix of the novel, along with Forty-four's sermons and dialogues. Meanwhile, Forty-four would continue to astonish the people of Petersburg with new miracles. Along the way, however, he would make his own astonishing discovery by falling in love with one of the village characters—possibly Hellfire Hotchkiss.

PUBLISHING HISTORY

After abandoning this story, Mark Twain attempted to develop its themes in other versions of the "MYSTERIOUS STRANGER" tales. He first returned to "The Chronicle of Young Satan," which he had started earlier, and then took up NO. 44, THE MYSTERIOUS STRANGER. Though those versions are both set in medieval Austria, each has elements closely akin to aspects of "Schoolhouse Hill." "Chronicle" in particular attempts to evoke the atmosphere of boys growing up in a village that characterizes the Huck Finn–Tom Sawyer stories.

The original manuscript of "Schoolhouse Hill" is held by the MARK TWAIN PAPERS project, which published the story for the first time in 1967 in *Hannibal, Huck & Tom*, a collection edited by Walter BLAIR. Two years later the project published the story again in *The Mysterious Stranger*, a collection of all the tales edited by William M. Gibson. An amended edition of Gibson's edition of the text also appeared in the 1989 Mark Twain Papers publication *Huck Finn and Tom Sawyer among the Indians*. Each edition contains extensive notes on the story's text and background.

Schurz, Carl (March 2, 1829, Liblar, Germany–May 14, 1906, New York, New York) Politician and journalist. The leading German-American spokesman of his time, Schurz fled GERMANY because of his involvement in the 1848 revolutionary movement. He reached the United States in 1852 and settled in Wisconsin a few years later. There he was admitted to the bar and

became involved in the abolition movement and Republican Party politics. After campaigning in Abraham LINCOLN's senatorial and presidential races, he was made U.S. minister to Spain. When the CIVIL WAR began, he returned to accept a commission as a brigadier in the Union army. Though lacking military training, he saw considerable action and proved one of the most capable politically appointed officers.

After the war, President Andrew JOHNSON had Schurz tour the South to study the political condition of black people. Schurz then became Washington correspondent for Horace GREELEY's NEW YORK TRIBUNE, edited a Detroit newspaper and moved to ST. LOUIS to run a local German-language newspaper, the *Westliche Post*. In 1868, Missouri elected him to the U.S. Senate. Though a Republican, he criticized U. S. GRANT's administration and pushed for civil service reform. In 1872, he helped organize the Liberal Republican Party that ran Greeley against Grant. Later, he was Rutherford Hayes's secretary of the interior.

During the early 1880s, Schurz edited the *New York Evening Post* and the *Nation*. He helped lead the mugwump revolt against James Blaine's nomination in 1884—probably the year that he met Mark Twain. In October, Mark Twain introduced Schurz at a Hartford mugwump rally. Schurz also bolted the Republican Party in 1900 over the question of American imperialism in the Philippines—another issue on which he sided with Mark Twain. In 1905 Mark Twain nominated Schurz for membership in the American Academy of Arts and Letters. Through these years, the two men were occasionally on speaking platforms together. In January 1906, for example, they both appeared with Booker T. WASHINGTON at a fund-raising event in Carnegie Hall. When Schurz died four months later, Mark Twain eulogized him in HARPER'S MAGAZINE. He admired Schurz's mastery of the English language and his opposition to all forms of tyranny, slavery and humbug. Schurz's *Reminiscences* appeared posthumously.

science fiction   As a literary genre, science fiction is the realistic—as opposed to fantasy—treatment of stories with elements not known to be scientifically possible at the time of writing. Science fiction treats themes almost unimaginably broad: from explorations of the inner mind to the outer universe, encompassing fabulous inventions, time travel, aliens, far-traveling, future history, super powers and a host of other ideas—many of which Mark Twain employed. Though Mark Twain is not generally recognized as a science fiction pioneer— as were Jules Verne and H. G. Wells—he wrote much that not only meets the genre's definition, but employed original ideas. As early as 1874, for example, he wrote about interstellar flight in "A CURIOUS PLEASURE EXCURSION." The best-known and perhaps clearest example of his science fiction, however, is *Connecticut Yankee* (1889). While Hank MORGAN's journey from the 19th century to the sixth century may smack of fantasy, it is what

Hank *does* once he gets there that makes the novel powerful science fiction. Mark Twain poses the question of what might happen if modern technology and political ideas were transplanted to medieval England. Later writers have explored similar themes. In L. Sprague de Camp's *Lest Darkness Fall* (1939), for example, a 20th-century man goes back to the Roman Empire in the sixth century and tries to avert the Dark Ages.

A theme that especially fascinated Mark Twain is instantaneous communication. His 1877 story "THE LOVES OF ALONZO FITZ CLARENCE AND ROSANNAH ETHELTON" is about a romance conducted over long-distance telephone lines; it qualifies as science fiction because he wrote it nearly 40 years *before* long-distance telephones existed. During the 1890s, he wrote two essays exploring what he called "Mental Telegraphy"—the notion of human beings communicating thoughts over great distances—a subject that fascinated him through the rest of his life. His 1898 story "FROM THE 'LONDON TIMES' OF 1904," uses a communications device called the telelectroscope, which anticipates television.

One of Mark Twain's wildest stories is "CAPTAIN STORMFIELD'S VISIT TO HEAVEN," which deals with far-traveling, aliens and teleportation. He left unfinished several other ambitious works dealing with strange voyages, such as "THE GREAT DARK" and "Three Thousand Years Among the Microbes." Much more conventional, even by the standards of its time, is *Tom Sawyer Abroad* (1894), in which Tom, Huck and Jim cross the Atlantic and North Africa in a balloon made by a mad PROFESSOR.

Modern science fiction writer Philip José Farmer (1918–) not only incorporates many themes and ideas from Mark Twain's writings into his *Riverworld* trilogy, he uses Mark Twain himself as a character. In David Carkeet's novel *I Been There Before* (1985), Mark Twain returns to life when HALLEY'S COMET revisits the Earth in 1985.

Scotland In 1873, Mark Twain and his family vacationed in Scotland. After spending late July and most of August in Edinburgh, they passed through Glasgow to IRELAND. On this trip, Mark Twain made a pilgrimage to Sir Walter SCOTT's Abbotsford home and the whole family became friends with Dr. John BROWN. They planned to revisit Brown in Scotland at the end of their 1878–79 trip to Europe, but poor weather and exhaustion encouraged them to go directly home from Liverpool in early September.

Scott, Sir Walter (August 15, 1771, Edinburgh–September 21, 1832, Abbotsford, Scotland) Prolific Scottish author who pioneered the historical novel. Through such works as *The Heart of Midlothian* (1818) and *Ivanhoe* (1820) Scott romanticized medieval chivalry—ideas that Mark Twain called the "Walter Scott disease" and credited with helping to bring on the CIVIL WAR. *Life on the Mississippi* accuses Scott of doing "more real and lasting

harm, perhaps, than any other individual that ever wrote" (chapter 40) and blasts Scott for restoring the "medieval chivalry-silliness" that CERVANTES had swept away (chapter 46). Though Mark Twain uses *Life on the Mississippi* as a platform to attack Scott's romanticism, the same book subtly romanticizes river life by overlooking its violence and vice. Ironically, an episode in *Huckleberry Finn* that alludes to vice on the river gives the name WALTER SCOTT to the derelict steamboat found by Huck and Jim that has "killed herself on a rock" (chapter 12).

Mark Twain also pokes fun at Scott in *The American Claimant*, in which Sally SELLERS attends a useless institution called Rowena-Ivanhoe College at which everything is "named out of Sir Walter Scott's books" (chapter 4). This place resembles the Southern "she-college" described in chapter 40 of *Life on the Mississippi*. In *Tom Sawyer Abroad*, Huck attributes Tom's proclivity for wild ideas from his reading of Scott's books (chapter 1). In "THOSE EXTRAORDINARY TWINS," a character named Rowena Cooper is a silly romantic.

Despite Mark Twain's attitude toward Scott, he visited Scott's Abbotsford home while he was in Scotland in 1873 and spent considerable time searching for a rare edition of Scott's works. Mark Twain's career resembled Scott's in striking ways. Both men started publishing companies that helped drive them to BANKRUPTCY at advanced ages, and both worked themselves out of debt and repaid their creditors in full. Scott's success in climbing out of bankruptcy during the 1820s was frequently called to Mark Twain's attention when he was in financial difficulty during the 1890s. In an 1895 interview in Seattle, Washington, Mark Twain explicitly compared himself with Scott, but pointed out that while Scott worked himself out of bankruptcy at a similar age only to write himself to death, his own solution, LECTURING, would make him healthier, rather than weaker.

scrapbook, self-pasting Invention patented by Mark Twain. Tired of assembling scrapbooks with mucilage and glue, Mark Twain got the idea of preprinting strips of glue on pages that users could dampen. He outlined this idea in a letter to his brother Orion Clemens in August 1872. After patenting his "Improvement in Scrapbooks" on June 24, 1873, he took the idea to his friend Dan SLOTE, whose company produced and distributed the product as "Mark Twain's Patent Self-Pasting Scrap Book." The books were sold in more than 30 sizes and models, including specially designed books for photographs, newspaper clippings and druggists' prescriptions.

The scrapbook was the only invention Mark Twain patented that made money—an ironic result, since the books contained a facetious notice in which Mark Twain claims to have invented them "*not* to make money," but "to economize the profanity of this country." He sold about 25,000 scrapbooks in 1877, earning about

$12,000, but rapidly falling sales in succeeding years made him suspect Slote's honesty. Nevertheless, his success in this venture encouraged him to invest in KAOLA-TYPE with Slote a few years later.

Screamers: A Gathering of Scraps of Humor, Delicious Bits & Short Stories Pirated collection of Mark Twain material published in London in 1872 by John Camden HOTTEN. The unauthorized book contains several Mark Twain items in their first book publication, as well as several sketches attributed to Mark Twain that he did not write.

The Secretary Character in *Roughing It.* The book opens with the narrator stating that his brother has just been appointed to the majestic post of Secretary of NEVADA Territory. The "Secretary" is modeled on Mark Twain's brother, Orion Clemens—who is never named in the book—but much that is ascribed to him is exaggerated or invented. For example, his depiction as a self-sacrificing drudge forced to pay many petty expenses out of his own pocket is contradicted by Orion's records of his actual relationship with the federal government. The book also mentions the Secretary in chapters 1–4, 13, 21–22, 25 and 30.

Seelye, John (January 1, 1931, Hartford, Connecticut–) Scholar and novelist. Seelye's fiction includes *The True Adventures of Huckleberry Finn* (1970; revised, 1987) and *The Kid* (1972), a western satire that he originally conceived as a continuation of Mark Twain's *Huckleberry Finn.* His scholarly work includes *Prophetic Waters: The River in Early American Life and Literature* (1977) and *Mark Twain and the Movies* (1977), an illustrated essay on Mark Twain's public image.

Seelye's *True Adventures* is not so much a pastiche as a revision of Mark Twain's *Huckleberry Finn.* In trying to reshape the original novel to satisfy the "consensus" of critics, Seelye has written a book that is both a work of imaginative fiction and an exercise in criticism. The bulk of its text leaves Mark Twain's original prose unaltered. Seelye concentrates on tightening the narrative around Huck and Jim's journey down the river. He truncates or deletes episodes that many regard as out of place in the original—such as the digressions about Tom Sawyer's GANG. He also occasionally supplies minor details missing in the original, such as a name—"Riverton"—for Peter WILKS's town. Finally, he relaxes Mark Twain's self-censorship by having Huck use coarser language and by introducing sexual innuendo and allusions to natural bodily functions. He changes Mark Twain's "ROYAL NONESUCH" episode by restoring Jim GILLIS's "Burning Shame" version.

Seelye modifies several characters. Huck, for example, is sexually more mature. He has a girlfriend in ST. PETERSBURG, he enjoys kissing Joanna WILKS and he is highly aroused by revealing glimpses of Mary Jane WILKS. The con man known as the KING is nastier and more lecherous. Always ready to slit Huck's throat, he closely monitors Huck's whereabouts—giving Huck and Jim a more cogent reason not to try getting away from him. When the King discovers that Wilks's gold is stolen, he proposes selling the Wilks girls to a New Orleans whorehouse, where he would be the first customer.

In Seelye's effort to preserve Jim's dignity, Tom Sawyer is the first casualty. As in *Huckleberry Finn,* Tom tries to trick Jim into thinking that witches moved his hat while he was asleep; however, Jim simply brushes off the incident without building it into a celebrated mystery. Tom's elaborate "EVASION," which dominates the end of *Huckleberry Finn,* simply never happens. The second casualty is Miss WATSON, who dies *before* Jim runs off. Finally, the omission of Tom's "evasion" episode also eliminates Aunt Sally PHELPS and reduces Silas PHELPS to a redneck Louisiana farmer.

Seelye's most important changes concern Huck and Jim's relationship. While Jim is spared the comic buffoonery that he endures in *Huckleberry Finn,* he is more demanding of Huck's attention and loyalty. Huck, on the other hand, agonizes louder and longer over the morality of helping a slave to escape. The novel ends abruptly near PIKESVILLE, with Jim drowning in the river while fleeing bounty-crazed rednecks. Only then does Huck fully appreciate the value of Jim's friendship.

Sellers, Isaiah (Captain Sellers) (c. 1802, Iredell County, North Carolina–June 3, 1864, Memphis, Tennessee) Mississippi steamboatman from whom Mark Twain claimed to take his PEN NAME. Sellers began working on Lower Mississippi River STEAMBOATS around 1825 and may have been on keelboats even earlier. By 1828, he was a PILOT. Over the next 35 years, he made at least 460 round-trips between New Orleans and other ports and was responsible for several navigational innovations, such as a system of signaling between boats.

When Mark Twain began his own piloting career in 1857, Sellers was the river's "only genuine Son of Antiquity" (*Life on the Mississippi,* chapter 50). No matter what any other pilot had done—or however long ago he had done it—Sellers had a story topping his. His anecdotes oozed such precise details and so many names of long-disappeared places that younger pilots ridiculed him as an old bore. In July 1858, Mark Twain may have clerked aboard the WILLIAM M. MORRISON—a steamboat that Sellers is known to have piloted at that time. An anonymous account published in 1880 claims that Sellers earned Mark Twain's animosity by hitting him in the face during a wake-up call aboard this steamboat.

Life on the Mississippi recalls how Sellers wrote brief items about the river for the *New Orleans Picayune* and claims that Sellers signed them "MARK TWAIN." Other pilots mocked these squibs, inspiring Mark Twain (then known as Sam Clemens) to BURLESQUE them in a piece that he signed "Sergeant Fathom." This spoof describes a river voyage in 1763 with a Chinese captain and a Choctaw crew and cites ludicrously precise details of river conditions over the years. Mark Twain's fellow pilots had the piece published in the *New Orleans Crescent* in May 1859, embarrassing Sellers so much that he stopped writing for newspapers and focused his detestation on the spoof's author.

In *Life on the Mississippi* and elsewhere, Mark Twain claims to have appropriated his famous pen name while he was a journalist on the Pacific coast—where he heard about Sellers's death. This story is, however, suspect in its most important particulars. While Sellers is known to have published river reports in New Orleans newspapers, there is no record of his ever signing them "Mark Twain." Furthermore, Samuel L. CLEMENS first used "Mark Twain" as a pen name himself in February 1863—more than a year *before* Sellers died.

Sellers, Mulberry (Colonel Sellers) (a.k.a. **Eschol** and **Beriah**) Character in *The Gilded Age* and *The American Claimant*. One of Mark Twain's most enduring creations, Sellers is a warm-hearted, generous optimist whose resilience and enthusiasm for grandiose schemes never flag. He is first mentioned in the opening of *The Gilded Age*, when Si HAWKINS receives a letter from him urging Hawkins to come to Missouri. Although Hawkins has previously lost money in Sellers's speculations, he accepts his advice (chapter 1). Sellers himself first appears in chapter 5, when the Hawkinses reach Murpheysburg (identified by name in chapter 18), where Sellers lives in a one-room cabin with his wife of one week, Polly (whose name is first given in chapter 7). Sellers's embarrassed admission that his wife calls him "Colonel" suggests that he has only recently adopted this honorific title; however, earlier in the same chapter Washington HAWKINS refers to him as "Colonel Sellers" *before* his family even reaches Murpheysburg. Chapter 6 of *The Gilded Age* jumps the narrative ahead a decade, by which time Sellers has eight children, including two sets of twins, and is living in HAWKEYE. Always the romantic, he has given his children names such as Lafayette, Roderick Dhu and Marie Antoinette (chapter 11). Little more is said about these children, however, and by the time *Claimant* begins all but one of them are dead (chapter 2). Sellers's age is never specified, but it may be close to that of Si Hawkins, who is about 35 at the beginning of the narrative. Since *The Gilded Age* unfolds over about 23 years and *The American Claimant* opens about 15 years later, Sellers is probably in his early seventies by the time of the latter novel.

As a central character in *The Gilded Age*, Sellers is a crucial link among the other major characters. He encourages Washington Hawkins in his delusions about his family's TENNESSEE LAND; along with coauthor C. D. WARNER's character Henry Brierly, he is a major player in the abortive scheme to develop STONE'S LANDING; he is an unofficial ally of Senator DILWORTHY and he accompanies Laura HAWKINS as a chaperon when Dilworthy invites her to come to Washington, D.C. Sellers flourishes in the national capital, where "for the first

time in his life his talents had a fair field" (chapter 40). Though he never actually accomplishes anything, he gets to know everyone in the government, including President GRANT, who enjoys hearing him talk (chapters 40 and 44).

At the end of *The Gilded Age*, after every scheme with which Sellers is connected collapses, he decides to go into law and shoot for the chief justiceship of the United States (chapter 61). By the time *Claimant* opens, however, he and his wife Polly live in a poor black neighborhood of WASHINGTON, D.C. (chapter 2). Signs in front of his shabby house proclaim him an "Attorney at Law and Claim Agent," as well as "a Materializer, a Hypnotizer, a Mind-Cure Dabbler, and so on." When his old friend Washington Hawkins arrives, Sellers explains that he returned to Washington to take up an ambassadorial appointment to England, but arrived a day too late. Over the ensuing years, he occasionally prospered, only to give his money away. He counts many great men among his friends, including Grant, SHERMAN, Sheridan and Lee. He also dabbles with inventions, including one that actually has commercial worth—a mechanical game called "Pigs in the Clover." Most of his ideas are of dubious value—such as schemes to materialize the dead, use sewer-gas for home lighting and manipulate sunspots to alter the earth's climate. His ideas, however, are always more important to him than money. Though Sellers is still promoting commercial schemes in *Claimant*, this book's central theme is his claim to be the rightful Earl of ROSSMORE. By the end of the narrative, however, he happily abandons this claim when his daughter Sally SELLERS marries the current earl's son, Lord BERKELEY.

Mark Twain modeled Sellers closely on his mother's cousin James LAMPTON, whom his AUTOBIOGRAPHY describes as a "person who could not be exaggerated." Like Sellers, Lampton forever saw vast riches around the corner and always said of the Clemens family's TENNESSEE LAND that "there's millions in it!" Mark Twain claimed that many of the strange behaviors attributed to the fictional Sellers—such as the turnip and water banquet of *The Gilded Age* (chapter 11)—actually occurred. Sellers also borrows traits from other people, notably Mark Twain's father—who tinkered with a perpetual motion machine when Mark Twain was young—and who matched Sellers's fierce pride in his VIRGINIA birth. Like Mark Twain's brother Orion Clemens, Sellers changes religions frequently, but is a consistent teetotaller. Sellers is also like Mark Twain himself in his fascination with inventions and his weakness for financial speculation.

Although Sellers was Mark Twain's own invention, his coauthor Warner suggested his "impossible" name, "Eschol Sellers"—which he borrowed from a man he met in the West years earlier. Warner suggested this name because it was quaint, but Mark Twain was probably already aware of its biblical significance, as he had earlier mentioned Palestine's "Eschol" (or Eshtaol) in

Innocents Abroad (chapter 46). Shortly after *The Gilded Age* came out, a real Eschol Sellers appeared and objected to seeing his name in the novel, so the authors renamed their character "Beriah"—another biblical name meaning "unfortunate." Mark Twain tells how he and Warner made this change in his autobiography, in chapter 47 of *Life on the Mississippi* and in the introduction to *Claimant*. In *Claimant*, he further altered the name to "Mulberry," or "Berry"—an adaptation of Beriah with a hint of "HUCKLEBERRY." Colonel Mulberry Sellers is also the name of a character in "Three Thousand Years Among the Microbes."

Shortly after publication of *The Gilded Age*, John T. RAYMOND played Sellers in a dramatic adaptation of the novel that proved so popular that the play was soon renamed *Colonel Sellers*.

Sellers, Polly   Minor character in *The Gilded Age* and *The American Claimant*. The dutiful wife of Colonel Mulberry (Beriah) SELLERS, Polly occasionally persuades Sellers to behave more sensibly—in matters such as putting baskets of human ashes on display in their home—but is generally unobtrusive. Although she recognizes that the world regards her husband as a failure, she regards him as a success because of his kindness, generosity and optimism. At the end of *Claimant* she goes to England alone, as Sellers remains behind to work on a new scheme.

Sellers, Sally ("Lady Gwendolen")   Character in *The American Claimant*. The daughter of Colonel SELLERS, Sally is first mentioned when Sellers calls her home from Rowena-Ivanhoe College (chapter 4). Thinking that he is now the Earl of ROSSMORE, Sellers dubs her "Lady Gwendolen." Never comfortable with this aristocratic pretension, Sally drops the name altogether after meeting and falling in love with BERKELEY in chapter 20. In chapter 22, she says, "My name is Sally Sellers— or Sarah, if you like." The name "Sarah" does not otherwise appear in the narrative. Unlike her father, Sally is sensible and levelheaded; once she is home, she starts designing and making clothes and becomes the family's financial mainstay.

Senior, F. M. (*fl.* 1890s)   Illustrator. Along with C. H. WARREN, Senior illustrated the first edition of *Pudd'nhead Wilson and Those Extraordinary Twins* (1894). Senior's work adorns virtually every page of all but five chapters of *Wilson* (11, 16, 20, 21 and conclusion), as well as all the chapters of "THOSE EXTRAORDINARY TWINS." Senior's *Wilson* drawings are generally more whimsical than those of Warren, and his "Twins" drawings are essentially comic cartoons. The *New York Times* praised his work for multiplying the book's drollery and comedy.

Senior also contributed at least 13 illustrations to *Following the Equator* (1897). This work, scattered throughout the book, depicts scenes in Hawaii, Australia and India. (The list of illustrators on page 19 of the first edition misspells his name as "Seinor.")

Sevastopol (Sebastopol)   City in southwestern CRIMEA. Mark Twain spent a day at Sevastopol when the QUAKER CITY landed there on August 21, 1867. During the Crimean War a dozen years earlier, the city had been nearly destroyed by a long siege. In chapter 35 of *Innocents Abroad*, Mark Twain calls Sevastopol the "worst battered town" he has ever seen, but he also finds it to be the most hospitable toward Americans. Three years after his visit, RUSSIA renounced a treaty demilitarizing Sevastopol and began rebuilding it as its Black Sea naval base. It has been under Ukrainian control since 1992.

Shackleford, Abner   Minor character in *Huckleberry Finn*. In chapter 24 Tim COLLINS names Shackleford and his wife as friends of the late Peter WILKS. In the next chapter, Shackleford introduces the KING to Dr. ROBINSON as "Harvey WILKS."

Shakespeare, William (c. April 23, 1564, Stratford, England–April 23, 1616, Stratford)   Mark Twain was familiar with Shakespeare's writings from an early age and their imprint is visible throughout his own work. Though not commonly performed, Shakespearean drama was popular on the western frontier as Mark Twain grew up and he occasionally saw itinerant actors perform bits from Shakespeare's plays. In *Life on the Mississippi* (chapter 51), for example, he recalls seeing two actors perform the sword fight from RICHARD III— a scene that he later had the DUKE and KING recreate in *Huckleberry Finn*.

Mark Twain's richly autobiographical IS SHAKESPEARE DEAD? (1909) describes the long hours he spent as a cub PILOT listening to George EALER recite Shakespeare and argue about the authorship of his plays during the 1850s. As a journalist during the 1860s, he often worked Shakespearean references into his writing. His most elaborate example is a parody, "THE KILLING OF JULIUS CAESAR 'LOCALIZED'" (1864), which draws all its characters from Shakespeare's play.

Mark Twain's interest in Shakespeare grew stronger during the 1870s. He visited Shakespeare's birthplace in July 1873 and read Shakespeare's plays as part of his research for *The Prince and the Pauper*, which he set in Tudor England just before Shakespeare's time. In 1876, he wrote *1601*, a scatological experiment with 16th-century dialogue that uses Shakespeare himself as a minor character. After completing *The Prince and the Pauper* (1878), he wrote a BURLESQUE of HAMLET. This effort did not lead to publication, but gave him more background on Shakespeare, which he used in *Huckleberry Finn*. In that novel, his two con men, the KING and DUKE, pose as the Shakespearean actors David GARRICK "the Younger" and Edmund KEAN and propose to stage a "Shaksperean Revival" in riverfront towns (chapter 20). The highlight of their repertoire—which includes scenes from *Hamlet, Richard III* and ROMEO AND JULIET—is a fractured version of Hamlet's SOLILOQUY. The novel also reenacts the theme of star-crossed lovers from *Romeo and Juliet* in earlier chapters in which members of the feuding GRANGERFORD and SHEPHERDSON families elope.

In addition to making Shakespeare a character in *1601*, Mark Twain has Oliver Hotchkiss call him up in a seance in "SCHOOLHOUSE HILL" (chapter 4) and he makes Shakespeare a heavenly prophet in "CAPTAIN STORMFIELD'S VISIT TO HEAVEN." *Following the Equator* has a long story about P. T. BARNUM's reputed purchase of Shakespeare's birthplace (chapter 64).

Sheffield City in central ENGLAND, about 140 miles north–northwest of LONDON. In *Huckleberry Finn*, Sheffield is mentioned as the home of Harvey and William WILKS—whom the KING and DUKE pretend to be (chapters 24–29). Since they introduce Huck as their English servant "ADOLPHUS," he is also presumed to be from Sheffield. Huck reveals his ignorance about Sheffield when Joanna WILKS grills him about England (chapter 26). Mark Twain may have passed through Sheffield in July 1873 when he visited York.

Shepherdson Fictional family in *Huckleberry Finn*. Five or six branches of the aristocratic Shepherdsons live a few miles north of the GRANGERFORDS, with whom they have been engaged in a deadly feud for about 30 years. They attend the same church as the Grangerfords and use the same steamboat landing. Huck sees Shepherdsons at both places, but mentions only two by name: Harney and Baldy SHEPHERDSON. At the end of chapter 18, the Shepherdsons kill all the men in the branch of the Grangerford family with whom Huck is living.

Shepherdson, Baldy Background figure mentioned in *Huckleberry Finn*. In chapter 18, Buck GRANGERFORD tells Huck that Baldy Shepherdson, an "old man," shot his cousin Bud three months earlier. Within a week, the Grangerfords killed Baldy. In an earlier incident, Shepherdson killed two of three Grangerfords in a gunfight.

Shepherdson, Harney Minor character in *Huckleberry Finn*. Harney is the secret lover of Sophia GRANGERFORD. In chapter 18, Huck sees Buck GRANGERFORD ambush Harney, who makes no attempt to retaliate after spotting who is shooting at him. Huck later unwittingly carries a message from Harney to Sophia. The next day Harney and Sophia elope, precipitating a deadly battle between the two feuding families.

Sherburn, Colonel Character in *Huckleberry Finn*. A prosperous merchant in BRICKSVILLE, Arkansas, Sherburn is proud-looking, about 55 years old and the town's best-dressed man. Huck arrives just before a drunk named BOGGS provokes Sherburn into shooting him (chapter 21). Afterward, a mob goes to Sherburn's house to lynch him, but he quietly stares them down, then scatters them simply by cocking his gun. Sherburn is modeled partly on William Perry OWSLEY, a Hannibal merchant who shot a man named Samuel SMARR in 1845.

Sherman, General William Tecumsah (February 8, 1820, Lancaster, Ohio–February 14, 1891, New York, New York) Union general in the CIVIL WAR. Famous for his march through Georgia, Sherman was the most celebrated passenger scheduled to sail on the QUAKER CITY in 1867. In late March, Sherman publicly affirmed that he would join the excursion with his daughter, but canceled two months later when his responsibilities in the war department demanded his attention. Sherman's withdrawal left Mark Twain as the cruise's biggest celebrity, as well as the recipient of the cabin originally intended for Sherman.

After U. S. GRANT became president in 1869, Sherman assumed command of the entire United States Army—a position that he held until November 1883. Mark Twain finally met him at a Chicago banquet honoring Grant in November 1879. Both men also spoke at a dinner for the Army of the Potomac in Hartford on June 8, 1881. The next day they traveled by train to West Point together; along the way, Sherman had Mark Twain wear his uniform and step onto the platform to speak. Five and a half years later, Sherman heard Mark Twain read an early draft of *Connecticut Yankee* in New York.

Mark Twain regarded Sherman as second only to Grant as a military hero. Even so, he turned down a travel book that Sherman submitted to Charles L. WEBSTER & COMPANY in 1885; however, the company republished his *Memoirs* (1885) in 1890. Chapter 3 of *The American Claimant* (1892) mentions Sherman as a friend of Colonel SELLERS.

Shillaber, Benjamin P[enhallow] (July 12, 1814, Portsmouth, New Hampshire–November 25, 1890, Chelsea, Massachusetts) Editor and humorist. Between editorial stints on the staffs of the *Boston Post* (1840–50) and *Saturday Evening Gazette* (1856–66), Shillaber founded and edited the CARPET-BAG (1851–53), in which Mark Twain published "THE DANDY FRIGHTENING THE SQUATTER" anonymously in May 1852. While at the *Post*, Shillaber began writing sketches about a character named "Mrs. Ruth Partington." He continued her adventures in the *Carpet-Bag* and in such books as *Rhymes with Reason and Without* (1853), *Life and Sayings of Mrs. Partington* (1854) and *Partingtonian Patchwork* (1873). Mark Twain probably read the *Carpet-Bag* carefully, as the HANNIBAL JOURNAL often quoted from it during the time he worked on the paper.

Shillaber's stories about Mrs. Partington and her impish nephew Ike challenged the long-popular "MODEL BOY" literature and influenced Mark Twain's writing of *Tom Sawyer*. Ike, like Tom Sawyer, is mischievous but basically good-hearted. Ike even anticipates Tom by styling himself the BLACK AVENGER when he plays pirates. The character Mrs. Partington shares many similarities with Tom's Aunt POLLY. For example, both are tenderhearted widows raising orphaned nephews; both favor patent medicines; and both are Calvinists. True WILLIAMS even took his portrait of Aunt Polly that appears in the last chapter of *Tom Sawyer* from Shillaber's *Life and Sayings*. It is possible that the borrowing was done by permission. Mark Twain met Shillaber at least six years before he wrote *Tom Sawyer*, and Shillaber published a congratulatory poem on Mark Twain's marriage in 1870. *Roughing It* alludes to Shillaber's Mrs. Partington in its description of a character named BALLOU as having a "Partingtonian fashion" (chapter 27).

Siamese twins Popular term for physically conjoined or xiphophagic twins—that is, twins attached to each other. Such twins are always identical, the products of ova that fail to divide completely in early embryonic stages. Each year about five sets of conjoined human twins are born in the world. Until the 20th century, however, few survived infancy. Even so, recorded instances of conjoined twins reaching adulthood go back a thousand years. The most famous such twins were Chang and Eng Bunker (1811–1874). Born in Siam, they were taken to Europe and America as teenagers and celebrated as the "Siamese Twins"—a nickname subsequently applied to all conjoined twins. Their nickname is ironic; though born in Siam, Chang and Eng were ethnically almost purely Chinese and were known in their own country as the "Chinese Twins." In the

According to Mark Twain, the Siamese twins' habit of going everywhere together had its drawbacks when they both fell in love with the same woman.

early 1840s, they gave up touring, became American citizens, married American women and settled permanently in North Carolina.

After the CIVIL WAR, Chang and Eng returned briefly to show business and worked for Phineas T. BARNUM. In 1869, Mark Twain wrote a brief sketch about them, "The Personal Habits of the Siamese Twins," for *Packard's Monthly*. It was known that the brothers disagreed on issues such as religion and drinking and reputedly even fought occasionally. Mark Twain's sketch explores what it could mean to people who do not get along to be literally stuck to each other. Claiming to know the twins "intimately," he says that although they "have not always lived in perfect accord," they still share a bond that makes them "unwilling to go away from each other and dwell apart." He then touches on the comic possibilities arising from their differences over drinking, smoking and religion. Most interesting—but historically least accurate—is the claim that the twins fought on opposite sides of the Civil War. The sketch concludes with the remark that one twin is 51, the other 53.

A year after Chang and Eng died, Mark Twain's sketch about them reappeared in SKETCHES, NEW AND OLD (1875). That same year, another pair of celebrated Siamese twins—the Tocci brothers—were born in Turin, Italy. Whereas the bodies of Chang and Eng were separate, except for a ligament connecting their chests, the bodies of Giovanni and Giacomo Tocci were separate only halfway down their rib cages. Above the sixth rib, they had separate bodies; below, they had one body.

Mark Twain saw the Toccis on exhibit in 1891. A few years later, while living in FLORENCE, he wrote "THOSE EXTRAORDINARY TWINS," a novel about Angelo and Luigi CAPELLO, Italian brothers physically similar to the Toccis. Eventually, he recast the Capellos as ordinary twins and rewrote his novel as *Pudd'nhead Wilson*. Later, he described his original effort as having "no purpose but to exhibit that monstrous 'freak' in all sorts of grotesque lights."

The genesis of the Capello twins can be seen in the 25-year-old "Siamese Twins" sketch. Angelo and Luigi differ in almost every important way. Angelo is a pious, nonsmoking teetotaler, while Luigi is a freethinking, smoking and hard-drinking rake. Even their politics are different. While the Tocci brothers provided the physical model for the Capellos, they were poor models as a functional unit. Since each Tocci brother controlled one leg of their shared body, they could never coordinate their movements in order to walk. To solve this problem, Mark Twain borrowed a lesson from Chang and Eng. Although these brothers could function independently, they alternated overall "mastery" to get through day-to-day activities without argument. By mutual agreement, each brother "controlled" both bodies for three days. In "Those Extraordinary Twins" the Capellos alternate control for *exactly* seven days—not by voluntary agreement, but by some natural force of nature. The BURLESQUE possibilities arising from this system are fully realized in the fifth chapter's trial scene—in which witnesses cannot determine which brother is responsible for kicking someone—and in the next chapter's DUEL, which ends abruptly when control switches suddenly from one brother to the other.

Mark Twain was not the only writer of his time to exploit Siamese twin themes. Chang and Eng inspired voluminous sentimental poetry, including a book-length ode by Edward Bulwer-Lytton in 1831. Herman Melville alludes to the twins in *The Confidence Man* (1857), and an English humorist, Gilbert Abbott à Beckett (1811–1856), wrote a play about them that ran in London and New York during the 1850s.

In 1889, Mark Twain introduced James Whitcomb Riley and Edgar Wilson Nye at a Boston banquet as "Chang Riley" and "Eng Nye." In December 1906, he delivered a burlesque speech in New York City in which he and another man were tied together as if they were Siamese twins. As his "brother" drank, Mark Twain lectured on temperance while growing increasingly tipsy—much like Angelo Capello's experience in chapter 9 of "Those Extraordinary Twins."

1601 ([Date, 1601] Conversation As It Was by the Social Fireside in the Time of the Tudors) Parody of Elizabethan manners. In the summer of 1876, Mark Twain began studying 16th-century English history to prepare for writing *The Prince and the Pauper*. Fascinated by indelicacies in old English speech and court language, he wrote *1601* to experiment with Elizabethan dialogue and to amuse his friend Joseph TWICHELL.

In Mark Twain's 2,300-word manuscript, Queen ELIZABETH's CUPBEARER describes an august company of men and women at court who politely discuss matters such as flatulence, sexual intercourse and masturbation—with neither embarrassment nor any sense of impropriety. Indeed, Mark Twain was intrigued with how differently people of that time perceived "moral" behavior. While he wrote *1601* for fun, he regarded it as representative of the kind of conversations that actually took place in Elizabeth's time. In addition to helping him prepare for *The Prince and the Pauper*, writing *1601* anticipated several scenes in *Connecticut Yankee*. In that novel, the page-boy CLARENCE assumes the role of *1601*'s disapproving cupbearer when he hears MERLIN bore the court (chapter 3). Later, at Queen MORGAN LE FAY's banquet, Hank MORGAN overhears a conversation risqué enough to make "Elizabeth of England hide behind a handkerchief" (chapter 17).

SYNOPSIS

Queen Elizabeth's cupbearer describes a gathering at court attended by Lord (Francis) BACON, Sir Walter RALEIGH, Ben JONSON, Francis Beaumont, SHAKESPEARE, the Duchess of BILGEWATER, the Countess of Granby and her daughter the Lady Helen, the Lady Margery Bothby and the Lady Alice Dilbeery. As they talk, some-

one breaks wind, releasing a mighty stink. The queen asks the perpetrator to confess, but each person denies responsibility until Raleigh admits that he did it. Calling the effort unworthy of notice, he promises to do better, then issues forth a more powerful blast with an even worse stench.

Conversation then turns to the sexual customs of different peoples. Raleigh tells about a remote people in America whose men remain virgins until they are 35 (the age at which Mark Twain married) and women until they are 28. Raleigh's remarks move the queen to tease 15-year-old Lady Helen about preserving her virginity. When Helen confesses that she has already sprouted pubic hair, the queen tries taunting young Beaumont into an indiscretion, then tells of meeting Rabelais when she herself was 15. Raleigh adds a story from Boccaccio.

As conversation turns to religion, Luther is mentioned, then poetry is discussed. Shakespeare elicits praise when he reads from *Henry IV* and "Venus and Adonis," but the cupbearer remains unimpressed. After Raleigh begins breaking wind again, conversation shifts to how clever Nicholas Throgmorton had been during Queen MARY's reign to save himself from condemnation; the queen recalls, however, that he could not save his daughter from being debauched. Her remark makes the cupbearer reflect on the debaucheries of the entire company. Conversation shifts to Rubens and CERVANTES and concludes with Raleigh telling a story about a lecherous old archbishop.

BACKGROUND AND PUBLISHING HISTORY

While Mark Twain wrote *1601* for his own and Twichell's amusement, he later claimed to have anonymously submitted it to a magazine whose editor had wished for a modern-day Rabelais—only to have it rudely rejected. The experience may have been on his mind when he later wrote *A Tramp Abroad* (1880), which asks why writers are not allowed the same license to express indecencies that artists are (chapter 50).

Mark Twain gave the manuscript to Twichell, who circulated it privately for several years. When John HAY got hold of it in July 1880, he had four unbound copies printed in Cleveland. Pressed by requests for more copies, Mark Twain took the manuscript to Lt. Charles Erskine Scott Wood (1852–1944) at WEST POINT in April 1882 and had him print 50 more copies. With Mark Twain's approval, Wood altered spellings to reflect late–16th-century forms, set the text in old-fashioned type and printed it on artificially aged linen to give it an authentic appearance. Since then, dozens of editions of *1601* have been printed. In the absence of an authoritative text, punctuation and spellings have varied greatly, as has the sketch's title.

David GRAY also admired *1601* so much that he encouraged Mark Twain to publish it openly. He thought that it would be remembered longer than *Innocents*

Abroad; however, Mark Twain never publicly admitted authorship of *1601*.

Sketches, New and Old, Mark Twain's (1875)

Collection of sketches and short stories originally issued as a SUBSCRIPTION BOOK by the AMERICAN PUBLISHING COMPANY. Mark Twain began assembling material for this volume in early 1871, but set the project aside until after several pirated collections of his sketches had been published. The first edition's cover was stamped "Sketches Old and New"; however, the title page reads "Mark Twain's Sketches, New and Old." Since Mark Twain's name appears in the title, the book is usually listed simply as *Sketches, New and Old.* Although Mark Twain thought little of the volume's contents, the book was later reissued many times in standardized editions.

Most of the book's 63 selections are brief, averaging less than 1,500 words. Of 56 previously published items, about 10 come from Mark Twain's early western journalism; these include "CURING A COLD," "AURELIA'S UNFORTUNATE YOUNG MAN" and "THE KILLING OF JULIUS CAESAR 'LOCALIZED.'" The book also reprints the JUMPING FROG STORY, adding a French translation from a French magazine and Mark Twain's excruciatingly literal English retranslation. Several items from New York newspapers include "THE FACTS CONCERNING THE RECENT RESIGNATION" and "A CURIOUS PLEASURE EXCURSION."

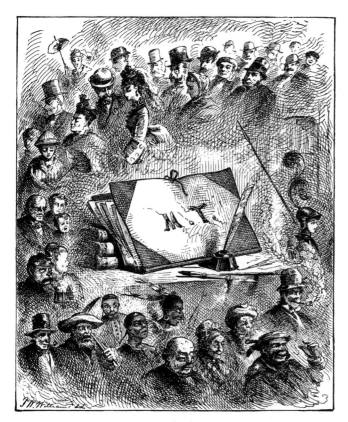

True Williams's frontispiece to Sketches, New and Old.

About a third of the selections come from the GALAXY. These include "MY LATE SENATORIAL SECRETARYSHIP," "HOW I EDITED AN AGRICULTURAL PAPER ONCE" and "POLITICAL ECONOMY." Fifteen items from the BUFFALO EXPRESS include "JOURNALISM IN TENNESSEE," "THE CAPITOLINE VENUS," "A MEDIEVAL ROMANCE," "A GHOST STORY" and "A CURIOUS DREAM." Other important selections include "CANNIBALISM IN THE CARS," "A TRUE STORY" and "Experience of the MCWILLIAMSES with Membranous Croup."

True WILLIAMS drew 130 illustrations for the book. When he illustrated *Tom Sawyer* a year later, he used similar designs for chapter openings and adapted several characters from the earlier book. His drawings of Tom—especially his frontispiece for *Tom Sawyer*—are almost identical to the character that he drew for "THE STORY OF THE BAD LITTLE BOY" in *Sketches*. He adapted his picture of Huck Finn for chapter 35 of *Tom Sawyer* from an illustration that he drew for "THE STORY OF THE GOOD LITTLE BOY" in *Sketches*.

Slade, Joseph Alfred (Jack) (1829?, Clinton County, Illinois–March 10, 1864, Virginia City, Montana)

Western outlaw. The son of Charles Slade (d. 1834), an English-born U.S. congressman, Slade grew up in a respectable Illinois family and served as a U.S. Army private in the Mexican War. Around 1850, he left Illinois for the West, after reportedly killing a man. By the late 1850s, he was working as a wagon boss on the Overland Trail and is said to have killed a teamster around 1860. He then became a STAGECOACH driver on the Overland line, which made him superintendent over its roughest territory, between JULESBURG, Colorado and South Pass, Wyoming. Combining administrative skill with lethal ruthlessness, Slade cleaned up the district, allegedly littering it with the corpses of troublemakers. His most notorious deed was capturing a crooked Overland agent named Jules Beni (or Reni), whom he slowly shot to death.

Details of Slade's bloody career are colored by legend, but he clearly was greatly feared. At the same time, however, he charmed people with his soft-spokenness and excellent manners and had numerous loyal friends. Mark Twain met Slade in southeastern Wyoming during a breakfast stop on his overland stagecoach journey in August 1861. *Roughing It'*s description of their encounter describes Slade as "so friendly and so gentle-spoken that I warmed to him in spite of his awful history" (chapter 10). It goes on to recall the narrator's trepidation in accepting Slade's offer of the last cup of coffee in a pot. This anecdote is fanciful, however, as Mark Twain and his brother did not know about Slade's reputation until *after* meeting him.

In 1862, the Overland stage company fired Slade after he went on a drunken rampage, and he followed a new gold rush to southwestern Montana, where he ran a freighting business. Though never accused of killing anyone in Montana, he persistently terrorized

Roughing It's tenderfoot narrator hesitates about accepting the last cup of coffee from Slade, fearing that if the notorious desperado has not killed anybody this morning, he might still need diversion.

Virginia City, Montana with drunken shooting sprees and was eventually hanged by vigilantes.

Mark Twain published a brief piece on Slade in the BUFFALO EXPRESS on January 22, 1870. When he wrote the passage about meeting Slade for *Roughing It* a little over a year later, he relied on a letter from his brother giving details of their meeting. Chapter 11 of *Roughing It* draws heavily on Thomas J. DIMSDALE's *Vigilantes of Montana* (1866) to reconstruct Slade's last days.

Slote, Dan (1828?–c. February 13, 1882)   Friend and business associate of Mark Twain. Mark Twain met Slote in June 1867, just before the QUAKER CITY cruise, on which they became close friends. Slote is the fun-loving sinner called "Dan" in *Innocents Abroad* (chapters 7, 10–14, 23, 27, 30, 45, 56 and 58). A partner in a New York banking firm, Slote was about 39 at the time of the cruise. He and Mark Twain were originally assigned to room together, but they ended up in separate cabins. Nevertheless, Slote is the "room-mate" to whom chapter 35 of *Innocents Abroad* alludes. Slote was with Mark Twain on the side trip to TANGIER and on journeys through FRANCE and ITALY. When the *Quaker City* went to Russia, Slote remained in CONSTANTINOPLE while Mark Twain borrowed his passport. Slote evidently enjoyed his long stay in the Turkish capital, as Mark Twain noted that he filled his stateroom with "rubbish," including a tombstone with his name incised in Turkish. Slote was also Mark Twain's tent-mate

throughout the HOLY LAND expedition. When the *Quaker City* left EGYPT, Slote stayed behind in order to spend a few more months touring Europe.

After the cruise, Slote and Mark Twain remained friends and were partners in several business deals. After patenting his self-pasting SCRAPBOOK in 1873, Mark Twain arranged with Slote's firm, Slote, Woodman and Company, to produce and market the books. Slote's company also published the first book edition of PUNCH, BROTHERS, PUNCH! in 1878, and Slote was involved in the KAOLATYPE process in which Mark Twain invested heavily in 1880. After this venture failed, Mark Twain came to regard Slote as a crook.

Slote's full name is used for a character in "CANNIBALISM IN THE CARS" (1868).

Slovenly Peter / Der Struwwelpeter   German children's book translated by Mark Twain. While staying in BERLIN in October 1891, Mark Twain discovered *Der Struwwelpeter,* a popular book of GERMAN verses about naughty children written in 1845 by August Heinrich Hoffman (1798–1874). Enthralled by the cleverness of Hoffman's jingles, Mark Twain translated the slim book into English as a Christmas present for his daughters. He wanted Charles L. WEBSTER & COMPANY to publish his translation right away, but Fred HALL balked, so the manuscript was set aside. The Limited Editions Club finally published it in August 1935, with a foreword by Clara Clemens; HARPER's issued a trade edition several weeks later.

Hoffman was a politician whose song *Deutschland, Deutschland über Alles* (1841) became Germany's national anthem in 1919. In contrast to the expansionist spirit with which his song was later identified, Hoffman composed it merely as an appeal for pan-German unification.

"Small-pox Hut"   This title of chapter 29 of *Connecticut Yankee* refers to the house of a destitute English peasant family whom Hank MORGAN and King ARTHUR meet on the day the mother, her husband and her two daughters succumb to smallpox. At great peril to the king—who unlike Hank has never had smallpox—the men ease the woman's sufferings and wait with her until she dies, leaving the house just before her three adult sons return. The sons are freshly escaped from ABBLASOURE's manor house prison and know nothing of their family's troubles until this moment. In the next chapter, Abblasoure's lord is murdered and his house burned down. Suspicion immediately falls on friends and relatives of the "Small-pox Hut" family, and the murdered lord's retainers wreak a terrible vengeance. Meanwhile, Hank and the king find hospitality in the home of the family's relative MARCO—who has escaped the purge.

Smarr, Samuel (ca. 1788–January 22, 1845, Hannibal, Missouri)   Missouri cattleman and neighbor of Mark Twain. Smarr was shot to death in Hannibal by a local merchant, William OWSLEY, when Mark Twain was nine. Mark Twain saw Smarr die in a drugstore near his home, and his father, John M. Clemens, took depositions from witnesses. The incident inspired the episode of Colonel SHERBURN's murder of BOGGS in chapter 21 of *Huckleberry Finn.* Like Smarr, the fictional Boggs dies in a drugstore with a Bible on his chest. In his AUTOBIOGRAPHY, Mark Twain recalls having nightmares about Smarr's struggling to breathe under the weight of the Bible while onlookers did nothing.

Smiley, Jim Character in the JUMPING FROG STORY. A former resident of ANGEL'S CAMP, Smiley was notorious for being willing to take either side of any bet, and he was uncommonly lucky. He once even offered odds to the Parson Walker that the parson's wife would not recover from her illness. Smiley owned many animals on which he wagered, including a broken-down horse known as the "fifteen-minute nag," a fighting dog named ANDREW JACKSON, chicken cocks and tomcats. His prize possession, however, was his jumping frog, DAN'L WEBSTER, which he spent three months teaching to jump. He often took the frog with him to town on the chance of getting up a bet—which is how he came to wager with the stranger of the story.

According to Simon WHEELER, Smiley also owned a yellow, one-eyed cow without a tail, but we never learn what he did with this animal. When Mark Twain first heard the jumping frog story from Ben COON, the Smiley character was called Coleman.

Smiley, Reverend Leonidas W. Name mentioned in the JUMPING FROG STORY. The story's narrator (Mark Twain himself in the first published version) visits ANGEL'S CAMP at the request of an eastern friend (originally Artemus WARD) to look up a boyhood chum named Leonidas W. Smiley. When the narrator asks Simon WHEELER about him, Wheeler launches into a long narrative about someone named *Jim* SMILEY. The narrator concludes that *Leonidas W.* Smiley never existed, and was merely an invention of his friend to draw him into being bored to death by Wheeler.

Smith, F[rancis] Berkeley (August 24, 1868, Astoria, New York–1931) Illustrator. The son of author F[rancis] Hopkinson Smith (1838–1915), Smith practiced architecture until 1896, when he turned to illustrating. He drew the African elephant for the cover of *Following the Equator* (1897) and contributed at least seven pictures to the first half of the book; several are caricatures at the ends of chapters. Smith himself later wrote travel books about Europe.

Smith, Henry Nash (September 29, 1906, Dallas, Texas–May 30, 1986, Elko, Nevada) Editor of the MARK TWAIN PAPERS (1953–64, 1979). Just eight and a half months younger than Dixon WECTER, Smith succeeded the latter as literary editor of the Mark Twain

Estate in 1953. He had previously earned a doctorate in English at Harvard and taught at Southern Methodist University (1927–41), the University of Texas (1941–46) and the University of Minnesota (1947–53).

As editor of the Mark Twain Papers, Smith added to the project's document collection, began planning its long-term publication program and signed an exclusive publication contract with the University of California Press. After resigning this post in 1964, he served on the project's editorial board and taught English at the University of California until 1974. When Frederick ANDERSON died suddenly in early 1979, Smith resumed general editorship of the Mark Twain Papers on an interim basis until Robert H. HIRST replaced him the next year.

One of the most distinguished scholars to serve as an editor of the Mark Twain Papers, Smith wrote the award-winning *Virgin Land: The American West as Symbol and Myth* (1950), *Democracy and the Novel: Resistance to Classic American Writers* (1978) and other works. He was coeditor of *Mark Twain of the Enterprise* (1957) and *Mark Twain–Howells Letters* (1960)—which set a new editing standard for Mark Twain letters—and edited *Mark Twain: A Collection of Critical Essays* (1963). He also wrote *Mark Twain: The Development of a Writer* (1962) and *Mark Twain's Fable of Progress: Political and Economic Ideas in "A Connecticut Yankee"* (1964).

Smith, John Character in "THE CAPITOLINE VENUS" (1869). A lifelong friend of the sculptor George Arnold and a resident of ROME, Smith makes Arnold rich by pulling off a careful HOAX. He takes Arnold's statue of a woman, hammers off its nose and other parts, buries it in a plot of land that he buys near Rome and registers in Arnold's name, then digs up the statue five months later. The newspaper *Il Slangwhanger di Roma* ("The Roman Rebuker") praises "John Smitthe" for making the discovery.

One of Mark Twain's favorite stock names, "John Smith" is the name of at least two dozen of his characters, including a Nevada miner in *Roughing It* (chapter 46), the captain of a fictitious steamboat in *Life on the Mississippi* (chapter 15) and a man whom Wilson fingerprints in *Pudd'nhead Wilson* (chapter 2). *Innocents Abroad* retells the "Legend of the Seven Sleepers," one of whom is called "Johannes Smithianus" (chapter 40).

Mark Twain dedicated his first book to "John Smith," thanking him for the help he had rendered. He evidently hoped that this tribute would encourage the country's thousands of "John Smiths" to buy the book.

Smith, Lucretia Borgia Character in "LUCRETIA SMITH's SOLDIER." A native of Bluemass, Massachusetts, Lucretia is the sweetheart of Reginald de Whittaker, whom she wants to enlist to fight in the CIVIL WAR. When Whittaker comes to tell her that he *has* enlisted, however, she drives him off without letting him speak. She learns the truth only after he marches off the next morning, then suffers because no soldier is carrying her name into war. She seeks redemption for her rash behavior by heroically nursing a badly wounded soldier named "R. D. Whittaker" for three weeks, only to discover that he is the *wrong* Whittaker.

Lucretia's selfishness and imperious insincerity reflect Mark Twain's feelings about her namesake, the Italian noblewoman Lucrezia Borgia (1480–1519), who was notorious in the 19th century for her alleged vice and cruelty. *Innocents Abroad* comments on "the facility with which she could order a sextuple funeral and get the corpses ready for it" (chapter 19). His 1872 speech to "The Ladies" alludes to the "gentle ministrations, the softening influences, the humble piety of Lucretia Borgia."

Smyrna   City in TURKEY now called Izmir. A major port on Anatolia's Aegean coast, Smyrna has roots going back several millennia. After enduring several waves of foreign conquest, it fell under the Ottoman Empire in the early 15th century and was one of its biggest cities when the QUAKER CITY visited it on September 5, 1867. The ship was there only through the following night, but Mark Twain's description of Smyrna fills most of chapters 38–39 in *Innocents Abroad*. After describing Smyrna's dark, uncomfortable houses, cramped streets, dirt and stenches, he sums up his feelings with "such is Oriental splendor!"

Mark Twain later claimed that when the *Quaker City* was anchored in Smyrna's harbor, he first saw his future wife, Livy, in an ivory miniature carried by her brother, Charles J. LANGDON.

Smythe, Carlyle Greenwood (September 16, 1865, Ambala, India–December 15, 1925, Nice, France) Australian LECTURE agent. Smythe grew up in Melbourne and had a brief journalism career, during which he edited the *Belgian Times* in Brussels. After joining the lecture bureau of his father, Robert S. SMYTHE, in Melbourne, he personally managed Mark Twain's tour through AUSTRALIA, NEW ZEALAND, INDIA and SOUTH AFTICA. He was with Mark Twain from September 1895, when he met him at Sydney, until mid-July 1896, when the tour ended in Cape Town, South Africa. Mark Twain's book about the tour, *Following the Equator*, mentions Smythe in chapters 34, 36, 37 and 48, and MARK TWAIN'S NOTEBOOK adds anecdotes about Smythe in South Africa. Smythe's own account of the tour, "The Real Mark Twain," appeared in *Pall Mall Magazine* in September 1989. Other figures for whom Smythe later managed tours included Arthur Conan Doyle and the explorer Roald Amundsen.

Smythe, Robert Sparrow (March 1833, London–May 23, 1917, Deepdene, Australia) Australian LECTURE agent. After organizing major lecture tours of H. M. STANLEY and others, Smythe invited Mark Twain to

undertake a world tour. Mark Twain received Smythe's letter in early 1895, around the same moment that he was writing to Smythe on the same subject. Mark Twain regarded this coincidence as an instance of "mental telegraphy" and described it in "Mental Telegraphy Again," an essay published in HARPER'S MAGAZINE in September 1895. Meanwhile, he met Smythe in Paris in April 1895 and contracted with him to organize a tour for later that year that Smythe's son, Carlyle SMYTHE, personally managed.

Snodgrass, Quintus Curtius   Between January 21 and March 30, 1861, 10 letters signed "Quintus Curtius Snodgrass" appeared in the *New Orleans Crescent*. Their unknown author—who probably took his pen name from Alexander the Great's Roman biographer, Quintus Curtius Rufus—addressed himself to someone named Charles Augustus Brown, relating his experiences in a new military unit drilling for the coming CIVIL WAR. Most of his letters are subtitled "Hints to Young Campaigners."

Mark Twain was in NEW ORLEANS several times in early 1861 while working as a steamboat PILOT and he had published at least one pseudonymous sketch in the *Crescent* (about Isaiah SELLERS) in 1859. Still earlier, he used "Thomas Jefferson SNODGRASS" as a pen name. In later years, he used other "Snodgrass" names in various writings, such as *The American Claimant*, in which Washington HAWKINS claims that Lord BERKELEY's real name is "Spinal Meningitis Snodgrass" (chapter 24).

Convinced that Mark Twain was "Q. C. Snodgrass," Minnie M. Brashear printed four Snodgrass letters in *Mark Twain, Son of Missouri* in 1934; 12 years later, the press of Southern Methodist University published all the letters in *The Letters of Quintus Curtius Snodgrass*, identifying Mark Twain as the author. Ernest Leisy edited the slim volume, drawing on equally slim circumstantial evidence to establish Mark Twain's authorship. Mark Twain, however, was almost certainly *not* the author of these letters. Aside from the fact that no noncircumstantial evidence supports his authorship, several of the letters allude to events in New Orleans that occurred when he was not there. Furthermore, word-frequency analysis suggests that he did not write them. Most telling, however, is that nothing about the style or content of the letters resembles anything else that Mark Twain ever wrote.

Snodgrass, Thomas Jefferson   Early PEN NAME. During his last half year as a journeyman printer, Mark Twain wrote three humorous letters from ST. LOUIS and CINCINNATI that were published under the byline "Thomas Jefferson Snodgrass" in the KEOKUK *Post* (November 1 and 29, 1856 and April 10, 1857). Following the conventions of many contemporary southwestern humorists, he makes "Snodgrass" a country bumpkin with atrocious spelling and grammar (a style called cacographic) who comments disdainfully on big-city life.

The letters are collected in *The Adventures of Thomas Jefferson Snodgrass* (Chicago, 1928), a 48-page, limited-edition book edited by Charles Honce.

"Sociable Jimmy" Sketch published in the *New York Times* on November 29, 1874. On the last day of December in 1871, Mark Twain was resting in a hotel in Paris, Illinois during a lecture tour, when he met the "most artless, sociable and exhaustless talker" he ever encountered. "Jimmy," a black 10-year-old hotel employee, told him about his family, his fellow employees and the town; nothing he said was remarkable or memorable, but his irresistible enthusiasm moved Mark Twain to record his entire conversation and publish it three years later as "Sociable Jimmy." As Mark Twain's first published work dominated by a child's voice, the article anticipated the narrative voice he was to give Huckleberry Finn a few years later. A similarly loquacious character appears in chapter 27 of *A Tramp Abroad*.

In 1943, the TWAINIAN reprinted "Sociable Jimmy" with little comment and without knowing its original source; Paul Fatout also reprinted it in *Mark Twain Speaks for Himself* in 1978. The sketch's importance was not recognized until years later, however. In mid-1992, it received national attention when the *New York Times* published a front-page story about Shelley Fisher Fishkin's then-forthcoming book, *Was Huck Black?* Fishkin puts "Sociable Jimmy" at the center of her thesis that African-American voices played a powerful role in Mark Twain's art, particularly in his creation of Huck Finn's speech patterns. The challenging assertion that Huck himself owed his voice to a black person started a new national debate among scholars about *Huckleberry Finn*.

Soldier Boy Title character of "A HORSE'S TALE." An example of a stolidly unimaginative animal that is morally superior to most human beings, Soldier Boy is the sole narrator of chapters 1 and 14 and a primary conversationalist in chapters 6, 7 and 9. When the narrative opens, he is Buffalo Bill CODY's veteran scout horse. A fast and noble steed whose mother was a Kentucky thoroughbred and father a bronco, he considers himself well educated, but is given to using words that he does not understand, such as "acrimonious" and "antiphonal." In chapter 6, he mentions that the only person who has ridden him for several months is young Cathy ALISON, to whom he is devoted. When he later saves Cathy from wolves, Buffalo Bill gives him to her (chapter 9).

When Cathy returns to Spain, she persuades her uncle to take Soldier Boy along (chapter 13). Shortly after they arrive, Soldier Boy is stolen, then spends the next five or six months being passed around among disreputable owners until he is a bony scarecrow. By the final chapter, he is reduced to working in a bullfight ring, where he is horribly gored. Cathy—who has been searching for him—reaches his side just before he dies. Then she, too, is fatally gored.

soliloquy *Soliloquy* and *monologue* are nearly synonymous. While the roots of the first are in Greek and those of the latter are in Latin, both derive from words for "speech" and "alone." In literary terminology, however, a "soliloquy" is regarded as a variety of a "monologue." In contrast to dialogue, a monologue is a speech delivered without a response from another character. A soliloquy is a monologue that a character delivers to himself alone. Soliloquy was a popular device in Elizabethan drama; perhaps the most famous example is HAMLET's soliloquy beginning with "To be, or not to be"—which *Huckleberry Finn* burlesques. In the absence of an external audience, the soliloquy becomes a kind of internal debate that poses moral alternatives and expresses one's inner thoughts. Since the person speaking is entirely alone, he presumably speaks the full truth.

Mark Twain had a lifelong interest in separating truth from falsehood, so it is not surprising that he occasionally employed soliloquy as a device for squeezing truth out of his characters. The most extended examples are KING LEOPOLD'S SOLILOQUY and "THE CZAR'S SOLILOQUY," polemics that he wrote in 1905. Around the same time, he also wrote "ADAM's Soliloquy"; this piece, however, lacks the strong internal debate of a true soliloquy. Minor soliloquies appear elsewhere in Mark Twain's writings. In chapter 17 of *Tom Sawyer*, for example, Becky Thatcher "soliloquises" over Tom's apparent death by drowning.

Solomon, King One of the most frequently mentioned biblical figures in Mark Twain's writings, Solomon was an Old Testament Hebrew king purported to have 700 wives—a subject often joked about in American folk humor. One of Mark Twain's best-known passages about Solomon appears in *Huckleberry Finn*, when Huck tells Jim that Solomon had "about a million wives" and was the wisest man who ever lived. Jim objects, however, arguing that no truly wise man would have that many wives. He also questions Solomon's proposing to split a baby in half, suggesting that Solomon would not have been so wasteful with children if he did not have about five million of his own (chapter 14). Mark Twain often read this passage to audiences when he was on the lecture circuit with G. W. CABLE in 1884–85.

"Some National Stupidities" Essay written around 1891–92 and first published in EUROPE AND ELSEWHERE (1923). Mark Twain puzzles over the nearly universal failure of nations to borrow superior ideas from other countries. America, for example, has failed to adopt the wonderful German stove. Conversely, European nations have failed to adopt such superior American ideas as the typewriter, the fountain pen, fair-dealing in shops, improved railroad methods and especially the improved elevator—which will make possible the vertical development of cities. When America does borrow European ideas, such as gas lighting and the railroad, it generally improves on them. Europe does just the opposite.

Where Americans tend to develop borrowed ideas *forward,* Europe develops American ideas *backward.* Its history of doing this goes back 300 years, when the Spanish failed to adopt precolonial Peru's excellent postal system.

"Some Rambling Notes of an Idle Excursion" (also called "Random Notes of an Idle Excursion") Sketch about a trip to BERMUDA that Mark Twain and Joseph TWICHELL made in 1877. On May 16, 1877 they took an overnight boat from New Haven, Connecticut to New York City, from which they sailed aboard the steamship *Bermuda* the next day. They spent three days at sea sailing in each direction, and four days loafing on Bermuda, mainly around Hamilton. Twichell is the former Civil War chaplain to whom Mark Twain alludes as "the Reverend" throughout the sketch.

The approximately 15,000-word sketch is aptly named. Much of it is simply random gossip and overheard conversations, such as that of two brothers discussing cemetery plots on the overnight boat. Aboard the *Bermuda* many of the anecdotes revolve around a dreary young passenger, known simply as "the Ass," who spoils every conversation with a dull question or remark. One of the best-known parts of this segment is a long anecdote about Captain Hurricane JONES—in actuality a caricature of Captain Edgar WAKEMAN, who had nothing to do with this journey. Mark Twain works in the anecdote on the premise that "Jones" was a subject of gossip aboard the ship. Another anecdote, apparently taken from Twichell's Civil War experiences, concerns two dying soldiers competing for a pine coffin.

Once the travelers reach Bermuda, Mark Twain raves about the island's peace and quiet, cleanliness, general prosperity and beauty. At a moment when his opinion of ENGLAND and the British Empire was at a peak, he praises British rule in Bermuda. He also admires the scarcity of dogs, while remaining unsure about the abundance of cats. He tells several cat anecdotes, has a great deal to say about onions in Bermuda, and curses the day that the telegraph will reach Bermuda and spoil its tranquility.

The sketch first appeared in the ATLANTIC MONTHLY from October 1877 through January 1878 and was first collected in book form in PUNCH, BROTHERS, PUNCH! (1878). In 1882 it appeared in THE STOLEN WHITE ELEPHANT with "THE INVALID'S STORY" tacked on as an extension. This latter story was separated in later collections.

"Some Thoughts on the Science of Onanism" Speech delivered at Paris's Stomach Club in spring 1879. As a risqué text, "Onanism" ranks with Mark Twain's *1601.* Mark Twain uses the speech to warn the private club's artists and writers against a form of self-abuse to which he perceives they are addicted, namely, masturbation. He builds his case with invented quotations from ancient and modern writers who have struggled with this problem, such as Homer, whose *Iliad* says "Give me masturbation or give me death." In his *Commentaries,* CAESAR admits to "times when I prefer it to sodomy." (DEFOE'S) *Robinson Crusoe* "cannot describe what I owe to this gentle art" and Queen ELIZABETH regarded it as "the bulwark of virginity." In mentioning Michelangelo as a representative of the old masters, he points out that "old masters" itself is an abbreviation. He also mentions Benjamin FRANKLIN, SOLOMON, Galen, (Adam?) Smith and DARWIN.

To assist his audience, he points out signs of excessive indulgence: a disposition to eat, drink, smoke, meet together convivially, laugh, joke and tell indelicate stories and, especially, a yearning to paint pictures. "Of all the various kinds of sexual intercourse," he concludes, "this has the least to recommend it. As an amusement, it is too fleeting; as an occupation, it is too wearing; as a public exhibition, there is no money in it." Cultured society has, unfortunately, banished it and degraded it to "brotherhood with flatulence."

Mark Twain kept his manuscript of the speech, and 50 copies of it were privately printed as a pamphlet in 1942. It has since been published in *Playboy* and in modern collections of his speeches.

South Africa A unified, independent country since 1910, South Africa was made up of four distinct political units when Mark Twain visited it in 1896. Natal and the Cape were British colonies, while the Orange Free State and the Transvaal ("South African Republic") were independent republics ruled by white Afrikaners ("Boers"). In just over 10 weeks, Mark Twain traveled through all four territories, giving 32 lectures in 15 different towns.

Mark Twain's interest in South Africa began in 1870, when the discovery of diamonds in the Cape attracted worldwide attention. Buoyed by the success of *Innocents Abroad* and excited about writing *Roughing It,* he was keen to write the first book on the diamond fields. Unable to go there himself, he paid John H. RILEY to go as his proxy to collect material that he would write up in a book. Riley went to South Africa, but Mark Twain never used his notes.

In 1896, South Africa was the final leg of Mark Twain's round-the-world lecture tour. After a two-week rest on MAURITIUS with his wife and daughter Clara, he sailed to Natal on the *Arundel Castle,* stopping briefly in Mozambique before landing at Durban on May 6, 1896. He spent a week lecturing and sightseeing around Durban, then left his family behind to tour the country with his Australian manager Carlyle SMYTHE. A zigzag itinerary took them to Pietermaritzburg, Johannesburg, Pretoria, Bloemfontein, Queenstown, King William's Town, East London and Port Elizabeth—where Mark Twain rejoined his family on June 10. From there, he went to Grahamstown, Cradock and Kimberley before officially ending his tour in Cape Town on July 15. The next day, he sailed for England with his family aboard the steamship *Norman.*

Mark Twain arrived in South Africa four months after Dr. L. S. Jameson led a filibustering expedition into the Transvaal. Jameson and his men were ignominiously captured, and Cecil RHODES—the Cape Colony's prime minister and southern Africa's leading power broker—was implicated in the affair. At the time of Mark Twain's visit, Rhodes was facing another crisis in present-day Zimbabwe, where Africans were rising against the administration of his chartered company. It was a tumultuous period in South African politics, and Mark Twain tried to learn all he could. He twice visited Pretoria's prison to meet Jameson's men, and he had private meetings with the lieutenant-governor of Natal, the Transvaal's president Paul Kruger and the Free State's president Martinus Steyn. His greatest disappointment was not meeting Rhodes himself.

South Africa came last both in Mark Twain's tour and in *Following the Equator,* his account of his trip. Both the traveling and the writing left him physically and mentally drained. Consequently, *Following the Equator*'s South Africa chapters are comparatively brief and somber. Although Mark Twain spent more time in South Africa than he did in INDIA, his book gives it only a fourth of the space devoted to the latter—a fraction that might have been even smaller. He wanted to end the book with India and save his South African material for a possible second book; however, when he discovered that what he had written was insufficient to fill out his first book, he hurriedly added chapters on South Africa. These chapters (64–69 and Conclusion) contrast with those on Australia and India in giving only a vague picture of his travels through the country, while focusing on Rhodes and the Jameson raid. A useful supplement to these chapters is MARK TWAIN'S NOTE-BOOK, which contains extracts from his original journals.

South America   South America is the only inhabited continent that Mark Twain never visited—an ironic omission on his part, since his first plan to travel outside the United States was to go to Brazil. While working in KEOKUK, Iowa in 1856, he was enthralled by William Lewis Herndon's and William Francis Lynch's *Exploration of the Valley of the Amazon* (1853) and wanted to go to Brazil himself. He still hoped to reach Brazil when he boarded the steamboat PAUL JONES in Cincinnati in February 1857. *Life on the Mississippi* recalls his plan to sail from New Orleans to South America, where he "would go and complete the exploration of the Amazon" (chapter 5). After reaching New Orleans, however, he abandoned that quest and got a position as an apprentice steamboat PILOT. In "THE TURNING POINT OF MY LIFE," he tells of wanting to be a coca trader in the Amazon.

An echo of Mark Twain's early dream of reaching Brazil is heard in *Huckleberry Finn,* in which Huck and the KING meet a young man named Tim COLLINS, who is going down the Mississippi, headed for "Ryo Janeero" (chapter 24). Like the young Sam Clemens, this character with the phonetically similar name evidently hopes

to take passage for Brazil in New Orleans. A more substantial story relating to South America appears in *Roughing It*'s yarn about Ned BLAKELY's hanging a murderer in the Chincha Islands off Peru (chapter 50).

Although Mark Twain never set foot on South America's mainland, he did traverse Central America three times. At the end of 1866 he crossed NICARAGUA. In 1868 he twice crossed the Isthmus of PANAMA—when Panama was still part of the South American nation of Colombia.

Spain   When the cruise ship QUAKER CITY landed at GIBRALTAR, a British enclave on the southern coast of Spain, on June 29, 1867, several passengers left the ship to travel through Spain to France. Mark Twain nearly joined this group, but stayed behind and instead visited TANGIER. The original itinerary for the *Quaker City*'s return voyage 15 weeks later called for stops at Majorca and Valencia, from which passengers could go overland to Madrid, rejoining the ship at Gibraltar. This plan was never carried out. On October 17, the ship stopped instead at Malaga, a port south of Valencia, where Mark Twain and Captain DUNCAN went ashore under guard to ask permission to land. Malaga was quarantining *all* foreign ships out of fear of CHOLERA, so the *Quaker City* continued to Gibraltar.

Since overland travel was difficult and there was little time for side trips, most passengers stayed with the ship through the next week. As soon as he could, however, Mark Twain left Gibraltar with Dr. Abraham JACKSON, Julia NEWELL, Julius MOULTON and a Spanish guide, Michael Benuñes, as well as several other passengers who turned back when complications arose. After a lightning tour of Andalusia by horseback and train, they rejoined the *Quaker City* at Cadiz on October 24 and the ship sailed the next morning.

Mark Twain evidently kept no notes during this trip and wrote no letters about it. He did, however, write a chapter about Spain for *Innocents Abroad,* but he left it out of the book at the suggestion of Bret HARTE, who apparently thought it repetitious and in poor taste. It remarks, for example, on Spaniards staring at the "short traveling dress" of the narrator's unnamed female traveling companion (Julia Newell). It also repeats the well-worn guide-baiting gag of earlier "FERGUSON" passages and includes long mock critiques of works by the 17th-century painter Murillo. Chapter 59 of *Innocents* merely says that the narrator's experiences in Spain "were too varied and numerous for a short chapter and I have not room for a long one."

Four decades later, Mark Twain used Spain as a setting for the conclusion of his bull-fighting story, "A HORSE'S TALE."

Spanish Island   Fictional Mississippi River location in *Huckleberry Finn.* Spanish Island is a wooded island a few miles below PIKESVILLE where Huck hides the RAFT after learning that the KING has sold Jim (chapter 31). He spends the night there, then returns to Pikesville by canoe. In chapter 40, Huck, Tom Sawyer and Jim flee to the island after completing Jim's escape. Once there, Tom reveals that he has been shot in the leg. Huck leaves to fetch a doctor. The island is not identified by name until the next chapter, when Huck tells a Pikesville doctor where to go to treat Tom. Jim emerges from hiding to help the doctor and is soon recaptured on the island.

Sphinx (Sphynx) Egyptian monument. Of the thousands of stone sphinxes in EGYPT, the most famous is the colossal stone figure that Mark Twain saw at Gizeh during a day-trip from nearby Cairo on October 5, 1867. In ancient Egyptian mythology, sphinxes were

Huck and Tom swoop down on the Sphinx to rescue Jim in chapter 12 of Tom Sawyer Abroad.

beasts with human faces and animal bodies that typically symbolized pharaohs. The word *sphinx* itself comes from Greek mythology, in which sphinxes were winged beasts that killed people who could not answer their riddles. The phrase "riddle of the sphinx" now connotes two things: the Greek notion of monsters that pose insoluble riddles, and the Egyptian image of a great silent beast whose face suggests ageless mysteries.

Eight months after leaving Egypt, Mark Twain composed a description of the Great Sphinx for chapter 58 of *Innocents Abroad* that was calculated to evoke the deep riddle of its sad face, patiently watching as untold aeons roll by. Reviewers praised this reverent passage, which was also a favorite with Mark Twain's "AMERICAN VANDAL ABROAD" lecture audiences. The *Innocents* passage ends jarringly, however, mentioning the attempt of a fellow American passenger to chisel a piece off the sphinx as a "specimen." Mark Twain's notes indicate that the offending person was Dr. William GIBSON. Mark Twain also evokes the "riddle" notion in the second chapter of *Roughing It,* which describes a woman sitting silently in a stagecoach as a "grim sphynx." Chapter 12 of *Tom Sawyer Abroad* makes more dramatic use of the Great Sphinx; Jim is stranded on its top, while an angry crowd climbs up after him. The moment recalls Mark Twain's own 1867 experience atop the Pyramid of Cheops, where he was harassed by an army of hustlers and beggars demanding BAKSHEESH.

The sheer size of Egypt's pyramids also impressed Mark Twain; in *Innocents,* he compares them favorably to the puny mountains he thought huge during his youth—such as Holliday's (CARDIFF) Hill. In chapter 73 of *Roughing It,* a description of Hawaiian ruins leads into a discussion of how Egypt's pyramids were built.

Sprague, Reverend Mister Minor character in *Tom Sawyer.* Sprague is the minister of a ST. PETERSBURG church, whose congregation regards him as a "wonderful reader." Mark Twain had a professional interest in public reading; he often criticized ministers as a group as being poor readers. In chapter 5, he puts Sprague to a severe test. The minister delivers a long, wordy Calvinist sermon that threatens to put his congregation to sleep. Tom meanwhile plays with a beetle that gets loose and pinches a stray dog. The dog then runs wildly through the aisles, yelping and bringing welcome relief to the congregation—without stopping Sprague from finishing his sermon. Though not mentioned by name again, Sprague is probably the "clergyman" in chapter 17 who delivers the funeral sermon for Tom, Huck and Joe Harper, who are presumed dead.

stagecoaches In July 1861, Mark Twain and his brother Orion Clemens began a three-week stagecoach trip from Missouri to NEVADA that is the subject of most of the first 20 chapters of *Roughing It.* While the book embellishes many incidents, it presents a generally accurate outline of Mark Twain's route. After leaving St. Joseph, his coach followed the first part of the Oregon Trail and passed through parts of Kansas, NEBRASKA, Colorado, Wyoming, UTAH and Nevada before arriving in CARSON CITY. During his years in the Far West, Mark Twain also made many shorter stagecoach trips, particularly between Nevada and SAN FRANCISCO—a journey that *Roughing It* claims that he made 13 times (chapter 20).

Stagecoach transportation began in England in the late 17th century and reached its highest development in western America in the mid-19th century. It takes its name from a system of pulling carriages with teams of horses that are changed at regular stations, or "stages," along set routes. During the 19th century, stagecoach transportation was the fastest way for travelers to cross the American continent until the first transcontinental railroad line was completed in 1869. As railroad lines expanded, stagecoach lines gradually disappeared.

Stanley, Henry Morton (January 28, 1841, Denbigh, Wales–May 10, 1904, London) British-American explorer and journalist. Born John Rowlands in Wales, Stanley fled from a workhouse as a teenager and later shipped from Liverpool as a cabin boy. In 1858 he jumped ship in NEW ORLEANS, where he was adopted by Henry Morton Stanley, an American merchant whose name he took. During this same period, Mark Twain was visiting New Orleans regularly while piloting steamboats on the Mississippi River. The outbreak of the CIVIL WAR in 1861 launched both men on new careers. Pressured by Southern friends, Stanley joined the Confederate army, in which he fought against U. S. GRANT at Belmont, Missouri in November 1861. The following April he was captured at the Battle of Shiloh. Stanley's Northern captors persuaded him to join the Union army under a special policy for foreign-born prisoners, but he was soon discharged because of illness. He then went to Cuba, where he learned that his adoptive father had died, and then revisited Britain. On his return to America, he joined the Union navy—becoming perhaps the only person to serve in the Confederate and Union armies and the Union navy. While in the navy, he began writing for newspapers, and after the war he was in demand as a traveling newspaper correspondent.

In 1867 the *St. Louis Missouri-Democrat* sent Stanley west to cover cavalry campaigns against the Plains Indians. He was in ST. LOUIS, Missouri when Mark Twain was lecturing there in March–April 1867. Stanley reported on Mark Twain's lecture on the Sandwich Islands in such detail for the *Missouri-Democrat* that Mark Twain could not use the same material again in the region. Stanley's usurpation of the lecture text angered Mark Twain, but the two men later became fast friends.

The popularity of Stanley's reports won him European and African assignments from the NEW YORK HERALD, whose proprietor, James Gordon Bennett, sent him to East Africa in 1871 to find the Scottish missionary-

explorer David Livingstone. After locating Livingstone in Tanzania, he returned to England to confront public skepticism that he had accomplished what he claimed. Mark Twain was at the Royal Geographical Society dinner in the fall of 1872, when the society's president publicly apologized to Stanley for having earlier ridiculed his claims. Mark Twain later paraphrased Stanley's famous remark from his meeting with Livingstone in *Huckleberry Finn*—in which Tom Sawyer appears at the Phelpses' home and says, "Mr. Archibald NICHOLS, I presume?" (chapter 33). Meanwhile, with his fame now assured, Stanley launched a new career as a lecturer. His success on the lecture circuit moved James REDPATH to encourage Mark Twain to make a similar tour at about this same time.

Stanley led further African expeditions that would establish him as one of the giants of African exploration. After traversing the central part of the continent in 1874–77, he published *Through the Dark Continent,* coining a nickname for Africa that stuck. From 1879 into the early 1880s, he explored the Congo River and played a major role in establishing the Congo Free State for Belgium's King LEOPOLD II.

Over the next several years, Stanley traveled widely on profitable lecture tours. In December 1886, he spoke at an engagement in Boston at which Mark Twain introduced him. Later that year, Mark Twain tried to persuade him to write an autobiography for Charles L. WEBSTER & COMPANY, but the project never came to anything. Stanley returned to northeastern Africa for a final epic journey in 1887–89. In 1892 he reestablished his British citizenship and was elected to Parliament three years later.

Meanwhile, Stanley's lecturing success during these years encouraged Mark Twain to undertake a world tour in 1895–96. He consulted Stanley and used Stanley's Australian agent, R. S. SMYTHE, to organize his own tour. When Mark Twain passed through London in April 1895, Stanley gave a dinner in his honor. After his world tour, Mark Twain spent over a year near London and occasionally got together socially with Stanley. In the spring of 1897, London's Savage Club elected Stanley, Mark Twain and the Prince of Wales (EDWARD VII) as honorary lifetime members.

After Stanley's health began failing in 1899, Mark Twain, again living in London, encouraged Stanley's wife to put him under the care of Dr. J. H. KELLGREN, a Swedish physician who had been treating the Clemens family. Mark Twain was living in Florence when he learned about Stanley's death in May 1904. He kept the news from his wife Livy, who died four weeks later. In 1909, Stanley's wife published his unfinished autobiography. This work, largely a compilation of previously published materials, does not mention Mark Twain. Stanley's other writings include *My Kalulu* (1873), a children's book on Africa from which Mark Twain possibly took the name of the character Kalula in his story "THE ESQUIMAU MAIDEN'S ROMANCE" (1893).

Stavely, Butterworth (Butterworth I) Character in "THE GREAT REVOLUTION IN PITCAIRN" (1879). An American settler in tiny Pitcairn's island, Stavely foments a revolution that throws off English rule, replaces universal suffrage with a system of nobility, and gets himself crowned "Emperor Butterworth I." Soon, however, he is overthrown and the island reverts to its previous condition.

In his desire to find trouble where none exists, Stavely resembles Tom Sawyer, particularly the Tom of "TOM SAWYER'S CONSPIRACY." More significantly, he is a rehearsal for Hank MORGAN, the modern American of *Connecticut Yankee* who revolutionizes sixth-century England. Stavely, however, is a kind of mirror image of Morgan—who seeks to destroy the established church and replace hereditary nobility with universal suffrage.

Life on the Mississippi mentions a real Hannibal resident named John Stavely (chapter 55). "Stavely" is also the name of characters in several of Mark Twain's unfinished stories.

steamboats Mark Twain's name is inextricably linked to steamboats, with good reason. After growing up in a Mississippi River town whose lifeblood was steamboat commerce, he became a PILOT during the greatest era of steamboating. By the time he established himself as a writer, the great age of steamboats had already passed, but he helped to preserve its memory in *Life on the Mississippi, Huckleberry Finn* and other works.

The idea of using steam engines to propel vessels was first tried on rivers; it became a practical reality with James Watt's invention of an improved steam engine in 1769. A decade later, primitive steamboats were starting to sail on France's Saône River and Pennsylvania's Delaware River. By the beginning of the 19th century, paddle-driven steamboats were operating profitably on New York's Hudson River. The term steamboat—which

Mark Twain favored over "riverboat"—applies to large steam-powered vessels used on inland waterways. Steamboats differed from oceangoing steamships in several ways. Designed to draw as little water as possible, they used paddle-wheel propulsion long after ocean vessels began adopting screw propellers.

Steamboats happened to develop as a practical form of river transportation just after the Louisiana Purchase doubled the size of the United States in 1804. For America to expand westward, improved transportation systems were urgently needed. At the beginning of the 19th century, the vast Mississippi Valley was sparsely developed; much of its commerce was floated downstream on keelboats and rafts. Such vessels sufficed to move goods and people downstream, but were useless for carrying anything *up*stream. In 1811, steam power arrived on the Mississippi when Robert Fulton's associate Nicholas Roosevelt took a round-bottomed boat from Pittsburgh to New Orleans in a perilous three-month voyage. He left this boat on the Lower Mississippi to run between New Orleans and Natchez. Other steam-powered boats soon followed, but the fast-moving, shallow and unstable channels of the Mississippi and its tributaries called for a different kind of boat than those being developed on the East Coast and in Europe. The full commercial potential of steamboats was assured only after boats with high-pressure engines were introduced a few years later. Over the next two decades, a basic steamboat design evolved, favoring straight-sided and flat-bottomed boats, with paddle wheels. With their boilers above the main deck, many large boats had drafts as shallow as two feet. Stern-wheelers, with their paddle wheels in the rear, were cheaper to build, but side-wheelers offered greater maneuverability, and they predominated. The "classic" Mississippi River steamboat was essentially a raft with an elaborate and typically ornate superstructure—a kind of giant floating wedding cake or swan.

By the mid-1830s, when Mark Twain's family settled in Missouri, the Mississippi and its major tributaries were being worked by more than 200 boats—a number that doubled in the 1840s and again in the 1850s. By the eve of the CIVIL WAR, nearly a thousand boats plied these rivers, carrying more cargo than all the nation's oceangoing vessels combined. Mark Twain, meanwhile, watched this growing traffic pass by his Hannibal home and reveled in the daily landings of local "packets." At age 10, he made his first steamboat journey, to St. Louis—a trip that *A Tramp Abroad* mentions (chapter 10). Afflicted with the ambition to be a steamboatman—an ambition common to boys of that time and place—he achieved his dream in early 1857, when he became an apprentice pilot. Over the next four years, he served on at least 18 different boats, all flat-bottomed side-wheelers.

The following list of the boats on which Mark Twain served has been reconstructed by scholars from Mark Twain's correspondence and NOTEBOOKS, contemporary

Horace Bixby's Baton Rouge, *the last steamboat on which Mark Twain sailed on the lower Mississippi.*

newspapers and other sources. From February 1857 through April 1859, he was a cub; from May 1859 to May 1861 he was a fully licensed pilot (there is an individual entry for each boat and each boat is entered under its full name).

Colonel Crossman (February–March 1857)

Crescent City (April–June 1857)

Rufus J. Lackland (July–August 1857)

John J. Roe (August–September 1857)

William M. Morrison (October 1857)

Pennsylvania (November 1857, February–June 1858)

D. A. January (December 1857)

New Falls City (January 1858, October–December 1858)

Alfred T. Lacey (July 1858, May 1859)

John H. Dickey (August–October 1858)

White Cloud (October 1858)

Aleck Scott (December 1858–April 1859)

J. C. Swon (June–July 1859)

Edward J. Gay (August–October 1859)

A. B. Chambers (October 1859–February 1860)

City of Memphis (March–July 1860)

Arago (July–August 1860)

Alonzo Child (September 1860–May 1861)

Mark Twain's piloting career was entirely on the Lower Mississippi, but he also had some experience as a passenger on steamboats on other rivers. For example, his first trip on the PAUL JONES began on the OHIO RIVER. In July 1861—after his piloting career ended—he and his brother Orion Clemens rode a MISSOURI RIVER steamboat, the *Sioux City*, from St. Louis to St. Joseph—a journey briefly described in the first chapter of *Roughing It*. His next steamboat experiences were in CALIFORNIA, where an important steamboat traffic was developing on the Sacramento River system. In February 1866, for example, he went from San Francisco Bay to Sacramento aboard a steamboat. In 1882, he returned to the Mississippi, going from St. Louis to New Orleans and back, and then to Minnesota. The boats on which he traveled during that trip included the GOLD DUST, *Charles Morgan*, CITY OF BATON ROUGE, *Gem City* and *Minneapolis*. When he took his family to Iowa for a Fourth of July reunion in 1886, they traveled from St. Paul to Keokuk by steamboat. During his last visit to the Mississippi River in 1902, he helped dedicate a St. Louis harbor boat that was renamed the "MARK TWAIN" in his honor.

The obvious economic importance of steamboats and their stately splendor made steamboating glamorous in many ways; however, steamboating also had its dark sides. Gambling, prostitution and violence were endemic on the river, and the steamboats themselves had notoriously short lives. During their glory years, new boats could pay for themselves in five months. Speed, shallow draft and ornate decor counted for more in their design than safety and durability. As a consequence, the boats did not stand up well to the rivers' many hazards. Shipboard fires, boiler explosions, rocks, snags and collisions took heavy tolls; the average boat met a disastrous ending within five years. Mark Twain himself came close to being in disasters several times. In February 1858, for example, he chanced not to be working with his usual mentor pilot, Horace BIXBY, when the latter's boat, the *Colonel Crossman*, exploded and burned near New Madrid, Missouri. Five months later, Mark Twain was put ashore from the *Pennsylvania* shortly before that boat exploded in an accident that killed his brother Henry Clemens and the pilot William BROWN. In 1882, he traveled on the *Gold Dust* just four months before it exploded and took 17 lives.

Mark Twain's most important writing about steamboats is in *Life on the Mississippi*. Most of the first part of this book is adapted from "OLD TIMES ON THE MISSISSIPPI," a memoir of his cub piloting days. The balance of the book derives from his return to the river in 1882, when he wanted to see how much steamboating had changed in two decades.

Steamboats figure into much of Mark Twain's fiction. His first novel, *The Gilded Age*, documents the role of steamboats in westward migration and gives the fullest account of what it was like to travel on a steamboat that appears in his fiction. Si HAWKINS takes his family to Missouri aboard the *Boreas*. In an otherwise uneventful voyage, the boat races against the AMARANTH, which blows up. Although *Tom Sawyer* is another of the icons associated with Mark Twain, no true steamboats appear in it. Even the word "steamboat" appears in just one chapter—the second—when Ben ROGERS impersonates the "Big Missouri" (a real boat alluded to in chapter 4 of *Life on the Mississippi*). Otherwise, the nearest thing to a steamboat in the story is the town's "steam ferry boat" that is used to search for the bodies of Tom, Huck and Joe Harper when they are believed to have drowned (chapter 14). Later, the same boat conveys children downriver for Becky Thatcher's picnic (chapter 29). This St. Petersburg ferryboat is presumably the same one that hunts for Huck's body in chapter 8 of *Huckleberry Finn*.

Steamboats play important roles throughout the narrative of *Huckleberry Finn*. A substantial portion of its narrative takes place on the Mississippi River, where Huck and Jim constantly see steamboats as they themselves drift downstream on a raft. Many passages become lyrical. At night, for example, Huck describes seeing a steamboat slipping along in the dark, and now and then "she would belch a whole world of sparks up out of her chimbleys, and they would rain down in the river and look awful pretty; then she would turn a corner and her lights would wink out and her pow-wow shut off and leave the river still again" (chapter 19).

A reminder of the hazards of steamboating occurs in chapter 12, in which Huck and Jim explore the derelict WALTER SCOTT—which has "killed herself on a rock." This episode and other passages reveal Huck as having more steamboat knowledge than one might expect from a boy with his background. He is, for example, familiar with the major parts of boats and understands how pilots choose their channel crossings. At the end of chapter 16, another steamboat plows into Jim and Huck's raft, forcing Huck and Jim ashore. When Huck meets the GRANGERFORD family, he tells them that he fell off a passing steamboat while traveling as a deck passenger. In chapter 20, he invents another steamboat story in order to explain to the KING and DUKE why he and Jim are on their raft together.

In chapter 24, Huck, the King and the Duke take a short ride aboard the steamboat SUSAN POWELL in order to make a proper entrance to the town of the late Peter WILKS—whose brothers the con men claim to be. Another steamboat arrives in town in chapter 28, bringing rival Wilks brother claimants down from Cincinnati. In an allusion to one of the minor hazards of steamboat travel, the newcomers report that their luggage was put ashore at the wrong landing. Later, when Huck arrives at the PIKESVILLE farm of Sally and Silas PHELPS, they think he is Tom Sawyer, freshly arrived from St. Petersburg (chapter 32). To explain his delay, he says that a cylinder-head on his steamboat blew up. Aunt Sally then recalls how Silas had once been traveling on the LALLY ROOK when a similar accident occurred. Tom Sawyer himself arrives on a boat shortly afterward. In the final chapter, Huck learns of Tom's desire to return Jim to St. Petersburg "in style" aboard a steamboat.

Tom Sawyer Abroad picks up where *Huckleberry Finn* ends, with Huck recalling the glory that he and Jim enjoyed when they returned home from their raft journey aboard a steamboat. Their glory was, however, tame compared to that of Tom: "We only went down the river on a raft and came back by the steamboat, but Tom went by the steamboat both ways. The boys envied me and Jim a good deal, but land! they just knuckled to the dirt before Tom." In *Tom Sawyer, Detective*, Tom and Huck return to Pikesville aboard an unnamed sternwheeler, on which they meet Jake DUNLAP, who is hiding out in the next stateroom (chapters 2–5). In "TOM SAWYER'S CONSPIRACY," Tom and Huck ride a steamboat a short distance down the river while trying to catch up with murder suspects; Huck encounters his former nemeses, the KING and DUKE, aboard the boat (chapters 7–8).

Steamboats also play a prominent part in *Pudd'nhead Wilson*. DAWSON'S LANDING is a busy port, with boats stopping almost constantly. The character Tom DRISCOLL uses steamboats frequently to visit St. Louis. When the slave woman ROXANA is freed in chapter 4, she goes "chambermaiding on a steamboat." Over the next eight years she works on the GRAND MOGUL, a packet following the same Cincinnati–New Orleans route as the real *Paul Jones*. During the winter months, she works on an unnamed Vicksburg packet on the Lower Mississippi.

Mark Twain's original draft of *Pudd'nhead Wilson* contains a description of the *Grand Mogul* that is richer in details on passenger life aboard steamboats than anything he wrote elsewhere. However, the published version of the novel reduces Roxy's steamboat experiences to a few lines in chapter 8. Nevertheless, Roxy, like Mark Twain himself, discovers that "if there was anything better in this world than steamboating, it was the glory to be got by telling about it." Later, Roxy escapes from an Arkansas plantation, happens upon the *Grand Mogul* and hitches a ride home.

Additional references to steamboats can be found throughout Mark Twain's writings. Even *Connecticut Yankee* mentions them. In chapter 27, Hank kills several knights with a dynamite bomb, whose blast he compares to a "steamboat explosion." Chapter 40's list of Hank's improvements in sixth-century England include "a steamboat or two on the THAMES." Shorter works that involve steamboats include the Civil War tale "A CURIOUS EXPERIENCE," in which a boy claims to have escaped from New Orleans on a steamboat called the *Duncan F. Kenner*—named after Louisiana Confederate leader Duncan Farrar Kenner (1813–1887).

Despite the unhappy outcome of the racing in *The Gilded Age*, Mark Twain loved steamboat races, which he thought the most enjoyable of all races (*Life on the Mississippi*, chapter 45). He recaptures some of their excitement in "CAPTAIN STORMFIELD'S VISIT TO HEAVEN," in which Stormfield's race against a comet through the cosmos is described as if it were a steamboat race (chapter 3).

Stedman, Edmund Clarence (October 8, 1833, Hartford, Connecticut–January 18, 1908, New York, New York)   A poet and influential critic in his time, Stedman corresponded for the *New York World* during the CIVIL WAR, after which he was a banker and stockbroker while continuing to write and edit. He advised Mark Twain on the manuscript of *Connecticut Yankee* (whose "CLARENCE" may borrow Stedman's middle name). Around the same time, he helped edit the *Library of American Literature* (1888–90) for Charles L. WEBSTER & COMPANY, which also employed his son Arthur Stedman (1859–1908) as an editor.

Stephens, Henry Louis (1824, Philadelphia, Pennsylvania–1882, Bayonne, New Jersey)   Illustrator.   A leading caricaturist of his time, Stephens drew for *Leslie's* and HARPER's magazines in the 1850s and 1860s. Elisha BLISS reused several pictures that Stephens drew for Albert RICHARDSON's *Beyond the Mississippi* in Mark Twain's *Roughing It*. In 1871 Stephens illustrated Mark Twain's BURLESQUE AUTOBIOGRAPHY with pictures that

Edmund Clarence Stedman, who believed that the sun rose merely to admire his poetry—according to Mark Twain. (W. D. Howells, *Literary Friends and Acquaintance,* 1902)

satirize some of the political scandals of the era. He also contributed several illustrations to *The Gilded Age,* but these can no longer confidently be identified because they are unsigned.

Stewart, William Morris (August 9, 1827, Galen, New York–April 23, 1909) NEVADA politician. Drawn to California by the GOLD RUSH in 1850, Stewart studied law there and became an expert in mining litigation. By 1854 he was the state's acting attorney general. Five years later, silver discoveries drew him to NEVADA, where he practiced law and won fame defending the original claimants to the COMSTOCK Lode. Mark Twain knew Stewart well during this period and relates an anecdote about him in chapter 44 of *Roughing It.* Stewart's *Reminiscences* (1908) charge *Roughing It* with unfairly accusing him of cheating Mark Twain, and call True WILLIAMS's caricature of him "scurrilous."

After Nevada gained statehood on October 31, 1864, Stewart and James W. NYE were elected its first senators. During his first two terms of office (1864–1875), Stewart promoted legislation favoring miners' rights and aligned

William Morris Stewart regarded his portrait in Roughing It *as "scurrilous."*

with the Radical Republicans on Reconstruction issues. His greatest distinction was writing the Fifteenth Amendment, which guaranteed voting rights to former slaves (1869). When Mark Twain returned from the QUAKER CITY excursion in November 1867, he became Stewart's private secretary and briefly roomed with him in WASHINGTON, D.C. They soon had a falling-out, however. Mark Twain quit after just two months and then publicly satirized himself in "MY LATE SENATORIAL SECRETARYSHIP." When Mark Twain visited Washington in July 1870, Stewart introduced him to President U. S. GRANT.

After leaving the Senate in 1875, Stewart resumed practicing law in California. He returned to Nevada in 1886 and was elected to three more terms in the U.S. Senate (1887–1905). As a champion of remonetizing silver—an issue crucial to Nevada mining interests—he earned a reputation as a narrow sectionalist.

Still-house branch Stream near Hannibal. A small tributary of the Mississippi River located north of CARDIFF HILL, this stream is mentioned in *Tom Sawyer* as the locale of the HAUNTED HOUSE. It took its name from a local distillery that used its water.

Stillman, Archy Central character of "A DOUBLE-BARRELED DETECTIVE STORY." The son of a woman who calls herself "Mrs. Stillman," Archy is born shortly after his father, Jacob FULLER, abandons his mother in 1880. Archy has the tracking powers of a bloodhound, possibly because his father set hounds on his mother when she was pregnant with him. When Archy is 16, his mother explains how his father brutalized her and he vows revenge. The story then follows his three-and-a-half-year pursuit of his father in the Far West. Despite the fact that Archy has grown up without friends and willingly sacrifices his youth to torment his father, he has a kind and generous nature and seems to get along well with people he encounters.

Stoddard, Charles Warren (August 7, 1843, Rochester, New York–April 23, 1909, Monterey, California) Poet and travel writer. Stoddard went to SAN FRANCISCO as a teenager in 1855 and later wrote poetry for the GOLDEN ERA under the pen name Pip Pepperpod. He and Mark Twain met in the mid-1860s and became life-long friends. In November 1873, he went to England with Mark Twain as his personal secretary, though Mark Twain later claimed to have paid his passage merely to have company. Stoddard later taught literature at Notre Dame (1885–86) and Washington, D.C.'s Catholic University (1889–1902). He and Mark Twain saw each other occasionally and corresponded through 1904. Stoddard died on the same day as Senator William M. STEWART—almost exactly a year before Mark Twain's DEATH. His writings include *Poems* (1867), several books on Pacific islands, notably *South-Sea Idyls* (1873), the autobiographical *A Troubled Heart* (1885) and a novel, *For the Pleasure of His Company* (1903).

Stoker, Bram (Abraham) (November 8, 1847, Dublin, Ireland–April 20, 1912, London, England) Irish novelist and theater impresario. After studying at the University of Dublin, Stoker spent a decade as a civil servant and wrote drama critiques for the *Dublin Mail*. He met the actor Henry IRVING (1838–1905) in 1878, then managed Irving's LONDON theater and business affairs for nearly three decades. He accompanied Irving on his tours and met Mark Twain through him—possibly in London in mid-1879—beginning a long friendship. At some point Stoker invested money in the PAIGE COMPOSITOR, but Mark Twain later returned it to him when it was clear the machine had failed. Mark Twain saw Stoker regularly while he was living in LONDON and writing *Following the Equator* in 1896–97, and he had Stoker act as his British agent for the book, which CHATTO published in England as MORE TRAMPS ABROAD in 1897. He last saw Stoker in 1907 and corresponded with him until the end of his life.

In 1897, the same year in which *Following the Equator* appeared, Stoker's *Dracula* was published. A chilling novel about a Transylvanian vampire, it became a horror classic. His other novels include *The Shoulder of Shasta* (1895), which is set in northern California.

Stoker, [Jacob] Richard (Dick) (1820–1898) California prospector. Originally from Kentucky, Stoker went into business in southern Illinois before serving in the Mexican War, then joined the GOLD RUSH to CALIFORNIA, settling in TUOLUMNE COUNTY'S JACKASS HILL in late 1849. There he built a cabin in which he spent the rest of his life pocket-MINING, and he took in Jim and William GILLIS as partners. Mark Twain stayed at Stoker's cabin from December 1864 through late February 1865. During this interlude, Jim Gillis often told outrageous tales featuring Stoker as a man who communed with animals, while Stoker listened quietly and smoked. Mark Twain adapted several of Gillis's tales, renaming their hero "Dick BAKER" in *Roughing It* and "Jim Baker" in *A Tramp Abroad*. Toward the end of his life, Stoker struck a rich "pocket" that allowed him to spend his last years in comfort.

"The Stolen White Elephant" Short story written in 1878. A BURLESQUE of detective fiction, "The Stolen White Elephant" is a FRAME-STORY narrated by an unnamed "chance railway acquaintance," an unmistakably honest man over 70 years old who once was in INDIA's civil service. Five years earlier, when Britain and Siam resolved a frontier dispute, Siam's king wanted to atone for being in the wrong by giving the queen of England (presumably Queen VICTORIA, who is not named) a sacred white elephant.

Deputed to convey the elephant to England aboard a special ship, the narrator stops at Jersey City, near New York City, to rest the animal. When it is reported stolen two weeks later, he immediately enlists the help of the chief of New York's detective force, Inspector Blunt. Blunt begins by taking a full deposition on the missing animal, whose name is JUMBO, and has his assistant, Alaric, distribute 50,000 copies to every detective and pawnbroker on the continent. He suggests that the narrator offer a $25,000 reward and assigns all his best detectives to the case: five men to shadow the elephant, six to shadow the thieves and 30 to guard the site of the crime. Additional plainclothes detectives are assigned to every transportation depot in Jersey City, while others cover railway stations and telegraph offices between Jersey City and Canada, Ohio and Washington, D.C. Stressing that everything be done with the utmost secrecy, Blunt confidently predicts that the elephant will be found, filling the narrator with admiration. The next morning, however, newspapers report every detail of Blunt's plans, posing 11 different theories about the crime and naming 37 suspects, including Blunt's two principal suspects. Questioned about the secrecy he promised, Blunt explains that publicity is the detective's bread and butter.

Over the next few days, the narrator gives Blunt more money for expenses as they await news. One night, messages begin pouring out of the telegraph from detectives all over the East, reporting on havoc caused by the elephant in separate (and mostly fictitious) towns. One telegram relays an offer from BARNUM to buy advertising space on the elephant; another reports that people fired small cannon balls at the elephant after it killed mourners at a funeral. The telegrams stop coming when a dense fog sets in. The next morning's papers sum up the gory details: 60 persons dead and 240 injured. The elephant is evidently hiding in the fog. The publicity pleases Blunt.

Several days pass without news, so Blunt recommends doubling the reward. After two weeks pass, the narrator raises the reward to $75,000. The newspapers are turning against the detectives, but Blunt is unperturbed. After three weeks pass, Blunt proposes compromising with the thieves by offering $100,000—half of which customarily goes to the detectives. He relays the offer through the wives of his two prime suspects, only to be told that both suspects have long been dead. He next publishes an encrypted message to lure the thief to a rendezvous. The following night, the narrator brings the $100,000 reward. When Blunt goes into the vast basement of his headquarters where his detectives sleep, he trips over something in the dim light—the dead body of the missing elephant! Now the hero of the hour, Blunt gleefully distributes the reward money among his detectives, pocketing a share for himself. The narrator must be restored with carbolic acid. His priceless charge is dead, his reputation is ruined and he is personally out $142,000. Nevertheless, his admiration for Blunt is undimmed.

BACKGROUND AND PUBLISHING HISTORY

Mark Twain wrote this 4,420-word story while staying in BERLIN in late November or December 1878. His purpose was to BURLESQUE a well-publicized investigation then underway in New York City, where Alexander Turney Stewart's body was stolen from its tomb. The story parallels the Stewart investigation in many lurid details. It also draws on ideas about "sacred white elephants" that Mark Twain had when he wrote about a character named Eckert in chapter 7 of *Roughing It.* He originally intended this new story for *A Tramp Abroad,* but instead made it the title story of *The Stolen White Elephant, Etc.,* a collection published by James R. OS-GOOD. The book appeared in June 1882—a few months after P. T. Barnum achieved tremendous publicity by importing a real elephant named "Jumbo" from England. The book combines the title story with all the items that had appeared in *Punch, Brothers, Punch!* (1878), as well as several other sketches, including two on the "MCWILLIAMSES." Most of its contents were later incorporated into *Tom Sawyer Abroad; Tom Sawyer, Detective and Other Stories* (1896) in standard editions.

Stone's Landing   Fictional village in *The Gilded Age.* Located 10 miles from HAWKEYE, Missouri, Stone's Landing is a collection of about a dozen cabins standing on the muddy bend of Goose Run (chapter 16). Colonel SELLERS wants to develop Stone's Landing into a metropolis called "Napoleon" by bringing in a railroad and transforming the crooked stream into the navigable "Columbus River." Neither Stone's Landing nor Napoleon is mentioned after chapter 28, when a decision is made to route the railroad through Hawkeye instead of Stone's Landing; however, later chapters occasionally mention the "Columbus River" scheme in retrospect (chapters 31, 40, 46 and 50).

A reference to "Napoleon" in chapter 4 is apparently to NAPOLEON, Arkansas.

Stormfield   Nickname of Mark Twain's last home near REDDING, Connecticut (1908–10). In 1906, Mark Twain bought 248 acres of farmland on Redding Road, three and half miles from Redding's train station. A year later, he engaged John Mead HOWELLS to design a house for him. The result was an 18-room, two-story Italianate villa built on a hill overlooking the Saugatuck Valley, with fine views in all directions and two trout streams running through the property. A natural spring supplied the estate's water, a steam generator supplied heat and an acetylene plant powered electric lights.

Mark Twain bought the property sight unseen, on the advice of his biographer A. B. PAINE, who owned land nearby. Mark Twain's daughter Clara Clemens selected the location for the house, and she and his secretary Isabel LYON helped Howells supervise its construction and they oversaw its decoration and furnishing. Mark Twain's only specific instructions were that the house have rooms large enough for his orchestrelle (an organlike instrument similar to a player piano) and for his BILLIARD table, and that he not have to visit the house until it was complete down to the cat purring by the hearth. He thus did not see the site until the day he

Mark Twain at the piano of his Stormfield home in 1908, with his daughter Clara (left) and her friend Marie Nichols. (Courtesy, Library of Congress, Pictures & Prints Division)

moved in—June 18, 1908. His arrival was naturally an anxious moment for everyone who helped design and prepare the house, but he found everything satisfactory and immediately felt entirely at home. Before he moved in, he had intended this house to be only a summer residence, but one day in Redding's tranquil countryside convinced him to give up his NEW YORK CITY apartment.

Mark Twain initially intended to call his new home "Autobiography House" since it was built with $30,000 that he earned from publishing chapters of his AUTOBIOGRAPHY in the NORTH AMERICAN REVIEW. By the time he moved in, however, he was calling it "INNOCENCE AT HOME"—a name to which Clara fiercely objected because of its connection with his "ANGELFISH" girls. In October, he renamed the house "Stormfield," after "CAPTAIN STORMFIELD'S VISIT TO HEAVEN," whose sale helped finish the house, which cost about $60,000 to build and furnish. He thought the name "Stormfield" especially apt because he could see storms approaching from all directions.

Stormfield was the first residence that Mark Twain owned after leaving Hartford in 1891. Years of travel and the bustle of New York City life made it a welcome change. He was largely content with his surroundings, even though a BURGLARY disrupted the calm three months after he arrived. The main storms that he weathered during his last two years there were strained relationships with his daughters and a growing distrust of Lyon and his business adviser Ralph ASHCROFT.

On October 6, 1909, Clara married Ossip GABRILOWITSCH at Stormfield and left for Europe. Late in December, shortly after Mark Twain returned from a trip to BERMUDA, his youngest daughter, Jean Clemens, died suddenly at Stormfield. Two weeks later he returned to Bermuda, but his own health was failing so rapidly that Paine brought him home a week before his DEATH at Stormfield on April 21, 1910. By then, Clara and Gabrilowitsch were back from Europe. They remained at the house through August, when Clara gave birth to Mark Twain's only grandchild, Nina GABRILOWITSCH. Afterwards she and housekeeper Katy LEARY closed down the house.

Stormfield burned down on July 25, 1923. A similar house later built on its foundations is now a private property, not open to visitors.

Stormfield, Captain Eli (Ben) Narrator and central character of "CAPTAIN STORMFIELD'S VISIT TO HEAVEN." A ship's captain who dies at sea when he is at least 65 and then spends 30 years hurtling through space, Stormfield expects to land in hell. He is delighted, however, to arrive in heaven and to learn that it is nothing like the tediously pious place he learned about in Sunday school.

Stormfield is modeled on Edgar WAKEMAN, a veteran sailor who during the 1860s told Mark Twain about a vivid dream he had of going to heaven. Like Wakeman, Stormfield is a big, blustering man, profoundly innocent

of formal education, but an enthusiastic and imaginative student of the Bible. A subtext of the "Extract" portion of his narrative is his running lecture on Bible matters to someone named PETERS. Mark Twain may also have put a bit of his tycoon friend H. H. ROGERS in Stormfield, who comes from "Fairhaven"—presumably Rogers's home town, Fairhaven, Massachusetts (Wakeman himself came from Connecticut). The image of Stormfield's speeding through the heavens, racing a comet also evokes Mark Twain's own personal identification with HALLEY'S COMET.

The truncated version of this story that Mark Twain published in 1909 gives the character's full name as "Captain Eli Stormfield" from SAN FRANCISCO. Posthumously published chapters call him "Captain Ben Stormfield of Fairhaven and 'Frisco."

"The Story of the Bad Little Boy" Short story originally published in the CALIFORNIAN (December 23, 1865) as "The Christmas Fireside for Good Little Boys and Girls." The 1,370-word story explores one of Mark Twain's favorite themes: the difference between Sunday-school morality and real life, in which sin is rarely punished. In contrast to the "bad boys" in Sunday-school literature, the story's title character, Jim, has a tough mother who would rather spank him to sleep than kiss him. Despite the spankings, however, Jim never feels guilt or remorse when he commits such crimes as stealing jam. Everything about him is curious—no matter what he does, he never suffers grief or serious punishment. He is not even drowned when he goes boating on a Sunday. When he grows up, he marries, raises a large family and brains them all with an ax. He gets wealthy through cheating and rascality. Though the biggest scoundrel in his village, he is universally respected and belongs to the legislature.

The story was first collected in THE CELEBRATED JUMPING FROG OF CALAVERAS COUNTY, AND OTHER SKETCHES and SKETCHES, NEW AND OLD.

"The Story of the Good Little Boy" Story first published in the GALAXY (May 1870) and reprinted in SKETCHES, NEW AND OLD. This 1,900-word tale deals with one of Mark Twain's favorite themes: the futility of modeling one's behavior on goody-goody Sunday-school books. The fate of its hero anticipates those of Edward Mills in "EDWARD MILLS AND GEORGE BENTON: A TALE" and DUTCHY in *Life on the Mississippi*.

SYNOPSIS

A good little boy named Jacob Blivens always obeys his parents, is never late to Sabbath school and never plays hookey. Ridiculously honest, his fondest ambition is to be put in a Sunday-school book. Since he realizes that the boys in such books always die, he prepares a moving dying speech and dreams about his sad funeral. Nothing goes right for Jacob, however. Unlike the boys in his books, he never has fun and constantly has bad luck. For example, when he warns Jim Blake against stealing apples because bad boys always fall out of the tree, Blake falls on him. Similar mishaps occur when Jacob assists a blind man and a lame dog, and he nearly drowns while warning bad boys against sailing on Sunday. His final disaster occurs when he tries to help dogs that other boys have tied to nitroglycerin cans. Blown to bits by the nitroglycerin, Jacob never gets to deliver his dying speech.

Stowe, Harriet Beecher (June 14, 1811, Litchfield, Connecticut–July 1, 1896, Hartford, Connecticut) The sister of Reverend Henry Ward BEECHER and author of *Uncle Tom's Cabin* (1851–52), Stowe was Mark Twain's next-door neighbor in Hartford after 1886. After she died, Mark Twain made gentle fun of her in the first chapter of "TOM SAWYER'S CONSPIRACY," an unfinished novella set around 1850. After Tom drops his proposal of starting a "civil war" as a summer diversion, Huck laments the fact that "Harriet Beacher Stow

Harriet Beecher Stowe during the years when Mark Twain was her neighbor. (Courtesy, National Archives, Still Picture Branch)

and all them other second-handers gets all the credit of starting that war" instead of Tom Sawyer.

Mark Twain's AUTOBIOGRAPHY recalls that during Stowe's last years her mind "had decayed," leaving her a pathetic figure who wandered through the neighborhood, even into houses, uninvited, occasionally sneaking up behind people to startle them with war whoops. Stowe's Hartford home is now maintained as a museum by the Stowe-Day Foundation next door to Mark Twain's former home.

Strothmann, Fred (September 23, 1879, New York, New York–May 1958) Illustrator. Trained in Berlin and Paris, Strothmann was noted as a humorous illustrator. In 1903, he illustrated the first book devoted solely to Mark Twain's JUMPING FROG STORY, a HARPER'S book titled *The Jumping Frog*. The following year, he illustrated EXTRACTS FROM ADAM'S DIARY. Harper's wanted him to do EVE'S DIARY in 1906, but Mark Twain wanted a humorless treatment, so the assignment instead went to Lester RALPH.

Styles, Robert Character in *Life on the Mississippi*. A PILOT on the GOLD DUST, Styles is a composite character based mostly on Lemuel Gray (c. 1838–1882), a real *Gold Dust* pilot whom Mark Twain had known during his own piloting days. In chapter 24 of *Mississippi*, Styles regales the narrator—who is traveling incognito—with outlandish talk about the hazards of navigating in "alligator water." After stumbling over his own lies, he reveals that he recognized the narrator (presumably Sam Clemens) all along. Styles's speedy unmasking of the narrator's attempt to disguise his identity "ended the fictitious-name business" of the latter, but not entirely, as the name "Styles" itself is fictitious.

Mark Twain's notebooks indicate that both Lemuel Gray and his brother and fellow pilot, Edmund Gray, quickly identified him—not only by his face and voice, but by his habit of running a hand through his hair. The way that they exposed his incognito probably helped inspire a moment in the last chapter of *Tom Sawyer, Detective;* in that book, Tom exposes Jubiter DUNLAP's disguise when he recognizes Dunlap's old habit of tracing crosses on his cheek with a finger. In *The Prince and the Pauper*, Tom CANTY's mother uses a similar method to prove Tom's true identity.

Mark Twain used Lem Gray's real name in his manuscript of *Life on the Mississippi*, but substituted "Styles" after learning that Gray had died in the *Gold Dust*'s explosion in August 1882—an incident described in chapter 37. Another change that Mark Twain made after Gray's death was to omit a passage from chapter 24 in which Styles claims to have been blown up nine times in steamboat accidents. Three of the alleged accidents occurred at Walnut Bend, where he always fell through the roof of the same house. During one of these incidents, Styles took the boat's wheel with him— a passage reminiscent of chapter 18 of *Innocents Abroad*, in which Mark Twain recalls taking a window sash with him while fleeing a room in which he discovers a corpse.

The 1944 film THE ADVENTURES OF MARK TWAIN adapts Styles's alligator yarn by having Sam Clemens himself tell similar lies to Charlie LANGDON. Philip José Farmer uses Robert Styles as a character in his science fiction novel *The Fabulous Riverboat* (1971).

subscription-book publishing System of marketing books that flourished during the 19th century. While trade publishers sold books through retail stores, subscription houses used armies of agents to sell their books door-to-door—usually in communities isolated from regular book markets. Working on commission, agents canvassed communities, persuading customers to "subscribe" to books before they were published. The system thrived on aggressive sales techniques, fostered by rewarding agents with up to 50 percent of a book's selling price. Since agents generally promoted one title at a time, their books had to command comparatively high prices to be profitable. High prices in turn required the books to be large and heavily illustrated to justify their cost. Agents carried attractive prospectuses containing title pages, tables of contents, lists of illustrations, sample text and specimens of optional binding materials. Canvassers became notorious for misrepresenting what actually would go into the books; and subscription publishers generally had poor reputations within the publishing world because of the poor quality of their books, their questionable marketing practices and their refusal to let retail stores sell their books. They were also resented by newspapers and magazines, since they rarely advertised or distributed review copies.

Before the CIVIL WAR, the most typical subscription books were Bibles and medical and legal self-help books—similar to what Huck Finn sees in the GRANGERFORDS' home in *Huckleberry Finn*. After the war, the industry changed dramatically. There was a huge demand for books about the war itself, as well as for autobiographies, travel books and books on sensational topics—such as MORMON polygamy. The war also unleashed legions of jobless veterans willing to be canvassers. By 1874, about 50,000 men representing Hartford publishers alone were canvassing the country.

Subscription publishing played a critical role in Mark Twain's writing career. Though he returned from the QUAKER CITY excursion in 1867 with a national reputation as a humorist, he thought little about writing books until Elisha BLISS invited him to write one about his voyage for the AMERICAN PUBLISHING COMPANY. Impressed by the advance-sales figures Bliss showed him on A. D. RICHARDSON's *Beyond the Mississippi*, Mark Twain agreed. Out of that agreement came *Innocents Abroad*—probably the best-selling travel book of the 19th century. Its success encouraged the subscription industry to broaden its horizons, while convincing Mark Twain that subscription publishing was the only sensible way to market his books. Thereafter, he measured the success

of each of his books against *Innocents Abroad*. So enamored with subscription publishing was he that he later told W. D. HOWELLS that "any other means of bringing out a book is privately printing it." After he left the American Publishing Company in the early 1880s, he persuaded James R. OSGOOD to open a subscription-book branch to market his books; then he formed his own firm, Charles L. WEBSTER & COMPANY.

The subscription market's voracious appetite for bulky, informative books often forced Mark Twain to struggle to bring his books up to subscription-book length. More than once, he was still adding pages to a book that agents were already promoting. The need to write by the pound magnified his natural tendency to digress, lending an even greater formlessness to much of his book writing. Had he written for regular trade publishers, his books might have been quite different.

One of the changes that Mark Twain personally brought to subscription publishing was the introduction of fiction. *The Gilded Age* (1873), which he coauthored, was the first novel ever published by a subscription house. Most of his other novels were marketed the same way. And while he brought fiction to subscription publishing, he also did the reverse. In 1881, he wrote a burlesque of HAMLET, to which he added a new character, Basil Stockmar, a subscription-book canvasser who observes the tragedy from a fresh perspective.

Susan Powell STEAMBOAT in *Huckleberry Finn*. In chapter 24, Huck, the KING and the DUKE board a big CINCINNATI steamboat about four or five miles above the village in which the WILKS family lives so that when they land at the village, they will give the appearance of having come all the way down the river from Ohio. In chapter 29 the King identifies the boat as the *Susan Powell*.

Sweden From early July through September 1899, Mark Twain was in Sweden with his family. They spent most of their time at J. H. KELLGREN's Sanna institute, near Jönköping at the southern tip of Lake Vättern, about 175 miles southwest of Stockholm. Aside from noting Sweden's fine sunsets, Mark Twain paid scant attention to the country and wrote little beyond "MY BOYHOOD DREAMS" and "HOW TO MAKE HISTORY DATES STICK" while he was there.

Swift, Jonathan (November 30, 1667, Dublin, Ireland– October 19, 1745, Dublin) An Irish-born English clergyman and satirist, Swift is best known for *Gulliver's Travels* (1726). A powerful SATIRE on human nature, *Gulliver's Travels* is a fantastic picaresque novel whose protagonist learns to appreciate the essential pettiness of humankind while living among both tiny and gigantic humans, civilized horses, and other beings. Similarities between Mark Twain's wit and often savage satire and that of Swift—who shares his birthday—are abundant, Dozens of direct allusions to Swift's works can be found in Mark Twain's own writings.

Mark Twain first read *Gulliver's Travels* as a boy and seems to have been particularly taken by its technique of altering scale to place petty human concerns in perspective. His unfinished novel "Three Thousand Years Among the Microbes" explores this theme by reducing the beings of entire worlds to the size of microbes—one of whom is named Lemuel Gulliver. In chapter 3 of *Roughing It,* the narrator imagines himself a Brobdignagian resting among lilliputian flocks and herds, while "waiting to catch a little citizen and eat him." This latter idea also recalls Swift's *A Modest Proposal* (1729), a pamphlet that proposed to deal with the surplus of poor Irish children by selling them as food.

Switzerland   Mark Twain spent about four months in Switzerland during three extended visits. On his first trip to Europe with the QUAKER CITY in 1867, some of his fellow passengers traveled through Switzerland, but he himself merely stepped over the border to spend several hours in Chiasso while he was staying at COMO, Italy. His first extended Swiss sojourn began on August 12, 1878, when he and Joseph TWICHELL joined his family at LUCERNE after tramping through GERMANY's BLACK FOREST. He and Twichell then toured the ALPS, visiting WEGGIS, INTERLAKEN, ZERMATT and other Swiss villages before rejoining the family at Geneva at the end of August. Over the next two weeks, they all shuttled between Geneva, Lausanne and Mont BLANC in FRANCE before moving on to ITALY. This month of travel in Switzerland forms the basis for most of chapters 25–42 and 47 of *A Tramp Abroad*—much of which deals with burlesque mountaineering adventures.

Mark Twain spent another three weeks in Switzerland with his family in September 1891. While staying at Interlaken, he wrote "Switzerland, the Cradle of Liberty" in Interlaken for the NEW YORK SUN (March 15, 1892), praising the wholesomeness of the country and its 600-year history of freedom. He then began a boat trip down the RHONE RIVER. The following June, he passed through Lucerne while going from Germany to Italy. In 1897, he and his family stayed at Weggis from mid-July through mid-September.

Syria   In mid-September 1867, Mark Twain entered what is now the Republic of Syria from LEBANON. He spent two days at DAMASCUS and camped overnight at BANIYAS in the Golan Heights before continuing into what is now Israel. At that time, all these territories were under TURKEY's Ottoman Empire and were collectively known by the region's historical name, Syria—the term used throughout chapters 41–52 of *Innocents Abroad* for all the eastern Mediterranean regions that Mark Twain visited.

Hank Morgan's list of royal baseball players in chapter 40 of *Connecticut Yankee* includes the "Sowdan of Syria."

Szczepanik, Jan (1872–1926)   Polish inventor. The subject of Mark Twain's essay "THE AUSTRIAN EDISON KEEPING SCHOOL AGAIN," Szczepanik was a schoolmaster who invented a primitive form of television that he called a *fernseher* (for "far seeing") or "telelectroscope," and a process for photographically transferring patterns to woven textiles. When Mark Twain lived in VIENNA, Szczepanik visited him often and demonstrated his carpet-pattern process. Anxious to invest in this invention, Mark Twain wrote to H. H. ROGERS on the subject in March 1898. Rogers investigated the commercial possibilities for carpet-weaving and concluded that it had little practical value.

Mark Twain used Szczepanik's telelectroscope device in "FROM THE 'LONDON TIMES' OF 1904," in which Szczepanik himself is a minor character believed to have been murdered by an American army officer, John Clayton.

Tahoe, Lake   The largest freshwater lake in the western United States, Tahoe straddles the California–Nevada border, covering 193 square miles of a Sierra Nevada basin 6,225 feet above sea level. The lake was known only to local Indians—who called it *Tahoe,* for "big water"—until John Frémont found it in 1844. Eight years later, the new state of CALIFORNIA dubbed it Lake Bigler—after Governor John Bigler (governor, 1852–58), but allowed its name officially to revert to Tahoe

Fire wipes out the Tahoe timber ranch of the narrator and his companion in chapter 23 of Roughing It.

during the CIVIL WAR, when Bigler's secessionist sympathies became suspect.

Mark Twain first visited Tahoe while he was living in CARSON CITY, Nevada in September 1861. He staked timber claims along its shores, but these came to nothing. Meanwhile, he fell in love with the lake's beautiful setting and incomparably clear waters. After his last visit in August 1863, he wrote his mother a letter calling Tahoe the "masterpiece of the universe." Throughout his later travels, he carried fond memories of Tahoe. In a footnote in *Innocents Abroad,* he explains that he measures all lakes by Tahoe because it is nearly impossible to speak of lakes and not mention it (chapter 48). For this same reason, *Innocents* devotes 850 words to Tahoe amidst a description of Italy's Lake COMO (chapter 20). Likewise, its discussion of the Sea of GALILEE gives Tahoe another 450 words (chapter 48). Mark Twain's most thorough treatment of Tahoe, however, appears in *Roughing It* (chapters 22–23).

"Taming the Bicycle"   Essay written in 1884. Ever fascinated with machinery, Mark Twain joined his friend Joseph TWICHELL in bicycle-riding lessons in May 1884. His apprenticeship was painful and short-lived; afterward, he wrote this humorous essay describing how he trained in his backyard with an "expert." For eight days, he suffered many minor humiliations and painful falls—especially when mounting his ungainly bicycle with an enormous front wheel. After investing considerable time in polishing the 3,400-word essay, he found it unsatisfactory and set it aside. It was posthumously published in *What Is Man? and Other Essays.* Meanwhile, Mark Twain put bicycles in sixth-century England in *A Connecticut Yankee in King Arthur's Court* (1889). In chapter 38 of that novel, Hank Morgan and King Arthur are rescued from execution by 500 knights in armor who arrived mounted on bicycles.

Tangier   North African seaport. Now part of Morocco, Tangier faces the Atlantic Ocean at the western end of the Strait of Gibraltar. On June 30, 1867, the day after the QUAKER CITY landed at GIBRALTAR, Mark Twain disregarded warnings against visiting the allegedly dangerous Muslim town and took a steamer across the strait, accompanied by Dan SLOTE, Jack VAN NOSTRAND, Dr. Abraham JACKSON, Julius MOULTON and Major James G. Barry. Their only adventure, however, was

Sixth-century chivalry meets 19th-century transportation in chapter 38 of Connecticut Yankee. *The knight is riding a bicycle similar to the one ridden by Mark Twain.*

stopping Barry from entering a mosque—an episode embellished and attributed to "BLUCHER" in *Innocents Abroad.* After three weeks at sea and the more conventional sights of Gibraltar and the AZORES, Mark Twain was so delighted by Tangier's exotic nature that he collected more notes than he could squeeze into two letters to the SAN FRANCISCO ALTA CALIFORNIA; with only minor changes, these letters became chapters 8–9 of *Innocents Abroad.*

Tanner, Bob Figure mentioned in chapter 16 of *Tom Sawyer* as a friend who Tom expects would be jealous if he knew that Tom and Joe Harper have learned how to smoke.

Tarrytown NEW YORK residential community located about 20 miles north–northeast of Manhattan. In April 1902, while Mark Twain and his family were living in a rented house in RIVERDALE, his wife Livy contracted to buy a house on 19 acres of land near Tarrytown for $45,000. The sale went through, but the decline of

Livy's health prevented the family from occupying the house, which Mark Twain resold in December 1904.

Tauchnitz, Baron Christian Bernhard von (August 25, 1816–1895) German book publisher. The heir to a large printing firm, Tauchnitz founded a Leipzig publishing house in 1837 that specialized in reprinting American and British authors. His list of cheap English-language editions sold well at railroad stations and exceeded 4,000 titles by the end of the century. In 1876, he began publishing Mark Twain's work with an edition of *Tom Sawyer* that preceded the first American edition. Though not required by international copyright law to do so, Tauchnitz paid royalties to authors—a fact that won Mark Twain's praise and a warm reception when Tauchnitz visited him in Paris in early 1879. Tauchnitz eventually published most of Mark Twain's books, and Mark Twain himself later used Tauchnitz's edition of *Huckleberry Finn* in his public readings.

Taylor, Bayard (January 11, 1825, Kennett Square, Pennsylvania–December 19, 1878, Berlin, Germany)

Bayard Taylor, perhaps America's most famous travel writer before Mark Twain. (W. D. Howells, *Literary Friends and Acquaintance,* 1902)

A popular travel writer, Taylor began writing letters to the NEW YORK TRIBUNE from Germany at age 19 and published the first of 10 travel books at age 21. He then worked as a newspaper editor in New York, covered California's GOLD RUSH as a reporter, traveled in Europe and Asia, and was a CIVIL WAR correspondent. He also published poetry, several novels and a distinguished translation of Goethe's *Faust* (1870–71). *Roughing It* hints at the breadth of Taylor's writing by suggesting that his works even include a version of the famous Horace GREELEY–Hank MONK anecdote (chapter 20); however, no such passage actually appears in Taylor's writings.

In 1878 Taylor was appointed a United States minister to GERMANY. Mark Twain had begun corresponding with him the previous year and spoke at a banquet in his honor in April 1878—just before they both sailed to Europe aboard the HOLSATIA. They became good friends in Germany, where Taylor died later that year. Taylor's untimely death helped lower Mark Twain's opinion of the U.S. State Department's niggardly treatment of its consular officials; Mark Twain was probably thinking about Taylor when he wrote "DIPLOMATIC PAY AND CLOTHES" and when he described a squalid American consulate in "THE BELATED RUSSIAN PASSPORT." A passage about a tail-less raven in *A Tramp Abroad* alludes to Taylor's sensitive understanding of animals (chapter 18). Chapter 59 of *Following the Equator* quotes Taylor's description of the Taj Mahal.

Taylor, Benny Figure mentioned in *Tom Sawyer* as a friend of Tom. In chapter 33 Tom "hooks" Benny's wagon to carry the gold that he and Huck have found in McDougal's CAVE.

Temple, Alfred Character in *Tom Sawyer*. Introduced in chapter 1 only as a "new-comer" from St. Louis, Alfred immediately gets into a fight with Tom. Though taller than Tom, he loses and vows vengeance. His name is first given in chapter 18, in which Becky THATCHER flirts with him to make Tom jealous. When Alfred realizes how he has been used, he pours ink on Tom's spelling book to get him in trouble. Tom learns what Alfred has done at the end of chapter 20. He plans vengeance, but Alfred is not heard from again. Mark Twain modeled Alfred on a childhood neighbor, Jim Reagan, whom he recalled as the "new boy" from St. Louis.

Tennessee State that was the home of Mark Twain's family during the decade before he was born. Around 1825, his parents settled in GAINESBORO. A few years later, they moved to FENTRESS COUNTY, where they bought around 75,000 acres that the family dubbed their "TENNESSEE LAND." They lived successively in JAMESTOWN, THREE FORKS OF WOLF RIVER and PALL MALL before moving to Missouri in 1835. All five of Mark Twain's older siblings were born in Tennessee. Mark Twain would later use his family's time in Tennessee in the early chapters of *The Gilded Age* (1873).

Mark Twain himself first visited Tennessee in early 1857 when he went by steamboat down the Mississippi to New Orleans. Over the next four years he worked on the river as a PILOT and stopped at Tennessee ports frequently; during this period, he developed a particular fondness for MEMPHIS. In June 1861, Tennessee became the last state to secede from the Union. By then, Mark Twain had left the river and it would be another 21 years before he again visited Tennessee.

Tennessee Land When Mark Twain's father, John M. Clemens, lived in TENNESSEE during the 1820s and 1830s, he accumulated more than 70,000 acres of land—for less than $500—in FENTRESS COUNTY, mostly in the Knobs of the Cumberland Mountains, between the Cumberland and Tennessee rivers. Clemens believed that this "Tennessee Land" would be the salvation of his impoverished family, and he died admonishing his family to hold on to it. Far from bringing prosperity, the land handicapped the family with what Mark Twain's AUTOBIOGRAPHY calls the "curse" of beginning life "poor and *prospectively* rich." *Roughing It* alludes to the "Tennessee Land" as a symbol of illusory wealth (chapter 41), and Mark Twain recreates his family's unhappy experience with the land in *The Gilded Age*, in which Si HAWKINS buys 75,000 acres in eastern Tennessee. Like John Clemens, Hawkins tells his family "never lose sight of the Tennessee Land" (chapter 9). This land becomes a focus of the narrative, as Washington HAWKINS, Colonel SELLERS and Senator DILWORTHY try to get a bill through Congress for the federal government to buy the land for the "Knobs Industrial University" for former slaves. After that scheme collapses, Hawkins finally resolves to let the land go for taxes and start his life over with "good solid work" (chapter 61).

The best chance that the Clemenses had to profit from their land came in the 1860s, when a man who wanted to create a colony of European wine makers offered $200,000 for it. Since Mark Twain's brother, Orion Clemens, was then in an abstemious mood, he declined the offer. Orion's poor management of the land eventually caused Mark Twain to disavow his own interest in it. Orion sold off the last of the land in 1887.

Tennyson, Alfred, Lord (August 6, 1809, Lincolnshire, England–October 6, 1892, Haslemere, England) England's poet laureate (1850–92), Tennyson began reading MALORY's *Le Morte d'Arthur* as a boy and later drew on it and other sources to create his own Arthurian epic. Between 1859 and 1885, he published *Idylls of the King*, a series of poems that begin hopefully with the rise of KING ARTHUR and build toward the tragic destruction of his kingdom caused by LAUNCELOT and GUENEVER's adultery. The immense popularity of Tennyson's *Idylls* began an Arthurian renaissance in England that spilled over into America, helping to inspire

Mark Twain—who met Tennyson in 1873—to write a parody. That idea evolved into *Connecticut Yankee,* whose illustrator, Dan BEARD, used photographs of Tennyson to draw MERLIN's face.

Texas   Three months after Mark Twain was born in Missouri, Texas declared its independence from Mexico; it joined the Union in December 1845. Mark Twain never visited Texas, but mentions it in several books. In *Tom Sawyer,* for example, INJUN JOE and his partner plan to escape to Texas (chapter 26); their perception of Texas as a criminals' refuge suggests that it is not yet part of the Union at the time the story takes place. By contrast, it appears that Texas *is* a state when the events of *Huckleberry Finn* take place. Both this novel and *Life on the Mississippi* use the word "texas" frequently as a term for the steamboat deck containing officers' cabins. Since parts of steamboats were traditionally named after *states,* "texas" could not have been used on steamboats before 1845. Therefore, unless Mark Twain uses "texas" anachronistically, 1845 is the earliest year in which *Huckleberry Finn* could be set.

Thames   One of ENGLAND's largest rivers, the Thames rises in the southwest and flows through LONDON to the North Sea. In *The Prince and the Pauper,* Tom CANTY lives in OFFAL COURT, a slum near the river's LONDON BRIDGE. Like Tom Sawyer—who lives equally close to the Mississippi River—Canty grows up swimming and playing in the Thames. After switching places with Prince EDWARD, he participates in two grand pageants on the Thames: barge rides from WESTMINSTER Palace to Dowgate (chapter 11) and from the palace to the Tower of London (chapter 32).

The Thames is one of the rivers to which Mark Twain compares the Mississippi in the first chapter of *Life on the Mississippi*—which says that the American river discharges 338 times as much water. In chapter 40 of *Connecticut Yankee,* Hank Morgan mentions that he has placed "a steamboat or two" on the Thames.

"That Day in Eden"   Sketch about the Fall, written around 1990 and first published in EUROPE AND ELSEWHERE. One of the ADAMIC DIARIES, this 250-word piece is subtitled "Passage from Satan's Diary." Satan recalls visiting ADAM AND EVE in the Garden of Eden to help them understand certain moral concepts. However, he fails to explain such ideas as "pain" and "fear," because *he* cannot experience them. Likewise, he cannot explain "eternal," which Eve cannot experience. After failing to find common ground on "good," "evil," and "morals," Satan explains that the moral sense is something that they should be glad they do not have.

As they talk, Eve eats an apple from the forbidden tree and visibly changes. She suddenly becomes modest. Adam is puzzled until he tastes an apple and undergoes a similar change. He gathers boughs to cover their nakedness and they walk away, "bent with age."

Thatcher, Becky (Rebecca)   Character in *Tom Sawyer.* Blonde and blue-eyed, Becky is modeled closely on Mark Twain's childhood sweetheart, Laura HAWKINS—whose Hannibal home has been preserved as the BECKY THATCHER HOUSE. Becky's age is not specified, but she seems to be about nine years old in *Tom Sawyer.* An earlier story that anticipates *Tom Sawyer* provides a clue. Mark Twain's "BOY'S MANUSCRIPT" has a character named "Amy" who is a clear prototype of Becky; her age is specified as just over eight.

While Becky is arguably Mark Twain's most famous female creation, he gave her little to do beyond reacting to Tom Sawyer. By the time he wrote *Huckleberry Finn,* he even forgot her name. As a character, she represents little more than an idealization of the innocence of young girls.

Becky first appears in chapter 3 of *Tom Sawyer,* when Tom sees her at her cousin Jeff THATCHER's house. Until then, Tom is devoted to another girl named Amy LAWRENCE. Immediately smitten by Becky, he performs elaborate stunts to impress her. He learns who she is in the next chapter, when he sees her at Sunday school with her father, Judge THATCHER, who is visiting from

Becky flirts with Alfred Temple to make Tom jealous in chapter 18 of Tom Sawyer.

nearby CONSTANTINOPLE. Tom finally meets Becky face-to-face in chapter 6, when she turns up at his school. No reason is ever given for why she is starting school in ST. PETERSBURG late in the year, while her family lives in Constantinople.

Tom's romance with Becky begins when he contrives to have himself punished so that he must sit next to her in class. He professes his love so quickly that Becky accepts his "engagement" proposal at lunchtime; however, she turns against him when he carelessly mentions that he was once "engaged" to Amy. When Becky is home sick from school in chapter 12, the fear that she might die saps Tom's energy. He is overjoyed when she returns, but she ignores him. His resulting heartbreak contributes to his decision to run off to JACKSON'S ISLAND with other boys in the next chapter. Tom finally wins Becky's devotion in chapter 20, when he takes a whipping in her place at school.

After spending most of the summer with her parents in Constantinople, Becky reappears in chapter 29 to host a picnic at the CAVE near St. Petersburg. In one of the novel's most dramatic episodes, she and Tom spend several days lost in the cave, until Tom's calmness and ingenuity save them.

Becky is also mentioned in two stories that Mark Twain wrote after *Tom Sawyer*, but never again as Tom's sweetheart. In *Huckleberry Finn*, Huck sees her among the people on the ferryboat searching the river for his body. When Mark Twain wrote this passage—not long after he finished *Tom Sawyer*—he was already forgetting Becky's name and wrote "Bessie Thatcher." His notes indicate that he later intended to correct this mistake, but the error slipped into the published book and remained uncorrected until the first MARK TWAIN PAPERS project edition of *Huckleberry Finn* in 1985. Becky also makes a perfunctory appearance in "SCHOOLHOUSE HILL."

In contrast to the teenage boys who have portrayed Tom in films, girls playing Becky have consistently been much younger. Among those who have portrayed her on screen are 10-year-old Mitzi Green (1930–31), who twice played opposite Jackie Coogan; 11-year-old Anne Gillis (1938); and 11-year-old Jodie Foster (1973).

Thatcher, Jeff Minor character in *Tom Sawyer*. A friend of Tom Sawyer and a cousin of Becky THATCHER, Jeff is introduced in chapter 3 as the son of a ST. PETERSBURG lawyer. In the next chapter he arouses the envy of his peers when he is called up in front of the Sunday school to stand beside his uncle, the great Judge THATCHER. Jeff takes his name from Laura HAWKINS's brother Jefferson, who died during childhood.

Thatcher, Judge Character in *Tom Sawyer* and *Huckleberry Finn*. The father of Becky THATCHER and brother of an unnamed ST. PETERSBURG lawyer, Thatcher is a prominent judge based at the county seat in nearby CONSTANTINOPLE. It is generally believed that Mark Twain modeled Thatcher partly on his own father, John M. Clemens, who was a justice of the peace. Thatcher first appears in chapter 4 of *Tom Sawyer*, when he visits Tom's Sunday school. He is "a fine, portly, middle-aged gentleman with iron-gray hair . . . a prodigious personage . . . altogether the most august creation these children ever looked upon." He does not make another significant appearance until near the end of the narrative. Chapter 23 mentions a "judge" who presides over Muff POTTER's murder trial, but it gives no indication that this judge is Thatcher. Thatcher finally reappears in chapter 32, when he tells Tom that he has had the entrance to the CAVE sealed after Tom and Becky were lost inside. Later, the judge expresses his admiration of Tom for his ingenuity in escaping from the cave and predicts a great future for him. At the end of the novel, Thatcher gets Aunt POLLY's approval to invest and manage Tom's share of the fortune that Tom and Huck find in the cave.

When *Huckleberry Finn* begins, the Thatchers are clearly residents of St. Petersburg and the judge—not the Widow DOUGLAS—is managing Huck's money, along with Tom's. In chapters 4 through 6, Huck's father, Pap FINN tries to pressure Thatcher into turning Huck's money over to him. Thatcher resists, and even tries to gain legal custody of Huck for himself or the Widow Douglas, but fails. Pap initiates a suit against Thatcher to get control of the money, and it is not until the last chapter of the novel that Huck learns that his father failed in his effort.

Thatcher appears briefly in "TOM SAWYER'S CONSPIRACY," in which he is still managing Tom and Huck's money.

Third House Mock legislative body in NEVADA. When Mark Twain was a VIRGINIA CITY TERRITORIAL ENTERPRISE reporter during the early 1860s, Nevada journalists organized a burlesque "Third House" every year, as the territory's real legislative sessions ended—a tradition that lasted into the 20th century. Holding meetings anywhere they could—from saloons to the formal legislative chambers—they carried on burlesque deliberations, debates and roll calls. On December 11, 1863, the Third House elected Mark Twain president as Nevada's Constitutional Convention was adjourning in CARSON CITY. In this capacity he presided over mock legislative sessions, delivered the "Third Annual Message to the Third House" and was addressed as "Governor Twain." On January 27, 1864, he repeated his Third House address before the first paying audience of his speaking career, filling a courthouse to capacity for a church-building fund.

"The $30,000 Bequest" Short story written in 1904 about a hard-working young couple who ruin their lives with dreams of vast wealth that they will earn from money that they expect to inherit. Similar in mood and resolution to "THE MAN THAT CORRUPTED HADLEYBURG"

(1899), this story likewise deals with greed, illusory wealth, vindictive practical joking and empty vanity. Powerful themes from Mark Twain's own life can be read into the story. The struggle between a practical, provident wife and an irreverent and less responsible husband seems to reflect Mark Twain's relationship with his own wife. Further, the couple's debilitating expectations from wealth that never materializes recall the Clemens family's expectations of their TENNESSEE LAND. Finally, the story ends with the husband warning against allowing the snare of "vast wealth, acquired by sudden and unwholesome means" to entice one away from the true happiness possible in a sweet and simple life. The statement seems to sum up Mark Twain's many failed quests for easy riches.

SYNOPSIS

For 14 years, Saladin and Electra FOSTER have diligently toiled in the pleasant western town of Lakeside. By day, "Sally"—as he is called—plods through his bookkeeping job, while "Aleck" efficiently manages the household and some modestly profitable investments. By night, they read romances to each other and dream of living as royalty. Their romantic bent can be seen in the names they have given their daughters, Gwendolen and Clytemnestra FOSTER.

One day, Sally receives a stunning letter from his only surviving relative, Tilbury Foster, who lives 500 miles away. Tilbury says that he will shortly die and leave Sally $30,000. To collect this bequest, however, Sally must satisfy Tilbury's executors that he has not discussed the bequest, inquired after Tilbury's condition or even attended his funeral. Aleck immediately subscribes to a newspaper in Tilbury's town, the *Weekly Sagamore,* and she and Sally vow never to jeopardize the bequest while Tilbury lives.

As Aleck dreams about investing the $30,000, Sally dreams about how to spend it. Sally agrees, however, to hold off all spending until the principal has had a chance to grow from Aleck's investments. Aleck's projections of the rate of financial growth they can expect make Sally's head swim. By the time Aleck goes to bed, she has worked their capital up to a half million dollars in her head. For more than a week, the Fosters anxiously await their first copy of the *Weekly Sagamore,* only to be crushed when they do not find Tilbury's obituary notice in its pages. Unbeknownst to them, Tilbury died earlier in the week, but thanks to an accident in the *Sagamore*'s print shop, the paper will *never* mention his death.

As weeks and months drag by without news, Aleck's imaginary investments amass a fortune. As more time passes, Aleck works ever harder on her phantom portfolio, while Sally keeps pace with plans for spending the phantom profits. When the couple finally conclude that they are legitimately "rich," they want to celebrate, but are unsure how they can, without giving away their secret. They settle on throwing a party to celebrate the discovery of America. It is a success, but some guests sense that the Fosters are becoming uppity. Afterward, Aleck and Sally begin considering the problem of choosing suitable husbands for their daughters.

After the fantasy fortune hits a million dollars, it takes off at a dizzy rate. Two years later, the Fosters are worth $380 million. When the figure reaches $2,400 million, they pause to take stock. Breaking the Sabbath for the first time, they inventory their wealth and find that they now can realize a steady income of $120 million a year. Aleck at last agrees to retire from "business" and allow Sally to spend freely.

Meanwhile, the mundane facts of real life intrude. Late-night imaginary spending sprees drive Sally to pilfer candles from his employer; these petty thefts lead to others. The Fosters continue to plod through their "restricted fact life," while their dream life settles them into a palace in Newport, Rhode Island. Aleck's philanthropy becomes prodigious; every Sunday she builds new hospitals and universities, while Sally blows millions in gambling and riotous living. The disparity between his dissolute extravagances and Aleck's well-meaning charity drives him to confess. Aleck forgives him, but no longer trusts him. Aleck has also been behaving dishonorably, however. She has broken their compact by secretly going back into business. Without consulting Sally, she invests their entire fortune in a purchase of *all* the country's railroads and coal and steel companies on margin, then nervously awaits developments.

It is now five years since the Fosters first learned of their bequest. Sally suggests they reconsider the question of their daughters' marriages. After having turned down a dentist and a lawyer, then sons of rich businessmen and politicians, and even members of the aristocracy, he thinks it time to let the girls themselves choose. Aleck then knocks him silly with the news that she is arranging *royal* marriages! For several days, the Fosters walk on air with these happy thoughts and Aleck's new investments start booming. As her imaginary brokers urge her to take her profits and sell, she breaks the good news to Sally. He joins in the chorus to sell, but Aleck insists on holding on a bit longer—a decision that proves fatal. The next day a historic crash reduces their entire fortune to nothing.

Aleck is devastated, but Sally comes down to earth and reminds her that nothing they have lost was real, and that his uncle's bequest is still coming. At that moment, the *Weekly Sagamore*'s editor arrives to collect on their unpaid subscription. He not only reports that Tilbury has been dead for five years, but that he died a pauper. Aleck and Sally never recover from the shock. Two years later, they both die on the same day.

BACKGROUND AND PUBLISHING HISTORY

Mark Twain wrote this 12,220-word story during the winter of 1903–4 at an unhappy time in his life. He had moved his family to FLORENCE, Italy for the sake of his wife's health; her condition did not improve and his work was constantly interrupted by unpleasant distractions. "The $30,000 Bequest" proved to be the longest piece of fiction that he finished and published during the remainder of his life. The story first appeared in HARPER'S WEEKLY on December 10, 1904. In 1906, it was made the title story of a new collection, *The $30,000 Bequest and Other Stories*, which became a volume in HARPER'S uniform sets. Other notable pieces in this collection include "A DOG'S TALE," "Was It Heaven? Or Hell?," "EXTRACTS FROM ADAM'S DIARY" and "EVE'S DIARY."

Thompson and Rogers   Characters in *Life on the Mississippi*. The last two-thirds of this book recount Mark Twain's 1882 journey on the Mississippi River with James R. OSGOOD and Roswell PHELPS, neither of whom is mentioned by name in the book. Chapter 22 alludes to them as a "poet" and a "stenographer," while other chapters merely hint at their presence as travel companions. Chapter 32 finally gives them names; "Thompson" is evidently the "poet," leaving "Rogers" to be the stenographer (the "Rogers" mentioned in chapter 22 is unrelated). Both men argue violently with the narrator over what to do with $10,000 that he expects to find in NAPOLEON, Arkansas, thanks to Karl RITTER's instructions.

Thompson, Ben   Minor character in *Huckleberry Finn*. Thompson is mentioned once, as one of the lazy BRICKSVILLE tobacco chewers whom Huck describes in chapter 21. Other loafers are mentioned only by first names. They include Andy, Bill, Buck (HARKNESS?), Hank, Jack and Joe.

Thompson, William   Alias used by Tom Sawyer in *Huckleberry Finn*. In chapter 33 Tom turns up at the farm of his aunt Sally PHELPS and playfully introduces himself as "William Thompson" of HICKSVILLE, Ohio, claiming to be looking for their neighbor Archibald NICHOLS. At dinner Tom changes his story and says that he is actually Sid SAWYER—his half-brother.

Mark Twain may have borrowed Tom Sawyer's pseudonym from a historical figure. There is evidence that his early travel letters were influenced by the work of the Southern humorist William Tappan Thompson (1812–1882), who—like Tom's invented character—originated in Ohio. Thompson wrote several popular books about a Southern hick named "Major Jones," one of whose letters is in MARK TWAIN'S LIBRARY OF HUMOR.

"Those Extraordinary Twins"   Original title of the novel that became *The Tragedy of Pudd'nhead Wilson*, as well as the title of an incomplete 10-chapter fragment published simultaneously with *Pudd'nhead Wilson* in 1894. The full title of the AMERICAN PUBLISHING COMPANY's first book edition is *The Tragedy of Pudd'nhead Wilson and the Comedy Those Extraordinary Twins*. The words "the Comedy" were probably intended as a description, not as part of the title. A subhead preceding the first chapter heading is "The Suppressed Farce."

Mark Twain began writing this story as a grotesque farce. Inspired by SIAMESE TWINS from Italy who shared a single torso and a single pair of legs, his original intention was to explore the comic possibilities of brothers with opposing personalities sharing such a body. His original central characters were Angelo and Luigi CAPELLO, a similar set of Siamese twins with separate heads and arms and a common torso and legs. By the time this story neared completion, he found it had shifted from farce to tragedy as new characters intruded. The slave woman ROXANA, her son Tom DRISCOLL and the lawyer David WILSON were taking center stage, turning his "twin-monster" and other characters into irrelevant encumbrances. To solve the problem, Mark Twain trimmed about 30,000 words from his original 85,000-word manuscript and—by his own words—"dug out the comedy and left the tragedy." The Capello brothers remained as minor characters, but were recast as ordinary twins in separate bodies. The published version of *Pudd'nhead Wilson* is thus a revised distillation of a more complex story in which the Siamese twins play a major part.

SYNOPSIS

The published version of this story consists of 10 chapters of uneven length totaling 19,800 words—including summaries of several omitted portions, with comments and references to *Pudd'nhead Wilson*. An 11th chapter contains Mark Twain's comments on the manuscript. The first five chapters make up nearly 70 percent of the total text, with chapter 5 twice the length of any other chapter. In contrast to *Pudd'nhead Wilson*, the published fragment of this story begins in the year 1853.

Chapter 1
The Capello twins write to Patsy COOPER about renting a room in her DAWSON'S LANDING house. She is thrilled by the fact that they are Italians who have traveled the world. Even before they appear, her romantic daughter, Rowena COOPER, becomes infatuated with Angelo Capello. On the following Thursday, the twins arrive near midnight. They present a "stupefying apparition—a double-headed human creature with four arms, one body, and a single pair of legs." Patsy and Rowena are paralyzed into immobility until their stunned slave Nancy drops a tea set. The brothers introduce themselves as "Count Angelo" and "Count Luigi" and retire to their room. Patsy and Rowena discuss the new arrivals and speculate on their personality differences.

As the twins prepare for bed, they bicker. Angelo complains about the tight shoes that Luigi wears, suggesting that only one of them commands the body at once. Angelo also complains about Luigi's smoking. As Angelo tries to sing the hymn "From Greenland's Icy Mountains," Luigi drowns him out with a loud and vulgar song. Before they nod off, Luigi downs a whiskey and Angelo takes a pill to prevent a headache.

Chapter 2
At breakfast the next morning, Rowena raves about how cultured the twins are. After the twins sit down, Angelo explains that their "natures differ a good deal from each, and our tastes also." The twins bewilder the women by using their arms interchangeably to feed themselves. They explain how they operate, point out various advantages of sharing a body and tell about their family background.

Chapter 3
After breakfast, townspeople crowd into the Coopers' house to see the twins. Judge York DRISCOLL shows them the town. That night the judge takes the twins to a meeting of his FREE-THINKERS' SOCIETY. Angelo feels slighted by the judge's attentions to his brother and ponders his condition as a Siamese twin.

Chapter 4
At dinner that night, Patsy Cooper entertains the twins and her friend Aunt Betsy Hale. Patsy perceives that Angelo's spirits are low. After she suggests that he retire to bed, Angelo explains that he and his brother alternate control over their body. Some mysterious force gives each of the brothers utter and indisputable command over their body for a week at time; the change occurs exactly at midnight on Saturday, regardless of where they are in the world. Luigi adds to the women's amazement by explaining that although he and Angelo were born at the same time, he is six months older than Angelo, adding, "We are no more twins than you are." He asks the women not to tell others, knowing that this deliberate lie will burden them with wonderful gossip that they cannot pass on.

When the twins rise to greet a visitor in the parlor, Betsy asks about Rowena's relationship with Tom Driscoll, who writes to her from St. Louis. Patsy confides to Betsy that Rowena has become romantically interested in Angelo. Betsy congratulates her. Meanwhile, the Reverend Hotchkiss talks to Angelo about his wish to become a Baptist.

Chapter 5
(A bracketed aside summarizes Angelo and Luigi's argument over religion and other matters, including events described in chapter 11 of *Pudd'nhead Wilson*, concluding with Luigi's kicking Tom Driscoll at the Sons of Liberty meeting.) The text of the chapter proper opens with the town learning the startling news that David WILSON has his first law case: He is defending the Capellos against Driscoll's assault and battery charge.

Judge Sim ROBINSON presides over the ensuing trial, while Robert Allen represents Tom Driscoll. After Harkness, the chairman of the Sons of Liberty, testifies that the Capellos kicked Driscoll, Wilson asks him if he saw *both* Capellos kick Driscoll, or just one. Harkness cannot answer. Wilson proceeds to discredit the other witnesses in order.

Judge Robinson intervenes to insist that the guilty party not go unpunished. When Wilson protests Robinson's unprecedented suggestion to bring separate charges against the Capellos, the judge dismisses his objection. John Buckstone is called to testify about how the twins control their body, but his testimony is inconclusive. Patsy Cooper is called next. She has trouble testifying coherently and insists on speaking familiarly with the judge. Meanwhile, her friend Betsy repeatedly tries to butt in until the judge throws her evidence out.

When the twins testify, they admit that control of their legs passes from one to the other regularly, but do not reveal which brother was in control at the meeting. The judge wants to force them to answer, but even the prosecuting attorney demurs. The baffled jury concludes by asking to be discharged. The judge grumblingly dismisses the defendants and charges court costs to the plaintiff. The twins and Wilson emerge popular heroes.

Chapter 6
(In a summary of action retained in *Pudd'nhead Wilson*, a deputation invites Wilson to run for mayor of Dawson's Landing, which is soon to gain a city charter. Meanwhile, Judge Driscoll challenges Angelo Capello—who Tom believes to be the brother who kicked him—to a duel after Tom declines. Angelo likewise declines, but Luigi accepts in his place.)

The chapter proper begins late Saturday night, at the vacant lot next to Wilson's house where the duel is to take place. Luigi must complete the affair before midnight. Pembroke HOWARD is the judge's second. Each time shots are exchanged, Angelo faints or lurches, causing Luigi to miss. Angelo himself is wounded several times, as are Wilson and Howard. When the duel is over, Luigi asks for another round, since he has not had a fair chance to shoot. The moment a new round is to begin, midnight strikes. Now in control of the twins' body, Angelo races away.

Chapter 7
Dr. Claypool returns to Aunt Patsy's house, where everyone is attending to the wounded Angelo. The doctor's inscrutable diagnosis throws everyone into despair, and Luigi offers to take a barrel of pills on Angelo's behalf. Angelo insists that he must be baptized that afternoon. His resolution raises him in everyone's opinion.

Chapter 8
The next day, the town divides into pro-Luigi and pro-Angelo parties over the question of who is the greater hero: Luigi, for trying to stand his ground at the duel, or Angelo, for having the courage to follow his conscience. Angelo's determination to be baptized despite his wounds adds to his reputation, and a crowd gathers at the river to see his baptism. Angelo sleeps well that

night, but Luigi is kept awake by having to take regular doses of medicine.

Chapter 9
Over the next several days, both twins grow seriously ill. Only when the doctor is summoned out of town do they recover. By Friday, they are back in circulation. The local Democrats nominate Luigi for the new city council, while the Whigs nominate Angelo to run against him. Both twins campaign hard as Wilson runs for mayor unopposed on the Democratic ticket.

As the campaign develops, troubles arise because of the contradictory behavior of the twins. When Luigi controls the legs, he takes Angelo to rum shops, horse races and other disreputable entertainments. When Angelo is in control, he drags Luigi to church meetings and other moralistic gatherings. The night before the election, Angelo is scheduled to head a Teetotalers' Union march and speak at a rally. Luigi drinks enough whiskey beforehand to make Angelo drunk, ensuring that Angelo's great speech is a flop. Getting drunk causes Angelo not only to lose the election, but also Rowena. He protests that he does not drink, but Rowena replies, "You get drunk, and that is worse."

Chapter 10
A week after the election, Angelo's reputation is ruined. Luigi is elected an alderman, but cannot be sworn in since his brother cannot be admitted to the board meetings. The matter is taken to court. Meanwhile, the remaining aldermen are gridlocked. The legal case gets nowhere, and frustrations in town mount. The townspeople solve the problem by hanging Luigi.

"1002d Arabian Night"   Story written in 1883 and first published in 1967. Mark Twain had a lifelong interest in the ARABIAN NIGHTS; while finishing *Huckleberry Finn* in mid-1883, he wrote "1002d Arabian Night" as a BURLESQUE conclusion to the Near Eastern classic. The original tales of the Arabian Nights are FRAME-STORIES told by a bride named Scherezade, who postpones her execution for 1,001 consecutive nights by beginning a new tale each night to distract her husband, Sultan Shahriyar. Mark Twain's burlesque begins on the 1,002nd night, when the sultan orders Scherezade to report to his executioner.

To gain another reprieve, Scherezade begins a new story. Her complex tale is about a boy and a girl whose sexual identities are reversed at birth by a witch, who parts their hair in ways to make people think the boy is a girl and the girl a boy. A sultan's son is thus raised as Fatima, a "girl" interested only in masculine activities, while a vizier's daughter grows up as an effeminate "boy" named Selim. Separated as infants, the children meet again when they are 17 and fall in love. After considerable confusion, they are permitted to marry two years later. Under the sultan's dictate, however, the "bride" Fatima expects to be executed if he bears a child.

Amazingly, however, Selim bears twins, so everyone is happy.

When Scherezade's tedious tale ends, the relieved Shahriyar calls for his executioner. However, the tale has taken so long that the executioner has died. Scherezade resumes her tale, prolonging it until the sultan dies as well.

After finishing this 18,000-word story, Mark Twain was eager to publish it, but first sent a copy to W. D. HOWELLS. In September 1883, Howells reported back that while he thought the story's opening extremely funny, the rest was as tedious to him as it is to Shahriyar. Mark Twain put his manuscript aside and forgot about it. It was finally published in SATIRES & BURLESQUES in 1967.

Three Forks of Wolf River   TENNESSEE village in which Mark Twain's family lived before he was born. A tiny FENTRESS County postal station, Three Forks stood about six miles south of the Kentucky border, on the south bank of the Wolf River. Around 1831, John M. and Jane L. Clemens moved there from Jamestown, nine miles farther south, and bought nearly 200 acres of land. After about three months, they relocated to PALL MALL across the river.

Tichborne Claimant   Subject of a celebrated trial in ENGLAND. In 1866, Sir Alfred Joseph Tichborne died, ending a line of English baronets going back 240 years. Soon afterward, an Australian butcher named Thomas Castro stepped forward claiming to be the baronet's missing brother, Roger Charles Tichborne—who had been lost at sea off Brazil in 1854, when he was 25. Endorsed by Tichborne's mother—who had never accepted that Roger was dead—Castro claimed the family's large estate. He was subjected to a long trial until his case collapsed in March 1872. The following year, he was charged with perjury and another long trial began.

Mark Twain was in London during the second trial, which made the "Tichborne Claimant" a *cause célèbre*. Fascinated by claimants such as his own relative Jesse LEATHERS, he had assistants compile clippings on the trial for him. In June 1873, he attended the trial himself and interviewed Castro. The following February, "Castro" was proven to be an Englishman named Arthur Orton and was sentenced to 14 years in prison. Released after 10 years, Orton confessed his imposture in 1895. He died as Mark Twain was writing *Following the Equator*, which summarizes Orton's story in chapter 15 (chapter 17 of MORE TRAMPS ABROAD contains a longer account). Mark Twain also mentions the Tichborne Claimant in part 1 of IS SHAKESPEARE DEAD? Meanwhile, Orton's attempt to claim the baronetcy helped inspire Mark Twain to write *The American Claimant* (1892), in which Colonel SELLERS claims to be an English earl.

Tom Quartz   Animal character in a tale related by Dick BAKER in chapter 61 of *Roughing It*. A large gray cat that Baker owned for eight years, Tom Quartz was a remarkable animal whose only interest in life was MINING. He always supervised pocket-miners closely. After quartz-mining came to the region, Tom Quartz happened to be sleeping on a gunny sack inside a shaft the first day that miners did blasting. After setting their charge, they ran to safety before remembering that Tom Quartz was in the shaft. The ensuing blast sent Tom Quartz tumbling end over end through the sky. He landed covered with soot, threw everyone a disgusted look and stalked off. After that, he was the most prejudiced cat there ever was against quartz-mining.

Mark Twain adapted Tom Quartz's story from a tale that Jim GILLIS related in California in late 1864 or early 1865. Gillis modeled Baker on his partner Dick STOKER, but the cat never existed, according to Mark Twain himself. Mark Twain's first, unpublished version of the story, "The Remarkable Sagacity of a Cat" (1865), calls the cat "George Billson." He published a revised version of the story in the BUFFALO EXPRESS in December 1869.

Tom Sawyer, The Adventures of **(1876)** The first novel that Mark Twain wrote without a coauthor, *Tom Sawyer* is also his most clearly autobiographical novel. It concerns a long summer in the life of an ordinary young boy living in Missouri in the early 19th century. It is set in a village modeled closely on Mark Twain's hometown and most of its characters are taken from life. Its narrative is enlivened by extraordinary and melodramatic events, but it is otherwise a realistic depiction of the experiences, people and places that Mark Twain knew as a child.

Tom Sawyer arrived at a momentous time in American history. Its first edition was issued in England on June 9, 1876. Sixteen days later, Indians annihilated George Armstrong Custer's Seventh Cavalry at Little Big Horn. Nine days after that, America celebrated the centennial of its birth. Publication of *Tom Sawyer* was little noticed in the United States at the time. The book has, however, proved to be one of the most durable works in American literature. By the time Mark Twain died, it was his top-selling book. It has been in print continuously since 1876, and has outsold all other Mark Twain works. It has been issued in hundreds of editions in at least three dozen languages.

SYNOPSIS

The novel is 76,000 words in length and is divided into 35 chapters, plus a brief epilogue. Its plot follows five distinct story lines, which overlap considerably. The loosest story line, beginning in chapter 1, concerns Tom's relationship with his family and his school and church activities. A second story line follows Tom's infatuation with Becky THATCHER, whom he meets in chapter 3. In a third story line, an episode contained within chapters 13–17 has Tom, Huck Finn and Joe HARPER spend a week playing PIRATES on JACKSON'S ISLAND. A fourth story line begins in chapter 9, when Tom and Huck see INJUN JOE murder a man in the graveyard; after the Jackson's Island interlude, this story line culminates with the trial of Muff POTTER in chapter 23, when Injun Joe is revealed as the true murderer and disappears. The final and most complex story line ties together the search for Injun Joe, Tom and Huck's quest for treasure, and Tom and Becky's adventure in a CAVE.

Chapter 1
The narrative opens in the shabby little village of ST. PETERSBURG, on the right bank of the Mississippi River. (Clues here and elsewhere indicate that it is Friday, June 14—a date that occurred in the year 1844). Aunt POLLY is searching for her impudent nephew, Tom Sawyer, the son of her deceased sister. She finds him and is about to put a switch to him, but he escapes. That afternoon, Tom cuts school to go swimming. At supper that night, his half-brother, Sid SAWYER, calls Polly's attention to a thread in Tom's shirt that reveals that he removed the shirt in order to swim. Tom silently vows revenge on his priggish brother. After supper, Tom goes out and gets into a fight with a new village boy (later identified as Albert TEMPLE), whom he chases away. When Tom returns home disheveled, Aunt Polly determines to put him to work the next day.

Chapter 2
Saturday morning finds Tom burdened with the task of whitewashing a huge FENCE. Just as he tries enticing a young black boy named JIM into helping, a sudden smack from Aunt Polly ends his negotiations. After Polly leaves, Tom persuades Ben ROGERS, Billy FISHER, Johnny MILLER and other boys to paint the fence for him. The other boys not only whitewash the fence, they pay for the privilege.

Chapter 3
Tom reports to Aunt Polly that he has finished painting the fence. Astonished to find the fence whitewashed three times over, Polly rewards Tom with an apple and dismisses him. As Tom leaves, he pelts Sid with dirt clods, then joins his pal Joe HARPER commanding boys in a mock military battle.

Tom returns home past Jeff THATCHER's house, where he sees a new girl in the garden (later identified as Jeff's cousin Becky THATCHER). Instantly falling in love with this new girl, Tom forgets his previous sweetheart, Amy LAWRENCE, and hangs about Jeff's house showing off. He arrives home in a happy mood that becomes ecstasy when Sid accidentally breaks a sugar-bowl. When Aunt Polly discovers the wreckage, she smacks Tom without stopping to ask who is responsible. When his cheerful cousin Mary (SAWYER?) returns home from a week in the country, Tom leaves in order to sulk. That evening, he returns to Jeff Thatcher's house, hoping to catch a glimpse of the new girl. When he steals quietly near the house, a bucket of water is dumped on his head from an upper-story window.

Chapter 4

Sunday morning begins with Tom struggling to master Bible verses for Sunday school, a place that he hates. Mary coaches him and encourages him with the unexpected gift of a pocketknife. At the entrance to the Sunday school, Tom accosts boys as they come in and trades the items amassed the day before for "tickets" that they have earned for memorizing Bible verses; he collects enough to claim one of the Bibles awarded to pupils who memorize 2,000 verses.

Mr. WALTERS, the Sunday-school superintendent, conducts the session and introduces several visitors. The most important of these is Jeff Thatcher's uncle, Judge THATCHER. The judge is accompanied by his wife and daughter—the very girl with whom Tom is enthralled. Anxious to impress his visitors, Walters wants to "exhibit a prodigy" by awarding a Bible prize. Tom presents the requisite number of tickets and demands a Bible. Walters is stunned, as are Tom's friends, who sold him the tickets that have made his moment of glory possible. As Tom accepts his Bible, the judge asks him to display some of his knowledge by naming the first two disciples. After Tom stammers "David and Goliah," the curtain of charity is drawn over the rest of the scene.

Chapter 5

Later that morning, Tom sits with Sid, Mary and Aunt Polly in the church during the Reverend Mr. SPRAGUE's sermon. The congregation includes all the village worthies, including the Widow DOUGLAS, the mayor, the postmaster and Willie MUFFERSON, the village's MODEL BOY. Tom fights off boredom by playing with a pinch-beetle. A stray poodle that is roaming the aisles sits on the beetle and is pinched. It raises a huge ruckus that delights the congregation, but the minister bravely carries on.

Chapter 6

As morning breaks on Monday, Tom looks for a malady that will keep him home from school. All he can come up with is a loose tooth that Aunt Polly yanks out. On his way to school, he encounters the village pariah, Huckleberry Finn, who is carrying a dead cat. After discussing the supposed wart-curing properties of dead cats, the boys agree to meet that night at the graveyard to test it. Meanwhile, Tom persuades Huck to swap a tick-bug for his freshly extracted tooth.

When Tom arrives at school late, the master (later identified as Mr. DOBBINS) demands an explanation. Tom is about to lie, but when he spots the new girl in the classroom, he startles everyone with the truth: that he was talking with Huck Finn. Dobbins whips him and sends him to sit with the girls. Tom is delighted to find himself sitting next to Becky. He shows off his drawing prowess and writes "I love you" on a piece of paper. At that moment, Dobbins takes him by his ear back to his regular seat, next to Joe Harper.

Chapter 7

Bored with schoolwork, Tom releases his tick-bug so that he and Joe can play with it on a slate. While the tick-bug engrosses them, Dobbins tiptoes down the aisle and whacks both of them. Tom spends the noon break with Becky at the empty schoolhouse, where they draw pictures and chat. Tom persuades Becky to become "engaged," but then upsets her by mentioning that he was once engaged to Amy Lawrence. He offers her his treasured brass andiron knob, but she knocks it to the floor. Tom leaves and does not to return to school that day.

Chapter 8

Tom goes to CARDIFF HILL. Consumed with self-pity, he wishes he could die, *temporarily*. His spirits lift, however, as he considers simply going far away and not returning. He fantasizes about becoming a clown, or a soldier, or, better still, a PIRATE with the name BLACK AVENGER OF THE SPANISH MAIN. In preparation for his new life of adventure, he invokes an incantation designed to round up all the marbles he ever lost, but this spell fails. Joe Harper, another truant, then appears and the boys play Robin Hood games the rest of the afternoon.

Chapter 9

Late the same night, Huck calls for Tom. They go to the graveyard outside of town, where they happen on INJUN JOE, Muff POTTER and Dr. ROBINSON in the act of robbing Hoss WILLIAMS's grave. Injun Joe starts an argument that develops into a scuffle. Potter is momentarily knocked out and Joe stabs Robinson to death with his knife. The boys flee. Injun Joe robs Robinson's corpse before Potter regains consciousness, then persuades Potter that *he* has killed the doctor. Drunk, as usual, Potter accepts Injun Joe's story and begs Joe to stand by him. Both men then leave.

Chapter 10

After running to the old tannery, Tom and Huck sign a blood-oath, swearing that they will never reveal what they have just seen. They hear snoring in the building and find Muff Potter asleep.

The next morning Tom oversleeps. Instead of rebuking him, Aunt Polly weeps over him for breaking her heart again, making Tom feel worse than he would after a whipping. He arrives at school in a gloomy mood. He and Joe Harper are flogged for the previous day's hookey. Tom's despair is complete when he finds that Becky has returned his brass knob.

Chapter 11

At noon, word of the murder electrifies the village. Tom joins the flow of townspeople to the graveyard, where he sees Huck. Muff Potter appears and is arrested because his knife was found at the scene of the crime. Injun Joe gives his version of what happened the previous night, leaving Huck and Tom dumbfounded that the man is not struck dead for lying. Agonizing over his secret knowledge of the murder, Tom has trouble sleeping through the next week. Friends and family members notice a marked change in his behavior. To ease his conscience, he regularly visits the jailhouse in order to smuggle goodies to Potter.

Chapter 12
Tom's interest in the murder case lessens as a new concern occupies his thoughts. Becky is ill and out of school. Aunt Polly, concerned about Tom's deteriorating spirits, fills him up with patent medicines and quack cures. These fail, so she orders a large supply of "Painkiller," which tastes like "fire in a liquid form." Tom persuades her to let him dose himself and gradually pours the medicine through a crack in the floor. One day, he gives his dose to Aunt Polly's cat Peter, which springs into the air and runs through the room wildly. Aunt Polly arrives as the cat does double somersaults and flies out the window. Tom explains what he has done and Aunt Polly thumps him. He expresses bewilderment, pointing out that he has only done for the cat what she has been doing for him.

At school that day, Tom is thrilled to see Becky again, but he fails to get her attention.

Chapter 13
Tom now believes that he has no alternative but to run away. Joe Harper shares his feelings of being put upon by the world, so they swear to stick together. Joe wants to become a hermit, but accepts Tom's plan to be pirates. Huck Finn soon joins them. Each boy steals supplies to begin their careers in crime. At midnight, they rendezvous two miles upriver and commandeer a raft to take them to JACKSON'S ISLAND. Tom again styles himself the "Black Avenger of the Spanish Main." The boys quietly float down the river and land on a bar at the north end of the island. They use an old sail for a makeshift tent, but sleep in the open.

Chapter 14
The boys spend the next morning swimming, skylarking and fishing. After eating, they explore the island, stopping to swim every hour. Despite their fun, the solitude gradually weighs on them. A booming sound catches their attention. Upstream, a ferryboat crowded with people and surrounded by skiffs is firing a cannon over the water. Tom explains that the boat must be searching for someone who has drowned. Suddenly he realizes that the boat is looking for *them*. The boys return to camp excited, but as night falls, their spirits sag. Joe hints that they might consider going home, only to have Tom deride him.

After his companions are asleep, Tom writes messages on bark. One piece he leaves in Joe's hat along with his personal treasures, the other he tucks into his jacket before sneaking off to the sand-bar.

Chapter 15
Tom wades and swims to the ILLINOIS shore, which he follows upstream to the ferryboat dock opposite St. Petersburg. He swims to the skiff towed behind the ferryboat and rides it across the river to the village and sneaks home. There he peeks inside and sees Aunt Polly, Sid, Mary and Joe Harper's mother talking. He slips in unobserved and listens to their conversation from beneath the bed in the parlor. He overhears that the raft that he and his friends used was found five or six miles below village, and that he and the others are believed drowned. If their bodies are not found by Sunday, a funeral service will be held for them on that day.

After the others leave, Aunt Polly goes to sleep on the bed. Tom emerges from his hiding place. He starts to place his sycamore-bark message by his aunt's bedside, but then thinks better of it. He kisses Polly and leaves. He detaches the skiff from the idle ferryboat, rows across the river and reaches camp just after daybreak, just as Huck and Joe are debating what to do with the possessions he left behind. Tom relates his adventure, then sleeps till noon.

Chapter 16
That night, the boys collect turtle eggs, on which they breakfast the next two mornings. Friday morning they devote to frolicking, but Joe's and Huck's spirits sink to a new low. Both want to go home, but Tom makes fun of them. As they start to leave, Tom springs a great secret on them that renews their spirits and persuades them to stay. After dinner, Huck teaches Tom and Joe how to smoke corncob pipes. Both boys profess to love smoking, but as their spitting reaches prodigious levels, they disappear to sleep off their new experience.

At midnight a lightning storm rocks the island, keeping the boys awake all night. They build a roaring fire when the storm abates. At daybreak on Saturday, they sleep on the sandbar and get sunburned. Joe and Huck's spirits again flag; Tom invigorates them by suggesting that they play Indians.

Chapter 17
The scene switches back to the village, where the families of Joe and Tom are in mourning. Becky Thatcher mopes about the schoolhouse, regretting her harsh treatment of Tom. Other children arrive and speak reverently about Tom and Joe. The next morning, the largest crowd in memory fills the church for the funeral service. Aunt Polly, Sid, Mary and the Harper family enter dressed in black. As the minister delivers a sermon extolling the boys for their overlooked virtues, the church door creaks open and the three boys march up the aisle. They have come down from the gallery, where they listened to their own funeral sermon. The families throw themselves on the restored boys and the congregation shakes the rafters with joyous singing. This is the proudest moment of Tom's life.

Chapter 18
As circumstances of how the boys made it from the island to the church are told, it is revealed that the chance to attend their own funeral was the secret that Tom saved for Huck and Joe earlier.

On Monday morning Mary and Aunt Polly are attentive to Tom, but Polly chides him for making her suffer by allowing her to think him dead. Tom tries to make her feel better by telling her that he dreamt about her while he was away. To prove it, he recounts every detail he remembers from the night that he sneaked into the house. Aunt Polly is immensely pleased with his amazing "dream." As the children go to school, Aunt Polly heads for Mrs. Harper's.

Now a hero, Tom decides that he no longer needs Becky—unless she is willing to make up. When she arrives, Tom ignores her, but makes sure that she sees him flirting with Amy Lawrence. Becky works on Tom's jealousy by extending picnic invitations to everyone but him and Amy. At recess, Tom continues flirting with Amy, but with waning enthusiasm, because Becky is flirting with the new boy, Alfred Temple. After Tom leaves at noon, Becky dismisses Alfred sharply. Realizing that he has been used, Alfred enters the schoolhouse and pours ink on Tom's spelling book. Becky happens to see him do it, but resolves to let Tom be punished.

Chapter 19
At home, Tom finds Aunt Polly in an angry mood. She has just learned from Mrs. Harper the truth about Tom's Wednesday night visit to the house. Tom insists that he had came home to leave a message written on bark for her, but she remains skeptical. After he leaves, she takes his jacket out of the closet, hesitates, then finds Tom's bark with the message that he wrote for her. She is so elated she would forgive him any sin.

Chapter 20
Near the school, Tom meets Becky and suggests that they make up, but she snubs him. Becky then enters the empty schoolhouse. Dobbins has left the key in his desk drawer. Becky opens the drawer and finds a mysterious book that Dobbins often furtively reads—an anatomy textbook, which she opens to a picture of a naked human. At that moment, Tom enters the room, so startling Becky that she tears the page almost in half. As she replaces the book in the desk, she tearfully turns on Tom, berating him because she expects that he will tattle on her. She adds that something bad is about to happen to him. She stalks off, leaving Tom perplexed.

After class resumes, Tom's damaged spelling book earns him another whipping. Eventually, Dobbins discovers the damage to his anatomy book and demands to know who caused it. No confession is forthcoming, so he starts challenging pupils, one at a time. Tom senses Becky's growing panic; he knows that she will crumble when Dobbins calls her name. Just as her turn comes, Tom jumps up and shouts, "*I done it!*" Dobbins gives Tom the most merciless flaying he has ever admin-

istered and makes Tom stay after school for two hours. Later, Tom and Becky reach a complete reconciliation. Tom goes to sleep that night planning vengeance against Alfred Temple.

Chapter 21
As vacation approaches and Dobbins prepares pupils for "Examination Day," the frequency and severity of his whippings increase and his victims plot an elaborate revenge. Dobbins is known to drink before these occasions, so the son of the sign-painter in whose house he lives does something to Dobbins while he naps before the big evening. At the school program that night, youngsters parrot speeches and young ladies read predictably melancholic compositions. Tom Sawyer's recitation of the "liberty or death" speech breaks down when stage fright overwhelms him.

The climax to the evening comes when a tipsy Dobbins mounts the stage to draw a map on the blackboard for a geography lesson. He hears the audience tittering, but has no idea what they are tittering about. Meanwhile, a boy lowers a cat on a rope toward Dobbins's head from an opening in the ceiling. The cat snags Dobbins's wig, revealing the fact that his head is gilded. The boys are avenged. Vacation has begun.

Chapter 22
Tom begins the summer vacation by joining the CADETS OF TEMPERANCE, but is quickly disillusioned. Various events and entertainments pass through the village: minstrel shows, a circus, a phrenologist and a mesmerizer. The Fourth of July is a partial flop; its parade is rained out and the featured speaker, Senator BENTON, proves a disappointment. Meanwhile, Becky is with her parents in CONSTANTINOPLE. The secret of Dr. Robinson's murder continues to weigh on Tom.

After measles keep Tom bedridden for two weeks, he emerges to find that the village has experienced a religious revival. Joe Harper is studying a Testament; Ben Rogers is ministering to the poor; Jim Hollis has become pious. Even Huck is quoting scripture. Tom fears that of all the village residents, he alone is lost. That night a terrible storm convinces him that his end is near. The next day he suffers a relapse and begins another three weeks in bed. This time he emerges to find that the effects of the revival have worn off and his friends have returned to their sinful ways.

Chapter 23
As Muff Potter's murder trial approaches, Huck and Tom consider springing Potter free, but instead merely pass tobacco and matches to him through his cell window. His pitiful gratitude magnifies their feelings of guilt. When the trial begins, the boys hang about the courtroom, lacking the resolve to enter. By the end of the second day, word is out that Injun Joe's evidence is holding firm, and that the verdict seems certain. That night Tom is out late and comes home too agitated to sleep.

The next day in court, the prosecution examines witness after witness. When Potter's attorney fails to cross-examine anyone, a murmur of discontent is heard. However, after the prosecution rests its case, Potter's attorney moves to withdraw Potter's original temporary insanity plea and calls Tom as a surprise witness. Without mentioning Huck's name, Tom tells what he saw at the graveyard the night of Dr. Robinson's murder. Just as he is about to reveal that Injun Joe stabbed the doctor, Injun Joe springs out the window and disappears.

Chapter 24
Once again, Tom is a hero. Nevertheless, nightmares of Injun Joe so haunt him that he hesitates to go out at night. Huck also is afraid; Tom's violation of their sacred oath has obliterated his confidence in the human race. Meanwhile, a detective from St. Louis arrives to investigate Injun Joe's disappearance, but he leaves after merely announcing that he has found a clue.

Chapter 25
After an unspecified period of time passes, Tom persuades Huck to hunt for buried treasure, exciting Huck's greed with predictions of the wealth they might find. They begin digging near the HAUNTED HOUSE just outside the village. After a few fruitless hours, they move to a spot near the Widow Douglas's house on Cardiff Hill. This spot also proves fruitless, so they decide to return at midnight to see where the shadow of a tree limb falls. That night, they mark the spot of the limb's shadow and dig again. Further failure moves them to consider yet another spot and Tom suggests that they try the haunted house itself. Agreeing to return during daylight, they boys give the house a wide berth as they go home.

Chapter 26
At noon the next day, they return to the tree where they left their tools. Tom remembers it is Friday—an unlucky day to enter haunted houses—so they spend the afternoon playing Robin Hood. On Saturday they finally enter the house and even venture to go upstairs. Two men then enter the house. One is "the old deef and dumb Spaniard" recently seen around the village. The other is a stranger. The boys are shocked to hear the "Spaniard" speak and even more shocked to recognize Injun Joe's voice. Joe and his unknown partner are discussing a job they intend to pull, after which they intend to escape to TEXAS.

Tom and Huck remain where they are as Injun Joe and his partner nap. When the criminals awaken, they discuss burying their "swag." Injun Joe digs into the dirt floor with a knife and strikes a box. The box is filled with gold coins. Injun Joe and his partner speculate that it is a treasure left by MURRELL's gang. Joe's partner suggests that they no longer need to pull the job they have been planning, but Joe insists on carrying out his plan because it is revenge.

Injun Joe wants to take the gold to his den, located at "Number Two-under the cross." The men find Huck and Tom's tools and become suspicious. To the boys' dismay, Injun Joe starts climbing the stairs, but he stops when the stairway crumbles. As the boys determine to track Injun Joe to his hiding place, they also wonder if his revenge plan is directed at them.

Chapter 27
That night Tom dreams about the treasure Injun Joe has found. The next morning he and Huck discuss the previous evening's adventure. Tom argues for tracking Injun Joe to his hiding place. They try to figure out what Injun Joe means by "Number Two." Tom guesses that it is a room in one of the village's temperance taverns. After he investigates the tavern, he and Huck plan to spy on Injun Joe that night.

Chapter 28
Over the next several nights Tom and Huck hang around the tavern, watching for Injun Joe. On Thursday night Tom enters a room in the tavern, where he finds Injun Joe asleep on the floor, drunk, and nearly steps on his hand. Tom runs out and alerts Huck, who suggests that it might be a good moment to search the room for the treasure box. However, neither boy is up to taking the risk, so they decide to keep watching Injun Joe's room until he is gone.

Chapter 29
The next day Tom learns that Judge Thatcher's family has returned to town. Becky persuades her mother to organize the long-promised picnic. On Saturday, Tom, Becky, many other children and a few young chaperons ride a chartered steam ferry downriver to the landing by the CAVE. Becky arranges with her mother to stay overnight at Susy Harper's, rather than journey home late. The ferry delivers them at a landing near the cave. Armed with candles, the picnickers stream inside to explore.

Huck, meanwhile, remains in town, watching the temperance tavern. Two men come out carrying a box. Huck quietly follows them to Cardiff Hill. He overhears Injun Joe talking to his unidentified partner about a "revenge job." Joe explains that when the Widow Douglas's husband was justice of the peace, the man treated him so badly that he now wants revenge. His plan is to mutilate the widow's face. When the partner objects, Injun Joe threatens to kill him. Huck runs down the hill to the house of JONES THE WELCHMAN and reports what he has overheard, begging not to have his own role in the affair revealed. Jones and his sons go off to protect the widow. Huck hears gunfire and a scream and he runs down the hill.

Chapter 30
The next morning, Sunday, Huck returns to Jones's house to learn what happened the night before. Jones welcomes him and explains that the assailants were chased off in the dark. He tries to get a description of

the men out of Huck, who makes a further demand of secrecy. Finally, Huck reveals that the mysterious "Spaniard" is actually Injun Joe. Someone comes to the door, so Huck hides. It is the Widow Douglas, coming to thank Jones and his sons.

At church later that morning, Mrs. Thatcher discovers that Becky did not spend the night at Susy Harper's as planned and Aunt Polly learns that Tom's whereabouts also are not known. Word spreads that Tom and Becky must still be in the cave, where 200 searchers soon converge to begin working through the night. The next morning, Jones returns home to find Huck sleeping in his house, delirious with fever. The Widow Douglas comes to take care of him. Meanwhile, the search for Becky and Tom in the cave continues for three days.

Chapter 31
At the start of the picnic, Tom and Becky go off on their own in the cave, not noticing that they are becoming separated from the other picnickers. Tom eventually concludes that they are lost. He leads Becky to a fresh-water spring, where he insists that they remain as their candles burn out. Using a kite string to find his way back to this spot, Tom keeps searching for a way out of the cave. When he sees Injun Joe walking through the cave with a torch, he cries out, but Joe seems not to notice him.

Chapter 32
On Tuesday, St. Petersburg goes wild when word is received that Tom and Becky are safe. Tom explains how he found a speck of light in the cave that proved to be an opening through which he and Becky escaped. He then learned from boatmen who picked them up that they were five miles south of the cave's main entrance.

Tom spends two weeks recovering from his exhaustion, then goes to visit Huck. When he stops at the Thatchers', he learns that the judge has had the entrance to the cave sealed with an iron door to prevent other people from getting lost. Tom pales, then announces that Injun Joe is inside the cave.

Chapter 33
People again rush to the cave, where they find Injun Joe lying dead behind the new door, surrounded by grisly evidence of his slow starvation. His body is buried near the cave's entrance.

The next day, Tom and Huck finally catch up on each other's adventures. Tom startles Huck with his revelation that the missing treasure must be in the cave. That afternoon, they go to the cave, entering it through the opening that Tom has kept secret since his escape with Becky. As they enter, Tom outlines his plans for a robbers' gang, which is also to include Ben Rogers and Joe Harper. Inside the cave, Huck's nerve starts to fail; he fears meeting Injun Joe's ghost. The boys persist, however, and find Injun Joe's cache of weapons and

treasure. Back in the village, they encounter Jones, who excitedly rushes them off to the Widow Douglas's, where they find Aunt Polly, the Thatchers, the Harpers and many others awaiting them. The boys are sent off to change into new clothes that have been purchased for Huck.

Chapter 34
Away from the crowd, Huck suggests fleeing, but Tom persuades him to stay. Sid arrives and explains that Jones is planning some kind of surprise. Downstairs, the widow announces her intention to provide Huck with a permanent home and later start him in business. Tom interrupts, however, saying that Huck does not need that, since he is already rich. The announcement stuns the crowd into silence. Tom then brings in the gold coins and pours them on a table. The coins add up to just over $12,000, which Tom says that he and Huck will split.

Chapter 35
After word of Tom and Huck's treasure gets out, every "haunted" house in the region is dismantled by treasure seekers. The Widow Douglas invests Huck's money for him, and Judge Thatcher does the same with Tom's money. Now under the widow's protection, Huck suffers the close attention of her servants, who keep him clean and neat. He hates having to eat with utensils, attend church and speak properly. After three weeks, he bolts and disappears for 48 hours. Tom finds Huck in an empty hogshead near the abandoned slaughter-house. He tells Huck that he will not be allowed to join his robber gang if he is not respectable. Huck agrees to go back and try living with the widow for another month. Tom promises to have an initiation meeting that night.

Conclusion
An epilogue of just over a hundred words explains that the narrative must end because it is "strictly a history of a *boy*." It cannot continue without becoming the history of a *man*. The narrator assures us that "most of the characters . . . still live, and are prosperous and happy," and suggests he might take up their story as adults later.

BACKGROUND AND WRITING

Mark Twain prefaced *Tom Sawyer* with the claim that "most" of its adventures "really occurred." This statement must be put in perspective. The events in the novel that Mark Twain personally experienced or observed as a child are mostly the minor ones. He was a mischievous boy at school; he did show off for Laura HAWKINS when she moved to his street; his brother Henry Clemens did break a sugar bowl, and so on. The major events, however, such as the grave-robbing and murder scene, getting lost in the cave and finding the treasure, are pure invention.

Tom (Jack Pickford) and Huck (Robert Gordon) reveal the treasure they have found in the cave in Huck and Tom, *the second film adapted from* Tom Sawyer.

During his years as a journalist, Mark Twain wrote about some of the incidents and themes that he would later use in *Tom Sawyer*. His early essays and sketches occasionally evoke his memories of Sunday school, the Cadets of Temperance, "Examination Day," childhood romance, and other matters that later figure into *Tom Sawyer*. Around 1868, he completed a short story, posthumously titled "BOY'S MANUSCRIPT," that clearly anticipates *Tom Sawyer*. In February 1870, he wrote a letter to his childhood friend Will BOWEN recalling many details of their boyhood together that he would use in *Tom Sawyer*.

Tom Sawyer was Mark Twain's first attempt to write a novel on his own. It is nearly impossible to pinpoint the exact dates that he worked on the manuscript. He may have begun work on the book as early as 1872. After writing about 400 pages of manuscript, he stopped. In early 1873, he joined with his neighbor, C. D. WARNER, to write another, much different novel, *The Gilded Age*. He returned to *Tom Sawyer* during the summer of 1874, most of which he spent in ELMIRA, New York.

In July 1875, Mark Twain wrote to W. D. HOWELLS, reporting that he had finished *Tom Sawyer*. Later that month, he arranged copyright for his own dramatic adaptation of the story. He gave a copy of the novel's manuscript to Howells for reading. Howells liked the book greatly, but upset Mark Twain by recommending that it be presented as a boys' book. Mark Twain conceded the point when his wife Livy agreed with Howells's view. The role of Howells and Olivia Clemens—to whom he dedicated *Tom Sawyer*—in the editing of the book has given rise to a theory that Mark Twain was constrained by their censorship. Close examination of the various manuscript texts has, however, revealed only minor, and mostly stylistic, changes. There is no reason to believe that the book that was published was something other than what Mark Twain intended it to be.

PUBLISHING HISTORY

On November 5, 1875, Mark Twain delivered his manuscript to his American publisher, Elisha BLISS, who turned it over to True WILLIAMS for illustration. For various reasons—not all of which are clear—it would be over a year before Bliss's AMERICAN PUBLISHING COMPANY finally issued the first American edition. In January 1876, Mark Twain had Moncure CONWAY take a corrected copy of his manuscript to England, where Conway arranged for its publication with CHATTO and Windus. Chatto issued an unillustrated edition on June 9, 1876. Other foreign editions followed quickly. BELFORD Brothers, a Canadian publisher, issued an unauthorized edition in late July, pouring perhaps 100,000 cheap copies of the book into the United States. Around October, Bernhard von TAUCHNITZ issued an English-language edition of the book in Leipzig, Germany. Another Leipzig publisher soon issued the first German translation of the book.

Around December 8, 1876, Bliss's company finally issued the first American edition, which was also the first illustrated edition. The company reissued the book in approximately the same format until HARPER AND BROTHERS became Mark Twain's exclusive American publisher in 1903. Harper's then issued all the authorized editions of *Tom Sawyer* in America until 1931, when its copyright expired. That event launched a spate of new editions, many with fresh illustrations, including an edition illustrated by Norman Rockwell in 1936. Since the book's original publication, it has never gone out of print.

MANUSCRIPTS

Mark Twain's original manuscript of *Tom Sawyer,* extending to 876 handwritten pages, is held by Georgetown University in Washington, D.C. In 1982 the university's library published it as a two-volume photo-facsimile edition. Shortly after completing the manuscript, Mark Twain had a secretarial, or amanuensis, copy written out by scribes. Howells read this copy and wrote his corrections on it; then Mark Twain added his own revisions. Mark Twain attempted to reconcile the two copies of the manuscript before Conway took the secretarial copy to England, but slight differences slipped through. The American edition drew on Mark Twain's original manuscript; the English edition drew on the secretarial copy. The original English edition also differs from the American edition in having somewhat different chapter numbers.

Mark Twain personally made additional corrections and revisions on the American edition's proof pages, but did not read proofs for the English edition. Chatto and Windus returned its copy of the manuscript to Conway and it eventually found its way to the museum in MARK TWAIN STATE PARK near Florida, Missouri.

In 1980 the MARK TWAIN PAPERS project published the first edition of *Tom Sawyer* based directly on the original manuscript that attempts to reconcile Mark Twain's corrections in the secretarial copy manuscripts and the first American edition.

***Tom Sawyer,* dramatizations of** Mark Twain's interest in creating a play out of *Tom Sawyer* developed along with the novel itself. His interest became even greater after his play based on *The Gilded Age* was a hit on the New York stage. In July 1875, he copyrighted a synopsis of a "Tom Sawyer" drama, but apparently set this project aside in order to concentrate on other plays, including AH SIN; *Cap'n Simon Wheeler, the Amateur Detective;* and *Colonel Sellers as a Scientist.* He finally completed

Tom Sawyer, A Play in 4 Acts in 1884 and then pushed his publisher, Charles L. WEBSTER, to find a backer to produce it. Meanwhile, the first dramatization of *Tom Sawyer* to be produced may have been an amateur play in Wichita, Kansas that Mark Twain gave permission to stage.

Miles and Barton produced Mark Twain's own play in Yonkers, New York and in Hartford, in May and June 1885, with a few performances in other towns. The problem of finding professional actors to play a boy was solved by casting women in the lead. Mollie Ravel played Tom in the play's initial run; Kitty Rhoades played him in road-show productions in 1888. Other productions of this play, as well as occasional BURLESQUES, were staged in New York City during the early 1890s.

Later in the 1890s, Mark Twain sold dramatic rights to *Huckleberry Finn* to the theatrical production team of Klaw and Erlanger. The musical play that they produced with this name in 1902 turned out to be based mostly on *Tom Sawyer.* Mark Twain was credited with coauthorship, but it appears that a Southern writer named Lee Arthur was its primary writer. Klaw and Erlanger's three-act production featured a cast of 80 and elaborate set-pieces. The scenes included several episodes from *Tom Sawyer,* such as the FENCE WHITEWASHING, but its central story line was original. Huck and his father are suspected of committing burglaries, but the real thieves are exposed when Huck and Tom rescue girls kidnapped by the thieves. The fact that Huck Finn is given a love interest—Amy LAWRENCE—suggests that Mark Twain himself was not directly involved in the production. As in the Miles and Barton production, adults played the leads. The play ran for a week each in Hartford, Philadelphia and Baltimore in late 1902, then closed permanently.

Meanwhile, impresario Paul Kester had the rights to dramatize *Tom Sawyer.* His slowness in developing a script may have contributed to Mark Twain's allowing Klaw and Erlanger's *Huckleberry Finn* production to draw heavily on *Tom Sawyer.* Kester's play was not copyrighted until 1914, and was not given a first-class production in New York until 1931. Expiration of the original copyright on *Tom Sawyer* that same year led to dozens of new unauthorized dramatizations of the story. Most of these were written for juvenile audiences. The handful of four-act plays to reach publication include Sara Spencer's *Tom Sawyer* (1935) and Charlotte B. Chorpenning's *The Adventures of Tom Sawyer* (1956). In 1957 LIVIN' THE LIFE, a musical based on *Tom Sawyer* and Mark Twain's other Mississippi writings, was staged in an off-Broadway theater.

***Tom Sawyer,* screen adaptations of** Jesse L. Lasky, who earlier adapted *Pudd'nhead Wilson* to film, was the first producer to make a movie from *The Adventures of Tom Sawyer.* He released his production in two parts, with Jack Pickford (1896–1993) playing Tom Sawyer in both.

Tom Sawyer (1917) covered the incidents in the first half of the novel, leaving the rest of the story to the following year's HUCK AND TOM.

The first sound film came in 1930, with Jackie Coogan (1914–1984) starring as Tom in Paramount's *Tom Sawyer*. Paramount immediately followed this production with *Huckleberry Finn*, using the same principals in both films: Junior Durkin played Huck, Clara Blandick was Aunt Polly, Jane Darwell was the Widow Douglas and Mitzi Green was Becky.

David O. Selznick produced the first color film adaptation of *Tom Sawyer* in 1938, the year before he released *Gone With the Wind*. His production team created a stir by visiting Hannibal to scout locations. The town's altered riverfront and modern look made it an unsuitable location for early 19th-century scenes, so the production was taken back to California. The cast of *The Adventures of Tom Sawyer* included Tommy Kelly (1928-) as Tom, Jackie Moran as Huck, May Robson as Aunt Polly, Walter Brennan as Muff Potter, Victor Jory as Injun Joe, Nana Bryant as Mrs. Thatcher and Margaret Hamilton as Mrs. Harper.

Tom Sawyer was not adapted to film again until 35 years later. In the meantime, numerous adaptations of the story appeared on television. In 1973, *Reader's Digest* and United Artists released a musical version of the story, with songs by Richard and Robert Sherman. Much of this film was shot on Missouri locations. The cast included Johnnie Whitaker (1959–) as Tom, Jeff East as Huck, Warren Oates as Muff Potter and Jodie Foster as Becky Thatcher. The same year, a major television adaptation of *Tom Sawyer* starred Josh Albee as Tom, Vic Morrow as Injun Joe, Buddy Ebsen as Muff Potter and Jane Wyatt as Aunt Polly. In 1985, ABC-TV broadcast a "girls' " version, "The Adventures of Con Sawyer and Hucklemary Finn," with Drew Barrymore and Brady Ward. In 1982, Soviet television made a three-hour adaptation of *Tom Sawyer*.

Tom Sawyer Abroad (1894)   Mark Twain's third published story about Tom Sawyer and Huck Finn is a short novel that begins soon after *Adventures of Huckleberry Finn* concludes. From allusions to actual historical events within these stories, we can surmise that the events in

The route of the "erronorts" in Tom Sawyer Abroad.

Tom Sawyer Abroad occur around 1850. Mark Twain first published it as a serial that ran from November 1893 to April 1894, then released it as a book in New York and London.

Although Huck's narration sets the story up as a sequel to events in *Huckleberry Finn*, the story's mood makes it more of a sequel to the earlier story *The Adventures of Tom Sawyer*. Mark Twain's apparent shift in focus seems to have been reflected in his shifting titles for the story. Originally he planned to call it "Huck Finn in Africa," but was soon calling it "Huckleberry Finn and Tom Sawyer Abroad," or "Huck Finn Abroad." These last two titles and the final title, *Tom Sawyer Abroad*, recall Mark Twain's first travel book, *Innocents Abroad*, which recounts his own actual visit to North Africa in 1867.

Aside from the fact that much of the action takes place over the Sahara Desert and around the pyramids of Egypt, it has little to do with Africa. There is in fact an emptiness about the story in that aside from Tom, Huck and Jim, the only character with dialogue is the PROFESSOR, who disappears in chapter 4. Virtually all other characters are faceless figures observed from a distance. The action scenes in the book are brief and episodic, and a substantial part of the text is devoted to lengthy arguments between Tom and Huck and Jim.

Mark Twain evidently intended the story as the first part of a series of foreign travel adventures narrated by Huck. He seems to have been heading the adventure toward some kind of special plot device, but nothing extraordinary ever occurs. Indeed, the jarringly abrupt ending suggests that he ended the story in the middle of something longer. It may be that he intended to publish the rest if the first part proved popular, which it did not.

SYNOPSIS

Containing 34,000 words in 13 chapters narrated by Huck Finn, this story is a simple narrative of a fantastic balloon voyage. Tom, Huck and Jim go to ST. LOUIS to see a balloon craft on display. While they are inside the craft, the PROFESSOR, its unstable inventor, takes off before his visitors can get off. After teaching Tom how to work the craft's simple controls, the Professor directs the craft toward England. Somewhere over the Atlantic, he gets into a fight with Tom and falls overboard. The involuntary passengers continue the voyage and make their first landing in AFRICA's Sahara Desert. They continue across North Africa to the Sinai Peninsula, where the story abruptly ends.

Chapter 1
Tom Sawyer finds himself growing restless. The reputation he earned in his previous adventure as a distant traveler is wearing thin, and he resents seeing the town's elderly postmaster, Nat Parsons, regain his former glory as ST. PETERSBURG's greatest traveler. Parsons, it seems, went to WASHINGTON, D.C. 30 years earlier to ask the

president to pardon him for not being able to deliver a letter. After he returned from this magnificent adventure, people came from miles around just to hear his story.

Tom chafes at everything robbing attention from him: a horse race, a burning house, a circus, a slave auction, an ECLIPSE and a religious revival. He tries to figure out ways to make himself famous again and proposes to Huck and Jim, the former slave, that they launch a "Crusade."

Chapter 2
As one adventure scheme after another collapses, Tom despairs until he reads about a balloon in ST. LOUIS that is to sail to Europe. When he learns that Parsons plans to go there, he persuades Jim and Huck to accompany him to see the balloon. As they reach the strange contraption, they find a crowd making fun of the balloon's inventor. The PROFESSOR, as Huck calls him, grows irate when his efforts to talk back to the disrespectful crowd backfire.

Tom, Jim and Huck join the crowd inspecting the craft, which is like a small ship suspended from a giant oblong balloon with wings. They make a point of being the last to leave—especially since Parsons is aboard—but just as they are about to get off, a shout alerts them

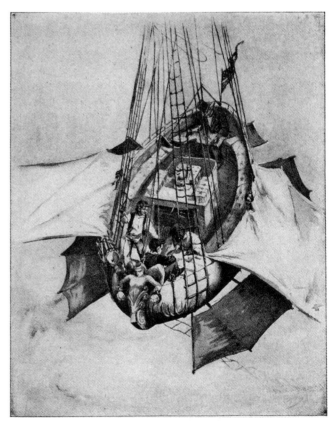

The mad Professor plots his course in chapter 4 of Tom Sawyer Abroad.

to the fact that the balloon is loose, and they are still on board as the craft rises. While the Professor crows about his success and his secret source of power, he makes Tom learn how to operate his ship and says that no one may get off. During the night, Tom tries to overpower the Professor, but gives up when he accidentally awakens him.

Chapter 3

The next morning, Tom, Huck and Jim argue over their location as they eat breakfast. With his newly acquired school learning, Huck insists that the different states that they fly over should have the same colors that they have on maps, bringing down Tom's derision. They also argue about time zones. When they realize that they are about to fly over the Atlantic Ocean, they beg the Professor to turn around, only to have him pull a pistol on them.

Chapter 4

As the balloon crosses the ocean, Tom, Jim and Huck nervously avoid the Professor, who says they will be in London in a day. Suddenly he challenges his passengers to admit that they want to leave him, and then goes to the other end of the ship and gets drunk while a storm builds up. He is overheard mumbling something about changing his course, away from England.

Out of the darkness of the storm, a flash of light reveals the Professor crawling toward Tom, threatening to throw him overboard. The sky darkens again the moment that he lunges at Tom, and then Huck sees Tom's head disappear over the edge of the ship. The Professor leaps after Tom. Jim and Huck hear screams from a great distance. When lightning flashes again, Tom's head reappears over the edge; the Professor does not return. Tom has been on a rope ladder, and explains that he was slow to climb back until he learned who had gone overboard. The storm continues.

Chapter 5

When Tom, Huck and Jim awaken the next morning, the storm is over. They decide to continue to England, since the craft is well stocked with food, clothes and trinkets—even money. Tom teaches the ship's simple controls to the others.

When they finally sight land the next morning, they are puzzled to see nothing but sand. Tom and Huck climb down the ladder to the land, where they are immediately chased by a lion. They make it back to the ladder, but in his panic Jim forgets how to operate the ship and there is a moment of great uncertainty until Tom climbs aboard and takes control. Meanwhile, Huck remains dangling over the lion, and more lions are approaching as the balloon slowly moves along. Tom and Huck face a dilemma: Huck does not want to climb the ladder, for fear that he will slip and let his leg dangle within the lions' reach, and Tom does not want to ascend too high, lest Huck get dizzy and fall. Tom finally shoots a lion so that Huck can scurry up the

ladder as the other lions turn on their wounded comrade.

Chapter 6

Once Huck is back on the ship, everyone is engulfed in fleas. Tom takes the balloon higher, until they reach air cool enough to drive the fleas away. Tom then realizes that they are in AFRICA's Sahara Desert. Huck sees a line on the ground that he thinks must be a line of longitude, but it turns out to be a camel caravan. When they descend for a closer look, caravan members fire on them, so they return to watch from a safer altitude. Meanwhile, horsemen swoop down on the caravan, and a terrific battle ensues. As the caravan repels the attack, a fleeing horseman snatches a baby from a woman's arms. The grief-stricken mother does not notice as Tom steers the airship into the kidnapper, knocking him off his horse. Jim lands to collect the baby and returns it to its mother, who rewards him with a gold chain.

Chapter 7

The balance of the day is spent arguing about such matters as fleas and the ARABIAN NIGHTS, and Huck muses over the pleasant similarities between life on the airship and life on a RAFT.

Chapter 8

The next morning they come across a caravan, all of whose members are dead. They help themselves to the weapons and valuables that they find and wonder what happened to the caravan as they leave it behind.

The mounting heat of the desert drives the party to search for water, but they only sight one mirage after another. Arguments over the existence of mirages lead into an argument about how much Catholic clerics cuss. By the time Jim and Huck have given up on finding water, Tom steers the ship over a lake in a real oasis. Tom, Huck and Jim take turns descending to swim, until more lions come along. Once again, Jim panics while at the helm, this time taking Tom and Huck to a high altitude as they hang on the rope ladder. Tom gets back in the ship and takes control, but Huck still hangs from the ladder, too exhausted to climb after him. Tom steers the ship back to the lake, where he instructs Huck to drop into the water to rest, while the lions busy themselves destroying the clothes that Tom, Huck and Jim left on shore, as well as each other.

Chapter 9

Tom, Huck and Jim haul a dead lion and a tiger cub aboard and use them for bait to fish from the balloon. Afterward they feast on lion and tiger steaks, fried fish, corn pone and dates plucked off the tops of palm trees. Tom lectures Huck and Jim on the size of the Sahara and gets into an argument with Jim about whether God would create something without value.

Chapter 10

Tom tells Huck and Jim a story from the Arabian Nights about a wandering dervish who tricks a greedy camel driver out of all his animals and wealth. When Jim suggests that the man learned a lesson from this experience, Tom argues that the lesson is useless, as Jim falls asleep. Tom then impresses Huck by piloting the ship to the exact hill in the desert that contains the treasure cave of the dervish story. They stop nearby to tan their animal hides in a salt pond.

Chapter 11

After a day or two of idle cruising, Tom, Huck and Jim come across another caravan that they observe from a distance for several days. Eventually, a sand storm comes along that engulfs both the balloon and the caravan. When the storm abates, the caravan is completely buried in sand-explaining the mystery of the dead caravan that they encountered earlier. In expressing the grief that they feel for the loss of the caravan, Huck reveals that while Tom, Huck and Jim were following the caravan, they closely observed its activities and assigned names to its members such as Elexander Robinson and Harryet McDougal.

The next day, they feel better, and they debate what to do with the tons of sand they have taken on. Jim suggests taking it home to sell; Tom counters by suggesting that there would be big money in selling it as *Sahara* sand, but then turns the argument around to point out that import duties would wipe out their profit. Once they agree to clean the sand from the ship, Tom suggests that in view of their different ages, he and Huck should each remove a fifth, and Jim the other three-fifths. Jim argues that it would be fairer if Huck and Tom each removed a *tenth*. Huck and Tom laugh over Jim's inverted math, but eventually help him do his share of the work.

Chapter 12

The ship eventually reaches EGYPT's pyramids, where Jim is overcome with emotion at being in the land of Moses. They maneuver through a thick fog until they find themselves at the SPHINX. After sailing around it, Tom lands Jim atop its head with an American flag to plant and then flies off to observe the effect with the benefit of "perspective." When Tom and Huck realize that angry people are trying to get at Jim, they rapidly return in the balloon, scattering his assailants.

As Tom, Huck and Jim cruise around the pyramids, Tom is moved by the antiquity of the surroundings to tell another story from the Arabian Nights, which leads to an argument about whether a bronze horse could actually have flown.

Chapter 13

As Jim pilots the balloon, Tom and Huck explore a pyramid and visit a nearby bazaar. Tom again amazes Huck when he finds the only surviving brick from a long-vanished house described in an Arabian Nights tale. Later, they hire a young man to be their guide and fly to the Red Sea and Mount Sinai.

When Tom's corncob pipe gives out on him, he decides to send Jim and the Egyptian guide back to St.

Petersburg to fetch another pipe from Aunt POLLY's house. He instructs Jim how to find his way home and back, gives him a note to leave for Aunt Polly, and sends Jim and the guide on their way as he and Huck relax on Mount Sinai. Two days later Jim returns with the pipe, but also with Aunt Polly's order to return home immediately. They comply and the story ends abruptly.

BACKGROUND AND PUBLISHING HISTORY

Mark Twain drafted notes for a balloon adventure in his NOTEBOOK as early as 1868, but evidently abandoned the idea a year later after learning that Jules Verne had published *Five Weeks in a Balloon*. Ironically, although Mark Twain appears to have originated this SCIENCE FICTION idea before he heard about Verne's story, several scenes in *Tom Sawyer Abroad* nearly duplicate episodes from Verne: the oasis scenes, the encounters with lions, the rescues from a suspended ladder, and the caravan buried by a sandstorm.

Mark Twain apparently wrote *Tom Sawyer Abroad* in response to a $5,000 offer from Mary Elizabeth Mapes DODGE for a boy's story for ST. NICHOLAS MAGAZINE, which she edited. The offer came at a moment when he was desperate for cash, so he began writing the story quickly while living in GERMANY in August 1892. He wrote half the book in five days.

After completing and revising the story, Mark Twain sent his typescripts to Frederick J. HALL, the head of his own publishing house, Charles L. WEBSTER & COMPANY, in the fall of 1892. He had it published in ST. NICHOLAS MAGAZINE, in which the story appeared in six installments between November 1893 and April 1894. Dan BEARD drew 29 pictures for the story, all but two of which were used in *St. Nicholas*.

Concerned about the possibility of offending his young readers, Mark Twain gave Dodge a free hand to edit his manuscript; he was too distracted by other matters to monitor the story's publication himself. However, while he was willing to accept Dodge's deletions—which were substantial—he was outraged by her substituting text for what she had removed. Dodge cleaned up Huck's grammar, removed or softened allusions to death, drunkenness, perspiration and swearing, and deleted a 650-word passage in chapter 8 about Roman Catholic clerics "cussing." Anxious not to offend racial sensitivities, Dodge permitted Jim to call black people "NIGGERS," but allowed white characters only to say "darkies." She even had Beard redraw several pictures to put shoes on the characters. According to Beard, Mark Twain entered the magazine's editorial office after the first installment appeared and proclaimed that while an editor could remove anything from his writings that she chose, "God Almighty Himself has no right to put words in my mouth that I never used!"

Mark Twain instructed Hall not to use the *St. Nicholas* text for the book edition, but by the time the book publisher received this order, type for the first nine chapters had already been set. Thus, only the last four chapters of the book had text that Mark Twain approved. Mark Twain's London publisher, CHATTO and Windus, prepared its edition from a carbon copy of his original typescript. Chatto's edition escaped Dodge's blue pencil, but did not incorporate all of Mark Twain's own final revisions.

Chatto and Windus issued the English edition on April 14, 1894, and Charles L. Webster issued the first American edition on April 18, 1894. The last book published by Webster, *Tom Sawyer Abroad* was, coincidentally, issued the day that the company filed for BANKRUPTCY. Two years later the story was republished by HARPER AND BROTHERS in a combined edition with *Tom Sawyer, Detective*—with which it has appeared in most subsequent editions.

Until 1980, when the University of California Press published an edition of *Tom Sawyer Abroad* corrected by the staff of the MARK TWAIN PAPERS project, no edition of the story had ever been faithful to Mark Twain's original intent. All American editions of the story had drawn on Dodge's bowdlerized version—the one still used by publishers seeking to take advantage of the original text's public domain status.

The earliest original manuscript of *Tom Sawyer Abroad* is in the New York Public Library. Complete notes on the corrected text can be found in the University of California editions.

Mark Twain's idea for a fantastic journey in a balloon was adapted to a motion picture, THE ADVENTURES OF MARK TWAIN (1985), which uses an airship modeled on that of *Tom Sawyer Abroad*. Animated by a technique called "claymation," Mark Twain himself pilots the airship, and his passengers are Tom, Huck and Becky Thatcher.

***Tom Sawyer Abroad; Tom Sawyer, Detective and Other Stories* (1896)**   Collection of short works first published by HARPER'S in 1896 and later reissued in many standard sets. Except for *Tom Sawyer, Detective*, all the items were published in earlier books. The collection incorporates most of THE STOLEN WHITE ELEPHANT (1882), including its title story and everything previously published in PUNCH, BROTHERS, PUNCH! (1878). Its contents include "SOME RAMBLING NOTES OF AN IDLE EXCURSION," "THE FACTS CONCERNING THE RECENT CARNIVAL OF CRIME IN CONNECTICUT," "THE GREAT REVOLUTION IN PITCAIRN," "THE CANVASSER'S TALE" and "THE LOVES OF ALONZO FITZ CLARENCE AND ROSANNAH ETHELTON."

Tom Sawyer Days, National   Annual Hannibal festival begun in the mid-1950s. A major tourist attraction staged over several days around the Fourth of July, the event includes a FENCE-painting contest, a frog-jumping competition and Tom Sawyer and Becky Thatcher lookalike contests.

***Tom Sawyer, Detective* (1896)**   Novella first published as a magazine serial. One of several sequels to *Huckle-*

Tom tells Aunt Polly that he does not want to go to Arkansas in chapter 1 of Tom Sawyer, Detective.

berry Finn, this story is set shortly after that earlier narrative, and like its predecessor, is narrated by Huck. Drawing on elements of a dramatic criminal trial held in Denmark in the 17th century, Mark Twain wrote this story to capitalize on the growing popularity of detective fiction stimulated by Arthur Conan Doyle's Sherlock HOLMES. *Tom Sawyer, Detective* uses many of Mark Twain's favorite themes: twins, switched identities, sleepwalking, a counterfeit deaf-and-dumb character and a murder trial. The narrative interweaves several mysteries that Tom Sawyer cleverly unravels in a climactic trial.

SYNOPSIS

The narrative contains 23,400 words divided into 11 chapters, with 30 percent of the text falling in the final chapter. It begins in Tom and Huck's hometown—presumably ST. PETERSBURG, though it is not mentioned by name—from which Tom and Huck travel to ARKANSAS to visit Sally and Silas PHELPS. After a STEAMBOAT journey lasting perhaps 10 days, they arrive in Arkansas on the first of September (although the first chapter sets the time as "spring"). The narrative concludes in mid-October.

The Phelpses are feuding with an unpleasant neighbor, Brace DUNLAP, who wants to marry Benny PHELPS. Shortly after Tom and Huck arrive, Brace's brother Jubiter DUNLAP disappears. It happens that during their steamboat trip to Arkansas, the boys meet Jubiter's long-missing twin brother, Jake DUNLAP, who is being pursued by fellow criminals whom he has double-crossed. About the same moment that Jubiter disappears, Jake is murdered by his former partners before anyone else knows he has returned home. When Tom and Huck meet Jubiter wearing the disguise that Jake planned to use, they believe him to be Jake.

Later, Tom and Huck discover the buried body of a man who is assumed to be Jubiter. Silas is arrested for Jubiter's murder, since he struck Jubiter shortly before his disappearance. When he goes to trial, his case looks hopeless, and he makes things worse by confessing. In a flash of brilliant deduction, however, Tom sorts out all the mysteries, identifies the true murder victim and his murderers, and earns a big reward for finding the stolen diamonds.

Chapter 1

During the spring following the time that Tom and Huck freed Jim from his imprisonment (in *Huckleberry Finn*), the boys are restless. They itch to travel, but Tom is reluctant to suggest going on a trip to his Aunt POLLY. One day, however, she surprises him with the news that his Aunt Sally PHELPS wants him and Huck to visit her in Arkansas. Sally hopes the boys will be a "diversion" from troubles that she and her husband Silas are having with a neighbor, Brace DUNLAP, who wants to marry their daughter Benny. While discussing this problem with Polly, Tom and Huck tell her about Brace's brothers, the twin, Jake and Jubiter DUNLAP.

Chapter 2

Tom and Huck take a STEAMBOAT down the Mississippi on a "thousand mile" trip to Arkansas. The boat has few passengers, who are mostly sleepy old people; it runs aground so often that it takes four days to reach the lower river. Meanwhile, the boys become interested in a passenger who locks himself in the next cabin. Determined to learn the man's secret, Tom bribes the waiters to let him and Huck enter the man's cabin in their place. The next day, the boys enter the cabin of the mysterious man. Tom immediately recognizes the man as Jubiter Dunlap, but the man nervously confesses that he is actually Jubiter's twin brother, Jake. Calling himself a "hard lot," Jake explains that he is hiding from pursuers. He is thrilled to learn from the boys

that folks in Arkansas already think that he is dead, as this will permit him to return home unrecognized. He gets the idea of pretending to be deaf and dumb from Tom's suggestion that his voice might give him away if he speaks.

Chapter 3

As the voyage continues, Huck and Tom spend most of their time with Jake to keep him company, and they describe everyone aboard the steamboat to him. Their information leads Jake to conclude that his pursuers are aboard, so he tells the rest of his story. Through a confidence trick, he and two partners, Bud Dixon and Hal Clayton, stole two diamonds worth $12,000 from a ST. LOUIS jewelry store. As they fled upriver on a steamboat, they realized that they could not trust each other. Unable to divide their two diamonds three ways, they had to stay together, but each man was afraid to go to sleep, for fear of being betrayed by the other two. When Dixon finally fell asleep, Jake and Clayton seized the paper containing the diamonds and left, only to discover that Dixon had substituted sugar lumps for the gems. After they returned to the cabin, Jake correctly guessed that Dixon was hiding the diamonds inside his boot heel.

Chapter 4

Jake continues his story. After the three criminals left the steamboat in northern Missouri, they took a room and gambled until the heavy-drinking Dixon fell asleep. Jake and Clayton removed their boots and Dixon's in order to search for the diamonds quietly. After failing to find anything, Jake casually slipped on Dixon's boots in place of his own, then fled north on foot, hoping that it would take Clayton a while to realize he had been conned. At Elexandria, Jake boarded the steamboat on which he has met Tom and Huck.

Jake now thinks that Clayton and Dixon are laying for him aboard the boat, which slowly moves down the river, stopping frequently for repairs. One night, it lands at a woodyard (identified as FLAGLER'S LANDING in chapter 11) about 40 miles north of the Phelpses'; the moment that a storm breaks, Jake slips ashore. Seconds later, the boys see two men rushing after him. Meanwhile, the boys have arranged to meet Jake at a sycamore grove near the Phelpses after they land and learn where Jake's brothers are.

Chapter 5

After further delays for repairs, the steamboat finally lands on the evening of September 2 and Huck and Tom go ashore. They rush to their rendezvous point, anxious to tell Jake why they are late. As they near the sycamore grove, they see men running into the woods and hear screams for help. Moments later, two other men enter the woods; then two men run out, chased by the other two. As the boys nervously watch from a hiding place, yet another figure emerges from the woods—a strange, tall man whom they take to be Jake Dunlap's ghost, wearing Jake's false whiskers and "goggles." After this specter walks by, other strollers appear: Bill and Jack Withers, and Lem Beebe and Jim Lane.

Chapter 6

Tom and Huck trail behind Lane and Beebe until they reach the Phelpses. Meanwhile, Tom points out that since the "ghost" was wearing boots, the thieves must not have removed Jake's boots before they fled. The diamonds must therefore still be in the real boots, which Tom proposes to buy at the auction that is certain to be held after the murder inquest. At the Phelpses' house, Aunt Sally greets the boys warmly, but Huck fails to provide a convincing explanation of why they were so long in getting to the house from the boat.

Chapter 7

At supper, Benny asks after Tom's family. Uncle Silas is visibly agitated—especially when Brace Dunlap's slave Billy comes to the door to ask where Jubiter is. After supper, Tom and Huck retire to a watermelon patch to talk and smoke. Later that night, as thoughts of murders and ghosts make sleep difficult, the boys look out their window and see a man in the yard carrying a shovel on his shoulder; because of his clothes, they assume it is Uncle Silas sleepwalking. A storm kicks up.

Before dawn, the boys awaken. Tom wonders why no one is discussing Jake's murder. They rise early and go out to listen for news, then visit the sycamore grove to see if Jake's boots are still on his body. Huck's nerve fails him, so Tom enters the grove alone, only to discover that the body is gone.

Chapter 8

Breakfast is not cheerful. Brace Dunlap's slave returns to ask after Jubiter, leaving Silas in a sorry state. Tom and Huck return to the woods, where they again see Jake's ghost. Tom soon deduces that the specter is not really a ghost, but Jake himself, still alive. He talks to the man, who initially acts irritated, but then gradually becomes pleasant. Afterward, the boys run into "some of Steve Nickerson's people," who ask all about the new stranger. They then visit a school, where the deaf-and-dumb stranger is already a subject of gossip.

Chapter 9

Over the next several days, the deaf-and-dumb man becomes popular in the area and Brace Dunlap wins public approval by taking him in. Meanwhile, search parties fail to turn up the missing Jubiter. After everyone else gives up, Tom borrows Jeff Hooker's bloodhound to continue the search with Huck. At the Phelpses', the dog finds a fresh grave in a tobacco field. With the help of passersby, they dig up Jubiter's body. When Tom rushes home to brag about his discovery, Uncle Silas nearly faints.

Chapter 10

Silas groans miserably, "I done it!" He explains that Jubiter so aggravated him that he finally "sort of lost his mind" and hit him over the head with a stick. Jubiter

ran off, but Silas is convinced that he has killed the man. Tom tells Silas that *he* could not have killed Jubiter; however, no one can imagine who else might have done it. The question of who buried Jubiter also nags at Huck and Tom, who recall seeing Silas with a shovel the night that Jubiter disappeared. Meanwhile, the sheriff arrests Silas and takes him to the town jail. Tom wants to organize an elaborate escape, but Silas squelches the idea. In order to be close to her husband, Aunt Sally goes into town to stay with the jailer's wife until the October trial, leaving the boys and Benny to manage the household.

Chapter 11

Each day, Tom and Huck visit Silas, but the old man is not holding up well and Tom tries to think of ways to help him. In mid-October, when the trial starts, the courtroom is jammed. Tom sits with Silas's "back-settlement lawyer," helping him wherever he can. After the jury is sworn in, the prosecuting attorney opens strongly, promising eyewitnesses who will testify to seeing Silas threaten, kill and bury Jubiter Dunlap. When witnesses testify about "bad blood" between Silas and Jubiter, Silas's lawyer is helpless, but Tom himself cross-examines them and trips them up on contradictions and inconsistencies.

Silas's case deteriorates rapidly after Lem Beebe testifies that he saw Silas killing Jubiter. Meanwhile, Tom

Tom astounds the court by revealing that a supposedly murdered man is alive in their midst in Tom Sawyer, Detective.

unaccountably drops into a "brown study," seemingly oblivious to the testimony. Jim Lane backs up Beebe's story, then Bill and Jack Withers testify that they saw Silas carrying Jubiter's body. When Brace Dunlap adds that he saw Silas bury Jubiter, Silas cries out, "It's true, every word—I murdered him in cold blood!"

Silas's sensational announcement fails to faze Tom. When Silas starts to explain how he killed Jubiter, however, Tom interrupts him. A murder *was* done, Tom announces, but Silas had no part in it. With the judge's permission, Tom outlines what really happened. After mentioning a reward poster for stolen diamonds that he has seen posted outside, he accuses Brace Dunlap of conspiring with his brother Jubiter to torment Silas. He pauses, then asks the court to consider how people who become lost in thought often do things unconsciously with their hands—such as drawing figures on their faces. As listeners nod in assent, Tom takes his narrative back to the night before the murder.

Without mentioning names, Tom tells about the diamond thieves aboard the steamboat that stopped at Flagler's Landing. About the same moment that Silas was striking Jubiter, he says, one of the jewel thieves was putting on a disguise in the sycamore grove. Moments later, the partners he betrayed fell on him and beat him to death. Two passersby heard the screams, chased the murderers away and returned to the scene of the crime. One of these men switched clothes with the murder victim in order to assume the dead man's disguise. That man was Jubiter Dunlap. Meanwhile, his companion lugged the murder victim away to Silas Phelps's property, where he took Silas's shovel and old work shirt and buried the murder victim in the tobacco field.

After a dramatic pause, Tom reveals that the dead man was *Jake* Dunlap and that the man who buried him was Brace Dunlap. He then announces that the deaf-and-dumb stranger sitting in the courtroom is *Jubiter*—which he proves by pulling off Jubiter's glasses and false beard. As listeners sing out Tom's praises, he supplies a motive for Brace and Jubiter's actions and denounces the prosecution witnesses as Brace's paid liars. He then adds a tantalizingly incomplete explanation of how he figured out the deaf-and-dumb stranger's true identity and waits for the crowd to insist that he complete his story. He recognized Jubiter, he explains, by his habit of tracing crosses on his cheek with a finger.

Praised by the judge, Tom modestly attributes his deductions to "just an ordinary little bit of detective work." Finally, he adds that there is a thief in the court with $12,000 worth of stolen diamonds on him. When he identifies Jubiter as the thief, Jubiter admits to all of Tom's other charges, but denies being a thief. The sheriff searches Jubiter, but turns up nothing. Tom then creates yet another sensation by extracting two big diamonds from Jubiter's boot.

The judge has Brace and his cohorts nabbed; a month later, they are tried and sent to jail. Meanwhile, Silas's reputation is restored and people flock to his church to hear his sermons. When Tom receives a $2,000 reward for recovering the diamonds, he gives half of it to Huck.

BACKGROUND AND PUBLISHING HISTORY

In late 1894, while he was living in FRANCE, Mark Twain drafted a story with the working title "Tom Sawyer's Mystery." By December he was living in Paris, where the wife of a Danish diplomat outlined for him the plot of the novel *The Minister of Veilby* (1829), by Steen Steensen Blicher (1782–1848) about a famous 17th-century murder case in Denmark. The details of that story so fascinated him that he completely rewrote his own mystery story in January, working in details from Blicher's novel. In an indirect effort to credit his source, he inserted this partly inaccurate footnote at the beginning of chapter 1:

> Strange as the incidents of this story are, they are not inventions, but facts—even to the public confession of the accused. I take them from an old-time Swedish criminal trial, change the actors, and transfer the scenes to America. I have added some details, but only a couple of them are important ones. — M. T.

Tom Sawyer, Detective was first published in HARPER'S MAGAZINE in August and September 1896, with 21 illustrations by A. B. FROST. The story's first book publication came in November 1896, when Harper's published it in *Tom Sawyer Abroad; Tom Sawyer, Detective and Other Stories*. CHATTO and Windus published the first British edition as *Tom Sawyer, Detective, as Told by Huck Finn and Other Tales* in December. *Tom Sawyer Abroad* and *Tom Sawyer, Detective* are often published together, but the latter—unlike the former—has never been issued as a book by itself.

In 1980 the MARK TWAIN PAPERS project issued a corrected edition of *Tom Sawyer, Detective*—along with *Tom Sawyer Abroad*—drawing on Mark Twain's original manuscripts and the story's first published versions. This edition is also the first since the original magazine serialization to incorporate all of Frost's drawings. The original handwritten manuscript is held by the Mark Twain Papers project in Berkeley; Mark Twain's own revised typescript is at the University of Kansas.

In 1938 Louis King directed a Paramount film, *Tom Sawyer, Detective*, with Billy Cook as Tom, Donald O'Connor as Huck, Porter Hall as Silas, Elizabeth Risdon as Sally, William Haade as Jake and Jubiter, and Clara Blandick in her third film portrayal of Aunt Polly.

"Tom Sawyer's Conspiracy" Unfinished short novel begun in 1897. One of the last stories of the Tom Sawyer / Huckleberry Finn cycle, "Conspiracy" opens shortly after *Tom Sawyer, Detective* (1896) concludes and about a year after the events of *Huckleberry Finn*. Back home looking for ways to stir up excitement, Tom,

Huck and Jim are accidentally caught up in the midst of a murder. The story reflects Mark Twain's interest in detectives. He models many minor characters on people he knew in Hannibal and makes fun of their misreading of clues. After the slave dealer is murdered, for example, Detective Flacker suspects that John MURRELL's gang (called "Burrell" here) is behind the crime.

While the story alludes to many characters and events from earlier Tom and Huck tales, its inconsistencies indicate that Mark Twain paid scant attention to certain details. For example, Miss WATSON—who dies in *Huckleberry Finn*—is alive and well here. In chapter 7, Huck encounters his former nemeses, the KING and DUKE. He expects them to be mad at him for costing them money when he freed Jim in Arkansas; however, the escape episode in *Huckleberry Finn* actually has nothing to do with them. Mark Twain's confusion about the ending of *Huckleberry Finn* is ironic, since he originally considered climaxing that novel with a trial scene in which Tom dramatically saves Jim from being convicted for Huck's murder—an ending he reworked for "Conspiracy."

SYNOPSIS

This story narrated by Huck contains about 29,000 words in 10 chapters. To enliven the coming summer, Tom, Huck and Jim plan to conduct a "conspiracy" that will shake up the town (presumably ST. PETERSBURG) with a phony abolitionist scare. After Tom disguises himself as a runaway slave, Huck will sell him to a slave dealer, from whom Tom will then escape in order to make it appear that abolitionists have struck. The scheme unravels when real criminals pull a similar trick on the slave dealer and murder him. Tom and Huck learn where the murderers are hiding, but after Jim is charged with the murder, Tom wants to take his time catching the criminals in order to rescue Jim in a dramatic trial. Once the criminals get away, however, Jim's situation becomes perilous. Huck accidentally meets the King and Duke, who offer to get Jim out of Missouri with forged papers and then take him downriver and sell him back into slavery. Figuring that they can rescue Jim later, Huck and Tom accept the plan; however, Jim's peril intensifies when the scoundrels fail to return until his trial is nearly over.

Chapter 1
Huck is again living with the Widow DOUGLAS, for whom Jim—no longer a slave—now works on salary. As summer approaches, Huck goes to JACKSON'S ISLAND with Jim and Tom Sawyer to discuss how they will spend their time. Huck is content to let things happen, but Tom wants to get up a "civil war." Jim objects to the absurdity of calling any war "civil," so Tom suggests starting a "revolution" instead. This time Jim objects because a proper revolution requires a king to overthrow—and he had his fill of kings the previous summer. Everyone rejects Tom's proposal to start an

"insurrection" because the idea is too hazy, but all three agree to get up a "conspiracy."

Chapter 2
Tom suggests creating an abolitionist scare in town. After setting up rendezvous points at scattered places, the conspirators make the island cave in which Jim and Huck hid the previous year their headquarters. In their first official meeting, Tom proposes beginning the conspiracy by running off a slave. Since they cannot run off any real slave, Tom suggests making a fake one—namely himself. He will put on blackface, pretend to be deaf and dumb, and hide in the HAUNTED HOUSE as if he were a runaway, so that Huck can betray him to the slave trader Bat BRADISH. After Bradish announces that he has a runaway, Jim and Huck will free Tom to launch the conspiracy.

Chapter 3
Back in town, Tom writes up a handbill, describing himself—as he will appear in disguise—as a runaway Arkansas slave with a $100 reward on his head. He and Huck then ride a canoe down to HOOKERVILLE to have handbills printed which they hang at the post office at night. Afraid that his brother Sid SAWYER might interfere with the conspiracy, Tom decides to catch measles from Joe HARPER so that Aunt Polly will send Sid away to their uncle Fletcher's farm. The trick works; however, Tom contracts not measles, but scarlet fever—which nearly kills him.

Chapter 4
After Tom recovers fully, the conspirators meet again in their island cave. Tom chisels a cryptic call to arms from the "Sons of Freedom" on a block of wood, which he uses to print a handbill. The printed bill unexpectedly reads backwards, but Tom decides that its message is more mysterious this way. The morning after he and Huck post this message in town, Aunt Polly and others are panicked by the prospect of an abolitionist invasion. Detective Jake Flacker takes charge of the investigation, and Colonel Elder is elected to command troops to guard the town. Huck wonders how the conspirators will get around with soldiers everywhere, but Tom accurately predicts that he will be appointed a spy because of his reputation in the (Jubiter) DUNLAP case. To allay Aunt Polly's growing fears, Tom posts a message from the "Sons of Freedom" on her house and others, ordering that no harm befall them. News of the conspiracy spreads as far as ST. LOUIS.

Chapter 5
After the boys post more runaway-slave bills around town, Huck tells Bradish that he knows where the "runaway" is. However, since Bradish has just paid someone else $200 for another runaway with a $500 reward on him, he is not ready to take on a second captive slave. Tom sneaks onto Bradish's property to examine the sleeping runaway, whom he discovers to be a disguised white man. Since the fake slave has a key hidden in his

shoe, he obviously plans to escape that night. Huck wants to call the sheriff to prevent this impending crime, but Tom wants to let matters unfold so that they can have fun helping to catch the criminals later. Meanwhile, they continue their original plan by having Jim blow a horn that night as their make-believe abolitionist signal.

Chapter 6
Before dawn, the boys return to Bradish's, where the slave dealer lies murdered and the fake runaway is gone. Tom finds the footprints of four men, including Jim—who he thinks must have gone for help. As the boys follow the tracks of the fake slave and his accomplice, Tom sees signs indicating that one of them has broken his leg, and he concludes that the fugitives must still be nearby. At the haunted house, Tom crawls under the floor and overhears the criminals talking.

Excited by how this real crime will improve his original conspiracy plans, Tom is even more pleased when he hears that Jim has been arrested for Bradish's murder. The news appalls Huck, but Tom is confident that Jim will go free and end up a hero. When the boys visit Jim in jail, Tom upsets him by trying to invent a motive explaining why Jim would kill Bradish; he figures that getting Jim charged with first-degree murder will make his later rescue an even bigger triumph. Since Bradish once arranged with Miss Watson to sell Jim down the river, Tom suggests revenge as Jim's motive for killing Bradish and makes sure that the district attorney hears about it.

Chapter 7
With most townspeople thinking that Jim is linked with abolitionists, there is talk of lynching him. Huck wants to save Jim immediately, but Tom insists on using the month that it will take before Jim's trial starts to nab the true culprits. After the boys find that the criminals have left the haunted house, however, Tom finally realizes how great Jim's peril is. Now remorseful, Tom gets Huck to rush downriver with him to catch up with the STEAMBOAT on which the criminals must be fleeing. Aboard the boat, Huck stumbles into the KING and DUKE—the scoundrels he knew a year ago. When he describes Jim's plight, they suggest selling Jim down the river as an alternative to hanging.

Chapter 8
The Duke proposes that he and the King go to St. Louis to have the forged documents that they are carrying modified to show that Jim has murdered someone elsewhere; they will then use these papers to get Jim out of Missouri so they can take him downriver and sell him. Huck agrees to the plan, confident that he and Tom can later rescue Jim and take him to ENGLAND to be free. Though Tom does not see the King and Duke himself, he approves their scheme after he later goes ashore with Huck. For once, Tom wants to use the *quickest* means to free Jim, instead of the showiest.

Though not pleased with the new plan, Jim agrees to trust the boys. That night at Aunt Polly's house, Detective Flacker spins theories about the murder, which he thinks was perpetrated by Burrell's gang.

Chapter 9
The next day, the boys search futilely for the tracks of the real murderers. Despairing of capturing the criminals, Tom gets a new idea: He and Huck will accompany the King and Duke as they convey Jim downriver; then, when they reach CAIRO, Illinois, he will buy Jim's freedom from the scoundrels for $1,000—an offer they will not refuse. Thrilled with this plan, Huck insists on paying half; the plan also cheers up Jim. The next day, each boy draws $800 from the money that Judge THATCHER manages for them.

With Jim's trial set for three weeks later, the boys become uneasy when the King and Duke fail to return as promised, so they go to St. Louis to look for them. After four days of fruitless searching, they return home and try to keep Jim cheerful.

Chapter 10
When Jim's trial finally opens, the prosecution presents a strong case. Huck testifies on Jim's behalf, but no one believes his story about the fake "conspiracy." Tom is more convincing, however, and the crowd's sympathies shift toward Jim until the judge asks Tom why he did not tell his story immediately after the murder. After Tom cannot answer, the jury swiftly returns a guilty verdict. As the judge is about to pronounce a death sentence on Jim, the King and Duke suddenly enter the courtroom. The moment they speak, Tom jumps up to denounce *them* as the murderers, saying that their voices are the same ones that he heard in the haunted house. The story ends just as he starts to produce his proofs— a drawing of the King's shoe-print and a set of false teeth that he took from the fake runaway slave's mouth.

BACKGROUND AND PUBLISHING HISTORY

Mark Twain began this story while living in SWITZERLAND in 1897. After tinkering with it for several years, he abandoned it suddenly, though it appears to be nearly complete. It was first published in *Hannibal, Huck & Tom* (1969), a volume of the MARK TWAIN PAPERS project edited by Walter BLAIR. It also appears in *Huck Finn and Tom Sawyer Among the Indians* (1989), edited by Blair and Dahlia Armon.

***A Tramp Abroad* (1880)** The third of Mark Twain's five travel books, *A Tramp Abroad* is the only one that he wrote about a trip that he made solely for the purpose of writing a book. He was in Europe from April 1878 until August 1879. The book covers only about the first third of the 16½ months of his journey.

In April 1878, Mark Twain sailed to GERMANY with his wife and daughters, a German nursemaid named Rosina (Rosa) Hay, and Livy's friend Clara Spaulding.

The narrator struggles to write A Tramp Abroad *in True Williams's frontispiece.*

They spent four months in HEIDELBERG and BADEN-BADEN, where Joseph TWICHELL joined them in August. From there, they went to SWITZERLAND, where Mark Twain and Twichell spent a month touring the ALPS together. After Twichell returned home in September, the Clemenses spent two months in ITALY, three months in MUNICH and nearly four months in PARIS. They then made quick visits to BELGIUM and HOLLAND and spent a month in ENGLAND before returning home in August 1879.

Most of *A Tramp Abroad* pertains to the time Mark Twain spent in southwestern Germany and Switzerland, with a few chapters on eastern France and northern Italy. As with his other travel books, he slips in stories not integrally related to his travels. These include Jim Baker's BLUEJAY YARN, "THE MAN WHO PUT UP AT GADSBY'S" and a tale about Nicodemus DODGE. The book also relates many German legends, including several of Mark Twain's own invention.

While most of the incidents in *A Tramp Abroad* mirror Mark Twain's real European experiences, the book's narrator is a different persona. Apart from a burlesque anecdote in chapter 8, in which he signs a note "Mark Twain," the narrator never identifies himself beyond the fact that he is an American who is anxious to travel through Europe on foot, study art and learn GERMAN. He travels with an "agent," Mr. HARRIS—whose background is even murkier. The narrator never mentions having a family and appears to be a young bachelor, particularly when he alludes to taking a woman to a ball (chapter 18).

The narrator's mask tends to fall away as his story unfolds, and he increasingly resembles veteran European traveler Mark Twain. He alludes to having been on a Mississippi STEAMBOAT as a boy (chapter 10), working in a printing office in Missouri (chapter 23), being near NEVADA silver mines (chapter 42), and being with the "INNOCENTS ABROAD" (chapter 47). Chapter 49 reveals more of his background by listing American dishes he craves. In addition to numerous "Southern-style" items, he specifies dishes from Baltimore, Boston, Illinois, Missouri, New Orleans, Philadelphia, San Francisco, the Sierra Nevada, Tahoe, the Mississippi and Virginia—all places Mark Twain had been, with the exception of Virginia, where his father was born.

Although Mark Twain went to Europe intending to write a book about his trip, he was unclear about the approach he should take until he was well into his manuscript. Even then, he lacked a clear focus. The book's title reflects his inconsistency: "A Tramp" could be either a journey on foot or a vagabond. A central theme of the book is a running joke about unfulfilled goals. While the narrator constantly proposes to undertake ambitious *walking* journeys, he invariably ends up *riding*—on anything from donkey carts and rafts to steamboats and trains. The "tramp" that never quite materializes ties in to several other jokes. The travelers carry a pedometer that registers wildly inaccurate distances. When they "climb" in the Alps, they encounter exaggerated perils. For example, an easy afternoon ascent of the RIFFELBERG becomes a huge week-long expedition (chapters 37–40). Later, the narrator ascends Mont BLANC by telescope (chapter 44).

The travelers also never get around to learning German or mastering painting. They give up on the language when they discover that most Germans speak English (chapter 11). Their study of art and music leads the narrator to the conclusion that "high" art cannot be appreciated without training, since no one can like it naturally. As the narrative nears its end, it offers increasingly harsh views on Europe that reflect the fatigue that overcame Mark Twain as he wrote. He is especially critical of European manners (chapters 27 and 47), water (chapter 46), and food (chapter 49).

A minor theme throughout the book is the narrator's frequent encounters with talkative Americans, including Cholley ADAMS (chapter 20), a playful woman (chapter 25) and two unnamed garrulous young men (chapters 27 and 38).

While the narrator of *A Tramp Abroad* never hints that he is married, one might read into the narrative Mark Twain's gentle teasing of his wife in the narrator's playful mockery of studying art (chapters 11, 14, 42 and 48) and collecting bric-a-brac (chapters 20–22)—activities to which Livy and Clara Spaulding devoted much of their time during the trip. The book also contains a surprising number of tales about lovers destroying each other (chapters 15, 16 and 19).

SYNOPSIS

The 50 numbered chapters and six appendixes of *A Tramp Abroad* contain 157,000 words of text. The narrative moves unevenly and has little relationship to how Mark Twain distributed his time during his actual travels. The first half of the book is set in southwestern GERMANY. Chapters 1 through 20 cover the narrator's arrival and stay in HEIDELBERG. Within this section are discussions of Heidelberg student life and DUELING (chapters 4–7), music and drama in MANNHEIM (chapters 9–10) and an expedition on the NECKAR River (chapters 11–19). Chapter 3 contains the unrelated BLUEJAY YARN and chapter 8 discusses French dueling. In chapter 20, the narrator shifts his base to BADEN-BADEN, whence he and Harris tour the BLACK FOREST (chapters 22–24).

Most of the second half of *A Tramp Abroad* covers the narrator's alpine experiences in SWITZERLAND and eastern France (chapters 25–47). After an interlude at LUCERNE (chapters 25–27), the travelers visit the RIGI-KULM (chapters 28–29), then go from Lucerne to ZERMATT and the MATTERHORN, by way of INTERLAKEN and the JUNGFRAU (chapters 31–41). The book's most dramatic adventure is the ascent of the RIFFELBERG (chapters 37–40). From Zermatt, the narrator goes to Lake Geneva and Mont BLANC, where he spends several days at Chamonix (chapters 42–46), concluding his time in Switzerland at Geneva (chapter 47).

The last three chapters cover visits to cities in northern ITALY, with brief remarks about Rome, Munich, Paris, Holland, Belgium, England and sailing home to America (chapters 48–50). The appendixes include discussions of hotel *portiers*, Heidelberg's castle and "college prison," the GERMAN language and German newspapers.

The first 29 chapters of both one- and two-volume editions of *A Tramp Abroad* have the same numbers. Chapters in the second volume of two-volume editions are numbered 1 through 21; this synopsis gives both sets of chapter numbers. All text that does not come directly from the book's chapters is enclosed in parentheses.

Chapter 1
In March 1878, the narrator of this book believes that it is time for another young man to travel through Europe on foot. To accompany him as his agent, he hires Mr. HARRIS, who shares his eagerness to study art

and GERMAN in Europe. In April, they sail aboard the HOLSATIA. After arriving in GERMANY, they rest briefly at Hamburg, then take an express train south, halting at Frankfurt. The narrator buys a copy of F. J. Kiefer's *The Legends of the Rhine*, translated by L. W. Garnham—who builds English sentences on the German plan, punctuating them with no plan at all. An example of Garnham's toothsome translation is "The Knave of Bergen"—a legend about an executioner who attends a royal masquerade ball disguised as a mysterious knight. After he dances with the queen, his identity is revealed and the outraged king orders his execution. The man saves himself by suggesting that the king knight him to remove the dishonor he has brought on the queen.

Chapter 2
At another stop, the narrator becomes interested in the official called the *portier*, a kind of first-mate of the hotel (also discussed in Appendix A). Meanwhile, the hotel makes elaborate preparations for the arrival of the Grand Duke and Duchess of Baden and the Empress of Germany.

In HEIDELBERG, Harris and the narrator take rooms at the Schloss Hotel, from which they have a serene view of Heidelberg Castle. The charm of the lofty hills around the town is enhanced by the legends and fairy tales that the narrator has been reading. One day he gets lost in the woods and imagines that the ravens are talking about him. Animals *do* talk to each other; however, the only man who truly understands them is a California miner named Jim BAKER, whom he quotes at length on the language of bluejays.

Chapter 3
Baker began learning jay language seven years earlier, when his last neighbor left. One day Baker saw a jay land on the roof of his neighbor's vacant cabin, on which the jay found a hole. Congratulating himself on his luck, the jay began filling the hole with acorns. While he worked, he muttered about the disappearance of his acorns into the hole, and vowed to fill the hole if it took a hundred years. As his frustration mounted, he became profane. When a passing jay stopped to investigate, the first jay showed him the hole and explained how many acorns he had put in it. Other jays arrived, examined the hole and discussed the mystery. They called in still more jays, until perhaps 5,000 were jawing and cussing. Each one expressed a chuckle-headed opinion about the hole, until one of them found the cabin's open door. When they all realized that the jay had been trying to fill up a house, they laughed heartily. Every summer over the next three years jays revisited the famous hole.

Chapter 4
During the summer semester, students are common figures around Heidelberg. Most do not wear badges or uniforms, but a tenth of them wear caps denoting five social organizations called "corps" that are famous for

DUELING with swords. Although German university life puts few restraints on students, the vast majority work hard and get solid educations. The students have excellent manners, but the elaborate and rigid etiquette of the corps forbids members from showing any courtesies to rival corpsmen.

Chapter 5
The narrator visits a dueling place on a day when the Red Cap Corps is taking on challengers in one of the twice-weekly combats. A White Cap corpsman acts as his host for the proceedings. Duelists wear goggles, ear protectors and heavy padding over their bodies, but use razor-sharp blades and fight with lightning intensity as a surgeon stands by. The first duel ends with both men bloodied and too weary to continue, but does not "count" because it is a draw lasting less than 15 minutes. In the second duel, a White Cap corpsman upsets a man considered a superior swordsman.

Chapter 6
The third and fourth duels end quickly when the surgeon intervenes to treat badly wounded combatants. The fifth duel is unusual in being an affair of "satisfaction" between students not affiliated with any corps. Through all this fighting, the narrator sees men receive hideous wounds, but never hears a victim wince or moan.

Chapter 7
In addition to their many laws, the corps also have customs that have the force of law. For example, the laws may not require a member to fight in certain circumstances in which custom dictates that he *must*. It is said that duelists prefer facial wounds because the scars show well, and that they deliberately even make their wounds heal badly. Whether or not this is true, many young German men have grim scars.

Chapter 8
The modern French duel may be ridiculed, but it is actually dangerous. Since it is always fought outside, combatants are nearly certain to catch cold—which is how the famous duelist Paul de Cassagnac (1843–1904) became an invalid.

When the narrator hears of trouble between his old friend GAMBETTA and Fourtou in the French assembly, he goes straight to Gambetta to be his second. However, he acts under a French name—which is why newspapers allude to Gambetta's second as a Frenchman. After having Gambetta draw up a will, the narrator proposes weapons to Fourtou's second—signing his note "Mark Twain." He suggests axes, but Fourtou's second shudders and says that the French code disallows them. The code also forbids rifles and COLT revolvers. Eventually, Fourtou's second produces dainty pistols and proposes a distance of 65 yards between the duelists; however, the narrator talks him down to 35 yards. The morning of the duel, the duelists cannot see each other in the

heavy fog, so the narrator has to stand behind Gambetta to holler out his position. After both men fire, Gambetta collapses on top of the narrator. Gambetta is unhurt, but the narrator has several broken bones and crushed organs—making him the only man hurt in a French duel in 40 years.

Chapter 9
One day, the travelers visit MANNHEIM to see SHAKESPEARE's *King Lear* performed in German, but do not understand a single word. On another visit to Mannheim, they hear the opera *Lohengrin* (by Richard WAGNER), which the narrator finds unbelievably and painfully noisy. He wonders whether others in the audience naturally like such noise, or if they learn to like it.

Chapter 10
Three or four hours is a long time to sit, yet Wagner operas lasting six hours leave some people actually wishing for more! A German woman explains that one must *learn* to like Wagner's music. After she praises a tenor who has lost his voice, the narrator realizes that Germans appreciate singers for what they *were* as much as for what they are. Why do we regard Germans as stolid and phlegmatic when the opposite seems to be true? Germans also have some admirable customs in their theaters—such as dimming the house lights as the curtain rises. In MUNICH concerts, late-comers are not seated while music is playing. On the other hand, our custom of scattering applause is better than the German custom of saving it up until an act ends.

Watching an old German actor rage around the stage with no audience response makes the narrator think how sick and flat the actor must feel. It reminds him of a moment on a Mississippi STEAMBOAT years earlier when a 10-year-boy awakened excitedly from a troubled sleep to sound the alarm for a fire. Instead of rousing everyone into action as he expected, he was merely advised to dress more warmly. That boy was the narrator.

Chapter 11
During Heidelberg's pleasant summer days, the travelers train for pedestrian tours and make satisfying progress in their German and art studies. After the narrator paints "Heidelberg Castle Illuminated," he and Harris open a studio. As they await orders, they decide to travel up the NECKAR to HEILBRONN with X and Z. They all wear slouch hats, blue army shirts and overalls and carry knapsacks, opera glasses, canteens, ALPENSTOCKS and sun-umbrellas. Harris also takes a pedometer. Downtown, they board a train, reasoning that they can do their walking on the way back. At picturesque Wimpfen, they eat dinner and nap before setting out again. This time they ride a peasant cart into Heilbronn, where they stay at an inn in which the robber-knight Götz von BERLICHINGEN stayed four centuries earlier. Harris and the narrator share a huge room with beds at opposite

ends and a round table as large as King ARTHUR's in the middle.

Chapter 12
Heilbronn's most picturesque Middle-Age architecture is the *Rathhaus,* or municipal building, whose archive contains a letter written by von Berlichingen. The travelers hire von Berlichingen's own hack and horse to visit a feudal castle noted for withstanding a great siege during the Middle Ages. After the castle finally surrendered, the victorious commander ordered all its men to be killed; however, when the castle's women begged for mercy, he granted one grace—that each woman could remove whatever she could *carry* away. As the castle gates swung open the next day, the women marched out carrying their husbands on their backs.

Chapter 13
At the hotel, the narrator winds Harris's pedometer and pockets it as both men retire early. Harris falls asleep immediately, but the narrator frets and cannot drop off. Later he throws whatever he can find at a noisy mouse, waking up Harris with a shoe and breaking a mirror. The mouse goes away, but new disturbances rob his sleep. Convinced that he will never sleep, he rises to go outside and dresses himself in the dark. In a prolonged search for a missing sock, he bumps into much more furniture than he remembers being in the room. After giving up on the sock, he makes for the door, but cannot find it. He now realizes he is lost; he cannot even find the door by feeling his way along the wall. He retreats to the middle of the room, intending to use the table as a base of departure, only to remember that its round shape makes it useless for orientation. Wandering about randomly, he knocks things down until he rouses the whole house. When X and Z enter with candles, the fresh illumination reveals that he has been circling the same chair all night. According to the pedometer, he has traveled 47 miles.

Chapter 14
Already impressed by the fact that Harris and the narrator are "artists," the landlord is even more impressed to hear that they are on a walking tour of Europe. He explains the road to them, provides them with a lunch and sends them off in von Berlichingen's carriage. When the narrator sees men assembling log rafts, he announces his intention of returning to Heidelberg on a raft. Though his companions fear the dangers of the deep, he charters the longest and finest raft available and its crew.

Chapter 15
As the raft drifts down the gentle river, the travelers watch people work the fields and they gossip with men who hop aboard. As the day grows hotter, the travelers shed their garments, dangle their legs overboard and watch boys swim out to the raft. They pass a steamboat pulling itself on a chain and they see many keelboats. Ashore they buy beer and chickens to eat on the raft.

When they pass von Berlichingen's old castle at Hornberg, they hear the legend of "The Cave of the Specter":

> Seven hundred years ago, beautiful young Lady Gertrude loved her poorest suitor, a Crusader named Sir Wendel Lobenfeld. Insisting that Gertrude choose someone worthier, her father locked her up, but she escaped to a cave down the river. Every midnight, she emerged to sing a plaintive love song that Wendel had composed, causing superstitious peasants to think her cave haunted. When Wendel finally returned from the Crusades, Gertrude's repentant father welcomed him as a son, but Wendel was so broken-hearted by losing Gertrude that he wanted only to find a worthy death for himself. Answering the peasants' plea to rid the haunted cave of its dragon, he boated downstream at midnight and fired his crossbow at the white figure emerging from the cave.

Chapter 16
Germany is rich in folk songs, including the popular "LORELEI," about a legend of the Rhine which the narrator likes so much that he reprints Garnham's translation:

> Lore was a beautiful water nymph who sat atop a rock above the Rhine called Lei, luring boatmen to their destruction with her plaintive songs. After falling hopelessly in love with Lore, young Count Hermann boated out to the Lei to offer her his songs. As he sang, the rock erupted in flames and the fairy rose above it, beckoning to him as she called forth waves to destroy his boat. Since then, the fairy has not been seen, but her sorrowful voice is still heard from her crystal castle.

For 40 years, Heinrich Heine's "The Lorelei" has been a favorite German song. The narrator prints its score and original German lyrics, along with his own translation and Garnham's—which is as succinct as an invoice. Garnham is a poet whom he wishes to make known in America; however, even he has a rival. In Munich, Mr. X bought *A Catalogue of Pictures in the Old Pinacotek,* containing such happy English captions as "St. Bartholomew and the Executioner with the knife to fulfil the martyr."

Meanwhile, the raft moves on.

Chapter 17
Near Eberbach they see a crumbling ruin known as the "Spectacular Ruin," whose legend the captain relates:

> During the Middle Ages, a fire-breathing dragon so terrorized the region that the emperor promised to grant whoever destroyed it anything he asked. After the dragon consumed many renowned knights, however, heroes became scarcer and panic spread. Finally, a poor knight from a distant country, Sir Wissenschaft ("Sir Science"), took up the challenge. Though his arrival provoked derision, he calmly went forth armed only with a knapsack. When the dragon

attacked him, he took a modern fire-extinguisher from his sack and quenched the dragon's flames, killing it. For his reward, Wissenschaft asked for a monopoly on making and selling spectacles. Though outraged, the emperor granted his request. However, Wissenschaft then reduced spectacle prices so much that a crushing burden was lifted from the nation and the grateful emperor decreed that everyone must buy and wear spectacles whether they needed them or not.

After the Spectacular Ruin, the raft passes a pile of castellated buildings, whose legend the narrator does not repeat because he doubts the truth of some of its details. The travelers also pass Italian laborers blasting a path for a new railway, but they can do little to dodge the resulting showers of stones.

The captain wants to stop for the night, but the narrator insists on continuing on to Hirschhorn. When the sky grows overcast, everyone else wants to land, but the narrator again orders that they go on. In the growing dark, the wind rises and the crew jumps to meet the storm. With the sea running "inches high," the mate reports that the raft has sprung a leak! Only a miracle will save them now. As the captain orders men forward to bail, cries of "Man overboard!" and "Breakers ahead!" are heard. All is saved, however, when a man jumps ashore and passes a line around a tree. Near midnight, they reach Hirschhorn's "Naturalist Tavern," which takes its name from its display cases of stuffed wildlife specimens.

Chapter 18

The next morning, they breakfast in the garden and encounter the living portion of the tavern's vast menagerie. A pitiable old raven catches the narrator's attention, but he admits that only Bayard TAYLOR can understand an animal's moral nature. After breakfast, they climb to Hirschhorn's decaying ancient castle and try to hire a skiff to take them to Neckarsteinach. The narrator cannot make himself understood in German, but Mr. X gets results simply by asking (in English), "Can man boat get here?" They decide against taking a boat, however, after the raftsmen discover that the raft's "leak" is merely a crack between its logs.

Bowing courteously to strangers at tables is a German custom that foreigners have trouble mastering. The narrator almost missed a train once because he was uncertain whether to bow to women before leaving his table. Germans also have a winning friendliness. Once, for example, Harris and the narrator exchanged bows with two young women and a man at a BLACK FOREST inn. Later, these same people treated them like old friends in Allerheiligen and helped them plan their route. Later still, the narrator was at a ball in Baden-Baden with a young American woman whose dress was somehow not up to standard. They were spared embarrassment when an elegant German woman whisked his companion away for a proper outfitting.

One of the hikers they met earlier, this helpful woman turned out to be a duchess.

Chapter 19

At Neckarsteinach, the travelers dine and plan a visit to the quaint village of Dilsberg across the river. Dilsberg's inhabitants are all blood-kin, but the narrator sees no idiots among them; the captain explains that the government carts them off to asylums. The village's chief pride is an ancient well, which legend claims had a subterranean passage through which supplies were brought to the village during sieges. Under an old linden tree, the captain recites the "Legend of Dilsberg Castle":

In old times, Dilsberg Castle had a haunted chamber in which anyone who slept would not wake up for 50 years. When a superstitious young knight, Conrad von Geisberg, proposed dismantling this dangerous chamber, friends decided to play a prank on him. His betrothed, Catharina, begged him to spend a night in the haunted chamber. When he woke up, the room was cobwebby and moldy, his clothing was decayed and he felt weak with age. Outside the room, he met strangers who explained that many years had passed. When told that Catharina had died of heartbreak 50 years earlier, Conrad vowed that he too would die of grief. Then young arms surrounded him and Catharina revealed that it was all a jest—he had only been drugged for one night. It was too late; Conrad could not be brought out of his daze.

After hearing this story, the travelers resume their voyage to Heidelberg.

Chapter 20

At Heidelberg, the narrator learns that his trunk has finally arrived from Hamburg and warns readers that when Germans say "immediately," they mean about a week. In preparing for his departure from town, the narrator's chief concern is his ceramics collection, which includes an Etruscan tear-jug and an Henri II plate. Although many people regard bric-a-brac hunting as an activity not suitably robust for a man, the narrator is proud of being a bric-a-brac hunter and "ceramiker."

After a day or two in farewell visits, the travelers take a train to BADEN-BADEN in the Rhine Valley. They get off at Oos and walk the remaining distance—aside from a lift on a passing wagon. They encounter an American minister who is an old friend. As they talk, a young American named Cholley ADAMS floods them with questions and ends up spending the evening with the minister.

Chapter 21

Situated in beautiful hills, Baden-Baden attracts visitors with hot baths famous for curing rheumatism. An unpleasant encounter with an imperious servant girl at the baths typifies the bad manners of local shopkeepers. Though an inane town, filled with sham and petty

No expert is needed to identify which part of this picture was drawn by Mark Twain and which by Walter Francis Brown in chapter 21 *of* A Tramp Abroad.

fraud, Baden-Baden has good baths and the narrator is pleased to leave his rheumatism there. The travelers stay at the Hôtel de France, which unfortunately is filled with inconsiderate, noisy people keeping long hours. The travelers wander into neighboring villages and particularly enjoy the early 18th-century La Favorita Palace.

Chapter 22
In the Black Forest, the travelers find suggestions of mystery and the supernatural, as well as the quaint kinds of farmhouses and villages that they had expected. One house big enough to be a hotel is ringed by heaps of manure; it appears that a man's station in life can be measured by the size of his manure pile—a feature never adequately stressed in Black Forest stories. To correct this deficiency, the narrator outlines his own Black Forest novel:

The central character, Huss, is a rich old farmer who owns an immense pile of manure. His neighbor, Paul Hoch, is a suitor for his daughter Gretchen, but

Hoch's real interest is Huss's manure. Gretchen only loves Hans Schmidt, who has no manure and is not welcome in Huss's house. Heartbroken, Schmidt goes off to die. Eventually, Huss offers Gretchen's hand to Hoch, but on the day of the wedding, his bookkeeper proves that manure missing from his pile is in Hoch's pile. As Hoch is arrested, Schmidt reappears and reveals that he has struck a great manure mine—a Golconda, a limitless Bonanza. Huss then gives Schmidt his daughter.

After lunch in Ottenhöfen, the travelers follow the carriage road up the valley. Along the way, the narrator studies ants and concludes that their reputation for intellect and industry is exaggerated. From the summit they admire the beautiful Allerheiligen gorge.

Chapter 23
The next day, Harris and the narrator head for Oppenau. The true charm of pedestrianism is not in the walking, but in the *talking*. Their conversation goes in many directions: from writers to dentistry to doctors, death and skeletons. The narrator recalls his Missouri boyhood, when the printing office for which he worked hired an ignorant country boy named Nicodemus DODGE who village smarties thought would be a perfect foil for their pranks. As Harris and the narrator drift into the subject of fossils, the sound of a boy tumbling down a hill disturbs them. The boy is unhurt, but they are left wondering how farmers can live safely on such steep slopes. In the evening, they reach Oppenau—11 hours and 146 miles from Allerheiligen, according to the pedometer.

Chapter 24
The next morning, the travelers return to Baden-Baden on a train filled with a Sunday crowd. At a church service, they sit behind a plainly dressed old woman who must be embarrassed at being in so conspicuous a pew. Angered by the thought of other people laughing at the old woman's poverty, the narrator plans to win some respect for the woman by taking her home in his fine carriage. When she rises, however, he discovers that she is the empress of Germany (Empress Augusta, 1811–1890).

That evening, a vast crowd fills the public grounds to hear the *Fremersberg*, a musical story about a medieval nobleman lost in the mountains until saved by a monastery bell. The narrator concludes that the *Fremersberg* must be low-grade music because *he* enjoys it. There seem to be two kinds of music—one which one feels, and another sort that requires a higher faculty.

The travelers' present business in Baden-Baden is to join the courier they have hired for their trip to Italy.

Chapter 25
The next morning they go by train to SWITZERLAND and arrive in LUCERNE at night. Discovering that the lake's

beauty is not exaggerated, the narrator finds Lucerne a charming place. He also discovers that much romantic nonsense has been written about the Swiss CHAMOIS. Most travelers carry ALPENSTOCKS as their trophies.

Half of Switzerland's summer horde is English; most of the rest are Germans and Americans. During dinner at the Schweitzerhof Hotel, the travelers try to guess other diners' nationalities and they argue about the age of a young American woman. To settle the dispute, the narrator decides to ask the woman her age. As he approaches her, she acts as if she already knows him. As he struggles to remember *how* he knows her, she helps him along with remarks about experiences they once shared, but his memory remains blank. Everything he says draws him in deeper, magnifying his embarrassment. Finally, he contradicts himself so obviously that the woman confesses that she has been taking him in because he pretended to know her.

Chapter 26
Tourists flock to concerts at Lucerne's Hofkirche, which has the biggest and loudest organ in Europe. The city's commerce consists mainly of souvenir knickknacks—especially miniature carvings of the Lion of Lucerne, a colossal monument carved into a rock cliff. The monument reminds the narrator how lucky France's LOUIS XVI was to become a martyr instead of dying in bed. The most pitiable act in his unroyal career was letting his Swiss Guard be massacred in Paris on August 10 (1792) in order to save himself.

For years, the narrator's pet aversion has been the cuckoo clock. Now that he is in the creature's very home, he buys one for someone he does not like.

Watching people fish in front of hotels reminds the narrator of an incident from the time he was a newspaperman in WASHINGTON (D.C.) in 1867. He was with (John H.) RILEY when he was accosted by a man named Lykins, who was anxious to push through his appointment to San Francisco's vacant postmastership. When Lykins said that he should wrap up the whole matter by the next day, Riley cornered him and told him a cautionary tale about "THE MAN WHO PUT UP AT GADSBY'S." After waiting nine hours to see a fisherman catch something, the narrator suggests that anyone willing to tarry there may as well "put up at Gadsby's" and be comfortable.

Chapter 27
After admiring Lake Lucerne for several days, the travelers go to Fluelen on a steamboat and admire the wonderfully tall mountains surrounding the lake. On the boat the narrator meets an 18- or 19-year-old American boy who barrages him with questions about what ship he came on, where he is staying, and so on, repeating himself several times. The boy is learning German while preparing to enter Harvard. Each time he repeats a question, the narrator answers him differently, but the boy overlooks the discrepancies. Later, the narrator overhears the boy having the same conversation with several women.

Chapter 28
The travelers go by steamboat to WEGGIS, where at noon they begin hiking up RIGI-KULM, from which they want to see an alpine sunrise. By six, they are high enough for a fine view of the lake and mountains. Since their guidebook says that it should take only three and a quarter hours to reach the summit, they are surprised to learn that they have actually only *begun* their ascent. They take rooms at an inn, intending to rise in time to see the sunrise, but sleep like policemen and do not get up until late morning. After several more hours of hiking, they encounter a yodeler, whom they give a franc to yodel some more. Soon they meet another yodeler, whom they give half a franc to yodel. After that, they meet yodelers every ten minutes and start paying them *not* to yodel. They stop at the hotel at Kaltbad station, eat and hurry to bed so as not to miss the next sunrise. They awaken excitedly but find that it is already late afternoon. Their spirits lift, however, when they learn that hotels at the summit awaken guests for sunrises with alpine horns. As they climb higher, they get lost in the dark and fog. Afraid of stepping over a precipice, they huddle together, shivering and abusing each other for their stupidity, until the fog thins enough for them to see that they are in front of a hotel at the mountain's summit. They check into the hotel.

When a horn blast awakens the men, they snatch their blankets, rush outside and ascend a scaffolding for the best possible view of the sunrise. They discover, however, that the sun is well above the horizon and is going *down*. What they are seeing is not the sun*rise*, but the sun*set*. After dark, they slink back to their room.

Chapter 29
The next morning, the travelers finally awaken *before* sunrise, but while they dress, Harris gets the happy idea of watching it from the comfort of their warm room. As the sky lightens, they sense that something about this sunrise is wrong. Gradually they realize they are looking in the same direction they looked when they watched the previous night's sunset. By the time they reach the summit observation deck, the sun is already well up.

They return to Weggis on a slow, peculiar train whose locomotive and passenger seats tilt back sharply to compensate for the steepness of the tracks.

Chapter 30 (volume 2: chapter 1)
After returning to Lucerne by boat, the narrator wants to rest up for his arduous walking tour. Since he is determined not to do things by halves, he thinks it essential that he visit the Furka Pass, Rhone Glacier, Finsteraarhorn and the Wetterhorn. He therefore instructs his agent to visit these regions with the courier

and report on them. A week later Harris returns with a long report. The narrator admires Harris's work but thinks it much too learned and asks the meaning of some of its many foreign words, such as *dingblatter*—which Harris says is Fiji for "degrees." Other words include *gnillic,* Eskimo for "snow"; *mmbglx,* Zulu for "pedestrian"; and *bopple,* Choctaw for "picture."

Chapter 31 (2:2)
After preparing to walk from Lucerne to INTERLAKEN, the travelers instead hire a four-horse carriage and leave in the morning. Along the way, they see where Pontius Pilate supposedly threw himself into the lake and where Santa Claus was born. They pass majestic mountains, endless limpid lakes, and green hills and valleys, and see an unbroken procession of fruit-peddlers and tourist carriages. On the highway, their driver maintains a comfortable trot, but he tears through villages, aware of the admiration in which he is held. In the heart of William Tell country, they join numerous tourist carriages stopping for dinner at a hotel below the Brünig Pass. A conversation with several Englishmen inflames their desire to see Meiringen from the pass. During an intoxicating ascent up a smooth road, however, both men fall asleep and the narrator awakens angrily to find they have missed an hour and a half of scenery. They sullenly complete their trip through Brienz and reach Interlaken around sunset.

Chapter 32 (2:3)
After dinner at the huge Jungfrau Hotel, the travelers retire to the great drawing room, where a young American bride drives everyone away by playing on the world's worst piano. No one likes mediocrity, but we all reverence perfection—which is what her terrible music is.

Europe has changed immensely. Napoleon was the only European of his time who could be called a traveler. Now everybody goes everywhere and Switzerland buzzes with restless strangers. In the morning, a wonderful sight greets the travelers through their hotel window: the giant form of the JUNGFRAU.

When a picture in a shop window attracts the narrator, he sends his courier to ask its price without identifying himself—thinking that a native will get the best price. The price the courier reports, however, is a hundred francs too high. When the narrator later visits the shop himself and is asked a hundred francs less for the same picture, the shopkeeper explains that this price does not include the courier's commission. The courier's deception explains how men in his trade can afford to work for just $55 a month and fares. Despite the extra cost that couriers add to traveling, the narrator would never consider traveling without one. A courier who might fairly be called perfection is Joseph N. Verey.

Chapter 33 (2:4)
The narrator wants to visit beautiful Giesbach Fall on Lake Brienz's opposite shore, but does not, since a boat trip would violate his private contract to travel through

Europe on foot. Meanwhile, an even grander sight is at hand—the mighty dome of the Jungfrau.

After a brief stop at an open-air concert, the narrator begins planning a formidable walking trip to ZERMATT. He gets directions and puts his courier in the care of someone going to Lausanne, but when it appears that it will rain the next morning, he hires a buggy for the trip. With the road to themselves, the journey is exceedingly pleasant, even though their driver gets drunk, and they stop for the night in Kandersteg.

Chapter 34 (2:4)
The guide they hire is over 70, but has strength to spare as they begin their ascent. Though they take great interest in wildflowers, they think little of edelweiss, the ugly Swiss favorite. They stop at a little inn and find a chance for real alpine adventure when the nearby Great Altels beckons to them. After sending Harris to arrange for guides and equipment to climb the mountain, the narrator reads (Thomas Woodbine) Hinchliff's *Summer Months Among the Alps* (1857) to learn about mountain climbing. Hinchliff's description of a particularly perilous ascent raises the narrator's excitement level. The moment he reads about a member of Hinchliff's party falling, Harris enters to announce that arrangements are made for their climb. Admitting that alp-climbing is different from what he supposed, the narrator declines, but instructs Harris to have the hired guides follow them to Zermatt.

Chapter 35 (2:6)
The narrator leaves the inn feeling exhilarated. They descend down corkscrew curves on a colossal precipice whose path is often little more than a groove. Near the bottom, Harris's hat blows off. They spend several hours searching for it, but all they find is pieces of an opera glass. When they try to find its owner's remains, they argue about what they will do with them once they find them.

At Leukerbad, they wade through liquid fertilizer. Covered with hungry irritating "chamois," Harris refuses to stop at the Chamois Hotel. Instead, they stop at the Hôtel des Alpes, which has the largest woman the narrator has ever seen; she has come to Leuk to shed her corpulence in the baths. The next morning, they hike to the famous Ladders on the perpendicular face of giant cliffs. The narrator orders Harris to climb one so he can record the feat in his book; Harris obliges by using a subagent. The next morning, they drive to the RHONE Valley and catch a train to Visp, whence they head for Zermatt on foot. At St. Nicholas, they wade ankle-deep in fertilizer-juice and stop at a hotel where all the tourists have their clothes baked. Afterward, their laundry is scrambled and everyone appears at dinner wearing other guests' clothes.

Chapter 36 (2:7)
At St. Nicholas they are awakened early by irritating church bells. The church should heed its own advice to

reform by dropping such practices as bell-ringing and reading "notices" from the pulpit. After breakfast, the travelers head for Zermatt. When the narrator admires a glacier, Harris surprises him by finding fault with it. A rabid Protestant, Harris has snarled for days about the superiority of Protestant cantons (administrative districts) over Catholic ones. He claims that Protestant cantons are less muddy when it rains and that everything in them is better—their church bells, dogs, roads, goats, chamois, flower-boxes—even their glaciers.

Later, they see a young Swiss girl just miss slipping over a precipice to her death. Harris irritates the narrator by going on and on about how glad he is that the girl was not hurt. He is heedless of the needs of the narrator—who might have profited from being able to write about rescuing the girl if she had slipped.

Near Zermatt, they approach the MATTERHORN. Nature here is built on a stupendous plan; *everything* is magnificent. At three in the afternoon, they reach Zermatt, where they know they are in real alp-climbing country when they encounter Mr. Girdlestone himself (Arthur Gilbert Girdlestone, English author of *The High Alps Without Guides*, 1870). While there may be no pleasure equal to climbing a dangerous alp; it is a pleasure confined to those such as Girdlestone, who has spent the summer trying to break his neck.

The guides whom the travelers hired earlier are waiting for them at Zermatt, so the narrator devotes his evening to studying up on climbing. Several books teach him the importance of strong shoes, good-quality equipment and having enough rope to tie the entire party together. He also reads a fearful passage by Mr. WHYMPER, describing a time when he fell 200 feet in seven or eight bounds.

The cover of the English edition of A Tramp Abroad *mixes Mark Twain's sketches with W. F. Brown's silhouettes from chapter 37. (Courtesy, Kevin Bochynski)*

Chapter 37 (2:8)
Intoxicated by his reading, the narrator announces that he will ascend the RIFFELBERG. Though startled, Harris vows to stand by him unto death. Everyone in Zermatt helps prepare for the expedition, which consists of 154 people, 51 mules and cows, and tons of equipment, including 143 pairs of crutches, 27 kegs of paregoric (an opiate), 154 umbrellas and 2 miles of rope. The men include 17 guides, 15 barkeepers, 4 surgeons, 3 chaplains and a host of other specialists. The narrator has all the men and animals arranged in a single file, lashed together on one strong rope, creating a procession 3,122 feet long. Harris and the narrator, the only persons mounted, take up the dangerous position at the extreme rear, with each man tied to five guides. Out of respect for tourists they will encounter, they wear full evening dress.

After starting in the afternoon, the expedition camps in a meadow. They rise at two in the morning, but wait until nine to start again. In the afternoon, the guides call a halt to admit they are lost. They are not certain that they are lost, however, because none of them has ever been in the region before. Troubles multiply when

the expedition comes up against a great rock. The narrator maintains morale by assuring everyone that they will be saved. With the help of paregoric, everyone gets through the night.

The next day the party uses ladders to scale the rock; the problem of getting the animals over it is solved by blowing it up with nitroglycerin. After bridging the resulting hole, they push on. The following day, new obstacles convince everyone that they truly are lost. To counter the growing demoralization, the narrator attaches a three-quarter-mile-long rope to a guide and sends him off to find the road. When the rope later jerks frantically, the expedition excitedly follows it for half a day, only to find it tied to a ram.

Chapter 38 (2:9)
The expedition camps where the ram has led it. After supper, the narrator again doses the men with paregoric and beds them down. The next morning, Harris brings a Baedeker map that proves that they are not lost—the summit is lost. After trying to determine the altitude,

the narrator faces a new crisis when a porter shoots the expedition's Latinist while aiming at a chamois. A rumor sweeps the camp that a barkeeper has fallen over a precipice, but happily it turns out to be only a chaplain.

The next morning, the party moves on in good spirits. When they encounter another big rock, they blast it away with dynamite, then discover it had a chalet on its top. After having the chalet rebuilt, the narrator retires inside with Harris to correct his scientific journals. A young man then enters and introduces himself as the grandson of a once-notable American and begins a long, vacuous conversation with Harris about his personal connections with European courts and other matters. He ranks with the innocent chatterbox on the lake (chapter 27) as one of the most interesting specimens of young Americans the narrator has met in his travels.

The caravan starts off again, following the zigzag mule road. After a lost umbrella causes a delay, they reach the summit the next day at noon. Exulting in having demonstrated the possibility of the impossible, Harris and the narrator march proudly into the great dining room of the Riffelberg Hotel and receive an admiring welcome from the tourists—mostly women and children.

Chapter 39 (2:10)
Baedeker's guidebook contains strange statements about the ascent to Riffelberg, but the narrator sends him corrections—instead of three hours, it takes seven days to make the trip.

With the men's strength restored, the problem now is getting them back *down* the mountain. Since balloons are not available, the narrator proposes descending on the great Gorner Glacier, which begins 1,200 feet below the summit. Objecting to the narrator's proposal to have everyone descend at once by umbrella to the glacier, Harris suggests having one man try this alone. However, Harris refuses to *be* that man. Unable to find anyone willing to take Harris's place, the narrator marches the men overland to the glacier and settles them in its middle—which Baedeker says moves the fastest. That night, the men pitch camp; the narrator paregorics them and retires, leaving orders to be called when Zermatt is sighted.

The next day, they still have not budged. Suspecting that the glacier may have run aground, the narrator rigs spars on each side to break it loose, but meets no success. After learning from Baedeker that the glacier moves less than an inch a day, he calculates that it will take them 500 years to get to Zermatt, so he decides to walk. After breaking camp, the men reach Zermatt in the evening.

Chapter 40 (2:11)
Having learned much more about glacial movement since taking passage on the Gorner Glacier, the narrator shares his knowledge and relates a story about mountaineers who disappeared into the glacial crevices on

Mont BLANC in 1864. Another Mont Blanc story concerns the disappearance of three men into a glacier in 1820. The English geologist Forbes (James David Forbes, 1809–1868) predicted that at the rate the glacier was moving, it would deliver the missing men's bodies to the foot of the mountain in about 35 or 40 years. In 1861, some of their remains finally appeared.

Chapter 41 (2:12)
The Alps' most memorable disaster occurred on the Matterhorn in July 1865, during Whymper's ninth attempt to scale the mountain. The chapter quotes at length from Whymper's account of how four men lost their lives.

Chapter 42 (2:13)
Switzerland is a large rock covered with a grass skin too valuable to waste on any but the living. As a result, Zermatt's graveyard is small and occupation is temporary. The travelers leave Zermatt by wagon in a rainstorm. At St. Nicholas, they strike out for Visp on foot. A scene of children playing at mountaineering reminds the narrator of children playing silver-mining in NEVADA. It also reminds him of a young boy whose preacher father disapproved of his playing such things as steamboat captain and army commander on Sundays, and told him instead to play only things suitable to the Sabbath. The next Sunday he found his son impersonating God, casting other children out of Eden.

After a night in Visp, the travelers go by train to Brevet, then by boat to Ouchy and Lausanne (on Lake Geneva). Long moved by BYRON's *Prisoner of Chillon* (1816), the narrator takes a steamer to the Castle of Chillon to inspect the dungeon where Bonnivard was a prisoner (1530–36). The visit removes some of the sympathy he has felt for Bonnivard when he finds Bonnivard's dungeon roomier and more comfortable than a private St. Nicholas dwelling. The travelers next go by train to Martigny and Argentière, from which they see Mont Blanc. Then they take a wagon to Chamonix.

Chapter 43 (2:14)
Everyone in Chamonix is out of doors, where Mont Blanc's looming presence overshadows everything and presents spectacular views. At the Exchange of Chamonix, which oversees all Mont Blanc expeditions and issues diplomas to climbers, the narrator tries to buy a diploma for an invalid friend, but finds no sympathy. The office also contains a book listing every fatal accident on Mont Blanc.

Chapter 44 (2:15)
After breakfast the next morning, the travelers study Mont Blanc though a telescope. When climbers come into view, the narrator hits on the idea of using the telescope to ascend the mountain in the climbers' company. At first, Harris is afraid to join him, but is finally persuaded. After a last look at his pleasant surroundings, the narrator boldly puts his eye to the glass and

follows the climbers to the summit, where he shares in their triumph.

In August 1866, Chamonix residents witnessed a frightful tragedy on Mont Blanc through their telescopes when three English climbers fell 2,000 feet. Amazingly, two men survived the fall and were seen trying to help the third. They then spent hours making their perilous descent. The next chapter copies (Stephen) D'Arve's account of one of the most mournful of all mountaineering calamities from his *Histoire du Mont Blanc*.

Chapter 45 (2:16)

On September 5, 1870, 11 climbers reached the summit of Mont Blanc, where they disappeared within a cloud. Help was sent eight hours later, but a raging storm prevented anything from being done for a week. When rescuers finally reached the summit, they found 10 bodies; the 11th person was never found. One body had a diary recording the climbers' grisly end. Hopelessly lost in the storm, they had wandered aimlessly within a tiny area until cold forced them to lie down and slowly die.

Chapter 46 (2:17)

With guides and porters, Harris and the narrator ascend to the Hôtel des Pyramides near the top of the Glacier des Bossons. After studying the glacier from within a long tunnel hewn inside it, they ask their chief guide to organize guides and porters to ascend the Montanvert, only to be advised that an ambulance would be more suitable. The next day they climb to the Montanvert's summit hotel and view the famous Mer de Glace. They cross this glacier safely, but worry about its yawning crevices.

In the blazing heat, the parched travelers slake their thirst in cold mountain streams—the *only* water in Europe capable of quenching thirst. Away from the mountains, European water is flat and insipid compared to American water.

After more climbing, the travelers return to their hotel, and they leave for Geneva the next morning.

Chapter 47 (2:18)

During several restful days at Geneva, they find the city's many little shops manned by irritatingly persistent clerks asking maddeningly elastic prices. Geneva has few "sights." After failing to find the homes of Rousseau and Calvin, the narrator gets lost among streets with such unlikely names as "Hell," "Purgatory" and "Paradise." The sight of young men deliberately obstructing pedestrians convinces the narrator that Americans are generally superior to Europeans in manners, particularly in their treatment of women.

The travelers prepare to walk to ITALY, but find the road so level that they instead take a train, stopping overnight at Chambèry. The next morning they leave for Turin on a railroad rich in tunnels. They share a compartment with a ponderous Swiss woman who stretches her legs to the opposite seat, crowding an American passenger. When the man politely asks her to move her feet, she sobs about being an unprotected lady who has lost the use of her limbs. Though the man apologizes profusely, the woman sobs until the train enters Italy, where she springs from her seat and strides away.

Turin is a fine city with everything built on a large scale. The narrator has read that tourists should expect to be cheated by Italians, but he experiences just the opposite. After a Punch and Judy show, for example, he gives a small coin to a youth who tries to return it because it is too much. The incident reminds the narrator how he once mistakenly gave a five-dollar gold piece to a blind woman in an ODESSA church and later stole it back.

Chapter 48 (2:19)

In MILAN the narrator visits the great cathedral and other regulation sights to see what he has learned in 12 years. He finds that his old idea about copies of Old Masters' paintings being superior to their originals is wrong. In VENICE he concludes that the Old Masters really do contain a subtle *something* that does not lend itself to reasoning, just as certain women may have indefinable charm invisible to strangers. He calls an Old Master that particularly fascinates him the "Hair Trunk"; it is a painting by Bassano in the Doge's Palace titled "Pope Alexander III and the Doge Ziani."

Chapter 49 (2:20)

Venice's St. Mark's Cathedral is such perfection in its nobly august ugliness, it is difficult to stay away from. Nearly 450 years ago, a noble named Stammato robbed the cathedral in a manner out of the ARABIAN NIGHTS. After months of methodically spiriting priceless treasures through a secret passage, he discovered that he could not enjoy his collection alone. He swore a fellow noble to secrecy and showed him his collection, only to be promptly betrayed and hanged.

In Venice, the travelers enjoy a rare luxury—dinner in a private home. European hotel fare is so awful that anyone accustomed to American cooking who is condemned to live on this fare would waste away. One first learns to do without the customary morning meal. What passes for coffee in Europe resembles the real thing as hypocrisy resembles holiness. A European dinner is better than the breakfast, but is monotonously unsatisfying. Starved for a nourishing meal, the narrator lists American dishes he wants to have waiting for him at home.

Chapter 50 (2:21)

Why is art allowed as much indecent license as in earlier times, while literature's privileges have been sharply curtailed in this century? Every European gallery has hideous pictures of blood and carnage, alive with every conceivable horror in dreadful detail, but no one complains. If a writer described such things, critics would skin him alive.

Titian's Venus of Urbino may defile its gallery; however, his "Moses" (actually a painting by Giorgione) glorifies it. It has no equal among the works of the Old Masters, apart from Bassano's divine Hair Trunk. The narrator goes to FLORENCE to see this painting and arranges to have it copied for his book (the frontispiece of *A Tramp Abroad* is actually adapted from an unrelated picture of Moses).

After visiting Rome and other Italian cities, the travelers go to MUNICH, PARIS, HOLLAND and BELGIUM, working in Spain and other regions through agents to save time. Finally, they cross to ENGLAND, whence they return home on the *Gallia*. Nothing that the narrator has experienced abroad compares with the pleasure of seeing New York harbor again. Europe has some advantages that we lack, but they do not compensate for what exists only here. To be condemned to live the way an average European family lives would make life a heavy burden to the average American family.

Appendix A
A hotel official with no precise American equivalent, the European *portier* serves as an intermediary between guests and the hotel, providing services and answering questions that one might be reluctant to ask a hotel clerk. The secret of the portier's devoted service is that he gets fees and no salary. No matter how long you stay in a hotel, you do not pay the portier until you leave.

Appendix B
This 2,560-word description of Heidelberg Castle emphasizes its special attractiveness when illuminated at night.

Appendix C
Subtitled "The College Prison," this essay discusses the special legal status of German students, who can only be tried and punished by their own universities. Convicted students can even choose when they serve their prison time.

Appendix D
"THE AWFUL GERMAN LANGUAGE" examines the perplexities of GERMAN.

Appendix E
"Legend of the Castles" is the story of two old bachelor twins known as Herr Givenaught and Herr Heartless. When Germany's most renowned scholar, Franz Reikmann, faces financial ruin after a speculator cheats him, his daughter Hildegarde dreams that the Virgin has instructed her to ask the brothers to bid on Reikmann's books at an auction. The brothers refuse, but both appear at the auction in disguise. Givenaught not only bids enough to pay off Reikmann's debts and leave him with a generous profit, but he returns Reikmann's books to him.

Appendix F
A survey of German newspapers finds them to be the dreariest of human inventions. They contain little more than "telegrams" and letters concerning political news and market reports. Compared to an average daily American paper, which has between 25,000 to 50,000 words of reading matter, a typical Munich newspaper has exactly 1,654 words.

BACKGROUND AND PUBLISHING HISTORY

In March 1878, Mark Twain secretly signed a contract with Frank BLISS to write a book about Europe. A month later, he sailed with his family to Germany, beginning the trip that would become the basis of *A Tramp Abroad*. Why he made this trip when he did is not fully clear. Perhaps the embarrassment he suffered after delivering a speech on WHITTIER's birthday in December made him want to leave the country. Also, he had not completed a major book since *Tom Sawyer* (1876) and he regarded a travel book as something he could write comparatively easily.

Mark Twain on the eve of publishing A Tramp Abroad *in 1880*. (Courtesy, National Archives, Still Picture Branch)

Shortly after reaching Germany in April 1878, Mark Twain began writing experimentally, but accomplished little for some months. The arrival of his friend Joseph TWICHELL in August and the time they spent together gave Mark Twain the spark he needed. After Twichell left, he hit on the idea of building the book around a man and his "agent" undertaking a walking tour that never quite gets going. Twichell was with Mark Twain only in the BLACK FOREST and the Alps, but the HARRIS character based on him travels with the narrator through most of *A Tramp Abroad*.

Mark Twain completed virtually all the traveling that he described in *A Tramp Abroad* by mid-November 1878, when he settled in MUNICH with his family. He then got down to serious writing. By January, he had completed 20 chapters, but was having trouble staying interested—especially after discovering that he had seriously overestimated the amount of work that he had finished. After adding another five chapters quickly, he took his family to Paris in late February 1879. His writing grew increasingly difficult, but he persevered until he returned home in September. In January 1880, he finished his manuscript. By then, he had arranged to publish with Elisha BLISS, instead of Bliss's son, and the AMERICAN PUBLISHING COMPANY issued *A Tramp Abroad* on March 13, 1880.

Though Mark Twain feared he would never write enough to fill the book, he eventually wrote so much that he had to make substantial cuts. Many deleted chapters had little to do with his European travels. Much of this material appeared in THE STOLEN WHITE ELEPHANT, ETC. (1882), whose title story he originally wrote for *A Tramp Abroad*. Other omitted material that found its way into that collection includes "Concerning the American Language," "Paris Notes," "Legend of Sagenfeld in Germany" and "THE GREAT REVOLUTION IN PITCAIRN." "THE PROFESSOR'S YARN" and a chapter about DUTCHY and Lem HACKETT later appeared in *Life on the Mississippi* (1883). "The French and the Comanches" finally appeared posthumously in LETTERS FROM THE EARTH. Deleted material still awaiting publication includes chapters on French marriage customs, Hamburg, Munich and Rome, as well as a brief passage on Ivan Turgenev, whom he saw in Paris in 1879.

Mark Twain's extensive notes from his 1878–79 trip are published in the second volume of the MARK TWAIN PAPERS project edition of his NOTEBOOKS. The project has tentatively scheduled a new edition of *A Tramp Abroad* for 2008; that edition will contain Mark Twain's complete working notes and the deleted chapters.

While *A Tramp Abroad* has never been as popular as Mark Twain's earlier travel books, it has generally remained in print. Modern editions, however, have ignored the book's original illustrations—which are an integral part of its humor. The first edition has 328 pictures, of which Walter Francis BROWN drew more than a third. Brown's illustrations are scattered throughout the volume and are mostly signed "W. F. B." It is difficult to identify who did many of the unsigned pictures, as Brown's work resembles that of True WILLIAMS, who contributed at least 40 pictures. Benjamin Henry DAY added 22 pictures—all clearly signed (chapters 2, 35–37, 39–40, 42–44, 46–48)—and William Wallace DENSLOW did six pictures initialed "W. W. D." for chapter 47's episode about a Swiss woman on a train. Mark Twain himself added at least nine pictures (chapters 11, 14, 15?, 19–21, 31–32 and 48). Other illustrations were adapted from previously published work by J. C. Beard, Roswell Morse Shurtleff and Edward Whymper.

Traum, Philip Pseudonym used in "THE CHRONICLE OF YOUNG SATAN." After the angel SATAN meets Theodor FISCHER and his friends, he tells them to call him "Philip Traum" around other people (chapter 2). When a villager later remarks on how the name Traum "fits him," Fischer parenthetically explains that "Traum is GERMAN for Dream" (chapter 4). Fischer's narrative usually calls the character "Satan," and does not use the name "Traum" after chapter 6.

"Traveling with a Reformer" Sketch written and published in 1893. Years of tedious railroad travel gave Mark Twain strong feelings about the poor manners of railroad employees. In *The Gilded Age*, he got his coauthor, C. D. WARNER, to use an incident that he had once observed, when a conductor threw a man off a train for defending a mistreated woman (chapter 29). Mark Twain seems to have had particularly bad experiences on trips to CHICAGO, including one he made with Frederick HALL to see the World's Fair in early 1893. Later that year, he got revenge by writing "Traveling with a Reformer" for COSMOPOLITAN. After the story appeared in December, the president of the Pennsylvania Railroad retaliated by refusing to grant Mark Twain complimentary passes when he returned to Chicago with H. H. ROGERS.

When the 5,500-word story first appeared in *Cosmopolitan*, it was illustrated by Dan BEARD. It was first collected in *How to Tell a Story and Other Essays* (1897), which was later issued as LITERARY ESSAYS (1899).

SYNOPSIS

While traveling to the Chicago World's Fair, the unnamed narrator is joined in New York by a serene but humorless man whom he calls the "major." Though illness prevents the narrator from actually seeing the fair, he picks up useful "diplomatic tricks" from the major, who is a passionate advocate of reforming petty public abuses. The major thinks that citizens should watch how laws are executed and work to prevent unfair abuses. When skylarking telegraph operators are slow to serve him, for example, he writes a telegram inviting Western Union's president to dinner, so that he can tell him "how business is conducted in one of your branches." Seeing these words makes the operator pale and promise to reform. The major admits to the narrator that he does not know the president of Western Union and explains the wonders that gentle diplomacy can work.

In the course of their journey, the major uses similar tactics to correct other abuses that he encounters. Meanwhile, he is not above using force when necessary, and he helps throw three roughs off a horse-car. Aboard a train, he later claims that his brother-in-law is a company director, and he not only gets a conductor to make a brakeman apologize to a man he has mistreated, he moves the conductor to *thank* him for complaining. On a "Pennsylvania [Rail]road" train to Chicago, he persuades a conductor to ignore the company's prohibition against Sunday card-playing. On the return train, he secures a sleeper stateroom by threatening to sue the company for violating its contract, and he gets the dining-car staff to serve him a dish not listed on the menu after he sees a railroad employee eating the same meal.

"A True Story" Story written and published in 1874. Subtitled "Repeated Word for Word as I Heard It," this 2,200-word FRAME-STORY is based on a story told by Mary Ann CORD, a former slave who worked for Mark Twain's sister-in-law in ELMIRA. Most of the story is narrated in an African-American dialect that Mark Twain worked hard to make authentic.

After writing this story in mid-1874, Mark Twain made it his first submission to the ATLANTIC MONTHLY, which published it in November. It was later collected in SKETCHES, NEW AND OLD.

SYNOPSIS

One summer evening, the narrator, Misto C- (Clemens?), sits on the farmhouse porch watching the colored servant Aunt Rachel—who sits at a respectfully lower level—being mercilessly teased. Impressed by her easy, hearty laughter, he asks how she has lived 60 years without seeing any trouble. Startled by this naive question, Rachel tells her story.

Born among slaves, she was raised in Virginia. Her mother, who was from Maryland, often went into tantrums, proclaiming, "I wa'nt bawn in de mash to be fool' by trash! I's one o' de ole Blue Hen's Chicken's, I is!" Rachel and her husband had seven children to whom they were devoted, but by and by, their mistress sold all her slaves at auction in Richmond. As Rachel says this, she rises to tower above the narrator. Chained and put on display for buyers, she watched her husband and most of her children being sold, then seized her young son Henry and threatened to kill anyone who touched him. Henry whispered for her not to worry, as he would escape to the North and return to buy her freedom. Since that day, 22 years ago Easter, Rachel has not seen her husband or six of her children.

Rachel's new owner took her to Newbern (New Bern, North Carolina?) and made her his family cook. Eventually, the war came and he fled before Union troops, who took the town and made his house their headquarters. While cooking for the Union officers, Rachel asked after her son Henry, in case they saw him in the North. Unbeknownst to her at the time, Henry had fled north and become a barber. Later, he hired himself out to Union officers and scoured the South looking for her.

One night a black regiment held a ball at the house. While Rachel was working, a spruce young man danced into her kitchen with his partner. When Rachel ordered him out, he shot her a surprised look. When more men came in, she straightened up to proclaim that she "wa'nt bawn in the mash to be fool' by trash," causing the young man to stare. The next morning, the young man returned to the kitchen early. As Rachel removed biscuits from the oven, the man leaned over to look in her face. Recognizing Henry by scars he had acquired as a child, Rachel realized that at last she had her own again.

Trumbull, J[ames] Hammond (December 20, 1821, Stonington, Connecticut–August 5, 1897, Hartford, Connecticut) Scholar and friend of Mark Twain. A former secretary of state of CONNECTICUT (1861–66) and the brother-in-law of William PRIME, Trumbull was a resident of Hartford's Nook Farm and a cofounder of the MONDAY EVENING CLUB. He wrote widely on history and philology and had a particular interest in American INDIANS; he contributed the diverse foreign-language chapter headings in *The Gilded Age* (1873). Mark Twain also drew on Trumbull's *True-Blue Laws of Connecticut and New Haven and the False Blue-Laws* (1876) for background material for *The Prince and the Pauper*, which cites Trumbull by name.

Tuckey, John S. (July 27, 1921, Washington, D.C.–September 4, 1987) Mark Twain scholar. After taking his doctorate at Notre Dame in 1953, Tuckey spent his entire career teaching literature at Purdue University's Calumet Campus. He became the leading authority on Mark Twain's post-1895 writings and discovered how much A. B. PAINE and Frederick DUNEKA had bowdlerized Mark Twain's writings to create THE MYSTERIOUS STRANGER (1916). He outlined his findings in *Mark Twain and Little Satan* (1963) and later edited *Mark Twain's "The Mysterious Stranger" and the Critics* (1968). Tuckey also edited WHICH WAS THE DREAM? AND OTHER SYMBOLIC WRITINGS OF THE LATER YEARS (1967), FABLES OF MAN and NO. 44, THE MYSTERIOUS STRANGER (1982) for the MARK TWAIN PAPERS project.

Tuolumne County East-central CALIFORNIA region between CALAVERAS and Mariposa counties, extending from the foothills to the crest of the Sierra Nevada, including the northern half of Yosemite National Park. In the heart of California's Mother Lode during the

GOLD RUSH, Tuolumne supported mostly small-scale mining when Mark Twain lived with friends at JACKASS HILL from late 1864 to early 1865—a period described in chapter 60 of *Roughing It.* The county also contains the resort town TWAIN-HARTE.

Turkey The Turkish, or Ottoman, Empire was a Muslim sultanate that arose in Asia Minor in the late 13th century and gradually replaced the Byzantine Empire as the major eastern MEDITERRANEAN power. At its peak, it controlled all of modern Turkey, the Balkans, SYRIA, LEBANON, PALESTINE, EGYPT, Iraq, the Barbary states of North Africa and parts of RUSSIA and Hungary. By the mid-19th century, however, its imperial government was weak and it was losing ground to Russia and to regional movements for autonomy within its own empire. When Mark Twain visited the eastern Mediterranean in 1867, Turkey still controlled Syria, Lebanon, Palestine and other Near Eastern territories, but this empire would last only 50 more years.

Five weeks before he even reached Turkey, Mark Twain saw its ruler, ABDUL AZIZ, in Paris. Chapter 13 of *Innocents Abroad* contains a negative description of the sultan that Mark Twain wrote *after* visiting the Turkish Empire, where he observed the effects of Ottoman rule. He spent about nine days in Turkey itself during stops of the cruise ship QUAKER CITY at CONSTANTINOPLE (August 17 and 29) and SMYRNA (September 5) and recorded his observations about these places in chapters 33–34 and 38–40 of *Innocents Abroad.* He then went to BEIRUT, whence he traveled overland through Turkish-ruled territories for about three weeks. His disdain for Ottoman rule can be read on almost every page of the chapters in *Innocents* concerning this trip. Chapter 42, for example, comments on the "inhuman tyranny of the Ottoman empire" and suggests that it would be a good idea to "let Russia annihilate Turkey . . . enough to make it difficult to find the place again without a divining-rod or a diving-bell."

Turner, Ab Minor character in *Huckleberry Finn.* Turner is one of two men who "helped to lay out the late Peter WILKS for burying." In chapter 29, Turner and his unnamed partner cannot recall seeing any kind of tattoo on the deceased's body.

Turner, Bill Figure mentioned in chapter 14 of *Tom Sawyer* as having drowned the previous summer—presumably in the Mississippi. A cannon was fired over the water in an attempt to raise his body, in accordance with the folk beliefs of the time.

Turner, Jim Minor character in *Huckleberry Finn.* In chapter 12, Huck sees Turner on the derelict steamboat WALTER SCOTT. A murderer, Turner has recently killed someone called "old Hatfield." Now, his former partners, Jake PACKARD and BILL, want to kill him, fearing that he will turn state's evidence and betray them for some unnamed affair. They decide to leave him tied up on the steamboat, however, expecting it to sink within two hours. In the next chapter, they are about to get off the steamboat, but return for Turner's money, leaving Huck and Jim to snatch their skiff. Turner and the others presumably drown when the steamboat later sinks. An early draft of *Huckleberry Finn* indicates that if the boat did not break up, Bill was prepared to return and tie Turner to a rock to make sure he drowned.

"The Turning Point of My Life" Essay published in 1910. An important adjunct to Mark Twain's AUTOBIOGRAPHY, this essay arises from the deterministic philosophy that he espouses in WHAT IS MAN? Though he submitted this piece in response to a magazine's invitation to write on the title subject, the essay is essentially a revision of a dictation that he made three years earlier, shortly after publishing *What Is Man?*

SYNOPSIS

Mark Twain begins by rejecting the idea of a single turning point in his life, arguing instead that a chain of 10,000 links has determined his life. He cites Julius CAESAR's crossing of the Rubicon—one of history's most celebrated turning points—as merely the last link of a long chain. As Caesar hesitated to cross the river, an impulsive act by his trumpeter suddenly moved him to decision. That tiny link affected virtually every event that has followed in Western history.

Since Mark Twain sees literature as the most important feature of his life, his own most important turning point must therefore be the link that turned him in that direction. To find that link, he goes back to when he was 12. At that time, a measles epidemic so scared him that he deliberately contracted the disease to end the suspense. After he got well, his mother—who was tired of trying to keep him out of mischief—took him out of school and apprenticed him to a printer; that was the first link. Later, his printing work took him to IOWA, where he read about the Amazon and planned to go there. His plan meant nothing by itself, however, until *circumstance* stepped in. When he found a $50 bill, he used it to go down the Mississippi River to NEW ORLEANS in order to ship out to SOUTH AMERICA. Since there were no ships to take him to the Amazon, he instead became a steamboat PILOT, until the CIVIL WAR intruded. This time, circumstance got his brother appointed secretary to NEVADA Territory; he followed his brother to the West, where he used what printing work had taught him about literature to become a reporter for the VIRGINIA CITY TERRITORIAL ENTERPRISE. Later, the SACRAMENTO UNION sent him to the SANDWICH ISLANDS. This gained him such notoriety that he took up LECTURING in SAN FRANCISCO and began earning the wherewithal to see the world and join the QUAKER CITY excursion. This, in turn, led to his writing *Innocents Abroad,* that made him a member of the literary guild.

He can therefore truthfully state that he entered the literary profession because he had the measles when he was 12.

What interests Mark Twain about these details is that he foresaw none of them, while circumstance did his planning for him, with the help of his temperament. He sees little difference between a man and a watch, except that the man is conscious and the watch is not. He goes on to argue that the real turning point of his and everyone else's life was the Garden of Eden, where ADAM AND EVE forged the first link that would lead him into literature by eating the forbidden apple. He cannot help but wonder what would have happened if God had put Martin Luther and JOAN OF ARC in the Garden instead. If they had been ordered not to eat the apple, they would not have eaten it, and there would be no human race and he would never have gone into literature.

BACKGROUND AND PUBLISHING HISTORY

In October 1906, Mark Twain received a letter that moved him to dictate an autobiographical passage on the "accidents" in his life that became the basis for this essay (the passage appears in MARK TWAIN IN ERUPTION). After drafting the present 3,670-word essay twice in 1909, he published it in HARPER'S BAZAAR in February 1910, two months before he died. Seven years later, A. B. PAINE republished it in the *What Is Man? and Other Essays*. Paul Baender published a corrected version in the MARK TWAIN PAPERS project edition *What Is Man? and other Philosophical Writings* in 1973.

Tuxedo Park   New York resort community on the Ramapo River, near the New Jersey border, about 30 miles northwest of Manhattan. From May to October 1907, Mark Twain interrupted his residence in NEW YORK CITY by renting William Voss's Tuxedo Park house, near the home of Harry Rogers, the son of H. H. ROGERS.

Twain   Small town in CALIFORNIA's Plumas County, on State Highway 70. Established in 1907 as a Western Pacific station, it was named in honor of Mark Twain.

Twain, John Morgan   Character in Mark Twain's BURLESQUE AUTOBIOGRAPHY. A purported ancestor, "John Morgan Twain" allegedly came to America in 1492 as a passenger with COLUMBUS. Possibly taking his name from the PIRATE Henry Morgan, Twain was an inventive con man who in some ways anticipates *Connecticut Yankee*'s Hank MORGAN. When he boarded the ship, he carried everything he owned in an old newspaper; when he left, he had four trunks, a crate and several champagne baskets and he even suggested searching other passengers' luggage because some of his own things were missing. After making himself unpopular by constantly complaining, he was thrown overboard. Even then, he managed to steal the ship's anchor and sell it to Indians. Twain was the first white person to try civilizing the Indians—by building a jail and a gallows—and was also the first white man hanged in America.

Twain boarded Columbus's ship with four monogrammed items that pose interesting deciphering challenges, if the initials mean anything. He had a handkerchief marked "B. G." ("brigadier general"?); a sock marked "L. W. C."; another sock marked "D. F." ("defender of the Faith"?); and a night-shirt marked "O. M. R." ("old man river"?).

Twain-Harte   Mountain resort town in CALIFORNIA's TUOLUMNE COUNTY, on State Highway 108, about 10 miles northeast of Sonora. Named after Mark Twain and Bret HARTE in 1924, it has no significant connection with either man apart from its name.

Twainian   Journal devoted to Mark Twain. The *Twainian* began in January 1939 as the newsletter of Chicago's 30-member Mark Twain Society, which humorist George Ade (1866–1944) had founded the previous year. Later, the society changed its name to the Mark Twain Association of America and moved to Elkhorn, Wisconsin along with the *Twainian*'s editor George Hiram Brownell (1875–1950), a journalist and Mark Twain collector. In 1947, the organization was reconstituted as the Mark Twain Research Foundation. After Brownell died in 1950, Chester L. Davis (1903–1987) moved the journal and foundation to his home in Perry, Missouri, near Mark Twain's FLORIDA birthplace. Over the remainder of his life, Davis published the *Twainian* as often as six times a year, filling it with an eclectic mixture of original documents, articles contributed by scholars, antiquarian features and generous quantities of material reprinted from books and other journals. It suspended publication after its December 1989 issue. By then, its foundation claimed 400 members. In November 1993, the *Twainian* resumed publication as a quarterly.

Twichell, Joseph Hopkins (May 27, 1838, Southington, Connecticut–December 20, 1918)   Friend of Mark Twain. The son of a Congregationalist deacon, Twichell graduated from YALE in 1859 and entered Union Theological Seminary. When the CIVIL WAR began, he suspended his studies to join the 71st New York State Infantry as a chaplain and began his service in late April 1861. For three years, he was in the midst of some of the war's heaviest fighting—from Fredericksburg through Gettysburg. Sharing chaplain duties in his rough, mainly Catholic regiment with a Jesuit priest broadened his views on people and religion, transforming him into a remarkably tolerant and open-minded man. After mustering out of the army in July 1864, he completed his studies at Andover Theological Seminary. Meanwhile, Hartford Congregationalists were building a new church in the prosperous Asylum Hill neighborhood. On the recommendation of Dr. Horace Bushnell—

Mark Twain's friend Joseph Twichell, whom he called "one of the best of men, although a clergyman." (Courtesy, Mark Twain Papers, the Bancroft Library)

whom Twichell had met while on leave during the war—they offered the attractive pastorate to Twichell. Twichell married Julia Harmony Cushman (1843–1910) in November 1865; a month later, he took up the pastorate, which he kept for 45 years.

Twichell's church was across the street from the home of publisher Elisha BLISS, whom Mark Twain visited in early 1868. When Bliss's wife introduced Mark Twain to him, Twichell bristled slightly at the man's dubbing his congregation the "Church of the HOLY SPECULATORS," but when Mark Twain next visited Hartford, he was the Twichells' guest. This period began a close friendship that endured through Mark Twain's life and involved Twichell deeply in the Clemens family's most important events. In 1870, Twichell officiated at Mark Twain's MARRIAGE along with Thomas K. BEECHER. In later years, he and Beecher occasionally swapped pulpits while visiting each other's towns.

Twichell's friendship with Mark Twain grew stronger after the Clemenses moved to Hartford in 1871, particularly after they settled in NOOK FARM near Twichell's

home and their families became close. Twichell and Mark Twain themselves belonged to the same organizations, such as the MONDAY EVENING CLUB, and often walked and talked together. While the Clemenses never formally joined Twichell's church, they rented a pew and attended the church regularly during the entire time they lived in Hartford.

Twichell's impact on Mark Twain's writing can be measured in many ways. He encouraged Mark Twain through difficult periods, and fed him ideas and shared experiences that his friend wrote about. In 1874, for example, Twichell went to Peru with another friend, Yung Wing, to investigate conditions of Chinese workers. While sailing on the Pacific, he had a serendipitous encounter with Mark Twain's salty old friend Captain Ned WAKEMAN. Anecdotes that Twichell collected in that encounter found their way into "SOME RAMBLING NOTES OF AN IDLE EXCURSION" and "CAPTAIN STORMFIELD'S VISIT TO HEAVEN"—both of which depict Twichell himself as "Reverend PETERS." Twichell is also the "Rev. Mr. —" of "PUNCH, BROTHERS, PUNCH!" (1876). A conversation with Twichell in the mid-1870s spurred Mark Twain to write "OLD TIMES ON THE MISSISSIPPI," which metamorphosed into *Life on the Mississippi.*

One of the many things that drew these men together was their shared sense of humor. Relishing the fact that Twichell could laugh even at bawdy humor, Mark Twain wrote *1601* largely to amuse him. In May 1877, they sailed to BERMUDA together on the trip described in "Rambling Notes." The following year, Twichell went to Europe at Mark Twain's expense, joining him for six weeks in GERMANY and SWITZERLAND. *A Tramp Abroad,* Mark Twain's book about that trip, converts Twichell into the agent "HARRIS." Though Twichell was with Mark Twain for only a fraction of the time that the latter was in Europe, he had a catalytic effect on *A Tramp Abroad.* Mark Twain acknowledged that without the six weeks he spent with Twichell, he could not have written his book. In later years, he credited Twichell with introducing him to Conan Doyle's Sherlock HOLMES.

Twichell lent strength to Mark Twain in the family crises that tormented his last 15 years. In August 1896, Susy Clemens became seriously ill in Hartford while Mark Twain and Livy were in England. The moment that Twichell learned of Susy's illness, he ended his vacation in the Adirondacks to rush to her side, and was with her when she died. He then went to New York City to convey the tragic news to Livy and Clara as they arrived from England. Twichell officiated at both Susy's funeral and Livy's, eight years later.

Twichell and Mark Twain enjoyed happier times in early 1907, when they finally made the return visit to Bermuda that they had promised themselves three decades earlier. It was also a happy moment when Twichell officiated at Clara's wedding to Ossip GABRILOWITSCH in October 1909. Two and a half months later, however, Mark Twain's third daughter, Jean, died and

Twichell conducted her funeral in Elmira. Mark Twain himself died the following April. Twichell officiated at his funeral service in New York City, then returned home in time to see his wife just before she too died. Soon after these disasters, Twichell retired from his pastorate. He spent his last eight years in the Hartford home that his congregation had given him in 1888, and he died in 1918 with all nine of his children still alive.

"Two Little Tales" Short story that Mark Twain wrote while living in LONDON in fall 1900. The title alludes to its story-within-a-story structure. The first story is set in London in February 1900, when Britain was busy fighting the South African (Boer) War. The unidentified narrator tells of a friend who has another friend who cannot get the attention of the War Office; this man has invented a boot that would be invaluable to British troops in South Africa. Even the narrator's friend, who is "not unknown," cannot get through to the director-general of the Shoe-Leather Department.

This story follows certain dialogue conventions. As the friend explains his difficulties, the narrator exposes the fallacies of his arguments, asserting that he knows better because he is "very old and very wise." He explains how to break through the government bureaucracy by means of a parable: "How the Chimney-sweep Got the Ear of the Emperor." This second story concerns the emperor of an unnamed realm vexed by the "plague of dysentery" devastating his army. The emperor himself becomes afflicted; nothing can be done, despite the efforts of the greatest physicians of the land.

Meanwhile, Tommy, a lowly 16-year-old assistant cesspool cleaner, has a younger chimney-sweep friend, Jimmy, who says he can cure the emperor. He learned from an old Zulu man that eating a slice of ripe watermelon will quickly cure any case of dysentery. Tommy conveys the idea to the emperor by telling it to a butcher, who in turn tells a chestnut-seller, and so on. Finally, the message reaches the Lord High Chamberlain and the emperor himself. Tommy explains that everyone has a special friend willing to pass on a message; one only has to find the *first* friend to get the message started.

After the emperor is cured, he wants to give a suitable reward. Responsibility for the message is traced all the way back down to Jimmy. The emperor sends Jimmy his reward: a pair of his own boots. They are too big for Jimmy, so he gives them to the old Zulu. After the narrator finishes the story, his friend approaches a friend of the director-general. The army soon adopts his friend's boots.

BACKGROUND AND PUBLISHING HISTORY

Mark Twain's immediate inspiration for this 4,100-word short story appears to have been the success of the makers of PLASMON in getting the British army to adopt the diet supplement during the South African War. His point seems to be that bureaucracy is blind even to useful truths, unless it is penetrated by personal contacts. The story first appeared in London's *Century* magazine in November 1901.

U

Unionville NEVADA town located about 135 miles due northeast of Lake TAHOE. Founded as "Dixie" after silver was discovered in the nearby HUMBOLDT Mountains in August 1861 and soon renamed "Unionville" by Unionists, the town experienced a minor boom and was made the seat of Humboldt County (it is now in Pershing County). In December 1861, Mark Twain went there with three companions to prospect. *Roughing It* describes Unionville as having "eleven cabins and a liberty-pole" (chapter 28). During two weeks of futile prospecting, Mark Twain lived in a canvas-roofed shelter built against the side of a crevice. This "Humboldt house" is also described in chapter 27 of *Innocents Abroad.*

The Unreliable Stooge name that Mark Twain used for a rival reporter, Clement T. RICE, in articles he wrote for the VIRGINIA CITY TERRITORIAL ENTERPRISE in the early 1860s. By contrast, he called himself "The Reliable." The only allusion to Rice in *Roughing It* calls him "Boggs" (chapter 43).

Utah When Mark Twain passed through Utah in August 1861, its people lived under two governments. A federal territory since 1850, Utah was also a theocracy under the rule of Brigham YOUNG, who as president of the MORMON Church had settled the region and named it Deseret in 1847. From 1850 through 1857, Young was also the territorial governor, leaving no uncertainty as to where power lay. However, President James BUCHANAN removed Young from office in 1857 in order to assert firmer federal control and sent troops to oc-cupy the territory—which was then much larger than the modern state. War was averted, but the question of who really ruled Utah remained and was one of several questions on Mark Twain's mind when he arrived. Although he was in Utah just four or five days, *Roughing It* devotes about the same space to it that it does to CALIFORNIA, where he spent more than two years (chapters 13–18, appendixes A and B).

Mark Twain and his brother Orion entered what is now Utah on August 5, 1861, by STAGECOACH, following the same route as modern Interstate Highway 80 from southwestern Wyoming. They spent two days in SALT LAKE CITY—where they met the acting governor, Francis H. Wootton (mistakenly identified in Mark Twain's autobiography as Frank FULLER), then resumed their journey south through Camp Floyd, from which they turned west into the southern fringe of the Great Salt Lake Desert, entering NEVADA through GOSIUTE Indian land on about August 9.

Utah applied for statehood as early as 1850 but because of the suspect loyalty of its predominantly Mormon residents and federal opposition to their practice of polygamy, its applications were denied until 1896—six years after the Mormon Church renounced polygamy.

Utterback, Sister Minor character in *Huckleberry Finn.* She is one of several nosy PIKESVILLE neighbors who visit the Phelpses after Jim's escape attempt in chapter 41.

Mark Twain's AUTOBIOGRAPHY recalls a Mrs. Utterback who was a farmer's wife and a faith healer when he was a child.

Valley of Holiness Fictional place in *Connecticut Yankee*. A monastic center located near the Cuckoo Kingdom, the Valley of Holiness appears to be about 75 miles south of CAMELOT. After completing their mission of rescuing damsels from ogres, Hank MORGAN and SANDY enter the valley with a band of PILGRIMS, who are anxious to cleanse their sins in water from the valley's holy fountain. Coincidentally, the fountain stops flowing about 10 days before Hank arrives. He discovers that the fountain is an ordinary well with a leak, which he repairs; then he restarts its water beneath a spectacular fireworks display (chapter 23). After this "miracle," he contracts a bad cold and stays in the valley to rest. Meanwhile, King ARTHUR arrives with part of his court; then he and Hank begin a journey disguised as freemen, leaving the valley in a direction that takes them farther from Camelot (chapter 27).

Originally an arid site, the valley's importance as a religious center began several hundred years earlier when ascetic monks established a monastery. When a stream miraculously appeared, they built a bath and the water stopped flowing. After the abbot destroyed the bath, however, the waters returned and the valley became famous. At the time of Hank's visit, it has a population of several hundred monks and nuns and an unspecified number of holy hermits, as well as a large transient population of pilgrims. Mark Twain drew some of his ideas for the valley's holy fountain and ascetic hermits from the writings of W. E. H. LECKY.

Van Nostrand, Jack (1847?–1879, New Mexico) One of Mark Twain's closest friends on the QUAKER CITY cruise, Van Nostrand is the "Jack" of *Innocents Abroad*, which depicts "Jack" as a cheerful, carefree and gullible youth whom everyone likes (chapters 4, 8–10, 17, 33–34, 43–45, 47 and 55–58). About 20 at the time of the cruise, Van Nostrand came from Greenville, New Jersey. His previous travel experience included a Western stagecoach journey to which *Roughing It* alludes (chapter 6).

The Jack of *Innocents* is only loosely based on Van Nostrand. Chapter 47, for example, tells an almost certainly invented anecdote about Jack's wanting to clod a mud turtle for refusing to sing. Several incidents attributed to Jack in *Innocents* were originally attributed to "BROWN" in Mark Twain's earlier SAN FRANCISCO ALTA CALIFORNIA letters.

The only major side trip on which Van Nostrand accompanied Mark Twain during the *Quaker City* cruise was the expedition through the Holy Land. Earlier, he was with the small party that met GARIBALDI in Italy, but he missed the meeting with Czar ALEXANDER II when he remained in CONSTANTINOPLE with Dan SLOTE. In later years, Van Nostrand contracted tuberculosis and went west hoping to find relief. In 1875, he wrote to Mark Twain from Colorado, reporting that *Innocents Abroad* was making him a celebrity wherever he went.

"CANNIBALISM IN THE CARS" (1868) has a character called "John A. Van Nostrand of New Jersey."

Vanderbilt, "Commodore" Cornelius (May 27, 1794, Staten Island, New York–January 4, 1877, New York, New York) Transportation tycoon. After starting a Staten Island ferry service as a teenager, Vanderbilt entered the shipping business and went on to become one of America's richest men. During California's GOLD RUSH, he developed a profitable steamship route between New York and the Pacific Coast that included an overland crossing of NICARAGUA. He then got into transatlantic shipping and the railroad industries and became head of the New York Central Railroad. After he died, his son William Henry Vanderbilt (1821–1885) and grandson Cornelius Vanderbilt (1843–1899) expanded his transportation empire.

Mark Twain regarded Vanderbilt as a greedy, soulless man and was offended by the obsequious praise heaped on him. In March 1869, he published "An Open Letter to Commodore Vanderbilt" in *Packard's Monthly* (reprinted in NEIDER's *Life As I Find It*), in which he appealed to Vanderbilt to surprise the country by doing something truly worthy of praise. Vanderbilt's name appears occasionally in Mark Twain's writings as an icon of wealth. "THE ESQUIMAU MAIDEN'S ROMANCE," for example, mentions Vanderbilt several times and calls the Eskimo owner of 22 fish-hooks a "polar Vanderbilt." Chapter 28 of *Following the Equator* has a tall tale about Vanderbilt and a man named Ed JACKSON.

Venice A powerful Italian merchant state during the Middle Ages, Venice is built on scores of islets separated by canals that have made it famous. In the late 18th century, Venice fell under Austrian rule; it became part of the new kingdom of ITALY only in 1866—the year before Mark Twain's first visit. He arrived there by train on July 20, 1867 and stayed for two days. Drawing mostly on his memory and guidebooks, he wrote chapters 22–23 of *Innocents Abroad* about Venice, offering a detached and essentially negative depiction. To him, the city's glory was gone, leaving it to stand among "stagnant lagoons, forlorn and beggared." His only fresh anecdote about Venice concerns his guide—a former American slave. The chapters say so little about Venice's vast collections of art that Mark Twain's lack of interest is obvious. Nevertheless, he developed a lecture on Venice that he delivered successfully in California in 1868. After returning to the East Coast, he incorporated parts of his Venice material into his "AMERICAN VANDAL ABROAD" lecture.

In late September 1878, Mark Twain returned to Venice with his family and stayed three weeks. During this visit, he and his wife bought an ornately carved bed that later became familiar in photographs of Mark Twain. Chapters 48–49 of *A Tramp Abroad* cover this visit and give a much more positive account of Venice's art than does *Innocents Abroad*. Mark Twain and his family also spent two weeks there in May 1892.

Vesuvius, Mount   An active volcano in southern ITALY, Vesuvius rises about 4,000 feet above the sea and stands 10 miles east of central NAPLES. Mark Twain visited Vesuvius during a midnight hike on August 9–10, 1867, reaching its crater at dawn. From there, he and his companions went to POMPEII. Chapter 30 of *Innocents Abroad* describes the Vesuvius visit, calling the volcano a "poor affair compared to the mighty volcano of KILAUEA" on Hawaii. Chapter 74 of *Roughing It* makes a similar comparison.

Though the eruption that buried nearby Pompeii in A.D. 79 is its most famous, Vesuvius has had several more devastating eruptions. A 1631 eruption, for example, killed over 18,000 people. On April 24, 1872—just five years after Mark Twain peered into its crater—Vesuvius suddenly erupted and killed dozens of tourists. More deadly eruptions occurred in 1905, 1929 and 1944.

Despite Mark Twain's higher regard for Hawaii's Kilauea, "Vesuvius" is the volcano whose name he most often uses in his imagery. Chapter 57 of *Life on the Mississippi,* for example, compares the orator Henry Clay DEAN to "another Vesuvius." In chapter 18 of *Connecticut Yankee,* Hank Morgan calls MORGAN LE FAY "a Vesuvius" compared to her husband, who is "but an extinct volcano." Hellfire Hotchkiss is a "Vesuvius, seen through the butt-end of a telescope," and India's city Benares is a "religious Vesuvius" (*Following the Equator,* chapter 51).

Vicksburg   MISSISSIPPI city that Mark Twain visited many times. Vicksburg stands at the confluence of the Yazoo and Mississippi rivers, due west of Jackson, the state capital. Mark Twain first saw the town when he took the PAUL JONES to New Orleans in February 1857.

Over his next four years as a steamboat pilot, he went past Vicksburg frequently, often stopping. In 1882 he returned to Vicksburg aboard the GOLD DUST—a journey described in *Life on the Mississippi.* On that trip, he learned that the Mississippi had shifted its channel six years earlier, leaving Vicksburg "a country town," until engineers rerouted the lower Yazoo to make it again accessible by steamboat.

During the CIVIL WAR, Vicksburg was a key to control of the Mississippi River. Union troops began bombarding it on May 18, 1863. On July 4, just as Robert E. Lee was withdrawing from Gettysburg, Vicksburg finally fell. Chapter 55 of *Roughing It* mentions how Mark Twain learned of the event while he was in Nevada and chapter 35 of *Life on the Mississippi* gives poignant details of how residents lived through the bombardment. Omitted portions of the latter book include additional passages on Vicksburg during the war.

Victoria (May 24, 1819, London, England–January 22, 1901, Isle of Wight)   Queen of Britain (1837–1901). The reigns of Victoria and her son, EDWARD VII, nearly

Dan Beard adapted a photograph of Queen Victoria for the troublesome old sow called "your highness" in chapter 20 of Connecticut Yankee.

coincided with Mark Twain's life span. Victoria became queen on June 20, 1837, a year and a half after Mark Twain's birth, and Edward died two weeks after Mark Twain's death. Mark Twain never met Victoria, but he mentions or alludes to her in many writings. *Huckleberry Finn,* for example, vaguely alludes to her succeeding her uncle WILLIAM IV on the throne (chapter 26). The unfinished "TOM SAWYER'S CONSPIRACY" alludes to her more directly; when Jim faces the possibility of being sold back into slavery, Tom Sawyer proposes to buy Jim himself, then take him to England to "hand him over to the Queen" to become a servant (chapter 8).

In December 1887, Mark Twain published "A Petition to the Queen of England" in HARPER'S MAGAZINE, twitting Victoria for unfairly taking income tax out of his English royalties. *Connecticut Yankee,* which he published two years later, contains Dan BEARD's caricature of Victoria as an old sow in chapter 20. In June 1897, Mark Twain covered the celebration of the queen's 60th anniversary jubilee in London for the *New York Journal.* In a 1909, an unknown publisher privately printed his reports in a bound booklet titled *Queen Victoria's Jubilee.* On the occasion of the queen's birthday in 1908, Mark Twain delivered a tribute to Victoria at a British banquet in New York City, offering what he called a "colossal eulogy."

Victoria Kamamalu (November 1, 1838, Hawaii–May 29, 1866, Honolulu, Hawaii) Hawaiian princess. The sister of King KAMEHAMEHA V, Victoria was next in line to the Hawaiian throne when she died suddenly on Oahu, a few days after Mark Twain sailed from the island. After he returned, he attended her funeral dirge on June 23, 1866 and her formal funeral a week later. He describes these ceremonies at length in his 14th letter to the SACRAMENTO UNION, comparing them to funerals of earlier times, which he calls "funeral OR-GIES." Much of this account appears in chapter 68 of *Roughing It.* His posthumously published remarks in his NOTEBOOK indicate that Victoria died while "forcing" her seventh abortion.

Vienna Capital of AUSTRIA. On September 27, 1897, Mark Twain and his family arrived in Vienna from SWITZERLAND, beginning a residence that would last 20 months. The next day, they rented a spacious suite in the Hotel Metropole on Franz-Josefs-Kai near the Danube River. They stayed there through the following May, then spent the summer of 1898 in KALTENLEUT-GEBEN, a short commute southwest of Vienna. In mid-October, they moved back inside the city, renting rooms in the new Hotel Krantz (now Hotel Ambassador) at Neuer Markt 6, where they remained until leaving for ENGLAND on May 26, 1899.

Then capital of the sprawling Austro-Hungarian Empire, Vienna was a bustling cultural center in which Mark Twain was lionized. Invited to countless social events, he met the empire's leading cultural figures,

spoke before many groups and was interviewed by numerous newspapers. The desire of his daughter Clara to study piano contributed to the family's staying there longer than they might otherwise have done, and in the course of her studies, she met her future husband, Ossip GABRILOWITSCH.

"Villagers of 1840–3" Informal notes on Mark Twain's Hannibal neighbors. While summering in WEGGIS, Switzerland, in 1897, Mark Twain wrote roughly 8,000 words about everyone he could remember from his childhood, drawing on his memories and an 1884 book on MARION COUNTY containing biographical sketches. He recorded these notes largely for his own satisfaction around the same time that he began writing "Hellfire Hotchkiss" and "TOM SAWYER'S CON-SPIRACY." "Villagers of 1840–3" is Mark Twain's own title, but he probably intended the second date to be "1853"—the year that he left Hannibal.

First published in the MARK TWAIN PAPERS project's *Hannibal, Huck and Tom* (1969), edited by Walter BLAIR, "Villagers" provides a trove of information on Mark Twain's early life and the people who inspired many characters in his Tom Sawyer and Huckleberry Finn stories. His notes are particularly rich on the Clemens family. He calls his father "Judge Carpenter," his brother Orion "Oscar Carpenter" and himself "Simon Carpenter."

Virginia Mark Twain's paternal grandparents were Virginians, and his father, John M. Clemens, was born in Virginia's Campbell County, near Lynchburg. Mark Twain himself grew up acutely aware of his father's pride in being a Missourian of Virginian birth. He satirizes this attitude in *The Gilded Age,* whose Missourian Colonel SELLERS considers himself a "Virginia gentleman." In *Pudd'nhead Wilson,* Judge DRISCOLL is another Missourian who believes that his highest duty in life is to keep his great inheritance as a member of the "First Families of Virginia" (F.F.V.) unsmirched (chapter 12). Mark Twain's own attitude was different. *Roughing It* alludes to his personal discovery that his father's "sumptuous legacy of pride in his fine Virginian stock" was not enough to live on by itself (chapter 42). Virginia pride is also central to "A DOUBLE-BARRELLED DETEC-TIVE STORY."

Mark Twain probably first entered Virginia during one of his many visits to WASHINGTON, D.C. In 1907, he visited Jamestown, Virginia twice aboard H. H. ROGERS's yacht KANAWHA. In April 1909, he spoke at a dinner in Rogers's honor in Norfolk.

Virginia City Western NEVADA town. One of America's great "boom towns," Virginia City grew from nothing to rival SAN FRANCISCO in culture and financial clout. It then slid back to near nothingness, saved from oblivion only by exploiting memories of its former greatness.

Virginia City, Nevada in Mark Twain's time. (*Roughing It,* chapter 43)

The town was built on the steep eastern slope of 7,820-foot high Mount Davidson, amid rugged hills 12 miles northeast of CARSON CITY. It began as the "Ophir Diggings" mining camp when the COMSTOCK Lode was discovered in mid-1859 and was soon renamed "Virginia City"—reportedly after James Fenimore, a popular miner nicknamed "Old Virginia." Over the next several years, it grew apace with the local mining industry and became the seat of Storey County. During the 1860s, its buildings inched up Mount Davidson in terraced streets, while a vast labyrinth of subterranean mining tunnels spread out below it and the region surrounding it was stripped of timber.

When Mark Twain arrived in September 1862, Virginia City had nearly 10,000 residents and was entering the "flush times" described in *Roughing It* (chapters 42–55). As he took up his reporting duties for the VIRGINIA CITY TERRITORIAL ENTERPRISE, he was drawn into daily contact with leading miners, businessmen and politicians, as well as touring celebrities, such as Adah Isaacs MENKEN and Artemus WARD. He also became familiar with the town's many saloons, desperadoes and other seamy aspects. On July 27, 1863, he lost all his personal possessions when the White House hotel burned down (an incident fictionalized in chapter 7 of *The American Claimant*). He later roomed with Dan DE QUILLE at 25 North B Street. Apart from several trips to California, he remained in Virginia City until late May 1864, when he moved to San Francisco. During his time in Virginia City, he began using the name "MARK TWAIN" and established his reputation as a professional writer.

Mark Twain returned to Virginia City twice. In late October 1866, he lectured there on Hawaii, but left abruptly after friends played an unwelcome joke on him by holding him up at gunpoint. His last visit was in early May 1868, when he stayed several days after delivering two lectures on the HOLY LAND in April. He reportedly witnessed a hanging during this visit.

Virginia City began declining in the late 1860s, but enjoyed its greatest boom after new silver strikes were made in the early 1870s. During that decade, its population rose to more than 20,000—possibly as many as 30,000—residents. It boasted substantial schools, several daily and weekly newspapers, fine restaurants and hotels, an opera house, meeting halls, benevolent societies and a business section built largely of brick and stone. Gas lit its streets, omnibuses connected it to adjacent GOLD HILL and there were plans for streetcars. Attracting the leading entertainers and lecturers of the time, it lacked few amenities that San Francisco could provide and its mine owners were major players in the Pacific Coast's financial world.

Shortly after recovering from a devastating fire in its business district on October 26, 1875, Virginia City reached its apogee. Around 1878, however, its mines began their final decline. By 1900, the town had shrunk to just 2,700 residents. Fifty years later, barely 500 persons remained. Since then, however, the town has experienced modest growth by developing its historic resources into a tourist attraction. Emphasizing its Mark Twain heritage along with its mining history, it has restored many 19th-century buildings, including Piper's Opera House and the *Enterprise* building, which now houses a Mark Twain museum.

Virginia City Territorial Enterprise NEVADA's leading newspaper during the 19th century, the *Enterprise* began as a weekly on December 18, 1858 in Genoa, 13 miles south of CARSON CITY, where it relocated in November 1859. A year later, it moved again, to VIRGINIA CITY, where it struggled to survive until Joe GOODMAN and Denis MCCARTHY bought into it in March 1861. Its whole operation, as well as its staff living quarters, were then housed within a squalid one-story building. As the local mining industry boomed, however, so did the *Enterprise*. Goodman and McCarthy found larger quarters for the

NEVADA'S FIRST NEWSPAPER
Established 1858

The revived Territorial Enterprise *celebrates the memory of Mark Twain and Dan De Quille.*

paper and began publishing it as a daily in September 1861. It prospered so rapidly that they moved it into a new three-story brick building with steam-powered printing presses in July 1863. Still standing on South C Street, that building now houses a Mark Twain museum in its basement.

Mark Twain began his association with the *Enterprise* while he was prospecting at AURORA. Around April 1862, he started sending the paper humorous letters signed "JOSH." Goodman thought enough of his writing to offer him a job at $25 a week—a figure that later rose to $40. Aside from Mark Twain's evident writing talent, the fact that his brother, Orion Clemens, was secretary to the territorial government may have influenced Goodman's decision. Goodman knew that Mark Twain was familiar with the workings of the territorial government, and that Orion was responsible for ordering government printing jobs. In any case, the paper's top writer, Dan DE QUILLE, was planning a long leave of absence and Goodman needed someone to fill in for him.

In late September, Mark Twain arrived in Virginia City to begin his first real job as a newspaper reporter. With the guidance of Goodman, De Quille and Rollin DAGGETT, he began learning his trade. He covered local news and territorial legislature sessions and wrote humorous sketches. A lively, intelligent paper respected for both its news and wit, the *Enterprise* was an ideal workshop in which Mark Twain could develop his talent. Goodman encouraged him to be creative and irreverent, and allowed him considerable freedom. This he was quick to use, as proved by his PETRIFIED MAN HOAX, published only a month after his arrival. Goodman also tolerated his occasional lapses, such as when he published his MASSACRE HOAX a year later. The 17-month period that Mark Twain spent with the paper was one of the happiest and busiest of his life; chapters 42–45 of *Roughing It* recall it with relish.

In May 1864, Mark Twain resigned abruptly and went to San Francisco with his friend Steve GILLIS, an *Enterprise* compositor. According to his AUTOBIOGRAPHY, he had charge of the paper while Goodman was out of the state and got into a dispute with the rival VIRGINIA CITY UNION's owner, whom he challenged to a duel. The duel did not come off, but he left to avoid arrest under an anti-dueling law. After resettling in California, he spent four months reporting for the SAN FRANCISCO CALL, then became the *Enterprise*'s Pacific Coast correspondent. His last known sketch for the *Enterprise* appeared in December 1865. His formal association with the paper ended, but he retained his friendships with several staff members.

In later years, the *Enterprise*'s fortunes followed those of the Comstock, which experienced its biggest boom in the early 1870s. Goodman, by then the paper's sole owner, sold out in early 1874. As the Comstock's mines played out, Virginia City's population shrank so drastically that the *Enterprise* finally had to close down in 1893. It was later revived as a weekly, largely to serve tourists.

No complete run of the *Enterprise* still exists; the last known collection was destroyed when San Francisco's public library burned down in the 1906 earthquake. Many of Mark Twain's *Enterprise* articles are now known only through reprints in other western newspapers; some—including his Josh letters—are lost altogether. Selections of his *Enterprise* material have been collected in *Mark Twain of the Enterprise*, edited by Henry Nash SMITH (1957), and in the first two volumes of the MARK TWAIN PAPERS project's edition *Early Tales & Sketches* (1979 and 1981), edited by Edgar Marquess Branch and Robert H. Hirst.

Virginia City Union NEVADA newspaper. A rival to the VIRGINIA CITY TERRITORIAL ENTERPRISE. The daily *Union* began in CARSON CITY as the weekly *Silver Age* after the *Enterprise* relocated from there to Virginia City in 1860.

In November 1862—shortly after Mark Twain joined the *Enterprise*—new owners moved the weekly to Virginia City and renamed it the *Daily Union,* indicating their Northern bias during the CIVIL WAR. As COMSTOCK mines boomed, the *Union* and *Enterprise* waged a lively competition, often attacking each other in print. Nevertheless, one of Mark Twain's closest Virginia City friends was Clement T. RICE, a *Union* reporter whom he calls Boggs in *Roughing It.* A *Union* editor, Thomas FITCH, is the "Mr. F." of chapter 51. In early 1864, when Mark Twain had charge of the *Enterprise* during its editor's absence, he accused the *Union* in print of not living up to its SANITARY COMMISSION pledges. The *Union*'s proprietor, James Laird, then running his paper in the absence of his regular editor, responded in kind. According to Mark Twain's AUTOBIOGRAPHY, their feud became so vicious that he challenged Laird to a duel and ended up leaving Nevada to avoid arrest.

A new owner bought the *Union* in 1868 and changed its name to the *Trespass.* After that it went through a series of ownership and name changes and was eventually moved to California.

Chapter 42 of *Roughing It* mentions an unrelated newspaper called the *Esmeralda Union,* which was published in AURORA, Nevada from March 1864 to November 1867.

W

Wagner, Richard (May 22, 1813, Leipzig, Germany–February 13, 1883, Venice, Italy) German composer. A major innovator in opera, Wagner was one of the most influential composers of Mark Twain's time. Mark Twain disliked opera and especially disliked Wagner's operas. In May 1878, he attended Wagner's *Lohengrin* (1847) in MANNHEIM—a painful experience he describes in *A Tramp Abroad* (chapters 9–10). Told that the ability to appreciate music such as Wagner's requires methodical training, he implies that no one could like such music naturally.

Mark Twain heard Wagner's opera *Parsifal* (1882) when he revisited Germany in 1891. "At the Shrine of St. Wagner," written for the NEW YORK SUN (December 6, 1891), describes his visit to Bayreuth, where Wagner founded a musical festival in 1876.

Mark Twain has been credited with a famous quip expressing the sentiment that "Wagner's music is better than it sounds." The remark actually comes from Bill Nye (1850–1896), a contemporary humorist whom he quotes in his autobiography.

Wakeman, Captain Edgar (Ned) (1818, Connecticut–May 8, 1875, Oakland, California) Sea captain. One of the most colorful people whom Mark Twain ever knew, Wakeman was the model for several fictional characters and the subject of many anecdotes in Mark Twain's NOTEBOOKS and AUTOBIOGRAPHY. Wakeman's forceful personality, storytelling ability, life experiences and rich imagination had an immense impact on Mark Twain's imaginative writings.

According to Wakeman's own memoirs, he was born on a Connecticut farm, went to sea at 14 and traveled the entire world. He lacked formal education, but—as Mark Twain liked to stress—"knew the Bible by heart." He had been sailing the Pacific Coast for 17 years when Mark Twain was his passenger on the steamer *America* in December 1866. By then, Wakeman was married, had two daughters and lived in Oakland, California. Mark Twain mentions Wakeman by name in his first travel letter to the SAN FRANCISCO ALTA CALIFORNIA from the *America;* later letters call the ship the *Columbia* and Wakeman himself "Captain Waxman" (these letters are reprinted in MARK TWAIN'S TRAVELS WITH MR. BROWN). Mark Twain met Wakeman a second time in PANAMA in mid-1868. Contrary to some accounts, Mark Twain sailed with Wakeman just once; their second meeting was at a Panama City hotel.

After Wakeman suffered a debilitating stroke in 1872, Mark Twain published an appeal in the *Alta* for contributions to help his family. Two years later, Wakeman asked him to help write his life story; Mark Twain replied with the suggestion that his brother, Orion Clemens, help instead, but this scheme came to nothing. In mid-1874, Mark Twain's friend Joseph TWICHELL had a chance encounter with Wakeman while both were sailing along the Pacific Coast. Three years after Wakeman's death, Wakeman's daughter published his memoirs as *The Log of an Ancient Mariner* (1878). The book recounts some of the episodes that Mark Twain fictionalized, but says nothing about Mark Twain himself.

Mark Twain's first major characterization of Wakeman appears in *Roughing It*, in which Wakeman becomes Captain Ned BLAKELY, who hangs a murderer near Peru (chapter 50). Mark Twain's later sketch "SOME RAMBLING NOTES OF AN IDLE EXCURSION," incorporates anecdotal material that Twichell gathered from his meeting with Wakeman. In this story, Wakeman becomes Captain Hurricane JONES and Twichell is the Reverend PETERS.

"CAPTAIN STORMFIELD'S VISIT TO HEAVEN" evolved out of a story that Wakeman told Mark Twain in 1868 about a dream he had of going to heaven. The story features a loosely drawn Wakeman as Captain Eli STORMFIELD, who differs from Wakeman in having been born at sea and having reached the age of 65. Other characters whom Wakeman helped to inspire include Captain Saltmarsh in *The American Claimant*, Captain Davis in "THE GREAT DARK," Admiral Abner Stormfield in "The Refuge of the Derelicts" and Judge Sim ROBINSON in "THOSE EXTRAORDINARY TWINS."

Walter Scott Fictional STEAMBOAT that Jim and Huck explore in chapters 12–13 of *Huckleberry Finn*. The *Walter Scott* is a wreck "that had killed herself on a rock." Its position on the Mississippi River appears to be somewhere between Thebes, Illinois and Commerce, Missouri, perhaps 25 miles northwest of CAIRO, Illinois. Against Jim's advice, Huck insists on boarding it during a storm. Inside, he hears two men, Jake PACKARD and BILL, discussing whether to kill a third man, Jim TURNER, who is tied up. Huck wants to strand these murderers aboard the wreck by cutting their skiff loose, and then find a sheriff to arrest them. However, Jim discovers that their own raft has drifted away, so they take the murderers' skiff themselves. When Huck goes ashore to find help for the stranded men, he learns that the steamboat is called the *Walter Scott.* The boat breaks up before a local FERRYBOATMAN gets to it.

Steamboat names associated with romantic literature, such as "Ivanhoe" and "Lady of the Lake," were common on the Mississippi River during Mark Twain's time. *Walter Scott* was the name of a real NEW ORLEANS–based side-wheeler during the 1830s. Mark Twain evidently chose the name for his fictional steamboat as a subtle dig at the Scottish writer Sir Walter SCOTT.

Walters, Mister Minor character in *Tom Sawyer.* "A slim creature of thirty-five with a sandy goatee and short sandy hair," Walters is the earnest superintendent of Tom's Sunday school. In chapter 4, Walters wants to impress the visiting Judge THATCHER by awarding a Bible to someone who has mastered 2,000 Bible verses. Shocked when Tom Sawyer steps forward to claim a Bible, he correctly suspects that something is wrong.

"Wapping Alice" Posthumously published story. In 1877, while Mark Twain was living in Hartford, Lizzie Wells, a family maid, tripped the burglar alarm, revealing the fact that she was admitting a secret lover named Willie Taylor. When Mark Twain and Joseph TWICHELL later confronted Wells, she claimed that Taylor had made her pregnant, and they pressured him into marrying her. Over the next 30 years, Mark Twain wrote about this incident intermittently. After first using real names, he rewrote the story around 1897 as fiction and set it in LONDON's Wapping district. This version retained many real details of the Wells incident, but added a surprising twist: After the fictional Alice marries her lover, she announces that she is actually a man.

After failing to sell the story to HARPER'S MAGAZINE in 1907, Mark Twain set it aside. It was first published in 1981 by the Friends of the Bancroft Library—with which the MARK TWAIN PAPERS project is affiliated. A special booklet edited by Hamlin Hill includes all of Mark Twain's "Wapping Alice" manuscripts, several letters to his wife and the text of "The MCWILLIAMSES and the Burglar Alarm."

"The War Prayer" Short story written in early 1905 and published posthumously. An outgrowth of Mark Twain's increasing opposition to war and imperialism, "The War Prayer" expresses the horrible implications of war by spelling out the full meaning of military victory. The story's single incident may go back a moment described in *Life on the Mississippi,* in which an apparently deranged man delivers a speech that leaves

his audience thinking that he is an archangel (chapter 57).

SYNOPSIS

The setting could be any Christian country during any war. Patriotism is rampant, soldiers are marching off and churches everywhere are asking God to support their cause. The scene narrows to a single church packed with people whose young men will leave the next day. After the pastor delivers a long, eloquent prayer, asking God to bless their arms and grant them victory, a strange elderly man in a robe advances to the pulpit and motions him aside. Calling himself a messenger from the Throne, the stranger explains that the prayer just delivered is actually two prayers: one uttered, the other *unuttered.* God will grant the uttered prayer if the parishioners wish it, he promises—but only after he articulates for them the unuttered prayer behind their request for "victory." He then asks God to tear the enemy to bloody shreds, devastate his homes, leave his unoffending widows grief-stricken and his children homeless. After the man finishes, everyone concludes that he is a lunatic because there is no sense in what he has said.

PUBLISHING HISTORY

According to A. B. PAINE, Mark Twain had no intention of trying to publish this story in his lifetime; however, he did submit it to HARPER'S BAZAAR, which rejected it as unsuitable. Paine himself included a long extract in *Mark Twain: A Biography* (1912), and he published the entire story in EUROPE AND ELSEWHERE (1923). Frederick ANDERSON later included a corrected text in *A Pen Warmed-up in Hell* (1972).

The television play MARK TWAIN: BENEATH THE LAUGH-TER (1979) depicts Mark Twain reading the manuscript of "The War Prayer" to his shocked daughter Jean. As he reads, the scene cuts to a 19th-century Protestant church, in which the story is acted out with Richard Moll as the stranger. Another dramatization of "The War Prayer" is appended to the end of the television play "THE PRIVATE HISTORY OF A CAMPAIGN THAT FAILED" (1981).

Ward, Artemus (April 26, 1834, Waterford, Maine– March 6, 1867, Southampton, England) Pseudonym of the popular American humorist Charles Farrar Browne. Though Ward's life was short, it paralleled that of the slightly younger Mark Twain in many ways. Just 13 when his father died, Ward went to work as a printer, entered journalism and traveled throughout the East. By the early 1850s, he was setting type and writing for Boston's CARPET-BAG—the first eastern magazine in which Mark Twain published a story. Ward then drifted to Ohio, where he became a columnist on the *Cleveland Plain Dealer.* In 1858, he started writing

Artemus Ward, whom Mark Twain thought "one of the kindest and gentlest men in the world," as well as one of the funniest. (Don C. Seitz, *Artemus Ward*, 1919)

letters to the paper in the persona of "Artemus Ward," an illiterate but shrewd YANKEE showman traveling with a wax museum. By the time he left Cleveland for New York City in 1860, his letters had earned him a national reputation and he was known primarily by his pen name. He continued writing sketches and launched a new career as a humorous lecturer.

During a western tour, Ward spent the last three weeks of December 1863 in VIRGINIA CITY, Nevada, where he and Mark Twain became friends. Eight years later, Mark Twain recorded a fanciful account of their meeting in "First Interview with Artemus Ward," which was later reprinted in SKETCHES, NEW AND OLD (1875). Ward encouraged Mark Twain to return to the East and later asked him to contribute a sketch to a book he was compiling for George W. CARLETON. This invitation led to the JUMPING FROG STORY, whose first published version is told in the FRAME of a letter from Mark Twain to Ward.

Ward's success on the LECTURE circuit also inspired Mark Twain to take up this vocation a few years later. In fact, Mark Twain was lecturing in the Midwest in March 1867, when Ward, not yet 33, died of tuberculosis while on his own triumphant tour of England. Ward's early death left Mark Twain as America's premier humorist, but Mark Twain was still a few years away from the national renown that *Innocents Abroad* bring him.

Fascinated by wordplay, Ward based much of his written humor on puns and exaggerated misspellings (cacography). His style, which was comparatively fresh during his time, enjoyed a brief vogue, but his work was soon mostly forgotten. Except in his early Thomas Jefferson SNODGRASS letters, Mark Twain never followed this style, preferring instead to recreate authentic vernacular voices. The extent to which Ward influenced Mark Twain's writing has been a subject of debate. Both humorists often exaggerated the naïveté of their narrators, created logical confusion in their plots and employed anticlimax and understatement. While specific examples of Ward's influences on Mark Twain's work have been demonstrated, it has been argued that the similarities may simply arise from the fact that both men drew on the same traditions in American humor. It is more generally acknowledged, however, that Ward had a direct influence on Mark Twain's lecturing style. Both were adept at the deadpan delivery of humorous stories and both were expert at making effective use of dramatic pauses in their delivery.

Mark Twain retained a high opinion of Ward as both a friend and a humorist. During the 1871–72 lecture season he delivered a lecture on Ward. In 1880, he called Ward "one of the kindest and gentlest men in the world" and described his famous "Babes in the Wood" lecture as the funniest thing he had ever heard. Chapter 9 of *Connecticut Yankee* alludes to Ward as one of the humorists who have told the same tired joke throughout history. Nine pieces by Ward appear in MARK TWAIN'S LIBRARY OF HUMOR (1888).

Warner, Charles Dudley (September 12, 1829, Plainfield, Massachusetts–October 20, 1900, Hartford, Connecticut) New England journalist and author. After graduating from college, Warner spent a year and a half as a railroad surveyor in Missouri, then worked in business in Philadelphia while studying law. He earned his legal degree in 1858, and practiced in Chicago until J. R. HAWLEY invited him to become assistant editor of the *Hartford Evening Press* in 1861. Hawley's CIVIL WAR duties left Warner effectively the newspaper's editor—a position that Warner kept when Hawley entered politics after the war. The *Evening Press* consolidated with the *Courant* in 1867 and Warner was its coeditor for the rest of his life. Meanwhile, he also traveled broadly, wrote popular books about Europe and published collections of humorous essays.

After Mark Twain became Warner's neighbor in Hartford's NOOK FARM neighborhood, their families became close. Drawing on their different experiences in Missouri, Warner and Mark Twain coauthored what was the first novel for each—*The Gilded Age* (1873). Warner did not write more long fiction until 1889, when he began a trilogy of serious novels about the corruption of wealth. He also wrote biographies of Washington Irving and Captain John Smith and was a contributing editor to HARPER'S MAGAZINE (1884–98), on which he succeeded W. D. HOWELLS as author of "The Editor's Study" column. He later coedited the 31-volume *Library* of the World's Best Literature (1896–97) with his brother, George H. Warner (1833–1919).

After a five-year sojourn abroad, Mark Twain returned to the United States in October 1900, five days before Warner died. The painful task of attending Warner's funeral in Hartford evidently contributed to his decision not to live in that city again.

Life on the Mississippi mentions Warner twice: as coauthor of *The Gilded Age* (chapter 47) and as the skeptic who questions the authenticity of the Charlie WILLIAMS story (chapter 52).

Warren, C. H. (*fl.* 1890s)   Illustrator. Along with F. M. SENIOR, Warren illustrated the first American edition of *Pudd'nhead Wilson* (1894). He drew the marginal illustrations for chapters 11, 16, 20 and 21 and the conclusion. He also contributed at least nine illustrations to *Following the Equator* (1897), mostly of scenes in India.

Warrimoo   Steamship on which Mark Twain crossed the PACIFIC in 1895. The *Warrimoo* left British Columbia, CANADA on August 23 and stopped at HAWAII and FIJI before reaching Sydney, AUSTRALIA on September 16. Repairs delayed its Canadian departure because its young captain had run it aground near Vancouver on his first voyage. Mark Twain was on the *Warrimoo* for 24 days—one of the longest periods he spent on any ship except the QUAKER CITY. He enjoyed a generally calm and rainless voyage and regarded the *Warrimoo* as reasonably comfortable. *Following the Equator* alludes to the *Warrimoo* several times without mentioning its name (chapters 1–9).

Warwick   City in ENGLAND. Standing on the Avon River, about 20 miles southeast of Birmingham, Warwick is a popular tourist town because of its proximity to SHAKESPEARE's birthplace and its well-preserved 14th-century castle. Mark Twain visited Warwick in September 1872, and may have returned in 1873 or 1879. *Connecticut Yankee* opens in Warwick Castle, where the frame-narrator (probably Mark Twain himself) meets the Yankee while on a tour. Their guide points out Sir SAGRAMOUR LA DESIROUS's sixth-century suit of armor with a bullet hole in it, giving the Yankee the starting point for his tale. The novel ends in the nearby Warwick Arms hotel. Though Warwick is far north of where CAMELOT appears to be, Mark Twain probably chose it as a setting because of his familiarity with the castle's armor collection. Nothing in the real castle's collection, however, goes back as far as the sixth century.

Warwickshire, the county surrounding Warwick, is also apparently the site of the Earl of ROSSMORE's fictional Cholmondeley Castle in *The American Claimant*.

Washington, Booker Taliafero (c. 1856, Franklin County, Virginia–November 14, 1915, Tuskegee, Alabama)   Black educator. Perhaps the most influential black American of his time, Washington was the princi-

pal of Tuskegee Institution (1881–1915), an Alabama trade school that drew much of its funding from northern philanthropists, such as Andrew CARNEGIE, John D. Rockefeller and H. H. ROGERS. Mark Twain greatly admired Washington and helped support his work; they first met at Ambassador Joseph H. Choate's Fourth of July reception in LONDON in 1899. Washington briefly mentions this meeting in his autobiography, *Up From Slavery* (1901), while Mark Twain comments on it at greater length in his own AUTOBIOGRAPHY. The two men later met socially and at such public functions as a Lotos Club dinner welcoming Mark Twain home from Europe on November 10, 1900; Woodrow Wilson's installation as president of Princeton on October 25, 1902; and benefits for Tuskegee in January 1906 and January 1908. After Mark Twain died, Washington wrote a tribute that praised him for his sympathetic treatment of the slave Jim in *Huckleberry Finn* and for his work for Congo reform.

Washington, D.C.   America's capital city was little developed when Mark Twain first saw it in 1854. Then an 18-year-old journeyman printer working in PHILADELPHIA, he vacationed for about four days in Washington in mid-February that year and wrote a detailed letter home about the city that his brother Orion published in the MUSCATINE JOURNAL.

When Mark Twain next visited Washington in late 1867, both he and the city had changed considerably. Now 32 years old, he had a national reputation as a writer and he was private secretary to Nevada's Senator W. M. STEWART. Washington itself was booming as the country emerged from the CIVIL WAR, and Congress was on the verge of impeaching President Andrew JOHNSON. In the midst of political intrigue and corruption, Mark Twain quickly became disenchanted with national politics. By March 1868, he was out of Washington and moving his career in other directions. Meanwhile, he wrote several sketches satirizing politics and government, including "MY LATE SENATORIAL SECRETARYSHIP," "CANNIBALISM IN THE CARS," "THE MAN WHO PUT UP AT GADSBY'S," "The Facts in the Case of the Great Beef Contract" and "THE FACTS CONCERNING THE RECENT RESIGNATION." A few years later, he and C. D. WARNER made Washington a principal setting in *The Gilded Age* (1873). In the sequel to that story, *The American Claimant* (1892), Washington is the novel's primary setting. Colonel SELLERS assumes that Washington HAWKINS has come to the capital to make a claim against the government, since he can think of no other reason a person go there; however, aside from the fact that Hawkins has come to Washington as a hopeful congressional delegate, the city itself has little relevance to the story.

After early 1868, Mark Twain never again lived in Washington, but he visited it frequently between 1869 and 1891. In July 1870, while he was there to lobby for his father-in-law's business interests, Mathew Brady photographed him. In May 1877, Mark Twain was in

Washington for the opening of AH SIN, the play he wrote with Bret Harte. He and G. W. CABLE lectured there in November 1884 and closed their long tour there the following February. A year later, Mark Twain made his first formal appearance before Congress when he testified on copyright to a Senate committee. After visiting the city several times in 1890 and 1891, he appears not to have returned again until November 1905, when he dined at the White House with Theodore ROOSEVELT. The following year, he testified on copyright before Congress in January and December. During the latter occasion, he made his debut in a WHITE SUIT.

Washoe Former name for NEVADA. Taken from the name of an Indian community near Lake TAHOE, "Washoe" was a popular nickname for the region among settlers when Mark Twain lived in Nevada in the early 1860s. It applied particularly to the area between Tahoe, CARSON CITY and VIRGINIA CITY that contains the Washoe Mountains, Washoe Valley and Washoe Lake. *Roughing It* introduces the term in its description of the "Washoe ZEPHYR" (chapter 21). When Nevada joined the Union in 1864, the federal Committee on Territories overruled residents who wanted to call the new state "Washoe" because it thought the name undignified. Washoe is now the name of a county in northwestern Nevada that extends from Reno to Oregon along the California border.

Watson, Miss Character in *Huckleberry Finn*. A "slim old maid," Miss Watson is a recent arrival to ST. PETERSBURG, where she lives with her sister, the Widow DOUGLAS, and helps to raise Huck. Huck finds her a more severe and pious guardian than her sister, and hankers to get away from her control. At the beginning of *Huckleberry Finn*, Miss Watson owns the slave Jim. For financial reasons, she decides to sell him; when he overhears her plans, he flees to JACKSON'S ISLAND, where he joins Huck. Through the ensuing chapters, Huck is troubled by the idea that he is harming Miss Watson by stealing her slave. To ease his conscience, he finally writes her a letter, telling her where Jim is. However, his affection for Jim proves stronger than his conscience, so he tears up the letter and resigns himself to going to the "bad place" that Miss Watson has warned him against (chapter 31). Meanwhile, Miss Watson has died—a fact that Huck learns from Tom Sawyer in chapter 42. Before she died, she repented her decision to sell Jim and freed him in her will.

Mark Twain's tendency to forget details about his characters was particularly evident in his allusions to Miss Watson. His prelude to the "RAFT CHAPTER" in *Life on the Mississippi* alludes to Jim as belonging to the Widow DOUGLAS (chapter 3). He later started a sequel to *Huckleberry Finn*, "TOM SAWYER'S CONSPIRACY," in which Miss Watson is still alive. Another unfinished sequel, "HUCK FINN AND TOM SAWYER AMONG THE INDI-

ANS," mentions "old Miss Watson" as Jim's former owner.

Mark Twain modeled Miss Watson on an early schoolteacher, Mary Ann NEWCOMB. In the 1939 film adaptation of *Huckleberry Finn*, Miss Watson was played by Clara Blandick, who had previously appeared as Aunt POLLY in three films. One of the fullest portrayals of Miss Watson was by Anne Shropshire in the 1986 PBS television miniseries.

Webb, Charles Henry (January 24, 1834, Rouses Point, New York–May 24, 1905, New York, New York) Humorist, editor and inventor. A close contemporary of Mark Twain, Webb had a similarly diverse life. He went to NEW YORK CITY as a teenager, but interrupted his journalistic career by spending four years as a whaler and working in Illinois before returning to become a columnist for the *New York Times*. In April 1863, the *Times* sent him to California as a correspondent. On his way west, he stopped at VIRGINIA CITY, Nevada, where he met Mark Twain. After reaching San Francisco, Webb joined the staffs of the SAN FRANCISCO BULLETIN and the GOLDEN ERA, then founded the CALIFORNIAN, an influential literary weekly that published Bret HARTE's best work and many of Mark Twain's early sketches. After losing money in mine investments, Webb returned to New York in 1866. The following year he helped Mark Twain meet local newspaper people and became the publisher of Mark Twain's first book, THE CELEBRATED JUMPING FROG OF CALAVERAS COUNTY (1867). Through these years, Webb also wrote his own burlesques and plays.

In the early 1870s, Webb worked in banking and finance on Wall Street, then began writing letters to the NEW YORK TRIBUNE under the pen name "John Paul." Webb later concentrated on writing verses and working on inventions, including an adding machine that suffered the same long gestation and ultimate fate as the PAIGE COMPOSITOR in which Mark Twain invested heavily; both inventions went bust in 1893. Mark Twain eventually turned against Webb, whom he called a "liar and thief." He later described Webb's prose and poetry as puerile and attributed Webb's death to "over-cerebration."

Webster, Charles L. (September 24, 1851–April 26, 1891, Fredonia, New York) Mark Twain's business manager and nephew by marriage. Webster grew up in FREDONIA, New York, where as a child he accidentally killed an infant girl while playing with a gun. He later became a civil engineer and married Annie Moffett (1852–1950), the daughter of Mark Twain's sister Pamela Clemens MOFFETT, in 1875.

In March 1881, Mark Twain brought Webster to New York City to investigate the management of his KAOLATYPE Company and soon put him in complete charge. As Webster tried to salvage the doomed company, Mark Twain continually added to his responsibilities until Webster was his general business manager. Meanwhile, Mark Twain got James R. OSGOOD to bring Webster into his firm to organize a SUBSCRIPTION-BOOK department.

When Mark Twain started his own publishing firm in May 1884, he put Webster in charge and named the firm "Charles L. WEBSTER & COMPANY" after him. Webster became a full partner in March 1885 and was given additional financial authority the following January. The early successes of *Huckleberry Finn* and U. S. GRANT's *Memoirs* quickly elevated Webster to one of the nation's leading publishers; however, the company's fortunes soon waned, causing Mark Twain to grow impatient with Webster's management. In early 1888, Mark Twain made him take a leave of absence for health reasons and replaced him with Frederick HALL. By the end of the year, Webster was completely out of the company. With his health broken, he retired to Fredonia and died before reaching 40.

In a letter to his brother in 1889, Mark Twain said that he had never hated anyone as much as he hated Webster, whose vanity and ignorance he despised. He may have taken a subtle shot at Webster in *Connecticut Yankee* by having Hank MORGAN complain about ignorant people who never admit that they do not understand a big word (chapter 18)—a charge that Mark Twain made against Webster. Much of the invective that he pours out against Webster in his AUTOBIOGRAPHY was published in MARK TWAIN IN ERUPTION in 1940. Webster's son Samuel Charles Webster (1884–1962) replied to that book with *Mark Twain, Business Man* (1946), which documents Mark Twain's own responsibility for many of the business problems he blamed on Webster.

Webster & Company, Charles L. ("Websterco") Mark Twain's own publishing firm. Unhappy with most of his PUBLISHERS, Mark Twain established his own SUBSCRIPTION-BOOK company in May 1884, naming it after his junior partner and manager, Charles L. WEBSTER. His initial goal was simply to publish his own books, and he began successfully with *Huckleberry Finn* in 1885. Almost fortuitously, he got the contract to publish U. S. GRANT's *Memoirs* (1886)—a huge success. Now transformed into a major publisher, Webster & Company signed many new authors, but it never again matched its early successes. Its list included more memoirs by Civil War generals—Crawford, Hancock, McClellan, Sheridan and SHERMAN. It also published books by Irving Bacheller, John Kendrick Bangs, Dan BEARD, Poultney Bigelow, Matt Crim, Elizabeth Custer, Hawaii's King David Kalakaua, Leo Tolstoy and Walt Whitman. Aside from Grant's *Memoirs*, Mark Twain's own books remained Webster's most profitable titles. The firm reissued many of his earlier books and was the first publisher of *Connecticut Yankee* (1889), MERRY TALES (1892), *The American Claimant* (1892), *The £1,000,000

Bank-Note and Other New Stories* (1893), *Pudd'nhead Wilson* (1894) and *Tom Sawyer Abroad* (1894). The company also enjoyed some success with the anthology MARK TWAIN'S LIBRARY OF HUMOR (1887).

Webster's problems began in 1887. That year, Mark Twain thought that the company outdo Grant's book with an authorized biography of Pope LEO XIII that every Roman Catholic would want; however, the book barely broke even. Early the same year, the company paid $5,000 to Henry Ward BEECHER for his autobiography—two months before he died. Later that year, the firm discovered that its bookkeeper had embezzled $25,000. Meanwhile, it was sinking cash into the *Library of American Literature* (1887–90), an 11-volume anthology that later sold moderately well, but brought in cash on agonizingly slow subscription-payment plans.

Inclined to blame Webster for all the firm's problems, Mark Twain forced him out of the company in 1888 and replaced him with Frederick HALL. Hall increased the firm's publication rate and transformed it into a trade publisher. Meanwhile, Mark Twain weakened the firm by diverting a large part of its assets to the PAIGE COMPOSITOR. By the early 1890s, Webster & Company was in serious financial trouble. Mark Twain was living in Europe and had to commute frequently across the ATLANTIC to check on his business interests; he spent seven months in the United States in late 1893 and early 1894, trying to save the company. Although he was helped by H. H. ROGERS, it was too late. On April 18, 1894, a bank called in its loans and Webster filed for BANKRUPTCY.

Wecter, Dixon (January 12, 1906, Houston, Texas–June 24, 1950, Sacramento, California) Mark Twain scholar and editor. In 1946 the directors of the MARK TWAIN COMPANY, who included Clara Clemens, appointed Wecter to succeed Bernard DEVOTO as the estate's literary editor. An English professor at the University of California at Los Angeles, Wecter also chaired the research staff at the Huntington Library in San Marino, California, and was associate editor of the *Literary History of the United States*. His publications included *The Saga of American Society* (1937), *Edmund Burke and Kinsmen* (1939) and *When Johnny Comes Marching Home* (1944).

Wecter was born the same week that Mark Twain's first literary editor, A. B. PAINE, approached Mark Twain for permission to be his official biographer. Two days before Wecter was born, Paine moved into Mark Twain's house and began organizing his papers—one of the tasks that Wecter would later continue. Wecter also developed the first long-range publishing plan for the MARK TWAIN PAPERS.

In the fall of 1949 Wecter accepted a chair in history at the University of California at Berkeley, where he moved the project. That same year he published two collections of Mark Twain letters. *Mark Twain to Mrs.

Fairbanks drew on the Huntington's collection of Mark Twain correspondence with Mary FAIRBANKS. *The Love Letters of Mark Twain* encompasses correspondence between Mark Twain and Olivia Langdon Clemens and other family members, drawing on manuscripts owned by Clara Clemens.

Wecter saw the need to improve on Paine's multivolume biography of Mark Twain. One of his major goals was to write a definitive new biography, using the vast manuscript resources under his management. While attempting to retrace Mark Twain's wide travels, Wecter even boated down the Mississippi River reading Mark Twain's NOTEBOOKS. He completed his study only through the first 18 years of Mark Twain's life, however, before he died during a visit to California's mining country. His widow, Elizabeth Wecter, published what he had completed as *Sam Clemens of Hannibal* in 1952. Later that same year, Harper's published Wecter's *Report from Paradise*, the fullest version of Mark Twain's "CAPTAIN STORMFIELD'S VISIT TO HEAVEN" published up to that time. Henry Nash SMITH succeeded Wecter as editor of the Mark Twain Papers.

Weekly Occidental Nevada literary journal published by Thomas FITCH from March to April 1864. Little is known about the *Occidental*, which apparently lasted just six issues. Chapter 51 of *Roughing It* contains a colorful account of the ambitious paper's brief history, claiming that "Mr. F." (Fitch) engaged all the literary people in VIRGINIA CITY to write for it. They put particular energy into creating a serialized novel, for which each person was to write a chapter. *Roughing It* uses the episode as an excuse to present a BURLESQUE romance as the purported synopsis of the novel, claiming that when a drunken contributor wrote an unpublishable chapter, the *Occidental* went to press without it and the paper consequently died. An attempt was made to revive the paper with an apt new title, the "Phenix," but a sarcastic reporter suggested that "Lazarus" be more appropriate, provoking the townspeople to laugh the paper into permanent oblivion.

Roughing It also presents Mark Twain's burlesque poem "THE AGED PILOT MAN," which he claims to have written for the *Occidental* just before it folded.

Weggis (Wäggis) Resort town on the north shore of SWITZERLAND's Lake LUCERNE. In mid-August 1878, Mark Twain used Weggis as a base for climbing RIGI-KULM—an episode burlesqued in chapter 28 of *A Tramp Abroad*. He also spent several days there in September 1891. In mid-July 1897, he returned with his family and spent two months writing intensively before moving on to AUSTRIA. Most of the stories he began at Weggis on this last visit remained unfinished and were published posthumously—such works as "TOM SAWYER'S CONSPIRACY," "NO. 44, THE MYSTERIOUS STRANGER," "THE GREAT DARK" and "Hellfire Hotchkiss."

Westminster Central LONDON borough on the north shore of the THAMES. The district is the historic seat of English government and its Palace of Westminster—which was rebuilt several times—served as the primary residence of English monarchs from the mid-11th century until 1529, when HENRY VIII moved to nearby Whitehall Palace. In 1547, the old palace became the permanent seat of Parliament. After it burned down in 1834, new parliament buildings were built on the site. Although *The Prince and the Pauper* is set in 1547, it has King Henry living in the Palace of Westminster when Tom CANTY wanders onto its grounds in chapter 3. After Tom switches clothes with Prince EDWARD, he spends most of the next three weeks within the palace. Chapter 32 is set in nearby Westminster Abbey, the site of most of the English royal coronations since the 11th century. The next chapter returns to the Palace of Westminster, with Edward on the throne as king.

Mark Twain describes his June 1873 visit to the abbey in the posthumously published sketch "A MEMORABLE MIDNIGHT EXPERIENCE."

West Point Popular name for the United States Military Academy at West Point, New York, on the Hudson River, 35 miles north of NEW YORK CITY. Founded in 1802, the academy has long stressed engineering and mathematics curricula. Between 1881 and 1890, Mark Twain visited West Point at least six times, often reading to audiences there from his own work. In June 1881, he took a special train there with General SHERMAN. After an early 1882 visit, he arranged with the academy's Lieutenant C. E. S. Wood to print the first edition of *1601* in a West Point print shop.

In *Connecticut Yankee* "West Point" is the name of Hank MORGAN's sixth-century academy. He first mentions it in chapter 10 as a secret military academy he is keeping out of sight until he is ready to launch his civilization. Hank later plans to create a standing army and is disappointed to learn that King ARTHUR has already started staffing it with nobles instead of his highly trained West Pointers. In a competitive exam held in chapter 25, a cadet named Webster (possibly after Charles L. WEBSTER) displays his expertise in military, mathematical and other sciences.

What Is Man? Book published in 1906. In the last decades of his life, Mark Twain adopted a mechanistic and deterministic philosophy that he called his private "gospel," which he sums up in *What Is Man?* Published only anonymously during Mark Twain's lifetime, this 27,500-word volume is a Socratic dialogue in which an "Old Man" spends several days converting a "Young Man" to his philosophy, whose essential idea is that man is a machine controlled by outside forces, such as heredity, environment and training. Further, man creates nothing, acts only to satisfy his own needs, and should neither be praised for good acts nor be condemned for bad ones. Free will, heroism, genius, virtue

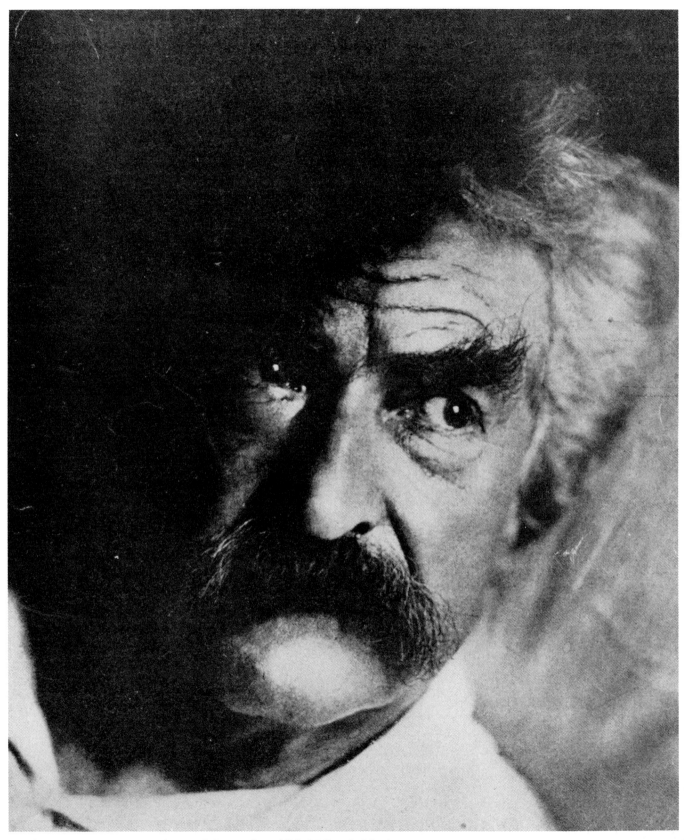

Mark Twain in a pensive mood around the time he published What Is Man? (Courtesy, Mark Twain Memorial)

and vice are all merely man's delusions. While the origins of Mark Twain's ideas are complex, two particularly important sources may have been W. E. H. LECKY and a man named MACFARLANE whom Mark Twain claimed to know when he was younger.

Mark Twain began articulating his private gospel during the early 1880s and first gave it public expression in "What Is Happiness?," a paper delivered to Hartford's MONDAY EVENING CLUB in February 1883. His gospel received fuller expression in *Connecticut Yankee* (1889), a novel that builds to a grimly deterministic ending. Midway through its narrative, for example, its hero Hank MORGAN decides that reasoning with Morgan Le Fay is pointless because of her training. He explains that "training is all there is *to* a person. We speak of nature; it is folly; there is no such thing as nature; what we call by that misleading name is merely heredity and training. We have no thoughts of our own, no opinions of our own; they are transmitted to us, trained into us" (chapter 18).

Though Mark Twain never publicly acknowledged his authorship of *What Is Man?*, he expressed many of its core ideas in "THE TURNING POINT OF MY LIFE," which HARPER'S BAZAAR published three months before he died. Other writings that deal with similar themes include his MYSTERIOUS STRANGER stories, "CORN-PONE OPINIONS" and "THE DERVISH AND THE OFFENSIVE STRANGER."

SYNOPSIS

(Remarks within parentheses derive from sources outside this dialogue.)

Part 1
As an Old Man (O.M.) and a Young Man (Y.M.) converse, the O.M. asserts that a human being is merely a machine. Objecting to this, the Y.M. demands proof, thus beginning their dialogue. Prodded by the O.M., the Y.M. defines a "machine." The O.M. then demonstrates how this definition applies to human behavior, showing that man is an impersonal engine. Whatever a man is, is due to his make and the influences of his heredity, habitat and associations. Commanded by *exterior* influences, man *originates* nothing, not even a thought. The O.M. goes on to argue that even the first man, ADAM, had no original thoughts. Only gods have them. Even SHAKESPEARE created nothing. He merely imitated people whom God had created.

Part 2
The O.M. dismisses acts of "self-sacrifice" that appear to demonstrate love, philanthropy or patriotism as motivated solely by the desire for self-approval that is trained into man. We help others because it gratifies *us;* we regret hurting others only because the guilt disturbs *us.*

Part 3
To prove his Gospel of Self-Approval, the O.M. challenges the Y.M. to cite an example of a totally selfless act.

The Y.M. suggests an example from a novel (Florence Wilkinson, *The Strength of the Hills,* 1901) in which a lumberman sacrifices his worldly interests to save souls for the glory of God and Christ, solely for duty's sake. The O.M. counters that the lumberman is acting only for self-approval; furthermore, he is indifferent to the hardships that his actions produce for his own family.

Later the Y.M. offers the sinking of the *Berkeley Castle* as an example of selfless sacrifice. At their colonel's command, a thousand unprotesting soldiers went down with the troopship so that women and children could be saved on its few lifeboats (an allusion to the H.M.S. *Birkenhead,* which sank off of South Africa in 1852, drowning about 450 people). The O.M. dismisses their heroism, however, as purely a product of their military training.

Part 4
The O.M. defines "training" as not merely formal instruction, but *all* outside influences that a person encounters from cradle to grave. To make his point, he asks why people adhere to certain religious sects and not to others. The answer lies in the cultures with which a person is associated.

To challenge the O.M.'s assertion that a man always acts to please his interior master, the Y.M. asks why it is that he scolds a servant, even though he *wants* to control his temper. The O.M. explains that there are two kinds of pleasure: primary and secondary. Scolding gives the Y.M. short-term primary pleasure, while mastering his temper provides long-term secondary pleasure.

Part 5
To further his case that man is a machine, the O.M. reminds the Y.M. how the mind sometimes works by itself all night, keeping one awake and restless, despite one's trying to make it stop. He challenges the Y.M. to command his mind not to wander. Several days later, the Y.M. reports back, conceding that he could not control his mind even once in 10 experiments. In one instance, for example, he could not clear his head of the popular song "The Sweet Bye and Bye." Other examples of man's inability to control his own mind include moments when he blurts out words without knowing that they are coming.

To defend his assertion that no man ever originates or creates anything, the O.M. argues that those we call "inventors" are merely discoverers who observe things and add to what others have already seen. The process is the same even in the creation of a Shakespearean play. Men observe and combine, just as a rat does when his observation of a smell leads to his discovery of a cheese.

Part 6
The Y.M. dislikes the fact that the O.M.'s theories strip away man's dignities and grandeurs, which the O.M. calls mere shams. The Y.M.'s objection to having man

reduced to the level of a rat leads to discussion of intellect and instinct. The O.M. argues that intellect works the same in both man and the animals; the difference is a matter only of capacity.

The O.M. flatly denies the existence of free will—untrammeled power to *act* as one pleases. He believes that there is only "free choice"—the ability to choose between options.

Conclusion

At their final meeting, the Y.M. asks the O.M. if he intends to publish his ideas. Challenged to answer this question himself, the Y.M. concedes that publishing this philosophy would be harmful. He finds it desolate and degrading, as it denies man glory, pride or heroism, turning him into a mere coffee mill. While the Y.M. frets that this philosophy must make a person wretched, the O.M. points out that he himself has an inborn temperament to be cheerful, despite his convictions. And it is differences in temperament that explain why different people may respond so differently to the same experiences. The O.M. sees no point in publishing his philosophy, since mankind generally *feels* rather than *thinks* and not respond to it.

BACKGROUND AND PUBLISHING HISTORY

After completing *Following the Equator* in 1897, Mark Twain began writing stories that might help him understand the disasters that were befalling his family. He left most of these manuscripts—such as "WHICH WAS THE DREAM?" and "THE GREAT DARK"—unfinished and was hesitant to express his opinions publicly. Between April and July 1898, while he was living in AUSTRIA, he wrote the first half of *What Is Man?* After setting the manuscript aside, he went back to it around late 1901 or early 1902, then tinkered with it over the next three or four years, while testing its ideas on members of his household and close friends. After deciding to publish the book, he deleted several chapters. One of them argues that man's "moral sense" places him below the animals because it enables him to do wrong; two others examine God's attitude toward man and argue that God is a cruel and vindictive being.

Mark Twain completed *What Is Man?* in the fall of 1905 and decided to publish it anonymously the following spring. To make it difficult for his authorship to be recognized, he deleted several passages that might be associated with him—such an allusion to the jingle in "PUNCH, BROTHERS, PUNCH!" He maintained his anonymity by having Frank N. Doubleday serve as his go-between with DeVinne Press, a New York City firm that published 250 copies of the book in August 1906. Issued without an author's name, the book was copyrighted under the name of J. W. Bothwell, DeVinne's superintendent.

What Is Man? received little notice after it was published. The NEW YORK SUN and *New York Times* found merit in its wit and clarity, but dismissed its arguments as old. Mark Twain later regretted publishing the book, since it attracted so little interest. Two days after he died, the NEW YORK TRIBUNE revealed his authorship of the book in an article containing long extracts. Later that year, an unauthorized edition of *What Is Man?* with Mark Twain's name on it was published in England. The first authorized edition with his name appeared in 1917, when HARPER's published *What Is Man? and Other Essays.* Edited by A. B. PAINE, this volume's 16 essays also include "At the Shrine of St. WAGNER," "THE DEATH OF JEAN," "ENGLISH AS SHE IS TAUGHT," "HOW TO MAKE HISTORY DATES STICK," "IS SHAKESPEARE DEAD?," "A Scrap of Curious History," "SWITZERLAND, The Cradle of Liberty," "TAMING THE BICYCLE," "THE TURNING POINT OF MY LIFE" and "William Dean HOWELLS."

In 1973, the MARK TWAIN PAPERS project issued a corrected edition of *What Is Man?* edited by Paul Baender. Drawing on Mark Twain's original manuscripts—all of which survive—this edition shows Mark Twain's textual changes and incorporates his omitted chapters. The same volume also includes CHRISTIAN SCIENCE, LETTERS FROM THE EARTH and other shorter writings relating to religion and philosophy.

Wheeler, Simon Character in the JUMPING FROG STORY. The tale opens in a dilapidated mining camp tavern, where Wheeler is found dozing. Though it is not clear whether he works in the tavern, he is clearly a long-term camp resident. Old, bald, fat and garrulous, he is good-natured but tediously boring.

The earliest published version of the story opens with the FRAME narrator (Mark Twain himself) asking Wheeler about a friend of Artemus WARD. Wheeler then corners the narrator and tells him a long story about someone else—Jim SMILEY, a notorious local gambler who owned a champion frog. Lacking a sense of humor, Wheeler drones on, oblivious to the comic absurdity of his story. His deadpan delivery and attention to detail are modeled on Ben COON, a tavern keeper who told Mark Twain the frog story at ANGEL'S CAMP in 1865.

Mark Twain also uses the name "Wheeler" in several other works. It appears once in *Roughing It* (1872); Jim BLAINE's "Old Ram's Tale" of chapter 53 mentions a Wheeler who was woven into a carpet in a factory. "Simon Wheeler" is also the central character in "Cap'n Simon Wheeler, the Amateur Detective. A Light Tragedy," a burlesque drama on detectives that Mark Twain wrote around 1877. After failing to get this play produced, he started rewriting it as a novel to be called "Simon Wheeler, Detective." Aside from the name, however, the Wheeler of these stories has little in common with the character in the jumping frog story. The play describes Wheeler as brave and gentle, but uneducated and simple-minded enough to have the confidence that a detective needs to succeed.

The name "Simon Wheeler" itself is curiously similar to "Simon Carpenter"—the name that Mark Twain assigns to himself in "VILLAGERS OF 1840-3."

Which Was the Dream? and Other Symbolic Writings of the Later Years, Mark Twain's (1967)   Collection of unfinished stories edited by John S. TUCKEY for the MARK TWAIN PAPERS project and published by the University of California Press. Mark Twain wrote the volume's 11 stories between 1896 and 1905. Seven of the fragments are substantial pieces: "Which Was the Dream?," "THE ENCHANTED SEA WILDERNESS," "An Adventure in Remote Seas," "THE GREAT DARK," "Indiantown," "Which Was It?" and "Three Thousand Years Among the Microbes." The four briefer fragments—placed in an appendix—are titled "The Passenger's Story," "The Mad Passenger," "Dying Deposition" and "Trial of the Squire." Aside from "The Great Dark" and a small part of "Three Thousand Years," all the stories in the volume are published for the first time.

Most of the stories are narrated by men similar to Mark Twain himself who have thought themselves lucky until they find themselves in the midst of nightmarish failures. Each narrator poses the same question: Is he living in a dark dream from which he will awaken, or is his nightmare the reality, with the happiness he previously knew the dream?

Tuckey's *The Devil's Race-Track: Mark Twain's Great Writings* (1980) is a popular edition selecting what Tuckey regards as the best stories from *Which Was the Dream?* and FABLES OF MAN.

Whipple, Bill   Name mentioned in *Huckleberry Finn.* In chapter 13 Huck invents a story for a FERRYBOATMAN about being with a group of people who got stranded on the derelict steamboat WALTER SCOTT. He names "Bill Whipple" as a person who died heroically in the accident.

Whistler, James (July 10, 1834, Lowell, Massachusetts–July 17, 1903, London, England)   American painter who spent most of his adult life in Europe. Mark Twain met Whistler at a dinner party in London in July 1879. According to a possibly apocryphal story told by William Lyon Phelps, Mark Twain visited Whistler's studio, where he pretended to touch his gloved finger to a wet painting. When Whistler cried out in horror, Mark Twain told him not to worry, since he was wearing *old* gloves. A more definite joke that Mark Twain played on Whistler can be read in chapter 17 of *Huckleberry Finn* (1884), in which Huck learns that teenage poetaster Emmeline GRANGERFORD died of a broken heart after failing to come up with a rhyme for the name "Whistler."

White Cloud   STEAMBOAT on which Mark Twain apprenticed as a PILOT. Built in McKeesport, Pennsylvania in 1857, the *White Cloud* replaced the JOHN H. DICKEY on the St. Louis–Memphis run in late October 1858, when Mark Twain apparently cubbed during one trip. He probably worked under the pilot Sam BOWEN and Captain Daniel Able.

White River   River mentioned in *Huckleberry Finn.* In chapter 32, Huck tells the PHELPSES—who think that he is Tom Sawyer—that his steamboat was three days late reaching PIKESVILLE because it blew a cylinder-head "at the mouth of the White River." The White is a real tributary of the Mississippi River. Nearly 700 miles long, it rises in northwestern ARKANSAS, enters Missouri, then returns to Arkansas and flows southeast, meeting the Mississippi just above the latter's confluence with the much larger Arkansas River. Most of the Missouri portion of the river now passes through MARK TWAIN NATIONAL FOREST.

white suit   A dominant modern image of Mark Twain is that of an elderly man with wildly flowing white hair, wearing a white suit. From the frequency in which he is depicted in white suits, one might conclude that he never wore anything else. In fact, Mark Twain did not begin wearing white suits in public until he was 71. He began dramatically, however, by appearing before a congressional committee on copyright in December 1906—in the dead of winter—wearing a dazzling white suit. Afterward, he occasionally wore such suits in public, but never regularly. And though Hal HOLBROOK and other Mark Twain impersonators have built careers on portraying Mark Twain as a white-maned, white-suited

Mark Twain wearing his signature white suit.

lecturer, Mark Twain himself wore a white suit while speaking just once—in a speech *about* white clothes before London's Savage Club in July 1907.

Many reasons have been suggested for Mark Twain's adoption of white suits during his last years. One was what his friend W. D. HOWELLS called his "keen feeling for costume" and his enjoyment of shocking people. Indeed, Mark Twain called his white suit his "dontcareadamn suit" and enjoyed wearing it to express his freedom. He also had an apparently compulsive need to feel clean, and had long liked to wear clothes whose cleanliness was visible.

Whiteman (Mr. W.) (d. 1883?)   Historical figure mentioned in *Roughing It.* Nevada mining traditions recall Gideon F. Whiteman as a prospector who spent years searching the eastern slopes of the Sierra Nevada for a fabulously wealthy vein of gold in a "cement mine." According to *Roughing It,* Whiteman learned about the mine from the lone survivor of three German brothers who stumbled on it more than 20 years earlier (chapter 37). Whenever Whiteman is sighted passing through ESMERALDA district, men turn out to follow him. Although Whiteman has suffered and starved for 12 or 13 years with nothing to show for his quest, other men persist in stalking him. In chapter 41, the narrator's partner HIGBIE blows a chance for riches on his "BLIND LEAD" claim when he cannot resist chasing off after Whiteman again, instead of working the claim.

Roughing It makes it appear that Whiteman spent years searching for the cement mine before the narrator even arrives in Esmeralda. The historical Whiteman did spend nearly two decades in his futile quest; however, he only *began* in 1861. He is believed to have continued his quest until 1880 and to have died about three years later. The search for his mine continued into the 20th century, doubtless inspired partly by *Roughing It* itself.

Whitmore, F[ranklin] G[ray] (1846–1926)   Mark Twain's business agent. The son of a prominent New York businessman, Whitmore settled in Hartford in 1880 and went into real estate and insurance. He was a neighbor and friend of Mark Twain and handled most of his minor business affairs from around 1887 through 1903, when he sold the Clemenses' Hartford house. He was especially busy with Mark Twain's Hartford affairs in the 1890s, during most of which Mark Twain was out of the country.

Whittier, John Greenleaf (December 17, 1807, Haverhill, Massachusetts–September 7, 1892, Hampton Falls, New Hampshire)   New England journalist and poet. Mark Twain's connections with Whittier were slight except for one moment that had a pivotal impact on his life. On December 17, 1877, he spoke at a banquet honoring Whittier's 70th birthday given by the ATLANTIC MONTHLY at Boston's Hotel Brunswick. Accustomed to giving well-received humorous speeches,

Mark Twain determined to outdo himself on this occasion. Before nearly 60 distinguished literary figures, he presented a BURLESQUE description of a visit he made to a lonely Nevada miner 13 years earlier:

After Mark Twain identified himself, the miner reluctantly admitted him to his cabin, complaining that four "littery" men in 24 hours were too much. The miner then described being visited the previous evening by LONGFELLOW, EMERSON and Oliver Wendell HOLMES—each of whom was an uncouth ruffian who insulted him with quotations from their famous works. Holmes, for example, examined the man's cabin critically, telling him, "Build thee more stately mansions." After nearly getting into a brawl, the men made the miner sing all night. When they finally left the next morning, they stole his boots. Mark Twain protested that these men were impostors, but the miner asked him, "Ah! impostors, were they? Are you?"

W. D. HOWELLS, who introduced Mark Twain at the banquet, recalled the speech as a "disaster" that froze the audience into embarrassed silence. Contemporary newspaper reviews, however, suggested that the audience generally reacted favorably. Mark Twain himself regarded the speech as a catastrophe and immediately wrote apologies to Emerson, Holmes and Longfellow—none of whom had taken offense. Nevertheless, the speech continued to haunt him and probably helped prompt him to take his family to Europe the following spring. In later years, Mark Twain concluded that the problem with his speech lay mostly in his audience. As Howells pointed out, he failed to appreciate the "religious veneration" in which the targets of his burlesque were held. A few years before he died, Mark Twain considered delivering the speech again, but never did.

Known variously as "The Whittier Birthday Speech" and "A Littery Episode," the text of this speech has been frequently reprinted in collections of speeches and sketches.

Whymper, Edward (April 27, 1840, London–September 16, 1911, Chamonix, France)   British mountaineer. After achieving some distinction from climbing in the French Alps, Whymper tried six times to climb Switzerland's MATTERHORN during the early 1860s. On July 14, 1865, he was one of seven British and Swiss men who became the first climbers to conquer that mountain. During their descent, four men fell to their deaths, leaving Whymper the only British survivor. His book about the expedition, *Scrambles Amongst the Alps* (1871), went through many editions and made both him and the Matterhorn famous. Mark Twain became interested in Whymper when he saw the Matterhorn from ZERMATT in August 1878. *A Tramp Abroad* quotes liberally from Whymper on the 1865 Matterhorn disaster (chapters 36, 40 and 41) and borrows seven pictures from his book—including several showing the imprint of Whymper's own London engraving company. In later years Whymper climbed in the Ecuadorian Andes and Canadian Rockies and continued to write and lecture about mountaineering.

Wiley, Strother (*fl.* **1850s–1880s**) Steamboat PILOT and friend of Mark Twain. Wiley was evidently Horace BIXBY's copilot on the CRESCENT CITY when Mark Twain was the latter's apprentice in mid-1857. Wiley may also have piloted with Samuel A. BOWEN when Mark Twain cubbed on the JOHN H. DICKEY from early August to mid-October 1858.

Wiley appears in several anecdotes in *Life on the Mississippi*. He is the "Mr. W." of chapter 8 who reports late to his watch; the "Stephen W." of chapter 14 who takes a piloting job at half wages when he is down on his luck; and the carefree money borrower named "Stephen" of chapter 17. Despite the book's generally flippant portrayal of Wiley, Mark Twain had a high opinion of him both as a pilot and as a person. In 1875, when he was trying to persuade W. D. HOWELLS to accompany him on a trip to the Mississippi, he suggested Wiley as a third traveling companion—possibly because Wiley wrote to him as "OLD TIMES ON THE MISSISSIPPI" installments were beginning to appear. It was also around this time that Dan DE QUILLE published a sketch titled "Pilot Wylie" in the VIRGINIA CITY TERRITORIAL ENTERPRISE about a drunken steamboat pilot who wrecks Sam Bowen's *Bully Arabia*. De Quille sketch may have been based on stories about Wiley that Mark Twain had told him years earlier.

Wilhelm II (January 27, 1859, Berlin, Germany–June 4, 1941, Doorn, Holland) Emperor of GERMANY and king of Prussia (1888–1918). A year and a half before Mark Twain came to BERLIN, Wilhelm dismissed Bismarck as his chancellor and began policies that culminate in Germany's defeat in World War I and his own abdication. Meanwhile, he arranged to meet Mark Twain through one of his generals, who was married to Mark Twain's cousin. On February 20, 1892, Mollie Clemens von Versen and her husband staged a private banquet at which Mark Twain dined with the emperor and many members of his staff. On this occasion, Wilhelm praised *A Tramp Abroad*—which has an anecdote about his mother, Empress Augusta (chapter 24)—and called *Life on the Mississippi* his favorite American book. Mark Twain's AUTOBIOGRAPHY recalls an "indiscretion" that he committed that evening by remarking on a dish before the emperor tasted it. Wilhelm evidently did not discuss *Connecticut Yankee*, in which Dan BEARD used his face for one of his "chucklehead" nobles (chapter 24). Beard also put Wilhelm's face on a more respectful picture of a knight in armor (chapter 28).

Mark Twain's essay "To the Person Sitting in Darkness" (1901) criticizes Wilhelm's China policy, charging him with contributing to the Boxer Rebellion by demanding excessive compensation for the deaths of two German missionaries killed in a riot.

Wilks, Harvey and William Names used in *Huckleberry Finn*. Harvey and William Wilks are the English brothers and heirs of the recently deceased Peter WILKS. A "dissenting minister," Harvey is about Peter's age; deaf-and-dumb William is in his early thirties. In chapter 24, the KING learns from Tim COLLINS that these brothers are expected in Peter's town. Since no one there has ever met them, the King decides to pose as Harvey, while the DUKE poses as William. At the end of chapter 28, two more men claiming to be Harvey and William Wilks arrive. Huck accepts them as the genuine brothers; however, they, too, may be impostors. The fact that the King and Duke are not perturbed by the newcomers' arrival suggests that they recognize kindred scoundrels. Furthermore, the newcomers seem to be suspiciously unmoved by Peter's death.

The newcomers arrive with no proof of their identity; however, they are content to retire immediately to a hotel to await mishandled luggage that will prove who they are. The townspeople do not want to wait, however. They collect all four claimants at an inn to determine which two are the real brothers. Huck thinks that "anybody but a lot of prejudiced chuckleheads" should see that the newly arrived Harvey "was spinning truth" and the King "lies."

Levi BELL, who has letters from the real Wilks brothers, administers a handwriting test that quickly proves the King and Duke to be frauds; however, the test also appears to indict the two newcomers. The one claiming to be Harvey writes in an illegible scrawl, then claims that William is the actual scribe of all the letters sent in his name to Peter. "William," however, cannot produce a handwriting specimen because his writing arm is broken and in a sling. "Harvey" then offers irrefutable proof that he is Peter's brother by describing a tattoo on Peter's chest. This proves nothing, either. Ab TURNER and another man who prepared Peter's body for burial cannot remember seeing *any* tattoo on him. Finally, the angry townspeople march all four claimants off to the graveyard to examine Peter's body for the tattoo. The scene ends before the examination is made, so the presumed Harvey's assertion is never verified. Thus, no proof is ever adduced that the real Harvey and William Wilks appear in the novel.

Wilks, Joanna (Joe) Character in *Huckleberry Finn*. At 14, the youngest of the three Wilks sisters, Joanna has a harelip and is devoted to "good works." In chapter 26 she quizzes Huck about England, but is forced to apologize to him by her older sisters, Mary Jane and Susan WILKS. Joanna is about the same age as Huck, but E. W. KEMBLE's illustrations in the first edition misleadingly show her towering over him.

Wilks, Mary Jane Character in *Huckleberry Finn*. Mary Jane is the oldest of the three WILKS sisters left orphaned by George Wilks and his wife. When the KING and DUKE arrive in her town and claim to be her English uncles, Harvey and William WILKS, she immediately accepts them at face value and dismisses the doubts of Dr. ROBINSON. Huck is so taken by Mary Jane's beauty and innate goodness that he cannot stand the thought of seeing her and her sisters cheated by the scoundrels, particularly when he sees how upset she is by the King's callous separating and selling of the family slaves. In chapter 28, he finally tells Mary Jane the full story of the frauds' chicanery. First, however, he makes her promise to leave town immediately so that she will not accidentally give away the fact that something is wrong. She leaves before the frauds are publicly exposed. Huck never sees her again, but says that he subsequently thought of her "many a million times."

One of the few strong female characters in Mark Twain's writings, Mary Jane Wilks has provided screen roles for Charlotte Henry (1931), Lynne Carver (1939), Florence Henderson (TV, 1957), Sherry Jackson (1960), Kim O'Brien (1974) and Patty Weaver (TV, 1975).

Wilks, Peter Background figure in *Huckleberry Finn*. Wilks was a prosperous tanner in an unnamed town who died after a three-week illness. The next day, Huck and his raftmates stop near Wilks's unnamed town. The KING learns about Wilks from a neighbor named Tim COLLINS, who is on his way out of the country. As young men, Peter and his brother George came to America from England. Wilks has died a bachelor; his only living relatives are brothers in England, Harvey and William WILKS, and George's daughters, who live in his town.

Wilks has left a letter directing the division of his money and properties between his brothers and nieces. It reveals where $6,000 in gold coins is hidden. For reasons never explained, this hoard is $415 short of $6,000. The King and Duke pretend to be Wilks's brothers and move into the house with his nieces.

Wilks, Susan Character in *Huckleberry Finn*. The 15-year-old sister of Mary Jane and Joanna WILKS, Susan appears in chapters 25–26 and 28, but plays almost no individual role in the narrative.

William IV (August 21, 1765, London–June 20, 1837, Windsor Castle, England) King of Great Britain (1830–37) when Mark Twain was born. In chapter 26 of *Huckleberry Finn* Huck tells Joanna WILKS that "William Fourth" is England's current monarch, even though "I knowed he was dead years ago"—a solid clue to the time in which *Huckleberry Finn* takes place. William's niece, VICTORIA, succeeded William as monarch in 1837.

William M. Morrison STEAMBOAT on which Mark Twain may have PILOTED. Limited evidence suggests that Mark Twain cubbed on this year-old boat on a round-trip between St. Louis and New Orleans in October 1857—most likely under the pilot Horace BIXBY. He also may have clerked on this boat during a trip in early July 1858, when Isaiah SELLERS was its pilot.

Williams Character in *Roughing It*. A cheerful passenger aboard the AJAX, Williams distinguishes himself in chapter 62 by breaking the power of the Old ADMIRAL, whose overbearing political arguments wear everyone else out. Williams is the only passenger whom the Admiral cannot goad into an argument, until a day when he unexpectedly reopens one of the Admiral's arguments and turns his lies against him. After pretending to accept the old man's invented pre–Civil War history about outrages against Southern women, Williams comes back at him with "clean, pure, manufactured history, without a word of truth in it," calmly getting the Admiral to swallow it. Thereafter, Williams is a hero aboard the ship; whenever the Admiral starts an argument, he is fetched to cow him into submission. Eventually the Admiral stops discussing politics.

Williams, Charlie Fictitious name of a character in *Life on the Mississippi*. In a tale subtitled "A Burning Brand" in chapter 52, "Charlie Williams" is the alias of a burglar serving nine years in prison. He forged a letter to himself from a nonexistent fellow convict, "Jack Hunt," dated June 9, 1872 (exactly one week after the death of Langdon Clemens—a curious coincidence in view of the similarity of the character's alias to the name of the dead baby Charles William ALLBRIGHT of the "RAFT CHAPTER"). The son of a minister, "Williams" is apparently a Harvard graduate; the warden at his unnamed state prison (evidently some distance from St. Louis) describes him as a "dissolute, cunning prodigal."

Williams's bogus letter tells a heartrending story of Hunt's experiences outside of prison, culminating in his finding God and winning the trust and support of a St. Louis grain merchant named Brown. "Hunt" attributes his success to what he learned from Williams while in prison. The key passage in the letter is Hunt's allusion to Williams's bleeding lungs—a hint that the ostensibly saintly Williams was dying in prison.

Widely circulated and read in church sermons, the letter wins over everyone who hears it until C. D. WARNER questions its authenticity. The narrator of *Life on the Mississippi* says that he had planned to write an article about this letter until he learned it was a fake. Williams smuggled it out of prison with the evident intention that it be publicized and help lead to his being pardoned. The narrator had long intended to look up the benevolent Mr. Brown when he reached St. Louis, but now feels no need to do so.

Williams, Hoss (Horse) Figure whose grave is robbed in *Tom Sawyer*. The narrative of *Tom Sawyer* begins on a

Friday. Hoss Williams is buried the next day—a fact revealed in chapter 6. The same chapter implies that Williams was a "wicked man," since Huck Finn expects devils to visit his grave at midnight to carry him away. Three chapters later, Tom and Huck happen to be in the graveyard on Monday night, when they see INJUN JOE and Muff POTTER dig up Williams's body and place it in a wheelbarrow for Dr. ROBINSON. A similar grave-robbing scene occurs in Charles DICKENS's novel *A Tale of Two Cities* (1859), which Mark Twain is known to have read several times before he wrote *Tom Sawyer*.

Tom Sawyer's original illustrator, True W. WILLIAMS, had a little fun in his picture showing the townspeople at Hoss Williams's grave the day after the murder. In a corner of the picture he drew a tombstone with his own name on it.

Williams, Sarah Mary Alias used in *Huckleberry Finn*. In chapter 12, Huck is disguised as a girl when he meets a woman named Judith LOFTUS. He tells her his name is "Sarah Williams." When she later asks him to repeat his name, he answers "*Mary* Williams." Loftus catches the inconsistency, prompting Huck to explain, "Sarah's my first name. Some calls me Sarah, some calls me Mary." Under pressure, Huck finally admits that he is a boy and gives George PETERS as his name. He later has a similar problem remembering the "George JACKSON" alias that he gives to the GRANGERFORD family.

Williams, True W. (*fl.* 1860s–1870s) Illustrator. True Williams ranks as the most prolific illustrator of Mark Twain's books, but little is known about him. During the 1860s and 1870s he lived in Hartford boarding-houses and worked frequently for Elisha BLISS's publishing company. Mark Twain admired the raw humor in Williams's pictures and appreciated the fact that the untrained artist worked cheaply; however, Williams drank heavily and was not always reliable. Williams did not sign all his work, but many of his pictures can be identified by either his clear script signature or his "T. W. W." monogram.

Williams illustrated most of Mark Twain's early SUB-SCRIPTION BOOKS. For *Innocents Abroad* he did most of the illustrations not copied from photographs. He also contributed many pictures to *Roughing It*, as well as all the pictures in *The Gilded Age*, except for 16 full-page prints done by August HOPPIN. In 1875 he drew 130 pictures for *Sketches, New and Old*. Though Williams could generally choose his subject matter, Mark Twain gave him specific instructions for several of this book's illustrations. For example, Mark Twain wanted the PET-RIFIED MAN to be depicted thumbing his nose, and he had strong ideas about how the JUMPING FROG should appear. Williams satisfied this latter demand by making the frog resemble its namesake, Daniel Webster.

Even before finishing *Sketches*, Williams began illustrating *Tom Sawyer*. The two books consequently have

Having to illustrate Roughing It*'s clever liar "Williams" gave True Williams a perfect opportunity to draw a picture of himself.*

similar designs, and several sets of unrelated characters that he drew for the two books look almost identical. For example, Williams made Tom Sawyer resemble a character named Jim in "THE STORY OF THE BAD LITTLE BOY." His Huck Finn closely resembles Jacob Blevins in *Sketches*'s "THE STORY OF THE GOOD LITTLE BOY."

Of Williams's 200 *Tom Sawyer* pictures, 161 appeared in the original American editions of the book. Several curious examples of his irreverent sense of humor can be seen in these drawings. A graveyard scene in chapter 11 of *Tom Sawyer*, for instance, shows Williams's own name on a headstone labeled "SACRED TO THE MEMORY OF T. W. WILLIAMS." An illustration for chapter 21's "Examination Night" contains a small sign with the motto, "THE PEN IS MIGHTIER THAN THE SWORD"; Williams's lettering allows suspiciously little space between the second and third words.

Williams's final major job for Mark Twain was more than 40 illustrations for *A Tramp Abroad* (1880). These pictures are scattered through the volume, with particular concentrations in chapters 17–26 and 31–35. After completing this assignment, Williams himself seems to have disappeared from historical record.

Wilson, David ("Pudd'nhead Wilson") Character in *Pudd'nhead Wilson*. Born in New York, Wilson is 25 years old when he comes to DAWSON'S LANDING in February 1830 to seek his fortune. He arrives in the same month in which Tom DRISCOLL and CHAMBERS are born.

Wilson studies his fingerprint collection while preparing for the trial in chapter 21 of Pudd'nhead Wilson.

"Homely, freckled, sandy-haired . . . with an intelligent blue eye," he is college-educated and has completed a course at an eastern law school.

On his arrival, Wilson makes a "fatal remark." Annoyed by a barking dog, he utters a wish to own *half* the dog. Why? So that he could kill his half. SOLOMON might have said the same thing, but those who overhear Wilson say this merely think him daft, and his ironic remark earns him the nickname "PUDD'NHEAD." Years later, his reputation is further damaged when his friend Judge York DRISCOLL shows samples of his ironic MAXIMS to uncomprehending town leaders. The maxims of PUDD'NHEAD WILSON'S CALENDAR reveal Wilson's intellectual and emotional complexity, but further distance him from other townspeople. Apart from Driscoll, the only person in town who respects Wilson's intellect is ROXANA. She not only thinks him the smartest man in town, she suspects he may even be a witch. To some, perhaps he is. He ultimately wins respect by performing what many townspeople think a miracle.

Wilson arrives in Missouri with enough money to buy a house at the western edge of town, near Judge Driscoll's home. He also opens an office in town and hangs a shingle advertising himself as "Attorney & Counselor-at-law." Like Mark Twain's brother Orion Clemens, however, Wilson never gets a case. Eventually, he removes his shingle and concentrates on surveying and bookkeeping, while filling his considerable idle time with such hobbies as palmistry, collecting FINGERPRINTS and writing his calendar.

Despite his pudd'nhead reputation, Wilson is well liked in town. He is such a gentleman that even the treacherous Tom Driscoll can count on a gracious reception at his home. Wilson seems totally lacking in guile or ambition. After he discovers the terrible truth about Driscoll, in chapter 20, he takes no satisfaction in knowing that the man will hang—despite the fact that he murdered Wilson's best friend.

Meanwhile, Wilson's fortunes improve after Angelo and Luigi CAPELLO arrive in town in 1853. They increase his paltry stock of intelligent friends and serve as cata-

lysts in his life. Luigi launches Wilson's law career by engaging him to defend him against Tom Driscoll's assault charges in chapter 5. Immediately afterward, Wilson is asked to run for mayor. His reputation rises even higher when he serves as Luigi's second in a DUEL in chapter 14. Finally, his defense of Luigi in the climactic murder trial lifts him to heroic stature. By the end of the narrative, the Capellos are gone, but Wilson's future is apparently secure.

Mark Twain himself evidently thought little of Wilson. In January 1894, he wrote to his wife, "I have never thought of Pudd'nhead as a *character,* but only as a piece of machinery—a button or a crank or a lever, with a useful function to perform in a machine, but with no dignity above that." Some of this is true. Despite Wilson's evident compassion, his dimensions are limited. Not only is he satisfied to wait two decades to take up his law career, he is content to remain an ascetic bachelor. He seems to devote his life to developing the arcane knowledge that will prove essential for one extraordinary trial, in which pieces of several diverse puzzles fall together simultaneously. It is not an achievement that he could ever hope to repeat.

What most interested Mark Twain about Wilson is his being "an example of that unfortunate type of human being who, misunderstood at the moment of entering a new community, may spend a lifetime trying to live down that blunder, especially if he gets cataloged by some ridiculous nickname." During the long years that Wilson goes without legal cases, he keeps up with the law, confident that his chance will come. Until his climactic triumph, he is merely an example of unrecognized talent—a theme explored in "CAPTAIN STORMFIELD'S VISIT TO HEAVEN," featuring such unappreciated talents as Absalom Jones.

There are obvious flaws in Wilson's characterization. For example, while his philosophical maxims are often bitterly non-conformist, he has a strongly conventional side. Though not a Southerner by birth or upbringing, he empathizes with the South's archaic code of honor. In chapter 13 he astounds Tom Driscoll by saying that he rather not get his first case than see Judge Driscoll suffer the humiliation of Tom's settling an affair of honor in court instead of in a duel. Later, he serves as Luigi Capello's second in a duel.

Though in many ways astute, Wilson seems remarkably blind to many things happening around him. For example, he never notices Roxy and Tom's many meetings at the nearby HAUNTED HOUSE. Further, he apparently never thinks to compare the infant fingerprints of Chambers and Tom Driscoll with their adult prints until an accidental discovery alerts him to Tom's guilt in the murder case.

In the published version of "THOSE EXTRAORDINARY TWINS," Wilson is first mentioned in chapter 3 as a member of the FREE-THINKERS' SOCIETY. Nothing is said about his background. In chapter 5, Wilson defends the

Capello brothers—here SIAMESE TWINS—against Tom Driscoll's assault charge. He wins the case and emerges popular, admired and happy. In *Pudd'nhead Wilson* this scene is reduced to an offstage trial that Wilson loses; however, the case still serves to launch his legal career.

The unfinished story "Hellfire Hotchkiss" quotes Wilson as describing Hellfire as "the only genuwyne male man in this town." In "A DOUBLE-BARRELLED DETECTIVE STORY" (1902), "David Wilson" is one of the aliases used by Jacob FULLER.

A likely real-life model for Wilson was the distinguished Missouri attorney Samuel Taylor GLOVER, whom the people of Hannibal regarded as a "chucklehead" despite his accomplishments. When *Pudd'nhead Wilson* was serialized in 1893–94, many people thought that a New York Stock Exchange officer named Theodore Wilson was Mark Twain's model.

Ken Howard portrayed Wilson in PBS's 1983 television adaptation of *Pudd'nhead Wilson*. Oddly, this adaptation overlooks the basis of Wilson's nickname. When it begins, Wilson appears to have an active law practice.

Winn, Deacon   Figure mentioned in *Huckleberry Finn*. In chapter 3, Huck tries to understand the purpose of prayer and wonders why Deacon Winn cannot recover money he has lost on pork by simply praying for it.

Wolfe (or Wolf), Jim (c. 1833–?)   Childhood friend of Mark Twain who came to Hannibal from a remote Missouri village in the late 1840s. Wolfe worked as a printer's devil on Orion Clemens's *Hannibal Journal* in the early 1850s, when he became the subject of Mark Twain's earliest-known published sketch, "A GALLANT FIREMAN." During this period, he lodged with the Clemens family, sharing a room with the slightly younger Mark Twain, who enjoyed taking advantage of his simple, trusting nature. On one occasion, Mark Twain talked Wolfe into climbing out on an icy ledge from which the desperately bashful boy fell into the midst of a group of girls. Mark Twain later described the incident in "Jim Wolf and the Cats," a sketch he published in the *New York Sunday Mercury* in 1867. A long passage in his AUTOBIOGRAPHY retells the original story and recalls how his sketch was later pirated. Wolfe also appears as "Nicodemus DODGE" in chapter 23 of *A Tramp Abroad*, which recounts incidents that actually happened to him. Mark Twain's "VILLAGERS OF 1840–3" reports Wolfe as having died before 1897.

Woodlawn Cemetery   ELMIRA, New York, cemetery in which Mark Twain and all the members of his immediate family are buried. His family plot—adjacent to that of the Jervis LANGDON family—also includes the graves of his only grandchild, Nina GABRILOWITSCH, and Clara's two husbands, Ossip GABRILOWITSCH, Jacques SAMOSSOUD (unmarked). Mark Twain's parents and two of his brothers are buried in MOUNT OLIVET CEMETERY in Hannibal.

X

X, Mr. Pseudonym for many characters. Mark Twain often uses single letter pseudonyms for real persons. In *Life on the Mississippi,* for example, "X" is the sleep-walking pilot who steers a steamboat through treacherous low water (chapter 11). In *A Tramp Abroad,* "X" and "Z" accompany the narrator from HEIDELBERG to Heilbronn (chapters 11–18). A speaker of peculiar GERMAN who makes himself understood despite turning sentences inside out, Mr. X is based on Edward M. Smith—the American consul at MANNHEIM who was Mark Twain's real companion on this trip. Mr. Z, a younger man who speaks German properly, is based on another Smith who traveled with them. *Following the Equator* alludes to "Mr. X," a missionary (chapter 12), "Professor X" from YALE (chapter 26) and "Dr. X" in South Africa (chapter 68).

Mark Twain also occasionally uses "Blank" as a pseudonym. For example, the narrator's political opponents in "RUNNING FOR GOVERNOR" are Mr. John T. SMITH and "Mr. Blank J. Blank." *Following the Equator*'s narrator goes on a fox hunt with "the Blanks," friends of "F." (chapter 20). In Bendigo, AUSTRALIA, the narrator is entertained by "Mr. Blank," the sole member of the "Mark Twain Club" (chapter 25). *The Gilded Age* alludes to a "Senator X" in Chapter 19 and a "Miss Blank" and "Senator Blank" in chapter 42.

Y

Yale University   Private liberal arts college founded in New Haven, Connecticut in 1701. The first university to bestow an honorary degree on Mark Twain, Yale made him a master of arts in 1888 and a doctor of literature in October 1901. The year after receiving each degree, Mark Twain spoke at Yale alumni meetings in Hartford. Mark Twain knew many Yale graduates and faculty members—such as Joseph TWICHELL and William Lyon Phelps—and he quietly paid the tuition of two black students at Yale's law school, Warner McGuinn and Charles W. Johnson.

Mark Twain's "VILLAGERS OF 1840–3" recalls Neil Moss, a Hannibal schoolmate who went off to Yale—"a mighty journey and an incomparable distinction." When Moss returned, he dressed as an eastern swell until local ridicule forced him to change his ways. Mark Twain's meeting with Moss in Nevada—by which time Moss had become "a graceless tramp"—is described *Roughing It* (chapter 55), and the fictional Tom DRISCOLL duplicates Moss's Yale experience in *Pudd'nhead Wilson.* Another character who attends Yale is Alfred Parrish, in "THE BELATED RUSSIAN PASSPORT." An unpublished portion of *Life on the Mississippi* indicates that the professor of "THE PROFESSOR'S YARN" is from Yale.

When Clara Clemens revised her will in 1958, she stipulated that all of Mark Twain's papers were to go to the University of California, except a manuscript of *Joan of Arc* that was to go to Yale. The university also received half the principal of Nina GABRILOWITSCH's trust fund on her death in 1966.

Yalta   Resort town on the southern coast of CRIMEA. Now within Ukraine, Yalta was part of RUSSIA when Mark Twain visited it with the QUAKER CITY in 1867. The ship landed there on August 25; the next day, he and many other passengers went a few miles inland to meet Czar ALEXANDER II at his winter palace. On August 28 the ship departed for CONSTANTINOPLE. Chapter 37 of *Innocents Abroad* describes Yalta's forested setting as a vision of California's Sierra Nevada. Chapter 38 of *Innocents* recalls a young and pretty Russian woman with whom Mark Twain was taken at Yalta.

Yankee   Now a popular nickname for an American, especially a Northerner, "Yankee" goes back to the mid 18th century, when British soldiers used the name to insult New Englanders. Its origin is uncertain, but it may have come from Dutch *Janke,* for "Little John." Over time, "Yankee" grew respectable and was applied more widely. By the CIVIL WAR era it was a popular Southern nickname for Northerners generally.

Mark Twain used "Yankee" to refer specifically to New Englanders, and called himself "a Connecticut Yankee by adoption" in an 1881 speech. He saw the defining characteristic of "Yankees" as their alleged shrewdness in business enterprises. A prime example is the stranger of the JUMPING FROG STORY who fills the frog with shot. While this story does not itself call the man a Yankee, an essay that Mark Twain wrote in 1894 makes it clear that he was thinking of a Yankee when he wrote the story.

Mark Twain's best-known Yankee is Hank MORGAN—the title character of *Connecticut Yankee* (1889). In the novel's prelude, Hank describes himself as "a Yankee of the Yankees—and practical; yes, and nearly barren of sentiment." Hank sees almost everything in business terms; he craves to control every enterprise in sixth-century England and tries to find profits in everything from chivalrous tournaments to an ascetic hermit whom he uses to power a sewing machine (chapter 22). Lest there be uncertainty as to how Mark Twain regards Hank's Yankee zeal, chapter 25 uses the term to describe unscrupulous London aldermen of a later age who manipulated the law to extort fines from religious dissenters.

A Yankee at the Court of King Arthur   Title under which CHATTO and Windus published the English edition of *A Connecticut Yankee in King Arthur's Court* in London in December 1889. "A Yankee *in* the Court of King Arthur" is stamped on the spine and front cover of early American editions. While Chatto dropped "Connecticut" from the title to avoid confusing British readers, the American edition evidently dropped the word in order to save space.

Yokel   Minor character in *The Prince and the Pauper.* A member of the RUFFLER's criminal gang, Yokel is a once-prosperous farmer who fell on hard times after his mother was burned as a witch because a patient she nursed died. Reduced to begging, Yokel and his wife were lashed from town to town until his wife died, his

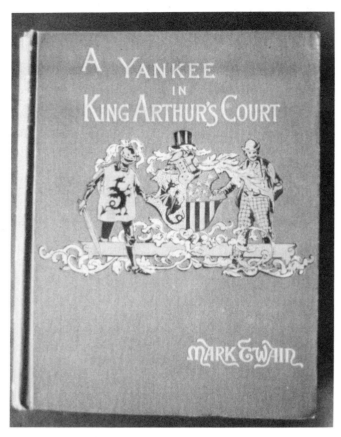

The first American edition of A Connecticut Yankee in King Arthur's Court. *(Courtesy, Kevin Bochynski)*

children starved and he was sold as a slave and branded. When King EDWARD VI—who gang members think is a common beggar boy—hears Yokel's sad story, he jumps up to declare the unjust law ended (chapter 17). In chapter 22, Yokel saves the king from an attempt by

HUGO and the Tinker to burn a scar on his leg. After Edward later regains his throne, he has Yokel found and provided with "a comfortable livelihood."

Yonge, Charlotte Mary (August 13, 1823, Otterbourne, England–March 24, 1901, Otterbourne) English author of 160 novels, histories and other works for juveniles. In 1908, Mark Twain admitted to getting his idea for *The Prince and the Pauper* from Yonge's *Little Duke* (1854), which he once read at QUARRY FARM. Set in 10th-century France, Yonge's book is a moralistic tale showing how the youthful Duke of Normandy becomes a tolerant and gentle ruler after escaping from political imprisonment and struggling to claim his rightful throne with the aid of an older protector. Another Yonge book that probably influenced the title of *The Prince and the Pauper* is *The Prince and the Page* (1865). In this romance, a cousin of England's King Edward I spends several years disguised as a blind beggar.

York Harbor Seaside town at MAINE's southern tip where Mark Twain stayed with his family in a riverfront house from mid-June to mid-October 1902. Through the same summer, his friend W. H. HOWELLS was staying at nearby Kittery Point. After Livy's health declined in mid-August, H. H. ROGERS sent his yacht KANAWHA to stand by in the harbor to carry her away, but Mark Twain instead took her back to RIVERDALE, New York in a special railroad car.

Young, Brigham (June 1, 1801, Whitingham, Vermont–August 29, 1877, Salt Lake City, Utah) The second president of the MORMON Church (1844–77), Young led the Mormon migration to UTAH and served as the territory's first governor (1849–57). When Mark Twain visited Salt Lake City in early August 1861, Utah was quieting down after having nearly gone to war against the federal government four years earlier, when Young was dismissed as governor. Since Utah's loyalty

Even Brigham Young has trouble sleeping amid 72 snoring wives in chapter 15 of Roughing It.

to the Union was suspect after the CIVIL WAR started, Mark Twain's brother Orion Clemens, in his capacity as a federal officer, interviewed Young to learn what he could about Mormon attitudes toward the Confederacy. Mark Twain attended Orion's interview—which is facetiously described in *Roughing It* (chapter 13). The book also has several other anecdotes about Young (chapters 14–16, 21 and 25).

Like many Americans, Mark Twain was curious about Young's reputation as a polygamist. In *Roughing It,* a man named Johnson tells about a private meeting with Young that was constantly interrupted by wives demanding breast-pins like the one he had given to wife "No. 6." In a 1,300-word monologue, Young bemoans the fact that the original $25 breast-pin will end up costing him $2,500—a figure suggesting that he has 100 wives. Young also complains about how he tried to save money by using a single giant bed to accommodate 72 wives at once, but found sleep impossible when they all snored at the same time (chapter 15). In chapter 14, a non-Mormon telegraph contractor named Street (based on the real James Street) recalls a time when he could not get his Mormon subcontractors to fulfill their contracts and went to Young for help. After Young simply ordered the Mormons to fulfill their contracts, Street never had trouble again, and he declared that "Utah is an absolute monarchy and Brigham Young is king!"

When Mark Twain visited Italy six years later, he wrote a letter to the SAN FRANCISCO ALTA CALIFORNIA describing the women of Genoa as so beautiful that it would be difficult to select a wife from among them, adding that if "Brigham" spent just one day in Genoa, "he would discharge those eighty-five miraculously ugly women who vegetate in his harem now." He omitted this passage when he revised the letter for chapter 17 of *Innocents Abroad*. His 1879 speech "SOME THOUGHTS ON THE SCIENCE OF ONANISM" calls Young an "expert of incontestable authority" on masturbation.

zephyr, Washoe Named after a Greek wind god, a *zephyr* is normally a gentle wind—usually from the west. In northwestern NEVADA, especially during the spring and fall prevailing westerly winds often develop into powerful gales known as "Washoe zephyrs." The steep mountains surrounding towns—particularly VIRGINIA CITY—upset normal wind flow, creating whirlwinds and strong vertical currents. The ferocity of these gales during Mark Twain's time was the subject of tall tales, to which he contributed in *Roughing It.* In chapter 21, for example, the narrator arrives in CARSON CITY and is greeted by a Washoe zephyr that creates a "soaring dust-drift about the size of the United States" flecked

A Washoe zephyr stirs things up in Carson City on Mark Twain's arrival.

with hats, chickens, signs, shovels, cats, children, wheelbarrows and "emigrating roofs and vacant lots." Later in this chapter, a zephyr blows a roof into the narrator's boardinghouse, setting loose the boarders' collection of pet tarantulas in the middle of the night.

Zermatt Resort town in southern SWITZERLAND. Located in a valley 5,315 feet above sea level, Zermatt is a few miles northeast of the MATTERHORN. After Edward WHYMPER climbed the Matterhorn in 1865, Zermatt became a mountaineering center and a popular summer tourist resort, especially among the English. Mark Twain and Joseph TWICHELL spent several days there at the end of August 1878, during which they also visited the nearby RIFFELBERG. *A Tramp Abroad* describes Zermatt in chapters 33–37, 39 and 41–42.

Zola, Emile (April 2, 1840, Paris, France–September 29, 1902, Paris) French novelist. Born into poverty, Zola turned to writing in his late twenties and went on to create a 20-volume cycle, "The Rougon-Macquart," realistically exploring French society. Mark Twain was troubled by what he regarded as "filth" in Zola's novels, but nevertheless admitted to their fundamental honesty. His brief essay on Zola's novel about peasant life, *La Terre* (1887), appeared posthumously in LETTERS FROM THE EARTH.

Zola's greatest fame came after 1898, when he published *J'accuse,* attacking the French general staff for persecuting Alfred DREYFUS. Sentenced to prison for libel, Zola escaped to England until a general amnesty was declared in France. Despite Mark Twain's squeamish ambivalence toward Zola's fiction, he called Zola "the manliest man in France" and ranked him in greatness with JOAN OF ARC.

BOOKS BY MARK TWAIN

This is a listing of first editions of books that Mark Twain published during his lifetime, as well as significant posthumous publications that contain previously uncollected writings, letters and speeches. The list excludes many pamphlets, minor collections of letters and revised editions of previously published books. Entries on most of the titles that were published during Mark Twain's lifetime can be found within *Mark Twain A to Z*.

NOVELS, TRAVEL BOOKS, SKETCHES, STORIES, ESSAYS AND AUTOBIOGRAPHICAL WRITINGS

1867   *The Celebrated Jumping Frog of Calaveras County and Other Sketches.* New York: C. H. Webb.

1869   *The Innocents Abroad, or The New Pilgrims' Progress; Being Some Account of the Steamship Quaker City's Pleasure Excursion to Europe and the Holy Land.* Hartford: American Publishing Co.

1871   *Eye Openers.* London: John Camden Hotten.

1871   *Mark Twain's (Burlesque) Autobiography and First Romance.* New York: Sheldon.

1872   *Roughing It.* Hartford: American Publishing Co.

1872   *Screamers.* London: John Camden Hotten.

1873   *Choice Humorous Works of Mark Twain.* London: John Camden Hotten.

1874   *The Gilded Age: A Tale of To-day.* Hartford: American Publishing Co. Coauthor Charles Dudley Warner.

1874   *Number One: Mark Twain's Sketches.* New York: American News Co.

1875   *Sketches, New and Old.* Hartford: American Publishing Co.

1876   *The Adventures of Tom Sawyer.* Hartford: American Publishing Co.

1877   *A True Story and the Recent Carnival of Crime.* Boston: James R. Osgood.

1878   *Punch, Brothers, Punch! and Other Sketches.* New York: Slote, Woodman.

1880   *A Tramp Abroad.* Hartford: American Publishing Co.

1880   *[Date, 1601] Conversation as It Was by the Social Fireside in the Time of the Tudors.* [privately published; titles vary in different editions]

1881   *The Prince and the Pauper: A Tale for Young People of All Ages.* Boston: James R. Osgood.

1882   *The Stolen White Elephant, Etc.* Boston: James R. Osgood.

1883   *Life on the Mississippi.* Boston: James R. Osgood.

1885   *Adventures of Huckleberry Finn.* New York: Charles L. Webster.

1889   *A Connecticut Yankee in King Arthur's Court.* New York: Charles L. Webster.

1892   *Merry Tales.* New York: Charles L. Webster.

1892   *The American Claimant.* New York: Charles L. Webster.

1893   *The £1,000,000 Bank-Note and Other New Stories.* New York: Charles L. Webster.

1894   *Tom Sawyer Abroad.* New York: Charles L. Webster.

1894   *Pudd'nhead Wilson and Those Extraordinary Twins.* Hartford: American Publishing Co.

1896   *Tom Sawyer Abroad; Tom Sawyer, Detective and Other Stories.* New York: Harper.

1896   *Personal Recollections of Joan of Arc.* New York: Harper.

1897   *How to Tell a Story and Other Essays.* New York: Harper.

1897   *Following the Equator: A Journey Around the World.* Hartford: American Publishing Co.

1898   *More Tramps Abroad.* London: Chatto and Windus.

1899   *The American Claimant and Other Stories and Sketches.* New York: Harper.

1899   *Literary Essays.* New York: Harper.

1900   *English As She Is Taught.* Boston: Mutual Book Co.

1900   *The Man That Corrupted Hadleyburg and Other Stories and Essays.* New York: Harper.

1902 *A Double-Barrelled Detective Story.* New York: Harper.

1903 *My Début as a Literary Person and Other Essays and Stories.* Hartford: American Publishing Co.

1904 *A Dog's Tale.* New York: Harper.

1904 *Extracts from Adam's Diary.* New York: Harper.

1905 *King Leopold's Soliloquy: A Defense of His Congo Rule.* Boston: P. R. Warren.

1906 *Eve's Diary.* New York: Harper.

1906 *What Is Man?* New York: De Vinne Press.

1906 *The $30,000 Bequest and Other Stories.* New York: Harper.

1907 *Christian Science.* New York: Harper.

1907 *A Horse's Tale.* New York and London: Harper.

1909 *Is Shakespeare Dead? from My Autobiography.* New York: Harper.

1909 *Extract from Captain Stormfield's Visit to Heaven.* New York: Harper.

1916 *The Mysterious Stranger, A Romance.* New York: Harper.

1917 *What Is Man? and Other Essays,* ed. Albert Bigelow Paine. New York: Harper.

1919 *The Curious Republic of Gondour and Other Whimsical Sketches.* New York: Boni and Liveright.

1919 *Saint Joan of Arc.* New York: Harper.

1922 *The Mysterious Stranger and Other Stories,* ed. Albert Bigelow Paine. New York: Harper.

1923 *Europe and Elsewhere,* ed. Albert Bigelow Paine. New York: Harper.

1924 *Mark Twain's Autobiography,* ed. Albert Bigelow Paine. New York: Harper.

1928 *The Adventures of Thomas Jefferson Snodgrass,* ed. Charles Honce. Chicago: Pascal Covici.

1935 *Slovenly Peter: Der Struwwelpeter.* New York: Marchbanks Press. Translated by Mark Twain.

1940 *Mark Twain in Eruption: Hitherto Unpublished Pages About Men and Events,* ed. Bernard DeVoto. New York: Capricorn Books.

1952 *Report from Paradise,* ed. Dixon Wecter. New York: Harper.

1957 *Mark Twain of the Enterprise: Newspaper Articles & Other Documents, 1862–1864,* ed. Henry Nash Smith and Frederick Anderson. Berkeley and Los Angeles: University of California Press.

1958 *Traveling with the Innocents Abroad: Mark Twain's Original Reports from Europe and the Holy Land,* ed. Daniel Morley McKeithan. Norman: University of Oklahoma Press, 1958.

1959 *The Autobiography of Mark Twain, Including Chapters Now Published for the First Time,* ed. Charles Neider. New York: Harper.

1961 *Contributions to the Galaxy, 1868–1871, by Mark Twain,* ed. Bruce R. McElderry, Jr. Gainesville, Fla.: Scholars' Facsimiles and Reprints.

1961 *The Portable Mark Twain,* ed. Bernard DeVoto. New York: Viking.

1961 *Mark Twain: Life As I Find It,* ed. Charles Neider. Garden City, N.Y.: Hanover House.

1962 *Letters from the Earth,* ed. Bernard DeVoto. New York: Harper.

1963 *Mark Twain's San Francisco,* ed. Bernard Taper. New York: McGraw-Hill

1967 *Mark Twain's Satires & Burlesques,* ed. Franklin R. Rogers. Berkeley and Los Angeles: University of California Press.

1967 *Mark Twain's Which Was the Dream? and Other Symbolic Writings of the Later Years,* ed. John S. Tuckey. Berkeley and Los Angeles: University of California Press.

1969 *Clemens of the Call: Mark Twain in San Francisco,* ed. Edgar M. Branch. Berkeley and Los Angeles: University of California Press.

1969 *Mark Twain's Hannibal, Huck & Tom,* ed. Walter Blair. Berkeley and Los Angeles: University of California Press.

1969 *Mark Twain's Mysterious Stranger Manuscripts,* ed. William M. Gibson. Berkeley and Los Angeles: University of California Press.

1972 *Mark Twain's Fables of Man,* ed. John S. Tuckey. Berkeley and Los Angeles: University of California Press.

1973 *What Is Man? and Other Philosophical Writings,* ed. Paul Baender. Berkeley and Los Angeles: University of California Press.

1978 *Mark Twain Speaks for Himself,* ed. Paul Fatout. West Lafayette, Ind.: Purdue University Press.

1979 *Early Tales & Sketches,* vol. 1, *1851–1864,* ed. Edgar Marquess Branch and Robert H. Hirst. Berkeley and Los Angeles: University of California Press.

1981 *Early Tales & Sketches,* vol. 2, *1864–1865,* ed. Edgar Marquess Branch and Robert H. Hirst. Berkeley and Los Angeles: University of California Press.

1990 *Mark Twain's Own Autobiography: The Chapters from the North American Review,* ed. Michael J. Kiskis. Madison: University of Wisconsin Press.

1992 *Collected Tales, Sketches, Speeches, & Essays, 1853–1890,* ed. Louis J. Budd. New York: Library of America.

1992 *Collected Tales, Sketches, Speeches, & Essays, 1891–1910,* ed. Louis J. Budd. New York: Library of America.

1995 *The Bible According to Mark Twain,* ed. Howard G. Baetzhold and Joseph B. McCullough. Athens: University of Georgia Press.

LETTERS, SPEECHES AND NOTEBOOKS

1910   *Mark Twain's Speeches,* ed. Albert Bigelow Paine. New York: Harper.

1917   *Mark Twain's Letters,* ed. Albert Bigelow Paine. 2 vols. New York: Harper.

1935   *Mark Twain's Notebook,* ed. Albert Bigelow Paine. New York: Harper.

1937   *Mark Twain's Letters from the Sandwich Islands,* ed. G. Ezra Dane. Palo Alto, Calif.: Stanford University Press.

1940   *Mark Twain's Travels with Mr. Brown,* ed. Franklin Walker and G. Ezra Dane. New York: Alfred A. Knopf.

1949   *The Love Letters of Mark Twain,* ed. Dixon Wecter. New York: Harper.

1949   *Mark Twain to Mrs. Fairbanks,* ed. Dixon Wecter. San Marino, Calif.: Huntington Library.

1960   *Mark Twain–Howells Letters: The Correspondence of Samuel L. Clemens and William D. Howells, 1872–1910,* ed. Henry Nash Smith and William M. Gibson. Cambridge, Mass.: Harvard University Press.

1967   *Mark Twain's Letters to His Publishers, 1867–1894,* ed. Hamlin Hill. Berkeley and Los Angeles: University of California Press.

1969   *Mark Twain's Correspondence with Henry Huttleston Rogers, 1893–1909,* ed. Lewis Leary. Berkeley and Los Angeles: University of California Press.

1975   *Mark Twain's Notebooks & Journals,* vol. 1: *1855–1873,* ed. Frederick Anderson, Michael B. Frank, and Kenneth M. Sanderson. Berkeley and Los Angeles: University of California Press.

1975   *Mark Twain's Notebooks & Journals,* vol. 2: *1877–1883,* ed. Frederick Anderson, Lin Salamo and Bernard L. Stein. Berkeley and Los Angeles: University of California Press.

1976   *Mark Twain Speaking,* ed. Paul Fatout. Iowa City: University of Iowa Press.

1979   *Mark Twain's Notebooks & Journals,* vol. 3: *1883–1891,* ed. Robert Pack Browning, Michael Frank and Lin Salamo. Berkeley and Los Angeles: University of California Press.

1988   *Mark Twain's Letters,* vol. 1, *1853–1866,* ed. Edgar Marquess Branch, Michael B. Frank and Kenneth M. Sanderson. Berkeley and Los Angeles: University of California Press.

1990   *Mark Twain's Letters,* vol. 2, *1867–1868,* ed. Harriet Smith, et al. Berkeley and Los Angeles: University of California Press.

1991   *Mark Twain's Aquarium: The Samuel Clemens Angelfish Correspondence, 1905–1910,* ed. John Cooley. Athens: University of Georgia Press.

1992   *Mark Twain's Letters,* vol. 3, *1869,* ed. Victor Fischer, Michael B. Frank and Dahlia Armon. Berkeley and Los Angeles: University of California Press.

1995   *Mark Twain's Letters,* vol. 4, *1870–1871,* ed. Victor Fischer, et al. Berkeley and Los Angeles: University of California Press.

SUGGESTED READING

The literature on Mark Twain is immense. This list contains only a representative sampling of books that address the most interesting issues in Mark Twain's life and writings. For additional bibliographical information, see Thomas Tenney's annotated *Mark Twain: A Reference Guide* (1977) and its annual supplements in *American Literary Realism* (1977–83) and the *Mark Twain Circular* (1984–). J. R. LeMaster and James D. Wilson's *The Mark Twain Encyclopedia* contains bibliographies keyed to individual topics.

In the list below, titles of special reference value are marked with asterisks (*). The names of authors who are subjects of entries in *Mark Twain A to Z* are printed in SMALL CAPS.

Agor, Stewart, and Barbara Agor. *Samuel Clemens and Mark Twain.* New York: Regents Publishing Co., 1986.

Allen, Jerry. *The Adventures of Mark Twain.* Boston: Little, Brown, 1954.

Andrews, Kenneth R. *Nook Farm: Mark Twain's Hartford Circle.* Cambridge, Mass.: Harvard University Press, 1950.

Asselineau, Roger. *The Literary Reputation of Mark Twain from 1910 to 1950: A Critical Essay and a Bibliography.* Paris: Marcel Didier, 1954.

Ayres, Alex, ed. *The Wit & Wisdom of Mark Twain.* New York: Harper & Row, 1987.

Baetzhold, Howard G. *Mark Twain and John Bull: The British Connection.* Bloomington: Indiana University Press, 1970.

*Baldanza, Frank. *Mark Twain: An Introduction and Interpretation.* Totowa, N.J.: Barnes & Noble, 1961.

BEARD, Dan. *Hardly a Man Is Now Alive: The Autobiography of Dan Beard.* New York: Doubleday, Doran & Co., 1939.

*Beaver, Harold. *Huckleberry Finn.* London: Unwin Hyman, 1988.

Bellamy, Gladys Carmen. *Mark Twain as a Literary Artist.* Norman: University of Oklahoma Press, 1950.

Benson, Ivan. *Mark Twain's Western Years.* New York: Russell & Russell, 1966 (orig. publ., 1938).

Berger, Sidney E. *Pudd'nhead Wilson and Those Extraordinary Twins.* New York: W. W. Norton, 1980.

Berret, Anthony J. *Mark Twain and Shakespeare: A Cultural Legacy.* Lanham, Md.: University Press of America, 1993.

BLAIR, Walter. *Native American Humor (1800–1900).* Boston: American Book Co., 1937.

———. *Mark Twain & Huck Finn.* Berkeley and Los Angeles: University of California Press, 1960.

Branch, Edgar M. *The Literary Apprenticeship of Mark Twain.* Iowa City: University of Iowa Press, 1950.

———, ed. *Clemens of the Call.* Berkeley: University of California Press, 1969.

Bridgman, Richard. *Traveling in Mark Twain.* Berkeley and Los Angeles: University of California Press, 1987.

BROOKS, Van Wyck. *The Ordeal of Mark Twain.* New York: Dutton, 1920.

Budd, Louis J. *Mark Twain, Social Philosopher.* Bloomington: Indiana University Press, 1962.

———, ed. *Critical Essays on Mark Twain, 1867–1910.* Boston: G. K. Hall, 1982.

———, ed. *Critical Essays on Mark Twain, 1910–1980.* Boston: G.K. Hall, 1983.

———. *Our Mark Twain: The Making of His Public Personality.* Philadelphia: University of Pennsylvania Press, 1983.

———, ed. *New Essays on "Adventures of Huckleberry Finn."* Cambridge, England: Cambridge University Press, 1985.

Cardwell, Guy. *The Man Who Was Mark Twain.* New Haven, Conn.: Yale University Press, 1991.

———, ed. *Discussions of Mark Twain.* Boston: D. C. Heath, 1963.

Champion, Laurie, ed. *The Critical Response to Mark Twain's "Huckleberry Finn."* Westport, Conn.: Greenwood Press, 1991.

CLEMENS, Clara. *My Father: Mark Twain.* New York: Harper & Bros., 1931.

CLEMENS, Susy. *Papa: An Intimate Biography of Mark*

Twain, ed. Charles Neider. Garden City, N.Y.: Doubleday, 1985.

Covici, Pascal Jr. *Mark Twain's Humor: The Image of a World*. Dallas: Southern Methodist University Press, 1962.

Cox, James M. *Mark Twain: The Fate of Humor*. Princeton, N.J.: Princeton University Press, 1966.

Cummings, Sherwood. *Mark Twain and Science: Adventures of a Mind*. Baton Rouge: Louisiana State University Press, 1988.

David, Beverly R. *Mark Twain and His Illustrators, vol. 1 (1869–1875)*. Troy, N.Y.: Whiston Publishing Co., 1986.

Davis, Sara deSaussure, and Philip D. Beidler, eds. *The Mythologizing of Mark Twain*. Tuscaloosa: University of Alabama Press, 1984.

DEVOTO, Bernard. *Mark Twain's America*. Boston: Little, Brown, 1932.

———. *Mark Twain at Work*. Cambridge, Mass.: Harvard University Press, 1942.

Dolmetsch, Carl. *"Our Famous Guest": Mark Twain in Vienna*. Athens: University of Georgia Press, 1992.

Doyno, Victor A. *Writing "Huck Finn": Mark Twain's Creative Process*. Philadelphia: University of Pennsylvania Press, 1992.

Duckett, Margaret. *Mark Twain and Bret Harte*. Norman: University of Oklahoma Press, 1964.

Eble, Kenneth E. *Old Clemens and W. D. H.: The Story of a Remarkable Friendship*. Baton Rouge: Louisiana State University Press, 1985.

*Ehrlich, Eugene, and Gorton Carruth. *The Oxford Illustrated Literary Guide to the United States*. New York: Oxford University Press, 1982.

Emberson, Frances Guthrie. "Mark Twain's Vocabulary: A General Survey," *University of Missouri Studies* 10, 3 (July), 1935.

Emerson, Everett. *The Authentic Mark Twain*. Philadelphia: University of Pennsylvania Press, 1984.

Ensor, Allison. *Mark Twain & the Bible*. Lexington: University of Kentucky Press, 1969.

Evans, John D. *A Tom Sawyer Companion: An Autobiographical Guided Tour with Mark Twain*. Lanham, Md.: University Press of America, 1993.

Ewing, Raymond P. *Mark Twain's Steamboat Years*. Hannibal, Mo.: Cave Hollow Steamboat Landing, 1981.

Fatout, Paul. *Mark Twain on the Lecture Circuit*. Bloomington: University of Indiana Press, 1960.

———. *Mark Twain in Virginia City*. Bloomington: Indiana University Press, 1964.

Faude, Wilson H. *The Renaissance of Mark Twain's House: Handbook for Restoration*. Larchmont, N.Y.: Queens House, 1978.

Ferguson, DeLancey. *Mark Twain: Man and Legend*. New York: Bobbs-Merrill, 1943.

Fishkin, Shelley Fisher. *Was Huck Black? Mark Twain and African-American Voices*. New York: Oxford University Press, 1993.

Foner, Philip S. *Mark Twain Social Critic*. New York: International Publishers, 1958.

Foote, Bud. *The Connecticut Yankee in the Twentieth Century: Travel to the Past in Science Fiction*. New York: Greenwood Press, 1991.

Frear, Walter Francis. *Mark Twain and Hawaii*. Chicago: Lakeside Press, 1947.

French, Bryant Morey. *Mark Twain and *The Gilded Age: *The Book That Named an Era*. Dallas: Southern Methodist University Press, 1965.

*Gale, Robert L. *Plots and Characters in the Works of Mark Twain*. 2 vols. Hamden, Conn.: Archon Books, 1973.

Ganzel, Dewey. *Mark Twain Abroad: The Cruise of the "Quaker City."* Chicago: University of Chicago Press, 1968.

Geismar, Maxwell. *Mark Twain: An American Prophet*. New York: Houghton Mifflin, 1970.

Gerber, John C. *Mark Twain*. New York: Twayne Publishers, 1988.

Gibson, William M. *The Art of Mark Twain*. New York: Oxford University Press, 1976.

Giddings, Robert, ed. *Mark Twain: A Sumptuous Variety*. London: Vision; Totowa, N.J.: Barnes & Noble.

Gillman, Susan. *Dark Twins: Imposture and Identity in Mark Twain's America*. Chicago: University of Chicago Press, 1989.

———, and Forrest G. Robinson. *Mark Twain's "Pudd'nhead Wilson": Race, Conflict, and Culture*. Durham, N.C.: Duke University Press, 1990.

*Gribben, Alan. *Mark Twain's Library: A Reconstruction*. 2 vols. Boston: G. K. Hall, 1980.

———, and Nick Karanovich, eds. *Overland with Mark Twain: James B. Pond's Photographs and Journal of the North American Lecture Tour of 1895*. Elmira, N.Y.: Center for Mark Twain Studies at Quarry Farm, 1992.

*Harnsberger, Caroline Thomas, ed. *Mark Twain at Your Fingertips*. New York: Beechhurst Press, 1948.

———. *Mark Twain: Family Man*. New York: Citadel Press, 1960.

———. *Mark Twain's Clara, or What Became of the Clemens Family*. Evanston, Ill.: Ward Schori, 1982.

Harris, Susan K. *Mark Twain's Escape from Time: A Study of Patterns and Images*. Columbia: University of Missouri Press, 1982.

Hayes, John Q. *Mark Twain and Religion: A Mirror of American Eclecticism*. New York: Peter Lang, 1989.

Henderson, Archibald. *Mark Twain*. London: Duckworth & Co., 1911.

Hill, Hamlin. *Mark Twain and Elisha Bliss*. Columbia: University of Missouri Press, 1964.

———. *Mark Twain/God's Fool*. New York: Harper & Row, 1975.

Hillyer, Katharine. *Young Reporter Mark Twain in Virginia City*. Sparks, Nev.: Western Printing & Publishing Co., 1964.

Hoffman, Andrew Jay. *Twain's Heroes, Twain's Worlds.* Philadelphia: University of Pennsylvania Press, 1988.

HOWELLS, William Dean. *My Mark Twain: Reminiscences and Criticisms.* New York: Harper & Bros., 1910.

Inge, M. Thomas, ed. *Huck Finn among the Critics: A Centennial Selection.* Frederick, Md.: University Publications of America, 1985.

Jerome, Robert D., and Herbert A. Wisbey, eds. *Mark Twain in Elmira.* Elmira, N.Y.: Mark Twain Society, 1977.

Johnson, James L. *Mark Twain and the Limits of Power: Emerson's God in Ruins.* Knoxville: University of Tennessee Press, 1982.

*Johnson, Merle. *A Bibliography of the Works of Mark Twain: A List of First Editions in Book Form and of First Printings in Periodicals and Occasional Publications of.* New York: Harper & Bros., 1935.

Kahn, Sholom J. *Mark Twain's Mysterious Stranger: A Study of the Manuscript Texts.* Columbia: University of Missouri Press, 1978.

Kaplan, Justin. *Mr. Clemens and Mark Twain.* New York: Simon & Schuster, 1966.

———. *Mark Twain and His World.* New York: Simon & Schuster, 1974.

*Kinch, J. C. B., comp. *Mark Twain's German Critical Reception, 1875–1986: An Annotated Bibliography.* New York: Greenwood Press, 1989.

Knoper, Randall. *Acting Naturally: Mark Twain in the Culture of Performance.* Berkeley and Los Angeles: University of California Press, 1995.

Krause, Sydney J. *Mark Twain as Critic.* Baltimore: Johns Hopkins Press, 1967.

Kruse, Horst H. *Mark Twain and "Life on the Mississippi."* Amherst: University of Massachusetts Press, 1981.

Lauber, John. *The Making of Mark Twain: A Biography.* New York: Noonday Press / Farrar, Straus & Giroux, 1985.

———. *The Inventions of Mark Twain.* New York: Hill & Wang, 1990.

Lawton, Mary. *A Lifetime with Mark Twain: The Memories of Katy Leary, for Thirty Years His Faithful and Devoted Servant.* New York: Harcourt, Brace & Co., 1925.

Leary, Lewis. *A Casebook on Mark Twain's Wound.* New York: Thomas Y. Crowell, 1962.

*LeMaster, J. R., and James D. Wilson, eds. *The Mark Twain Encyclopedia.* New York: Garland, 1993.

Lennon, Nigey. *Mark Twain in California: The Turbulent Years of Samuel Clemens.* San Francisco: Chronicle Books, 1982.

———. *The Sagebrush Bohemian: Mark Twain in California.* New York: Paragon House, 1990.

Leonard, James S., Thomas A. Tenney, and Thadious M. Davis. *Satire or Evasion? Black Perspectives on "Huckleberry Finn."* Durham, N.C.: Duke University Press, 1991.

*Long, E. Hudson, and J. R. LeMaster. *The New Mark Twain Handbook.* New York: Garland, 1985.

Lorch, Fred W. *The Trouble Begins at Eight: Mark Twain's Lecture Tours.* Ames: Iowa State University Press, 1968.

Lynn, Kenneth S. *Mark Twain and Southwestern Humor.* Boston: Little, Brown, 1959.

———. *William Dean Howells: An American Life.* New York: Harcourt Brace Jovanovich, 1973.

*Machlis, Paul, ed. *Union Catalog of Clemens Letters.* Berkeley and Los Angeles: University of California Press, 1986.

*———, and Deborah Ann Turner, eds. *Union Catalog of Letters to Clemens.* Berkeley and Los Angeles: University of California Press, 1992.

Mack, Effie Mona. *Mark Twain in Nevada.* New York: Charles Scribner's Sons, 1947.

Macnaughton, William R. *Mark Twain's Last Years as a Writer.* Columbia: University of Missouri Press, 1979.

Maik, Thomas A. *A Reexamination of Mark Twain's Joan of Arc.* Lewiston, N.Y.: Edwin Mellen Press, 1992.

Marotti, Maria Ornella. *The Duplicating Imagination: Twain and the Twain Papers.* University Park: Pennsylvania State University Press, 1990.

Masters, Edgar Lee. *Mark Twain: A Portrait.* New York: Charles Scribner's Sons, 1938.

McBride, William M. *Mark Twain: A Bibliography of the Collections of the Mark Twain Memorial and the Stowe-Day Foundation.* Hartford, Conn.: McBride Publishing, 1984.

McKeithan, Daniel Morley. *Court Trials in Mark Twain and Other Essays.* The Hague, Netherlands: Martinus Nijhoff, 1958.

Meltzer, Milton. *Mark Twain Himself.* New York: Thomas Y. Crowell, 1960.

NEIDER, Charles. *Mark Twain and the Russians: An Exchange of Views.* New York: Hill & Wang, 1960.

———. *Mark Twain.* New York: Horizon Press, 1967.

Norton, Charles A. *Writing Tom Sawyer: The Adventures of a Classic.* Jefferson, N.C.: MacFarland & Co., 1983.

PAINE, Albert Bigelow. *Mark Twain, A Biography: The Personal and Literary Life of Samuel Langhorne Clemens.* 3 vols. New York: Harper & Bros., 1912.

———. *The Boys' Life of Mark Twain.* New York: Harper & Bros., 1916.

———. *A Short Life of Mark Twain.* New York: Harper & Bros., 1920.

Pettit, Arthur G. *Mark Twain & the South.* Lexington: University of Kentucky Press, 1974.

Powers, Ron. *White Town Drowsing.* Boston: Atlantic Monthly Press, 1986.

Quick, Dorothy. *Enchantment: A Little Girl's Friendship with Mark Twain.* Norman: University of Oklahoma Press, 1961.

Quirk, Tom. *Coming to Grips with Huckleberry Finn: Essays on a Book, a Boy, and a Man.* Columbia: University of Missouri Press, 1993.

*Ramsay, Robert L. "A Mark Twain Lexicon," *University of Missouri Studies* 13, 1 (January), 1938.

Regan, Robert. *Unpromising Heroes: Mark Twain and His Characters.* Berkeley and Los Angeles: University of California Press, 1966.

Robinson, Forrest G. *In Bad Faith: The Dynamics of Deception in Mark Twain's America.* Cambridge, Mass.: Harvard University Press, 1986.

*Rodney, Robert M. *Mark Twain International: A Bibliography and Interpretation of His Worldwide Popularity.* Westport, Conn.: Greenwood Press, 1982.

———. *Mark Twain Overseas: A Biographical Account of His Voyages, Travels, and Reception in Foreign Lands, 1866–1910.* Colorado Springs, Colo.: Three Continents Press, Inc., 1993.

Rogers, Franklin R. *Mark Twain's Burlesque Patterns as Seen in the Novels and Narratives, 1855–1885.* Dallas: Southern Methodist University Press, 1960.

———, ed. *The Pattern for Mark Twain's "Roughing It": Letters from Nevada by Samuel and Orion Clemens, 1861–1862.* Berkeley and Los Angeles: University of California Press, 1961.

Salomon, Roger B. *Twain and the Image of History.* New Haven, Conn.: Yale University Press, 1961.

Salsbury, Edith Colgate, ed. *Susy and Mark Twain: Family Dialogues.* New York: Harper & Row, 1965.

Sanborn, Margaret. *Mark Twain: The Bachelor Years.* New York: Doubleday, 1990.

Sanderlin, George. *Mark Twain as Others Saw Him.* New York: McGann & Geoghegan, 1978.

Sattelmeyer, Robert, and J. Donald Crowley. *One Hundred Years of "Huckleberry Finn": The Boy, His Book, and American Culture.* Columbia: University of Missouri Press, 1985.

Scharnhorst, Gary, ed. *Critical Essays on The Adventures of Tom Sawyer.* New York: G. K. Hall, 1993.

Schmitter, Dean Morgan, ed. *Mark Twain: A Collection of Critical Essays.* New York: McGraw-Hill, 1974.

Scott, Arthur L. *On the Poetry of Mark Twain, With Selections from His Verse.* Urbana: University of Illinois Press, 1966.

———. *Mark Twain at Large.* Chicago: Henry Regnery Co., 1969.

Seelye, John. *Mark Twain in the Movies: A Meditation with Pictures.* New York: Viking, 1977.

Sewell, David R. *Mark Twain's Languages: Discourse, Dialogue and Linguistic Variety.* Berkeley and Los Angeles: University of California Press, 1987.

Shillingsburg, Miriam Jones. *At Home Abroad: Mark Twain in Australasia.* Jackson: University Press of Mississippi, 1988.

Skandera-Trombley, Laura. *Mark Twain in the Company of Women.* Philadelphia: University of Pennsylvania Press, 1994.

Sloane, David E. E., *Mark Twain as a Literary Comedian.* Baton Rouge: Louisiana State University Press, 1979.

———, ed. *Mark Twain's Humor: Critical Essays.* New York: Garland, 1993.

Smith, Henry Nash. *Mark Twain: The Development of a Writer.* Cambridge, Mass.: Harvard University Press, 1962.

———, ed. *Mark Twain: A Collection of Critical Essays.* Englewood Cliffs, N.J.: Prentice-Hall, 1963.

———. *Mark Twain's Fable of Progress: Political and Economic Ideas in "A Connecticut Yankee."* New Brunswick, N.J.: Rutgers University Press, 1964.

Stahl, J. D. *Mark Twain, Culture and Gender: Envisioning America Through Europe.* Athens: University of Georgia Press, 1994.

Steinbrink, Jeffrey. *Getting to Be Mark Twain.* Berkeley and Los Angeles: University of California Press, 1991.

Stone, Albert E. Jr. *The Innocent Eye: Childhood in Mark Twain's Imagination.* New Haven, Conn.: Yale University Press, 1961.

Stoneley, Peter Nicholas. *Mark Twain and the Feminine Aesthetic.* Cambridge, England: Cambridge University Press, 1992.

Strong, Leah A. *Joseph Hopkins Twichell: Mark Twain's Friend and Pastor.* Athens: University of Georgia Press, 1966.

Sundquist, Eric J., ed. *Mark Twain: A Collection of Critical Essays.* Englewood Cliffs, N.J.: Prentice Hall, 1994.

Taper, Bernard, ed. *Mark Twain's San Francisco.* New York: McGraw-Hill, 1963.

*Tenney, Thomas Asa. *Mark Twain: A Reference Guide.* Boston: G. K. Hall, 1977.

Tuckey, John S. *Mark Twain and Little Satan: The Writing of "The Mysterious Stranger."* West Lafayette, Ind.: Purdue University Press, 1963.

———. *Mark Twain's The Mysterious Stranger and the Critics.* Belmont, Calif.: Wadsworth Publishing, 1968.

Vallin, Marlen Boyd. *Mark Twain: Protagonist for the Popular Culture.* Westport, Conn.: Greenwood Press, 1992.

Wagenknecht, Edward. *Mark Twain: The Man and His Work.* 2d ed. Norman: University of Oklahoma Press, 1967.

Walker, Franklin, ed. *The Washoe Giant in San Francisco.* San Francisco: George Fields, 1938.

Wallace, Elizabeth. *Mark Twain and the Happy Island.* Chicago: A. C. McClurg, 1913.

Webster, Samuel Charles, ed. *Mark Twain, Business Man.* Boston: Little, Brown, 1946.

Wecter, Dixon. *Sam Clemens of Hannibal.* Boston: Houghton, Mifflin, 1952.

Welland, Dennis. *Mark Twain in England.* London: Chatto & Windus, 1978.

———. *The Life and Times of Mark Twain.* New York: Crescent Books, 1991.

Wiggins, Robert A. *Mark Twain: Jackleg Novelist.* Seattle: University of Washington Press, 1964.

Williams, George, III. *On the Road with Mark Twain in California and Nev.* Dayton, Nev.: Tree by the River Publishing, 1993.

Willis, Resa. *Mark and Livy: The Love Story of Mark Twain and the Woman Who Almost Tamed Him.* New York: Atheneum, 1992.

*Wilson, James D. *A Reader's Guide to the Short Stories of Mark Twain.* Boston: G. K. Hall, 1987.

Wonham, Henry B. *Mark Twain and the Art of the Tall Tale.* New York: Oxford University Press, 1993.

Zall, Paul M. *Mark Twain Laughing: Humorous Anecdotes by and about Samuel L. Clemens.* Knoxville: University of Tennessee Press, 1985.

Zwick, Jim, ed. *Mark Twain's Weapons of Satire: Anti-imperialist Writings on the Philippine–American War.* Syracuse, N.Y.: Syracuse University Press, 1992.

INDEX

This index is designed to be used in conjunction with the many cross-references in the A-to-Z entries; it thus does not attempt to be exhaustive. Page references to titles, names and terms that have their own A-to-Z entries are **boldfaced** below; for additional references see their text entries. Other titles, names and terms that are not the subjects of A-to-Z entries are generally given fuller citiations here. *Italicized* page references indicate illustrations; *c* following the page locators indicate the chronology.

A

A. B. Chambers (steamboat) **1**, 41, 441

A, Brother *see* Brother A and Brother B

Abblasoure, England (fictional village) **1**, 94

Abdul Aziz (sultan of Turkey) **1**, 15

Abel (biblical character) 132–133, 281

Abelard and Héloise (Peter Abelard and Héloise) **1**, 237

Able, Daniel 512

Abner Dilworthy, Senator (fictional character) *see* Dilworthy, Senator Abner

Abner Moore (fictional character) *see* Moore, Abner

Abner Shackleford (fictional character) *see* Shackleford, Abner

abolitionism
family and friends: Clemens, John Marshall (father) 78–79; Langdon, Jervis (father-in-law) 275; Redpath, James 388
historical figures: Conway, Moncure D[aniel] 99; Douglass, Frederick 117; Gillette, Francis 176; Glover, Samuel Taylor 176
places: Indian Territory 232–233; Marion City, Missouri 302
writings on: *Huckleberry Finn* 221, 227, 232; "Scrap of Curious History" 302; "Tom Sawyer's Conspiracy" 474–476

Aborigines 115, 148–149

"About All Kinds of Ships" (essay) 26, 33

"About Play Acting" (essay) **1**

"About Smells" (essay) **1**

Abraham (Maltese guide) **2**, 138, 241–242

Ab Turner (fictional character) *see* Turner, Ab

Acropolis (Athens, Greece) 18

actors (who have portrayed Mark Twain) **2**

Adair County, Kentucky 269

Adam, Ronald 2

Adam and Eve (biblical characters) 2, **2–3**
"Captain Stormfield's Visit to Heaven" 60
Clemens, Olivia (Livy) 81
Eve's Diary 132–133
"Eve Speaks" 132

Extracts from Adam's Diary 133
Innocents Abroad 243
"Letters from the Earth" 281
"Monument to Adam" 322
"That Day in Eden" 453

Adamic Diaries **3**, 132–133

Adams, Brooke 245

Adams, Cholley (fictional character) **3**, 481

Adams, George Jones **3**, 243, 271, 325

Adams, Henry (Hal) (fictional character) **3**, 315–316

Adams, Joseph 371

Adams, Wm. R. (fictional character) 54

"Adam's Diary, Extracts from" (souvenir publication, 1893) 337

Adam's Diary, Extracts from (sketch) *see Extracts from Adam's Diary*

"Adam's Soliloquy" (sketch) **3–4**

adaptations and dramatizations
Adventures of Mark Twain (1985) 5
Big River 33
"Captain Stormfield's Visit to Heaven" 62
Connecticut Yankee 98
"Death Disk" 108
Eve's Diary 133
Gilded Age 175–176
Huckleberry Finn 229–230
Innocents Abroad 245
jumping frog story 266
Life on the Mississippi 292
"Man That Corrupted Hadleyburg" 301
"£1,000,000 Bank-Note" 317
No. 44, The Mysterious Stranger 342
Prince and the Pauper 370
"Private History of a Campaign That Failed" 371
Pudd'nhead Wilson 379
Roughing It 407–408
Tom Sawyer 466–467
Tom Sawyer Abroad 471
"War Prayer" 503

Ade, George 492

Adelaide (fictional ship) 128

Adeler, Max (pen name) *see* Clark, Charles Heber

Adler, Private Franz (fictional character) **4**

Admiral, the Old (fictional character) **4**, 117, 404

Adolf, Father (fictional character) 69–71, 329, 340–341

Adolphus (alias of fictional character) **4**, 223

adultery 28

Adventures in the Apache Country (John Ross Browne) 407

Adventures of Colonel Sellers (novel) **4**, 175

Adventures of Huckleberry Finn see Huckleberry Finn, Adventures of

Adventures of Mark Twain, The (film) (1944) **4–5**

Adventures of Mark Twain, The (film) (1985) **5**

Adventures of Tom Sawyer, The see Tom Sawyer, The Adventures of

Africa **5** *see also specific countries* (e.g., South Africa); *cities* (e.g., Pretoria)

African Americans
derogatory terms for: nigger 338
fictional characters: Betsy **32**; Chambers **66**, 373–374, 377–378; Driscoll, Tom 119–120, 373–378, *408*, 457; Jack 222, *250*; Jake, Uncle **251**; Jasper **252**, 353; Jim (in *Huckleberry Finn*) 106, 186, 214–215, 217–223, 225–228, *228*, **252–254**, *253*, 283, 385–386, 468–470, 475–476; Jim (in *Tom Sawyer*) **252**, 459; Jinny, Aunt, and Uncle Dan'l 10, 160, **254**, 283; Lize 286, **293**; Nat 226–227, **332**; Roxana (Roxy) 373–378, *408*, **408–409**
historical figures: Cord, Mary Ann 100; Daniel, Uncle 106; Douglass, Frederick 117; Griffin, George 186; Lewis, John T. 283; Washington, Booker T. 505
slavery *see* slavery
writings on: "Corn-pone Opinions" 100–101; "Golden Arm" 177; "Sociable Jimmy" 435; "True Story" 490

"Aged Pilot Man, The" (poem) **5–6**

Agent, the (fictional character) *see* Harris (Mr. Harris, the Agent)

Agravaine, Sir (fictional character) 97

Aguinaldo, Emilio 159

Ah Sin, The Heathen Chinee (Twain/Harte play) 6

Ah Song Hi (fictional character) 178

Aileen Mavourneen (fictional dog) **6**, 114

"Aix, the Paradise of the Rheumatics" (article) 6

Aix-les-Bains, France **6**

Ajax (steamship) 4, **6**

Alaric (fictional character) 444

Albee, Josh 467

Albert, Eddie 98, 325

Albertson, Frank 75

Alden, Henry Mills **6**, *34*, 262

Alden, Jean François (fictional character) **6–7**, 255

Aldrich, Thomas Bailey (friend) **7**, 18, 195, 327

Aleck Foster (fictional character) *see* Foster, Electra (Aleck)

Aleck Scott (Alexander Scott) (steamboat) **7**, 35, 441

Alexander II, Czar of Russia **7**, 104, 241

Alexandria, Egypt 243

Alexandria, Missouri 127

Alfred T. Lacey (steamboat) **7–8**, 40–41, 45, 124, 287, 441

Alfred Temple (fictional character) *see* Temple, Alfred

Alger Jr., Horatio 320

Algiers, Algeria 5, 68, 244, 382

Ali, Muhammad (Mehemet) 127

Alison, Catherine (Cathy) (fictional character) **8**, 84, 209–210

Alison, Brigadier General Thomas (fictional character) 209–210

Allbright, Charles William (fictional character) **8**, 386

Allbright, Dick (fictional character) **8**, 386

Allen (fictional character) 11

Allen, A. D. 400

Allen, Helen 14

Allen, Robert (fictional character) 457

Allman, Elvia 355

Almanzar, James 355

Alonzo Child (steamboat) **8**, 35, 41, 73, 441

alpenstock **8**

Alps **8–9**

Alta (newspaper) *see San Francisco Alta California*

Amaranth (fictional steamboat) **9**, 168

Amazon 285, 334, 358, 437, 491

Ambassadors, The (Henry James) 251

Ament, Joseph **9**, 191–192

America (steamship) 502

American Claimant, The (novel) **9–13**
fictional characters: Berkeley, Lord Kirkcudbright Llanover Marjoribanks (Howard Tracy) 31; Hawkins, (George) Washington 200–201; Jinny, Aunt, and Uncle Dan'l 254; Lathers, Simon 275; Rossmore, Earl of 394; Sellers, Mulberry (Colonel Sellers) 426; Sellers, Polly 427; Sellers, Sally ("Lady Gwendolen") 427
historical figures: Arnold, Matthew 16; Cody, William Frederick ("Buffalo Bill") 85
lecture tour 279
satire 419
setting: Washington, D.C. 505

American Publishing Company **13**, 38

"American Vandal Abroad, The" (lecture topic) **13–14**, 18, 438, 497

Amy (fictional character) 43

Amyas le Poulet (fictional character) *see* Clarence

Amy Lawrence (fictional character) *see* Lawrence, Amy

Andersen, Tobias 35, 304

Anderson, Frederick 6, **14**, 307–308, 379

Anderson, Maxwell 229

Andrew, Father (fictional character) **14**, 364–365

Andrew Jackson (fictional dog) **14**, 265

Andrews, Blake (fictional character) 367–368

Andrews, Dr. Edward ("the Oracle") 235, 345

Andrews, Harry 203, 370

Angelfish (girls' club members) **14**, *34*, 342

Angelo Capello (fictional character) *see* Capello, Angelo and Luigi

angels 60

Angel's Camp (Angels Camp), California **14–15**, 265–266, 404

Anglo-Boer War (1881) 153

anti-Semitism *see* Jews